CW01390874

Numbers

BAKER COMMENTARY *on the* OLD TESTAMENT

PENTATEUCH

Bill T. Arnold, EDITOR

Volumes now available

Genesis, John Goldingay
Numbers, Mark A. Awabdy

Numbers

Mark A. Awabdy

B
Baker Academic
a division of Baker Publishing Group
Grand Rapids, Michigan

To Leslie,
love of my life,
one of five daughters
(Num. 27:1)

© 2023 by Mark A. Awabdy

Published by Baker Academic
a division of Baker Publishing Group
Grand Rapids, Michigan
www.bakeracademic.com

Printed in the United States of America

Library of Congress Cataloging-in-Publication Data
Names: Awabdy, Mark A., 1981– author.
Title: Numbers / Mark A. Awabdy.
Description: Grand Rapids, Michigan : Baker Academic, a division of Baker Publishing Group, 2023. | Series: Baker commentary on the Old Testament: Pentateuch | Includes bibliographical references and index.
Identifiers: LCCN 2023009233 | ISBN 9780801035746 (cloth) | ISBN 9781493439904 (ebook) | ISBN 9781493439911 (pdf)
Subjects: LCSH: Bible. Numbers—Commentaries.
Classification: LCC BS1265.53 .A93 2023 | DDC 222/.1407—dc23/eng/20230518
LC record available at https://lccn.loc.gov/2023009233

Unless otherwise indicated, all Scripture quotations are the author's translation.

Baker Publishing Group publications use paper produced from sustainable forestry practices and post-consumer waste whenever possible.

23   24   25   26   27   28   29   7   6   5   4   3   2   1

Contents

Illustrations

Figures

Maps

Tables

Series Preface

If the ancient books we call the "Old Testament" were studied simply as witnesses to a bygone era, they would still merit continued scrutiny and analysis. Were they merely works of great antiquity, reflecting the thoughts, actions, and worldviews of writers from a faraway world, they would still garner great interest. They would arouse our curiosity about the history, society, and culture of that long-ago period of human civilization. And if these ancient volumes were also of high literary quality—as the books of the Old Testament certainly are—an entirely separate field of investigation would no doubt be needed to understand and appreciate those qualities and rhetorical properties.

Of course, today we have texts from ancient Babylonia, such as the Enuma Elish, the Gilgamesh Epic, and others, as well as similarly soaring belles lettres from Egypt, Syria-Palestine, Greece, and Rome. Surely Israelite literature is among the greatest ever produced—with its tales of homeless ancestors trekking across ancient lands while following the deity's call to be a blessing to all the world, a covenant-making deity in love with a people of little political significance, and divinely ordained kings and prophets rising and falling with the fortunes of the nation. If such were all that the books of the Old Testament offered, we would certainly continue to acknowledge their great worth. And for many readers, this is all that the Old Testament books represent.

However, this is not the whole story. The truth is that these books are considered by millions of readers through the centuries as much more—as the Word of God. We mean by this that the books of the Old Testament have a divine origin, they are divinely inspired, and somehow they say what God intended for them to say. Of course, there are as many different ways of explaining what this means and of understanding inspiration as there are believers in the truthfulness of these books. But in general, Christians turn to these writings as trustworthy and authoritative expressions of God's will.

Fascination with the books of the Old Testament has not diminished for two thousand years. It is safe to say with some degree of confidence that these books will continue to command our attention. As long as there are believers in the Jewish and Christian traditions of faith, there will be a need for fresh readings and attractively presented commentaries to aid in the interpretation of these ancient documents.

The Pentateuch is the fountainhead from which the Bible's "Torah" (its teaching) flows. From this source—Genesis, Exodus, Leviticus, Numbers, and Deuteronomy—we are given to understand the very nature of God, creation, humankind, sin, salvation, atonement, sacrifice, holiness, and righteousness. All these themes find rootage and are in fact defined in the pages of the Pentateuch. Today's believers want and need reliable resources for reading these important texts.

The Baker Commentary on the Old Testament (BCOT): Pentateuch series represents one attempt to address this need in the church. The volumes in the series are critically informed and respect the integrity of the original discourse as well as the theological dimensions of the text. That is, the commentaries consider not merely what God originally said through the authors of the Torah but also what God is saying today through these ancient books.

The need for a commentary series on the Pentateuch that is both critically engaged and sensitive to the theological contributions of the text is especially pressing given that the relationship between law and gospel has been a perennial problem for the church. Moreover, advances have been made in the past twenty years on the relationship between law and narrative in the Pentateuch, on the way the various legal corpora of the Pentateuch relate to each other diachronically, and on the Pentateuch's contribution to theological studies more generally. These factors have not yet found expression in the type of comprehensive textual treatment possible only in a detailed commentary. Fortunately, a growing number of scholars are engaging in a critical investigation of the text, especially in methodologies that arise naturally and appropriately from the biblical documents themselves and can be combined with sensitivity to the theological contours of the text.

Each commentary in this series not only highlights the distinctive features unique to each biblical book but also reflects the unique approach of the one commenting on it. Each volume provides a fresh translation of the Hebrew text along with section-by-section comments. Each contributor carefully attends to (1) the meaning and significance of the ancient discourse and, where appropriate, (2) its reception in Jewish and Christian tradition, (3) the text's relation and contribution to the canon of Scripture as a whole, and (4) the text's implications for our contemporary setting. In this way, these commentaries not only lay bare the perspectives of the ancient human authors but also bring their voices into dialogue with other words that God has spoken—and is speaking—through Scripture and tradition, doing so in a way that dignifies the relevance of the Pentateuch as a contemporary word from God rather than merely an ancient, dusty book from antiquity. It is our hope that these BCOT: Pentateuch volumes will enable us all to hear this word from God afresh for the benefit of the church universal.

Bill T. Arnold
Paul S. Amos Professor of Old Testament Interpretation
Asbury Theological Seminary

Author's Preface

Occasionally a faithful Bible reader, even a pastor, will admit to me that they struggle with boredom or confusion when they arrive at the dwelling-place instructions in Exod. 25–40, the books of Leviticus and Numbers, or the legal core of Deuteronomy. This has grieved me for twenty years and counting, not because I have never shared those feelings (!), but because I have been captivated by the mystery and beauty of Yahweh through the literary world of the Torah. Some are repelled especially by Numbers because it seems pedantic and redundant in its censuses (chaps. 1, 26), layout of the wilderness camps (chap. 2), dedication of the altar (chap. 7), and sacrificial calendar (chaps. 28–29), to name a few texts. It is precisely this scrupulous repetition, however, that reveals how contextual Yahweh is—resolved to make himself known to people embedded in culture—by using ANE conventions of literary repetition to stress the authors' theological convictions.[1] Others dismiss the rituals of Numbers as obscure and antiquated, or overturned by Christ. But the book's textualized rituals are latent with formative symbolism for the people of God throughout time, and we must grapple with what it means that Christ came not to destroy these rituals but to fulfill them (Matt. 5:17). Other Bible readers are put off by its depressing stories of rebellion and a wrathful God (chaps. 11–25). If only the satirical Balaam Cycle (chaps. 32–34) and the episodes about the courageous daughters of Zelophehad (chaps. 27, 36) opened the book instead of the esoteric Priestly instructions (chaps. 1–10)! Such a wish, however, distorts the brilliant editorial design, which stresses first the centrality of Yahweh's desert shrine and servants amid his people (chaps. 1–10) before exalting Yahweh's holiness (divinity), which necessitates the purging of ingratitude, insubordination, and physical contagions from his covenant people (chaps. 11–25), whom he is relentless in leading toward

---

1. E.g., see the repetition in the Sumerian King List and the Ugaritic Baal Cycle.

Canaan to actualize his land promise to the patriarchs (chaps. 26–36). As I write these words, I pray that this present study will ignite or reignite a resolve to know and make known God through the text of Numbers.

I have approached each dimension of this commentary as an evangelical and critical student of Numbers. My translation style vacillates between formal-equivalence ("Yahweh said to Moses") and dynamic-equivalence ("the ark containing the witness") to communicate the form and function of the Hebrew text in perspicuous, contemporary English. The translation footnotes provide a guide to textual criticism, lexicology, and syntactical and discourse analysis as a gateway to ascertaining meaning and theology.[2] To write the commentary proper, I first sought to suspend a priori theological and ecclesial convictions in order to explain the text as an ANE artifact, comparing and contrasting its forms, ideations, and theologies with those of Israel and Judah's neighbors. To explain the text on its own terms, I maneuvered between methodologies: literary structural analysis (not structuralism); form, source, and redaction criticism; narrative criticism; innerbiblical exegesis; ancient Near Eastern comparative research (literature, iconography, material culture); historical geography; other apropos sciences (botany, metallurgy, psychology, etc.); and reception in the Hebrew Bible, NT, and some rabbis and early church fathers.

For some readers, this commentary will be their first exposure to the scrupulous reflections of German, French, and English critical scholars. For these readers, I call attention to the initial footnotes of the "Overview" section in each chapter, in which I present the primary proposals for the different sources and redactions that can be identified in the distinct contours (clusters of verses) in the composition of the text. To be clear, perceiving in the text different literary layers with distinct theological perspectives and suspending a priori personal convictions does not mean undermining theology or the authority of the text as the Word of God in our lives today. On the contrary, my resolve is to allow each discursive unit to speak on its own terms, in its own cultural context, in order to appreciate how its own distinct theology contributes to the redemptive metanarrative of the whole canon. Rather than flatten the witness of the composition into a monotone, I have tried to make way for the polyphony of voices about Yahweh, his covenant people, and his world to sing their independent parts in a more complex chorus of glory to Yahweh. The "Implications" essays at the end of most chapters became, to my surprise, my favorite aspect of this writing project.

I thank Bill Arnold and Jim Kinney for giving me the rich experience of writing the Numbers volume for this series. I am grateful to those who have

---

2. References reflect English Bible versification; where the Hebrew numbering differs, it follows in square brackets (e.g., Ps. 51:1 [3]). Letters accompanying verse numbers (e.g., v. 1a, v. 1b) refer to subdivisions of the verse and generally correspond to the MT markings.

supported me so faithfully along the way: Bill Arnold for trusting me with this project and mentoring me graciously and wisely; Christian Frevel and Reinhard Achenbach for conversations with me in Helsinki that left me mesmerized by Numbers; Brad Haggard for digitally scanning endless chapters and articles; Becky Vijay for judiciously copyediting the manuscript; Wells Turner, David Garber, and other members of the Baker team for their stellar editorial work; my wife, Leslie, and our kids, extended family, and friends for cheering me on at every turn; and God for sustaining me with the joy of his presence. The non-Israelite diviner Balaam captures my experience throughout this study:

Yahweh their God is with them, acclaimed as king among them. (Num. 23:21*)

Abbreviations

Bibliographic and General

*	after a numeral, it indicates selected verses within a chapter or selected portions of a verse; before a transliterated Hebrew word, it indicates the root form of the word
/	alternative
//	parallel passage
§	section
≈	When a reading in another language is equivalent in the relevant details, or two numbers are roughly equal
>	greater than
≥	greater than or equal to
<	less than
≤	less than or equal to
a.k.a.	also known as
Akk.	Akkadian
ANE	ancient Near East(ern)
ANET	*The Ancient Near East: An Anthology of Texts & Pictures*. Edited by James B. Pritchard. Princeton: Princeton University Press, 2011. Reprint, 2021
Ant.	Josephus, *Jewish Antiquities*
b.	Babylonian Talmud
BCE	before the Common Era
BHRG	*A Biblical Hebrew Reference Grammar*. Edited by Christo H. J. van der Merwe, Jacobus A. Naudé, and Jan H. Kroeze. 2nd ed. New York: T&T Clark, 2017
BHS	*Biblia Hebraica Stuttgartensia*. Edited by Karl Elliger and Wilhelm Rudolph. Stuttgart: Deutsche Bibelgesellschaft, 1983
ca.	circa, around/approximately

CAD	*The Assyrian Dictionary of the Oriental Institute of the University of Chicago.* Edited by A. Leo Oppenheim et al. 21 vols. Chicago: The Oriental Institute of the University of Chicago, 1956–2006
CAL	The Comprehensive Aramaic Lexicon. https://cal.huc.edu
CE	Common Era
CEB	Common English Bible
cent.	century/centuries
cf.	*confer*, compare
chap(s).	chapter(s)
COS	*The Context of Scripture.* Edited by William W. Hallo and K. Lawson Younger Jr. 4 vols. Leiden: Brill, 1997–2016
CSB	Christian Standard Bible
DCH	*Dictionary of Classical Hebrew.* Edited by David J. A. Clines. 9 vols. Sheffield: Sheffield Phoenix Press, 1993–2014
DJD	Discoveries in the Judaean Desert (series)
DNWSI	*Dictionary of the North-West Semitic Inscriptions.* Jacob Hoftijzer and Karen Jongeling. 2 vols. Leiden: Brill, 1995
ea.	each
EA	El-Amarna tablets. According to the edition of Jørgen A. Knudtzon. *Die el-Amarna-Tafeln.* Leipzig: Hinrichs, 1908–15. Repr., Aalen: Zeller, 1964. Continued in Anson F. Rainey, *El-Amarna Tablets*, 359–79. 2nd rev. ed. Kevelaer: Butzon & Bercker, 1978
EBA	Early Bronze Age
ed(s).	editor(s), edition, edited by
e.g.	*exempli gratia*, for example
Eng.	English (versions and their versification)
esp.	especially
EST	Esarhaddon's Succession Treaty
ESV	English Standard Version
et al.	*et alii*, and others
etc.	*et cetera*, and so forth, and the rest
EÜ	*Einheitsübersetzung* [Unified Translation] of the Bible into German
F	Fahrenheit (temperature)
fig.	figure
formally	i.e., literal translation of the Hebrew forms
GBHS	*A Guide to Biblical Hebrew Syntax.* Bill T. Arnold and John H. Choi. 2nd ed. New York: Cambridge University Press, 2018
GELS	*A Greek-English Lexicon of the Septuagint.* Takamitsu Muraoka. Rev. ed. Leuven: Peeters, 2009
Gk.	Greek
GKC	*Gesenius' Hebrew Grammar.* Edited by Emil Kautzsch. Translated by Arther E. Cowley. 2nd ed. Oxford: Clarendon, 1910

HALOT	*The Hebrew and Aramaic Lexicon of the Old Testament.* Ludwig Koehler, Walter Baumgartner, and Johann J. Stamm. Translated and edited under the supervision of Mervyn E. J. Richardson. 4 vols. Leiden: Brill, 1994–99
hapax	hapax legomenon: a word occurring only once in the Bible
Hb.	Hebrew language
HB	Hebrew Bible
Hist. eccl.	Eusebius, *Historia ecclesiastica* (*Ecclesiastical History*)
IBHS	*An Introduction to Biblical Hebrew Syntax.* Bruce K. Waltke and M. O'Connor. Winona Lake, IN: Eisenbrauns, 1990
i.e.	*id est*, that is
Iron	Iron Age (I–III)
JLAT	Jewish Literary Aramaic, Targumic
Joüon and Muraoka	Joüon, Paul. *A Grammar of Biblical Hebrew.* Translated by Takamitsu Muraoka. 2nd ed. Paperback single volume. Rome: Pontifical Biblical Institute, 2006
kg	kilogram
KTU	*Die keilalphabetische Texte aus Ugarit.* Edited by Manfried Dietrich, Oswald Loretz, and Joaquín Sanmartín. Münster: Ugarit-Verlag, 2013
LBA	Late Bronze Age (I–II)
lbs.	pounds
LEH	Lust, Johan, Erik Eynikel, and Katrin Hauspie, eds. *Greek-English Lexicon of the Septuagint.* Rev. ed. Stuttgart: Deutsche Bibelgesellschaft, 2003
m.	Mishnah
mg	milligram
NASB	New American Standard Bible
NET	New English Translation
NETS	*A New English Translation of the Septuagint.* Edited by Albert Pietersma and Benjamin G. Wright. New York: Oxford University Press, 2007; corrected to 2014. https://ccat.sas.upenn.edu/nets/edition
NIV	New International Version (2011)
NJPS	*The Tanakh: The Holy Scriptures: The New JPS Translation according to the Traditional Hebrew Text* (1985)
NLT	New Living Translation (2007)
no(s).	number(s)
n.p.	no page/no place/no publisher
NRSV	New Revised Standard Version
NRSVUE	New Revised Standard Version, Updated Edition
NT	New Testament
OT	Old Testament
PB	Priestly Blessing (Num. 6:24–26)
pl(s).	plate(s)
prb.	probably
SAA	State Archives of Assyria
s.v.	*sub verbo*, under the word

ThB	*Theokratischen Bearbeitung*, a theocratic/hierocratic community ruled by the high priest
trans.	translator, translated by, translation
vs.	versus
VTE	Vassal Treaties of Esarhaddon

Grammatical and Syntactical

act.	active	obj.	object
adv.	adverb	pass.	passive
const.	construct	pers.	person
fem.	feminine	pl(s).	plural
fut.	future	prep.	preposition
gen.	genitive/genitival	pron.	pronoun
impf.	imperfect	ptc(s).	participle(s)
impv.	imperative	sg.	singular
inf.	infinitive	subst.	substantive/substantival
masc.	masculine	suf.	suffix
nom.	nominative		

Text-Critical Sigla

⌐...⌐	from LXX^ed and/or Qumran; absent from MP, SP
[. . .]	encloses what is conjectured for a damaged scroll
col.	column
D	Deuteronomistic source
Dtr	Deuteronomistic (History; writer); Deuteronomist
DtrL	land-conquest narrative in Deut. 1 to Josh. 22, with a preexilic redaction of Deuteronomy
E	Pentateuch source using the name Elohim (*'ĕlōhîm*)
H	Holiness Code, esp. Lev. 17–26, yet also elsewhere
Hb.	Hebrew; Hebrew text agreement/versification: Qumran MSS, MT, SP
HB	Hebrew Bible
J	Pentateuchal source using the name Yahweh (*yhwh*)
KD	Deuteronomistic composition
KP	Priestly composition that incorporates non-P material
LXX	Septuagint (the Greek OT)
LXX^A	Codex Alexandrinus of the LXX
LXX^B	Codex Vaticanus of the LXX
LXX^C	The C (catena) group of LXX manuscripts
LXX^ed	Göttingen critical edition of the LXX of Numbers: *Numeri*. Edited by John William Wevers. Septuaginta 3/1. Göttingen: Vandenhoeck & Ruprecht, 1982. 2nd ed., 2020
LXX^L	The Lucianic text (recension) of the LXX

LXX^O The O recension of Septuagint manuscripts
majority   most versions
M^L Masoretic text in Codex Leningradensis B 19^A
MS(S)   manuscript(s)
MT   Masoretic Text
MT^{ketiv} *ketiv* = "what is written" in the main text of the MT
MT^L Leningrad Codex of the Masoretic Text (1008 or 1009 CE)
MT^{mss} manuscripts of the Masoretic Text
MT^{qere} *qere* = "what is (should be) read," as suggested in the margin of the MT
P   Priestly writing(s)
P^g groundwork of Priestly source of the Pentateuch
P^{ge} supplement to the Priestly source, including some of Exod. 16
P^s secondary additions to the Priestly source of the Pentateuch
SP   Samaritan Pentateuch
Syr   Syriac (Peshitta)
Tg   Targum, a reading shared by the major Aramaic versions of Numbers (see next)
Tg^{Neo} Targum Neofiti
Tg^O Targum Onqelos
Tg^{PJ} Targum Pseudo-Jonathan
Vulg   Latin Vulgate
Vulg^{ed} Latin Vulgate, a critical edition of Jerome's Vulgate in *Biblia Sacra iuxta Vulgatam Versionem*. 5th ed. Stuttgart: Deutsche Bibelgesellschaft, 2007

Old Testament / Hebrew Bible

Gen.	Genesis	Neh.	Nehemiah	Hosea	Hosea
Exod.	Exodus	Esther	Esther	Joel	Joel
Lev.	Leviticus	Job	Job	Amos	Amos
Num.	Numbers	Ps(s).	Psalm(s)	Obad.	Obadiah
Deut.	Deuteronomy	Prov.	Proverbs	Jon.	Jonah
Josh.	Joshua	Eccles.	Ecclesiastes	Mic.	Micah
Judg.	Judges	Song	Song of Songs	Nah.	Nahum
Ruth	Ruth	Isa.	Isaiah	Hab.	Habakkuk
1–2 Sam.	1–2 Samuel	Jer.	Jeremiah	Zeph.	Zephaniah
1–2 Kings	1–2 Kings	Lam.	Lamentations	Hag.	Haggai
1–2 Chron.	1–2 Chronicles	Ezek.	Ezekiel	Zech.	Zechariah
Ezra	Ezra	Dan.	Daniel	Mal.	Malachi

New Testament

Matt.	Matthew	Acts	Acts
Mark	Mark	Rom.	Romans
Luke	Luke	1–2 Cor.	1–2 Corinthians
John	John	Gal.	Galatians

Eph.	Ephesians	Heb.	Hebrews
Phil.	Philippians	James	James
Col.	Colossians	1–2 Pet.	1–2 Peter
1–2 Thess.	1–2 Thessalonians	1–3 John	1–3 John
1–2 Tim.	1–2 Timothy	Jude	Jude
Titus	Titus	Rev.	Revelation
Philem.	Philemon		

Old Testament Apocrypha/Deuterocanonical Books

Add. Dan.	Additions to Daniel (= Pr. Azar., Sg. Three, Sus., and Bel)
Add. Esth.	Additions to Esther
Bar.	Baruch
Bel	Bel and the Dragon
1–2 Esd.	1–2 Esdras
Jdt.	Judith
Let. Jer.	Letter of Jeremiah (= Baruch chap. 6)
1–4 Macc.	1–4 Maccabees
Pr. Azar.	Prayer of Azariah (often cited as part of the Song of the Three Jews)
Pr. Man.	Prayer of Manasseh
Ps. 151	Psalm 151
Sg. Three	Song of the Three Jews
Sir. (Ecclus.)	Sirach (Ecclesiasticus)
Sus.	Susanna
Tob.	Tobit
Wis.	Wisdom (of Solomon)

Qumran/Dead Sea Scrolls

Qumran documents cited in the text are identified by cave number + Q + document number. Scrolls cited by letter/abbreviation are listed below.

CD	Damascus Document from Cairo Genizah
Hev	Naḥal Ḥever
Hev/Se	Naḥal Ḥever documents formerly attributed to Wadi Seiyal
1QM	War Scroll (*Milḥamah*)
Mur	Murabaʿat
Q	Qumran

Introduction

Title and Hebrew Manuscripts

The title "Numbers" is arguably the worst misnomer in the entire Bible, and at least in recent decades, it has grievously deterred English readers from engaging this essential book.[1] This title comes from the Greek *Arithmoi* (ΑΡΙΘΜΟΙ, source of the English word "arithmetic"), which is not attested until the Septuagint (LXX) codices of the fourth centuries CE and later.[2] This name was adopted into English translations at least by John Wycliffe (1382–95) and famously by the King James Version (1611). The beauty of the Greek and English Bibles notwithstanding, the title "Numbers" is not divinely inspired and gives the wrong impression by suggesting that this book is the Hebrew stepchild of Babylonian and Egyptian mathematics or that it contains lots of genealogies, like what we find in Gen. 5–11 but from the time of Moses. This is not the case. In fact, out of thirty-six chapters, only four contain numerical records (chaps. 1–3 and 26), and even these are not mathematics or genealogies or esoteric to the original audience but instead resemble the ancient literary genre of a military census. More important, these rare numerical sections of the book are acutely *theological*. For instance, the signal military census (chap. 1) was vital for conscripting eligible Israelite young men for war service in Canaan in order to take hold of Yahweh's land promise to the patriarchs and matriarchs. That exodus generation died tragically in the wilderness for their rebellion (chaps. 11–25), rendering the first census obsolete and necessitating

---

1. See Strawn, *Old Testament Is Dying*, 33–34.
2. Namely, Codex Vaticanus (B, 4th cent. CE); Alexandrinus (A, 5th cent. CE); Ambrosianus (F, 5th cent. CE); Coislinianus (M, 7th cent. CE); Venetus (V, 8th cent. CE); see Wevers, *Numeri*, 47. In Codex Vaticanus (B), for example, ornamentation, diacritics, and textual notations were added in the Middle Ages: Šagi, "Codicis B," 3–29; Birdsall, "Codex Vaticanus," 34; Payne and Canart, "Text-Critical Symbols," 106.PP. 89f.

a fresh count of the military troops from the second generation (chap. 26) to inherit the land of promise. The tribal arrangement (chap. 2) centralized Yahweh's dwelling among them (2:17), and the cultic census (chap. 3), still using military terminology, validated the authority of the priests, the sons of Levi, and defined their service in Yahweh's meeting tent to make life with this holy and dangerous God possible.

By contrast, the Jewish title, "In the wilderness" (במדבר, bəmidbar), which dates back to the late Second Temple period or earlier, is quite fitting.[3] This title raises the right kinds of expectations for readers precisely because it is the incipit, the opening words, of Numbers from an original editor, "Then Yahweh spoke to Moses *in the Sinai wilderness* [bəmidbar sînay] inside the meeting tent" (Num. 1:1). This setting distinguishes Numbers from Leviticus, which is self-contained by its own superscription and subscriptions (Lev. 1:1; 26:46; 27:34), which prepares readers for the central wilderness motif in Num. 10:11–21:35.[4] The phrase "in the Sinai wilderness" (bəmidbar sînay) first occurs in Lev. 7:38, where it localizes Yahweh's sacrifices and offerings. The phrase appears eight more times in the OT, all in the book of Numbers, suggesting that Num. 1:1 signals the most important segment of this motif in the Pentateuch.[5] In Numbers, the noun *midbar* refers to one or another "desert," but the translation "wilderness" may offer a slight conceptual advantage since the English word often points to "an area of land that has not been used to grow crops or had towns and roads built on it, especially because it is difficult to live in as a result of its extremely cold or hot weather or bad earth."[6] This is a good start for the geography of Numbers, if we are careful not to think of the wonder of forests or grasslands but of the stigma of desolation and death.[7] In the context of the ANE, the deserts of Sinai, Paran, Zin, and Transjordan were like the primordial chaos, "formless and empty" (tōhû wābōhû, Gen. 1:2). By residing, leading, providing, punishing, and showing immeasurable grace to his covenant people, Yahweh would shape and fill these places, making them suitable for life.[8] *In the Wilderness* is, therefore, a fitting title for the book.

---

3. The heading of the Qumran Numbers scrolls is broken off, but the Jewish title of Genesis, "In the Beginning" (bršyt) is attested in 4QGen^h-title (50–25 BCE) and 4QGen^b (br'šyt, 30–100 CE) and 4QGen^g (br'šyt, late Hasmonean); see Webster, "Chronological Index," 351–446; and Ulrich, ed., *Qumran Scrolls*, 1.

4. See Nihan, *Priestly Torah*, 70–74. Otto ("Ende der Toraoffenbarung," 191–201, esp. 197) argues that Num. 1:1 reflects a post-Pentateuchal redaction, assuming Exod. 33:7–11 and introducing, after the Lev. 27:34 colophon, a Sinai wilderness collection that extends the Mosaic revelation up to the Israelites' departure from the mountain in Num. 10:12.

5. Num. 1:1, 19; 3:4, 14; 9:1, 5; 26:64; 33:15.

6. Cambridge Dictionary, https://dictionary.cambridge.org/dictionary/english/wilderness.

7. See Leal, *Wilderness*, 67–72.

8. See Brueggemann, *Land*, xiv, 27–33.

The primary Hebrew manuscripts of the book of Numbers are the Leningrad Codex of the Masoretic Text (MT[L], 1008 CE);[9] the Samaritan Pentateuch codices (SP, 12th–14th cent. CE);[10] and the scrolls and fragments from the Judean Desert, known popularly as the Dead Sea Scrolls, that contain part of every chapter of Numbers except chaps. 6 (Nazirite vow and Priestly Blessing) and 14 (Israel fears the people of Canaan).[11] The scrolls were discovered in caves 1, 2, and 4 of Khirbet Qumran, a settlement on the northwestern shore of the Dead Sea; a cave in Naḥal Ḥever, a wadi (seasonal stream) near the western shore of the Dead Sea; and a cave in Wadi Murabba‘at (Naḥal Darga), a wadi that runs just southwest of Jerusalem past the Herodium down to the Dead Sea. The two most extensive Numbers scrolls from the Judean Desert come from Qumran and are numbered 4Q23 and 4Q27. The first, 4Q23, is labeled 4QLev-Num[a] (ca. middle to late 2nd cent. BCE)[12] and contains parts of Leviticus together with part of every chapter in Num. 1–5*, 8–13*, 22*, 26*, 30*, 32–33*, 35*.[13] The second, 4Q27, is labeled 4QNum[b] (ca. latter half of the 1st cent. BCE) and contains Num. 11–13*, 15–36*.[14] A theory that many scholars have either adopted or adjusted is that the texts found in the Judean Desert can be classified into four groups based on their alignment or nonalignment with the major text forms of the MT, SP, and LXX.[15] Of 46 Torah texts long enough to serve as a testable sample, 48

---

9. The Aleppo Codex (ca. 930 CE), the earliest Masoretic Text of the Hebrew Bible, is broken and so today does not contain Gen. 1:1–Deut. 28:17.

10. For a clear overview of the SP and its manuscripts (Codex Add. 1846 [1100 CE]; Codex B [1345/46 CE]; Manuscript E [1219 CE]; Abisha‘ [12th–13th cent. CE]), see VanderKam and Flint, *Dead Sea Scrolls*, 93–95.

11. See Ulrich, "Index," 113–29, esp. 121–23.

12. R. Kugler and Baek, *Leviticus at Qumran*, 3.

13. The asterisk denotes select verses within a chapter.

14. There are other extant Qumran manuscripts containing smaller portions of the book of Numbers. 1Q3 (1QpaleoLev, ca. 125–75 BCE) appears to contain parts of Leviticus and Num. 1* and 36* written in paleo-Hebrew script; 4Q121 (4QLXXNum, ca. late 1st cent. BCE–early 1st cent. CE) contains Num. 3* and 4* in Koine Greek, arguably reworking the original LXX (Old Greek) to align with a text form close to MT; 2Q6/7/8/9 (2QNum[a, b, c, d?], ca. late Herodian, 1st cent. CE or post-Herodian) contain Num. 3*, 4*, 7*, 18*(?), and 33*; 5/6ḤevNum. 1a (5/6ḤevNum[a], ca. 50–68 CE) contains Num. 20*; XḤev/Se 1, 2 (XḤev/SeNum[a,b], ca. 50–68 CE) contains Num. 19*, 27*, and 28*; Mur 1 (MurNum, ca. 115 CE) contains Num. 34*, 35*, and 36*; and 4Q365 (4QRP[c] = 4QReworked Pentateuch[c], ca. 40–10 BCE) contains idiosyncrasies: jumping unbroken from 4:49 to 7:1, juxtaposing the stories of the daughters of Zelophehad (Num. 27 and 36), and attaching Deut. 16:13–14 to Num. 29. Another scroll, 4Q65, reflects a Qumran scribal practice and, while close to SP, does not display the "editorial manipulations of SP" (Tov, *Textual Criticism: Collected Essays*, 54). See Ulrich, "Index," 121–23; Bernstein, "4QReworked Pentateuch," 36–37, 42.

15. Tov (*Textual Criticism* [3rd ed.], 107–10) concludes that we have enough unbroken evidence to classify 121 of the 210–12 biblical scrolls. Tov originally spoke of a fifth group, Qumran scribal practice, but now concedes that those texts reveal "diverse textual backgrounds, and not one common typology" (109). Critiquing Tov is Segal, "Hebrew Bible," 5–20.

percent align with the MT or the MT/SP (22 of 46 texts); 11 percent with the pre-SP, that is, the SP text form prior to the insertions of its ideological readings (5 of 46); 2 percent with the presumed source of the LXX (1 of 46); and 39 percent are nonaligned, that is, they do not match the MT, SP, or LXX (18 of 46).[16]

The debate will continue over how to classify each Qumran scroll and fragment of the book of Numbers—that is, whether it resembles the text form of the MT or MT/SP, the SP, the LXX, a mixture of these, or none of these. In my study of the Qumran texts of Numbers, six scrolls do not provide any exegetically significant variants (1Q3; 2Q8; 2Q9; 4Q121; 5/6ḤevNum. 1a; Mur 1), and 4Q365 is idiosyncratic. The other important Numbers scroll, 4Q27, appears to have harmonized (assimilated) to the context or to idiomatic usage in at least fifteen readings,[17] while 4Q23, 11Q19, and 2Q7 appear to have harmonized in at least one place each.[18] Errors due to homophony (words with same sounds) and haplography (omission of a word or letter) as well as clarifying additions and omissions appear in the Numbers Qumran scrolls but not with high frequency.[19] Scribal efforts to clarify the meaning of the text appear in at least nine places in 4Q27.[20] It can be difficult to determine whether one is looking at a secondary reading that is a harmonization to the context (style, phraseology, or content) or an original reading that fits well within its context.[21]

The Qumran scribes formatted four of the extant Numbers scrolls with section or paragraph divisions (4Q23, 2Q6, 2Q7, 4Q27). These divisions reveal some of the most ancient interpretations of the book. By indenting the opening words on a line (about fifteen to twenty letters/spaces to the left of an otherwise justified column) and by writing a line in red ink instead of black, the Qumran scribes reveal their thinking that the text has begun a new discursive unit, however large or small. By leaving a space within a line and by not starting a new sentence but leaving the remainder of a line blank (in an otherwise justified column), the Qumran scribes reveal their conception of a break in the flow of the discourse. Unfortunately, our comprehension of these early scribal hermeneutics is limited because of the fragmentary nature of the extant texts and because we are sometimes left to speculate on why scribes marked paragraphs where they did or did not mark paragraphs where we expect them.

16. Tov, *Textual Criticism* (3rd ed.), 108.
17. Num. 11:32; 16:8; 18:30; 27:22; 29:11, 28; 30:8; 31:48; 32:1, 25, 29; 35:21, 23; 36:1, 4.
18. See 4Q23 in 5:3; 11Q19 in 29:11, 17 (omission); and 2Q7 in 33:52 (omission).
19. In 4Q27 there is possible homophony in 24:6 and clarifying omission in 18:26; in 4Q23 and 4Q365 there is possible homophony in 13:22; and 4Q23 exhibits possible haplography in 1:38; 4:49 (with MT[L]).
20. See 12:6 (2×); 18:26, 28, 31; 22:12, 17, 33; 32:30; 35:27(?).
21. Tov, "Textual Theories," 1:34.

Table Intro.1. Early Section Divisions by Qumran Scribes
(following Ulrich, *Qumran*, 138–74)

	4Q23 (4QLev-Num[a])	2Q6 (2QNum[a])	2Q7 (2QNum[b])	4Q27 (4QNum[b])
First line indented	Num. 5:1; 9:9		Num. 33:50	Num. 22:21; 25:7; 26:4b; 26:12 (? broken text), 15, 63; 29:17 (? broken text); 29:26 (? broken text); 32:16 (? broken text); 33:50 (? broken text)
Blank line				*Between* Num. 35:21 and 35:22
After a sentence, the rest of the line is left blank (the next sentence begins on the line below, either justified right or indented)	*After* Num. 3:4; 3:51 (before 4:1); 4:49 (before 5:1)	*After* Num. 3:39; 3:51 (before 4:1)	*After* Num. 33:49	*After* Num. 11:35 (before 12:1); 15:41 (before 16:1); 16:7 (entire line below is blank before 16:8 begins); 16:15 (? probably, but broken text, may be insignificant because not much space on the line to begin 16:16); 16:50 (before 17:1 = Hb. 17:15 before 17:16); 18:32 (before 19:1); 20:21; 21:12b; 21:20; 22:5a; 22:6; 24:2; 25:6; 26:11; 27:5, 7, 21dβ; 28:15, 31 (? broken text); 29:11 (? broken text); 29:28, 39; 30:16 [30:17]; 31:24, 30, 36, 47, 54 (? broken text); 32:4, 5 (? broken text), 24, 42; 33:20; 35:34 (before 36:1)
After a sentence, a space on the line separates the next sentence (but the next sentence begins on the same line)	*Between* Num. 3:10 and 3:11; 5:4 and 5:5; maybe unintentionally, 11:19 and 11:20 (? broken text)			*Within* 20:13[gloss] (= SP ≠ MT LXX); *Between* 21:11 and 21:12a; 24:10a–b and 24:10c; 26:18 and 26:19; 26:22 and 26:23; 26:25 and 26:26 (? broken text); 26:27 and 26:28; 26:65 and 27:1; 27:17 and 27:18; 27:21 and 27:22; *within* 27:22 (*between* w and the rest of the wayyiqtol form y'ś); Between 27:23 and 27:23[gloss] (= SP ≠ MT LXX)
Written in red ink (no indention or spaces; the column remains justified)				20:22–23 (1.5 lines of text); 21:21[gloss] (1 line = SP ≠ MT LXX); 22:21a–c (indeterminate how much is in red ink because lines below are missing); 23:13a–b (1 line); 23:27 (? probably all of v. 27 is written in red ink, but the line above is missing, so only v. 27d is extant); 31:25 (? maybe through most of v. 26a, but mainly broken); 31:37–38a (? broken text); 31:48 (one line, not entire verse); 32:25; 33:1–2aα

The Samaritan Pentateuch (SP) manuscripts that we have today all date to the medieval period,[22] but the translations of the SP into other languages and other Samaritan literature indicate that the SP goes back much earlier. The Samaritan ideological additions may have arisen from a scribal adherent to the Mount Gerizim sacrificial cult in the second century BCE.[23] These additions are few[24] and can be easily isolated and set aside.[25] What remains is a form of the Pentateuch, often called pre-SP, that predates the Samaritan revision and matches around 11 percent of the testable Qumran Torah manuscripts.[26] In the book of Numbers, the SP includes eight interpolations, which are derived from the historical prologue of Deuteronomy. These primarily transform Moses's first-person speech (Deuteronomy) into third-person narration (SP Numbers):

Deut. 1:6–8	→	SP Num. 10:10
Deut. 1:20–23a	→	SP Num. 12:16
Deut. 1:27–33	→	SP Num. 13:33
Deut. 3:24–28 and 2:2–6	→	SP and 4Q27 Num. 20:13
Deut. 2:9	→	SP and 4Q27 Num. 21:11
Deut. 2:17–19	→	SP and 4Q27 Num. 21:12
Deut. 2:24–25	→	SP and 4Q27 Num. 21:20
Deut. 2:31	→	SP Num. 21:23

Surprisingly, these adaptations from Deut. 1–3 into Numbers were not the work of Samaritan scribes but belonged to the pre-SP form of the text. The best evidence for this is that 4Q27 contains four of the same interpolations in Num. 20–21* (with some spelling differences), and because 4Q27 is broken today with only Num. 11–13*, 15–36*, we can reasonably infer that it originally contained the interpolations in Num. 10, 12, 13.[27]

The pre-SP text form of Numbers must be taken seriously as a witness, which I attempt to do in my text-critical analyses. An important caution, however, is that before the popular SP text came about, the pre-SP text form

---

22. Codex Add. 1846 (1100 CE); Codex B (1345/46 CE); Manuscript E (1219 CE); Abishaʿ Scroll (12th–13th cent. CE); see VanderKam and Flint, *Dead Sea Scrolls*, 93–94.

23. Gallagher, "Samaritan Pentateuch," 105.

24. Tov, "Samaritan Pentateuch," vii–viii.

25. SP inserts "(Mount) Gerizim" as the centralized place of worship (after Exod. 20:17; Deut. 5:18; in Deut. 27:4) and changes "the place Yahweh will choose to put his name" to "the place Yahweh has chosen to put his name" (Deut. 12:5, 14).

26. Tov, *Textual Criticism* (3rd ed.), 108.

27. Also, Tov affirmed to me in an email conversation (07/16/20) that he is not aware of any sectarian SP interpolations in Numbers; see the earlier note on SP inserting "Gerizim" in Exodus and Deuteronomy.

already displayed a harmonizing tendency.[28] This includes (1) linguistic corrections, removing unusual forms and spellings and adapting the text grammatically, and (2) minor alterations in content, interchanging individual letters or entire words.[29] The pre-SP readings vacillate between (1) agreeing with the LXX against the MT, giving us the actual Hb. *Vorlage* of the LXX (this is common); (2) agreeing with the MT against the LXX, strengthening the likelihood of the primacy of an MT reading (common); (3) providing a unique reading, especially the addition or omission of waws and shifts in number (sg./pl.) (common); and (4) agreeing with a Qumran reading against the MT, either with or against the LXX, probably giving us reason to question the MT reading (uncommon).

Although I normally find that the MT reading explains the other variants as secondary, there are instances where I prefer the reading attested in some or most of the other witnesses (esp. 4Q27 SP LXX[ed] Vulg[ed]) against the MT.[30]

Early and Modern Translations

The early translations of Numbers can help us to reconstruct an early Hebrew edition of Numbers and, perhaps more importantly, give us some of the earliest interpretations of the book. The most significant is the Septuagint, the Koine Greek translation, called the Old Greek when referring to the putative (nonextant) first Greek translation of the Pentateuch, probably by Jews in Alexandria, Egypt, in the third century BCE.[31] The Greek translation of Numbers has rightly been characterized as showing "a taste for consistency and harmonisation and a tendency toward clarification and elaboration, involving sometimes major differences from the MT in the arrangement or structure of specific passages."[32] These tendencies, however, are not all the result of interpretive changes by the Greek translator: it has been argued persuasively that harmonizations were already present in the translator's Hebrew source (*Vorlage*) and then were perpetuated by the translator.[33] The textual notes of the translation in this commentary extensively illustrate the harmonizing and clarifying character of the Greek text of Numbers and likely of its Hebrew source.[34] Yet, with the obvious exception of the harmonizations and dynamic renderings, the default translation

---

28. Tov, "Samaritan Pentateuch," ix.
29. Tov, "Samaritan Pentateuch," ix.
30. See 11:4; 12:8; 13:24; 14:21; 18:31; 19:3; 21:30; 22:11; 23:3, 10; 24:3; 26:23; 30:7; 35:5.
31. See B. Wright, "Letter of Aristeas," 322–25.
32. Evans, "Numbers," 64.
33. Tov, "Septuagint of Numbers," 181–201.
34. See translation notes.

technique of LXX Numbers comes closest to a formal-equivalence rendering of its source.[35]

The text of Num. 4 illustrates the harmonization apparent in LXX Numbers. Throughout the chapter we find that all the Hebrew witnesses—Qumran (4Q23[vid]), the MT, and SP—read that the Levites eligible for Yahweh's tent service must be "from thirty to fifty years old" (vv. 3, 23, 30, 35, 39, 43, 47). However, the LXX throughout chap. 4 consistently states that the Levites should be "from *twenty-five* [*eikosi kai pente*] years and above to fifty years" (LXX[ed]). The Greek translator could have expanded the age span to from twenty-five to fifty to match 8:24–25, which begins the Levites' service at age twenty-five.[36] More likely, however, this harmonization was already present in the Hebrew *Vorlage* that the Greek translator was using.[37] To illustrate the dynamic-equivalent renderings in LXX Numbers, consider the report of the ten explorers about the locals in Canaan: "All the people we saw there are huge. We saw the Nephilim there" (13:33c–34a LXX). The term "Nephilim" is transliterated in English translations since it reflects the name of a legendary people group (Gen. 6:4), but the Greek translator, presumably thinking that such a transliteration would not be understood by his readers, describes them as "giants" (*tous gigantas*, v. 34a), a synonym of the preceding genitive "very tall" (*hypermēkeis* for Hb. *middôt* "great stature," v. 32c). In this example, the dynamic rendering "giants" can also be seen as a harmonization to LXX Gen. 6:4, which set a precedent of replacing Nephilim with "giants" (*hoi gigantes*).[38] Finally, let me illustrate what I see as the default "translation technique" of LXX Numbers, formal equivalence. Consider Moses's ruling by the word of Yahweh for Zelophehad's daughters: "What the tribe of the Josephites is saying is right" (36:5b). The Greek translator mistook the adjective *kēn* I (correct, right, accurate)[39] for its homonym, the adverb *kēn* II (thus, in the same manner, so).[40] Instead of attempting a dynamic rendering based on the context, the Greek translator opts for awkward formality: "*Thus* [*houtōs*] Ioseph's sons' tribe are saying."

After the Septuagint, the Aramaic versions of Numbers are next in importance. To the surprise of some, the Aramaic translations of the Hebrew Scriptures, called targums (Hb. *targumim*), characteristically represent the original Hebrew form, word for word, but not always the meaning,[41] and Numbers is no exception to this. All the various targums—Onqelos (Tg[O]), Pseudo-Jonathan (Tg[PJ]), Neofiti (Tg[Neo])[42]—have literal renderings as their

---

35. See Aejmelaeus, "Translation Technique," 531–52.
36. Wevers, *Notes*, 55.
37. Tov, "Textual Harmonization," 1–16; Tov, "Septuagint of Numbers," 181–201.
38. With Wevers, *Notes*, 209.
39. See "*kēn* I," *HALOT* 2:482.
40. See "*kēn* II," *HALOT* 2:482.
41. Flesher and Chilton, *Targums*, 27.
42. In some passages, like Num. 20*, there are Neofiti marginalia, Galilean Targum, et al.

default. For example, Tg^PJ of Num. 22:1–3 represents a one-to-one verbal correspondence with the Hebrew word order but also swaps out a few individual words with meanings that differ from the Hebrew words.[43] The text of Num. 11:34 is illustrative. After the Israelites complain and suffer Yahweh's judgment, the narrator concludes, "So the name of that place was called Kibroth Hattaavah (Graves of Craving), because there they buried the people who had a craving." The Greek and Latin (≈ Syriac) versions do not transliterate Kibroth Hattaavah but instead represent the Hebrew meaning closely as "Tombs of Craving" and "Graves of Lust," respectively (see the second translation note on 11:34). Targums Onqelos and Pseudo-Jonathan translate the genitive more dynamically: "Graves of *the Demanders* [*dimša'ălê*] (Tg^O, my trans.) and "Graves of *the Desirers of the Flesh* [*dmšyyly byšr'*] (Tg^O, my trans.). There are, of course, occasional targumic insertions that explicate difficult texts, such as the one at Num. 16:1. Korah either "took" men as an implied object (many versions) or "took" Dathan and Abiram, but both options have an unclear meaning (undisputed is the verb "took" *wylqḥ* 4Q27 MT SP). Targum Onqelos swaps out the verb so that Korah, with Dathan and Abiram, "made a division" (*w'tplyg*), which makes perfect sense contextually (16:2–3). Targum Pseudo-Jonathan, however, inserts an object so that Korah "took his robe, which was all of hyacinth" (*wnsyb gwlyytyh dkwl' tykl'*), before rising up against Moses (16:2).

Other important early versions include Jerome's Latin Vulgate (late 4th cent. CE) and the Syriac version (a.k.a. Peshitta, ca. 2nd cent. CE). The earliest Arabic translations of the Pentateuch (9th cent. CE) were based on the Syriac.[44] Our study indicates what is true for other biblical books: the Syriac and Vulgate were sometimes influenced by the LXX. For example, in Num. 25:3a the Hebrew narrator writes, "So Israel joined themselves to Baal [*ba'al*] of Peor." The Syriac translator selected the verb, "And Israel *completed itself* [from **šmly*] to Baal Peor," which makes no sense in conventional Syriac usage but makes perfect sense in later Greek usage: "And Israel *was initiated* [*etelesthē*] to Beel-Phegor" (NETS)."[45] Investigation of the Latin Vulgate reveals that its Hebrew source was nearly identical to the MT; although Jerome was careful to represent that source, he was frequently influenced by the exegesis of the LXX and its recensions (Symmachus, Aquila, and Theodotion).[46] Once we isolate the LXX-influenced readings in the Syriac and Latin versions, we then discover that although they were produced later chronologically than the other witnesses (Qumran, MT, SP, LXX), they attest to countless original readings. Their primary value is in giving us a polyphony of early interpretive voices.

43. Flesher and Chilton, *Targums*, 24–26.
44. Griffith, *Bible in Arabic*, 129–32.
45. Weitzman, *Syriac Version*, 71.
46. Tov, *Textual Criticism* (2nd ed.), 153.

There are many reliable modern translations of the book of Numbers. For pragmatic reasons, in this commentary I will interact primarily with seven, produced by translators from three backgrounds—Jewish (NJPS), Protestant/ecumenical (ESV, NET, NIV, NLT, NRSV), and Roman Catholic (EÜ). These seven range from formal equivalence, preserving the Hebrew word order and syntax when possible, to dynamic equivalence, conveying the meaning of the text in common English syntax, style, and idiom.[47]

Formal Equivalence			↔		Dynamic Equivalence	
ESV	NRSV	NJPS	NET	EÜ	NIV	NLT

One potential fallacy that pastors, teachers, and students alike can fall into is thinking that by simply evaluating an array of English translations on a given passage, they are then equipped to choose the best variants (textual criticism) and translational meanings (exegesis). As post-Renaissance interpreters, however, we must rigorously return to the primary sources to ascertain the best text and interpretation. The apostle Paul is an exemplar. Already saturated in the Hebrew and Aramaic Scriptures, Paul expressed a desire while imprisoned to regain possession of the scrolls, probably containing biblical sources, and parchments of either papyri or vellum for his writing (2 Tim. 4:13). The textual notes in this commentary provide an entry into the ancient and modern witness for all who by their "labor of love" (1 Thess. 1:3) study to be "approved by God" in rightly dividing the word of truth (2 Tim. 2:15) so that they are prepared to "preach the word" (2 Tim. 4:2) in season and out.

Literary Genre and Structure

The book of Numbers, as we have said, is not fundamentally a book of numbers but an unfolding story containing an anthology of literary forms through which Yahweh reveals himself and his will. The importance of literary genres cannot be overstated, even if we cannot always reconstruct the oral prehistory of a genre (*Gattung*) in its original life setting in society (*Sitz im Leben*), as Hermann Gunkel and his enduring form-critical school endeavor to do (*gattungsgeschichtliche Schule*).[48] As one teacher has claimed: "You cannot understand what a text means unless you understand how a text means."[49] What a text means, its message, is bound up with how a text means, its literary form.

47. See van der Louw, *Transformations*, 10.
48. See Gunkel's *Sagen der Genesis* (1901) and *Psalms* (1930).
49. John I. Lawlor, 2007, in the course "Hebrew Exegesis: Pentateuch," Grand Rapids Theological Seminary.

The question of the genre of Numbers operates on two basic levels, the book as a whole and the individual units that compose it, but the distinction is not clean. The individual units, or genres of discourse, in Numbers are embedded in one another, so that the interpreter must aim to distinguish each concentric ring of genre based on its form and content.[50]

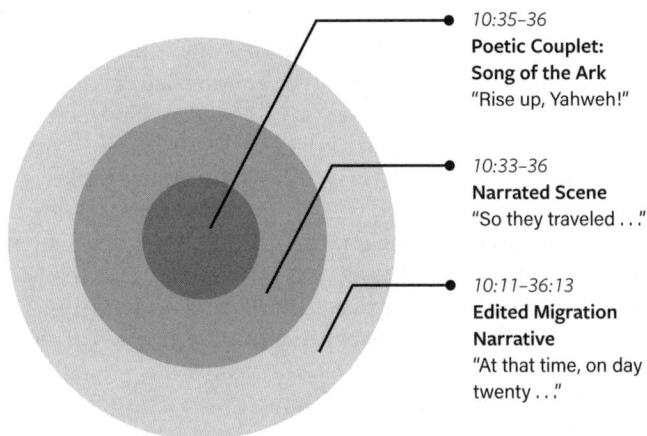

10:35–36
Poetic Couplet:
Song of the Ark
"Rise up, Yahweh!"

10:33–36
Narrated Scene
"So they traveled . . ."

10:11–36:13
Edited Migration
Narrative
"At that time, on day twenty . . ."

Figure Intro.1. Embedded Discourse Genres (I)

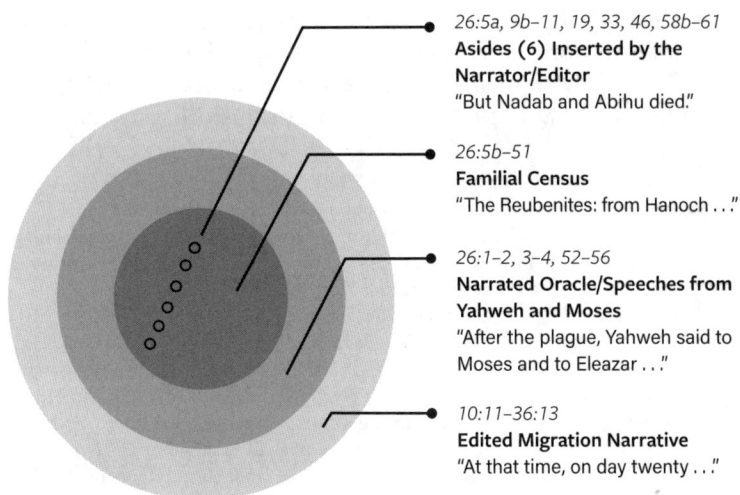

26:5a, 9b–11, 19, 33, 46, 58b–61
Asides (6) Inserted by the
Narrator/Editor
"But Nadab and Abihu died."

26:5b–51
Familial Census
"The Reubenites: from Hanoch . . ."

26:1–2, 3–4, 52–56
Narrated Oracle/Speeches from
Yahweh and Moses
"After the plague, Yahweh said to Moses and to Eleazar . . ."

10:11–36:13
Edited Migration Narrative
"At that time, on day twenty . . ."

Figure Intro.2. Embedded Discourse Genres (II)

50. In figure Intro.2, the "Asides (6) Inserted by the Narrator/Editor" are not one unit but six units dispersed throughout the familial census.

11

These individual units have also been strategically positioned so that together they build the entire structure of Numbers. As a whole, Numbers is a composite, yet essentially coherent, Hebrew narrative[51] and warrants using narrative-critical tools to make sense of it.[52] What are the perspectives and convictions of the storyteller, the so-called implied narrator? How do they[53] withhold and reveal knowledge between characters and readers to create curiosity and suspense? How do they use characterization to advance the story line? How do they use repetition and variation, evaluation (explicit) or representation (implicit) of characters, and other limiting features to guide readers to interpret characters? The Numbers story line is driven by monologues and dialogues, principally from Yahweh to the Israelites through Moses (see 1:1) and from Moses to the people (see 31:14). Many other speakers, however, saturate the story line.[54] One could conceive of Yahweh's monologues as dialogues cut short for readers, if one imagines Moses lingering and responding to Yahweh in the tent, with his ear against the inner curtain (Num. 7:89). In an oral culture, the speeches are critical to advancing the narrative,[55] revealing not just divine *tôrâ* (instruction) but also the characterization of the personae throughout the book.

Moreover, the narrative details of Numbers have led some to support its historicity, some to reconstruct its history, and some to reject its historicity altogether. Persons of faith will generally accept the Numbers accounts as reliable, even though many details cannot be confirmed with archaeological and epigraphic data.[56] Other believers interpret Numbers as a theological narrative, whose transformative power substantiates its divine nature. Those holding to a naturalistic worldview will read Numbers, with its hyperbolic stories and talk of Yahweh as supreme among the gods of the ancient world, as unreliable. Regardless of what one concludes about the historicity of the accounts, the

51. See Frevel, *Desert Transformations*, 23–52.

52. See Alter, *Biblical Narrative* (1981); and Sternberg, *Poetics* (1985).

53. "They" is used for the implied narrator: although scribal education was largely restricted to the male upper class, in Mesopotamia, for instance, princesses and a few other elite females could learn to write (van der Toorn, *Scribal Culture*, 55).

54. Speakers include Yahweh; Moses; unclean men at Passover (9:7); Hobab, Moses's father-in-law (10:30); the Israelites (11:4; 14:2, 4, 7; 16:34; 17:12; 20:19; 21:2); Joshua (11:28); Miriam and Aaron (12:2); Aaron (12:11); Joshua and Caleb (13:30; 14:6–9); the discouraging explorers (13:31); Dathan and Abiram (16:12–14); a collective Edom (20:18, 20); the Moabites (22:4); Balaam, Balak, the Moabite officials, Balaam's donkey, the angel of Yahweh, and Elohim (chaps. 22–24); Moses and Eleazar together (26:3–4); Zelophehad's daughters (27:2–4); Eleazar the high priest (31:21–24); Israel's military officers (31:49); the Gadites and Reubenites (32:2–5, 16–19); and the leaders of Israel's patriarchal families (36:1–4).

55. Alter, *Biblical Narrative*, 79–110.

56. There is no extrabiblical archaeological evidence of Israel's migration and campaigns from Sinai to Moab, only broad Late Bronze Age and Iron Age parallels, including cultural trends, toponyms, onomastics, archaeological surveys, religious parallels (see Hoffmeier, *Ancient Israel*; Wenham, *Numbers*, 81–91).

composition of Numbers presents itself as "assumed historiography"—that is, as a narrative that *claims* to record historical individuals and events, and we should take that claim seriously if we want to read the story on its own terms.[57]

It will continue to be debated whether we can classify the book of Numbers as a *specific form* of historiographic narrative within its ANE literary world. Is it a saga; legend (irrespective of its historicity); report of a campaign, migration, pilgrimage, or procession; or some combination of these?[58] Few would disagree that the book presents "a prophetic or theological history in that it interprets Israel's founding events in terms of God's promises made to the patriarchs."[59] Furthermore, the bipartite structure of Numbers does not mean it conveys essentially two genres—*tôrâ* (instruction) at Sinai (1:1–10:10) versus migratory campaign to the desert valleys of Moab (10:11–36:13). This is because the instructions of part 1 are crafted as a narrative that anticipates the migration, and the migratory story of part 2 is infused with *tôrâ* and concluded by the colophon, "These are the commandments and the decisions that Yahweh commanded the Israelites by the authority of Moses, in the desert valleys of Moab by the Jordan River across from Jericho" (36:13).[60] In its bipartite structure one can see a parallel with the so-called royal novellas of Egypt: "The Egyptian accounts about campaigns and the construction of temples and tombs, mainly contained in the Royal Novellas, frequently consist of two parts, one about the preparation, especially the deliberation in Pharaoh's council, and the other about the actual execution of the campaign or construction."[61]

The first part of Numbers (1:1–10:10) is like the pharaoh's council in the royal novellas: Yahweh as the divine king and Moses as his prophet are preoccupied with preparing for Israel's migration toward and conquest of Canaan. The New Kingdom pharaohs were optimally concerned with subjugating the land of Canaan,[62] and now Yahweh orients his people specifically to conquer Canaan. In the second part (10:11–36:13), the story line turns out to be a migratory campaign on the way to the land,[63] and in that sense it reflects the second part of the royal novella genre. Perhaps more important, the entire composition of 10:11–36:13 is premised on the reader's expectation that the story line should instead be about Israel's conquest of Canaan (10:36b–11:1aα;

---

57. Sternberg, *Poetics*, 25–26; contra Alter's "prose fiction" (*Biblical Narrative*, 23–24).

58. See Knierim and Coats, *Numbers*, 17–23.

59. Wenham, *Numbers*, 29.

60. In 10:10–36:13, Douglas (*Wilderness*, 103, 123) thinks there are alternating law and story sections, but this is unpersuasive.

61. Knierim and Coats, *Numbers*, 21–22. Egypt's royal novellas are not paralleled in Mesopotamian reports that appear to restrict their content to the campaigns themselves.

62. Redford (*Egypt, Canaan, and Israel*, 192–213) notes that Nubia to the south, after the Hyksos age, could be more easily colonized and Egyptianized, but Canaan posed a far greater challenge.

63. See W. Lee, *Migratory Campaign*.

13:30–31; 20:12b; 26:1–2). Israel's definitive conquest, part 2 of the royal novella form, is subverted by the rebellious Israelite community, which takes a generation-long detour to the south and east of the land. At the same time, although the war campaign in Canaan is deferred until the Hexateuch's consummative book of Joshua, the antecedent battles in Numbers—against the Canaanite king of Arad, Sihon, Og, the Midianites, and the Transjordan towns (Num. 21, 31–32)—function rhetorically to assure the audience that Yahweh's power to conquer Canaan is indisputable. Also, the Reubenites and Gadites reimagine that the conquest of the land promised to Abraham did not have to be restricted to Canaan proper (Cisjordan) but could include the Transjordan territories Yahweh had already defeated (Num. 32). In other words, the conquest of the land begins internally within Numbers prior to Joshua. By one reading of Numbers, the Pentateuch's editors imagined Num. 25–36 as a replacement for the book of Joshua,[64] and even if we do not find this persuasive, it points toward an internal coherence to Numbers' plotline of conquest and land inheritance. Finally, the writers of Numbers are skilled in employing ANE genres, and the editors of Numbers have organized the materials in the narrative for compelling reasons, increasing the probability of an overarching literary form, like Genesis as a family history (*tôlədōt*) or Deuteronomy as a political treaty (cf. Esarhaddon's).

Within the bipartite structure of preparation (1:1–10:10) and migratory campaign (10:11–36:12), the thematic movement operates from obedience (chaps. 1–10) to disobedience (chaps. 11–25), so that a strong thematic break occurs not at 10:11 but at 11:1.[65] The thematic cycle of travel→rebel→death dominates chaps. 11–25, so that the geographic (migration) notices form only softer transitions, including the final notice at 22:1b, on Israel's arrival in the Desert Valleys of Moab. On the literary level, the two censuses form an *inclusio* in chaps. 1 and 26, so that the break between 25 and 26 is slightly harder than between 20 and 21 but softer than between 10:10 and 10:11. The effect of the *inclusio* is primarily twofold: the old generation dies in judgment along their journey from Sinai through the wilderness to Moab (Num. 11–25), but a new generation with renewed hope in Yahweh and his land promise emerges from the ashes (Num. 26–36).[66] While interpreters can detect this overarching compositional unity, it is only natural that readers will be mentally preoccupied with the book's substructure: the individual units of discourse, which the editors collect into multiunit segments that share a related theme, whether travel, war, cult, ethics, or land. This chart exhibits the geographical shifts, overarching structure, and substructure of the composition.

---

64. Albertz, "Pentateuchal Redaction," 220–33.

65. Olson, *Death of the Old*, 121–22; Leveen, *Memory*, 81. Wenham (*Numbers*, 13) sees a literary unity with five parts: 1:1–10:10 (Sinai); 10:11–12:16 (Sinai to Kadesh); 13:1–19:22 (forty years near Kadesh); 20:1–22:1 (Kadesh to Moab); 22:2–36:13 (Moab).

66. See Olson, *Death of the Old*, 55, 198; Leveen, *Memory*, 37–39.

Exod. 19:1		Josh. 3←
→ 1:1→Mt. Sinai→10:10	10:11→Migration→22:1a	22:1b→Desert Valleys of Moab→36:12
1:1–10:10/10:36 **Preparations for the Canaan Campaign by Divine Instruction** *Old generation prepares militarily, cultically, ethically	**10:11/11:1–25:18** **Migratory Campaign: Phase I** *Old generation's cycle of travel→rebellion→death (11-25*) *Anticipatory wars (21)	**26:1–36:13** **Migratory Campaign: Phase II** *Campaign and settlement begins in Transjordan (31-32; 34:13-14; see 36:10-12 *New generation prepares familially, cultically, geographically
1 1st CENSUS	OLD GENERATION (EXODUS→WILDERNESS→MOAB)	**26** 2nd CENSUS — NEW GENERATION (MOAB)

1-2 Travel/War	3-4 Cult	5-6 Ethics/Cult a	7:1-9:14 Cult	9:15-10:36 Travel/War	11-12 Ethics	13-14 Travel/War	15 Cult	16-17 Ethics/Cult	18-19 Cult/Ethics	20-21 Ethics/Travel	22-25 Cult/Ethics	26 Travel/War	27 Land	28-30 Cult	31-35 Land	36 Land
1st Census, Camp Arrangement	Levites Belong to Yahweh, Levites in the Meeting Tent	Remove Impurity, Restore Wrongs, Adultery Ritual, Nazirite Vow, Priestly Blessing	Chieftains Dedicate Meeting Tent Altar, Tent Lamps, Consecrate Levites	Passover, Cloud and Fire, Trumpets, Israel Departs from Mt. Sinai	Complaining–Burning–Death in the Camp, Miriam–Aaron Speak against Moses	Explore Canaan, Report Discouraging, Israelites Complain, Invasion Fails	Offerings, Violating Sabbath, Tassels	Korah–Dathan–Abiram Rebel, Aaron's Staff Produces Almonds	Liability and Portion of the Levites, Red Cow Ritual	Israelites Complain, Moses–Aaron Rebel, Edom Hostile, Aaron Dies, Serpent, Defeat of Sihon–Og	Arrival at Moab, Balaam Narrative, Israel Worships Ba`al of Peor	2nd Census	Daughters of Zelophehad Inherit Land, Moses Disinherited, Joshua Succeeds Moses	Sacrificial Calendar, Vows to Yahweh	Midian War, Transjordan Inheritance, Itinerary, Cisjordan Borders, Levite–Refuge Towns	Daughters of Zelophehad Keep Land, Colophon

a. Contra Seybold (*Der Segen*, 61), who sees Num. 6–7 as P's disordered junk pile, a concentric structure of chaps. 1–10 is identifiable (Leveen, "Variations," 208).

Figure Intro.3. Structure of the Book of Numbers

When teaching or preaching from or through Numbers, it is helpful to explain concisely the location of the text within (1) the Hexateuch epic (creation→conquest), (2) the Moses story (Exodus→Deuteromy), (3) the Sinai pericope (Exod. 19:1–Num. 10:10), (4) part 1 (1–10:10/10:36) or part 2 of the book (10:11/11:1–36:13), and finally (5) after the first census (1:1–25:18) or the second (26:1–36:13). This latter category indicates whether the Israelites in view experienced the exodus and will rebel and die in the wilderness (chaps.

1–25) or did not experience the exodus but anticipate life with Yahweh in the promised land (chaps. 26–36).

Composition

Our study of literary genres and structure can be called *synchronic* because we examine Numbers "with time," that is, in its final form now frozen in time. Our study of the book's composition can be called *diachronic* because we examine how Numbers developed "through time," that is, how sources and editorial activity shaped the contours of the book over centuries. Both approaches have value for the Jewish and Christian scholar, teacher, and pastor.[67] Jesus, Paul, and Peter teach that the Torah, Prophets, and Writings were composed by human authors who were guided by the Holy Spirit to write the very words of God.[68] With this as our interpretive boundary, there is no biblical evidence that Moses *composed* the book of Numbers.[69] Instead, Numbers is written in the third person, that is, it presents itself as the product of later scribes, who not only transmitted the words of Yahweh through Moses but also conveyed many short stories and other literary forms (see "Literary Genre and Structure" above) associated with Israel's experience from Sinai to the desert valleys of Moab (1:1a; 12:7). Only rarely do the scribes reveal their inherited sources: "That is why it is said in *The Scroll of the Wars of Yahweh*, 'Waheb in Suphah and the wadis . . .'" (21:14). How, then, did the scribes decide what to include and what to exclude? This is impossible to answer definitively. Communicating the teachings (*tôrôt*) and cherished stories (or testimonies, *ʿēdəwōt*) of Yahweh's character and actions must have been a determining factor (see "Theology" below), but sometimes Numbers gives the impression of being more like an anthology of materials belonging to the Mosaic wilderness tradition.

The scribes of Numbers have left clues throughout their work that they did not belong to the wilderness era: "*When the Israelites were in the wilderness*, they found a man gathering wood on the Sabbath day" (15:32; also 22:4c). So from the text itself, the hermeneutical question arises: In what historical eras did the Hebrew scribes write and later edit the book of Numbers? Contrary to the opinion of some, the way we answer this question does not drastically affect interpretation. The reader can capture the imagery and message of Homer's epic poem *The Iliad*, about the purported Trojan War (13th or 12th

---

67. For a canonical interpretation that appreciates both dimensions of text formation, see Childs, *Old Testament as Scripture*, 60–83.

68. E.g., Matt. 22:29; John 5:39; 2 Pet. 1:20–21; 2 Tim. 3:16–17.

69. As a shorthand citation device, Second Temple scribes began to refer to the whole Pentateuch, from Genesis before Moses through the record of Moses's death, as "the book of Moses" (2 Chron. 25:4; 35:12; Ezra 6:18; Neh. 13:1; Mark 12:26; Tob. 6:13; 7:11–12; 1 Esd. 1:11; 5:49; 7:6, 9) or "the law of Moses" (many times).

cent. BCE), but remain clueless about Homer's own life, his historical context, and the transmission of this epic traditionally attributed to him. Yet there will be some trace effects, just as the writers and producers of today's historical dramas seek to make their films relevant to their contemporary audiences by including themes of interest to them.

Some characteristics in the text can be interpreted as either revealing different sources or stylistic variation by a single author. For instance, scholars will continue to debate whether the interchange of the divine names/appellatives God (*'ĕlōhîm*), Yahweh (*yhwh*), and El (*'ēl*), as in the Balaam Cycle (Num. 22–24), indicate separate sources or stylistic variation. Similarly, redundancy can point toward interwoven sources (Num. 16) or emphasis within a single source (Num. 17). However, three characteristics cannot be explained away as stylistic variation and indicate distinct sources or contributions by subsequent redactors:

1. Competing information: Did Yahweh's cloud, word, ark, or Hobab guide the Israelites in their departure from Sinai (10:11–36; see chart below)?
2. Ideological and perspectival differences: How can Moses be called the most humble man on earth (Num. 12:3) and yet rebel against Yahweh by not honoring Yahweh as holy (deity) in the eyes of the people (20:10–12)?
3. Name and phraseology preferences: Is Moses's father-in-law named Reuel (Exod. 2:18), Jethro (Exod. 18), or Hobab (Num. 10:29–30; Judg. 4:11)?[70]

There is a basic consensus today that the internal evidence from Numbers points toward vacillation between non-Priestly (traditionally JE) and Priestly materials.[71] The Priestly materials are identified generally as P or *Priesterschrift*, "Priestly writing," or particularly as the Priestly *Grundschrift*, "foundational writing" (P^g), and Priestly supplements (P^s).[72] Further analysis of the language of each discursive unit suggests that the compositional process was more complex and included Holiness (H) contributions from the same scribes who wrote Lev. 17–26 and editorial work in two phases: first a Hexateuch redaction (Hex^R), then a Pentateuch redaction (Pent^R). Conceivable but debatable is the theory that the Torah was perfected by three late revisions (Num. 1–10*, 26–36*), which emphasize Israel as a theocratic and hierocratic community ruled by the high priest (*Theokratischen Bearbeitung* = ThB).[73] Similar Priestly revisions are posited by other scholars.[74] A Deuteronomistic composition or redaction in Numbers is also

70. See Baden, "Documentary Hypothesis," 13–33.
71. Even Wenham (*Numbers*, 79), who stresses a unified composition, holds to a fragmentary hypothesis.
72. See two-source (JE and P) of de Vaulx, *Nombres*, and Levine, *Numbers* (2 vols.).
73. See Achenbach, *Vollendung*, 635–38. For a critique, see Nihan, review of R. Achenbach (2006).
74. E.g., PB$^{1–5}$ proposed by Albertz, *Pentateuchstudien*, 471–85.

unclear.[75] Scholars will endlessly debate the date, provenance, and literary parameters (verses and parts of verses) of each source and redaction. Interpreters will also take many different paths to explain how Numbers was integrated into the Pentateuch.[76] The scholarly conflict, however, does not discredit the overwhelming evidence of identifiable sources and unifying redactions.[77] My own approach in this commentary is to note common attributions of sources and redactions but not to speculate about the social and political context of the scribes involved.

The evidence within the book of Numbers indicates a composition that has incorporated available sources, composed new texts, and redacted diverse materials to unify them. How can such a deeply human process correlate with an orthodox view of divine revelation and inspiration? Without assigning dates to the transmission process, of which I am far less confident, below I offer a sketch of the model to which I hold:

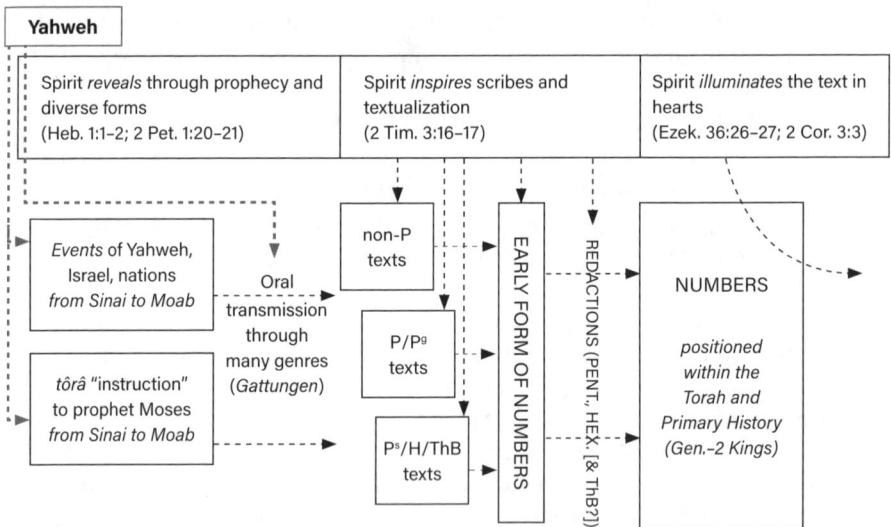

Figure Intro.4. Scripture as Divine-Human Communication

Evangelicals, as well as many Jews and Catholics, believe that the origin of the Scriptures is fully human and fully divine, trustworthy to communicate through human forms the very Word of God. Therefore, the fundamental question is

---

75. See Schmid, *Der sogenannte Jahwist* (1976), positing a Deuteronomistic composition from creation to the fall of Judah; and Erhard Blum, *Komposition des Pentateuch* (1990), arguing for a pre-P D-*Komposition* (KD) in the Moses story. Also unclear is Thomas Römer, "De la périphérie" (2008), with Numbers created to be a bridge between the priestly texts of the Tritoteuch and Deuteronomy (and the Dtr traditions); see critique by Frevel, "Book of Numbers," 20–22.

76. See Frevel, *Desert Transformations*, 53–142.

77. On this logical fallacy, see Wible, "Inflation of Conflict," 280–81.

not whether the oral transmission and textualization of Numbers was a fully human process; the evidence indicates that it was. Rather, the question is How much freedom did the Spirit give to the post-Moses storytellers (oral), scribes, and editors (textual) to shape traditions and sources creatively, even create new texts or redactionally unify diverse materials for theological purposes? If we readily acknowledge the creative genius of books like Job, Jonah, and Esther, why would we not say the same is true of artfully fashioned materials in Numbers? More important, why could the Creator not inspire creative and diverse literature that still faithfully reveals his nature and actions in the world?

Finally, let me offer five points on how the pastor-teacher, even the evangelist, can teach sources and redactional layers in Numbers (or the Pentateuch) for the edification of the body of Christ and glorification of the head, Christ himself (Eph. 4:11–16).

1. When exegeting a passage, *identify intertexts* with the same phraseology, ideations, and theology between the passage and other parts of the Pentateuch (or Hexateuch). Group these together and succinctly describe their unique focus and perspective.

2. *Identify contrasting materials*, apparently from other sources, and find their intertexts elsewhere in the Pentateuch. Scholars have not solved many source and editorial mysteries, so you can make your own observations about the distinct materials in the text.

3. *Summarize the discrete theology of each layer*, whether it is an oral form (originally), source, or redaction. Try to capture each layer's convictions about Yahweh/God and what he desires for his covenant people.

4. When preaching or teaching your passage, *clearly describe the different theologies* coexisting in tension within a given text. Omit scholarly jargon, which will probably confuse and frighten the audience. Each theology can be fruitfully traced throughout the canon to its culmination in the NT witnesses to the Messiah. This step can be compared to appreciating the contribution of each tile in a mosaic.

5. *Explain the overarching theological message* that emerges from the composite form of the text. This is like appreciating the complete image of a mosaic.

While the gospel of Jesus Christ (*euangelion Iēsou Christou*) is singular and not complex (1 Cor. 15:3–4), the gospel can be clarified when the teacher does not conflate the disparate textual layers to say only one thing but allows the polyphonic discourse to bear testimony to God in Christ from different perspectives. A diamond in a dark room looks monochromatic, still lovely, but its beauty is more fully appreciated when sunlight is refracted through its many facets. The following survey of Num. 10 illustrates this approach.

Table Intro.2. Divine Guidance in Numbers 10: From Sources to Theologies to Theology

Verses	Description	Plausible Source	Intertexts (same or related sources)	Theologies	Composite Theological Message
10:11–12 10:13–28, 34	Tent cloud guides the Israelites	P or post-P[a]	Intertexts: →Exod. 13:21–22; 14:19–24; 40:36–38 and Num. 9:15–23*; 14:14 depict customary tent cloud guidance →*Inclusio* with camp departure in Num. 2	Yahweh's cloud in his dwelling place is the source that guides his people to the promised land.	Sovereign Yahweh, by any mode he (not Moses) chooses, has resolved to guide Israel into the land he promised to their ancestors.
10:13	Word of Yahweh, by the authority of Moses, guides the Israelites	P (a second concept)[b]	Intertexts: →Num. 9:18a–b, 20b–c, 23	Yahweh's word by his intermediary Moses is the source that guides his people to the promised land.	
10:29–32	Moses asks Hobab to guide the Israelites through the desert	a non-P[c], self-standing fragment[d], pre-Dtr[e]	Intertexts: →Judg. 4:11 with Hobab as Moses's father-in-law Independent texts: →Jethro as Moses's father-in-law (Exod. 3:1; 4:18; 18*), but in Exod. 18, like Num. 10:29–32, Jethro, not Yahweh, meets Moses's need (contra Num. 11) →Reuel as Moses's father-in-law (Exod. 2:18; cf. Num. 10:29)	Moses does not depend on Yahweh's guidance, but asks his non-Israelite father-in-law, Hobab, to guide the Israelites through the desert.	
10:33	Ark searches for a resting place for the Israelites	non-P[f], *maybe* Dtr[g]	Intertexts: →*Possibly* Josh. 3–4, 6; 1 Sam. 3:3–7:2; 2 Sam. 6; Ps. 132:8	The ark, containing Yahweh's covenant, guides and fights for the Israelites.	
10:35–36	Song of the Ark				

a. Numbers 10:11–28 as P: Gray, *Numbers*, 90–92; de Vaulx, *Nombres*, 141–43; Levine, *Numbers*, 1:303; Seebass, *Numeri*, 2:12–13; but 10:11 not ending P[g] (Frevel, *Mit Blick*, 50, 77–82). Many see vv. 11–12 as P's superscription of vv. 13–28 (Schmidt, *Numeri*, 13). Others distinguish vv. 13–28 from 2:1–31(P) and see vv. 13–28 as post-P (Noth, *Numbers*, 76–77); similarly, Achenbach (*Vollendung*, 635) attributes these verses to his post-P ThB and PentR.

b. But still P or P[g], as Boorer (*Priestly Narrative*, 72) notes the "word of Yahweh through Moses" is characteristic of P[g].

c. JE: Gray, *Numbers*, 92–97; Levine, *Numbers*, 1:311.

d. Seebass, *Numeri*, 2:8.

e. Achenbach (*Vollendung*, 635) also splices vv. 29–32 into PentR and HexR.

f. Römer, "L'Arche," 98–99; Van Seters, *Life of Moses*, 329, 344.

g. Utzschneider, *Heiligtum*, 122.

Ancient Near Eastern Background

Not just words, literary forms, and editorial techniques but the very contents of Numbers bear the marks of the ANE and Mediterranean world.[78] That world has become increasingly clear to us through the history of research in four primary domains: historical geography, archaeology, literature, and iconography.[79]

Historical geography is important because the land, it has been said, functions like the chessboard on which the game of the biblical narrative is played.[80] Consider, for instance, the major expanse of the Hexateuch story when Israel encamps at the edge of the promised land, from Num. 22 through Josh. 3, "along the Jordan River across from Jericho," in what the Hebrew narrator consistently calls the *'arbôt mô'āb*. The great majority of English translators still default in following the KJV's "the plains of Moab," which perpetuates the meaning of the Latin Vulgate, *"campestribus Moab"* (so NRSV, ESV, NASB, NLT, NIV, CEB, CSB). I am convinced that when most readers arrive mentally at the "the plains of Moab" in the story, they imagine flat grasslands without mountains in view. The NJPS supplies a different term, "steppes of Moab," but this gives the same connotation, since a steppe is "a large area of land with grass but no trees, especially in eastern Europe, Russia, and Central Asia."[81] By contrast, what the narrators in the Hexateuch story pictured comes much closer to "the desert valleys of Moab,"[82] since the Israelites encamped on the east bank of the Jordan River basin, of the Jordan Rift Valley, which put them right in the middle of the visible Transjordan (east) and Cisjordan (west) mountain ranges. The adjective *desert* valleys does not appear explicitly in the Hebrew phrase, but it provides additional clarity because the specific area north of the Dead Sea where the Israelites camped is classified as a desert, with only from zero to four inches of annual rainfall.[83] The place Israel camped in Moab stood in contrast to their future home, now visible to them in the form of the spring-fed oasis of Jericho, later called "the city of palms" (*'îr hattəmārîm*; Judg. 1:16; 3:13).

Archaeology is important for many biblical scholars since it provides an independent source for reconstructing the history reflected in the biblical text.[84] This commentary will reflect on the material cultures left behind by Israel's

---

78. Mesopotamia (Iraq, Kuwait, Syria, western Iran), Anatolia (Turkey), the Levant (Syria, Lebanon, Israel), the Arabian Desert (Jordan, Saudi Arabia, and the other Arabian Peninsula countries), Egypt, and the Mediterranean (primarily Greece).

79. See Greer, Hilber, and Walton, *Behind the Scenes of the Old Testament.*

80. Rasmussen, "Encountering the Holy Land."

81. Cambridge Dictionary, https://dictionary.cambridge.org/dictionary/english/steppe.

82. Num. 22:1; 26:3, 63; 31:12; 33:48, 49, 50; 35:1; 36:13; Deut. 2:8; 34:1, 8; Josh. 13:32. For more, see the translation note on 22:1.

83. Rasmussen, *Atlas*, 30.

84. Grabbe, *Ancient Israel*, 6–11.

neighbors insofar as they illuminate Israel's story. For example, the English reader of Num. 33:51–52 may wonder what exactly Yahweh has in mind when he demands: "Speak to the Israelites and tell them, 'When you cross the Jordan into the land of Canaan, you must drive out all the land's inhabitants before you. Destroy all their *carved images* [*maśkît*], destroy their *cast images* [*ṣalmê massēkōt*], and demolish all their *high places* [*bāmôt*].'" Archaeology has revealed many such carved and cast images—humanlike (anthropic), animallike (theriomorphic), and part human- and part animallike (anthropomorphic)—as well as high places (open-air cult platforms) in Canaan and its neighboring lands in the Bronze and Iron Ages.[85] These cultic sites and objects, known to us today through archaeological discoveries, help us to imagine how they enticed the ancient Israelites (cf. 2 Kings 17) and how countercultural it was for Israel to demolish them and remain loyal to Yahweh alone (cf. 2 Kings 23).[86]

Literature and *iconography* from the diverse yet intersecting cultures of the ANE are the most significant extrabiblical domains for interpreting the book of Numbers. Yahweh's, Moses's, and Israel's words and actions can be compared and contrasted with discovered writings (literature) and pictures, cult statues, figurines, and other symbols (iconography) produced by societies contiguous to Israel. The best comparisons will be not just *analogous*, but what Jack Sasson has called *homologous*, comparisons between cultures close in their location, language, and time.[87] Comparing texts or images with a "functionally equivalent genre" is also optimal.[88] Unfortunately, since we cannot verify the time span when or the locations where Numbers was composed and edited,[89] we do not know if we are reaching the ideal of homologous comparisons (location-language-time) of the same genre. However, because there are textual and iconographic trends across the empires of the ANE and over the *longue durée* (long term) of its history, we will find many analogies—some will be homologies—that are germane to reading Numbers in its cultural context. Finally, because literature and iconography always communicate some aspect of the worldview of its culture, temple, or royal institutions, we can often discern when Numbers is assuming, adapting, or rejecting the ethical values and theologies of Israel's neighbors.

Theology

In the commentary proper, I try to answer two questions: (1) How does Numbers portray the nature or character of Yahweh in each of its units of discourse

85. See Hess, *Israelite Religions*, 81–140; Stern, *Archaeology*, 1:478–513.
86. See the "Implications" essay in chap. 30, "Canaanite Cultic Sites."
87. Sasson, "'Mari and the Bible,'" 97–123.
88. Hallo, "Compare and Contrast," 13.
89. See "Literary Genre and Structure" and "Composition" above.

and in its collections of discourse (Num. 1–10, 11–25, 26–36)?[90] (2) How does Numbers compare and contrast Yahweh with the deities depicted in the literature and iconography of the ANE?

The *nature of Yahweh*[91] is arguably disclosed in the literary structure (see above) and in every discursive unit of Numbers. The narrator explains that Yahweh, who sits enthroned between the cherubim, would customarily speak in his meeting tent with his chosen liaison, Moses (7:89). Yahweh reveals himself through a polyphony of voices, which can be briefly illustrated here.

First, as a reminder to obey the covenant terms, the Israelites were to wear tassels on the edges of their clothes (15:38–40), but as a motivation to obey, God self-identifies in the formula now circumscribed by *inclusio* (v. 41):

> I am Yahweh your God,
>> who brought you out of the land of Egypt to be your God.
> I am Yahweh your God.

In the frames, the divine speaker repeats the copula-complement to self-identify by the name Yahweh (*yhwh*),[92] Israel's national deity;[93] in the center, Yahweh explains that he rescued Israel out of Egypt for the purpose of entering into a covenant relationship with them. Thus Yahweh presents the Sinai covenant (Exod. 19–24) as the telos of the exodus (Exod. 1–15).

Yahweh's actions toward his covenant people also communicate his nature. One of several negative examples appears in chaps. 13–14, where ten of the twelve explorers discourage the community from inheriting the promised land, and Yahweh responds by cursing the entire exodus generation to die in the wilderness, outside the land (14:28–35). Does this episode, building on Israel's complaining and insubordination (chaps. 11–12), reveal the limit of Yahweh's patience? Or is it that failing to trust Yahweh to fulfill his patriarchal land promise is so offensive to Yahweh, and a defiant contravention of the covenant, that it invokes Yahweh to exterminate the very Israelites he has just redeemed (cf. Exod. 32–33; Lev. 26:14–39)? Yahweh's actions, even his lack of action, toward *nonelect* nations also reveal his nature.[94] Yahweh

---

90. On thematic and kerygmatic approaches to the book's theology, see Wenham, *Numbers*, 92–102.

91. For this commentary, the vocalization "Yahweh" was selected for reading, teaching, and preaching purposes; otherwise, a vowelless spelling (Yhwh) is better since we still do not know how the divine name was vocalized. Tropper ("Divine Name," 1–21) has made a convincing case that Yhwh was a nominal lexeme of the *qatl*-pattern, with a basic form *yahw (> yahû ≈ Late Babylonian ia-a-ḫu-ú) and a name form with an absolute case ending -a marked by the final h as a mater lectionis, yahwa(h) (≈ ia-a-wa₆).

92. See *GBHS* 9–10, §2.1.2.

93. See the translation note on 10:9.

94. See Kaminsky, "Election," 397–425.

does not order Israel to attack Edom, Moab, or Ammon (Num. 20:14–21; 21:10–20, 24), so do the authors assume the Deuteronomistic theology that Yahweh has given specific territories to these Transjordan peoples (Deut. 2)? Likewise, Yahweh's actions toward the *anti-elect* nations display his nature: he responds favorably to Israel's vow and enables the Israelites to completely destroy (*ḥrm hiphil stem) the Canaanite king of Arad and his towns in the Negev (Num. 21:1–3). Through this abridged scene, both Israel's and Yahweh's loyalty to their word is displayed.

Words to and about Yahweh from the lips of Moses can also communicate theology. In Exod. 34:5–7, Yahweh pronounces his name, Yʜwʜ, and "a virtual exegesis of this name"[95] in a rich creed about his character. Moses innerbiblically prays this creed, with some adjustments, in Num. 14:17–20, and Yahweh responds congruously with his gracious nature by forgiving the Israelites. Moses's theological logic here is rooted in the conviction that Yahweh, as he revealed himself in Exod. 34, is internally predisposed to bless his people.[96] Yahweh affirms this perhaps nowhere more majestically than through the Priestly or Aaronic Blessing (Num. 6:24–26). Similarly, Aaron's plea to Moses on behalf of their skin-diseased sister reveals Aaron's conviction that Yahweh and his intermediary, Moses, are merciful toward repentant sinners (12:11). Other covenant members by their words and actions reveal their beliefs about Yahweh, which, if not questioned or rejected, could be taken as theologically sound. Israel's officers, for instance, believe that Yahweh will be pleased and that atonement can be accomplished on their behalf without a blood sacrifice by their impressive war tribute of gold jewelry (31:48–50). Moses and Eleazar accept this tribute and bring it into Yahweh's meeting tent as a memorial, which implies that they, too, believed Yahweh would accept the bloodless atoning offering (31:51–54; cf. Lev. 5:11–13). Since Torah readers know that Yahweh does reject aberrant offerings (Exod. 32; Lev. 10:1–3), Yahweh's silence in this instance implies his acceptance of the officers' sacrifice and, with it, their theological appropriation of an offering method.

The rituals in Numbers also promulgate Yahweh's nature insofar as the participants embody the values that Yahweh espouses: the consecration of the Levites shows that they belong uniquely to Yahweh (Num. 3, 8, 18); the adultery ritual and vows underscore Yahweh's passion for fidelity (Num. 5, 30); the Nazirite vow beautifully embodies total devotion to Yahweh (Num. 6); the chieftains' lavish altar dedication stresses Yahweh's worthiness to receive extravagant worship (Num. 7); perpetually burning lamps symbolize the light of Yahweh's presence (Num. 8; cf. 6:24–26); trumpets signal movement toward Yahweh's promised land, to fight for Yahweh and worship him (Num. 10); individual sacrifices and the cultic calendar orient Israel toward a

---

95. Fretheim, *Exodus*, 301.
96. See the "Implications" essay in chap. 14, "Exegeting and Applying Yahweh's Character."

lifestyle of Yahweh worship (Num. 15, 28–29); tassels dangling from clothes visually remind the Israelites to obey their deity (Num. 15); the budding of Aaron's staff elevates him and his sons as Yahweh's sole priestly intermediaries (Num. 17); the red-cow ritual enacts Yahweh's demand for purity, physical and spiritual (Num. 19); the raised bronze serpent accentuates Yahweh as the one who provides the means of healing and survival for his rebellious and wounded people (Num. 21); and the leadership-transfer ritual presents Joshua as Moses's divinely appointed successor (Num. 27).

Why should we think the words of non-Israelites about Yahweh's nature should be dismissed a priori? There are no biblical grounds for this.[97] However, the Hebrew storytellers do caution readers against uncritically adopting non-Israelite theology and guidance. Balaam is a perfect case in point (Num. 22–24). He is the Moabite prophet who fails to see the angel of Yahweh in the road (22:21–34), so it is only natural for the reader to question if Balaam's self-introductions are presumptuous, even ironic: "The prophecy of Balaam, Beor's son, the prophecy of *the man whose eye is opened, who sees a vision* from the Almighty, falling flat on the ground *with eyes uncovered*" (24:3–4; also 24:15–16).[98] However, the narrator gives us no clear reason to question the theological perspectives in Balaam's oracles that fit within the guardrails of the Hebrew canon: "I see him, but not now. I look at him, but not near. A star will come out of Jacob, and a scepter will rise out of Israel. . . . One from Jacob will reign" (24:17–19*; see Gen. 49:10; Ps. 2:9; et al.). This stands in contrast to the claims of Job's friends, which the reader must critically appraise since Yahweh in the end says, "You have not spoken about me what is right, as my servant Job has" (Job 42:7c). Can animals, if given a voice, convey theological truths? In a scene of incisive dramatic irony, Balaam's donkey sees and rightly fears the angel of Yahweh in the road, but Balaam, the visionary prophet, does not see or fear (22:21–34).[99] His donkey rebukes him, saying, "What have I done to you that you would beat me these three times?" This retort marks Balaam as a man of questionable character who mistreats an animal, for which God cares.[100] Balaam's way is "perverse" before the angel of Yahweh, while Balaam's reliable donkey saves his life and receives praise and protection from the angel of Yahweh (22:30, 33).

Theological reflection by the authors of Numbers is not confined to the book's own internal discourse but interacts with the conceptions of deity prevalent in the ANE. By *comparing and contrasting* Numbers with the

---

97. Non-Israelite sages in Proverbs include King Lemuel (31:1–9) and Agur (30:1–33) (see Waltke, *Proverbs*, 465); Prov. 22:17–24:22 borrows from the Instruction of Amenemope (see Römheld, *Wege der Weisheit*, 1–12); cf. Dan. 1:4; Acts 7:22; 17:27–28.

98. See the "Implications" essay in chap. 22, "The Irony and Satire of the Balaam Cycle."

99. In dramatic irony, the audience knows the fuller significance of a character's words or actions, but the character remains in the dark (Garmendia, *Irony*, 6).

100. See Prov. 12:10; Jon. 4:11; Matt. 10:29; 12:11.

theologies of ANE literature and iconography, we find fascinating similarities and meaningful differences. As a whole, Numbers consistently mirrors the distinctive worldview of the Hebrew Scriptures that Yahweh, Israel's deity, is transcendent, ontologically distinct from and sovereign over his creation.[101] By contrast, the cultures of the ANE held on to a worldview of continuity: that gods emerge from and ontologically extend the creation.[102] Illustrating this continuity are the cosmogonies of Mesopotamia, Enuma Elish and Atra-Ḥasis, and of Egypt, Memphite Theology. In the book of Numbers, one finds a dominant worldview of divine transcendence, but this appears variously to be contextualized into the surrounding world of divine continuity.[103] For example, Yahweh does not hypostatically inhabit a cult image, but he does place his name—his essence or presence?—on his people (6:27),[104] and the ark comes curiously close to being a tangible extension of Yahweh himself (10:33–36).

Or consider when Aaron and Miriam act insubordinately to Moses, and Yahweh retorts in anger: "I speak with him [Moses] face-to-face, in an appearance and not in riddles, and he looks at the form of Yahweh" (12:8a–b). If "face-to-face" can be explained as an idiom for unmediated, interpersonal communication (as in Exod. 33:11), the synonymous parallelism of "in an appearance" and "the form of Yahweh" most straightforwardly implies that Yahweh takes on a physical form when revealing himself to Moses,[105] perhaps echoing the episode of Yahweh's visible appearance in Exod. 24:9–11. The implication, in view of other aniconic orders (Exod. 20:4–6), is that Israel must not create a form for Yahweh, but Yahweh holds the prerogative to create a form for himself.

One also thinks of Balaam's oracle: "Yahweh their God is with them, acclaimed as king among them. God brought them out of Egypt, *like the horns of a wild bull for them*" (Num. 23:21c–22). The reference to Egypt and Yahweh like a bull draws an association with the Apis bull, one of the earliest gods worshiped by the Egyptians, and the Canaanite and Phoenician god El, who held a common epithet, "Bull El his Father."[106] El, Baal, and other gods were frequently represented iconographically in pictures, cult statues, and figurines as a bull in order to replicate their divine form, symbolize them, or display them with superhuman virility (see the translation note on 23:22).

---

101. J. Oswalt, *Bible among the Myths*, 63–84.

102. J. Oswalt, *Bible among the Myths*, 47–62.

103. On various approaches to ancient Israel's religious and theological contextualization, see Cross, *Canaanite Myth*; Machinist, "Question of Distinctiveness"; Smith, *Monotheism*; Smith, *History of God*; Niehaus, *Themes*; Hess, *Israelite Religions*; Sparks, "*Enūma Elish*"; Sparks, *God's Word*; Enns, *Inspiration and Incarnation*; Arnold, "Singular Israel"; Hilber, *Divine Accommodation*.

104. Cf. Mettinger, *Dethronement of Sabaoth*.

105. See the "Implications" essay in chap. 12, "Did Moses See Yahweh?"

106. Ugaritic: *ṭr ʾil ʾabh* (*KTU* 1.3 V 35–36; 1.4 I 4–15, etc.).

The simile in Num. 23:21–22 comes from the lips of a non-Israelite, who later is killed in divine judgment (31:8, 16); yet as I suggested earlier, it is not at all clear that the narrator reporting his oracle intends for readers to dismiss Balaam's imagery as syncretic. Yahweh, who defeated the Apis bull and the other gods of Egypt (33:4b), is now supplanting the position of El and Baal of Canaan (see the excursus in chap. 22).

Canon and Reception

What can we say about when Numbers was incorporated into the canon of the Hebrew Scriptures? One Numbers scroll from Qumran on the Dead Sea (4QLev-Num[a]) dates to the middle-to-late second century BCE.[107] Also, most Septuagintalists date the Old Greek (original LXX) translation of the Pentateuch to the third century BCE, and Numbers was no doubt included among "the scrolls" (*ta teuchē*) mentioned in the Letter of Aristeas (line 310).[108] This means that Second Temple Jews considered Numbers to belong to the canon of Hebrew Scriptures *before* the mid-third century BCE (*terminus ante quem*). Although we cannot speak precisely regarding the date of the whole composition, we can say that *well before* the third century BCE various textual traditions now incorporated into the book of Numbers were honored in ancient Israelite and Judahite societies. The two silver amulet scrolls inscribed with the Priestly Blessing (Num. 6:24–26) come from Jerusalem around the seventh or sixth century BCE. They were probably used in a private apotropaic ritual,[109] suggesting that common, preexilic Judahites venerated the Priestly Blessing.

Since Gabriel Barkay and his team discovered these amulets by accident, it is not unreasonable to postulate that other Sinai and wilderness stories and instructions were also honored in preexilic Judahite and Israelite societies. Based on analogies of textualization in other ANE cultures, it is conceivable that these texts may have begun as part of a scribal school curriculum and eventually were arranged into the scroll of Numbers and incorporated into the sacred library of the Jewish nation.[110] This theory, which stresses the human role in including some traditions and excluding others from the book, is compatible with divine inspiration. As a NT analogy, the evangelists were highly selective in composing their Gospels (Luke 1:1–4; John 20:30–31; 21:25).

What, then, were the scribes' guidelines for selecting, omitting, and editing the Sinai and wilderness materials to compose the Numbers scroll? We can only guess. But we can invert the question and answer it with confidence: How

---

107. R. Kugler and Baek, *Leviticus at Qumran*, 3.
108. See de Troyer, "Pentateuch," 269–86, esp. 278.
109. See Smoak, *Priestly Blessing*; and chap. 6 in the commentary below.
110. See van der Toorn, *Scribal Culture*, 244–64.

do the materials that made it into the Numbers scroll now contribute to the narrative and theology of the canon of the two Testaments? We can begin to answer this by summarizing nine narrative and theological realities that culminate in the NT witnesses to Jesus the Messiah and the new-covenant people of God that Jesus is creating through his life, death, and resurrection.

1. The final Sinai instructions of Num. 1–10 stress the centrality of Yahweh's presence in the middle of Israel's camps (Num. 2:2, 17; 9:15–23).[111] His presence was itself the ultimate blessing for his covenant people (Lev. 26:11–12; Num. 6:24–27).
   → *John 1:14; Rev. 21:3*

2. After a continuum of Israelite obedience from Lev. 25—when they stone the one who cursed the Name (Lev. 24)—through Num. 10, the reader expects Num. 11 to narrate how Israel follows Yahweh's cloud-fire and moves toward the promised land. Instead, Num. 11 introduces the horrific cycle of journey→camp→complain and rebel→death, which recurs throughout Num. 11–21 and 25.
   → *Matt. 4:1 (cf. Mark 1:12; Luke 4:1); Heb. 3:7–11, 15–19; 4:15–16*

3. When the people of Yahweh slander him or his appointed leaders, this profoundly offends Yahweh, and he righteously punishes them for it (Num. 11–12, 14, 16–17, 20, 21).
   → *Phil. 2:14–15; 1 Tim. 5:17; Heb. 13:17; 2 Pet. 2:9–10*

4. The sins of ingratitude, idol worship, and sexual infidelity transgress Yahweh's boundaries, reflecting his own nature, and must be purged from the community of Yahweh's people (Num. 11–12, 14, 16–17, 20, 25; Lev. 18–20).
   → *Rom. 1:21–25, 32; 1 Cor. 5:1–2, 12–13; 10:1–11*

5. Yahweh's great prophet, Moses, and high priest, Aaron, do not enjoy impunity. Even they fail to honor Yahweh as holy (as deity) in the eyes of his covenant people and thereby forfeit their inheritance in the promised land (Num. 20, 27; Deut. 32).
   → *Rom. 14:10–12; 2 Cor. 5:10; James 3:1*

6. After magnifying his righteous judgment against the old (exodus) generation who rebel against the covenant (Num. 11–25),[112] Yahweh is relentless in his covenant faithfulness to bring the new generation into the land, which he promised long ago to Abraham, Isaac, and Jacob.
   → *Heb. 4:1; 11:8–10; 2 Pet. 3:13*

7. Israel must never put Yahweh to the test by their unbelief and complaining. Even though Yahweh does not tempt his people to sin, he does lead

---

111. See Frevel, *Desert Transformations*, 143–54.
112. Except for Caleb and Joshua (Num. 14).

them into situations where they are tested and tempted (Num. 14:22; cf. Exod. 16–20).[113]

→*Matt. 4:1, 7; 6:13; Rom. 8; 1 Cor. 10:13; Gal. 5; James 1:13*

8. God's people must not fear scarcity or the lethal powers or the unknown future (Num. 11–20), but must trust him to provide everything they need for life with him living in their midst (Num. 6:24–26; chaps. 26–36; cf. Lev. 26:1–13).

→*Matt. 7:11; Rom. 8:35–39; Phil. 4:19; Heb. 13:5–6*

9. Yahweh provides Israel with the sacrificial means to bring him delight, make atonement for their sins, avert his own wrath, and be forgiven (Num. 5, 6, 7, 15, 16, 25, 28–29, 31).

→*Rom. 3:22–25a; 6:23; Heb. 7:26–27; 1 Pet. 2:5*

Finally, if readers today might prefer to skip over Numbers and its companion, Leviticus,[114] it is not because Numbers was overlooked by later biblical authors, rabbinic Jews, or Christian interpreters at any time in the history of the church. Rather, the earliest Israelite, Judahite, and Jewish faith communities received and, by the Spirit's inspiration, shaped the composition of Numbers to convey the dynamic word of God to his people.[115] The student-scribes of preexilic Israel and Judah, exilic Babylon, and Persian Yehud were also being shaped by the Sinai and wilderness texts that they were shaping. In Mesopotamia, Egypt, and Greece, there was a common practice of enculturating the literate elite through oral and written mastery of their cultures' canonical works, like the Epic of Gilgamesh, the Instruction of Dua-Kheti, and the Iliad and Odyssey.[116] In a similar way, the scribes of ancient Israel, Judah, and Yehud fluidly drew upon Numbers and other sacred texts to craft their own works. Sometimes they did this through innerbiblical exegesis and application of Numbers,[117] but sometimes they drew upon other historical sources that differ from the accounts in Numbers.[118] It may be true, however, that most later scribes reused Numbers texts from memory, consciously and subconsciously.[119] Of the countless reflections on the book of Numbers and its enduring power in the lives of individuals and faith communities throughout history, this sampling must suffice.[120]

113. The testing theme emerges predominantly in later reflection on Numbers (Deut. 8:2–3; Pss. 78:18, 40–41; 106:14; Heb. 3:8).

114. See Strawn, *Old Testament Is Dying*, 33–34.

115. See Childs, *Old Testament as Scripture*, 127–35, 194–200.

116. Carr, *Writing*, 287–93.

117. E.g., Fishbane (*Biblical Interpretation*, 329–34) explores the haggadic exegesis of the Priestly Blessing of Num. 6:24–26.

118. E.g., Choi (*Traditions at Odds*, 127–31) discusses the discrepancies between the narrative poem of Ps. 106 and the stories of Num. 11, 14, 16, 20, 25.

119. On memorized reuse, see Bergland, *Reading*, 102–6.

120. See index of Beale and Carson, *Commentary*, 1168–69; also Wenham, *Numbers*, 103–21.

So Moses made a bronze snake and put it on a pole, so that if a snake had bitten someone, when they looked at the bronze snake, they lived. (Num. 21:9)[121]

He [Hezekiah] also crushed the bronze snake that Moses had made, because up until that time the Israelites had been burning incense to it. It was called Nehushtan. (2 Kings 18:4)

And Mōysēs made a bronze snake and set it up on a sign, and it so happened that when a snake was biting a person and they looked at the bronze snake, then they lived. (Num. 21:9 LXX)

But your children were not conquered even by the fangs of venomous serpents, for your mercy came to their help and healed them. (Wis. 16:10 NRSV; cf. 16:5–13)[122]

Just as Moses lifted up the snake in the wilderness, so must the Son of Man be lifted up, so that everyone who believes in him will have eternal life. (John 3:14–15 NRSV; cf. 12:32–34; 19:37)

We should not put Christ to the test, as some of them tested [the Lord], and were destroyed by snakes. (1 Cor. 10:9)[123]

He promises that he would deliver from the bites of the serpent (that is, evil actions, idolatries, and other sins) all those who believe in him who was put to death by this sign, namely, the cross. (Justin Martyr)[124]

So Moses made the bronze snake and put it in a suspended place, and it so happened that when a (the) snake bit a (the) man and he looked at the bronze snake, and he set his heart to the name the word of Y— [Yahweh], then he lived. (Tg[PJ])[125]

To be made whole of a serpent is a great sacrament. What is it to be made whole of a serpent by looking upon a serpent? It is to be made whole of death by believing in one dead. (St. Augustine)[126]

G'd's purpose in commanding Moses to make a snake and for the people to focus on it was to show them that it was not the snake that causes death but the sin. (Bachya ben Asher)[127]

121. MT SP ≈ Vulg, no Qumran MSS. My translations of Num. 21:9, Hb. and LXX; 2 Kings 18:4; 1 Cor. 10:9; Tg[PJ]; and Seebass, *Numeri*, 2:327.
122. Wisdom of Solomon (1st cent. BCE) in the Apocrypha.
123. Possible biblical allusions: Jer. 8:17; Mark 16:18 (Byzantine); Luke 10:19; Acts 28:3–6.
124. Justin Martyr, ca. 100–165 CE (Lienhard, *Numbers*, 242–43).
125. Aramaic Targum Pseudo-Jonathan (4th cent. CE). Targum Onqelos (early 2nd cent. CE) does not include the final phrase about the word of Yahweh.
126. Saint Augustine of Hippo (4th–5th cent. CE) (Lienhard, *Numbers*, 243).
127. Jewish commentator on the Torah (13th–14th cent. CE), https://www.sefaria.org/Rabbeinu_Bahya%2C_Bamidbar.21.9.

Sistine Chapel mural (Michelangelo)

For, just as no healing was conveyed from the serpent to any who did not turn their eyes towards it, when set up on high, so the look of faith only causes the death of Christ to bring salvation to us. (John Calvin)[128]

That hereby he may purchase salvation for all believers: all those who look to him by faith recover spiritual health, even as all that looked at that serpent recovered bodily health. (John Wesley)[129]

One of the principal truths of Christianity, a truth that goes almost unrecognized today, is that looking is what saves us. The bronze serpent was lifted up so that those who lay maimed in the depths of degradation should be saved by looking upon it. (Simone Weil)[130]

As soon as the people asked for forgiveness, God was ready to make this goal possible again. Yet, as an exception, he did not choose to abolish the evil, but to separate the people from the evil by looking at a symbol that would not allow them to forget their failure. (Horst Seebass)[131]

So Moses made a metal snake,
And nailed it to a pole
Sent out the saving word so they would know
That the symbol of their suffering was now the focus of their faith
And with a faithful glance, the healing power would flow. (Michael Card)[132]

128. Calvin, *Harmony*, 137.
129. On John 3:15, from Wesley, *Wesley's Notes*, 197.
130. See the 20th cent. French philosopher and activist Weil, *Waiting for God*, 192–93.
131. Seebass, *Numeri*, 2:327, my trans.
132. Song by Michael Card, "Lift Up the Suffering Symbol" (2012), https://www.invubu .com/music/show/song/Michael-Card/Lift-Up-the-Suffering-Symbol.html.

1

Military Census of the First Wilderness Generation

(1:1–54)

꧁꧂

Overview

Within the Hexateuch narrative, from the creation of the world to the conquest of the land, Num. 1:1–10:10 supplies the final segment of the so-called Sinai Pericope (Exod. 19:1–Num. 10:10). Surprisingly, Num. 1:1–10:10 does not continue the sacrificial and other rituals of Leviticus but rather resumes the instructions of Exod. 25–40 regarding Yahweh's meeting tent, its furnishings, and the priesthood—thus forming an *inclusio* around the book of Leviticus.[1] Even so, the opening chapter of Numbers begins with a superscription (1:1) that continues Yahweh's revelatory speeches from Mount Sinai to the Israelite community below—or to Moses, Aaron, or his sons—primarily but not exclusively mediated through Moses. The Qumran scribes of the second century

---

1. Blum, *Komposition des Pentateuch*, 301. Ruwe (*"Heiligkeitsgesetz,"* 42) contends that the institutions of Num. 1–10*—the tribal census (Num. 1) and arrangement around the meeting tent (Num. 2); the census, tasks, location and consecration of the Levites (Num. 3, 4, 8); and the votive offerings of the chieftains at the sanctuary's consecration (Num. 7)—are all subordinate to the primary institutions of the meeting tent in Exod. 25–40*. The consensus sees Num. 1–10* as growing out of a priestly environment (Cardellini, *Numeri 1,1–10,10*, 44), but many have more specifically assigned it to the Priestly writing (see, i.e., Kellermann, *Priesterschrift*), a Priestly *Grundschrift* "foundational writing" (P^g), or a P-*Komposition* (KP) (Blum, *Komposition des Pentateuch*, 287–32). Others see Num. 1–10* as containing post-P/P^g materials, called supplements (P^s) (Gray, *Numbers*, 1–89), Holiness writings related to Lev. 17–26 (H) (Knohl, *Sanctuary*, 105), a theocratic revision of the Torah (ThB) (Achenbach, *Vollendung*, 638), or other post-P explanations (see Boorer, *Priestly Narrative*, 70–71).

BCE perceived this continuum, and surely other connections, when they copied Leviticus and Numbers together onto a single scroll (4QLev-Numᵃ).[2] In Num. 1:2–16, Yahweh commands Moses directly and Aaron in the third person, with the assistance of the head of each of the twelve tribes, to take a census of the Israelite males, twenty years old and upward, who could fight in Israel's campaigns in Canaan. In vv. 17–19, the narrator recounts the people's obedience to Yahweh in registering themselves and then in vv. 20–43 supplies the census. The chapter closes in vv. 44–54 with the sum of military personnel (vv. 44–46) and an explanation for why the Levites are exempted from going to war: they are to stay back and guard Yahweh's dwelling place (vv. 47–53). The remark that Israel obeys "as Yahweh commanded Moses" (v. 54) recurs at the ends of the subsequent three chapters and editorially unifies Num. 1–4.[3]

Translation

1Then Yahweh spoke to Moses in the Sinai wilderness inside[4] the meeting tent,[5] on day one of the second month in the second year after their exodus from the land of Egypt:[6]
   2"Take a census[7] of the entire Israelite community by their families,[8] by their patriarchs' households,[9] counting the name of every individual male.[10] **3**You and Aaron must enlist[11] everyone eligible for military service,[12] twenty years old and up, by their divisions. **4**A man from each tribe, each the head[13] of his patriarchal household, will assist

---

2. See "Title and Hebrew Manuscripts" in the introduction.

3. Num. 1:54; 2:34; 3:51; 4:49; see Leveen, *Memory*, 34–35.

4. A spatial *b* marking the location within an area (*IBHS* §11.2.5b); cf. *m-* for *min* in Lev. 1:1, "*from out of* the meeting tent."

5. LXXᵉᵈ: "tent of witness"; Tgᴼ: "dwelling place/tent of assembly."

6. Throughout my translation of Numbers, a colon will often represent the complementizer "saying" (*lē'mōr*), which marks reported speech (*BHRG* §20.1.5).

7. Formally, "lift up a head."

8. "Families" (*mišpāḥôt*) is often translated "clans" (NRSV, ESV, NIV, NLT, NJPS), but that term today can have a divisive or even racist connotation (KKK). The Hebrew term refers simply to an association of "very large families" (King and Stager, *Life*, 36).

9. Formally, "by the house of their fathers"; see Stager, "Archaeology," 1–35; Schloen, *House of the Father*.

10. Formally, "by the number of names of every male, by their skulls."

11. Throughout Num. 1–4*, "enlist" renders the verb **pqd*, which in Hebrew and a few Semitic and cognate languages frequently means "'to enroll' or 'to muster' in association with militaristic and/or cultic activities" (Spencer, "PQD," 546).

12. Formally, "all who go out for war [or, in the army]"; LXXᵉᵈ: "everyone who goes out in the force of Israel."

13. "Head" (*rō'š*) refers to a tribal leader, which LXXᵉᵈ captures well by "rulers" or "princes" (*archontōn*). Staubli (*Levitikus, Numeri*, 208, 389) sees a possible resemblance in an Egyptian depiction of a donkey-riding tribe driver in central Sinai.

you.[14] [5]Now these are the names of the men who will assist you.[15] From Reuben, Shedeur's son Elizur.[16] [6]From Simeon, Zurishaddai's son Shelumiel. [7]From Judah, Amminadab's son Nahshon. [8]From Issachar, Zuar's son Nethanel. [9]From Zebulun, Helon's son Eliab. [10]From Joseph's sons: from Ephraim, Ammihud's son Elishama; from Manasseh, Pedahzur's son Gamaliel. [11]From Benjamin, Gideoni's son Abidan. [12]From Dan, Ammishaddai's son Ahiezer. [13]From Asher, Ocran's son Pagiel. [14]From Gad, Deuel's son Eliasaph. [15]From Naphtali, Enan's son Ahira." [16]These were the ones chosen[17] from the community, chieftains[18] of their ancestral tribes. They were the leaders of Israel's thousands.

[17]So Moses and Aaron took these men who were mentioned by their names,[19] [18]and they assembled the entire community on day one of the second month.[20] The people registered themselves[21] by families and patriarchs' households, and the men twenty years old and up were listed individually by name, [19]just as Yahweh commanded Moses. So he enlisted them in the Sinai wilderness. [20]They were as follows:

The descendants of Reuben, Israel's firstborn: according to the family history[22] of their families and patriarchs' households, every male[23]

---

14. Formally, "there must be with you."

15. Formally, "will stand with you."

16. The syntax of vv. 5–15 repeats the pattern: "From/with regard to tribe A [*l* of class, *IBHS* §11.2.10d]: proper name B, namely, the son of C." The format, "Shedeur's son Elizur," calls attention to the ANE societal importance of identifying every son by his father's name.

17. Formally, "the called/named ones."

18. Speiser ("*nāśî'*," 111–17) argues persuasively that *nāśî'* was used by the Priestly authors to designate a pre-monarchic leader who could suitably be called a chieftain, not a prince, and who was responsible for normal administrative processes. The Deuteronomic authors prefer the term *šōpēṭ* (judge) for a political authority relied on in times of crisis.

19. Formally, "who were marked by names"; the niphal verb "were marked" (*niqqəbû*) has a passive sense: their names were acted on by Yahweh in vv. 5–13 (*IBHS* §23.2.2a).

20. LXX[ed], possibly to adjust to Num. 1:1, reads "on the first of the month of the second year."

21. This root in the hithpael stem (*wayyityalədû*) probably indicates a direct-reflexive force whereby the people acted to have their own names recorded on an ancestral list (*IBHS* §26.2c; "*yld*," *HALOT* 2:411–12; "register genealogy," *DCH* 4:213–20).

22. "Family history" (gloss no. 3 of "*tôlədōt*," *DCH* 8:604–5) communicates more closely the meaning of what is often translated as "descendants, successors" ("*tôlədōt*," *HALOT* 4:1699–1700). LXX[ed] seems to perceive this nuance, "according to kindred" (LEH) or "according to families" (NETS). This Hebrew *Leitwort* in Num. 1 creates a literary continuity with the primeval and patriarchal "family histories" (*tôlədōt*) that organize the book of Genesis and that appear later (Exod. 6:16, 19; Num. 1:20, 22, 24, 26, 28, 30, 32, 34, 36, 38, 40, 42). The precise formula in Genesis "these are the *tôlədōt* of" recurs with the progenitors Aaron and Moses in Num. 3:1. See Arnold, "Holiness Redaction"; Tengström, *Toledotformel*; Weimar, "Toledot-Formel," 65–93; Scharbert, "Toledot-Formel," 45–56; Thomas, "*Toledot*" *Formula*, 96–103.

23. In this census "every male" (*kol-zākār*) qualifies only the descendants of Simeon and Reuben (see the descriptor in 1:2) for no apparent reason (Kellermann, *Priesterschrift*, 10).

twenty years old and up, everyone eligible for military service,[24] was listed individually[25] by name. [21]Those who were enlisted from the tribe of Reuben came to 46,500.[26]

[22]From the descendants of Simeon: according to the family history of their families and patriarchs' households, every male (of those who were enlisted)[27] twenty years old and up, everyone eligible for military service, was listed individually by name. [23]Those who were enlisted from the tribe of Simeon came to 59,300.

[24]From the descendants of Gad: according to the family history of their families and patriarchs' households, the men twenty years old and up, everyone eligible for military service, were listed by name. [25]Those who were enlisted from the tribe of Gad came to 45,650.

[26]From the descendants of Judah: according to the family history of their families and patriarchs' households, the men twenty years old and up, everyone eligible for military service, were listed by name. [27]Those who were enlisted from the tribe of Judah came to 74,600.

[28]From the descendants of Issachar: according to the family history of their families and patriarchs' households, the men twenty years old and up, everyone eligible for military service, were listed by name. [29]Those who were enlisted from the tribe of Issachar came to 54,400.

[30]From the descendants of Zebulun: according to the family history of their families and patriarchs' households, the men twenty years old and up, everyone eligible for military service, were listed by name. [31]Those who were enlisted from the tribe of Zebulun came to 57,400.

[32]From the descendants of Joseph, the descendants of Ephraim: according to the family history of their families and patriarchs' households, the men twenty years old and up, everyone eligible for military service, were listed by name. [33]Those who were enlisted from the tribe of Ephraim came to 40,500.

[34]From the descendants of Manasseh: according to the family history of their families and patriarchs' households, the men twenty years old and up, everyone eligible for military service, were listed by name. [35]Those who were enlisted from the tribe of Manasseh came to 32,200.

---

24. Probably "everyone eligible for military service" (*kōl yōṣē' ṣābā'*) is appositional, describing the condition "every male twenty years old and up" (*kol-zākār mibben 'eśrîm šānâ wāma'lâ*); *IBHS* §12.3.

25. Formally, "by their skulls" (see 1:2); like "every male," this phrase qualifies only Simeon and Reuben. "Every male" and "individually" may belong to a later redaction (Kellermann, *Priesterschrift*, 10), or the writer felt no need to repeat this phrase throughout the rest of the census (Judah to Naphtali in 1:26–43).

26. The verb is a qal pass. ptc. from *pqd* (*HALOT* 3:959; *DCH* 6:737–45, gloss 3b) with a subject suffix that functions as a predicate adjective: "*The ones who were enlisted of them* [*pəqudêhem*] of the tribe of Reuben were 46,500."

27. "Of those enlisted" (*pəqudāyw*) occurs in this census only here and may indicate a redactor who clarified the referent as not every male but only those enlisted—but why here and not in 1:20?

36From the descendants of Benjamin: according to the family history of their families and patriarchs' households, the men twenty years old and up, everyone eligible for military service, were listed by name. **37**Those who were enlisted from the tribe of Benjamin came to 35,400.

38From the descendants[28] of Dan: according to the family history of their families and patriarchs' households, the men twenty years old and up, everyone eligible for military service, were listed by name. **39**Those who were enlisted from the tribe of Dan came to 62,700.

40From the descendants of Asher: according to the family history of their families and patriarchs' households, the men twenty years old and up, everyone eligible for military service, were listed by name. **41**Those who were enlisted from the tribe of Asher came to 41,500.

42From the descendants of Naphtali: according to the family history of their families and patriarchs' households, the men twenty years old and up, everyone eligible for military service, were listed by name. **43**Those who were enlisted from the tribe of Naphtali came to 53,400.

44These were the men whom Moses, Aaron, and the twelve Israelite chieftains enlisted, each one representing[29] his[30] patriarchal household. **45**All the Israelite men twenty years old and up, everyone eligible for Israel's military service, were enlisted according to their patriarchs' households.[31] **46**All those who were enlisted came to 603,550. **47**But[32] the Levites, representing their ancestral tribe,[33] were not enlisted among them.[34] **48**Yahweh had said to Moses, **49**"Only the tribe of Levi you must not enlist or count[35] with the other Israelites. **50**But you must appoint the Levites over the dwelling place of witness,[36] over all its

28. 4Q23 reads sg., "From the descendant of Dan" (*lbn dn*), probably due to haplography since this Q fragment elsewhere matches the MT plurals (*lbny '[šr]*, 4Q23 Num. 1:40; Ulrich, *Qumran*, 138).

29. "Representing" interprets the preposition as a *l* of class (*IBHS* §11.2.10d), but the *l* may also be used here to avoid a three-term const. chain (*IBHS* §11.2.10f).

30. SP and LXX[ed] add "his tribe and the tribe of." This may be an early scribal gloss to describe only the chieftains (see 1:4). Instead, MT's "each one representing his father's household" (*'îš 'îš-'eḥād lǝbêt-'ăbōtāyw*) describes all the men who were enrolled in the census (vv. 20–43).

31. Against MT (= Tg° Vulg) "by the households of their patriarchs," SP and LXX[ed] read "by/with their divisions/forces." This reading form creates an *inclusio* with 1:3 that highlights the fulfillment of Yahweh's census stipulation, "by their divisions."

32. "But" (*wǝ*) marks the contrast with v. 46 (*IBHS* §39.2.3b).

33. Formally, "by the tribe of their fathers," in contrast to all other Israelite men who were enrolled "according to their partriarchs' households" (v. 45).

34. LXX[ed] specifies "among *the sons of Israel*," probably to clarify that the Levites were not counted among the Israelite men enrolled in the census.

35. Formally, "you must not enlist, and their head you must not lift up."

36. The head noun, "*The dwelling place* [*miškan*] of witness," is often translated "tabernacle" ("*miškan*," *DCH* 5:527–31, gloss 1: "[tent] tabernacle as dwelling place of Y"; *HALOT* 2:646–47, gloss 4). Whereas "tabernacle" can be archaic in some sociolects of English today, the metonym "dwelling place" draws immediate attention to its primary function in the ancient Near East, which the Priestly authors of the Pentateuch understood, as an abode or dwelling place for the Deity, Yahweh. The metonym, "meeting tent" or "tent of meeting" (*'ōhel mô'ēd*), connotes the

utensils, over all its belongings. They will carry the dwelling place and all its utensils, and they will attend to it,[37] and they will camp all around[38] the dwelling place. [51]Whenever the dwelling place is to set out on a journey, the Levites must take it down; and whenever the dwelling place is to camp, the Levites must set it up. But[39] the unauthorized person[40] who encroaches must be put to death. [52]The Israelites must camp each man with his company, and each man with his division of troops.[41] [53]But the Levites must camp around the dwelling place of witness, so that wrath will not fall on the Israelite community. So the Levites must protect[42] the dwelling place of witness." [54]The Israelites did everything Yahweh commanded Moses. Indeed, they did.[43]

Interpretation

1:1. The two subscriptions of Leviticus doubly concluded Yahweh's instructions from Mount Sinai (Lev. 26:46; 27:34), so this superscription surprisingly restarts the divine revelation that will extend up until the Israelites depart from Sinai (Num. 10:11–12).[44] Numbers 1:1 matches the design of Lev. 1:1 but with some key differences. In Exod. 40:35, even Moses, who spoke directly with Yahweh on Sinai, could not enter Yahweh's presence in the meeting tent (*ʾōhel môʿēd*), the very place a deity in the ANE was supposed to meet with his people.[45] Moreover, in the Priestly texts of the Pentateuch, the meeting tent refers to Yahweh's sanctuary as the place where cultic rituals were performed.[46] So in Lev. 1:1, with Moses outside, Yahweh speaks *from* inside the meeting tent to institute the sacrificial system and thereby provide a means to gradually break

---

place where the Deity, Yahweh, would meet with his people: see Hundley, "Tabernacle or Tent of Meeting?," 3–18. Also see the "Implications" essay in chap. 7, "The Yahweh-Moses Relationship."

37. Formally, "they will serve/minister (at) it."

38. *lə* + *sābîb* meaning, "*All around* the dwelling place" (*BHRG* §39.18e).

39. Fronting activates an identifiable entity in contrast with the entity in v. 51a–b: "the Levites must set it up. *But the unauthorized person who encroaches* must be put to death" (*BHRG* §47.2.1[a]*b*; *IBHS* §39.2.3b).

40. "The unauthorized person" (*hazzār*), elsewhere translated "stranger," in the Priestly literature often refers to a non-priest not authorized to approach the divine dwelling.

41. Formally, "according to his division by their troops." SP: "according to his hand." The rare word *dgl* (division) occurs in the HB only in Numbers (9× in Num. 1–2; 4× in Num. 10) and Song of Songs (1×) (Num. 1:52; 2:2, 3, 10, 17, 18, 25, 31, 34; 10:14, 18, 22, 25; Song 2:4). See the translation note on 2:2.

42. A cognate accusative, formally, "The Levites must guard the guard of" (*wəšāmərû halwiyyim ʾet-mišmeret*).

43. The second proposition of v. 54, "thus they did" (*kēn ʿāśû*), is redundant and emphatic: "Indeed, they did."

44. Otto, "Ende der Toraoffenbarung," 197.

45. See the first translation note on 1:50.

46. See Rhyder, *Centralizing the Cult*, 119.

down the divine-human separation.[47] There is some ambiguity in Num. 1:1: Is Moses now *inside* the meeting tent with Yahweh, listening in the divine presence as he used to do?[48] Locating the place of revelation not on Mount Sinai[49] but "in the Sinai *wilderness*" (*bəmidbar sînay*, Num. 1:1) prepares the reader for the book's major theme of wilderness wanderings (Num. 10:11–22:1).[50] The chronological marker (1:1) giving the date Num. 1:1–10:10 was delivered[51] presents this block of revelation as the next scene in Israel's history, which indelibly began with Yahweh delivering Israel from Egypt. One year after the exodus, Yahweh's dwelling place was set up at Sinai (Exod. 40:17), followed by the month-long revelation of Leviticus (no chronological marker) and then by the nineteen-day revelation of Num. 1–10 (see Num. 1:1; 10:11). Yahweh's grace and power exhibited in his redemption of Israel from Egypt injects the Priestly instructions of Num. 1–10 with theological import.

1:2–16. Yahweh instructs Moses and Aaron to take a census of all the Israelite men eligible to serve in the military, those twenty years old and up (vv. 2–3). Census lists are widespread in the ancient world: from Old Kingdom Egypt, whose army staff counted their troops and pharaohs who issued biennial and annual surveys of land ownership,[52] to Mari (Syria), Ras Shamra (Syria), and Alalakh (Turkey/ancient Syria); from Rome and Greece to India, Japan, and China.[53] These census lists were primarily intended either to levy and collect taxes or to enlist men who were obligated to serve in the military.[54] The census of the exodus generation in Num. 1 and of their surviving children in Num. 26 was not for taxation but for military conscription, as indicated by the recurring qualifier, "everyone eligible for military service" (throughout chap. 1; 26:2).[55] The census does not cover every family member, which one might wrongly infer from the phraseology (v. 2, 18a–bβ), but was specified further as recording only the names of the men qualified to serve in Israel's military, twenty years and older (v. 3, 18bγ).[56] In Exod. 18, rather than consulting with Yahweh, Moses follows the advice of a Midianite priest, his father-in-law, in appointing leaders to assist in adjudication (cf. Num.

---

47. Nihan, *Priestly Torah*, 90–91.

48. See the first translation note on 1:1.

49. Since Exod. 19, "Mount Sinai" (*har sînāy*) has been the central toponym for the Sinai revelation (cf. Num. 3:1; 28:6).

50. See Nihan, *Priestly Torah*, 70.

51. Cf. Brenner, "Introduction," 1.

52. Valbelle, "Les recensements," 37–49, esp. 46.

53. Olson (*Death of the Old*, 73) observes that the Babylonian and Egyptian census lists stem from a centralized administration, whereas the lists from Mari, like Num. 1 and 26, record "manpower among tribal groups."

54. Mendenhall, "Census Lists," 53–54.

55. Contra Albertz (*Israelite Religion*, 2:485), who thinks Num. 1 and 26 are for taxation (Exod. 38:25–26; cf. the temple tax in Exod. 30:11–16).

56. Ashley, *Numbers*, 49.

11:14–17).[57] Here, by contrast, Yahweh preemptively designates by name a patriarchal leader from each of the twelve tribes, who probably functioned like a chieftain over "Israel's thousands" (v. 16),[58] to assist in carrying out this military census, which would be an overwhelming task for Moses and Aaron alone (vv. 4–16).[59] A Mari letter (18th cent. BCE) from Terqa governor Kibri-Dagan to King Zimri-Lim, illustrates the use of assistants in generating a military census.[60] An oath taken by the governor's assistants is not paralleled in Num. 1:5–15, but illuminates the reality that if Israel's tribal leaders were responsible to register their respective tribes, they must have carried this out with a measure of independence, and in their task they proved to be dependable (vv. 18, 44–45).[61]

1:17–43. The same day that Yahweh orders the census, a full thirteen months after the exodus (vv. 1, 18), Moses, Aaron, and the named assistants initiate the census by gathering the people (vv. 17–19), but the narrator credits the people themselves with obeying Yahweh precisely (v. 19; see the second translation note on 1:18). The military census of Israelite males twenty years old and up who can fight for Israel is recorded, tribe by tribe (vv. 20–43). The order in which the tribes are listed differs among the biblical traditions (note the items shaded gray in the table below):[62]

Table 1.1. Order of the Tribes Compared

Birth Order (Gen. 29–30, 35)	Jacob Blesses Sons (Gen. 49)	Prologue to Exodus (Exod. 1)	Chieftain Assistants (Num. 1:1–16)	Military Census (Num. 1:20–43)	Number of Warriors (20+)
Reuben	Reuben	Reuben	Reuben	Reuben	46,500
Simeon	Simeon and Levi	Simeon	Simeon	Simeon	59,300
Levi		Levi			
Judah	Judah	Judah	Judah	Gad	45,650
Dan	Zebulun	Issachar	Issachar	Judah	74,600
Naphtali	Issachar	Zebulun	Zebulun	Issachar	54,400
Gad	Dan	Benjamin	Sons of Joseph: Ephraim Manasseh	Zebulun	57,400

57. Moses's father-in-law is called variously Jethro, Hobab, and Reuel; see "Composition" in the commentary introduction.

58. See the translation note on "ancestral tribe" in 1:47.

59. The Hebrew names in vv. 5–15, and throughout Numbers, have original meanings, which Ambrose (4th cent. CE) interprets allegorically (Lienhard, *Numbers*, 205).

60. Sasson, *Mari Archives*, 189.

61. Sometimes village leaders were resistant or unreliable in carrying out the census: Saggaratum's governor Yaqqim-Adad bemoans that he had to deal severely with the leaders and make them "swear a powerful 'oath of the gods'" to execute their task (Trimm, *Warfare*, 105).

62. See Frevel, *Desert Transformations*, 189–208.

Birth Order (Gen. 29–30, 35)	Jacob Blesses Sons (Gen. 49)	Prologue to Exodus (Exod. 1)	Chieftain Assistants (Num. 1:1–16)	Military Census (Num. 1:20–43)	Number of Warriors (20+)
Asher	Gad	Dan	Benjamin	Sons of Joseph: Ephraim Manasseh	40,500 32,200
Issachar	Asher	Naphtali	Dan	Benjamin	35,400
Zebulun	Naphtali	Gad	Asher	Dan	62,700
[Dinah]					
Joseph	Joseph	Asher	Gad	Asher	41,500
Benjamin	Benjamin	Joseph	Naphtali	Naphtali	53,400
				Total	603,550

The round numbers indicate neither falsification nor specificity but a substantial conscription of soldiers and the respective size of Israel's tribes: Judah (largest), Dan, Simeon, Zebulun, Naphtali, Reuben, Gad, Asher, Ephraim, Benjamin, Manasseh (smallest). All men twenty years old and older were conscripted.[63] It is surprising that there are no stated physical qualifications or exemptions, which one finds elsewhere in the Torah[64] and in the ANE.[65]

The sheer number of registered warriors from the Israelite tribes could be a temptation for self-dependence, boasting, or royal propaganda,[66] but this is not the stress of the narrator in Num. 1, who instead presents Israel's inventory of its military personnel as an act of obeying and therefore trusting Yahweh (vv. 19, 54). This positive perspective contributes to the larger narrative. First, the military size envisions a now populous Israelite tribal confederacy,[67] which implies that Israel has obeyed the Priestly command in Gen. 1:28, and the resultant divine blessing of fertility while in Egypt still describes their present condition in the Sinai wilderness: "But the Israelites were fruitful, increased greatly and multiplied, and became extremely strong" (Exod. 1:7a–c).[68] The

---

63. See the first translation note on 1:3.

64. Deuteronomy 20:5–8 exempts from war: new homeowners who have yet to dedicate their house (v. 5); farmers who have planted a vineyard but have yet to harvest any grapes (v. 6; ca. three years before a vineyard yields grapes); men engaged but not yet married (v. 7); and soldiers afraid of the war (v. 8).

65. See Sasson, *Mari Archives*, 189.

66. See esp. Judg. 7:2, but also, e.g., Deut. 17:16; Jer. 9:23; Ps. 20:7; Zech. 4:6.

67. The census lists of Num. 1 and 26 indicate a tribal alliance in early Israel (see D. Fleming, *Legacy*, 19).

68. On the link between the multiplication formula in Exod. 1:7 and Num. 1*, see Pola, *Priesterschrift*, 145. Furthermore, Exod. 1:7 (*pārû . . . wayyirbû . . . wattimmālēʾ*) echoes the language of Gen. 1:28 (*pərû ûrəbû ûmilʾû*), which corresponds to the creation theology of the so-called Holiness Code of Lev. 17–26; see Tucker, *Holiness Composition*, 70–73, 110–13, 187; Arnold, "Genesis 1," 332–44.

warriors are registered by their family histories (*tôlədōt*), which recalls the family-history (*tôlədōt*) structure of Genesis that correlates with the motif of descendants and Yahweh's resolve to bless all the families of the earth through Abraham's family (Gen. 12:3).[69] Yahweh's promise of fertility to the patriarchs is manifested in Israel's tribal population.[70]

Second, Israel's sizeable army is now poised to overthrow Canaan's inhabitants and actualize the fulfillment of Yahweh's promise of land to the patriarchs.[71] The exodus generation witnessed Yahweh single-handedly defeat Egypt, its deities, and the watery chaos, and they sang, "Yahweh is a warrior; Yahweh is his name" (Exod. 15:3); but Yahweh's omnipotence does not prevent him from often appointing human agents, here Israel's military divisions, to accomplish his redemptive purposes (see Gen. 22:17 and the "Implications" essay below, "Counting the Army").

1:44–54. Verses 44–46 form an *inclusio* with vv. 17–19, which encloses the military census as a unit (vv. 20–43). The stated size of the army, 603,550 strong, equals the sum of the eligible warriors from each tribe (v. 46 = vv. 20–43) and correlates with the 600,000 men of all ages, not counting their dependents, who exited Egypt (Exod. 12:37). If each male soldier had a wife and an average of three children, Israel's exodus generation would exceed two million, a huge number, spawning various reinterpretations of the data.[72] In my view, the Priestly historiographers followed an ancient source, indicated by the randomness of the sum of each tribe's warriors,[73] while they also designed the census literarily to stress the fulfillment of the divine blessing of fertility and military power to possess the promised land of Canaan. It is plausible that the Priestly writers presented Num. 1 and 26 as a taunt of the military censuses of the great Late Bronze Age armies through a literary technique known as elite emulation, in which a peripheral culture's scribes (Israel's)

69. See the first translation note on 1:20.

70. Kellermann, *Priesterschrift*, 16.

71. Gen. 12:1–3; 13:14–17; 15:18–21; 22:16–18; 24:60; 26:2–5; 35:11–12. See Douglas, *Wilderness*, 99–100.

72. The *Vetus Testamentum* journal was a center for this debate between Mendenhall, Barnouin, E. Davies, Humphreys, and Heinzerling. Developing the view of W. M. Flinders Petrie (*Researches in Sinai* in 1906), Mendenhall ("Census Lists," 66) argued that *ʾlp* (normally rendered "thousand") originally referred to a division of a tribe, which drastically reduces the Israelite population to modern sensibilities (see Kitchen, *Reliability*, 264–65). Mendenhall's view is unlikely because the author could have simply supplied the word for "troop" (*ṣābʾā*) or "division" (*degel*) but did not (both are used throughout Num. 2). Jerry Waite ("Census," 487–91) takes *ʾlp* as "troop," but the second part of the number as the men: instead of 46,000 enlisted from Reuben, read "46 troops and 500 men" (v. 21); and instead of a total of 603,550, read "603 troops and 550 men." However, Waite's construction unnaturally bifurcates the typical formation of a Hb. number, and the number of divisions/troops is not reciprocal, as one would expect, with the number of men. For example, Gad would have 59 troops and 300 men, while Benjamin would have 35 troops and 400 men.

73. Mendenhall, "Census Lists," 63.

symbolically mimic the imperial cultures that threaten it (chiefly Egypt and Anatolia, i.e., Turkey).[74] The New Hittite Kingdom to the north loomed large, and the Canaanite city-states were an extension of the enduring New Kingdom Egypt, while a nomadic tribal Israel was camping in a life-threatening desert and afraid of Canaan's inhabitants.[75] The great army of Rameses II (13th cent. BCE) is estimated to have reached 100,000 males, with a field army on the ground made up of divisions of 5,000 men each.[76] The coalition forces of the Hittite vassal states were formidable, although the Hittite army itself may have been only 6,000 strong.[77] Unlike the Deuteronomic portrayal of Canaan's "seven nations more numerous and powerful than you" (Deut. 7:1), the Priestly writers offer a mimicry or even a mockery: the "very, very strong" Israelites in Egypt (*wayya'aṣmû bim'ōd mə'ōd*, Exod. 1:7) now have over six hundred thousand registered male fighters, none of them mercenaries, making the Ramesside and Neo-Hittite forces look impotent and no match for Yahweh's blessed people.

Numbers 1 next turns abruptly to distinguish the Levites because they were not listed with the twelve tribes in the census (v. 47). Joseph's sons, Ephraim and Manasseh, are now independent tribes, converting the original twelve tribes with Joseph and Levi (Gen. 29:32–30:24; 35:16–19) into twelve fighting tribes plus Levi, making thirteen. The divine speech in vv. 48–53 serves as a literary bridge from the census report devoid of Levites (1:2–47) to the wilderness camp arrangement with the Levites and meeting tent at the center (2:1–34).[78] Yahweh explains to Moses the occupational and theological reasons they were exempted from military service (vv. 48–53). Their vocation is to maintain and transport Yahweh's dwelling place, deconstructing and reconstructing it with all its accoutrements during Israel's migration from Egypt into the land of Canaan.[79] If accompanied by holiness, Israel's priests would effectively safeguard Yahweh's presence among his people, a crucial

74. On this technique by P, see Sparks, "*Enūma Elish*," 625–48.

75. See their fear in Num. 13:22–29 and in the stories of scarcity that frame the Sinai pericope in Exod. 16–17 and Num. 11.

76. Gabriel, *Great Armies*, 6. The Wilbour Papyrus, dating to Ramesses V (12th cent. BCE), measures land zones in Middle Egypt for taxation purposes, and the Egyptian male warriors numbered 510,000 within a total population in that region of three million, but scholars believe the numbers are inflated and that the troops there came closer to 75,000 (Spalinger, *War in Ancient Egypt*, 264–65).

77. Gabriel, *Great Armies*, 75.

78. Kellermann, *Priesterschrift*, 32. Numbers 1:48–54 is intertextually connected to 3:5–10; both texts describe the special task of Levi's tribe in service to Yahweh's tent and its equipment. See Achenbach (*Vollendung*, 78–79), who further argues that Num. 1–4* initiates the first layer of a high-priestly theocratic revision of the Torah.

79. In Canaan the Levites continued transporting the ark containing the covenant until Solomon's temple was constructed (2 Sam. 15:24; 1 Kings 8:4; 1 Chron. 15:2, 14). Their function in the second temple, including gatekeeping, was complex (see 1 Chron. 9*; Leuchter and Hutton, *Levites and Priests*).

responsibility first assigned in the Sinai narrative to Aaron and his sons (Lev. 8–16, 21–22), and then expanded to the Levites (Num. 1–4, 7–8, 18, 31, 35).[80] The particulars of how the Levites must protect and maintain the meeting tent, which will affect the entire community, are specified later, in Num. 3–4.[81] Across the ancient Near East, not only priests but also others protected the deity's temple. Egypt's pharaohs, represented by giant stone statues (colossi) at the monumental gate (pylon), protected the temple from chaos and so preserved *ma'at*. In Canaan, basalt guard lions flanked the entrance to the Area H temple in Hazor.[82] In Assyria, protective deities (*kāribu*), a storm bird (*anzû*), and terrifying creatures like colossal lions were stationed in front of the portals and the inner sanctuary of the deity dwelling within. By contrast, winged statues of lions or bulls with human heads (*lamassu*) typically guarded Assyrian palaces. Along with statues of frightening creatures that defended the sacred space, the Hittites also considered the temple door, door bolt, and hearth as deities or spirits that deterred evil.[83] In Num. 1, neither human leaders, nor creatures, nor the meeting tent itself was deified, but the Levites were appointed as professional guardians of the physical space of Yahweh's dwelling, an integral function of cultic personnel in the ANE.[84]

The narrator closes the unit in v. 54 with the second statement of Israel's obedience, which this time is redundant and emphatic (see the translation note on v. 54). With a formidable army (vv. 20–46) and Yahweh's presence guarded by his priests, who cared for, transported, and protected his dwelling place (vv. 47–53); with the leaders enacting their orders (vv. 17–19, 44); and with people responding to Yahweh in full obedience (vv. 19, 54), nothing but geography stands in Israel's way of conquering and inhabiting Canaan with divine blessing.

Implications

Counting the Army: Trusting in Human Power or in God?

In the story of the Pentateuch, the censuses of Num. 1 and 26 register soldiers for war to fight for and occupy the land of Canaan as the fulfillment of Yahweh's promise to the patriarchs.[85] The military census of Num. 1, however,

---

80. See Nihan, *Priestly Torah*, 90, 93; Knohl, *Sanctuary*, 152.

81. Cardellini, *Numeri 1,1–10,10*, 96.

82. Keel, *Die Welt*, 110.

83. Hundley, *Gods in Dwellings*, 39, 43, 65–66, 73, 97, 101.

84. For the Hittite priesthood, with two guarding functions similar to the Levites (outer precinct) and priests (inner precinct), see Milgrom, "Shared Custody," 204–9; Taggar-Cohen, "Covenant Priesthood," 22.

85. Militant imagery appears in Gen. 22:17 and is echoed in 24:60; the land promise appears in Gen. 12:1; 15:13–21; 17:8.

presents a narrative twist because the exodus from Egypt was held up as the pattern for the conquest of Canaan: Yahweh alone, without Israel's armies, fought to bring Israel out of Egypt (Exod. 14:14; 15:17), so also Yahweh would bring Israel into the land of Canaan by sending his "hornet" to defeat and disinherit Canaan's inhabitants (Exod. 23:27–31; 33:1–2; 34:11; cf. Ps. 44:1–3). Later Yahweh told Gideon to dramatically thin out the number of his warriors against Midian, so that Israel would not boast, "Our own strength has delivered us" (Judg. 7:2). In a notoriously enigmatic text, Yahweh incites David and then punishes him for counting all the people, but the narrator's remark reveals that David's interest, and therefore pride, was in the number of "soldiers" and "warriors who could handle a sword" (2 Sam. 24:9).[86] So which is it in the book of Numbers? Israel takes Canaan through huge numbers of warriors (Num. 1; 26), with the temptation of arrogance and amnesia of the exodus? Or Yahweh alone fights for Israel and takes all the glory?

Later in Numbers it becomes clear that these approaches are not mutually exclusive. After Israel departs from Sinai and explores the land of Canaan (Num. 10–13), Caleb stresses their human capacity to conquer (13:30), while Joshua and Caleb also stress the cruciality of divine backing (14:6–9). Furthermore, the pattern of a divine promise achieved through a mobilized, powerful army is found elsewhere in ANE literature. For example, from LBA Ugarit comes an epic in which the god 'Ilu informs King Kirta that his future child-bearing wife would be a war captive. 'Ilu announces that Kirta will dispatch an army of formidable size to capture his wife in order to bring about the fulfillment of his promised child.[87] Or consider the divine-human symbiosis in war, for example, when Assurnasirpal II (883–859 BCE reign) rides into battle with his stretched bow while the god Assur, represented as a winged disc, fights in unison in the sky.[88]

So also in Num. 1, and later in 26, it is a false dichotomy to pit divine promise and sovereignty against human forces in the fulfillment of Yahweh's redemptive purposes, but this highlights the fine line that God's people often face when God himself finally, usually after some agonizing delay, makes his people powerful and directs them to use their power for his appointed ends. The NT authors use this divine-human collaboration in warfare as a metaphor for the obedient and victorious Christ-follower. Hebrews venerates

---

86. David's census, 2 Sam. 24 (2 Chron. 2:17), is difficult to interpret (Park, "Census and Censure," 21–27), but violates the spirit of the law of the king in Deut. 17:14–20, which commands the king to read the *tôrâ* and prohibits the king from multiplying horses (military power), gold (glory), or wives (foreign alliances, sexual and spiritual infidelity).

87. "The Kirta Epic," COS 1.102:334. Kirta's army, "three hundred myriads" (*tlt . mat . rbt*: Parker, ed., *Ugaritic*, 15). This could refer to a countable three million (Rendsburg, "Additional Note," 393) or to myriads times three, which better fits with the ensuing synthetically parallel lines of incalculable soldiers and archers (see Num. 23:10).

88. Stone relief from Northwest Palace at Kalhu (Nimrud) (British Museum, rooms 7–8).

Gideon, Barak, Samson, Jephthah, and David—war machines of controversial character—alongside godly Samuel and Israel's honored prophets, all as those who conquered enemies by faith (Heb. 11:32–34). To the Corinthians, Paul explicates the divine source of their power and the spiritual nature of their warfare for Christ, who alone is worthy of obedience requiring a disciplined and submissive mind (2 Cor. 10:3–6).[89]

89. See also Rom. 7:23; 2 Cor. 12:9; Eph. 6:10–20; 1 Tim. 1:18; 6:12; 1 Pet. 2:11; James 4:1. *Christus Victor* is in John 16:33; Eph. 1:20–23; Col. 2:13–15; 1 Cor. 15:54–57; 1 Pet. 3:22; Rev. 5:5. God and his forces fight victoriously in Rev. 2:16; 12:7; 19:11, 14.

2

Military Arrangement
of the Wilderness Camps

(2:1–34)

⁓◦⁓

Overview

After the narrator's commentary (1:44–54), Yahweh continues speaking, this time to Moses and Aaron (cf. 1:1) regarding the arrangement of the tribes and the order in which the tribes would set out to travel, implicitly from the Sinai wilderness to Canaan (2:2–31). So far the Moses story has not been concerned with these details in Israel's travels from Egypt to Sinai (Exod. 15–18/19*) or during their stay at the base of Mount Sinai (Exod. 19:2–Num. 1:54), but now for over a month they have lived with Yahweh's freshly constructed meeting tent stationed ambiguously somewhere in their midst (see Exod. 40:17; Num. 1:1). Numbers 2 eliminates this ambiguity by giving Yahweh's meeting tent pride of place as the geographical center of Israel's tribes. The divine instructions for the tribes' military formation and their order of departure for Canaan (Num. 2:3–31) are preconditioned by the command "They must camp facing and surrounding the meeting tent" (v. 2). The core location and departure of the Levites with the meeting tent (v. 17)—along with the narrator's disjunctive, "But the Levites were not enlisted among the Israelites" (v. 33), a variation of 1:47—has led some to see only a soft break between Num. 1 and 2 and appreciate the literary unity of Num. 1:48–2:34 in distinguishing the Levites in their exceptional station and role.[1] As in 1:19,

---

1. See Kellermann, *Priesterschrift*, 17–32. Seebass ("Eigene Komposition," 88–89) argues that Num. 1–2 and 36 begin and end a self-standing, edited story that only prepares for, but

47

54, here again the narrator concludes the unit with the Israelites' response of precise obedience to Yahweh (2:33–34).

Translation

1Then Yahweh spoke to Moses and Aaron: **2**"The Israelites must camp, each in his division[2] by the banners of their patriarchs' households. They must camp facing and surrounding[3] the meeting tent.

3Those camping to the east, toward the sunrise, will be the division of Judah's camp by their troops. The chieftain of the people of Judah is Amminadab's son Nahshon. **4**Those who were enlisted in his troop came to 74,600. **5**Those camping next to them will be the tribe of Issachar. The chieftain of the people of Issachar is Zuar's son Nethanel. **6**Those who were enlisted in his troop came to 54,400. **7**Next[4] will be the tribe of Zebulun. The chieftain of the people of Zebulun is Helon's son Eliab. **8**Those who were enlisted in his troop came to 57,400. **9**All those who were enlisted in relation to[5] Judah's camp, by their troops, came to 186,400. They will travel first.

10On the south will be the division of Reuben's camp by their troops. The chieftain of the people of Reuben is Shedeur's son Elizur. **11**Those who were enlisted in his division came to 46,500. **12**Those camping next to them will be the tribe of Simeon. The chieftain of the people of Simeon is Zurishaddai's son Shelumiel. **13**Those who were enlisted in his division came to 59,300. **14**Next will be the tribe of Gad. The chieftain of the people of Gad is Deuel's son Eliasaph. **15**Those who were enlisted in his division came to 45,650. **16**All those who were enlisted in relation to Reuben's camp, by their troops, came to 151,450. They will travel second.

---

does not initiate, the land and its capture. Knohl (*Sanctuary*, 83) posits 1:48–54 and chap. 2 as late Holiness additions to a so-called Levite Treatise.

2. SP has the pl., "divisions" (*dglyw*). This military term, appearing first in 1:52, occurs in Northwest Semitic inscriptions to denote "a subdivision of a military colony (detachment < standard, banner), consisting of foreign reserve-troops" ("*dgl*," *DNWSI* 1:240–41). In Numbers the term seems to be restricted to Israelites, since each division associates with "the households of their patriarchs" (2:2), with no mention of foreigners or immigrants (cf. *gēr*, "immigrant," in chaps. 9 [2×], 15 [7×], 19 [1×], 35 [1×]).

3. I interpret "facing" (*minneged*) and "surrounding" (*sābîb*) asyndetically as two distinct modifiers of the camps' relative position to the meeting tent (similarly NRSV, ESV, EÜ). "Facing" (*minneged*) correlates with the Israelites' custom of watching Moses enter the meeting tent while "they would stand at the entrance of their tents" (Exod. 33:8; see 40:38).

4. "Next" clarifies the asyndeton (MT Tg[O]; conj. in SP LXX[ed]).

5. "*Of* the camp of Judah" (LXX[ed] has *ek*; NRSV, NET) is misleading for *l* since the number is the summation of Judah, Issachar, and Zebulun together (vv. 3–9). Rather, it is a specification *l*, "in relation to" or "with regard to" (*IBHS* §11.2.10d; see nos. 18–19).

[17]Then the meeting tent will travel with[6] the Levites' camp in the middle of the camps. Just as they camped, so they will travel by their divisions,[7] each one in his position.[8]
[18]On the west will be the division of Ephraim's camp by their troops. The chieftain of the people of Ephraim is Amihud's son Elishama. [19]Those who were enlisted in his division came to 40,500. [20]Next to them will be the tribe of Manasseh. The chieftain of the people of Manasseh is Pedahzur's son Gamaliel. [21]Those who were enlisted in his division came to 32,200. [22]Next will be the tribe of Benjamin.[9] The chieftain of the people of Benjamin is Gideoni's son Abidan. [23]Those who were enlisted in his division came to 35,400. [24]All those who were enlisted in relation to Ephraim's camp, by their troops, came to 108,100. They will travel third.
[25]On the north will be the division of Dan's camp by their troops. The chieftain of the people of Dan is Ammishaddai's son Ahiezer. [26]Those who were enlisted in his division came to 62,700. [27]Those camping next to them will be the tribe of Asher. The chieftain of the people of Asher is Ocran's son Pagiel. [28]Those who were enlisted in his division came to 41,500. [29]Next will be the tribe of Naphtali. The chieftain of the people of Naphtali is Enan's son Ahira. [30]Those who were enlisted in his division came to 53,400. [31]All those who were enlisted in relation to Dan's camp came to 157,600. They will travel last, by their divisions.
[32]These are the Israelites, enlisted according to their patriarchs' households. All those who were enlisted in the camps, by their divisions, came to 603,550. [33]But[10] the Levites were not enlisted among the Israelites, as Yahweh had commanded Moses. [34]The Israelites did[11] everything that Yahweh had commanded Moses. This was how they camped by their divisions and how they traveled, each by his family and with[12] his patriarchal household.

Interpretation

2:1–2. Yahweh now speaks to both Moses and Aaron, which occurs less frequently than speaking to Moses alone, although in the Pentateuch it

6. "With" marks the anacoluthon of accompaniment (*b*, et al.; cf. LXX[ed], "and") or agency (*l*); *GBHS* §4.1.

7. "By" (*l*) subdivides the tribal camp into smaller parts (also 2:31, 34; "normative," *GBHS* §4.1.10.i).

8. Formally, "each upon his hand."

9. "Benjamin" (*binyāmin*, son of the right hand) is spelled Benjamim (*bn ymym*, son of days) in SP Genesis and Numbers.

10. "But" (*wə*) marks the contrast with v. 32 (*IBHS* §39.2.3b).

11. The wayyiqtol "the Israelites *did*" (*wayyaʿăśû*) likely expresses Israelite obedience to the whole divine speech (2:1–33; as 1:54).

12. "With" for an accompaniment *l* (*GBHS* §4.1.16g).

occurs most frequently in Numbers.[13] Yahweh orders Moses and Aaron, apparently without requiring help from the tribal leaders as occurred in 1:4–17, to direct the Israelites (1) to camp in their military divisions, which contained a cluster of patriarchal households marked by a banner, and (2) to station their camps "facing and surrounding the meeting tent" (see the second translation note on 2:2). In this military camp formation, Israel's orientation toward and around Yahweh's meeting tent may seem counterintuitive, given that their sights were set externally northward in anticipation of their war campaign in Canaan. The centripetal function of the meeting tent, however, would be a constant visual reminder that meeting with their deity, Yahweh, in his tent was more important than, yet also essential for, overcoming external threats to their survival in the wilderness, such as water and food shortage (Exod. 15:22–17:7), attacks from foreign armies (Exod. 17:8–16), adjudicating conflict in the community (Exod. 18:1–27), or even swiftly inheriting the promised land.[14] In effect, the Priestly text of Num. 2 restructures Israel's wilderness society to exhibit the preeminence of Yahweh's presence, which was already underscored in the Yahweh-Moses dialogue in the aftermath of the golden-calf apostasy: "My presence will go with you, and I will give you rest," to which Moses responded, "If your presence does not go [with us], do not bring us up from here" (Exod. 33:14–15).

2:3–16. In the core of the unit, Yahweh orders the tribe of Judah, followed by Issachar and Zebulun, to camp to the east and depart first when Israel migrates to its next location (vv. 3–9). These tribes in the signal position total 186,400, the most formidable grouping (cf. group totals in vv. 15, 24, 31). In the next group, Reuben, followed by Simeon and Gad, must camp to the south and depart second (vv. 10–16). Like the military census of Num. 1, the recurring language used here is martial: (1) the Israelites are to camp in their tribal *divisions*, each by a *banner* (v. 2);[15] (2) each tribe's eligible fighters are divided into *troops*, and each tribe is collectively called a *troop* (vv. 3–31);[16] and (3) these terms set the context so that *camping* evokes the image of an army camp, with *chieftains* as tribal commanders.[17] The summation of eligible soldiers, given in Num. 1:20–46, is repeated again here, probably

---

13. Exod. 6:13; 7:8; 9:8; 12:1, 43; Lev. 11:1; 13:1; 14:33; 15:1; Num. 2:1; 4:1; 4:17; 14:26; 16:20; 19:1; 20:12, 23.

14. "As heaven on earth, the welfare of the [Mesopotamian] temple and its resident was deemed absolutely essential for the welfare of the nation and its residents" (Hundley, *Gods in Dwellings*, 77).

15. See the first translation note on 2:2 about "division"; "banner" occurs frequently in war contexts (Exod. 17:15, *Yhwh nissî*).

16. *Ṣāb'ā* (troop, standard) elsewhere refers to military service, an army, or war, sometimes with nonmilitary meanings.

17. On "chieftain," see the second translation note on 1:16; contextually *nāśî'* referred to tribal officers in wartime (Josh. 9:15–21; 13:21; 22:30, 32). *Maḥăneh* (camp) often occurs in

not reflecting separate sources but clarifying that these camps—now with an assigned chieftain, camping position, and order of departure—are composed of the same warriors just registered in Num. 1.[18] The military quarters are not separated from the community; instead, the warriors, alongside their civilian families and the Levites, are to camp and march together northward to the great battlefields of Canaan.[19]

2:17. Breaking the literary pattern of vv. 3–16 and vv. 18–24, in v. 17 the opening subject is not the Levites but the meeting tent, which will travel with the Levites' camp in the center of all the camps.[20] The next qualification for the Levites is also unparalleled: "Just as they camped, so they will travel by their divisions, each one in his position" (v. 17b). When Israel journeys, the Levites must stay in the same positions, with their divisions, in which they camp. Their precise stations around the meeting tent with Moses and Aaron will be supplied later (3:23, 29, 35, 38). Whether moving or stationary, the Levites in their divisions are to retain the same positions in order to transport and protect the building materials and furnishings of the meeting tent, which Yahweh ordered in 1:53 (see the comments there). The centralized tent of Yahweh, tended and guarded by the Levites, may replicate the ANE tradition of a king pitching his tent in the center of his military camp (see the "Implications" essay below, "The Centrality of God's Presence"). In any case, the weight of the divine residence in Israel's encampment renders the Levites' circumscribing presence and cultic vocation both prodigious and mysterious.

2:18–31. After v. 17 breaks the literary flow, the pattern resumes in vv. 18–31 as Ephraim, followed by Manasseh and Benjamin, is commanded to camp to the west and depart third (vv. 18–24). Finally, Dan, followed by Asher and Naphtali, must camp to the north and depart last (vv. 25–31). The combined divine instructions from Num. 2–3 envision the following camping arrangement and marching order:[21]

---

war contexts; see *ḥnh qal for armies camping in position to fight in Judges (6:4, 33; 7:1; 9:50; 10:17 [2×]; 11:18, 20; 15:9; 18:11–12; 20:19).

18. Numbers 1 and 2 are interconnected, and the lack of any mention of sanctuary preparations may distinguish Num. 1–10 from what one would expect in a putative base layer of P^g (Pola, *Priesterschrift*, 78; Achenbach, *Vollendung*, 485). Achenbach (*Vollendung*, 638) attributes Num. 1–2 to the first layer of the theocratic revision of the Torah, which centers on Yahweh's sanctuary, Israel's order, and its claim on the land.

19. Through the Negev (13:17); but Israel's rebellion (13:28–14:45) results in a circuitous migration, eventually to enter Canaan from Moab, in the east (Num. 16–36).

20. Cf. Ezekiel's temple city, with the prince and faithful Levites in the center (48:21–22).

21. Cf. Buis, "Livre des Nombres," 11. Against the basic sense that Levi moves collectively in 2:17, Buis thinks Gershon-Merari departed with the dwelling place after Judah-Issachar-Zebulun, and Kohath departs with the sanctuary after Reuben-Simeon-Gad.

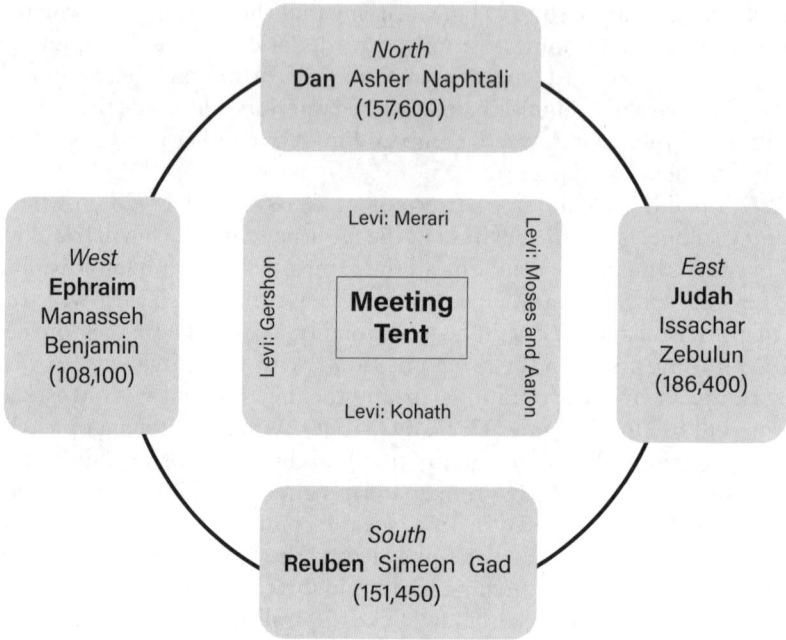

Figure 2.1. Camp Positions

The four clusters of three tribes may be laid out in the general location of the tribes in Canaan: Dan, Asher, and Naphtali in the north of Canaan (see Judg. 18*); Manasseh, Ephraim, and Benjamin would be west and central, but here the Levites alone must inhabit the center with the meeting tent; Reuben and Simeon are southern tribes with Gad on Reuben's northern border. The grouping that does not neatly fit this schema is Judah, Issachar, and Zebulun, but it could be explained as assimilation to prior lists in which these three are frequently contiguous.[22] Also, Leah's sons Judah, Issachar, and Zebulun on the east counterbalance Rachel's sons, Joseph (Ephraim, Manasseh) and Benjamin, on the west.[23] The layout exhibits a series of concentric rings that function as multiple protective layers around the divine presence, which is stationed above the atonement lid of the ark containing the covenant inside the most holy place:[24] radiating outward from the divine presence, the sequence is cherubim [→ incense, Lev. 16:13] → inner curtain → incense → outer curtain → bordered courtyard → Levites → twelve tribes. Moses and Aaron are stationed to the east of the meeting tent for pragmatic reasons, giving

22. Judah, Issachar, Zebulun (Gen. 35:23; 46:12–14; Exod. 1:2–3; Num. 1:7–9, 26–31); Judah, Zebulun, Issachar (Gen. 49:8–15); Issachar, Zebulun (Gen. 30:18–19).
23. Douglas, *Wilderness*, 100.
24. See Exod. 25:22; 30:6, 36; 40:34–35; Lev. 16:2.

them ease of access to the courtyard gate on the east side (Exod. 27:13–14; 38:13–15; the temple gate is also on the east side: Ezek. 8:16). In addition, the reason could be symbolic: the meeting tent faces eastward, toward the rising sun, reminding Israel of the illuminating divine presence resident among them (Num. 6:25; Ps. 84:10–11).

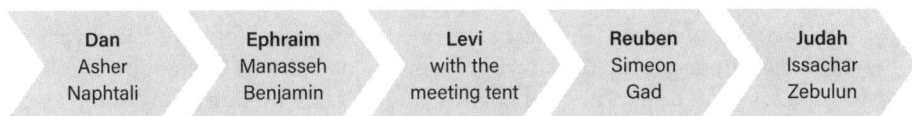

Dan	Ephraim	Levi	Reuben	Judah
Asher	Manasseh	with the	Simeon	Issachar
Naphtali	Benjamin	meeting tent	Gad	Zebulun

Figure 2.2. Travel Order

The order in which the tribes depart and travel (see fig. 2.2 above) does not follow any other OT order for Israel's tribes,[25] but one might surmise that Jacob's prominent sons were assigned the signal positions. Judah is a fraternal leader and warrior king (Gen. 37–49*, esp. 49:8–12; notable in 1 Chron. 12:24; Rev. 7:5);[26] Reuben is the firstborn (Gen. 29:32; 49:3). Jacob blessed Joseph's younger son, Ephraim, in place of Manasseh, the older (48:13–20), and he blessed Dan as a judge and warrior associated with divine deliverance (49:16–18).

2:32–34. After Yahweh stops speaking, the narrator summarizes and formally encloses the camp arrangement and order of departure (vv. 3–31). This recalls the narrator's parallel language in 1:45–54, which brought closure to the military census of chap. 1:

Numbers 1:45–54	Numbers 2:32–34
[45]All the Israelite men twenty years old and up, everyone eligible for Israel's military service, were enlisted according to their patriarchs' households.	[32]These are the **Israelites**, enlisted according to their patriarchs' households.
[46]All those who were enlisted came to 603,550.	All those who were enlisted **in the camps, by their divisions,** came to 603,550.
[47]But the Levites, **representing their ancestral tribe,** were not enlisted among them.	[33]But the Levites were not enlisted among the Israelites, **as Yahweh had commanded Moses.**
[48]Yahweh had said to Moses, [49]"Only the tribe of Levi you must not enlist. . . . [53]But the Levites must camp around the dwelling place of witness, so that wrath will not fall on the Israelite community. So the Levites must protect the dwelling place of witness."	

25. See table 1.1, "Order of the Tribes Compared"; and Olson, *Death of the Old*, 56–57.

26. On a historiographical relationship between the royal tribe of Judah and the prominent sons of Aaron, see Galil, "Sons of Judah," 488–95.

Numbers 1:45–54	Numbers 2:32–34
[54]The Israelites did everything Yahweh commanded Moses. **Indeed they did.**	[34]The Israelites did everything that Yahweh had commanded Moses. **This was how they camped by their divisions and how they traveled, each by his family and with his patriarchal household.**

The theological reason why the Levites were not enlisted for military service (1:48–53) is alluded to by the citation formula "as Yahweh had commanded Moses" (2:33).[27] The exceptional Levites, however, are offset by the emphasis on the participation of all Israel in community life with Yahweh.[28] The primary stress of 2:32–34, illuminated by the unique text (in bold), is that the military personnel registered in the Num. 1 census are to camp and travel in their divisions, with their families and extended families. Living with their kindred is an ever-present reminder to all that this war campaign is also a mass migration of families onto foreign soil. Unlike Israel's patriarchs and matriarchs, who lived in or near Canaan's urban centers as landless immigrants (Gen. 23:4) and occasionally fought to defend themselves (Gen. 14), Yahweh now leads the Israelite families to become revolutionary immigrants, whose husbands and fathers and sons would fight for their families, to control and occupy the homes, cities, vineyards, and cisterns belonging to other people groups.[29] In the end, Yahweh's promise to give Canaan to Israel as an inheritance, repeatedly announced at Sinai,[30] along with the continuum of the Israelites' total obedience (Num. 1:19, 54; 2:34) generates the expectation in characters and readers alike that camping and traveling will soon reach its forecasted end in Canaan.[31]

Implications

The Centrality of God's Presence

By analogy to the layout of Israel's encampment, the army of Rameses II, while campaigning against the Hittites, camped in a rectangular formation around his royal tent.[32] A relief in the Abu Simbel temple (bordering modern Sudan) displays Rameses's centralized tent with several similarities to Yahweh's: the main room is veiled by curtains (cf. Exod. 26:33; 35:12); in the anteroom, some people plead for help against the invading Hittites (cf.

27. See Fishbane, *Biblical Interpretation*, 163. Origen believed the Levites' exclusion from the twelve tribes pointed to their eminence over Israel (Lienhard, *Numbers*, 206).
28. Olson, *Death of the Old*, 110–11.
29. Cf. Lev. 14:34; Deut. 6:10–12; 7:1; 8:7–10.
30. Exod. 32:13; 33:1; Lev. 14:34; 18:3; 23:10; 25:2, 38.
31. See Sternberg, *Poetics*, 376–78.
32. Gressmann, *Texte und Bilder*, 2:33n50; de Vaulx, *Nombres*, 71.

Exod. 33:8–17; "facing" in Num. 2:2); and apparently the royal tent was the largest (cf. Exod. 26*; 27:9–21).[33] Later the Greek historian Xenophon (ca. 431–354 BCE) described Cyrus the Great's tent in the middle of Persia's army camp in several ways that would have been true of Yahweh's tent as well: Cyrus's tent was luxurious (cf. Exod. 35–36*), in the most secure location encompassed by "his most trusty followers" (cf. Num. 2:17) and armed soldiers (cf. martial imagery of Num. 1–2*), and surrounded by identifiable and accessible officers (cf. named chieftains in Num. 2:3–31).[34] Against this backdrop, there are two ways to interpret Num. 2:17: (1) the sanctuary and not the king is to be the center of Israel's society;[35] or (2) in light of the glory of Yahweh that fills and appears from the meeting tent,[36] Yahweh is the king who has taken up residence in the center of his people's military encampment. Either way, if Yahweh not only possesses Israel as his people (Lev. 20:26) but also created the heavens and earth (Exod. 19:5; 20:11; 31:17), then wherever he pitches his tent becomes the *axis mundi* (axis of the world), a continuum that extends from heaven through earth and into the abyss below.[37] When encountered in history or grasped by faith, the presence of Yahweh in time and space reorients everything.

Yet God's localized presence, around which the social fabric of his people must revolve, has taken a dramatically different form according to the New Testament authors. The dwelling place of God is no longer a chosen mountain, tent, or temple but is the incarnate Son of God, Jesus of Nazareth.[38] God's glory no longer inhabits the most holy place, but by the Spirit indwells, both individually and collectively, his new covenant people, the church.[39] At the same time, the Son today is physically with the Father, interceding for his holy ones and preparing a place for them,[40] while the sealing "Holy Spirit . . . is the *down payment* of our inheritance, *until the redemption of God's own possession*" (Eph. 1:13–14 NET, italics mine). In other words, both the Son and the Spirit together are even now orienting us toward the consummation of all things, when God will come to live forever, tangibly and geographically amid his people in the new Jerusalem of the new heavens

33. The royal tent may have also contained the army's sanctuaries (Gressmann, *Texte und Bilder*, 2:33). On tent parallels and historicity, see Homan, *To Your Tents*, 89–185.

34. See Trimm, *Warfare*, 503–4.

35. Albertz, *Israelite Religion*, 2:485. Noth (*Stämme Israels*) thought the pre-monarchic league of twelve tribes organized around a central shrine resembled the later Delphi (Greek) and Italian amphictyonies.

36. *Kəbôd yhwh* in the meeting tent in Exod. 40:34–35; Lev. 9:6, 23; Num. 14:10 (cf. vv. 21–22); 16:19, 42; 20:6.

37. Levenson (*Sinai & Zion*, 122–25) applies *axis mundi* from Eliade, *Comparative Religion*, 375. See Hundley, *Gods in Dwellings*, 3–4.

38. John 1:14, 18; 4:19–24; Col. 1:15, 19; Heb. 1:1–3.

39. 1 Cor. 3:16–17; 6:19; 2 Cor. 6:16; Eph. 2:21.

40. Rom. 8:34; John 14:1–3.

and the new earth.[41] What are we supposed to do with this already-not-yet tension? While we must never represent God in the form of any image,[42] we have freedom in Christ to benefit from aesthetics, architecture, and rituals that pull our affections forward to the day when the residential arrangement of Num. 2 becomes a permanent reality for God and his people: "Look! *God's tent [hē skēnē tou theou] is among the people. He will live among them [skēnōsei met' autōn], and they will be his people, and God himself will be with them*" (Rev. 21:3; cf. v. 22).[43] Religious traditions that stress the importance of liturgical symbolism can help us in this regard. To offer one illustration, Joseph Cardinal Ratzinger addresses the relatively recent liturgical renewal, in the aftermath of Vatican II, that rearranged the Eucharist to be *versus populum* (toward the people), in which the priest and congregation face each other without obstructions in the communal meal. Ratzinger argues that this is a misreading of the Last Supper layout, and I would add, departs from the God-centered orientation of the people and the Levites illustrated in our passage, with the camp "facing and surrounding the meeting tent" (Num. 2:2). Today the officiating priest and congregants watch each other while the altar cross and the Lord it symbolizes have been decentralized, but to what end?

> Moving the altar cross to the side to give an uninterrupted view of the priest is something I regard as one of the truly absurd phenomena of recent decades. Is the cross disruptive during Mass? Is the priest more important than Our Lord? This mistake should be corrected as quickly as possible; it can be done without further rebuilding. The Lord is the point of reference. He is the rising sun of history.[44]

41. See Wolters, *Creation Regained*; Wittmer, *Heaven*; Beale, *Temple*; Middleton, *New Heaven*.
42. Exod. 20:4–6; Deut. 6:8–10; Acts 17:16, 29–31; 2 Cor. 6:16; 1 Thess. 1:9; 1 John 5:21. See Beale, *Idolatry*.
43. Alluding to LXX Pentateuchal language of Yahweh's "tent" (*skēnē*; Awabdy, *Leviticus*, 23–28).
44. Ratzinger, *Spirit of the Liturgy*, 84.

3

The Levites Belong to Yahweh

(3:1–51)

Overview

The narrative has already established the Levites' exclusion from Israel's military service, their special service to Yahweh's meeting tent, and their special camping position around the centralized meeting tent (Num. 1:47–53; 2:17, 33). Those instructions all marked off the Levites as the exception to Israel's overarching tribal structure, but now the narrator turns to the Levites as the exclusive subject of chaps. 3–4. This shift into an extended discourse on the Levites (Num. 3–4) suggests that the sporadic Levite remarks of chaps. 1–2 were not superfluous but the seedbed for the editor's primary interest in the Levites in Num. 1–4. The unit begins with the initial family history (*tôlədōt*) of Aaron (vv. 1–4), which is a display of his importance in the history of Yahweh's people. In vv. 5–10, Yahweh appoints the tribe of Levi to assist Aaron and his sons in executing the responsibilities of the meeting tent. In vv. 11–13, Yahweh explains that he has chosen the Levites for himself as a surrogate for Israel's firstborn sons. The ensuing Levite census of vv. 14–38 may surprise readers since the Levites were not to be listed among the other tribes, which is somewhat ambivalent (Num. 1:47–49; 2:33). The stress of the census, unlike Num. 1, is not on numbers per se but on the separate tasks in and around the meeting tent that Yahweh designates for Gershon (vv. 21–26), Kohath (vv. 27–32), and Merari (vv. 33–37). Through a series of framing devices, the narrator slows down the closure of the unit (v. 10//v. 38; v. 15//v. 39; vv. 11–13// vv. 40–43). Yahweh's final two speeches to Moses in vv. 40–43 innerbiblically revise prior, foundational firstborn legislation by counting the Levites and their livestock as substitutes for Israel's firstborn sons and livestock.[1] This unit is then augmented by Yahweh's speech in vv. 44–51 prescribing the giving of redemption money, which resolves the problem of 273 firstborn Israelites who exceeded the number of Levites.

Translation

[1]Now these are the family histories[2] of Aaron and Moses when Yahweh spoke with Moses on Mount Sinai. [2]These are the names of Aaron's sons: Nadab, the firstborn, and Abihu, Eleazar, and Ithamar. [3]These are the names of Aaron's sons, the anointed[3] priests, whom he had ordained to serve as priests.[4] [4]Nadab and Abihu died before Yahweh when they offered strange fire before Yahweh in the Sinai wilderness. They had no children, so[5] Eleazar and Ithamar served as priests with[6] Aaron their father.

[5]Then Yahweh spoke to Moses: [6]"Bring the tribe of Levi near, and stand them before Aaron the priest so that[7] they may serve him [7]and keep his responsibilities and the responsibilities of the whole community before the meeting tent, by performing the dwelling-place service.[8] [8]They must care for the furnishings of the meeting tent and for the responsibilities of the Israelites, by performing the dwelling-place

1. See Exod. 13:2, 11–15; 22:29–30; 34:19–20; Lev. 27:26.

2. "These are the family histories" (*'ēlleh tôlədōt*) occurs as a structuring formula throughout Genesis to introduce a genealogy of or narrative about a progenitor's descendants (2:4; 5:1 [with *spr*, scroll]; 6:9; 10:1, 32; 11:10, 27; 25:12, 19; 36:1, 9; 37:2; outside Genesis and Num. 3:1, see Ruth 4:18; 1 Chron. 1:29; cf. similar phrases in Exod. 1:1; 6:16, 19). Kellermann (*Priesterschrift*, 46) contends that P in Num. 3:1 augments the final *'ēlleh tôlədōt* clause in Gen. 37:2 to close out the continuum, putting Moses and Aaron in continuity with the patriarchs. On the Holiness origins for this formula in Genesis and Num. 3:1, see Arnold, "Holiness Redaction"; Knohl, *Sanctuary*, 105.

3. "Anointed" (*hamməšūḥîm*) is an attributive qal pass. ptc. that indicates a completed action (*GBHS* §3.4.3).

4. Formally, "whom he filled their hand to serve as a priest" (*'ăšer-millē' yādām ləkahēn*), with Aaron as the implied agent of the piel factitive verb, "*he* filled." To what this refers is unclear since Moses, not Aaron, was the agent who ordained Aaron and his sons (Lev. 8; Exod. 28:41). This problem is nonexistent in the pl.: see 4Q23 ("their hands *were* filled [vocalized *mill'û*]") and LXX[ed] ("whose hands *they had fulfilled*"); cf. Lev. 7:36, with Yahweh as possible agent. Either 3:2 innerbiblically revises to stress Aaron's authority or refers to Aaron's sacrifices for himself and his family at the ordination (Lev. 9:2, 7–14).

5. The wayyiqtol "so they served as priests" (*wayəkahēn*) appears to indicate the result of the childlessness of Nadab and Abihu (*GBHS* §3.5.1b; NLT).

6. Formally, "before/above/opposite the face of," not precluding Aaron's priestly work (as 3:3); hence "with" (NLT; cf. dynamic "lifetime" NRSV, NJPS, ESV).

7. This weqatal "so that they may serve him" (*wəšērətû 'ōtô*) follows the impv. "stand them before Aaron" (*GBHS* §3.5.3b).

8. A cognate accusative, formally, "*by serving the service* [*la'ăbōd 'et-'ăbōdat*] of the dwelling place" (also v. 8).

service. **9**You must assign the Levites to Aaron and his sons; they will be assigned exclusively[9] to him from among the Israelites.[10] **10**You must appoint Aaron and his sons so that they protect[11] their priesthood; but the unauthorized person who approaches must be put to death."

11Then Yahweh said to Moses: **12**"Look, I myself have taken the Levites from among the Israelites[12] in place of[13] every firstborn of the womb[14] among the Israelites.[15] So the Levites will belong to me, **13**since all the firstborn are mine. When I destroyed all the firstborn in the land of Egypt, I set apart for myself all the firstborn in Israel, from human to animal. They belong to me. I am Yahweh."

14Then Yahweh said to Moses in the Sinai wilderness: **15**"List the Levites by their patriarchs' households and their families; every male a month old and up you must list."[16] **16**So Moses listed them according to the word of Yahweh,[17] just as he was commanded.[18] **17**These were Levi's sons by their names: Gershon, Kohath, and Merari. **18**These were the names of Gershon's sons by their families: Libni and Shimei. **19**Kohath's sons by their families were Amram, Izhar, Hebron, and Uzziel. **20**Merari's sons by their families were Mahli and Mushi. These were the Levite families by their patriarchs' households.

21To Gershon belonged[19] the Libnite family and the Shimeite family; these were the Gershonite families. **22**Those of them who were listed, counting every male a month old and up, came to[20] 7,500. **23**The Gershonite families were to camp behind the dwelling place to the west. **24**The chieftain of the patriarchal household of the Gershonite family was Lael's son Eliasaph. **25**And the responsibilities of the Gershonites

---

9. The pass. ptc. is repeated, "they are given, given (to him)" (*nətûnim nətûnim*), to indicate that the Levites were "given exclusively for his service" (GKC §123e).

10. Probably SP harmonizes to 8:16, "given *to me*"; LXX^ed may also smooth its source, "*the priests*; these have been given *as a gift to me*" (Wevers, *Notes*, 36).

11. The weqatal, following the yiqtol, is probably consequential: "Aaron and his sons [pre-verbally stressed], you must appoint [impf.] *so that they protect* [*wəšāmərû*] their priesthood" (*GBHS* §3.5.2b).

12. "From among the Israelites" (*mibənê yiśrā'ēl*, MT^L) vs. "among the Israelites" (*bbny yśr'l*, 4Q23 M^mss).

13. "In place of" (*taḥat*, commonly "under") indicates substitution (*GBHS* §4.1.18d).

14. Formally, "every firstborn opening of a womb"; cf. 18:15.

15. After "among the Israelites," SP and LXX^ed add, "They will be their redemption" ("ransom," NETS). This longer reading replaces expected substitute lambs with the Levites by recalling Yahweh's *redemption* [Hb. *pdh*] of the Israelite firstborn sons with the lambs in Egypt (Exod. 13:15) and Israel's requirement to redeem their firstborn with lambs (13:13; 34:20).

16. Here "list" (*pəqōd*, qal impv. *pqd*), whereas in 1:49 the Levites were not to be *enlisted* (same verb) in the Israelite military census.

17. Formally, "according to the mouth of Yahweh"; LXX^ed: "by the voice of Yahweh."

18. LXX^ed and SP read "just as Yahweh *commanded him/them*."

19. The *l* probably marks a gen. relationship (*GBHS* §4.1.10g; with NJPS, NRSV, ESV) rather than source (NET).

20. "Came to" renders the second "those enrolled of them" (*pəqudêhem*).

in the meeting tent involved[21] the dwelling place,[22] the tent, its cover, the curtain at the entrance to the meeting tent, [26]the hangings of the courtyard, the curtain for the entrance to the courtyard, which is around both the dwelling place and the altar, with their tent ropes—regarding all their needed service.[23]

[27]To Kohath belonged the Amramite family, the Izharite family, the Hebronite family, the Uzzielite family; these were the Kohathite families. [28]The number of every male a month old and up came to 8,600; these attended to the responsibilities of the sanctuary.[24] [29]The Kohathite families were to camp on the south side of the dwelling place. [30]The chieftain of the patriarchal household of the Kohathite families was Uzziel's son Elizaphan. [31]Their responsibilities included the ark, the table, the lampstand, the altars,[25] the sanctuary utensils with which they ministered, the curtain, along with[26] all their needed service. [32]Now the chieftain over[27] the Levite chieftains was Eleazar son of Aaron the priest, appointed over those responsible for the sanctuary.

[33]To Merari belonged the Mahlite family and the Mushite family; these were the Merari families. [34]Those of them who were listed, numbering every male a month old and up, came to 6,200. [35]Now the chieftain of the patriarchal household of the Merari families was Abihail's son Zuriel. They were to camp on the north side of the dwelling place. [36]The appointed responsibility of the Merarites involved the frames of the dwelling place, its crossbars, its tentpoles, its bases, its utensils, along with all their needed service, [37]and the tentpoles around the courtyard, with their bases, their tent pegs, and their ropes.

[38]But[28] those camping in front of the dwelling place to the east, in front of the tent of meeting, were Moses, Aaron, and his sons, who protected the responsibilities of the sanctuary for[29] the responsibilities

---

21. "Involved" expresses the relationship of the subject to its predicate nominatives.

22. In vv. 25–38, the repeated article ("*the* dwelling place," etc.) is anaphoric (*GBHS* §2.6.1), presuming knowledge of sacra from Exodus–Numbers or personal experience.

23. Formally, "for all its service," with a specification *l* focusing on the obj. (*GBHS* §4.1.10h).

24. A cognate accusative, "who guarded what is to be guarded [*šōmərê mišmeret*] of the sanctuary."

25. "The altars" (*hammizbəḥōt*) of burnt offering and of incense are known not from Num. 1–3 but from Exodus (27:1–8; 38:1–8; 30:1–10; 37:25–28).

26. "Along with" renders a conjunctive *w* (*GBHS* §4.3.3), as v. 36; but cf. *l* in v. 26.

27. "Over" communicates the relationship of a "superlative part" (the chieftain) to the "divided whole" (the Levite chieftains); *BHRG* §25.4.3(2).

28. "But" (*wə*) marks a break from the literary pattern of Gershon, Kohath, and Merari in vv. 21–37 (*IBHS* §39.2.3b).

29. "For" (*l*) may mark the deverbal "obligations" (*mišmeret*) as the purpose (*GBHS* §4.1.10[e.1]); the leaders were to ensure that the sanctuary was maintained properly *so that* the Israelites could fulfill their cultic obligations.

of the Israelites, but any[30] unauthorized person who came near was to be put to death. [39]All the listed Levites, whom Moses and Aaron had listed according to the word of Yahweh, by their families, every male a month old and up, came to 22,000.

[40]Then Yahweh spoke to Moses: "List all the firstborn males[31] belonging to the Israelites a month old and up, and take the number of their names. [41]You must take[32] the Levites for myself—I am Yahweh—in place of all the firstborn among the Israelites, and the Levites' livestock in place of all the firstborn among the Israelites' livestock."[33] [42]So Moses listed[34] every firstborn Israelite, just as Yahweh had commanded him. [43]All the firstborn males, by the number of the names a month old and up, came to 22,273.

[44]Then Yahweh spoke to Moses: [45]"Take the Levites in place of all firstborn Israelites, and the Levites' livestock in place of their[35] livestock. So the Levites will be mine. I am Yahweh. [46]For the redemption of the 273 firstborn Israelites who exceed the number of the Levites, [47]you must collect for each individual five shekels[36] in the currency of the sanctuary shekel[37] (this shekel equals[38] twenty gerahs).[39] [48]Then give the money for the redemption of the excess number of them to Aaron and his sons." [49]So Moses collected the redemption money from the ones who exceeded those redeemed by the Levites. [50]From the firstborn Israelites he collected the money, 1,365 shekels, according to the value of the sanctuary shekel. [51]Then Moses gave the redemption money to Aaron and his sons, according to the word of Yahweh, just as Yahweh had commanded Moses.

---

30. Article for a class of persons, "any" (BHRG §24.4.4[4]).

31. The Hb. is sg. here (kōl bəkôr zākār, every firstborn male; also vv. 40, 41, 42, 43, 45, 46, 50) but rendered as pl. for smoother Eng.

32. The weqatal assumes the imperatives' force in v. 40 (GBHS §3.5.2c).

33. "All the firstborn [kol-bəkôr] among the Israelites' livestock" probably implies male firstborn animals since the Israelites are qualified twice in the context as "male" (zākār, vv. 40, 43), the animals in Exodus may be male (13:2, 12–15; 34:19–20), and the fem. form (bəkîrâ, firstborn female) was not given as an alternative.

34. "So [Moses] listed" (wayyipqōd) is sequential (GBHS §3.5.1a), reporting Moses's obedient response to Yahweh's command in v. 40.

35. Verse 45 repeats v. 41 but expands the redeemed obj. from "the firstborn among the Israelites' livestock" (v. 41) to "their [presumably all of the Israelites'] livestock." Seebass (Numeri, 1:98) identifies this revision as modifying an already authoritative mandate.

36. Formally, "you must receive/take five, five shekels for the skull."

37. "In the currency of the sanctuary shekel" dynamically renders b as realizing the action as a "mode of quality" (BHRG §39.6.3[4]).

38. "This shekel" conveys an anaphoric article (IBHS §13.5.1d); formally, "the shekel takes."

39. Five shekels—for every firstborn Israelite who exceeds the number of Levites—is approximately two ounces of silver. A šeqel was "a measurement of weight and later became the term for a coin. As the basic unit of the Israelite weight system, it equaled 11.4 grams of silver. The Hebrew šāqel means 'to weigh' in the sense 'to pay.' Pieces of silver were weighed by using shekel weights" (King and Stager, Life, 198).

Interpretation

3:1–4. The formula "these are the family histories of Aaron and Moses" (*wə'ēlleh tôlədōt 'ahărōn ûmōšeh*) appeared last in the biblical narrative as a structuring device in the book of Genesis to introduce a genealogy of or narrative about a progenitor's descendants (see the translation note on 3:1). This has the rhetorical effect of elevating Aaron into the same story line of the great family histories (*tôlədōt*) of Abraham, Isaac, and Jacob.[40] Although the formula introduces the line or sagas of "Aaron and Moses" (v. 1), surprisingly only Aaron's sons, not Moses's, are recounted (vv. 2–4).[41] This exhibits the narrative's transition from prophet Moses to priest Aaron. Yahweh continues communicating with Moses alone.[42] Moses, Aaron, and his sons together are the first line of defending the meeting tent from intruders (v. 38), but the role of sacrificial mediator has passed from Moses (Exod. 24:5–8) to Aaron and his four sons, and then to Aaron and his surviving sons, Eleazar and Ithamar (Lev. 1–10*, 16*, 21–22*; Num. 3:3–4, 10). There is some ambivalence about Moses's ability or right to enter Yahweh's sacred dwelling (Exod. 40:34–35 and Lev. 1:1 *versus* Exod. 33:11; Num. 1:1; 7:89), whereas Aaron and his primogenital successors were given the prerogative to enter the most holy place annually (Lev. 16:1–2, 32–33).

The priests who work in proximity to Yahweh do not have impunity, however. The narrator could simply have said that Nadab and Abihu died and then moved on to Eleazar and Ithamar. Instead, as in Lev. 16:1, their violation is put on display: "Nadab and Abihu died before Yahweh when they offered strange fire before Yahweh in the Sinai wilderness."[43] The shame is reinforced by the detail that "they had no children," which was considered a stigma or even a curse.[44] Their childlessness restricted the priestly line to Eleazar and Ithamar, leaving Aaron without their assistance in the dwelling place or in the home. They failed to be ideal sons, which required both cultic and filial devotion, as Ugaritic King Danel envisioned for his sons.[45] Furthermore, the information in vv. 1–4 is known from Exodus and Leviticus,[46] but vv. 1–4 are presented as an independent source, as if Numbers' readers were not aware of Aaron's children or the Nadab and Abihu catastrophe. The purpose of this text is to show that Nadab and Abihu did not invalidate Aaron's family and that Eleazar and Ithamar have become the patrilineal inheritors of the

40. Olson, *Death of the Old*, 98–114.

41. Moses's wife was Zipporah, and their two sons were Gershom and Eliezer (Exod. 2:21–22; 18:2–4).

42. Five speeches: 3:5–10, 11–13, 14–39, 40–43, 44–51.

43. "When they offered strange fire before Yahweh" matches LXX Lev. 16:1, whereas MT Lev. 16:1 reads, "when they came before Yahweh" (see Awabdy, "Nadab and Abihu," 580–93).

44. King and Stager, *Life*, 46.

45. "The 'Aqhatu Epic," *COS* 1.103:345.

46. Exod. 6:23; 28:1; Lev. 8–10*.

priesthood. In a context that stresses Levi (Num. 1:47–49; 2:33; 3:5–4:49), it is surprising that vv. 1–4 do not mention Levi, from whom Eleazar and Ithamar descended. This distinguishes the Aaronides' priestly service to Yahweh from the service of the Levites, and their proximity to Yahweh from that of the surrounding Israelite tribes and even Moses.[47]

3:5–10. More than a month has passed since the construction of Yahweh's dwelling, and the priests have begun their work.[48] The reader can imagine that Aaron and his surviving sons, Eleazar and Ithamar, have already been confronted with a work overload in and around Yahweh's meeting tent. Ongoing priestly work, including sacrifices and other rituals, within a war camp away from the soldiers' homeland is attested in the ancient Near East.[49] In response, Yahweh designates the tribe of Levi to support Aaron in maintaining and transporting the divine abode (vv. 6–9). I interpret vv. 7–8 together as modifying "so that they may serve him [Aaron]," and v. 8 as restating v. 7, so that the Levites' dwelling-place service supports Aaron in two ways: (1) the Levites keep Aaron's tent responsibilities, caring for the furnishings of the meeting tent, and (2) they keep the responsibilities of the whole community, the Israelites, probably referring to their sacrifices and offerings (Lev. 1–7*, esp. 7:38). In this context about Levi, v. 10 seems displaced: Aaron and his sons must protect the priesthood, and any unauthorized person who approaches the meeting tent must be killed (also v. 38). However, the placement of v. 10 is sensible if it refers to Aaron and his sons protecting the priesthood *even from the Levites*. This correlates with the death penalty demanded explicitly for the Kohathites, of the tribe of Levi, if they touched or even looked at the holy things (4:15, 20), which would apply by extension to the Gershonites and Merarites (4:21–33). The division between (1) the Levites guarding the tent's outer precincts and (2) the Aaronic priests guarding the tent's inner precincts is analogous to the two classes of (prebiblical) Hittite temple guards (see the "Implications" essay below, "Is There a Hierarchy?").

3:11–13. Yahweh explains to Moses the innovation of his choice of Levi: the Levites, who belong to Yahweh, have become a substitute for Israel's firstborn sons and livestock, who also belong to Yahweh (see the translation notes on v. 12). In the Moses story, Yahweh commands Moses to declare to Pharaoh: "This is what the LORD says, 'Israel is my firstborn son; . . . since

---

47. Cf. Moses's distance (Exod. 40:34–35; Lev. 1:1) with the proximate service of Aaron's family (Lev. 8–10*) and Aaron (Lev. 16:12–17, 32–34; see Leveen, *Memory*, 52. The ascendency of the Aaronides over Moses, Levi, and the rest of the tribes in Num. 3, 8, 18 demonstrates the theological-conceptual concerns of the editors (Blum, *Komposition des Pentateuch*, 270; Achenbach, *Vollendung*, 488–95). However, Frevel ("High Priest," 148–50) rightly questions the textual evidence often put forward (Num. 16) to claim an underlying conflict between the Levites and priests in Numbers.

48. Exod. 40; Lev. 24; Lev. 8–10; Num. 1:1.

49. For Neo-Assyrian examples, see Trimm, *Warfare*, 501–3.

you have refused to let him go, I will kill your firstborn son'" (Exod. 4:22–23). This foreshadows Yahweh's final sign against Egypt, the death of all Egyptian firstborn males,[50] which becomes the etiological basis for sacrificing firstborn animals to Yahweh and redeeming firstborn sons from Yahweh (Exod. 13:15; Num. 3:13). The law of the firstborn is adapted over the course of the narrative. I mark the innovations in bold below:

Exod. 13:2, 11–15	Exod. 22:29–30	Exod. 34:19–20	Lev. 27:26	Num. 3:11–13, 40–43
*Firstborn males belong to Yahweh.	[*unstated]	*Firstborn males belong to Yahweh.	*Firstborn animals belong to Yahweh.	*Levites also belong to Yahweh.
→ Israel must sacrifice every firstborn male animal to Yahweh.	→ Israel must give firstborn oxen and sheep to Yahweh when they are eight days old.	→ Israel must give firstborn to Yahweh.	→ Therefore, one cannot consecrate, as a voluntary gift, a firstborn ox or sheep to Yahweh.	→ Yahweh has taken the Levites in place of Israel's firstborn sons.
→ Israel must redeem firstborn donkeys and boys, that is, buy them back from Yahweh and not sacrifice them.	→ Israel must give to Yahweh firstborn sons.	→ May redeem donkey with a lamb, if not, then break its neck. Must redeem firstborn sons, not appearing before Yahweh empty-handed.		→ Israel must take the Levites' livestock in place of Israel's firstborn livestock.

In light of these preceding texts in the narrative flow, the basic sense of Num. 3:11–13, 40–43 (51) is that Yahweh regards the Levites as quasi-vicarious firstborn sacrifices in place of Israel's firstborn.[51] However, unlike the firstborn animal sacrifices that were slaughtered and offered to Yahweh, the Levites were not sacrificed but ordained to serve Yahweh in and around the meeting tent (Num. 1–4*; see 3:6–9). The Levites insulate the threat of Yahweh's judgment: Egypt's firstborn were slaughtered (v. 13), and Aaron's firstborn, Nadab and Abihu, were also killed by Yahweh (v. 4), but the Levites now insulate both the Israelite community and Aaron's priestly family from the threat to their firstborn sons.[52]

3:14–39. Yahweh speaks to Moses again, this time expressly "in the Sinai wilderness" (3:14), which links this speech to the incipit of Numbers—"Then Yahweh spoke to Moses in the Sinai wilderness inside the meeting tent"—and

---

50. Exod. 11:5; 12:12, 29.
51. Achenbach, *Vollendung*, 156.
52. Leveen, *Memory*, 115–17.

anticipates the central *wilderness* motif of Num. 10:11–21:35.[53] Yahweh commands Moses to take a census of the Levites, by—probably meaning under the heading of—their patriarchal households and their families. For the other tribes, only Israelite men twenty years and older were counted because they had to be capable of fighting (Num. 1:3, 18–46); here the Levite males a month old and up are counted because neither their boys nor men will go to war (3:15). The requirement that those counted be at least one month of age could be because (1) circumcision was performed on the eighth day (Gen. 17:12; Lev. 12:3) and would have taken another ten or more days to heal; and (2) the mortality rate for infants in the ancient world was extremely high, with most infant deaths occurring in the perinatal period (0–7 days after birth),[54] so infants surviving their first month were more likely to continue to thrive. Where the nursing mothers or other Levite wives camped is unstated; the maleness of the Levites, Aaronic priests, Moses, and their firstborn sons is foregrounded.[55] Moses obeys Yahweh exactly in listing the Levites by name (v. 16). That exhaustive census is not preserved in the text (cf. vv. 21–37), which instead begins with a truncated genealogy of Levi (vv. 17–20), apparently resuming the source of 3:1–4. The genealogy is not vertical; that is, it does not trace a direct line from Levi to a single descendant (as Gen. 5:3–32; 11:10–26). Instead, it is horizontal, naming all of Levi's sons and grandsons (as Gen. 10:1–32):

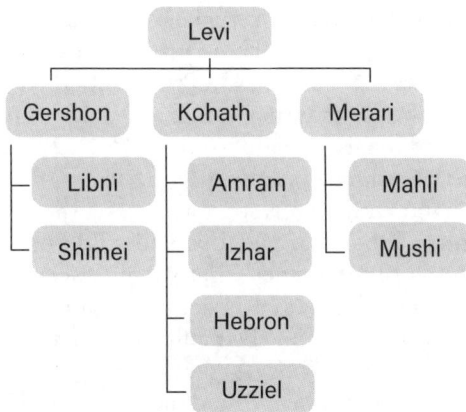

Figure 3.1. Horizontal Genealogy

53. Nihan, *Priestly Torah*, 70–74.
54. Garroway, *Growing Up*, 223–24; cf. King and Stager, *Life*, 41. For infants less than one year old, compare an estimated mortality rate in ancient Israel approaching 50 percent to 0.55 percent of live births in the US in 2019 (US Department of Health and Human Services, "Infant Mortality in the United States, 2019," *National Vital Statistics Reports* 70, no. 14, December 8, 2021, https://www.cdc.gov/nchs/data/nvsr70/nvsr70-14.pdf).
55. See Shectman, "Social Status," 90.

The core of the chapter, vv. 21–39, is trifurcated into the extended families who trace their origins back to Levi's three boys, Gershon (vv. 21–26), Kohath (vv. 27–32), and Merari (vv. 33–37). Although Moses took a census (v. 16), what has been preserved is only a synopsis, which includes five elements for the Gershonite, Kohathite, and Merarite families: (1) their children (Levi's grandchildren) as extended families; (2) the number of their males one month old and older; (3) their camping position immediately surrounding Yahweh's dwelling place (see fig. 2.1, "Camp Positions"); (4) their current chieftain; (5) their responsibilities in and around Yahweh's meeting tent, which are vague now but expounded later in Num. 4:4–20 (Kohathites), 4:21–28 (Gershonites), and 4:29–33 (Merarites). The meeting-tent work was distributed, but on what basis remains unclear: the 7,500 Gershonites were responsible for the protective curtains of the dwelling place and courtyard; the 8,600 Kohathites were responsible for the furniture; the 6,200 Merarites were responsible for the meeting tent's wooden framework on which the curtains were hung. The narrator marks off the special status of Eleazar, Aaron's oldest surviving son: although he was numbered and thereby accountable to Moses and Aaron, he was granted the high status of chieftain over the tribe of Levi and responsibility for the most sacred furnishings of Yahweh's tent.

Why do the Priestly historians feel compelled to include all these details? The image created is that the Levites, who will not fight with Israel's soldiers (1:3, 47; 2:33), will nonetheless play a crucial role in the fight for Canaan insofar as they faithfully serve, surround, and protect the dwelling place of their warrior deity, Yahweh (1:47–53; 2:17, 33). Principally, their position is central within the military camp so that they can service and guard the residence of Yahweh, who will lead them and fight for them (3:23, 29, 35).[56] This reciprocal relationship between honoring the meeting tent and ark containing the covenant, on one hand, and victorious warfare, on the other, is later made explicit at the seams of the Sinai pericope and wilderness narrative (Num. 10:3, 33–36). It is only sensible, then, that while Israel's twelve other tribes had chieftains who were "leaders of Israel's thousands" (1:16), the Levites had their own named chieftains for their cultic service (4:24, 30, 35; see comments there).

By resuming two literary frames around the core of vv. 17–38, the narrator slows down the closure of the unit in vv. 38–39:

> Aaron and his sons must "**protect** their priesthood; but the unauthorized person who approaches must be put to death" (3:10)
>> "'List the Levites by their patriarchs' households and their families; every male a month old and up you must list.' So Moses listed them

---

56. See the "Implications" essay in chap. 1, "Counting the Army."

according to the word of Yahweh, just as he was commanded."
(3:15–16)

Genealogy of Levi and synopsis of the Levite census (3:17–38)

"All the listed Levites, whom Moses and Aaron had listed according
to the word of Yahweh, by their families, every male a month old
and up, came to 22,000." (3:39)

Moses, Aaron, and his sons "**protected** the responsibilities of the sanctuary, . . . but any unauthorized person who came near was to be put
to death" (3:38)

The frames (v. 10//v. 38 and vv. 15–16//v. 39) stress Moses and Aaron's exact
obedience in completing the Levite census and Aaron and his sons' vital role
to insulate Yahweh's sacred space from neglect and from intruders, who must
be executed for encroaching.

3:40–43. Yahweh commands Moses to take a census of all Israel's firstborn
males, but instead of sacrificing those counted firstborn animals to Yahweh
and redeeming the boys and men from Yahweh (Exod. 13, 22, 34; Lev. 27),
the Levites have now become a substitute. Forming another frame around
the core of vv. 14–39, vv. 40–41 reiterate the theology of vv. 11–13, without
repeating the etiology of the firstborn (Passover in Egypt), but with three
additions (emboldened below): (1) Moses must list and number the Israelite
males; (2) Moses must emulate Yahweh's action by taking the Levites; and
(3) the Levites' livestock will also be a substitute for the firstborn of the Israelites' livestock:

Numbers 3:11–13	Numbers 3:40–41
[11]Then Yahweh said to Moses: [12]"Look, I my-self have taken the Levites from among the Israelites in place of every firstborn of the womb among the Israelites. So the Levites will belong to me, [13]since all the firstborn are mine. When I destroyed all the firstborn in the land of Egypt, I set apart for myself all the firstborn in Israel, from human to ani-mal. They belong to me. I am Yahweh."	[40]Then Yahweh spoke to Moses: "List all the firstborn males belonging to the Israelites a month old and up, and take the number of their names. [41]You must take the Levites for myself—I am Yahweh[57]—in place of all the firstborn among the Israelites, and the Le-vites' livestock in place of all the firstborn among the Israelites' livestock."

Just as all Levites, not just the firstborn, become substitutes for Israel's firstborn males, so also all the Levites' animals, not just the firstborn, become
substitutes for Israel's firstborn animals. Since the Levites have already been
counted in v. 39 (22,000), Yahweh orders the logical next step of counting the
firstborn Israelite males, and Moses obeys flawlessly (v. 42), counting 22,273

---

57. "I am Yahweh," characteristic of Lev. 17–26, may reflect H influence in Num. 3 (Knohl,
Sanctuary, 53; Awabdy, "Priestly Blessing," 46–47).

firstborn Israelites, not including their livestock. One may wonder how this Levite innovation of the firstborn law could be enacted at this later stage in the Exodus-Leviticus-Numbers narrative: Haven't the Israelites already dedicated the firstborn of the exodus generation to Yahweh? The Moses story suggests that they have not yet done this, making this radical, novel Levite theology possible to implement in the wilderness or when they arrive in Canaan.[58]

3:44–51. The difference between the number of Levites (22,000; v. 39) and the number of firstborn Israelites (22,273; v. 43) leaves 273 firstborn males in Israel without a Levite designated to Yahweh to take their place. Yahweh redresses this disparity by mandating that Moses exact a redemption cost of 5 shekels from each of the additional 273 Israelite firstborn males. This would be about 2 ounces of silver (5 shekels), totaling close to 34 pounds of silver (1,365 shekels), a huge stockpile of precious metal given exclusively to Aaron and his sons (v. 47; see the last translation note there).[59] It remains unclear which firstborn Israelites were the 273 extras who had to pay (v. 49), whether those who just happened to be counted last in the census (vv. 40–43) or those who simply volunteered to pay the ransom fee (see Exod. 35:29), but probably not just the rich (Exod. 30:15; cf. 38:25). The concluding statements of faithful obedience are redundant and thereby emphatic: "according to the word of Yahweh, just as Yahweh had commanded." They appear to modify both Moses's action of collecting the redemption money and his giving it to Aaron and his sons (vv. 50–51). This significant collection given to the Aaronic priests is distinct from Num. 18:20–32, in which Yahweh designates "every tithe" from the Israelites for not just Aaron's household but the entire Levite tribe.[60] In Num. 3, instead, Aaron and sons form an *inclusio* around the integral Levite tribe of vv. 5–47: Aaron's priestly family is validated (vv. 1–4) and Aaron's priestly family is supplied with a substantial quantity of silver (vv. 48–51).

58. Exodus 13:2 mentions no implementation of this firstborn ritual, while Exod. 13:11–15 anticipates "when Yahweh brings you into the land of the Canaanites." Exodus 22:29–30 is ratified by the people's oath but without record of enactment (24:3). Exodus 34:19–20 was communicated (34:32) but without an account of Israel's obedience.

59. Thirty-four pounds of silver represents a lucrative collection. Although the value of precious metals such as gold, silver, and copper fluctuated over the LBA and Iron Age, they were always desirable (Moreno García, "Economies," 1–39).

60. With Kellermann (*Priesterschrift*, 46), 3:14–39 reflects an original core collection of diverse materials; with Achenbach (*Vollendung*, 160), it does appear that 3:11–13, 40–51 were added later to vv. 14–39 because the Levite-firstborn innovation is not even hinted at in Num. 18, which is bound intertextually to Num. 3–4*. Also, the choosing of Levi (3:5–10) and the Levite census (vv. 14–39) flow coherently, whereas vv. 11–13 introduce a radically new firstborn theology absent in vv. 14–39 but resumed in vv. 40–51. Knohl (*Sanctuary*, 72–73) thinks 8:5–22 provides a bridge within the H continuum of Num. 3, 8, and 18, but this does not solve why 18:15–18 does not exhibit awareness of the Levite substitution in 3:11–13, 40–51.

Implications

Is There a Hierarchy within the People of God?

This question has divided churches, denominations, Catholics, Orthodox, and Protestants through the ages. After quoting Num. 3:6, Origen writes in his commentary on the Song of Songs, "Do you see how here too he both speaks of the priests as superior to the Levites, and once more makes the Levites appear as more eminent than the children of Israel?"[61] His point is actually that this priestly order illustrates the supremacy of Christ (figurally represented by King Solomon) over the church (represented by Solomon's lover). From one perspective, Origen was correct to identify a hierarchical organization in the Priestly historiography of Num. 3. In practice, both Levi and Aaron's family held prerogatives denied to others, and the large group of Levites were subject to the Aaronides as they cared for, maintained, and transported Yahweh's tent, while Aaron's family engaged in the sublime work[62] of mediating between God and the people in the exercise of worship. This pecking order in Israel was a contextualization of other ancient Near Eastern societies. For example, in pre-biblical Anatolia (Turkey), one finds two classes of Hittite priests with distinct, gradated roles in guarding the temple.[63] Ada Taggar-Cohen describes their two types of protective service: "The guarding of the inner parts of the temple by the priests, patrolling the temple grounds in shifts and sleeping through the night inside the temple at the door to the shrine (indicated in the texts as 'sleeping with the god'), and guard duty outside the temple by *ḫaliyatalla-men* ('watchers'), who were troops assigned by the king to guard the temples in certain towns."[64] Similarly, Israel's priests protected the inner precinct of Yahweh's tent (Num. 3:4, 7, 10, 32, 38) while the Levites protected the outer precinct (Num. 3:6–9, 11–39), and the community at large was banned from entry (Num. 3:10, 38).

Whatever is true in Origen's claim, he has committed a non sequitur by concluding that because of their privileged roles, priests were qualitatively superior to Levites and Levites to the common people. This obfuscates the distinction between each covenant member's *gradated function* but *equal value* before God. Yahweh's choice of the priests and Levites afforded them a special, vital function in the community, and as a result they possess both ascribed honor, inherited by patrilineal descent (3:1–4), and acquired honor.[65] In the NT, Paul acknowledges that he, too, should have honored the high priest (Acts 23:5) and later that church elders who lead well should "be considered

---

61. Origen, *Song of Songs*, 54.
62. Cardellini, *Numeri 1,1–10,10*, 43.
63. Milgrom ("Shared Custody," 204–9) saw this parallel in a text named The Instructions for Hittite Temple Officials.
64. Taggar-Cohen, "Covenant Priesthood," 22.
65. The ascribed and acquired honor of the Levites, especially the Aaronic priests and Moses, is stressed in Num. 12–18 (see Moxnes, "Honor and Shame," 20, 27–28).

worthy of double honor, especially those who labor in preaching and teaching" (1 Tim. 5:17 ESV).[66] At the same time, in the theology that comes to fruition in Lev. 17–26, every Israelite—not just the priests, meeting tent, and sacrifices—belongs to a holy Yahweh and therefore must live a holy life in the community (Lev. 19:2). In distinction from the Priestly theology of silent rituals enclosed in Yahweh's meeting tent (Exod. 25–31*, 35–40*; Lev. 1–16), the Holiness theology is expansive: "The holiness of God expands beyond the Sanctuary to encompass the settlements of the entire congregation of Israel, in whose midst God dwells."[67] This means that ancient Israel's leaders were valued by God not because of their superior status or function but because as humans they were marked with the divine image[68] and because they mediated God's covenant relationship with the people. On the positive side, this implies that "only a careful separation and ordering of priests, Levites and laity could make certain that the cult brought atonement and blessing for the whole community."[69] On the negative side, it implies that Yahweh's great prophet, Moses, and high priest, Aaron, were judged severely for not honoring Yahweh in the sight of the Israelites, to whom he has given the promised land (20:12, 24; 27:14).[70] The NT affirms the sanctity of the community of God's people, who have been purchased by their High Priest's own blood and have been collectively made into royal priests and inheritors of the promised land.[71]

In sum, the priests' and Levites' location and work were not intrinsically valuable but instrumentally valuable. The proximity of the Aaronic priests and Levites to Yahweh, their task to protect the divine dwelling, and Aaron's family's atonement rituals in the sanctuary were all divine prerogatives and not to be manipulated for their own intrigue, lust, or glory;[72] nor were they an ultimate end, the Good or the Supreme Good in Aristotelian terms.[73] Rather, their lives were to be bound up in service to Yahweh *for the supreme good of Yahweh's name and people.* This instrumental (extrinsic) value saturates both Testaments as the grounds for exhorting and judging the shepherd leaders of God's people (Ezek. 44:10–11; Jer. 23:1; Acts 20:28–29). Regardless of one's thinking about Roman Catholic theology, we can all appreciate the charge given by Pope Francis to seminary students in Sicily on November 24, 2018: "Clericalism, my dear ones, is our ugliest perversion. The Lord wants you to be shepherds; shepherds of the people, not clerics of the state."[74]

66. Also 1 Thess. 5:12; 1 Pet. 5:5.
67. Knohl, *Sanctuary*, 185.
68. Tucker, *Holiness Composition*, 6, 40n19.
69. Albertz, *Israelite Religion*, 2:486; Knohl, *Sanctuary*, 192–96.
70. Awabdy, "Holiness Contribution," 251–56.
71. Exod. 19:5–6; 1 Pet. 2:9; Heb. 9:11–15; 13:9–16; Rev. 1:5–6; 5:9–10; 20:6.
72. See Lev. 10:1–3; 1 Sam. 2:12–17.
73. Aristotle, *Nicomachean Ethics* 1.2.
74. Holy See Press Office, "Audience with Seminarians," https://cruxnow.com/vatican/2018/11/clericalism-is-ugly-perversion-pope-tells-seminarians.

4

Meeting-Tent Service
of the Levite Families

(4:1–49)

⁓⁓

Overview

Within the Num. 1–10 instructions, which complement the meeting-tent
instructions of Exod. 25–40, chapter 4 culminates the Num. 1–4 segment,
which centers on Israel's military preparations by orienting their lives *around*
and, for the Aaronides and Levites, *within* Yahweh's meeting tent. In Num.
4, Yahweh orders the fourth census of the book so far: the Israelite men,
twenty years old and above, eligible for army service (1:2–46); the Levites, a
month old and up, belonging to Yahweh for meeting-tent service (3:14–39);
the firstborn Israelite males (3:40–43); and now the thirty-to-fifty-year-old Levites from each extended family, the Kohathites, Gershonites, and Merarites.
The first Levite census was to be exhaustive (3:14–39), whereas the second
homes in on the middle- and upper-aged Levite patriarchs with the physical capacity to carry the deconstructed parts and furniture of Yahweh's
meeting tent from Sinai to Canaan (see 4:1–3). The Kohathites must wait
for Aaron and his sons to cover and extract the sacred furniture and cultic
implements (4:4–14) before they can carry that furniture by their poles and
avoid a catastrophic death (4:15–20). Levi's other descendants, the families
of the Gershonites and Merarites, are likewise to be counted and delegated
the tasks of carrying the curtains, coverings, and ropes (Gershonites, vv.
21–28), and framework and related tools (Merarites, vv. 29–33). Israel's
leaders obey Yahweh's orders (from vv. 1–2) and complete the census with

a count of each of the three Levite families (vv. 34–45), forming an *inclusio* around the extended discourse on their different tasks (vv. 4–33). The unit is doubly closed by the addition of the second *inclusio* of vv. 46–49, which likewise stresses the leaders' obedience and gives the combined total number of Levites now ready to begin their service in and for the divine dwelling (vv. 46–49). The composition of Num. 4 indicates that Yahweh highly values the priestly rituals, maintenance, and transport of the tent where he dwells in the center of his people.

Translation

1Then Yahweh spoke to Moses and Aaron: **2**"Take a census[1] of the Kohathites from among the Levites, by their families, by their patriarchs' households, **3**from thirty to fifty years old,[2] each one who qualifies[3] for the cultic service[4] to do the work in the meeting tent. **4**The service of the Kohathites inside the meeting tent involves the holiest things. **5**When the camp sets out to travel, Aaron and his sons must come and take down the covering curtain[5] and must cover with it the ark containing the witness.[6] **6**Next they must put on top of it a

---

1. Formally, "lift up the head of the sons of Kohath" (imperatival inf. *nāśōʾ*; *IBHS* §35.5.1; cf. 1:2, 49, 50; 4:22; 26:2; 31:26, 49).

2. Against 4Q23[vid] MT SP, throughout chap. 4 LXX[ed] reads, "from twenty-five [*eikosi kai pente*] years and above to fifty years." This probable harmonization to 8:24–25, which starts the Levites' service at age twenty-five, likely arose not from the LXX translator (Wevers, *Notes*, 55), but from his Hb. source (Tov, "Textual Harmonization," 1–16; "Septuagint of Numbers," 181–201).

3. Formally, "comes to the cultic service." Anarthrous 2Q6 and MT, perhaps "each and every one who comes" (*kol-bāʾ* 2Q6 MT; *BHRG* §36.5.1). Articular SP substantival ptc. (*kl hbʾ*): "all who come" (assimilating to 4:23, 30, 35, 39, 43, 47).

4. *Ṣābāʾ*, attested 36× in Num. 1–2 (not in chap. 3), has a martial connotation (so "military service") but here in chap. 4 (6×) has the nuance of *cultic* service (with "*ṣābāʾ* I," *DCH* 7:64–69, gloss 9; notice the subset "military service > service in the cult" in *HALOT* 3:994, gloss A.6).

5. The gen. construction *pārōket hammāsāk* (the covering curtain; Exod. 35:12; 39:34; 40:21) is probably not partitive (ESV: "the veil of the screen") because *pārōket* (covering)—in Numbers only here and 18:7 (cf. 3:25, 26, 31)—was a metonym for the curtain itself (appearing without *hammāsāk* 10× in Exod. 26–40, 7× in Lev. 4–24). Instead, as an epexegetical gen. (*IBHS* §9.5.3c), the curtain (*hammāsāk*) is characterized by its function as a covering (*pārōket*; "screening curtain" NJPS, NRSV, NET, but not the nuance of "inner curtain," NLT).

6. This dynamic rendering of a gen. of container content (*ʾărōn hāʿēdut*; *BHRG* §25.4.6[5]) reflects Exod. 25:16, "You must put *into the ark* [*ʾel-hāʾārōn*] *the witness* [*ʾēt hāʿēdut*] *that I will give to you*" (here and in 25:21, "the witness" is marked as the direct obj.; see Dozeman, *Exodus*, 50–51). After 25:21, "the ark of the witness" becomes the favored metonym in the narrative. "Witness" (*DCH* 6:279–80, gloss 1) reflects its function as a visible witness to the covenant, as in ANE diplomatic treaties.

covering of dolphin skin[7] and spread on top of that[8] a completely blue cloth; then they must insert its poles. [7]But on the table of the Presence[9] they must spread a blue cloth and put on it the dishes, the pans, the libation bowls, and the pitchers for pouring,[10] and the bread displayed continuously[11] must be on it. [8]They must spread over them[12] a scarlet cloth and cover that with a covering of dolphin skin; and they must insert its poles.[13] [9]They must take a blue cloth and cover the lampstand for the light, with its lamps, its wick-trimmers, its firepans,[14] and all its vessels for oil, with which they supply it. [10]Then they must put it with all its utensils in a covering of dolphin skin and put it on a carrying

---

7. Probably a possessive gen., "covering of a skin *of a dolphin* [*taḥaš*]." In Numbers this term occurs only in chap. 4 (vv. 6, 8, 10, 11, 12, 14, 25; also Gen. 22:24; Ezek. 16:10; pl. *'ōrōt taḥāšîm* in Exod. 25–39), and there is no consensus on its meaning: "vermillion" (*ssgwn* Tg[O], as in CAL); "blue" (*yakinthinon* LXX[ed]; *GELS* 692); "violet [sealskin]" (*ianthinarum* [*pallium*] Vulg); "dolphin" (NJPS); "goat(skin)" (ESV); "sheep(skin)" (both goat- and sheepskin, RSV [Noth, *Numbers*, 28–29]); "badger(s' skins)" (KJV); "durable (leather)" (NIV); "fine (leather)" (various translations); "fine goat(skin)" (NLT); left untranslated by Budd (*Numbers*, 42–43); transliterating or parenthesizing *taḥaš* (Cardellini, *Numeri 1,1–10,10*, 129; de Vaulx, *Nombres*, 84; Seebass, *Numeri*, 1:62; EÜ). The Akkadian loanword from Hurrian *taḥ-si-a* (leather-colored) might be a cognate (Levine, *Numbers*, 1:166–67); not cited in *CAD* or *HALOT*. The Egyptian *tḥś*, "stretch a skin," if analogous, may suggest "fine leather imported from Egypt" (*HALOT* 4:1720, glosses 1b, 1d). The possible Arabic cognate "dolphin" (*d/tuḥas*, porpoise, a dolphin species, *HALOT* 4:1720, glosses 1a, 1c) is followed by Driver ("dugong," *Exodus*, 265–66), Childs (*Exodus*, 523n5), Ashley (*Numbers*, 96–98), and Walton and Matthews (*Genesis–Deuteronomy*, 180), who render 4:6 as "hide of sea cows," noting that dolphins and sea cows are found in the Red Sea. Most important, Levine (*Numbers*, 1:166–67) reminds us that dolphin skins were used broadly in ANE cults, and in a Mediterranean context, home to several dolphin and whale species, Cross (*Epic to Canon*, 89) recalls: "'El's abode 'in the midst of the sea' at the 'fountain of the double-deep' provides the proper setting for a tent of dolphin skins. The dolphin is, of course, a favorite motif in Phoenician art, both on the mainland and in the Punic colonies, where it is associated with 'El and Tannit."

8. "On that" in SP and LXX[ed], but implied in MT.

9. "The table of the Presence" (*šulḥan happānîm*) is a hapax metonym for "the table" (*haššulḥan*) in the holy place on which the "bread of the Presence" (*leḥem happānîm*) was arranged (Exod. 25:30; 35:13; 39:36). I capitalize "the Presence" (*happānîm*) since it implies the divine presence, which is explicit in the wordplay, "bread of *the Presence* [*pānîm*] *before me* [*ləpānay*]" (Exod. 25:30). This substantive may be a euphemism to avoid naming Yahweh as Israel's deity seated at his table to eat in contrast to ANE deities who were believed to eat meal offerings put before their cult images (but cf. "bread of God" 6× in Lev. 21–22 KJV); see Oppenheim, *Ancient Mesopotamia*, 183–98.

10. A gen. of purpose: pitchers intended for pouring (*qəśôt hannāsek*; GBHS §2.2.8).

11. A substantivized adjective, formally, "the continual bread" (*leḥem hattāmîd*, from "*tāmîd*," *HALOT* 4:1747–48, gloss 2f).

12. SP "*coverings* [*kswy*] of garments" may be influenced by 4:6, 14.

13. SP direct obj. marker (*'t*).

14. SP spelling may be an error or variant (*mḥtytyh* vs. *mḥttyh* 4Q23 MT); see Ulrich, *Qumran*, 140.

frame,[15] [11]but over the golden altar[16] they must spread a blue cloth and cover it with a covering of dolphin skin; and they must insert its poles. [12]Then they must take all the service utensils, with which they serve in the sanctuary, put them in a blue cloth, cover them with a covering of dolphin skin, and put them on a carrying frame. [13]Then they must remove the fatty ashes[17] from the altar and spread a purple cloth over it. [14]They must put on it all its utensils with which they serve—the firepans, the meat forks, the shovels, the basins, with all the containers of the altar—and they must spread on it a covering of dolphin skin; then they must insert its poles. ⌜They must take a purple cloth and cover up the washbasin and its base. Then they must put them in a covering of dolphin skin and put it on a carrying frame⌝.[18]

[15]When Aaron and his sons have finished covering[19] the sanctuary and all the furnishings of the sanctuary, when the camp sets out to travel,[20] then the Kohathites will come to carry them. But[21] they must not touch the holy things[22] or they will die. These are what the

---

15. "Carrying frame" (*môṭ* II) occurs 3× in Numbers (4:10, 12; 13:23 as "pole"), once in Nah. 1:13 as "rod" (*DCH* 5:172; *HALOT* 2:555).

16. This gen. of material, "the altar *made out of* gold" (*GBHS* §2.2.10), is definite and refers to the golden altar, which is not mentioned in Numbers or Leviticus but is in Exodus (30:1–10; 37:25–28; 39:38; 40:5, 26). This creates a narrative coherence by enclosing the Sinai materials (*BHRG* §24.4.4.2b).

17. This piel (*wədiššnû*) is a denominative (from *dšn*, fat) and privative, *removing* the fatty ashes; cf. qal: to become fat; also piel: to consider as fat; pual: to be made fat; *IBHS* §24.4f; "*dšn*," *HALOT* 1:234, piel gloss 2; but "*dšn* II," *DCH* 2:477.

18. SP and LXX[ed] share this plus (i.e., textual addition) between ⌜ ⌝, which is absent in the MT Tg° 4QLXX Num (see Cardellini, *Numeri 1,1–10,10*, 132n137). This plus may have been a scribal insertion to incorporate "the washbasin and its base," because these were integral sacra well-known from Exod. 30–Lev. 8 (8× together, 2× "washbasin" alone in Exod. 40:7, 30). I include the reading in brackets (trans. SP/retroverted LXX[ed]) because (1) it is contextual, preserving the pattern in vv. 5–14; (2) the washbasin and its stand were anointed and sanctified and called "most holy," like the other furnishings (Exod. 30:26–29; 40:3–11; Lev. 8:11), contra Milgrom (*Leviticus*, 1:515), who sees the description of the altar as "most holy" in Exod. 40:10, marking its status as higher than the basin/laver in 40:11, but no one would say that the ark is not "most holy" even though, like the basin, it is not explicitly called most holy in this particular unit (see Exod. 30:26–29); (3) it is improbable that the Priestly historiographers forgot the washbasin; and (4) MT could have omitted this reading by haplography (from waw to waw), which admittedly is also improbable for the Masoretes.

19. This weqatal (*wəqillâ*, finished) is a factitive piel (cause producing a state; *GBHS* §3.1.3a) complemented by the inf.

20. The inf. const. *binsōaʿ* (when [the camp] set out) with a *b* is simultaneous with the first main verb ("finished covering"; *GBHS* §3.4.1b1).

21. "But" (*wə*) marks the prohibition in contrast to the Kohathites' sanctioned role of transporting sacra in v. 15a (*IBHS* §39.2.3b).

22. They were not to touch "the holy things" (sg. *haqqdōš*, that which is holy), which probably refers to "the most holy things" (*qōdeš haqqŏdāšîm*, v. 4) of vv. 5–15. Milgrom (*Numbers*, 28) infers that this includes touching *covered* sacred objects as well. The consequence of death intensifies the gravity of accidentally, let alone intentionally, touching the primary sacra (ark,

Kohathites must carry in the meeting tent. [16]Eleazar son of Aaron the priest is appointed over the oil for the light, the spiced incense, the routine grain offering, and the anointing oil. He is also appointed over the entire dwelling place with all that is in it, in the sanctuary[23] and in its utensils."[24] [17]Then Yahweh said to Moses and Aaron: [18]"Do not let the tribe of the families of the Kohathites be destroyed[25] from among the Levites, [19]but do this for them, so that they will live and not die when they approach the holiest things: Aaron and his sons will go in and assign to each of them[26] his service and what he must carry. [20]But[27] the Kohathites[28] must not go in to look at the holy things for even a moment,[29] or they will die."

[21]Then Yahweh said to Moses: [22]"Take a census of the Gershonites also, by their patriarchs' households and by their families. [23]Count them from thirty to fifty years old, each one who qualifies to perform

---

table, lampstand, golden altar, [washbasin and base], although they were to touch utensils). Caution to not touch the primary objects was essential when covering, inserting poles, and transporting the objects by grasping the inserted poles (vv. 6, 8, 11, 14) and carrying frames (vv. 10, 12); later Aminadab's son Uzzah died when touching the ark (2 Sam. 6:6–7; 1 Sam. 7:1 indicates that Uzzah's brother Eleazar had been consecrated to oversee the ark).

23. The Kohathites were responsible for the bronze altar (also washbasin?) in the courtyard (vv. 4–16), which belongs to the "entire dwelling place" (*kol-hammiškān*), but also for the cultic objects within the "sanctuary" (anarthrous *qōdeš*), referring to the smaller tent with an outer (table-lampstand-golden altar) and inner room (ark) (contra Cardellini, *Numeri 1,1–10,10*, 133, who translates "sanctuary" as a synonym for "the dwelling place"). In chap. 4, "the meeting tent" (*'ōhel mô'ēd*) is coextensive with "the dwelling place/tabernacle" (*hammiškān*), although the former connotes the place where Yahweh meets with his people, and the latter, the place where Yahweh resides (Hundley, "Tabernacle or Tent of Meeting?," 3–18).

24. LXX[ed]: "in all the works."

25. The Hebrew euphemism "*cut off from among* the Levites" (**krt* + *mittôk*) is characteristic of H in Lev. 17–26 (17:10; 20:3, 5, 6; 26:22; 26:30; also Exod. 8:5; Deut. 12:29; 19:1). Knohl (*Sanctuary*, 105) attributes Num. 1:48–5:10 to H. The specific or immediate prohibition, "Do not let x be cut off" (*'al-takrîtû*; *'al* + jussive, *GBHS* §4.2.3), is a hiphil causative with one direct obj. (*GBHS* §3.1.6.a2).

26. "Each of them" (*'îš 'îš*) does not appear in SP (*'îš*), perhaps due to haplography (cf. *'îš 'îš* in SP/MT in 1:4, 44; 4:49; 5:12; 9:10). LXX[ed] Numbers renders this distributive formally (*andres anēr*, 1:44; similarly, 4:49; 5:12; 9:10) and contextually (**hekastos* for prb. *'îš 'îš* SP/MT in 1:4; 4:19).

27. "But" (*wә*) contrasts the general or permanent prohibition (*lō'* + impf.; *GBHS* §4.2.11) with the Kohathites' service in v. 19.

28. The gentilic "Kohathites," absent in Hb., is supplied for clarification (NRSV, NLT, NET, NIV).

29. The permanent prohibition "They must not go in *to look at the holy things for even a moment* [*lir'ôt kəballa' 'et-haqqōdeš*]" is rhetorical, with the adverbial inf. "for even a moment" (formally, "as a swallowing," i.e., "the time it takes to swallow": Ashley, *Numbers*, 106; Job 7:19). Not looking intensifies not touching (v. 15), possibly revealing v. 20 as an editorial addition to vv. 17–19 by which the Kohathites were banned from their service (Kellermann, *Priesterschrift*, 59–60). On the high-priestly role to restrict the Levities in chap. 4, see de Vaulx, *Nombres*, 87; Achenbach, *Vollendung*, 497; Budd, *Numbers*, 51.

the cultic service, to do the work[30] in the meeting tent. **24**The service of the Gershonite families involves serving and carrying. **25**They must carry the curtains for the dwelling place and the meeting tent with its covering, the covering of dolphin skin that is on top of it, the curtains for the entrance of the meeting tent, **26**the hangings of the courtyard, the curtain for the entrance of the gate of the court, which is around both the dwelling place and the altar, with their ropes, along with all the furnishings for their service; and with these they must do everything that needs to be done.[31] **27**All the service of the Gershonites will be at the direction of Aaron and his sons, concerning all they carry and every way that they serve. You must assign them to their responsibilities, all they must carry. **28**This is the service of the Gershonite families in the meeting tent. Their responsibilities will be under the authority[32] of Ithamar son of Aaron the priest. **29**As for the Merarites,[33] you must number them by their families and by their patriarchs' households. **30**Count them from thirty to fifty years old, each one who qualifies for the cultic service to do the work of the meeting tent. **31**This is what they are responsible to carry[34] as their complete service in the meeting tent: the frames of the dwelling place, its crossbars, its tentpoles, its bases, **32**and the tentpoles of the surrounding courtyard with their bases, tent pegs, and ropes, with all their furnishings and everything for their service. You all must assign[35] by names the objects that they are responsible to carry. **33**This is the service of the Merarite families, their complete service in the meeting tent, under the authority of Ithamar son of Aaron the priest."

34So[36] Moses, Aaron, and the chieftains of the community listed the Kohathites by their families and by their patriarchs' households,[37]

---

30. Cognates accusative, formally, "to serve the cultic service" (*liṣbōʾ ṣābāʾ*) and "to work the work" (*laʿăbōd ʿăbōdâ*).

31. Formally, "and with all that is done by them, so they must do." LXX[ed] omits "the curtain for the entrance of the gate of the court," perhaps by homoeoteleuton (Wevers, *Notes*, 69). LXX[ed] closes, "and they shall handle as many as those with which they minister" (NETS), which may harmonize to 4:12.

32. Formally, "by the hand of Ithamar," where "hand" is a metaphor for a "(sphere of) power, rule, control . . . authority (e.g., Gen. 41:35)" ("*yād* I," *DCH* 4:82, gloss 4a).

33. By left dislocation, the subject is activated as the primary topic of the subsequent clause: "*As for the Merarites*, by their families and by their patriarchs' households *you must number them*" (*BHRG* §48.2.1).

34. Formally, "this is the responsibility of their load/burden" (see "*maśśāʾ* I," *DCH* 5:495, gloss 2, whereas gloss 6 is "responsibility").

35. The yiqtol command "You all must assign" (*tipqǝdû*, *GBHS* §3.2.2.d.4) is distinctively pl. (SP LXX[ed] and 1:3) since the sg. is predominant (Num. 1:49; 3:10, 15; 4:23, 29, 30; jussive in 27:16) and Yahweh is speaking here to Moses alone (vv. 21–33; cf. to Moses *and* Aaron in vv. 1–16, 17–20).

36. The wayyiqtol "So Moses . . . listed" (*wayyipqōd*) foregrounds the sequence (*BHRG* §21.2.1.1[1]) from Yahweh's command (v. 32) to Moses's obedience (v. 33). See J. Cook, "Wayyiqtol and Weqatal," 247–73.

37. As in 3:16, 42, the wayyiqtol "So Moses . . . listed" (*wayyipqōd*) provides Moses's obedient response to Yahweh's command in v. 2 (sequential, *GBHS* §3.5.1a).

35from thirty to fifty years old, each one who qualified for the cultic service for the work in the meeting tent. **36**Those listed by their families came to 2,750³⁸—**37**these were the ones listed from the Kohathite families, each one who served in the meeting tent, whom Moses and Aaron listed according to the word of Yahweh by the authority of Moses.³⁹ **38**They were listed from the Gershonites,⁴⁰ by their families and by their patriarchs' households, **39**from 30 to 50 years old, each one who qualified for the cultic service for the work in the meeting tent. **40**Those listed by their families, by their patriarchs' households, came to 2,630—**41**these were the ones listed from the Gershonite families, each one who served in the meeting tent, whom Moses and Aaron listed according to the word of Yahweh.⁴¹ **42**They were listed from the Merarite families, by their families, by their patriarchs' households, **43**from thirty to fifty years old, each one who qualified for the cultic service for work in the meeting tent. **44**Those listed by their families came to 3,200—**45**these were the ones listed from the Merarite families, whom Moses and Aaron listed according to the word of Yahweh by the authority of Moses.

46All who were listed from the Levites, whom Moses, Aaron, and the Israelite chieftains listed by their families and by their patriarchs' households,⁴² **47**from thirty to fifty years old, each one who qualified to do the work of service and the work of carrying in the meeting tent—**48**those of them listed came to 8,580. **49**According to the word of Yahweh they were listed, by the authority of Moses, each one according to his service and according to what he was to carry. So they were listed by him, just as⁴³ Yahweh had commanded Moses.

Interpretation

4:1–14. After the monetary collection for the firstborn Israelites who exceeded the number of Levites (3:44–51), Yahweh speaks again, this time to both

---

38. SP "and" (*w*) in the cardinal number (first occurrence) aligns the *w* in vv. 40, 48 (MT/SP).

39. Formally, "by the hand of Moses," where "hand" is a metaphor for a "(sphere of) power, rule, control . . . authority (e.g., Gen. 41:35)" ("*yād* I," *DCH* 4:82, gloss 4a).

40. LXX^ed "Gedson" (*gedsōn*) probably mistook the Hb. *r* for *d* (letters that look similar in Hb.).

41. "By the hand of Moses" is added in LXX^ed, T^J and MT^mss, aligning to Num. 4:37, 41, 45, 49 (also 9:23; 10:13; 15:23; 17:5 [LXX^ed = 16:40]; 33:1; 36:13; in 27:23: 4Q27 MT SP, but not LXX^ed).

42. The Yahweh-Moses discourse (vv. 21–33) and incorporation of Aaron in vv. 1, 34, 37, 41, 45, 46 may indicate an editorial layer that stresses Aaron's important role (Kellermann, *Priesterschrift*, 61–62).

43. "Just as" in LXX^ed (*on tropon*), SP and MT^mss (*k'šr*) may be preferred to "*which* ['šr]" in 4Q23 MT^L. Although *'šr* (4Q23 MT^L) could be motivational ("because," *BHRG* §36.3.1.1.d–e), this reading instead may have resulted from haplography because the parallel relative clauses in Numbers always modify an antecedent, "(according to) *everything that* Yahweh commanded Moses" (1:54; 2:34; 8:20; 9:5; 15:23; 30:1) and "This is/these are *the X that/whom* Yahweh commanded" (19:2; 30:2, 17; 31:21; 34:13, 29; 36:6, 13).

Moses and Aaron (as 2:1), to mandate a census of the Kohathite families, descendants of Levi, who were eligible to serve in Yahweh's tent (4:1–2). The choice of terms is martial: just as other tribal men qualify by age to serve in the military service, so the Levites qualify by age "for the cultic service" in Yahweh's tent (see the third translation note on 4:3). The qualifying age for the other tribesmen to serve in Israel's military was twenty and up (1:3, 18–45), and the age of the Levite substitutes for Israel's firstborn was one month and up (3:15, 22–40), while the age of the Levite patriarchs qualified for the cultic service in Yahweh's meeting tent was thirty to fifty years old (4:3). This twenty-year age span is later expanded to twenty-five years (8:23–26; see comments there), but here initially may reflect two ancient realities. On the one hand, a thirty-to-fifty-year-old male would be able to carry the heavy furniture, coverings, and framework of the meeting tent; on the other hand, a life expectancy in ancient Israel of forty to fifty years would make it unreasonable to require any men over fifty years old to perform this manual labor.[44]

Rather than immediately sending Moses and Aaron to take the count, Yahweh offers an expanded discourse for the Kohathites, who are responsible to transport the tent's holiest objects (4:15–20). As a prerequisite to the Kohathites' involvement, however, Aaron and his sons alone must cover those holiest objects—the ark, table, lampstand, golden (incense) altar, sanctuary utensils, (bronze) altar, and utensils—because Aaron and his sons are allowed to touch them (vv. 4–14).[45] Only then can the Kohathites execute their task of entering the sanctuary to transport the holy furniture by handling their carrying poles (and a carrying frame, v. 10) to avoid touching the furniture even accidentally through their coverings. This divine tent furniture is given the superlative metonym "the holiest things" (superlative gen. in v. 4), which comes from the verb "to be holy" (qdš qal stem). The meaning of "the holiest things" is the cultic objects *that belong to the deity*, Yahweh. To explain this, it is useful to quote the definition of qdš by David Clines, which applies not only to the tent furniture of Num. 4 but also to correlative forms and appearances of qdš throughout Numbers:

> I would advocate instead an inductive approach, based on the typical and most frequent occurrences of the term. Such an approach has led me to the view that qdš is a term for the deity's status or quality (i.e. God is holy), and for what

---

44. Eng, *Our Years*, 40.

45. The inner curtain that divided the sanctuary was repurposed as a cover for the ark, with no mention in Num. 4:5 of "the atonement cover" (*hakkappōret* in Exod. 25–40*; Lev. 16:2–15*; Num. 7:89). Gurtner ("'Atonement Slate,'" 396–98) suggests that the function of the curtain in Num. 4:5 to conceal the ark was recognized by the LXX translator of Exod. 26:34, who renders "*You must put the atonement cover [wənātattā 'et-hakkappōret]* on the ark containing the covenant" (MT/SP) as "*and you must conceal with the curtain [kai katakalypseis tō katapetasmati]* the ark of the testimony" (LXX[ed], my trans.).

belongs to or is in the realm of the deity, whether persons or objects (e.g. holy priests, holy temple). When God is said to be [*qādôš*], no other characteristic or quality is in view than his deity, i.e. his being God. When a person or thing is [*qādôš*], it means it belongs to the deity, no more than that. The natural English equivalent for *qdš* is "holy," but "divine" and "sacred" are usually also appropriate translations. Such a definition can be applied to all the occurrences of the root *qdš* in the Hebrew Bible, I believe. It fits equally well the use of [*qādôš*] for the deity personally and for persons and things that belong to his realm.[46]

Yahweh's possession of the dwelling-place furniture corresponds to the divine-human relational purpose of each piece (see the "Implications" essay below, "The Holiness of God Is Lethal"). Inserting poles into the sacred ark, table, golden altar, and sacrificial altar for transportation (vv. 6, 8, 11, 14) is paralleled elsewhere in the ANE. For example, a scene on the reliefs in the Ramesseum in Thebes (13th cent. BCE) depicts the Egyptian priests handling poles to elevate and transport the sacred bark (boat).[47] By inserting the carrying poles and covering the sacred furniture and their utensils (vv. 5–14), Aaron and his sons mitigated the risk of damage, excessive desert dust, and looting, but also restricted the Israelites and Levites from touching or even seeing the furniture, which must have increased the aura of mystery and danger surrounding their deity, Yahweh.

4:15–20. A soft break occurs in Yahweh's discourse in vv. 2–16 at v. 15: after Aaron and his sons cover the sacred furniture and tools of the sanctuary and the courtyard altar (vv. 2–14), the Kohathites must then begin their work of carrying these cultic accoutrements. Binding together the close of Yahweh's speech in vv. 15–16 and Yahweh's subsequent speech in vv. 17–20 are the key recurring terms (*Leitwörte*) "touch" and "die." The divine warning to the Kohathites of their sure death if they touch the sacred furniture is emphatic, not simply because it is highly redundant in this cluster of verses (vv. 15, 18, 19, 20) but also because of the evocative and contrastive language: "*Do not let* the tribe of the families of the Kohathites *be destroyed*" (v. 18; see the translation note there); and they "must not go in *to look* at the holy things *for even a moment*" (v. 20; see the third translation note there); and three disjunctives (*wə*), two marking prohibitions (vv. 15b, 20a), one making provision so that the Kohathites would not die (v. 19a). In contrast to Mesopotamia, where a non-priestly oath-taker would grasp and lift the cult image of a god in the temple, here in Num. 4 presumably touching even covered sacred objects or catching a glimpse of them uncovered would ensure one's sudden death.[48] The ominous divine warning, repeated four times here in vv. 15–20, suspends the reader until one of Kohath's sons, Korah, with

46. Clines, "*Qdš*," 481–502.
47. Sprinkle, *Leviticus and Numbers*, 203.
48. Milgrom, *Leviticus*, 1:45; see Greengus, *Laws*, 54–55.

his followers oversteps the divine boundaries and is put to death.[49] No such warnings are given to the other two Levite families enlisted in the chapter, the Gershonites and Merarites, since they work outside the most sacred space of the sanctuary, not handling the holy cultic objects but rather the curtains and framework (vv. 21–33). Aaron's oldest son, Eleazar, is appointed as the supervisor over all daily Yahweh worship in the insulated sanctuary (v. 16).[50] The only significant domain outside Eleazar's authority is the altar of burnt offering, in the courtyard, the place where Israelites offer all spontaneous and discretionary burnt offerings, grain offerings, and sacrifices of greetings (Lev. 1–3) but also where they execute the initial blood rituals of the purification and reparation offerings (Lev. 4:1–6:7). The hierarchy manifest in vv. 15–20 could lead to the Kohathites' resentment because Aaron and his sons counted them (implying that the Kohathites are accountable to the Aaronides and ultimately to God),[51] Eleazar is their immediate authority, and the Aaronides alone handle and gaze on the sancta of Yahweh's tent.[52] Resentment is not the only option for the Kohathites, however; the psalmist was content to serve outside Yahweh's sanctuary (Ps. 84:10).

4:21–33. Yahweh commands Moses to take a census of the Gershonites, delegate to them the work of carrying the curtains, coverings, and ropes (vv. 21–28), and take a census of the Merarites, who are assigned the work of carrying the tent's framework and related furnishings (vv. 29–33). Their censuses, like that of the Kohathites (vv. 2–3), are to be organized and recorded by their patriarchal families but restricted to thirty-to-fifty-year-olds who can physically serve in Yahweh's tent (see discussion on 4:3 above). In distinction to the expanded instructions for the Kohathites assigned to work with the sacred cultic furniture (vv. 4–20), the instructions for the Gershonites and Merarites are grouped together in the text in four ways: First, they are expressed as a single divine speech (vv. 21–33). Second, these Levite families will carry no cultic objects but only the curtains, framework, and related tools. In the context, the terms "serving" and "service work" (vv. 24, 28, 30, 33) imply that along with carrying, they are responsible for dismantling and reassembling the tent structure.[53] Third, Ithamar, Aaron's fourth son, has authority over both families (vv. 28, 33; cf. Eleazar in v. 16; see the translation note on

---

49. Douglas (*Wilderness*, 130) spots the theme of danger/death six more times in the rebellion of Kohath's son, Korah (Num. 16).

50. Frevel ("High Priest," 156–57) rightly observes that while Aaron is the most prominent figure, the narrative slowly unfolds the ascendancy of Eleazar as chief priest (3:32→17:2→20:25–28).

51. Leveen, *Memory*, 72–73.

52. Leveen, *Memory*, 117–18.

53. Knohl (*Sanctuary*, 84–85) argues that this task assigned to the Levites was added by H. In any case, we see the conspicuous absence of the Levites in Lev. 1–16 and Exod. 25–40, except for Exod. 32:26–29 (golden-calf judgment) and the terse statement in Exod. 38:21—"the work of the Levites under the authority of Ithamar the son of Aaron the priest"—which is anachronistic because Ithamar is appointed to this role in Num. 4:28, 33 (Frevel, "High Priest," 142).

4:28). Fourth, in v. 29 the asyndeton (no conjunction) and left dislocation are to activate a new but related subject, the Merarites, linking vv. 29–33 to vv. 21–28: "*As for the Merarites*, you must number them" (see the translation note on 4:29). The language of vv. 27–28 and vv. 32b–33 is imprecise but seems to imply that Aaron and his sons (v. 27), maybe limited later exclusively to Ithamar (vv. 28, 33), delegated specific tasks to each Gershonite and Merarite and ensured that they executed their tasks faithfully. The absence of any warnings about the deadly fate of violating their job parameters renders their work less frightening and precarious than that of the Kohathites (cf. vv. 15–20). Although safer and thus more desirable, their work is more distant from the locus of the divine dwelling than the Kohathites, who themselves are more distant than the Aaronides.[54]

4:34–45. In obedience to Yahweh's word, Moses, Aaron, and the chieftains faithfully list the eligible meeting-tent servants in the three families of Levi's tribe (vv. 34–45). The unit repeats the pattern for each family, Kohathites, Gershonites, then Merarites: (1) the leaders listed by their patriarchal households, the thirty-to-fifty-year-olds qualified to serve in the meeting tent (vv. 34–35, 38–39, 42–43); then (2) the narrator gives the total for each family—2,750 Kohathites, 2,630 Gershonites, 3,200 Merarites (vv. 36, 40, 44); (3) inclusion with the listing language of step 1 but augmenting it with a statement of their precise obedience to Yahweh's orders (vv. 37, 41, 45), the first and last statements frame the unit (vv. 37, 45) and affirm Moses as the authorized mediator of the divine orders (see the translation notes on vv. 37 and 41). Maybe the workloads of each Levite family (vv. 4–33) are assigned in proportion to their respective sizes: the smallest family, the Gershonites with 2,630 capable servicemen, carries the folded cloth curtains and ropes (awkward to carry); the medium family, the Kohathites with 2,750, carries the solid tent furniture; while the largest family, the Merarites with 3,200, carries the heavy piles of framework.

4:46–49. The narrator closes out the unit by reiterating their obedience and calculating the sum of Levi's eligible workers (vv. 46–49). Verses 46–48 perpetuate the pattern of vv. 34–45 but now add up the eligible meeting-tent workers for a sum of 8,580 (= totals of vv. 36, 40, 44) to give the impression of a more than adequate, indeed a powerful, task force for constructing, dismantling, and transporting Yahweh's dwelling through the wilderness into Canaan, heading for a heretofore unspecified, yet presumably more stable,

---

54. De Regt ("Partial Repetition," 420–21) argues further that the phraseology in Num. 4 hints at this hierarchy between the three Levite families: "to do work in the meeting tent" applies only to the Kohathites (v. 3), whereas the other two Levite families are in a more submissive posture, commanded "to serve" (vv. 23, 30; also vv. 15, 24). Also, the Merarites may have been asked to assume a more submissive posture than the Gershonites (cf. v. 31 with v. 24): the Gershonites serve under the direction of Aaron and his sons (v. 27), but no such authorization is stated for the Merarites (vv. 29–33).

resting place. Verse 49 is redundant, but for the rhetorical purpose of again reinforcing the reality of Moses and the leaders' obedient execution of the divine directive of listing the qualified Levite workers. The closing in vv. 46–49 functions as an *inclusio* with vv. 2–3 (also culminating vv. 29–30 and 22b–30) but is also an *inclusio* with the faithful enactment of the census of the other eleven Israelite tribes in Num. 1:44–46, 54b–c.[55] The implication is that now, because of the obedience of Israel's leaders, all military personnel (Num. 1–2*) and all divine tent personnel (Num. 3–4*) are registered and strategically primed to march northward, with their satisfied deity residing in their midst, to capture and inherit the land of Canaan from the polities inhabiting it. These framing devices formalize the new sociology of Israel—once only a cultic community (Exod. 25–40) but now a *militant* cultic community on the precipice of a war campaign (Num. 1–4).[56]

Implications

The Holiness of God Is Lethal

The Kohathites, charged with transporting the most sacred furniture of Yahweh's dwelling, lived a precarious existence. If they even touched the covered furniture or glimpsed the uncovered furniture, they had to die (Num. 4:15–20). With no mention of human agents to execute the perpetrator (as there were in Lev. 24:14–16; Num. 15:32–36), the implication is that Yahweh himself would kill any and every guilty Kohathite (as in Lev. 10:2; Num. 16:31–35; et al.). This is vividly illustrated by the story of Uzzah, presumably a Kohathite, whom Yahweh struck dead when he grabbed the ark to keep it from hitting the ground (1 Sam. 7:1; 2 Sam. 6:3–8; 1 Chron. 13:7–11). Is not this punishment much too harsh? Dawkins would certainly say so: among other things, he calls the God of the Old Testament "vindictive, bloodthirsty" and a "capriciously malevolent bully."[57] As offensive as his words may be to believers, I appreciate his critique for its power—like David Hume's "Of Miracles" or Friedrich Nietzsche's *Thus Spoke Zarathustra*—to reveal the perspective of unbelievers whom we are called to love and to compel us to reexamine the OT witnesses to determine whether his reading is essentially correct or misguided. Much could be said in response,[58] but here I simply call attention to the fact that Dawkins has conveniently omitted two descriptors

---

55. See Douglas, *Wilderness*, 110. Obedience to Yahweh's command closes each of the first four chapters in 1:54; 2:34; 3:51; 4:49 (Leveen, *Memory*, 35).

56. Pola (*Priesterschrift*, 51–146, esp. 145) argues the original Priestly layer (P^g) in Exod. 25–40 is distinguishable from the supplement (P^{ge}) that includes Num. 1–4; 10:11–12; 13–14; and Exod. 16*.

57. Dawkins, *God Delusion*, 51.

58. See A. McGrath and J. McGrath, *Dawkins Delusion?*

that saturate the OT story line: Yahweh is both "holy" (*qādôš*) and "your God" (*'ĕlōhêkā*). Yahweh is ontologically *holy*, meaning he is divine,[59] and this implies for the Priestly scribes of the Torah that he is not able to coexist with sin, guilt, or ritual impurity (Lev. 4:1–6:7; 16:16). At the same time, Yahweh is *your God*, the covenant deity of Israel, meaning he has bound himself to this people to love, protect, and satisfy them as he takes up residence in their midst, eventually in the land of Canaan. The Pentateuch's scribes demand that the reader filter any absurd, painfully difficult, even humanly offensive saga about Yahweh's behaviors through the lens of the *antinomy* of his undefilable deity (holiness) and his intimate bond with Israel (covenant).[60] Consequently, any divine act that aims to protect a human or creature from Yahweh's holiness must be perceived as an act of extraordinary grace (cf. Gen. 6:11–13 with Jon. 3:10; 4:2, 11).

This explains why the Kohathites' work was so ominous: the sacred furniture represented the tent where the Divinity, the Holy One, met with his covenant people.[61] This is the literary backdrop of Num. 4:4–14, which good readers of the Moses story so far (Exodus–Leviticus) have picked up incrementally. Here I offer a survey of the meeting-tent furniture that illuminates Yahweh's profound goodness in making a way for his covenant people to survive, to avoid their oft-deserving annihilation, with their holy deity residing in the middle of their encampment.

The "covering curtain" restricts access to Yahweh's dwelling place (see the first translation note on 4:5) and serves to keep it out of sight and free from contagions, which incite divine wrath.[62] Behind that curtain, "the ark containing the witness" functioned as a visible witness to the Yahweh-Israel covenant (see the second translation note on 4:5), which was a common function of international treaty tablets similarly deposited in the temple of the deities and in the palaces of the two kings entering the contract.

This (treaty) was made into seven tablets and sealed with the seals of the sun-goddess of Arinna and the storm-god of Ḫatti. One tablet was placed before the sun-goddess of Arinna, one before the storm-god of Ḫatti, one before Lelwani, one before Ḫebat of Kizzuwatna, one before the storm-god of lightning, and one in the king's house before Zitḫariya. And Kurunta, king of Tarḫuntašša, keeps one in his house.[63]

---

59. Clines, "*Qdš*," 481–502.

60. See Frevel, "Unvollkommenheit," 225–26, 243–44.

61. See Hundley, "Tabernacle or Tent of Meeting?," 3–18.

62. Curtains sequestering the deity in the inner sanctuary are found in Mesopotamia and Canaan. In Mesopotamia, linen curtains were hung for the deity to eat privately, then removed when the meal was finished (Hundley, *Gods in Dwellings*, 69n59, 112n24, 274–75).

63. "The Treaty of Tudḫaliya IV with Kurunta of Tarḫuntašša on the Bronze Tablet Found in Ḫattuša," *COS* 2.18:106.

In distinction, the bilateral treaty between Yahweh and Israel, presumed in Num. 4,[64] was inscribed on two tablets,[65] both of which were deposited before Yahweh in his tent dwelling. The ark was also envisioned as the throne of the invisible, aniconic (without a cult image) presence of Yahweh. The blue cloths and possible dolphin skin covers (vv. 6, 8, 10, 11, 12, 14) were not only protection against a touch from the Levites or other non-Aaronic Israelites but also portrayed Israel's deity as a god of the sea, like Ugarit's 'El, who resided "in the midst of the sea" (see the first translation note on 4:6). Perhaps also the blue signifies the sky or heavens, insofar as the aniconic (unrepresentable) Yahweh was nonetheless glorified as the one who fashioned the sky.[66] I capitalize the genitive in the hapax descriptor, "table of the Presence" (v. 7), where "Presence" is a metonym for Yahweh. The imagery is of Yahweh seated at a table in his dwelling place, but the anthropomorphism is restricted in that an expected (ANE) accompanying libation is absent, and the priests, not Yahweh, eat the bread (see the first translation note on 4:7).[67] The stress, instead, is on Yahweh as creator and sustainer, who rests in his abode communing with his covenant people.[68] The almond-tree-shaped lampstand (Exod. 25:31–35) probably reflects the ancient sacred tree of life in Mesopotamian, especially Sumerian and Assyrian iconography,[69] but now, burning in the meeting tent, this candelabrum signifies that Yahweh illuminates and gives life to Israel (see Num. 6:24–26).[70] The golden incense altar removed foul smells and surrounded the Deity with an aroma absorbed by officiating priests.[71] The altar was intended for Israelite sacrificial expressions of devotion and gratitude to

64. In the Sinai narrative, the tent furniture ensues from the Yahweh-Israel covenant (Exod. 20–24, 34), and Num. 1–4 may reflect H influence (Knohl, *Sanctuary*, 71–73, 172–75, 189–96).

65. Exod. 24:12; 31:18; 32:15–19; 34:1–4, 28–29.

66. The Decalogue forbids imaging Yahweh (Exod. 20:4), but from another source comes the claim that Moses, Aaron, Nadab, Abihu, and seventy elders "saw the God of Israel. Under his feet there was something like a pavement of blue lapis lazuli, as clear as the sky itself" (Exod. 24:10, my trans.). Theodoret of Cyr (5th cent.) thought the blue cloth of Num. 4 symbolized the sky and heaven, while purple signified the kingdom of God (Lienhard, *Numbers*, 207).

67. Mesopotamian temple priests generally sought to maintain the impression that the god consumed the meal in his dwelling (Hundley, *Gods in Dwellings*, 257).

68. Gane, "'Bread of the Presence,'" 179–203.

69. Staubli, *Levitikus, Numeri*, 233. Eagle-winged genies are often found attending the tree of life on the reliefs of Assyrian palace walls. Yarden (*Tree of Light*, 35–36, 40–42) argues that the menorah in the tent/temple of Yahweh (1) reflects Israel's reformulation of the Mesopotamian mythology of the cosmic Tree of Life; (2) incorporates the ANE, Aaronic, and Mosaic notions of the budding almond tree and burning bush (Exod. 3; Num. 17); and (3) offers a response to tree fertility cults and Asherah images. On the tree of life in Scripture, see Gen. 2:9; 3:22, 24; Prov. 3:18; Rev. 2:7; 22:2, 14, 19.

70. See also Pss. 4:6; 18:28; 27:1; 36:9; 43:3; 44:3; 56:13; 89:15; 90:8; 97:4; 104:2; 118:27; 119:105, 130.

71. In Egyptian temple worship, "Incense removes any olfactory impurity, surrounding the deity, its space and its priests with the divine aroma. Alongside radiance, aroma is a primary sign of divinity" (Hundley, *Gods in Dwellings*, 179).

Yahweh (Lev. 1–3) and for purification and reparation offerings (Lev. 4:1–6:7). Covering and preparing to transport the washbasin, which was not merely hygienic but essential to removing ritual impurities from the sacred priests and implements that belonged to Yahweh,[72] has a disputed textual basis (v. 14 SP/LXX). I am inclined to regard this step as original because its omission in vv. 4–26 (presuming either the Kohathites or Gershonites had to carry it) would be a glaring absence (see the translation note on 4:14).

In sum, the furniture of Yahweh's meeting tent had to be guarded by the Aaronic priests and Kohathites not merely because it was lethal upon physical or visual contact but also because it was a gift of immeasurable proportion that made possible the enduring presence of Yahweh with his incessantly defiling, but well-loved, covenant people.

---

72. The holy, associated with life, cannot coexist with impurity, associated with death (Milgrom, *Leviticus*, 1:46–47).

5

Remove Impurity; Restore Wrongs; Ritual for Adultery

(5:1–31)

❦

Overview

After the closure of the first block of discourse (Num. 1–4), which oriented Israel's military forces and cultic life around Yahweh's dwelling, the subsequent three divine speeches to Moses in Num. 5 cohere under the common theme of *removing impurity from the Israelite community*, whether it is impurity transmitted bodily through contagions (vv. 1–4), communally through wrongdoing (vv. 5–10), or sexually through infidelity (vv. 11–30).[1] The unit of vv. 1–4 contributes to the dominant theme in Num. 1:1–10:10 of preparing to march into Canaan.[2] Yahweh directs Moses to command the Israelites to send outside their encampment all physically unclean people (à la Lev. 11–15), and the narrator tells us that the Israelites immediately obeyed. The next two speeches in vv. 5–10 and 11–30 seem to depart thematically from the march preparations of 1:1–10:10,[3] and linguistically they are connected not to vv. 1–4 but to each other by the language of "unfaithfulness" (*ma'al) to Yahweh (v. 6) and to one's husband (vv. 12, 27). In vv. 5–10, Yahweh orders

---

1. Stuabli (*Levitikus, Numeri*, 220) sees 5:1–6:27 as a single Priestly scroll, starting with expelling impurity from the people (5:1–4) and ending with the Aaronic blessing of the people (6:22–27). For Achenbach (*Vollendung*, 499–508, 638), within the theocratic revision of the Torah (in Num. 1–10, 15–19, 26–36), Num. 1–4 belongs to the first layer, with Num. 5–6 starting the second layer, which focuses on purity laws and ritual regulations.
2. Seebass, "Eigene Komposition," 90–92.
3. Seebass, "Eigene Komposition," 106.

Moses to instruct the Israelites to make full restitution for their sins against others resulting in unfaithfulness to Yahweh. Finally, in vv. 11–28, Yahweh's lengthy discourse supplements the sexual code for Israelite males revealed in Lev. 18 and 20: now Yahweh also expressly demands the sexual faithfulness of married Israelite women and adapts an ancient water ritual to expose marital infidelity and remove such impurity from the community. Finally, the narrator in vv. 29–31 concludes the last speech (vv. 11–28) by summarizing the purpose of the law and the water ritual for a woman suspected of infidelity.

Translation

1Then Yahweh spoke to Moses: **2**"Command[4] the Israelites to send out[5] of the camp everyone with a skin disease,[6] everyone with a discharge, and everyone defiled by a corpse. **3**You must send out both male and female.[7] You must send them outside the camp so that they will not defile their camps in which I live."[8] **4**So the Israelites did this and sent them outside the camp. Just as Yahweh had spoken to Moses, so the Israelites did.

5Then Yahweh said to Moses: **6**"Speak to the Israelites, 'When a man or a woman commits any sin against another person, resulting in

---

4. SP: "*He commanded* the Israelites" (*ṣwh*, vocalized *ṣiwwāh* piel qatal; some SP^mss read *ṣwy* [also in SP 20:13; 34:2; 35:2], the meaning of which is questioned: Ulrich, *Qumran*, 141). The 2nd masc. sg. impv. "Command" (MT) appears for the first time in Numbers here and is less common (5:2; 28:2; 34:2; 35:2), while SP probably harmonized to conventional usage (36× in Num. 1–36).

5. The weqatal "send out" (*wîšalləḥû*) assumes the impv. force of the opening verb (command) and is a piel factitive, which, if obeyed, would cause the state of being sent out (*GBHS* §3.1.3a).

6. This qal pass. ptc. "who is skin diseased" (*ṣārûaʿ*) is often translated "leprous" or "leper" (ESV, NRSV, KJV, NET), but this is misleading. Since the late nineteenth century, "leprosy" has medically been referred to as Hansen's disease, the symptoms of which are reflected in records from India from 600 BCE and maybe as early as 1400 BCE (Bennett, Parker, and Robson, "Leprosy," 198–99); *contra* Walton and Matthews (*Genesis–Deuteronomy*, 187), who claim no attestation prior to Alexander the Great. However, the verb *ṣrʿ* (noun *ṣāraʿat*) in Lev. 13–14 signifies not leprosy but various types of skin disease (NLT, NIV, NJPS); the same is true for the Greek *lepros*, which was confused with what we call *leprosy* today (see Awabdy, *Leviticus*, 275). What Naaman and Gehazi suffer from in 2 Kings 5:1–27 is indeterminate. In Akkadian, *saḥaršuppû* (*CAD* 15:36–37) refers to the skin disease, the person afflicted with it, and the scaly symptoms, offering an analogy to Num. 5:2 and other Pentateuch texts (Exod. 4:6; Lev. 13–14*; 22:4; Num. 12:10; Deut. 24:8).

7. Formally, "from male *to* [*d*] female" (MT^L SP LXX^ed), but 4Q23 (and MT^mss SP^mss Tg^PJ Syr) includes "from male *even to* [*wd*] a female" (as 6× in chap. 4 "even to fifty years"; also see 6:4; 14:11, 19).

8. See excursus below.

unfaithfulness to Yahweh,[9] and that[10] person is found guilty, [7]then they must confess their sin that they committed and make full restitution, add one fifth to it, and give it to the one he wronged. [8]But if the wronged person has no close relative to whom restitution can be made, the restitution must be paid to Yahweh for the priest, in addition to the ram of atonement by which atonement is made for him.[11] [9]Every tribute[12] of all the Israelites' holy things that they bring to the priest will be his. [10]Every person's holy things will be[13] his; whatever any person gives the priest will be his.'"

[11]Then Yahweh said to Moses: [12]"Speak to the Israelites and tell them, 'If any man's wife goes astray and is unfaithful to him,[14] [13]and a

---

9. A verb and adverbial cognate, "for unfaithfully acting unfaithfully against Yahweh" (*lim'ōl ma'al bayhwh*). The *l* + inf. const. likely indicates the result: "commits any sin against another person, *resulting* in unfaithfulness to Yahweh" (*GBHS* §3.4.1d). 4Q23 might include a direct obj. marker between the inf. and noun (Ulrich, *Qumran*, 141).

10. The MT spelling of this 3rd fem. sg. far demonstrative (21× in Numbers) is idiosyncratic in the Pentateuch (*hahiw'*) versus 4Q23 SP (vocalized *hahî'*).

11. "The ram of atonement" ('*êl hakkippurîm*), meaning the ram that atones (subjective gen., *GBHS* §2.2.3) or ram intended to atone (purpose, *GBHS* §2.2.8), with an anaphoric article, which arguably refers to the atonement ram in Lev. 5:15–19, but now Num. 5:5–10 adapts the prior law (see comments on 5:5–10). This first occurrence of the verb **kpr* in Numbers is a piel resultative (of **kpr* qal transitive; see Gen. 6:14, "cover it," *DCH* 4:455–56). The priest is the implied agent (see Lev. 5:6, 10), the ram is the means, and the offender is the beneficiary (advantage '*al: IBHS* §11.2.13c): "with which [the ram] he [the priest] makes atonement by it [the ram, resumptive pron.] on behalf of him [the offender]." The piel of **kpr* (to make atonement, to atone for) in Numbers means "to make expiation (for)" (*DCH* 4:455; later S. Wong, "Notion of [*kpr*]," 81) adds that in the Priestly literature, **kpr* piel expiates or purges by means of a *kōper* (ransom); the blood sacrifice "rescues the impure person or sinner from the judgment of the Lord." Expiating—purging or removing sin, guilt, or ritual impurity—is distinct from the frequent LXX rendering of **kpr* as *exilaskomai* (middle voice), which means "to propitiate, appease" the deity or the Lord (as **kpr* is used initially in Gen. 32:21 [20 Eng.]): Büchner, "Appeasing God," 237–60.

12. Instead of overinterpreting the morphology of *tərûmâ* as a "raised offering" (deverbal from **rwm*, to raise; Seebass, *Numeri*, 1:114; NET), the noun refers generically to a "contribution" (*DCH* 8:675) or "tribute" (*HALOT* 4:1788–90, gloss 3c–d). Similarly, in Akkadian the probable verbal cognate *riāmu* means "to present, to grant, to deed an estate" ("*râmu* B," *CAD* 14:146), and its substantive noun probably originally meant "gift" (*HALOT* 4:1788–90, drawing on von Soden, "Mirjām-Maria," 269–72). I prefer "tribute": (1) "contribution" (most versions) and "donation" (Levine, *Numbers*, 1:387) can give the impression that the Israelites are somehow contributing toward a need that Yahweh has, which *tərûmâ* does not imply; (2) *tərûmâ* in Num. 31 is an improper synonym of *mekes* (tribute), which appears in the OT only in Num. 31 (*mekes*: vv. 28, 37, 38, 39, 40, 41; *tərûmâ*: vv. 29, 41, 52). The translation "tribute" is similar to "levy" or "dues" (for de Vaulx, *Nombres*, 208; EÜ; Schmidt, *Numeri*, 76).

13. SP sg. "*it will be* his" (*lw yhyh*) perhaps harmonizing to vv. 9, 10.

14. A cognate adverbial inf.: "and she unfaithfully acts unfaithfully against him." In Numbers, **m'l* occurs only in this chapter (5:6, 12, 27), functioning as a submotif meaning "to be untrue, violate one's legal obligations" (*HALOT* 2:612) or "transgress, esp. commit sacrilege, as redressed by the ['*āšām*] *reparation offering*" (*DCH* 5:400).

man has sex with her[15] without her husband knowing it, and it is hidden that she has defiled herself, and there is no witness against her, that is,[16] she was not caught, **14**but then jealous feelings[17] come over him and he becomes jealous of his wife who has defiled herself,[18] or jealous feelings come over him and he becomes jealous of his wife though[19] she had not defiled herself, **15**then the man must bring his wife to the priest, and he must bring the offering required for her:[20] one tenth of an ephah[21] of barley flour. He must not pour olive oil on it or put frankincense on it because it is a grain offering[22] for jealousy, that is, a memorial grain offering for remembering iniquity.[23] **16**Then the priest will bring her near and have her stand before Yahweh.[24] **17**The priest will take holy water in a clay jar and take[25] some of the dust that is on the floor[26] of the dwelling place and put it into the water. **18**Then the priest will have the woman stand before Yahweh, and he will let down the woman's hair[27] and put in her hands the grain offering for remembering, which is the grain offering for jealousy. The priest will hold in his hand the bitter[28] water that brings

15. Formally, "and a man lies with her in a bed of semen/seed."

16. The conjunction *w* may be epexegetical (*GBHS* §4.3.3d) since "there is no witness against her" explains "she was not caught."

17. Formally, "a spirit of jealousy" (*rûaḥ-qinʾâ*), an attributive gen. with "jealousy" as an attribute of his "spirit" or "feelings" (*GBHS* §2.2.5).

18. This niphal verb *niṭmāʾâ* is likely a reflexive, "has defiled herself" (NRSV, NLT, ESV; *GBHS* §3.1.2), which is supported by her active role in her unfaithfulness (v. 12), rather than a passive or stative, "is defiled/impure" (NIV, NET).

19. "Though" renders a *w* marking the circumstances of this second scenario (*GBHS* §4.3.3e).

20. Formally, "her offering upon her," with "upon her" (*ʿāleyhā*) marking her obligation (*GBHS* §4.1.16b) or, less likely, "on her behalf" (NLT), indicating that her husband offers this for her benefit.

21. The "ephah" (*ʾēpâ*), a dry measure for cereals, was a tenth of a homer (*ḥōmer* = 150 liters), about 15 liters (King and Stager, *Life*, 200). One-tenth of an ephah of barley flour would be about 1.5 liters, not quite "two quarts" (NLT).

22. LXX[ed] "sacrifice" (*thysia* in chap. 5: vv. 15 [2×], 18 [2×], 25 [2×], 26) conceals the nuance of this "grain offering" (*minḥâ*).

23. The raw grain offering required olive oil and frankincense (Lev. 2:1–3), whereas this variation for jealousy is qualified as "a memorial grain offering" (*minḥat zikkārôn*), which, formally, "causes remembering iniquity" (*mazkeret ʿāwōn*, hiphil attributive participial phrase) and thus conveys its purpose "*for* remembering iniquity."

24. "Before Yahweh" (*lipnê yhwh*, vv. 16, 18, 25, 30) here refers to a location proximate to Yahweh's altar of burnt offering, as suggested by the only previous use (3:4, Nadab and Abihu) and is clarified later 5:25–26.

25. For the sake of style, the restated subject, "the priest" (*hakkōhēn*), is untranslated.

26. "Floor" (*qarqaʿ*) occurs only here in the Pentateuch and six other times in the OT, where it refers to the floor of the temple, throne room, or seabed (*HALOT* 3:1148; *DCH* root I, 7:330; cf. Akkadian *qaqqaru* in *CAD* 13:113, gloss 1, "ground, soil"; and 10, "floor").

27. This weqatal has an impv. force; the root (*prʿ* I) appears in Numbers only here and means to let hair down (*HALOT* 3:970, gloss 2a) or hanging loose (*DCH* 6:772, gloss 1b).

28. In vv. 18, 19, 23 [2×], 24, 27, the gen. noun **mar* probably does not mean "strength" (Sasson, "Numbers 5," 249–51) or "instruction" (Brichto, "*šōṭā*," 59). With support from an

a curse.[29] [19]Then the priest will put the woman under oath and say to her,[30] 'If no other[31] man has had sex with you, and if you have not gone astray and defiled yourself while under your husband's authority, may you be immune[32] from this bitter water that brings a curse. [20]But if you have gone astray while under your husband's authority, and if you have defiled yourself and a man other than your husband has had sex with you . . .' [21]Then the priest must have the woman take the oath of the curse and say to her,[33] 'May Yahweh make you a sworn curse[34] among your people, if Yahweh makes your hips collapse and your womb swell,[35] [22]then[36] this water that brings the curse will enter your intestines and make your womb swell up and your hips collapse.' Then the woman must say, 'Yes, let it be.'[37] [23]Then the priest will write these curses on a scroll and wipe them off into the bitter water.[38] [24]He will make the woman drink the bitter water that brings a curse, and the water that brings a curse will enter her to cause bitter pain. [25]Then the priest will take the grain offering of jealousy from the woman's hand, elevate[39] the grain offering before Yahweh, and bring it to the altar. [26]The priest will

---

Ugaritic text (*mr), Pardee ("Mārîm," 112–15) argues convincingly that it means "bitterness," which is coextensive with "illness."

29. The attributive piel ptc. might convey a fut. tense: "the bitter waters *that will curse* [ham'ărārîm]" (aspect and tense of attributive ptcs. are contextually determined; *GBHS* §3.4.3a).

30. The Hb. word order, "Then the priest will put *her* under oath and say to *the woman*," was interchanged for Eng. style.

31. "Other" is added in this translation for clarification.

32. A niphal impv. (hinnāqî) here meaning "to be free (from harm)" ("nqh," *DCH* 5:749, gloss 6) but not precisely "to be free . . . from guilt" (*HALOT* 2:720).

33. Formally, "and the priest must say to the woman."

34. I render this as a hendiadys with two uses of *l* that mark two products, formally, "into an oath and into a curse" (lə'ālâ wəlišbu'â; *GBHS* §4.1.10e.2).

35. I render the double accusatives, "Yahweh makes your *hips collapse* ['et-yərēkēk nōpelet] and your *womb swell* ['et-biṭnēk ṣābâ]," because maternal physiology is in view (yārēk, hip, thigh; bṭn, womb, stomach: *DCH* 4:299, gloss 1; 2:141, gloss 1). Most likely, Num. 5 does not refer to a miscarriage (Garroway, *Growing Up*, 39–40), since there is (1) no mention of a baby; (2) the language is of fertility and infertility, not effects on a current pregnancy. Rather, the positive outcome in v. 28—"She will be immune and *able to conceive a child* [wənizrə'â zāra']"—implies that the negative outcome in v. 27 would make her infertile (Seebass, *Numeri*, 1:141–42; Cardellini, *Numeri 1,1–10,10*, 251). Womb swelling appears to reflect an enlarged uterus possibly caused by endometriosis, fibroids, adenomyosis, PCOS, endometrial cancer, early menopause, ovarian remnant or cysts, or another malady. Hips collapsing might reflect pelvic failure possibly caused by musculoskeletal problems, pelvic floor dysfunctions, chronic pelvic inflammatory disease, hypothalamic dysfunction, or other malady.

36. The weqatal marks the logical result, the apodosis, of the condition, "*then* . . . will enter" (ûbā'û; *GBHS* §3.5.2d).

37. With "may it be, may it be!" (NETS for LXX^ed); formally, "Amen, Amen."

38. LXX^ed adds, "the water of reproof *that brings the curse*" (NETS).

39. See the first translation note on 6:20.

take[40] a handful of the grain offering as its memorial portion, burn it on the altar, and afterward make the woman drink the water. **27**When he has made her drink the water,[41] then, if she has defiled herself and been unfaithful to her husband, the water that brings a curse will enter her to cause bitter pain. Her womb will swell up, her hips will collapse, and the woman will become a curse among her people. **28**But if the woman has not defiled herself and is pure, then she will be immune and able to bear children."

29This is the jealousy law, when a wife, while under her husband's authority, goes astray and defiles herself, **30**or when jealous feelings come over a man and he becomes jealous of his wife. He must have the woman[42] stand before Yahweh, and the priest will apply this entire law to her. **31**Then the man will be free from iniquity, but that woman will suffer for her iniquity.[43]

Interpretation

5:1–4. Divine words continue to come from the meeting tent (1:1), but the subject matter shifts from Yahweh's meeting tent as the center of Israel's military arrangement and priestly mediation to removing physical impurities that threaten to contaminate the Israelite camp (vv. 1–4). Yahweh's imperative to Moses, "*Command* to send out of the camp," replaces the typical "speak to the Israelites," suggesting now an urgent problem that must be remedied (see the first translation note on 5:2). The three contagions that need to be expelled from the camp are named but without any detail about their nature (v. 2), probably since they were already extensively described in the Sinai instructions of Leviticus: various cases of "skin disease" (*ṣrʿ) are detailed in Lev. 13–14 (see the third translation note on 5:2); genital "discharge" (*zwb), male and female, in Lev. 15; and "corpse" defilement (*ṭmʾ lnpš, lit., "defiled by a life/corpse") in Lev. 11* and 21–22*.[44] This triad, which appeared in a slightly longer form only in Lev. 22:4, may serve as a shorthand for all the contagions of Lev. 11–15 and 21–22.[45] Yahweh makes explicit the reason why the Israelites must remove these physically impure people from their camp: "so that they will not defile their camps in which I live." In the Moses story,

40. SP: "The Priest *will take up* [*whrym*] some of the grain offering," probably assimilating to the wording of Lev. 2:9.

41. "When he has made her drink the water" (MT SP) is absent in LXX[ed], possibly due to homoeoteleuton (*hmym*, "the water," also ends v. 26; Wevers, *Notes*, 91).

42. LXX[ed] clarifies as "*his* wife."

43. Formally, "will carry her iniquity/guilt."

44. Defilement by carcasses of scurrying creatures in Lev. 11:31–32, but more precisely in Num. 5:2 of a human corpse, as in Lev. 21:1, 11; 22:4.

45. Frevel ("Book of Numbers," 32) rightly questions how Num. 5:1–4 relates to the impurity laws of Num. 19:11–22.

Yahweh's enduring residence among his people is always one of the central aims of his covenant with his people.

Excursus: Yahweh Lives among His People

The participle in v. 3, "so that they will not defile their camps in which *I live* [*šōkēn*]," expresses a continuous action simultaneous with Yahweh's present speech (*BHRG* §20.3.3[1]). This belongs to the dwelling motif in the Sinai pericope (Exod. 19:1–Num. 10:10): Yahweh's glory, covered by the cloud, resides on the mountain, where he meets with Moses (Exod. 24:16), orders the construction of his dwelling place (*miqdāš*) "so that I may live in their midst" (Exod. 25:8, *wəšākantî bətôkām*; similarly 29:45–46), and then takes up residence in his dwelling (Exod. 40:34–35). In Leviticus, this dwelling "resides with them in the midst of their uncleannesses" (Lev. 16:16), necessitating annual cleansing by atonement. After Sinai, the cloud moves and resides (**škn* qal) to direct the Israelites where they must camp in the wilderness (Num. 9:17, 18, 22; 10:12), but in Numbers an *inclusio* with Num. 5:3 is formed in 35:34, where Yahweh demands, "Do not defile the land where you will live, *in which I live* [*'ăšer 'ănî šōkēn bətôkāh*], because *I Yahweh live among the Israelites* [*'ănî yhwh šōkēn bətôk bənê yiśrā'ēl*]." The language differs in Deuteronomy: Yahweh places *his name to reside* in the place that he will choose out of Israel's tribes (12:5, 11; 14:23; 16:2, 6, 11; 26:2).

Although Yahweh continues to live among his people, he cannot coexist with the impurity caused by sin or guilt (Lev. 4:1–6:7; 16); now he makes clear that he cannot coexist with bodily impurities either.[46] It is essential to clarify that physical impurities are not equivalent to, or the result of, any particular sin, iniquity, or rebellion;[47] however, they do contribute to the defilement of Yahweh's dwelling, as Milgrom explains for Lev. 14–16: "The individual's ethical 'wrong' . . . , the impurity of the person with scale disease (chap. 14) or abnormal discharge (chap. 15), and the physical impurities and moral iniquities of collective Israel (chap. 16) have this in common: they are responsible

---

46. This conceptuality in Num. 5 underlies Qumran's Temple Scroll (ca. late 1st cent. BCE/early 1st cent. CE), which excludes physically impure persons from the temple city: "And the city which I will sanctify to cause my name and my sanctu[ary to dwell within it] shall be holy and pure from every type of impurity by which they can become impure; everything else which shall enter it shall be pure" (11Q19 XLVII, 3–6): Harrington, "Intermarriage," 466–67.

47. Relevant to 5:1–4 are Milgrom's (*Leviticus*, 1:926) remarks on Lev. 15:15: "One bearing physical impurities, even the most severe kind, is not accused of sin; his sacrifice is not *mēḥaṭṭā'tô* 'for his wrong' (4:26). Above all, the purpose of the sacrifice is not *wənislaḥ lô* 'that he may be forgiven' (4:31, 35)." Theodoret of Cyr (5th cent. CE) sees this distinction but infers that there were levels of uncleanness (Lienhard, *Numbers*, 208).

for the pollution of the sanctuary."[48] Probably the reason is that skin disease, genital discharge, and corpse contact are impure contagions that belong to the realm of death—dead skin, genital discharges (blood/semen life force) not bringing about a new human life, and dead bodies—and this realm is dangerous because Yahweh is entirely for life and is ontologically incompatible with death.[49] Nothing is said of those whose skin and genitals heal, wash themselves, perform the correct purification ritual, and are pronounced clean by the priest, but the source text of Lev. 13–15 already granted them permission to resume their lives in the community.[50]

Following the pattern of Num. 1–4, the narrator closes by explaining Israel's obedience in a three-part repetition: "[1] So the Israelites did this, [2] and sent them outside the camp. [3] Just as Yahweh had spoken to Moses, so the Israelites did." Consequently, the unit's legacy is to underscore the Israelites' expeditious removal of impurities that threaten to defile their camps, in the middle of which Yahweh resides.

5:5–10. Yahweh communicated the preceding speech to redress a present Israelite issue, unremoved contagions, that Yahweh as deity *was witnessing* (vv. 1–3). This next speech returns to the norm of Yahweh *anticipating* issues to come: "When a man or woman commits any sin against another person, resulting in unfaithfulness to Yahweh." An offense against another human requires full restitution of the losses or damages plus a fifth (vv. 7–8), but it is simultaneously regarded as an act of unfaithfulness to Yahweh and therefore also requires a ram for atonement (v. 8; see the translation note there).[51] The notion that interpersonal sin is fundamentally against God appears frequently in the OT, such as the psalmist confessing his murder to God (Ps. 51:14, attributed to David), or Joseph's conviction that adultery is a vertical offense: "So how could I do such a great evil and sin against God?" (Gen. 39:9). Regarding Num. 5:5–10, the notion that sin against other members of the covenant (treaty) community is tantamount to unfaithfulness to Yahweh echoes from the ancient Near Eastern contractual literature.[52] By analogy, in the Assyrian king Esarhaddon's Succession Treaty (EST and VTE), loyalty to the future king demands loyalty to the king's brothers also. Fidelity to the divine king, Yahweh, necessitates fidelity to his covenant people, Israel.[53]

---

48. Milgrom, *Leviticus*, 1:926.

49. Frevel, "Unvollkommenheit," 226; Milgrom, "Impurity," 107–11; Milgrom, *Leviticus*, 1:46; Douglas, *Leviticus*, 176–94.

50. See Lev. 13:13, 17, 37, 39, 40, 41. The adverbial phrase is limiting: "*All the days they have the disease*, they will be unclean" (Lev. 13:46*).

51. Frevel, "Unvollkommenheit," 230–31.

52. "Every hostile action against a co-vassal is hostility against the king himself" (Mendenhall, "Covenant Forms," 59).

53. "SAA 02 006. Esarhaddon's Succession Treaty [EST and VTE]," §8, http://oracc.museum.upenn.edu/saao/saa02/corpus.

The primary contribution of the divine speech in Num. 5:5–10, delivered at Sinai (assumed from 3:14), can be seen in how it innerbiblically expands prior divine revelation from Sinai in Lev. 6:1–7.[54] The bold text marks distinct language, while the underlined text marks shared language (intertexts), which may best be described as an allusion in Num. 5* to Lev. 6*:

Leviticus 6:1–7 [5:20–26] (my trans.)	Numbers 5:5–10
[1]Then Yahweh spoke to Moses:	[5]Then Yahweh said to Moses: [6]**"Speak to the Israelites,**
[2]"When a person sins and so acts in unfaithfulness to Yahweh by deceiving one of his own people with regard to a deposit or a pledge, or something stolen, or by defrauding one of his own people, [3]or found something lost but denies it and swears falsely about anything that a person might do to sin,	[6]**'When a man or a woman** commits any sin **against another person,** resulting in unfaithfulness to Yahweh,
[4]and so it happens that he **sins** and he is found guilty, **then he must return what he stole, or what he defrauded, or what he held as a deposit, or the lost thing that he found,** [5]**or anything about which he swears falsely.**	and that person is found guilty,
He must restore it fully and add one fifth to it, and he must give it to its owner when he **is found guilty. [6]Then he must bring his reparation offering to Yahweh,** a ram **without blemish from the flock, in your estimation as a reparation offering** to the priest. [7]**So the** priest will make atonement for him **before Yahweh, and he will be forgiven for whatever he has done to become guilty."**	[7]**then they must confess their sin that they committed** and make full restitution, add one fifth to it, and give it **to the one he wronged. [8]But if the wronged person has no close relative to whom restitution can be made, the restitution must be paid to Yahweh for the priest,** in addition to the ram of atonement by which atonement is made for him. [9]**Every tribute of all the Israelites' holy things that they bring** to the priest **will be his. [10]Every person's holy things will be his; whatever any person gives the priest will be his.'"**

There is no indication that Num. 5:5–10 was intended to be a replacement, since it includes the core elements of Lev. 6:1–7—interpersonal sin, unfaithfulness to Yahweh, found guilty, full restitution plus one-fifth, and the ram of atonement—and Num. 5:8 employs a subtle citation device to teach that the atonement ram detailed in Lev. 6:6–7 is still required: *"in addition to [millǝbad] the ram of atonement by which atonement is made for him."* If one reads Num. 5:5–10 by itself, one is left wondering which primary offenses in

54. Knohl (*Sanctuary*, 86–87) identifies H style (à la Lev. 17–26; Num. 18) in Num. 5:5–10 but not in Lev. 5:21–26; see Cardellini, *Numeri 1,1–10,10*, 233–41; Seebass, *Numeri*, 1:115–19; Frevel, "Rituals," 143–45.

view result in unfaithfulness to Yahweh and how one can "make full restitution" for them (Num. 5:6–7). The answers are clear from the source text of Lev. 6:2–4: the offender must restore anything taken deceptively or by fraud in various ways, such as stealing items, deposits, and pledges; keeping lost property; and swearing falsely. Furthermore, the priest's reparation offering ritual expiates or purges the sin of vv. 6–7, and this removal, the source text of Lev. 6:7 has made clear, allows Yahweh to forgive—that is, not to direct his punitive anger against the offender (see the translation notes on 5:8 and 6:12).

The intertextual revision of Num. 5:5–10 modifies Lev. 6:2–4 in three distinct ways. First, Num. 5* is more egalitarian and possibly also more expansive, including immigrants who were held to the same standard elsewhere in Numbers (*gēr*, immigrant; 11× in Num. 9–35*). So "when a person sins" (Lev. 6:2) is rewritten as "when a man or a woman commits any sin" (Num. 5:6), and the twofold mention of deceiving or defrauding "one of his own people" (Lev. 6:2) appears to be replaced by the more inclusive "against another person" (Num.5:6).[55] Second, indemnity without remorse is seen as insufficient, so Num. 5 demands that the offender start by verbally confessing the sin to the offended and maybe implicitly also to Yahweh (see Num. 5:6; Lev. 16:21; 26:40; 1 John 1:9).[56] Third, not only is the meat of the atonement ram of the reparation offering designated for the male Aaronic priests (Lev. 6:6; csp. 7:6–7; Num. 5:8), but now presumably if the offended person dies with no close relative, the restitution must be paid *to Yahweh for the priest* (Num. 5:8). This is then expanded even further in the over-specified vv. 9–10 as the primary communicative stress of the 5:5–10 unit: every tribute from all the Israelites now belongs to the priests for their consumption or use.[57] The "tribute" and "holy things" (vv. 9–10) are two generic metonyms for various Israelite offerings and sacrifices, but the reader must wait for the divine speech in Num. 18:8–13 to discover which types are specifically designated for the Aaronic priests.

5:11–31. Yahweh's preceding speech (5:5–10) and this speech (5:11–28) are conjoined by a disdain for Israelite *unfaithfulness* (esp. vv. 5–6, 12, 27). Yahweh is deeply concerned that his covenant people are marked by loyalty: the Israelites must not sin against each other because this is tantamount to *unfaithfulness* to God, and a wife must not have sex with another man because this is tantamount to *unfaithfulness* to her husband. The deceptive offenses among the Israelites—listed in Lev. 6:2–5, the source text presumed in Num.

---

55. The addressees ("Speak to *the Israelites*," 5:6) could encompass immigrants living in the community (9:10, 14; 15:2, 14–16, 18, 26–30; 19:2, 10; 35:10, 15).

56. Hithpael **ydh* (confess) occurs four times in the Pentateuch: Num. 5:7 and its source, Lev. 5:5; on the Day of Atonement, Aaron confesses Israel's iniquities, transgressions, and sins to Yahweh (Lev. 16:21); and exiled Israel confesses iniquity to Yahweh (Lev. 26:40).

57. With Cardellini (*Numeri 1,1–10,10*), vv. 9–10 are likely a clarification by the Priestly editors; cf. Achenbach, *Vollendung*, 503–4.

5:6—are continued here with deceptive infidelity by the wife (5:12, 27). The
verbal root for "unfaithful," used in both units, conveys a formal breach of
loyalty (on *m'l, see the translation note on 5:12), which is analogous to formal
breaches of loyalty in the ancient Near Eastern contractual literature.[58] Verses
11–31 are not only connected by "unfaithfulness" to vv. 5–10 but also return
with over-specificity to the *Leitwort* of defilement or impurity (forms from
ṭm') from vv. 1–4: the Israelites must purify their own human defilement
caused by physical contagions (vv. 2–3) and by a wife's adultery (vv. 13–29).[59]

In vv. 11–31, when a husband has jealous feelings (see the first translation
note on v. 14) and becomes suspicious that his wife has had sex with another
man, whether the husband's suspicion of her infidelity is correct or not (vv.
12–14), he must bring her with the accompanying offering to the priest (v. 15),
who then will direct the woman to enact a holy-water drinking ritual explicitly in Yahweh's presence (vv. 16–28).[60] Elsewhere in the Torah, adulterers
are sentenced to death on the testimony of witnesses, so the loophole that
this ritual fills is that when human witnesses are lacking,[61] the community
can ascertain *from Yahweh* whether the wife was unfaithful by observing if
she experiences a divine curse manifested in her presumably instantaneous
physiological deformation (vv. 15–28). The ritual has ten steps by one count,[62]
but may be collected into five phases:

1. *The husband brings his wife suspected of adultery to Yahweh's dwelling with an accompanying grain offering* (vv. 15–16). The suspicious
   husband leads his wife to the priest, presumed to be stationed in the
   courtyard around or even inside the meeting place (4:16, 28, 33; 5:8, 16),
   and the priest guides the woman to "stand before Yahweh" (v. 16), which
   likely refers to the courtyard (no non-priest was to enter the sanctuary:
   3:38; 4:20), but putting her in the presence of the divine amplifies the
   gravity of the situation (see the translation note on 5:16). Accompanying
   his wife, the husband brings a new form of the raw grain offering, which
   resembles Lev. 2 and 6 but is revised as "a grain offering *for jealousy*,
   that is, *a memorial* grain offering *for remembering iniquity*" (see the
   last translation note on 5:15). In Lev. 2:1–3 and 6:14–18, the devotee

---

58. See comments on 20:24; 27:14 for the improper synonym *mrh* (rebel).

59. In v. 2, the adj. *ṭāmē'* (defiled) occurs, followed in v. 3 with *ṭm'* piel (defile); *ṭm'* niphal
(defile oneself) occurs in vv. 13, 14 [2×], 20, 27, 28, 29; and the adj. *ṭum'â* in v. 19.

60. For a robust study of 5:11–31, see Cocco, *Women*, 7–115. Traditionally this unit was
called the Sotah law, from *śôṭâ*, a Mishnaic Hebrew term for a woman "who goes astray" (*śṭâ*
in 5:12).

61. Witnesses (two or three in Deut. 19:15) were needed to bring accusations of adultery in
Deut. 22:22; Lev. 19:20; 20:10 (Frevel, "Unvollkommenheit," 233–34; Fishbane, "Accusations,"
25–26, 39).

62. Kellermann, *Priesterschrift*, 79.

can voluntarily bring to Yahweh an undefined amount of an undefined type of raw grain, mixed with olive oil and frankincense, and from this grain the priest burns a handful to Yahweh on the altar of burnt offerings but eats the rest in the courtyard. By contrast, the Num. 5* grain offering is obligatory; a measured amount, roughly 1.5 liters, of barley; and *without* olive oil or frankincense "because it is a grain offering for jealousy," intended to evoke the bitter memory of the sexual perversion and thus not to function like a normal grain offering as "a pleasing scent to Yahweh" (Lev. 2:2, 9, 12; 6:15, 21). While diverging from Lev. 2* and 6*, the ritual innovation of the grain offering for jealousy does appear to adapt Lev. 5:11,[63] which accommodates so that a poor person can offer roughly 1.5 liters of raw grain as a purification offering, but in that case it is used by the priest to effect atonement (without blood! Lev. 5:13).

2. *The priest prepares the ritual elements, guides the woman to display her vulnerability before Yahweh, and administers an oath* (vv. 17–22). The source of the "holy water" (a hapax construction, v. 17) is unstated, but most simply is the washbasin, which has been recently consecrated to Yahweh (Lev. 8:11). Into a container with this water the priest adds "dust that is on the floor of the dwelling place"—not that this dust has been sanctified by the priests (in Exod. 35–40; Lev. 8–9) but that the floor of the deity's dwelling (see the second translation note on Num. 5:17) is probably regarded as sacred by proxy (as Exod. 3:5) and, in any case, is incorporated into the ritual to ascertain Yahweh's verdict.[64] Dirt from the floor can represent the very walking place of Yahweh, like his garden temple in Eden (Gen. 3:8),[65] which is imagined in ANE temples such as at 'Ain Dara', where giant footprints were carved into the floor as a walking path from outside directly into the sanctuary.[66] The priest then positions the woman before Yahweh and lets her hair down (see the first translation note on v. 18), which is not clearly a symbol of mourning or shame[67] but rather of her vulnerability in the presence of the divine judge.[68] For Yahweh and his priest to see her unbound hair was to encounter her beauty, as her husband does.[69] Yahweh will see this vulnerable woman

---

63. Frevel, "Rituals," 145–46.
64. The Urim and Thummim were also divinely sanctioned: Exod. 28:30; Lev. 8:8; Num. 27:21; Deut. 33:8; 1 Sam. 14:41; Ezra 2:63; Neh. 7:65.
65. With Beale, *Temple*, 66–75; but cf. Block, "Eden," 3–30.
66. Hundley, *Gods in Dwellings*, 154, 362.
67. Contra Walton and Matthews (*Genesis–Deuteronomy*, 181), mourning is more precisely linked with disheveled or unkempt hair (Lev. 10:6; 21:10). For the connotation of a shameful exposure, one would expect nudity (Lev. 20:17), and while it was shameful for a woman to have her hair shaved (Isa. 3:24; King and Stager, *Life*, 283) and dishonorable to uncover her hair, at least later in NT worship (1 Cor. 11:6), this text says nothing of disheveled, cut, or uncovered hair.
68. Frymer-Kensky, "Strange Case," 25.
69. Song 4:1; 5:2; 7:5; 2 Kings 9:30; Ezek. 16:7; 1 Cor. 11:15.

in the wilderness, as he saw a vulnerable Hagar in the wilderness (Gen. 16:13), and if she is innocent, Yahweh will protect her honor and capacity to bear children (Num. 5:28). The priest then immerses her hands in the grain offering "for remembering" and "for jealousy" (v. 18), which again underscores her vulnerability and generates suspense for her husband and the priest,[70] leaving only her and Yahweh to know if her conscience is clear or accusing her while the grain engulfs her hands. Holding the bitter water that brings a curse (see the third translation note on v. 18), the priest places her under an oath, which is a performative speech act that activates either her immunity to the cursing water if she is innocent (see the third translation note on v. 19) or her suffering of the curse if she is guilty (vv. 19–20; for ANE laws, see the "Implications" essay below, "A Misogynistic or Optimal Ritual to Counter Infidelity?"). The woman then takes the oath of the curse, meaning she herself, if guilty, will become "a sworn curse" (see the second translation note on v. 21) among her people as Yahweh, by means of the bitter water that she drinks, deforms and thereby sterilizes her procreative organs (vv. 21–22; see the third translation note on v. 21).[71] The language of the priest's words and her words is highly over-specified, which slows down the discourse to magnify how precarious that moment is for her.[72]

3. *The priest writes the oath curses on a scroll and wipes them into the bitter water* (vv. 23–24). In the ancient Near Eastern context where writing down texts had a numinous power as a "gift of the gods,"[73] the priest writes onto a scroll the words of the curses that he just pronounced (v. 21) and that the woman affirmed (v. 22), then wipes them off into the bitter water that brings a curse (v. 23). Yahweh announces that the priest is going to make her drink it (v. 24, actualized in v. 26).[74] An analogy to this can be seen in an Old Babylonian ritual at Mari (eastern Syria) that involved "eating the oath," that is, one accused of perjury had to swallow herbs that would become poisonous if they were guilty.[75]

---

70. See Sternberg, *Poetics*, 265–67.

71. In distinction from P's impersonal punishments, H directly attributes punishment to God, as in v. 21 (Knohl, *Sanctuary*, 88). Lipton ("Bitter Waters," 121–39) argues that the *bitter waters* ritual in Num. 5 utilizes the structure, imagery, and theology of the *flood waters* in Gen. 6–9 to show how the husband/wife relationship is apropos to the divine/human relationship, but the evidence is unconvincing.

72. See Runge, *Discourse Grammar*, 387.

73. Schniedewind, *Bible Became a Book*, 24–34, here 24.

74. Yahweh orders some of his prophets to eat the scroll that contains his revelation (Jer. 15:16; Ezek. 3:3). Van Seters (*Life of Moses*, 305) recalls that Yahweh commands his people to drink "poisoned water" because of their sin (Jer. 8:14; 9:15; 23:15), but rightly points out that the similarity with Exod. 32 is limited to drinking the water with the remains of the golden calf.

75. Sasson, "Numbers 5," 249–51. Staubli (*Levitikus, Numeri*, 222) and Walton and Matthews (*Genesis–Deuteronomy*, 181) see a parallel from a Mari letter, depicting a human who

4. *The priest takes the woman's grain offering of jealousy, raises a handful before Yahweh, burns it on the altar, then makes her drink the water* (vv. 25–26). The priest takes the grain offering from the woman's hand, elevates it before Yahweh (see the first translation note on 6:20), and burns it on the altar in typical fashion as a memorial portion; but instead of eating the rest of the grain as one expects (Lev. 6:16), the priest makes the woman drink the bitter water (v. 26).

5. *When she drinks the water, she will either be immune, revealing her faithfulness, or will suffer physiologically, revealing her unfaithfulness* (vv. 27–28). After drinking the water, which is now loaded with the divine power to curse her (by virtue of vv. 19–23), then if she has defiled herself and been unfaithful to her husband, her body will degenerate, immediately one presumes, rendering her infertile and accursed; but if she has been faithful, then she will be immune and fertile (vv. 27–28).

The editorial subscript in vv. 29–31 summarizes only the bitter water ritual for the wife suspected of adultery (vv. 11–28). Restating key terms from the unit, two elements are unique in this subscript: the husband, not merely the priest, has the woman stand before Yahweh (cf. vv. 16, 18, 30), the exclusive judge of the matter, and the final word stresses the innocent husband's freedom from iniquity but his guilty wife's suffering (v. 31; see the "Implications" essay below, "A Misogynistic or Optimal Ritual to Counter Infidelity?"). Verse 29 appropriates the formula of subscripts known so far in the Pentateuch only from the Priestly laws in Lev. 1–16: "This is the law of X" (*zō't tôrat* + genitive).[76] The rhetorical effect of employing this formula in Num. 5:29–31 is to present the bitter-water ritual for exposing a woman's adultery (vv. 11–28) as an extension of Lev. 1–16—that is, *as legislation pertaining to the priestly cult of Yahweh's dwelling*. For a wife to defile herself by a sexual act of disloyalty to her husband, echoing the motif of disloyalty to Yahweh (5:6, 12), defiles the dwelling of Yahweh, which means that the grain offering for jealousy, the wife's infertility, and the curse she embodies (vv. 15, 18, 25, 27) do not nullify her contribution to the layers of impurity amassing on the divine dwelling that must be purified through the annual Yom Kippur ritual: "So he must make atonement for the (most) holy place from the impurities of the Israelites and from their transgressions with regard to all their sins. So he must do this for the meeting tent, which resides with them in the middle of their impurities" (Lev. 16:16, my trans.).

---

saw the gods drinking a potion containing dirt from the city gate as they vowed to guard the city of Mari (Sasson, "*Apocalypticizing*," 151–67).

76. In the Pentateuch, "This is the law of X" can serve as a superscription or subscription to a law, ritual, or collection of speeches. Prior to Num. 5, all occurrences come from Lev. 1–16 (6:9, 14, 25; 7:1, 11, 37; 11:46; 12:7; 13:59; 14:2, 32, 54, 57; 15:32). Occurrences after Num. 5 are as follows: Num. 6:13, 21; 19:14; Deut. 4:44; 19:4; Ezek. 43:12.

Implications

A Misogynistic or Optimal Ritual to Counter Infidelity?

If read in isolation, the bitter water ritual of Num. 5:11–31 can give the impression of being a primitive and obsolete ordeal, or worse, a misogynistic weapon used by the priest to humiliate and control women and the entire community.[77] This has led some to resort to an allegorical reading informed by prophetic dramas like the book of Hosea: the unfaithful woman in Num. 5* is the unfaithful Israel, and the just and jealous, yet compassionate, husband is Yahweh.[78] Such an approach, however, fails to read this ritual in its Pentateuchal and ancient Near Eastern legal context.

First, in the Pentateuch, Num. 5* has been placed after the Sinai instructions already delivered by Yahweh in Lev. 18–20 that emphatically subordinated Israelite *patriarchs* and *young men* to a sexual code that aligned with the holy nature of Yahweh (Lev. 19:2) and protected the purity of the covenant community and of their future home, the land of Canaan (Lev. 18:1–5, 24–30; 20:22–24). Specific sexual prohibitions (Lev. 18) and their correlating punishments (Lev. 20) are almost exclusively directed to Israelite males,[79] so that one could conceive of Num. 5* as answering the question "What about females who initiate adultery but there are no witnesses? What if someone's wife is secretly promiscuous?"[80] The opening protasis, indeed, depicts a scenario in which the wife is the initiator (5:12c), while the common, androcentric idiom indicates that her lover was complicit (5:13a), yet the stress falls on her defiling action (5:13c): "*If any man's wife goes astray and is unfaithful to him*, and a man has sex with her without her husband knowing, and it is hidden that *she has defiled herself*" (vv. 12b–13c); and again later in the ritual oath, "and if you have not gone astray and defiled yourself" (v. 19).

Second, when compared with the ancient Near Eastern laws and rituals, the Num. 5* ordeal is redemptive in that it gives more power and honor to accused women. Several studies have come to conclude that the Num. 5* ritual was formulated not to trap and punish guilty women but to protect innocent

---

77. Leveen, *Memory*, 74–75.

78. Douglas, *Wilderness*, 168–69.

79. Specific sexual prohibitions directed to males: Lev. 18:6, 7, 8, 9, 10, 11, 12, 13, 14, 15, 16, 17, 18, 19, 20, 22, 23a; 19:20–22, 29; the sole sexual prohibition directed to females is Lev. 18:23b. Although both the man and woman (or another man [20:13] or animal [20:15]) are subject to the death penalty for their perversions, the protases focus on the sexual agency and culpability of the man (Lev. 20:10, 11, 12, 13, 14, 15, 17, 18, 19, 20, 21); only one of twelve protases or prohibitions is directed to a woman (Lev. 20:16).

80. Similar questions could also be raised about the Num. 25 story, which indicates that although the Moabite/Midianite women initiated the infidelity (v. 2), it was the Israelite men who were to be executed (v. 5). The execution of the Moabite/Midianite women who had ritual sex with the Israelite men came later in the unfolding narrative at Moab in Num. 31:17.

women.[81] This claim cannot be validated, but what is clear, especially in the ANE context, is that the ritual transfers the social power of the male priests to Yahweh, who alone reveals his verdict and sentence, either accusing and punishing the woman or acquitting and liberating her.[82] Like drinking the curse-producing waters (Num. 5:18–19), other ANE laws demand that the accused woman be thrown into the turbulent waters of the divine River god: if she survives, she is exonerated, but if she drowns, she was obviously guilty.[83] These ordeals, with demonstrable divine verdicts, had the power to silence false (and thereby oppressive) accusations. However, other ANE laws required some form of retribution for accusations of adultery that were proved false or thought to be proved false.[84] The Num. 5* ritual is, in this way, superior in that a husband's misguided suspicions or accusations were not punishable, encouraging the community's recourse to expose infidelity, but were invalidated categorically by Yahweh, which would restore the woman's honor in the community: "But if the woman has not defiled herself and is pure, then she will be immune and able to bear children" (v. 28). Conversely, if guilty, her infertility would be a stigma and curse, so that she became the embodiment of a deterrent to sexual unfaithfulness.[85]

Finally, in the Code of Hammurapi (Hammurabi) §131, an accused woman's oath by a god is adequate to acquit her: "If her husband accuses his own wife (of adultery), although she has not been seized lying with another male, she shall swear (to her innocence by) an oath by the god, and return to her house."[86] Such an oath would be taken seriously by the woman and her husband, but without the judgment of the River god, her husband could question her veracity and harbor jealousy when she returns home. Those lingering feelings would not be possible in the Israelite household after an accused woman escapes the Num. 5* ordeal with immunity, for even though her innocence embarrasses her unjustifiably jealous husband, in the end it gives him grounds for renewed trust in her.

In continuity with the intent of the Num. 5* bitter-water ritual, and with the faithful life and teachings of Jesus of Nazareth,[87] the body of Christ, the church, is likewise to be marked by fidelity and therefore called to expose marital infidelity. It is only becoming of the sons of light who are united to

---

81. Sasson, "Numbers 5," 249–51; Brichto, "śōṭā," 55–70; Milgrom, "Suspected Adulteress," 69–75; Feinstein, "'Bitter Waters,'" 300–306; Roi, "Law of the Sotah," 161–79.

82. Frymer-Kensky, "Strange Case," 25.

83. The River god ordeal(s) for accusations of adultery are found in Urnamma Laws §14; Code of Hammurapi §132; Middle Assyrian Laws §A 17 (see Greengus, *Laws*, 53–58).

84. Greengus (*Laws*, 53–59) discusses Deut. 22:13–21; Middle Assyrian Law §A 17, 18; and the Code of Hammurapi §127.

85. See King and Stager, *Life*, 46.

86. "The Laws of Hammurabi," *COS* 2.131:344.

87. See Matt. 5:27–32; 15:19–20; 19:9, 18; Mark 7:22; 10:11–19; Luke 16:18–20; John 8:3–4 (secondary tradition).

the holy, resurrected Lord Jesus Christ to expose darkness in his body, his visible manifestation on earth (Eph. 4:11–14).[88] The fundamental problem the church has with the Num. 5* ritual is not how to expunge its misogynistic elements (which I hope I have shown to be a misguided view of it), but rather, shockingly, the opposite: *How do we expose infidelity effectively and honorably without the benefit of ancient Israel's foolproof bitter-water ritual?* That ritual had the ideal capacity not only to punish and deter infidelity but also to publicly invalidate all false accusations. In these matters, the church of Jesus must throw itself, again and again, on the grace and wisdom of our holy Lord, the great shepherd of the sheep, who is perfecting his sheep and enabling us to do God's will and please him in every painfully difficult path we must tread (Heb. 13:20–21).[89]

---

88. Also Rom. 2:22; 13:9; 1 Cor. 5:1–13; James 2:11; 2 Pet. 2:14; Rev. 2:22.

89. This correlates with the vision of a ritual like 5:11–31 to perfect the imperfect people of a holy and dangerous God (Frevel, "Unvollkommenheit," 243–44).

6

Nazirite Vow and Priestly Blessing

(6:1–27)

∽◦◦◦

Overview

Following the formulaic (Leviticus-like) subscript of 5:29–31, which closed off instruction for the bitter-water ritual (5:5–28), Yahweh speaks again to Moses in the meeting tent in the Sinai wilderness (1:1). Again, the message is intended for the entire Israelite community (6:1–20), and again the editors employ the formulaic subscript (6:21) to circumscribe the law in the same way that the editors characteristically distinguished the collections of sacrificial and dwelling-place instructions in Lev. 1–16*. This time, Yahweh extends a unique prerogative to Israelite men and women alike (v. 2): if any Israelite, female or male, desires to devote themselves wholly to Yahweh, they can do so by taking a Nazirite vow for a set period of time (6:1–21).[1] This was the common, non-priestly Israelite's opportunity to become consecrated to Yahweh, just as the Levites and Aaronic priests were (3:10, 11–51), but only temporarily. After the subscript of 6:21, Yahweh orders Moses to instruct Aaron precisely how to perform the powerful speech act of verbally blessing the Israelite people (6:22–27). Employing a salutary blessing form well known in ANE epistolary correspondence and common anthropomorphic imagery, the so-called Priestly or Aaronic Blessing centers on the benefits of

---

1. Staubli (*Levitikus, Numeri*, 224, my trans.) identifies:
    A   Introduction (6:1–2)
      B   Prohibitions (6:3–8)
         X (Corpse) Defilement (6:9–12)
      B¹ Fulfillment (6:13–20)
    A¹ Subscript (6:21)

the life-giving divine presence of Yahweh in the center of his covenant people, illustrated most recently and clearly by the covenant blessings in Lev. 26:1–13. Some have seen the arrangement of Sinai materials in Num. 1:1–10:10 as an editorial "junkyard," pointing in particular to the seemingly arbitrary order of 6:1–21 (Nazirite law), 6:22–27 (Priestly Blessing), and then 7:1–89 (chieftains dedicating Yahweh's altar).[2] In contrast to chaps. 3–4, however, these units are interconnected in centering on the inclusion of non-priestly Israelites in Yahweh worship: the prerogative for any non-priestly Israelite to be consecrated to Yahweh (6:1–21) is followed by the priestly transmission of Yahweh's blessing on every Israelite (6:22–27), followed by the non-priestly chieftains taking center stage in the grand ceremony to consecrate Yahweh's altar (7:1–89).[3]

Translation

¹Then Yahweh spoke to Moses: **²**"Speak to the Israelites, and tell them: When a man or a woman performs the wonder[4] of taking a Nazirite vow in order to consecrate themselves[5] to Yahweh, **³**they[6] must separate themselves from wine and brandy.[7] They must not drink vinegar made

---

2. Seybold, *Der Segen*, 61.

3. On the organization, see Seebass, "YHWH's Name," 43–50; Seebass, *Numeri*, 1:169–70; Berlejung, "Gesegnete Mensch," 43–44.

4. Due to the context here, many translate **pl'* hiphil as "make a difficult vow" (*DCH* 6:685) or "take/make a special vow." Elsewhere, however, it means "to do something wonderful" (*HALOT* 3:927–28). I prefer the latter meaning because the modifying construction (*l* + inf. const. + internal adjunct) already means "by vowing a Nazirite vow" (*lindōr neder nāzîr*), showing *DCH* to be redundant: "He makes a difficult vow by vowing a Nazirite vow." Several versions try to adapt the "wonder" nuance: "take/make a *special* vow of a Nazirite."

5. The *Leitwort* of 6:2–21 is **nzr*, which as a substantive, "(the) Nazirite" ([*han*]*nāzîr*, vv. 2, 13, 18, 19, 20, 21), could be a stative "one who is consecrated" (similarly *DCH* 5:649) or reflexive "one who consecrates oneself" (qāṭil pattern: *IBHS* §5.3c). The root **nzr* in chap. 6 (vv. 2, 3, 5, 6, 12) is always in the hiphil with a reflexive meaning and an expressed or implied *l* of advantage, "consecrate oneself to Yahweh" (see *DCH* 5:651; *GBHS* §4.1.10.e.1); the verb can also have a denominative connotation, "to be a Nazirite" (*HALOT* 2:684; *DCH* 5:651). The nominalized segolate *nēzer* (consecration) is used throughout this unit to refer to the Nazirite's period of separation to Yahweh (vv. 4, 5, 7, 8, 9, 12 [2×], 13, 18 [2×], 19, 21 [2×]).

6. Throughout vv. 1–21, I use they/them/their for 3rd-pers. masc. sg. verbs because the vow can be taken by either gender: "When a man or a woman" (v. 2).

7. This OT dyad, "wine and brandy" (*yayin wəšēkār*), is fronted here as the focus (*BHRG* §47.2.1[2a]). While "wine" (*yayin*) production and consumption are well-known (McGovern, S. Fleming, and Katz, *Origins*, 321–32), identifying *šēkār* is more difficult, although King and Stager (*Life*, 101–2) offer a convincing possibility: "The pomace of the grape was 'distilled' into grappa, a brandy. The simple technology for its production was available in the Bronze Age. It is probably this brandy, with an alcoholic content of 20 to 60 percent, that was known in Hebrew as *šēkār*, giving rise to the verb *šākar*, 'to be drunk.' . . . Based on this passage in Numbers [chap. 6], *šēkār* cannot refer to 'beer' (as it does in Mesopotamia) but can only be

from wine or vinegar made from brandy,[8] and they must not drink any grape juice[9] or eat fresh grapes or raisins. **4**During[10] their consecration, they must not eat anything that is produced from the grapevine, from seed to skin. **5**During their vow of consecration, no razor may be used on their head until the period that they consecrated themselves to Yahweh is finished.[11] They will be holy. They must let the hair on their head grow long.[12] **6**While they consecrate themselves to Yahweh, they must not go near a dead body.[13] **7**They must not defile themselves[14] for their father or mother, brother or sister, if they die, because their consecration to God is visible on their head.[15] **8**During their consecration they must be holy to Yahweh. **9**If anyone dies suddenly beside them and they defile their consecrated head, then they must shave their head when it is purified—on the seventh day they must shave it. **10**On the eighth day they must bring two turtledoves or two young pigeons to the priest at the entrance to the meeting tent. **11**Then the priest will offer one as a purification offering[16] and the other as a

---

a grape product. . . . At Ashkelon it is second on a list of beverages after 'red wine' (*yayin 'ādōm*)."

8. Genitives of material/source: "They must not drink vinegar *made from wine* or vinegar *made from brandy*" (*ḥōmeṣ yayin wǝḥōmeṣ šēkār*; IBHS §9.5.3d).

9. This const. noun with a gen. of source, "juice from grapes" (*mišrat 'ănābîm*), is an OT hapax (*DCH* 5:567). Its meaning as a synonym for *'āsîs*—unfermented juice exuded from stone-crushed grapes or the weight of the grape pile (King and Stager, *Life*, 98, 101)—may be inferred since wine and vinegar have already been covered and now "they must not drink any grape X" (see *šrh II, "soak," but no obvious Semitic cognates: *HALOT* 3:1354). SP with an aleph (*mš'rt*) may have confused this uncommon word for "juice" with "kneading trough" (*miš'eret*), which occurs elsewhere in the Pentateuch (Exod. 7:28; 12:34; Deut. 28:5, 17) and could make sense in 6:3, "they must not drink anything from *a trough of grapes*."

10. Formally, "all the days."

11. Formally, "until the fulfillment of the days that they consecrated."

12. The asyndetic piel inf. const. assumes the imperatival force of the prior main verb (*GBHS* §3.4.2d). "Long hair" ("*pera'* I," *DCH* 6:773) appears only here clearly and in the reinterpreted law for Zadokite priests in Ezek. 44:20, where the redundant gen. "long hair *of hair*" is absent; debatable are Deut. 32:42 and Judg. 5:2, which might use the homonym, "leader" ("*pera'* II," *DCH* 6:773; *HALOT* 3:971).

13. The construction (*'al-nepeš mēt lō' yābō'*) could contextually mean "must not contact a dead body" (NET), which would resemble Lev. 22:4, where priests must not touch a dead body (with "touch," **ng'*). However, one might prefer the formal "must not go near a dead body" (NRSV, ESV, NLT, NJPS, NIV) because of the Lev. 21:11 parallel, which apparently prohibits priests from even approaching corpses. This would suggest, in a canonical reading, that Samson as Nazirite should not have even turned aside to see (Judg. 14:8), let alone touch (v. 9), the lion's carcass.

14. The hithpael factitive is reflexive, meaning: "They must not put themselves into a defiled state" (*GBHS* §3.1.3a; 3.1.5a).

15. "Visible" (like "symbol," NIV, NLT) is added to clarify the formal expression "The consecration of his God is on his head" (*nēzer 'ělōhāyw 'al-rō'šô*), which is shorthand for v. 5.

16. Rendering *ḥaṭṭā't* as "purification offering" (NET) rather than the more common "sin offering" (*HALOT* 1:306, gloss 2) conveys the removal of impurity caused by sin but also by

burnt offering, and make atonement for them, because they sinned with regard to the corpse. So, they must sanctify[17] their head that same day [12]and consecrate themselves to Yahweh during their consecration and bring a year-old male lamb as a reparation offering,[18] but the previous days will not be counted because their separation was defiled."

[13]"This is the Nazirite's instruction: When the period of their consecration is finished, they must be brought to the entrance of the meeting tent, [14]and they must present their gift to Yahweh: one male lamb a year old without blemish as a burnt offering, one ewe lamb a year old and without blemish as a purification offering, one ram without blemish as a sacrifice for peace,[19] [15]and a basket of bread made without yeast, cakes of fine flour mixed with olive oil, wafers made without yeast and smeared with olive oil, with their grain offering and their libations. [16]The priest must present all these[20] before Yahweh and offer his purification offering and his burnt offering. [17]He must offer the ram as a sacrifice for peace to Yahweh, along with the basket of bread made without yeast. The priest must also offer his grain offering and his libation. [18]Then the Nazirite must shave their consecrated head at the entrance to the meeting tent and take the hair from their

---

contagious ritual impurities (i.e., after childbirth, skin diseases, bodily discharges in Lev. 12, 14, 15). As Milgrom (*Leviticus*, 1:760) concluded, "The *ḥaṭṭā't* is [also] prescribed for persons and objects who cannot have sinned"; also Goldstein, "Women," 47–65.

17. Rather than regarding it as an improper synonym of *nzr hiphil (as in "reconsecrate," NET; "consecrate . . . again," NIV), I chose to render *wəqiddaš*—a factitive piel meaning "put into a holy state"—as "sanctify" because this is the first and only time the verb occurs in chap. 6.

18. The noun *'āšām* (HALOT 1:96, gloss 3; DCH 1:415, gloss 1)—which occurs in Numbers only here and in 5:7, 8 (2×); 18:19—is here translated "reparation offering" (de Vaulx, *Nombres*, 100; Cazelles, *Nombres*, 43; Ashley, *Numbers*, 136; Budd, *Numbers*, 68; NET) with a connotation of reparation from 5:7–8 (Cardellini, *Numeri 1,1–10,10*, 221, transliterates). The conventional rendering, "guilt offering" (Levine, *Numbers*, 1:217; Seebass, *Numeri*, 1:151; EÜ), can give the wrong emphasis on legal or psychological guilt, which is secondary to the damaged relationship with both divine and human parties.

19. This sacrifice, appearing nineteen times in Numbers (thirteen in chap. 7), is conventionally translated "peace offering(s)" (ESV, NLT, NET), formally "the sacrifice of peaces [pl.]" (*zebaḥ haššəlāmîm*, of *zebaḥ* I DCH 3:79; HALOT 1:262–63, gloss 3), or dynamically "the sacrifice of well-being" (NRSV, NJPS). The rendering "sacrifice for peace" (a gen. of purpose) was chosen to reflect the Akkadian "gift of peace/greeting" (*šulmānu*), which was presented while pronouncing "Peace!" Also, in the Ugaritic Keret epic a besieged king sends a tribute (*šalāmūma*) to pacify his attacker (Levine, *Numbers*, 1:224–25; cf. Jacob's gifts to pacify Esau: Gen. 32:3–21; 33:8–11). Conceptually, I follow Levine, but his word choice, "sacred gifts of greeting," has a weaker connotation today, like a sacrifice to say "Hi" to God. The Israelites ate the blood-drained meat of the sacrifice for peace, Yahweh metaphorically consumed the fats, and the priests ate the breast (Lev. 7:15–17, 29–36; cf. Lev. 21:6, "offerings by fire to Yahweh, the food/bread of their God"); such a communal meal also supports the connotation of "sacrifice for peace" (similarly, "sacrifices of communion," for Seebass, *Numeri*, 1:179; de Vaulx, *Nombres*, 108; Cazelles, *Nombres*, 46; "sacrifices of shared offerings," Budd, *Numbers*, 78).

20. The elliptical obj. "all these," referring to all sacrificial animals and elements in vv. 14–15, is supplied for clarity.

consecrated head and put it on the fire where the sacrifice for peace is burning.[21] [19]The priest must take the boiled shoulder of the ram, one cake made without yeast from the basket, and one wafer made without yeast, and put them in the Nazirite's hands after they have shaved their consecrated head. [20]Then the priest must elevate them as an elevation offering[22] before Yahweh—they are a holy portion for the priest, along[23] with the breast of the elevation offering and the thigh of the tribute offering.[24] After that the Nazirite may drink[25] wine."

[21]This is the instruction for the Nazirite who vows their offering to Yahweh in addition to their consecration, as well as[26] whatever else they

21. Formally, "on the fire that is under the sacrifice for peace."

22. The "elevation offering" (*tənûpâ*; NRSV, NJPS; Milgrom [see below]; de Vaulx, *Nombres*, 102; Leveen, *Memory*, 118–20) in Num. 6:20 (2×); 8:11–21 (4×); 18:11, 18 is often rendered "wave offering" (ESV, NIV, NET, RSV; Noth, *Numbers*, 53) but sometimes "special offering" (NLT; Budd, *Numbers*, 69), "presentation offering" (Levine, *Numbers*, 1:276; Cazelles, *Nombres*, 20), "dedication offering" (Seebass, *Numeri*, 1:151, Ashley, *Numbers*, 137), "shaking offering" (rendering Cardellini, *Numeri 1,1–10,10*, 224), or dynamically, "moves back and forth" (for EÜ). The noun is deverbal, derived from and used as a cognate obj. with the verb *nwp, which in cultic settings occurs in the hiphil and is thought to mean (1) "wave an offering, in presenting it at the altar" ("*nwp* I," *DCH* 5:646, gloss 3) or "move backwards and forwards in front of the altar" ("*nwp* I," *HALOT* 2:682, gloss 2a); (2) "bring something while holding it up" toward the deity in the sacred space ("*nwp* I," *HALOT* 2:682, gloss 2b); or (3) from a different root, "treat as a special contribution" ("*nwp* IV," *DCH* 5:646). Levine (*Numbers*, 1:276) conflates meanings 1 and 2, which is improbable, while meaning 3 has been argued on the basis of the Neo-Babylonian noun *nūptu* (additional payment, present; *CAD* 343), yet there is no evidence that a *nūptu* was ever offered to a deity. Meaning 1 is based on the hiphil, meaning "wave back and forth" (*HALOT* 2:682), but I prefer meaning 2. Milgrom ("Alleged Wave-Offering," 33–38; *Leviticus*, 1:461–73) has shown that the predominant connotation of the verb is not "to wave" but "to elevate," and "elevate" makes more sense of a number of texts that are often translated "to wave" or "to wield" (i.e., Isa. 10:15b; 11:15; 13:2; 19:16; Exod. 20:25; Deut. 23:26; 27:5; Milgrom *sic*.: Exod. 20:24 [22]; Deut. 27:4; Josh. 8:31). Whereas the Hittite and Mesopotamian waving rituals were not sacrificed to a deity, distancing them from the biblical *tənûpâ*, the Egyptians practiced a rite of elevating offerings to Amen-Ra' or another deity (i.e., Karnak temple relief), so Milgrom argues that "'elevate . . . before the face of the God' is the exact equivalent of *hēnîp tənûpâ . . . lipnê YHWH*" ("Alleged Wave-Offering," 36; *Leviticus*, 1:472). Additional support for rendering *tənûpâ* as "elevation offering" may come from the cult at Ugarit: de Tarragon proposes a possible gesture of elevating a sacrifice to Baal in "A Ritual for a Day and a Night" (*KTU* 1.39, lines 9b–10). My translation differs slightly from Pardee's (*Ritual and Cult*, 67–68): "*dtt*-grain and emmer, fifteen full measures of each *as a presentation offering* [*šnpt*], half of this. A ram for *Ba'lu* of *Ṣapunu*" (*dtt . w kšm . ḥmš 'šrh . mlun . šnpt . ḥsth . b'l*; text from de Tarragon, *Culte à Ugarit*, 64–66). Noting the Ugaritic corresponding term, Smith ("Ugarit," 162) also uses "elevation offering" for this offering in Numbers.

23. The SP copula "*it will be* [*yhyh*] in addition to the breast" may have been to clarify.

24. Elsewhere *tərûmâ* refers generically to what the Israelites offer to Yahweh as a tribute (see the translation note on 5:9), but here a particular tribute is in view, namely, the thigh of a sacrifice for peace that is designated as food for the Aaronic priests; see "the thigh of the tribute" (*šôq hattərûmâ*) in Exod. 29:27; Lev. 7:34; 10:14, 15.

25. Permissive, "may drink" (*yište*, *GBHS* §3.2.2[d.2]).

26. The twofold *'al* is additive: "in addition to" and "as well as" (*GBHS* §4.1.16g).

can provide. According to the precise vow[27] that they take, they must follow the instruction for their consecration.

[22]Yahweh spoke to Moses: [23]"Tell Aaron and his sons: This is the way[28] you are to bless the Israelites. Say to them:

> [24]Yahweh[29] bless you[30] and protect you;
> [25]Yahweh shine[31] his face upon you and be gracious to you;
> [26]Yahweh lift up his face upon you and give you peace.

[27]So[32] they will put my name on the Israelites, and I will bless them."[33]

Interpretation

6:1–12. The editor's superscript, which introduces Yahweh's next speech through Moses *to the Israelites* (vv. 1–2b), is fitting because the law is egalitarian: Yahweh explicitly gives to Israelite men and women alike (v. 2c) the prerogative to take a Nazirite vow as a means of consecrating themselves to Yahweh (v. 2).[34] I preserve the formal sense "perform the wonder," indicating a wonderful act that puts on display one's self-consecration to Yahweh (see the translation notes on v. 2). This was the common, non-priestly Israelite's opportunity to become consecrated to Yahweh, just as the Levites were (3:11–51) and as the Aaronic priests were (3:1–10),[35] yet without the Nazirite having to transfer the location of their home and vocation around Yahweh's dwelling

---

27. Formally, "according to the strength of his vow."

28. "This is the way" (*kōh*) expresses the manner in which the Aaronic priests are to pronounce the blessing (*GBHS* §4.2.8a).

29. Each of the six jussive verbs in vv. 24–26 convey a benediction whereby a superior, a priest, speaks of God as the subject to annunciate a blessing for the Israelites (*GBHS* §3.3.1[c]). "*May* Yahweh bless" is acceptable (NLT), but "Yahweh bless" (ESV, NJPS, NRSV, NET, NIV) reflects colloquial use, like "God bless you" and "The Lord be with you."

30. The piel factitive *yəbārekkā* means "May Yahweh put you into a blessed state" (*GBHS* §3.1.3a).

31. This hiphil transitive means "Yahweh *shine* [*yā'ēr*] his face [direct obj.]."

32. The weqatal (*wəśāmû*) form could be volitional, or more likely indicates the result of the priest's pronouncement of blessing: "So [as a result] they will put my name" (*GBHS* §3.5.2).

33. The simple *w* with an emphatic subject, "and I" (*wa'ănî*), followed by a cohortative of resolve "I will bless them" (*'ăbārăkēm*), is not a verbal sequence with v. 27a (*GBHS* §4.3.3). This might indicate that Yahweh's blessing is not mechanistic; that is, he is not manipulated by the priestly speech act. LXX^ed, probably using a distinct Hb. source, places this verse at the end of v. 23, but it is an overstatement to say that this "ensures that the blessing will be effective" (Wevers, *Notes*, 106). LXX^ed "and I *the Lord* [*egō kyrios*] will bless them" might assimilate to "I the Lord" (*egō kyrios*) well-known from Lev. 17–26 and Num. 3 (Awabdy, "Priestly Blessing," 29–49).

34. Contra Cartledge ("Nazirite Vows," 409–22), who argues that the Nazirite vow must have been a conditional act. See the "Implications" essay below, "Taking a Nazirite Vow Today."

35. See Achenbach, *Vollendung*, 509–11; Seebass, "Eigene Komposition," 91.

place.[36] This envisions a new dimension of holiness now possible beyond the boundaries of the official sanctuary cult.[37] The governing term (*Leitwort*) of the unit, vv. 2–21, is the root *nzr: the Nazirite (*nāzîr*), meaning either "one who is consecrated" or "one who consecrates herself/himself," is the agent who performs the action *nzr to "consecrate oneself to Yahweh" (hiphil + *l* of adv. in vv. 2, 3, 5, 6, 12), and they do this for a period of "consecration" (*nēzer*, 13× in vv. 4–21; see the second translation note on v. 2). The Nazirite's consecration to Yahweh could presumably be for any length of time that they choose up front (vv. 12–13). Their devotion to Yahweh becomes apparent to all by their new lifestyle of abstaining from consuming grapes in any form (vv. 3–4), not cutting any hair on their head (v. 5), and not touching a corpse (v. 6). The prohibition of these three in particular is intriguing since grape products were associated with fertility, hair with sympathetic magic, and corpse defilement with the cult of the dead.[38]

In vv. 3–4, the prohibition of consuming grapes could have been stated succinctly (i.e., "no grape nor grape product may enter your mouth") but instead is over-specified: no wine, brandy, vinegar from wine or brandy, no grape juice, fresh grapes, raisins, or any other product from any part of the grape (see the translation notes on 6:3). Why the Nazirite must abstain from grapes and grape products is never stated, but the simplest explanation is that abstaining from a ubiquitous source of palatable food and drink symbolized the Nazirite's pronounced devotion to Yahweh. Grapes and their derivatives (juice, wine, brandy, vinegar) were desirable for their taste, nutrition, and intoxication and so were commonly enjoyed in daily life and celebrations[39] by the wealthy, the middle class, and the poor alike: from the Pharaoh in his palace (Gen. 40:10–11)[40] to Israelite vineyard owners (Deut. 23:24; 24:21) and the landless gleaners in their vineyards (Lev. 19:10; Deut. 24:21–22). Crushed, worm-eaten, and sour grapes symbolized bloodshed, a divine curse, and Israel's covenant unfaithfulness, respectively (Gen. 49:11; Deut. 28:39; 32:32; Isa. 5:2–4), whereas healthy grapes in the land of Canaan were a sign of its exceptional fertility (Num. 13:20–24; Deut. 6:11; Josh. 24:13), of Yahweh's goodness (Deut. 32:14), and of the blessing that ensued from Israel's obedience to the covenant (Lev. 26:5). The Nazirite vow afforded to any Israelite the opportunity to become, for a time, like a Levite or a priest, belonging uniquely

---

36. Samuel, by contrast, was consecrated to Yahweh after he was weaned, and he joined the dwelling place service under Eli the high priest (1 Sam. 1:11, 22–28; 2:18–21).

37. Nihan, "Priestly Laws," 129; Frevel, "Book of Numbers," 30.

38. Walton and Matthews, *Genesis–Deuteronomy*, 182.

39. Harvesting grapes was often coupled with a joyful celebration of singing and shouting (Judg. 9:27; Isa. 16:10; Jer. 48:33; King and Stager, *Life*, 99).

40. Egyptian grape harvesting and pressing appears in a wall painting on the tomb of one scribe, Nakht, in the Valley of the Nobles, Thebes, from the New Kingdom (18th dynasty): https://nl.pinterest.com/pin/335658978472164697/.

to Yahweh. As the Levites were consecrated to Yahweh but did not enjoy an inheritance of the land because Yahweh was their inheritance (Num. 3:40–45; 18:20–21; Deut. 18:2), so any Israelite woman or man could consecrate themselves to Yahweh but, as an expression of their devotion to Yahweh, would not enjoy a choice fruit of the land.[41] Likewise, as the consecrated priests were to abstain from "wine and strong drink" when serving in the meeting tent (*yayin wəšēkār*, Lev. 10:9), so every Israelite consecrated to Yahweh by a Nazirite vow was to abstain from "wine and strong drink" (*yayin wəšēkār*, Num. 6:3). Like the psalmist, a Nazirite could sing to Yahweh "You put more happiness in my heart than when their grain and wine abound" (Ps. 4:7).

The second restriction on the Nazirite (v. 5) was not to use a razor on the head but to let the hair grow long during the period of consecration (see the second translation note on v. 5). For a female, whose hair would likely already be long, allowing the hair to continue to grow during the Nazirite vow would not obviously signal her consecration to Yahweh.[42] For men, although excessively long hair might be disgraceful in some contexts,[43] long hair was not considered effeminate but was typically regarded as handsome and virile,[44] even a life force.[45] In an Egyptian manual for interpreting dreams, when a man dreams of his own long hair, it is a good omen that he will experience something delightful.[46] Also, while Egyptian priests famously shaved or plucked all their hair for purification, other priests in the ancient Near East grew their hair long.[47] Hair entirely untouched by a razor goes above and beyond the Holiness prohibition against trimming sideburns and beard edges (Lev. 19:27; Jer. 9:26)[48] and thereby was a signal to the Israelite community that the Nazirite belonged to Yahweh ("They will be holy," Num. 6:5).

In vv. 6–12, Yahweh provides the final and most extensively developed Nazirite prohibition: they must not go near a dead body, let alone touch it (see the translation note on 6:6). Like the first two prohibitions against grapes and haircuts (vv. 3–11), this echoes the restriction put on the anointed Aaronic priests not to make contact with a dead body (Lev. 22:4) and more precisely

---

41. As consecrated persons, Nazirites belong to the realm of their Deity, Yahweh; see comments on 4:1–14 for quotation of Clines, "*Qdš*," 481–502.

42. See note contra Walton and Matthews in comments on 5:18; cf. Song 4:1; 5:2.

43. In Nebuchadnezzar's degeneration "his hair grew like (the feathers of) an eagle" (Dan. 4:33).

44. Judg. 13:5; 16:13–22, 28 (Samson); 2 Sam. 14:25–26 (Absalom); Song 5:11 (male lover).

45. Milgrom, *Leviticus*, 2:1691.

46. The text reads: "His hair having become long. Good. It means something at which his face will light up" ("Dream Oracles," *COS* 1.33:53).

47. A Neo-Assyrian relief depicts either a priest or a priest-like genie grasping a poppy flower and nurturing a sacred tree (ca. 722–705 BCE, Dur-Sharrukin, modern Khorsabad, Iraq, capital of Sargon II's empire): https://archaicwonder.tumblr.com/post/141050104278/neo-assyrian-relief-of-a-genie-or-a-priest-holding.

48. Milgrom (*Leviticus*, 2:1689–92) lucidly argues that Lev. 19:27 associates the trimming of sideburns and beard edges with cutting one's body for the cult of the dead.

for the high priest not even to approach a dead body (Lev. 21:11//Num. 6:6). This adds further weight to the view that during the period of consecration, Nazirites resembled the Aaronic priests in their holiness (belonging) to Yahweh, even though Nazirites never experienced the priests' exclusive privilege of serving Yahweh in his dwelling place. The Aaronic priests and the Nazirites were both holy to Yahweh (Lev. 21:6–8; Num. 6:5, 8), yet the Aaronic priests were allowed to defile themselves by burying the corpses of their immediate family members, though not other relatives (Lev. 21:1–4), while Nazirites were not allowed to handle the corpse of even their immediate family members (Num. 6:6–12), the same heightened restriction placed on the high priest in Lev. 21:10–12.[49] In comparing these laws, the boldface words are distinct, while the words with Hb. in brackets are identical (intertexts), and the underlined words are conceptual parallels:

Leviticus 21:10–12	Numbers 6:6–8
[10]The priest who is exalted above his brothers,	[6]While they [female or male Nazirite, v. 2]
on whose head the anointing oil has been poured and who has been consecrated to wear the garments, must not dishevel his hair, nor tear his garments.	consecrate themselves to Yahweh,
[11]He must not go near any dead body [*wa'al kol-napšōt mēt lō' yābō'*]. He must not defile himself for his father or mother [*la'ābîw ûla'immô lō' yiṭṭammā'*].	they must not go near a dead body [*'al-nepeš mēt lō' yābō'*]. [7]They must not defile themselves for their father or mother [*la'ābîw ûla'immô . . . lō'-yiṭṭammā' lāhem*] **brother or sister if they die,**
[12]He must not go outside the sanctuary and thus defile the sanctuary of his God,	
because the consecration of the anointing oil of his God is upon him. I am Yahweh.	because their consecration to God is visible on their head. [8]During their consecration they must be holy to Yahweh.

The anointed high priest held unparalleled responsibility in cultic mediation (Lev. 16:32–34) and was not to participate in conventional mourning rites (21:10), whereas Num. 6* does not explicitly prohibit a Nazirite from mourning by disheveling hair and tearing clothes (Num. 6:6). Both the high priest and Nazirite were consecrated to Yahweh, which was visibly symbolized on their head.[50] The Num. 6* ritual appears to augment the Lev. 21 restriction by adding "brother or sister if they die" to clarify that sibling corpses would also defile and nullify the Nazirite's vow (Num. 6:7; see the first translation note there). More important, the realm that is polluted by contact with a

49. Zuckschwerdt, "Literarischen Vorgeschichte," 195–97; Frevel, "Rituals," 148.
50. In the case of the high priest, anointing oil (Lev. 8:6–12; 21:10, 12); in the case of the Nazarite, long hair (see the translation notes on Num. 6:5).

111

corpse differs: the high priest would defile the divine dwelling (Lev. 21:12), whereas the Nazirite would defile their own consecrated head (Num. 6:7–8).

The other non-high priests and Israelites were permitted to touch a corpse for funeral rites and interment, and although they had to undergo purification afterward, their defiling action was not a sin that needed to be forgiven (see the note to the comments on 6:11; see also the comments on 5:1–4). Defilement by a human corpse could stand in as a synecdoche for "anything by which they can become unclean" (Num. 5:3). By contrast, the high priest and Nazirite must avoid contact altogether with a corpse, a contagion of death, because they were consecrated to Yahweh, who cannot coexist with anything belonging to the realm of death.[51] Consequently, one may infer from 6:9–12 that any corpse contact by a Nazirite (and implicitly a high priest) was a sin (v. 11) that nullified their vow: "but the previous days will not be counted because their separation was defiled" (v. 12). The scenario of v. 9 is not entirely clear, but two indicators suggest that the Nazirite could have avoided contact with one who dies suddenly nearby. First, the syntax suggests that they are active agents, who put their own head into a defiled state, "and they defile their consecrated head."[52] Second, although the required purification offering is sometimes prescribed to purify contagions that do not arise from sin (see the translation notes on 6:11), the basic sense of v. 11 is that the Nazirite broke their orders, "because they sinned with regard to the corpse." As a result, the Nazirite invalidates their vow (see v. 12) and must perform a multistep atonement and re-consecration process: (1) whereas one undergoing purification from a skin disease had to shave first, wait seven days, then shave again (Lev. 14:8–9), the defiled Nazirite must wait seven days and then shave once (Num. 6:9);[53] (2) on the eighth day they must bring two turtledoves or pigeons to the priest at the meeting tent (v. 10), who (3) offers one as a purification offering (see the translation notes on 6:11) and the other as a burnt offering—which resembles the accommodating atonement ritual for cleansing a *less affluent* defiled person[54]—and make atonement for the Nazirite's violation, resulting implicitly in forgiveness[55] and in fulfilling the precondition for (4) consecrating

---

51. Frevel, "Unvollkommenheit," 226; Milgrom, "Impurity," 107–11.

52. An act. and factitive piel, like hithpiel usage in context; see the first translation note on 6:7.

53. With Frevel ("Rituals," 148), the Nazirite law is innovative in that the defiled Nazirite does not *confess* their corpse defilement (as Lev. 5:3, 5), but their shaved hair could serve as a substitute for confession as a public display of their defilement. In my translation of Num. 6:9, the em dash marks the attributive prepositional phrase, formally "shave their head on the day of their purification, *that is, on the seventh day [bayyôm haššəbîʿî]* they must shave it." Kellermann (*Priesterschrift*, 88, 94) sees a clarifying addition in 9bβ–21* that centers on the sacrificial rituals.

54. Such as a person who touches a contagion (among other violations, Lev. 5:7–10), a postpartum mother (Lev. 12:8), a person with a skin disease (Lev. 14:22, 30), or man or woman with an unclean discharge (15:14, 29).

55. For removing sin (*ḥaṭṭāʾt*) and guilt (*ʾāšām*), making atonement (**kpr*) explicitly results in *divine forgiveness* of the offender (Lev. 4:20, 26, 31; 5:10, 13, 16, 18; 6:7), but for removing

their head again to Yahweh (see the second translation note on 6:2), which now also requires a reparation offering (v. 11; see the translation note on 6:12). In the book of Judges, Samson, who was uniquely devoted to Yahweh as a Nazirite from birth (13:4–5), violated at least two and maybe all three of the Nazirite restrictions: (1) he approached and touched the dead bodies of those he killed in battle;[56] (2) his hair was cut (16:17–20); and (3) he may have drunk wine at the wedding party he hosted (14:10, 17). Yahweh's spirit empowered Samson to deliver Israel from the Philistines by means of his long hair (16:22–30), in spite of Samson's chronic failure to protect his Nazirite consecration to Yahweh.

6:13–20. The clause "This is the Nazirite's instruction" (v. 13), continuing Yahweh's words, marks a transition in the ritual from the three prohibitions for the consecrated Nazirite—grape consumption, hair cutting, corpse touching (vv. 3–12)—to the Nazirite's presentation of their multifaceted gift to Yahweh at the tent of meeting (vv. 13–20). After finishing their period of consecration, a length of time perhaps fixed in advance with the priests (see vv. 12–13), the Nazirite offers specific types of six offerings—burnt, purification, greetings, bread basket, grain, and libation (vv. 13–17)—followed by shaved hair and elevation offerings (vv. 18–20b). These variegated offerings to Yahweh audibly, visually, and aromatically display different aspects of the Nazirite's consecration to Yahweh. The burnt offering (*'ōlâ*, v. 14), a year-old, umblemished male lamb, ascends into Yahweh's nostrils as a "sweet savor" (Lev. 1:9, 13, 17) and is entirely burnt up for Yahweh as an expression of the Nazirite's total and costly devotion (see Lev. 1:3–17). The purification offering (*ḥaṭṭā't*, Num. 6:14), a year-old, unblemished ewe lamb, purges any known or unknown impurity caused by the Nazirite's sin or bodily contagions (see the first translation note on 6:11). The sacrifice for peace (*zebaḥ haššəlāmîm*, cf. vv. 14, 17–18), an unblemished ram, is a communal meal shared by Yahweh (fats), the priests (breast), and the Nazirite (the remaining meat; see Lev. 3*; 7:15–17, 29–36). The sacrifice for peace may have been the Nazirite's declaration of peace to Yahweh, analogous in the ANE to a besieged king who would send a peace tribute to pacify his attacker (see the translation note on 6:14). The basket of bread (v. 15) is a derived type of grain offering—oven-baked cakes made of fine flour, olive oil, and no yeast and smeared with olive oil (as Lev. 2:4)—which the Nazirite brings to the priest, who burns a handful of it as a memorial portion on the altar as a "sweet savor" to Yahweh (Lev. 2:2, 9) and then keeps the rest for himself and his sons (Lev. 2:8–10). The referential phrase "with their grain offering and their libations" (v. 15), not specified in Numbers, must refer to fixed formulations of raw grain and wine (probably),

---

physical impurities, atonement results in a pronouncement of *cleansing* (**ṭhr*) of the offender (Lev. 12:7, 8; 14:18–20, 29–31, 53; probably implied in Lev. 15:15, 30).

56. Judg. 14:19; 15:7–8, 14–16; also, a lion's carcass (14:5–9) and donkey's jawbone (15:15–17).

maybe like the offerings for the Feasts of Firstfruits and Weeks (Lev. 23:13, 18).[57] In any case, giving cakes, fine flour, and wine (v. 15) to Yahweh demonstrates the Nazirite's gratitude for Yahweh's gracious provision of land and for the strength to farm, bake, and enjoy life.[58] The mediating priest presents the Nazirite's array of offerings to Yahweh in this order: purification offering, burnt offering, sacrifice for peace, unleavened bread basket, grain offering, and libation (vv. 16–17). Other texts suggest that each offering was placed or poured out on top of the preceding offerings.[59] A similar combination of offerings, but without the libation mentioned in Num. 6:15, 17, was presented at the inauguration of the Aaronic priests—first, by Moses for Aaron and sons (Lev. 8:18–28), and later by Aaron for the Israelites (9:15–21).

The Nazirite then shaves their consecrated head at the entrance to Yahweh's meeting tent and burns their hair clippings on the same altar fire that is burning the sacrifice for peace (v. 18; see the translation note there).[60] Rather than seen as a shameful punishment to cut off their hair, as in some ANE laws,[61] this human hair sacrifice is an ideal symbol of the Nazirite's very personal and physical devotion to Yahweh[62] and has parallels elsewhere in the ANE. For instance, in Cyprus (9th cent. BCE), at the fulfillment of a vow, one removed their hair and dedicated it to the goddess Astarte.[63] Here in vv. 14–17, in the process of burning the sacrifices on the altar, the Aaronic priest extracts various parts: he places the ram's boiled shoulder, one unleavened cake, and an additional unleavened wafer (as Lev. 8:26) into the shaved Nazirite's hands (v. 19), which[64] the priest then raises up as an elevation offering to Yahweh (v. 20; see the first translation note there). This echoes the elevation offering at the inauguration of Yahweh's priests: Moses placed similar elements into the hands of Aaron, who then raised the offering to Yahweh (Lev. 8:25–27). Once

57. The grain offering consists of two-tenths of an ephah of fine flour mixed with olive oil; the libation, a fourth hin of wine (Lev. 23:13).

58. The theology of praise to Yahweh for the good land and strength to produce wealth is developed in Deut. 8:7–18.

59. Lev. 4:35; 5:12; 8:26, 28; 9:14.

60. Cf. Acts 18:18; 21:23–26.

61. For accusers of various scenarios who cannot bring proof "they shall cut off his hair" ("The Middle Assyrian Laws," COS 2.132:355 §18, §19; also cf. plucking out their hair in §44, §59); or "they shall flog that man before the judges and they shall shave off half of his hair" ("The Laws of Hammurabi," COS 2.131:344 §127).

62. Paterius (6th cent. CE) interprets the cultivating and shaving of Nazirite hair tropologically (Lienhard, Numbers, 210).

63. Staubli, Levitikus, Numeri, 225. He also points to Lucian's On the Syrian Goddess (2nd cent. CE), which depicts the earlier Syrian temple cult in Manbij, Syria, where a puberty initiation ritual involved consecrating the great Syrian Goddess with holy curls (or first hairs) in precious vessels inscribed with their name.

64. The masc. pl. obj. "Then the priest must elevate them" (wəhēnîp 'ōtām hakkōhēn) in v. 20 could refer to the offerings of v. 19a–b alone but could include the Nazirite's two hands (kappê, fem. dual construction) holding the offerings.

again, the Nazirite, a common Israelite woman or man, resembles Yahweh's priests. These elements are not consumed by fire but are handed back to the priest as his provision, as implied by "they are a holy portion for the priest," in addition to other cuts of meat designated for the priests (see the translation note on 5:9 and the first translation note on 6:20).

After a Nazirite finishes their period of consecration (6:2–13b) and presents offerings to Yahweh (6:13c–20b), they are free to drink wine again (v. 20c; see the last translation note there), which is likely a synecdoche meaning that they can resume their normal, pre-consecration lifestyle, including consuming any form of grapes, cutting their hair, and handling the corpses of relatives and other neighbors. However, the imperfective verbal form could mean "After that the Nazirite will/must drink wine," which would be an imperative to celebrate the fulfillment of their vow in Yahweh's presence (see vv. 13, 18) while Yahweh also metaphorically imbibes his drink offering (vv. 15, 17).[65]

6:21. The subscript—which I interpret as editorial and so do not put into quotations as Yahweh's words—serves three main literary purposes. First, it distinguishes this law from chap. 5 and from 6:22–27 by reviewing the Nazirite's instructions in an inverted order: first vv. 13–20, then vv. 2–12. That is, the Nazirite "who vows their offering to Yahweh" (v. 21) summarizes the diversity of offerings just given in vv. 13–20 and, "in addition to their consecration" (v. 21), summarizes their initial period of consecration marked by tripartite abstinence (grape-hair-corpse) in vv. 2–12. Second, the subscript creatively expands the Nazirite law in two ways: (1) "as well as whatever else they can provide" now surprisingly compels the Nazirite to go above and beyond the prescribed offerings (of vv. 13–20), which effectively enhances the priests' supply (see the first translation note on v. 21); and (2) "according to *the precise vow* that they take, they must follow the instruction for their consecration" seems to clarify the ambiguity of duration. Apparently a woman or man could choose how long they remain consecrated to Yahweh as a Nazirite (see the second translation note on v. 21). Third, the subscript reproduces the formula used in Lev. 1–16 and so marks the Nazirite instructions as a law that pertains *to the priestly cult of Yahweh's dwelling place* (see the comments on 5:29 and the note there). This is fitting in that the Nazirite's lifestyle resembles that of the officiating priests of Yahweh (see above on vv. 1–12), and Yahweh's meeting place and presence ("before/to Yahweh") are over-specified as the centripetal location of the Nazirite's culminating offerings (vv. 13, 14, 16, 17, 18, 20).

6:22–27. Yahweh's next speech is doubly mediated *through* Moses and *through* Aaron and his sons for the Israelites (vv. 22–23). That is, this instruction is given not to increase the power of a cultic aristocracy over the common folk but to teach Yahweh's priestly intermediaries how to verbally bless his

---

65. See the "Implications" essay in chap. 26, "Does Yahweh Eat the Sacrifices of His People?"

covenant people (see the translation note on 6:23). Four quotative frames (vv. 22–23) delay, and so increase anticipation for,[66] the formal poetic blessing known as the Priestly or Aaronic Blessing (vv. 24–26). In Ketef Hinnom, Jerusalem, Gabriel Barkay and his archaeological team found this blessing inscribed onto two silver amulet scrolls that date to the seventh or sixth century BCE and were likely used in private apotropaic ritual at that time. This is the earliest text of the Hebrew Scriptures ever discovered![67] By six Hebrew jussives, Aaron, a superior figure, articulates his desire for Yahweh to bless the Israelites (see first translation note on v. 24). The blessing is artistically composed of three bicolons (poetic sentences) in which the second colon in every verse (vv. 24, 25, 26) continues and completes the first colon: "Yahweh bless you *and* [Yahweh] protect you." These bicolons have an incrementally increasing number of Hebrew words: three words (v. 24) → five words (v. 25) → seven words (v. 27). The poetic unit is framed by Yahweh's intention for both an Aaronic verbal blessing (v. 23b) and Yahweh's blessing, implying his divine response to bring about their blessed condition (v. 27):

> Yahweh spoke to Moses: (v. 22)
>
>   "Tell Aaron and his sons: (v. 23a)
>
>   This is the way <u>you are to bless the Israelites</u>. (v. 23b)
>
>   Say to them: (v. 23c)
>
>   Yahweh bless you   and protect you; (v. 24)
>
>   Yahweh shine his face upon you   and be gracious to you; (v. 25)
>
>   Yahweh lift up his face upon you and give you peace. (v. 26)
>
>   So they will put my name on the Israelites, <u>and I will bless them</u>." (v. 27)

The genre of the unit is probably an expanded form of salutary blessing, well-attested in formal Middle Hittite, Ugaritic, and Akkadian letters.[68] For instance in Ugaritic: "May the gods guard you, may they keep you well, may they strengthen you, for a thousand days and ten thousand years, through the endless reaches of time."[69] Most likely the Priestly Blessing of Numbers Yahwistically reformulates (6:24) and then expands (6:25–26) the bicolon of salutary blessing that was widespread in ANE correspondence: "May the gods [of Ugarit] guard you, may they keep you well."[70]

Perhaps supplying the content of the Aaronic and Mosaic blessing in Lev. 9:22–23, here the PB (Priestly Blessing) is presented as a performative

---

66. Miller-Naudé and Naudé, "Quotative Frames," 249–69.

67. See Smoak, *Priestly Blessing*; see also Ngo, "Miniature Writing."

68. For similar blessings in Akkadian, Hittite, and Ugaritic letters, see Awabdy, "Priestly Blessing," 36–38.

69. "A Scribe Shows Off," *COS* 3.4500:115.

70. Awabdy, "Priestly Blessing," 38.

speech act by Aaron and his sons.[71] We have already discussed the locutionary act, the syntax, and genre of *what is said*. The perlocutionary act, or *the intended effect*, is expressed in the closing frame of v. 27: Yahweh resolves within his power to bring about the blessing of his people, after, but not as a mechanistic consequence of, Aaron's obedience to perform the speech act (on the grammar, see the translation notes on v. 27). By virtue of the PB, the priests place Yahweh's name onto the Israelites (v. 27), which may envision a hypostasis of Yahweh in his dwelling place,[72] but the priests cannot manipulate Yahweh's presence, even though Yahweh is inclined toward blessing his people. In my view, the illocutionary act (*what is meant by what is said*) has two main dimensions. First, as in the ancient Near East, the PB is anthropomorphic in its imagery of how the deity, here Yahweh, puts his people into a state of blessing (see the second translation note on 6:24). In the ANE, many parallel divine facial expressions represent the deity's one-directional favor: in Ugaritic, "the face shines"; in Akkadian, "to make (one's) face shine," "to direct the face (toward)," "to turn the face (toward)," "to lift the head (toward)"; and in Egyptian, "The face of the Great God will be Gracious over you."[73] However, unlike the PB, in the rest of the ANE the deity shines not directly on the populace but on the king or the priests, who then mediate the divine presence to the people. For example, from the El-Amarna royal tomb, Pharaoh Akhenaten, Queen Nefertiti, and their daughters worship and bask in the rays of the sun disk, Aten, but only Akhenaten, son of Aten, "was the direct manifestation of the sun and the world's only mediator of the divine presence."[74] Likewise, King Hammurapi calls himself the "mighty king, solar disk of the city of Babylon, who spreads light over the lands of Sumer and Akkad."[75] This worldview stands in contrast to the blessing of Num. 6:24–26, which envisions Yahweh *directly* illuminating his people by his presence.

The second dimension to what is meant by the PB, its illocutionary force, can be seen in the nomenclature and ideology that it shares with the H collection in Lev. 17–26.[76] In distinction from the Priestly system that affects the divine presence by faithfully executing sacrificial ritual (e.g., Lev. 9:22–10:3; 16*), the divine presence and associated blessings in H ensue from the obedience

---

71. See Austin, *Do Things with Words*, 4–11, and other places.

72. Mettinger, *Dethronement of Sabaoth*. Contra de Boer ("Numbers VI 27," 3–13), who emends the MT vowels from "put my name *on* ['*al*] the Israelites" to "name me *the Most High* ['*ēl* ≈ '*elyôn*] of the Israelites." Also, there is no evidence that "put my name" means writing the divine name on the hand or forehead of the Israelites being blessed (cf. *ktb, "write" in Deut. 6:9; 11:20): contra Meir Bar-Ilan ("They shall put my name," 19–31), Num. 6:27 has *wǝśāmû 'et-šǝmî*; see the translation notes on v. 27.

73. Cohen, "Priestly Blessing," 232–36; Keller, "Egyptian Analogue," 338–45.

74. LeMon, "Egypt," 176–77.

75. "The Laws of Hammurabi," COS 2.131:337.

76. Knohl, *Sanctuary*, 89; Awabdy, "Priestly Blessing," 41–49.

of Yahweh's covenant people. In its present location (6:22–27), the PB gives the impression that it operates irrespective of human obedience or disobedience, as a blessing without conditions.[77] The simple fact that Yahweh orders Aaron to pronounce the PB reveals that Yahweh is predisposed to bless his people. While true, not only the words chosen throughout the PB but also its literary placement after Lev. 17–26* indicate that covenant obedience is a prerequisite to divine blessing. The opening bicolon, "Yahweh bless you and protect you" (v. 24), already richly illustrates the covenant blessings ensuing from obedience in the land of Canaan: the *blessing* of abundant fertility in Lev. 26:4–5c, and *protection* from enemies in Lev. 26:5d–8. "Yahweh shine his face upon you and be gracious to you" (see the translation note on v. 25) and "Yahweh lift up his face upon you" (v. 26a) are metonyms for the life-giving and gracious divine presence as illustrated by the Edenic imagery of Lev. 26:11–12: "I will put my dwelling place among you, and I will not abhor you. I will walk among you. I will be your God, and you will be my people."[78] Finally, the closing colon, "and give you peace" (v. 26b), echoes the covenant blessing, "I will give peace in the land" (Lev. 26:6). The Aaronic blessing must be performed, but for Yahweh to unleash the goodness of his presence, his covenant people must also be living in fellowship with him. Paul's blessings, of a Greco-Roman epistolary form, may also echo the Priestly Blessing (e.g., Rom. 1:7). So also on the new earth, those whose names are written in the Lamb's book of life by faith marked by obedience (Rev. 3:4–5; 21:27) are those who will experience the PB in the fullest measure: "They will see his face, and his name will be on their foreheads" (Rev. 22:4 NIV).

Implications

Taking a Nazirite Vow Today

The Nazirite vow seems obscure to many of us today. Akin to Samson, John the Baptizer was dedicated to God from birth (Luke 1:15), with echoes of a Nazirite's vows, but these two men are presented as exceptional cases among God's people. After meeting the risen Christ, the apostle Paul still took presumably Nazirite vows (Acts 18:18). He also paid for the purification offerings of four men who had fulfilled their (likely) Nazirite vows (Acts 21:23–26), although this was to pacify his opponents in Jerusalem who believed Paul was ordering the Gentiles to break the Torah. After Paul, the Nazirite vow drops out of use for the post-temple followers of Jesus, but was this more for pragmatic than theological reasons?

---

77. Berlejung, "Gesegnete Mensch," 44.
78. In light of other texts, to "lift up his face on/to you" may imagine Yahweh, the divine king, receiving the one being blessed (Geiger, "Synergie," 51–72).

What would it look like for a woman or man who loves God to take a Nazirite vow today, and why would they even want to do so? Jesus seems to uphold that one can fulfill the intention of a vow to God without making a dangerous, verbal pledge, swearing an oath (Matt. 5:33–37). Considering the nature of a *ritual* may help us further here: "A ritual is a privileged activity system that is believed to carry out a transformation process involving interaction with a reality ordinarily inaccessible to the material domain."[79] If we believe that the ancient rituals God prescribed for Israel were *transformative*, and if we believe that God has prescribed for Jesus's disciples at least the transformative rituals of baptism and the Passover-Eucharist (Matt. 28:19; Luke 22:1–20; 1 Cor. 5:7–8), then are there enduring elements in rituals like the Nazirite vow that could be used by the Spirit to transform God's people into the image of Christ and to advance the gospel?[80] To answer this question, we might be inclined to define the Nazirite ritual in a generic way, such as temporarily depriving oneself of food to redirect one's affections toward God. The problem is that every self-denial ritual—including the Nazirite vow in ancient Israel, Jesus's teaching on fasting (Matt. 6), and Lent in the Christian calendar—is highly contextual. Any common definition that these rituals could share is, by nature, a generalization that downplays the very particular, enculturated shape of the beliefs and performance of each ritual. Catherine Bell, therefore, moves us to think in another direction: "Under what circumstances are such activities distinguished from other forms of activity? How and why are they distinguished? What do these activities do that other activities cannot or will not do?"[81] What, then, distinguishes the Nazirite vow from other ancient sacrificial vows as well as from the self-denial rituals of Christian fasting and Lent?

First, in contrast to other vows (*nədārîm*) in the Bible that can be conditional (Gen. 28:20–22) or unconditional (14:22) and vows in the ANE (outside the Bible) that are "consistently conditional,"[82] the ritual textualized in Num. 6:1–21 leaves no room for the Nazirite to place conditions or expectations on Yahweh.[83] That is, the Nazirite vow has no telic clause ("so that") or protasis ("if . . . then") like, for example, Jacob's: "Then Jacob made a vow [*neder*], saying, '*If* God is with me and protects me on this journey, . . . *then* Yahweh will become my God'" (Gen. 28:20–21; so also Num. 21:2). Neither Samson

---

79. Gane, *Cult and Character*, 15.
80. See Acts 18:18; 21:23–24; 1 Cor. 9:19–27.
81. Bell, *Ritual Theory*, 70.
82. Cartledge, *Vows*, 134–35.
83. Against Cartledge ("Nazirite Vows," 409–22, quotations from 422), who imposes data from vows in the ANE and Bible and later tradition onto Num. 6:1–21 to argue that the Nazirite vow was conditional, paying one's dues to the Deity, Yahweh, "in prospect of answered prayer." Rather, none of the elements in Num. 6 should be called "legalistic" or a "payment of sacrifices" or require conditionality.

nor Samuel consecrated themselves to Yahweh as Num. 6* envisions; rather, their mothers consecrated these boys before birth or after weaning (Judg. 13:4–7, 13–14; 1 Sam. 1:11). Hannah's conditional vow (1 Sam. 1:11) is not tantamount to a Nazirite vow, but *precedes* her dedication of Samuel (1 Sam. 1:26–28).[84] In sum, the lack of conditions sets the Nazirite vow apart from conditional vows but resembles the rituals in the Leviticus frames: the burnt offering, grain offering, and sacrifice for peace (Lev. 1–3) and personal vows (Lev. 27). All these are discretionary, but none afford Israelites the chance to put conditions on Yahweh. A Nazirite vow today, likewise, must be voluntary, not an obligation of one's faith community (as in some Lenten traditions), and must not be taken for ulterior motives (as hypocritical fasting in Matt. 6).

Second, the combination of the three aspects of self-denial for the Nazirite (Num. 6:1–12) is without known parallel in the Bible or ANE, but these elements are curiously all associated with ancient mechanisms of manipulating the gods or spirits: grapes were connected with fertility, hair with sympathetic magic, corpse defilement with the cult of the dead.[85] Furthermore, the absence of grapes or grape products meant no enjoyment of Yahweh's gift of a common fruit of the land of Canaan but also meant emulating the lifestyle of the officiating Aaronic priests (see the comments above). Not cutting one's hair or having long hair was symbolic of one's virility and life force but also visibly flagged the Nazirite as belonging markedly to Yahweh, who is ontologically opposed to the realm of death (see above). Touching or even approaching a corpse, then, is prohibited since that would defile the Nazirite's consecrated head, just as the same action by the high priest would defile the divine dwelling (see above). This restriction means that the Nazirite and priests (esp. high priest), because they are Yahweh's alone, cannot physically engage in caring for their family members at their death. Any contemporary Nazirite vow would carefully distance the devotee from manipulating God or other spirits (for fertility, etc., through magic or through a cult of the dead). The three prohibitions also would be put on display in one's daily life: (1) abstaining from some aspect of enjoyment of God's gifts of eating and drinking; (2) marking one's physical appearance as belonging to God, which is different than God-centered fasting, which Jesus teaches should be self-effacing (Matt. 6:16–18); and (3) not touching the physical contagions associated with the realm of death. This third restriction, I would argue, has been overturned by Jesus, who is "the resurrection and the life" (John 11:25–26) and who, by the power of the Spirit of God, touches and regenerates human corpses, both physical and spiritual (Ezek. 37:1–14; Mark 5:41–42; Eph. 2:5–6). Not touching a corpse is

---

84. Neither the story of Samson nor Samuel uses the technical term "consecrate oneself to Yahweh" or "to be a Nazirite" (*nzr*; see the second translation note on 6:2), and with other narrative details, we cannot determine the nature of the connection with the textualized law of the Nazirite in Num. 6.

85. Walton and Matthews, *Genesis–Deuteronomy*, 182.

replaced by not engaging in "dead works," sinful thoughts, words, and actions that defile both body and soul before the holy God (Col. 3:5; Heb. 6:1; 9:14).

Third, the entrance to the dwelling place of Yahweh holds a sort of centripetal force that demands the presence of the consecrated Nazirite with his array of sacrifices (Num. 6:13–20).[86] This aspect is, of course, more difficult for disciples of Jesus to appropriate because the designated place of worship has shifted from the temple in Jerusalem to Jesus's own body, which is mysteriously now in some way coextensive with the body of Christ, the church, on earth (John 4:21–24; Eph. 1:22–23; 2:19–22). Even so, taking a Nazirite vow today must be consciously oriented toward the presence of God residing amid his people (Ps. 84:2). A Nazirite offered a wide array of sacrifices to Yahweh (vv. 13–20), which symbolized total devotion (burnt offering), cleansing from sin and physical contagions (purification offering), a peacemaking meal with Yahweh (sacrifice for peace), gratitude for divine provision (bread basket, grain, and libation), physical purity (shaved hair), and worship (elevation offerings). Beyond the real, spiritual offerings of the NT that believers still offer,[87] we may consider how to express, at the fulfillment of a period of intense devotion to God, the purpose of these different sacrifices.

Fourth, although other rituals had a democratizing effect, the Nazirite perhaps exemplifies this best of all. The Priestly rituals of the Pentateuch, surprisingly, do not fundamentally enhance the power of the priests but of the people, who now are invited to participate meaningfully in cultic worship. Nonprofessionals are given responsibility and "a degree of autonomy in their ritual negotiation of the sacred."[88] As I have argued throughout vv. 1–21 (above), the Nazirite vow afforded to Israelite women and men the remarkable chance to consecrate themselves to Yahweh just as the cultic professionals—the Levites and Aaronic priests—were consecrated to Yahweh (3:1–10, 11–51). In the church, every woman, man, and child—not just leaders—who trusts in the Messiah is made holy and has access to the very presence of God (1 Cor. 6:11; Eph. 3:11–12).

Thus a modern Nazirite vow will somehow visualize the condition of personal consecration to God, taking down the façade of a sacred hierarchy between clergy and laity in the church. This must never become legalistic or cultish, but can offer Jesus's followers a creative way to exhibit their loyalty to and affection for the God who recuses them by his love and resides in them by his Spirit.

---

86. With Frevel ("Rituals," 141), who diagrams the spatial dimension of the rituals of Num. 5:5–6:22 as internally oriented toward Yahweh's dwelling place.

87. Awabdy, *Leviticus*, 24–25.

88. Bell, *Ritual Theory*, 181; Bibb, *Ritual Words*, 157.

7

Israel's Chieftains
Dedicate Yahweh's Altar

(7:1–89)

∽∾

Overview

Numbers 7:1–10:10 contains by one count at least ten different literary units, but all can be subsumed under the theme of cultic preparations for Israel's departure for Canaan.[1] Together, 7:1–88, the dedicatory offerings from the twelve tribes, and 8:5–26, the investiture of the Levites, reveal the need for a functioning sanctuary with clear relations between the priests/Levites and the rest of the Israelites.[2] Establishing Yahweh worship was a prerequisite for Israel to take hold of the promise of land. Contrary to popular assumption, the Num. 7 dedicatory offerings, like many ritual texts in the Torah and the majority of ritual texts in Ugaritic and especially Babylonian sources, were not *prescriptive* but *descriptive* of the ritual event performed by Israel's representatives.[3] Numbers 7:1–88 contains four units bound together by the generous giving of the twelve chieftains. First, the chieftains give carts and oxen, which Yahweh directs Moses to distribute to the Levite families for transporting the dwelling place (vv. 1–9). Then in twelve successive days, the twelve chieftains, each representing the people of their tribe, give twelve identical sacrificial gifts to dedicate the bronze altar of Yahweh (vv. 10–83).

---

1. See de Vaulx, *Nombres*, 106–7. Achenbach (*Vollendung*, 529–56) attributes 7:1–10:1* to the third phase of the theocratic revision of the Torah, which expanded and added to the preexisting legends.
2. Cardellini, *Numeri 1,1–10,10*, 332.
3. Levine and Hallo, "Offerings," 17–58.

The priestly historiographers carefully add the sum of the precious metals and sacrificial animals (vv. 84–88). The chapter shifts abruptly to the fulfillment of Yahweh's promise in Exod. 25:22: Moses enters Yahweh's meeting tent for his exceptional, mysterious custom of listening to the divine voice (v. 89).

Translation

1When Moses had finished setting up the dwelling place,[4] he anointed it and consecrated it and all its furnishings, and he anointed and consecrated the altar and all its utensils. **2**Then[5] Israel's chieftains, the heads of their patriarchs' households, presented an offering. They were the chieftains of the tribes; they were the ones in charge[6] of those who were enlisted. **3**They brought their offering before Yahweh: six covered carts and twelve[7] oxen—one cart for every two chieftains, and an ox for each one—and they presented them in front of the dwelling place. **4**Then Yahweh spoke to Moses: **5**"Accept these gifts[8] from them, that they may be used in the work of the meeting tent. You must give them to the Levites, to each one as his service requires." **6**So Moses accepted the carts and the oxen and gave them to the Levites. **7**Two carts and four oxen[9] he gave to the Gershonites, as their service required; **8**and four carts and eight oxen he gave to the Merarites, as their service required, under the authority of Ithamar[10] son of Aaron the priest. **9**But[11] to the Kohathites he did not give any, because they were responsible for the service of the holy things, which they carried on their shoulders.
  10Then the chieftains presented gifts to dedicate the altar[12] when it was anointed. So the chieftains presented their offering before the altar.

4. Formally, "*On the day of* the finishing by Moses of setting up the dwelling place" (cf. NLT, NRSV, ESV, NJPS) does not necessarily mean on that precise day, but is idiomatic for an event concurrent with the main verb (*GBHS* §3.4.1[b.1]; NET, NIV; e.g., the Gen. 2:17 idiom allows for deferred death in 3:23–24; 5:3–5).

5. Even with a shift of subject (Moses to chieftains), this wayyiqtol in v. 7 ("Then they presented," *wayyaqrîbû*) continues the sequence of the prior four wayyiqtols, presenting the chieftains' offerings as following Moses's anointing and consecration of the dwelling place (Exod. 40; Lev. 8).

6. "In charge" (*'al*) marks the rank or responsibility of the chieftains over the men who were enrolled for military service in chaps. 1–2 (*GBHS* §4.1.16c).

7. SP absolute *šᵊnêm 'āśār* vs. MT const. *šᵊnê 'āśār*.

8. "These gifts" (NET) clarifies the elliptical obj.

9. "Two carts and four oxen" are fronted as the focus of the sentence (*BHRG* §47.2.1[2]).

10. Formally, "by the hand of Ithamar," where "hand" is a metaphor for a "(sphere of) power, rule, control, . . . authority (e.g., Gen. 41:35)" ("*yād* I," *DCH* 4:82, gloss 4a).

11. "But" (*wᵊ*) marks the contrast of the negated verbal clause of v. 9 with vv. 6–8 (*IBHS* §39.2.3b).

12. Formally, "dedication of the altar" (*ḥᵃnukkat hammizbēaḥ*), where "the altar" is the obj. of the verbal idea of the const. (*GBHS* §2.2.4). "The dedication" (*'ēt ḥᵃnukkat*) is the

11For Yahweh had said[13] to Moses, "They must present their offering, one chieftain for each day, for the dedication of the altar."

12The one who presented his offering on the first day was Amminadab's son Nahshon, from the tribe of Judah. **13**His offering was one silver plate weighing 130 shekels and one silver sprinkling bowl[14] weighing 70 shekels, both according to the sanctuary shekel, both filled with fine flour mixed with olive oil as a grain offering; **14**one gold pan weighing 10 shekels, filled with incense; **15**one young bull, one ram, and one male lamb a year old, for a burnt offering;[15] **16**one male goat for a purification offering;[16] **17**and for the sacrifice for peace:[17] two bulls, five rams, five male goats, and five male lambs a year old. This was the offering of Amminadab's son Nahshon.

18On the second day Zuar's son Nethanel, chieftain of Issachar, presented his offering.[18] **19**He offered for his offering one silver plate weighing 130 shekels and one silver sprinkling bowl weighing 70 shekels, both according to the sanctuary shekel, both filled with fine flour mixed with olive oil as a grain offering; **20**one gold pan weighing 10 shekels, filled with incense; **21**one young bull, one ram, and one male lamb a year old, for a burnt offering; **22**one male goat for a purification offering; **23**and for the sacrifice for peace: two bulls, five rams, five male goats, and five male lambs a year old. This was the offering of Zuar's son Nethanel.

24On the third day Helon's son Eliab, chieftain of the Zebulunites, presented his offering. **25**His offering was one silver plate weighing 130 shekels and one silver sprinkling bowl weighing 70 shekels, both according to the sanctuary shekel, both filled with fine flour mixed with olive oil as a grain offering; **26**one gold pan weighing 10 shekels, filled with incense; **27**one young bull, one ram, and one male lamb a year old, for a burnt offering; **28**one male goat for a purification offering; **29**and for the sacrifice for peace: two bulls, five rams, five male goats, and five male lambs a year old. This was the offering of Helon's son Eliab.

---

verbal obj., "The chieftains presented *the dedication* of the altar," which I render contextually "presented gifts to dedicate the altar" in view of vv. 12–88.

13. The past narrative is rendered contextually as Eng. past perfect, "*For* Yahweh had said" (*wayyōʾmer yhwh ʾel-mōšeh*), since Yahweh's directive is dischronologized, appearing after the narrator's remark that the chieftains offered the dedicatory gifts in v. 10b (NIV, NET, EÜ; see Seebass, *Numeri*, 1:191).

14. "Sprinkling bowl" (*mizrāq*) is deverbal from *zrq (to sprinkle; HALOT 1:283, gloss 2); with two possible exceptions (Amos 6:6; Neh. 7:69), the other thirty OT occurrences refer to a cultic object used for manipulating oil or blood inside the meeting tent or temple.

15. Throughout this passage, SP and LXX[ed] express "and," while MT is more often asyndetic.

16. On the "purification offering," see the first translation note on 6:11.

17. On the "sacrifice for peace," see the translation note on 6:14.

18. "Presented his offering" is added for clarity throughout (vv. 18, 24, 30, 36, 42, 48, 54, 60, 66, 72, 78) since the text elides a derivation of v. 12, "The one who presented his offering" (*hammaqrîb . . . ʾet-qorbānô*).

[30]On the fourth day Shedeur's son Elizur, chieftain of the Reubenites, presented his offering. [31]His offering was one silver plate weighing 130 shekels and one silver sprinkling bowl weighing 70 shekels, both according to the sanctuary shekel, both filled with fine flour mixed with olive oil as a grain offering; [32]one gold pan weighing 10 shekels, filled with incense; [33]one young bull, one ram, and one male lamb a year old, for a burnt offering; [34]one male goat for a purification offering; [35]and for the sacrifice for peace: two bulls, five rams, five male goats, and five lambs a year old. This was the offering of Shedeur's son Elizur.

[36]On the fifth day Zurishaddai's son Shelumiel, chieftain of the Simeonites, presented his offering. [37]His offering was one silver plate weighing 130 shekels and one silver sprinkling bowl weighing 70 shekels, both according to the sanctuary shekel, both filled with fine flour mixed with olive oil as a grain offering; [38]one gold pan weighing 10 shekels; [39]one young bull, one ram, and one male lamb a year old, for a burnt offering; [40]one male goat for a purification offering; [41]and for the sacrifice for peace: two bulls, five rams, five male goats, and five lambs a year old. This was the offering of Zurishaddai's son Shelumiel.

[42]On the sixth day Deuel's son Eliasaph, chieftain of the Gadites, presented his offering. [43]His offering was one silver plate weighing 130 shekels and one silver sprinkling bowl weighing 70 shekels, both according to the sanctuary shekel, both filled with fine flour mixed with olive oil as a grain offering; [44]one gold pan weighing 10 shekels; [45]one young bull, one ram, and one male lamb a year old, for a burnt offering; [46]one male goat for a purification offering; [47]and for the sacrifice for peace: two bulls, five rams, five male goats, and five lambs a year old. This was the offering of Deuel's son Eliasaph.

[48]On the seventh day Ammihud's son Elishama, chieftain of the Ephraimites, presented his offering. [49]His offering was one silver plate weighing 130 shekels and one silver sprinkling bowl weighing 70 shekels, both according to the sanctuary shekel, both filled with fine flour mixed with olive oil as a grain offering; [50]one gold pan weighing 10 shekels, filled with incense; [51]one young bull, one ram, and one male lamb a year old, for a burnt offering; [52]one male goat for a purification offering; [53]and for the sacrifice for peace: two bulls, five rams, five male goats, and five lambs a year old. This was the offering of Ammihud's son Elishama.

[54]On the eighth day Pedahzur's son Gamaliel, chieftain of the Manassites, presented his offering. [55]His offering was one silver plate weighing 130 shekels and one silver sprinkling bowl weighing 70 shekels, both according to the sanctuary shekel, both filled with fine flour mixed with olive oil as a grain offering; [56]one gold pan weighing 10 shekels, filled with incense; [57]one young bull, one ram, and one male lamb a year old, for a burnt offering; [58]one male goat for a purification offering; [59]and for the sacrifice for peace: two bulls, five rams, five male

goats, and five lambs a year old. This was the offering of Pedahzur's son Gamaliel.

[60]On the ninth day Gideoni's son Abidan, chieftain of the Benjaminites,[19] presented his offering. [61]His offering was one silver plate weighing 130 shekels and one silver sprinkling bowl weighing 70 shekels, both according to the sanctuary shekel, both filled with fine flour mixed with olive oil as a grain offering; [62]one gold pan weighing 10 shekels, filled with incense; [63]one young bull, one ram, and one male lamb a year old, for a burnt offering; [64]one male goat for a purification offering; [65]and for the sacrifice for peace: two bulls, five rams, five male goats, and five lambs a year old. This was the offering of Gideoni's son Abidan.

[66]On the tenth day Amishaddai's son Ahiezer, chieftain of the Danites, presented his offering. [67]His offering was one silver plate weighing 130 shekels and one silver sprinkling bowl weighing 70 shekels, both according to the sanctuary shekel, both filled with fine flour mixed with olive oil as a grain offering; [68]one gold pan weighing 10 shekels, filled with incense; [69]one young bull, one ram, and one male lamb a year old, for a burnt offering; [70]one male goat for a purification offering; [71]and for the sacrifice for peace: two bulls, five rams, five male goats, and five lambs a year old. This was the offering of Amishaddai's son Ahiezer.

[72]On the eleventh day Ocran's son Pagiel, chieftain of the Asherites, presented his offering. [73]His offering was one silver plate weighing 130 shekels and one silver sprinkling bowl weighing 70 shekels, both according to the sanctuary shekel, both filled with fine flour mixed with olive oil as a grain offering; [74]one gold pan weighing 10 shekels, filled with incense; [75]one young bull, one ram, and one male lamb a year old, for a burnt offering; [76]one male goat for a purification offering; [77]and for the sacrifice for peace: two bulls, five rams, five male goats, and five lambs a year old. This was the offering of Ocran's son Pagiel.

[78]On the twelfth day Enan's son Ahira, chieftain of the Naphtalites, presented his offering. [79]His offering was one silver plate weighing 130 shekels and one silver sprinkling bowl weighing 70 shekels, both according to the sanctuary shekel, both filled with fine flour mixed with olive oil as a grain offering; [80]one gold pan weighing 10 shekels; [81]one young bull, one ram, and one male lamb a year old, for a burnt offering; [82]one male goat for a purification offering; [83]and for the sacrifice for peace: two bulls, five rams, five male goats, and five lambs a year old. This was the offering of Enan's son Ahira.

[84]This was the dedication for the altar from the chieftains of Israel, when it was anointed: 12 silver plates, 12 silver sprinkling bowls, and 12 gold pans. [85]Each silver plate weighed 130 shekels, and each silver sprinkling bowl weighed 70 shekels. All the silver of the vessels weighed 2,400 shekels, according to the sanctuary shekel. [86]The 12 gold pans

19. On SP spelling of Benjamin, see the translation note on 2:22.

filled with incense weighed 10 shekels each, according to the sanctuary shekel;[20] all the gold of the pans weighed 120 shekels. [87]All the cattle for the burnt offering were 12 young bulls, 12 rams, 12 male lambs a year old, with their grain offering, and 12 male goats for a purification offering. [88]All the cattle for the sacrifice for peace were 24 young bulls, 60 rams, 60 male goats, and 60 lambs a year old. This was the dedication for the altar after it was anointed.

[89]Now when Moses went into[21] the meeting tent to speak with Yahweh,[22] he heard the voice speaking[23] to him from above the atonement cover[24] that was on the ark containing the witness, from between the two cherubim. And he spoke with him.[25]

Interpretation

7:1–9. The narrator begins by explaining that this new scene—the dedicatory giving of the chieftains in 7:2–88—was a continuation of the dwelling-place narrative of Exod. 25–Lev. 9. For rhetorical purposes, the narrator in v. 1 has removed the time lapse between setting up, anointing, consecrating, and the chieftains' gifts, since originally we were told that Moses *anointed* the dwelling place and its furniture (**mšḥ*, Exod. 40:9–16), then it was set up (one year after the exodus; Exod. 40:17), but only a few days into the thirty-day revelation of Leviticus do we learn that Moses *consecrated* it (**qdš*, Lev. 8:10–11),[26] and

---

20. "Weighed 10 shekels each, according to the sanctuary shekel" (*ʿăśārâ ʿăśārâ hakkap bašeqel haqqōdeš*) is absent in LXX[ed] (but under Hexapla asterisk), perhaps by haplography already in the Hb. source (even Wevers, *Notes*, 115–16, admits this).

21. "When Moses went into" is simultaneous with the main verb, "he heard" (*GBHS* §3.4.1[b.1]). This is a strange start to the new unit (v. 89) unless the narrator is not referring to a single event but to Moses's custom. Asyndetic LXX[ed] moves from v. 88 into v. 89 with an inf. clause contemporaneous with the subsequent verb, "When Moyses went into . . . , then he heard."

22. The *l* + inf. const. indicates the reason why Moses entered: "*in order to* speak with Yahweh" (*GBHS* §4.1.10[d]). For the Hebrew "speak *with him* [*ʾittô*]," the referent "Yahweh" is supplied since he is the assumed interlocutor, forming an *inclusio* with the 1:1 superscription.

23. With Levine (*Numbers*, 1:258), the hithpael ptc. of **dbr* (*middabbēr*) probably has an iterative force, meaning "he repeatedly spoke."

24. This sole occurrence of "the atonement cover" (*hakkappōret*) in Numbers has a solitary article, which marks it as unique and implies that readers know about it from Exod. 25–40 (18×) and Lev. 16 (7×); elsewhere only 1 Chron. 28:11; *GBHS* §2.6.4, and "referential article" within P: *GBHS* §2.6.1.

25. Yahweh is clearly the implied referent in v. 89aα, "When Moses went into the meeting tent to speak *with him* [*ʾittô*]," yet the final sentence of v. 89b, "And he spoke with him" (*waydabbēr ʾēlāyw*), is ambiguous. Did Moses speak with Yahweh (as v. 89aα), did Yahweh speak with Moses (inferred from v. 89aβ: NLT, NIV, NJPS), or did the voice of Yahweh speak to Moses (continuing the subject of v. 89aβ: ESV, NRSV)?

26. The thirty-day revelation is deduced from Exod. 40:17 and Num. 1:1. There is no such marker in Leviticus.

then, using the past narrative tense to indicate a basic sequence, the chieftains *presented* their offerings to the front of the dwelling place (vv. 2–3; see the first translation note on 7:2).[27] In a way, this democratizes the worship of Yahweh by elevating the participation of the people's representatives, the chieftains, onto the level of Yahweh's holy cultic representatives, Moses and the Aaronic priests. The naming of the twelve chieftains in vv. 12–83 confirms that the chieftains in view throughout vv. 1–10, who are tribal leaders over Israel's troops (v. 2; see the second translation note on 7:2), are the same chieftains who had already (Num. 1:4–16) assisted Moses and Aaron in counting the eligible warriors.

In v. 3, the narrator recounts that every two chieftains brought a covered cart to the entry to Yahweh's dwelling place, and every chieftain brought an ox, totaling six carts and twelve oxen. Why does the storyteller narrate that the chieftains gave their gifts (v. 3) prior to any orders from Yahweh (v. 4)? One could conceive that the editor intentionally dischronologized the events: perhaps Yahweh did direct them first, but the chieftains appear first to stress their generosity. Alternatively, the view I take is that the chieftains took the unsolicited initiative to give, and then only in response does Yahweh order Moses: "Accept these gifts from them" (v. 5; see the translation note there). Yahweh resourcefully (!) directs Moses to receive the carts and oxen and give them to the Levites to use in their meeting-tent service (v. 5), and Moses, in obedience, distributes them judiciously among two of the three Levite families "as their service required" (2×, v. 7). He gives two carts and four oxen to the Gershonites since they need to transport the dwelling-place curtains, ropes, and related equipment (Num. 4:22–28) and four carts and eight oxen to the Merarites since they need to transport the even heavier framework of the dwelling place (4:29–33). Moses gives none to the Kohathites because they are required to carry all the holy furniture on their shoulders (v. 9; 4:2–20). Without carts and oxen, the Kohathites' unparalleled privilege of conveying the most sacred objects is also the most physically taxing.

7:10–83. Israel's twelve tribal chieftains, on twelve consecutive days, each present an identical combination of offerings to dedicate Yahweh's altar. The chieftains are tribal representatives, which means that, effectively, each tribe gives offerings to Yahweh by the agency of their chieftain. Continuing the importance of the tribes' role in establishing the priestly cult in vv. 1–4 (above), the narrator in v. 10 also explicitly marks the altar dedication as an "all-Israelite"[28] democratic activity beyond the priestly aristocracy (see the translation note on v. 10).[29] Repeating the pattern of human action followed by

---

27. See Achenbach, *Vollendung*, 529–31.
28. Knohl (*Sanctuary*, 85) attributes chap. 7 to the more egalitarian H.
29. Douglas (*Wilderness*, 182) admits that chap. 7 betrays "egalitarian principles enshrined in the enclave culture" but then surmises that there is probably some political explanation.

divine orders (vv. 2–4), two times the narrator tells us first that the chieftains presented their dedication offerings at the altar (v. 10) before the clarifying divine orders are interjected: "For Yahweh had said to Moses, 'They must present their offering, one chieftain for each day, for the dedication of the altar'" (v. 11; see the translation note there).

Every chieftain, the patriarchal leader of their tribe, was already listed by name as the census assistants of Moses and Aaron (Num. 1:4–16), but that list differs in the twelve-day order of their dedicatory offerings here.

Table 7.1. Order of the Chieftains Compared

Numbers 1:5–15	Numbers 7:12–83*
1. Reuben → Shedeur's son Elizur	Judah → Amminadab's son Nahshon
2. Simeon → Zurishaddai's son Shelumiel	Issachar → Zuar's son Nethanel
3. Judah → Amminadab's son Nahshon	Zebulun → Helon's son Eliab
4. Issachar → Zuar's son Nethanel	Reuben → Shedeur's son Elizur
5. Zebulun → Helon's son Eliab	Simeon → Zurishaddai's son Shelumiel
6. Ephraim → Ammihud's son Elishama	Gad → Deuel's son Eliasaph
7. Manasseh → Pedahzur's son Gamaliel	Ephraim → Ammihud's son Elishama
8. Benjamin → Gideoni's son Abidan	Manasseh → Pedahzur's son Gamaliel
9. Dan → Ammishaddai's son Ahiezer	Benjamin → Gideoni's son Abidan
10. Asher → Ocran's son Pagiel	Dan → Ammishaddai's son Ahiezer
11. Gad → Deuel's son Eliasaph	Asher → Ocran's son Pagiel
12. Naphtali → Enan's son Ahira	Naphtali → Enan's son Ahira

The reordering of Num. 7* exactly follows the camping organization around Yahweh's dwelling place (Num. 2:1–31). The chieftains successively move in a centripetal rotation toward the dwelling place with their sacrificial gifts, beginning with the tribes to the east (Judah→Issachar→Zebulun), then to the south (Reuben→Simeon→Gad), to the west (Ephraim→Manasseh→Benjamin), and to the north (Dan→Asher→Naphtali). This ordering, in Num. 2, 7, and 10, promotes Judah, possibly revealing a social connection between Judah and the cultic leaders of Levi (for the other tribes, see comments on 2:18–31).[30] Levi is excluded from both lists because his tribe has now been subsumed into a consecrated lifestyle oriented around Yahweh's meeting-tent service and exempted from military service (Num. 1:47–53). Although Reuben was the firstborn, he had sex with his father's concubine (Gen. 35:22; 49:4), and in his place Judah was granted the signal position in view of the poetic intimations at his royal power (Gen. 49:8–12; Deut. 33:7) and the future rise to prominence of the tribe of Judah and its famous kings, David and Solomon. Thus, in the reordering of Num. 2, 7, and 10, unlike the northern tribes of Israel, the ascendancy of the tribe of Judah is clearly evident.[31]

---

30. See Rhyder, *Centralizing the Cult*, 126–27, 163.
31. See Rhyder, *Centralizing the Cult*, 128.

One wonders how the Israelites, now over thirteen months in the hostile Sinai desert, had acquired all these sacrifices. Although Moses is convinced that the Israelites do not have enough flocks and herds to slaughter to feed the whole nation (Num. 11:22), the chieftains of Num. 7* belong to the same generation who emigrated from Egypt with "a very large number of cattle" in tow (Exod. 12:38; cf. v. 32). This fits within a broader collection of stories, beginning with Abraham through Moses and beyond, that paint Israel's early culture as a pastoralist more than an agrarian subsistence.[32] This would explain the 252 sacrificial animals in their possession (see totals below), while the thirty-six utensils of silver and gold can be traced, in the narrative, back to the silver and gold that the Egyptians gave the Israelites when they departed (Exod. 12:35–36). In the context of the chieftains' gifts for the Levites to use in the meeting tent (vv. 1–9), and now to dedicate the altar (vv. 10–88), their gifts of silver plates and sprinkling bowls and gold pans not only contained the fine flour form of a grain offering (Lev. 2:1–3) and incense as a pleasing aroma to Yahweh;[33] the utensils must also have been intended for future priestly use at the bronze altar, either alongside or replacing the bronze-coated instruments already in use (Exod. 27:3; 38:3; see Num. 4:7; see the translation note on 7:13). Going beyond a single land animal required for a burnt offering (Lev. 1:1–13), each chieftain offered the combination of a bull, ram, and lamb, any of which would have been equally "a pleasing aroma to Yahweh" (Lev. 1:9, 13, 17). Likewise the sacrifice for peace was not one animal (Lev. 3:1–17) but was composed of two bulls, five rams, five male goats, and five male lambs a year old for a great pacifying communal meal in Yahweh's presence (see the translation note on 6:14). The purification offering, by contrast, was single, for removing sin, transgression, and impurity (see the first translation note on 6:11).

Why, over the course of eighty-four verses (!), does the narrator repeat the same pattern of offerings for each one of the twelve chieftains? This feels highly redundant to us, but it played several important rhetorical purposes: (1) every chieftain's offering was identical, so that neither Judah nor any other tribe could claim supremacy in their devotion to Yahweh; (2) with a history of apostasy at Sinai (Exod. 32–34*), they are excessive in their sacrifices as an unmistakable display of loyalty to Yahweh;[34] (3) the list in vv. 10–88 gives the impression of being a "bookkeeping list," a sort of record of the gifts and supplies coming to the priests;[35] and (4) in the context of the ancient Near East, the known pattern was to dedicate a deity's new dwelling with a surplus of diverse sacrifices. In the Ugaritic Baal cycle, after Kothar-wa-Khasis constructs Baal's temple in seven days, Baal (also called Hadad) furnishes it, then slaughters an array of animals and feeds them to the gods in a housewarming

---

32. D. Fleming, *Legacy*, 162–70.
33. The chieftains' incense would not have been placed on the incense altar (Exod. 30:34–38).
34. Levine, "Descriptive Tabernacle," 317.
35. Rainey, "Order of Sacrifices," 490.

feast: "He slaughters bovids [and] caprovids, he fells bulls [and] fattened goats, yearling calves, lambs (and) great numbers of kids."[36] The Israelite chieftains' sacrifices are equally or more impressive. Rather than Yahweh feasting with seventy other gods, it may be that he feasted metaphorically with the chieftains, as their daily sacrifice for greetings involved a pacifying meal with seventeen slaughtered animals (see Lev. 7:15–17, 29–36).

7:84–88. The narrator recapitulates vv. 10–83 by giving the sum of the weight of the precious metals (vv. 84–86) and number of sacrificial animals (vv. 87–88) that the chieftains presented to dedicate Yahweh's altar. This unit of summations is framed by *inclusio* (v. 84a//v. 88b). This leaves the lasting impression of a formidable accumulation of desirable gifts, particularly for ancient readers who knew that a shekel approximated 11.4 grams in weight (see the last translation note on 3:47).

Utensils for altar service	12 silver plates (130 shekels ea. = ca. 3.2 pounds ea.)
	12 silver sprinkling bowls (70 shekels ea. = ca. 1.75 pounds ea.)
	(2,400 shekels = ca. 60 pounds of silver)
	12 gold pans with incense (10 shekels ea. = ca. ¼ pound)
	(120 shekels = ca. 3 pounds of gold)
Burnt offerings	12 young bulls
	12 rams
	12 male lambs a year old with their grain offering
	12 male goats for a purification offering
Sacrifices for Peace	24 young bulls
	60 rams
	60 male goats
	60 lambs a year old

More precisely, vv. 84–88 give totals for six items: (1) silver bowls; (2) silver basins; (3) gold ladles; (4) herd animals for burnt offerings; (5) goats for sin offerings; (6) herd animals for sacrifice.[37] The totals in the text are accurate, as one would expect from the tendency toward careful bookkeeping in archival documents of the ANE and priestly texts in the Hebrew Bible (so also Exod. 38:24–30).[38] In fact, vv. 84–88 may have originally been formatted to be read in two parallel columns with totals for each item/animal, a format well-attested in Old Babylonian and Mesopotamian records.[39] In addition to the 6 carts and 12 oxen (vv. 2–3), the chieftains gave a total of approximately 60 pounds of silver, 3 pounds of gold, 48 animals for burnt offerings, and 204 animals for sacrifices for peace. This was a formidable gift to dedicate

36. "The Baʿlu Myth," COS 1.86:261–62; a "housewarming party" (Walton and Matthews, *Genesis–Deuteronomy*, 184).
37. Levine, "Descriptive Tabernacle," 315.
38. Milgrom, "Decoding," 131–32.
39. Levine, "Descriptive Tabernacle," 315–18.

Yahweh's bronze altar, which only underscores the magnitude of Solomon's dedicatory offerings for the first temple—22,000 cattle and 120,000 sheep and goats for sacrifices for peace (1 Kings 8:63; 2 Chron. 7:5)—and even of the people's dedicatory offerings for the second temple: 100 bulls, 200 rams, 400 lambs, and 12 male goats for all Israel's sin (Ezra 6:17). Considering the chieftains' life situation, having already survived over thirteen months in the arid, ecologically sparse Sinai desert,[40] one might argue that their offering was qualitatively even more impressive (cf. Mark 12:41–44; Luke 21:1–4).

7:89. Shifting abruptly from the chieftains' dedicatory gifts, the narrator describes Moses's unparalleled custom of entering the meeting tent to meet and speak with Yahweh, who resides above the atonement cover, between the cherubim (on the customary aspect, see the first translation note on 7:89). The syntax further expresses that the reason Moses enters the meeting tent is specifically to speak with Yahweh (see the second translation note on 7:89). Moses's communion (meeting and speaking) with Yahweh is a fulfillment of Yahweh's promise in Exod. 25:22, and this prerogative for Moses stands in distinction from Aaron and his sons' reason for entering the tent's holy place: to serve at the table, lamp, and incense altar and to bear the names and decisions of the Israelites on Aaron's heart before Yahweh (Exod. 28:30; 30:22–38; Lev. 24:1–9). Moses alone enters the outer room of the tent to talk with and receive revelation from Yahweh, whereas Aaron alone enters the inner room of the tent, the most holy place, to make atonement annually (Lev. 16). Through various twists and turns, the Yahweh-Moses relationship continues to revolve around their spatial proximity and spoken communication (see the "Implications" essay below, "The Yahweh-Moses Relationship").

Implications

The Yahweh-Moses Relationship: Veiled Presence but Audible Word

You cannot see my face. For no one can see me and live.

Yahweh to Moses (Exod. 33:20)

To my mind the Infinite comes in the signifyingness of the face [of another person]. The face signifies the Infinite.

Emmanuel Levinas[41]

The Infinite affects thought by devastating it and at the same time calls upon it.

Emmanuel Levinas[42]

---

40. Chronology (Exod. 40:17; Num. 1:1); harsh Sinai conditions (Exod. 17:1–3; Num. 11:4–6; 16:13).

41. Levinas, *Ethics and Infinity*, 105.

42. Levinas, "God and Philosophy," 162.

The narrator's abrupt remark in 7:89 leaves us, perhaps intentionally, with many questions. One of them is What was Moses feeling and thinking when he lingered in the divine presence in the meeting tent?[43] The very name "meeting tent" matches one of the ancient Near Eastern purposes of a divine dwelling—that is, for the deity to meet with his people.[44] Moses repeatedly entered directly into the cloud and smoke that surrounded the divine presence on Mount Sinai,[45] and inside the mysterious, makeshift (?) "meeting tent" of Exod. 33:7–11, Moses met directly with Yahweh while Yahweh guarded the entrance with a pillar of cloud. The narrator shockingly remarks that "Yahweh would speak to Moses face-to-face, the way someone speaks to a friend" (v. 11a, my trans.). This is an idiom for intimate communication (not visualizing Yahweh's face), which would destroy any mortal being (Exod. 33:20). At the installation of the great meeting tent, however, "Moses was not able to enter into the meeting tent because the cloud had settled on it, and the glory of Yahweh had filled the dwelling place" (Exod. 40:35). This divine-human distance continues through Lev. 1:1–9:22 as Moses stays outside the tent, but Yahweh begins to break down the separation by his communication and the gift of the sacrificial system (Moses and Aaron enter in Lev. 9:23).[46]

At the inception of Numbers, there is a subtle shift in language: "Yahweh spoke to Moses in the Sinai wilderness *inside the meeting tent* [*bəʾōhel mōʿēd*]" (1:1aα–β). In my view, Num. 7:89 explicates this terse introduction, so that readers now not only know that Moses is indeed able to enter, but readers also begin to imagine what it was like for Moses. Through an innerbiblical allusion to Exod. 25:22, the narrator in Num. 7:89 indicates that Yahweh has begun to fulfill his remarkable promise to commune personally with Moses in the tent.[47] The claim of an innerbiblical allusion is supported by the shared language and by the fact that the atonement cover (*hakkappōret* in Numbers only here), ark, and cherubim are unintelligible apart from Exod. 25:17–22 (see also the fourth translation note on Num. 7:89). However, there is one subtle distinction: Exod. 25* gives the impression that Moses will *meet* Yahweh in the most holy place of the meeting tent, but Num. 7* is immovably stationed after Lev. 16*, which bars all but Aaron, so the fulfillment of Exod. 25:22 takes the twist of Moses listening to the voice of Yahweh *through a curtain*. So "the meeting tent" (*ʾōhel mōʿēd*) of Num. 7:89 refers metonymically to

43. Paterius (6th–7th cent. CE) infers that Moses, a model for pastors, contemplated the mysteries of God while inside the tent, but outside the tent he bore the burdens of weak sinners (Lienhard, *Numbers*, 211).

44. See the first translation note on 1:50; and Hundley, "Tabernacle or Tent of Meeting?," 3–18.

45. Exod. 19:16–20; 24:18.

46. See comments on 1:1; and Nihan, *Priestly Torah*, 90–91.

47. Achenbach, *Vollendung*, 537–38; Seebass, *Numeri*, 1:198–200. Kellermann (*Priesterschrift*, 108–9, 111) sees 7:89 as an insertion into Num. 1–10 to report the fulfillment of Exod. 25:22.

the entire bipartite tent, the dwelling place or tabernacle (*miškan*), of which Moses enters only the first room.[48]

Even so, the stress of this narration is not on separation, but on verbal communication by Yahweh to Moses, which the narrator over-specifies:[49] Moses enters in order "to speak with Yahweh," he hears Yahweh's "voice speaking to him," and if we still did not catch it, "he spoke with him." The second in this sequence is probably an iterative; that is, Moses hears the voice continually speaking to him (see the third translation note on 7:89). The subject of the final clause is, I think, intentionally elusive: Is it that Yahweh speaks with Moses, Moses speaks with Yahweh, or both? (see the last translation note on 7:89). In any case, Exod. 25:22 and the phrase in Num. 7:89 that Moses "heard the voice speaking to him from above the atonement cover" stress the audible divine voice that spans the physical divide between Yahweh and Moses. Azzan Yadin has made a compelling case that the voice (*qôl*) of Yahweh in Num. 7:89, among other texts,[50] represents a *mediating hypostasis* of Yahweh himself.[51]

Echoes of this phenomenon—revelatory divine word or voice crossing the divine-human separation—abound in the NT writings, depicting the intermediation of Jesus the Messiah, the Son of God.[52] Unlike Moses, who could not enter the most holy place, and unlike Aaron, who entered while fearing for his life (Lev. 16:2), all of Jesus's followers now "have confidence to enter the Most Holy Place by the blood of Jesus, by a new and living way opened for us through the curtain, that is, his body" (Heb. 10:19–20 NIV).

48. While the tent is bipartite, the entire edifice with the courtyard is tripartite, resembling MB and Iron Age Syro-Palestinian tripartite temples (see Arnold, "Singular Israel," 4–5).
49. See Runge, *Discourse Grammar*, 387.
50. Exod. 19:19; 20:18–19; Deut. 4:12; cf. *dbr* hithpael in Ezek. 2:2; 43:6.
51. Yadin, "[Qwl]," 601–26.
52. Mark 15:37–39; John 1:14, 18; Heb. 1:1–3; 2 Pet. 1:17–18; Rev. 1:12–18.

8

Craft Seven Lamps;
Consecrate the Levites

(8:1–26)

❧

Overview

Moses, Israel's first cultic mediator, is now engaging with Yahweh outside the curtain of Yahweh's dwelling (7:89), which signals that his authoritative social role is in the process of being transferred to the Aaronic priests (8:1–4) and even, to a lesser extent, to the Levites (8:5–26).[1] In place of Moses, who originally set up the lampstand in the holy place (Exod. 25:37; 40:4b, 25), the Aaronic priests now hold this prerogative and must orient the lamps to shine toward the tent's entrance (8:1–4). The core of the chapter, Yahweh's extended speech, centers on the purification and consecration of the Levites to Yahweh, to belong exclusively to Yahweh and become servants to Aaron and his sons in the meeting tent (8:5–22). In chap. 7, the chieftains gave gifts for the Levites to serve in the meeting tent and many more gifts to dedicate the meeting tent. Now in chap. 8, Yahweh gives the Levites as a gift to Aaron and his sons to support their service in the meeting tent.[2] The consecration of the Levites (8:5–22) literarily and conceptually holds a Janus function of looking backward to the initial choice of the Levites as substitutes for Israel's firstborn and servants in Yahweh's meeting tent (3:5–51) and forward to the implication of the Levites' consecration, that they are worthy to receive Israel's

---

1. Hess, *Israelite Religions*, 186n49.
2. Douglas, *Wilderness*, 103, 186–87.

sacrificial gifts (18:2–7).[3] The narrator is emphatic that Moses, Aaron, and the entire Israelite community dedicated the Levites to Yahweh and to his tent service precisely as Yahweh commanded Moses (8:20–22). Finally, presumably to meet the demands of the meeting tent with a smaller demographic of Levites in society, Yahweh expands the eligible working-age range of the Levites to begin at twenty-five years old (8:23–26) instead of thirty (Num. 4*).

Translation

[1]Then Yahweh spoke to Moses: [2]"Speak to Aaron and tell him, 'When you set up the lamps, seven lamps must give light toward the area in front of the lampstand.'"[4] [3]So Aaron did this. He set up the lamps toward the area in front of the lampstand, as Yahweh commanded Moses. [4]Now this is how the lampstand was made: It was a hammered work of gold; from its base to its flowers, it was hammered work. According to the pattern that Yahweh had shown Moses,[5] so he made the lampstand.

[5]Then Yahweh spoke to Moses: [6]"Take the Levites from among the Israelites and purify them. [7]Do this to them in order to purify them: Sprinkle water of purification on them, and have them shave their whole body and wash their clothes, so that they will purify themselves.[6] [8]Then they must take a young bull with its grain offering of fine flour mixed with olive oil, and you must take a second young bull for a purification offering. [9]You must bring the Levites in front of the meeting tent and assemble the entire Israelite community. [10]Then you must bring the Levites before Yahweh,[7] and the Israelites must lay their hands on the

---

3. Knohl (*Sanctuary*, 71–73) attributes all three texts to a single Levite treatise by H. However, this is called into question: Achenbach (*Vollendung*, 160) rightly notes that the Levite substitution for Israel's firstborn is not even intimated in Num. 18. Reconstructing Levite history is complex (cf. Levine, *Numbers*, 1:279–90; Leuchter and Hutton, eds., *Levites and Priests*).

4. Following Levine (*Numbers*, 1:269), but the position of the seven illuminating lamps in relation to the lampstand can be debated due to the stacking of three Hebrew prepositions in v. 2: formally, "toward opposite before [*'el-mûl pәnê*] the lampstand"; hence, the variations "from the side in front of" (NETS of LXX[ed]); "before the face of" (Tg[O]: *lqbyl 'py*); "in (at the) front of" (NRSV, ESV, NJPS); "(falls) forward in front of" (NLT, EÜ); "the area in front of" (NIV; Cardellini, *Numeri 1,1–10,10*, 308); "toward the front" (Seebass, *Numeri*, 1:202; de Vaulx, *Nombres*, 118).

5. A hiphil causative, *her'â* (had shown) with the cognate accusative *mar'eh* (pattern; appearance, visible form; DCH 5:474).

6. This reflexive hithpael weqatal does not indicate a fourth directive, but provides the purpose for obeying the orders (also weqatal) of sprinkling, shaving, and washing: "*so that* they will purify themselves" (*wәhittehārû*; GBHS §3.5.3b).

7. "*Then you must bring* [*wәhiqrabtā*] the Levites before Yahweh" (NET, NIV, NJPS) reflects a sequential weqatal (*GBHS* §3.5.2a), not as a dependent, temporal clause (ESV, NRSV). Bringing the Levites before Yahweh (v. 10a) appears to be a second act after bringing the Levites before the tent and community (v. 9).

Levites, [11]and Aaron must elevate the Levites before Yahweh as an elevation offering[8] from the Israelites, so that they may do the work of Yahweh. [12]Then the Levites will lay their hands on the heads of the bulls, and you must offer the one for a purification offering and the other for a burnt offering to Yahweh, to make atonement for the Levites.[9] [13]You must have the Levites stand before Aaron[10] and his sons, and then elevate them as an elevation offering to Yahweh. [14]So you will separate the Levites from among the Israelites, and the Levites will be mine. [15]After this, the Levites will enter to do the work of the meeting tent.[11] So you must purify them and elevate them as an elevation offering.

[16]"For they are given exclusively[12] to me from among the Israelites. I have taken them for myself in place of all who open the womb, the firstborn sons of all the Israelites.[13] [17]For every firstborn male among the Israelites is mine, both human and animal. When I destroyed all the firstborn in the land of Egypt, I set them apart for myself. [18]So I have taken the Levites in place of all the firstborn sons among the Israelites. [19]I have given the Levites as a gift[14] to Aaron and his sons from among the Israelites, to do the work for the Israelites in the meeting tent, and to make atonement for the Israelites, so that there will be no plague among the Israelites[15] when the Israelites come near the sanctuary."

[20]So Moses and Aaron and the whole Israelite community did this with the Levites.[16] According to everything Yahweh commanded Moses concerning the Levites, this is what the Israelites did with them. [21]The

---

8. See the first translation note on 6:20.

9. LXX[ed] 3rd masc. sg., "he must offer (do) . . . for them" (*poiēsei . . . peri autōn*) refers to Aaron (Dorival, *Nombres*, 611). This is a legitimate reading of the consonantal Hebrew text (Wevers, *Notes*, 123); "for them" is more difficult than stating "for the Levites," but it could be an assimilation to 8:21.

10. LXX[ed] includes "And you shall stand the Leuites *before the Lord and [enanti kyriou kai]* before Aaron" (NETS), assimilating to vv. 10, 11, 12, which may reflect the translator's (or *Vorlage*'s) desire "that Israel's God was not neglected in the ceremony" (Wevers, *Notes*, 124).

11. Formally, "to work/serve the meeting tent" (MT), whereas SP and LXX[ed]—probably to assimilate to vv. 11, 19, 22—read "to work/serve *the work(s)/service(s) of* the meeting tent."

12. An intensifying repetition of the pass. predicate ptc.; formally, "they *are given, are given* [*nətunîm nətunîm*]."

13. Perhaps to assimilate to 3:12, SP reads "in place of *every firstborn who opens the womb among* the Israelites."

14. A substantivized pass. ptc., formally, "what is given" (*nətunîm*), whereas in v. 16 they "are given exclusively" (*nətunîm nətunîm*) to Yahweh. In Ugaritic, a cognate term (*ytnm; KTU* 4.93 1) likewise refers to the servants devoted to the deity who serve at the temple and cultic sites in the city of Ugarit (Hess, *Israelite Religions*, 111).

15. LXX[ed] omits "plague among the Israelites" (cf. *negep*, "plague," in 16:46–47 [17:11–12]). Dorival (*Nombres*, 611) notes that the MT of 8:19 implies that the Israelites were permitted to approach the sanctuary. Wevers (*Numbers*, 127), therefore, conjectures that the LXX omission was the translator's interpretation that the Israelites were not to encroach at any time.

16. "With the Levites" (NRSV, NJPS, NET, NIV, EÜ) renders a specification *l* (*GBHS* §4.1.10h; Cazelles, *Nombres*, 54; Levine, *Numbers*, 1:270; Ashley, *Numbers*, 168), rather than quasi-datival *l* ("to the Levites," ESV; Budd, *Numbers*, 89) or interest *l* ("for the Levites": Cardellini,

Levites purified themselves and washed their clothing. Then Aaron elevated them as an elevation offering before Yahweh, and Aaron made atonement for them to purify them. [22]After this, the Levites went in to do their work in the meeting tent before Aaron and before his sons. As Yahweh had commanded Moses concerning the Levites, so they did with them.

[23]Then Yahweh spoke to Moses: [24]"This applies to the Levites: Those twenty-five years old and up[17] are qualified to serve[18] in the work of the meeting tent, [25]and at fifty years old they must retire[19] from their service and may not work anymore.[20] [26]They may assist their brothers in the meeting tent, to keep their responsibilities,[21] but they must not do any work. This is what you must do regarding the Levites and their responsibilities."

Interpretation

8:1–4. In obedience to Yahweh's orders through Moses, Aaron sets up seven lamps to illuminate the area in front of the lampstand. The anaphoric articles in Yahweh's orders, "*the* lamps" and "*the* lampstand" (v. 2), point back to Exod. 25:31–40, which contains the original blueprint for the lampstand (*mənôrâ*) on which seven lamps (*nērōt*) were positioned and lit with oil.[22] For those unaware or forgetful of the lampstand's design from Exod. 25:31 and 37:17, the editor in v. 4 gives a synopsis (using synecdoche) of its composition under the auspices of Moses.[23] Likewise, Yahweh's instruction in vv. 1–2 is not new but reaffirms from Exod. 25:37 that the lamps on the lampstand must be positioned to shine in a certain direction, toward the area in front of the

---

Numeri 1,1–10,10, 314; de Vaulx, *Nombres*, 122; *GBHS* §4.1.10e.1), since the Levites themselves are also agents in the consecration ritual (vv. 7, 8, 12).

17. Throughout chap. 4, LXX[ed] expands the lower number of the Levite census age span from thirty to twenty-five years old (see the first translation note on 4:3).

18. The precise phrase (only here) is permissive, "may come to serve in the service" (*yābô' lišbō' ṣābā'*; *GBHS* §3.2.2d2), which alludes to chap. 4's language of the Levite families qualified for cultic service (4:3, 23, 30, 35, 39, 43).

19. Formally, "return from service."

20. Contextually, a general prohibition (*GBHS* §4.2.11), which I translate more softly as "and may not work anymore" (*wəlō' ya'ăbōd 'ôd*) because of the exception in v. 26 allowing them to assist after the age of fifty.

21. Formally, "they may serve with their brothers in the meeting tent," followed by the purpose inf. containing the cognate accusative well-known from chaps. 3–4, "to guard the guarded things and the service" (*lišmōr mišmeret wa'ăbōdâ*).

22. For Leon Yarden's view of the lampstand symbolism, see the note to the "Implications" essay in chap. 4, "The Holiness of God Is Lethal."

23. Contra B. Robinson ("Moses," 120–21), who unpersuasively argues that "the *pattern* [*mar'eh*] that Yahweh had shown Moses" (8:4) refers to the vision Moses saw at the burning bush (Exod. 3).

lampstand.[24] Moses was initially responsible to orient the seven lamps,[25] but Exod. 27:21 and Lev. 24:3 assign the continual task to the high priest, Aaron.[26] However, these texts are ambiguous about the direction of the lamps: one could interpret "before Yahweh" as illuminating the area nearest to Yahweh's presence, which would be *behind* the lampstand and toward the curtain concealing the most holy place. Numbers 8:1–2 now makes clear that, like Moses (Exod. 25:37), Aaron also must position the lamps to illuminate the area *in front of* the lampstand (see the translation note on 8:2). As a result of Aaron's exact obedience to the blueprints revealed to Moses (v. 3; see the translation note on 8:4), this light throughout the holy place enables Aaron to execute his regular assignments at the bread table and incense altar (Exod. 30:1–10; Lev. 24:5–9). The redactional placement of 8:1–4 immediately after 7:89 is intriguing, as both fulfill the roles Yahweh promised in Exodus for Moses and Aaron.[27] In these roles, there would also be a symbiotic relationship. On one hand, Aaron (8:1–4)—not Moses, who lingers near Yahweh (7:89)—now mediates the illumination of Yahweh's presence to the people (as in 6:22–27).[28] On the other hand, Moses's custom of entering the holy place to listen to Yahweh's voice behind the curtain implies that the lamps Aaron adjusted would also brighten Moses's space as he remains close to the divine presence.[29]

8:5–19. Yahweh directs Moses, Aaron, and all the Israelites to play distinct roles in purifying and consecrating the Levites to Yahweh for their meeting-tent service (vv. 5–15). Multiple steps are required:

1. Moses sprinkles purification water on the Levites (v. 7).
2. The Levites shave their whole body and wash their clothes to purify themselves (see the translation note on v. 7).[30]

---

24. Levine, *Numbers*, 1:271.

25. Exod. 25:37; 40:4b, 25.

26. Knohl (*Sanctuary*, 89–90) assigns Exod. 27:21; Lev. 24:1–4; and Num. 8:1–4 to H. Albertz (*Israelite Religion*, 2:458) claims, without textual evidence from the Second Temple period, that the seven-branched lampstand of the Priestly writings of the Pentateuch reflects the second temple's adaptation of the earlier ten-branched lampstand in Solomon's temple (1 Kings 7:49; 2 Chron. 4:7).

27. Cardellini (*Numeri 1,1–10,10*, 346–47) observes that "just as the word spoken in Exod. 25:22 is fulfilled in Num. 7:89—that the LORD would manifest himself above the ark between the cherubim—so also the command given in Exod. 25:37 is fulfilled in Num. 8:2b–3, as it was never implemented (as expected) in Exod. 37:17–24" (my trans.).

28. Achenbach, *Vollendung*, 539.

29. De Vaulx (*Nombres*, 117) notices that among the Second Temple depictions of the lampstand are those with a symbolic, sacred character: "the lampstand of the light" (1 Macc. 1:21) and "the eyes of Yahweh, which cross the whole earth" (Zech. 4:2, 10).

30. Likewise, Egyptian priests shaved all their head and body hair in their purification rituals (Walton and Matthews, *Genesis–Deuteronomy*, 184).

3. The Levites take a young bull, with its grain offering, for a whole burnt offering (v. 8; see v. 12).

4. Moses takes a second young bull for a purification offering (v. 8).

5. Moses brings the Levites to the front of the meeting tent and assembles the whole Israelite community (v. 9).

6. Moses brings the Levites before Yahweh (see the translation note on v. 10), and the Israelites lay their hands on the Levites (vv. 9–10).

7. Aaron elevates the Levites before Yahweh as an elevation offering, so they can do Yahweh's work (v. 11).

8. The Levites lay their hands on the bulls' heads, symbolically transferring their impurities caused by sin, guilt, and bodily contagions, and Moses offers his bull as a purification offering and their bull as a burnt offering. Both bulls collectively make atonement, purging the Levites' impurities from them in Yahweh's sight (v. 12; see v. 8; Lev. 1:4; 4:1–5:13).

Elsewhere in the Hebrew Scriptures, only cuts of animal meat, grains, and materials belonging to the meeting tent are to be physically lifted up to Yahweh as an "elevation offering" (see the first translation note on 6:20).[31] The only humans on record to be raised to Yahweh as an elevation offering are the Levites, and one could argue that this was the central component of their consecration ritual (repeated mention in vv. 11, 13, 15, 21; for more detail, see the "Implications" essay below, "The Levites, a Living Sacrifice"). Forming an *inclusio* with the language of separating and purifying the Levites in v. 6, Yahweh in vv. 14–15 explains that the purpose of the multistep ritual with the Levites (vv. 7–12) is to separate them to belong uniquely to Yahweh, resulting in their installation in Yahweh's meeting-tent service (v. 15).[32]

Continuing the same speech, in vv. 16–19, Yahweh then reviews the theological basis, which he laid down in Num. 3:6–46* and will later reframe in Num. 18*, for why the Levites must be consecrated to Yahweh. Here we find a device called Seidel's Law, which is used to mark an innerbiblical reformulation of a prior source text.[33] That is, through Yahweh's second speech on the Levites' election in 8:16–19, *he abridges and reverses* the order of the elements in the first speech (3:5–16). The meaningful differences are in bold font:

---

31. Leveen, *Memory*, 118.

32. As Seebass (*Numeri*, 1:217) observes, v. 15b duplicates v. 13b, both ultimately attributing to Moses, rather than Aaron (v. 11), the cleansing and elevating of the Levites to Yahweh.

33. Levinson, *Deuteronomy*, 18–19.

Table 8.1. Numbers 3 and 8 Compared

Numbers 3:6–13, 41–46*	Numbers 8:16–18
⁶Bring the tribe of Levi near, and stand them before Aaron the priest so that they may serve him ⁷and keep his responsibilities and the responsibilities of the whole community before the meeting tent, by performing the dwelling place service. ⁸They must care for the furnishings of the meeting tent and for the responsibilities of the Israelites, by performing the dwelling place service. ⁹**You must assign** the Levites to Aaron and his sons; they will be assigned exclusively to him from among the Israelites. ¹⁰You must appoint Aaron and his sons **so that they protect their priesthood; but the unauthorized person who approaches must be put to death.** ¹²Look, I myself have taken the Levites from among the Israelites in place of every firstborn of the womb among the Israelites. So the Levites will belong to me, ¹³since all the firstborn are mine. When I destroyed all the firstborn in the land of Egypt, I set apart for myself all the firstborn in Israel, from human to animal. They belong to me. I am Yahweh. ⁴¹**You must take** the Levites for myself—I am Yahweh—in place of all the firstborn among the Israelites, and the Levites' livestock in place of all the firstborn among the Israelites' livestock. [Also vv. 45–46]	¹⁶For they [the Levites] are given exclusively to me from among the Israelites. **I have taken** them for myself in place of all who open the womb, the firstborn sons of all the Israelites. ¹⁷For every firstborn male among the Israelites is mine, both human and animal. When I destroyed all the firstborn in the land of Egypt, I set them apart for myself. ¹⁸So I have taken the Levites in place of all the firstborn sons among the Israelites. ¹⁹**I have given** the Levites as a gift to Aaron and his sons from among the Israelites, to do the work for the Israelites in the meeting tent, **and to make atonement for the Israelites, so that there will be no plague among the Israelites when the Israelites come near the sanctuary.**

From all the Israelites, Yahweh has selected the Levites to belong exclusively to himself (see the first translation note on 8:16). The Levites and their livestock are transformed, in Yahweh's estimation, into surrogate firstborn sacrifices in place of every firstborn Israelite boy and animal, who were devoted to Yahweh when he destroyed Egypt's firstborn but preserved Israel's (vv. 16b–18; see the comments in chap. 3). Yahweh's great redemption of Israel, his firstborn, from Egypt substantiates the unfolding obligations that Yahweh, Moses, and Aaron will place on the Levites and Israelites.[34] In chap. 3, Yahweh stressed Moses's agency in consecrating and giving the Levites to Aaron: "You must assign" and "You must take" (3:9, 41, in bold font above). Since Moses

34. Leveen, *Memory*, 45, 74.

essentially executed these tasks (3:42, 49–51), now in chap. 8 Yahweh speaks of his own completed works: "I have taken" and "I have given" (8:16, 19, bold font above).[35] Since the Levites belong to Yahweh, he holds the prerogative to give them to Aaron and his sons (vv. 16, 19; see the first translation note on 8:19).[36] Now, aside from their self-purification, bringing sacrifices to Aaron and entering the tent to begin their service (vv. 7–8, 21–22), the Levites never act independently, but only under the authoritative direction of the Aaronic priests.[37] Through the Num. 8* ritual, the Levites simultaneously became liminal, belonging honorably to Yahweh and protecting his dwelling, and marginal, subordinate to the Aaronides.[38] The Levitical services, according to Yahweh in 3:9, are to support Aaron and sons, who need to protect their priesthood and prevent unauthorized persons, non-priests, from encroaching on the sacred space; anyone who encroaches must be executed. By contrast, in the innerbiblical reformulation of 8:19, the Levites support the Aaronic priests for the benefit of non-priests—that is, to atone for the Israelites and prevent them from encroaching, thus protecting them from divine wrath in the form of a plague (see bold text above).[39]

8:20–22. The narrator reports Moses, Aaron, and the whole community's faithful response to purify and devote the Levites to Yahweh, and this results in the Levites starting to work in Yahweh's meeting tent. This report is framed by an *inclusio* of general statements portraying the careful obedience of Moses, Aaron, and the whole community (vv. 20, 22b; see the translation note on 8:20). Within this framing device, v. 21 lists the specific actions that were faithfully performed: (1) the Levites purified themselves and washed their clothes, as Yahweh ordered in v. 7; (2) Aaron elevated the Levites as an elevation offering, as Yahweh ordered in vv. 9–11; and (3) Aaron made atonement for the Levites, as Yahweh ordered in vv. 8 and 12. Absent in v. 12 but added subtly here is the purpose for the atonement, not explicitly for forgiveness for known sin or guilt, but for cleansing from physical contagions (v. 21; see the note near the end of the comments on 6:1–12 on the removal of sin, guilt, and physical impurities).

8:23–26. By this divine speech, Yahweh expands the original age span (chap. 4) of active Levite service from ages 30–50 to ages 25–50 (see Num. 4:3, 23, 30, 35, 39, 43, 47). To harmonize with this larger age span, the Septuagint

---

35. The Levite theology of Num. 8, in which the Levites are honored yet subordinated to the Aaronic priests, anticipates the rebellion of a faction of the Levites, Korah and company, in Num. 16 (Frevel, "High Priest," 149–50; Nihan, "Priestly Laws," 120–22).

36. Douglas, *Wilderness*, 138.

37. Frevel, "High Priest," 139.

38. Christian, "Middle-Tier Levites," 176.

39. See 16:46–48. The Levites' role in protecting the Israelites against divine judgment is paralleled in Hittite and Babylonian appeasement rituals (Walton and Matthews, *Genesis–Deuteronomy*, 184).

throughout chap. 4 reads twenty-five to fifty years of age (see the first translation note on 4:3). Instead, the Hebrew manuscripts reflect the original text, and the logical inference one draws is that the earlier, thirty to fifty age span did not supply enough eligible Levites to transport, or to transport efficiently, Yahweh's meeting tent (see the first translation note on 8:24). Retirement age stayed the same at fifty (see the comments in chap. 3 and the translation notes on 8:25). Levites 50 and older could still assist but "not do any work," presumably not transport anything (see the translation note on 8:26).

Two indicators suggest that vv. 23–26 were a later Priestly insertion into the Num. 1:1–10:10 collection, I believe under the inspiration of the Spirit, in order to supply more Levites to care sufficiently for Yahweh's dwelling place.[40] First, vv. 23–26 are placed *after* the narrative of the Levites' consecration (vv. 20–22), not with Yahweh's speech in vv. 5–19, where it would fit more naturally. Second, without an underlying shortage of personnel, there would be no need for this revision, since the Israelites in the story line are still stationed at Mount Sinai (through Num. 10:10) and presumably would not yet know whether the number of thirty-to-fifty-year-old Levites would be adequate. In summary, vv. 23–26 offer us a good example (1) of underlying sociopolitical realities that influence the shape of biblical law, and (2) of Yahweh's constant willingness to revise, sometimes even overturn, his prior instruction for the sake of the present situation of his covenant people.

Implications

The Levites, a Living Sacrifice

The elevation offering in the Hebrew Bible could consist of animal thighs, breasts, barley, wheat, or dwelling-place materials, with one exception: the Levites. The Levites are the only humans recorded in the biblical narrative to have been raised to Yahweh as a personal form of this technical sacrifice.[41] Human sacrifice of adults, not just infanticide, was practiced in the ancient Near East, although its frequency is debated due to the issues of interpreting the skeletal remains in the archaeological record, the ambiguities of iconography, and the ideological shape of the textual evidence.[42] In the case of the Levites, however, they were never slaughtered ritually[43] but were a form of living sacrifice to

---

40. Kellermann, *Priesterschrift*, 120–24; Noth, *Numbers*, 69–70; Seebass, *Numeri*, 1:106, 220; Achenbach, *Vollendung*, 545. Scharbert (*Numeri*, 39) notes that in the early postexilic period, in contrast to many priests who returned to Judah (973 in Neh. 7:39), only a few Levites returned (74 in Neh. 7:43).

41. Leveen, *Memory*, 118.

42. Recht, "Human Sacrifice," 168–80.

43. Offering the Levites contrasts with the human sacrificed in the ANE substitutionary king rituals (Walton, *Ancient Near Eastern Thought*, 98–99).

Yahweh, something akin to the scapegoat that is sent off into the desert on Yom Kippur (Lev. 16:7–10, 20–22) or the living bird, coated in a slaughtered bird's blood, released to fly away into the field for the purification of the person with a skin disease (Lev. 14:6–7). Even so, the Levites as an elevation offering do not effect atonement or cleansing (rather, see Num. 8:12). In the ancient world, perhaps the closest parallel to the elevation offering is found, not in the Hittite and Mesopotamian waving rituals, which were not actually offered to the gods, but in the Egyptian rite of elevating sacrifices to Amun-Re or to other deities, and probably the Ugaritic gesture of presenting offerings to Baal (see the first translation note on 6:20). How, then, could Aaron (8:11, 21), even if he had Moses's help (8:13, 15), conceivably pick up and lift the Levites into the air before Yahweh? Numbers 8:13—possibly belonging to the base layer of the composition,[44] now in its final placement in 8:5–22—answers this question: in lieu of the traditional elevating gesture, Moses would have them simply "stand" before Aaron as an elevation offering to Yahweh.

So what does this actually mean for the Levites? In dramatic rituals associated with a change of leadership, one frequently finds that the prospect, here the Levites, is humbled by a "structural inferior," here the Israelites who lay their hands on the Levites, just before the prospect is raised to their new status.[45] The Levites do not effect atonement, but they do become a living sacrificial substitute for all of Israel's firstborn males, animal and human, and they do become Yahweh's holy tribe. As glamorous as this might sound, it was not a lifestyle of sublime transcendence for the Levites. Rather, they were hereditary servants, with their active duty from twenty-five to fifty years old consuming the prime of their lives until or slightly before their time to die.[46] Under the authority of the Aaronides, the Levites could not assert their individualism: daily they had to submit their will to the priests, who directed the Levites' rigorous, physical labor of transporting the meeting tent and who restricted the Levites from accessing Yahweh's presence and from even glimpsing the most holy sacra (Num. 4*). The Levites rebelled only to their own destruction (Num. 16*). There was one dimension of their existence, however, that could inspire joyful contentment and galvanize them in their work: they were Yahweh's inheritance, his own possession, and they lived and worked ultimately for Yahweh (8:11). With Aaron's permission, they were among the few who could potentially tarry in Yahweh's tent as Moses's assistant did: "Nun's son Joshua did not leave the tent" (Exod. 33:11c). Beyond what every Israelite could celebrate in their covenant with Yahweh, the Levites could sing with another layer of depth: "Yahweh is the portion of my inheritance and my cup. You hold my lot" (Ps. 16:5).

44. Kellermann, *Priesterschrift*, 118, 122; Seebass, *Numeri*, 1:216–17.
45. Leveen (*Memory*, 118–19) applies this observation from Turner, *Ritual Process*, 171.
46. On the forty-to-fifty-year life expectancy in the ANE, see the comments on 4:1–14.

After the Levites in ancient Israel, another polity of living sacrifices has arisen out of the people of God, believers who in response to God's mercies present their bodies to God as a "living sacrifice" (*thysian zōsan*, Rom. 12:1). Where does Paul get this image of a living, human-body sacrifice? Keener is right to point out its innovative nature: "Old Testament sacrifices, involving inanimate things or slain animals, were not described as living. Paul adapts the OT image of sacrifice in a new direction as believers embrace Christ's death even while living."[47] The Levites are the one exception. It is, therefore, plausible that the Levites as an elevation offering provided the figural soil for Paul's innovation. The conceptual analogy with Rom. 12:1 is apparent as Aaron and Moses presented the Levites bodily as a living sacrifice to God (Num. 8:9–11, 13, 15, 21), and they were acceptable to God (Num. 8:15–19, 22). Linguistically also, the believers' bodily sacrifice must be "holy" (*hagian*, Rom. 12:1), even as the Levites by their purification ritual in Num. 8 were made holy to God: "For they [the Levites] are given exclusively to me. . . . When I destroyed all the firstborn in the land of Egypt, *I set them apart* [*hēgiasa*, Israel's firstborn sons, v. 17a LXX] for myself. So I have taken the Levites in place of all the firstborn sons among the Israelites." In the compound nature of the body of Christ portrayed in Rom. 12:1, multiple bodies (*ta sōmata hymōn*) form a single sacrifice (*thysian*), just as multiple Levites (always pl. in Num. 8) form a single sacrifice (elevation offering, always sg.: Num. 8:11, 13, 15, 21). The Christ-followers' living sacrifice is their "spiritual worship"[48]—or, more formally, "reasonable service" (*tēn logikēn latreian*, NET)—even as the Levites entered the meeting tent "to serve in their service" (*leitourgein tēn leitourgian*, Num. 8:22 LXX; cf. vv. 11, 15, 19).[49] As Rom. 12:1–2 envisions, the Levites were, with all Israelites, called to be ethically holy within the holy covenant community.[50] The crucial difference was that the Levites' bodily sacrifice was demanded because of their tribal heritage, whereas the believer's bodily sacrifice is voluntary and self-giving because of the mercies of God in Christ.[51]

---

47. Keener, *Romans*, 143.

48. Witherington, *Romans*, 284n16.

49. Paul envisions that living sacrifices serve God and God's people (Rom. 12:3–21), just as the Levites "do the work of Yahweh" (Num. 8:11), which enables the priests "to do the work for the Israelites" (8:19).

50. As Nihan (*Priestly Torah*, 99) has shown, Lev. 18–20, with 19:2 in the center, functions as a *tôrâ* for Yahweh's holy people. Paterius, a bishop of Brescia, Italy (6th cent. CE), interpreted the Levites' consecration to Yahweh tropologically: shaving all their hair (8:7) referred to cleansing their carnal thoughts in God's eyes, while the twenty-five-to-fifty-year age span (8:24–25) restricted their eligibility to serve as young men (twenty-five) who blossomed into victors over temptation until the jubilee age of inner peace (fifty) (Lienhard, *Numbers*, 211–12).

51. See Betz, "Das Problem," 209–11, 215.

9

Passover; Cloud and Fire; Trumpets

(9:1–10:10)

∽∾

Overview

As the last major segment of discourse at Sinai, Num. 7:1–10:10 is bound together under the theme of supplying various *meeting tent materials*[1] *and personnel* necessary for Yahweh's cult to be fully operational prior to Israel's departure from Sinai: offering carts, pans, and offerings to support the Levites and dedicate the altar (7:1–88); positioning the lamps, for Moses and Aaron, in Yahweh's holy place (7:89–8:4); consecrating and offering the Levites for service (8:5–26); observing the first wilderness Passover (9:1–14); narrating the divine guidance through the cloud-fire of the meeting tent (9:15–23); and constructing and blowing silver trumpets for cultic assemblies, travel, and war (10:1–10).[2] The chronological markers at 9:1 and 9:15, and the decisive break from Sinai at 10:11, along with internal features, suggest that the 9:1–10:10 collection was added at a later point to the meeting-tent instructions from Sinai (Exod. 25–Num. 10*).[3] This collection begins with a divine call to celebrate the first Passover in the Sinai wilderness, a year after the exodus from Egypt, and Israel does so faithfully (9:1–5). However, an unanticipated scenario arises as men unclean from corpse contact express their desire to bring Yahweh's Passover offering (9:6–8). Through Moses, Yahweh addresses

---

1. Cardellini, *Numeri 1,1–10,10*, 32.
2. Douglas (*Wilderness*, 124) sees Num. 7–9 as a thematic unit, which wrongly dissociates trumpets (10:1–10) from the priestly cult (see 10:2, 7–8, 10).
3. Achenbach (*Vollendung*, 547–56) identifies 9:1–14, 15–23; 10:1–10 as expansions in the final phase of the theocratic revision of the Torah.

this situation with a case law applicable for future generations (vv. 9–14). In vv. 15–23, the implied narrator innerbiblically expands the description in Exod. 40* to underscore Israel's obedience to Yahweh's cloud-fire guidance. Finally, 10:1–10 holds pride of place as the last word before Israel departs from Sinai for Canaan: Yahweh orders the fashioning and functioning of the silver trumpets for various purposes, now the most important being to direct Israel's travels and warfare.

Translation

1Yahweh spoke to Moses in the Sinai wilderness in the first month of the second year after their exodus from the land of Egypt:
2"The Israelites[4] must observe the Passover at its appointed time. **3**On day fourteen of this month, at twilight,[5] you are to observe it at its appointed time. You must observe it by following[6] all its statutes and all its customs." **4**So Moses instructed the Israelites to observe the Passover, **5**and they observed the Passover on day fourteen of the first month at twilight in the Sinai wilderness.[7] The Israelites did everything just as Yahweh had commanded Moses. **6**But at that time[8] there were some men[9] who had become unclean[10] by touching a human corpse,[11] so they could not observe the Passover on that day. They came before Moses and Aaron on that day. **7**And those men said to Moses,[12] "We have become unclean by a human corpse. Why are we kept[13] from offering Yahweh's offering at its appointed time among

---

4. LXX[ed] includes, "*Speak [eipon], and let the sons of Israel keep . . .*" (NETS).

5. Formally, "between the two evenings"; LXX[ed] "*toward evening*" (*pros hesperan*); 4Q23 reads "on the day" (*bywm*), then the text breaks off (Ulrich, *Qumran*, 142).

6. "By following" (*k . . . k*) indicates an agreement in Yahweh's norm (*IBHS* §11.2.9b).

7. LXX[ed] does not mention twilight: "When the month began, on the fourteenth day, in the wilderness of Sina" (NETS).

8. "But" contrasts the exceptional case(s) in vv. 6–14 with the Passover custom in vv. 1–5. The copula introduces foregrounded events, "But/and at that time" (*wayhî*, BHRG §21.2.1.1.2ba), whereas the SP and LXX[ed] pl. agrees with the pl. subject, "*But/and there were* certain men who were unclean."

9. The pl. *'ănāšîm* appears to refer only to the male gender; cf. Exod. 35:22, "both men and women" (*hā'ănāšîm 'al-hannāšîm*); Num. 5:6, "a man or woman" (*'îš 'ô-'iššâ*); in contrast to the undefined gender of "person, life" (*nepeš*) or "person" (*'îš*).

10. The English pluperfect "had become unclean" (*hāyû ṭəmē'îm*) renders a qatal stative (*GBHS* §3.2.1b).

11. Formally, "by a (dead) person" (*lənepeš*), with a *l* of agency (*GBHS* §4.1.10[l]). "Touching" was added (many versions) to clarify that contact with the unclean contagion of a corpse is implied (Lev. 21:1; Num. 5:2; 9:6, 7, 9).

12. "To Moses" was added to clarify "*to him*" (*'ēlāyw*).

13. The niphal incomplete pass. "*are kept [niggāra'] from offering*" (*IBHS* §23.2.2e) nonetheless implies the men's assumption that Yahweh or the Israelite leadership restricted them from observing Passover.

the Israelites?'" **8**So Moses said to them, "Stay here while I hear[14] what Yahweh commands concerning you." **9**Yahweh spoke to Moses: **10**"Tell the Israelites, 'If any of you[15] or your descendants become unclean by touching a corpse, or are away on a journey, then you may still observe[16] a Passover for Yahweh.[17] **11**They may observe it on day fourteen of the second month at twilight. They must eat it with bread made without yeast and with bitter herbs. **12**They must not leave any of it until morning, nor break any of its bones. They must observe it by following every Passover statute.[18] **13**But anyone[19] who is clean and not on a journey, yet fails to keep the Passover, that person must be cut off from their people. Since they did not bring Yahweh's offering at its appointed time, that person must bear their sin. **14**If an immigrant lives among you[20] and wants to observe[21] a Passover for Yahweh, he must do so following the Passover statute, following its custom. You must have the same statute for the immigrant and for the native.'"

14. "*While* I hear" (*wə'ešmə'â*) reflects a circumstantial *w* (*GBHS* §4.3.3e), as the men obeyed the command to wait (formally, "stand," *'imdû*) while Moses would listen to Yahweh.

15. In contrast to the unclean men (*hā'ănāšîm*, v. 7), here in v. 10 Yahweh's response includes both men and women (*'îš*, somebody; *HALOT* 1:43–44, gloss 9), with a distributive "any person" (*'îš 'îš*; GKC §123.d1). I supply "any of *you*" to align stylistically with "or *your* descendants" (*'ô lədōrōtêkem*).

16. The weqatal "*then* you may observe" (*wə'āśâ*) is apodictic (*GBHS* §3.5.1[d]), but the context indicates not a logical result but a concessive meaning: "If any of you . . . become unclean . . . , then you may *still* observe a Passover for Yahweh" (NIV, NLT, NRSV, ESV). The weqatal could here convey a permissive aspect, "*You may* observe a Passover for Yahweh" (*GBHS* §3.2.2[d.2], §3.5.2), making an exception to the divine precedent in 5:2–4 of expelling those defiled by a corpse (*kōl ṭāmē' lānāpeš*).

17. This construction (*pesaḥ lyhwh*) can mean "observe *a Passover belonging to Yahweh*" ("Yahweh's Passover," NLT, NIV = possession: *GBHS* §4.1.10f). However, more naturally, the fientive verb "observe" (*wə'āśâ*) is modified by a *l* of advantage, "observe a Passover *for Yahweh*" or "observe a Passover *to Yahweh*" (quasi-datival: *GBHS* §4.1.10e1; NET, ESV, NJPS; cf. Exod. 12:11, 48; Lev. 23:5; Num. 9:14; 28:16; Deut. 16:1, 2). Support comes in other places where the qualifier "Yahweh, *your God*" makes possessive *l* awkward: "You must observe Yahweh your God's Passover" (Deut. 16:1; also vv. 2, 10, 15; translations render these as a *l* of advantage).

18. As v. 3, "by following every Passover statute" (*kəkol-ḥuqqat happesaḥ*) is a dynamic rendering (*IBHS* §11.2.9b).

19. "But" (*wə*) marks the exception to vv. 10–12 (*IBHS* §39.2.3b). "But anyone" comes closer to the anarthrous witnesses "but a person who" (SP LXX^ed Tg^O), which matches 5:10 (2×), although MT is still sensible with a cataphoric article, "but the person who" (*wəhā'îš*).

20. "Immigrant" (*gēr*) indicates one who resides within Israel's settlements ("who lives among you," *yāgûr 'ittəkem*) and whose solidarity with native Israelites in the vision of H (Lev. 17:1 [or 16:29]–26:46) must be protected through a single standard (Num. 9:14b), in contrast to D's legal accommodation of the law to benefit the immigrant (Awabdy, *Immigrants*, 220–26). In the Pentateuch, the noun *gēr* occurs twice in Genesis (15:13; 23:4), twelve times in Exodus (chaps. 2–23), twenty-one times in Leviticus (chaps. 16–25), eleven times in Numbers (9:14 [2×]; 15:14, 15 [2×], 16, 26, 29, 30; 19:10; 35:15), and twenty-two times in Deuteronomy (chaps. 1–31).

21. As a substitute for the imperfective aspect (*GBHS* §3.5.2), this contextual rendering of the weqatal as "wants to observe" (*wə'āśâ*) indicates a nonperfective of desire (*IBHS* §31.3h; EÜ; Levine, *Numbers*, 1:294; NRSV, NLT, NET).

15On the day that the dwelling place was set up,[22] the cloud covered the dwelling place—the tent containing the witness[23]—and from evening until morning a fiery appearance[24] was over the dwelling place. **16**This is the way it always used to be: The cloud would cover it by day, and there was a fiery appearance by night. **17**Whenever[25] the cloud lifted[26] from the tent, then after that the Israelites would begin to travel, and wherever the cloud settled, the Israelites would camp. **18**At Yahweh's command the Israelites would begin to travel, and at Yahweh's command they would camp. As long as the cloud stayed over the dwelling place, they would camp. **19**When the cloud stayed over the dwelling place many days, then the Israelites kept Yahweh's[27] orders and did not travel. **20**When the cloud was over the dwelling place only a few days,[28] at Yahweh's command they camped, and at Yahweh's command they traveled. **21**And if the cloud stayed[29] only from evening until morning, when the cloud lifted in the morning, then they traveled on. Or for a day or a night, when the cloud lifted, then they traveled. **22**Whether it was for two days, or a month, or a year that the

22. Following the pass. SP LXX[ed] Tg[O] "was set up" (SP: vocalized *hûqam*; LXX[ed]: *estathē*; Tg[O] hithaphel *dəʾittāqam*). This may be a harmonization to Exod. 40:17 to remove the difficulty of the MT causative (hiphil) in Num. 9:15 with an unidentifiable agent, formally, "On the day that *he set up* [*hāqîm*] the dwelling place"; of course, Moses could be imported from Exod. 40.

23. As with "the ark *containing* the witness," this metonym for the dwelling place, "the tent *containing* the witness" (*ʾōhel hāʿēdut*; also 17:7–8 [22–23]; 18:2), reflects a gen. of container content (*BHRG* §25.4.6[5]). By analogy to the Neo-Hittite suzerain-vassal treaties, provision was made to deposit the treaty tablets in the temple (Mendenhall, "Covenant Forms," 50–76). Moreover, by analogy to Esarhaddon's Succession Treaty (EST), nine copies of this treaty were deposited in the throne room of Nabu's temple, the Ezida, in Nimrud, where the *akītu* ceremony of the gods Nabu and Tašmet was enacted, and another copy of EST was found in 2009 in a temple in the Assyrian provincial capital of Tell Tayinat. Lauinger ("Neo-Assyrian *adê*," 113–14) argues that the temples in which these treaty copies were deposited were chosen because they were locations where the vassal states would deliver tribute to the governor outside the Assyrian heartland.

24. "As an appearance of fire" (*kəmarʾē-ʾēš*) is rendered as "a fiery appearance," an attributive gen. (*GBHS* §2.2.5). Staubli (*Levitikus, Numeri*, 237) reminds us that on Sinai Yahweh was compared to a furnace (Exod. 19:18), and in the covenant ritual with Abraham, his appearance was compared to the fire and smoke of an oven (Gen. 15:17).

25. "Whenever" renders the idiom "and by the mouth" (*ûləpî*; cf. Lev. 25:16; Num. 21:24; 26:54; 35:30).

26. "The cloud lifted" (*hēʿālōt heʿānān*) renders the niphal (inf. const.) as a middle voice (*GBHS* §3.1.2b), which comes closer to the active agency of the cloud in v. 17b, "the cloud settled (there)" (*yiškān[-šām] heʿānān*). Readers still infer that Yahweh was the ultimate cause of the cloud's activity of lifting and settling.

27. LXX[ed]: "God's."

28. "Only a few days" reads formally, "days, number" (*yāmîm mispār*). This appositional nom. in 4Q23 and MT (similarly LXX[ed]) appears only here in the OT (*IBHS* §8.3d), suggesting that SP smoothed the text by adding "days *in* number."

29. "Stayed" is supplied for style but derives from the context in which the cloud would *škn (stay, dwell, remain, settle; vv. 17, 18, 22).

cloud stayed over the dwelling place,[30] the Israelites camped without traveling, but when it lifted, they traveled. [23]At Yahweh's command they camped,[31] and at Yahweh's command they traveled on. They kept Yahweh's orders according to Yahweh's command, by Moses's authority.

[10:1]Yahweh spoke to Moses: [2]"Make two trumpets out of silver. You must make them as hammered work.[32] You will use them for assembling the community and for directing[33] the camps to travel. [3]When they blow them both, the whole community must meet you at the entrance of the meeting tent. [4]But if they blow one trumpet, then the chieftains, the heads of the thousands of Israel, must meet you. [5]When you blow a signal, the camps on the east side[34] should begin to travel. [6]When you blow a second signal, the camps on the south side[35] should begin to travel. ⌜When you blow a third signal, the camps on the west side should begin to travel. When you blow a fourth signal, the camps on the north side should begin to travel.⌝[36] A signal must be sounded for their travels. [7]But when you assemble the community, you must blow, but do not sound a signal. [8]Aaron's sons, the priests, must blow the trumpets, and they will be to you a permanent statute throughout your generations.[37] [9]When you go to war in your land against an adversary who is hostile toward you, you must sound a signal with the trumpets; then you will be remembered by Yahweh your God,[38] and you will be

---

30. Probably a *l* + inf. const. of purpose: "the cloud was over the dwelling place *in order to dwell* [*liškōn*] over it" (*GBHS* §3.4.1c).

31. LXX[ed] omits "At Yahweh's command they camped" (also v. 23 diverges).

32. "Out of/from" is supplied for clarity. *Miqšâ* I (hammered work; *DCH* 5:472) is fronted for stress: "*As hammered work* you must make them" (*BHRG* §46.1.2[2]b).

33. "For assembling" (*ləmiqrā'*) and "for directing" (*ləmassaʿ*) are infinitives const. of purpose (*GBHS* §3.4.1c), the second of which can also be rendered "for breaking camp" (from *massaʿ* II; see *DCH* 5:369; *HALOT* 2:607, gloss 1).

34. A cognate noun and verb with a directive *hē*, formally, "the camps who are camping toward the east" (*hammaḥănôt haḥōnîm qēdəmâ*).

35. SP, "on the north (side)."

36. The text in half-brackets derives from LXX[ed] but is absent from MT and SP (see Cardellini, *Numeri 1,1–10,10*, 329n166). MT/SP of v. 6 includes only the trumpet-initiated departure of the camps on the east and south sides, with nothing said of the west and north sides. This sits uncomfortably after chap. 2, where the wilderness camps circumscribe the meeting tent on the east (2:3–9), south (vv. 10–16), *west* (vv. 18–24), *and north* (vv. 25–31). The issue is solved by the longer LXX[ed] text. This plus (textual addition) may reflect an LXX supplement to the truncated instructions (Wevers, *Notes*, 148; for Rabbi Ibn Ezra, see Milgrom, *Numbers*, 74), but if the MT/SP reading resulted from parablepsis (scribal skip), the longer text would be preferred, with instructions to signal the departure of all four encamped sides, as one would expect from P's preference for more detail (Budd, *Numbers*, 105n6b; following Paterson, *Numbers*, 47).

37. "Enduring statute throughout your generations" (*ḥuqqat 'ōlām lədōrōtêkem*) occurs frequently in P and in Numbers is the first of three identical constructions (10:8; 15:15; 18:23) and five similar constructions (18:8, 11, 19; 19:10, 21).

38. Formally, "*before* Yahweh your God" (*lipnê yhwh 'ĕlōhêkem*; LXX[ed]; ESV, NRSV, NET) has been rendered dynamically "by Yahweh" (NIV) to convey a perceptual *lipnê*, indicating that Israelites will be brought to Yahweh's attention (*GBHS* §4.1.12c). An argument can be made for

rescued from your enemies.[39] [10]Also whenever you are rejoicing[40] at your appointed festivals or at the beginnings of your months, you must blow your trumpets along with[41] your burnt offerings and with your sacrifices for peace, so that they will become a memorial for you before your God. I am Yahweh your God."[42]

Interpretation

9:1–14. Still in the opening month of the new year after the exodus (Num. 1:1; 9:1), Yahweh orders the Israelites to celebrate their first annual Passover outside Egypt (vv. 1–5), as Exod. 12* anticipated, but an unanticipated problem

the lower case, "Yahweh *your god* [*'ĕlōhêkem*]," and this should not be automatically branded as syncretism or heresy. In the progressive revelation of God, before the *monotheism* expressed in texts like Isa. 40–55 and Ps. 96:5 was the ancient Israelite worldview of *henotheism*, according to which Israel's loyalty belonged to one deity, Yahweh, among many competing deities; for example, "You must have no *other gods* [*'ĕlōhîm 'ăḥērîm*] before my face" (Exod. 20:3; Deut. 5:7; *not* "There are no other Gods," *or* "You must not have idols/cult images/statues/ idols before my face"). This conceptuality explains references to Yahweh's divine council (Job 1:6; Ps. 82:1; 1 Kings 22:19; cf. Pss. 8:6; 86:8; 138:1) and "the sons of Elohim," which in the ANE literature often depicts subordinate deities in a pantheon (see H. Robinson, "Council of Yahweh," 151–57; Cooke, "Sons," 22–47; Tsevat, "God and the Gods," 123–37). Deuteronomy 4:7 illustrates an instance in which a morphologically pl. *'ĕlōhîm* may best be understood, when applied to Yahweh, not as a sg., proper name, but as a sg., common noun (and thus lowercase): "For what great nation is there that has *a god/gods* [*'ĕlōhîm*] so near to it as Yahweh *our god* [*'ĕlōhênû*] is whenever we call on him?" (rendering *'ĕlōhîm* as sg.: LXX[ed] [*theos*] Tg[O] [*'ălâ*]; ESV, NRSV, NLT, NET; contra NIV). Similarly, in Num. 10:9, 10; 15:40, 41, the presumption of Israel's covenant relationship with their deity, Yahweh, is manifested in the enclitic pronoun on *'ĕlōhîm*, which could be rendered: "Yahweh your god," focusing on the personal or national deity, or "Yahweh your God," focusing on *'ĕlōhîm* as Israel's unique formulation—distinct from El (*'ēl*)—of Israel's personal and national deity. Proper names are self-determinative, so one does not expect them to be modified by an enclitic pronoun (e.g., nowhere do we find "your Yahweh"; see Tropper, "Divine Name," 18). This suggests that *'ĕlōhîm* + enclitic was regarded as a common noun, which we do not capitalize in English. Balaam self-identifies as a devotee of Israel's deity, Yahweh: "I could not go beyond the command of *Yahweh my god/God [yhwh 'ĕlōhāy]*" (Num. 22:18). Similarly, Yahweh says of Phinehas, "because he was jealous *for his god/God [lē'lōhāyw]*" (Num. 25:13), in contrast to other Israelite men who, with the Moabite women, sacrificed to and worshiped "their gods" (*'ĕlōhêhen*, 2× in 25:2). With these considerations in mind, I adopt the Jewish (NJPS), Protestant/ecumenical (all versions), and Roman Catholic (EÜ) translation choice of "God," even when it has a proclitic pronoun.

39. The weqatal, "then you will be rescued" (*wanôša'tem*), gives the logical result when Yahweh remembers Israel, while the niphal pass. implies Yahweh as the agent of the deliverance (*IBHS* §23.2.2a).

40. SP: "Also when *I cause you to rejoice*" (*śmḥtykm*).

41. Rather than the somewhat ambiguous "You must blow your trumpets *over* [*'al*] your burnt offerings and *over* [*'al*] your sacrifices" (LXX[ed]; NLT, NJPS, NRSV, ESV, NET, NIV; Seebass, *Numeri*, 1:237), "along with" (*'al*) communicates that the trumpet blast *accompanies* the sacrifices (*GBHS* §4.1.16g; EÜ; "during" for Cazelles, *Nombres*, 59).

42. After v. 10, SP interpolates a passage adapted from Deut. 1:6–8.

arises with a group of disqualified celebrants (vv. 6–8), so Yahweh addresses this by amending the prior Exodus law (vv. 9–14). By a superscription that differs slightly from 1:1, the narrator presents the Num. 1–9 divine speeches and its unfolding plotline as occurring within the first month of the second year after the exodus from Egypt (9:1)—more specifically, after the Israelites celebrated this Passover on the fourteenth of the month (vv. 3–5)—and vv. 6–14 are connected temporally to the Passover (see below). As a result, all of Num. 1:1–9:14 occurs narratively in the first two weeks of the new year. Yahweh orders this first annual Passover celebration "at its appointed time" (vv. 2, 3), which refers back to the time fixed in Exod. 12:6, that is, the Israelites must slaughter their household lamb at twilight on the fourteenth day of the first month (see the first translation note on 9:3).[43] Yahweh uses anaphoric pronouns and the citation formula "by following all its statutes and all its customs" (see the second translation note on 9:3) to summon the Israelites to obey the Passover protocols imparted in Exod. 12*,[44] and the narrator stresses that they did obey entirely as Yahweh had commanded (v. 5).

In vv. 6–14, we encounter an "oracular novella," a form of Priestly historiography that contains a short story (vv. 6–8) followed by a divine oracle containing a case ruling and formal legislation (vv. 9–14).[45] In v. 6, as if in the same breath from v. 5, the narrator turns our attention to a loophole that was exposed on the very day the Israelites celebrated the Passover ("on that day" 2× in v. 6; see the first translation note there). Some men who had become unclean by touching a corpse, presumably while caring for the body of a deceased relative (see Num. 6:7; see last three translation notes on 9:6), expressed to Moses their desire to still celebrate the Passover. Their question in the passive voice, "Why are we kept from offering Yahweh's offering at its appointed time among the Israelites?" does not assign blame but implies someone or a deficient jurisprudence was inhibiting their good desire to show their loyalty to Yahweh and the nation of Israel (see the second translation note on 9:7).[46] In light of his custom, detailed in Num. 7:89, Moses presumably entered the tent to hear the divine adjudication (v. 8; see the translation note there). In this brief story, the narrator leaves various gaps in the reader's knowledge, which generates curiosity.[47] Not least, within the two-week time span of Num. 1:1–9:14 (see the preceding paragraph), Moses had already

---

43. Num. 9 is linked to Exod. 12, while Lev. 23:5–8 is linked to Num. 28:16–25 (Otto, "Priesterschrift," 48; cf. Knohl, *Sanctuary*, 22).

44. See Köckert, *Leben*, 95–96. As secondary to Exod. 12, Num. 9:1–5 is often assigned to the Priestly supplements (Pˢ): Frevel, *Mit Blick*, 110. On deictic terms and citation formulae in Pentateuchal legal exegesis, see Fishbane, *Biblical Interpretation*, 44, 170–87.

45. Chavel, *Oracular Law*. See also Lev. 24:10–23; Num. 15:32–36; 27:1–11.

46. Zeelander ("Closural Conventions," 335) stresses Passover's power to enculturate one into Israel's national identity.

47. Sternberg, *Poetics*, 265–67.

expelled those who were unclean by corpses (5:1–4), and we do not know what happened to them. Are the unclean men of 9:6–7 exempt from expulsion, or at some point are they, likewise, removed from Israel's encampment to undergo their purification process?

Yahweh responds without delay to Moses with a legal ruling (vv. 9–14). As a result, the scenario of vv. 6–8 becomes an etiology that explains how the legal precedent arose.[48] At the seam in v. 9, the narrator signals that the story is coming to a close by transitioning from the *present request* of the unclean men who wanted to observe Passover (vv. 6–8) to Yahweh's instruction (*tôrâ*) for *future* Passover celebrants (vv. 9–14).[49] Everyone, woman and man, who has become unclean by a corpse and everyone on a journey away from the festival community may celebrate the Passover for Yahweh at twilight exactly one month later (vv. 10–12; see the first and third translation notes on 9:10). The context of vv. 10–11 suggests that for unclean persons a deferred Passover was an *option* but not an obligation: in contrast to v. 13, there is no mention of punishment for unclean or traveling Israelites who do not observe Passover a month later (see the second translation note on 9:10).[50] A month would be adequate time to complete their period of isolation from the camp and perform purification rituals (Lev. 5:1–13; Num. 5:1–4). Any deferred Passover celebration must presumably follow all the protocols of Exod. 12*, although Yahweh refers to only a few of the components (metonymy) in vv. 11–12: the Israelites must eat (1) bread without yeast and bitter herbs, reminding them of their hasty departure from Egypt (Exod. 12:8), and (2) consume "it," referring to the lamb or goat, in its entirety that evening, not breaking any of the animal's bones (cf. Jesus's bones in John 19:36), perhaps because that very night, not the next morning, Yahweh struck down Egypt's firstborn (Exod. 12:10, 29–31, 46). Everything else from Exod. 12* not mentioned by Yahweh here is embedded in the demand to follow "every Passover statute" (see the translation note on Num. 9:12), which meant slaughtering a one-year-old male lamb or goat—or several of them, depending on the household size—performing the doorframe blood ritual, not boiling but roasting the meat, burning the remainder until morning, and eating in travel attire (Exod. 12:3–11).

Yahweh's oracle refines the Passover law further by condemning all clean and present Israelites who neglect to keep the Passover (v. 13). When such persons abstain from Passover, they exhibit malice toward the divine command, whereas the unclean men who abstained were motivated by a resolve to obey

---

48. Kellermann, *Priesterschrift*, 133; Zeelander, "Closural Conventions," 335.

49. Zeelander, "Closural Conventions," 339, 343. Baker ("Law," 494) asserts that no biblical text refers to the legal precedent fixed in vv. 9–14; however, Hezekiah's delayed Passover due to ritual uncleanness in 2 Chron. 30 (not attested in 2 Kings) may indicate a postexilic tradition shared with Num. 9:1–14.

50. Schenker ("Expiatory Sacrifices," 699) does not supply any textual support for his claim that the unclean and traveling Israelite is *obligated* to make up their Passover obligation.

a divine commandment (vv. 6–8; cf. Num. 6:1–4).[51] Finally, Yahweh grants immigrants, nonindigenous residents, the prerogative to observe Passover, provided they do so according to the same norms demanded of the Israelites (v. 14; see the first translation note there). The parlance of this additional instruction (vv. 13–14) reflects that of the Holiness corpus of Lev. 17–26.[52] As in Lev. 19–22*, only here in 9:13 and 18:22 do we find that in the apodosis of a conditional, these two idiomatic penalties are stacked together:[53] the negligent Israelite "must be cut off from their people" (i.e., expelled from one's tribe or land)[54] and "must bear their sin" (i.e., endure punishment).[55] More specifically, the "immigrant who lives among you" is not accommodated with a reduced standard, as in Deuteronomy's legal core, but rather is subject to "the same statute" as the "native" Israelite.[56] The language reverberates from Exod. 12:48–49,[57] where Yahweh grants the immigrant freedom to celebrate this distinctively Israelite ritual, Passover, on the condition that he subject all the males in his household to the rite of circumcision, the sign of Yahweh's covenant with Abraham and Israel.[58]

9:15–23. For unknowing or forgetful readers, the narrator depicts the customary phenomenon, already described in Exod. 13–14 and 40, of how Yahweh's cloud and fire guided the Israelites to encamp and travel toward the land they would inherit. More specifically, Exod. 13:21–22 and 14:19–24 depict the cloud-fire mode of divine guidance from Goshen, Egypt, to Mount Sinai, whereas Exod. 40 and Num. 9 recollect Israel's migratory campaign from Sinai forward. Several questions arise: Why does the narrator in Exod. 40 and in Num. 9 anachronistically describe this phenomenon, since the Israelites were still camped at Sinai, until the cloud lifts in Num. 10:11? Also, why expand the Exod. 40 narration with great redundancy in Num. 9:15–23?

51. Schenker, "Expiatory Sacrifices," 699.

52. I am not persuaded that all of Num. 9:1–14 is Holiness (Knohl, *Sanctuary*, 90), but maybe vv. 5–14 are (Staubli, *Levitikus, Numeri*, 235–36). Even Frevel ("Book of Numbers," 16), who with Nihan ("Priestly Laws," 114–19, 132–34) is hesitant to assign Numbers passages to H, respects the argument for assigning vv. 13–14 to H.

53. Feucht, *Heiligkeitsgesetz*, 57–58.

54. Levine, *Numbers*, 1:466.

55. It can mean the death penalty (Lev. 22:9; 24:15–16) but includes other forms of public punishment (Lev. 5:1–13).

56. Awabdy, *Immigrants*, 187, 214–15, 220–26. Nihan ("Priestly Laws," 116, 118) observes that the immigrant-native dyad is characteristic of H but sees Num. 9:14; 15:29, 30 as late additions of P that postdate Lev. 17–26. Achenbach (*Vollendung*, 47–49, 511–28; "Complementary Reading," 220) posits that the immigrant-native egalitarianism in Num. 9:14; 15:14–30*; 19:10; and 35:15 are post-Lev. 17–26 and belong to the theocratic revisions that perfected the Torah.

57. Kellermann, *Priesterschrift*, 127–29, 133.

58. Gen. 17:9–27; Exod. 4:24–26; Lev. 12:3. For Exod. 12:48–49 as H, see Awabdy, *Immigrants*, 199–200; cf. Frevel, "Book of Numbers," 16.

Table 9.1. Exodus 40 and Numbers 9 Compared

Exodus 40:17, 33–38	Numbers 9:15–23
[17]In the first month of year two, on day one of the month, the dwelling place was set up.	[15]On the day that the dwelling place was set up,
[34]The cloud covered the meeting tent, and the glory of Yahweh filled the dwelling place. [35]But Moses was not able to enter the meeting tent because the cloud settled on it, and the glory of Yahweh filled the dwelling place.	the cloud covered the dwelling place—the tent containing the witness[a]—and from evening until morning a fiery appearance was over the dwelling place.
[36]Whenever the cloud lifted from the dwelling place, the Israelites would begin to travel on each of their journeys, [37]and if the cloud did not lift up, then they would not begin to travel until the day that it lifted.	[16]This is the way it always used to be: The cloud would cover it by day, and there was a fiery appearance by night.
[38]For the cloud of Yahweh was on the dwelling place by day, and fire was in the cloud by night, before the eyes of the whole house of Israel in all their journeys.	[17]Whenever the cloud lifted[b] from the tent, then after that the Israelites would begin to travel, and wherever the cloud settled, the Israelites would camp.
	[18]*At Yahweh's command* the Israelites would begin to travel, and *at Yahweh's command* they would camp. As long as the cloud stayed over the dwelling place they would camp. [19]When the cloud stayed over the dwelling place many days, *then the Israelites kept Yahweh's orders* and did not travel. [20]When the cloud was over the dwelling place only a few days, *at Yahweh's command they camped*, and *at Yahweh's command they traveled*. [21]And if the cloud stayed only from evening until morning, when the cloud lifted in the morning, then they traveled on. Or for a day or a night, when the cloud lifted, then they traveled. [22]Whether it was for two days, or a month, or a year that the cloud stayed over the dwelling place,[c] the Israelites camped without traveling, but when it lifted, they traveled. [23]*At Yahweh's command* they camped, and *at Yahweh's command* they traveled on. *They kept Yahweh's orders according to Yahweh's command, by Moses's authority*.

a. See the second translation note on Num. 9:15.
b. See the translation notes on Num. 9:17.
c. See the translation note on Num. 9:22.

On an editorial level, it is possible that these texts in Exod. 40*, Num. 9*, and Num. 10:11–12 are late Priestly additions to the Pentateuch, especially because, surprisingly, there is no record of the divine cloud guiding the Israelites to move and settle to named places after they left Sinai (Num. 11–36).[59] Although Num. 9:15–23 recalls similar depictions of Yahweh with Abraham (Gen. 15:17) and with Moses on Sinai (see the last translation note on 9:15), Num. 9 functions as a sort of "repetitive resumption" of Exod. 40*, which circumscribes the meeting-tent law narrative of Lev. 1:1–Num. 9:14.[60] Even so, the repetition is not identical, and the differences are telling. The Num. 9* narrator has no interest in repeating Moses's inability to enter the shrouded meeting tent (Exod. 40:34–35), which aligns with the narration in Num. 7:89 stressing Moses's proximity, not distance, behind the curtain. Most important, although Num. 9:15–17 succinctly establishes the Israelites' obedience to Yahweh's cloud-fire guidance, the narrator was not content. Instead, by the almost poetic[61] expansion of vv. 18–23, unparalleled in Exod. 40*, the narrator inordinately over-specifies to inculcate this single rhetorical point: wherever and whenever the cloud settled or rose to move, the Israelites followed it in habitual obedience to Yahweh's command (see bold italicized text in table 9.1).[62] The anachronistic report of Exod. 40 recasts the divine presence inhabiting the dwelling place as the sole director of Israel's migratory campaign.[63] The Num. 9* narrator affirms this, but now underscores that Israel assiduously obeyed their divine director in all their travels from Sinai onward. This serves a "primacy effect," preconditioning readers to expect that an obedient Israel will beeline toward Canaan and inherit the divine land grant promised to the patriarchs.[64] This expectation will soon be shattered by Israel's long detour of rebellion and death in the wilderness (Num. 11:1–25:18). At this juncture in Num. 9, however, an ideal image of the divine-Israel relationship is celebrated, unifying the people and creating social order.[65]

59. Frankel, "Priestly Conceptions," 32. Elliger ("Sinn und Ursprung," 133) reads Exod. 40:36–38 and Num. 9:15–18 as Priestly supplements (P^s) to the base layer of the account in Num. 10:11. Pola (*Priesterschrift*, 217) sees Exod. 40:36–38 as a later addition that presupposes Num. 9:15–23. Although Num. 14:14 and Deut. 1:33 theologically reflect on the cloud's divine guidance of Israel through the wilderness, these texts do not name any places on the route as Num. 10:11–12 (Sinai → Paran).

60. Cf. Seebass, *Numeri*, 1:234–35; Seebass, "Eigene Komposition," 92; Staubli, *Levitikus, Numeri*, 237. See Kuhl, "Wiederaufnahme," 1–11.

61. Seebass, "Eigene Komposition," 99.

62. In 9:18–23, LXX^{ed} presents God, not the narrator, as the speaker who commands the Israelites as in vv. 2–3, 10–14, which resolves the anachronism (Evans, "Alleged Confusions," 247).

63. Scharbert, *Numeri*, 41–42.

64. What a storyteller first tells the reader "creates expectations in the reader—a primacy effect—that is fulfilled, modified, or even shattered by what comes later in the narrative—the recency effect" (Resseguie, *Narrative Criticism*, 209).

65. Leveen, *Memory*, 75–76.

10:1–10. In preparation for Israel to set out on its migratory campaign toward the southern entrance into Canaan (see Num. 13–14) and for Israel's future life in the land, Yahweh orders Moses to make two silver trumpets to blow for the purpose of assembling and directing the Israelites (see the second translation note on 10:2). This divine speech is composed of four subunits: (1) make two trumpets of hammered work (see the first translation note on 10:2); (2) blow both to assemble the whole community, but blow one to assemble leaders only (vv. 3–4); (3) the first trumpet blast will launch the departure of Israel's tribes camped east of the meeting tent, the second for the tribes to the south, the third for tribes to the west, and the fourth for tribes to the north (vv. 5–6; see the second translation note on 10:6); and (4) clarifications that a simple trumpet blast rather than a signal must be used to assemble the Israelites, and Aaron and his sons will forever be the sole trumpeters (vv. 7–8). The trumpet would also be used to call to war (v. 9) and to announce Israel's calendrical worship (v. 10). As Moses's cultic intermediary role has shifted, so also now we see that Aaron's sons, the priests, alone will forever hold the office of blowing the trumpets (see the translation note on 10:8). This signifies the authority of the Aaronic priests, not Moses or the Levites, over multiple sectors of Israelite society: community gatherings, travel, military, festivals, and the sacrificial cult.[66] Later, priests blew trumpets at the first temple's dedication (Solomon) and rededication (Hezekiah), while repentant non-priests blew trumpets and horns at its purification (Asa).[67]

Making Aaron's sons the trumpeters is a natural conclusion to the unit (v. 8), so vv. 9–10 give the impression of being a supplement by specifying two more purposes for the trumpet:[68] (1) the trumpet must also signal when Israel's military attacks their enemies in the land, resulting in Yahweh's remembrance and deliverance (see the second translation note on 10:9), and (2) the trumpet sound must accompany every burnt offering and sacrifice for peace presented to Yahweh at Israel's joyful festivals and at the beginning of every month (see the second translation note on 10:10; cf. Num. 28:11–14). In subsequent biblical stories and in reliefs from ancient Egypt and Syria, trumpeters are active on the battlefront (Num. 31:6; Josh. 6*; Judg. 7*; Jer. 51:27; see the relief in the temple of Ramses II at Abydos).[69]

In distinction from vv. 2–8, where Yahweh is implicit, the undercurrent of vv. 9–10 is the explicit victory and sacrificial acceptance by Israel's deity, whose name is Yahweh. In the context of the ancient Near East, when the Israelite and Jewish audiences of Numbers heard the enclitic pronouns in

---

66. Achenbach, *Vollendung*, 555.

67. De Vaulx (*Nombres*, 129) cites 2 Chron. 5:12–13; 15:8–14; 29:26–28; Ezra 3:10. One would expect Deut. 20:2–4 to mention the priest's trumpet call into battle, although it could be that Deut. 20:2–4 supplements Num. 10:9, showing what the priests must do after they blow the trumpets (Kilchör, *Mosetora*, 242).

68. Kellermann, *Priesterschrift*, 144–47.

69. Trimm, *Warfare*, 200, 202, 414.

the expressions "Yahweh *your God*," "before *your God*," and "I am Yahweh *your God*" (vv. 9–10), they thought not of a personal name but of their own national deity with whom they had entered into a covenant relationship (see the last translation note on 9:10). Finally, the literary placement of 10:1–10 is clear: this divine speech supplies the last prerequisite for Israel's obedient departure from Mount Sinai, telling Yahweh's cultic representatives how to trumpet the way for Yahweh, their deity, to lead them decisively and victoriously into the great unknown land of promise.

Implications

Numbers 9:9–14 in the Progressive Theology of Passover

The Passover and exodus events, narrated in Exod. 12:21–42, and the derived rituals of Passover and Unleavened Bread, initially prescribed in Exod. 12:1–20, 43–51, have accrued many rich layers of theological reflection and adaptation. We can now ask: How does Yahweh's legal innovation in Num. 9:9–14 contribute to the progressive theology of Passover? To summarize our study above, Yahweh's addendum in Num. 9:9–14 makes three contributions to the progressive theology of the Passover: (1) Yahweh flexes his festival calendar so that unclean people and travelers can still choose to celebrate divine redemption of Israel from Egypt and as an expression of Holiness thought, (2) Yahweh issues judgment on all who with evil intent neglect the Passover, but (3) Yahweh welcomes immigrants as Passover celebrants as long as they follow the same protocols. Now we can see how Num. 9* fits into Passover theology.[70]

A household ritual meal in Egypt
(Exod. 12*; 34:25)[71]

Israel's elders slaughter a lamb or goat, smear its blood on the doorposts and lintels of their house, and eat it with their families to commemorate the night when Yahweh's lethal wrath destroyed Egypt's firstborn but was averted from his own firstborn, Israel, by the lamb's blood smeared on Israel's doorposts and lintels. Immigrants who had their household males circumcised could celebrate.

↓

A centralized meeting tent ritual in the wilderness
(Lev. 23:4; Num. 28:16–25; cf. Exod. 12:1–19)[72]

Fortifying the connection of Passover and Unleavened Bread,[73] Israel celebrates a weeklong festival of sacrifices to Yahweh at his portable meeting tent.

↓

70. This is not an attempt to reconstruct the underlying history of Passover in ancient Israel and Judaism (cf. Albertz, *Israelite Religion*, 2:410–11).
71. Cf. Josh. 5:10–11; Heb. 11:28.
72. Cf. Ezra 6:19–20; Ezek. 45:21.
73. See Levinson, *Deuteronomy*, 53–97.

Num. 9:9–14 Addendum

Deferred Passover for the unclean and travelers, judgment for the negligent, inclusion of immigrants

↓

A centralized ritual at the place where Yahweh chooses to put his name

(Deut. 16:1–8; 2 Chron. 30:1–20; 2 Kings 23:21–24; 2 Chron. 35:1–19)

Again interconnecting Passover and Unleavened Bread—at Yahweh's central shrine, presumably at the first temple in Jerusalem—Israel/Judah's patriarchs offer and eat a Passover sacrifice in the evening and eat bread without yeast for six/seven days.[74]

↓

A confession about Yahweh's servant as a slaughtered lamb

(Isa. 52:13–53:12)[75]

A guilty "we" confess that the servant of Yahweh was slaughtered as a lamb in their place, securing a second exodus.[76]

↓

A decentralized ritual meal with Jesus as the slaughtered lamb

(Matt. 26:17–29; Mark 14:12–26; Luke 22:7–20; 1 Cor. 5:7–8; 11:17–34)[77]

Jesus's first and subsequent disciples celebrate the combined Passover-Unleavened Bread[78] Festival by eating the bread of Jesus's body and drinking the wine of Jesus's shed blood of the new covenant, for the forgiveness of sins. This ritual meal was decentralized for the first disciples (occurring in an upper room of a home outside the temple precincts) and for subsequent disciples (occurring in diaspora gatherings across the world).

↓

The centralized, consummative feast in the presence of Jesus as the slaughtered lamb

(Rev. 19:6–9)[79]

The church, the bride of the Lamb, will rejoice in God at a feast to celebrate their marriage consummation with the slaughtered Lamb.

---

74. Levinson (*Deuteronomy*, 93) infers that Passover pilgrims were to eat the sacrifice in the evening at the central cultic site (Deut. 16:1–2, 5–7) and then immediately the next day observe Unleavened Bread back in their hometowns (vv. 7–8).

75. Cf. Jer. 11:19; Zech. 12:10–14.

76. Brendsel, *Isaiah*, 56; cf. Isa. 52:12 and Exod. 12:11. Contra J. Schipper ("Lamb Imagery," 315–25), who, because Isa. 52–53 presents the servant as an animal physically unsuitable as a sacrifice, wrongly concludes that Second Isaiah must not be drawing imagery from the Passover lamb (Exod. 12) or Day of Atonement scapegoat (Lev. 16; see Zimmerli, "Jes 53," 213–21).

77. Jesus and the Passover occur in the same literary contexts also in Matt. 26:2; Mark 14:1; Luke 2:41; John 2:13, 23; 11:55–57; 13:1; 18:39; 19:14; Jude 5 (some MSS).

78. See Morgenstern, "'Suffering Servant,'" 327, 329.

79. See Rev. 1:5; 5:6, 9, 12; 6:9; 7:14; 12:11; 13:8.

Each of the three contributions of Num. 9:9–14, I suggest, lay an ideational foundation for the NT writers in their adaptation of the Passover ritual in light of Jesus the Messiah. (1) Yahweh makes a way for individuals who are *unclean and distant physically* to celebrate the exodus from Egypt (vv. 10–12), even as Jesus makes a way for individuals who are *unclean and distant spiritually* to celebrate the exodus from spiritual exile and sin: "This cup is the new covenant in my blood, which is poured out for you" (Luke 22:20; cf. Mark 14:24; Jer. 31*; Ezek. 36*), even "for the forgiveness of sins" (Matt. 26:28). Also, like travelers who defer their Passover observance, Jesus, while away with the Father, is deferring his own Passover observance until the kingdom comes in its fullness (Luke 22:15b–16). (2) The pronouncement of divine judgment against those who, by their evil, fail to observe Passover (Num. 9:13) sets a precedent for Paul to pronounce divine judgment against those who, by their evil, abuse the Lord's Supper (1 Cor. 11:27; also 5:7–8). (3) Last but not least, the inclusion of immigrants in Israel's Passover celebration (Exod. 12:48; Num. 9:14) can now be seen as the embryonic form of God's massive, redemptive vision to incorporate every tribe, language, people, and nation in the worship of the slaughtered Lamb (Rev. 5:9–10; 7:9–10).[80]

---

80. A "redemptive-movement hermeneutic" (see Webb, *Slaves, Women, and Homosexuals*) cannot be claimed for every theological and social issue in Scripture, but here it seems to be a fair description of the immigrant trajectory from Exod. 12:48//Num. 9:14 through the canon to Rev. 5 and 7.

10
Israel Departs from Mount Sinai

(10:11–36)

∽∞∾

Overview

At last, after living at Sinai for one year, one month, and twenty days, the cloud lifts and Israel begins the journey for Canaan (Num. 10:11). This encloses the Sinai narrative (Exod. 19:1–Num. 10:10), but also with the date given at Num. 1:1, this verse encloses the first ten chapters of Numbers and so divides Numbers into two main sections: (1) nineteen days of events and instructions at Sinai (Num. 1:1–10:10); (2) about thirty-nine years of events and instructions between Sinai and the desert valleys of Moab (Num. 10:11–36:13; see date at 33:38).[1] In 10:11–28, the narrator describes Israel's departure for the Paran wilderness led by Israel's named chieftains. Israel follows the tribal order of travel, which Yahweh commanded in 2:3–31, but the order is slightly adapted to enable the Levite families to deconstruct, transport, and reconstruct the dwelling place (cf. 2:17; 10:17, 21). In vv. 29–32, an abrupt dialogue between Moses and his father-in-law, Hobab, takes place. Moses seeks Hobab's guidance through the wilderness, which raises serious questions in the context of Yahweh's cloud-fire and ark as the exclusive mode of guiding Israel (10:11–28; 10:33–36). In vv. 33–36, the narrator returns to zoom in on vv. 12–13, the first leg of the Israelites' journey, in order to specify the three-day length of Israel's first trip (v. 33), the personified ark as Israel's guide (v. 33), the cloud's position above Israel when they travel (v. 34), and Moses's war chant summoning King Yahweh to terrify his enemies; then the narrator returns to his people, Israel (vv. 35–36).

1. W. Lee, *Migratory Campaign*, 91.

Translation

11At that time,[2] on day twenty of the second month, in the second year, the cloud lifted[3] from the dwelling place of witness. **12**So the Israelites set out on their travels from the Sinai wilderness, and the cloud settled in the Paran wilderness. **13**This was the first time they set out according to the word of Yahweh, by the authority of Moses. **14**The division of the Judahite camp set out first by their companies, and over his company[4] was Amminadab's son Nahshon. **15**Over the company of the Issacharite tribe was Zuar's son Nethanel, **16**and over the company of the Zebulunite tribe was Helon's[5] son Elion. **17**Then the dwelling place was dismantled,[6] and the Gershonites and Merarites set out, carrying the dwelling place.[7] **18**Then the division of the camp of Reuben[8] set out by their companies, and over his company was Shedeur's son Elizur. **19**Over the company of the Simeonite tribe was Zurishaddai's son Shelumiel, **20**and over the company of the Gadite tribe was Deuel's son Eliasaph. **21**Then the Kohathites set out, carrying the items of the sanctuary. The dwelling place was to be set up[9] before they arrived. **22**Then the division of the Ephraimite[10] camp set out by their companies, and over his company was Ammihud's son Elishama. **23**Over the company of the Manassite tribe was Pedahzur's son Gamaliel, **24**and over the company of the Benjaminite[11] tribe was Gideoni's son Abidan. **25**Then the division of the Danite camp set out, which was the rear

2. "At that time" (*wayhî*) introduces the foregrounded events of v. 11 (*BHRG* §21.2.1.1.2ba).

3. Similar to 9:17, "the cloud lifted" (*naʿălâ heʿānān*) renders the niphal as a middle voice (*GBHS* §3.1.2b). Yahweh is the implied ultimate cause of the cloud's activity of lifting and settling.

4. The same term is used in the sg. and pl.—"by their companies, and over his company" (*ləṣibʾōtām wəʿal-ṣəbāʾô*)—suggesting that the sg. "his company" (*ṣəbāʾô*) is a metonym for "the division of the Judahite camp" (*degel maḥănēh bənê-yəhûdâ*).

5. "Halon" (*ḥyln*) in 4Q23 and SP (see Ulrich, *Qumran*, 143).

6. The weqatal "Then . . . was dismantled" (*wəhûrad*) occurs sequentially after the wayyiqtol in v. 14, "set out" (*wayyissaʿ*; *GBHS* §3.5.2a). "Was dismantled" (NET) dynamically renders the hophal causative pass. "to be taken down" ("*yrd* I," *HALOT* 2:434–35, gloss 1; *DCH* 4:289; *GBHS* §3.1.7a).

7. The ptc. is substantival; formally, "the Gershonites and Merarites, *who carry/were carrying* [*nōśəʾê hammiškān*] the dwelling place, set out" (see 4:21–45). For style, I opt for "set out, carrying" (NLT, NET).

8. I follow "Reuben" (*rʾwbn*) in 4Q23 MT[L] SP[ms] LXX[ed], since the phrase "sons of Reuben" (*bny rʾwbn* MT[mss] SP LXX[mss] Vulg) is probably adapted to the "sons of X" in vv. 14, 15, 16, 17 (2×), 19, 20, 22, 23, 24, 25, 26, 27, 28.

9. The weqatal command is a hiphil causative with an impersonal pl. subject, "they must set up" (*wəhēqîmû*), meaning, "was to be set up."

10. "Ephraimite" renders "sons of Ephraim" (*bny ʾprym*) in 4Q23 MT[L] SP; "sons" (*bny*) is absent from MT[mss] LXX[ed] Syr.

11. As was noted in the translation of 2:22, the SP spelling of Benjamin (*binyāmin*, son of the right hand) is Benjamim (*bn ymym*, son of days).

guard[12] of all the camps by their companies, and over his company was Ammishaddai's son Ahiezer. [26]Over the company of the Asherite tribe was Ocran's son Pagiel, [27]and over the company of the Naphtalite tribe was Enan's son Ahira. [28]These were the traveling arrangements[13] of the Israelites by their companies when they traveled.

[29]Now Moses said to Hobab son of Reuel the Midianite, Moses's father-in-law,[14] "We are traveling to the place of which Yahweh said, 'I will give it to you.' Come with us, and we will treat you well, for Yahweh has promised good things for Israel." [30]But Hobab[15] said to him, "I will not go. Instead, I will go to my own land and to my own people."[16] [31]Moses said, "Please do not leave us, because you know where we should camp[17] in the wilderness, and you can be our guide.[18] [32]And if you come with us, whatever good things Yahweh gives to us, we will share with you."[19]

---

12. The piel ptc. *mə'assēp* means "to form the rearguard" ("*'sp*," *HALOT* 1:74, gloss 3; *DCH* 1:349), portraying the Danite tribe as *gathering* all the camps (**'sp* qal, "to gather"; piel, "to glean").

13. Formally, "these were the departures."

14. Three discrete names appear to have been given to Moses's father-in-law (*ḥōtēn mōšeh*): Jethro (*yitrô*) in Exod. 3–18 (3:1; 4:18; 18:1, 2, 5, 6, 9, 10, 12); Hobab (*ḥōbāb*) here and in Judg. 4:11 (also LXX[ed] Judg. 1:16: *Iobab* = "Iobab" NETS); and Reuel (*rə'û'ēl*) in Exod. 2:18. One explanation is that *ḥōtēn*, a male in-law, can describe both Moses's father-in-law (Jethro) and brother-in-law (Jethro's son, Hobab) (Walton and Matthews, *Genesis–Deuteronomy*, 185). However, this goes against the plain meaning of *ḥōtēn* as father-in-law (*HALOT* 1:364; *DCH* 3:337). Another explanation, without textual support, is to say that "father-in-law of Moses" (*ḥōtēn mōšeh*) was a later gloss (Levine, *Numbers*, 1:315). The simplest explanation is that the different names come from different sources. The name Jethro bookends Exod. 3:1–4:18, which likely belongs to a single non-Priestly base text in Exod. 1–15* and is assumed by 18:1–12, where Jethro plays a central role in what could have been the work of the Hexateuch redactor unifying Genesis through Joshua as a narrative whole (see Gertz, "Miracle," 93–95; Albertz, "Wilderness Material," 159; Albertz, "Hexateuch Redaction," 58–62). The name Reuel in Exod. 2:18 is enigmatic but should not be branded an error in the modern sense (contra Schmidt, *Numeri*, 15–16); Num. 10:29 probably revises it to Hobab, the name also used in Judg. 4:11 (Schmidt, *Numeri*, 15–16). The self-standing unit of Num. 10:29–32 reflects a non-Priestly perspective, seeking guidance in the wilderness from a Midianite priest, Hobab, rather than by Yahweh's cloud-fire (P: Exod. 40:36–38; Num. 9:15–23; 10:33–36) or by the Israelite priests whom Yahweh has identified as holy (cf. Urim and Thummim for direction in the Priestly text of Num. 27:21; also Exod. 28:30; Lev. 8:8; similarly Seebass, *Numeri*, 2:8; assigning vv. 29–32 to J: de Vaulx, *Nombres*, 144; Schmidt, *Numeri*, 15–16; Scharbert, *Numeri*, 45; Seebass, *Numeri*, 2:9; but assigning it to the non-Priestly K[D]: Blum, *Komposition des Pentateuch*, 137–44). LXX[ed] may attempt to eliminate the problem of multiple names for Moses's father-in-law by calling Iobab (Gk. for Hobab) Moses's "brother-in-law" (NETS for *tō gambrō*).

15. "Hobab" from v. 29 is added to clarify the subject (NLT, NET).

16. Or "my own *relatives*" ("*môledet*," as *HALOT* 2:556, gloss 2) or "my own *kindred*" (*DCH* 5:174, gloss 2), referring to the Midianites (Exod. 2:15, 16; 3:1; 4:19; 18:1; Num. 10:29).

17. "We *should* camp" (*ḥănōtēnû*) conveys this obligation in order to survive in the wilderness (*GBHS* §3.4.1e).

18. Formally, "and you will be our two eyes."

19. Formally, "and that good with which Yahweh does good with us, we will do good for you."

³³So they traveled from the mountain of Yahweh²⁰ for three days. The ark containing the covenant with Yahweh²¹ was traveling before them for those²² three days to search for a resting place for them. ³⁴The cloud of Yahweh was over them by day, when they traveled from the camp. ³⁵Whenever the ark traveled, Moses would say, "Rise up, Yahweh!²³ May your enemies be scattered, and may those who hate you flee before you!" ³⁶Whenever it came to rest,²⁴ he would say, "Return, Yahweh, to the many thousands of Israel!"

Interpretation

10:11–28. After the great expanse of narrative laced with divine instruction through Moses at Mount Sinai (Exod. 19:1–Num. 10:10), the narrator describes the Israelites' obedient and orderly departure for Canaan (vv. 11–28). The chronological notation fixes Israel's departure "from the Sinai wilderness" at one year, one month, and twenty days after Israel left Egypt (10:11). This is the closing frame around the Sinai narrative, with Exod. 19:1 as the opening frame, when Israel arrived at the "Sinai wilderness" three months after the exodus.²⁵ The cloud, directed by Yahweh only implicitly (vv.

---

20. "The mountain of Yahweh" (*har-yhwh*, also Gen. 22:14; Ps. 24:3; Isa. 2:3//Mic. 4:2; Isa. 30:29; Zech. 8:3) is probably a non-Priestly writer's toponym (commonly J: Schmidt, *Numeri*, 16) for the same "mountain of God" (Exod. 3:1; 4:27; 18:5; 24:13; once thought to be E's term: Seebass, *Numeri*, 2:16), famously known as Mount Sinai (Exod. 19 [4×]; 24; 31; 34 [4×]; Lev. 7; 25–27 [3×]; Num. 3:1; 28:6; but cf. Deut. 33:2), but called Horeb by the Deuteronomists (Deut. 1:2, 6, 19; 4:10, 15; 5:2; 9:8; 18:16; 29:1; also non-P Exod. 3:1, see Gertz, "Miracle," 93–95; and Exod. 17:6; 33:6). Others see this three-day journey as an editor's narrative bridge that recalls the three-day wilderness journey before Mount Sinai in Exod. 15:22 (Achenbach, *Vollendung*, 206).

21. "The ark containing the covenant with Yahweh" (*'ărôn bryt-yhwh*) appears here for the first time in the Hexateuch, then in Num. 14:44, in Deuteronomy's frames (10:8; 31:9, 25, 26), and in Josh. 1–8 (3:3, 17; 4:7, 18; 6:8; 8:33). As with "the ark/tent containing the witness," "the ark *containing* the covenant" indicates a gen. of container content (*BHRG* §25.4.6[5]; Exod. 25:16). Here in Num. 10:33 and in 14:44, the addition of the name of Israel's Deity exhibits the bilateral nature of covenant treaties in the ancient Near East. I avoid "Yahweh's covenant," which can denote a covenant merely belonging to Yahweh, and prefer "with Yahweh" to connote Israel's oath-sworn covenant treaty with Yahweh (Otto, "Covenant," 2047–51).

22. "Those" clarifies that the same three days of v. 33a are in view in v. 33b; the ptc. is read as a past tense with continuous aspect, "was traveling" (*nōsēaʿ*; *GBHS* §3.4.3).

23. The impvs. "*Rise up*, Yahweh" (*qûmâ*, v. 35) and "*Return*, Yahweh" (*šûbâ*, v. 36) are urgent *requests* to Yahweh but are valid only for the occasion at hand (*GBHS* §3.3.2a).

24. SP: "And in its resting place"; LXXᵉᵈ: "And when it came to rest."

25. Many believe P contributed these and other framing notations at Exod. 19:1 and Num. 10:11 (Ruwe, *Heiligkeitsgesetz*, 39). The chronological system in the Moses story spans Exod. 16:1–Num. 10:11. Even so, departing from Sinai would be an incomplete ending for the P composition (Frevel, *Mit Blick*, 77–78).

15–28), is the acting subject that lifts up and settles in the Paran wilderness (vv. 11–12; see the second translation note on 10:11).[26] The arid region of Paran was north of the Sinai wilderness, south of Judah, and west of Edom, probably including Kadesh Barnea, as Num. 33:36 LXX indicates.[27] Israel's three-day journey (10:33) northward to Paran, the edge of Canaan, gives the impression that this was either the penultimate or antepenultimate trip before Israel crossed into Canaanite territory to begin Yahweh's war.[28] By contrast, Exod. 40* and Num. 9* suggest many legs to Israel's migration. Even so, by the cloud's action in v. 11 and Israel's action in vv. 12–13, readers are meant to perceive that the custom of Yahweh's cloud-fire guidance and Israel's habitual obedience in Exod. 40* and Num. 9* has now begun to occur in the plotline.

For the third time, the same chieftains over each tribe are named (Num. 2*, 7*, 10*), ascribing to them status[29] and signifying their military command over the companies in their tribe (vv. 12–27; see the translation note on 10:14). The order in which the Israelite tribes depart from Sinai (vv. 12–27) follows Yahweh's command in 2:3–31, and that order is also replicated in the chieftains' dedicatory sacrifices for Yahweh's altar (7:12–83). One difference, however, is that the tent transportation by Levi's three families (the Gershonites, Merarites, and Kohathites) prevents the tribe of Levi from traveling together in the center—after the first six tribes and before the remaining six tribes—as 2:17 envisions. Instead, the dwelling place, a metonym for the meeting tent and courtyard (4:21–33), must be dismantled, transported, and set up by the Gershonites and Merarites *before* the Kohathites arrive with the sanctuary furniture (10:17, 21; see the translation notes on these verses). Consequently, Levi's families transporting the tent and sancta needed to be staggered:

---

26. Based on linguistic features, Pola (*Priesterschrift*, 13, 145–46) argues that 10:11 and the following, along with Num. 1–4, 13–14 and Exod. 16*, are supplements to the Priestly base layer (*Ergänzung zu P*ᵍ); relatedly, Elliger ("Sinn und Ursprung," 133) argues that 10:11 is the editorial work of Pˢ to Pᵍ. More simply, Frevel (*Mit Blick*, 145; cf. Boorer, *Priestly Narrative*, 72) rather attributes 10:11a, 12a to P. Achenbach (*Vollendung*, 196–202) assigns 10:11, 13–28, 34 to the first phrase of the theocratic revision of the Torah, which stressed the import of the sanctuary, Israel's order, and its claim to the land.

27. Simkins, "Paran," 1009.

28. No one today knows where Mount Sinai was, but the popular identification of Jebel Musa, where the Monastery of St. Catherine is located, is improbable since (1) the P and non-P historiographers were not ignorant of the geography, and (2) Google Maps yields a walking trip of 240 miles (385 km) from Jebel Musa through Eliat to Nitzanei Sinai (Kadesh Barnea), requiring Israel to walk 80 miles per day for three days. According to Deut. 1:2, the route from Horeb (Sinai) by way of Mount Seir (Edom) to Kadesh Barnea took eleven days.

29. "A name confers being, even status, without defining personality" (Sternberg, *Poetics*, 330).

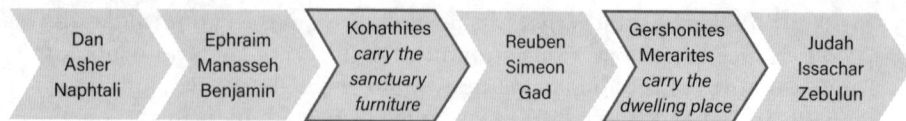

Figure 10.1. Order of Travel

Unlike Num. 2*, here in 10:3–31 it is less clear that four groups of three tribes departed together—each with a tribal forerunner (Judah, Reuben, Ephraim, Dan)—from the east of the meeting tent, south, west, and north. Yet this does seem to be implied: "the division of" applies only to Judah, Reuben, Ephraim, and Dan; the Danites, not Naphtali, are called "the rear guard" (see the translation note on 10:25). The narrator's précis in v. 28 closes off the unit.

10:29–32. In this quick but loaded exchange, the very last episode at Mount Sinai, Moses requests that his father-in-law, Hobab, guide Israel through the wilderness, but Hobab refuses (see the translation note on 10:29). This is the closing frame around the Sinai narrative, since the very first episode at Sinai also involved guidance given by Moses's father-in-law (called Jethro), but there his father-in-law initiated and supplied wisdom to alleviate Moses's adjudication overload (Exod. 18:13–27).[30] Hobab's skill set fits within with an ancient tradition of local guides in the Sinai region,[31] and Moses attempts to cajole him by four enticements. (1) Yahweh is giving the land to Israel, implying that Hobab could live with his daughter and son-in-law in a new divinely granted land (v. 29b). (2) Israel will treat Hobab well out of the bounty that Yahweh gives to Israel (v. 29c). At this point in the narrative, before Num. 25* and 31*, Midian is neither elect (Israel) nor anti-elect (Amorites, inhabitants of Canaan) but nonelect,[32] so Moses can extend God's benevolence to the Midianites as an expression of the Abrahamic blessing (Gen. 12:3).[33] But Hobab rejects Moses's offer in a resolve to return to his own land and people (v. 30; see the second translation note there), which is honorable in the Deuteronomic conviction that Yahweh has given land to Israel's neighbors as well.[34] Moses is unrelenting and proffers two more enticements. (3) Without Yahweh, Hobab is wanted, even needed: Hobab can use his trekking prowess to guide the inexperienced Israelites (v. 31; see the first translation note there). (4) Moses repeats that Israel will share Yahweh's bounty with Hobab (v. 32). Surprisingly, at this point the narrator lops off the conversation before we hear

---

30. On the parallel stories, see Römer, "Egypt Nostalgia," 69.

31. Representing an Egyptian iconograph, Staubli (*Levitikus, Numeri*, 389) draws a donkey-riding tribal leader, with an ax as a sign of his ability, accompanied by two servants. The inscription indicates that he led the Egyptians to the turquoise mines in central Sinai.

32. See Kaminsky, "Election," 397–425.

33. See de Vaulx, *Nombres*, 145. Achenbach (*Vollendung*, 181–83) claims that the issue of tolerance and the integration of non-Israelites underlies the Hobab-Moses story.

34. Deut. 2:5 (Edom), 9 (Moab), 19 (Ammon).

Hobab's response, creating an ambivalence about whether Hobab gave in to Moses.[35] Only later do readers infer that Hobab may have joined Moses, since his descendants, the Kenites, took up residence in Canaan with Judah.[36] In the end, the greatest ambiguity is not about whether Hobab chose to accompany Moses but why Moses sought a human guide when the surrounding context stressed that Yahweh alone, by cloud-fire and ark, was Israel's exclusive guide through the wilderness (vv. 11–27, 33–36).[37]

10:33–36. Earlier, in vv. 12–13, the narrator from a panoramic view reported Israel's migration from Sinai to Paran; now the narrator zooms in to specify the length and nature of Israel's journey. This terse unit differs linguistically from vv. 12–13[38] and centers on Yahweh, both the places where he locates his presence (his mountain, ark, and cloud; vv. 33–34) and his military power to scatter his enemies and defend his people, Israel (vv. 35–36). In v. 33, the narrator tells us that Israel's migration to Paran took three days, but rather than repeating "from the Sinai wilderness" (v. 12), an uncommon, non-Priestly metonym for the divine mountain is used: "So they traveled from *the mountain of Yahweh* for three days" (see the first translation note on 10:33). The point is theological: even though Israel left Yahweh's mountain, they did not leave Yahweh behind. In the ancient world, deities were connected to a cult site or mountain dwelling, such as Baal to Mount Zaphon and the Greek gods to Mount Olympus.[39] In some cases, the linkage was so strong that it was thought to be heretical, even impossible, to move the deity's temple away from the deity's mountain. For instance: "Assur, the god of the mountain peak of Assur, was so intimately allied to that particular physical location that neither he nor the cosmic axis his home represented could be safely moved."[40] By contrast, Yahweh leaves his mountain to travel with his covenant people through the vehicle of the ark, as the storyteller narrates: "The ark containing the covenant with Yahweh was traveling before them for those three days to search for a resting place for them" (v. 33b; see the second translation note there). Here the ark is personified as the active agent by which Yahweh, who dwells above it, searches for the optimal place for Israel's next encampment.[41] As implied by 9:15–23, the cloud of Yahweh had lifted from the dwelling place and now hovered over the Israelites as they

---

35. Seebass ("Num X 33f.," 111) is right about this ambivalence but then offers his reconstruction of vv. 33–36.

36. Seebass ("Num X 33f.," 111); also Milgrom, *Numbers*, 80. Knierim and Coats (*Numbers*, 163–64) see this Judg. 4:11 tradition as the missing link that explains Num. 10:29–31.

37. See the "Implications" essay below, "Yahweh or Hobab?"

38. Gray, *Numbers*, 92–93.

39. See Smith, *Monotheism*, 28.

40. Hundley, *Gods in Dwellings*, 83.

41. See the first translation note on 13:2 concerning **twr*, the same root as here in 10:33. In Num. 13 the twelve do not spy but explore the land of Canaan, Israel's future resting place.

traveled (10:34). In contrast to 9:15–23, however, the agent of guidance in this unit is not the cloud but the ark, as twice more—in addition to v. 33—the narrator depicts the ark, the throne of Yahweh, as Israel's trekking guide: "Whenever the ark traveled . . . Whenever it [the ark] came to rest" (vv. 35–36). Depending on whether the ark is traveling or stationary, Moses develops a custom of invoking Yahweh with urgent, antithetical requests (vv. 35–36; see the translation note on v. 35):

> [35]Whenever the ark traveled,
>   Moses would say,
>   "Rise up, Yahweh!
>   May your enemies be scattered,
>   and may those who hate you flee before you!"
> [36]Whenever it came to rest,
>   he would say,
>   "Return, Yahweh, to the many thousands of Israel!"

Moses's direct speech in vv. 35 and 36 forms a poetic couplet of antithetical parallelism, often called the Song of the Ark, which may have belonged to a more expansive saga of the life of Moses.[42] The sequence of v. 35 occurs in Ps. 68:1, "God attacks! His enemies disperse! His foes flee from his presence!"[43] Numbers 10:36 finds a parallel in Ps. 90:13, which also invokes Yahweh to return to his people, "Return, Yahweh! How long? Have compassion on your servants" (my trans.). Psalm 132:8 seems to combine the two notions, "Rise up, Yahweh, to your resting place, you and the ark of your strength!" (my trans.).[44] Moses's custom in Num. 10:35–36 features the ark, not as the container of the tablets of the law (Exod. 25:21), but as a symbol of the divine presence (Num. 7:89) powerful in battle, similar to what we find in the Deuteronomistic historiography of Joshua and Samuel.[45] In particular, the ark is envisioned here and in Num. 14:44 as an "emblem of the divine warrior, who is invisibly enthroned over the ark, fighting for his people."[46] In the ANE, kings gave credit to the gods for ordering and empowering them to scatter their enemies. Sennacherib publicizes: "By the word of the god Ashur, the great lord, my lord, I advanced into their midst like a fierce arrow and defeated their armies. I scattered their concentrations (and) I shattered

---

42. Milgrom, *Numbers*, 81.

43. Levine, *Numbers*, 1:318; see Deut. 20:3–4; Judg. 5:12; Pss. 10:12; 17:13.

44. Staubli, *Levitikus, Numeri*, 241.

45. Römer, "L'Arche," 98–99; Van Seters, *Life of Moses*, 329, 344. Some see 10:33–36 as Deuteronomistic (Utzschneider, *Heiligtum*, 122).

46. W. Lee, *Migratory Campaign*, 85.

their troops."[47] By contrast, the presence of the divine warrior, Yahweh, with or without any human agents, terrifies and scatters his enemies but then turns around to provide a comforting presence to his people. In this regard, the Song of the Ark resonates with the Song of the Sea (Exod. 15*), which likewise exalts Yahweh as the unparalleled warrior, who not only fights for his people but also leads them to a resting place where he will live with them (Exod. 15:6, 13).

Implications

Yahweh or Hobab: Who Will Guide Israel?

In contrast to Yahweh's cloud-fire and ark as the only sanctioned mode(s) of guidance through the wilderness (Exod. 40*; Num. 9*; 10:1–12, 33–36), Num. 10:29–32 shows Moses trying to persuade his Midianite father-in-law to guide Israel through the wilderness.[48] Milgrom sees the ark as Israel's exclusive guide and Hobab as a legitimate advisor (as Exod. 18),[49] whereas Douglas sees Moses's request to Hobab as "very dubious": "It was certainly somewhat strange under the guidance of the cloud to ask for guidance from a human."[50] So, which is it? Could Yahweh allow Hobab to be Israel's guide, formally Israel's eyes (v. 31; see the second translation note there), but at the same time demand that Israel go only where Yahweh's cloud and ark go? Since I am convinced that "context is king," Douglas's view is preferred, and I lay out the following supporting evidence.

Yahweh's ark, which alone searches for Israel's resting place (v. 33b), implies that "the Israelites were not dependent on a man who knew the desert."[51] A look at the larger context also calls Moses's request to Hobab into question. In biblical narrative, it has been argued that a narrator's *representation* of a character (actions, words, thoughts) and *evaluation* of that character (narrator's or Yahweh's explicit critique) are inversely proportional.[52] The reader knows how to make sense of a character's actions because, if representation is high, there is no need for evaluation, and vice versa. In vv. 29–32, I argue that there is no need for the narrator to explicitly evaluate Moses's request to Hobab because the narrator has already more than adequately represented Moses's exclusive dependence on Yahweh's guidance as the only normative path (Num. 7:89; 9:8–9a, 18). In Wisdom literature, divine guidance and wise

47. "Sennacherib: The Capture and Destruction of Babylon," *COS* 2.119E:305. See Niehaus, *Themes*, 62–81.
48. See Seebass, *Numeri*, 2:7–8.
49. Milgrom, *Numbers*, 80.
50. Douglas, *Wilderness*, 58, 190.
51. Schmidt, *Numeri*, 14 (my trans.).
52. Sternberg, *Poetics*, 54.

human counsel are compatible (Prov. 3:5–6; 11:14), but Yahweh's cloud-fire guidance is incompatible with Moses's plea to Hobab: "Please do not leave us, because you know where we should camp in the wilderness, and you can be our guide" (Num. 10:31). In addition to guidance, Moses seeks Hobab's presence, "Please do not leave us," which echoes and undercuts his prior appeal to Yahweh, "If your presence does not go with us, do not take us up from here" (Exod. 33:15). In short, the Israelites were not to depend on the prowess and presence of a man, a non-Israelite at that, to lead them through the wilderness to the promised land.[53]

This short exchange between Moses and Hobab likely reflects a non-Priestly source (vv. 29–32), not only by its openness to guidance from a human and foreigner, as Wisdom literature would allow, but also by the use of the name Hobab for Moses's father-in-law, instead of Jethro or Reuel (see the translation note on 10:29). Now in its canonical form, the redactional placement of vv. 29–32 between two pericopes that foreground exclusive divine guidance (vv. 11–27 and 33–36) has a rhetorical effect: none of Yahweh's prophets, not even Moses, is immune from wrongly seeking out skilled humans in place of God.[54] As Jeremiah, a prophet like Moses, would come to say, "Thus says Yahweh: 'Cursed is the man who trusts in human beings and makes flesh his strength, but who turns his heart away from Yahweh.'"[55] Ironically, it is Hobab's refusal that spares Moses from misplaced trust, but Moses's solicitation hints at a fissure in his character that will eventually be exposed in his rebellion and loss of the land.[56] As a full-fledged character, acting and emoting in ways with which we as readers can identify,[57] we are relieved that Moses did not get what he wanted. In the book of Numbers, there is no mention of Moses actually depending on Hobab's guidance during Israel's wilderness wanderings. Yet some will wonder if Moses's insistence on a human guide foreshadows something ominous on the horizon for the Moses-Yahweh relationship.

---

53. See Schmidt, *Numeri*, 14.
54. Compare the Islamic, esp. Shia, notion of the prophets' immunity from sin (*'iṣma*).
55. Seitz, "Prophet Moses," 3–27, citing Jer. 17:5.
56. Num. 20:12; 27:14; Deut. 32:48–52.
57. Berlin, "Characterization," 78.

11

Complaining, Burning, and Death in the Camp

(11:1–35)

∞

Overview

After Israel's consistent obedience in preparation for Canaan (1:1–10:10) and their successful first migration (10:11–34), culminating with the conquering war chant, the so-called Song of the Ark (10:35–36), the reader expects the Israelites to progress faithfully on their Yahweh-led journey toward the land he promised to the patriarchs.[1] But at 11:1, the dominating cadence of Israel's hopeful obedience is broken.[2] In a tragic turn of events, the Israelites in back-to-back stories deeply offend Yahweh and provoke him to destructive judgment (vv. 1–3, vv. 4–35). In the first story, the people complain, and Yahweh metaphorically burns with anger and physically with fire through the wilderness camp (vv. 1–3). The second story contains what seems to have been two originally independent stories, now woven together thematically: "Moses, the people, and plague" (vv. 4–15, 18–24a, 31–35) and "Moses, the elders, and prophecy" (vv. 16–17, 24b–30).[3] Now in its final form, vv. 4–35

---

1. See "Literary Genre and Structure" in the introduction.

2. Olson, *Numbers*, 121–22; Leveen, *Memory*, 81.

3. Sommer, "Redaction," 601–24; Reis ("Numbers XI," 207–31), however, perceives a single story line and attempts to harmonize the contrasts. Numbers 11 is often viewed as JE (de Vaulx, *Nombres*, 148–49; Cross, *Canaanite Myth*, 315) or a core Yahwistic (J) story that was supplemented (Noth, *Numbers*, 83; Schmidt, *Numeri*, 21; Seebass, "Num. XI," 214–23) and bound with Num. 12 (J, E, or JE) by the travel notice of 11:35 (Knierim and Coats, *Numbers*, 177). Many see the Hobab story (10:29–32) with Num. 11–12 as the opening pre-Priestly stories in the book with Num. 13–14, 16–17, 20–25 (Frevel, "Alte Stücke," 281; Frevel, "Purity

comprise four major scenes by one count.[4] In the opening scene, an Israelite mob is nostalgic for the food they allegedly enjoyed in Egypt, so Yahweh becomes angry; meanwhile Moses complains to Yahweh that the people have become a great burden (vv. 4–15). In response, Yahweh commands Moses to bring seventy elders to the meeting tent so Yahweh can put his spirit on them to relieve Moses's burden. At the same time, he also promises to give the nostalgic Israelites so much meat that it makes them nauseous (vv. 16–20). Moses doubts Yahweh's ability to provide meat for 600,000 Israelites, for which Yahweh rebukes him. Yahweh then proceeds to put some of the spirit that was on Moses onto the elders, who as a result, prophesy (vv. 21–30).[5] In the final scene, Yahweh sends a wind that brings in an abundance of quail, which the Israelites eat apparently without giving thanks, so Yahweh becomes angry again and strikes the people with a deadly plague (vv. 31–35). The stories, vv. 1–3 and vv. 4–35, complement each other to illustrate from different angles that ingratitude by members of the vassal nation, Israel, is heinous to the great king, Yahweh, and punishable by death.

Translation

[1]But at that time,[6] when the people complained in Yahweh's ears about their hardship, Yahweh heard them and his anger burned, and fire from Yahweh burned among them and consumed some of the outer parts of the camp. [2]Then the people cried out to Moses, so he[7] prayed to Yahweh, and the fire died out. [3]So he called[8] the name of that place

---

Conceptions," 378). Janowski (*Gottes Gegenwart*, 299–301) sees an older, pre-Priestly "tent of meeting" tradition in Num. 11–12 (with Exod. 33:7–11; traditionally E: see D. Wright, "Profane," 148n50), and many see Pg/P as adapting this tradition (Boorer, *Priestly Narrative*, 356). Römer ("Nombres 11–12," 487–91, 496) attributes Num. 11 to a prophetic redaction that knew the Deuteronomic and Priestly stories of revolt. Achenbach (*Vollendung*, 635) subdivides Num. 11 between (1) a pre-Deuteronomic source and (2) the Hexateuch and Pentateuch editors (cf. Scharbert, *Numeri*, 46).

4. Staubli (*Levitikus, Numeri*, 242) sees vv. 4–34 as concentric, with Moses's unbelieving reaction in the center (vv. 21–22). Ashley (*Numbers*, 206–7; but cf. W. Lee, *Migratory Campaign*, 127–28) sees three cycles: food theme→transition→leadership theme (vv. 4–13, 14–15, 16–17// vv. 18–20, 21–23, 24–30//vv. 31–34, 35; 12:1–15).

5. This scene with the spirit-empowered elders could be classified as a "heroic saga" (Knierim and Coats, *Numbers*, 177).

6. "But" interprets the contrast of the hopeful story line: (1) Israel obeys (Num. 1–10), the cloud finally moves (10:11), Israel moves (10:12) as Moses gives a Yahweh-centered war cry (vv. 33–36); with (2) Israel's complaining and Yahweh's judgment (11:1–34). "But/and at that time" (*wayhî*) introduces the foregrounded events of v. 1 (*BHRG* §21.2.1.1.2ba).

7. The Hb. repeats "Moses" (*mōšeh*).

8. As in v. 34, MT is act., "So he called" (*wayyiqrā'* ≈ Tg⁰ Tg^Neo Vulg), and there is no need to make the verb pass. with LXX^ed (and ESV, NRSV, NLT, NIV, NJPS) since the Moses of v. 2 can function as the subject who names the location (NET, EÜ).

Taberah (Place of Burning)[9] because fire from Yahweh burned among them there.

4Now the mob[10] among them had a craving,[11] so the Israelites sat down and wept,[12] saying, "Who will give us meat to eat? **5**We remember the fish we used to eat at no cost in Egypt, the cucumbers, melons, leeks, onions, and garlic. **6**But now our throats[13] are dry, and we see nothing but this manna!"[14] **7**(The manna was like coriander seed and looked like gum resin.[15] **8**The people went around and gathered it, and ground it in mills or crushed it in mortars. They baked it in pans and made cakes out of it. It tasted like a cake made with oil.[16] **9**And when the dew came down on the camp at night, the manna came down with

---

9. "Taberah" (*tab'ērâ*) may not originally have been a deverbal noun from "to burn" (*b'r* I: *DCH* 2:242) but a phonetic wordplay on that root in vv. 1, 3 (see Ross, "Paronomasia").

10. *'Āsapsup* (mob, rabble) is an OT hapax (*DCH* 1:350). In 1 Sam. 17:1, the verbal form refers to assembling fighting forces (Levine, *Numbers*, 1:321). Many unverifiably equate this subgroup in Israel with the "mixed multitude" (*'ēreb*) of Exod. 12:38, that is, the "non-Israelites who joined the Hebrews at the time of the Exodus" (*HALOT* 2:878, gloss 1; NET, "mix. mult."; Albertz, *Israelite Religion*, 1:44). It is a deverbal formation from the passive "gathered" (*'āsûp*, a qataltūl; see Joüon and Muraoka §88Jb); *'sp* (to gather) occurs 18× in Numbers, 6× in chap. 11 alone: vv. 16, 22, 24, 30, 32 (2×); also substantivized "ingathering, harvest": "*'sp*₂," *DNWSI* 1:89; "*'āsîp*," *HALOT* 1:73. This may indicate that it was a *gathered* faction, a mob, that incited the larger Israelite community to complain (v. 4); similarly, de Vaulx, *Nombres*, 148; Seebass, *Numeri*, 2:28; Levine, *Numbers*, 1:312.

11. Hithpael reflexive, "the Israelites had a craving" (*hit'awwû*; *GBHS* §3.1.5a). The internal adjunct of the same verbal root—"the mob among them *craved a craving*" (*hit'awwû ta'ăwâ*)—probably has "no semantic meaning" (*BHRG* §33.3[5]). Thus, simply craving, not an *intense* craving, contra "insatiable appetites" (Levine, *Numbers*, 1:312), "craved fiercely" (Seebass, *Numeri*, 2:28), "strong craving" (RSV; Noth, *Numbers*, 81); "seized by greed" (de Vaulx, "Nombres," 148; EÜ).

12. Most uncritically adopt the MT pointing, "*they returned* and they wept" (*wayyāšubû*), meaning "they wept *again*," which was probably an aural error. Without changing the consonants, the preferred reading is found when the vowels are repointed to mean "*they sat down* and wept" (*wayyēšəbû*), which is the meaning of LXX^ed (*kathisantes*) and Vulgate (*sedens*). Beirne ("Numbers 11,4") has made a strong case that (1) "they sat down" removes the problem of finding a prior story of weeping to which "they wept again" refers, and (2) sitting and weeping is a well-known funeral rite, as well as a custom during times of great sadness and national calamity (Ps. 137:1).

13. Here *nepeš* means not "life" or "soul" but "throat" ("*nepeš* I," *DCH* 5:724–25, gloss 1).

14. A referential article, "*this* manna" (*hammān*), recalling Yahweh's provision of manna in Exod. 16 (*GBHS* §2.6.1).

15. "Gum resin" (*habbədōlaḥ*)—frequently identified as "bdellium" (*DCH* 2:96), a yellowish, fragrant gum from a south Arabian tree (*HALOT* 1:110)—occurs only here and Gen. 2:12, which depicts the land of Havilah into which the Pishon River flowed from Eden. This gum resin is known in Akkadian (*budulḫu*) as a common aromatic (*CAD* 2:305–6) and is attested in Phoenician ("*bdlḥ*," *DNWSI* 1:145). Less likely, DeGuglielmo ("Manna," 116–17) sees the LXX "rock-crystal" (*krystallos*) as correctly identifying *bədōlaḥ* as a glistening or sparkling precious stone.

16. A gen. of material, "a cake *made with* oil" (*ləšad haššāmen*; *GBHS* §2.2.10; EÜ). However, the meaning of "cake" (*lāšād*) is disputed since it occurs lucidly only here in the OT (maybe

it.)[17] [10]Moses heard the people weeping among their families, everyone at the entrance of their tent. The anger of Yahweh burned severely, and Moses was displeased. [11]So Moses said to Yahweh, "Why have you hurt your servant?[18] Why have I not found favor in your sight, that you put the burden of this entire people on me? [12]Did I conceive this entire people? Did I give birth to them, that you should say to me, 'Carry them in your arms,[19] as a nurse[20] carries a nursing baby,' to the land which you swore in an oath to give[21] to their fathers? [13]Where will I get meat to give to this entire people, since they cry to me, 'Give us meat so we can eat!'? [14]I am not able to carry this entire people alone because they are too heavy[22] for me! [15]But if you must treat me like this, then kill me now. If[23] I have found favor in your sight, then do not let me see my misery."

[16]Yahweh said to Moses, "Gather to me seventy of Israel's elders,[24] whom you know are officiating elders among the people,[25] and bring them to the meeting tent. Let them stand there with you. [17]Then I will

---

in Ps. 32:4, "strength") and could refer instead to moisture or a delicacy (*DCH* 4:576; "rich cream," NJPS).

17. Verses 7–9 are parenthesized (NET) since they are not part of the story line, but the mention of manna in v. 6 prompted a supplement (vv. 7–9) to explain its nature and use to unfamiliar readers (Schmidt, *Numeri*, 23–24). The description differs, not irreconcilably, from Exod. 16:31 (see Van Seters, *Life of Moses*, 230).

18. "Why *have you hurt* [*hărēʿōtā*] your servant?" uses the hiphil of the root "to do evil, treat badly" ("*rʿʿ*," *HALOT* 3:1269–70; *GBHS* §3.1.6a.2), indicating that Moses is not questioning Yahweh's character, "Why are you evil?" (requiring *rʿʿ* qal). See Yahweh as agent of a hiphil *rʿʿ* in Exod. 5:22; Josh. 24:20; Ruth 1:21; 1 Kings 17:20; Ps. 44:2 [44:3 MT]; Jer. 25:6 [implied?]; 25:29; 31:28; Mic. 4:6; Zeph. 1:12 [implied?]; 8:14).

19. This is a dynamic rendering of *ḥêq* (lap, bosom), that is, the "lower, outer front of the body where loved ones (infants and animals) are pressed closely" (*HALOT* 1:312, gloss 1; cf. *DCH* 3:216).

20. This substantive ptc. (*hāʾōmēn*) can refer to a female "nurse" (Ruth 4:16; 2 Sam. 4:4), gender-neutral "guardian" (2 Kings 10:1, 5), or male "guardian" or "foster father" (Esther 2:7; Isa. 49:23).

21. "You swore in an oath to give" (*nišbaʿtā*) renders a single niphal reflexive (*GBHS* §3.1.2c). The background is the oath-sworn contracts, treaties, and loyalty oaths in the ANE (Otto, "Covenant," 2047–51).

22. This sg. stative "it is (too) heavy" (*kābēd*) could imply "burden" or "load" as its subject (an ellipsis of *maśśāʾ* from v. 11; NLT, ESV, NIV; Budd, *Numbers*, 122); or in keeping with the v. 12 metaphor of a nurse (Moses) carrying a nursing infant (Israel), the grammatical subject could be the preceding collective "all this people" (*kol-hāʿām hazze*, v. 14α); hence, "*they are too heavy for me*" (NRSV).

23. SP "and if" (*wʾm* ≈ Vulg[ed] "and") was probably added to connect the conditionals.

24. Formally, "seventy men from the elders of Israel"; cf. seventy elders of Israel who, with Moses, see the Mount Sinai theophany (Exod. 24:1–11).

25. The formal phrase, "elders of the people and the officials of them [the people]" (*ziqnê hāʿām wašōṭərāyw*), is probably not two separate subcategories, but a nominal hendiadys: "officiating elders" (*GBHS* §4.3.3a, g.1).

come down and speak with you there, and I will set aside[26] some of the spirit that is on you and put it on them, so they will carry some of the burden of the people with you, and you will not carry it alone. [18]Say to the people, 'Consecrate yourselves[27] for tomorrow, and you will eat meat, because you cried and Yahweh heard you,[28] saying, "Who will give us meat to eat, for life was good for us in Egypt?"[29] Now Yahweh will give you meat, and you will eat. [19]You will eat, not one day, or two days, or five days, or ten days, or twenty days, [20]but a whole month, until it comes out your nose and makes you nauseous,[30] because you have rejected[31] Yahweh who is among you and cried before him, saying, "Why did we ever leave Egypt?"'"

[21]Moses said, "There are 600,000 people on foot around me,[32] but[33] you say 'I will give them meat to eat for a whole month!' [22]Would they have enough if flocks and herds[34] were slaughtered for them? Would they have enough if all the fish in the sea were caught for them?" [23]Yahweh said to Moses, "Is Yahweh's hand too short? Now[35] you will see if my word to you will come true or not!"[36] [24]So Moses went out and told the people what Yahweh had said.[37] He gathered seventy elders of

---

26. This verb (*'ṣl* I) occurs five times (Gen. 27:36; Num. 11:17, 25; Eccles. 2:10; Ezek. 42:6) and means "withhold, set aside" in the qal stem (*DCH* 1:363). SP: "I will take away" (*wḥṣlty* = hiphil of *nṣl*); similarly LXX[ed]: "I will remove" (**aphaireō* rendering hiphil of *nṣl* in Gen. 31:9, 16, but never *'ṣl* I), probably an aural mistake, using the rare verb for the more common verb (25× in the Pentateuch, etc.): *wəhiṣṣaltî* (vocalized SP; see Exod. 6:6) for *wə'āṣaltî* (MT).

27. The hithpael impv. "consecrate yourselves" (*hitqaddəšû*) is reflexive and factitive-resultative, commanding the Israelites to put themselves into a consecrated state (*GBHS* §3.1.3a, 3.1.5a). This exact form, demanding communal self-consecration, occurs in the Hexateuch only here, Josh. 3:5 (before crossing the Jordan), and 7:13 (after the sin of Achan); cf. injunctive forms of **qdš* hithpael in Exod. 19:22; Lev. 11:44; 20:7.

28. Formally, "in the two ears of Yahweh" (*bə'oznê yhwh*), with Yahweh as the subjective gen. of the verbal notion "to hear" (*'zn*; *GBHS* §2.2.3).

29. "Life" clarifies the text, formally, "for it was good for us in Egypt."

30. *Zārā'* is an OT hapax meaning "abhorrence, nausea; something disgusting" (*DCH* 3:134) ≈ LXX[ed] "nausea" ("cholera," *GELS* 734).

31. Or "spurned" or "despised," often found in religious contexts with Yahweh either rejecting or being rejected ("*mā'as* I," *DCH* 5:120). The perfective aspect of this fientive verb calls attention to the Israelites' state of mind enduring into the present: "you have rejected Yahweh" or even "you reject Yahweh" (*mə'astem*; *GBHS* §3.2.1c).

32. Formally, "the people whom I am in the midst of are 600,000 on foot."

33. "But" (*wə*) marks a contrast with v. 21a–b (*IBHS* §39.2.3b).

34. SP "and *the* herds" (*wḥbqr*) probably arose by mistaking (or interpreting) the interrogative *hă* as a definite article; a question can still be implied, but with referential articles: "Would they have enough if the [Israelites' present] flocks and the [Israelites' present] herds were slaughtered for them?" (*GBHS* §2.6.1).

35. SP states the pronoun as the constituent focus: "*You* ['*th*] will see" (*BHRG* §36.1.1.3[1]). Probably SP confuses the gutturals: '*th* "you" (SP) for '*th* "now" (MT = *ēdē* LXX[ed]; *k'n* Tg[O]).

36. Formally, "if my word meets [encounters/happens to] you or not."

37. Formally, "the words of Yahweh" (*dibrê yhwh*), a subjective gen., "what Yahweh had said" (*GBHS* §2.2.3).

the people and had them stand around the tent. **25**Then Yahweh came down in the cloud and spoke to them, and he set aside[38] some of the spirit that was on him[39] and put it on the seventy elders. When the spirit rested on them, they prophesied, but did not do so again.[40] **26**But two men remained in the camp—one's name was Eldad, the other's name was Medad. And the spirit rested on them. They were among those registered but had not gone out to the tent. So they prophesied in the camp. **27**And a young man ran and told Moses,[41] "Eldad and Medad are prophesying in the camp!" **28**Then Nun's son Joshua, who had been Moses's assistant from his youth, said, "My lord Moses, stop them!" **29**Moses said to him, "Are you jealous[42] for me? I wish that all Yahweh's people were prophets, that Yahweh would put his spirit on them!"[43] **30**Then Moses and Israel's elders returned to the camp.

31Then a wind went out from Yahweh and brought[44] quail[45] from the sea, and let them fall near the camp, about a day's journey on this side and a day's journey on the other side, all around the camp, and about three feet deep on the ground's surface. **32**And the people[46] stayed

---

38. See the translation note on 11:17.

39. The referent of "some of the spirit that was *on him* [*'ālāyw*]" might be intentionally ambiguous, either "on Moses" (NLT, NET, NIV [implied])—as in v. 17 "some of the spirit that is on you"—or "on Yahweh"—since Yahweh is the implied agent of the main verb "and he set aside" (*wayyāʾṣel*) and since in v. 29 the spirit belongs to Yahweh ("his spirit," *rûḥô*). Therefore, I leave the referent unspecified, "on him" (with LXX[ed]; NRSV, ESV, EÜ; de Vaulx, *Nombres*, 154; Schmidt, *Numeri*, 19; Seebass, *Numeri*, 2:29; Levine, *Numbers*, 1:313).

40. SP "but they had not been gathered" (*yʾspw*, *ʾsp*) conflicts with v. 24 since Moses had just gathered them around the tent (*ʾsp*); probably homophonic error: *yēʾāspû* (vocalized SP; see Gen. 29:8) for *yāsāpû* (MT = LXX[ed] "and *they* no longer *added* [*prosethento*]").

41. This comma represents the redundant quotative frame "and told . . . *and he said* [*wayyōʾmar*]."

42. The piel predicate ptc. implies a present tense, "Are you jealous?" (*hamqannēʾ ʾattâ*). In Numbers, this root in the piel "to be jealous" (*qnʾ*) is the response to infidelity, depicting the husband who suspects his wife has been unfaithful (5:14 [2×], 30) and Phinehas the priest, whose response averts Yahweh's wrath against Israel for cultic prostitution with the Moabite women and their deity, Baal of Peor (Num. 25:11, 13).

43. See the translation note on 24:2.

44. The wayyiqtol "brought" (*wayyāgāz* from *gwz*) is a root that occurs three times in the OT, two of those in the MT occur in the qal (here and Ps. 90:10), but the word is probably the niphal of *gwz* (to be passed) in Nah. 1:12 (*DCH* 2:329). Since the qal means something like "to pass," many ancient and modern versions point the vowels (against MT) to read as the hiphil *wayyāggez*, meaning "bring, transfer" (*DCH* 2:329). LXX[ed] uses the hapax "to carry out" ("*ekperaō*," *GELS* 214); Vulg[ed] "drove in" (*arreptas*); Tg[O] "made fly" (*waʾapraḥ*, haphel causative of "*prḥ*," CAL gloss C2).

45. This noun (*śalāw*) appears four times in the OT (Exod. 16:13; Num. 11:31, 32; Ps. 105:40) and probably refers to common quail (*Coturnix* [genus], *coturnix* [species]: *DCH* 8:156; *HALOT* 3:1331). SP *ślwy* has no pl. inflection (*m*), probably by conflating the two nasals (mm→m); see SP in v. 32 (*hślwy* SP vs. *hślw* MT, without *y*).

46. 4Q27 "*all* the people" (*kwl hʿm*) is hyperbolic, but so is "the people" (MT SP LXX[ed]), which refers to the entire community (*GBHS* §2.6.1).

up all that day, all that night, and all the next day,[47] and gathered the quail. Those who gathered the fewest gathered ten homers,[48] and they spread them out[49] for themselves all around the camp. [33]But when the meat was still between their teeth, before they chewed it, Yahweh's anger burned against the people, and Yahweh struck the people with a very severe plague. [34]So the name of that place was called[50] Kibroth Hattaavah (Graves of Craving),[51] because there they buried the people who had a craving. [35] [35a]From Kibroth Hattaavah the people traveled[52] to Hazeroth (Settlements).[53]

Interpretation

11:1–3. Prior to Num. 11, the story line has been totally positive, beginning with a lengthy segment of supplementary meeting-tent instructions accompanied by Israel's repeated obedience (1:1–10:10), then Israel's successful first leg of its journey (10:11–34), and finally a victorious war chant, the Song of

47. Anarthrous MT, "all *day* of the next" (*kōl yôm hammāḥŏrāt*), is preferred grammatically since only the gen. noun should be articular (*hammāḥŏrāt*), whereas the articular "*the* day" (*hywm* 4Q27 SP) probably assimilates to the prior two articular, attributed nouns (LXX[ed] "all the next day"). See *BHRG* §36.5.1(3).

48. "Ten homers" (*ʿăśārâ ḥŏmārîm*) is typically a dry measure equal to about 400 liters, or ten ephahs, or ten baths of liquid measure (Ezek. 45:11, 13–14; see "*ḥōmer* III," *HALOT* 1:330, gloss 1; "*ḥōmer* III," *DCH* 3:259 notes that it is used as a liquid measure of wine in the Arad ostracon 2:5). "Homer" (*ḥōmer*) occurs in Numbers only here.

49. A wayyiqtol with a cognate adverbial inf., formally, "they spread them out, spreading *for themselves*" (*wayyišṭəḥû lāhem šāṭôaḥ*; *GBHS* §3.4.2b.2). Instead of "spreading" (*šāṭôaḥ*), SP reads "slaughtering" (*šḥwṭ* vocalized as *šāḥôṭ* from **šḥṭ*, to slaughter). The rarity of **šṭḥ*, "to spread out" (only in Num. 11:32; 2 Sam. 17:19; Job 12:23; Ps. 88:9 [10]; Jer. 8:2), may have predisposed SP to transpose *ṭ* and *ḥ*.

50. MT has an act. verb and direct obj., "So he called the name of that place . . ." (*wayyiqrāʾ ʾet-šēm-hammāqôm hahûʾ* ≈ Tg[O]), which is often reconfigured by modern translations as a passive. The omission of the direct obj. marker in SP allows for a passive vocalization of the verb, "So the name of that place was called" (≈ LXX[ed] Vulg[ed]). Ulrich (*Qumran*, 144) reconstructs 4Q27 as the SP reading.

51. Ancient versions: "Tombs of Craving" (NETS for *Mnēmatōn epithymias*); "Graves of Lust" (Vulg: *sepulchra Concupiscentiae* ≈ Syr); "Graves of the Demanders" (Tg[O]: *qibrê dimśaʾălê*); "Graves of the Desirers of the Flesh" (Tg[PJ]: *qybry dmśyyly bśrʾ*).

52. The pl. predicate "traveled" (*nāsʿû*), of a collective sg. noun "the people" (*hāʿām*), is acceptable grammatically (*BHRG* §35[3]), but thinking the construction to be incongruent might explain the sg. reading in 4Q27 (*nsʿ*) and LXX[ed] (*exēren*, which Ulrich [*Qumran*, 144] accidentally lists as pl.).

53. Hazeroth (*ḥăṣērôt*, pl. of *ḥāṣēr* II) denotes settlements or villages (*DCH* 3:296), maybe more specifically without walls (*HALOT* 1:345). 4Q27 does not include the verse's first mention of "Hazeroth" (*ḥăṣērôt* MT SP [with article] Tg[O] LXX[ed]: "for/to Haseroth," *eis Asērōth*), which may have been an attempt to remove the ostensible redundancy of the copula, "*and they were* at Hazeroth" (see 12:16; 21:10–33:49). I therefore read 11:35b with 12:1 (with NRSV, NLT, NJPS, EÜ).

the Ark (10:35–36). All now expect that Israel will obediently move to its next encampment enroute to the land. Those hopes are deflated for the first time in the book by the opening of the new scene: "But at that time, when the people complained in Yahweh's ears about their hardship, Yahweh heard them" (11:1a–c; see the translation note there). The narrator lifts the heavenly curtain for the reader: while the Israelites think their complaining (*'nn hithpolel) about the hardship or evil (ra')[54] they have suffered is confined to themselves, Yahweh has been listening attentively to them all along (2× in v. 1: "Yahweh's ears" and "Yahweh heard"). This is not the first time since the exodus that they have complained (Exod. 16:2). Here Yahweh responds by burning with anger (metaphorically) and with fire (physically) among the people, consuming some of the outer parts of the camp. To modern readers, this may seem like the opposite of Yahweh's self-claim that he is "slow to anger" (Exod. 34:6; Num. 14:18), but in the ancient Near East, those who complain against the great king or his heir have violated the covenant and deserve to be annihilated.[55] With the death penalty as the standard, Yahweh's burning in this instance appears mild: his fire burns only on the periphery, and the narrator does not refer explicitly to the death of people as in the ensuing episode (vv. 33–34). Is this only a divine warning, without death, to demonstrate to the people that Yahweh hears everything they say and that, by burning the outskirts, he is not confined to his centralized tent? Or does Yahweh actually prune the complainers from the camp by fire?[56] In either case, the story as it now stands functions as an etiology for why the place is named, probably by Moses, Taberah (Place of Burning)—that is, "because there fire from Yahweh burned among them" (v. 3; see the translation notes there). While Taberah's location is unknown today,[57] positioned somewhere in the Sinai desert between the also unidentified Mount Sinai and the Paran desert to the north, the name has forever become textualized as a theological warning to God's covenant people (Deut. 9:22).

11:4–15. As a mob of Israelites long nostalgically for the food of Egypt, Yahweh burns with anger, and Moses complains about the burden of the people. The mob (see the first translation note on 11:4), also called the Israelites, acts as the collective agent whose "whole personality gets crammed into one or two adjectives, with clear evaluative import but little else."[58] They sit down and weep, as if mourning at a funeral or a national disaster (v. 4; see the third translation note there). Compare the Canaanite god El, who gets off his throne, sits on the ground, and mourns for Baal, who has died. When

54. Alternatively, "complained *bitterly*," since *ra'* is not the obj. of an expected prep. *'al* (about; Milgrom, *Numbers*, 82; NJPS).

55. See the "Implications" essay below, "Complaining as Covenant Violation."

56. Dozeman, "Numbers," 111.

57. Rasmussen, *Atlas*, 104, 300.

58. Sternberg, *Poetics*, 327.

reflecting on life in exile, the Hebrew poet writes, "By the waters of Babylon, there we sat down and wept when we remembered Zion" (Ps. 137:1).[59] No one has died (even the story in vv. 1–3 does not say this), and no one is in exile. On the contrary, they have just been liberated from bondage in Egypt, which turns their sitting and weeping with a craving into a satire. Their craving (v. 4; see the second translation note there) at first may seem purely physiological, but the narrator makes clear that it is also psychological: "Who will give us meat to eat? We remember the fish we used to eat at no cost in Egypt, the cucumbers, melons, leeks, onions, and garlic. But now our throats are dry, and we see nothing but this manna!" (vv. 4d–6; cf. 1 Cor. 10:6). Their food craving echoes the cry for "pots of meat" in the Exod. 16 story, and their complaining echoes the story of complaining about having no water in Exod. 17 (later Num. 20:3–5).[60] These and related Israelite complaints, spanning Exod. 14–Num. 21, have often been called "Egypt nostalgia."[61] The psychology of craving (addiction) can help us to probe slightly deeper. Looking through the lens of a dual-effect model, we see the exodus generation's collective "memory networks that store information on the stimuli that trigger the craving system."[62] This model posits that the stimuli activating a craving are either positive (celebratory mood) or negative (depression, anger, etc.), but not both at the same time.[63] For the mob, a negative emotional response seems most likely: they yell "Our throats are dry" as they try to survive in the Sinai desert and "we see nothing but this manna!" as they are repulsed by their monotonous diet (v. 6). In what may strike the reader as satire, the Israelites absurdly revise their history, omitting the memory of their suffering in Egypt (Exod. 1:8–14:12). Yet even with no record of Israel eating the named Egyptian delicacies since Jacob's sojourn there (Gen. 46–Exod. 12), Israel's cry here makes the most sense if they had become accustomed to eating tastier food in Egypt, which they are now nostalgically embellishing in their own memory.[64]

59. Beirne, "Numbers 11,4," 202–3.

60. See Baden, "Violent Origins," 110.

61. Römer ("Egypt Nostalgia," 70–71) charts the parallel phrases from the texts in which the people are critical that they have been led out of Egypt: Exod. 14:11–12 (also 13:17b); 16:3; 17:3; Num. 11:18–20 (also v. 5); 14:2–4; 16:12–14; 20:3–5; 21:5.

62. Tiffany, "Concepts of Craving," 219.

63. Tiffany, "Concepts of Craving," 219.

64. Every food category of vv. 5–6 can be identified in the Moses story: meat from livestock (Exod. 9:6–7); fruits and vegetables (Exod. 10:15; Deut. 11:10); and fish (Exod. 7:18–21) "at no cost," that is, they must have fished the distributaries of the Nile Delta (Tel ed-Dabʿa/Avaris = Rameses? Tell er-Retabah = Pithom? See Rasmussen, *Atlas*, 102–3). Some of the produce mentioned are attested in Egyptian texts and wall paintings (Walton and Matthews, *Genesis–Deuteronomy*, 186). Even in modern Egypt (ca. 1900), poor inhabitants in Egypt have subsisted on all of these and other specific fruits, vegetables, and fish but excluding meat (Gray, *Numbers*, 104; Milgrom, *Numbers*, 83). The Israelites of the exodus now have livestock (Exod. 12:38; Num. 11:22), but they would surely have been hesitant to butcher these for meat apart from special celebrations (Walton and Matthews, *Genesis–Deuteronomy*, 186).

Asiatic prisoners and forced laborers, something akin to the Israelites' status after Exod. 1:8, were typically disdained by the Egyptians. However, the concept that God gave food to foreigners and Egyptians alike is attested in Akhenaton's form of monotheism: "All men, cattle and wild game, . . . thou hast provided for their needs, each one with his food" (cf. Ps. 145:16).[65] The Israelites do not deny that the divine creator and sustainer, Yahweh, continues to provide food for them, but they are no longer satisfied with or thankful for *how* Yahweh is providing for them. They forget that in their recent past, when they complained of having no food or water, Moses interceded, and Yahweh immediately and graciously supplied it for them (Exod. 16–17).

The description of manna is placed in parentheses as a narrator's aside or editor's insertion for later readers unfamiliar with it (vv. 7–9; see the translation notes on vv. 7–9). It differs (italicized below) from the description in the parallel manna episode in the Sin wilderness, between Egypt and Sinai:

Exodus 16*	Numbers 11:6b–9
[14]. . . *a thin flaky texture, thin like frost on the ground.*	
[31]The house of Israel called it manna.	[6b]". . . we see nothing but this manna!"
It was like coriander seed, *white,* and its taste *was like wafers with honey.*	[7]The manna was like coriander seed *and looked like gum resin.*
[16:4–5, 8, 12, 16–30 = The people gather manna like dew *in the morning, not to be left for the next morning. Gather twice as much on the sixth day for the seventh.* Bake and boil it *on the sixth day in preparation for the Sabbath.*]	[8]The people went around and gathered it, *and ground it with mills or crushed it in mortars.* They baked *it in pans and made cakes out of it. It* tasted like *a cake made with oil.* [9]And when the dew came down on the camp at night, the manna came down with it (see the translation notes on vv. 7–9).

It is simplest to infer that the scribes of each episode drew from different sources,[66] but whether the manna was flaky and sweet like honey (Exod. 16)* or savory like an oil cake but viscous like gum resin (Num. 11), or somehow both, we are at a loss to determine (see the translation notes on 11:6–7). Nonetheless, the shared descriptor coriander seed was used to flavor food and vegetables,[67] which should have inspired Israel in both stories to thank

---

65. See Redford, *Egypt, Canaan, and Israel*, 221–31 (231).

66. Contra Van Seters (*Life of Moses*, 189), who assigns both to J. While Exod. 16:31 is probably not P[g]/P, its origins are debated (Boorer, *Priestly Narrative*, 58). Some have identified vv. 7–9 as E (Eissfeldt, *Hexateuch*, 161), others as J (Budd, *Numbers*, 125) or the Hexateuch editor, who in distinction from Exod. 16 narrates the manna story as an outline of the desert season from Moses to Joshua (see Exod. 16:35; Josh. 5:12; Achenbach, *Vollendung*, 227).

67. King and Stager, *Life*, 107.

Yahweh that his daily provision was not insipid.[68] Through the Deuteronomic scribes, Moses explains how Yahweh is working for the Israelites by
supplying strange manna: "He humbled you by letting you hunger, then by
feeding you with manna, with which neither you nor your ancestors were
acquainted, in order to make you understand that one does not live by bread
alone, but by every word that comes from the mouth of the LORD" (Deut.
8:3 NRSV). Even more strange to God's people was his provision of Jesus,
"the true bread from heaven," who forever satisfies the hunger of those who
trust him (John 6:32, 35).

Rather than gratefully relying on Yahweh's spiritual bread (word) and
physical bread (manna), the people weep at their tents, implicitly in dis-
satisfaction and disappointment. Moses now, like Yahweh in v. 1, overhears
them; Yahweh burns in anger, while Moses is displeased (v. 10). Immediately,
Moses directs his prayer to Yahweh (vv. 11b–15), beginning with four accusing questions (vv. 11 [2×], 12, 13). Moses does not explicitly show concern
for Yahweh's reputation or character (cf. Exod. 32:11–13; Num. 14:17–20 à
la Exod. 34:5–7). He only wants relief from the people, so his prayer comes
across as egocentric: "your servant . . . on me" (v. 11); "I . . . I . . . to me . . .
'your [Moses's] arms'" (v. 12); "I . . . to me" (v. 13); "I . . . alone . . . for me"
(v. 14); and "me . . . me . . . I . . . me . . . my misery" (v. 15). Was Moses bearing
the burden of the people alone, or was he so overwhelmed by the people that
he forgot the many judges adjudicating cases and alleviating his burden (Exod.
18)?[69] Even as self-focused as Moses's prayer is, the fact that he is aiming his
vehement criticism at Yahweh stands in sharp contrast to his reliance on his
father-in-law, a non-Israelite priest, for wisdom (Exod. 18; Num. 10:29–32).
By an offhand retort with two metaphors and a simile, Moses challenges
Yahweh to remain faithful to his land promise to the patriarchs: "[metaphor
1] Did I give birth to them, that you should say to me, [metaphor 2] 'Carry
them in your arms, [simile] as a nurse carries a nursing baby,' [concrete] *to
the land which you swore in an oath to give to their fathers?*" (v. 12; see the
first translation note there). Moses implies that Yahweh is the one who gave
birth to Israel, who has delivered Israel from Egypt and entered into a covenant
with them (Exod. 1–24) and carries his child in his arms as a nursing mother
or wet nurse carries her baby—that is, the one who lovingly and protectively
will lead Israel to the land he promised to Abraham, Isaac, and Jacob (Josh.

---

68. Milgrom (*Numbers*, 84) associates this with a flakey, sweet formation from the sap of
the tamarisk tree in northern Arabia, also in the Sinai Peninsula, but he admits that the text
identifies manna as a miracle.

69. Referring to himself as the sole burden-bearer might intimate this story's independence
from the Exod. 18 tradition, where Moses, at the advice of his father-in-law, installs Israelite
leaders to alleviate the burden of adjudicating all the people's cases. However, see Num. 11:16.
Later, Deut. 1:9–18 appears to reflect on Num. 11 and/or Exod. 18.

24:17–18).[70] Similar motherly metaphors for Yahweh birthing, nurturing, and protecting Israel appear elsewhere in Scripture.[71]

In a manner like Job and the psalmists, Moses accuses Yahweh of hurting him with the wearisome Israelites and even pleads with Yahweh to put him out of his misery (vv. 11–15).[72] Moses's opening question, "Why *have you hurt* [*hărē'ōtā*] your servant?" or "Why have you done evil/harm to your servant?" is not identical to questioning Yahweh's character, requiring a different construction, "Why are you evil? (see the translation note on 11:11). Moses's raw honesty about Yahweh's painful/evil treatment is here linked lexically by the narrator to his own feelings in v. 10: "and Moses was displeased" (formally, "and in the eyes of Moses it was *evil* [*rā'*]"). In v. 15, the direct object, "Do not let me see *my misery*" (*bərā'ātî*), includes a feminine form of the same root "evil" (*rā'[â]*) and thus culminates this recurring motif in the chapter (1:1, 10, 11 [verb **r''*], 15). Moses's unwillingness to endure this evil from Yahweh can be contrasted with Job's incisive response to his wife: "'Should we accept good from God, but not accept *evil* [*hārā'*]?' In all this Job did not sin with his lips" (Job 2:10c–d). Like Job, Moses believes that Yahweh is sovereignly responsible for both good and harm in his life (as Job 1:21; 2:10). Yet Moses also reveals his belief that he did not have the right to take his own life, but he could beg Yahweh, who holds the power of life and death, to take his life (v. 15; see the translation note there), as Elijah later would (1 Kings 19:4). Moses is clearly angry with the people because they are acting like ungrateful, selfish children, craving and crying because they do not get what they want (vv. 1–3, 4–9).

11:16–20. Yahweh acts immediately to redress the problem of the burdensome people, first by ordering Moses to gather seventy elders so Yahweh can put his spirit on them, then by pledging to give the nostalgic Israelites so much meat that they will become sick. Yahweh's orders to gather seventy of Israel's elders to the meeting tent (v. 16) is reminiscent of the day Yahweh ordered seventy elders, Aaron, Nadab, and Abihu, to accompany Moses, albeit from afar, in worshiping Yahweh, but astonishingly they "saw the God of Israel" (Exod. 24:1–2, 9–10). The number seventy symbolizes fullness,[73] meaning that

---

70. See the first two translation notes on 11:12.

71. See Yahweh/God as a nurturing mother (Hosea 11:3–4), a mother bear robbed of her cubs (Hosea 13:8), an eagle hovering over its young (Deut. 32:11–12), a rock that gave birth to Israel (32:18), a mother of a weaned child (Ps. 131:2), a laboring mother (Isa. 42:14), a nursing mother (49:15), and a comforting mother (66:13). See Yahweh as a father who carries his son (Deut. 1:31) and Jesus as a hen (Matt. 23:37; Luke 13:34); also cf. Ps. 123:2–3; Luke 15:8–10; 1 Thess. 2:7.

72. E.g., Job 3; 6:1–9; Pss. 13; 82:2; 119:84.

73. Gen. 11:26 (Terah's age when fathering Abram); 46:27 (Jacob's family; also Exod. 1:5); 50:3 (days mourning for Jacob); Exod. 15:27 (palm trees at Elim); 24:1, 9 (elders); 38:29 (talents of bronze for the dwelling place); and Num. 7:13–85 (shekel weight of the chieftains' altar gift of sprinkling bowls).

the chosen elders will be sufficient to meet the needs of the people. The next descriptor of these elders, "whom you know are officiating elders among the people" (v. 16; see the second translation note there), differs from Exod. 18, but in a canonical reading, one can imagine these elders as coextensive with the men whom Moses appointed to administer justice for the people (18:25–26). An echo of Jethro's "burden" language (Exod. 18:18, 21–22) can also be heard here in Num. 11:11, 14, 17. Whether Num. 11 fixes Exod. 18 so that Yahweh by the "spirit" remedies the deficiency of a Midianite priest's system or whether Num. 11 is an independent story where Moses is truly alone in his leadership burden, the story is clear that Yahweh is the source of this auxiliary system of traditional tribal leadership to address Moses's inadequacy.[74]

Yahweh promises to put "some of the spirit" (*min-hārûaḥ*) that is on Moses onto the seventy elders to empower them to share Moses's load of caring for the Israelites (cf. 2 Kings 2:9, 15). We should resist superimposing later biblical pneumatology onto this text (see discussion of v. 29), but this does not diminish this text's own rich theology: Yahweh alone holds the prerogative to distribute this spirit to care generously for Moses and his entire covenant people. Yahweh next, through Moses, addresses his complaining people (vv. 18–23). They must consecrate themselves before receiving Yahweh's meat provision the next day (v. 18; see the first translation note there), just as they had consecrated themselves at Mount Sinai before the theophany (Exod. 19:10, 22). These orders should frighten them, not only because of the potential of an imminent, terrifying manifestation of Yahweh (Exod. 19; Lev. 9:24), but because "it also intimates that the coming sacrifice will be Israel" (Num. 11:33–34).[75] Yahweh has heard and interpreted their cry as a failure to depend on him and as an ungrateful, irrational nostalgia for Egypt: "*Who will give us meat to eat, for life was good for us in Egypt?*" (v. 18e–f). These two sins are reiterated by Yahweh in v. 20 to explain his judgment: "[1] You have rejected Yahweh, who is among you, and you cried before him, saying, [2] 'Why did we ever leave Egypt?'" (see the second translation note on v. 20). Yahweh's patience toward Moses is contrasted with his impatience toward the people when he expresses his intent to nauseate the Israelites with an overwhelming quantity of meat (vv. 18e–20; see the first translation note on v. 20). The situational irony becomes obvious: "We craved meat without turning to Yahweh, and now Yahweh has given us so much meat that we want to vomit."[76]

11:21–30. After an interchange in which Yahweh forcefully declares his sufficiency to a doubting Moses, Yahweh puts some of the spirit that was on

---

74. See Reviv, "Traditions," 570–72. Kilchör (*Mosetora*, 204, following Pearce, *Words of Moses*, 46–48) sees the laws for installing a local judiciary in Deut. 16:18–20 as a continuation of both Exod. 18:13–27 and Num. 11:14–17.

75. Milgrom, *Numbers*, 88.

76. See Garmendia, *Irony*, 5.

Moses onto the seventy elders, who then meet with Yahweh and prophesy. To Yahweh's acrimonious speech (vv. 16–20), Moses retorts with his doubts that Yahweh can feed 600,000 Israelites in the desert: "But you say 'I will give them meat to eat for a whole month!" (cf. Mark 8:4).[77] His questions in v. 22 are hyperbolic and imply a negative answer: Would slaughtering flocks and herds provide enough food? Would catching all the fish in the sea be sufficient to feed them?[78] In a canonical reading, it seems that Moses has repressed his memory of Yahweh's powerful signs and wonders in Egypt, the exodus and provision of quail and manna in the Sin wilderness (see below). Yahweh does not put Moses to death for his brazen faithlessness, but he does silence him: "Is Yahweh's hand too short? Now you will see if my word to you will come true or not!" (v. 23). An echo can be heard from the time Moses questioned Yahweh's power to deliver the Israelites: "Now you will see what I will do to Pharaoh!" (Exod. 6:1b). Jesus, likewise, rebukes his followers: "You of little faith, why did you doubt?" (Matt. 14:31 NRSV).

Moses then tells the people what Yahweh said and obediently gathers the seventy elders and stations them around Yahweh's tent (Num. 11:24).[79] Yahweh descends in the cloud and speaks to them, just as he had been accustomed to doing with Moses (v. 25).[80] After setting aside some of the spirit on Moses and putting it on the seventy elders, that spirit rested on them, and they prophesied at that time but never again (v. 25; see the second translation note there). The same verbal form of "prophesy" used here appears also when Saul turned into a different person in a prophetic frenzy (hithpael of *nb'),[81] but here there is no evidence that the elders who prophesied entered into an ecstatic experience (Num. 11:25).[82] Rather, this nonrepeatable ritual functioned as a rite of passage for the elders, with prophecy as the "ritual mark" through which they were "reborn" into their new function in Israelite society.[83] Understanding this prophesying as a ritual mark, the intent of the rite was not to convert the elders into prophets[84] but to publicly validate their Mosaic (same spirit) authority to "carry some of the burden of the people" (v. 17). In the HB, only here and in 2 Kings 2, where Elisha receives a double

---

77. The number is 600,000 in Exod. 12:37; cf. 603,550 in Num. 1 and 601,730 in Num. 26; see Olson, *Death of the Old*, 79.

78. Does "the sea" (*hayyām*) here refer to the Sea of Reeds (Red Sea?), Mediterranean or Salt (Dead) Sea, or most likely the Gulf of Aqaba/Elath (cf. Ps. 78:20; Milgrom, *Numbers*, 92)?

79. Alleviating the leadership burden (vv. 16–17, 24–30) may be secondary to the original food problem that frames the whole account (vv. 4–9, 31–34): Knierim and Coats, *Numbers*, 175.

80. Exod. 19:18, 20; 24:15–18; 34:5; also Num. 12:5.

81. 1 Sam. 10:6, 10–13; Jer. 29:26; cf. *muhhu*, the Mesopotamian title for an ecstatic prophet (Walton and Matthews, *Genesis–Deuteronomy*, 186).

82. Levison, "Prophecy," 503–21; contra Albertz, *Israelite Religion*, 2:479.

83. Vartejanu-Joubert, "Les 'anciens du peuple,'" 542–63.

84. Similarly, Saul's prophetic activity did not make him a prophet, but it served to validate his kingship (1 Sam. 10).

portion of "the spirit of Elijah," does a personal spirit serve as the source of conferring authority on new leadership (cf. John 20:22–23).[85] However, since Moses's communicative relationship with Yahweh remained unparalleled (Exod. 33:11; Num. 7:89),[86] the elders became something akin to scribes insofar as they were to "govern by interpreting and applying the revelation received by Moses to Israel's life in the camp."[87]

The narrator next describes a surprising turn of events. Two men, identified by name as Eldad and Medad, were not with the seventy elders at the meeting tent but were somewhere in the surrounding camp with the rest of the Israelites with whom they had been registered in the first census (v. 26).[88] "The spirit rested on them" as well is the same expression that described the elders' experience (qal *nwḥ* + *ʿălêhem hārûaḥ*, vv. 25, 26). The determinate subject "the spirit" (*hārûaḥ*, v. 26) is anaphoric and refers back to "some of the spirit that was on him [Moses]" (v. 25). Like the seventy, the two men also prophesy (v. 26), but unlike the seventy, they prophesy *in the Israelite camp*. The suspense of this anomaly builds: Is Yahweh behind this, or will his anger burn hotter still (vv. 1, 10, 18–20)?

The scene intensifies further with the insertion of two foil characters whose interjections reveal their strong concerns.[89] The first character, unnamed, functions as an Aristotelian agent, acting only to advance the plot:[90] "And a young man ran and told Moses, 'Eldad and Medad are prophesying in the camp!'" This young man (*naʿar*) was not among the elders (*hazzəqēnîm*), and because he *ran* from the camp, we may infer that his remark was exclamatory. The next interjector, however, is not only an agent but also a stereotype of loyalty to Moses and Yahweh: "Then Nun's son Joshua, who had been Moses's assistant from his youth, said, 'My lord Moses, stop them!'" (v. 28).[91] Unlike the runner (v. 27), Joshua is inferably stationed at Moses's side with the elders. Nun's son Joshua is not only named, honoring him, but also described as a lifelong assistant to the great prophet Moses, recalling for the reader his devotion to Moses and Yahweh since his appearance in the post-exodus stories before and at Sinai.[92] There we are told that after Moses finished meeting with Yahweh in the (antecedent) meeting tent, "his assistant, Nun's son Joshua, a young man, did not leave the tent" (Exod. 33:11). In light of Joshua's trustworthiness, the narrative suspense is thick (v. 28). The scenes of vv. 1–3 and vv. 4–23 are now compounded with the

---

85. Weisman, "Personal Spirit," 225–34.
86. See Gunneweg, "Das Gesetz," 175.
87. Dozeman, "Numbers," 112.
88. See Num. 1–2 for the census and meeting-tent-centric arrangement.
89. Alter, *Biblical Narrative*, 87.
90. See Berlin, "Characterization," 73.
91. See Berlin, "Characterization," 76–78.
92. Exod. 17:9–13; 24:13; 32:17.

interjections of these two distraught loyalists, signaling that the future of Eldad and Medad is ominous.[93]

Astoundingly, instead of affirming Joshua, Moses rebukes him:[94] "Are you jealous for me? I wish that all Yahweh's people were prophets, that Yahweh would put his spirit on them!" (v. 29). Moses seems to perceive Joshua's good intentions, a jealousy for the benefit of Moses's honor.[95] That is, Joshua apparently concluded that Eldad and Medad received not "some of the spirit" that was on Moses (v. 25) but some other negative spirit.[96] However, good intentions based on wrong thinking are still wrong. Here Moses reveals his true character, showing that although he was a charismatic (spirit-empowered) leader, he was not an elitist (cf. Num. 12:3).[97] He wished all the Israelites could experience the privilege of serving as true prophets animated by Yahweh's own spirit (v. 29; cf. 1 Cor. 14:5). In the minds of Moses and the authors of this story, the "spirit" (*rûaḥ*) of Yahweh is not the Third Person of the Trinity clarified later in biblical revelation but a force emanating from Yahweh that comes upon and possesses an individual who, consequently, delivers Yahweh's prophetic message (see the translation note on 24:2). This story teaches that Yahweh's spirit and the prophetic office cannot be institutionalized: Yahweh is open to democratizing access to his spirit by his own sovereign choice.[98]

In the biblical narrative, Moses's desire for all of God's people to be spirit-filled prophets is actualized when God fulfills Joel's prophecy in a surprising way on the day of Pentecost in Jerusalem (Acts 2:17; Joel 2:28–29). In alignment with Moses's conviction, Jesus teaches the advantage of the Spirit, and Luke presents the Spirit's prophetic ministry through God's people.[99] As Moses challenged Joshua, so Jesus challenged his close disciple, John, who was similarly concerned about spiritual activity in Jesus's name outside Jesus's cohort of disciples: "'Do not stop him. . . . For whoever is not against us is for us'" (Mark 9:39–40* NET).

Moses and the elders return to the camp, which closes out the scene but also finalizes their Mosaic authority in the estimation of the Israelites looking on (v. 30).

93. See Sternberg, *Poetics*, 265–67.

94. "Him" refers here to Joshua because of the sg. pronouns: "*to him* [*lô*], '*Are you jealous* [*hamqannē' 'attâ*]?'"

95. Like Phinehas later; see the first translation note on 11:29.

96. I.e., a spirit of the dead (Lev. 20:27); a spirit that stirs hostility from Yahweh (Judg. 9:23; Jer. 28:11); a deceiving spirit (1 Kings 22:21); a spirit of idolatry (Hosea 5:4); an evil spirit from God/Yahweh (1 Sam. 16:14–15; 18:10; 19:9).

97. On charismatic leadership in Numbers, see Frevel, *Desert Transformations*, 379–424.

98. See Christian, "Middle-Tier Levites," 192n78. Albertz (*Israelite Religion*, 2:480) sees democratization as a possibility only for the distant future, but he notes a similar vision for all Israel as "a kingdom of priests" (Exod. 19:6).

99. E.g., John 16:7–15; Acts 1:5–8. For connecting the Spirit and prophecy, see, e.g., Acts 11:28; 19:2–6; 1 Cor. 12–14.

11:31–35. Yahweh sends a wind that drops an incalculable number of quail, which the Israelites consume, and Yahweh again burns in anger and sends a lethal plague. Now the reader can perceive that the basic plotline of the stories in Exod. 16 and 18 is distributed across the two stories of Num. 11:1–3 and 4–35:

Table 11.1. Exodus 16 and 18 and Numbers 11 Compared

Exodus 16 and 18	Numbers 11
Israelites complain (16:2)	Israelites complain (v. 1)
Israelites crave foods they ate in Egypt (16:3)	Israelites crave foods they ate in Egypt (vv. 5–6)
Yahweh promises manna (16:4–5)	Manna mentioned, described, Israel gathers (vv. 6b–8)
Theophany announced (16:6–7)	
Moses announces meat, reprimands them for complaining (16:8–9)	People weep and Yahweh and Moses get angry (v. 10),
Theophany before the community (16:10)	
Yahweh promises and provides quail and bread (16:11–12)	
Israel gathers, manna described, *Sabbath condition and memorial manna (16:13–36)*	
Israel eats manna 40 years until Canaan (16:35)	
Moses explains his burden of the people to Jethro, who advises Moses to appoint judges to mediate cases (Exod. 18)	Moses prays his burden to Yahweh, who appoints 70 elders, who receive the spirit and prophesy (vv. 16–17, 24–30)
	Yahweh promises, provides quail (vv. 18–23, 31–33)
	40 years until Canaan (Num. 14:33–34; Josh. 5:12)

Although Num. 11 overlaps thematically and sometimes lexically with Exod. 16, the narrator gives no sense that Yahweh had provided quail before, so at least this scene in vv. 31–34 must be read on its own terms.[100] Yahweh had placed a *rûaḥ* (spirit) on Moses and had set aside some of it to place on

---

100. Boorer (*Priestly Narrative*, 377–83) argues that Pᵍ drew from Num. 11:4–34* to formulate Exod. 16, whereas Römer ("Egypt Nostalgia," 76) sees Num. 11* as midrashically continuing the manna-quail story of Exod. 16 to stress the people's permanent rebellion. Similarly, Frevel ("Alte Stücke," 298) sees in Num. 11–12, 16–17, 20, 31 indications of haggadic exegesis of texts in Exod. 15–19, 32–34, and Lev. 10, without differing significantly; cf. Scharbert, *Numeri*, 47; Van Seters, *Life of Moses*, 189–91.

the elders.[101] Now a *rûaḥ* (wind) sourced in Yahweh sets out and brings quail from the sea,[102] probably the Gulf of Aqaba (v. 31; on "the sea," see the note to the comments on 11:22). The Red Sea is also a possibility, as even today "Small, plump migratory quail often come through the Sinai on their way north from the Sudan to Europe, usually in the months of March and April. They generally fly with the wind and are driven to the ground (or water) if caught in a crosswind."[103] In the story, the wind forces the quail to fly in from the sea, drop a day's journey from the camp on every side, and pile up three feet deep on the ground (v. 31; see the translation notes there). The people gather quail all day, through the night, and through the next day; those who gathered the fewest collected the equivalent of 400 liters of quail![104] The point is that Yahweh had provided a huge surplus, which should have prompted the Israelites to stop to give thanks and rejoice in Yahweh, but instead the people are preoccupied with gathering excessive quantities of quail and spreading them out all around the camp "for themselves" (*lāhem*), for their own benefit (v. 32; see the last translation note there).[105] They begin to sink their teeth into the meat, "but when the meat was still between their teeth, before they chewed it, Yahweh's anger burned against the people, and Yahweh struck the people with a very severe plague" (v. 33). By casting the people like ravenous animals, presumably tearing into the raw quail meat with their teeth, the narrator has formed a plot *inclusio* with the craving mob among them who yelled "Who will give us meat to eat!'" (v. 4). In narrative poetic verse, the psalmist reflects on this and related sagas as a negative motivation to trust and obey Yahweh who has shown his power to rescue and provide for his covenant people (Ps. 78:18–32; cf. 105:40). God does "spread a table in the wilderness" (Ps. 78:19), more like an incomparably prodigious feast for which his people should burst out with thanksgiving and song: "To the one who gives food/meat to every living thing, for his loyal love endures forever! Give thanks to the God of heaven, for his loyal love endures forever!" (Ps. 136:25–26, my trans.).

Just as naming the site Taberah (Burning) reframed vv. 1–3 as an etiology—how it came to be so named—and as an enduring warning against complaining, so also naming the place Kibroth Hattaavah (Graves of Craving) "because there they buried the people who had a craving" (v. 34) forms an *inclusio* with v. 4 and reframes vv. 4–34 as an etiology and a warning against craving with

---

101. *Rûaḥ* in vv. 17, 25 [2×], 26, 29.

102. *Min* of source (*GBHS* §4.1.13).

103. Walton and Matthews, *Genesis–Deuteronomy*, 186. Aristotle (*History of Animals* 8.2; in *Works of Aristotle*, 1:934) explains how quail fly comfortably with northerly winds, but southerly winds adversely affect their ability to fly because of their heavy bodies, making it an ideal time for trappers. Pliny the Elder (1st cent. CE) also describes quail swarms (Staubli, *Levitikus, Numeri*, 247).

104. See the third translation note on 11:32.

105. Quasi-datival *l* of advantage (*GBHS* §4.1.10.e.1).

ingratitude (see the second translation note on 11:34; cf. 1 Cor. 10:6).[106] Upon arriving at v. 34, the reader now sees most fully that the redactional juxtaposition of Num. 10 and 11 illuminates a contrast of competing memories of Israel's past, as shown by Leveen:[107]

Table 11.2. Numbers 10 and 11 Compared

Numbers 10	Numbers 11
The present anticipating the future	The past
The voice of God and Moses	The voice of the people raised in complaint
An unfamiliar, new life of Israelite law and practice	The familiar old life
The promised land	Egypt (its food as the desired object)
God's protection of the people	God's attack on the people
Rewards	Punishments
Life	Death

Moving from chap. 10 to chap. 11 raises serious questions about Israel's future life with Yahweh. At the same time, Yahweh's care for his people in sustaining them, maintaining peace and order among them, endures.[108] This theological focus of Num. 11, not geographic or otherwise, is also seen in the placement of the geographic notes of vv. 34–35. Until v. 34, the reader did not know that the Israelites had moved from Taberah (Burning), and now in v. 35 the people travel to Hazeroth (Settlements; see the second translation note on 11:35a).[109] What is perhaps most striking is the absence of any mention of either the cloud (10:12) or the ark of the covenant (10:33–36), raising the question: Is Yahweh still leading his people, or has Israel, even before the curse of 14:20–35, already begun their forty years of wandering aimlessly without Yahweh's guidance, only to die off in the desert?

Implications

Complaining as Covenant Violation

The first story in Num. 11 depicts the Israelites as *complaining* in Yahweh's ears about their hardship (v. 1). The reciprocal force of the verb "complain"

---

106. W. Lee, *Migratory Campaign*, 127–29.

107. Leveen, "Variations," 220.

108. Wellhausen, *Prolegomena*, 346.

109. As Frevel (*Mit Blick*, 256) notes, Deut. 1:9–18 presents the Num. 11 account as occurring while Israel is still at Horeb (Sinai). This becomes clear only when reading the travel notice of Num. 12:16 in light of 10:12–28 (see the comments on 12:16).

189

('*nn* hithpolel)[110] means they complained among themselves.[111] The second story describes the people *craving* (v. 4; see the second translation note there), complaining of being "dried up" (v. 6), *weeping* with nostalgia for Egypt (v. 10), and disgusted by their monotonous diet from Yahweh: "We see nothing but this manna!" (v. 6; see the second translation note there). Then, when Yahweh does lavishly provide quail, the people stockpile the birds and begin to tear into the meat without a word of thanks to Yahweh (vv. 32–33). To the modern reader, these displays of ingratitude may seem rude at best, repulsive at worst. Such actions from a child today invite a parent's verbal rebuke, followed by some form of discipline. So why, then, does Yahweh respond so violently toward the complainers, burning them to death in the first saga, infesting them with a mortal disease in the second? One could jump to the conclusion that Yahweh's holiness has almost instinctively incited his wrath, and this may well be true. But unlike cultic passages such as 4:15–20, which required the Kohathites to be executed if they were even to glimpse the sacred furniture uncovered, here nothing is said of sacred objects or holy places.[112]

The best explanation for Yahweh's deadly anger toward the complaining Israelites comes from Yahweh's own lips in Num. 11:20, "because you have *rejected* [*m's*] Yahweh who is among you and cried before him, saying, 'Why did we ever leave Egypt?'"[113] This question, found only here as Yahweh's interpretive paraphrase, reveals that "the people rejected the exodus and thus their God."[114] The severity of complaining against their deity's goodness—against his redemption from Egypt and ongoing providential care in the desert—is clarified by the ANE political context. Among Israel's neighbors was a well-established practice of drafting contracts and treaties in which the king would pledge on oath to assassinate his subjects who complain against him or his heir. For example, in a treaty with the Aziru (14th cent. BCE), Šuppiluliuma, king of Hatti, pronounces the curse of the oath's gods to destroy any subject (even a Hittite), along with their family members, who maligns the king or fails to depend on him for provision.[115] Mendenhall elucidates at least the first of these stipulations: "The vassal must hold lasting and unlimited trust in the [Hittite] King; he must not entertain malicious rumors that the King is acting disloyally toward the vassal ("since man is depraved"), nor must he permit any evil words against the King, for this is the beginning of rebellion."[116] The tradition evolves into Neo-Assyrian treaty and loyalty oath forms. In the

110. See "'*nn*," *DCH* 1:344; *HALOT* 1:72.
111. *GBHS* 58, §3.1.5b.
112. For the "holy" (**qdš*) objects as a submotif in 4:2–20, see vv. 4, 15, 19, 20; also "holy place" (*qōdeš*, 4:16). See the "Implications" essay in chap. 4, "The Holiness of God Is Lethal."
113. See Leveen, *Memory*, 84.
114. Römer, "Egypt Nostalgia," 77.
115. "Treaty Between Šuppiluliuma and Aziru," *COS* 2.17A:95.
116. Mendenhall, "Covenant Forms," 59.

Accession Treaty of Esarhaddon (7th cent. BCE), the king demands that his subjects swear allegiance to him, not just in their actions, but also in their words: "I [will] be [his servant] and speak good of him, I [will be] loyal to him and [. . . the *fa*]*ce* of Esarhaddon my lord, [. . .]."[117] As in Num. 11:33, one of the curses for breaking this oath is a divine plague that afflicts his people: "[May Nergal, *the strongest among the gods*,] destroy [his] people through plague and pestilence [. . .]"[118] An Aramaic treaty from Sefire (mid-8th cent. BCE) also indicts malicious speech that incites an attack against the king, "[And if] one of (the) kings [should speak a word] against me, . . . you will have been unfaith[ful to the trea]ty which is in this inscription,"[119] and the unfaithful person will be cursed and variously destroyed by the gods.

These few examples suffice to show that speaking maliciously against the sovereign king was regarded as a breach of the treaty or of the loyalty oath. This likely forms the ideological backdrop of Num. 11. Israel had entered into a covenant treaty (*bᵊrît*) with their divine king Yahweh (Exod. 19–24),[120] and the scribes who composed Num. 11 assume that this covenant relationship was operational.[121] Perhaps the Israelite subgroups thought they had impunity because their actions—complaining (v. 1), craving Egypt's foods and disdaining manna (vv. 4–9), weeping (v. 10), and consuming without giving thanks (v. 33)—were known only to themselves. However, the narrator makes clear for the first story (vv. 1–3), and it is implied in the second (vv. 4–34), that the people "complained evil in Yahweh's ears, and Yahweh heard" (v. 1). In effect, the Israelites were communicating disdain for Yahweh and would rather get what they wanted, when they wanted it, and how they wanted it. Whether or not they maligned Yahweh's name audibly (as in Lev. 24:11), the evil words they articulated offended their sovereign deity, provoking him to judgment. The story of Num. 11 is connected to Exod. 16:2–36,[122] where this theology was already made plain: "Your grumbling is not against us, but against Yahweh. . . . Come before Yahweh because he has heard your grumblings" (Exod. 16:8–9*). In a canonical reading, complainers in Israel received several layers of divine grace in Exod. 16, but in Num. 11 Yahweh's patience runs out (cf. Exod. 34:6–7), and he begins to give Israel a taste of the curses for violating the covenant (Exod. 23:21; Lev. 26:14–39).

117. "SAA 02 004. Accession Treaty of Esarhaddon (JCS 39 187)," http://oracc.museum
.upenn.edu/saao/saa02/corpus.

118. "SAA 02 004. Accession Treaty of Esarhaddon (JCS 39 187)," http://oracc.museum
.upenn.edu/saao/saa02/corpus.

119. "The Inscriptions of Bar-Ga'yah and Mati'el from Sefire," COS 2.82:215.

120. Royal imagery in Exod. 19:3–6; cf. throughout the Song of the Sea (Exod. 15).

121. Achenbach (*Vollendung*, 635) subdivides Num. 11 into pre-Dtr source, the Hexateuchal and Pentateuchal redactions, all of which presumed the covenant (in contrast to P and the alleged theocratic revision); Levine (*Numbers 1–20*, 319) attributes Num. 11 to JE (similarly de Vaulx, *Nombres*, 148–49, who adds his L, popular etymologies).

122. Seebass, *Numeri*, 1:47–54.

It is crucial to see the distinction between Israel's complaining *to one another* implicitly or explicitly about God (Num. 11) and complaining or lamenting *to God* with the conviction that God has the power to rescue, sustain, and vindicate his covenant people (as in Ps. 44:17; Rev. 6:10b). Those who trust in and follow Israel's Messiah, Jesus of Nazareth, will ultimately never face divine condemnation for anything they do (commission) or do not do (omission) to violate the terms of the covenant (Rom. 8:1; Heb. 8:8–13). Yet just as in Num. 11, complaining to others, rather than crying out in distress to God, is a serious violation for the new-covenant community. Paul connects complaining (or grumbling) and arguing (or disputing) as blameworthy, affecting the church's light in the world and Paul's own experience on the day of Christ (Phil 2:14–16; cf. 1 Pet. 4:9). Unbelievers will be marked by complaining and ingratitude, understandably so, because they do not recognize God's overwhelming goodness in creation, redemption, or providential care in their daily lives.[123] The opposite habit, incessantly giving thanks to God through Christ, must characterize Christ's followers now and forever.[124]

---

123. E.g., Luke 6:35; Rom. 1:21; 2 Tim. 3:2.
124. E.g., Matt. 15:36; 26:27; Mark 8:7–8; 14:23; Luke 2:38; 17:16; 22:17, 19; John 6:11, 23; Acts 24:3; 27:35; Rom. 6:17; 7:25; 14:6; 16:4; 1 Cor. 1:4; 10:30; 11:24; 14:16–17; 15:57; 2 Cor. 1:11; 2:14; 4:15; 8:16; 9:11, 15; Eph. 1:16; 5:4, 20; Phil. 4:6; Col. 1:12; 2:7; 3:15–17; 4:2; 1 Thess. 1:2; 3:9; 5:18; 2 Thess. 1:3; 2:13; 1 Tim. 4:3–4; Rev. 4:9; 7:12; 11:17.

12

Miriam and Aaron
Speak against Moses

(12:1–16)

∽◯∾

Overview

On the very first leg of Israel's journey toward Canaan, as they set up camp in the Paran wilderness (10:12, 33), the community rebels by complaining, which results in Yahweh's burning anger and lethal judgment (11:1–34). Yahweh ordains elders to alleviate the burden that the people have become to Moses (11:16–17, 24–30). But gaps in the reader's knowledge persist. While complaining about hardships and cravings is clearly ruled out of bounds for the covenant community, might Yahweh condone some of Israel's leaders if they were to criticize Moses? Does Yahweh elevate the elders to Moses's own stratum of authority in the community? These questions are resolved by the saga of Num. 12.[1] With the Israelites now encamped at their second site after Sinai, Hazeroth (11:35), Moses's older siblings, Miriam and Aaron, speak against Moses because of his questionable marriage to a Cushite woman and their sense of being undervalued as Yahweh's intermediaries (12:1–2). By contrast, the narrator venerates Moses (v. 3), followed by Yahweh's affirmation of Moses in an unequivocal way, first by a theophany especially intended

1. Knierim and Coats (*Numbers*, 181) identify the genre of chap. 12 as a story of rebellion, but originally it was a legend. Numbers 12:1–15 was conventionally considered a composite JE (de Vaulx, *Nombres*, 158–59; Van Seters, *Life of Moses*, 234–39; Scharbert, *Numeri*, 51–53). While Römer ("Israel's Sojourn," 436, 440, 442–43) sees it as post-P, most view it as pre-P with P (or other) additions (Noth, *Numbers*, 93; Budd, *Numbers*, 133–34; Dozeman, "Numbers," 108–9; Levine, *Numbers*, 1:311, 333). Achenbach (*Vollendung*, 267–301, 635) divides Num. 12 between the Hexateuch and Pentateuch redactors.

for Miriam and Aaron (vv. 4–5) and then by a monologue about Moses's unequalled relationship to Yahweh (vv. 6–7). Ensuing from Yahweh's burning anger—a motif that has been accruing from chap. 11—Yahweh, one infers, subjects Miriam to a grotesque skin disease (v. 10); then Aaron pleads with Moses, and Moses with Yahweh, to heal her (vv. 11–13). Again, the reader infers that Yahweh does graciously heal her even though she must remain in seven-day isolation outside the camp according to purification law (vv. 15–16). The discursive unit is circumscribed by the *inclusio* of the travel notices in 11:35a (Kibroth Hattaavah→Hazeroth) and 12:16 (Hazeroth→Paran wilderness). This sojourn at Hazeroth teaches the Israelites that Moses is without peer in his remarkable relationship with Yahweh and in his status above the seventy elders and above Moses's siblings. Criticizing Yahweh's great prophet is something like scraping the apple of Yahweh's eye and provokes his divine wrath.

Translation

12:1 [11:35b]While they were at Hazeroth,[2] **[12:1]**Miriam and Aaron spoke against Moses[3] because of the Cushite woman he had married[4] (for he had married a Cushite woman).[5] **2**They said, "Has Yahweh spoken only through Moses? Hasn't he also spoken through us?" And Yahweh heard it. **3**Now the man Moses was very[6] humble,[7] more than anyone on the face of the earth.[8] **4**Immediately Yahweh spoke to Moses, Aaron, and Miriam: "You three come out to the meeting tent." So the three of them went out. **5**And Yahweh came down in a pillar of cloud, and he stood[9] at the tent's entrance. He called Aaron and Miriam, and they both came forward.

2. On reading "While they were at Hazeroth" (11:35b) as introducing 12:1–16, see the translation notes on 11:35a.

3. An adversative *b*, "spoke *against* Moses [*bəmōšeh*]" (*GBHS* §4.1.5d; see Num. 12:8; 21:5, 7; Jer. 31:20; Pss. 50:20; 78:19).

4. LXX^ed clarifies "whom *Moyses* [*Mōusēs*] had taken (married)" (> 4Q27 MT SP Tg^O).

5. Here the parentheses (NRSV, NET) mark the editor's explanation to readers, who were either aware of Zipporah's Midianite origins (Exod. 2–18*) or unaware that he married a Cushite (12:1a).

6. 4Q23 spells *məʾōd* (very) as *mʾdh* (reconstructed [*mʾ]dh*); cf. *mʾdh* in 4Q22 of Exod. 12:38.

7. MT^ketiv is *ʿānāw* (with SP), and MT^qere is *ʿānāyw*. The sense "bowed" down is lost (contra *HALOT* 2:855). Also, Moses was "humble, meek," not "poor" or "miserable" (*DCH* 6:502, gloss 2).

8. "On the face of the earth" (*ʿal-pənê hā'ădāmâ*) does not connote the globe, because only after the Greeks, maybe first Pythagoras (6th cent. BCE), did the earth begin to be thought of as a sphere. Instead, the ancient Israelites inherited the Mesopotamian conception that the earth was a flat disc that floated in the ocean, over which hung a hemispherical sky dome (Gen. 1:6–10, with *rāqîaʿ* [firmament] as the sky dome; Walton, *Ancient Near Eastern Thought*, 165–78).

9. Yahweh is the implied subject of this wayyiqtol, "and he stood" (*wayyaʿămōd*), as it follows sequentially after the wayyiqtol, "And Yahweh came down" (*GBHS* §3.5.1a). The anthropomorphism of Yahweh *standing* at the entrance of his dwelling place may be contrasted with

6Yahweh[10] said,[11] "Listen to my words: If there is a prophet of Yahweh among you, I will make myself known[12] to him in a vision. I will speak with him in a dream. **7**It is not this way with my servant Moses. He is entrusted with my whole house.[13] **8**I speak[14] with him face-to-face,[15] in an appearance[16] and not in riddles,[17] and he looks[18] at the form of Yahweh.[19]

---

the terrifying creatures (non-deities) that stood at the entrances of Mesopotamian temples to guard the deity's abode, or compared with statues of an Egyptian pharaoh, who incarnated the God Horus (then became Osiris after death), standing outside a temple's pylon, or with an ANE aniconic (imageless) standing stone that functioned as a point of access to the deity, seemingly "as a vessel of potential manifestation [of a deity] or more generally as an accessible element in the divine constellation" (Hundley, *Gods in Dwellings*, 27, 73, 347–49, 357).

10. "He said" (*wayyō'mer* MT SP LXX^ABC) is original, but in 4Q27 "*Yahweh* [*yhwh*] said" helpfully clarifies the subject (*kyrios*, LXX^L et al.).

11. 4Q27 and LXX^ed include "Yahweh said *to them*," possibly restricting the audience to Aaron and Miriam from v. 5c–d.

12. The hithpael is reflexive: "I will make myself known" (*'etwaddā'*; *GBHS* §3.1.5[a]). SP, probably by homophony, reads a 3rd masc. sg. "(Yahweh) will make himself known" (*htwd'*, vocalized *hitwaddā'*), which awkwardly shifts from Yahweh as the speaker (v. 5) and breaks the first-person parallelism (v. 6cβ).

13. **'Mn* niphal can be either a passive with a specification *b* ("he *is entrusted with* my entire house, *bəkol-bêtî ne'ĕmān hû'*) or stative with a spatial *b* ("he *is faithful in* my entire house"; *GBHS* §3.1.2a, d; §4.1.5a, e; *DCH* 1:314). I prefer "is entrusted with" (Seebass, *Numeri*, 2:58; Ashley, *Numbers*, 221; Budd, *Numbers*, 132; EÜ, NRSV) because everything else Yahweh says in vv. 6–8 concerns his self-directed communication with Moses, without mentioning Moses's character or actions (but see v. 3).

14. The yiqtol, "I speak" (*'ădabber*), has a customary force, meaning Yahweh customarily or frequently speaks with Moses (*GBHS* §3.2.2b).

15. Formally, "mouth to mouth" (*pe 'el-pe* ≈ LXX^ed *stoma kata stoma*; ESV, NJPS, EÜ; de Vaulx, *Nombres*, 160; Cazelles, *Nombres*, 68), but in contemporary English the phrase paints an awkward image, so "face-to-face" is preferred (NRSV, NLT, NET).

16. I prefer "in an appearance" (*bammar'â* 4Q27 MT^mss SP; *en eidei*, in visible form, LXX^ed) over either reading with a conjunction *w* (*wbmr'h* 4Q23; *wmr'h* MT^L, following Ulrich, *Qumran*, 144, who corrects the *BHS* error). Rather than convert this phrase into an adv. "clearly, openly, plainly" (many versions) to contrast with "in riddles," the rendering "in an appearance" (*bammar'â*) underscores the theophanic mode of communication (Schmidt, *Numeri*, 28; even "face to face" for EÜ; or adv. "visibly" for de Vaulx, *Nombres*, 160; but not "as a saying" for Seebass, *Numeri*, 2:58). If, however, one adopts *wbmr'h* (4Q23) or *wmr'h* (MT^L), then alternatives could be in view: "I speak with him face-to-face, *neither* in an appearance, *nor* in riddles, but he gazes at the form of Yahweh" (*BHRG* §40.23.4.1[2]; Ashley, *Numbers*, 221).

17. This is the only occurrence in the Pentateuch of "riddle, ambiguous saying" ("*ḥîdâ*," *HALOT* 1:309; pl. with instrumental *b*: "by means of riddles" *bəḥîdōt*). "Riddle" (*ḥîdâ*) occurs next as a *Leitwort* in Judges 14 (vv. 12, 13, 14, 15, 16, 17, 18, 19).

18. The hiphil "he looks" (*yabbîṭ*) is not necessarily an intensification ("beholds," ESV, NRSV, NJPS) but probably indicates that Moses looks in a particular direction, namely, *at* Yahweh's form (with "*nbṭ*," *HALOT* 2:661, gloss 2). There is no reason to interpret the yiqtol as fut. ("he will see," NET), since the synthetic parallelism is with Yahweh, who "speaks" customarily with Moses (v. 8a).

19. On "the form of Yahweh" (*təmunat yhwh*), see the "Implications" essay below, "Did Moses See Yahweh?"

Why then were you not afraid to speak against my servant Moses?"
⁹Yahweh's anger burned against them, and he left.

¹⁰When the cloud departed from above the tent, Miriam's skin had a disease²⁰ like snow. Then Aaron looked at Miriam, and she had a skin disease!²¹ ¹¹So Aaron said to Moses, "O my lord, do not hold this sin against us, which we have so foolishly committed! ¹²Do not let her be like a stillborn baby, whose flesh is half eaten away when it comes out of its mother's womb!" ¹³Then Moses cried to Yahweh, "O God,²² heal her now!" ¹⁴Yahweh said to Moses, "If her father had only spit in her face, would she not have been shamed²³ for seven days? She must be shut outside²⁴ the camp seven days, and afterward she can be brought back in again." ¹⁵So Miriam was shut outside the camp for seven days, and the people did not travel²⁵ until Miriam was brought back in.²⁶

¹⁶After that the people traveled from Hazeroth and camped in the Paran wilderness.²⁷

Interpretation

12:1 [11:35b]–5. Moses's older siblings, Miriam and Aaron, speak against Moses because of his questionable marriage, but Yahweh responds by appearing to them in a theophany at his meeting tent. Following their arrival at Hazeroth, a place name that means "settlements," the narrator probably

20. Pual ptc., formally, "Miriam was skin diseased" (*məṣōraʿat*). Not leprosy, perhaps eczema or psoriasis (Walton and Matthews, *Genesis–Deuteronomy*, 187). See the third translation note on 5:2.

21. Formally, "then Aaron turned to Miriam, and behold she was skin diseased."

22. On *ʾēl* (God), see comments on 12:13 below.

23. This verb occurs in the Pentateuch only here, meaning "be humiliated, be ashamed, be put to shame, be confounded" (niphal pass. of "*klm*," *DCH* 4:426; *HALOT* 2:480).

24. The niphal pass. of **sgr*, a form that occurs only here in vv. 14 and 15 in the Torah, is a yiqtol with the force of a strong injunction: "She must be shut (outside)" (*tissāgēr*; *GBHS* §3.2.2d.4). The typical agent, the priest, can be supplied from Lev. 13–14, where the priest alone was to shut out the diseased person whom he had examined (**sgr* hiphil occurs 11× in Lev. 13–14). Aaron the high priest has in effect examined Miriam's skin (vv. 11–12), but the narrator leaves it ambiguous whether Aaron personally shuts her out since he is indicted with her for speaking against Moses (vv. 1–9).

25. Possibly harmonizing to 11:35a, SP writes a pl. predicate, "they traveled" (vocalized *nāsʿū* ≈ pl. *nṭlw* Tg^Neo) for a collective sg., "the people" (*hāʿām*; *BHRG* §35[3]), while the sg. predicate occurs in MT LXX^ed Tg^O PJ.

26. SP (*h'sph*) is a solecism (niphal inf. const. not inflected for gender), and LXX^ed reads "and the people did not set out until *Mariam was cleansed* [*ekatharisthē Mariam*]" (NETS), which may interpret "Miriam was gathered" (*hēʾāsēp miryām*) in light of the skin disease protocol in Lev. 13:1–46, which demands cleansing (**katharizō* 28× in Lev. 13–14) before reentry into the camp (similarly Wevers, *Notes*, 191). Perhaps the homophony of *h'sp* (was brought back in) with *'zwb* (hyssop; Lev. 14 [5×]; Num. 19:6, 18) prompted this exegetical decision by the LXX translator.

27. After v. 16, SP interpolates a passage adapted from Deut. 1:20–23a.

begins the new scene with the geographical introduction "While they were at Hazeroth, Miriam and Aaron spoke against Moses" (see the translation notes on 12:1).[28] The reason for their criticism according to the narrator, and redundantly by the editor, is that Moses had married a Cushite woman (12:1). The feminine gentilic "Cushite woman" ('iššâ kušît) refers to a woman from Kush (cf. genealogies Gen. 10:6–7; 1 Chron. 1:9), which was the Egyptian name for Upper Nubia or all of Nubia (today southern Egypt to central Sudan). In that region, the Kerma kingdom (ca. 2500–1500 BCE) was the first known culture, followed by New Kingdom Egyptian control (from 1550 BCE), but the Kushite kingdom emerged only in the first millennium BCE and was divided into the Napatan (750–270 BCE) and Meroitic (270 BCE–320 CE) phases.[29] The LXX translator here reinterprets "Cushite woman" as "Ethiopian woman" (gynaika Aithiopissan), which is too far southeast, whereas Exodus identifies Moses's wife as Zipporah from Midian,[30] which was likely in the northwest of the Arabian Peninsula, on the eastern shore of the Gulf of Aqaba (Saudi Arabia), a region settled most fully in the eighth to seventh centuries BCE.[31] Two conclusions can be drawn from 12:1: the narrator (v. 1α) and editor (v. 1β) shared a tradition distinct from that of the Zipporah-of-Midian texts in Exod. 2–18*,[32] and they both highlight the perceived problem that Moses had married a foreigner.[33] Prohibition of intermarriage with foreigners is a well-attested issue later in Israel's history.[34] It is conceivable, then, that this story in which Yahweh sides with Moses confronts Aaronic ethnic prejudices.[35]

When one hears from Miriam and Aaron themselves, however, the issue of Moses's foreign marriage (v. 1) feels like a smoke screen for their real issue with Moses: "Has Yahweh spoken only through Moses? Hasn't he also spoken through us?" (v. 2a–b).[36] Since "They said" (v. 2a) has no indirect object, the

28. Miriam is called the sister of Aaron (Exod. 15:20) and the sister of Moses and Aaron (Num. 26:59).

29. Kuhrt, *Ancient Near East*, 2:632–34.

30. "Zipporah" (ṣippōrâ) in Exod. 2:21; 4:25; 18:2; spelled fully ṣpwrh in SP and 4Q22 [18:2].

31. Dever, *Early Israelites*, 34; cf. Frevel, *Desert Transformations*, 209–24.

32. Habakkuk 3:7 makes parallel "the tents of Cushan" and "the tent curtains of the land of Midian." See Schmidt, *Numeri*, 31.

33. Scharbert, *Numeri*, 51; Achenbach (*Vollendung*, 281–85) attributes most of 12:1–12* to the Pentateuch redactor.

34. Deut. 7:3–4; 23:3–6; 1 Kings 11:1–13; Ezra 10; Neh. 13. See Dozeman, "Numbers," 109–10.

35. Sparks, *Ancient Texts*, 303. Römer ("Mose in Äthiopien," 203–15) postulates Num. 12 as a late Persian story that, by accepting Moses's "Ethiopian" marriage, makes the Moses traditions available to a progressive Judaism living outside the land. Moses then, like Joseph in Egypt, becomes an identity figure for the diaspora. Contrarily, Gerhards ("Frau des Mose," 162–75) sees Moses's Egyptian name and non-Israelite (Midianite/Cushite/Qenite) wife as interests that do not belong to later times but indicate the origins of a historical Moses as a leader of the exodus and mediator of Yahweh.

36. Abela, "Shaming Miriam," 534.

impression is that this is their own private conversation, but they are fooling themselves because "Yahweh heard it" (v. 2c). On the one hand, Yahweh had spoken directly to Aaron without Mosaic mediation (Exod. 4:27; Lev. 10:8), and Miriam as a prophetess would also have received divine revelation.[37] In the Pentateuch, aside from Moses, only Abraham, Aaron, and Miriam are called "prophets."[38] Their inspiration to challenge Moses might come from Eldad and Medad, who also prophesied for God independently of Moses (Num. 11:26–29).[39] On the other hand, there is no record of Aaron and Miriam transmitting divine revelation for the whole Israelite community,[40] and readers already know that Yahweh has honored his chosen prophet Moses more highly than anyone else (Exod. 33:7–34:8).[41] So if the sin of Miriam and Aaron in v. 1 is racism, their sin in v. 2 is envy.[42]

The editorial insertion in v. 3 delays Yahweh's response, generating curiosity as to how he will respond to the siblings.[43] The editor inserts: "Now the man Moses was very humble, more than anyone on the face of the earth" (v. 3; see the third translation note there).[44] This veneration of Moses in 12:3, 6–8 aligns with the perspective of the Pentateuch editor in Deut. 34:10–12 and may theoretically be from the same hand.[45] The high honoring of Moses's character here will come into contrast with later texts that castigate the rebellious Moses and Aaron, who lose their land inheritance (see earlier note). At first glance, the editor's remark in v. 3 seems displaced, but rhetorically it serves at least two functions. In the editor's estimation, Moses's humility both overshadows concerns about Moses's Cushite wife and removes any suspicion that Moses may have become arrogant toward Miriam and Aaron because of his unparalleled role as Yahweh's designated intermediary. As a working definition, "Humility is selflessness before God and others. Such persons do not hoard power jealously;

---

37. Exod. 15:20–21; see other prophetesses in Judg. 4:4; 2 Kings 22:14; 2 Chron. 34:22; Isa. 8:3; Luke 2:36; Joel 2:28; Acts 2:17; 21:9; but some with a negative connotation: Neh. 6:14; Rev. 2:20.

38. Dozeman, "Numbers," 109. See Gen. 20:7; Exod. 7:1; 15:20.

39. Milgrom, *Numbers*, 93.

40. The instructions of Lev. 10:8–11 ensue from the Nadab and Abihu disaster and are restricted to Aaron and his male descendants; Num. 18 occurs after the Num. 12 episode.

41. Sperling ("Miriam," 39–55) conjectures that this story was fabricated in the Persian era to subordinate oral tradition (Miriam and Aaron) to written revelation (Moses), but this has no grounding in the story, which makes no mention of written *tôrâ* (cf. Exod. 24:24; 34:28; Deut. 31:9, 19, 22).

42. Sprinkle, *Leviticus and Numbers*, 258–63.

43. Sternberg, *Poetics*, 265–66.

44. This veneration of Moses in 12:3, 6–8 aligns with the perspective of the Pentateuch editor in Deut. 34:10–12, indicating that the same editor may have also contributed Num. 12:1–12* (Achenbach, *Vollendung*, 281–85; Schmidt, *Numeri*, 32–34). This perspective is sharpened by a contrasting collection of texts that castigate the rebellious Moses and Aaron, who lose their inheritance (see Num. 20:10–12, 24; Deut. 32:48–52: Awabdy, "Holiness Contribution," 247–58).

45. Achenbach, *Vollendung*, 281–85; Schmidt, *Numeri*, 32–34.

they give it away."[46] Moses recently displayed such humility in his response to Eldad and Medad: "Are you jealous for me? I wish that all Yahweh's people were prophets, that Yahweh would put his spirit on them!" (11:29b–c).

Immediately, Yahweh speaks to Moses, Aaron, and Miriam and directs them to come to his meeting tent, and they do so (v. 4). In many Canaanite myths, El dwells in a tent on the mount of assembly in the distant north, where he makes cosmic decisions.[47] By analogy, Yahweh, who also dwells in a tent, assembles Aaron, Miriam, and Moses to decide the verdict of this case (v. 4). By contrast, while other deities would self-isolate in the inner recesses of their dwellings out of sight, with creatures guarding their shrine's entrance,[48] here Yahweh descends in a pillar of cloud and anthropomorphically stands at the tent's entrance in plain sight (v. 5; see the translation note there).[49] Now he singles out Aaron and Miriam (inverted order of v. 1), they both come forward, and the suspense swells as all remember how Yahweh recently killed the complainers (Num. 11).

12:6–9. Through a monologue accompanied by his burning anger, Yahweh endorses Moses alone as his unparalleled prophet who deserves careful respect. Yahweh's speech opens with the imperative "Listen to my words" (v. 6a), a metacomment that slows down and so heightens anticipation for the discourse:[50]

> *Listen to my words*: (6a)
>> If there is a prophet of Yahweh among you, (6bα)
>>> in a vision to him I will make myself known.[51] (6bβ)
>>> in a dream I will speak with him. (6bγ)
>>>> It is not this way with my servant Moses; (7a)
>>>> with my whole house he is entrusted. (7b)
>>>>> face-to-face I speak with him, (8aα)
>>>>> in an appearance and not in riddles, (8aβ–γ)
>>>>> and the form of Yahweh he looks at.[52] (8b)
> *Why then were you not afraid to speak against my servant Moses?* (8c)

---

46. Dozeman, "Numbers," 112.
47. Cross, *Canaanite Myth*, 43.
48. Hundley, *Gods in Dwellings*, 84.
49. See Boorer, *Priestly Narrative*, 356–58.
50. Runge, *Discourse Grammar*, 386.
51. Staubli, *Levitikus, Numeri*, 249. Contra Cross (*Canaanite Myth*, 203n37), who repositions "Yahweh" to the beginning of v. 6, and contra many versions that remove the parallelism of the genitives "prophet of Yahweh" (v. 6bα) and "form of Yahweh (v. 8b) by the rendering: "If there is a prophet among you, *I Yahweh* will make myself known."
52. I try to preserve the Hb. word order, with fronted constituents, within the concentric structure seen by Cross, *Canaanite Myth*, 203–4; Kselman, "Numbers XXII 6–8," 500–505; Staubli, *Levitikus, Numeri*, 249; Seebass, *Numeri*, 2:70.

The concentric encomium that honors Moses (vv. 6b–8b) is framed, by *inclusio*, as a harangue to and against Aaron and Miriam (vv. 6a, 8c). In contrast to Miriam and Aaron, who *spoke* against Moses and believed that Yahweh *had spoken* through them as well (vv. 1–2), Yahweh's response "suggests a sense of divine irony: 'Hear then my words' (Num. 12:6), as if to say, if you really want to hear my words, I'll grant you that wish, but you will mightily regret it!"[53] Prophecy, by dreams and visions, was already widespread throughout the ancient Near East, most famously at Mari on the Euphrates (cf. Moabite Balaam in Num. 22–24).[54] In distinction from, formally, "*your* prophet of Yahweh" (*nəbîʾăkem yhwh*), to whom Yahweh conventionally reveals himself through the mediums of visions and dreams (v. 6; see the third translation note there), to "*my* servant Moses" (*ʿabdî mōšeh*) Yahweh speaks customarily, personally, visibly, and intelligibly (v. 8a; see the first four translation notes there).[55] Here Yahweh explicates the collective sum of Moses's phenomenal encounters with Yahweh and his service to Yahweh (e.g., Exod. 4:16; 19–24ff.*; 33:7–34:8; Num. 7:89). A second reflection on Moses's greatness will come not from Yahweh's lips, but from the final editors of the Pentateuch (Deut. 34:8–10).

By another *inclusio*, Yahweh makes two more claims, now with Moses as the verbal subject: "He is entrusted with my whole house" (v. 7b) and "he looks at the form of Yahweh" (v. 8b). For a discussion of how Moses looked at Yahweh's form, see the "Implications" essay below, "Did Moses See Yahweh?" As for the opening claim in v. 7b, Yahweh uses a divine passive, and the metonym "my whole house" (*kol-bêtî*) has royal overtones; that is, Yahweh has entrusted Moses with his whole kingdom (see the translation note on v. 7; cf. Heb. 3:2, 5). Conceivably, *house* could refer to Yahweh's dwelling, meaning Moses has authority over Aaron the high priest (Exod. 23:19; 34:26; Josh. 9:23; et al.). However, in light of usage in the HB, the addition of "*all my* house" suggests Yahweh's kingdom: Joseph oversaw Pharaoh's house, the Egyptian kingdom ("over my house," *ʿal-bêtî*, Gen. 41:40); Yahweh promised to give David an enduring house (2 Sam. 7), the dynastic kingdom of Judah, to which the Tel Dan Stele likely refers.[56] Yahweh applies the appellative "*my servant* Moses" (vv. 7a, 8c)[57] to a

---

53. Leveen, *Memory*, 86. Schmid (*Der sogenannte Jahwist*, 75–76) sees the language of vv. 6–8 as reflecting prophetic writings like Ezekiel, and "my servant" as Deuteronomic, whereas Seebass (*Numeri*, 2:63–64) prefers J.

54. See Nissinen, *Prophecy*.

55. Kilchör (*Mosetora*, 222–23) argues that Deut. 18:15–18 alludes to Num. 12:6–8 (also to Exod. 4 and Exod. 20/Deut. 5).

56. The "House of David" (*bytdwd*) in the Tel Dan Stele reasonably implies, "A century after King David lived there was a dynastic Davidic kingdom, known to an Aramean king, probably Hazael. This dynasty and its king ruled over a country mentioned together with Israel" (Hagelia, *Dan Debate*, 136).

57. "My servant Moses" occurs in Num. 12:7, 8; Josh. 1:2, 7; 2 Kings 21:8; Mal. 4:4.

few nonroyal exemplars,[58] but mainly to royals.[59] By this title Yahweh elevates Moses to the prestigious tier alongside "my servant Abraham" (Gen. 26:24) and "my servant David."[60] Yahweh confronts Aaron and Miriam with his logic that they should have deduced: Because of Moses's incomparable relationship with Yahweh, "Why then were you not afraid to speak against my servant Moses?" (v. 8c). Alluding to this text, the writer of Hebrews asserts the supremacy of Jesus the Messiah over even Moses himself: "Now Moses was faithful in all God's house as a servant, to testify to the things that would be spoken. But Christ is faithful as a son over God's house. We are of his house, if in fact we hold firmly to our confidence and the hope we take pride in" (Heb. 3:5–6 NET). The narrator's placement of Yahweh's burning anger in v. 9a, rather than after v. 2 as expected, means that readers can fully appreciate *why* Yahweh has become so angry: because berating Yahweh's beloved servant Moses is akin to scraping the apple of Yahweh's eye. Thus, when Yahweh leaves in anger (v. 9b), the reader, who has already traversed Num. 11, wonders when and how Yahweh will punish Aaron and Miriam or the Israelites as a whole.

12:10–16. Yahweh afflicts Miriam with a skin disease; after the pleadings of Aaron and Moses, Yahweh heals her, but she must still isolate outside the camp. This next scene in the story begins with the circumstantial clause "When the cloud departed from above the tent, Miriam's skin had a disease like snow" (v. 10).[61] No causal particle is used in the Hebrew, but the narrator implies that Yahweh has caused her skin disease, since this scene follows Yahweh's harangue (vv. 6–8) and anger (v. 8). Aaron confesses their sin (v. 11) while Moses begs Yahweh to heal her (v. 13). Aaron is shocked by the sight of his sister wasting away with some form of skin disease (v. 10; see the translation notes there).[62] Leprosy is not in view, but *psoriasis vulgaris* is a plausible diagnosis, with inflamed skin covered with scaly, silvery-white skin.[63] Did Yahweh afflict Miriam with such a skin disease merely as a visible sign to substantiate Moses's trustworthy authority[64] or to display God's

---

58. Caleb (Num. 14:24); Job (Job 1:8; 2:3; 42:7, 8 [3×]); Isaiah (Isa. 20:3); Eliakim (22:20).

59. King Nebuchadnezzar (Jer. 25:9; 27:6; 43:10); David (see refs. below); and with royal overtones: Jacob-Israel/Isaiah/Messiah (Isa. 41:8–9; 42:1, 19; 43:10; 44:1, 2, 21 [2×]; 45:4; 49:3, 6; 52:13; 53:11; Jer. 46:28; Ezek. 28:25; 37:25); Zerubbabel (Hag. 2:23); "the Branch" (Zech. 3:8); Jesus fulfilling Isaiah (Matt. 12:18; John 12:26).

60. 1 Sam. 16:22 (variation); 2 Sam. 3:18; 7:5, 8; 1 Kings 11:13, 32, 36; 14:8; 2 Kings 19:34 (variation); 20:6 (variation); 1 Chron. 17:4, 7; Ps. 89:3, 20; Isa. 37:35; Jer. 33:21, 22, 26; Ezek. 34:23–24; 37:24–25.

61. "When the cloud [*wǝheʿānān*]" explains the circumstances surrounding Miriam's skin disease (*GBHS* §4.3.3e).

62. Kazen ("Purity and Persia," 451n62) notes that skin disease (*ṣāraʿat*) is often associated with death: Num. 12:12; Job 18:13; Josephus, *Ant.* 3.264; m. Kelim 1.4; m. Negaʿim 13.7, 11; b. Nedarim 64b.

63. Schinkel, "Mirjam als Aussätzige?," 94–101.

64. Schinkel, "Mirjam als Aussätzige?," 94–101.

judgment?[65] There may be a *lex talionis* principle at work: if you attack Moses's character publicly, Yahweh will attack your body publicly (cf. Lev. 24:17–22).[66] Aaron turns not to Yahweh, but to Moses, addressing him as "my Lord" (*'ădōnî*) and submitting to Moses as the one who offers powerful intercessory prayers to Yahweh (v. 11).[67] There is no reason to lump Aaron's plea here with his pathetic excuse for constructing the golden calf (Exod. 32:22–24). Even if his outcry here lacks the language of repentance and seeking forgiveness,[68] Aaron's remorse is clear enough: "Do not hold this sin against us that we have so foolishly committed!" (v. 11). His confession is, nonetheless, motivated by compassion for his sister's health: "Do not let her be like a stillborn baby, whose flesh is half eaten away when it comes out of its mother's womb" (v. 12). Recently, Israel longed to eat Egypt's foods, which provoked Yahweh's fire to eat some of them in judgment, and now Miriam's flesh is "half eaten" by Yahweh.[69] This vivid language resembles that of "a list of Mesopotamian omens where a miscarriage is described as giving birth to individual body parts (i.e., not a whole child), or a membrane, or a membrane filled with blood."[70] Whether Aaron imagined a miscarriage (before the 20th week of pregnancy) or a stillbirth (after the 20th week), Miriam's body was decomposing before her brothers' eyes.

Without delay, Moses intercedes for her by crying out to Yahweh: "O God, heal her now!" He directs his address to *'ēl* (God), which is both the generic Semitic term for god (Akkadian *ilu*; Ugaritic *'il*; Phoenician *'l*) and also the personal name El, the high god of the Canaanite pantheon.[71] By imploring Yahweh as *'ēl*—whether meaning "deity" or replacing El—to heal Miriam, Moses's prayer resonates with the Akkadian name used by a probable mayor of Gubla, "My god/El is the healer" (*Ili-Rapiḫ*).[72] Moses does not take time

---

65. Ashley (*Numbers*, 227) notes this function for the skin diseases given to Moses (Exod. 4:6) and Elisha's servant, Gehazi (2 Kings 5:27).

66. Cross (*Canaanite Myth*, 204) conjectures: "The term 'Cushite' may also have had connotations of blackness derived from its [Hb.] homonym, 'Ethiopian,' rendering the whitened skin of Miriam a singularly fit punishment for her objections to the Cushite wife." Douglas (*Wilderness*, 196–215) unconvincingly argues that skin-defiled Miriam symbolizes religiously defiled Israel.

67. Lohfink (*Theology*, 68n99) also recalls Abraham (Gen. 20:7), the man of God (1 Kings 13:6), Elijah (1 Kings 17:19–21), et al.

68. E.g., Ps. 51; Neh. 1:4–11; Dan. 9:3–19; Luke 18:13.

69. Leveen, *Memory*, 145; see "eat" (*'kl) in 11:1, 4, 5, 13, 18 [3×], 19, 21; 12:12.

70. Garroway, *Growing Up*, 36, see 36–40.

71. See *'ēl* also in Num. 16:22; 23:8, 19, 22, 23; 24:4, 8, 16, 23. Smith (*Memoirs of God*, 114–15) theorizes a preexilic Israelite pantheon with four tiers: (1) Yahweh is associated with El alongside Asherah and/or the Queen of Heaven; (2) depersonalized sun, moon, stars; (3) ? [not named]; (4) messengers (angels) and servants. In the late monarchy, the hierarchy develops: (1) Yahweh-El alone; (2) nothing below them; (3) "the *satan* [adversary]" (Job 1–2; Zech. 3); (4) messengers (angels) and servants.

72. EA 128.21; 139.2; 140.3 (Moran, *Amarna Letters*, 208, 225, 226, 382).

to remind God of his patriarchal promises (Exod. 32:13; Num. 11:12) but is confident that God is the one who both afflicts and heals, as the Song of Moses will make explicit, "See now that I, even I, am he, and there is no God beside me; I kill and I make alive; I wound and I heal; and there is none that can deliver out of my hand" (Deut. 32:39 ESV). Perhaps Moses recalled when Yahweh had struck him with a skin disease when he questioned whether Pharaoh would listen to him (Exod. 4:6–7).[73] Yahweh responds to Moses with a curious rhetorical question and then a verdict (see v. 8): "If her father had only spit in her face, would she not have been shamed for seven days? She must be shut outside the camp seven days, and afterward she can be brought back in again" (v. 14). Yahweh ostensibly deflects Moses and Aaron's concern with Miriam's healing[74] by giving an analogy to an unknown custom: just as a father who spits on his daughter shames her and necessitates her isolation for seven days,[75] so Miriam should also be shamed for dishonoring Moses and be "shut outside" the camp for seven days (v. 14; see the translation notes there). The shaming probably resulted in both social and ritual diminishment,[76] yet in her humiliated state, Miriam also fulfills standard protocol, since the person healed of a skin disease must quarantine for seven more days, at which time the priest reexamines her to pronounce her clean.[77]

Why Miriam alone, and not also Aaron, was afflicted with a skin disease and shamed by isolation may be a by-product of Israel's patriarchal culture.[78] Yet the reason may also be revealed in the name order in 12:1. Listing Miriam the woman first with a feminine singular verb[79] seems to indicate that she was the instigator: "Miriam and Aaron spoke against Moses" (v. 1).[80] The narrator never reports Miriam's healing but clearly implies it because it would validate Moses's intercessory authority, the point of Yahweh's speech.[81] Also, her healing is indicated by reporting that she was put in isolation outside the camp for a week, and the people waited to travel until Miriam returned to

---

73. Douglas, *Wilderness*, 197.

74. Similarly, Yahweh deflects Job's concerns in Job 38–41.

75. Spitting to shame another occurs elsewhere (Deut. 25:9; Isa. 50:6; Job 30:10), but only here is this followed by a seven-day quarantine. Is this custom deduced from the woman's seven-day purification for her menstruation (Lev. 15:19, 28)?

76. Lynch, "'Shame' Terminology," 516; cf. Abela, "Shaming Miriam," 521–34. Kilchör (*Mosetora*, 276) sees "purge evil from your midst" (Deut. 17:7) as echoing Miriam being shut outside the camp for her evil speech against Moses.

77. Lev. 13:4, 5, 21, 26, 31, 33; but cf. Lev. 14:8; Num. 5:1–4; see Frevel, "Purity Conceptions," 386; Kilchör, *Mosetora*, 261–62.

78. See Douglas, *Wilderness*, 197–98. See the "Implications" essay in chap. 27, "Patriarchal Family Structure."

79. Scharbert, *Numeri*, 51.

80. Douglas, *Wilderness*, 196; cf. Korah in Num. 16:1–3. In the NT, Priscilla is listed before her husband, Aquila, likely indicating her primary role in instructing Apollos (Acts 18:18, 19, 26): Keener, *Acts*, 3:2808–11.

81. See Douglas, *Wilderness*, 196.

the camp (v. 15). The implication is that now that Aaron and Miriam have been restored spiritually (vv. 11–14) and physically (vv. 14–15), with Israel not departing prematurely (v. 15), the covenant people are back on track to inherit the divine promises. Two travel notices form an *inclusio* around this story: "From Kibroth Hattaavah the people traveled to Hazeroth" (11:35 [35a]) and "After that the people traveled from Hazeroth and camped in the Paran wilderness" (12:16).[82] Thus the editors distinguish this story (12:1 [11:35b]–15) from Num. 11 and 13–14 as the incident that characterized their stay at Hazeroth ("Settlements").[83] The narrator already reported that the cloud settled in the Paran wilderness in 10:12, so with the notice in 12:16, the editors re-chronologize the stories of the Sinai wilderness, with Kibroth Hattaavah (chap. 11) and Hazeroth (chap. 12) occurring before the cloud led Israel northward to the Paran wilderness (10:12).[84] The Paran wilderness formed the geographical border to the south of Canaan, meaning that Israel is now stationed for entry into the land.[85]

Implications

Did Moses See Yahweh?

The angel of Yahweh appeared to Moses in a flame of fire within a perpetually burning bush, but was that angel a coextension of Yahweh? And what did the flame look like (Exod. 3:2)? Since arriving at Mount Sinai, it has been Moses's custom to meet personally with Yahweh in a dense cloud on the mountain, in the cloud in Moses's meeting place, and in the cloud in the cleft of the rock.[86] A cloud, nonetheless, would have at least obfuscated Moses's visualization of Yahweh and at most would have completely hidden Yahweh's appearance. In Num. 7:89, the narrator describes Moses's later custom of meeting with Yahweh inside the tent to hear the divine voice, but presumably the inner curtain and the incense smoke separated and masked Yahweh, who remained solitary in the most holy place enthroned above the cherubim (cf. Lev. 16*). Based on these and other accounts, one can understand why the apostle John consistently claims in his writings that a human has never seen God. Formally, in the Greek word order, he says "God no one has ever seen" (John 1:18) and "God no one has ever looked at (intently)" (1 John 4:12). Both of the verbs John uses refer to the past, with ongoing effects into the

---

82. W. Lee, *Migratory Campaign*, 130–31.
83. Noth, *Numbers*, 97; Frevel, *Mit Blick*, 80.
84. Levine (*Numbers*, 1:311) sees 12:16 as P, and Schmidt (*Numeri*, 31) as the Pentateuch redactor; cf. Van Seters, *Life of Moses*, 156–58.
85. Frevel, *Mit Blick*, 367.
86. "In a dense cloud" (*ba'ab he'ānān*) in Exod. 19:9, and "*the* cloud" (*he'ānān*) refers to the same dense cloud in 24:15–18 (4×).

present. The latter verse refers to a subject: "no one" has ever been affected by the verbal action of seeing God.[87] Does this mean that God can never be seen, that he is invisible? Or does this mean that, in his ontological essence, "God is spirit" (John 4:24), and therefore no natural being has ever seen his essence? In any case, it cannot mean that humans have never seen *some form* of Yahweh, since Yahweh has chosen to appear many times in the Hebrew Bible in what we call theophanies.[88]

In his diatribe against Miriam and Aaron for their arrogance toward Moses, Yahweh uses striking language to describe his special mode of communication with Moses:

> I speak with him face-to-face,
>> in an appearance
>> and not in riddles,
> and he looks at the form of Yahweh. (12:8)

Speaking "face-to-face" (formally, "mouth to mouth," *peh 'el-peh*) indicates a direct interpersonal encounter,[89] but as an anthropomorphic Hebrew idiom, we should not contort this to mean that Moses laid eyes on Yahweh's mouth or face. Yahweh says elsewhere that Moses, and by extension no human, can see Yahweh and survive (Exod. 33:20). Thus Yahweh put Moses in a cleft in the rock and covered Moses's face so he would not see Yahweh's "face" (*pāneh/pānîm*, Exod. 33:20) or "glory" (*kābôd*, 33:22) but would see Yahweh's "back" (*'āḥôr*, 33:23). Here in Num. 12, Yahweh further qualifies the idiom of his communication with Moses as being "in an appearance and not in riddles"— that is, in a visible encounter, not in perplexing words. The final phrase is maybe the most astounding: "and he looks at the form of Yahweh" (see the fifth translation note on 12:8). The LXX renders this, "and he saw *the glory of the Lord [tēn doxan kyriou]*" (12:8).[90] In the Hebrew, the possessive genitive is definite, meaning "*the* form *belonging to* Yahweh" or "Yahweh's form" (*təmunat yhwh*).[91] The construct noun *təmûnâ* can be translated "form, likeness, representation"[92] or "manifestation";[93] it occurs ten times in the Hebrew Scriptures: in the prohibition of crafting an idol or *likeness* of anything in the

---

87. John 1:18 and 1 John 4:12 use combinative aspect verbs (have not seen and continue not to see) and the obj., "God" (*theon*), is fronted for emphasis.

88. *Theo* comes from *theos* (God) and *phanē* relates to "appearing."

89. The idiom "face-to-face" (*pānîm 'el-pānîm*) pertains to the Yahweh-Moses relationship (Exod. 33:11), whereas "eye with eye" (*'ayin bə'ayin*) pertains either to Yahweh-Moses or Yahweh-Israel (Num. 14:14). Also a NT Koine idiom: 2 John 12; 3 John 14.

90. Augustine interprets 12:8 anagogically (Lienhard, *Numbers*, 221).

91. *GBHS* §2.2.1.

92. See "*təmûnâ*," *DCH* 8:640.

93. See "*təmûnâ*," *HALOT* 4:1746–47.

heavens, earth, or waters beneath the earth (Exod. 20:4; Deut. 4:23, 25; 5:8), including a male or female figure (Deut. 4:16 [cf. 4:17–19]); seeing Yahweh's *form* (Num. 12:8; Ps. 17:15) or not seeing Yahweh's *form* (Deut. 4:12, 15); and an ambiguous *form* or *figure* that Eliphaz recounts to Job (Job 4:16). Here Moses's direct encounter of Yahweh may recall Exod. 24:9–11, where Israel's leaders climbed Mount Sinai and "saw the God of Israel" (*wayyir'û 'ēt 'ĕlōhê yiśrā'ēl*).[94] That theophany was terrifying, yet they ate and drank in God's presence! Yahweh shows up in other graphic ways later in the biblical narrative,[95] but presumably in the minds of the Hebrew scribes, each distinct theophany shows only how Yahweh chose to represent himself visibly at any given moment in time.

In the ANE—Mesopotamia, for example—the cult image enshrined deep inside the deity's temple structure was thought to be "a semipermanent theophany."[96] By contrast, the Israelites were never to represent Yahweh in any form (Exod. 20:4; Deut. 5:8–9), and they could not manipulate him by their ritual services. Yet, like the ANE deities, Yahweh holds the prerogative to take on any form he so chooses. He does this, we may infer, to contextualize his revelation of himself, to make himself known in ways that his image bearers can resonate with and even interpret in simplistic and symbolic ways.

For the NT writers, the fully human body of Jesus in the incarnation has become an eternal theophany of God's glory: "No one has ever seen God. It is God the only Son, who is close to the Father's heart, who has made him known" (John 1:18 NRSV; Col. 1:15, 19; Heb. 1:1–3). By believing the gospel, we know and experience God's glory in Christ (2 Cor. 4:4, 6). Yet at the same time, Jesus veiled his glory in his first coming to spare those who interfaced with him; presumably his transfiguration only partially unveiled his glory for Peter, James, and John (Matt. 17:2; Mark 9:2–3). What, then, of God's essence, his glory, will his redeemed children actually see on the new earth? While the answer remains unimaginable, together with Moses we will see far more than Moses ever saw in his lifetime: "But the throne of God and of the Lamb will be in it, and his servants will worship him; *they will see his face*" (Rev. 22:3b–4a).[97]

---

94. Cf. Gen. 32:30; Judg. 13:22; Isa. 6:1, 5; Ps. 17:15; John 1:18; Col. 1:15; 1 Tim. 6:16; Heb. 1:3; 1 John 4:12, 20.

95. E.g., Ezek. 1:4–28; 8:2–4; Ps. 18*; Dan. 7:9–10; Rev. 1:12–16.

96. Hundley, *Gods in Dwellings*, 84.

97. See also Titus 2:13; 1 John 3:2d; Phil. 3:21; 1 Cor. 13:12; Rev. 21:23.

13

Canaan Explored; Report Discouraging

(13:1–33)

$$\mathcal{O}\!\!\!\!\sim\!\!\!\!\mathcal{O}$$

Overview

In 10:12 Yahweh's cloud had settled in the Paran wilderness, but with the travel notice at 12:16 marking Israel's arrival in the Paran wilderness, the reader should reimagine the episodes of Num. 11 and 12 as occurring on the way to Paran—that is, on a geographical detour from the divinely directed path toward Canaan. The detour was also spiritual in nature, marked by the covenant people's complaints and death at Taberah (Num. 11) and envy and disease at Hazeroth (Num. 12). Now Israel is back on track geographically, encamped not far south of the southern border of Canaan, but is Israel back on track spiritually? To this question, the first three subunits of Num. 13 supply an affirmative answer, but in the third subunit, at v. 31, the narrator describes the beginning of the most serious spiritual disaster of the book, culminating in Yahweh's curse on the exodus generation to die in the wilderness and never enter the land (14:23, 29–37).[1] Thus, Num. 13–14 is pivotal in the plotline of

---

1. Num. 13–14 has been seen to integrate a J(E)/non-P story and a P story (Noth, *Numbers*, 101–3; de Vaulx, *Nombres*, 164–79; Seebass, *Numeri*, 2:84–101; Levine, *Numbers*, 1:347–49; Budd, *Numbers*, 141–44; McEvenue, "Source-Critical," 453–65), or it is assigned primarily to J/non-P with supplements, and Deut. 1:19–46 is literarily dependent on it (Schmidt, "Kundschaftererzählung," 40–58). Others see Num. 13–14 as post-Dtr, that is, after the synopsis of the explorers in Deut. 1 (Frevel, "Alte Stücke," 286; Van Seters, *Life of Moses*, 370–79), but containing an independent P source (Frevel, *Mit Blick*, 133, following Schart). The Pentateuch redactor, some think, combined the stories (Scharbert, *Numeri*, 54–61; cf. Schart, "Spy Story," 194). Kislev ("Joshua," 39–55) affirms an independent Priestly thread in Num. 13–14 and claims that the places where Joshua and Caleb appear together were added later. Boorer (*Priestly Narrative*, 71–77) sees Num. 13–14* as belonging to P^g, and she ("Numbers 13–14*," 45–63)

Numbers.[2] This discursive unit begins with Yahweh and Moses commanding twelve chieftains, representing each tribe (excluding Levi), to explore the land of Canaan, Yahweh's gift to Israel (13:1–16). Moses further enjoins the chieftains to travel through the Negev into the central hill country and discover specific ethnographic and demographic features of Canaan (vv. 17–20). The chieftains obediently explore Canaan's land and inhabitants, and the narrator highlights what they discover on their trek (vv. 21–25). They return and convey to the whole community a mixed report about Canaan, its fortified cities and residents, beginning to instill fear in the Israelites (vv. 26–29). Judah's chieftain, Caleb, seeks to inspire the Israelites with his conviction that they can and must conquer the land, but the other explorers (presumably minus Joshua) seek to discourage the Israelites with a bad report in which they obsess over the brutal and intimidating people who control the land (vv. 30–33).[3]

Translation

1Then Yahweh spoke to Moses: **2**"Send men to explore[4] the land of Canaan, which I am giving to the Israelites. You must send[5] one man

---

also contends that Num. 13–14* and 20:2–12 deliberately reverse and negate P[g]'s story of the creation of the nation and representation of its main leaders, Moses and Aaron, in Exod. 6– Num. 10 (esp. in Exod. 16). Artus (*Études*, 157) identifies P's influence in Num. 13–14, spanning through 20:13, as P distinguishes those who comply with Yahweh's law and are recognized as being worthy of belonging to his people from those who knowingly deviate from Yahweh's law, are condemned by Yahweh, and are separated as being unworthy of his people. Knohl (*Sanctuary*, 90–92) identifies 13:1–17a and 14:26–38 as H additions. Achenbach (*Vollendung*, 635) distributes Num. 13–14* across the pre-Dtr source, DtrL, Hexateuch and Pentateuch editors, and theocratic revision. Schart ("Spy Story," 164–200) argues for an oral spy-story version from which came two Yahwist versions (Num. 13–14*) and the earliest Deuteronomistic layer in Deuteronomy. Galbraith ("Interpellation," 29–48) interprets inconsistencies in the text, not as source and redactional layers, but as different ideologies among "the Judean and Samarian populace yet coalescing in their support of the text's ideology of a righteous remnant"; his view is pragmatically implausible. Philo of Alexandria reconstructs the Num. 13–14 story to position Moses in the center; see Feldman ("Philo's Version," 29–48).

2. See Olson, *Death of the Old*, 129–52; Ashley, *Numbers*, 229–31.

3. Milgrom (*Numbers*, 387–90) and Staubli (*Levitikus, Numeri*, 250) perceive a chiastic structure, but W. Lee (*Migratory Campaign*, 134) argues that it is artificial:

   A   The scouts' expedition (13:1–24)

      B   The scouts' report (13:25–33)

         X   The people's response (14:1–10a)

      B′   God's response (14:10b–38)

   A′   The people's expedition (14:39–45)

4. Following the impv., the simple *wǝ* with the yiqtol functions as a purpose clause: "send men *to explore*" (*GBHS* §3.5.3b); *ʾtwr* qal means "to search out" (*DCH* 8:610).

5. The opening impv. in v. 2a is sg., but here the MT imperatival yiqtol (*GBHS* §3.2.2d4) is pl., "You (all) must send" (*tišlāḥû*), which may have been adjusted back to sg. by SP and LXX[ed] (Wevers, *Notes*, 193).

from each ancestral tribe,[6] each one a chieftain among them." [3]So Moses sent them from the Paran wilderness at Yahweh's command. All of them were Israelite leaders. [4]These were their names: from the tribe of Reuben, Zaccur's son Shammua; [5]from the tribe of Simeon, Hori's son Shaphat; [6]from the tribe of Judah, Jephunneh's son Caleb;[7] [7]from the tribe of Issachar, Joseph's son Igal; [8]from the tribe of Ephraim, Nun's son Hoshea; [9]from the tribe of Benjamin,[8] Raphu's son Palti; [10]from the tribe of Zebulun, Sodi's son Gaddiel; [11]from the tribe of Joseph, that is,[9] the tribe of Manasseh, Susi's son Gaddi; [12]from the tribe of Dan, Gemalli's son Ammiel; [13]from the tribe of Asher, Michael's son Sethur;[10] [14]from the tribe of Naphtali, Vophsi's son Nahbi; [15]from the tribe of Gad, Maki's[11] son Geuel.[12] [16]These are the names of the men whom Moses sent to explore the land. And Moses gave Nun's son Hoshea the name Joshua.[13]

[17]When Moses[14] sent them to explore the land of Canaan, he told them, "Go up through the Negev, then go up into the hill country, [18]and see what the land is like, and if the people who live in it are strong or weak,[15] few or many, [19]and if the land they live in is good or bad, and if the cities they live in are like camps or fortified cities,[16] [20]and if the land is fertile or infertile,[17] and if there are forests in it or not. Be brave,[18] and

---

6. Formally, "by the tribe of their fathers." Unlike here, in chap. 1 this precise phrase depicts the Levites in contrast to all other Israelite men who are enrolled "according to their patriarchs' households" (1:45).

7. LXX[ed] switches the order: "of the tribe of Symeon, Saphat son of Houri; of the tribe of Ioudas, Chaleb son of Iephonne" (NETS).

8. On the SP spelling of "Benjamin" (binyāmin), see the translation note on 2:22.

9. "That is" (l) expresses the apposition of a prepositional obj. (IBHS §11.2.10h).

10. 4Q365 transposes v. 13 with v. 15.

11. "Maki" (mākî MT[L]), appearing only here, is pronounced differently by others: "Mika" (vocalizing 4Q27 as mîk'ā); "Miki" (vocalizing 4Q365 and SP as mîkî); and "Macchi" (NETS for makchi LXX[ed]).

12. "Geuel" (gəʾûʾēl: MT) is spelled differently in SP and could be vocalized "Goel" (gôʾēl), meaning "redeemer"; LXX[ed] "Goudiel" (Goudiēl).

13. SP repeats, "Joshua the name Joshua" (lyhwšʿ), but this is nonsensical and should not be chosen over "Hoshea the name Joshua" (lhwšʿ: 4Q27 MT LXX[ed]).

14. "Moses" (mōšeh MT 4Q27 [partial] LXX[ed]) is absent in SP, perhaps by haplography or a felt redundancy with v. 16.

15. 4Q27 has "they are weak"; 4Q365 has "they are strong or weak" (similarly LXX[ed]); SP has "strong, that is/or, the giants/Rapha [hrpʾ]" (see 1 Chron. 8:2; 20:6, 8; cf. MT, hărāpeh, weak).

16. MT basically agrees with 4Q27 (or whether) and LXX[ed] (walled or unwalled); there are slight variations in 4Q365, SP, and SP[mss] (Ulrich, Qumran, 146).

17. Formally, "fat or lean" (haššəmēnâ hiwʾ ʾim-rāzâ). 4Q27 reads "[and] or poor, whether it is fitting" ([w]ʾm rzh hyʾh; see *yʾh, hapax in MT Jer. 10:7), but this may have been an expansion on "or poor" (ʾm rzh: MT 4Q365 SP ≈ LXX[ed]).

18. "Be brave" (NET) dynamically renders this weqatal command, a reflexive hithpael, meaning "strengthen yourselves" (wəhithazzaqtem; GBHS §3.5.2c, §3.1.5a).

bring back some of the fruit of the land." (It was the season[19] for the first ripe grapes.[20])

21So they went up[21] and explored the land from the Zin wilderness to Rehob, near the entrance of Hamath.[22] **22**They went up through the Negev and came[23] to Hebron, where[24] Ahiman,[25] Sheshai, and Talmai,[26] descendants of Anak,[27] lived. (Hebron had been built seven years before Zoan in Egypt.)[28] **23**When they came to Wadi Eshcol,[29] they cut down from there a branch with one cluster of grapes,[30] and they carried it[31] on a staff between two men, along with some of the pomegranates

19. Formally, "and the days were days of the first ripe grapes"; LXX[ed] includes "and the days were the days *of spring [earos]* forerunners of the grape" (NETS for LXX[ed]), with no equivalent term in the Hebrew, so Origen marked it with the obelus symbol to indicate that it does not appear in the original Hebrew text (Wevers, *Notes*, 200).

20. Instead of "*the first ripe [bikkûrê] grapes*" (MT, from "*bikkûrîm*," DCH 2:172), 4Q27, 4Q365, and SP read, "*early figs*, grapes" (*bkwrwt*, from "*bikkûrâ*," HALOT 1:130; DCH 2:172; the Hb. source of the LXX[ed] is unclear, as *prodromoi* means "forerunner, herald": LEH 7508).

21. 4Q27 and SP read, "They came back" (verbal hendiadys from *wayyēlǝkû wayyābō'û*), which might be a harmonization to v. 26 inspired by a perceived redundancy with "they went up" in vv. 21 and 22.

22. Commonly, "Lebo Hamath," but LXX[ed] probably correctly understands the *l* + inf. const. "for entering Hamath" (*eisporeuomenōn Hemath*, with NET; Cazelles, *Nombres*, 71; Seebass, *Numeri*, 2:79); see Gen. 35:16, "(for entering) Ephrath" (*lābô' 'eprātâ*). SP probably has a *hē'* locale, "toward Lebo Hamath" (*lbw' ḥmtẖ*; BHRG §28.1; de Vaulx [*Nombres*, 166] combines the readings, "in the direction of Ḥamât").

23. In MT[L] and 4Q27, the shift to sg., "and (he) came up" (*wayyābō'*), could presume the men in vv. 5–16 as a collective subject (BHRG §35[3]), but my translation reflects other manuscripts that preserve the parallelism of two pl. verbs: "They went up . . . *and they came [wayyābō'û]*" (MT[mss] 4Q365 SP LXX[ed] [*elthon*]).

24. Formally, "and there" (*wǝšām*: MT SP ≈ LXX[ed] *kai ekei*); whereas 4Q23 and 4Q365 read "and toward there" (*wǝšammâ*, not sensibly vocalized as *ûšǝmāh*, "and its/her name"), which may have arisen due to homophony with the next word.

25. Pronounced "Ahimon" or "Ahimun" by 4Q365 (vocalized *'ăḥîmôn* or *'ăḥîmûn*).

26. "Talmai" (*talmay*: MT 4Q365 SP), pronounced "Tulmai" or "Tolmai" by 4Q27 (broken, Vulg[mss] Syr) and "Thelamin" (*thelamin*) by LXX[ed] (Ulrich, *Qumran*, 146).

27. Formally, "descendants of the Anak" (*yǝlîdê hā'ānāq*), not a gentilic morphology ("the Anakites"); SP and LXX[ed] are anarthrous.

28. LXX[ed] "Tanin of Egypt" (*Tanin Aigyptou*) probably refers to Tanis in the northeastern Delta, appearing first in Egyptian sources from the Nineteenth Dynasty (Wevers, *Notes*, 202). Na'aman ("'Hebron,'" 488–92) sees this as a late editorial comment that acclaimed Hebron's antiquity.

29. Traditionally, "the Valley of Eshcol" (*naḥal 'eškōl*), whose location today is uncertain, may more precisely be called "Wadi Eshcol" (NRSV, NJPS) insofar as this fertile depression was probably dry apart from the rainy season ("*naḥal* II," DCH 5:657, gloss 1).

30. Others clarify "with one cluster of grapes *on it [bh]*" (4Q365 4Q27 ≈ LXX[ed] [*ep' autou*] > MT SP).

31. SP lacks an obj. suffix but could imply it or use the *b* to mark the obj.: "they carried *it/a* staff [*wyś'w bmwt*]" (IBHS §11.2.5f).

and the figs. **²⁴**They called[32] that place Wadi Eshcol (Cluster), because of the cluster that the Israelites cut from there. **²⁵**They returned from exploring out the land after forty days. **²⁶**They came back[33] to Moses and Aaron and to the whole Israelite community in the Paran wilderness at Kadesh. They reported[34] to the whole community and showed them the fruit of the land. **²⁷**They explained to Moses,[35] "We went to the land where you sent us. It is indeed flowing with milk and honey, and this is its fruit. **²⁸**However,[36] the inhabitants are strong, and the cities are fortified and very large. We even saw the descendants of Anak there. **²⁹**The Amalekites live in the land of the Negev; the Hittites,[37] Jebusites, and Amorites live in the hill country; and the Canaanites live by the sea and along the banks of the Jordan."

³⁰Then Caleb silenced[38] the people before Moses, saying, "We must go up to possess it,[39] because we are definitely able to conquer it!" **³¹**But[40] the men who had gone up with him said, "We are not able to go up against those people[41] because they are stronger than us!" **³²**Then they presented the Israelites a bad report[42] about the land they had explored, saying, "The land that we passed through to explore is a land

32. The pl. act. voice, "They called" (*qr'w*, vocalized *qār'û*), has good manuscript support (4Q27 4Q365 SP LXX^ed [= v. 25, *epōnomasan*]) and is preferred to MT "he called" (*qārā'*), which requires one to render an act. qal stem as a pass.

33. "They came back" renders a verbal hendiadys; formally, "They walked/went and they came" (*wayyēləkû wayyābō'û*; GBHS §4.3.3g.2).

34. Hiphil **šwb*, formally, "they brought them back a word" (*wayyāšîbû 'ōtām dābār*).

35. Formally, "him," implying "Moses" (v. 30). "They explained to Moses" (*waysappərû-lô wayyō'mərû* ≈ LXX^ed) represents another verbal hendiadys, formally, "they reported to him and they said" (GBHS §4.3.3g.2).

36. The unique disjunction means "except that" (*'epes kî*; DCH 1:359, gloss 4b; also in Deut. 15:4; Judg. 4:9; 2 Sam. 12:14; Amos 9:8).

37. SP and LXX^ed include "and the Hivites," probably harmonizing with other lists (Exod. 3:8, 17; 13:5; 34:11; 13:29; Deut. 7:1).

38. "Then he silenced" (*wayyahas*), occurring twice in the OT ("*hsh*," DCH 2:579), is a hiphil factitive (cf. piel in Neh. 8:11), which brings about the people's *state* of silence (GBHS §3.1.6a.2; contra HALOT 1:253, marking this as a hapax without an attested piel form). The Akkadian stative "to be silent" ("*ḫesû* E," CAD 6:177–78) might be a cognate.

39. An inf. absolute of the same root (*'lh*) indicates Caleb's conviction that "going up" must happen (BHRG §20.2.2.2.1); in this cohortative of resolve, Caleb expresses his determination to take action in his ability: "We must go up!" (*'ālō na'āleh*; GBHS §3.3.3a). The purpose of going up: "to possess it" (*wəyārašnû*; GBHS §3.5.3b).

40. "But" (*wə*) contrasts the men and their speech with Caleb's charge in v. 30c–d (IBHS §39.2.3b).

41. Formally, "to the people," but the prep. indicates a disadvantage, "against" (estimative: GBHS §4.1.2b); the article is taken as referential, "those" (GBHS §2.6.1).

42. Without a separate adjective (bad), this rare word (9× in the OT)—repeated in Yahweh's indictment in Num. 14:36, 37—has a negative sense in the context: "evil report, gossip, defamation" ("*dibbâ*," DCH 2:383; a neutral report could be possible in other contexts requiring an adj.: HALOT 1:208).

that devours[43] its inhabitants. All the people we saw there are huge.[44] **33**We saw the Nephilim[45] there (the descendants of Anak came from the Nephilim),[46] and we seemed like grasshoppers[47] both to ourselves and to them."[48]

Interpretation

13:1–16. Yahweh orders and Moses directs twelve chieftains, one from each tribe, to explore the land of Canaan. The Israelites are now stationed in the Paran wilderness just south of the southern boundary of the Negev (south) in Canaan (12:16).[49] In other words, the people are poised to enter the promised land from the south. Yahweh sends the twelve expressly "to explore the land of Canaan, which I am giving to the Israelites," by which the authors here present Yahweh as initiating the realization of his land promise to Abraham, Isaac, Jacob, and eventually to Moses.[50] Contrary to popular thought, Yahweh did not send the twelve on a mission of reconnaissance;[51] rather, they

---

43. The present, predicate ptc. *'ōkelet* (is eating) expresses the land's ongoing consumption of its inhabitants (*GBHS* §3.4.3b).

44. "Huge" (cf. "giants," NLT; Budd, *Numbers*, 141; "enormous proportions," Levine, *Numbers*, 1:351) or "men of stature/size" (*'anšê middôt*; similarly rendered by NRSV, NET, NIV, NJPS; Schmidt, *Numeri*, 36; Seebass, *Numeri*, 2:80; Ashley, *Numbers*, 235); others confine this to their height, "very tall" (LXX[ed]: *andres hypermēkeis*; similarly: ESV; Cazelles, *Nombres*, 72; de Vaulx, *Nombres*, 168; EÜ).

45. LXX[ed], with NLT, renders this noun "giants" (*tous gigantas*), which probably comes from the description of Nephilim as "giants" (*hoi gigantes*) in Gen. 6:4 (Wevers, *Notes*, 209).

46. The gloss "the descendants of Anak came from the Nephilim" (*bənê 'ănāq min-hannəpilîm*) is parenthesized (ESV, NRSV, NET, NIV) because it breaks the flow of the verbal sequence (qatal, wayyiqtol). It functions as an aside to inform readers who, presumably, knew the Anakites but did not know the Nephilim, from whom they came (assigned to P by Schmidt, *Numeri*, 45). LXX[ed] omits this gloss, possibly by homoeoteleuton (of *hannəpilîm*: Wevers, *Notes*, 209), or a Hb. editor added the gloss for his readers at a very late stage (see Seebass, *Numeri*, 2:112–13; on this methodology, see R. Müller and Pakkala, *Insights into Editing*).

47. This type of grasshopper or locust ("*ḥāgāb* I," *DCH* 3:158) was edible according to the Priestly dietary code (Lev. 11:22) but is not named, yet it may be implied as edible in Deuteronomy's code (Deut. 14:19–20). The locust of the exodus plague, also edible (Lev. 11:22), had a different name ("*'arbeh*," *HALOT* 1:83) and was perhaps a migratory locust.

48. After v. 33, SP interpolates a passage adapted from Deut. 1:27–33.

49. See Rasmussen, *Atlas*, 106.

50. Frevel (*Mit Blick*, 355) sees Num. 13:2 as the realization of the land promise, especially from Gen. 17:8 and Exod. 6:8.

51. Olson (*Death of the Old*, 129–52), Van Seters (*Life of Moses*, 363–82), and many others call Num. 13–14 "The Spy Story." Milgrom (*Numbers*, 99) names it "The Reconnaissance of Canaan," Levine (*Numbers*, 1:351) "The Dispatch of the Spies," Ashley (*Numbers*, 229) "The Spies," and Kislev ("Joshua," 39–55) "the Priestly Spies Story." In an expansive diachronic and synchronic treatment of Num. 13–14, Knipping (*Kundschaftergeschichte*) calls it a "spy/scout story"; likewise, Wagner ("Kundschaftergeschichten," 255–69) argues for the existence of a "spy

were engaged in conspicuous exploration. Three pieces of evidence support this claim.

1. Yahweh expresses the purpose of their trip in v. 1 by a Hebrew verb (*twr*) that here means not "to spy out, reconnoitre"[52] but "to search out" or "explore" or "investigate."[53] This verb (*twr*) functions as a *Leitwort* (lead word), occurring twelve times in chaps. 13–14 alone.[54] Its first occurrence in the Pentateuch is in Num. 10:33, where the ark does not spy but searches for a resting place for Israel.[55] There is no mention in the Num. 13–14 story of spying or secrecy.[56] Krause has identified the parallel lexemes between the Josh. 2 Rahab story, Num. 13–14, and Deut. 1:19–46 but argues that Josh. 2 does not relate intertextually to these, and as an independent story focuses not on the people or the spies (who remain nameless) but on Rahab, the prostitute heroine.[57] The connotation of spying does appear in Deut. 1:24, which revisits the Num. 13–14 saga, but this Deuteronomic text belongs to the "relecture" of Deut. 1–3 with its distinct theological purposes.[58] By contrast, within the book of Numbers itself, Yahweh redescribes the purpose of Israel's expedition in Num. 13 as visualization without any hint of spying: "when I sent them from Kadesh Barnea (in order) *to see the land* [*lir'ôt 'et-hā'āreṣ*]" (Num. 32:8).[59]

---

stories" genre to which Num. 13–14 belongs, and Knierim and Coats (*Numbers*, 192) identify the genre as a spy report within a story.

52. See "*twr*," HALOT 4:1707–9, gloss 1; DCH 8:610, gloss 1a; ESV, NRSV; Cazelles, *Nombres*, 70–76; Budd, *Numbers*, 140–49; Ashley, *Numbers*, 231–53; ≈ "scout," NJPS and Levine, *Numbers*, 1:349–61.

53. See the first translation note on 13:2. For *twr* as "explore" in Num. 13–14, see: DCH 8:610, gloss 1b; Seebass, *Numeri*, 2:78–81; Schmidt, *Numeri*, 34–37; de Vaulx, *Nombres*, 164–76; EÜ, NLT, NIV, NET ("investigate").

54. See *twr* in Num. 10:33 ["search"]; 13:2, 16, 17, 21, 25, 32 [2×]; 14:6, 7, 34, 36, 38; 15:39 ["follow"].

55. Also, Deut. 1:33, the only other appearance of *twr* in the Pentateuch.

56. Unlike Josh. 2:1, which refers to sending *spies* (*məraggəlîm*, piel *rgl*) secretly (*ḥereš*); also see Josh. 6:22–25; 7:2.

57. Krause, "Aesthetics," 420–22.

58. "They came to Wadi Eshcol and *spied it out* [*wayraggəlû*]" (Deut. 1:24); also, cf. Josh. 14:7, both with the piel of *rgl* I, "spy (out)" (DCH 7:410). This verbal meaning is also found in Gen. 42 [7×] and Num. 21:32. These subsequent texts reflect the Deuteronomists' "relecture" of some form of Num. 13 to compel Israel and Judah to covenant faithfulness (See Gertz, "Kompositorische Funktion," 103–23).

59. See GBHS §3.4.1c. Similarly, Lohfink (*Theology*, 126–27) promotes the view that, in contrast to other traditions (Dtr), in the priestly account in Num. 13–14 "it is not a hostile troop of spies, but a sort of sacred group of land inspectors, who in the name of their people, are to look over the gift of God that lies before them."

2. The men cut down (harvest) and visibly export an impressive sample of fruit from Wadi Eshcol near Hebron (vv. 23–24), but the narrator gives no impression that they had to steal it or evade the notice of the locals (cf. Deut. 23:25; 2 Sam. 23:15–17; Prov. 9:17).

3. The twelve men may have been cautious, but they imply that they interfaced directly with the inhabitants: "We seemed like grasshoppers both to ourselves *and to them* [lit., "in their eyes," *bəʿênêhem*]" (13:33c).

What is the point of making this distinction? In contrast to the Deuteronomists and the Jericho story, with their own literary purposes, the theological point here is that Yahweh does not need secret intelligence from the twelve to plan out his military strategy. Yahweh already knows Canaan because he owns it (Lev. 25:23), and his presence alone scatters his enemies (Num. 10:35–36). Why, then, did Yahweh send the men to explore the land? The answer is *for the Israelites*, as Moses's specifying instructions (vv. 17–20), the expedition (vv. 21–25), and the competing reports (vv. 26–33) will reveal.

Yahweh specifies that the twelve explorers must include one man from each tribe, and Moses sends them in obedience (vv. 2–3a). Their social pedigree is stressed by Yahweh and the narrator: "men . . . one man from each ancestral tribe" (patriarchal culture), "a chieftain" and "Israelite leaders" (war officers, community leaders; vv. 2–3), whom the narrator then honors by naming them with their fathers (vv. 4–16).

Table 13.1. Lineage of the Chieftains Compared

Numbers 1:5–14; 7:12–83[a]	Numbers 13:4–15
1. Reuben → Shedeur's son Elizur	Reuben → Zaccur's son Shammua
2. Simeon → Zurishaddai's son Shelumiel	Simeon → Hori's son Shaphat
3. Judah → Amminadab's son Nahshon	Judah → Jephunneh's son Caleb
4. Issachar → Zuar's son Nethanel	Issachar → Joseph's son Igal
5. Zebulun → Helon's son Eliab	Ephraim → Nun's son Hoshea
6. Ephraim → Ammihud's son Elishama	Benjamin → Raphu's son Palti
7. Manasseh → Pedahzur's son Gamaliel	Zebulun → Sodi's son Gaddiel
8. Benjamin → Gideoni's son Abidan	Manasseh → Susi's son Gaddi
9. Dan → Ammishaddai's son Ahiezer	Dan → Gemalli's son Ammiel
10. Asher → Ocran's son Pagiel	Asher → Michael's son Sethur
11. Gad → Deuel's son Eliasaph	Naphtali → Vophsi's son Nahbi
12. Naphtali → Enan's son Ahira	Gad → Maki's son Geuel

a. There is a different tribal order in 7:12–83.

One can only conjecture why the tribal order in Num. 13 differs from that of other Pentateuchal lists (including the birth order in Gen. 29–30). As for why the named chieftains and their fathers differ from those in Num. 1 and 7, one can imagine multiple leaders per tribe (e.g., 25:14) or simply

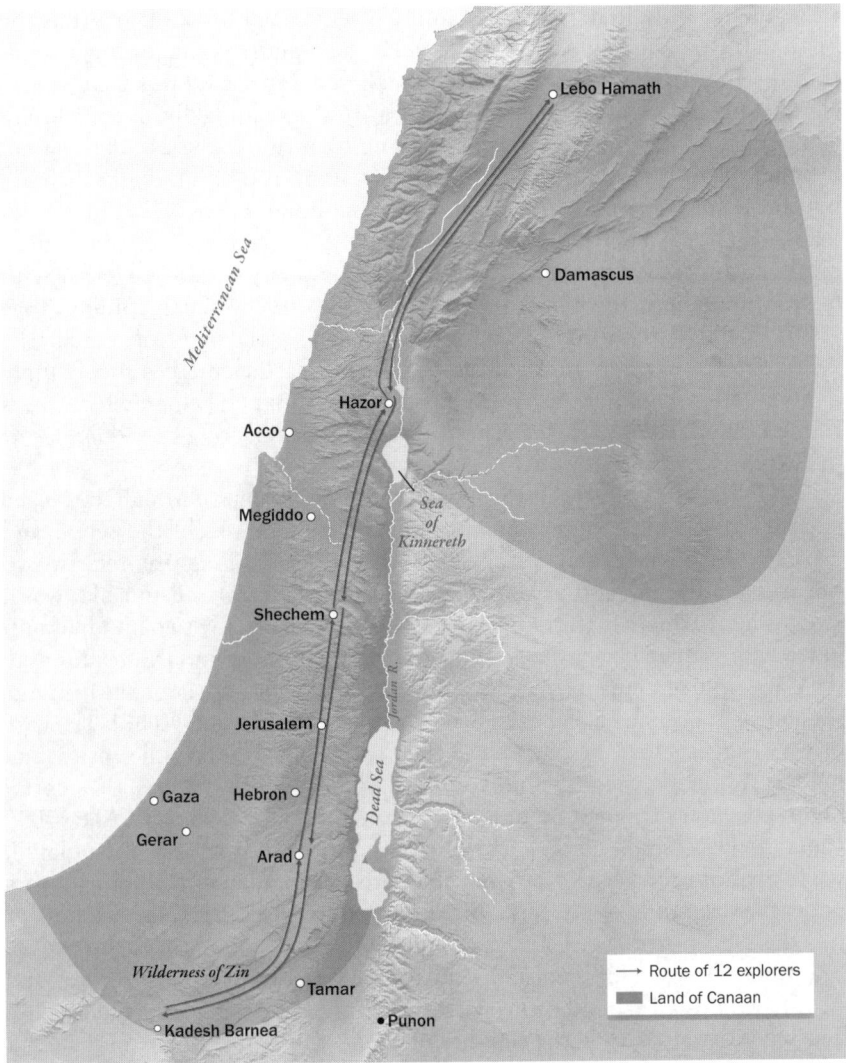

Map 13.1. Route of the Twelve Explorers

different sources.[60] Even so, as expected from the census and Levite theology of Num. 1–4, 7–8, the chieftains include no one from Levi, since they must remain stationed in and around Yahweh's tent, but two from Joseph. This marks the expedition as non-cultic military preparation for the conquest

60. Most see Num. 1:1–10:10 as P or P^g (see Kellermann's *Priesterschrift*), but on Num. 13–14, see the first note in this chapter.

of Canaan. Only here (vv. 8, 16) and in Deut 32:44 do we learn that the birth name of Nun's son, Joshua, was Hoshea, perhaps suggesting a tradition distinct from other Joshua texts. The narrator explains that Moses changes his name from Hoshea (*hôšēaʿ*, v. 16),[61] meaning "he saves" (hiphil causative), to Joshua (*yəhôšuaʿ*), meaning "Yah(weh) saves." As the great prophet of Yah(weh), Moses marks his assistant as a devotee of Yahweh,[62] but the name also anticipates Joshua's forthcoming role as war commander who enacts Yahweh's deliverance in Canaan.[63] In recent memory, the reader recalls Joshua's zeal for Moses's honor and authority (11:28); together with his renaming here, the narrator foreshadows his role in the upcoming story (14:6, 30, 38). By contrast, the naming of Caleb for the first time here in the Pentateuch (v. 6) offers no such foreshadowing, yet he emerges surprisingly as an even more influential protagonist than Joshua.[64] The name list here is framed by *inclusio*, with the repetition of *šəmôt* referring to the *names* of the explorers (vv. 4a, 16a).

13:17–25. Moses instructs the named chieftains to enter through the Negev (south) into the hill country and to survey the ethnography of the people and demography of their land (vv. 17–20). "The Negev" (*hannegeb*), referring to the arid southern region of Canaan, northeast of the Sinai Peninsula, was a strip of approximately thirty miles, with an average of only two hundred millimeters (less than 8 inches) of rainfall per year. The most important sites were the Canaanite settlements of Arad in the eastern Negeb and, later, the Iron Age settlement at Beersheba (Tel Beer-sheba) in the western Negeb.[65] The basic sense of v. 17 suggests that the purpose of their trip is not to survey the entire land but to sample its core, "the hill country" (*hāhār*; v. 17)—that is, the central highlands later occupied by Judah and Benjamin. In Late Bronze Age (LBA) Canaan, these highlands were considered frontier lands, sparsely populated, while various urban centers, vassal city-states, were ruled by chieftain mayors under the suzerainty of the New Kingdom Pharaohs (see the Amarna letters).[66] It is this LBA portrait of Canaan that colors Moses's directive to the twelve. They must discover, for themselves and for the Israelites, the nature of the land (v. 18), people (v. 18), land (v. 19), cities (v. 19), and once again, the land (v. 20). The repetitive stress is on the viability of *the land* not only for pastoralism but

61. This is the same spelling as Hosea the prophet.
62. See Exod. 17:9–13; 24:13; 32:17; see comments on 11:28.
63. Also, through v. 16b, the author brings "Hoshea" (v. 8) of this non-P name list into alignment with all other texts, which give his name as "Joshua": Exod. 17:9, 10, 13; 24:13; 32:17; 33:11; Num. 11:28; 13:16; 14:6, 30, 38; 26:65; 27:18, 22; 32:12, 28; 34:17.
64. Num. 13:6, 30; 14:6, 24, 30, 38; also as Jephunnah's son in Deut. 1:36. In another tradition, Othniel is called *Kenaz's son* and Caleb's younger brother (Judg. 3:9–11); see Greengus, *Laws*, 4.
65. Aharoni, *Land*, 26–27, 31, 201–2; Aharoni, "Beer-sheba," 111.
66. See Stager, "Forging an Identity," 90–93, 95–101; Stone, "Early Israel," 137–42; Moran, *Amarna Letters*.

also subsistence agriculture, as indicated by the alternatives, "good or bad," "fertile or infertile," forested or not (vv. 19–20).[67] This geographical focus is seen in Moses's final command to the twelve to act courageously and bring back some of the land's fruit (v. 20; see the second translation note there). The narrator or editor inserts that it was the beginning of the early grape harvest (v. 20; see the third translation note there), which starts in June or July and is followed by the vintage season in August and September.[68] This aside explains why Moses specifically requests a fruit sample and foreshadows what will soon transpire for the twelve (vv. 23–24).

The twelve must also discover the strength ("strong or weak"; see the translation note in v. 18) and population ("few or many") of the land's inhabitants as well as how vulnerable their settlements are to invasion (vv. 18–19). The contrast is between whether they live in open (exposed) villages, here called "camps" (*maḥănîm*), or "fortified cities" (*mibṣārîm*), which commonly would include "an encircling wall with towers."[69] Since the land's owner, Yahweh, knows the forces and fortifications of Canaan's people groups,[70] and since Yahweh has no rival power (10:35–36),[71] Moses's orders make the most sense as another test. In their living memory, the Israelites will recall when they camped in front of the sea but looked back in terror at Pharaoh's army rapidly approaching (Exod. 14:10–14; cf. 2 Chron. 20:12). Will the chieftains fixate on the warriors and fortresses of Canaan or put their trust in Yahweh, who recently rescued the Israelites from Egypt's ruthless forces?[72]

Without delay, the twelve chieftains obey Yahweh and Moses by exploring the land and its people (vv. 21–25; cf. Deut. 1:24–25).[73] The narrator offers no description here of the peoples' strength and cities' fortifications as Moses solicited (only later, in vv. 26–29, 32–33). Also, Yahweh and Moses direct the men to explore "the land of Canaan" (vv. 2, 17–18), but Moses seems to specify their destination as the hill country in particular (v. 17). However, the men opt to traverse through the Zin desert, which is part of the more expansive Paran desert,[74] and continue far north to Rehob, at the entrance to Hamath, which is the modern town of Hama, on the Orontes River in Syria (v. 21).[75] With these discrepancies aside, the narrator implies that the men executed their task faithfully, as the language of v. 22 indicates.

---

67. This seems to indicate movement away from Israel's early pastoralist origins (Abraham→ Moses) to the incorporation of agrarian subsistence (D. Fleming, *Legacy*, 162–70).

68. King and Stager, *Life*, 99.

69. King and Stager, *Life*, 231.

70. Exod. 19:5; Lev. 25:23; cf. Deut. 11:12; 2 Chron. 16:9; Prov. 15:3.

71. See the "Implications" essay in chap. 1, "Counting the Army."

72. Cf. Deut. 20:1–4.

73. Comparing Num. 13–14 and Deut. 1:19–46, see Schart, "Spy Story," 180–85.

74. Aharoni, *Land*, 199.

75. See Rasmussen, *Atlas*, 106.

They went up, as commanded, through the Negev and came to the critical southern outpost of the central highlands, Hebron, from which they drew their samples.

Hebron was the sacred burial ground of all Israel's patriarchs and matriarchs, excepting Rachel; there God first promised to give Abraham the land of Canaan.[76] The narrator highlights three men living in Hebron—Ahiman, Sheshai, and Talmai—all descended from Anak, about whom the Pentateuch reader knows nothing yet (v. 22; see the fifth translation note there). However, identifying them as "descendants of Anak" implies that the reader knows of Anak, possibly a prominent Hittite family (Gen. 23).[77] In an aside, the narrator explains that "Hebron had been built seven years before Zoan in Egypt" (v. 22), meaning that Hebron is even older and more impressive than the Egyptian region of Zoan, where by one tradition Israel had lived and Yahweh had displayed his wonders.[78] Again, will the twelve chieftains cower in fear or rise in faith?

In the highlands somewhere not far from Hebron, they arrive at a fertile wadi, a rain- or spring-fed riverbed (v. 23; see the first translation note there). They name it "Wadi Eshcol" (*naḥal 'eškōl*), meaning Wadi of Cluster, because of the impressive grape cluster they harvested there.[79] The scene is driven by "cluster" as its *Leitwort* and framed by *inclusio* (vv. 23a–b//v. 24):

> [23]When they came to Wadi *Eshcol* ['*eškōl*],
>> they cut down from there a branch with one *cluster* ['*eškōl*] of grapes,
>>> and they carried it on a staff between two men,
>>> along with some of the pomegranates and the figs.
> [24]They called that place Wadi *Eshcol* ['*eškōl*],
>> because of the *cluster* ['*eškōl*] that the Israelites cut from there.

The fecundity imaged in vv. 23–24 was not even the best of the land, since "the better soils around Hebron [of Judah] had their value reduced [compared to

---

76. Milgrom, *Numbers*, 103.

77. So Milgrom (*Numbers*, 103), who also notes the equating of the Anakites and Rephaites (Deut. 2:11), from whom giants later living along the Philistine coast had descended (Josh. 11:21–22; 1 Sam. 17 [Goliath]; 2 Sam. 21:18–22).

78. See Ps. 78:12, 43. Milgrom (*Numbers*, 103) notes that Zoan, in Hellenistic sources, is identified as Tanis, which is associated with Avaris, the Hyksos rulers' capital (18th–16th cent. BCE) and subsequent palace of Rameses II (13th cent.); cf. Zoan also in Isa. 19:11, 13; 30:4; Ezek. 30:14.

79. Curiously, Abram lived near Hebron "by the oaks of Mamre, the Amorite the brother of *Eshcol* ['*eškōl*] and Aner," allies of Abram by a parity treaty (Gen. 14:13, 24). Also, see clusters of grapes in Gen. 40:10; Song 1:14 [henna blossoms]; 7:8, 9; Isa. 65:8; Mic. 7:1. See reflections on Eshcol in Num. 32:9; Deut. 1:24; cf. Deut. 32:32.

Israel in the north] by low rainfall."[80] The Moses Story imagery of the promised land "flowing with milk and honey"[81] is a synecdoche for a fertile region. At the same time, the elements of milk and honey reveal the land's suitability for grazing herds and dairy farming (esp. goat milk)[82] and for cultivating apiaries (for bee honey) and date-palm groves (dates, date honey).[83] Here another image is added, namely, the land's viability for viticulture (grapes, wine) and orchard farming (pomegranates, figs).[84] Mentioning these lush fruit trees paints an Edenic image of life with Yahweh in his land.[85] Yahweh's presence and provision await his covenant people who trust and obey him. This orchard-divine dwelling remains the enduring hope for the church in the world to come (Rev. 2:7; 22:2, 14, 19).

The twelve return after forty days, a symbolic duration that implies a completed excursion, neither cut short nor prolonged (v. 25). Moses was on Mount Sinai for forty days and nights receiving Yahweh's commands (Exod. 24:18), and now, in obedience to Yahweh's recent command, the chieftains have explored the land over the same length of time.

13:26–29. The chieftains return and give the whole community a mixed report about the land, its fortified cities, and strong inhabitants, planting fear in the hearts of the Israelites. The reader knows that the Israelites are encamped in the Paran desert (10:12; 12:16; 13:3), but here for the first time the narrator specifies that the site to which the twelve return is the arid settlement of Kadesh,[86] elsewhere called Kadesh Barnea (v. 26; see the first translation note there).[87] Kadesh, probably about eighty kilometers (ca. fifty miles) south of Beersheba (Negev settlement), later became the southern border of Judah's territory. Kadesh Barnea was formerly believed to be the modern Israeli city of Nitzanei Sinai, but scholars today tend to identify it with the archaeological site Tel el-Qudeirat,[88] five miles from the modern town of Qusaymah, Egypt. Along with Ain el-Qudeirat, Kadesh is the "most fertile oasis in northern Sinai."[89]

---

80. Grabbe, *Ancient Israel*, 37.

81. *Zābat ḥālāb ûdəbāš*: see Exod. 3:8, 17; 13:5; 33:3; Lev. 20:24; Num. 13:27; 14:8; 16:13, 14; Deut. 6:3; 11:9; 26:9, 15; 27:3; 31:20; Josh. 5:6; Jer. 11:5; 32:22; Ezek. 20:6, 15; cf. Isa. 7:15, 22.

82. Signs of dairy production have been discovered in Anatolia (Turkey) as early as the Neolithic Age (7th millennium BCE).

83. King and Stager, *Life*, 103–6.

84. See Clement of Alexandria's christological reading (Lienhard, *Numbers*, 223).

85. Fruit trees are mentioned in Gen. 2:9, 16, 17; 3:1, 3, 6, 11, 12, 17, 22, 24.

86. Rasmussen, *Atlas*, 105.

87. Kadesh: Num. 13:26; 20:1, 14, 16, 22; 27:14; 33:36, 37; Deut. 1:46; 32:51; Judg. 11:16, 17; Ps. 29:8; Kadesh Barnea: 32:8; 34:4; Deut. 1:2, 19; 2:14; Josh. 10:41; 14:6, 7; 15:3. Meribath Kadesh: Ezek. 47:19; 48:28.

88. Milgrom, *Numbers*, 104. A 10th cent. (Iron Age II) fortress has been discovered there.

89. Redmount, "Bitter Lives," 67.

Mentioning that the twelve return not only to Moses and the community but also to Aaron probably marks the subordination of the twelve tribal chieftains to the tribe of Levi and particularly to Yahweh's Aaronic priests (v. 26). Showing the community their sample of the land's fruit, they then explain to Moses that they entered into the land where he had sent them (vv. 26b–27; see the translation note on v. 27). The twelve affirm that the land is "flowing with milk and honey" and prove it by showing off some of its fruit (v. 27; see *zābat ḥālāb* in the comments on vv. 23–24). In principle, their actions and their ensuing report convey what Moses enjoined them to discover (vv. 28–29):

Table 13.2. Exploration Commission and Report

Numbers 13:17–20	Numbers 13:27–29
[17]When Moses sent them to explore the land of Canaan, he told them, "Go up through the Negev, then go up into the hill country,	[27b]"We went to the land where you sent us.
[18]and see what the land is like,	It is indeed flowing with milk and honey, and this is its fruit.
and if the people who live in it are strong or weak, few or many,	[28]However, the inhabitants are strong, and the cities are fortified and *very* large.
[19]and if the land they live in is good or bad, and if the cities they live in are like camps or fortified cities,	We even saw the descendants of Anak there. [29]The Amalekites live in the land of the Negev; the Hittites, Jebusites, and Amorites live in the hill country; and the Canaanites live by the sea and along the banks of the Jordan."
[20]and if the land is fertile or infertile, and if there are forests in it or not. Be brave, and bring back some of the fruit of the land."	

The twelve effectively carry out Moses's orders, but three elements stand out as going beyond his instructions.

1. A strong disjunctive breaks the tone of their speech: "*However* [*'epes kî*], the inhabitants are strong" (v. 28; see the translation note there). Moses never suggested that strength, fortifications, or size was a problem, nor did he solicit the chieftains' feelings on the matter. This "however" colors everything reported in vv. 28–29 as aspects of the land about which the Israelites should be afraid.

2. Instead of choosing from Moses's proffered binary, "few or many," they report a third reality: the inhabited cities are "very large" (gədōlōt məʾōd, v. 28). This could also reflect their perception of the Canaanite city walls, which archaeology has shown to be 30–50 feet high and up to 15 feet thick.[90]

3. Moses did not ask for an ethnography of the land, but the twelve men conclude their speech with what seems like a preexisting, now calcified, phobia of the infamous people groups occupying their respective territories in Canaan (vv. 28d–29). The peoples who occupied the Negev, the southern desert (Amalekites), the central highlands (Hittites, Jebusites, Amorites), and the Mediterranean coast and Jordan River valley (Canaanites) are well-attested in ANE literature and biblical texts.[91] The illocution of their speech—what is meant by what is said—is that the land's fertility (v. 27) is irrelevant because the same land is also densely populated with powerful, fortified, and numerous people groups, whom they would have to face in battle (vv. 28–29).

13:30–33. In response, one of the explorers, Judah's chieftain, Caleb, silences the people in Moses's presence, and charges them: "We must go up to possess it because we are definitely able to conquer it!" (v. 30b; see the translation notes there). If read in isolation, Caleb's charge may seem self-reliant, even arrogant, but this overlooks the strong echoes of Yahweh's promises to Abram and Moses about conquering and possessing the land. The other explorers (excluding Moses's attendant Joshua, we presume)[92] mockingly invert Caleb's charge: "We are not able to go up against those people because they are stronger than us!" (v. 31b; see the second translation note there). In contrast to Caleb's optimism rooted in Yahweh's promises, the explorers discourage the Israelites by presenting "a bad report about the land" (dibbat hāʾāreṣ), fixating on their perception of the destructive power and gigantic stature of the land's inhabitants (vv. 32–33). Their report not only instills fear in the hearts of the exodus generation but also jump-starts a downward spiral of anthropocentric faithlessness that results in forty years of death in the wilderness (Num. 14:20–38).[93] In Num. 11, and now definitively in Num. 13–14, the death of the exodus generation has begun.[94]

90. Milgrom, *Numbers*, 105.
91. See Milgrom, *Numbers*, 105–6; Walton and Matthews, *Genesis–Deuteronomy*, 188–89.
92. Later Joshua is distinguished from the discouragers (14:6, 30, 38).
93. Blum (*Komposition des Pentateuch*, 329) rightly identifies Num. 13–14 as a comprehensive trial and disaster, leading to Israel's forgetting God, and yet Yahweh's loyalty remains unbreakable.
94. See Olson, *Death of the Old*, 144–52.

Implications

When You Trust and Fear God, You No Longer Fear People

In the Moses story, Judah's representative explorer, Caleb, is completely unknown prior to the list of explorers' names (vv. 4–16). Now, by the story-teller's prowess, he enters the scene prominently. Through his terse exhortation to the community in v. 30, he displays "a limited and stereotyped range of traits"; namely, he typifies the courageous warrior.[95] From what recesses in his soul does Caleb's bravery come? At first glance, based on his word choice, it might seem that Caleb is a proud, self-dependent fighter (contra Jer. 9:23; 2 Chron. 20:12). Such a reading, however, fails to recognize that Caleb's words echo the language that Yahweh famously directed first to Abraham and later to Moses to *go up* and *possess* the promised land of Canaan:

Yahweh: "I am Yahweh who brought you out of Ur of the Chaldeans to give you this land *to possess* [*yrš* qal]." (Gen. 15:7)[96]

Yahweh: "*Go up* [*ʿlh* qal] from here, you and the people whom you brought up out of the land of Egypt, to the land that I swore on oath to Abraham, to Isaac, and to Jacob." (Exod. 33:1)[97]

Caleb: "*We must go up* [*ʿlh* qal] *to possess* [*yrš* qal] it because we are definitely able to conquer it!" (Num. 13:30b; see the second translation note there)

Caleb's (and Joshua's) faith in Yahweh's power to conquer and fulfill the patriarchal land promise is made explicit as the saga unfolds (14:6–9, 24, 30, 38). Caleb never downplays the power of the enemy, but he fears Yahweh more, and he is ready to risk his life to actualize the covenant promises.

By contrast, the other explorers try to subvert Caleb's motivational speech by turning it into antithetical parallelism!

> We must go up to possess it
>> because we are definitely able to conquer it! (v. 30b)

> We are not able to go up against those people
>> because they are stronger than us! (v. 31b; see the second translation note there)[98]

---

95. See Berlin, "Characterization," 78.
96. See *yrš* qal + Canaan in Gen. 15:7, 8; 22:17; 28:4; Lev. 20:24.
97. See *ʿlh* qal + Canaan in Exod. 33:1, 3, 5; cf. 34:24.
98. The Hb. text can also be read as antithetical chiasm:
> We must go up to possess it
>> because *we are definitely able* to conquer it! (v. 30b)

They extrapolate their defeatist mindset in their slanderous report about the land (*dibbat hā'āreṣ*) in vv. 32–33. Their report is reminiscent of a lawsuit that distorts reality, particularly in legal settings,[99] and it has four basic premises.

1. They say the land they explored devours—formally, is *perpetually eating*—its inhabitants (v. 32; see the second translation note there). The blessing of eating the fruit of the land is converted into trepidation of being eaten by the land.[100]
2. They claim that all those living in Canaan are huge—formally, *men of stature* (v. 32; see the third translation note there).
3. They assert that they saw the Nephilim there, and the narrator or editor contextualizes this for his audience by an aside: the descendants of Anak came from the Nephilim (see the second translation note on v. 33). Apparently, in the context of what they say before and afterward, identifying the Nephilim as the ancestors of the Anakites would strike fear into the listeners' ears.
4. The men self-reflect on how they thought of themselves in comparison to the Nephilim, and they even project how the Nephilim thought about them: "and we seemed like grasshoppers both to ourselves and to them" (see the third and fourth translation notes on v. 33). This is a reversal of image, attested in the Ugaritic Legend of Keret (or Kirta Epic) and in Joel 1:4–7, of swarms of grasshoppers as a metaphor for a vast army of soldiers.[101] The cumulative implication of 13:31–33 is that the reporters, representing the exodus generation, are rejecting Yahweh's gift of land because of their unbelief.[102]

Their report inverts the logic of their craving at Kibroth Hattaavah: the Israelites exaggerated the delicious food of Egypt but ignored its oppressive forces (11:5); now they exaggerate Canaan's forces but ignore its delicious food (13:23–24, 27–29, 31–33). Ingratitude and the fear of people rather than God have the power to obfuscate one's mind and soul. Often Num. 12 is held up in preaching and teaching to illustrate the misplaced fear of people, worrying about what others think of you. This illustrates the hermeneutical proverb:

We are not able
to go up against those people because they are stronger than us! (v. 31b).

99. P. Guillaume, *Land*, 146. *Dbh* is used of Joseph's negative report to his father about his brothers (Gen. 37:2). Leveen (*Memory*, 86–87) notes that Joseph was eventually sold into slavery in Egypt; here the explorers want to return to Egypt.

100. P. Guillaume, *Land*, 146.

101. See Walton and Matthews, *Genesis–Deuteronomy*, 189.

102. Elliger, "Sinn und Ursprung," 140. Boorer (*Priestly Narrative*) sees the rejection of Canaan and other themes in Num. 13–14*, 20*, 27* as reversing Exod. 1–40*.

right theology, wrong text.[103] The explorers did not fear that the locals thought less of them as smaller and weaker men; rather, they feared that the locals had the power to slaughter them in battle (13:28–29, 31–33). The message is clear: *When you trust and fear God, you no longer fear what people can do to you.*

How, then, does one take this brave path of Caleb (and later Joshua) and avoid the paralyzing ditch the other ten chieftains fell into? First, when push came to shove with the other explorers, Caleb's words reveal how deeply the language of Yahweh's land promise to his people had taken root in his psyche (13:30). We too must saturate our minds with the language of God's promises to his covenant people so that we can rise above the temptation to dread other humans who can harm or kill us. This is immediately relevant to our persecuted brothers and sisters around the world[104] but is becoming more significant in the increasingly anti-Christian cultures of the northern hemisphere. Second, as Caleb and Joshua believed that God was fulfilling his promises *through them*, so we must understand ourselves as chosen agents contributing meaningfully within God's metanarrative of redemption (2 Cor. 2:14; 5:18–20). Third, Caleb and Joshua trusted not in their own muscle mass, martial arts, or military genius but in Yahweh's power alone: "He will bring us into this land and give it to us. . . . Yahweh is with us" (14:8–9*). Trusting in God's power not only liberated Caleb and Joshua from fearing the destructive power of other humans but also oriented them toward pleasing Yahweh, who was present with them, above everything else.[105] If we trust in God's power to deliver us—whether in this life or the next—from those who can harm and murder us physically, from the enslaving forces of sin, and from fear of eternal death, then our highest aim must be to fear and honor our Father in all things (Matt. 10:28).

---

103. On fearing God instead of fearing the perception of others, observe Jesus in many stories in the Gospels; also see 1 Sam. 15:24; 16:7; Prov. 29:26; Isa. 2:22; 51:7; Matt. 6:1–8; John 5:44; 12:42–43; Acts 4:19–20; 5:29; Gal. 1:10; 2:5–6, 11–16; Eph. 6:6; Col. 3:22–25; 1 Thess. 2:4; 1 Tim. 4:12; 2 Tim. 2:4.

104. See The Voice of the Martyrs, https://www.persecution.com.

105. "If Yahweh delights in us, . . . do not rebel against Yahweh" (14:8–9*).

14

Israelites Complain; Moses Intercedes; Invasion Fails

(14:1–45)

❧

Overview

Chapter 14 continues the aftermath of the story of the twelve explorers of Canaan (chap. 13), and this becomes clear from many thematic and intertextual references back to that expedition and its fallout.[1] Theoretically, if the community had rejected the report of the discouraging explorers in favor of Caleb's courageous vision (13:30–33), the script of chap. 14 would conceivably involve Israel's next leg of their journey toward or even into Canaan (they were already at the border). Putting the disastrous detours of chaps. 11–13 behind, the exodus generation would now be restored to favor in the presence of Yahweh, who will defend them as they capture their new homeland (Lev. 26:6–8; Num. 6:24–26; 10:35–36). Tragically, this is not how the story goes. With the negative report planted traumatically into their psyche, the community again expresses their nostalgia for Egypt and desire for a new leader, at which point Moses and Aaron fall flat on the ground while Joshua and Caleb urge the community to conquer the good land through the power of

1. W. Lee, *Migratory Campaign*, 131–35. The story genre threads together Num. 13–14 but not as tightly as a novella by a single author due to its editorial strata (Knierim and Coats, *Numbers*, 192). P. Guillaume (*Land*, 143–48) perceives "intense redactional activity" in Num. 13–14. Boorer (*Priestly Narrative*, 383–98) argues that P[g] in Num. 13–14*, as in Exod. 16, presents a paradigmatic scenario: Israelites complain, disputation speech, Yahweh's glory and speech, ensuing events. G. Kugler ("Threat of Annihilation," 632–47) argues that the annihilation-threat myth of the non-P portion of Exod. 32 and Num. 13–14 was secondary to these independent narratives and later than Ps. 78.

Yahweh (vv. 1–9). In response, the community colludes to stone Yahweh's four representatives, but Yahweh reveals his glory to all and informs Moses that he will destroy the Israelites and create a new people, starting with Moses as the new Abraham (vv. 10–12). Moses implores Yahweh to forgive his covenant people so that Yahweh can preserve his international reputation and prove his faithfulness to his revealed nature (vv. 13–19). Yahweh does forgive, but he swears an oath that the exodus generation, excepting Caleb and Joshua, will not inherit the promised land (vv. 20–25). To explicate this terse oath, Yahweh effectively curses the exodus generation to die in the wilderness, but promises that their children, alongside Joshua and Caleb, will survive and enter the land (vv. 26–35). The ten discouraging explorers are struck dead with a plague before Yahweh, so the community grieves and tries, without Yahweh, to conquer the Amalekites and Canaanites but is shamefully defeated.

Translation

1Then the whole community raised their voice,[2] and the people cried[3] that night. **2**And all the Israelites complained[4] against Moses and Aaron, and the whole congregation said to them, "If only we had died in the land of Egypt, or if only we had died in this wilderness! **3**Why is Yahweh bringing us into this land to fall by the sword? Our wives and our children will become war captives.[5] Wouldn't it better for us to return to Egypt?" **4**So they said to each other, "Let's appoint a leader and return to Egypt."[6] **5**Then Moses and Aaron fell facedown before the whole community gathering[7] of the Israelites. **6**And Nun's son Joshua

2. A verbal hendiadys: formally, "the whole community lifted and gave their voice" (*wattiśśā' kol-hā'ēdâ wayyittənû 'et-qôlām*; *GBHS* §4.3.3g.2).

3. MT: "the people, *they wept* [*wayyibkû*]" (cf. sg. SP and LXX^{ed}: "the people cried").

4. This niphal wayyiqtol (*wayyillōnû*) is probably "a pl. variation of the reflexive" (*GBHS* §3.1.2c), meaning "they complained among themselves." The Phoenician cognate, *lwn$_2$*, occurs in a reflexive stem, meaning "to growl, to grumble" (under "*lyn$_1$*," *DNWSI* 1:575). This root in the OT, often translated by the more archaic "murmur" (niphal of "*lwn* I," *DCH* 4:530; *HALOT* 2:524), occurs in Exod. 15–17 (7×), Num. 14–17 (9×), and Josh. 9:18. In this chapter, it becomes a *Leitwort* (Num. 14:2, 27 [2×], 29, 36 [2×]) and reappears in Korah's rebellion (16:11 [2×], 41 [17:6 MT]; 17:5, 10 [20, 25 MT]).

5. "War captives" (*baz*) appears first in the Pentateuch here, then in v. 31 (then 31:32; Deut. 1:39), and is typically translated with terms that are less common today, such as "booty" (NRSV) or "plunder, spoil" (*HALOT* 1:117; NLT, NET, NIV), or that are not particular to war, such as "prey" (*DCH* 2:132, gloss 2; ESV). My translation reflects the sense of "prey of enemies" (EÜ) and "be carried off" (NJPS).

6. SP lacks the cohortative morpheme (-*hâ*) on these verbs, but they can still be cohortative in meaning (cf. LXX^{ed} subjunctives), imperfective ("We will appoint a leader and will return to Egypt"), or obligatory ("We must appoint a leader and must return to Egypt"; *GBHS* §3.2.2a, d.3).

7. Formally, "gathering/assembly of the community" (*qəhal 'ădat*). My choice, "community gathering" (with EÜ), renders an attributed gen., "gathered community" (similarly NJPS, NET; epexegetical, *IBHS* §9.5.3c).

and Jephunneh's son Caleb, who were among those who had explored[8] the land, ripped their clothes.[9] [7]They said[10] to the whole Israelite community: "The land we passed through to explore is an exceptionally good land.[11] [8]If Yahweh delights in us, then he will bring us into this land and give it to us—a land that is flowing with milk and honey. [9]Only do not rebel against Yahweh,[12] and do not fear the people of the land, for they are bread for us. Their protection has turned away from them, but[13] Yahweh is with us. Do not fear them!"

[10]Then the whole community said to stone them.[14] But[15] the glory of Yahweh appeared[16] in the meeting tent to all the Israelites. [11]Yahweh said to Moses, "How long will this people revile me,[17] and how long will

---

8. SP, probably a homophonic error, reads, "from among *the Atharim* [*h'trym*]," which is a toponym near Arad (21:1).

9. In the ANE and Israel, tearing one's clothes (**qr* + obj. *bəgādîm*) was a sign of mourning (*DCH* 7:328, gloss 1; *HALOT* 3:1147–48, gloss 1a; Walton and Matthews, *Genesis–Deuteronomy*, 189) and of grieving the death of a close relative (Milgrom, *Numbers*, 108). Here it signifies their distress, fearing that the people might rebel and incite Yahweh's judgment. In 2 Kings 22:11 Josiah tears his clothes (*qr* + *bəgādîm*) in distress at Judah's rebellion and Yahweh's judgment.

10. Caleb and Joshua are the implied speakers (v. 6).

11. The absolute superlative *mə'ōd* is repeated for stress: "a good land, very, very" (*ṭôbâ hā'āreṣ mə'ōd mə'ōd*; *BHRG* §30.4.2c).

12. After the restrictive adv. *'ak* (only, but), focus is placed on Yahweh, the fronted constituent: "Only *against Yahweh* do not rebel" (*BHRG* §47.2.1[2a]). The two prohibitions (*'al* + jussive) are specific or immediate, "do not rebel . . . do not fear."

13. "But" (*wə*) marks the contrast with v. 9c (*IBHS* §39.2.3b).

14. Formally, "Then the whole community said to stone them with stones." This implies movement toward actually stoning Joshua and Caleb (ESV; Budd, *Numbers*, 148; Ashley, *Numbers*, 245). It goes beyond a verbal threat ("threatened": NRSV, NET, NJPS, EÜ; Levine, *Numbers*, 1:360), communal thought ("thought" for Schmidt, *Numeri*, 36; Seebass, *Numeri*, 2:80), or deliberation ("was talking about stoning them" for Cazelles, *Nombres*, 73; de Vaulx, *Nombres*, 172; NLT, NIV).

15. "But" (*ú*) distinguishes the "glory of Yahweh" (*kəbôd yhwh*) from the community's intent to stone Caleb and Joshua (*IBHS* §39.2.3b).

16. The possessive gen., meaning "the glory possessed by Yahweh" (*kəbôd yhwh*; *GBHS* §2.2.1), occurs in the Pentateuch only in the Moses story (Exod. 16:7, 10; 24:16, 17; 40:34, 35; Lev. 9:6, 23; Num. 14:10, 21; 16:19; 16:42 [17:7]; 20:6). In Exod. 40:30–45, "the glory of Yahweh *filled* [*mālē'*]" the meeting tent (qal transitive), restricting even Moses from entering (cf. the allusion in 1 Kings 8:11), but in Lev. 9:23 and here, "the glory of Yahweh *appeared* [*nir'â*]" to the whole Israelite community, yet from inside the meeting tent (*bə'ōhel mô'ēd*). The niphal "appeared" (*nir'â*) functions as a causative-reflexive, meaning "the glory of Yahweh made itself to be seen" (*IBHS* §23.4.h.23).

17. This is the first of the Pentateuch's five occurrences of **n'ṣ*, which in the piel means "have contempt (for), revile, spurn" (*DCH* 5:581) or "treat disrespectfully, discard" (*HALOT* 2:706). All five occurrences have covenant overtones (Num. 14:11, 23; 16:30; Deut. 31:20; 32:19). Achenbach (*Vollendung*, 635–36) attributes these verses in Num. 14 and 16 to the Pentateuch and Hexateuch redactors, both of whom stress Israel's covenant relationship with Yahweh. Thus I prefer "revile" (*DCH*) or even "treat with contempt" (NLT, NIV), a fientive verb of abusive criticism that could be exposed and punished as a covenant breach (vassals must not criticize

they not trust in me,[18] in spite of all the signs that I have done among them? [12]I will strike them with a plague, and I will disinherit them, but[19] I will make you[20] into a nation that is greater and stronger than they are!"

[13]Moses said to Yahweh, "Then the Egyptians will hear it, since you brought up this people by your power from among them, [14]and they will tell it to the inhabitants of this land. They have heard that you, Yahweh, are among this people, that you, Yahweh, appear personally,[21] and your cloud stands over them, and you go before them in a pillar of cloud during the day and in a pillar of fire at night. [15]If you kill[22] this entire people at one time,[23] then the nations that have heard of your fame[24] will say, [16]'Yahweh was not able to bring this people into the land that he swore to them, so he slaughtered them in the wilderness.' [17]Now let Yahweh's power be great, just as you have said,[25] [18]'Yahweh is slow to anger[26] and abounding in loyal love,[27] forgiving iniquity and rebellion,[28] but does not leave the guilty unpunished, punishing the

the suzerain), rather than "despise" (many versions) or "spurn," a stative verb that connotes wicked thoughts or feelings about Yahweh. As a piel factitive, it means, "How long will this people put me into a reviled state?" (GBHS §3.1.3a).

18. Commonly, "How long will they not *believe in me*?" which might connote a cognitive or confessional faith, but the contextual meaning here is that the Israelites failed to *trust* in Yahweh's goodness and power to secure the land for them (with Seebass, *Numeri*, 2:80; Levine, *Numbers*, 1:360).

19. Contextual "but" (*wə*) with a cohortative by which Yahweh determines to act within his ability, "But I will make you" (*wə'e'ĕśeh*).

20. SP and LXX^ed include, "But I will make you *and your father's house* into a great nation." This may aim to substantiate the divine approval of other members of Moses's father's house, namely Aaron, whose election by Yahweh as priest is validated in Num. 17 (in contrast to chap. 12). Verse 12 presents Moses as a potential new Abraham, alluding to Gen. 12:2, but this SP/LXX^ed expansion contrasts with Abraham, whom Yahweh commanded to "*Leave* your father's house" (contra Wevers, *Notes*, 217).

21. Formally, "appear *eye by eye*" (*'ayin bə'ayin*). A niphal pass. is possible, "are seen" (*nir'â*) (≈ LXX^ed, most modern versions), but the shift from Yahweh's glory (v. 10) to Yahweh here does not demand a shift from the causative-reflexive nuance of the same niphal verb (v. 10), so again I prefer "appear" (Seebass, *Numeri*, 2:80), meaning "You, Yahweh, *make yourself to be seen* personally" (de Vaulx, *Nombres*, 172; Cazelles, *Nombres*, 74) or "appear visible" (EÜ) or "appear to them in plain view" (Levine, *Numbers* 1:360).

22. An implied conditional weqatal, "If you kill" (*wəhēmattâ*), whereas LXX^ed renders this formally, "And you will wipe out this people."

23. Formally, "If you kill this entire people as one man," probably meaning as quickly as it takes to kill one person.

24. "Your fame" (ESV, NLT, NET, NJPS, EÜ) renders "the hearing of you" (*šim'ăkā*) as an objective gen., meaning "what others hear about you" (IBHS §9.5.2b).

25. Comma for "saying." See the third translation note on Num. 1:1.

26. Formally, "long of two nostrils," referring anthropomorphically to the long time it takes for Yahweh's nose to become red hot with anger.

27. "Loyal love" (*ḥesed*, NET)—which others translate "grace" (EÜ), "steadfast love" (ESV, NRSV), "unfailing love" (NLT), "kindness" (NJPS)—expresses Yahweh's faithfulness to his covenant people, not his love for the whole world (see Ps. 136:13–24).

28. SP and LXX^ed add, "iniquity, rebellion, *and sin*," probably to harmonize with Exod. 34:7.

iniquity of the fathers against the children until the third and fourth generation.' **19**Forgive the iniquity of this people according to your great loyal love, just as you have forgiven this people[29] from Egypt until now."

20Then Yahweh said, "I have forgiven them[30] as you asked.[31] **21**Nevertheless, as surely as I live and the glory of Yahweh fills the whole earth,[32] **22**indeed all the people who have seen my glory and my signs that I did in Egypt and in the wilderness have tested me[33] now these ten times and have not obeyed me,[34] **23**they will not see the land that I swore to their fathers,[35] nor will any of them who reviled me see it.[36] **24**Only[37] my servant Caleb, because he has a different spirit and follows me completely,[38] I will bring him into the land where he had gone, and his descendants will possess it. **25**(The Amalekites and the

29. LXX[ed], "just as you were merciful to them" (v. 19) and "I am merciful to them" (v. 20), which, without SP support, probably shows the translator's exegesis (Wevers, *Notes*, 221).

30. Improper synonyms in vv. 19–20 vary the style: "'*Forgive* [*slḥ] the iniquity of this people . . . just as *you have forgiven/pardoned* [**nś'*] . . .' Then Yahweh said, '*I have forgiven* [*slḥ] them.'"

31. Formally, "according to your word"; SP pl.: "according to your words."

32. MT points the verb as a niphal incomplete pass., "the whole earth *is/will be filled* [*wəyimmālē'*] with the glory of Yahweh" (≈ Vulg[ed]; Migsch, "Bedeutung," 79–83; *GBHS* §3.1.2a). The problem with this is that "the whole earth" is marked as the direct obj., so it is preferable to vocalize the Hebrew as a piel act. (*yəmallē'*) with the LXX[ed] fut. act., "the glory of the Lord will fill the whole earth" (with Wevers, *Notes*, 222), or as a present tense, "fills" (NIV, NJPS, EÜ). Related OT constructions, sometimes passivized in translations, are not passive: "his glory fills the whole earth" (Ps. 72:19, contra MT niphal) and "the fullness of the earth is his glory" (Isa. 6:3). See the third translation note on 12:3.

33. This piel factitive of *nsh, means "Put me into a tested state" (*GBHS* §3.1.3a). The root *nsh occurs in Numbers only here. Exodus and Deuteronomy have more extensively developed the theology of the wilderness generation as testing Yahweh or Yahweh as testing them (*nsh 5× in Exod. 15–20, and 8× in Deuteronomy).

34. Formally, "They have not listened to my voice."

35. SP "swore to their fathers *to give to them* [*ltt lhm*]" probably harmonizes with parallel texts (Deut. 10:11; 11:21; 31:7, 20), but this is unnecessary since variations of this formula occur with an ellipsis of "to give" (*ltt*: Num. 32:11; Deut. 31:21, 23; 34:4). The LXX[ed] plus harmonizes with 14:31; 32:11; and Deut. 1:39, which exempt the Israelite children from this judgment (Dorival, *Nombres*, 23n14; Wevers, *Notes*, 223). The plus is italicized here: "to their fathers. *Instead, their children who are with me here, as many as do not know good nor evil, every inexperienced younger person—to these I will give the land*, but all those who provoked me shall not see it" (NETS). Van der Meer ("Next Generation," 399–416) argues that this plus arose not from a separate *Vorlage* or early Hebrew revisions but from a later creative reformulation.

36. See the first translation note on 14:11.

37. Fronting activates an identifiable entity in contrast with the entity in vv. 23–24: "nor will any of them who despised me see it. *Only my servant Caleb*" (*BHRG* §47.2.1[a]*b*; *IBHS* §39.2.3b).

38. Formally, "because a different spirit is with him and he follows after me" ('*ēqeb hāytâ rûaḥ 'aḥeret 'immô waymallē' 'aḥărāy*), in which the second verb means "wholly follows me" (*DCH* 5:281, gloss 6).

Canaanites were living in the valleys.)³⁹ Tomorrow, turn and travel into the wilderness by the way of the Sea of Reeds."⁴⁰

²⁶Yahweh said to Moses and Aaron: ²⁷"How long will this evil community complain against me?⁴¹ I have heard the Israelites complaining against me.⁴² ²⁸Say to them, 'As I live, says Yahweh, I will do to you the very thing I heard you say.⁴³ ²⁹In this wilderness your dead bodies will fall—all those of you who were enlisted in the census, twenty years old and up, who have complained against me. ³⁰You will not enter into the land that I swore with a raised hand to settle you, except for Jephunneh's son Caleb and Nun's son Joshua. ³¹But your little ones,⁴⁴ whom you said would become war captives, I will bring in, and they will experience⁴⁵ the land that you have rejected. ³²But as for you, your dead bodies will fall in this wilderness, ³³and your children will be shepherds⁴⁶ in the wilderness forty years and suffer for your unfaithfulness,⁴⁷ until

39. This parenthetical sentence (NET) is the narrator's third-person aside to inform readers that the Amalekites and Canaanites, whom they knew or had heard of, had once lived in the valleys of the hill country (cf. Num. 13:29; 14:40–45; Deut. 1:44; so Gray, *Numbers*, 159–60; Seebass, *Numeri*, 2:121).

40. Famously, LXX^ed—still followed today by most English translations—identifies this body of water as "the Red Sea" (*thalassan erythran*, v. 25), but the Hebrew text uses the toponym, "Sea of Reeds" (*yam sûp*), probably originally denoting a gen. of container content, a sea *containing* reeds (BHRG §25.4.6[5]). A wordplay could also be possible: "The crossing of the sea signaled the end of the sojourn in Egypt and it certainly was the end of the Egyptian army that pursued the fleeing Hebrews (Exod. 14:23–29; 15:4–5). After this event at *yam sûp*, perhaps the verb *sôp*, meaning 'destroy' and 'come to an end,' originated (cf. Amos 3:15; Jer. 8:13; Isa. 66:17; Psa. 73:19). Another possible development of this root is the word *sûpah*, meaning 'storm-wind.' . . . The meanings 'end' and 'storm-wind' would have constituted nice puns on the event that took place at the *yam sûp*" (Hoffmeier, *Israel in Egypt*, 214). However, supporting the traditional interpretation, Num. 21:4 uses "Sea of Reeds" (*yam sûp*) for what is most reasonably the Gulf of Aqaba of the Red Sea (Mallon, "La Mer Rouge," 396–400).

41. Formally, "How long for this evil community who (they) are complaining against me."

42. The obj. is Israel's complaints, which is fronted for emphasis: formally, "*The complaints of the Israelites that they complained against me* I have heard" (BHRG §47.2.1[2]). LXX^ed, "which they have complained *concerning you*," that is, concerning or against Moses, probably to align with v. 1 (Wevers, *Notes*, 226).

43. Formally, "Just as you spoke in my ears, so I will do to you."

44. Fronting activates the identifiable entity in contrast with the entity in v. 30a: "You will not enter . . . , *but your little ones*" (BHRG §47.2.1[a]*b*; IBHS §39.2.3b).

45. Commonly, "they will know" (*wəyādᵉʿû*), but contextually, "be familiar with, experience" ("*ydᶜ* I," *DCH* 4:100, from gloss 2).

46. To "shepherds" (*rōʿîm*) some add "wander(ing)" (NLT, NET), but wandering is not obvious at this point in the story. Rather, the point is that they would continue surviving, and soon dying, as seminomadic pastoralists seasonally or rotationally grazing *in the wilderness*, instead of where they should be, in Canaan (with EÜ: "Your children must graze their cattle in the wilderness").

47. The deverbal noun, "unfaithfulness" (*zənût*), occurs only here in the Pentateuch, then eight times in the Latter Prophets (Jer. 3:2, 9; 13:27; 43:7, 9; Hosea 4:11; 6:10). Elsewhere it refers to "prostitution" (Jeremiah and Ezekiel) and derives from **znh* I, which most frequently means

you have fallen dead in this wilderness.[48] **34**According to the number of days you explored the land, forty days, you will suffer for your iniquities for forty years, one year for every day, and you will know my opposition.[49] **35**I, Yahweh, have said, "I will definitely do this to this entire evil congregation that has gathered together[50] against me. In this wilderness they will be finished off, and there they will die!""

36The men whom Moses sent to explore the land—who returned and incited the whole community to complain[51] against him by spreading a bad report about the land—**37**those men[52] who produced the bad report about the land, died by a plague before Yahweh. **38**But only[53] Nun's son Joshua and Jephunneh's son Caleb remained alive[54] among the men who went to explore the land.

39When Moses told these things to all the Israelites, the people mourned deeply. **40**Early in the morning they went up[55] to the summit of the hills,[56] saying, "Here we are. We will go up to the place that Yahweh has said, for we have sinned."[57] **41**But Moses said,[58] "Why are you now stepping over[59] Yahweh's command? It will not succeed![60] **42**Do not go up,[61] for

---

"prostitute oneself" or "commit fornication" but is also used figuratively, "to be unfaithful" in one's relationship with God (*DCH* 3:121–23; *HALOT* 1:275).

48. Formally, "and your corpses have fallen in this wilderness."

49. "My opposition" (*tənûʾātî*) could be a subjective gen., "I oppose you" (LXX^ed, "the wrath of my anger"; NRSV, NLT, NIV), or an objective gen., "you oppose me" (EÜ, NJPS, NET: "thwart me") (*GBHS* §2.2.3, 2.2.4).

50. The niphal attributive ptc. is reflexive, meaning "that has gathered (itself) together" (*hannôʿādîm; GBHS* §3.1.2c).

51. "*Incited* the whole community *to complain*" renders the Masoretes' suggested vocalization as a hiphil causative (MT^qere: *wayyallînû*), instead of the niphal they recorded, "they returned *and complained*" (MT^ketiv: *wayyillônû*).

52. A referential article, "*those* men" (*hāʾănāšîm; GBHS* §2.6.1).

53. Fronting activates the identifiable entity in contrast with the entity in v. 37: "Those men who produced the bad report . . . *But only Nun's son Joshua and Jephunneh's son Caleb remained alive*" (*BHRG* §47.2.1[a]b; cf. *IBHS* §39.2.3b).

54. Formally, "they were alive" (*ḥāyû*), but the qatal stative here expresses their present condition: "they remained alive" (*GBHS* 3.2.1b).

55. A verbal hendiadys, formally, "They got up early in the morning and they went up" (*GBHS* §4.3.3g.2).

56. Formally, "head of the hill/mountain" (*rōʾš-hāhār*), referring to the small mountains around Tel el-Qudeirat (modern Qusaymah), which some today identify as Kadesh Barnea (rather than modern Nitzanei, Israel).

57. SP inserts text derived from Deut. 1:42: "Then Yahweh said to Moses, 'Say to them: Do not go up or fight because I am not in your midst, lest you be defeated before your enemies.'"

58. "*But* Moses *said* [*wayyōʾmer*]" contextually renders the contrast of v. 40 and v. 41.

59. Formally, "crossing over" (*ʿōbərîm,* *ʿbr*), but figuratively, "overstep, transgress" (*DCH* 6:234).

60. The SP hiphil, "So he will not bring success" (*taṣlîaḥ* vs. MT qal *tiṣlāḥ*), can be explained as clarifying Yahweh as agent of this verb (see Deut. 28:29 parallel).

61. This does not mean "never go up" but rather prohibits this instance: "Do not go up [at this time]" (*ʾal-taʿălû*; see *ʾal* + jussive, *GBHS* §4.2.3).

Yahweh is not among you, and you will be defeated before your enemies.
43For the Amalekites and the Canaanites will face you there, and you will
fall by the sword. Because you have turned away from Yahweh, Yahweh will
not be with you." **44**But they presumed[62] to go up to the summit of the hill
country, although[63] neither the ark containing the covenant with Yahweh[64]
nor Moses left the camp. **45**So the Amalekites and the Canaanites who
lived in that hill country[65] came down, attacked, and beat them down[66] as
far as Hormah.[67]

Interpretation

14:1–9. The community longs to return to Egypt and replace Moses with
another leader, but Moses and Aaron drop to the ground, and Joshua and
Caleb implore the community to seize the good land by Yahweh's power.
As the scene opens, the Israelites raise their voice and cry that night, but
not to Yahweh, as distressed psalmists and other God-fearers do (v. 1; see
the first translation note there).[68] Ingratitude and craving created the Israelites' nostalgia for Egypt in Num. 11; here it is ingratitude and *fear* of their
doom in the land of Canaan. In v. 2, the Israelites *complain* (*lwn* I) to Moses
and Aaron, which becomes a *Leitwort* and motif in the chapter (vv. 2, 27,
29, 36) and reappears in Num. 16–17 (see the translation note on 14:2; cf.
1 Cor. 10:10). The discouraging report of the explorers has been implanted

62. This root (*'pl* I) is found in the OT here (hiphil), meaning "presume, dare," and Hab.
2:4 (pual), meaning "be swelled up, be puffed up" (*DCH* 6:513).
63. The concessive "although" (*w*) marks the circumstances surrounding their action of
going up (*GBHS* §4.3.3e).
64. After the first appearance in the Hexateuch in Num. 10:33, "the ark containing the
covenant with Yahweh" (*'ărôn bryt-yhwh*) occurs in Deuteronomy's frames (10:8; 31:9, 25,
26) and Josh. 1–8 (3:3, 17; 4:7, 18; 6:8; 8:33). As with "the ark containing the witness" and
"the tent containing the witness," so "the ark *containing* the covenant" indicates a gen. of
container content (*BHRG* §25.4.6[5]; Exod. 25:16), but here and in 10:33 the addition of the
name of Israel's deity exhibits the bilateral nature of covenant treaties in the ANE, so I prefer
"with Yahweh" to connote Israel's oath-sworn covenant treaty with Yahweh (Otto, "Covenant," 2047–51).
65. SP inserts a text adapted from the interpretive Deut. 1:44: "who lived in that hill country
came out against them and chased them just as bees do and totally crushed them."
66. In a wayyiqtol sequence or perhaps hendiatris—"came down, attacked, and beat them
down"—the third root (*ktt*) occurs in the hiphil only here and Deut. 1:44 and is normally
defined as "to scatter (enemies)" (*HALOT* 2:507) or "disperse" (*DCH* 4:478). This definition
unnecessarily departs from the basic sense of its other tenses—"crush" (qal) or "hammer into
pieces" (piel)—so I prefer "beat them down" (*wayyakkətûm*); similarly, "pounded them to
pieces" (Levine, *Numbers*, 1:362); "dealt them a shattering blow" (NJPS); "cut them down"
(LXX^ed); also, Cazelles, *Nombres*, 77; de Vaulx, *Nombres*, 176.
67. To explain how the Israelites got back to the Paran wilderness (there since 12:16), SP
and LXX^ed add "and they turned back to the camp."
68. Pss. 22:2; 42:8; 88:1; 92:2.

traumatically in their psyche (13:31–33); consequently, the people complain that they would rather have died in Egypt or in the Paran wilderness than enter Canaan where they and their families will face a terrifying foe (14:2c–3). Although their complaint may seem reasonable and innocuous, it exhibits a multidimensional rejection of Yahweh as their deity. (1) They are ungrateful for Yahweh's gracious and powerful deliverance from their life of oppression in Egypt (v. 2c).[69] They not only want the food of Egypt (11:4–6), but now they also want to reverse Yahweh's exodus into an *eisodos*, immigrating back into Egypt so they can die there (cf. Acts 7:39).[70] Their absurd nostalgia for Egypt is comparable to repeat offenders today who, just four to six weeks after their release, inflate the comforts of returning to prison over their current predicaments: "A dominant theme in their accounts was positive thinking about imprisonment combined with fatalism."[71] (2) By predicting that they will be slaughtered by the sword and their wives and children abducted as war captives (v. 3a–b; see the translation note on v. 3), the Israelite patriarchs are failing to trust in Yahweh's power to conquer the residents of Canaan (Lev. 26:6–8; Num. 6:24–26; 10:35–36). (3) They conspire to replace Moses with a leader who will guide them back to Egypt, but this is a direct affront to Yahweh, who appointed Moses to lead Israel not only out of Egypt but into Canaan (Exod. 3:10; 32:34; 33:1; Num. 11:12). The people should have remembered that assailing Moses is tantamount to assailing Yahweh: "It is not this way with my servant Moses. He is entrusted with my whole house. . . . Why then were you not afraid to speak against my servant Moses?" (12:7–8*).

Moses and Aaron fall prostrate before the gathered community (v. 5; see the translation note there), while the two courageous explorers, Joshua and Caleb, rip their clothes not merely to get the attention of the mob, but likely to signal their distress about pending divine judgment against the rebellious community (v. 6; see the second translation note there; cf. Matt. 26:65; Mark 14:63). Joshua and Caleb present their case for fighting for the promised land: (1) The land they just explored is exceptionally good, a truth claim even the discouraging explorers affirmed with the impressive fruit sample in their arms (v. 7; see the second translation note there; 13:27). Repeating the imagery of "the land flowing with milk and honey" (v. 8) reminds the Israelites of the prospect of an abundant, Edenic life with Yahweh in his land (cf. Ps. 16:11).[72] (2) Joshua and Caleb call the people to fear Yahweh and manifest that by their obedience and trust: "If Yahweh delights in us . . . Only do not rebel against Yahweh. . . . Yahweh is with us" (vv. 8–9; see

---

69. Römer ("Egypt Nostalgia," 77) sees Num. 14:4 as fulfilling Exod. 13:17.

70. Ashley (*Numbers*, 247) notes that the Latter Prophets use "returning to Egypt" as synonymous with rebelling against God (Isa. 30:1–7; 31:1–3; Jer. 2:18; Ezek. 17:15).

71. Howerton, R. Burnett, Byng, and Campbell, "Consolations," 439–40.

72. See the comments on 13:17–25.

the first translation note on v. 9). Assuming a binary covenant in which both parties have obligations,[73] these godly men assert that if the Israelites obey and fight, Yahweh will bring Israel safely into the land just as he promised (Exod. 23:20–23). (3) Fearing Yahweh cannot coexist with fearing the land's inhabitants (v. 9). There is a subtle jab at the Canaanite deities here: "Their protection," the gods of Canaan, "has turned away from them."[74] The idea, as attested in ANE iconography, is that Israel's deity covers the Israelites, but the protective shadow of the Canaanite gods has left the people of the land.[75] For Joshua and Caleb, overcoming the fear of harmful and even lethal people requires habitual meditation on and articulation of Yahweh's promises and his power to fulfill them.[76]

14:10–12. Apparently detesting Joshua and Caleb's words (vv. 6–9) and desiring Moses's elimination (v. 4), the community moves toward stoning probably all four leaders, including Aaron (v. 5; see the first translation note on v. 10). Yahweh prevents the stoning by causing his glory to appear inside the meeting tent to all the Israelites (v. 10; see the second and third translation notes on v. 10). The last such theophany, at Sinai, incited communal fear but did not prevent disobedience (Lev. 9:23–10:3).[77] Then Yahweh, in a private message to Moses, indicates that his patience with the Israelites has come to an end (v. 11). It appears that Yahweh adapts the form of an individual complaint (lament) psalm and directs it against Israel:[78]

Summons to Yahweh:	[Yahweh said to Moses]
Complaint:	[11]*How long* ['ad-'ānâ] will this people revile me, and *how long* ['ad-'ānâ] will they not trust in me,
Reasons Yahweh must act:	in spite of all the signs that I have done among them?
Petition/Conviction of being heard:	[12]I will strike them with a plague, and I will disinherit them, but I will make you into a nation that is greater and stronger than they are!"

Yahweh is the lamenter and lamented (deity), so he complains to Moses, his interlocutor, and in lieu of expressing a petition and conviction of being heard, Yahweh simply announces his judgment. Yahweh's complaint is remi-

---

73. Arnold, *Genesis*, 101–2.

74. Gray, *Numbers*, 154; Noth, *Numbers*, 108; Ashley, *Numbers*, 250.

75. Staubli (*Levitikus, Numeri*, 253, 394) illustrates 14:7 with iconography that features the winged sun disk, casting divine protective rays (or shadow).

76. See the "Implications" essay in chap. 13, "When You Trust and Fear God."

77. Douglas (*Wilderness*, 210) notes the motif of rebellion→Yahweh's anger→consuming fire of Yahweh/appearance of his glory (11:1–3, 31, 33; 12:12; 14:10–13).

78. See Ps. 13; Gunkel, *Psalms*, 33–36; Westermann, *Praise and Lament*, 68–69.

niscent of his response to the golden-calf apostasy (Exod. 32:7–14).[79] The language of reviling Yahweh has overtones of violating the covenant (see the first translation note on Num. 14:11), while not trusting Yahweh is perhaps an even more personal offense (see the second translation note on v. 11). For Israel not to fight for their great king, Yahweh, is to transgress the oath of the covenant. The Hittite king, for example, demanded that his vassals fight the king's enemies: "If (then) you, Aziras, on your own decision [do not] march out with troops (and) charioteers and on your own [decision] will not give battle, . . . you will transgress the oath."[80]

The hostile language resembles that of the covenant curses (Lev. 26:14–39; Deut. 28:15–68). At Sinai, in the wake of the golden-calf apostasy, Yahweh threatened to wipe out the Israelites and start over with Moses as the new Abraham.[81] Now, in v. 12, Yahweh vows to make Moses into an even greater nation than the one he built from Abraham![82]

14:13–19. In an act of love, Moses pleads with Yahweh to forgive his people because Yahweh must preserve his reputation in Egypt and Canaan and remain faithful to his nature.[83] Moses conjectures that if Yahweh were to follow through and destroy his covenant people, the Egyptians, from whom Yahweh rescued Israel, would hear about it and report it to the inhabitants of Canaan (vv. 13–14). A Late Bronze Age narrative setting is illuminative insofar as the pharaohs conceived of the Levant as an extension of Egypt, and correspondence flowed from Canaan to the motherland and back.[84] As Moses reminds Yahweh, the Egyptians have heard that Yahweh lives among his people, appears to them personally, marks his presence with a standing cloud, and guides them by day with a pillar of cloud and by night with a pillar of fire (v. 14; see the translation note there). The Assyrians conveyed emblems of their deities on a pole called *imittu* (Akk.), but the Hebrew cognate, *'ammûd*, here describes Yahweh's self-revelation rather than a graven image.[85] If Yahweh kills the Israelites all at once in the desert, the nations that have heard about Yahweh's fame—chiefly Egypt and Canaan, but also Midian and others[86]—will conclude

79. Sénéchal ("Quel Horizon," 609–29) argues for innerbiblical development from Deut. 9:12–14, 26–29 (creative Dtr), then Exod. 32:7–14, then Num. 14:11–25 (post-P, post-Dtr).

80. "Treaty of Suppiluliumas and Aziras of Amurru," *ANET* 206 (trans. Albrecht Goetze).

81. Exod. 32:9–10 (cf. 33:3, 5).

82. Genesis 12:2. The Abrahamic nation's greatness and strength is displayed in Exod. 1:7, 20; 12:37; Num. 1; 11:21; 22–24; 26.

83. Cyprian (3rd cent. CE) sees Moses's prayer for the ungrateful people as an act of mildness and patience (Lienhard, *Numbers*, 224). Contra Curzer ("Spies and Lies," 187–95), who argues that Moses distorted the history underlying Num. 13–14 to present himself as blameless and his opponents as faithless cowards.

84. See Redford, *Egypt, Canaan, and Israel*, 192–213; Moran, *Amarna Letters*.

85. Milgrom, *Numbers*, 110.

86. Exod. 18:1 (Midian); Josh. 9:3, 9 (Canaan); cf. nations hearing/seeing Yahweh and Israel's destruction in Num. 21:1; 22:2; 33:40; Deut. 29:24–28; Josh. 10:1; 11:1.

235

that Yahweh was too weak to bring his people into the land he promised them, so he just slaughtered them instead (see the first and third translation notes on v. 15). It was common for ancient Near Easterners to turn to their patron deities for help, and when a people lost in battle, their god's power was discredited, and the people would commonly abandon that god (cf. 1 Cor. 10:5).[87] Thus Moses begins the climax of his petition in v. 17 with "Now let Yahweh's power be great," to invoke Yahweh to protect the international fame of his power to preserve his people and give them the land. In vv. 17aβ–19, Moses concludes his argument with innerbiblical exegesis of the Yahweh creed from Exod. 34:6–7. He urges Yahweh to forgive his cov-

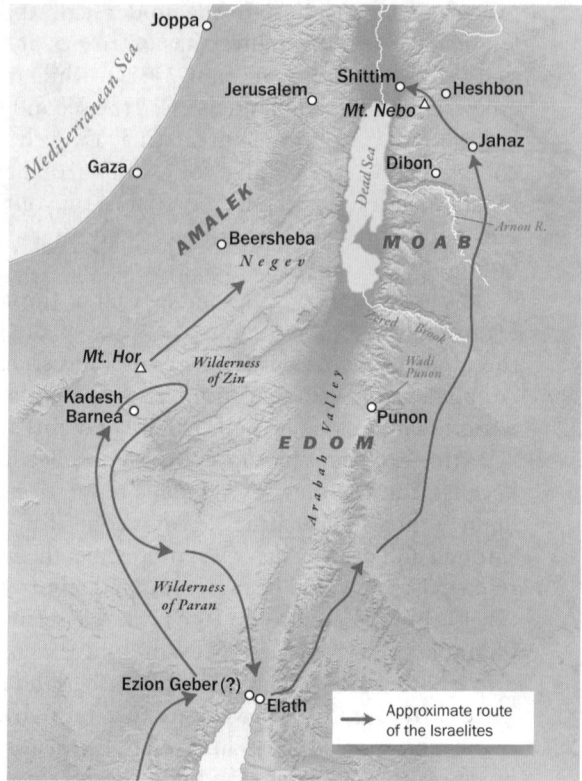

Map 14.1. Israel's Route from Kadesh to the Desert Valleys of Moab (12:16–22:1)

enant people on the basis of Yahweh's own previously revealed nature (see the "Implications" essay below, "Exegeting and Applying Yahweh's Character").

14:20–35. Yahweh forgives his people but swears an oath that the parents in the exodus generation, with the exception of Caleb and Joshua, will not enter the promised land. Yahweh listens to Moses's plea and, by a performative speech act, forgives the people (v. 20; see the translation notes there).[88] The implication is that Yahweh considers his international fame (vv. 13–16) and revealed nature (vv. 17–19) to be compelling reasons not to extinguish the rebellious community all at once. Forgiveness, however, does not overturn the consequences of their sin. To introduce his punishment in vv. 21–24 and vv. 27–35, Yahweh swears by the highest authority of himself and his pervasive glory (Heb. 6:13), formally taking a promissory oath to act in the

87. Walton and Matthews, *Genesis–Deuteronomy*, 189.
88. See Austin, *Do Things with Words*, 4–11, et al.

future against the Israelites: "Nevertheless, as surely as I live and the glory of Yahweh fills the whole earth" (v. 21; see the translation note there) and "As I live, says Yahweh, I will do to you the very thing I heard you say" (v. 28; see the translation note there). In the ANE, the promissory oath appears in various genres, such as the Neo-Assyrian vassal treaties,[89] but in my view Yahweh's oath here seems most analogous to a king's disciplinary action against those to whom he has granted land (see table 14.1).

The language of sin against the land-granting king, breaking the covenant, is lucid: "revile, evil, unfaithfulness, iniquities, evil generation." As Hattushilis III makes clear, the grantee can commit a violation that warrants death; Yahweh is now persuaded that the Israelites are worthy of death (cf. 1 Cor. 10:5; Heb. 3:11, 17, 18; Jude 5).[90] Yahweh's glory and signs in Egypt, the ten plagues, are inverted precisely by Israel's sin of testing Yahweh ten times (v. 22; see the first translation note there). It is not clear which stories from Exod. 15–Num. 14. add up to the ten tests against Yahweh,[91] but the rhetorical point is that for each of Yahweh's wonders (plagues) for Israel's benefit, Israel has recalcitrantly put Yahweh to the test, instead of trusting and obeying him (cf. Acts 7:36; 13:18; Jude 5; 1 Cor. 10:10). It is more than fair, then, that Yahweh responds with a *lex talionis* punishment,[92] in which his punishment matches the nature of the crime: the Israelites explored the promised land for forty days, and now they will suffer in the wilderness for forty years, one year for every day of exploring (v. 34).[93] This explains Yahweh's otherwise awkwardly placed command in v. 25b: "Tomorrow, turn and travel into the wilderness by the way of the Sea of Reeds" (see the second translation note on v. 25). In other words, your judgment of wandering and death in the wilderness begins tomorrow.[94] Also, the Amalekites and Canaanites—earlier said to be along the sea, Jordan, and Negeb (13:29)—are resident in the valleys, implying that all entrances into the land are obstructed (v. 25a).[95]

---

89. Promissory oaths were proleptic. Assertory oaths were the other major ANE type, declaring under oath that a certain action or state of affairs *had already been performed or occurred* (Wells, Magdalene, and Wunsch, "Assertory Oath," 13–14).

90. Sinners worthy of death: Gen. 3:12–24; Luke 13:1–5; John 3:18; Rom. 1:32; 3:10–23; 6:23; Eph. 2:1–3.

91. The Talmud (see Ashley, *Numbers*, 260–61) identifies these as the ten tests: the Sea of Reeds (Exod. 14:11–12), Marah (15:23), Sin wilderness (16:2), twice at Kadesh (16:20, 27), Rephidim (17:2), Sinai (32), Taberah (Num. 11:1), Kibroth Hattaavah (14:4), and this story (13–14).

92. See Lev. 24:10–23 and the "Implications" essay in chap. 16, *"Lex Talionis."*

93. See Leveen, *Memory*, 146–47. Caesarius of Arles (5th–6th cent. CE) applies this principle to every sinner: because of their countless sins, they deserve "ages and ages" of judgment (Lienhard, *Numbers*, 225).

94. Leveen, *Memory*, 88.

95. Milgrom, *Numbers*, 113. The literary placement of v. 25a is perplexing, but maybe as part of the Hexateuch redaction, it anticipates the victorious encounter Caleb (v. 24) will have with the Amalekites and Canaanites (Josh. 14:6–15:19; 21:12). Achenbach (*Vollendung*, 635) assigns v. 25a to the Pentateuch redactor and v. 25b to the Hexateuch redactor.

Table 14.1. Royal Land Grants

	Hattushilis III (or Tudhalyash IV) with Ulmi-Tesup of Dattasa[a]	Yahweh with the Patriarchs and Their Descendants[b]
Royal land grant to an individual and his descendants	After you, your son and grandson will possess it; nobody will take it away from them.	All the land which you see I will give to you and your descendants forever (Gen. 13:15; cf. 15:18; 22:17; 26:3). The land that I gave to Abraham and Isaac I will give to you [Jacob]. I will give the land to your descendants after you (Gen. 35:12).
Grantee's sin is punishable by death	If one of your descendants **sins** (*uasvtai-*), the king will prosecute him at his court. Then when he is found guilty . . . if he **deserves death, he will die.**	Indeed all the people who have seen my glory and my signs that I did in Egypt and in the wilderness have tested me now these ten times and **have not obeyed me**, they will not see the land that I swore to their fathers, nor will any of them **who reviled me** see it (Num. 14:22–23).[c] How long will this **evil community** complain against me? I have heard the Israelites complaining against me (v. 27).[d] your children . . . suffer for **your unfaithfulness** (v. 33*)[e] . . . for **your iniquities** (v. 34) . . . this entire **evil generation** that has **gathered together against me** (v. 35*).[f] First (exodus) generation, enlisted in Num. 1, will **die in the wilderness**, and children will wander as shepherds (vv. 29–30aα, 32, 33c, 35c–d).[g]
Yet the granted land remains the exclusive possession of the descendants	But nobody will take away from the descendant of Ulmi-Tesup either his house or his land in order to give it to a descendant of somebody else.	Only my servant Caleb, because he has a different spirit and follows me completely, I will bring him into the land where he had gone, and his descendants will possess it (Num. 14:24). except for Jephunneh's son Caleb and Nun's son Joshua (v. 30) But your little ones, whom you said would become war captives, I will bring in, and they will experience the land that you have rejected (v. 31).[h]

a. Translation is from Weinfeld, "Covenant of Grant," 189. He includes other similar examples: Muršilis and Kupanta-Kal; Tudḫaliyaš IV and Puduḫepa; a documented will from Nuzi.

b. My trans.

c. See the first translation note on v. 22 and the first translation note on Num. 14:11.

d. See the translation notes on Num. 14:27.

e. See the second translation note on Num. 14:33.

f. See the translation note on Num. 14:35.

g. See the first and third translation notes on Num. 14:33 and the translation note on Num. 14:34; see also Leveen, *Memory*, 73.

h. See the translation notes on Num. 14:31.

Although the forty-years-for-forty-days punishment is bound up with the explorer story (chaps. 13–14), mentioning that Israel tested Yahweh ten times (v. 22) suggests that Yahweh is disinheriting the exodus generation not just for the rebellion of the exploration (chaps. 13–14) but also for the accruing mass of covenant violations (Exod. 15–Num. 14; cf. Heb. 3:16–18).[96] Abusing and rejecting the gift of the land was the final provocation that pushed Yahweh over the precipice of his great patience.[97] At the same time, it also suggests that Yahweh has proven his patient character (14:18–19) by not executing the Israelites the first time they complained (Exod. 16:2), which he would have been justified in doing.[98] The exceptions are Caleb, Joshua, children below twenty years of age, and those born thereafter in the wilderness. Although they will suffer in the wilderness for their parents' sin in line with Yahweh's nature (14:18), they will—like the royal land grant illustrated above—possess the land that the great king, Yahweh, has granted to the descendants of the patriarchs. Caleb is stereotyped here as an exemplar of wholehearted devotion to Yahweh and is therefore an undisputed heir to the promises (v. 24; see the translation notes there).[99] Intriguingly, not even the great prophet Moses (Num. 12) or the high priest Aaron (Num. 3:5–10; 17) is mentioned alongside Joshua, Caleb, and the children whom Yahweh will lead to live in the promised land (Num. 14:30–31). This subtly foreshadows Moses and Aaron's rebellion on the near horizon (Num. 20:7–13).

14:36–45. Following Yahweh's destructive oaths (vv. 20–25, 26–35), the narrator recounts that the explorers who spread a bad report and incited the whole community to complain died by a plague in Yahweh's presence (vv. 36–37; see the translation notes there). Joshua and Caleb are the only explorers to survive the plague (v. 38; see the translation notes there).[100] Without an explicit evaluation of the characters in vv. 36–38, the narrator's representation of the plague as killing the negative explorers but sparing Joshua and Caleb is sufficient to imply Yahweh's judgment on the ten and blessing of the two.[101]

Moses proceeds to tell the Israelites "these things" (v. 39), which probably refers back to the entire dialogue: Moses's plea (vv. 13–19), Yahweh's oaths to curse to death the parents of the exodus generation (vv. 20–35), and the death of the ten explorers. The people mourn deeply (v. 39) but then arise the next morning to climb to the summit of the nearby hills, perhaps surrounding Ain el-Qudeirat (v. 40; see the translation notes there).[102] From the peak, they now profess their readiness to go up to the place Yahweh had

---

96. Cf. Olson, *Death of the Old*, 172.
97. Frevel, *Mit Blick*, 383.
98. See the "Implications" essay in chap. 11, "Complaining as Covenant Violation."
99. Noth, *Numbers*, 109; see Berlin, "Characterization," 78.
100. Frevel (*Mit Blick*, 77, 346) argues convincingly against finding the P^g ending in 14:38.
101. See Sternberg, *Poetics*, 54.
102. See the comments on 13:26.

239

promised, even acknowledging that they have sinned (v. 40). What here seem to be good intentions and even repentance are not enough: Moses retorts that by going up now, they will overstep Yahweh's command and will not succeed in their quest (v. 41; see the translation notes there). Moses prohibits them from going up because Yahweh will not be among them, and therefore their enemies—the Amalekites and Canaanites, standing for the whole population of Canaan (13:29)[103]—will kill the Israelites in the promised land (vv. 42–43; see the translation note on v. 42). Three separate times in vv. 41–43 Moses repeats that Israel's disobedience against Yahweh implies divine absence and battle defeat. His warning culminates with "Because you have turned away from Yahweh, Yahweh will not be with you" (v. 43c). Jesus teaches likewise: "Whoever is not with me is against me, and whoever does not gather with me scatters" (Matt. 12:30; cf. 10:32–33). Moses is not just saying that Yahweh will not fight for Israel *this time*, but because of Yahweh's oath to curse them to die in the wilderness (vv. 20–35), this exodus generation will always suffer defeat in Canaan.

Nevertheless, the Israelites presume to go up to the summit of the hill country—likely referring to Canaan's central highlands, which the explorers traversed (13:17, 22–24)—and the narrator names two realities that presage their downfall: "neither the ark containing the covenant with Yahweh nor Moses left the camp" (v. 44; see the translation notes there). The ark was the emblem of the terrifying presence of their warrior deity, Yahweh (10:35–36), and at this point in the narrative, Moses is still Israel's likely war commander. As expected, the hill-country residents—the Amalekites and Canaanites, who once struck fear into the ten explorers (13:29, 31–33)[104]—came down from the hills, attacked the Israelites, and beat them down all the way to Hormah, a Negev settlement perhaps not far from Beersheba (v. 45; see the second translation note there).[105] There is probably a wordplay on "Hormah" (*ḥormâ*), which fittingly means "destruction."[106] This tragic scene teaches that it is now too late. By fracturing their side of the covenant with their deity, those of the exodus generation have sealed their fate. They can never get back to a pre-Num. 14 state as heirs of the promised land, which provides a graphic OT image of the impossibility of postmortem repentance and salvation (Matt. 25:32–46; Luke 16:19–31). Their only reasonable course of action is, like Cain, to accept God's curse on their lives and maybe taste divine mercy along the way (Gen. 4:8–16).

---

103. Milgrom, *Numbers*, 117.

104. The tradition can be aligned with the v. 25 aside, which locates these two people groups *in the valleys* apparently of the hill country, but it appears to differ from 13:29, with the Amalekites in the Negev and with the Canaanites by the sea and along the Jordan.

105. Rasmussen, *Atlas*, 114, 166, 287.

106. Walton and Matthews, *Genesis–Deuteronomy*, 190. See the verbal cognate *ḥrm and Hormah in 21:1–3.

Implications

Exegeting and Applying Yahweh's Character

Moses urges Yahweh not to annihilate the Israelites, but why should Yahweh listen when his holiness and covenant curses justify deadly action against his rebellious and recalcitrant people?[107] Moses had assumed the societal role as Israel's supreme judge,[108] but now he becomes Israel's legal defender, even though he knows that Israel is exclusively the guilty party. As we have seen above, the thematic elements in Num. 14 resemble those in Exod. 32–34, although the sequence differs: Israel rebels,[109] Yahweh effectively says he will eliminate Israel and restart with Moses as the new Abraham,[110] Moses intercedes,[111] Yahweh relents/forgives and does not eliminate all the people.[112] However, in Exod. 32–33 the revelation of Yahweh's character was embryonic, still unfolding, and he had not yet expressed his nature through the Yahweh creed (Exod. 34:6–7). To persuade Yahweh to forgive Israel for the golden-calf apostasy (Exod. 32), Moses did not have the Yahweh creed at his disposal, but he does put an ultimatum to Yahweh: "If you do not forgive Israel, kill me" (cf. Exod. 32:32). Similarly, in the next exchange when Israel complains and Yahweh announces that his presence will leave his people so that he does not destroy them (33:3–6), Moses reminds Yahweh that his presence distinguishes Israel from the nations (33:16) and again places an ultimatum on Yahweh: "If your presence does not go with us, do not lead us into the promised land" (cf. 33:15). By the final exchange, which comes after the Yahweh creed, Moses appeals to Yahweh's nature to persuade him to maintain his presence among the Israelites (34:9).[113]

In this final exchange, Moses asks to see Yahweh's glory, to which Yahweh responds by hiding Moses in a cleft in the rock, allowing Moses to see only Yahweh's back (33:18–23) or, in another source, descending in the cloud and standing with Moses (34:5). In that spectacular moment, Yahweh pronounces his name twice, *yhwh yhwh*. Although we do not know how the tetragrammaton was or is to be pronounced, we could call this historic moment "a virtual exegesis of this name,"[114] because the theophany and duplicated divine name (v. 6a–d) are immediately followed by a rich creed about Yahweh's own nature (vv. 6e–7).

---

107. See the "Implications" essays in chap. 4 ("The Holiness of God Is Lethal") and chap. 11 ("Complaining as Covenant Violation").

108. Exod. 18:26; cf. Exod. 2:14; Num. 11:11–17.

109. Israel's rebellion is expressed in the golden calf (Exod. 32), complaining (Exod. 33), and wanting to return to Egypt and forgo Canaan (Num. 14).

110. Exod. 32:9–10; 33:3, 5; Num. 14:11–12.

111. Exod. 32:11–13, 31–32; 34:9; Num. 14:13–19.

112. Exod. 32:14, 33–34; 34:10; Num. 14:20.

113. See Levine, *Numbers*, 1:379–81.

114. Fretheim, *Exodus*, 301.

Table 14.2. Exodus 34 and Numbers 14 Compared

Exodus 34:6–7	Numbers 14:17–19
[6]Yahweh passed by before him and proclaimed: **"Yahweh, Yahweh,** a compassionate and gracious God [*'ēl*], **slow to anger and abounding in *loyal love* [*ḥesed*]** and faithfulness, [7]preserving loyal love for thousands, ***forgiving iniquity* [*nōśē' 'āwōn*] and rebellion** and sin [*wĕḥaṭṭā'â*], **but does not leave the guilty unpunished, punishing the iniquity of the fathers against the children** and children's children **until the third and fourth generation."** [8]Moses quickly bowed to the ground and worshiped, [9]and said, "Now if I have found favor in your sight, my Lord, let my Lord go among us, since this is a stiff-necked people. ***Forgive our iniquity* [*wĕsālaḥtā la'ăwōnēnû*] *and our sin* [*ûlĕḥaṭṭā'tēnû*], and take us as your inheritance."**	[17]Now let Yahweh's power be great, just as you have said, [18]**"Yahweh** **is slow to anger and abounding in *loyal love* [*ḥesed*],** ***forgiving iniquity* [*nōśē' 'āwōn*] and rebellion,** **but does not leave the guilty unpunished, punishing the iniquity of the fathers against the children until the third and fourth generation."** [19]***Forgive the iniquity* [*sĕlaḥ-nā' la'āwōn*]** of this people according to your great *loyal love* [*ḥasdekā*], just as you have forgiven this people from Egypt until now."

Note: All translations are mine.

By the citation formula, "just as you have said" (Num. 14:17aβ), Moses makes explicit that he is about to recite Yahweh's own soliloquy from Exod. 34:6–7.[115] The words in bold font show Moses's verbal reuse of the Yahweh creed;[116] the simplest explanation for his not reciting Exod. 34:6–7 verbatim is that Moses could refer to the whole creed by reciting most of it (synecdoche).[117] Moses holds Yahweh accountable to Yahweh's own self-claim that it takes a long time for his anger to heat up, and conversely, that he is governed by *ḥesed*, or covenant loyalty, toward his people (Num. 14:18; see the translation notes there). Even though Moses leaves out phrases from Exod. 34, he does not conveniently lop off Yahweh's just nature to punish the iniquity of the fathers in the lives of multiple generations of children (Num. 14:18). In both contexts, at Mount Sinai and in the Paran desert, Moses knows Yahweh is on the verge of abandoning or obliterating the Israelites (Exod. 34:9; Num. 14:11–12). While Moses begs for Yahweh's forgiveness on the basis of Moses's own self-sacrificing desire and the need to preserve Yahweh's reputation among the

115. On citation formulae, see Fishbane, *Biblical Interpretation*, 44, 170–87.
116. Cf. Achenbach, *Vollendung*, 152.
117. Krašovec ("'Collective Retribution,'" 88) argues the credo formula in Exod. 20:5–6 (Deut. 5:9–10); Exod. 34:6–7; Num. 14:18; Deut. 7:9–10; and Jer. 32:18 reflects "a consciousness of the collective effects of God's dealings with Israel."

nations,[118] Moses ultimately draws from the well of the creedal language that Yahweh uses to describe himself, as shown by the dashed arrows in the chart above: Forgive iniquity and sin (Exod. 34:9) compared with forgive iniquity because of your loyal love (Num. 14:19; see the translation note there).[119]

Pleading with Yahweh to forgive on the basis of his covenant loyalty (*ḥesed*) becomes critical not only for the restoration and survival of God's people[120] but also for his anointed king[121] and for individuals who have sinned against God and neighbor.[122] As God reveals himself progressively in the unfolding biblical narrative, Isaiah and NT writers make clear that God's covenant loyalty or faithful love is definitively, and now exclusively, available to those who trust in the substitutionary sacrifice of Yahweh's servant, the Messiah (Isa. 53:11; Mark 10:45; 1 John 4:10; Rom. 8:32, 39). Faith in the crucified and risen Messiah leads to what Moses sought for the nation, God's gracious forgiveness, but also to countless other eternal benefits.[123] One such benefit that is apropos here in the trajectory of Exod. 34 and Num. 14 can be found in the teaching of Jesus on prayer. Just as Moses pleaded with God on the basis of his name and revealed nature, and God answered powerfully and graciously (Exod. 34:6–9; cf. Num. 14:17–19), so Jesus's followers must plead with God on the basis of his Son's name and revealed nature, with confidence that God will always answer powerfully and graciously (John 14:13–14).

118. Exod. 32:32; 33:15–16; Num. 14:13–16.

119. For a study of innerbiblical interpretation between Exod. 34:6; Jon. 4:2; and Joel 2:13, see Dozeman, "Inner-Biblical," 207–23. Sakenfeld ("Divine Forgiveness," 317–30) argues that divine forgiveness began in Num. 14 as a conditional covenant tradition, stressing the people's existential threat, and was then enfolded into an everlasting covenant viewpoint, reinforcing the people's continuity.

120. See Ezra 3:11; 9:9; Neh. 1:5; 9:17, 32; Dan. 9:4; Hosea 2:21; Joel 2:13; Jon. 2:9; 4:2; Mic. 7:18, 20.

121. E.g., 1 Kings 3:6; 8:23; 2 Chron. 6:42; many psalms.

122. E.g., Pss. 51:1; 103:3, 8; and in humility, although without exposed sin: Neh. 13:22; Job 10:12; 37:13.

123. See Piper, *Fifty Reasons*.

15

Offerings; Violating Sabbath; Tassels on Clothes

(15:1–41)

⁂

Overview

The redactional placement of chap. 15—with its cultic, Sabbath, and mnemonic instructions (*tôrōt*) for the community—after the national disaster of chaps. 13–14 may seem arbitrary and misplaced. Chapter 15 would flow naturally after the chieftains' dedication of the altar (chap. 7), or alongside the offerings and festival calendar for the new generation in chaps. 28–29, which overlap with chap. 15 in their grain and libation formulations. Instead, by its location after chaps. 13–14, the content of Num. 15 indicates that rebellion, death, and disinheritance do not nullify Israel's calling to be "a kingdom of priests and a holy nation" for Yahweh (Exod. 19:6).[1] The children who will endure forty years in the wilderness for their parents' sins (14:20–35) must, even now, begin setting their hope on life with Yahweh in the land: "When you enter the land where you will live, which I am giving you . . ." (v. 2c), and "When you enter the land where I am bringing you . . ." (v. 18).[2] These children anticipate bringing delight to Yahweh through the cult (vv. 1–21), but the rest of the chapter is intended for them and their parents now, that is, to make atonement for forgiveness (vv. 22–31) and keep Sabbath and all

---

1. On the content of chap. 15 coming after chaps. 13–14, see Achenbach, "Complementary Reading," 206–7.
2. See Olson, *Death of the Old*, 89, 182, 197; Dozeman, "Numbers," 126.

Yahweh's commands (vv. 32–41). The chapter contains six discursive units,[3] the final two of which, as we will see, relate back thematically to the prior units:[4] supplementary sacrifices with grain offerings and libations (vv. 1–16); offering a bread tribute to Yahweh when Israel first eats some of the land's bread (vv. 17–21); presenting atoning sacrifices when the whole community does wrong inadvertently (vv. 22–26); presenting an atoning sacrifice for a person who sins inadvertently, while the defiant offender is cut off (vv. 27–31); a novella that ends in obediently stoning a man who gathered sticks on the Sabbath (vv. 32–36); and sewing tassels as mnemonic symbols to promote loyalty to Yahweh and his commands (vv. 37–41).[5]

Translation

[1]Then Yahweh said to Moses: [2]"Speak to the Israelites and tell them, 'When you enter the land where you will live, which I am giving you, [3]and you make an offering by fire to Yahweh—either a burnt offering or a sacrifice for fulfilling a vow or as a freewill offering or at your appointed feasts—to create a pleasing scent to Yahweh[6] from the herd or from

---

3. Knierim and Coats (*Numbers*, 195–96) identify the genres of a speech with introductory formula, ordinances, then ritual. The story of the wood gatherer on the Sabbath (vv. 32–36) can be called an oracular novella (Chavel, *Oracular Law*, 165–95).

4. Contra Noth (*Numbers*, 114), who sees the individual units of chap. 15 as having no connection to each other; instead, see Baden, "Structure and Substance," 351–67.

5. Wellhausen (*Composition*, 175) and Kuenen (*Hexateuch*, 96) see the affinities between Num. 15 and H in Lev. 17–26 and infer editorial theories. Knohl (*Sanctuary*, 53, 90) argues more pointedly that chap. 15 was composed by H (also Stackert, "Composition," 193n64). Even Frevel ("Book of Numbers," 16) and Nihan ("Priestly Laws," 109–10) concede to H influence in the chapter. Scharbert (*Numeri*, 61–65) sees Num. 15 as a Priestly tradent supplementing Lev. 6–7, so not P[s] (Seebass, *Numeri*, 2:136). Others regard it as supplementing P (P[s]) more generally (Levine, *Numbers*, 1:385; Cross, *Canaanite Myth*, 315; Budd, *Numbers*, 166–67), yet also integrating older texts (Gray, *Numbers*, 167). Achenbach (*Vollendung*, 517–25, 638) identifies chap. 15 with the second phase of the theocratic revision of the Torah, which supplied final purity laws and ritual regulations. Chavel ("Numbers 15:32–36," 45–55 [52]) argues that the wood gatherer story comes from Priestly oracular law with its later composition as "intertextual, based on the running Priestly work."

6. A *l* + inf. const. marks the purpose of these gifts: "to create a pleasing scent to Yahweh" (*laʿăśôt rêaḥ nîḥōaḥ lyhwh*). This "pleasing scent/aroma to Yahweh" (*rêaḥ nîḥōaḥ lyhwh*) occurs in Numbers for the first time here in chap. 15 (vv. 3, 7, 10, 13, 14, 24), then chaps. 18 (1×) and 28–29 (11×), but was already well known in the Pentateuch as a purpose for or result of the burnt offering: by Noah after the flood (Gen. 8:21); by Moses for the priestly installation of Aaron and his sons (Exod. 29:18, 25; Lev. 8:21, 28; and a combination as a *rêaḥ nîḥōaḥ* in Exod. 29:41); or by any Israelite (Lev. 1:9, 13, 17). The original formulation of the burnt offering both atones—probably for unknown or unexposed sin not covered in Lev. 4:1–6:7 (Milgrom, *Leviticus*, 1:172–77)—and generates this pleasing smell to Yahweh (Lev. 1:4, 9, 13, 17; 17:6), while the basic grain offering and sacrifice for peace—which are not for sin or guilt, but the Israelite's means of expressing devotion to Yahweh—also generate a pleasing scent to Yahweh

245

the flock, [4]the person who presents this offering to Yahweh must bring a grain offering containing one-tenth of an ephah[7] of finely ground flour mixed with one-fourth of a hin[8] of olive oil. [5]You must also prepare one-fourth of a hin of wine as a libation[9] with the burnt offering or the sacrifice, for each lamb.[10] [6]Or for a ram, you must prepare as a grain offering two-tenths of an ephah of finely ground flour mixed with one-third of a hin of olive oil, [7]and as a libation you must offer one-third of a hin of wine as a pleasing scent to Yahweh. [8]When you prepare a young bull as a burnt offering or a sacrifice for fulfilling a vow or for peace to Yahweh,[11] [9]then present, along with this young bull, a grain offering of three-tenths of an ephah of finely ground flour mixed with half a hin of olive oil, [10]and you must present as the libation half a hin of wine, an offering by fire, as a pleasing scent to Yahweh. [11]This is what is to be done for each ox, or each ram, or each of the male lambs or the goats. [12]You must do this for each one, depending on the number that you prepare.[12] [13]Every native Israelite must do these things in this way to present an offering by fire as a pleasing scent to Yahweh. [14]If an immigrant is living with you or is among you in generations to come,[13]

(grain as *rêaḥ nîḥōaḥ*: Lev. 2:2, 9, 12; 6:15, 21; greetings: Lev. 3:5, 16). The composite sacrifices in H (Lev. 17–26) presented as one's firstfruits or at the Festival of Weeks are also called a "pleasing scent" (Lev. 23:13, 18). When the sacrifice for peace is adapted as an offering for the unintentional sin of an individual, it is also called a pleasing scent (Lev. 4:31).

7. "Ephah" (*'êpâ*) is inferred (Num. 5:15). The ephah, used to measure cereals, equals a tenth of a homer (*ḥōmer* = 150 liters), about 15 liters (King and Stager, *Life*, 200). One-tenth of an ephah of finely ground flour is about 1.5 liters; two-tenths = 3 liters; three-tenths = 4.5 liters.

8. A "hin" (*hîn*) is a liquid measure of about 5.5 liters used for measuring olive oil (here; cf. Exod. 30:24) and wine (Exod. 29:40) (King and Stager, *Life*, 200). One-fourth of a hin of olive oil or wine is about 1.375 liters; one-third = 1.83 liters; a half hin = 2.75 liters.

9. The libation or drink offering, "*nesek* I" (*HALOT* 2:703; *DCH* 5:700), is mentioned most frequently in Numbers (i.e., 34 times; see chaps. 4, 6, 15, 28–29). One time in Genesis Jacob pours a libation on the standing stone (35:14). The word occurs three times each in Exodus (29:40–41, priestly inauguration; 30:9, prohibition) and Leviticus (23:13, 18, 37, firstfruits) and once in Deuteronomy (32:38, synonym *nāsîk* used in mocking other gods).

10. LXX[ed] adds, "so much as an offering, an odor of fragrance to the Lord" (NETS). This likely clarifies "that the amounts ordered in v. 4 are to apply in the case of the lamb" and to include the otherwise absent "pleasing scent" from vv. 10, 14 (Wevers, *Notes*, 239).

11. "For peace" is shorthand for "the sacrifice for peace" (*zebaḥ haššəlāmîm*), which is detailed in Lev. 3 and referenced most recently in Num. 6 (3×), 7 (13×), and 10:10. See the translation note on 6:14.

12. Formally, "according to the number [SP, "their number"] that you prepare, so you must prepare each one according to their number."

13. The "settler" (*tôšāb*) is not mentioned here, but simply "you" (vv. 14–16), meaning "the native" (v. 13) and the "immigrant" (*gēr*), a binary that belongs to the priestly texts in Exodus–Leviticus–Numbers, whereas the phrase "immigrant who is within your towns [gates], orphan and widow (and Levite)" is characteristic of Deuteronomy. For the descriptors used to qualify each *gēr* reference in the Pentateuch, see Awabdy, *Immigrants*, 117–18, 187. The noun *gēr* occurs in all books of the Pentateuch, including eleven times in Numbers (9:14 [2×]; 15:14, 15 [2×], 16, 26, 29, 30; 19:10; 35:15).

and prepares an offering by fire as a pleasing scent to Yahweh, he must do it the same way you do. **15**As for the assembly,[14] you and the immigrant who lives among you must have one statute, a permanent statute for generations to come. You and the immigrant will be alike before Yahweh. **16**You and the immigrant who lives alongside you will have one law and one custom.'"

17Yahweh said to Moses: **18**"Speak to the Israelites and tell them, 'When you enter the land where I am bringing you **19**and you eat some of the land's bread,[15] you must offer a tribute[16] to Yahweh. **20**You must offer a tribute of round loaves[17] from the first of your finest flour. You must offer it up the same way you offer a tribute from the threshing floor.[18] **21**You must give to Yahweh some of the first of your finest flour as a tribute for generations to come.'"

22"'But if you all do something wrong inadvertently[19] and do not observe all these commands that Yahweh has spoken to Moses— **23**everything that Yahweh has commanded you by the authority of Moses, from the day that Yahweh commanded and continuing for generations to come—**24**then if any inadvertent wrongdoing is

---

14. A left dislocation of a verbless clause in v. 15, "*As for the assembly*, you and the immigrant who lives among you . . ." (*BHRG* §48.1.3; with Seebass, *Numeri*, 2:131; Schmidt, *Numeri*, 53). This understanding that the immigrant and native are both constituents of the Yahweh-worshiping community is the concept of the Holiness (H) materials (Lev. 17–26; et al.) and is preferred contextually over SP, LXX[ed], and Cazelles (*Nombres*, 79), which interpret the noun (SP *hqhl* before the *sôf pāsûq* [end-of-verse mark]; LXX[ed] nom. *hē synagōgē*) as the subject of the closing verb in v. 14, "the same way the community does." EÜ adopts the Syriac, which omits "the assembly." On H's assimilation of the *gēr* into the Israelite community, see Awabdy, *Immigrants*, 184–226.

15. Or "land's food," since *leḥem* (root I) can mean food, bread, or a loaf of bread (*DCH* 4:534, glosses 1, 2). Here *bread* is preferred (ESV, NRSV, NJPS) since the ensuing tribute is round loaves of bread from fine flour (vv. 20–21).

16. See the translation note on 5:9.

17. With Levine (*Numbers*, 1:394): "The basic sense seems to be 'roundness' (the verb *ḥ-w-l*) rather than 'piercing' (the verb *ḥ-l-l* [sic, rather *ḥ-l-l*])."

18. Formally, "as a contribution of the threshing floor, so you must offer it up." This seems to presume readerly awareness of how to offer up a contribution *from the threshing floor* (*gōren*); by way of analogy, "Deut. 15:14 requires Israelites to give to the poor a part of what they process at the threshing floor and vat. Most cultic assessments of grain, fruits, and oil were collected at that stage, when natural products first become usable as food" (Levine, *Numbers*, 1:394–95). Nonetheless, the ritual protocols or regulations of Num. 15:20 remain elusive to us today. In Gen. 50:10, 11, the "threshing floor" (*gōren*) in Canaan was the site of mourning Jacob's death. The noun occurs twice in Num. 18 with similarly undefined references to this contribution (18:27, 30), and then, without additional clarity, appears twice in Deuteronomy as provisions for a freed slave (15:14) and as the seasonal marker to initiate the Feast of Booths (16:13). Numbers 15:20 may have been a later gloss to contextualize for readers who knew this custom (similarly, de Vaulx, *Nombres*, 183).

19. In contrast to *defiant* rebellion in vv. 30–31, illustrated throughout Num. 11–17.

committed without the community knowing,[20] the whole community must prepare a young bull as a burnt offering, a pleasing scent to Yahweh, along with its grain offering and its customary libation,[21] and a male goat as a purification offering. **25**And the priest will make atonement for the whole Israelite community, and they will be forgiven, because it was an inadvertent wrongdoing and they have brought their offering, an offering by fire to Yahweh, and their purification offering before Yahweh, for their inadvertent wrongdoing. **26**The whole Israelite community and the immigrant who lives among them will be forgiven, since all the people were involved in inadvertent wrongdoing."[22]

27"'If a single person sins inadvertently, then they must offer a one-year-old female goat as a purification offering. **28**The priest must make atonement for the person who sins inadvertently, when they sin inadvertently before Yahweh, to make atonement for them, and they will be forgiven.[23] **29**You must have one law for the person who does something wrong inadvertently, both for the native among the Israelites and the immigrant who lives among them. **30**But the person who acts defiantly,[24] whether a native Israelite or an immigrant, insults Yahweh.[25] That person must be cut off from among their people.[26] **31**Because they have despised[27] the word of Yahweh and have broken his command,[28] that person must be completely cut off. His iniquity will be on him.'"

20. Formally, "is done unintentionally *from the eyes of the community* [mēʿênê hāʿēdâ]," with a privative *min*, indicating, "*without* the eyes [i.e., knowledge] of the community" (*GBHS* §4.1.3g).

21. Formally, "its libation *according to the custom/standard* [kammišpāṭ]."

22. Formally, "since with respect to all the people, (they were) in the inadvertent wrongdoing."

23. LXX[ed] omits "and they will be forgiven," possibly by haplography from ʾlyw to lw (Wevers, *Notes*, 250).

24. By left dislocation, the subject is activated as the primary topic of the main clause: formally, "But *the person who acts with a high/raised hand*, . . . *that one* insults Yahweh" (*BHRG* §48.2.1).

25. Fronting the direct obj. makes Yahweh the focus: formally, "*Yahweh* he insults" (*BHRG* §47.2.1[2]). *Gdp* occurs only here in the Pentateuch (7× in the OT) and could mean "blasphemes" (Seebass, *Numeri*, 2:132; Schmidt, *Numeri*, 54; EÜ; *HALOT* 1:181, gloss 2) or "reviles" (*DCH* 2:326; many versions), but I prefer "insults" (NET), which calls attention to how the action affects Yahweh (similarly "outrages" for de Vaulx, *Nombres*, 184; Cazelles, *Nombres*, 80). Its piel ptc. form here (məgaddēp) is probably factitive, "puts Yahweh into an insulted state" (*GBHS* §3.1.3a), maybe with a continuous aspect ("is maligning YHWH": Levine, *Numbers*, 1:388). LXX[ed] "provokes God" (see Wevers, *Notes*, 251); cf. "God" in LXX 16:5, 11.

26. An imperatival weqatal: formally, "that life *must be cut off* [wənikrətâ] from among its people," a euphemism for "that person must be totally destroyed."

27. The root *bzh* ("despised"; *DCH* 2:132; *HALOT* 1:117) occurs in the Pentateuch only here and in Gen. 25:34: "so Esau *despised* [wayyibez] his birthright." This and its parallel verb here are qatal forms with a "recent perfective" aspect: "Because they *have despised* [bāzāh] the word of Yahweh and *have broken* [hēpar] his command" (*IBHS* §30.5.1).

28. SP and LXX[ed]: "his commands."

[32]When the Israelites were in the wilderness, they found a man gathering wood on the Sabbath day. [33]Those who found him gathering wood brought him to Moses, Aaron, and the whole community.[29] [34]They put him in custody, because it was not clear what should be done to him. [35]Then Yahweh said to Moses, "The man must be put to death. The whole community must stone[30] him outside the camp." [36]So the whole community took him outside the camp and stoned him to death,[31] just as Yahweh commanded Moses.

[37]Then Yahweh spoke to Moses: [38]"Speak to the Israelites and tell them to make tassels[32] for themselves on the corners of their garments for generations to come, and put a blue thread[33] on the tassel of the corners. [39]You must have this tassel so that you will see it[34] and remember all Yahweh's commands and obey them so that you will not follow after your own heart and your own eyes that lead you into infidelity[35]—[40]in order that you will remember and do all my commands so you will be holy to your God. [41]I am Yahweh your God, who brought you out of the land of Egypt to be your God. I am Yahweh your God."

---

29. LXX[ed]: "whole congregation *of Israel's sons*" may be a scribal gloss to remove the immigrant from the community's prerogative to execute retribution (Wevers [*Notes*, 253] calls this gloss "otiose"). Such translational exegesis would align with the LXX interpretation of "the assembly" as excluding the immigrant in 15:14–15 (see the translation note on v. 15 above).

30. Formally, "They must stone him with stones" (*rāgôm 'ōtô bā'ăbānîm*), with an inf. absolute assuming the imperatival force of the prior verb, modified by an instrumental *b* (*bā'ăbānîm*; GBHS §3.4.2d, 4.1.5c). Apparently SP clarifies this force by altering it to a masc. pl. impv., "stone him" (*rgmu*).

31. Formally, "and stoned him with stones and he died."

32. Of the four times this noun (*ṣîṣit*) occurs in the OT, three are in Num. 15 (vv. 38 [2×], 39), meaning "tassel" (*DCH* 7:119), and the other in Ezek. 8:3, where Ezekiel the priest, who knows the priestly *tôrâ* well, recounts how a figure escorted him by his "lock" or "mop of hair" to Jerusalem in visions from God ("lock," *DCH* 7:119; "mop o. h. [of hair]," *HALOT* 3:1024). Its probable Akkadian cognate (*ṣiṣītu*) refers to part of a weaver's loom, likely either its harness or heddle ("ṣiṣītu," *CAD* 16:214). SP and LXX[ed] adjust the collective noun to a morphological pl., "fringes" (also v. 39).

33. The gen., "thread *of blue*" (*pətîl təkēlet*), may have been a loanword from Phoenician (or Aramaic; see *HALOT* 4:1732–33) of the eastern Mediterranean coastal region, well-known for producing purple-colored dye extracted from different species of predatory murex snails or rock snails (*Muricidae*); see Astour, "Origin," 346–50. No Phoenician term is attested, but in Akkadian, *takiltu* refers to "a precious blue-purple wool" that could be used "for decorating garments" (*CAD* 18:70). Elsewhere in Numbers, *təkēlet* describes the "blue cloth" (*beged təkēlet*) used to cover the table, lampstand, golden altar, and utensils (4:7, 9, 11, 12).

34. SP and LXX[ed] "you will see *them*" agrees with their pl. "tassels" (v. 38).

35. Formally, "whom you are prostituting (yourselves) after them" (*'ăšer-'attem zōnîm 'aḥărêhem*; similarly Seebass, *Numeri*, 2:158). With the more dynamic rendering, "that lead you into infidelity," I seek to convey the implication that one's own heart and eyes *lead* or *cause* one to commit spiritual prostitution, to break covenant with Yahweh (metaphorical use of "znh," *HALOT* 1:275; with EÜ; Cazelles, *Nombres*, 81; de Vaulx, *Nombres*, 186; NET).

Interpretation

15:1–16. Through Moses, Yahweh instructs the Israelites, but by implication, only the children who have not been disinherited will be alive to enact
these words: "When you enter the land where you will live, which I am giving
you" (v. 2). The purpose of these instructions is to augment the protocols
revealed on Mount Sinai for voluntary offerings—not for sin or guilt, but to
show grateful devotion—with an accompanying grain offering and libation.
Clearly, these expressions of Yahweh worship—"*a burnt offering* [*ʿōlâ*] or *a
sacrifice* [*zebaḥ*] *for fulfilling a vow* [*ləpallēʾ-neder*] or *as a freewill offering*
[*bindābâ*] or *at your appointed feasts* [*bəmōʿădêkem*]" (v. 3)—presume the
reader's knowledge of the protocols already given at Sinai, especially from
Leviticus.[36] This discursive unit begins with three subunits of protocols (vv.
2c–5, 6–7, 8–10), followed by a précis in vv. 11–12, which develops the Sinai
protocols and can be summarized as follows:

At Sinai, the ram was designated as a reparation offering (Lev. 5:14–19)
but now is distinguished by its own portions of accompanying grain and libation. The quantities of accompanying grain and wine increase in proportion
to the value of the sacrificial animal (herd or flock→ram→young bull). The
grain offering was not for the ritual of the jealous husband (Num. 5:11–31)
or its original formulation with frankincense and salt (Lev. 2), but like the
original, it did signify the devotee's expression of gratitude for Yahweh's
agricultural bounty in the land (cf. Lev. 26:4–5, 10; Num. 15:2). The ritual
of accompanying grain offerings and libations is part of the Nazirite vow,
although without the specificity here; it is incorporated into the festival calendar (Num. 28–29) and is revisited by the Qumran scribes in the Temple
Scroll.[37] Of the books of the Pentateuch, Numbers by far most frequently
prescribes variations of a "libation" or "drink offering" ("*nesek* I," see the
first translation note on 15:5). The picture from the prior Sinai instructions
is that libations are contained in pitchers and bowls, positioned on the table
(inside the outer curtain), then poured out to Yahweh in his holy place, but
not on the incense altar.[38] Prior to the time of Moses, the Hittites, Mesopo-
tamians, Ugaritians, and Grecians all offered sacrifices coupled with libations.[39] In the Ugaritic epic that bears his name, King Keret (Kirta) offers a
sacrificial lamb, accompanied by offerings of bird, honey, and wine.[40] The

36. "Vow" (*neder*): Lev. 7:16; 22:18, 21, 23, 38; 27:2; Num. 6:2; 5, 21; "freewill offering"
(*nədābâ*): Lev. 7:16; 22:18, 21, 23, 38; "appointed feasts of Yahweh" (*môʿădê yhwh*): Lev. 23:2, 4,
37, 44. On intertextuality with Lev. 1–7, 23, see Achenbach, "Complementary Reading," 213–18.
37. G. Anderson ("Purification Offering," 17–35) argues that the Qumran Temple Scroll
(11Q19) follows the model of Num. 15:1–12 for the grain and drink offerings over that of
Num. 28–29.
38. Exod. 25:29; 30:9; 37:16.
39. Milgrom, *Numbers*, 118.
40. See de Vaulx, *Nombres*, 179.

Table 15.1. Types of Offerings

Sinai Protocols	Numbers 15 Classification	Grain Offering Mixture (approximations)	Libation (approximations)
Lev. 1:1–13; 6:9–13 Lev. 7:16–18; 22:21–23; 23:18, 21, 23; 27:9–13; Num. 6:1–21 Lev. 23	**vv. 2c–5** For every *herd or flock animal* as a → burnt offering → sacrifice for fulfilling a vow freewill offering → at your appointed feasts	1.5 liters of finely ground flour 1.375 liters of olive oil[a]	1.375 liters of wine
New subclassification	**vv. 6–7** For every *ram* as any of the above sacrifices (implied)	3 liters of finely ground flour 1.83 liters of olive oil	1.83 liters of wine
Lev. 1:1–9; 6:9–13 Lev. 7:16–18; 22:21–23; 23:18, 21, 23; 27:9–13; Num. 6:1–21 Lev. 3:1–17; 7:11–21	**vv. 8–10** For every *young bull* as a → burnt offering → sacrifice for fulfilling a vow → sacrifice for peace	7.5 liters of finely ground flour 2.75 liters of olive oil	2.75 liters of wine
	Précis: This is what is to be done for each ox, or each ram, or each of the male lambs or the goats. You must do this for each one, depending on the number that you prepare (vv. 11–12).[b]		

a. See the translation notes on 15:4.
b. See the translation note on 15:12.

mindset in Syria-Palestine was that, alongside other sacrificial forms, libation liquids, primarily oil and wine (but also beer, et al.), were offered in order to nourish and entertain the gods who shared in the sacred meal or banquet.[41] By contrast, Yahweh has no need for food or drink as nourishment (Deut. 32:37–38), yet here he invites gifts of sacrificial formulations of meat and now of supplementary grain and wine, but why?

One theory is that the priestly reform party of the second temple traced its line back to Aaron and wanted to increase its resources, even as Yahweh in Num. 18 designates to Aaron and his family every Israelite offering as food (vv. 8–19).[42] While we may contemplate underlying social influences, this view

41. See del Olmo Lete, "Sacrifice," 332–33.
42. Albertz, *Israelite Religion*, 2:461–62.

remains provisional because Num. 15 and 18 are not intertextually connected,[43] and 15:1–16 makes no mention of Aaron or the priests. The textual data, instead, stresses the fivefold recurrence of the intended purpose or result of the sacrifices to be "as a pleasing scent to Yahweh" (*rêaḥ nîḥōaḥ lyhwh*: vv. 3, 7, 10, 13, 14). Yahweh simply delights in the uncoerced gifts of sacrifice from his covenant people.[44] The literary placement of 15:1–16 here is intriguing: it stands after the nation's epic failure in chaps. 13–14 instead of after chap. 7 or before or after chaps. 28–29. Numbers 15 shows that Israel's recalcitrance and disinheritance do not abrogate Yahweh's purpose for Israel to be "a kingdom of priests and a holy nation" (Exod. 19:6). The children who will suffer in the wilderness for forty years for their parents' rebellion (14:20–35) must, even now, fix their gaze on life with Yahweh in the land (vv. 2, 17). Numbers 15 reaffirms that Yahweh is the same covenantal deity that he was at Sinai: just as Yahweh gave the exodus generation the high privilege of bringing him pleasure through their sacrificial gifts (Lev. 1–7), he now transfers this privilege to their children. Verses 13–16 function as a remarkable addendum, extending to resident immigrants the same prerogative of sacrificing the same voluntary offerings by fire "as a pleasing scent to Yahweh" (*rêaḥ nîḥōaḥ lyhwh*, v. 14).[45]

15:17–21. Through Moses, Yahweh directs the Israelites to bring a tribute of bread to Yahweh when they enter the land and eat some of its fruit. This is not to be confused with Israel's annual Festivals of Firstfruits and Weeks, both also attached to Canaan's agriculture.[46] Here, instead, the offering takes place one time in history, after Israel eats some of the land's bread (see the first translation note on v. 19), presumably made from the ripe wheat fields or grain stored in ceramic pithoi (see 13:23–24). From the most finely ground flour, the Israelites are apparently to form and bake round loaves of bread as the tribute (v. 20; see the first translation note there).[47] More accurate than "a raised offering," the offering was a "tribute" (*tərûmâ*), a more generic term that appears eighteen times in Numbers (chaps. 5, 6 [6:20, *šôq hattərûmâ*], 15, 18, 31), and only in Ezekiel does it appear more frequently (roughly 20 times; see the translation note on 5:9). The concept could be that the Israelites—as vassals of their great king, Yahweh, who has given them the land—are to give a tribute of the land's produce (also 18:27, 30), but also animal parts (6:20) and animal and human spoils of war (31:26–54). Neo-Assyrian emperors similarly received from their vassals various natural resources, crafts, animal parts (i.e., ivory), live animals, especially wild and exotic, chariots, and humans.[48] Israel must offer the bread loaves "the same way you offer a tribute

---

43. See intertexts of Num. 15 and 18 in Achenbach, *Vollendung*, 141–72, 517–25.
44. See the "Implications" essay in chap. 26, "Does Yahweh Eat the Sacrifices of His People?"
45. See the "Implications" essay below, "Immigrants Who Worship Yahweh."
46. Exod. 23:16; 34:22; Lev. 23:9–22; Num. 28:26–31; Deut. 26:1–15; cf. Rom. 11:16.
47. See Milgrom, *Numbers*, 121–22.
48. Kuhrt, *Ancient Near East*, 2:479–97.

from the threshing floor," which probably means following the Sinai protocols for the *bread* (*ḥallâ*) type of grain offering, made without yeast or honey but with olive oil and salt (v. 20; see the second translation note there).[49] Although their tribute was a one-time event, it would function vicariously "for generations to come" (v. 21). The Deuteronomists make explicit the theology of this tribute: when you enter and enjoy the land already developed with no help of your own—its cities, choice things, cisterns, vineyards, olive groves—then "be careful not to forget Yahweh your God who brought you out of Egypt, a house of slaves" (Deut. 6:12).

15:22–31. Yahweh continues the same speech to mandate that if, or when, the Israelite community (vv. 22–26) or a single person (vv. 32–36) sins inadvertently, they must offer sacrifices to make atonement, and the whole community will be forgiven. The verb *šgh* (v. 22) is used in Numbers only here, whereas its cognate noun (*šəgāgâ*) occurs fifteen times in the Pentateuch: six in Leviticus and nine in Numbers (vv. 24–29 [7×]; 35:11, 15). It refers to "inadvertent wrongdoing" committed by negligence (by accident) or by ignorance (in error), and it must be expiated by a purification offering (on *ḥṭ't*, see the first translation note on 6:11).[50] In v. 22, the verbs are plural, painting a scenario in which the entire community fails to observe all of Yahweh's permanently binding commands through Moses, which are mentioned emphatically three times (vv. 22–23). Although the community is ignorant of their own wrongdoing (v. 24; see the first translation note there), when they become aware of it,[51] they must perform the sacrificial ritual so that the priest can make atonement for them, and as a result, they will be forgiven. In v. 27, the violator shifts to a single individual, and their recompense is understandably smaller, a female goat. The wrongdoing of the community (v. 22) is the same quality as that of the individual (v. 27), since to "do something wrong inadvertently" (*šgh* or *śh* + *šəgāgâ*, vv. 22–29) is interchangeable with "sins inadvertently" (*ḥṭ'* + *šəgāgâ*, vv. 27–28).[52]

At Sinai, Yahweh already provided instructions for inadvertent wrongdoing (Lev. 4),[53] so why is a Kadesh supplement necessary in Num. 15:22–31? In Leviticus, following a generic introduction (4:2), the subclasses of wrongdoers include (1) the high priest (4:3–12), (2) the whole community (4:13–21), (3) a leader (4:22–26), and (4) another individual (4:27–35).[54] Comparing Lev. 4

---

49. Lev. 2:4, 11, 13; 7:12–13.

50. Milgrom, *Leviticus*, 1:228–29. Milgrom distinguishes this from sin committed *unintentionally*, which requires a "reparation offering" (*'šm*) to make atonement (Lev. 5:17–19; Num. 5:6–7). See also Frevel, "Purity Conceptions," 375–76.

51. As Lev. 5:3–4.

52. Demonstrated by the return to *śh* + *šəgāgâ* in 15:29 with a synonymous meaning.

53. See *šgh* in Lev. 4:13; *šəgāgâ* in Lev. 4:2, 22, 27; 5:15; 22:14.

54. A different scenario, which requires a reparation offering, involves a *trespass* (*maʿal*) of *sinning unintentionally* (*wəḥāṭ'â bišgāgâ*) against Yahweh's sacred objects, probably by defiling them unknowingly or carelessly (Lev. 5:15–19).

and Num. 15 regarding the community and individual laws illuminates the changes and additions of Num. 15 (differences appear in bold font).

Leviticus 4 (Sinai)	Numbers 15 (Kadesh)
Identification of inadvertent wrongdoing by the community (v. 13)	Identification of inadvertent wrongdoing by the community: **not obeying "all these commands, . . . everything that Yahweh has commanded" through Moses** (vv. 22–24a)
The assembly presents a [flawless; implied from 4:3, 23, 28, 32] young bull (vv. 14–21)	The whole community must prepare a young bull as **"a burnt offering, a pleasing scent to Yahweh, along with its grain offering and its customary libation, and a male goat"** (v. 24b)
as a purification offering.	as a purification offering.
They bring it before the meeting tent; the elders lay hands on the bull and slaughter it before Yahweh. The high priest sprinkles some of the blood toward the curtain, puts some on the altar's horns before Yahweh, and pours the rest at the base of the altar. The priest offers the fat on the altar and, following the protocols given earlier (vv. 8–10), offers particular organs on the fire, but burns the remaining carcass in a clean pile outside the camp (vv. 14c–20b).	
"So the priest will make atonement for them, and they will be forgiven" (v. 20c–d).	"And the priest will make atonement for the whole Israelite community, and they will be forgiven, **because it was an inadvertent wrongdoing and they have brought their offering, an offering by fire to Yahweh, and their purification offering before Yahweh, for their inadvertent wrongdoing"** (v. 25).
	"The whole Israelite community and the immigrant who lives among them will be forgiven, since all the people were involved in inadvertent wrongdoing" (v. 26).
Identification of inadvertent wrongdoing by an individual, **violating one of Yahweh's commands, pleading guilty or his sin is made known to him** (vv. 27–28a)	Identification of inadvertent wrongdoing by an individual (v. 27a)
Individual brings a **flawless** female goat as a purification offering (v. 28b).	Individual offers a **one-year-old** female goat as a purification offering (v. 27b).
Ritual protocols for the purification offering (vv. 29–31b; see vv. 14c–20b above)	

Leviticus 4 (Sinai)	Numbers 15 (Kadesh)
"So the priest must make atonement for him, and they will be forgiven" (v. 31c).	"The priest must make atonement for the person who sins inadvertently, when they sin inadvertently before Yahweh, to make atonement for them, and they will be forgiven. You must have one law for the person who does something wrong inadvertently, both for the native among the Israelites and the immigrant who lives among them" (vv. 28–29).
Option, and protocols, to bring a female sheep as the sin offering (vv. 32–35)	

Numbers 15:22–29 assumes the knowledge and practice of certain elements from Lev. 4.[55] The bull and female goat must be flawless (implied in Lev. 4:3, 23, 28, 32);[56] either the individual pleads guilty, or their wrongdoing is made known to them (4:27–28a; cf. 5:1–5); and the offender and priest must follow the ritual protocols for the purification offering (Lev. 4:14c–20b, 29–31b). Numbers 15 then contributes three new elements. (1) Yahweh stresses obeying *all* his commands through Moses, not just at the famous site of Sinai, "the mountain of Yahweh" (Num. 10:33), but even in the wilderness (15:23).[57] (2) The young bull serves not as a purification offering but as a burnt offering, pleasing to Yahweh, with its accompanying grain offering and libation (15:25 à la 15:8–11; see the second translation note on v. 24). The revision of Num. 15 first places the emphasis on pleasing Yahweh and then turns to the issue of purifying after the wrongdoing. (3) Just as he did for the voluntary sacrifices in 15:14–16, Yahweh here underscores that the native Israelite and immigrant must follow one standard, the same protocols, for the sacrificial rituals for inadvertent wrongdoing (15:26, 29).

With that said, the purification offering (*ḥaṭṭā't*) still atones for (**kpr*)—that is, it removes the inadvertent wrongdoing from—the individual or community, which results in Yahweh's forgiveness, in which he relinquishes his determination to punish the offender (see the translation notes and comments on 6:11). In contrast to inadvertent offenses that can be forgiven (vv. 22–29), Yahweh closes by over-specifying that the person who acts defiantly by despising Yahweh's word and insulting Yahweh must be cut off (**krt*), which refers either to extirpation from the community by execution or exclusion from participating in the afterlife (mortality; vv. 30–31; see the translation

---

55. The lacking details suggest innerbiblical dependence of Num. 15 on Lev. 4 (Schmidt, *Numeri*, 56–57; Achenbach, "Complementary Reading," 221–25; Ashley, *Numbers*, 284–85), not just an alternative tradition (Staubli, *Levitikus, Numeri*, 259).

56. In 15:27 the female goat is to be a year old but still implicitly flawless.

57. Brin ("Numbers XV 22–23," 351–54) argues that vv. 22–23 self-disclose as post-Moses material in the Pentateuch.

notes there).[58] There is no purification offering, atonement, or forgiveness for the one who insolently hates the commands of God. Even in Sumerian law, the son who denounces his father publicly is disinherited and may be sold into slavery.[59] The modern equivalent is something like "To hell with you, Yahweh." The golden-calf apostates and the blasphemer of the Name illustrate this kind of defiance (Exod. 32; Lev. 24), and the very next story, on the Sabbath stick collector, offers another example. Ostensibly extending the trajectory of 15:30–31 and others like it, Jesus announces: "But whoever blasphemes against the Holy Spirit *will never be forgiven, but is guilty of an eternal sin*" (Mark 3:29 NET). This sin centers on attributing the works of the Spirit to Satan (Luke 12:10; cf. 11:15–20). Yet, at the same time, for "the vilest offender who truly believes,"[60] it can and must be said that "there is therefore now no condemnation for those who are in Christ Jesus" (Rom. 8:1 NRSV).

15:32–36. This brief but vivid scene takes the form of an oracular novella, which is a Priestly subgenre that entails a short story with an unsolvable legal conflict (vv. 32–34) that Yahweh then addresses through an oracle with a case ruling (v. 35).[61] Unlike the other samples of this genre, here Yahweh gives no statutory law to the community going forward[62] (below I speculate on why this is so). As the story goes, sometime "when the Israelites were in the wilderness" during Num. 10:11–21:35, they discover "a man gathering wood on the Sabbath day" (v. 32). Those who catch him in the act escort him to Moses, Aaron, and the entire community, apparently to turn him in for his violation. But what is his crime? Apparently even Moses and Aaron are not sure, so they put him in custody and wait on Yahweh for his verdict (vv. 33–34).[63] There is an ambiguity or loophole in the Sabbath laws that Yahweh alone can clarify or fill.[64]

The opening cosmology of Gen. 1:1–2:3 lays the foundation for Sabbath, but its theological ritual develops throughout the Moses story.[65] Sabbath is a day that is holy, meaning that it belongs exclusively to Yahweh,[66] and the Israelites must never tamper with Yahweh's domain.[67] For the scribes of the Exodus Decalogue, this means rooting Sabbath rest in a collective memory (*zkr) of Yahweh as the six-day Creator, who rested on the seventh day (Exod. 20:8–11);

---

58. Milgrom, *Numbers*, 405–8.

59. Walton and Matthews, *Genesis–Deuteronomy*, 191.

60. "To God Be the Glory" (1875), lyrics by Fanny Crosby.

61. Chavel, *Oracular Law*, 165–95; Chavel, "Numbers 15:32–36," 45–55; cf. Lev. 24:10–23; Num. 9:6–14; 27:1–11.

62. Cf. Lev. 24:15–22; Num. 9:9–14; 27:8–11.

63. Cf. Lev. 24; Num. 9, 27, 36.

64. See Burnside, "'Sabbath-Gatherer,'" 45–62.

65. Gen. 2:1–3; Exod. 16:23–29; 20:8–11; 31:12–17; 35:2–3; Lev. 16:31; 23:3, 11, 15, 16, 32; 19:3, 30; 25:2–7; 26:2, 35; Num. 15:32–36; 28:9–10; Deut. 5:12–15.

66. Clines, "Qdš," 481–502.

67. Exod. 20:8; Deut. 5:12.

that is, Yahweh took up residence to reign from his newly constructed cosmic temple.[68] By contrast, the Deuteronomy Decalogue grounds the observance (*šmr) of Sabbath rest in Yahweh as Israel's Redeemer: Just as Yahweh powerfully redeemed them, so they must use their power so that their extended household and the vulnerable, landless residents in their towns can vicariously experience Yahweh's redemption, too.[69] The Decalogues do not prohibit every form of work ('ăbōdâ) but specifically forbid "all business" (kōl-məlā'kâ), a word that frequently refers to one's business, occupation, or trade.[70] The penalty for doing business on the Sabbath is execution (Exod. 31:15; 35:2). In Lev. 23 and later, in Num. 28–29, the sacred days of the festival calendar also prohibit "any business work."[71] In the narrative context, business work may refer to food production, specifically collecting and preparing manna.[72] Yahweh instructed the Israelites not to gather any manna on the holy Sabbath day of rest, and it was a struggle for Israel to obey (Exod. 16:5, 22–30).[73]

It is conceivable that the wood gatherer of Num. 15 was amassing his own resources, doing business, but how can his eyewitnesses or Moses, Aaron, or the community determine whether he was doing business, producing food, or taking care of his family or even the poor as prescribed in the Torah?[74] Moses may fear executing an innocent man (Exod. 23:7),[75] so he brings the wood gatherer to Yahweh for a clear judgment. If the man's motives did indeed need to be revealed by Yahweh, this would also explain why Yahweh does not issue a sweeping statute for the community (Prov. 16:2). Another possibility is that the man violated the Sinai law that says "You must not kindle a fire in any of your homes on the Sabbath day."[76] Does that law prohibit the prerequisite activity of gathering kindling, as the man was doing, or prohibit the intention to light a fire? Again, the legal ambiguity of the man's actions necessitates a new oracle from Yahweh. Yahweh demands that the community stone the man (v. 35; see the translation note there), implying that he did violate the Sabbath, though the reader is kept in the dark about how.[77] It may be suggestive that the editors have positioned this story (vv. 32–36) directly after extirpation (*krt) was issued for "the person who acts defiantly" and "insults Yahweh" (vv. 30–31). The wood gatherer illustrates what it looks like to defy the Sabbath, insult Yahweh, and suffer the consequences. The community, probably

---

68. See Walton, *Lost World*, 71–85.

69. Deut. 5:12–15; 15:15; 16:12; 24:18, 22. See Awabdy, *Immigrants*, 148–52.

70. "*Məlā'kâ*," *HALOT* 2:586, gloss 2; see the second translation note on 28:18.

71. *Kol-məle'ket 'ăbōdâ*: Festival of Passover-Unleavened Bread (28:18, 25), Firstfruits (28:26), Trumpets (29:1), Day of Atonement (29:7, w/o 'ăbōdâ), Festival of Shelters/Booths (29:12, 35).

72. See Burnside, "'Sabbath-Gatherer,'" 52, 56, 58, 60.

73. See Chavel, "Numbers 15:32–36," 48–49; cf. Frevel, *Desert Transformations*, 339–56.

74. Exod. 21:10–11; Deut. 15:7–8.

75. Cf. Num. 35:30; Deut. 17:6–7; 19:15.

76. Exod. 35:3, my trans.

77. Curiosity is stirred by this knowledge gap (Sternberg, *Poetics*, 265–67).

by the agency of the tribal representatives, stones the man precisely as Yahweh ordered them (v. 36; see the translation note there).[78] We hear an echo from the Sinai story of the blasphemer whom, by Yahweh's command, the community stoned (Lev. 24:10–23).[79] The end of the wood gatherer marks the end of the story[80] but not the end of his disobedience among future Israelites and Jews. Take, for example, the apparent business dealings on the Sabbath by members of the fifth-century BCE Jewish diaspora living in Elephantine, Egypt, on the Nile: "Now, behold, legumes I shall dispatch tomorrow. Meet the boat tomorrow on Sabbath."[81]

If Yahweh's capital punishment of the wood gatherer seems ruthless, that is because modern readers as well as ancient ones (e.g., at Elephantine) fail to grasp that the Sabbath day belongs exclusively to Yahweh.[82] Defying Sabbath means defying Yahweh, who owns it, and the death penalty must ensue.[83] Also, as Salvian (5th cent. CE) inferred, God shows his mercy by killing a single man to caution many others.[84] The religious elite were convinced that Jesus, by healing on the Sabbath, violated the holy day and, like the wood gatherer, must be put to death.[85] They were wrong. Jesus came not to abolish the law, but to fulfill it (Matt. 5:17). As Israel's redeemer, à la Deut. 5:15, Jesus gave life and true rest to his people (Luke 1:68; Matt. 11:28; John 10:10).

15:37–41. With the communal stoning of the wood gatherer fresh in the reader's mind (vv. 32–36), Yahweh next commands these Israelites and later generations to create tassels, incorporating blue thread, and to attach them to the corners of their clothes (v. 38; see the translation notes there). In Egyptian portrayals of foreign peoples like the Shasu and the Philistines, the residents of Canaan wear clothes with three tassels—two on the sides and one in the middle.[86] The tassels resemble a lock of hair[87] and were worn as amulets intended to avert evil and harm.[88] Here the tassels are not for style or show[89] but

---

78. Cf. Lev. 24:14, 23.

79. See Achenbach, "Complementary Reading," 225–27.

80. Zeelander, "Closural Conventions," 337.

81. "Instructions regarding Legumes and Barley, etc," *COS* 3.87:214; cf. Achenbach, "*Lex Sacra*," 101–10.

82. The weight of Sabbath distinguishes this from other scenarios: e.g., in certain Hittite instructions, the king kills one of the water carriers for letting a hair get into the king's water pitcher (Sparks, *Ancient Texts*, 209).

83. Basil (4th cent. CE) and John Cassian (4th–5th cent. CE) saw the fact that his one act of sin warranted death as comparable to the final judgment against every sin of every kind (Lienhard, *Numbers*, 227).

84. Lienhard, *Numbers*, 227.

85. Matt. 12:1–14; Mark 2:23–3:6; Luke 6:1–11; 13:10–17; 14:1–6; John 5:9–18; 7:22–25; 9:14–16; cf. Luke 4:16–21.

86. Staubli, *Levitkius, Numeri*, 261, 394; Sprinkle, *Leviticus and Numbers*, 281.

87. Milgrom, *Numbers*, 127.

88. Walton and Matthews, *Genesis–Deuteronomy*, 191.

89. Cf. Matt. 23:5.

are a visual reminder to the Israelites to remain loyal to Yahweh their God (vv. 39–40),[90] in contrast to the wood gatherer who embodied disloyalty.[91] When they see the tassel dangling from their own or another's clothes, they are to meditate on Yahweh's commands *and* be faithful to obey them (vv. 39, 40). The clauses of vv. 39–40 can be a string of imperatives, but more likely they convey purposes leading to results.[92] As a result of their obedience, they do not become the people of Yahweh, but they are deterred from infidelity and thus exhibit holiness, showing that they belong to Yahweh their God (see the second translation note on v. 39).[93] The language of *following* or *exploring* (*twr*) and *infidelity* (*znh*) reflects the language of the preceding explorers' story (14:33–34),[94] as if to say that the tassels will serve to keep the new generation from following in their parents' tragic footsteps. Verse 41 recalls that Yahweh had redeemed Israel from Egypt (Exod. 1–15), entered into a covenant with them (Exod. 19–24), and distinguished them as his holy people (Exod. 19:5–6; Lev. 17–26). Glimpsing the tassels, then, points them to realign their lives with the reality of their holy identity by means of meditating on and obeying the divine commands.[95] Blue-threaded tassels, however useful, will prove to be inadequate in ensuring Israel's covenant faithfulness (Judges–1 Sam. 15; 2 Kings 17, 24–25), but by his grace Yahweh promises to establish with his people a new covenant infused with his own divine power to know him intimately and walk obediently in his *tôrâ* (Jer. 31:31–34; Ezek. 36:24–28; Rom. 8:1–4).

Implications

Immigrants Who Worship Yahweh

Immigrants, just like native Israelites, must sacrifice a purification offering for any exposed inadvertent wrongdoing (Num. 15:29). They must also be extirpated (*krt*) from the community or the afterlife for defying and insulting Yahweh (v. 30).[96] What is perhaps most striking, however, is that here, more than in any other text in the Torah, Yahweh opens the door wide for immigrants

---

90. Leveen, *Memory*, 110–11; Deut. 22:12 omits the theological rationale for the tassels (see Kilchör, *Mosetora*, 252–53).

91. The placement of 15:37–41 provides a great thematic segue that highlights the violations of the wood gatherer (15:32–36) and Korah's rebellion (chap. 16). Contra Kline ("Structure," 263), who overinterprets this unit as the structure of the book where the four fringes of a garment represent four flag tribes of Israel, God's garment, which Israel wears.

92. Four weqatals of purpose/result (v. 39), then *ləmaʿan* + yiqtol of purpose/result, then two weqatals of purpose/result (v. 40): *GBHS* §3.5.2c, §4.1.11.

93. Clines, "*Qdš*," 481–502.

94. See Achenbach, "Complementary Reading," 228–29; Leveen, *Memory*, 109.

95. Compare, e.g., moving from Eph. 1–3 (identity in Christ) to 4–6 (praxis); Rom. 1–11 (identity in Christ) to 12–16 (praxis).

96. See Milgrom, *Numbers*, 405–8.

to bring him delight through sacrificial rituals offered by those who simply want to express their gratitude and loyalty to Yahweh (vv. 1–16). Yahweh gives the non-Israelite Yahweh-worshiper the prerogative to offer up to him any or all of the noncompulsory offerings—burnt, vow, freewill, appointed feast—with their ancillary grain offering and libation.[97] Insofar as vv. 2–10 are enclosed by the subscript in vv. 11–12, the equalizing of the immigrant in vv. 13–16 may be a supplement but is no less important. In v. 13, beginning a second subscript, a new term is introduced to the discourse: "Every *native Israelite* [hā'ezrāḥ] must do these things in this way to present an offering by fire as a pleasing scent to Yahweh." Why does Yahweh introduce a new metonym when other terms used in this discourse—the Israelites, you plural, the person—seemingly would have been adequate. It is done to set up a binary of the native Israelite and the immigrant. In v. 14, then, we encounter the lengthiest descriptor in the Torah for this class, "If an immigrant is living with you or is among you in generations to come," which points toward the present and future authority of this supplement as "a permanent statute for generations to come" (v. 15; see the translation note on v. 14). However, the immigrant does not just live among Israel now and into perpetuity. The syntax of v. 15 suggests that the hyponym classes, native *and* immigrant, were both included under the hypernym of the assembly: "*As for the assembly* [haqqāhāl], you and the immigrant who lives among you . . ." (v. 15; see the translation note there).[98] The purpose of the native-immigrant binary in Num. 15 is to place native and immigrant under the same cultic standard, a demand that is repeated as a submotif in slightly different ways throughout (vv. 14, 15 [2×], 16, 26, 29, 30). In anthropological terms, the ancient Israel reflected in the Moses story is an enclave society that protects its own people, so "it is out of line when it adds that the stranger [immigrant] who lives among them can get forgiveness too. This is atypical for the normal enclave religion which keeps its benefits for insiders."[99]

The countercultural immigrant inclusivity that marks Num. 15 is not a novelty within the Torah, however. In Egypt (Exod. 12:48–49) and at Sinai (Num. 9:14), Yahweh grants the immigrant (gēr) the freedom to observe Passover, a distinctly Hebrew-Israelite festival, provided that all the males in his household are circumcised. Moreover, in the H law collection (Lev. 16:29–26:46),[100] there is one cultic and ethical standard for native Israelites and immigrants alike, and this includes observing the day of atonement, purifying after eating unclean carcasses, practicing sexual holiness, loving the immigrant as yourself, celebrating the Festival of Shelters (and the others?), and suffering the death

97. On the immigrant as a non-Israelite and non-Judahite in Deuteronomy, with germane argumentation for Num. 15, see Awabdy, *Immigrants*, 110–16.
98. For v. 15 as a possible chiasm, see Staubli, *Levitikus, Numeri*, 259.
99. Douglas, *Wilderness*, 54.
100. With H influence in Lev. 16:29–34, the H instructions incorporating the immigrant extend from chaps. 16 to 26 of Leviticus (Knohl, *Sanctuary*, 27–28, 70).

penalty for misusing Yahweh's name.[101] By contrast, in Deuteronomy's legal core (chaps. 12–26), Yahweh accommodates the law of the land for the benefit of the immigrant-orphan-widow triad of persons and the Levite, landless classes predisposed to poverty and injustice.[102] A critical text is Deut. 23, which allows the Egyptian and Edomite, for their positive past relations with Israel (!), to enter the worshiping community of Yahweh. They represent all non-Israelite ethnic polities who have treated Israel favorably à la the Abrahamic blessing (Gen. 12:3) and have resided in Israel for three generations and can thus be integrated into the cult of Yahweh.[103]

In Num. 15, and I believe in Deut. 23 also,[104] it is the nonindigenous resident (*gēr*) who is granted the right to express their worship of Yahweh through the cult. Other later traditions focus on excluding immigrants, appropriating the opening prohibitions of Deut. 23 to delegitimize foreign marriages in postexilic Yehud (Judah),[105] or drawing from other Torah texts to bar foreigners, uncircumcised physically and spiritually, from entering the restored temple.[106] The holiness and purity of Yahweh's people and sacred space must be maintained. With that said, in the book of Isaiah, Yahweh reveals a shockingly new vision. He imagines a day when an even lower class of allochthonous people, foreigners (*bənê hannēkār*), enter covenant with Yahweh and joyfully pray and sacrifice to him in the restored Jerusalem temple (Isa. 56:6–7). One might conclude that this provocative new reality was embodied in Jesus the Messiah. In the context, Isa. 56:1–12 singlehandedly condemns the Jewish leaders and welcomes non-Israelite worshipers.[107] So also in Mark's Gospel, Jesus castigates Israel's religious elite, the self-proclaimed loyalists of Yahweh, and replaces them with foreigners, as envisioned in Isaiah:

> My house
> > a house of prayer
> > > will be called
> > > > for all nations,
> > > > but you
> > > > > have made
> > it
> a den of robbers. (Mark 11:17)[108]

---

101. See Lev. 16:29; 17:15; 18:26; 19:34; 23:42; 24:16, 22.
102. Awabdy, *Immigrants*, esp. 220–26.
103. Awabdy, *Immigrants*, 66–83; cf. Kilchör (*Mosetora*, 257–59), who sees Deut. 23 as innerbiblical text engaging with other Priestly texts.
104. Chart in Awabdy, *Immigrants*, 81.
105. Ezra 10; Neh. 13:1–2; cf. the comments on Num. 31:13–20.
106. Ezek. 44:7; see Awabdy, "Yʜwʜ Exegetes Torah," 685–703.
107. See de Hoop, "Comfort or Criticism," 671–95.
108. Based on the Greek word order (Awabdy and F. Long, "Mark's Inclusion," 239).

The Spirit of God has birthed the church, Jew and Gentile together as one, and continues to bring worshipers of Jesus into the family of God from the ends of the earth (Matt. 28:17–20; Acts 1:8; 10:44–48; Eph. 2:15–22). However, still today the global coalition of Jesus worshipers is missing precious representatives from multiple thousands of ethnolinguistic people groups.[109] Today, believing immigrants, refugees, internationals, and the church in the global south are beautifully leading those of us from the western and northern hemispheres in fulfilling the Great Commission of our Lord. We are ignited by the hope of uniting to worship and enjoy the Son of God forever.[110]

---

109. See https://joshuaproject.net.

110. Rev. 5:9. John Piper (*Nations Be Glad*, 15) rightly concludes: "Missions is not the ultimate goal of the church. Worship is. Missions exists because worship doesn't."

16

Korah, Dathan, and Abiram Rebel

(16:1–50)

∽◌∼

Overview

After the old generation is cursed to die in the wilderness (chaps. 13–14), Yahweh gives their children a renewed hope of life with him in the land: sacrificing to Yahweh for his pleasure in them (15:1–16) and making atonement to result in his forgiveness of them (15:22–27). Yet they have also learned from the wood gatherer on the Sabbath and the tassels on their clothing that, whether doomed to die (old generation) or anticipating the future (new generation), Yahweh trenchantly warns his people, now in the wilderness, to obey every command through Moses (15:32–41). The person who acts defiantly must be cut off from the community (15:30–31). Korah, Dathan, Abiram, and On do not heed God's warning.[1] Their story of discontentment and insubordination initiates a final collection of stories in chaps. 16, 20, 21, and 25 that eradicate all hope for this sinful generation.[2] The primary purpose of chaps. 16–18 is to validate Aaron's family above the Levites and prevent encroachment on the meeting tent by Levites and non-Levites alike.[3] In the opening scene, Korah the Levite along with the Reubenites Dathan, Abiram, and On rise up to challenge the authority and

1. The redactional placement of the Korah story in chap. 16 illustrates the defiant offense of 15:30–31 (Achenbach, "Heiligkeitsgesetz," 174).
2. Olson, *Death of the Old*, 149. Knierim and Coats (*Numbers*, 209) identify the composite form of Num. 16 as a rebellion story.
3. Milgrom, *Numbers*, 129. On Ezek. 44's interpretation of Num. 16–18, see S. Cook, "Innerbiblical Interpretation," 193–208. Findlay ("Priestly Ideology," 421–29) argues that the LXX

privileged roles of Moses and Aaron (vv. 1–3). Moses confronts Korah and his followers, but the insurrectionists publicly defame the Yahweh-led exodus from Egypt and *eisodos* into the land (vv. 4–15). In a rapid succession of events, Moses orders a ritual with altar fire in censers, Korah and his followers assemble the community against Moses and Aaron, Yahweh appears to the community and announces that he will destroy everyone, but Moses and Aaron intercede to spare the community (vv. 16–22). Yahweh then proceeds to validate Moses by causing the earth to swallow the rebels whole (vv. 23–35). Having validated Moses, Yahweh next validates Aaron as his only priest by reforging the censers of those who died into a covering for the altar so as to be an ever-present admonition not to take the path of the rebels (vv. 36–40). As soon as the story closes with the warning in v. 40, the people complain again, and Yahweh sends a plague to annihilate them, but Moses and Aaron take censers and spread the altar fire throughout the camp to avert Yahweh's wrath (vv. 41–50).[4]

---

translator of Num. 16–17 further accentuated an anti-Levitical (Korah) and pro-Aaronide ideology.

4. Gray (*Numbers*, 186–93) contends for three traditions integrated into chap. 16: a J(E) Reubenite rebellion (vv. 12–15, 25, 26b–34); a P[g] non-Levite Korah rebellion against the Levites, Moses, and Aaron (vv. 3–7, 18–24, 26a, 35); and some see a P[s] supplement turning Korah into a Levite (variations: Lehming, "Versuch," 291–321; Noth, *Numbers*, 120–21; R. Gordon, "Compositeness," 57–69; Seebass, *Numeri*, 2:165–213; Schmidt, *Numeri*, 63–76); but against a non-Levite-to-Levite Korah, see Ashley, *Numbers*, 301–3. Levine (*Numbers*, 1:405) distinguishes two layers: JE (vv. 1–2 rewritten by P; vv. 12–15, 25–34 with P insertions) and P (vv. 3–11, 16–24, 35; and chap. 17) (similarly Van Seters, *Life of Moses*, 239–44; de Vaulx, *Nombres*, 190ff.). Blum (*Komposition des Pentateuch*, 263–71) argues the Priestly composition (KP) interweaves the Deuteronomic (KD) story of Dathan and Abiram with a Priestly narrative of the 250 men. Scharbert (*Numeri*, 65–70) sees the Pentateuch redactor supplying the 250 chieftains. Knohl (*Sanctuary*, 73–85) argues that H brought together two independent stories, the revolt of Dathan and Abiram and the revolt of the chieftains, which were appended with the Korah-Levite rebellion. Dozeman ("Numbers," 135) argues that, to the original story of Dathan and Abiram, the priestly writers added the conflict of Korah, Moses, and Aaron concerning the priestly leadership, resulting in a new tripartite drama. Achenbach (*Vollendung*, 37–123) sees a composite chapter with a Korah-Levite revision, from phase one of the theocratic revision of the Torah, as rejecting the participation of the community in the priestly cult. Budd (*Numbers*, 188–90) speculates that "Korah represents Levitical opposition to the priestly hierarchy proposed by the settlers from Babylon," and that the writer's purpose in Num. 16 is to validate the priestly hierarchy over the Levites; similarly, Albertz, *Israelite Religion*, 2:487, but for a counterargument, see Douglas, *Wilderness*, 41. Jeon ("Zadokites," 318–411) conjectures that a post-P redaction by the Zadokites conveyed "their struggle for their priestly prerogatives in the Jerusalem temple against the elders of the community and the powerful Levites in the Persian period." Miller ("Korahites," 58–68) attempts to reconstruct the history of the Korahite tribal group in the pre-monarchic times of southern Judah.

Translation

1Now Izhar's son Korah—Izhar was Kohath's son who was Levi's son—took[5] Eliab's sons Dathan and Abiram,[6] and Peleth's son On, who were Reubenites,[7] **2**and they stood up to Moses, along with some of the Israelites, 250 of the community's chieftains, chosen from the assembly,[8] famous men. **3**They assembled themselves against Moses and against Aaron[9] and said to them, "You've gone too far![10] If the whole community is holy, every one of them, and Yahweh is among them, then why do you exalt yourselves above Yahweh's assembly?"

4When Moses heard this, he fell facedown. **5**Then he said to Korah and to all his followers,[11] "In the morning Yahweh[12] will make known who

---

5. Manuscript support for "took" in v. 1 is strong (*wylqḥ* 4Q27 MT SP), but making sense of it is a notorious problem, as evidenced by the interpretation of the early versions: "spoke" (LXX[ed]), "took his robe which was all of hyacinth" (Tg[PJ]), "made a division" (Tg[O]), or "Look, however" (Vulg[ed]). These versions seek to improve the hard reading (Wevers, *Notes*, 258). The issue is that if one reads the verbal root as the transitive *lqḥ* (to take X), a common verb in Numbers (70×), no obj. is either stated or implied: "Then Korah *took* [*wayyiqqaḥ*] . . ." Schmidt (*Numeri*, 60) gives an honest, if awkward, translation without an object, and de Vaulx (*Nombres*, 188) and Cazelles (*Nombres*, 82) insert an ellipsis. Readers, then, would need to come up with an obj., such as "took men" (ESV, NET; but cf. the direct obj. expressed in 1:17) or "took counsel" (Levine, *Numbers*, 1:407). Another solution is to read these same consonants as the hiphil of an extremely rare verb (*wayyōqaḥ* from **yqḥ*: DCH 4:273; HALOT 2:430), meaning "were impudent" (Budd, *Numbers*, 179–80), "became arrogant" (Ashley, *Numbers*, 298), or "became impertinent" (for Seebass, *Numeri*, 2:167). Yet another solution is to say that Korah took *the power of the priesthood*, which relies heavily on the context for this anacoluthon (see Leveen, *Memory*, 120–21). The solution I offer is, without emending the text, to interpret the series of Reubenite men as the direct objects (see the comments on 16:1 below).

6. Also spelled "Abirum" or "Abirom" (*'byrwm*; 4Q27) and "Abiron" (LXX[ed]).

7. MT[L] identifies Dathan, Abiram, and On all as "Reubenites" (*bənê rə'ûbēn*), which makes the most sense (since Korah's tribe, Levi, was given), whereas MT[mss], SP, and LXX[ed] identify only On (Gk. "Aun") as a "son of Reuben" (Hb. *bn*; Gk. *huiou*); it is not clear whether 4Q27 is sg. or pl. (Ulrich, *Qumran*, 147).

8. Rather than apposition (MT SP), 4Q27 and LXX[ed] add "*and* famous men," probably trying to improve the text.

9. This niphal wayyiqtol functions "as a pl. variation of the reflexive" (GBHS §3.1.2c) and is modified by a repeated, adversative *'al* phrase, meaning "*they complained among themselves* [*wayyiqqāhəlû*] against ['*al*] Moses and *against* ['*al*] Aaron" (also in 20:2, 10 [implied '*al*]; GBHS §4.1.6f).

10. Formally, "enough/great for you all" (*rab-lākem*, also in v. 7). This expression occurs 8× in the OT and can indicate that the speaker thinks their audience (1) has done enough of something already (Deut. 1:6; 2:3; 1 Kings 12:28; Ezek. 44:5; 45:9) or (2) possesses a lot of something (Deut. 3:19). The idea here and in v. 7 is the former, with Ezek. 45:9 as the closest parallel.

11. Formally, "and all his community/congregation," but "and all his followers" (NLT, NIV) is clearer since this does not refer to Korah's tribal community, Levi, and the group clearly excludes Aaron's family but refers to Korah's 250+ adherents, who are presumably from various tribes (16:1–2).

12. LXX[ed] "God" (also in 15:30; 16:5).

belongs to him. The person who is holy he will bring near[13] to himself, and the person he chooses[14] he will bring near to himself. **6**You, Korah, and all your followers, must do this: Take censers, **7**put fire in them, and set incense on them before Yahweh tomorrow, and the person Yahweh chooses will be holy. You've gone too far, Levites!"[15] **8**Moses said to Korah,[16] "Listen now,[17] you Levites! **9**Isn't it enough that the God of Israel has distinguished you[18] from the Israelite community to bring you near[19] to himself, to perform the services of Yahweh's dwelling place,[20] and to stand before the community to serve them? **10**He has brought you near and all your brothers, the Levites, with you, and now you are seeking the priesthood also! **11**Therefore you and all your followers have gathered together against Yahweh![21] And Aaron, what is he that you complain[22] against him?" **12**Then Moses sent for Dathan and Abiram, Eliab's sons, but they said, "We will not come. **13**Isn't it enough that you have brought us up out of a land that flows with milk and honey in order to kill us[23] in the wilderness? Are you now making yourself a prince over us? **14**Clearly you have not brought us into a land that flows with milk and honey, or

13. Against 4Q27, which does not include a prefixed *w* (similarly LXX[ACO]), the MT hiphil weqatal (*wəhiqrîb*) is more fitting, functioning as the second colon of a tricolon in Moses's discourse (MT weqatal ≈ SP hiphil impf. *yqryb*), but *kai* in LXX[ed] (following LXX[BL]) does not recognize the weqatal and so preserves the *kai* but renders an aorist: "and he brought them to himself."

14. By left dislocation, which reactivates this referent for readers (*BHRG* §48.1.1, 48.2.1), MT and SP are best translated as present tense, "the person *he chooses*" (*yibḥar*; not likely preterite, *GBHS* §3.2.2e). Maybe to express their view that Yahweh had already made his choice, implying Aaron, 4Q27 and LXX[ed] adjusted the text to the perfective: "whom he has chosen."

15. See the second translation note on 16:3.

16. Here 4Q27 adds "and] to all his followers" (*w*]*'l-kl-'dtw*), which was likely added to harmonize to v. 5 (see vv. 6, 11, 16).

17. LXX[ed] "Listen *to me*, sons of Leui" is probably an "ad sensum gloss" (Wevers, *Notes*, 263; also 20:10), but could also have arisen as an aural confusion of *šəmā'ûnî* (Gen. 23:8) for *šim'û-nā'* (here).

18. Instead of using a niphal reflexive of **bdl* to indict them as we might expect, "you have distinguished yourselves," Moses's rhetoric hinges on the hiphil transitive, which accentuates their discontentment in the face of the special action taken by Israel's covenant deity toward them in particular: "the God of Israel *has distinguished you* from the Israelite community" or "has separated you" (*hibdîl 'ĕlōhê yiśrā'ēl 'etkem*; *GBHS* §3.1.6a.2); dynamically, "has lifted you out" (EÜ); "has chosen you" (NLT).

19. LXX[ed] "and brought you near" may render an alternate source that had harmonized to v. 10a; see Tov, "Septuagint of Numbers," 181–201.

20. Formally, "to serve the services of the dwelling of Yahweh."

21. LXX[ed] "God"; see Wevers, *Notes*, 264–65.

22. Following the Masoretic proposed hiphil (*tallînû* MT[qere] from **lwn*, with defectively spelled SP *tlnw*), instead of an unattested niphal form (*tillônû* MT[ketiv]), which could be pointed as a hiphil of another root to mean "You will lend to him" (*talwennû*, as in Deut. 28:44, from **lwh*).

23. The *l* + hiphil inf. const. indicates Dathan and Abiram's perception of the *purpose* for which Yahweh brought the Israelites out of the Caanan-like paradise of Egypt: "*in order to kill us* [*lahămîtēnû*] in the wilderness" (*GBHS* §4.1.10d).

given us an inheritance of fields and vineyards. Do you think you can blind these men?[24] We will not come!" [15]Moses was very angry, and he said to Yahweh, "Do not accept their offering! I have not taken a single donkey[25] from them or harmed even one of them!"

[16]Then Moses said to Korah, "You and all your followers,[26] present yourselves before Yahweh[27] tomorrow—you and they and Aaron. [17]Each of you take his censer, put incense in it, and then each of you present his censer before Yahweh—250 censers, with you and Aaron, each of you with his censer." [18]So everyone took their censer, put fire in them, set incense on them,[28] and stood at the entrance of the meeting tent with Moses and Aaron. [19]But Korah assembled[29] the whole community against them at the entrance of the meeting tent, and the glory of Yahweh appeared to the whole community.[30] [20]Yahweh spoke to Moses and Aaron: [21]"Separate yourselves from this community so I can consume them at once." [22]Then they fell facedown and said, "O God, the god[31] of the breath of all living things, will you be angry at the whole community when only one man sins?"[32]

[23]So Yahweh said to Moses: [24]"Tell the community: 'Get away from around the dwelling place[33] of Korah, Dathan, and Abiram.'" [25]Then

---

24. Formally, "the eyes of these men are you gouging out?" A modern equivalent is "pull the wool over the eyes" (Milgrom, *Numbers*, 134).

25. Formally, "one donkey," which LXX[ed] renders as "what was desired" (*epithymēma*), probably mistaking *r* for *d* (Wevers, *Notes*, 267), that is, *ḥmwr* (donkey) for some form of *ḥmd*, perhaps *ḥāmûd* (what is desired, treasure); LXX *epithymēma* often renders forms of *ḥmd*.

26. In the place of "You and all" ('*th wkl* MT SP 4Q27 [broken], as v. 11; cf. vv. 5, 6), LXX[ed] substitutes the impv., "*Sanctify* [*hagiason*] your congregation, and be ready before the Lord." This probably stems from a separate Hb. parent text (Wevers, *Notes*, 267), perhaps influenced by the prerequisite of communal consecration for the Sinai theophany (Exod. 19:14–15).

27. Formally, "be before Yahweh."

28. The pl. collection of fem. censers is referred to by the masc. pronouns *'ălêhem* ("on them," 2×; see Joüon and Muraoka §149b). SP apparently was discontented with this and adjusted the pronouns to fem. along with the first preposition: "put fire *in them* [*bhn*], set incense *on them* ['*lyhn*]."

29. The causative hiphil wayyiqtol is rendered as a disjunctive based on the contrast with the neutral, if obedient, actions of Korah's followers in the prior verse: "*But* Korah *assembled* [*wayyaqhēl*] . . ."

30. We may infer from 14:10 and the community's proximity to the tent's entrance here that the theophany occurred inside the meeting tent. See the third translation note on 14:10.

31. Here *'ēl* is the personal name, "God," which is in apposition to, not a second personal name, but the appellative that describes what kind of deity *'ēl* is: "God, the god of the breath of all living things." See the first translation note on 10:9.

32. SP includes two additional definite articles (*h* + inferred doubling), probably changing the meaning slightly: "O God, the god of the breath of all *living things* [*hbśr*], *the one man* [*h'yš h'ḥd*] sins and you are angry at the whole community."

33. The basic meaning is "residence" (Levine, *Numbers*, 1:408) or "homes" (NET) or "residential town" (for Seebass, *Numeri*, 2:68)—or in light of v. 26, "*the tents* of these wicked men" ('*ohŏlê hā'ănāšîm hāršā'îm hā'elleh*)—refers to "tents" (de Vaulx, *Nombres*, 194; EÜ, NLT, NIV, et al.). Instead, "*the dwelling place* [*miškan*] of Korah, Dathan, and Abiram" conveys the

Moses got up and went to Dathan and Abiram, and Israel's elders went after him. ²⁶And he said to the community, "Move away from the tents of these wicked men,³⁴ and do not touch anything they own, or you will be swept away³⁵ because of all their sins."³⁶ ²⁷So they got away from the residence of Korah, Dathan, and Abiram on every side, and Dathan and Abiram came out and were standing in the entrances of their tents with their wives, their children, and their toddlers. ²⁸Then Moses said, "This is how you will know that Yahweh has sent me to do all these works, that it was not my own idea.³⁷ ²⁹If these people die a natural death and share in the fate of humanity,³⁸ then Yahweh has not sent me. ³⁰But if Yahweh creates something new,³⁹ and the earth opens its mouth and swallows them up along with everything they own, and they go down alive into the realm of the dead,⁴⁰ then you

---

Hb. wordplay that contrasts their dwelling place with Yahweh's (with Cazelles, *Nombres*, 84; Schmidt, *Numeri*, 61; ESV; "tabernacle," Budd, *Numbers*, 180). Noth (*Numbers*, 127) further observes, "The mention of 'the dwelling of Korah' is out of place, for Korah and his company are in front of the tent of meeting (vv. 18bα, 19a), . . . a completely secondary fusion of the two narrative variants." In the present shape of the text, the dwelling-place wordplay seems to take precedence over the ambiguity as to how the men changed locations.

34. Cf. 2 Tim. 2:19.

35. "Or you will be swept away because of all their sins" (*pen-tissāpû bəkol-ḥaṭṭō'tām*) is a metaphoric way of exclaiming to the community how they could die as a result of the sins of Korah, Dathan, and Abiram. The verb is a niphal pass., implying divine agency; **sph* is used 7× in the Pentateuch to refer to an impartial destruction: four times it refers to the righteous or Lot's family being swept away in the destruction of Sodom and Gomorrah (Gen. 18:23, 24; 19:15, 17), and twice it appears when Moses warns that breaking the covenant leads to the sweeping destruction of both the watered and parched ground alike (Deut. 29:19 [18]) and of his people (Deut. 32:23).

36. Without emending the original text, the vowels of the Hebrew noun can be re-pointed as sg., meaning "all *their sin*" (*ḥaṭṭā'tām*, as 15:25), with LXXᵉᵈ, presumably referring to the rebellious act of Korah and his followers (16:1–25).

37. Formally, "that it was not from my heart" (*kî-lō' millibbî*), where his heart is a metaphor not for the origin of his feelings, but of his thoughts and will ("mind, thinking, intention, understanding" in *DCH* 4:498).

38. Likely a verbal hendiadys (*GBHS* §4.3.3g.2), two expressions for natural death (called apposition in Cazelles, *Nombres*, 85; de Vaulx, *Nombres*, 194; Levine, *Numbers*, 1:408). The simple *w* is not alternative, "or" (many versions), but conjunctive, "and" (NIV, EÜ; Ashley, *Numbers*, 301; Schmidt, *Numeri*, 61). Formally, "if these die as the death of all humankind and the appointment/fate of all humankind is appointed to them."

39. The internal adjunct of the same verbal root—"but if Yahweh creates a creation" (*wə'im-bərî'â yibrā' yhwh*; Schmidt, *Numeri*, 61)—simply means "Yahweh creates something new" (NRSV, ESV; *BHRG* §33.3[5]), not "*entirely/totally/completely* new" (NLT, NET, NIV, EÜ). Probably by homophony, SP misspells "something new" (*bryh* for *bry'h*). Hanson ("BĀRĀ'," 353–59, esp. 355) argues that "creates a creation" means "splits open a crevice," which matches the parallel line of the splitting ground (v. 31).

40. "The realm of the dead" (NIV), similarly "underworld" (EÜ), is a dynamic translation for *šə'ôl*, which is known in Eng. by its transliteration, "Sheol" (ESV, NRSV, NJPS). I prefer this dynamic translation because Sheol is archaic, while "grave" (NLT; *qeber*; Num. 19:16, 18) and "pit" (NET; *bôr*; Exod. 21:33–34) have their own Hebrew terms and do not communicate

will know that these men have reviled Yahweh!"[41] [31]Just as he finished speaking all these words, the ground under them split open, [32]and the earth opened its mouth and swallowed them, with their households, and everyone belonging to Korah, and all their possessions.[42] [33]They and everything they owned went down alive into the realm of the dead, and the earth closed over them. So they perished from among the community. [34]All the Israelites who were around them fled at their voice,[43] for they said, "The earth could swallow us too!" [35]Then a fire went out from Yahweh and consumed the 250 men who were offering the incense.

[36 [17:1]]Yahweh spoke to Moses: [37 [17:2]]"Tell Eleazar, son of Aaron the priest, to remove the censers out of the flame, for they are holy, and then scatter the burning coals some distance away. [38 [17:3]]As for the censers of these people whose sinfulness cost them their lives,[44] make them into hammered sheets as a covering for the altar, because they were presented before Yahweh and they have become holy.[45] They will become a sign to the Israelites." [39 [17:4]]So Eleazar the priest took the bronze censers, which those who were burned up had presented, and he had them hammered out[46] as a covering for the altar. [40 [17:5]]It was a reminder[47] for the Israelites, so that no unauthorized person[48] who is not a descendant of Aaron should approach to burn incense before

---

any of the common meanings for *šə'ôl*: "netherworld, underworld, abode of the dead" (*DCH* 8:206; cf. *HALOT* 4:1368–69). "Hades" (*hades* LXX[ed]) is fitting as it points to "*the underworld as the abode of the dead*" (*GELS* 10).

41. On "reviled," see the first translation note on 14:11.

42. This generic term "possessions, property, goods, equipment" can consist of livestock, as in Num. 35:2 (*DCH* 7:491), which LXX[ed] apparently infers with "cattle."

43. Formally, "at their noise/voice."

44. An attributive adjective, so I follow Levine (*Numbers*, 1:409): "*those persons whose sinfulness* [*haḥaṭṭā'îm hā'ēlleh*] cost them their lives" (formally, "by their lives"). Ancient versions: "sinners" (LXX[ed] Vulg), or emphatically, "those guilty men who sinned" (Tg[O]). Similarly, "these sinners" for Seebass, *Numeri*, 2:168; de Vaulx, *Nombres*, 198; NRSV; Scharbert, *Numeri*, 62.

45. **Qdš* qal is stative, describing the resulting state or quality of these censers (v. 38a), so "they have become holy" (*wayyiqdāšû*; GBHS §3.1.1b), rather than "and sanctified them" (NET), which would require **qdš* piel or hiphil.

46. With NIV, contextually rendering the impersonal pl., "and they hammered them out" (*wayraqqə'ûm*).

47. I prefer "a reminder" (*zikkārôn*, many translations) over "a memorial" (NET), which connotes an object, site, or service intended to *commemorate* the dead. Rather, like the hiphil of the same root (**zkr*), "to remind," this hammered bronze altar cover was to serve the Israelites as a "reminder" (*zikkārôn*), a visible "sign" (*'ôt*, v. 38) of the lethal consequences of Korah's rebellion, so that they would avoid Korah's fate by not taking the cultic prerogatives that belong to Aaron and his sons (v. 40).

48. "Unauthorized person" (*zār*) refers metonymically to a non-Aaronid, a "lay Israelite" (subst. adj. of "*zwr* I," *DCH* 3:98, gloss c). This is preferred over the vague rendering, "outsider" (many versions). Elsewhere, when referring to a person, this substantivized adj. can refer to a stranger, foreigner, or an unfamiliar or unrelated person (*HALOT* 1:267; *DCH* 3:98).

Yahweh, so that he might not become like Korah and his followers, just as Yahweh had said to him by the authority of Moses.[49]

41 [17:6]But on the next day the whole Israelite community complained against Moses and against Aaron, saying, "You have killed Yahweh's people!" **42 [17:7]**When the community assembled against Moses and against Aaron, they turned toward the meeting tent, and suddenly the cloud covered it, and the glory of Yahweh appeared.[50] **43 [17:8]**Then Moses and Aaron stood[51] in front of the meeting tent. **44 [17:9]**Yahweh spoke to Moses: **45 [17:10]**"Get away from this community so I can consume them at once!" They fell facedown, **46 [17:11]**and Moses said to Aaron, "Take the censer, put burning coals from the altar in it, place incense on it, and go quickly[52] into the community to make atonement for them, for wrath has gone out from Yahweh.[53] The plague has begun!"[54] **47 [17:12]**So Aaron took it as Moses said and ran into the middle of the assembly,[55] where the plague had already started among the people. He placed the incense on the coals[56] and made atonement for the people. **48 [17:13]**He stood between the dead and the living, and the plague was stopped. **49 [17:14]**But 14,700 people died in the plague, in addition to those who died in the event with Korah. **50 [17:15]**Then Aaron returned to Moses at the entrance of the meeting tent after the plague had stopped.[57]

49. The instrumental *b*, "by the hand of Moses" (*bəyad-mōšeh*), where "hand" is a metaphor for a "(sphere of) power, rule, control, . . . authority (e.g., Gen. 41:35)" ("*yād* I," *DCH* 4:82, gloss 4a). To what the phrase, "just as Yahweh had said to him by the authority of Moses," refers is not obvious, maybe to Eleazar for taking, hammering (v. 39), or converting the bronze altar cover into a reminder to the Israelites (v. 40).

50. See the third translation note on 14:10.

51. Formally, "went."

52. SP can be read a piel impv., "Go, *hurry* [*mahēr*] into the community" (cf. MT adv., "*quickly* [*məhērâ*]").

53. "Wrath" (*haqqeṣep*) is the subject of the fientive verb, and Yahweh is the wrath's source (*mn* of source: *GBHS* §4.1.13a; generic article: *IBHS* 13.5.1g). "Wrath" (*qeṣep* I, 28× in the OT) occurs in the Pentateuch four times, three in Numbers (1:53; 17:11; 18:5), once in Deuteronomy's epilogue (29:28 [27]). The assumption here is not merely that Yahweh bursts out in "anger, wrath," but also initiates his "judgment, punishment" (*DCH* 7:283, gloss 1, definitions 1–2, and 3–4, respectively).

54. LXX[ed] free rendering, "for anger has gone out from before the Lord, and it has begun *to shatter the people* [*thrauein ton laon*]" (NETS), making Yahweh's anger the expressed verbal agent (Wevers, *Notes*, 282). The Greek verb (*thrauō*) and its nominal form in vv. 47–50 (*thrausis*) recast the plague of the Hb. text as a slaughtering or massacre (Dorival, *Nombres*, 647).

55. LXX[ed] "into the congregation" might have had a source that lacked "the middle of" (*twk* 4Q27 MT SP), which may be an adjustment to v. 11. Hexapla adds *mesēn* (in the middle) under the asterisk (Wevers, *Notes*, 282).

56. "On the coals" (NET) is supplied here for clarity.

57. In this circumstantial clause (*GBHS* §5.2.11, 4.3.3e), the simple *wə* with a niphal qatal as the predicate indicates anterior action, "*after/when* the plague *had stopped*" (*wəhammaggēpâ neʿĕṣārâ*; Schmidt, *Numeri*, 62; Levine, *Numbers*, 1:409; Cazelles, *Nombres*, 87; EÜ, NRSV), yet contemporaneous is plausible (ESV; Ashley, *Numbers*, 323). This is preferred over subsequence ("and the plague was stopped" for Seebass, *Numeri*, 2:169; NET; Budd, *Numbers*,

Interpretation

16:1–3. Just when the reader of the wilderness epic thought chap. 15 turned a page to a bittersweet phase of relationship with Yahweh—living under the curse, yet grateful for his goodness and leadership—four men incite another rebellion. The Hebrew of v. 1 is notoriously difficult (see the first translation note on 16:1). However, without emending the text, one can interpret the series of Reubenite men as the direct objects, with a waw initiating the series: "Korah . . . took [*w*] Dathan [*w*] and Abiram . . . [*w*] and On . . ."[58] If Korah the Levite is presented here as the exclusive agent acting on these Reubenites (see the third translation note on 16:1), he instigates their rebellion, which would explain why the narrator always lists Korah first when the men are named together (16:24, 27) and why, later in the book, Dathan and Abiram are said to belong to Korah's "following" (*ʿēdâ*) or "company" (26:9; cf. 27:3).[59] These four with 250 of Israel's chieftains, "chosen from the assembly, famous men," assembled themselves *against* Moses and *against* Aaron (v. 3; see the first translation note there). This repetition of "against" becomes important as the story unfolds and the rebels fire separate criticisms against Yahweh's prophet-leader (vv. 13–14) and against Yahweh's priest (see Moses's response in vv. 8–11). The insurgents exclaim: "You've gone too far!" (v. 3; see the second translation note there). However, their deductive argument as to why Moses and Aaron have gone too far is invalid as a non sequitur. Although the two independent premises are true, the conclusion does not follow from the premises:[60]

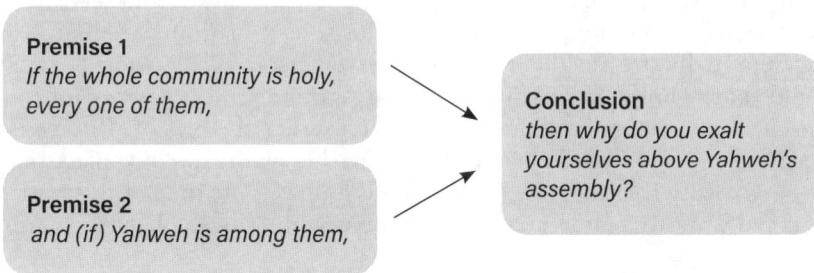

Premise 1
If the whole community is holy, every one of them,

Premise 2
and (if) Yahweh is among them,

Conclusion
then why do you exalt yourselves above Yahweh's assembly?

Figure 16.1. Korah's Rebellion

192) or causality ("since/for/because the plague had stopped" (de Vaulx, *Nombres*, 202; NJPS, NIV, NLT).

58. Joüon and Muraoka (§177): "Very occasionally the Waw is put before . . . the first of a series of nouns."

59. Indicating different traditions: after v. 1 the figure On drops out; Num. 26:11 explains the preservation of Korah's descendants; Deut. 11:6 and Ps. 106:17 mention only Dathan and Abiram, not Korah.

60. Their argument is unsound, since sound arguments not only have true premises but are also valid (Teall, *Logic*, 15–20).

At face value, both premises are true. In the theology of H (Lev. 17–26), the entire community, including every constituent member, is holy: every member belongs to Yahweh as his own possession.[61] In Exod. 19:6, Yahweh calls Israel "a holy nation,"[62] even as the people, not just the priests, must also choose to be holy through their obedience to Yahweh,[63] as they are becoming progressively more holy through Yahweh's action in and among them: "I am Yahweh who sanctifies you/him/them."[64] Also, Yahweh has repeatedly affirmed that his presence is among his covenant people. He has located his glory in his dwelling place (Exod. 40:34–35), which travels in the center of their camps (Num. 2:17; 10:11, 17, 21, 33–36). There is a special fellowship in Yahweh's presence when Israel obeys (Lev. 26:11–12). Even though Israel has repeatedly sinned (Exod. 16–19, 32; Num. 11–14), and even though Yahweh did not go up with the exodus generation to fight for Canaan (14:42), Yahweh still affirms his presence among them.[65]

But the conclusion the Levite and three Reubenites draw does not follow from either one of their premises. First, Moses and Aaron did not exalt themselves above Yahweh's assembly (v. 3).[66] Rather, Yahweh positioned them *over* the community *for* the community to transmit divine revelation for the people (Moses) and make atonement for them (Aaron).[67] Theoretically, the men could have tried to prove that Moses and Aaron had deceived everyone, that Yahweh had not appointed them after all, but there is no textual evidence that the opposition attempted this. Second, shared ontology does not imply shared function. Even if every member of the community belongs to Yahweh and lives in proximity to him as their resident deity (ontology), this does not mean that every member has the right to approach Yahweh and serve in his most sacred zones alongside Aaron and his sons (function). At Sinai, Yahweh repeatedly stressed that no unauthorized person (*zār*), no non-Aaronid, could eat the holy offerings belonging to Aaron or enter the holy (outside the curtain) or most holy (inside the curtain) sacred zones of the meeting tent.[68] Any unauthorized person who encroaches on the dwelling place must be put to death (Num. 3:38). Korah and his followers are tired of this restriction and want to democratize the community of Yahweh. The true nature

---

61. Milgrom (*Numbers*, 131; also Knohl, *Sanctuary*, 152–56, 189–92; Artus, "Numbers 32," 373) sees the conflict with P in which only the priests are holy. Here I follow the definition of *qdš* by Clines (see the comments on 4:1–14).

62. Exod. 19:6 as P: Dozeman, *Exodus*, 446.

63. Exod. 22:31; Lev. 11:44–45; 19:2; 20:7; Num. 15:40.

64. Lev. 20:8; 21:15; 21:23; 22:9; 22:16; 22:32; see Milgrom, *Leviticus*, vols. 2–3; Phil. 2:12–13.

65. Exod. 33:14; Lev. 9:23–24; 10:2; 16:16; Num. 7:89; 11:20; 14:10; implicit in ongoing speaking in 15:1–22 (for the land), and in the contents of 15:22–37 (for the wilderness and land).

66. "Yahweh's assembly" (*qəhal yhwh*) occurs in 16:3; 20:4; Deut. 23; see Kilchör, *Mosetora*, 257–59; Awabdy, *Immigrants*, 66–83.

67. See the "Implications" essay in chap. 3, "Is There a Hierarchy within the People of God?"

68. Exod. 29:33; Lev. 22:10–13; Num. 1:51; 3:10, 38.

of Korah's discontentment, however, becomes clearer only through Moses's two rejoinders that follow.

16:4–15. Hearing their invalid accusation, Moses falls facedown, just as he and Aaron did when the mutinous community complained against them after the explorers returned with the discouraging report (14:1–5). Then, in his opening rejoinder to Korah and his followers (vv. 5–7), Moses announces a contest to begin the next morning to allow Yahweh to make known who belongs to him.[69] The person who is holy, whom Yahweh chooses, Yahweh will bring near to himself (see the translation notes on v. 5). To distinguish the person who is holy for all to see, Korah and all his followers must take censers and put fire and incense in them before Yahweh. Moses closes by mimicking the rebels:

> Korah and followers (v. 3): You've gone too far!
>
> Moses (v. 7): You've gone too far, Levites![70]

In Moses's second rejoinder to Korah, vv. 8–11, he exposes the heart of the insurrection: in chap. 12 and 14:4 the people wanted to supplant Moses; here the Levite(s) want to supplant Aaron the priest. Moses addresses his speech specifically to the Levite Korah (v. 8a) and to all the Levites (v. 8b), not mentioning Korah's Reubenite followers as in v. 5. What is implicit throughout Moses's first speech is now explicit here: Since they left Sinai, the Levites have become discontented in their social rank and meeting-tent service work. Numbers 16 assumes the hierarchy of Num. 1–4 and 8,[71] and the Levites now want to overturn it. Of the three Levite family groups authorized to work in and around the meeting tent, the Kohathites (Korah's family) were authorized to carry the covered sancta by their poles (4:4–16). Unlike Aaron and his sons, however, the Kohathites were not permitted to touch the sancta or to see them uncovered or else they would be executed (4:17–20).[72] This distinction from the community and nearness to Yahweh are apparently not enough in their minds (see the first translation note on 16:9). They are jealous of Aaron's prestigious intermediary work and access to the most sacred zones and sacra of Yahweh. But Moses makes plain that mutiny against Aaron to gain the priesthood is tantamount to rebellion against Yahweh (v. 11). Contentment in the Levites' privileged role, which is subordinate to Moses's and Aaron's roles, is their only viable option. Like the first humans serving in the garden temple of Eden (Gen. 3:1–6), the Levites serving near the presence of God

---

69. Leveen, *Memory*, 123–24. Paul quotes Num. 16:5, "the Lord knows who belong to him," probably from the LXX, but replaces the LXX's *theos* (God) with *kyrios* (Lord), which aligns with the Heb. text *yhwh*. The rhetorical effect is that the Lord will reveal and punish false teachers as not belonging to God, just as Yahweh revealed and put to death Korah and his company.

70. See the second translation note on 16:3.

71. Frevel, "High Priest," 148–50.

72. See the "Implications" essay in chap. 4, "The Holiness of God Is Lethal."

have become discontented with God's good gifts to them, fixated on their one restriction, and this was a portent of things to come (cf. Gen. 3:7–24).

Moses, who has been talking most recently with Korah (v. 8; but cf. v. 5), sends for the Reubenites Dathan and Abiram, but with no mention of On (v. 1), and they refuse to come (v. 12c). The response of these men reveals that *their* core jealousy was not of Aaron, like Korah's envy, but of Moses, like the community on the way out of Egypt (Exod. 14), to Sinai (Exod. 17), and after departing from Sinai (Num. 14):[73]

Table 16.1. Israelite Complaint Texts Compared

Exodus 14–Numbers 14	Numbers 16
Is it because there are no graves in Egypt that you have taken us to die in the desert? What have you done to us by bringing us out of Egypt? (Exod. 14:11, also v. 12)	[13a]Isn't it enough that you have brought us up out of a land that flows with milk and honey in order to kill us in the wilderness?[a]
Why did you bring us up out of Egypt in order to kill us and our children and our cattle with thirst? (Exod. 17:3d)	
If only we had died in the land of Egypt, or if only we had died in this wilderness! Why is Yahweh bringing us into this land to fall by the sword? Our wives and our children will become war captives. Wouldn't it be better for us to return to Egypt? (Num. 14:2c–3)	
So they said to each other, "Let's appoint a leader and return to Egypt." (Num. 14:4)	[13b]Now you are making yourself a prince over us? [14]Clearly you have not brought us into a land that flows with milk and honey, or given us an inheritance of fields and vineyards. Do you think you can blind these men?[b]

a. See the translation note on Num. 16:13.
b. See the translation note on Num. 16:14.

In Nietzschean terms, the Reubenites are revolting in morality: their "ressentiment itself turns creative and gives birth to values," namely, the value of their power to say "yes" to themselves and "no" to Moses as their external master.[74] What is lacking in Nietzsche's claim is that he has no category for a volitional and joyful subordination to the divine Master who has liberated them (Matt. 16:24). These Reubenites have forgotten that Yahweh has redeemed them from

73. This is likely the reason the Reubenites are included in this story, not because their camp was proximate to the Kohathites (contra Leveen, *Memory*, 121). Each rebellion, the Levites' and the Reubenites', literarily brings the other into sharper focus (*with* Leveen, *Memory*, 121).
74. Nietzsche, *Genealogy of Morality*, 464.

slavery, is their new master, and loves them (Exod. 14–15; 19:4–6). They want the blessing of his presence (Exod. 33:14–16; Lev. 26:11–13; Num. 6:24–26), provision (Exod. 17:5–7), and protection (Num. 10:35–36) without Yahweh's exaltation of Moses as his unparalleled intermediary (Num. 12; 14:10–12) and Moses's intercession on their behalf (14:13–19).[75] Here they not only accuse Moses of failing to bring them into a land flowing with milk and honey (Canaan) but also slander Yahweh's patriarchal land promise by calling *Egypt* a land flowing with milk and honey.[76] Understandably, Moses is irate and enjoins Yahweh not to accept their offering (v. 15), probably referring to the incense they are to burn the next day (vv. 6–7). He tells Yahweh he has never robbed or harmed these men, implying that he does not deserve their diatribe (v. 15).

16:16–22. The story speeds up with a progression of events from the protagonists (Moses-Aaron-Yahweh) and antagonists (Korah and followers). As if specifying the contest he initiated in vv. 6–7, Moses now demands that each of the 250 chieftains who have joined Korah's rebellion (v. 2) must take a censer, place incense in it, and present it before Yahweh along with Aaron (vv. 16–17). The 250 enter this contest and stand at the entrance of the meeting tent with Moses and Aaron, but Korah, who is not among the chieftains, incites the entire community against Moses and Aaron at the meeting tent (vv. 18–19a; see the translation notes there). The insurrection site, Yahweh's meeting tent, symbolizes Korah's opposition to Moses, Aaron, and Yahweh.[77] Finally breaking the divine silence in the Korah story to this point,[78] Yahweh dramatically displays his opposition to those who oppose his leaders by causing his glory to be seen by all the people, for a second time at Kadesh (v. 19; see the third translation note on 14:10; cf. Lev. 9:23). As in Num. 14:11–12, 15, again Yahweh announces his intention to consume the entire community at once, so Moses and Aaron must separate themselves from the people to survive the mass execution (v. 20). In 14:13–19, Moses pleads with Yahweh not to annihilate the community so that Yahweh can preserve his reputation in Egypt and Canaan and remain true to his revealed gracious and forgiving nature (Exod. 34). By contrast, here Moses and Aaron together fall facedown[79] and collectively intercede to save the Israelites on the basis of the ethical problem of punishing the entire community "when only one man sins," that is, in light of the relatively minute number of rebels (254) compared to more than 600,000 Israelite men (1:46). Later, for example, Yahweh would punish the entire community for Achan's violation of the devoted things (Josh. 7) and for David's census (2 Sam. 24:10–17). But it seems to Moses and Aaron that

---

75. Römer ("Egypt Nostalgia," 78–79) contends that 16:13–14 belongs to a final post-P redaction, so it presupposes the other Egypt-nostalgia texts.

76. See the comments on 13:26–29.

77. Mirguet, "Numbers 16," 320–21.

78. W. Lee, *Migratory Campaign*, 145.

79. They also fall facedown prior to the theophany in 14:5.

God's justice is on the line, as Abraham once claimed (Gen. 18:25). Abraham challenged Yahweh not to destroy a righteous minority with the wicked in Sodom (18:16–33), and now Moses and Aaron challenge Yahweh not to destroy an innocent majority along with the wicked rebels. Like Abraham, who knew he was "but dust and ashes" (Gen. 18:27; cf. 18:30, 31, 32), they acknowledge their humble dependence on the one whom they are imploring: "O God, the god of the breath of all living things" (Num. 16:22; see the first translation note there; cf. Heb. 12:9).

16:23–35. In response to the mutinous community, Yahweh substantiates Moses's authority by causing the earth to swallow the insurgents whole (vv. 23–35; cf. Jude 11). Yahweh makes no statement of his forgiveness since the whole community has not sinned (cf. 14:20), and he answers Moses and Aaron's petition favorably by prompting the community to "get away from around *the dwelling place* [*miškan*] of Korah, Dathan, and Abiram" (v. 24). The command is rephrased, "Move away from *the tents* [from *'ōhel*] of these wicked men, and do not touch anything they own, or you will be swept away because of all their sins" (v. 26; see the translation notes there). The wordplay becomes clear: The dwelling place (*miškan*) and meeting tent (*'ōhel mô'ēd*) of Yahweh is indispensable and never to be a site of insurrection (v. 19),[80] but the dwelling place (*miškan*) and tent (*'ōhel*) of the wicked is dispensable and will become a site of destruction (see the translation note on v. 24).[81] The people get away, but Korah, Dathan, and Abiram, their wives, and children, including toddlers, stood at the entrances of their tents (v. 27).

In vv. 28–30, Moses presents a conditional to the community, probably the implied audience from v. 26, to substantiate his claim that Yahweh has sent him "to do all these works" and that it was not Moses's own idea to send himself (v. 28; see the translation note there). If the men die a natural death, then Yahweh has not sent him, but if Yahweh "creates something new" and the earth opens its mouth and swallows the men alive, then the men have reviled Yahweh (vv. 29–30; see the translation notes there). Scenario two unfolds precisely as Moses imagines: the anthropomorphic earth opens its mouth to swallow the men who opened their mouths to revile Moses and Aaron and Yahweh (vv. 31–34). The 250 chieftains burning incense before Yahweh were burned alive (v. 35). By *inclusio* of these 250 men (vv. 2, 35), the body of the Korah story has come to a close.[82] For more depth on the fitting punishments in vv. 30–35, see the "Implications" essay below ("*Lex Talionis*").

16:36–40 [17:1–5]. After substantiating Moses's honor and authority (vv. 23–35), Yahweh next validates Aaron as his only priest by directing his son

---

80. Utzschneider, *Heiligtum*, 127.
81. See Mirguet, "Numbers 16," 325–29; Leveen, *Memory*, 125–26.
82. Zeelander, "Closural Conventions," 333–34. Staubli (*Levitikus, Numeri*, 262) transposes vv. 34 and 35 to make a chiastic structure work.

Eleazar to reforge the censers of the 250 rebels into a covering for the altar in order to be an enduring warning against rebellion. This turn from the past events of the Korah story to the future with a new icon above the altar marks this subunit as an epilogue.[83] In Lev. 10, Yahweh spoke to Aaron and his remaining sons, Eleazar and Ithamar, but here the instructions through Moses are for Eleazar alone to carry out, even though Aaron is still alive (see 20:22–29). The reason is that Eleazar had been appointed over the sanctuary and its furnishings (3:32; 4:16). Eleazar must first remove the censers out of the flame because they are holy—they still belong to Yahweh even though they were handled by the rebels—and then scatter the burning coals at a distance (16:37 [17:2]). It is implied, but never stated, that Eleazar does this (cf. 16:39 [17:4]). The rest of the unit, 16:39–40 [17:4–5], mirrors 16:38 [17:3] in forward symmetry (ABCA′B′C′) to stress Eleazar's precise obedience and explicate the warning sign. One might think Yahweh would want his people to "forgive and forget" or that he would not want the stigma of Korah's rebellion to be attached to his bronze altar of burnt offerings. This is not the case. Yahweh has no interest in a putting on a façade that his covenant people have always been his loyal devotees, but he does whatever is needed to prevent his recalcitrant people from further acts of disobedience leading to their destruction. However, like the tassels of 15:37–41 that remind (*zkr) Israel to obey, the new bronze altar cover can serve only as a cognitive reminder (zikkārôn; see the first translation note on 16:40 [17:5]) and does not provide divine power to obey (Jer. 31; Ezek. 36; Rom. 8).

16:41–50 [17:6–15]. The warning of 16:40 [17:5] gives the impression of closing out the tragic story. To the reader's surprise, the nightmare continues. The community complains yet again against Moses and Aaron, accusing them of killing Yahweh's people (16:41 [17:6]). The accusation is absurd, as if Moses and Aaron, not Yahweh, had split open the swallowing earth and issued the consuming fire. While the people are assembling against Moses and Aaron, they turn toward the meeting tent, and the cloud covers it, and the glory of Yahweh appears yet again (16:42 [17:7]; see 16:19 and the third translation note on 14:10). Moses and Aaron stand before the meeting tent, but Yahweh tells Moses to get away from the community so that he can consume them at once, an echo of what Yahweh said he would do before he consumed the rebels (16:21; cf. 1 Cor. 10:10). Moses and Aaron fall facedown again (Num. 16:45 [17:10]; cf. 16:4, 22); this time Moses does not speak but directs Aaron, without Yahweh's explicit directive, to put burning altar coals into his censer, which alone remains (16:36–40 [17:1–5]), and quickly to burn the incense in the middle of the community (16:46 [17:11]). The plague has begun to spread among the people as an extension of Yahweh's wrath (see the second translation note on 16:46 [17:11]); the incense of holy altar

83. Zeelander, "Closural Conventions," 334–35.

fire can, Moses thinks, function as a bloodless means of making atonement and averting Yahweh's wrath (16:46 [17:11]; see the third translation note on 31:50). There is no *tôrâ* precedent for this exact ritual, but it is worth a shot (see 8:19).[84] Aaron obeys, running into the middle of the assembly, the epicenter of the epidemic, with the burning incense (16:47 [17:12]; see the translation notes there). The Egyptians burned censers to protect themselves from demonic forces.[85] To make atonement for the people and thereby terminate the spread of the outbreak, the narrator explains that Aaron "stood between the dead and the living" (16:48 [17:13]). Nothing can be done for the dead now, but Aaron as mediator using a sacred source, the incense on the altar coals, can theoretically block Yahweh's anger from killing off the remaining Israelites.[86] Many years later, Yahweh anoints another high priest, Jesus the Messiah, to show ineffable compassion by making atonement, not with incense but *with his own body*, averting God's wrath so that God's people can live with him forever.[87]

The plague is stopped, but sin has its consequences: 14,700 Israelite corpses (16:49 [17:14])—14,000 is double 7,000, then add 700 more, probably symbolizing the comprehensiveness of Yahweh's judgment.[88] When the plague ends, Aaron and Moses return to their honored station at the entrance of the meeting tent, marking the end of this catastrophe (16:50 [17:15]; see the translation note there).

Implications

Lex Talionis: *When the Punishment Mimics the Crime*

The climax of the Num. 16 narrative may be the appearance of Yahweh's glory as a portent of his imminence, intention, and power to kill the Israelites en masse (16:19–20). However, the only responses to that theophany worth mentioning, as far as the narrator is concerned, are those of Moses and Aaron, who intercede for the guilty community (16:22). Yahweh's appearance should have been enough to shock the community into repentance, but with no report of contrition, the plotline moves swiftly toward three acts of divine judgment against the rebels. (1) With the most detail, the earth opens its mouth and swallows Korah, Dathan, Abiram, and their families (16:23–33). (2) Tersely reported, Yahweh's fire consumes 250 of Korah's followers who are offering incense according to Moses's orders (16:16–18, 35). (3) Yahweh sends a

---

84. See Leveen, *Memory*, 133.
85. Walton and Matthews, *Genesis–Deuteronomy*, 192.
86. Cf. 2 Sam. 24:18–25; see Milgrom, *Numbers*, 142.
87. Heb. 2:17; 3:1; 4:14–16; 5:1, 5, 10; 7:26; 8:1; 9:11, 25–28; 13:11–12.
88. See the note in the comments on 11:16–20 on the number 70 in Gen. 11:26 (Terah's age); cf. Roscher, *Die Zahl 40*.

plague to ruin his complaining people (16:46–49 [17:11–14]). To understand the rhetorical and ritual function of these judgments, we can benefit from looking at the retributive justice principle of *lex talionis*.

From the Latin for "law of retaliation," *lex talionis* typically refers to a punishment that mimics the nature of the crime. So the most straightforward application of the *lex talionis* law requires killing a killer or amputating the same anatomical part that a perpetrator took from the victim: "But if there is serious injury, you are to take life for life, eye for eye, tooth for tooth, hand for hand, foot for foot, burn for burn, wound for wound, bruise for bruise" (Exod. 21:23–25 NIV).[89] It is more complicated than this, however. The scenario of this law in the Covenant Code (Exod. 21–23) does not *demand* amputation: a slaveholder who destroys the eye or tooth of his male or female slave must, as recompense, set the injured slave free (21:26–27). Thus, in practice, while the idiom "a life for a life" was carried out through the death penalty, in other cases "the talion [punishment] attributed to YHWH is not always precise."[90] This means that sometimes it is difficult to distinguish punishments that enact retributive justice more broadly from ones that operate on the principle of *lex talionis*. For example, Lev. 18:21 conveys not *lex talionis* but generic retribution. The community must stone, not burn, the worshiper of the Ammonite god, Molech, to whom children were burned in the fire.[91]

At other times when the connection between crime and punishment is not obvious to modern readers, it does not mean *lex talionis* is not operative. For example, in Lev. 24:13–23, where the *lex talionis* law ensues from the blasphemer story (24:10–12), how is stoning the one who has blasphemed the Name and cursed a fitting form of punishment? A semantic connection is conceivable. The Israelite-Egyptian not only cursed (**qll* piel) but metaphorically slandered or, more literally, bored holes through the name of Yahweh (24:11, *nqb** qal).[92] One can then see why Yahweh orders Israel to effectively put holes in the perpetrator by stoning him (*rgm**).[93] While this view cannot be proved, it challenges us to reconsider whether other punishments in the Moses story that typically have been considered unrelated in nature to their crimes may in fact represent to their earliest audiences an application of the *lex talionis* principle. For instance, twice in H, if a man has sex with his uncle's wife or his sister-in-law, he and the woman will both die "childless" (*ʿărîrîm*). Why are these H's only two instances of childlessness as divine punishment?

89. Cf. Lev. 24:18; Deut. 19:21; Matt. 5:38.

90. Milgrom, *Leviticus*, 3:2133.

91. See Lev. 18:21; 2 Kings 23:10; Jer. 32:35; maybe Isa. 30:33 (correcting MT *melek* "king" to *molek* "Molech"); cf. Lev. 20:2–5. Conversely, why *burn* the man who has sex with his wife and her mother (Lev. 20:14)?

92. "*Nqb*," *HALOT* 2:718–19, qal, gloss 1, "to bore through"; and pass., "to be full of holes"; and subset of gloss 3, "to slander."

93. Douglas, *Leviticus*, 207.

Is it because by their sexual intercourse "their hope is for children, and it will be frustrated by God"?[94]

In light of this, we can return to Num. 16 with a fresh set of questions. Could the earth swallowing Korah and associates, the fire burning the 250 chieftains, and the plague ravaging the community reflect the Sinai principle of *lex talionis*? For the first two, I would argue *yes*. It is not clear that the plague, which spread among the people, mimicked their complaining, which also spread contagiously among the people (16:41–50 [17:6–15]). But how does a swallowing earth and burning fire mimic the nature of their crimes? The most obvious is the fire, and the narration unfolds with dramatic irony: "Then a fire went out from Yahweh and consumed the 250 men who were offering the incense" (16:35). The story echoes that of Nadab and Abihu (Lev. 10:1–3). There the irony was dramatic, assuming that Aaron and Moses were not standing by watching: the priests called to burn Yahweh's sacrifices and incense were themselves burned alive.[95] Here the irony is situational, and the community can see the fuller significance of the event: The 250 chieftains, while burning incense to discover if they are equal with Aaron, are themselves burned alive by Yahweh's fire.[96]

Finally, at the center of the story line Moses says that this judgment will prove that Yahweh has sent him: "*If . . . the earth opens its mouth [ûpāṣtâ hā'ădāmâ 'et-pîhā] and swallows them up [ûbāl'â 'ōtām]* along with everything they own, and they go down alive into the realm of the dead, then you will know that *these men have reviled Yahweh!*" (16:30*; see the second translation note there). The storyteller includes a more concrete description of the event: "Just as he finished speaking all these words, the ground under them split open. . . . They and everything they owned went down alive into the realm of the dead, and the earth closed over them. So they perished from among the community" (16:31, 33). But the storyteller also reuses Moses's anthropomorphic language: "the earth opened its mouth and swallowed them, with their households, and everyone belonging to Korah, and all their possessions" (16:32; see the translation note there). In Ugaritic and Mesopotamian epics, the underworld is commonly depicted as a gaping mouth.[97] But why *use* and *reuse* this metaphor of an open mouth that swallows the men alive? The use of metaphor itself paints the image of a punishment that mimics the crime (*lex talionis*), and the reuse of the metaphor (16:32) underscores that Moses's verbal prediction came true exactly as he said (16:30). Moses

---

94. Milgrom, *Leviticus*, 2:1757.

95. In dramatic irony, the audience knows the fuller significance of a character's words or actions, but the character remains in the dark (Garmendia, *Irony*, 6).

96. Situational irony occurs simply because of the way an event happens or unfolds (Garmendia, *Irony*, 5). See the "Implications" essay in chap. 22, "The Irony and Satire of the Balaam Cycle."

97. Walton and Matthews, *Genesis–Deuteronomy*, 192.

says that the men have "reviled Yahweh" (16:30). This fientive (dynamic) verb denotes abusive criticism that could be exposed and punished as a covenant breach by vassals, who must not criticize the suzerain.[98] Korah, Dathan, and Abiram reviled Yahweh by means of two speeches (16:3 with On; 16:12–15). After their first speech, Moses delivers two diatribes (16:4–7, 8–11), but the men are still not persuaded to keep their mouths shut and repent. For this crime, a *lex talionis* judgment unfolds with poetic justice: For the men who opened their mouths to try to devour Aaron and Moses, the earth opens its mouth and swallows them whole. The response of the Israelites reinforces this reading: the rebels end their existence with their mouths open: "All the Israelites who were around them fled *at their voice*, for they said, "The earth could swallow us too!" (16:34; see the translation note there; cf. Rev. 12:16).

When Israel carries out Yahweh's *lex talionis* justice, the perpetrator, whether executed or maimed, embodies a divine warning to deter further acts of disobedience in the community. The punitive event itself, then, functions as formative public ritual (Lev. 24:14–16, 23), putting on display Israel's loyalty to its covenant deity: "For I am Yahweh your god" (24:22).[99] This is exactly the function that the incinerating fire and the swallowing earth of Num. 16 are intended to serve in the community. These punishments mimic the nature of the men's sins and continue to warn the people of God who refuse to repent today (Heb. 6:4–8; 10:26–27).

---

98. See the translation notes on 14:11, 23 and related comments; see also the "Implications" essay in chap. 11, "Complaining as Covenant Violation."

99. See the "Implications" essay in chap. 19, "The Formative Power of Purifying Rituals."

17

Aaron's Staff Produces Almonds

(17:1–13)

✦

Overview

In the preceding episode, the so-called Korah's rebellion, instigators from the tribes of Levi and Reuben publicly challenged the divinely authorized leadership of Moses and Aaron (16:1–3, 12–14). Their arrogance was silenced by divine judgment in three forms: a swallowing earth, consuming fire, and deadly plague (16:31–35, 46–50 [17:11–15]). One would think that this story has categorically established the unassailable status of Aaron and Moses in the community, but Yahweh and the editors who arranged Numbers see fit to insert the story of chap. 17 next because more persuasion is needed.[1] Yahweh has already validated Moses as his paragon prophet (Num. 12), and now Yahweh achieves a similar result for Aaron's priestly role and line.[2] In 17:1–5 [16–20], Yahweh directs Moses to receive the twelve staffs—one from each chieftain of the twelve tribes, including the tribe of Levi—to write the tribal leader's name on the staff, using Aaron's name for the tribe of Levi; and to place them in the meeting tent before the witness, the stones of the covenant. The staff that sprouts will reveal the man whom Yahweh has chosen, silencing

---

1. So Milgrom, *Numbers*, 142. Knierim and Coats (*Numbers*, 214) call chap. 17 an anecdote with a sign. De Vaulx (*Nombres*, 201) distinguishes the function of Aaron's staff, and therefore the genre of this story, from Romulus's spear and Hercules's club.

2. Traditionally 17:1–13 [16–28] has been assigned to P^g or P (Seebass, *Numeri*, 2:189; Budd, *Numbers*, 194; Levine, *Numbers*, 1:405–6). Many, however, see the text as post-P: Noth (*Numbers*, 130–31) sees it adopting P's style, while Scharbert (*Numeri*, 70–71) assigns it to the Pentateuch redactor using P, Achenbach (*Vollendung*, 126–29) to the first phase of the theocratic revision, and Knohl (*Sanctuary*, 73–85) to H.

further complaints against Yahweh's appointed leaders. In 17:6–12 [21–27], Moses follows these instructions, and Aaron's staff not only sprouts but also buds, blossoms, and produces almonds! This is emphatic and indisputable evidence of Yahweh's choice, not only of Levi but of Levi's descendant Aaron and his sons. Moses shows the blossomed staff to the community, and Yahweh honors Aaron and verbally threatens the people with death if they do not stop complaining. The Israelites take Yahweh's threat as an omen of their doom.

Translation

1 [16]Then Yahweh spoke to Moses: 2 [17]"Speak to the Israelites, and receive from them one staff for every tribe—one from every chieftain for their tribes—twelve staffs.[3] Write each man's name on his staff. 3 [18] Write Aaron's name on Levi's staff, for one staff is for the head of every tribe. 4 [19]Then place them in the meeting tent before the witness,[4] where I meet together with you.[5] 5 [20]The staff of the man whom I choose will sprout, so I will rid myself of the complaints of the Israelites, which they complain against you."

6 [21]So Moses spoke to the Israelites, and each of their chieftains gave him a staff, one for each chieftain, belonging to their patriarchs' houses, twelve staffs, and Aaron's staff was among their staffs. 7 [22] Then Moses placed the staffs before Yahweh in the tent containing the witness.[6] 8 [23]On the next day Moses entered the tent containing the witness, and Aaron's staff for the house of Levi had sprouted![7] It had even budded, blossomed, and produced almonds![8] 9 [24]Then Moses

3. Formally, "one staff for every *patriarch's house* [*bêt 'āb*]—one from every chieftain for their *patriarchs' house* [*bêt 'ăbōtām*]."

4. A referential article, "before *the witness*" (*hā'ēdût*), means before the tablets contained in the ark (see 4:5; 7:89).

5. *Y'd niphal is reflexive, perhaps reciprocal, while the imperfective aspect appears to denote regular or customary action, meaning "where I *often meet together* ['*iwwā'ēd*] with you" (*GBHS* §3.1.2c, 3.2.2b). MT's pl. seems peculiar and more likely original, "where I meet with *you all* [*lākem*]" (as Exod. 29:42), while the sg. SP and LXX[ed] restricts this to Moses, with whom Yahweh customarily meets and here speaks directly, "where I meet *with you*" (Exod. 30:6, 36).

6. As with "the ark *containing* the witness," the metonym for the dwelling place here and in 17:8 is rendered "the tent *containing* the witness" ('*ōhel hā'ēdut*; also 9:15; 18:2) to reflect a gen. of container content (*BHRG* §25.4.6[5]). There was a Neo-Hittite and Neo-Assyrian parallel practice of depositing a diplomatic treaty in a temple in the vassal state as a visible witness to the covenant (see the second translation note on 9:15).

7. Simple *w* + interjection (*wəhinnēh*), commonly "behold," is rendered with an exclamation point (NLT, NET). "And there" is too weak (EÜ; de Vaulx, *Nombres*, 204), while "indeed" (Ashley, *Numbers*, 329) unnecessarily diminishes the narrative climax, even though readers are expecting that Aaron's staff will sprout (17:3 [18], 6 [21], 8 [23], 10 [25]).

8. The qatal "Aaron's staff for the house of Levi *had sprouted* [*pārah*]" is followed by three wayyiqtols, which I interpret as epexegetical: "It had even budded, blossomed, and produced almonds!" (*wayyōṣē' peraḥ wayyāṣēṣ ṣîṣ wayyigmōl šəqēdîm*; *GBHS* §3.5.1d; NJPS, NRSV).

283

brought out all the staffs from before Yahweh to all the Israelites. They looked at them, and each one took his staff. [10 [25]]Yahweh said to Moses, "Bring back Aaron's staff before the witness to be preserved as a sign to the rebellious, so that you stop their complaints against me, or else they will die." [11 [26]]So Moses did it—he did it just as Yahweh had commanded him. [12 [27]]The Israelites said to Moses, "We are dead![9] We are destroyed! All of us are destroyed![10] [13 [28]]Anyone who even gets close to Yahweh's dwelling will die![11] Are we all to die?"

Interpretation

17:1–5 [16–20]. Following the rebellion of Korah and his followers (chap. 16), Yahweh orders Moses to receive twelve staffs, one from each tribal chieftain, and write the names of each chieftain on his own staff. A chieftain's staff was an insignia of his authority over his tribe.[12] The order reads formally, "One staff for every *patriarch's house* [*bêt 'āb*]—one from every chieftain for their *patriarchs' house* [*bêt 'ăbōtām*]" (17:2 [17]).[13] This does not refer to every patriarchal household, whose males twenty years old and up were enlisted for military service (1:2–3, 18–47), but refers metonymically to the twelve tribes, each of which had a patriarchal representative (1:4–17).[14] The Levites were enrolled, not for military service, but for service in Yahweh's dwelling place (1:47–53). Here Levi's staff, marked with Aaron's name, is emphatically included among the staffs of the other tribes (17:3, 6, 8, 10 [18, 21, 23, 25]). All prior (and future) chieftain lists in Numbers arrive at twelve tribes without Levi, who is devoted to Yahweh (Num. 1, 7, 13). It does not make sense that this text would refer to Joseph as a single tribe (Genesis–Exodus),[15] so it is simplest to see twelve conventional chieftain staffs (17:2 [17]), with Levi's being the exceptional thirteenth (17:3 [18]).[16] Naming Aaron as Levi's

---

9. Formally, "we have expired" (*gāwaʿnû*) from *gwʿ (expire, die; *DCH* 2:335, gloss 1).

10. The qal qatal of *ʾbd, emphatically repeated (2× in 17:12 [27]), "vividly and dramatically represents a future situation both as complete and as independent" (*IBHS* §30.5.1e): hence "We are destroyed! All of us are destroyed!" (*ʾābadnû kullānû ʾābādnû*) or "about to die, be in danger of death" (*DCH* 1:99, gloss 1b), but "We are lost! We are all lost" (*IBHS*) misses the deadly context.

11. Alluding to Exod. 19:12. If influenced by this text, SP hophal (*ywmt*, vocalized *yûmat*) would mean "must be put to death."

12. Cf. Gen. 38:18. Walton and Matthews, *Genesis–Deuteronomy*, 193; Ambrose (4th cent. CE; see Lienhard, *Numbers*, 232).

13. "Staff" (*maṭṭeh*) elsewhere can be a metonym for tribe, but not here in chap. 17, perhaps to distinguish the two and form a play on words (Ashley, *Numbers*, 331; Milgrom, *Numbers*, 143; Douglas, *Wilderness*, 140).

14. See Gray, *Numbers*, 215.

15. Cf. Gen. 29–30, 35; 48–49; Exod. 1:2–5.

16. Gray, *Numbers*, 214; Milgrom, *Numbers*, 144.

representative was established at Sinai, with the Levites subordinate to Aaron and his surviving sons, Eleazar and Ithamar, in Yahweh's tent service.[17]

Moses must place the staffs emphatically in Yahweh's presence (17:2b–4 [17b–19]), implying Yahweh's primacy in the ritual. This idea is reinforced in four ways. (1) "In the meeting tent" (17:4 [19]) denotes the place the deity, Yahweh, has designed purposefully to meet with his people.[18] (2) The qualifier redundantly reinforces this purpose, "where I meet together with you" (17:4 [19]). The Hebrew communicates Yahweh's custom of meeting not just with Moses but also with his covenant people (see the second translation note on 17:4 [19]).[19] (3) The unique phrase "before *the witness*" (*hāʿēdût*) refers to putting the twelve staffs before the tablets contained in the ark, which function as a witness to the covenant (17:4, 7; see the first translation note on 17:4 [19]). The qualifying words "where I meet with you" (17:4b) might suggest that Moses was not to break protocol and enter the holy of holies but instead to place the staffs outside the inner curtain where he was permitted to meet with Yahweh (7:89). The translation "the witness"[20] best indicates its function as a visible witness to the covenant treaty, as in the ANE diplomatic treaties (see Josh. 24:27). (4) Moses writes each man's name on his staff; in the ANE, writing was thought to have a numinous power: it was viewed as a gift from the gods and "used to communicate with the divine realm by ritual actions or formulaic recitations in order to affect the course of present or future events."[21] Here the point is that writing the names on the staffs not only identifies the owners but brings them into Yahweh's presence.

Then, in v. 5, Yahweh explains that the staff of the man whom Yahweh chooses will sprout like a tree, and this will serve to silence the Israelites' complaints against Moses, which began in Egypt (Exod. 14:11–12) and have been almost incessant from Num. 11 to 16.

17:6–13 [21–28]. Moses and the chieftains obey Yahweh and initiate this staff ritual, and the narrator inserts that "Aaron's staff was among their staffs" (17:6 [21]). This unnecessary aside may recall the miracle in Egypt that featured Aaron's staff becoming a snake and swallowing the magicians' snakes (Exod. 7:8–12). In any case, the aside here, compounded with "write Aaron's name on Levi's staff" (Num. 17:3 [18]), foreshadows that something special is going to happen involving Aaron. Moses places the staffs in the "tent containing the witness" (17:7, 8 [22, 23]), which is shorthand for the location described in 17:4 [19] but now draws an association with the Hittite and Assyrian parallel practice of depositing a diplomatic treaty in the temple of the vassal state as a visible witness to the covenant (see the translation note

17. Num. 3:5–10, 32; 4:16, 28, 33; see Milgrom, *Numbers*, 143.
18. Hundley, "Tabernacle or Tent of Meeting?," 3–18.
19. SP sg. restricts Yahweh's meeting to Moses (see 7:89).
20. *DCH* 6:279–80 in gloss 1.
21. Schniedewind, *Bible Became a Book*, 24–34.

on 17:7 [22] and the second translation note on 9:15). The next day, when Moses enters the tent (17:8 [23]), Aaron's staff representing the tribe of Levi has not only sprouted as Yahweh had said (17:5 [20]) but has also budded, blossomed, and produced almonds![22] The symbolism of this almond spectacle is debated.[23] A strong possibility is suggested by a wordplay on *maṭṭeh*, which can mean staff or tribe; a dry staff and tribe can be revitalized by the blessing of Yahweh's presence.[24] The ripe almonds, then, symbolize that, after a cycle of death in Levi's tribe (Nadab, Abihu, Korah and company), the surviving tribe will, through Aaron, be fertile and flourish in the future.[25] In any case, the miracle unmistakably confirms Yahweh's choice not just of the tribe of Levi, of which the rebel Korah had been a member (16:1), but also of Levi's descendant Aaron.[26] Moses removes the staffs from Yahweh's presence and shows them to the Israelites, and the chieftains take back their staffs (17:9 [24]). We might identify the moment when the difference between the chieftains' staffs and Aaron's is made clear as the climax of a continuous chap. 16–17: "The story of Aaron's rod is a symbolic reenactment of the rebellions against the priests and Levites described in Num. 16. The flowering of Aaron's rod when placed before the ark shows that priests can enter the tabernacle, whereas the lifelessness of the other rods shows laymen will die if they attempt to enter."[27]

Yahweh then tells Moses to return Aaron's staff before the witness as a present and future sign to the rebellious in order to stop the Israelites from their complaints against Yahweh (17:10 [25]).[28] Aaron's staff remained before the witness of the tablets in the desert tent of Yahweh but apparently not in the first temple (1 Kings 8:9; Heb. 9:4), and its prized location symbolized that only Aaron and the high-priestly line from him held the prerogative to

22. See the translation notes on 17:8 [23].

23. Walton and Matthews (*Genesis–Deuteronomy*, 193) see in it a symbol of God's power over creation, the fertility of the promised land, and Aaron's expected "diligence" (wordplay on the Hb. root *šqd*) as a priest. Ruprecht ("Zepter Jahwes," 57–60, 69) argues that the almond tree in Jer. 1:11 is to be understood as a royal scepter, but like Aaron's blooming staff in Num. 17, it serves as both a blessing and a weapon. Dozeman ("Numbers," 140) suggests that the almonds may symbolize watchfulness (Jer. 1:11), and their white buds represent purity and holiness (Isa. 1:18). The blossom as a warning fits with the Israelites' fear of impending doom expressed in vv. 12–13 (cf. Ezek. 7:10). Caesarius of Arles (5th–6th cent. CE) interprets the almonds tropologically: throw off the bitter shell of fleshly action, find the protective cover of doctrine and restraint, then discover the hidden nut of the mysteries of God's wisdom (Lienhard, *Numbers*, 234).

24. Milgrom, *Numbers*, 142; Ashley, *Numbers*, 331.

25. Leveen (*Memory*, 135) avers, "As the extension of the male holding it, the staff is a phallic symbol par excellence."

26. Budd, *Numbers*, 194.

27. Wenham, "Aaron's Rod," 281; Dozeman, "Numbers," 140; for other links between chaps. 16–17, see Blum, *Komposition des Pentateuch*, 267–75.

28. Formally, "rebellious children" (Ezek. 20:5–29); see Milgrom, *Numbers*, 145.

serve as priests in the holiest zone of Yahweh's presence.[29] Like the censers from the Korah rebellion, which were hammered into a bronze cover for the altar as a warning (16:39–40 [17:4–5]), Aaron's staff was also intended to deter rebellion and lethal divine wrath ("or else they will die"), suggesting that it was ultimately a good gift from Yahweh (see 1 Tim. 5:20). Moses obediently brings Aaron's staff back into Yahweh's presence (Num. 17:11 [26]), but the Israelites, who apparently overhear Yahweh's words to Moses (17:10 [25]), interpret them as an omen of their certain doom. The storyteller in 17:12–13 [27–28] gives the impression of a cacophony of shouts from the mob directed at Moses:

> We are dead!
> We are destroyed!
> All of us are destroyed!
> Anyone who even gets close to Yahweh's dwelling will die!
> Are we all to die?[30]

Standing in a vast wake of death spanning Num. 11–16, the Israelites are petrified. One way to read their death chant is that they love their lives more than they love obeying Yahweh and delighting in his glory and presence among them.[31] To be sure, a paralyzing fear of death (thanatophobia) can grip anyone not rooting their trust in Yahweh's promised seed, the Messiah.[32] On the other hand, their cries echo their experience at Mount Sinai, when they were terrified that Yahweh's presence would kill them (see the translation note on 17:13 [28]). In their cacophony of death, are the Israelites finally submitting to Yahweh's hierarchy: Aaron→Levites→Israelites?[33] Are they showing their recognition that divine and priestly holiness is inaccessible to them?[34]

Implications

Moses the Prophet, Aaron the Priest

Moses's primacy over his older brother, Aaron, in Yahweh's intermediary work for Israel has characterized the Moses story (Exod. 7:1; 17:12; 19:24; et al.).[35] Yahweh always speaks to Moses and Aaron, listed in that order when

---

29. Leveen, *Memory*, 134.

30. The stress on end of life in 17:12–13 [27–28] also functions as a closural device to end the story (Zeelander, "Closural Conventions," 337). See the translation notes on 17:12–13 [27–28].

31. Contrasted with Moses in Exod. 33:18–34:9; cf. Ps. 63:3; Dan. 3:16–18; Heb. 11:35b–39.

32. Gen. 3:15; 12:7; 13:15; 17:7; 24:7; Gal. 3:16; Heb. 2:14–15.

33. Leveen, *Memory*, 134.

34. Blum, *Komposition des Pentateuch*, 269.

35. Older is stated in Exod. 7:7 (Moses 80, Aaron 83) and implied in Exod. 6:20 (Aaron, Moses).

they appear together. But from Exod. 27:21 onward, a crucial priestly role emerges that is assigned not to Moses, but to his brother Aaron, and this role continuously develops throughout the Priestly materials about the dwelling place (Exod. 25–31, 35–40), the thirty-day revelation at Sinai called Leviticus, and throughout the book of Numbers. We cannot detail here the critical mediatory functions that Aaron and his sons are privileged to perform, which are featured most prominently in the intertextually related chapters of Exod. 28–30 and Lev. 1–16, 21–22. However, one text captures the weightiness of their service: "I will devote as holy Aaron and his sons so that they may serve as priests for me. I will live among the Israelites" (Exod. 29:44–45*). Aaron and his sons belong to Yahweh as holy in a way that Moses does not,[36] and they are central to ensuring that Israel is a suitable home for the divine presence. This clearly overlaps with the critical function of priests among Israel's neighbors.[37] The ANE worldview is altered for the aniconic worship of the one deity, Yahweh, who cannot be manipulated, but the importance of Yahweh's priests is, like other ANE cults, never in question. Against this backdrop, what are we to think when Moses cannot enter the freshly constructed meeting tent because the cloud of the divine presence has saturated the sacred space (Exod. 40:34–35)? Does this blockage mark a pivotal moment of a decrease in Moses's service in the tent and an increase in Aaron's, like the transition from harbinger John the Baptist to Jesus the Messiah, with John declaring, "He must increase. I must decrease" (John 3:30)?

The Yahweh-Moses distance of Exod. 40 persists throughout the sacrificial instructions (Lev. 1–7) until Moses enters the tent to anoint the dwelling place, but this is done not for his own prophetic mediation but for Aaron's priestly service (Lev. 8:10). Not Moses but Aaron and his sons sequester themselves in the meeting place for seven days and nights (Lev. 8:33–36), and then only with Aaron does Moses enter the meeting tent (9:23). Thus Leviticus narrates the transition from Moses to Aaron as the one authorized to serve in Yahweh's tent and dwelling place (10:7; 16*; 24:1–9). Probably as a consequence, in Leviticus Yahweh speaks to Moses not in the meeting tent but, surprisingly, back "on Mount Sinai" (*bəhar sînay*).[38] Most naturally, this means on top of Mount Sinai, not beside/at Mount Sinai, since it is the identical description for the mountaintop revelation in Exod. 19–34.[39] Then when we arrive at Numbers, a distinct composition, Moses is presumably back inside the

---

36. See Clines's definition of "holy" in my comments on 4:1–14.

37. Hundley, *Gods in Dwellings*, 365–66.

38. Lev. 7:38; 25:1; 26:46; 27:34. Other than Num. 28:6, recalling Lev. 1, *bəhar sînay* occurs in Numbers only after the *tôlədōt* formula of 3:1, which uses the deictic clause to locate this revelation back "on the day when Yhwh spoke to Moses on Mount Sinai" (3:1), which occurred before the Num. 1–10 instructions in the Sinai wilderness in the meeting tent (1:1).

39. For *bəhar sînay* as the place *on which* Yahweh spoke with Moses, see Exod. 31:18; 34:32; also see *bəhar sînay* as *on*, not *at*, Mount Sinai (Exod. 24:18; 25:40; 26:30; 27:8): *GBHS* §4.1.5.

meeting tent receiving more revelation from Yahweh (Num. 1:1), but never inside Yahweh's dwelling place (7:89).[40]

Although Moses holds pride of place over Aaron as Yahweh's unrivaled intermediary (Num. 7:89; 12) and agent of historic miracles (Deut. 34:10–12),[41] the episode of Num. 17, as we have seen, elevates Aaron from the tribe of Levi above all other chieftains, and in one sense even above Moses, who also hails from the tribe of Levi. In Numbers, surprisingly, explicit reference to the "high priest" does not appear until chap. 35, but the textual evidence hints that Num. 17 presents the installation of Aaron as Israel's high priest, and this is only reinforced by the high-priestly succession to Eleazar and the anticipation of Phinehas (20:25–28; 25:6–13; 27:19–22).[42]

In spite of all their wondrous acts of divine service, Moses and Aaron ultimately fall short of Yahweh's holy standard at the same site of Kadesh, this time featuring Moses's staff (Num. 20:7–13).[43] By contrast, in his first earthly ministry, Jesus of Nazareth served God perfectly in his role as prophet, priest, and king. In obedience as the suffering servant of Isa. 42–53, Jesus the Messiah displayed all the marks of being the greater-than-Moses *prophet*, the greater-than-Aaron *priest*,[44] and the divinely anointed, eternal *king*.[45]

40. See the "Implications" essay in chap. 7, "The Yahweh-Moses Relationship."
41. See the "Implications" essay in chap. 12, "Did Moses See Yahweh?"
42. Frevel, "High Priest," 150–52, 157–58.
43. On the intertexts of Num. 17 and 20, see Frevel, *Mit Blick*, 88, 320–22, 332–36.
44. Heb. 1:1–3; 3:2–6; 7:11–28; 9:1–28.
45. Gen. 49:8–12; 2 Sam. 7; Pss. 2; 110; throughout NT. On the threefold office, see Eusebius (ca. 260–340 CE) in *Hist. eccl.* 1.3.8 (Schaff, ed., *Eusebius Pamphilius*, 86).

18

Revising the Aaronides and Levites

(18:1–32)

‿✍◦‿

Overview

In the dramatic events of Korah's rebellion (chap. 16), Yahweh lucidly sub-ordinates the Levites to Aaron and the Israelite community to Moses and Aaron. The drama continues as Aaron's staff alone buds (chap. 17), validating the selection of Levi out of the tribes and of Aaron over Levi. What does all this mean pragmatically? The Sinai instructions in Num. 3–4 and 8 already explained the functions and interrelationship of the Levites, Aaronides, and community at large. After the events of chaps. 16–17, now 18:1–7 plays a critical role in confirming that the Sinai legislation is still binding, especially the subordination of the Levites to Aaron and his sons.[1] The remainder of Num. 18, however, is profoundly innovative:[2] it revises the Sinai legislation to protect the food supply for Aaron and his sons, on the one hand, and the Levites, on the other.[3] The discourse is divided into four subunits: three successive divine speeches to Aaron and one to Moses.[4] In vv. 1–7, Yahweh

---

1. Nihan, "Priestly Laws," 120.

2. Ashley, *Numbers*, 337.

3. Noth (*Numbers*, 134) believes that Num. 18 reflects the technical language of P but is an independent composition not belonging to the original P narrative. De Vaulx (*Nombres*, 204–13) identifies vv. 8–19* as pre-P (Deut. 18 connections, et al.); vv. 1–7 as P enforcing the Aaron-Levite relationship of Num. 1, 3–4; vv. 20–32 as Deuteronomistic theology; and vv. 8–19* (other parts) with a priestly editor binding with vv. 9, 11*. Budd (*Numbers*, 202–4) argues that vv. 1–7 align with P but sees vv. 8–32 as independent of P, that is, of Num. 3 and 8. Achenbach (*Vollendung*, 160–61) contends that Num. 18 belongs to the theocratic revision of the Torah, but 18:13–16 (on the firstborn) predates the revision of 3:11–13, 40–51 (Levites as substitute for the firstborn). Scharbert (*Numeri*, 72) assigns Num. 18 to a Pentateuch redactor bringing together materials from different tradents of the P-school. Knohl (*Sanctuary*, 53–55, 71–73) assigns Num. 17–18 to H, but Nihan ("Priestly Laws," 123–26) argues against this.

4. Knierim and Coats (*Numbers*, 215–16) identify these four divine speeches as centering on ordination (17:1–7), wages (vv. 8–19), inheritance (vv. 20–24), and ordination (vv. 25–32). W. Lee

speaks exclusively to Aaron and directs him and his sons to perform their priestly responsibilities, and the Levites must serve and support them, but any unauthorized person must not encroach on the sacred zones or they will be executed. In vv. 8–19, Yahweh addresses Aaron to expand the Sinai designation of the priestly cut of meat for the priests (Lev. 6–7, et al.) and now gives the priests all the Israelite offerings as their food. In vv. 20–24, Yahweh informs Aaron a final time (in the book) that he has given himself, Yahweh, to the Levites as well as giving them the tithes that the Israelites offer to Yahweh as tribute. In vv. 25–32, Yahweh teaches Moses to command the Levites to give Aaron a tithe, that is, a tenth, of Israel's tithe of their tribute to Yahweh.

Translation

1Then Yahweh spoke to Aaron:[5] "You and your sons and your ancestral house[6] with you must bear the iniquity attached to the sanctuary, and you and your sons with you must bear the iniquity attached to your priesthood.[7] **2**So bring with you your brothers, Levi's tribe, your father's tribe, so that they may join with you[8] and serve you while[9] you and your sons with you are before the tent containing the witness.[10] **3**They will care for your responsibilities and the responsibilities of the whole tent, but they must not come near the furnishings of the sanctuary or near the altar, or both they and you will die. **4**They must join with you, and they will care for the responsibilities of the meeting tent, for all the tent's service, but no unauthorized person may approach you. **5**You will care for the responsibilities of the sanctuary and the responsibilities

---

(*Migratory Campaign*, 148) suggests that even the order of these speeches reflects the primacy of the priests over the Levites.

5. LXX[ed] has "saying," which is lacking in the Hb., which moves abruptly into Yahweh's speech to Aaron (*BHRG* §20.1.5).

6. Formally, "your patriarch's/father's house." In 17:2 [17] this phrase means "tribe."

7. The genitives (*'āwōn hammiqdāš* . . . *'āwōn kₐhunnatkem*) are probably not objective— "iniquity committed against the sanctuary . . . iniquity committed against your priesthood"— since iniquity is against Yahweh, and the P or H historians do not present Yahweh as ontologically coextensive with his sanctuary or his priestly representatives (Lev. 17–26; Knohl, *Sanctuary*, 71–73; *GBHS* §2.2.4). Rather, I take the genitives as possessive (*GBHS* §2.2.1) with a contextual rendering: "the iniquity attached to the sanctuary . . . the iniquity attached to your priesthood." The word choice "attached" reflects the biblical and ANE concept of sin and cultic impurity moving aerially and attaching to Yahweh's sanctuary and demanding purification (Milgrom, *Leviticus*, 1:257).

8. This root in the niphal can mean "join, join oneself to, associate, be associated with, ally oneself with" ("*lwh* II," *DCH* 4:523). In the Pentateuch, this verb occurs in the niphal only here (18:2, 4 + prep. *'l*, "with") and Gen. 29:34 (+ prep. *'l*, "to").

9. "While" (*wₐ*) indicates the circumstances accompanying the tent work of the Levites (*GBHS* §4.3.3e).

10. See the translation note on 17:7 [22].

of the altar, so that wrath will no longer be on the Israelites.[11] [6]Look,
I myself have chosen[12] your brothers the Levites from among the
Israelites. They are given to you as a gift from Yahweh, to perform the
services of the meeting tent.[13] [7]But you and your sons with you must
exercise your priestly functions,[14] with regard to everything at the altar
and inside the curtain. You must serve. I give you your priestly functions
as a gift for service,[15] but the unauthorized person who approaches
must be put to death."

[8]Yahweh said to Aaron: "See, I have given you the responsibility
for tributes offered to me.[16] All the holy things of the Israelites[17] I have
given to you as your priestly portion[18] and to your sons as a permanent
share.[19] [9]This will be yours from all the holiest offerings[20] kept from the

11. On "wrath," see the second translation note on 16:46 [17:11]. Numbers moves thematically from the command given to the Levites to guard the tent to prevent Yahweh's wrath (1:53)
to Yahweh's wrath going out against the community because of the Levites (Korah and followers, 16:46 [17:11]). Although the plague has stopped (16:50 [17:15]), Yahweh here manifests
that his wrath has persisted but can be averted if Aaron, his sons, and his Levitical assistants
rightly execute their obligations in the tent (18:5: volitional weqatal, conditional *wə* + negated
yiqtol + *ʿôd*: *GBHS* §3.5.2c, 4.3.3e).

12. The subject pronoun marks Yahweh as the focus: "I *myself* (indeed) have chosen" (*wa'ănî
hinnē lāqaḥtî*; *BHRG* §36.1.1.3[1]).

13. Formally, "to serve the services of the meeting tent"; similarly 16:9.

14. Formally, "you must keep/guard your priesthood" (ESV; Ashley, *Numbers*, 338). Many
translate the verb dynamically: "take care of" (for Seebass, *Numeri*, 2:215); "provide for" (for
Schmidt, *Numeri*, 76); "enage in" (Budd, *Numbers*, 199); "carefully fulfill the charge of" (Levine,
Numbers, 1:437); "exercise" (for de Vaulx, *Nombres*, 208; EÜ). The meaning of "your priesthood" (*kəhunnâ* in 3:10; 16:10; 18:1, 7 [2×]; 25:13) is clarified as "you must exercise your priestly
functions" (and v. 7, with Cazelles, *Nombres*, 90).

15. Formally, "service of a gift" (*ʿăbōdat mattānâ*) can be understood as an explicative gen.,
"service, that is, a gift" (*GBHS* §2.2.12). This construction is fronted for emphasis: formally,
"*as a gift, service*, I give your priesthood" (*BHRG* §47.2.1[2]).

16. Formally, "my tributes" (pl. *tərûmōtāy*) is understood as an objective gen., meaning
"tributes that the Israelites offered to me" (*GBHS* §2.2.4). See the translation note on 5:9.

17. The dislocated constituent is reactivated as the primary topic: "*Regarding all the holy
things of the Israelites* [*ləkol-qodšê bənê-yiśrā'ēl*], to you I have given *them* [*nətattîm*] as your
priestly portion . . ." (*BHRG* §48.2.1).

18. "Priestly portion" (pointed *mošḥâ*), a second and complementary obj. ("[1] them [2] as
a priestly portion"), is an OT hapax from *mšḥ* (to anoint; *HALOT* 2:645–46), here meaning
"prescribed portion of priests from sacrifices" ("*mošḥâ* II," *DCH* 5:519; cf. related "*mišḥâ* I"
and "*mošḥâ* I," *DCH* 5:518–19).

19. Or "permanent statute" (*ḥoq-ʿôlām*, also vv. 11, 19; cf. variations in 10:8; 15:15; 18:23;
19:10, 21).

20. Formally, "the holy of holies" (*qōdeš haqqŏdāšîm* in 4:4, 19; 18:9 [2×], 10), which is
a superlative, "the most holy thing," and which I render contextually, "the holiest offerings"
(*GBHS* §2.2.13). SP and LXX[ed] are pl., which may reflect an attempt to improve the text since
multiple, edible offerings are implied: "holiest things [offerings]." Snaith ("Numbers XVIII 9,"
373–75) discusses the interpretive array of the early versions on the holiest gifts, but against
Snaith, not all the holiest offerings are brought into the holy place (the grain offering here and
Lev. 2:3, 10). With Snaith, portions of them are eaten by the officiating priest.

fire: Every offering of theirs—from every grain offering and from every purification offering and from every reparation offering—which they bring[21] to me will be holiest for you and for your sons. [10]As the holiest offering, you are to eat it.[22] Every male may eat it.[23] It will be holy to you. [11]This is also yours: the tribute they give as a gift,[24] along with all the elevation offerings of the Israelites. I have given them to you, to your sons and to your daughters with you as a permanent share. Every clean person in your household may eat them.[25] [12]All the best olive oil, the best new wine and grain, their firstfruits that they give to Yahweh, I have given to you. [13]The first ripe fruit in their land that they bring to Yahweh will be yours. Every clean person in your household may eat of it. [14]Everything devoted in Israel will be yours. [15]The firstborn of every womb[26] which they present to Yahweh, whether human or animal, will be yours. But you must redeem the firstborn sons, and the firstborn males of unclean animals you must also redeem. [16]As for their redemption price,[27] you must redeem them when they are a month old, in your estimation, for five shekels of silver according to the sanctuary shekel (which weighs twenty gerahs). [17]But you must not redeem the firstborn of a cow, the firstborn of a sheep or the firstborn of a goat.[28] They are holy. You must splash[29] their blood on the altar and burn their fat as an

21. Formally, "they return" (yāšîbû MT ≈ "they give back" LXX[ed]), misspelled by SP (y'šbw).

22. The superlative, qōdeš haqqŏdāšîm, probably does not refer to eating the sacrifices "in a/the most holy place" (≈ en tō hagiō tōn hagiōn LXX[ed]; ESV, EÜ; Seebass, Numeri, 2:215; Schmidt, Numeri, 76; Levine, Numbers, 1:438; Budd, Numbers, 199). Instead, the priests are to consume sacrifices "in a holy place" (bəmāqôm qādōš: Lev. 6:16, 26–27; 7:6; 10:13; 24:9). Continuing the language of v. 9, qōdeš haqqŏdāšîm serves as a metonym for Yahweh's sacrifices designated for priestly consumption, so it is preferable to read the preposition b as marking identity (IBHS §11.2.5e): "As the holiest offering(s) you are to eat it" (de Vaulx, Nombres, 210; Cazelles, Nombres, 90; NRSV, NLT, NET, NIV). However, b of manner remains plausible: "eat it in the way of the most holy things" (Ashley, Numbers, 345).

23. The first yiqtol expresses an obligation, the second, permission: "you are to eat it [tō'kǎlennû]. Every male may eat it [yō'kal]" (GBHS §3.2.2d.4, d.2). LXX[ed] supplies two nominatives of simple apposition, "every male shall eat them, you and your sons," which was probably inserted, based on vv. 1, 2, 7, to clarify that every male is restricted to Aaron and his male progeny.

24. Formally, "the tribute of their gift" (tərûmat mattānām), which can be understood as an objective gen., "the tribute they give as a gift" (GBHS §2.2.4).

25. The sg. 'ōtô (it) functions as a collective "them" (LXX[ed]), referring back to "I have given them" (nətattîm).

26. Formally, "every opening of a womb of all flesh," implying "firstborn" (bəkôr) as in 3:12.

27. This substantive pass. ptc. (pədûyāw, MT SP [defectively wpdyw] LXX[ed]) means contextually "its/their redemption price" (DCH 6:562 exception in gloss 4; most versions) rather than "his redeemed ones" (DCH 6:562, gloss 4; NET).

28. The fronted obj. activates an identifiable entity in contrast ('ak) with the redeemable animals in v. 15b: "But you must redeem the firstborn sons, and the firstborn males of unclean animals you must also redeem. . . . But the firstborn of a cow, the firstborn of a sheep or the firstborn of a goat you must not redeem" (BHRG §47.2.1[a]b).

29. This imperatival yiqtol "you must splash" (tizrōq), from *zrq (sprinkle; HALOT 1:283, gloss 2), depicts the Aaronic priests' manipulation of animal blood in Yahweh's tent (Pentateuch:

offering by fire for a pleasing scent to Yahweh. **¹⁸**And their meat will be yours, just as the breast that is elevated with the right thigh are yours.³⁰ **¹⁹**All the tributes of the holy things that the Israelites offer up to Yahweh, I have given to you, and to your sons and to your daughters with you, as a permanent share. It is a permanent covenant made by salt³¹ before Yahweh for you and for your descendants with you."

Exod. 9, 24, 29; Lev. 1–9, 17; Num. 18:17; 19:13, 20). Since "sprinkle" (many versions) can give the wrong impression of fine dripping or careful pouring onto an object or person, I prefer "splash" (Seebass, *Numeri*, 2:215; NIV, NET), "dash" (NJPS, NRSV; Levine, *Numbers*, 1:438), "scatter" or "toss" ("*zrq* I," *DCH* 3:144, gloss 1; Ashley, *Numbers*, 346; "throw," Budd, *Numbers*, 200), which implies an action involving gross motor skills with a messier result.

30. As already known from the divine instructions at Sinai (Exod. 19–Num. 10*), the Aaronic priests are designated to eat "the right thigh" (*šôq hayyāmîn*) and "the breast(s) that is elevated" (*ḥāzē hattənûpâ / heḥāzôt*) from the Israelites' sacrifices for peace (Lev. 7:31–34; 9:21; 10:14–15; Num. 6:18–20). The priests are not given the right thigh from the ram offered at their ordination, which is consumed by fire for Yahweh along with the burnt offering (Exod. 29:22, 25; Lev. 8:25–28), and the breast of that ordination offering goes to Moses (Exod. 29:26; Lev. 8:29).

31. Formally, "a covenant of salt forever" (*bərît melaḥ ʿôlām*; ESV), with two OT parallels: (1) "salt of the covenant of your God" (*melaḥ bərît ʾĕlōhêkā*, Lev. 2:13) in the context of adding salt to every grain offering to Yahweh, where *kol-qorbānkā* (all of your offerings) is contextually limited to grain offerings (so NLT, NET; but see Ezek. 43:24, which prescribes salt for burnt offerings in the future temple; also see Ezra 6:9; 7:22); and (2) "a covenant of salt" (*bərît melaḥ*) by which Yahweh gives David the kingship over Israel (2 Chron. 13:5; cf. Ezra 4:14, "We eat salt of the palace" as an indicator, perhaps a treaty, of loyalty to the Persian emperor). Enduring alliances were symbolized by salt in Babylonian, Persian, Arab, and Greek settings (Walton and Matthews, *Genesis–Deuteronomy*, 194). As with grain offerings (Lev. 2:13), the unique incense blend to be burned in Yahweh's meeting tent on the incense altar, but not to be replicated for secular use, is to be seasoned with salt (*məmullāḥ*, pual ptc., Exod. 30:35). Ancient West Asians produced salt (*melaḥ*) by evaporating seawater or harvesting it from the salt beds of the Salt (Dead) Sea; they used salt as a cleansing agent (Ezek. 16:4), seasoning (Job 6:6), and as a preservative (see King and Stager, *Life*, 106). Primarily it was valued as the best food preservative in antiquity (Milgrom, *Numbers*, 154). Elsewhere, salt is associated with the curse of death or desolation (Gen. 19:26; Deut. 29:23; Judg. 9:45; Job 39:6; Jer. 17:6; Ezek. 47:11; Zeph. 2:9), but sometimes the inverse, an instrument of life (2 Kings 2:20–21; cf. Ezek. 16:4; Fensham, "Salt as Curse," 48–50; on handling salt in an apotropaic Sumerian incantation, see Michalowski, "Carminative Magic," 4). Salt was pronounced in oaths as a curse, as in Mesopotamian law codes and Aramaic treaties: "May Hadad sow in them salt and weeds(?)"; "May his soil be salted"; and "They shall scour her mouth with one sila of salt" (respectively: "The Inscriptions of Bar-Gaʾyah and Matiʿel from Sefire," *COS* 2.82:214; "The Bukān Inscription," *COS* 3.89:219; "The Laws of Ur-Namma [Ur-Nammu]," *COS* 2.153:410). Concerning Lev. 2:13, Wenham (*Leviticus*, 71) is incorrect that "salt was something that could not be destroyed by fire or time or any other means in antiquity." Rather, salt dissolves in water, and its impermanence was known in antiquity, as for example in a Hittite military oath, "and like the salt may he disintegrate" ("The First Soldiers' Oath," *COS* 1.66:166). Nonetheless, salt typically endures, so Wenham is still right that "the addition of salt to the offering was a reminder that the worshipper was in an eternal covenant relationship with his God. This meant that the worshipper had a perpetual duty to uphold and keep the covenant law" (Wenham, *Leviticus*, 71). Similarly, here in 18:19, the lasting quality of salt symbolizes the lasting nature of Yahweh's covenant with the Aaronic priests, safeguarding the custom of designating certain sacrificial grains and meats as food for them and their families (cf. Budd, *Numbers*, 206; NLT: "eternal and unbreakable"). In the

20Yahweh said to Aaron:[32] "You will have no inheritance in their land,[33] nor will you have any portion among them. I am your portion and your inheritance among the Israelites. **21**See, I have given the Levites every tithe in Israel as an inheritance, as compensation for their service[34] that they perform, the service of the meeting tent. **22**No longer may the Israelites approach the meeting tent, or they will bear their sin and die. **23**But the Levites must perform the service of the meeting tent, and they must bear their iniquity. It will be a permanent statute throughout your generations[35] that among the Israelites the Levites have no inheritance. **24**Instead,[36] I have given to the Levites as an inheritance the tithes that the Israelites offer up to Yahweh as tribute.[37] That is why I said to them that among the Israelites they will not have an inheritance."

25Then Yahweh spoke to Moses:[38] **26**"Speak to the Levites and tell them, 'When you receive from the Israelites the tithe that I have given you from them as your inheritance, then you must offer up from it as tribute to Yahweh[39] a tenth of the tithe. **27**And your tribute will be counted[40] to you as though it were grain from the threshing floor or as new wine from the winepress. **28**So you are to offer up tribute to Yahweh[41] from all your tithes that you receive from the Israelites, and you must give Yahweh's tribute from it to Aaron the priest. **29**From all

---

ANE, one could ratify with a blood sacrifice, crossing a threshold, exchanging a daughter or son, planting a tree or pillar as a witness, and perhaps by salt (here and Lev. 2:13), suggesting a gen. of means in Num. 18:19: "a permanent covenant *made by* salt" (*GBHS* §2.2.9).

32. As in vv. 1 and 8, no complementizer "saying" (*BHRG* §20.1.5) moves quickly into Yahweh's discourse with Aaron.

33. A prepositional phrase and predicate are fronted: "*In their land*, you will have no inheritance in their land, *and a portion* you will not have among them" (*BHRG* §47.2.1[2a], 47.3.2).

34. The preposition *ḥēlep* I appears in the OT only here in vv. 21, 31, meaning "*in return for* their service" (*DCH* 3:239; *HALOT* 1:321; ESV); hence my rendering, "as compensation for their service" (similarly NLT).

35. See variations of "permanent statute throughout your generations" (*ḥuqqat ʿôlām lədōrōtêkem*) in 10:8; 15:15; 18:8, 11, 19, 23; 19:10, 21.

36. Rendering *kî* not as evidential ("because"; many versions) but as a disjunctive ("instead"; NIV) with a fronted obj. (*GBHS* §4.3.4b, g).

37. The fronted obj. activates the identifiable entity in contrast (disjunctive *kî*) with vv. 23–24: formally, "that among the Israelites the Levites will not inherit an inheritance. *Instead, the tithes of the Israelites that they offer up to Yahweh as tribute* I have given to the Levites as an inheritance" (*BHRG* §47.2.1[a]*b*).

38. The editor resumes the complementizer "saying" (see the third translation note on 1:1).

39. Probably to clarify the obj. and appositional relationship, 4Q27 adds the direct object marker and omits Yahweh, who is implied: "Then you must offer up from it *tribute* [*'t trwmt*], a tenth of the tithe" (cf. SP *'t trwmt yhwh*; MT *trwmt yhwh*; LXX[ed] "an advanced deduction to the Lord").

40. Here and in v. 30, this niphal weqatal incomplete pass.—"will be counted" (*wəneḥšab* from **ḥšb*; ESV), "will be credited" (NET), or "will be reckoned" (NIV, NRSV)—implies Yahweh as the subject (NLT; *IBHS* §23.2.2e).

41. 4Q27 and SP add the direct obj. marker for clarity: "So you are to offer up *tribute* [*'t (t) rwmt*] to Yahweh from all your tithes" (cf. LXX[ed] "from the advanced deductions").

your gifts, you must offer up every[42] tribute to Yahweh; from all the best of them,[43] a sacred offering.'[44] **30**Then say to them, 'When you offer up the best of it,[45] then it will be counted to the Levites[46] as though it were the product of the threshing floor or the product of the winepress.[47] **31**And you may eat it[48] in any place, you and your households,[49] since it is your wages in compensation for your service in the meeting tent. **32**You will not bear any sin because of it[50] when you offer up the best of it. But do not profane the holy things of the Israelites,[51] or else you will die.'"

Interpretation

18:1–7. Yahweh speaks to Aaron alone and commands him and his sons to exercise the responsibilities of the priesthood, while the Levites must serve the priests, but any unauthorized person who approaches the sacred zones must be put to death.[52] The governing concept of these sacred zones is that the most holy place, containing the ark, is the geographical center from which radiates "concentric zones of holiness, each with its requirements of levels of purity."[53] Earlier we saw that Num. 8:16–18 augmented 3:6–13, 41–46 to convey a new dimension of the Aaron-Levite theology (see the comments on 8:5–19). However, the relationship of Num. 18 to Num. 3 and 8 is more complex, not least because Num. 18 does not even hint at the theology of the Sinai texts (Num. 3, 8) that the Levites were chosen to become the living substitutes for the firstborn males in Israel.[54] The bold text below indicates the distinct teaching of each text:

42. MT[mss] and LXX[ed] omit "every," perhaps thinking tribute and gifts were synonymous, so "*every* tribute"; 4Q27 MT SP would preclude other gifts: "from all your gifts."

43. For "the best of them" (*ḥlbw* MT SP 4Q27[probably]), LXX[ed] reads "the firstfruits."

44. The semicolon represents asyndeton, the second comma, a verbal ellipsis; *miqdāš* normally means "sanctuary," but for "sacred offering," see *HALOT* 2:625–26, gloss 2.

45. For "the best of it" (*ḥlbw* 4Q27 MT SP), LXX[ed] reads "the firstfruit."

46. Probably to preserve the second-person address and harmonize to v. 27, 4Q27 reads, "*Your tribute* will be credited to *you*" (*lkmh trwmtkmh* 4Q27 ≈ Vulg[ed]).

47. Probably harmonizing to v. 27, 4Q27 reads "from the/a winepress" (*mn hyqb* ≈ LXX[ed]).

48. Probably to clarify the meaning of repeated meals, 4Q27 and LXX[mss] read, "And you may eat *them*" (*'w[t]mh* 4Q27 = LXX[FVOC]; cf. "it" [*'ōtô*], MT SP = LXX[ABL]).

49. Although the sg. noun in MT[L] could be original as the more difficult reading, "you [pl.] and your [pl.] household [sg.]" (*'attem ûbêtəkem*), this could reflect an aural error. I adopt the more sensible reading: "you and your *households* [*ûbāttêkem*]" (MT[mss]; *wbtykm*[*h*] 4Q27 SP ≈ LXX[ed]).

50. Interpreting the prepositional phrase (*'ālāyw*) as a causal, "because of it" (Schmidt, *Numeri*, 78; Cazelles, *Nombres*, 93; *GBHS* §4.1.16d).

51. The fronted obj. activates the identifiable entity in contrast with "the best of it" in v. 32a: formally, "You will not bear any sin because of it when you offer up the best of it. *But the holy things of the Israelites* do not profane, or else you will die" (*BHRG* §47.2.1[a]*b*).

52. On speaking to Aaron alone, see Milgrom, *Numbers*, 146.

53. Walton and Matthews, *Genesis–Deuteronomy*, 193.

54. See Frevel, *Desert Transformations*, 465–86.

Table 18.1. Textual Traditions of Levites and Priests

Numbers 3:5–13; 8:16–19	Numbers 18:1–7
3:5Then Yahweh spoke to **Moses:**	1Then Yahweh spoke to **Aaron:** **You and your sons and your ancestral house with you must bear the iniquity attached to the sanctuary, and you and your sons with you must bear the iniquity attached to your priesthood.**
6Bring the tribe of Levi near, and stand them before Aaron the priest so that they may serve him 7and keep his responsibilities and the responsibilities of the whole community before the meeting tent, by performing the dwelling-place service. 8They must care for the furnishings of the meeting tent and for the responsibilities of the Israelites, by performing the dwelling-place service. 9You must assign the Levites to Aaron and his sons; they will be assigned exclusively to him from among the Israelites. 10You must appoint Aaron and his sons so that they protect their priesthood;	2So bring with you your brothers, Levi's tribe, your father's tribe, so that they may join with you and serve you while you and your sons with you are before the tent containing the witness. 3They will care for your responsibilities and the responsibilities of the whole tent, **but they must not come near the furnishings of the sanctuary or near the altar,** or both they and you will die. 4They must join with you, and they will care for the responsibilities of the meeting tent, for all the tent's service,
but the unauthorized person who approaches must be put to death.	but no unauthorized person may approach you.
11Then Yahweh said to **Moses:**	5**You will care for the responsibilities of the sanctuary and the responsibilites of the altar, so that wrath will no longer be on the Israelites.**
12Look, I myself have taken the Levites from among the Israelites	6Look, I myself have chosen your brothers the Levites from among the Israelites.
in place of every firstborn of the womb among the Israelites. So the Levites will belong to me, 13**since all the firstborn are mine. When I destroyed all the firstborn in the land of Egypt, I set apart for myself all the firstborn in Israel, from human to animal. They belong to me. I am Yahweh.**	
18:16**For they [the Levites] are given exclusively to me from among the Israelites. I have taken them for myself in place of all who open the womb, the firstborn sons of all the Israelites.** 17**For every firstborn male among the Israelites is mine, both human and animal. When I destroyed all the firstborn in the land of Egypt, I set them apart for myself.** 18**So I have taken the Levites in place of all the firstborn sons among the Israelites.**	
19I have given the Levites as a gift to Aaron and his sons from among the Israelites, to do the work for the Israelites in the meeting tent,	They are given to you as a gift from Yahweh, to perform the services of the meeting tent. 7But you and your sons with you must exercise your priestly functions, with regard to everything at the altar and inside the curtain. You must serve. I give you your priestly functions as a gift for service,
and to make atonement for the Israelites, so that there will be no plague among the Israelites when the Israelites come near the sanctuary.	
	but the unauthorized person who approaches must be put to death.

For the first time in the book, Yahweh in Num. 18 speaks only to Aaron, whom he has just substantiated as the head of Levi above the other tribes (chap. 17). The generic orders of v. 1, to bear the iniquity attached to the sanctuary and to the priesthood, recall Aaron's priestly role in daily and annually purging the sanctuary, the people encircling it, and his own family of iniquities, transgressions, sins, and physical contagions (see the third translation note on 18:1).[55] Aaron and his male descendants need support in their daily atoning work, so Num. 18 shares the same general notion of Num. 3 and 8: Yahweh has chosen the Levites to assist Aaron as his supporting staff (vv. 2–3a, 6; see the translation notes for 18:2, 3, 6). In Num. 3 and 8, the encroacher was a broad referent: "*the unauthorized person* who approaches must be put to death" and "when *the Israelites* come near the sanctuary." By contrast, Num. 18 names the Levites in particular as the ones who must not approach the sanctuary furnishings, altar, or Aaron himself (vv. 3, 4, 7). To be clear, 4:15–20 did warn the Kohathite family of Levi's tribe that when they transport the sancta, they must not touch or see the sancta uncovered, or they would die. But 18:1–7 takes this one step further and emphatically prohibits any of the Levite families from *even approaching* these sancta. One explanation is that 18:1–7 belongs to a different stratum than 4:15–20, but now as it stands in the canon, Num. 18 intensifies the restrictions on the Levites, even if it makes the completion of their tent work equivocal. Their restriction is reinforced by the distinct material of 18:5, which stresses that Aaron and his sons[56] will care for the responsibilities of the sanctuary and the altar, the two sacred entities referenced in v. 3 that the Levites are expressly banned from approaching. In 8:19, the language suggested that atoning work, forestalling a plague among the Israelites, was carried out jointly by Aaron's males and their gift, the supporting Levites (see table 18.1 above). By contrast in 18:5–7, the gift of the Levites enables Aaron and his sons *alone* to perform their priestly functions "so that wrath will no longer be on the Israelites" (vv. 5, 7; see the translation notes there; cf. Heb. 9:6).[57]

The theological function of 18:1–7 in its present context now becomes clear. In the wake of the judgment on Korah and his followers, which established the authority of Aaron over the Levites (chap. 16), and the budding of Aaron's staff, which honored the Levites with Aaron as their head (chap. 17), Yahweh must increase restrictions on the Levites to ensure their subordination to Aaron.[58] The Levites must remain content not to draw near to the divine dwelling or perform any priestly functions but to empower Aaron and his

---

55. See Lev. 4–6, 16, 21–22; Num. 15.

56. The nearest antecedent of "you" (pl.) in v. 5 is "you" (pl.) in v. 4c, referring not to the Levites (vv. 4a–b), but to Aaron and his sons.

57. Wrath lingering presumably from the infractions of chaps. 11–16.

58. Kilchör (*Mosetora*, 215–20) argues that Deut. 18:1–8 presumes and expounds on Num. 18:2–20.

sons in their essential work. The Levites must serve faithfully under Yahweh's restrictive discipline because of their rebellion and in so doing show that they still belong uniquely to Yahweh (cf. Heb. 12:5–13).

18:8–19. Delivering a second speech to Aaron, Yahweh expands the Sinai designation of the priestly portion for Aaron and his sons, now giving them and their family every Israelite offering to eat. The unit is framed by the *inclusio* of vv. 8 and 19. The recurring term "tributes" (*tərûmōt*) is a hypernym inclusive of all of Israel's offerings to Yahweh, as a suzerain in the ANE would receive a diversity of tributes from his vassal states (see the first translation note on v. 8). The second repeated metonym for Israel's offerings is "the holy things," which is the nomenclature of Lev. 21–22,[59] where the Aaronic priests must be careful to eat Israel's sacred offerings according to Yahweh's instructions (see the second translation note on v. 8; cf. 1 Cor. 9:13). To be more precise, the Aaronides will eat the "priestly portion" as their "permanent share," and this portion comes from the Israelites' holiest offerings by fire: the grain offering, purification offering, and reparation offering (vv. 8–9, 19; see the third translation note on v. 8 and the first translation note on v. 9). The priestly portion in the Priestly corpus referred to the hind limb of the animal, but here it is expanded to include a portion of grain, as in other ANE cults.[60] Salt, regarded as the best preservative in the ANE,[61] symbolizes the binding nature of this law: Israel must always give their sacrifices for Yahweh *to* Aaron's descendants (v. 19; see the translation note there). This enduring "covenant of salt" Yahweh made with the Aaronic priests was probably not analogous to an ANE royal grant but more like "an administrative appointment with the expectation of total loyalty in return, as required from all the king's servants."[62]

The protocols for extracting the priestly portion from these offerings come not from Numbers, but from Lev. 1–7.[63] The language is also in the Priestly idiom (cf. Lev. 6:22; see the translation notes on Num. 18:10). The burnt offering is not listed because it was consumed by Yahweh, not eaten by the priest (Lev. 1; the priest keeps only the skin: 7:8). After Aaron burns a handful of the grain composition, a memorial portion, as a sweet savor to Yahweh, Aaron and his sons keep the remainder of the grain or loaves in a holy place, the court of the meeting tent (Lev. 2:3, 10; 6:16, 18). To officiate a purification offering, Aaron or his sons sprinkle, smear, and pour the blood of the animal on specific sancta; burn the organ fat, kidneys, and liver lobe; and burn the rest in a clean place outside the camp (Lev. 4:1–5:13). The innovation comes

59. Lev. 21:22; 22:2, 3, 4, 6, 7, 12, 15, 16.
60. Greer ("'Priestly Portion,'" 263) contends that, in contrast to P, another biblical tradition envisioned the hind limb as the priestly portion: D (Deut. 18:3–4), the LXX Priestly corpus (LXX of Exod. 29; Lev. 7–10; Num. 18), possibly Num. 6:19, but not v. 20.
61. Milgrom, *Numbers*, 154.
62. Taggar-Cohen, "Covenant Priesthood," 24.
63. See Meyer, "Ritual Innovation," 139–40.

later, where the officiating priest is ordered to eat the meat of the purification offering (Lev. 6:26, 29 [19, 22]; 10:14). It remains unclear how eating the meat coheres with burning the meat outside the camp (Lev. 4–5; esp. 4:12, 21). One possibility is that "the flesh of the ordinary purification offering is actually eaten by the officiating priest . . . , and the purification offering for severe impurities is incinerated outside the camp only because the fear of its lethal properties has survived."[64] The same discrepancy appears for the reparation offering (see 7:7).[65]

The sacrifice for peace, although not mentioned explicitly in Num. 18, may be assumed since it is the basis of the purification offering and is often noted in conjunction with the elevation offerings referenced here (v. 11).[66] The priest eats the choice portion (the right thigh) of the sacrifice for peace and the breast of the elevation offering.[67] The sons and daughters of the Aaronic priest may eat, providing they are ritually clean (v. 11).[68] Aaron and his sons also receive the firstfruits of the new olive oil, new wine, grain, and the first ripe fruit of the land, which the Israelites give initially to Yahweh (vv. 12–13).[69]

In vv. 14–18, Yahweh now shockingly gives the Aaronic priests the firstborn animals, which are to be devoted exclusively to Yahweh as his possession.[70] These verses appear to be antecedent to Num. 3 and 8; otherwise, we would have expected them to state that the Levites and their livestock have become substitutes for the firstborn Israelite males and their male livestock.[71] In 3:44–51 Aaron was given 1,365 shekels—5 shekels for each of the 273 firstborn Israelites that exceeded the number of Levites. But here in chap. 18, the 5 shekels must be paid to Aaron to redeem *every* firstborn man, not just those who exceed the number of Levites (18:15–16; see the translation note on v. 16).[72] Also, the Levite livestock are to serve as substitutes for the firstborn males of Israel's livestock, nullifying the need to sacrifice Israel's firstborn livestock to Yahweh (3:41, 45). The most persuasive explanation of 18:16–18 is that it exegetically expands the firstborn instructions of Exod. 34:19–20 and Lev. 27:6a, 9–10.[73] At last in Num. 18, Israel learns how to

---

64. Milgrom, *Leviticus*, 1:239.
65. Cf. no eating in Lev. 5:14–6:13 versus eating in 7:6–7.
66. Lev. 4:10, 26, 31, 35.
67. See Lev. 7:32–34; 10:14–15; and the translation note on Num. 18:18.
68. See Lev. 22:7, 12, 13.
69. Exod. 23:19; 34:26; Lev. 23:17, 20.
70. Exod. 13:2, 11–15; 22:29; 34:19–20; Lev. 27:26.
71. Num. 3:11–13, 40–51; 8:16–18. Some see Num. 18 as independent of Num. 3 and 8 (Budd, *Numbers*, 203) and regard 3:11–13, 40–51 as a later revision to 18:13–16 (Achenbach, *Vollendung*, 160; Meyer, "Ritual Innovation," 137–38).
72. Numbers 18:15 shares the conviction of Lev. 27:27 that every unclean firstborn animal must be redeemed (see Meyer, "Ritual Innovation," 138–39). Numbers 18 arguably assumes Num. 27 (Frevel, "Alte Stücke," 288, 297).
73. Nihan ("Priestly Laws," 126–28) makes this case for Num. 18 and Lev. 27.

perform their firstborn sacrifices of a cow, sheep, or goat like a sacrifice for peace as a pleasing scent to Yahweh (18:17).[74] The main purpose here is not this clarification, however, but an innovation that benefits Aaron. Every time Aaron officiates a sacrifice of Israel's firstborn livestock, excepting donkeys, the meat will belong exclusively to Aaron, just as the right thigh of the sacrifice for peace belongs to Aaron (v. 18; cf. v. 11 and Lev. 7:28–35). Aside from the burnt offering, Yahweh has effectively transferred everything over to Aaron, except the pleasing scent that arises from the burning sacrifices.[75] God the Father always nourishes his servants who rely on him to complete his sacred work: "Jesus said to them, 'My food is to do the will of him who sent me and to complete his work'" (John 4:34 NRSV).

18:20–24. Yahweh gives the Levites himself and the tithes the Israelites offer to Yahweh as tribute. By this point in the Moses story, the reader knows that the Levites will not fight with the other Israelite tribes because they belong uniquely to Yahweh as his meeting-tent servants (1:47–53; Num. 3–4, 7).[76] Also, the Jubilee law makes the curious statement that "the houses of the cities of the Levites are their property among the Israelites" (Lev. 25:32–34, esp. 33). Why is a special law of redemption given for the Levites in distinction from the other Israelites? At last, in these verses Yahweh finally makes clear that Aaron and the rest of the Levites will have no land inheritance in Canaan. Instead, the Levites have two other forms of inheritance, Yahweh and every tithe in Israel. The tithes here probably refer to one-tenth of the Israelites' annual produce from their vineyards, fields, and orchards, but the Torah traditions converge and diverge on how this is to be executed.[77] Like this tithe given to the Levites, the prophet Samuel warns that a future king, like those of the ANE, would exact a tenth of the Israelites' grain and flocks (1 Sam. 8:15, 17). Supporting this broadly, archaeologists have discovered the words "belonging to the king" (*lmlk*) stamped by seals onto the handles of storage vessels.[78]

The claim of no land inheritance, but Yahweh and tithe inheritance, is asserted emphatically through an opening counterpoint-point set (Num. 18:20), followed by two point-counterpoint sets (vv. 21–23c*, 24a–b):[79]

---

74. See Lev. 3:5, 16; see the translation notes on Num. 18:17.

75. Meyer, "Ritual Innovation," 142.

76. Contra Douglas (Wilderness, 138), who asserts that we do not know until 18:20–21 why the Levites were counted separately, but at least that much was made clear by their meeting-tent vocation in 1:47–53.

77. Cf. Num. 18:20–32 with Lev. 27:30–33; Deut. 12:17–19; 14:22–29; 26:12–15; Neh. 10:39. On intertextuality and/or independence of these texts, see Nihan, "Priestly Laws," 126–34; Kilchör, *Mosetora*, 83–88, 116–25; Levine, *Numbers*, 1:437; Shectman, "Social Status," 95–98; Staubli, *Levitikus, Numeri*, 272; Schmidt, *Numeri*, 82.

78. Staubli, *Levitikus, Numeri*, 271, 396.

79. See Runge, *Discourse Grammar*, 386.

> Counterpoint: You will have no inheritance in their land, nor will you have any portion among them.
> Point: I am your portion and your inheritance among the Israelites (v. 20; see the second translation note there).
>
> Point: See, I have given the Levites every tithe in Israel as an inheritance, as compensation for their service that they perform, the service of the meeting tent (v. 21; see the translation note there; cf. Heb. 7:5).
> Counterpoint: It will be a permanent statute throughout your generations that among the Israelites the Levites have no inheritance (v. 23c; see the translation note there).
>
> Point: Instead, I have given to the Levites as an inheritance the tithes that the Israelites offer up to Yahweh as tribute (v. 24a; see the translation notes there).
> Counterpoint: That is why I said to them that among the Israelites they will not have an inheritance (v. 24b).

In the centered counterpoint, the "permanent statute throughout your generations" stresses that neither the exodus, wilderness, nor future Levite generations will ever inherit land, and the integrity and continuity of this divine *tôrâ* will be maintained.[80] In the middle of these sets are vv. 22–23a, surprisingly resembling the elevated status of the Levites in Num. 3–4 and 8 but not 18:1–7, which emphasizes the restricted status of the Levites. Here the Israelites, not the Levites, are explicitly restricted from approaching the meeting tent, while the Levites serve in the tent to contribute to the priestly work of bearing the iniquity of the people (18:22–23). The conceptuality of vv. 22–23 aligns not with its direct context but with Num. 3–4 and 8, but now in their canonical placement these verses explicate why the Levites deserve to receive Israel's tithes as compensation: the Levites have a superior proximity to the Deity and perform priestly work for the benefit of the community. Later the Messiah—a Judahite and not a Levite—and Paul, a Benjaminite, may allude to these compensated Levite workers as a precedent in God's kingdom that "the worker deserves his pay."[81] Like the Levites and their subset, the Aaronic priests, as vocational ministers of the gospel, forfeit claims in this life because of their special calling from God.[82] Paul seems to draw his conviction specifically from Num. 18 that tithing is not to be regarded as a special gift but as the responsibility of all Christians (1 Cor. 9:13–14).[83] The author of Hebrews makes the argument for the superiority of Melchizedek and the Son of God over Abraham: "One might even say that Levi himself, who receives tithes,

80. Olson, *Death of the Old*, 97.
81. Luke 10:7; cf. Matt. 10:10; 1 Tim. 5:18.
82. Dozeman, "Numbers," 153.
83. Dozeman, "Numbers," 153.

paid tithes [to Melchizedek] through Abraham, for he was still in the loins of his ancestor when Melchizedek met him" (7:9–10).

18:25–32. Yahweh instructs Moses to tell the Levites that they must offer a tithe (tenth) of Israel's tithes as a tribute to Yahweh (v. 26). In the prior speech to Aaron, Yahweh informed his high priest that he has given, and thus Israel must give, every tithe in Israel to the Levites as compensation since the Levites have no land inheritance (vv. 20–24). Here the shift from Aaron (vv. 1, 8, 20) to Moses (v. 25) is curious but may have been to avoid the conflict of interest that would arise if Aaron were charged with telling the Levites to give *him* a tenth of the gifts they receive (v. 26).[84] Yahweh will consider these tithes that the Levites give as if they gave their own grain offering or libation, "as grain from the threshing floor or as new wine from the winepress" (vv. 27, 30; see the translation note on v. 27). In this instance, regifting is not a problem. In v. 28 Yahweh reiterates v. 26 but now inserts that the Levites must give this tithe-of-a-tithe, Yahweh's tribute, to Aaron the priest. Their gift is sacred, so they must give only the highest quality products of what they receive from the Israelites, and only then will it be counted as an acceptable grain or wine offering (vv. 29–30; see the translation notes for 18:29–30). In the Sinai instructions, the priests were told that they must eat their prescribed portion of Yahweh's grain, purification, and reparation offerings as well as the bread of the table *in a holy place* (i.e., the court of the meeting tent).[85] By contrast, the Levites and their families may eat Israel's tithes—that is, nine-tenths of them—"in any place" (v. 31; see the second translation note there). The priests symbolically bear Israel's sin and complete the atonement process by eating the purification and reparation offerings in the holy place (Lev. 10:17; cf. 22:15–16). By contrast, the Levites eat not to bear Israel's sin but to receive their compensation for their meeting-tent service (v. 31; cf. Matt. 10:10; 1 Cor. 9:13). They will not bear their own sin—that is, incur guilt—if they offer up the best of it to Aaron (v. 32a; see the first translation note there). If, however, they profane the holy things, the offerings, of the Israelites, they will die (v. 32b; see the second translation note there). They can profane the offerings if they, as non-Aaronides, eat the tithe designated for Aaron (Lev. 22:10, 14–15) or if they touch the tithe while they are unclean.[86] A day would come when the Aaronic priests would no longer hold the exclusive prerogative of eating the designated sacrificial offerings. Instead, God will grant to anyone who trusts in the sacrifice of his Son access to eat from an even greater altar (Heb. 13:10).

---

84. Blum (*Komposition des Pentateuch*, 270), admitting our lack of knowledge about the exilic and postexilic cult and social history, contends for theology and social conflict as underlying the Aaronide-versus-Levite hierarchy (cf. Albertz, *Israelite Religion*, 2:461). Seebass (*Numeri*, 2:237) sees Num. 18 as pointing to deep postexilic peculiarities that cannot be explained entirely by this text.

85. Lev. 6:16, 26; 7:6; 10:13; 24:9.

86. Extending the logic of Lev. 7:19–21; chaps. 11 and 15; 22:4–7.

19

Purifying Defilement by a Corpse

(19:1–22)

~~~

Overview

In the preceding speeches of Num. 18, Yahweh strengthened the subordination of the Levites to the Aaronides but also supplied a consistent food source for both the Aaronides and Levites. In other words, the Levite vocation, while adjusted in the aftermath of the Korah disaster, is still intact. At Sinai, the Levites were ritually purified for their service in and around the meeting tent (Num. 8:6, 7, 21). Since Israel left Sinai, the Levites and the whole community have been exposed to the corpses of their people, which defiles anyone ritually and hygienically (Num. 11, 14, 16). Yahweh's curse of the exodus generation has begun to unfold: "In this wilderness your dead bodies will fall; . . . your dead bodies will fall in this wilderness . . . until you have fallen dead in this wilderness" (14:29*, 32*; see vv. 37, 45). More recently at Kadesh, the Israelites were physically exposed to one human death after another—Korah the Levite, Dathan and Abiram, and their households swallowed by the earth; the 250 chieftains consumed by fire; and members of the community killed by plague (Num. 16). Does this mean that the formerly purified Levites have become defiled? What about the community? Are the Israelites obeying the Sinai protocols for contamination by a corpse (Lev. 5; Num. 5, 9)?[1] The narrative is silent on these questions,[2] but Num. 19 interjects a more robust ritual for purifying corpse-contamination than had previously been revealed at Sinai.

---

1. Milgrom (*Numbers*, 157) connects chaps. 16 [17] and 19 by corpse contamination and by the choice of Eleazar, no longer Aaron, as the primary priestly agent for the community (16:37–40 [17:2–5]; 19:3–22).
2. Leveen, "'Lo We Perish,'" 264.

In view of the content of Num. 11–18, it is not hard to see why the editors positioned the material of Num. 19 where they did.[3] In Yahweh's opening discourse (vv. 1–10), he orders Moses and Aaron to sacrifice an entire red cow and store its ashes in a clean place, available for creating purifying water for future use. Then Yahweh teaches that anyone who comes in contact with a corpse, by any means, will become unclean for seven days and must cleanse themselves with the purifying water on the third and seventh days (vv. 11–16). Finally, Yahweh elucidates how to purify someone defiled by a corpse and that if corpse-defiled persons do not purify themselves, they must be eliminated from the community because they have profaned Yahweh's sanctuary (vv. 17–22).[4] As we will see, the central concern of the chapter is not personal hygiene but a symbolic ritual purity that is essential because of the divine presence in Israel's midst.[5]

Translation

> [1]Then Yahweh spoke to Moses and Aaron:[6] [2]"This is the statute of the law that Yahweh has commanded: Tell the Israelites to bring you a red cow without blemish, which has no defect and[7] has never carried a yoke. [3]You must give[8] it to Eleazar the priest so that he can take it outside the camp,[9] and it must be slaughtered before him.[10] [4]Then

3. Ashley, *Numbers*, 361–62. Leveen ("'Lo We Perish,'" 262) sees Num. 19 responding to the death cries of the people after they interpret Aaron's budding staff as an ominous sign. She also draws several associations that link chaps. 18–19 (266). Contra those who see Num. 19 as displaced (Gray, *Numbers*, 241; Noth, *Numbers*, 139).

4. Milgrom (*Numbers*, 437–38; also Staubli, *Levitikus, Numeri*, 273) sees two structurally symmetrical panels of rituals, but W. Lee (*Migratory Campaign*, 150–51) shows that they are now obfuscated in the text's present form.

5. Historically, interpreters have identified Num. 19 as P (Gray, *Numbers*, 241), while others see it as an independent accretion either to P or to a form of the Pentateuch (Budd, *Numbers*, 209; Scharbert, *Numeri*, 76). De Vaulx (*Nombres*, 213) identifies Num. 19 as the composite product of the Priestly editor, while Knohl (*Sanctuary*, 92–94) attributes some verses to H (vv. 2a, 10b–13, 20–21a), and Achenbach (*Vollendung*, 525–29) places Num. 19 in the second phase of the theocratic revision of the Torah containing purity laws and ritual regulations.

6. Here and in v. 2, colons stand for "saying." See the third translation note on 1:1.

7. "And" (SP LXX[ed]) clarifies, but the original text was probably asyndetic (4Q27 MT).

8. 4Q27 and LXX[ed] are sg. ("you must give"), probably to maintain the 2nd pers. sg. address to Moses and Aaron as a unit from v. 1 but overlooking that Moses and Aaron were to speak to the pl. Israelites.

9. Probably to harmonize to v. 9, the LXX scribe (Wevers, *Notes*, 312) or Hb. source adds "to a clean place."

10. Eleazar is most naturally the agent of "so that he can take it" (*wǝhôṣîʾ*), and the next verb in MT/SP would also imply Eleazar—"and he must slaughter it before him" (*wǝšāḥaṭ ʾōtāh lǝpānāyw*)—which makes "before him" unnecessary. I follow 4Q27 and LXX[ed]—"they must slaughter" (*wšḥṭw / kai sphaxousin*)—pl. with an indefinite subject (*BHRG* §36.5.5), which can be rendered as a pass.: "and it must be slaughtered before him" (most versions).

Eleazar the priest is to take some of its blood with his finger,[11] and sprinkle some of the blood seven times directly in front of the meeting tent.[12] **5**Then the cow[13] must be burned[14] in his sight—its skin, its meat, its blood, and its dung is to be burned.[15] **6**The priest must take cedar wood, hyssop, and scarlet wool and throw them into the fire where the cow is burning. **7**Then the priest must wash his clothes and bathe himself in water, and afterward he may come into the camp, but the priest will remain unclean until evening. **8**The one who burns it must wash his clothes in water and bathe himself in water, and they will remain unclean until evening. **9**Then someone who is clean must gather up the cow's ashes and store them[16] outside the camp in a clean place. They must be kept for the Israelite community for use in the purifying water.[17] It is a purification offering. **10**The one who gathers the cow's ashes must wash their clothes, and they will remain unclean until evening. This will be a permanent statute both for the Israelites and the immigrant who lives among them.

11"Whoever touches the corpse of any person will be unclean for seven days. **12**They must purify themselves[18] with water on the third

11. LXX^ed lacks "with his finger," which could indicate that it was added (in 4Q27 MT SP) to align with the manipulation of blood "with his finger" nine times in Lev. 4–16 (see Wevers, *Notes*, 312).

12. Rather than "opposite/directly *in front* [*pǝnê*] of the meeting tent" (MT SP ≈ *tou prosōpou* LXX^ed), 4Q27 reads "opposite *the door* [*ptḥ*] of the meeting tent," which may reflect an intention to eliminate the seeming redundancy ("opposite" + "in front of") and match the common location in Numbers, "the door of the meeting tent" (*'l ptḥ '[w]hl mw'd*; 12× in Num).

13. LXX^ed "they must burn *it* [*autēn*]" continues using the pronoun already used in v. 4 (Wevers, *Notes*, 313).

14. An issue arises similar to that of v. 3 (see the third translation note there) regarding the *unidentified* agent of the 3rd masc. sg. verb: formally, "and he must burn the cow in his sight."

15. The em dash represents apposition (*IBHS* §12.3); the hyponyms "its skin, its meat, its blood, and its dung" (*'et-'ōrāh wǝ'et-bǝśārāh wǝ'et-dāmāh*) are subsets of the hypernym "the cow" (*'et-happārâ*). LXX^ed eliminates the apposition by adding "and," probably an interpretation rather than dittography (Wevers, *Notes*, 313). *To derma autēs* (its skin; LXX^ACL) appears as *'wrh* in 4Q27 and SP and as *'ōrāh* in MT, although LXX^B's *to derma* may reflect the original text with a possessive article (Hb. *h'wr*).

16. A hiphil volitional weqatal: formally, "and cause (them) to rest" (*wǝhinniaḥ*).

17. Formally, "waters of impurity" in vv. 9, 13, 20, 21 (*mê niddâ*; Schmidt, *Numeri*, 83; Ashley, *Numbers*, 363). The noun impurity (*niddâ*) occurs in the Pentateuch only in Leviticus (chaps. 12, 15, 18, 20) and Numbers (chaps. 19, 31), where it is used to describe a flow of blood (menstruation, postpartum discharge), unclean cultic objects (due to contact with such blood), and sexual intercourse with one's brother's wife. The implication of this gen. of purpose here is "waters *intended for removing* impurity" (*GBHS* §2.2.8; as "*niddâ* II," *DCH* 5:623), hence my rendering, "purifying waters" (similarly EÜ; Levine, *Numbers*, 1:459; "water of separation for disposal," Seebass, *Numeri*, 2:239; "the water for purification," Budd, *Numbers*, 208; less clear: "to make lustral water," Cazelles, *Nombres*, 94; and "to be kept as lustral water," de Vaulx, *Nombres*, 216).

18. The hithpael (*hû' yiṭḥaṭṭā'-bô*) is reflexive with a factitive sense and has a privative sense of removing impurity, meaning "They must effect the removal of impurity and so put themselves into a pure state" (with Sklar, *Sin*, 111; *IBHS* §24.4d; *GBHS* §§3.1.3a; 3.1.5a).

day and on the seventh day, and then they will be clean. But if they do not purify themselves on the third day and the seventh day, then they will not be clean. **13**All who touch a corpse, a body of a human[19] who has died, and do not purify themselves defile[20] Yahweh's dwelling place. That person must be cut off from Israel because the purifying water was not splashed on them.[21] He will be unclean—his uncleanness remains on him. **14**This[22] is the law for when someone dies in a tent: Anyone who enters the tent and all who are in the tent will be unclean for seven days. **15**And every open container with no cover fastened on it is unclean. **16**Whoever touches someone killed with a sword in the open fields, or someone who died a natural death,[23] or a human bone, or a grave, will be unclean for seven days.

17"For an unclean person, take some of the ashes burnt for purification and pour[24] fresh water[25] over them in a container. **18**Then a clean person must take hyssop, dip it in the water, and sprinkle it on the tent, on all its furnishings, and on the people who were there, or on the one who touched a bone, or someone who was killed or died of natural causes, or a grave. **19**The clean person[26] must sprinkle the unclean person on the third day and on the seventh day. On the seventh day, they must purify themselves, wash their clothes, and bathe in water, and then they will be clean in the evening. **20**But any

19. "Body of (the) human" (*nepeš hā'ādām*), likely an article of class (*IBHS* §13.5.1f), whereas SP is anarthrous, "a body of a human" (*npš 'dm*).

20. As in v. 20, the piel is factitive: "*put* Yahweh's dwelling place *into a defiled state* [*ṭimmē'*]" (*GBHS* §3.1.3a).

21. Verses 13, 20 employ the qal qatal pass., "was not splashed" (*lō'-zōraq*), from **zrq* (sprinkle). See the second translation note on 18:17.

22. SP and LXX[ed] add "*So*/*and* this is the law."

23. Formally, "who died" (*mēt*, qal ptc.) but understood contextually as one who died of natural causes in distinction from "someone killed with a sword in the open fields."

24. Two imperatival weqatals. I follow the pl. of SP and LXX[ed]—"they must take . . . *and they must pour*"—which could be secondary but preserves the parallelism and is superior to rendering the qal act. sg. of **ntn* as a pass. (Levine, *Numbers*, 1:460; ESV, NJPS, NRSV). This passivizing could work for a pl. with an unidentified agent, but for a sg. pass. of **ntn*, one expects a qal pass. or niphal. This allows one to understand both weqatals as 3rd pers. pl. act. verbs used with indefinite subjects (*BHRG* §36.5.5), which can be rendered contextually as "[You all/someone must] take . . . and [you all/someone must] *pour*" (NLT, NET, NIV, EÜ).

25. Formally, "living water" (*mayim ḥayyîm* ≈ LXX[ed]; Seebass, *Numeri*, 2:240; Schmidt, *Numeri*, 84; Levine, *Numbers*, 1:460; Cazelles, *Nombres*, 95; de Vaulx, *Nombres*, 281). The meaning is "fresh water" (many versions) or "spring water" (EÜ), but probably not "running water" (NET, NRSV; Gray, *Numbers*, 245; Budd, *Numbers*, 208) because (1) elsewhere in the Pentateuch *mayim ḥayyîm* refers only to spring/fresh water in a well (Gen. 26:19; Song 4:15) and, in the two-bird purification ritual, apparently to contained water, not flowing water (Lev. 14:5–6, 50–52); and (2) when *mayim ḥayyîm* is said to be flowing, other modifiers are supplied (Jer. 2:13; 17:13; Zech. 14:8; cf. modifiers for semantically similar constructions: Deut. 8:7; 21:4; Isa. 30:25).

26. A referential article, "*the* clean person" (*haṭṭāhōr*), refers to the same clean person who sprinkles the water in v. 18 (*GBHS* §2.6.1).

who are unclean[27] and do not purify themselves, those people must
be cut off from the community, because they have defiled Yahweh's
sanctuary.[28] The purifying water was not splashed on them, so they
are unclean. **²¹**This will be a permanent statute for them: The one who
sprinkles the purifying water must wash their clothes, and the one who
touches the purifying water will remain unclean until evening. **²²**And
whatever the unclean person touches will become unclean, and the
person who touches it will remain unclean until evening."

Interpretation

19:1–10. Yahweh commands Moses and Aaron to sacrifice a red cow in its
entirety, and its ashes must be stored in a clean place for formulating purifying
water on demand. As I suggested in the overview (above), the literary placement of Num. 19 is fitting as the solution to the implicit defilement by Israelite
dead bodies since Israel left Sinai (chaps. 11–16). The subunit of 19:1–10 is
circumscribed by the *inclusio* of the statutory nature of the divine instruction (vv. 2a, 10c).[29] A common legal standard that applies to the immigrant
as well as the native, this purification rite resembles the addendums to the
Passover law (9:14) and voluntary offerings (15:14–16). There is a mystery
here: "Numbers explicitly says that the sojourner [immigrant] is eligible for
the waters of purification (Num. 19:10). Who was he? Generally excluded
from the temple, here are non-Jews being included in ritual purifications and
even required to do them, like Jews."[30]

In the OT, only here in Num. 19 is there a ritual with a "red cow" (*pārâ
'ădummâ*), recalled, using the referential article, as simply "the cow" (vv. 5,
6, 9, 10).[31] Commonly this is translated red *heifer*,[32] which is a female cow
that has never become pregnant, milked, or been yoked to another animal to
plow or pull. However, the term in Hebrew (*pārâ*) is better translated "cow"
because, although here it has not been yoked (v. 2), it nonetheless may have
calved.[33] So why does Yahweh demand a red cow for this purification ritual?

27. Possibly adjusting the text to form a contrast with "the clean person" (*haṭṭāhōr*) in v. 19,
here SP (and Syr) is definite, "But *the person* [*h'yš*] who is unclean."

28. As in v. 13, a piel factitive, meaning "because *they* [*he*] *have put* Yahweh's sanctuary *into
a defiled state* [*ṭimmē'*]" (GBHS §3.1.3a).

29. This Priestly legal formula also occurs in 31:21 (Frevel, "Book of Numbers," 24; Knierim
and Coats, *Numbers*, 224).

30. Douglas, *Wilderness*, 167. On the non-Judahite and non-Israelite ethnicity of the immigrant (*gēr*), at least in Deuteronomy but with some data relevant to Num. 19, see Awabdy,
Immigrants, 110–16.

31. *Happārâ*; GBHS §2.6.1.

32. NIV, NET, ESV, NLT, NRSV.

33. NJPS, EÜ; with Gray (*Numbers*, 248), who notes references to a cow (*pārâ*) that has
borne calves (1 Sam. 6:7; Job 21:10; cf. Amos 4:1). Also, Ashley, *Numbers*, 363–64. By contrast,

Red refers not to an unnatural tone, but brown or reddish brown,[34] and it is conceivable that a red cow was thought to increase the amount of blood in the ashes, even if only symbolically.[35] The ritual is aimed at generating ashes to be stored for concocting purifying water—formally, "waters of impurity," meaning waters that remove impurity (v. 9; see the second translation note there). Yet the ritual is called "a purification offering" (*ḥaṭṭā't*, v. 9), suggesting that despite its uniqueness, it adapts the basic purification offering transmitted at Sinai (Lev. 4:1–5:13; 16*; cf. Heb. 9:10, 13, 19). A comparison is, therefore, warranted. Meaningful differences are marked with bold font.

Purification Offering (Lev. 4:3–12; 16:27–28)	Ashes for Purification Water (Num. 19:2b–10)
*Bull without blemish (v. 3)	*Red cow without blemish, no defect, **never yoked** (v. 2)
*Offender brings bull to meeting tent entrance, places hand on the bull, and slaughters it **before Yahweh** (v. 4).	*Eleazar the priest takes cow **outside the camp**, and the cow is slaughtered **before him** (v. 3; see the third translation note there)
*Priest brings some blood into the tent, dips his finger in it, and sprinkles it seven times in front of the sanctuary curtain before Yahweh (vv. 5–6).	*Eleazar takes some of its blood with his finger and sprinkles it seven times in front of the meeting tent (implicitly before Yahweh) (v. 4).
*Priest puts some blood on the horns of the incense altar before Yahweh and pours out the remaining blood at the base of the altar of burnt offering (v. 7).	
*Priest burns, on the altar, the bull's entrail fat, kidneys and their fat, and the liver's long lobe (vv. 8–10).	
*Priest burns outside the camp the remainder of the bull—its skin, meat, head, legs, entrails, and dung—on a clean place, an ash heap, on a wood fire (vv. 11–12).	*Cow **is burned** (outside the camp) in Eleazar's sight—its skin, meat, **blood**, and dung (v. 5; see the third translation note there).
	*Priest (initially Eleazar) throws cedar wood, hyssop, and scarlet wool into the fire where the cow is burning (v. 6).
Day of Atonement purification offering: [cf. Lev. 16:24]	
	*Priest washes his clothes, bathes in water, and afterward he may come into the camp but remains unclean until evening (v. 7).

---

cf. the heifer (*'eglat bāqār*) in Deut. 21:3, slaughtered for unsolved homicide (see Goodfriend, "Leviticus 22:24," 71).

34. Gray, *Numbers*, 248.
35. Milgrom, *Numbers*, 158.

Purification Offering (Lev. 4:3–12; 16:27–28)	Ashes for Purification Water (Num. 19:2b–10)
*One who burns it washes his clothes, bathes in water, and afterward he may come into the camp.	*One who burns it washes his clothes, bathes in water, and remains unclean until evening (v. 8).
	*Someone clean gathers the cow's ashes, stores them outside the camp in a clean place. They must wash their clothes and remain unclean until evening (vv. 9–10).

It is unclear whether Eleazar in Num. 19 would perform the additional steps of blood manipulation (Lev. 4:7) and fat and organ burning on the altar (Lev. 4:8–10).[36] It is only fitting that for creating the ashes for purifying water, Yahweh scrupulously emphasizes that the priest, burner, and gatherer must wash their clothes and bodies, remaining unclean until evening (19:7–10).

For the modern reader, perhaps the most striking question is how can *dirty* ashes, including incinerated cow excrement (!), be used to formulate *purifying* waters?[37] This question we will answer when discussing the protocols below (vv. 17–22). First, what is the purpose of adding cedar wood, hyssop, and scarlet wool to the fire burning the cow? Cedar wood, almost exclusive to Lebanon, was used by analogy in a Mesopotamian ritual for covering the kettledrum of the temple in which "the bull (whose hide would become the drumskin) was sprinkled with cedar balsam, burned with cedar wood, and buried in a red cloth."[38] Hyssop was a hairy, aromatic plant common in Canaan, used like a sponge in scrubbing and cleansing.[39] Even today it is burned as an essential oil with a purifying scent.

Second, what does this highly specific ash composition contribute symbolically to purifying water? We will contemplate this below as the ritual unfolds (vv. 17–18). Here we see that the officiating priest and the clean gatherer of the ashes must, logically, first launder their clothes and then bathe their bodies; otherwise their dirty clothes would recontaminate their bodies.[40]

19:11–16. Yahweh instructs that whoever touches a corpse will be unclean for seven days and must wash with the purifying water on days three and seven.[41] Yahweh expands the Sinai instructions, which are shown to be

---

36. Seebass (*Numeri*, 2:263) infers that the red-cow purification offering did not include these steps.

37. See Ezek. 4:12–15, where Ezekiel the priest accepts Yahweh's orders to eat food cooked over animal dung but not human dung.

38. Milgrom, *Numbers*, 169.

39. Milgrom, *Numbers*, 159.

40. Milgrom, *Numbers*, 159.

41. Washings on days three and seven indicate, among other points, that Num. 31:19–20, 24 was founded on the Num. 19 ritual (D. Wright, "Purification," 213–23).

incomplete to this point. In Leviticus, among a litany of unknown offenses later exposed, contact with "human uncleanness" probably includes touching a corpse (Lev. 5:3; cf. carcasses in 5:2). Yahweh requires a public confession and a specific purification offering, accommodating to the poor (5:5–13). No washing is mentioned. After touching animal carcasses, a man with genital discharges, a woman menstruating or discharging other blood, the defiled must wash their clothes and body, but nothing is said of touching corpses or using a special purifying water (Lev. 11, 15).[42] One declared clean from a skin disease must undergo a two-bird cleansing ritual, but there the cleansing agent is fresh water with bird blood (Lev. 14). Aaron the high priest was not permitted to touch the dead body of anyone, whereas his sons could touch only the corpses of their immediate family members, but nothing is said of how they must wash subsequently.[43] In the Holiness collection, Yahweh prohibits necromancy, which involved defiling contact with the spirits of the dead and possession by spirits of the dead, but for these rituals, washing can do nothing to stop the ensuing judgment.[44] In Num. 5:2–3, still at Sinai, Yahweh commanded the Israelites to expel from the camp anyone made unclean by a contagion, including "everyone defiled by a corpse" (*kōl ṭāmēʾ lānāpeš*). They do this, but nothing is said of how the defiled should purify themselves and gain access to reintegrate into the camp. In Num. 6:9–12, Nazirites who touch a corpse must undergo purification and rededicate themselves to Yahweh, but there is no mention of otherwise expected ritual washing.[45] In Num. 9, some men had become defiled by touching a dead body and so were not able to observe the Passover (9:6–8). In response, Yahweh delivers an oracular law that allows unclean Israelites to defer their Passover celebration until the next month, but he says nothing about their washing process to become clean (9:9–15).[46]

Filling this legal loophole, 19:11–16 illustrates different means of defilement by a corpse and days of requisite washing, vv. 17–20 elucidate the purification ritual and judgment for those who fail to purify themselves, and vv. 21–22 function as a subscript.[47] Everyone who touches a corpse will be unclean for seven days and must purify themselves with water on the third

---

42. This does not negate the possibility that Num. 19 and Lev. 11 are intertextually related (Frevel, "Purity Conceptions," 401).

43. Lev. 21:1–4, 11; 22:4. Frevel ("Alte Stücke," 288–89) contends that Lev. 21 presumes the ritual purification law of Num. 19.

44. Lev. 19:28, 31; 20:6, 27; Deut. 14:1; 18:10–11; 26:14.

45. Frevel ("Purity Conceptions," 373–74) sees a connection between 6:11 and 19:17–20.

46. Frevel ("Purity Conceptions," 399) argues that Num. 9 appropriates 19—both purify defiled persons inside the camp—but not 5:2, which puts defiled people outside the camp.

47. Gane ("Didactic Logic," 209) contends that childbirth impurity is the first type of impurity taught in the Torah (Lev. 12), with corpse impurity here being the last, suggesting a "birth-to-death cycle of mortality"; however, corpse and carcass impurities were taken up first (Lev. 5:2–3; 11:24–40).

and seventh day; then they will become clean (vv. 11–12; see the translation note on v. 12). The cleansing agent, water, has no anaphoric article (v. 12), but it contextually refers to "the purifying water" of v. 9, as v. 13 indicates. In v. 12c–d, the counterpoint, or inverse, that could have been deduced from v. 12a–b, is stated for emphasis.[48] Those who touch a corpse and do not purify themselves accordingly will "defile Yahweh's dwelling place" (v. 13). Putting Yahweh's dwelling into a defiled state is the essence of the infraction (see the second translation note on v. 13). In 5:3, by not expelling the corpse-defiled residents, the Israelites would "defile their camps in which I live," but now it is not just the camps but the divine dwelling that accrues contamination (see also Lev. 15:31). Yahweh is fundamentally opposed to death; so dead bodies and those who contact them would pollute the place where Yahweh resides (see the "Implications" essay below, "The Formative Power of Purifying Rituals"). The one defiled by a corpse must be eliminated from the community because the purifying water (v. 9) was not splashed on them, and they will remain unclean forever (v. 13b–c; see the third translation note on v. 13). In the last subunit (vv. 14–16), Yahweh illustrates seven modes of becoming unclean for seven days through contact with human death: be present in, enter, or handle (implied) an uncovered container in a tent in which someone has died (modes 1–3);[49] or touch someone killed with a sword in the open fields (mode 4), someone who died a natural death (mode 5; see the translation note on v. 16), a human bone (mode 6), or a grave (mode 7).[50] These are not intended to be exhaustive but illustrative. Later the prophet Elijah defiles himself by touching the corpse of the Zarephath widow's boy so that by Yahweh's power he might raise the boy to life (1 Kings 17:17–24), and later Elisha follows the example of his master (2 Kings 4:18–37). Ultimately, Num. 19:11–16 becomes critical to understanding the numerous times when Jesus, with great compassion, chose to defile himself by touching corpses in order to generate new life, physical and spiritual: "For just as the Father raises the dead and gives them life, so also the Son gives life to whomever he wishes" (John 5:21 NET).[51]

19:17–22. Yahweh finally explicates *how* to purify those defiled by a corpse. What follows is not a robust purification ritual like Lev. 14 but four primary

---

48. See Runge, *Discourse Grammar*, 386; see, i.e., 18:20–24.

49. Paterius (6th–7th cent. CE) read this tropologically: "For a vessel without a cover or seal is spoiled, like as in the case of one who devotes himself to ostentation and is not covered by any veil of silence" (Lienhard, *Numbers*, 237).

50. Noam ("Corpse-Blood," 243–51) argues that the Qumran Temple Scroll and the rabbinic Sifre Zuta had the addition "or blood" in their text at Num. 19:16, suggesting that contact with corpse-blood also defiled.

51. See Matt. 9:23–26//Mark 5:38–43//Luke 8:49–56; Matt. 10:8 (cf. Luke 7:22); 11:5; 23:27; Luke 7:11–15; cf. Mark 9:26–27; Luke 10:30–34; 17:37; John 5:25; 11:38–44 (avoiding defilement?); 12:1, 9, 17; Acts 20:9–10; Eph. 2:1–7; et al.

steps to cleanse the corpse-defiled person on days three and seven of their seven-day uncleanness (vv. 12, 19):

1. Moses and Aaron (implied from v. 1?) put some of the red cow's ashes (vv. 9–10) into a container and pour fresh water over them (v. 17; see the translation notes there).
2. A clean person dips hyssop—an evergreen herb used like a cleansing sponge—into the water and sprinkles it on the corpse-defiled tent, its furnishings, and residents (vv. 14–15) or on the one who has touched a bone, a dead body (whether killed or dying by natural causes), or a grave (v. 18).
3. The same clean person sprinkles the corpse-defiled person, who must wash their clothes and bathe in water (v. 19; see the translation note there).
4. On the seventh day, the sprinkler must also wash their clothes and bathe in water, and they will become clean in the evening (v. 21).

Though surprising to the modern reader, the ashes serve as the "ritual detergent par excellence," but the reason for this is that the ashes contain the blood of the purification offering that alone can expunge the impurity from the corpse-defiled person.[52] At the same time, there is also evidence that wood ashes containing potassium carbonate were used as a cleansing agent in antiquity and even in some developing contexts today.[53] Hyssop, burned earlier, was also useful at this ritual since its fuzzy branches could absorb the water like a sponge.[54] Ultimately, it was the concocted purifying water that was Yahweh's prescribed means of cleansing.[55] The reason for using water plus a distributed use of the ashes of a single purification offering may have secondarily been economic, since it would have been a financial burden for everyone near the corpse of a deceased family member to offer an individual sacrifice.[56]

In v. 20, Yahweh reiterates from v. 13 the punishment of failing to purify oneself, namely, elimination from the community. The reason for this retribution is that it renders Yahweh's dwelling place (19:13)—more precisely, his most holy place, the sanctuary (*miqdaš*, v. 20)—unfit for his presence.[57]

---

52. Milgrom, *Numbers*, 159, 160. As Frevel ("Purity Conceptions," 374) notes, it is not clear whether this is the same formulation of waters used to purify the Levites in 8:12. Wefing ("mit der roten Kuh," 341–64) conjectures that the Num. 19 ritual was originally a Canaanite sacrifice but was Yahwized in light of Num. 5:11–31 and Exod. 32:20.

53. King and Stager, *Life*, 71; Ruikar, Rajopadhye, Kale, and Masurkar, "Formulation," 1256–63.

54. Walton and Matthews, *Genesis–Deuteronomy*, 196.

55. Sklar, *Sin*, 111.

56. Sklar, *Sin*, 114n28.

57. Exod. 15:17; 25:8; Lev. 16:33; 21:12.

Defiling Yahweh's sanctuary leads to death.[58] The subscript of vv. 21–22, like that of the red-cow ritual (v. 10c), establishes this purification ritual (vv. 17–20) as a permanent statute in Israel. The subscript also subtly expands the law in two ways. First, why does the one who sprinkles the purifying water become unclean until evening? As in a Hittite purification ritual, the ritual in conjunction with the sacrificial concoction for the purification results in the priest's temporary impurity.[59] One view of Num. 19 is that everyone involved in the ritual must launder and bathe because they came closer to the sacred than they should have. That is, "when too high a degree of the sacred is in the wrong realms, defilement results," so they must purify to reduce their sanctity level and return to normalcy.[60] Instead, I am persuaded that the opposite is true. Just like the purification offerings of Lev. 4:1–5:13, *the blood* of the red cow, a type of purification offering, functions as the ritual detergent because it "absorbs the impurity of the sanctuary."[61] Therefore, the red cow's blood *pollutes* everyone who handles it at any and every stage: the sacrificing priest, burner, ash gatherer, and water splasher must all launder and bathe (vv. 7, 8, 10, 21). Second, the subscript renders unclean anyone who touches the corpse-defiled person, as one could have inferred from the defiling touch of the discharging man and bleeding woman (Lev. 15:4–12, 19–27). Therefore, in the Gospels not only was the hemorrhaging woman herself defiled, but she also defiled Jesus by touching his cloak to receive his healing.[62] In the same way, any relatives or friends who had touched the corpse of Jairus's little daughter or Lazarus or nameless others and had escorted Jesus into their home would also have defiled Jesus (Num. 19:22).[63] But for the Son of Man, compassion that engenders life always supplants a reductionistic application of Num. 19.

Implications

The Formative Power of Purifying Rituals

The Hittites of Anatolia (Turkey) were known for responding to defilement with ritual bathing, sacrifices, and a period of isolation.[64] The Babylonians practiced a seven-day purification ritual for corpse contamination. Anyone who touched the dust from a place of mourning for the dead had to offer sacrifices to Shamash the sun god, bathe, change clothes, and remain in

---

58. Sklar, *Sin*, 179.
59. Walton and Matthews, *Genesis–Deuteronomy*, 195.
60. With Baumgarten ("Paradox," 444–45, 449), who claims that the other means of deviating from the norm is when one is farther from the sacred than one should be.
61. Milgrom, "Confusing," 557; cf. Frevel, *Desert Transformations*, 261–88.
62. Matt. 9:20–22; Mark 5:25–34; Luke 8:43–48.
63. See the note at end of the comments on Num. 19:11–16.
64. See Walton and Matthews, *Genesis–Deuteronomy*, 196.

their house for a week.[65] Priests would perform complex purification rituals called NAM.BÚR.BI. Their apotropaic purpose was to avert the evil predicted whenever the actions of animals, stars, and other phenomena unfolded as recorded in the apodoses of the Akkadian omen literature.[66] The Sargonid Assyrian and Neo-Babylonian priests who executed these rituals were deeply concerned about corpse defilement: "What may have been of concern was a mixing of the two spheres of existence, the living and the dead. When a person came in contact with the dead, whether human or animal, contamination occurred."[67] The Babylonians would also purify the corpse out of fear that it might be attacked by demons.[68] More than this, the corpse-defiled individual, in trepidation that they had been infected with a deadly impurity, needed not only to launder, wash, and isolate but also to be exorcised through an incantation.[69]

Although the Yahweh who speaks in Num. 19 does not condone Akkadian or any other form of omen reading or exorcism, his instructions here are not focused on countering omen reading, necromancy, demonic possession, or other forms of black magic.[70] There is inadequate textual evidence to claim that Num. 19 contains a "vestige of a pre-Israelite rite of exorcism for the corpse contaminated"[71] or that "the hidden agenda of Num. 19 is the cult of the dead."[72] Why, then, is Yahweh so determined to ensure that his covenant people purify themselves after they have come into contact with a dead body? As we have discussed in the commentary at 5:1–4, bodily impurities are not tantamount to, or the product of, any specific sin, iniquity, or rebellion, yet like sin they do pollute Yahweh's dwelling place.[73] They pollute, most likely, because genital discharges, skin diseases, and corpse contact are all impure contagions that belong to the realm of death—the life forces of blood or semen that fail to engender life, the dead skin, and the lifeless bodies. Contact with the realm of death is dangerous because Yahweh is fundamentally for life and his nature is incompatible with death.[74] In the Priestly conception, the contagion of a corpse, when touched by the Israelites, travels aerially and fixes

---

65. Milgrom, *Numbers*, 160.

66. Caplice, "Namburbi Rituals," 346; Oppenheim, *Ancient Mesopotamia*, 226.

67. Walton and Matthews, *Genesis–Deuteronomy*, 196.

68. Gray, *Numbers*, 244.

69. Milgrom, "Paradox," 69. Kazen ("Purity and Persia," 455–56) notes that in Zoroastrianism, corpse impurity was considered the most dangerous, requiring various defenses and apotropaic purification rituals.

70. Contrasting with texts containing these prohibitions: Lev. 19:28, 31; 20:6, 27; Deut. 14:1; 18:10–11; 26:14.

71. Milgrom, "Paradox," 72.

72. Levine, *Numbers*, 1:472, see 468–79; also Dozeman, "Numbers," 149.

73. Milgrom, *Leviticus*, 1:926.

74. Frevel, "Unvollkommenheit," 226; Milgrom, "Impurity," 107–11; Milgrom, *Leviticus*, 1:46; Douglas, *Leviticus*, 176–94.

onto Yahweh's residence, which renders it antithetical to Yahweh's nature.[75] As Dozeman concludes, "Death is a power that is incompatible with the holiness of God, and thus it defiles."[76] Here the reader learns that failure to ritually wash corpse (death) contamination with the purifying water on days 3 and 7 defiles not only Israel's camps where Yahweh lives in a broad sense (5:3) or his dwelling place as a whole (19:13) but also his sanctuary (*miqdaš*), the most holy place, where Yahweh has localized his presence on earth (v. 20).[77] This explains why it would not be sufficient to wash oneself individually at the wadi, or privately in one's tent with fresh water drawn from the cistern or well. Contamination through one brings contamination to all encamped around Yahweh. After the public burning of the red cow outside the camp and watching Eleazer exit and reenter, a clean community member splashed the defiled with the purifying water. Failure to submit to this procedure resulted in being cut off from the community.

The corporate nature of the purification law of Num. 19 also relates to its power to spiritually and ethically form those who observe it or are mentally aware that it is taking place in their midst. It is commonly accepted that "the meaning inherent in a ritual is often acted out through overt symbolic expression."[78] Said another way, "Social dramas are embodied in ritual, where they have paradigmatic functions that make clear the deepest values of the culture."[79] The Num. 19 purification ritual dramatizes what Yahweh wants his covenant people to value deeply as he does. Yahweh is incompatible with death, and the red cow must die so that the corpse-defiled person who washes with its ashes need not die (vv. 13, 20). The ritual process, when witnessed, could also generate empathy for the person contaminated. Imagine a week of not physically greeting another human; not using household things; not bringing an offering of gratitude to Yahweh; not sleeping next to your spouse; not hugging your children, your father, mother, brother, sister, or friend.[80] Imagine never seeing your father again after he obstinately chooses to work the farm instead of undergoing the purification. On the other hand, imagine seeing the sacred water splash off a contaminated person's body on the designated days so that they will soon become ritually clean again, fully restored to Yahweh and the community.

By eliciting positive and negative emotional responses, the Num. 19 purification ritual had the power to shape the Israelites' motivations and social

75. Milgrom, *Leviticus*, 1:257.
76. Dozeman, "Numbers," 152.
77. Exod. 15:17; 25:8; Lev. 16:33; 21:12.
78. Hobson et al., "Psychology of Ritual," 261.
79. Bell (*Ritual Theory*, 41) draws from Turner, *Ritual Process*. For more depth on rituals in Numbers, see Frevel, *Desert Transformations*, 289–338.
80. By observing COVID-19 quarantine protocols, many of us have experienced the sense of isolation such social distancing brings.

behaviors away from unnecessary defilement or outright disobedience and so fostered trust in Yahweh, who loves life and provides for his people's purification.[81] Consequently, one can argue that Num. 19 lays the ideational groundwork for the purification rituals of the church, not only communion and baptism observed by all believers but also the footwashing ceremony practiced by some Christian traditions (see John 13; 1 Tim. 5:10). These Christian cleansing rites put on display the death and resurrection of Christ by which sin and death are purified from the believer, incrementally now and exhaustively someday soon.[82] Some similarities between OT and NT purification rituals are highlighted by the texts compared in table 19.1.

Table 19.1. Purification Rituals Compared

Numbers 19	Christian Purification Rituals
Contamination from a corpse, the realm of death, defiles God's dwelling, adversely affecting his people's relationship with him (19:13, 20; cf. 5:3).	Contamination from sin, which leads to death, adversely affecting all humans in their relationship with God.[a]
Yahweh provides the ritual by which his people may be purified (vv. 1–22). The priest serves as an intermediary agent for Yahweh by sprinkling the blood, burning the purification offering (red cow), preparing the purifying water (v. 17).	God provides the means by which people may be purified. Christ, the Son of God, as the definitive high priest serves as an intermediary agent for the Father by sprinkling his own blood, offering his own body, and purifying with his blood and his word people from sin, guilt, and shame.[b]
The defiled person who does not wash is eliminated from the community (vv. 13, 20).	The sin-defiled person who is not washed by Christ is eliminated from the community forever.[c]
A clean person must gather the ashes and wash the defiled person and objects, and the defiled person becomes clean (vv. 9–10, 18–19, 21).	The only clean person, the Lord Jesus Christ, washes sin-defiled people who trust in his death and resurrection.[d]

a. Pre-ritual defiled state: Matt. 15:11, 18–20; Mark 7:1–8, 20–23; 1 Cor. 7:14; 2 Cor. 6:17; Eph. 5:3, 5; Col. 3:5–6; Jude 23; Rev. 14:4; 21:27.

b. Salvific (or sanctifying) priestly work exhibited in baptism and communion: John 6:63; 15:3; Eph. 5:26–27; Heb. 2:17; 3:1; 4:14–15; 5:1, 5, 10; 6:20; 7:26; 8:1, 3; 9:7, 11, 25; 13:11.

c. Rejected, ritual defiled state: John 13:10–11; Rev. 21:27.

d. Salvific (or sanctifying) washing exhibited in baptism and communion: Acts 22:16; 1 Cor. 5:7; 6:11; 7:1; 2 Tim. 2:21; Titus 2:14; 3:5; Heb. 9:10, 13, 14, 19; 10:22; James 4:8; 1 Pet. 1:2; 3:18; 1 John 1:7, 9; Rev. 7:14; 22:14 (cf. Mark 1:39–44; John 9:7–15; Matt. 10:8).

Paul's words to the believers at Corinth, even those who struggled with destructive sin, apply to every believer today: "And that is what some of you were. *But you were washed*" (1 Cor. 6:11). However, the justified, pure state

---

81. On this shaping power of religious rituals, see Alcorta and Sosis, "Ritual," 323–59.
82. See Dozeman, "Numbers," 152–53; Seebass, *Numeri*, 2:263.

of the believer does not nullify Christ's ongoing work of washing his bride and preparing her to meet him in person (Eph. 5:26–27). Nor does it negate believers' recurring need, after every defiling sin, to purify themselves until they see Jesus when he returns in glory (1 John 3:2–3).

20

Israelites Complain; Moses and Aaron Rebel; Edom Is Hostile; Aaron Dies

(20:1–29)

❧

Overview

Although the evidence may be circumstantial, it is intriguing that the editor and narrator of Num. 20 opens with the themes of Num. 19, namely, a dead body and water: "Miriam died and was buried there. Now there was no water for the community" (20:1c–2a).[1] Even so, the narrator gives no impression whatsoever that the people want water to obey Yahweh's orders and purify themselves in the aftermath of Miriam's death (à la Num. 19). Instead, echoing the post-exodus stories, the Israelites here complain to Moses and Aaron that they have no water to quench their deadly thirst (Exod. 15:22–27; 17:1–7). In the notice of v. 1, the editor reestablishes Kadesh as the geographical setting and then reports Miriam's death and interment without interpreting these events. In the opening story of vv. 2–14, the people complain that they have no water, and Yahweh graciously supplies it, but in the process Moses and Aaron fail to honor Yahweh's holiness in the eyes of the community. Tragically, because of their rebellion, the two renowned leaders forfeit their inheritance in the promised land.[2] In vv. 14–21 the scene shifts to the next leg of Israel's

---

1. See Leveen, "'Lo We Perish,'" 266–68.

2. Classically, the materials have been divided as v. 1 (P, JE); vv. 2–13, 22–29 (P); and vv. 14–21 (JE) (Gray, *Numbers*, 259–71; Noth, *Numbers*, 143–54; Schmidt, *Priesterschrift*, 207–11; Levine, *Numbers*, 1:483–85). Baden ("Numbers 20–21," 634–52) delineates a P narrative (v. 1*, 2, 3b–4, 6–13, 22b, 23–29) and a non-P narrative (vv. 1*, 3a, 5, 14–21, 22a). Albertz ("Buch Numeri . . . Tiel I," 174, 183) assigns vv. 14–21, 23b* to a post-Priestly layer. Boorer ("Numbers

319

travels. Moses asks the king of Edom if Israel may pass through Edom's territory, but Edom regards this as trespassing and dispatches a huge military force to prevent the Israelites from entering their land. The scene shifts again in vv. 22–29 to a historic moment on Mount Hor, just outside Edom's border. On the mountain, Moses transfers Aaron's high-priestly authority to Aaron's oldest surviving son, Eleazar. Since the Korah rebellion, Eleazar's role has been expanding and Aaron's diminishing (16:37–40; 19:3–5).[3] Now, just as Yahweh foretold, Aaron dies, and all Israel mourns his death for thirty days. The chapter is thus bookended by the deaths of Moses's two siblings (vv. 1, 28–29),[4] which conveys the disheartening post-Eden reality for every human but also serves as a portent of things to come for Moses himself.[5]

Translation

1Then the whole Israelite community entered the Zin wilderness in the first month, and the people stayed in Kadesh. Miriam died and was buried there.

2Now there was no water for the community,[6] so they gathered themselves together against Moses and Aaron.[7] **3**The people contended[8] with Moses, saying, "If only we had died when our brothers died before Yahweh! **4**Why did you bring Yahweh's community into

---

13–14," 45–63) argues that in Num. 13–14 and 20:2–12 P[g] inverts the P[g] themes of the creation of the nation and its leadership in Exod. 6–14, 16, and 19ff. (Sinai). Specht ("Die Verfehlung," 273–313) marshals the evidence that 20:1–13 was an original Priestly narrative (perhaps with a foreign v. 3a) that is coherent and theologically dense. Blum (*Komposition des Pentateuch*, 271–76) attributes 20:1–13, 24; 27:12–14; and Deut. 32:48–52 to KP, whereas Knohl (*Sanctuary*, 94–96) and Awabdy ("Holiness Contribution," 251–56) assign these to H. Frevel (*Mit Blick*, 41, 381–82) contends for the death of Aaron (20:22–29) as P[g]. Achenbach (*Vollendung*, 302–44, 636) splits 20:14–21* between pre-Dtr and the theocratic revision and assigns 20:1–13*, 22b–29 to the Pentateuch redactor, with interspersed text from the Hexateuch redactor.

3. See Milgrom, *Numbers*, 157.

4. Cf. Leveen, *Memory*, 155.

5. Knierim and Coats (*Numbers*, 228–35) identify 20:1–13 as a story connected to the murmuring tradition, 20:14–19 as a negotiations report, and 20:20–29 as a death report.

6. "*Now (w) there was no water*" probably marks a disjunctive clause (*wəlōʾ-hāyâ mayim lāʿēdâ*; IBHS §39.2.3c).

7. Precisely as in Korah's rebellion in 16:3, this niphal wayyiqtol reciprocal serves "as a plural variation of the reflexive" (GBHS §3.1.2c) and is modified by a repeated, adversative *ʿal* phrase, meaning "*they complained among themselves* [*wayyiqqāhălû*] *against* [*ʿal*] Moses and *against* [*ʿal*] Aaron" (20:3; see v. 10). For English idiom, I follow LXX[ed] in not repeating the preposition.

8. The precise parallel of this wayyiqtol past narrative, "The people contended with Moses" (*wayyāreb hāʿām ʿim-mōšeh*), occurred in Exod. 17:2. The root *ryb (contend; always qal) occurs only twice in Numbers, here and in v. 13. Although it could be translated "quarreled" (ESV, NRSV, NIV, NJPS, EÜ; de Vaulx, *Nombres*, 220; Seebass, *Numeri*, 2:268; Schmidt, *Numeri*, 88; Levine, *Numbers*, 1:485), this could give the impression that Moses may have been in the wrong (and "strove" [DCH 7:478 first gloss of 2a] is archaic Eng. for this context). Rather, because

this wilderness so that we and our cattle should die here?[9] **5**Why did you bring us up out of Egypt only to bring us to this terrible place?[10] This is no place for grain or figs or vines or pomegranates,[11] and there's no water to drink!" **6**Moses and Aaron went from the presence of the assembly to the entrance of the meeting tent and threw themselves facedown, and the glory of Yahweh appeared to them.[12] **7**Then Yahweh spoke to Moses: **8**"Take the staff and assemble the community, you and your brother Aaron. Speak to that rock while in their presence,[13] and it will pour out its water.[14] Then you will bring them water from the rock; so you will give the community and their cattle water to drink."[15] **9**So Moses took the staff from Yahweh's presence, just as he had commanded him. **10**Then Moses and Aaron gathered the assembly together in front of the rock, and he said to them, "Listen, you rebels! Do we have to bring you water from this rock?"[16] **11**Then Moses raised his hand and struck the rock twice with his staff, and water gushed out.[17] So the community and their cattle drank. **12**Then Yahweh spoke to Moses and Aaron, "Because you both did not trust me by honoring me as holy[18] in the sight of the

---

the action is "unilaterally from the perspective of one of the parties" (*DCH* 7:478; i.e., Israel against Moses), I prefer "contended" (NET; or "attacked, lashed out" ≈ Cazelles, *Nombres*, 96).

9. The *l* of purpose + qal inf. const. modifying the main verb exposes what the community believes is Moses's lethal intention for them: "Why *did you bring* [*hăbē'tem*] Yahweh's community into this wilderness *so that* we and our cattle *should die* [*lāmût*] here?" (*GBHS* §4.1.10d).

10. Formally, "to this bad/evil place."

11. Polysyndeton (of *w*) slows down the discourse to emphasize each of the "apparent" alternatives, which compounds how desolate the Israelites think the place is (*BHRG* §40.23.4.1[2]; *GBHS* §4.3.3c).

12. This is the last of the four theophanies in Numbers that are presented with the same expression, "the glory of Yahweh appeared" (before in chaps. 14, 16, 17). See the third translation note on 14:10.

13. I take "while in their presence" (*la'ênêhem*, formally, "before their eyes") as an adverbial (with NLT, NJPS). Translating the articular prepositional obj. as "*the* rock" (*hassela'*; Seebass, *Numeri*, 2:268; Schmidt, *Numeri*, 88; Levine, *Numbers*, 1:485; EÜ, ESV, NRSV, NET, NJPS) might wrongly suggest to modern readers a rock already mentioned (anaphoric, *GBHS* §2.6.1). Rather, one imagines a proximate rock to which Yahweh refers Moses ("that rock"), in which case the article designates a particular "thing necessarily understood to be present or vividly portraying someone or something whose identity is not otherwise indicated" (*IBHS* §13.5e; Cazelles, *Nombres*, 97).

14. Formally, "and it will give its waters."

15. A hiphil causative, meaning "*so you will cause* the community and their cattle *to drink* [*wəhišqîtā*]."

16. Moses's rhetorical question uses a yiqtol obligation, "Do *we have to bring* [*nôṣî'*] you water from this rock?" (*GBHS* §3.2.2d.3). A mountain spring, such as Ain el-Qudeirat, could be the secondary cause of the miracle. The rocks of the region of Kadesh and Tel el-Qudeirat are marine sedimentary (Eocene) and a soft chalk (Senonian) (Aharoni, *Land*, 11–12; Monson, *Geobasics*, 12–13). See the comments at 13:26–29.

17. Formally, "and great waters came out."

18. The negated hiphil qatal could also be translated "believe (in me)" (ESV), but I prefer "trust (me)" (many versions) because the expression "believe in me" could give the wrong

Israelites, therefore you will not bring this community into the land I have given them." ¹³These are the waters of Meribah (contention),[19] because the Israelites contended with Yahweh, and he showed himself to be holy[20] among them.[21]

¹⁴Moses sent messengers from Kadesh to the king of Edom: "This is what your brother Israel says: 'You know all the hardships that we have experienced,[22] ¹⁵how our ancestors went down into Egypt, and we lived in Egypt a long time, and the Egyptians mistreated us[23] and our ancestors. ¹⁶We cried to Yahweh, and he heard our voice,[24] sent a

---

impression that Moses fails to believe that Yahweh exists. Rather, Moses fails to trust in Yahweh as he has revealed himself—especially in the Holiness collection of Lev. 17–26—as one who is holy and who has a covenant relationship, not merely with Moses, Aaron, and his sons, but also with the entire, holy Israelite community (hence, "in the sight of the Israelites"; for additional textual evidence that Holiness scribes contributed 20:1–13, 22–29 to the Hexateuch epic, see Awabdy, "Holiness Contribution," 251–56). The adverbial *l* + hiphil inf. const. (*ləhaqdîšēnî*) could indicate result (*GBHS* §3.4.1d), which one might infer from the variations of "to sanctify me" (*hagiasai me* LXX[ed] ≈ Schmidt, *Numeri*, 89; "to uphold/show/honor me as holy," ESV/ NET/NIV; "to show/demonstrate my holiness," NRSV/NLT/de Vaulx, *Nombres*, 226; "to affirm my sanctity," NJPS). The other possibility, which I prefer, is that it explains or provides the means of the preceding verbal action: "You both did not trust me *by honoring me as holy* [*ləhaqdîšēnî*]" (specification: *GBHS* §3.4.1g; similarly: "*which* would have affirmed my sanctity," Levine, *Numbers*, 1:486).

19. With LXX[ed] "water of dispute" (*hydōr antilogias*), I supply the otherwise hidden meaning of the toponym in parentheses: "Meribah (contention)" (similarly: "dispute water," EÜ; "which means arguing," NLT).

20. The wayyiqtol niphal (*wayyiqqādēš*) is not a stative, "he was holy"—an ontological reality that Yahweh already self-disclosed (Lev. 11:44–45; 19:2)—but a reflexive, not meaning "he sanctified himself/made himself holy" (already holy) nor exactly "he treated himself as holy" because Israel, Moses, and Aaron failed to do this (20:2–12) but rather "he showed himself to be holy among them" (*HALOT* 3:1072–75, gloss 2; *GBHS* §3.1.2c).

21. After v. 13, SP *and* 4Q27 interpolate a large passage, which shows that this Hebrew text form cannot be reduced to a late Samaritan revision. Nonetheless, the plus was secondary since the scribes adapt Deut. 3:24–28 and 2:2–6. The 4Q27 fragment is broken just before the bottom margin (col. XI of the scroll), then the next column (col. XII) is broken and lacks lines 1–12 but picks up only at v. 16 (MT), indicating that 4Q27 once likely contained the full plus appearing in the SP (see Ulrich, *Qumran*, 149). 4Q27 differs from SP in a few letters, mainly just fuller spellings than SP.

22. Formally, "all the hardships that have found us." "Hardships" (pl. of "*təlā'â*," *DCH* 8:635) appears four other times in the OT: Exod. 18:8; Neh. 9:32; Lam. 3:5; Mal. 1:13. Here in Num. 20:14–16, Moses narrates Israel's "hardships," referring foremost to their experience in Egypt. In the only other occurrence of "hardship" in the Pentateuch, the narrator remarks that Moses told his father-in-law of "all the hardship that had found them on the way" (*kol-hattəlā'â 'ăšer məṣā'ātam badderek*) just after Yahweh redeemed them out of Egypt (Exod. 18:8).

23. Formally, "*Egypt/Egyptians* [*miṣrayim*] mistreated us" (MT ≈ Tg[O PJ Neo] Syr), but the referential meaning is rightly conveyed by other witnesses: "*The Egyptians* mistreated us" (SP LXX[ed]).

24. LXX[ed] restates, ". . . the Lord and *the Lord* [*kyrios*] listened to our voice," probably influenced by Deut. 26:7.

messenger, and brought us out of Egypt.[25] Now we are here in Kadesh, a town on the edge of your territory. **[17]**Let us pass through your land.[26] We will not pass through a single field[27] or vineyard, nor will we drink water from any well.[28] We will follow the King's Highway.[29] We will not spread out[30] to the right or the left until we have passed through your territory.'" **[18]**But Edom said to him, "You will not pass through me, or I will come out to attack you with the sword."[31] **[19]**Then the Israelites said to him, "We will follow the highway,[32] and if we or our cattle drink your water,[33] we will pay for it.[34] We will only pass through on foot,[35] nothing else." **[20]**But he said, "You will not pass through."[36] Then Edom came out to attack them with a large and powerful force.[37] **[21]**Edom refused to give[38] Israel passage through their territory, so Israel turned away from them.

25. Contextually, the second, third, and fourth wayyiqtols indicate a string of results from the prior wayyiqtol action of the Israelites: "*We cried* [*wanniṣʿaq*] to Yahweh, *and* [as a result] *he heard* [*wayyišmaʿ*] our voice, *sent* [*wayyišlaḥ*] a messenger, *and brought us* [*wayyōṣiʾēnû*] out of Egypt" (consequential: *GBHS* §3.5.1b).

26. "*Please* let us pass through" (*naʿbərâ-nāʾ*; many versions) is not demanded by the particle *nāʾ* (Lambdin, *Biblical Hebrew*, 170).

27. Formally, "in/through a field or in/through vineyard" (also 21:22).

28. This source of water in Edom could be a well, pit, or cistern ("*bəʾēr* I," *DCH* 2:87). Probably due to homophony, SP wrote a synonym ("*bôr* I," *DCH* 2:129).

29. Formally, "we will go the road of the king" (*derek hammelek nēlēk*). The most important land bridge that connected Anatolia (Turkey), Egypt, and Mesopotamia (Iraq and Syria) was called "Way of the Sea" (*Via Maris*), an intracoastal route extending from Egypt through Canaan (today Gaza and Israel), Phoenicia (Lebanon), and Ugarit (Syria) to Anatolia (Turkey). Next in significance was the so-called King's Highway, or Transjordanian Highway, referred to first in the OT here in 20:17 (*derek hammelek*, then 21:22) and by the metonyms "(on) the highway" (*bamsillâ*, 20:19) and "the road to Bashan" (*derek habbāšān*, 21:33; Deut. 3:1). See Aharoni, *Land*, 54–57.

30. The formal meaning is sensible, "We will not spread out" (*lōʾ niṭṭeh*), but many ancient and modern translations adapt this to "We will not turn aside" (SP LXX[ed] 4Q27?; see Ulrich, *Qumran*, 149).

31. Formally, "or else with the sword I will come out to meet you."

32. "(On) the highway" (*bamsillâ*) is a metonym for the King's Highway referred to in v. 17 (see the fourth translation note there).

33. Formally, "and if your water we drink, I or my cattle." Perhaps to imply that Israel would not even touch Edom's water supply, other witnesses and most modern versions add a partitive "drink *any/of/from* of your water" (SP LXX[ed] 4Q27?; Ulrich, *Qumran*, 149).

34. Formally, "then I will give their price" (*wənātattî mikrām* MT 4Q27 SP). LXX[ed] "I will pay *you* a price" (*timēn soi*) could reflect a Hebrew variant (*mkr lkh*; so Ulrich, *Qumran*, 150), but Wevers (*Notes*, 331) calls it an ad sensum gloss by LXX[ed].

35. LXX[ed] here and earlier in the verse: "We will pass *along the mountain*" (see Wevers, *Notes*, 332).

36. 4Q27 includes "through me, or I will come out to attack you with the sword" ([*by p*]*n bḥ*[*r*]*b ṣʾ* [*lqr*]*ʾtk*[*h*]). This is probably a harmonization to v. 18 (LXX[ed] includes "through me").

37. Formally, "with a heavy and strong people"; see the second translation note on 21:23.

38. The verb "*refused* to give" (*waymāʾēn . . . nətōn*) occurs always in the piel (16× in the Pentateuch), and in Numbers it appears first here, then twice to recount, in Balaam's words

²²The whole Israelite community traveled from Kadesh and came to Mount Hor. ²³And Yahweh spoke to Moses and Aaron at Mount Hor, by the border of the land of Edom:³⁹ ²⁴"Aaron will be gathered to his people,⁴⁰ for he will not enter the land I have given to the Israelites because both of you rebelled against my word⁴¹ at the waters of Meribah.⁴² ²⁵Take Aaron and his son Eleazar, and lead them up Mount Hor.⁴³ ²⁶Remove⁴⁴ Aaron's garments and put them on his son Eleazar, and Aaron will be gathered to his people⁴⁵ and will die there." ²⁷So Moses did as Yahweh commanded, and they went up Mount Hor⁴⁶ in the sight of the whole community. ²⁸Moses⁴⁷ removed Aaron's garments and put them on his son Eleazar. So Aaron died there on top of the mountain. And Moses and Eleazar came down from the mountain. ²⁹When the whole community saw that Aaron had died, the whole house of Israel mourned for Aaron for thirty days.⁴⁸

---

and actions, when Yahweh refused to let him to go with Balak's officials (22:13, 14; "*m'n*," *DCH* 5:119).

39. After v. 21 the rest of the line is blank in 4Q27 (col. XII), and the next line and a half (all of vv. 22–23) is written in red ink, indicating that the scribe regarded v. 22 as beginning a new unit of discourse (Ulrich, *Qumran*, 150).

40. A euphemism for death, using a niphal incomplete pass., "Aaron *will be gathered* [*yēʾāsēp*] to his people" (*IBHS* §23.2.2e). The pass. voice does not necessarily imply human agency; natural causes instead would transport Aaron to his deceased ancestors, as in "from dust you are, and to dust you will return" (Gen. 3:19). Or Yahweh is the implied agent (1 Sam. 2:6; cf. Deut. 32:39; Ps. 139:8; Eccles. 12:7). 4Q27 and SP can read "Aaron will be gathered *to with him* [*ʾel ʾimmô*]," but the preferred translation is "to his people" (vocalized *ʾel-ʿammô* as in Exod. 1:9; see also SP Deut. 32:50; cf. here *ʾel-ʿammāyw* MT ≈ LXX*ᵉᵈ*).

41. Formally, "you [pl.] rebelled against my mouth" (*mərîtem ʾet-pî*). The root of this qal qatal is **mrh*, which occurs in the Pentateuch in Num. 20 and 27 and then again in Deuteronomy, especially in its frames (Deut. 1:26, 43; 9:7, 23, 24; 21:18, 20; 31:27).

42. In v. 13, LXX*ᵉᵈ* reads "water of *dispute* [*antilogias*]," but here in v. 24 it employs a synonym, "the water of reviling [*tēs loidorias*]."

43. Likely to assimilate to v. 27, LXX*ᵉᵈ* inserts "up Mount Hor *before all the congregation*."

44. Instead of simple *wə* + masc. sg. hiphil impv. (*wəhapšēṭ* MT ≈ LXX*ᵉᵈ*), 4Q27 and SP have a 2nd masc. sg. weqatal, still imperatival, "You must take off" (4Q27 is partial: *ṭth[whpš]*). This variant may have arisen to improve the syntax by harmonizing to the immediately following weqatal form, *wəhilbaštām* (and put them on; MT).

45. This Hebrew euphemism for death is in an abbreviated form, "and be gathered" (*yēʾāsēp*), but most modern translations supply "to his people," implied from Yahweh's word in the context in v. 24, "Let Aaron be gathered *to his people* [*ʾel-ʿammāyw*]."

46. Probably to sharpen the narration of Moses's obedience to the divine command (v. 27a), SP and LXX*ᵉᵈ* express a transitive (hiphil/aorist) and obj., "He [Moses] brought them up."

47. LXX*ᵉᵈ* "And *he* stripped" removes a redundancy with Moses as stated in v. 27 (Wevers, *Notes*, 336).

48. A qal fientive verb with Aaron as its direct obj.: formally, "the whole house of Israel *wept* Aaron [*wayyibkû ʾet-ʾahărōn*] for thirty days."

Interpretation

20:1–13. Israel has been stationed at Kadesh Barnea since 12:16 or 13:26, but in 20:1a–b the narrator indicates that they stopped at Kadesh in the Zin wilderness, contiguous to the southern boundary of Canaan if not actually inside Canaan (13:21; Josh. 15:1, 3).[49] There is no reason to take Kadesh as a location different from Kadesh Barnea;[50] the editors of 13:26 and 20:1 are simply working with independent Kadesh/Kadesh Barnea stories. Here Kadesh evokes the memory of a cursed place, marked by painful, formative events in the biblical witnesses.[51] Their arrival in "the first month" lacks a year (cf. Exod. 19:1), but it is reasonable to infer that it was the beginning of the fortieth year after the exodus.[52] The end of the exodus generation is pending (14:34). At Kadesh, Miriam dies and is buried there (v. 1c). After Yahweh delivered the Israelites from Egypt, Miriam the prophetess led the women in celebration through tambourines and dancing, and she sang to Israel in worship of Yahweh: "Sing to Yahweh! For he is highly exalted. The horse and its rider he has hurled into the sea!" (Exod. 15:21). After Israel left Sinai and came to Hazeroth, Miriam and Aaron criticized Moses, and she was struck with a skin disease, but through Aaron's begging and Moses's intercession, Yahweh healed her (Num. 12).[53] Mourning for Aaron's death closes out the chapter (20:28–29), but here at its opening, the fact that Miriam's death is included in the Torah suggests that she was a significant leader.[54]

The opening full story, vv. 2–13, echoes some of the language of Exod. 16,[55] but more so the language and plot of Exod. 17:1–7, before the Israelites reached Sinai. (In the comparison table, the actual wording of the text is italicized, and the bold font marks the meaningful differences.)

Exodus 17:1–7 (adapting NET)	Numbers 20:2–13
There was no water for the people to drink (v. 1).	There was no water for the community (v. 2).
	They gathered themselves against Moses and Aaron (v. 2; see the second translation note there).

---

49. The Zin desert (*midbar-ṣin*, 13:21; 20:1; 27:14; 33:36; 34:3, 4; Deut. 32:51) is not to be confused with the post-exodus Sin desert, between Elim and Rephidim (Exod. 16:1; 17:1); see Rasmussen, *Atlas*, 106, 302.

50. Rasmussen, *Atlas*, 289.

51. Buis, "Qadesh," 268–85.

52. Aaron dies, according to 33:38, on the first day of the fifth month. See Milgrom, *Numbers*, 164.

53. Miriam was already identified as Aaron's sister (Exod. 15:20) and will be identified as Aaron and Moses's sister in Numbers' second census (26:59; and 1 Chron. 6:3).

54. Seebass, *Numeri*, 2:304; Leveen, *Memory*, 150.

55. Otto ("Priesterschrift," 15–16) argues that Exod. 16 and Num. 20 form a frame around P.

Exodus 17:1–7 (adapting NET)	Numbers 20:2–13
The people contended with Moses (v. 2).	The people contended with Moses (v. 3a; see the translation note there).
"Give us water to drink!" Moses said to them, "Why do you contend with me? Why do you test Yahweh?" But the people were very thirsty there for water, and they complained against Moses and said, "Why did you bring us up out of Egypt—to kill us and our children and our cattle with thirst?" (vv. 2–3)	"If only we had died when our brothers died before Yahweh! Why did you bring Yahweh's community into this wilderness so that we and our cattle should die here? ⁵Why did you bring us up out of Egypt only to bring us to this terrible place? This is no place for grain or figs or vines or pomegranates, and there's no water to drink!" (vv. 3b–5; see the translation notes on vv. 4–5)
Moses cried out to Yahweh, "What will I do with this people? They are about to stone me!" (v. 4)	Moses and Aaron went to the meeting-tent entrance, threw themselves facedown, and Yahweh's glory appeared to them (v. 6; see the translation note there).
Yahweh tells Moses to go before the people **with some of the elders** and take the staff with which he struck the Nile (v. 5).	Yahweh tells Moses to take the staff and assemble the community **with Aaron** (v. 8).
"I will be standing before you there on the rock in Horeb, and you will strike the rock, and water will come out of it so that the people may drink" (v. 6).	
	"Speak to that rock while in their presence, and it will pour out its water. Then you will bring them water from the rock, so you will give the community and their cattle water to drink." (v. 8; see the translation notes there)
So Moses did this in the sight of **the elders** of Israel (v. 6).	
	Moses and Aaron rebel against Yahweh by not honoring Yahweh as holy in the sight of the community, but Yahweh still causes water to flow from the rock, from which the community and their cattle drank (vv. 9–12).
He called the name of the place **Massah (testing)** and Meribah (contention), because the Israelites contended with **and tested Yahweh**, saying, "Is Yahweh among us or not?" (v. 7)	
	These are the waters of Meribah (contention), because the Israelites contended with Yahweh, **and he showed himself to be holy among them** (v. 13; see the first translation note there).

Traditionally, source analysts have seen Num. 20 as a doublet of Exod. 17, providing two perspectives on the same event.[56] Thus, complaining of no water results in Yahweh's provision by Moses's staff and the identical toponym, Meribah, meaning "contention." However, Exod. 17 locates Moses's actions in the presence of the elders, whereas Num. 20 puts Moses in the presence of the entire community. The theological focus of Exod. 17 is that the Israelites put Yahweh to the test (*nsh), to which Num. 14:22 and Deuteronomy ostensibly allude.[57] By contrast, Num. 20 says nothing of testing Yahweh but culminates with both Yahweh's and the narrator's evaluation that Moses and Aaron failed to honor Yahweh as holy (deity), but Yahweh preserved his holy reputation in the community (vv. 12–13).[58] Of course, this is not the final word of the narrative of God, culminating in the NT witnesses to the Messiah. In the end, the reigning God and his Lamb will receive honor, not only in the eyes of his people, but also from every creature in heaven, on earth, and under the earth (Rev. 5:13). From Num. 20 also arises a second message, less overt, but present: In the face of the ingratitude and distrust of Yahweh's people (vv. 2–5), Yahweh still graciously provides for their survival (vv. 8, 11; see the third translation note on v. 8; cf. 1 Cor. 10:4).[59] Jesus likewise affirmed the Father's goodness toward his evil children (Matt. 7:11; Luke 11:13, giving the Holy Spirit). In fact, this is not restricted to his people, for even the unrighteous and unjust daily receive God's providential goodness (Matt. 5:45).

20:14–21. In this short story, the Israelites request to travel through Edom's territory, but Edom opposes the Israelites with force. Moses sends messengers from Kadesh to present this request to Edom's king (v. 14). Their message recapitulates Israel's history,[60] but it is highly selective for the purpose of compelling the Edomite king to grant the Israelites safe passage through his

56. JE/non-P in Exod. 17 and P in Num. 20 (Lehming, "Massa und Meriba," 71–74; Boorer, *Priestly Narrative*, 77–79; Baden, "Violent Origins," 115). De Vaulx (*Nombres*, 221–23) sees Exod. 17 as the base text, which underwent an Elohistic (perhaps) and Priestly redaction in Num. 20:2–13. Similarly, Ska ("Old and New," 108) and Römer ("Egypt Nostalgia," 79–81) see Num. 20 as rewriting Exod. 17. Garton (*Mirages*, 202–35) maintains that the earliest form of Num. 20:1–13 derived from the same oral tradition from which Exod. 17:1–7 came, but then Num. 20:1–13 underwent five more stages of literary growth (*Fortschreibung*). Scharbert (*Numeri*, 78) sees the Pentateuchal redactor as splitting one event into two, Exod. 17 (J) and Num. 20 (P). Frevel (*Mit Blick*, 124) and Römer ("Egypt Nostalgia," 81) argue that a redactor has linked the two stories, while Blum (*Komposition des Pentateuch*, 271–76) avers that KP has skillfully coordinated Num. 20 and Exod. 17 as two stories of a single Meribah setting.

57. See Num. 14:22; Deut. 6:16; 33:8; Heb. 3:8. Blum (*Komposition*, 276–77) takes Num. 20:1–13, 24 as a midrash on Deut. 33:8 (cf. God testing Israel: Deut. 8:2, 16; 13:3; Judg. 2:22; 3:1, 4).

58. There is an *inclusio* of the story by "water" (v. 3) and "waters of Meribah" (v. 13); see Zeelander, "Closural Conventions," 338.

59. Milgrom, *Numbers*, 163.

60. Cf. Deut. 26:5–9; see Gertz, *Tradition*, 39; Kilchör, *Mosetora*, 306.

domain, which spanned from the Dead Sea to the Gulf of Aqaba.[61] The message, therefore, stresses four points.

First, Israel is "your brother"; that is, Jacob/Israel's biological, older brother was Esau, progenitor of the Edomites.[62] After Jacob, the younger, gained ascendancy over Esau by taking Esau's birthright and blessing, Esau forgave Jacob, and they parted from each other peacefully (Gen. 33:15–16). In Deuteronomy, it is precisely, and maybe only, because Esau was Jacob's brother that third-generation resident Edomites could join the assembly of Yahweh (Deut. 23:7).[63] In the ANE, "hospitality, then, is directed at those relatively unknown travelers who are assumed to be members of one's larger community, but not immediately recognized as such."[64] By using the appellative "your brother," Israel's messengers are reminding the Edomites of their responsibility to show conventional hospitality.

Next, the messengers recount Israel's suffering as they lived a long time in Egypt, inferably as foreigners, and how the Egyptians mistreated them and their ancestors (vv. 14–15; see the translation notes there).[65] The subtext is that the messengers are appealing to the Edomite king to show empathy to his fellow humans.

Then the story turns to Israel's deity, Yahweh, who hears their cry and rescues them out of Egypt, intimating that Yahweh, a powerful deity, is on Israel's side (v. 16; see the second translation note there).[66]

Finally, they explain their current residence in Kadesh, "a town on the edge of your territory," implying that they had been living peacefully and unnoticed as Edom's proximate neighbors (v. 16).

Having made a strong case for kinship, empathy, deity, and proximity, the Israelites now submit their modest request: Permit us to pass through your territory. They promise to circumvent fields and vineyards (not trampling or stealing), abstain from drinking well water, and remain exclusively en route until they exit Edom (v. 17; see the translation notes there). Exposing their whereabouts at all times, the Israelites declare that they will traverse the famous King's Highway (a.k.a. the Transjordan Highway), an international

---

61. Walton and Matthews, *Genesis–Deuteronomy*, 197.

62. Gen. 25:30; 32:3; 36:1, 8, 16, 17, 19, 21, 31, 32, 43.

63. See Awabdy, *Immigrants*, 69–83; Kilchör, *Mosetora*, 259. Whereas W. Oswalt ("Revision des Edombildes," 218–32) reads 20:14–21 as a reinterpretation of Deut. 23, so that belligerent Edom moves from being accepted into Yahweh's assembly (Deut. 23:7) to being excluded like Amon and Moab (23:3–6).

64. Hobbs, "Hospitality," 24. Bridge ("Polite Israel," 77–88) applies politeness theory to this story to draw out the nuances of Israel's strategically polite request, which was met with Edom's impolite response, reinforcing the biblical depiction of Edom as Israel's "bad brother."

65. Exodus and pre-exodus generations (Exod. 1:8), but clearly not Jacob and Joseph's generations, when they lived favorably as immigrants (Gen. 46–Exod. 1:7).

66. In 20:16, the "angel" (*mal'āk*) who delivers Israel represents Yahweh (Stein, "Der Engel," 292).

route extending from the Transjordan highlands to the ancient city of Damascus, Syria.[67]

Instead of the expected favorable response, "Edom," now acting collectively as a stereotyped enemy,[68] delivers an ultimatum: If you pass through, I will attack you with the sword (v. 18). Formally, the wording is "or else with the sword I will come out to meet you"; instead of greeting the Israelites with hospitality, the Edomites will greet them with war (see the translation note on v. 18). The Israelites resubmit their request, reaffirming that they will stay on the highway (see the first translation note on v. 19) and adding that they will even purchase water for themselves and their cattle, implying a boost to the local economy (v. 19). They will go on foot, perhaps implying that they have no horses or chariots and thus are not a serious threat (cf. Ps. 20:7). Edom not only reasserts its ban but comes out to attack Israel with a powerful force (vv. 20–21; see the translation notes there). Unlike battles to come—in Transjordan against Sihon and Og (Num. 21) and in Canaan against its residents—Yahweh never orders the Israelites to fight the Edomites, so Israel retreats to take another route (cf. Deut. 2:3–8).[69] Edom's adversarial response seems to portend their own destruction (see Num. 24:18–19),[70] unless somehow Edom, Jacob's brother, is protected by Yahweh, who allotted Edom their specific territory.[71] As Edom keeps its word of ultimatum and comes out to attack the Israelites, the reader wonders when Yahweh will keep *his word* to Abraham's descendants: "The one who treats you lightly I will curse" (Gen. 12:3b; see Obadiah).

20:22–29. On Mount Hor, beside Edom's border, Moses transfers Aaron's high-priestly authority to his son Eleazar; then Aaron dies, and Israel mourns for one month. Since at least as far back as 13:26, the Israelites have known in Kadesh the tragedy of rebellion, disinheritance, and death. In the narrative flow, they seem to have returned to Kadesh (Num. 20:1), and now they will leave this site for good. They probably migrated northward—the quickest path into Canaan, which the explorers took through the Negev—and first came to stop at Mount Hor, by the border of the territory of Edom (vv. 22–23).[72]

---

67. See the fourth translation note on Num. 20:17 and Aharoni, *Land*, 54–57.

68. Cf. the collective mob in 11:4; Sternberg, *Poetics*, 327; Berlin, "Characterization," 78.

69. Sumner ("Israel's Encounters," 216–28) regards Num. 20:14–21 (JE) and Deut. 2:2–8, 29 (D) as too different to be related, whereas Glatt-Gilad ("Edomite-Israelite Encounter," 441–55) sees the Deuteronomist (Deut. 2) reworking the JE tradition (Num. 20) for ideological reasons. MacDonald ("Edom and Seir," 83–103) argues that 20:14–21 was composed based on the Sihon accounts in Num. 21:21–24 and Deut. 2:26–37. To these influences on 20:14–21, Van Seters (*Life of Moses*, 386–93) would add Judg. 11. Dozeman ("Geography," 187) notes that 20:14–21 does not correlate with 14:25 or 21:4 and so may have been a post-Priestly addition.

70. B. Anderson ("Edom," 38–51) argues that the two negative portraits of Edom, 20:14–21 and 24:18–19, are literarily connected.

71. See Deut. 2:4–8; cf. Awabdy, *Immigrants*, 147–48.

72. See Rasmussen, *Atlas*, 106.

At the mountain, Yahweh spoke to Moses and Aaron, foretelling that Aaron would die, euphemistically described as being "gathered to his people" (see the first translation note on v. 24), and that he would not enter the land Yahweh has given to the Israelites (v. 24). The reason for this disinheritance, Yahweh said earlier (v. 12), is because Moses and Aaron did not honor Yahweh as holy (deity) in the eyes of the people, which is reinforced here by the verdict "because both of you rebelled against my word at the waters of Meribah" (v. 24). In this theological reflection on vv. 10–13, Yahweh indicates that the great prophet and priest broke the covenant of the deity they worship and serve.[73] Although one might infer that for Aaron and Moses to be disinherited, they must also die outside the land (v. 12), here Yahweh announces, and then by implication actualizes, Aaron's death. Aaron's final journey is a mountain climb, just as Abraham thought Isaac's climb would be final (Gen. 22).

On this mountain peak, Moses transfers Aaron's high-priestly authority to his oldest living son, Eleazar. Divine orders are met with precise obedience, led by Moses (v. 27), in the prescribed order:

> Take Aaron and his son Eleazar and lead them up Mount Hor. (v. 25)
>   Remove Aaron's garments [and]
>   put them on Eleazar.
>   Aaron will die. (v. 26; see the first translation note on v. 24)
>   They went up Mount Hor in the sight of the community. (v. 27)
>   Moses removed Aaron's garments [and]
>   put them on Eleazar.
>   Aaron died on top of the mountain. (v. 28)

Moses takes the priestly garments with which he once clothed Aaron at the base of Mount Sinai and places them on Eleazar to confer his new status.[74] Since Sinai, Eleazar would have been wearing a tunic (wrapped with a sash) and a headband (Lev. 8:13), but Moses probably replaced these with Aaron's high-priestly tunic wrapped with a different sash (8:7). Most distinctively, Moses would have then clothed Eleazar with Aaron's robe and fastened the ephod with a decorated band (8:7). Over these, Moses would have hung a breastpiece into which the Urim and Thummim were inserted. Finally, he would have placed the turban on Eleazar and affixed a gold plate, the holy diadem, on its front side (8:8). These had already been anointed and consecrated (8:10), but it is conceivable that Moses anointed Eleazar for his new office of high-priestly service (as in Lev. 8:12). In Num. 20:29d, a new era begins, more bitter than sweet, as Moses and his nephew Eleazar descend the mountain

---

73. See the "Implications" essay below, "What Was the Sin of Moses and Aaron?"
74. See also Eleazar's role in Joshua's ordination ritual in 27:15–23.

without their brother and father (Aaron), and at the mountain base they will not be welcomed by their sister and aunt (Miriam). The old generation fades as the new rises.[75] The reader wonders when it will be Moses's turn to die, for he too rebelled and was disinherited (20:11–12).[76] For now, it is only fitting that for such a man as Aaron—divinely chosen, imperfect, but a servant of the Israelites for many years (Exod. 4:14)—the community mourns ritually, not just for the conventional seven days, but for thirty days (v. 29).[77] Yet the story does not end here, because God's promise to Abraham in Gen. 17 of a generational succession of children reaches beyond even Moses and Aaron.[78]

Implications

What Was the Sin of Moses and Aaron?

Since the earliest reception of the story that now appears as Num. 20:2–13, interpreters have struggled to identify the nature of Moses and Aaron's sin. Why was their violation so offensive to Yahweh that he would respond by disinheriting them? After all, this was Yahweh's unrivaled prophet (Num. 12) and undisputed high priest (Num. 17). And, yes, Yahweh does disinherit them. In Num. 18:20–26, the Levites, including Moses and Aaron, will not inherit territory among the tribes in Canaan because the tithes of the Israelites and Yahweh himself are their inheritance. By contrast, Num. 20:2–13, 20:23–29, and 27:12–14 present a different view: the Israelites of the new generation, with a few from the old (Joshua and Caleb), will receive from Yahweh the gift of the land, but Aaron and Moses, because of their rebellion, are disinherited and will die outside the land.

We might begin by asking whether Yahweh hunting down Moses in Exod. 4:24–26 provides any insight for us here. Indeed, there are several structural and thematic parallels with the obscure scene of Exod. 4:24–26, where Moses disobeys in the matter of circumcision, and Yahweh seeks to kill him,[79] but that story is literarily independent and does not explain the contravention of a different nature here. The question at hand is not why Yahweh—who is "slow to anger and abounding in loyal love, forgiving iniquity and rebellion"— punished these leaders, because Yahweh is justified in "punishing the children for the iniquity of the fathers" (Num. 14:18*). Rather, the question is why their infraction deserved this punishment, the devastating loss of their land share

75. Olson, *Death of the Old*, 93.
76. Schmidt ("P in Deuteronomium 34," 475–94) has argued that P's (better H's) account of Aaron's death prepares for Moses's death in Deut. 34.
77. As for Moses (Deut. 34:8). See the translation note on Num. 20:29; Walton and Matthews, *Genesis–Deuteronomy*, 197.
78. Seebass, *Numeri*, 2:304.
79. Burnside, "Moses Banned," 111–60.

promised long ago to the patriarchs. The Deuteronomists deflect this question by presenting Moses as blaming the Israelites for the loss of his inheritance: "But Yahweh was angry with me because of you and would not listen to me. . . . And Yahweh was angry with me because of you, and he swore that I would not cross the Jordan, and that I would not enter the good land that Yahweh your God is giving to you as an inheritance" (Deut. 3:26; 4:21–22). Jerome (4th–5th cent. CE) also minimizes their offense from a human point of view, deducing that if Aaron and Moses "seemed to waver" and lost their entry to the land, then the rest of us, "bent under the burden of sin, shall be far less able to cross the river Jordan."[80] While these perspectives are legitimate, the story itself raises a question that begs for an answer: What exactly did Moses and Aaron do wrong that caused Yahweh to disinherit them?

Historically, interpreters have identified the sin of Moses and Aaron as relating to (1) the speech of Moses, (2) abusing Aaron's staff, (3) shirking leadership responsibilities, (4) the speech Moses uttered while performing the water miracle, or (5) striking the rock.[81] These five primary views, with countless secondary views, suggest that the narrator may have deliberately left the precise sin of Moses and Aaron ambiguous, even as, for example, the sin of Nadab and Abihu was probably intentionally left ambiguous.[82] The ambiguity here stems from the fact that it was likely not just one action but a combination of things performed in the people's sight that constituted the devastating sin that led to their disinheritance: striking the rock twice, when Yahweh said to speak to it (vv. 8, 11), and verbally berating Israel (v. 10). As Rabbi Judah Loew ben Bezalel, Maharal of Prague (16th–17th cent. CE), deduced, "Behold, both acts—the declaration of 'hear now you rebels,' and striking the rock—are the opposite of faith. This is why you will find that sometimes our Sages say that the sin was in striking the rock twice, and sometimes in declaring 'hear now you rebels,' because they are one thing. At the moment when God did for them such a miracle, they [Aaron and Moses] should have grown in their faith and trust, and with that faith and trust there is no place for anger."[83]

This gets us closer to the sin of Moses and Aaron, but not close enough, because in v. 12 Yahweh himself explicates to Moses and Aaron the essence of their offense. The language and ideology that Yahweh employs here reflect that of the Holiness collection of Lev. 17–26.[84] There are basically two phrases in v. 12 that expose the nature of Moses and Aaron's sin. First, "You both did not trust me" (*lō'-he'ĕmantem*) is another way of saying, "You have broken my

---

80. Lienhard, *Numbers*, 239.

81. Lim, *Sin of Moses*, 106–33.

82. With G. Anderson ("Nadab and Abihu," 1–19), the ambiguity of the "strange fire" illustrated that the divine presence could not be conjured by some magic ritual.

83. Ben Bezalel, *Gur Aryeh on Bamidbar*, online.

84. See Awabdy, "Holiness Contribution," 251–56.

covenant" (v. 12; see the translation note there).[85] In the Hittite suzerain treaty stipulations, "The vassal must hold lasting and unlimited trust in the King,"[86] and this standard of trust is also presumed in the later (first-millennium) treaties. In three subsequent reflections on Moses and Aaron's collaborative sin, Yahweh introduces two additional terms with covenantal overtones: "because *both of you rebelled* [*mərîtem*] against my word" (20:24; see the second translation note there), and "because *both of you rebelled* [*mərîtem*] against me" (27:14), and "because *you both were unfaithful* [*məʿaltem*] to me" (Deut. 32:51).[87]

By analogy, unfaithfulness or disloyalty was a primary impetus for forming international treaties and loyalty oaths in the ANE. For instance, in Esarhaddon's Succession Treaty, nine times the king condemns future rebellion and insurrection against his son and successor, Assurbanipal.[88] Moses and Aaron have broken the covenant and therefore deserve to die in the land of their enemies, outside the promised land, as Yahweh indicated in the curses of Lev. 26:33, 38.[89] Yahweh will keep his word: Aaron dies among inhospitable Edomites (20:14–29) and belligerent Canaanites (21:1–3), and Moses dies in the land of Moab (Deut. 34:4–6).

Second, the way they did not trust Yahweh, how they broke the covenant, Yahweh says was "by not honoring me as holy in the sight of the Israelites" (Num. 20:12). Moses and Aaron failed to honor Yahweh *as deity* in the sight of the people,[90] and we see this in the story in three distinct ways. As a recurring motif, the storyteller and Yahweh are fundamentally concerned about Yahweh's reputation as a powerful and gracious deity *in the sight and presence of the community*.[91] (1) With the Israelites gathered and watching, Moses and Aaron did not obey Yahweh when they struck the rock twice instead of speaking to it as Yahweh specifically told them to do (vv. 8, 11). (2) Instead of gladly channeling Yahweh's grace to the people—grace that Yahweh alone holds the prerogative to give whenever and however he wants (14:17–20)—Moses cheapens this grace by his invective "Listen, you rebels!" (v. 10). (3) Yahweh never ordered Moses and Aaron to speak to the Israelites, and when they do, they subvert the status of Yahweh as deity: "Listen, you rebels! *Do we have to bring you water from this rock?*" (v. 10; see the translation note there). By these words, Moses, who is highly honored by Yahweh (7:89; chap. 12),

---

85. Novick ("[*hʾmyn*]," 577–83, esp. 580) argues that the meaning of the verb is assent: "You did not obey [my request] to sanctify me."

86. Mendenhall, "Covenant Forms," 59.

87. On **mʿl*, see the comments on 5:11–31.

88. Parpola and Watanabe, *Neo-Assyrian Treaties*, online.

89. See Awabdy, "Holiness Contribution," 254.

90. On Yahweh as deity and holy (**qdš*), see Clines's quotation in the comments on 4:1–14.

91. Explicitly in vv. 8 [2×], 10, 12, 13; see the first translation note on v. 8; Milgrom, *Numbers*, 166.

has foolishly elevated himself to a divine status: "Whether the 'we' reflects a triunity of Moses, Aaron, and Yahweh, or a dyad of Moses and Aaron acting independently of Yahweh, this condescending speech violates the conviction of H in Lev. 17–26 that not only Moses, Aaron, and the dwelling place but also the entire Israelite community and the divine land grant of Canaan are holy to Yahweh as well."[92] Also, the narration "Moses raised his hand" (v. 11) could be read figuratively as Moses's intention to display his power over Yahweh.[93] In fact, not just this subtle gesture but also a combination of details present Moses as an illustration of one who acts defiantly (with a high hand), insults Yahweh, and therefore must be cut off from the community (Num. 15:30–31).[94] In the narrator's evaluative conclusion, he asserts that Yahweh "showed himself to be holy among them" (v. 13; see the second and third translation notes there). By demonstrating his power to bring water from the rock and his grace to do it for his complaining people, Yahweh displays his holiness, his deity, to all the community.

What, then, was the catastrophic sin of Moses and Aaron? By their actions and words, and presumably their thoughts,[95] they committed the paradigmatic human sin of taking Yahweh's honor as deity (Gen. 3:4–7; Rom. 1:21a–b). In Num. 20 Yahweh is fundamentally concerned about his reputation as deity in the perception of his covenant people, and he alone is worthy to have this concern (Isa. 42:8). Therefore the medieval French Rabbi Rashi was probably right to infer that, although Moses's words in Num. 11:22 may have been more offensive to Yahweh in their content, because Moses spoke these words *where all Israel were standing by*, Scripture [God] does not spare him because of the Hallowing of the Divine Name."[96] So in the end, Jerome was wrong to state that Moses and Aaron merely "seemed to waver," but he was right to frighten us with our own propensity toward taking the glory that belongs to God alone, and thus he drives us to cling to Christ and not forsake our share in the eternal inheritance.

---

92. Awabdy, "Holiness Contribution," 252.
93. K. Wong, "Numbers 20,11," 397–400.
94. Sonnet, "NB 20,11," 535–43.
95. "For out of the overflow of the heart, the mouth speaks" (Luke 6:45).
96. Rashi, "On Numbers 20:12" (emphasis added).

21

Defeating Arad's King;
Healing by a Bronze Snake;
Defeating Sihon and Og

(21:1–35)

❧

Overview

The trauma of recent failure and death reverberates in the narrative. Miriam the prophetess has died (20:1), and Yahweh has disinherited his chosen leaders, Moses and Aaron, for their rebellion (20:2–13). Edom, Israel's brother (20:14), has denied Israel customary hospitality (20:14–21). Next, Aaron joins his sister among the dead, and in his place his son Eleazar is installed as Israel's new high priest (20:22–29). Aaron and Miriam symbolize the exodus generation doomed to die outside the promised land (14:20–35); Eleazar represents the new generation who will inherit the land (14:31). But the narrator's last word in the story line is devoted to mourning for Aaron for thirty days (20:29). Is there any present hope for the community, or is disinheritance and death their exclusive reality until the new generation fully replaces the old? To this painful question, Num. 21 interjects Yahweh's goodness toward his covenant people in each of the four scenes.[1] In the opening short story (vv. 1–3), Israel vows that if Yahweh delivers the Canaanite king of Arad into their hands, they will devote his cities to destruction (Hb. *ḥrm*). Yahweh listens to Israel and delivers them, and Israel obediently decimates the Canaanite cities for Yahweh.

---

1. Knierim and Coats (*Numbers*, 236, 241, 45) identify multiple genres in the chapter: etiology and battle report (vv. 1–3), story (vv. 4–9), itinerary related to royal annals with a song (vv. 10–20), battle report, victory song, and salvation oracle (vv. 21–34).

In vv. 4–9, Israel lapses into impatience and ingratitude, so Yahweh sends venomous snakes to kill the complainers. Surprisingly, the people confess that they have sinned, Moses intercedes for them, and Yahweh graciously supplies a means of healing, a bronze snake on a pole, for anyone bitten. In vv. 10–20, the narrator strings together a series of stops, including an ancient source and a song, to trace Israel's migration around Edom to arrive at a valley in Moab near Mount Pisgah. In vv. 21–35, the narrator recounts how Israel destroyed Sihon, king of the Amorites, and Og, king of Bashan, and remarks that Israel possessed their territories in Transjordan. Every one of the four scenes in Num. 21 reveals that Yahweh has not abandoned his recalcitrant people but is still predisposed to preserve them by grace (Num. 6:24–26; cf. 14:17–20).[2]

Translation

1When the Canaanite king of Arad, who lived in the Negev, heard that Israel was approaching along the road to Atharim, he attacked Israel and captured some of them.[3] **2**So Israel made a vow to Yahweh[4] and said, "If you will indeed deliver this people into our hand, then we will completely destroy[5] their cities."[6] **3**Yahweh listened to Israel's voice and delivered the Canaanites,[7] and they completely destroyed them and their cities. So they named that place Hormah (devoted to destruction).[8]

---

2. Historically, interpreters have associated vv. 1–3 with J (Noth, *Numbers*, 154); vv. 4–9 with E/non-P (Gray, *Numbers*, 274–78; Boorer, *Priestly Narrative*, 375–76); vv. 10–35 with JE and P (Gray, *Numbers*, 279–306) or vv. 10–20 as several unidentifiable sources, and vv. 21–35 as E (Noth, *Numbers*, 159–62). Achenbach (*Vollendung*, 636) rather assigns much of Num. 21 to unspecified pre-Dtr sources, whereas Van Seters (*Life of Moses*, 383–404) argues that 21:21–31 is a post-Dtr J composition dependent on Deut. 2 and Judg. 11 (similarly, Schmidt, "Sihon und Og," 314–33). Frevel ("Numbers 21," 111–35) argues convincingly that Num. 21, which functions as a pivot between chaps. 15–20 and 22–26, displays a collection of unidentifiable sources, probably oral in their most recent antecedent form, which were edited together by a redaction that implied the preexistence of a Hexateuch. In a similar vein, Scharbert (*Numeri*, 83) sees the Pentateuch redactor as combining multiple literary threads, and Römer ("Egypt Nostalgia," 81–83) takes 21:4–7 as a later redactional composition.

3. The second two wayyiqtol verbs are consequential (to the first), "When he heard . . . *then he fought* [*wayyillāḥem*] . . . *and he captured* [*wayyišb*]" (*GBHS* §3.5.1b).

4. Verses 1–2 contain two internals adjunct of the same verbal root, formally, "and captured some of them captive," and "and Israel vowed a vow to Yahweh," but these have no semantic value (*BHRG* §33.3[5]).

5. See the "Implications" essay below, "Devotion to Destruction."

6. Here, as in 20:19 et al., the speaker uses the 1st pers. sg. as the representative of his people or army, formally, "*into my hand* [*bəyādî*] *then I will totally destroy* [*wəhaḥăramtî*] their cities."

7. SP and LXX[ed] qualify the narration: "over the Canaanites into his hand/as subject to him."

8. "Hormah" (*ḥormâ*) relates to *ḥrm and *ḥērem, meaning "excluded from profane use and devoted to Yahweh for destruction" ("*ḥrm, ḥērem* I," *DCH* 3:317, 319). I supply the meaning in parentheses (with EÜ; cf. LXX[ed] "anathema, accursed").

4Then they traveled from Mount Hor along the route to the Sea of Reeds,[9] to go around the land of Edom, but the people became impatient along the way.[10] **5**And the people spoke against God and against Moses, "Why have you brought us up out of Egypt[11] to die in the wilderness, for there is no bread or water, and we detest this horrible food."[12] **6**So Yahweh sent venomous snakes[13] among the people, and they bit the people, and many people of Israel died. **7**Then the people came to Moses and said, "We have sinned because we spoke against Yahweh and against you. Pray to Yahweh[14] that he would take the

---

9. See the second translation note on 14:25.

10. An ingressive stative, idiomatically, "They *became*/*had become short* along the way" (*wattiqṣar nepeš-hāʿām baddārek*; *IBHS* §30.5.3b).

11. Perhaps influenced by Deut. 9:28, SP and LXX[ed] read "Why *have you brought us out* of Egypt" (*hwṣʾtnw* SP ≈ LXX[ed] vs. *heʿĕlîtunû* MT).

12. This attributive adjective is an OT hapax likely meaning "contemptible, worthless," which I render "horrible" (NLT; "*qəlōqēl* I," *DCH* 7:261), cognate to the verb, "to be light . . . be despised . . . viewed with contempt" (qal stative "*qll* I," *DCH* 7:256). This should not be confused with "cassia," a cinnamon-like spice ("*qəlōqēl*," *HALOT* 3:1106; "*qəlōqēl* II," *DCH* 7:261), attested in Ugaritic (*qlql*), Akkadian (*qulqull[i]ānu*), and Arabic (*qilqil*), since (1) this would require repointing the MT without the definite article to form a const., against the ancient versions with a definite adj. (LXX[ed] Vulg[ed] Tg Syr); and (2) this noun would generate a positive connotation, "cinnamon bread," which does not fit Israel's complaint in v. 5. The rendering "this dungheap bread" is plausible, based on an analogy to a curse formula discovered in an inscription from Tell Fekherye (Aster, "Num. 21:5," 341–58).

13. These "snakes" (*hannəḥāšîm*) that Yahweh has sent (piel factitive) are apposited by what I take to be their species (*haśśərāpîm*; *GBHS* §2.4.1). This species *śārāp* (seraph), found only a handful of times in the OT, means venomous snake, but maybe a fiery snake ("*śrp* I," *DCH* 8:197). It could relate to the homonym "seraphim" (*śərāpîm*, of "*śrp* II," *DCH* 8:197), known famously as Yahweh's celestial, six-winged creatures in Isa. 6:2, 6, and/or it could be a deverbal noun from **śrp* I (to burn; *HALOT* 3:1358–59). Elsewhere *śārāp* occurs only in Deut. 8:15 (probably an allusion to Num. 21) and in Isa. 14:29 and 30:6 (*śārāp məʿôpēp*, winged serpent). The word also occurs as a man's name in 1 Chron. 4:22 (see Goodman, "Seraphim," 213–15). For Num. 21:6, 8, Targum Onqelos prefers "burning snakes" (Tg[O] ≈ "fiery serpents," ESV), but this deverbal etymology is debatable. Instead, the context highlights the lethal bite of the snakes (vv. 6b–c, 8d, 9c), so I follow the lead of other ancient translations: "deadly snakes" (LXX[ed]) or "poisonous snakes" (Tg[PJ]; many modern translations). Venomous snakes local to Jordan and the northeastern Sinai Peninsula, the geographical setting of the Num. 21:4–9 episode, include the Arabian horned viper (*Cerastes gasperettii*), Palestine viper (*Daboia palaestinae*), Field's horned viper (*Pseudocerastes fieldi*), and black desert cobras (*Walterinnesia aegyptia*). The LD_{50} (lethal dose by which 50 percent of the test population dies) of the venom as an intraperitoneal injection [IP] from these four species is as follows: 1.285–1.75 mg per kg of body weight (Arabian horned viper); 1.9 mg/kg (Palestine viper); 0.675 mg/kg (Field's horned viper); and 0.45 mg/kg (black desert cobras); see Amr and Disib, "Venomous Snakes."

14. The hithpael stem of this impv. and of the subsequent wayyiqtol verb **pll* means "intercede" (*HALOT* 3:933–34, gloss 2a; "*pll* I," *DCH* 6:698, gloss 2), but "pray" expresses this in current idiomatic Eng. This verb appears in Numbers only here and in a parallel plot sequence in 11:2, in which Israel complains, Yahweh judges, and the people pray to Yahweh.

snakes away from us." So Moses prayed for[15] the people. [8]Yahweh said to Moses, "Make a venomous snake and put it on a pole.[16] When anyone who was bitten looks at it, they will live." [9]So Moses made a bronze snake and put it on a pole, so that if a snake had bitten someone, when they looked at the bronze snake, they lived.

[10]The Israelites traveled on and camped in Oboth. [11]Then they traveled from Oboth and camped at Iye Abarim, in the wilderness that faces Moab toward the sunrise.[17] [12]From there they traveled and camped in Wadi Zered.[18] [13]From there they traveled and camped on the other side of the Arnon, in the wilderness that extends into Amorite territory, since Arnon is the border of Moab, between Moab and the Amorites. [14]That is why it is said in "The Scroll of the Wars of Yahweh,"[19] ". . . Waheb[20] in Suphah and the wadis, the Arnon [15]and[21] the slope of the wadis that extends to the settlement of Ar,[22] and lie along Moab's border." [16]And from there they traveled[23] to Beer,[24] that is, the well where Yahweh told Moses, "Gather the people[25] so I can give them water." [17]Then Israel sang this song: "Spring up, O well! Sing to it! [18]The well that the tribal chiefs dug, the nobles[26] of the people opened with

15. The divine direct obj. implied in MT/SP is stated in LXX[ed], "Moses prayed *to the Lord* [*pros kyrion*] for the people," which draws attention to Moses's precise enactment of the people's request, "Pray to the Lord" (v. 7d).

16. Here and in v. 9 SP is definite: "on *the* pole."

17. Seebass ("Edom," 255–62) identifies a difficulty with "toward the sunrise" in the context of vv. 10–13 and suggests adopting LXX of v. 11 and viewing the last two words of MT as a gloss. After v. 11, 4Q27 and SP interpolate the standard superscription with a replication of Deut. 2:9.

18. After v. 12, 4Q27 and SP interpolate the standard superscription and Deut. 2:17–19.

19. Or "Chronicle of the Wars of Yahweh" (Levine, *Numbers*, 2:81). "*Book* [*sēper*] of the Wars of the LORD" (many versions) gives the impression of a codex (1st cent. CE and following), the precursor to our modern book, but the earliest source documents, which are now integrated into the Hebrew Scriptures, were likely written on individual sheets of papyrus and then later collected and joined to form a continuous scroll, usually containing one or sometimes two books (i.e., 4Q23). Of the Qumran scrolls, 8–13 percent were on papyrus, 85–90 percent on vellum (i.e., fine-grained animal skin), and 1.5 percent on bronze sheets; see van der Toorn, *Scribal Culture*, 9–26, 148–49; Arnold, "Number Switching," 171–72.

20. The ellipsis (. . .) is written (NIV, NJPS) because this clip from the scroll begins with the direct obj. marker without a verb, suggesting that the scroll contained the beginning of the sentence.

21. SP excludes "and" (*w*) but includes ". . . the Arnon. The slope of the wadis, *along with what* [*w'šr*] extends to the settlement of Ar."

22. Formally, "the dwelling of Ar" (*šebet 'ār*).

23. The verb here and in v. 18 is elided: formally, "And from there to Beer." It is possible that vv. 16 and 18 also imply encampment following the pattern of v. 13: "From there *they traveled and camped* [*nāsā'û wayyaḥănû*] on the other side of the Arnon."

24. "Beer" is a toponym, referring not to the drink but to a well, pit, or cistern ("*bə'ēr* I," DCH 2:87).

25. SP includes movement into Yahweh's proximity: "Gather the people *to me*."

26. The noun "nobles" (*nədîbê*) is in synonymous parallelism to "tribal chiefs" (*śārîm*, with "*śār* I," DCH 8:187, gloss 2.4, in a foreign land, but not clearly "representatives of the king":

their scepters, and with their staffs." From the wilderness they traveled to Mattanah, [19]and from Mattanah to Nahaliel, and from Nahaliel to Bamoth, [20]and from Bamoth to the valley that is in the region of Moab, near the top of Pisgah, which overlooks the wasteland.[27]

[21]Then Israel sent messengers to King Sihon of the Amorites,[28] saying, [22]"Let us pass through your land.[29] We will not spread out into a single field[30] or into a vineyard, nor will we drink water from any well, but we will follow the King's Highway[31] until we pass through your territory."[32] [23]But Sihon did not let Israel pass through his territory.[33] He gathered all his people[34] together and went out to fight Israel[35] toward the wilderness. When he came to Jahaz, he fought against Israel. [24]But Israel defeated him in battle[36] and took possession of his land from the Arnon to the Jabbok, as far as the Ammonites, since

---

HALOT 3:1350–52, gloss A1) and is modified by a partitive gen., "nobles [*who come*] *from the people*" (IBHS §9.5.1k). This noun (*nədîbê* from *nādîb*) occurs in the Pentateuch only here and with a different meaning in Exod. 35 (vv. 5, 22), where "all with *willing/generous* [*nədîb*] hearts" from the Israelites brought possessions for the construction of Yahweh's meeting tent (*DCH* 5:625).

27. "Wasteland" ("*yəšîmôn*," *DCH* 4:333, gloss 2), found in the Pentateuch three times (Num. 21:20; 23:28; Deut. 32:10), is not the common word for a desert or wilderness (*midbār*). Rather, the imagery of Deut. 32:10 suggests even here a negative image of desolation ("*yəšîmôn*," *DCH* 4:333). After v. 20, 4Q27 and SP interpolate the standard superscription with a replication of Deut. 2:24–25. In 4Q27 after v. 20 (col. XIII), the rest of the line is blank, and the next line is written in red ink, indicating that the scribe regarded v. 21 as initiating a new unit of discourse: "Then Yahweh said to Moses, 'Get up and cross Wadi Arnon. See, I have already delivered into your hands" (Ulrich, *Qumran*, 151).

28. SP and LXX[ed] add, "messengers . . . *with peaceful words*, saying."

29. Unlike the parallel language in 20:17, here the text reads, formally, "*Let me pass* [*'e'bərâ*] through your land. We will not spread out," where a single "Israel" begins by speaking as a collective voice (sg.).

30. See the second translation note on 20:17.

31. Regarding the King's Highway, see the fourth translation note on 20:17.

32. Derived from Deut. 2:27–29 and 2:8, SP supplies more detail: ". . . through your land. On the King's Highway I will go. I will not turn aside to the right or to the left. I will not spread out into any field or vineyard. You will sell me food for money, so that I may eat, and give me water for money, so that I may drink. Only let me pass through on foot, as the sons of Esau who live in Seir and the Moabites who live in Ar."

33. SP interpolates text drawn from Deut. 2:31.

34. In Num. 20:20, Edom's military is depicted formally as "a heavy and strong people," which most render "force" or "army," as with the text here, "entire army" (NLT, NIV) or "all his forces" (NET) or "all his men" (Budd, *Numbers*, 241). Instead, here and in vv. 33–35, I prefer to preserve the hyperbole, "He gathered *all his people* [*kol-'ammô*] together and went out to fight Israel" (with Seebass, *Numeri*, 2:346; de Vaulx, *Nombres*, 244; Ashley, *Numbers*, 415; ESV, NRSV, NJPS).

35. The *l* + inf. of purpose shows the goal of the main verb (formally, "and went out *to meet* Israel [*liqra't yiśrā'ēl*]"; GBHS §4.1.10d), but the rest of the verse makes clear that this implies "to meet Israel *with the sword*" (as 20:18).

36. Formally, "But Israel struck him down by the mouth of the sword." SP adds "But Israel defeated him in battle, *along with his sons and all his people*."

the Ammonite border was fortified.[37] **25**So Israel took all these cities, and Israel settled in all the Amorite cities, in Heshbon, and in all its villages, **26**since Heshbon was the city of King Sihon of the Amorites. He had fought against the former king of Moab and had taken all his land from his control,[38] as far as the Arnon. **27**That is why those who speak in proverbs[39] say, "Come to Heshbon! It is fortified! The city of Sihon is firmly founded![40] **28**But fire came out from Heshbon, a flame from the city of Sihon. It consumed Ar of Moab and owners of the high places of Arnon.[41] **29**Woe to you, Moab. You are destroyed, O people of Chemosh! He has made his sons fugitives, and his daughters war captives of King Sihon of the Amorites. **30**We have overpowered them. Heshbon has perished as far as Dibon. We demolished them until fire set Medeba ablaze."[42] **31**So the Israelites settled in the land of

37. Formally, "strong was the border/barrier of the Ammonites." For the settlement patterns of Ammon in the archaeological record (which is notoriously difficult to align with an LBA setting for Num. 20–21), and for Ammonite fortifications (mainly walls and gates), including the Amman Citadel (*Jabal al-Qal'a*), see: Tyson, *Ammonites*, 15–70. LXX[ed] translates "strong" (*'az*) as a toponym, apparently an aural error: "for *lazer* [*lazēr*] is the borders of Amman's sons" (NETS).

38. Formally, "from his hand" (*miyyādô*), which LXX[ed] translates as a toponym, apparently an aural error: "and they took all his land from *Aroer* [*Aroēr*] as far as Arnon" (NETS).

39. The substantivized ptc., "Those who speak in proverbs" (*hammōšəlîm*), comes from a verb that in the Pentateuch occurs only here and refers to a "teller of proverbs, sage, bard" (18× in the OT; "*mšl* II," DCH 5:537).

40. The niphal passives (*tibbāneh . . . wətikkônēn*) are often taken as jussives, meaning "let it be built . . . let it be established" (ESV, NRSV, NET) or, in light of the destruction in vv. 28–30, "let it be rebuilt . . . let it be reestablished" (de Vaulx, *Nombres*, 246; NLT, NIV; cf. EÜ). Yet the verbs can also be read as yiqtols, which, in view of the defeated city (vv. 25–26, 28–30), generates a wonderful verbal irony on the lips of the proverbial sages: "Come to Heshbon! It is fortified! The city of Sihon is firmly founded!" (similarly, Levine, *Numbers*, 2:83).

41. The common translation, "the heights of Arnon" (ESV, NRSV ≈ NLT), is improbable since the Arnon was a wadi (today Wadi Mujib), and even if this was a toponym, "Bamoth by the Arnon" (NJPS), it had a meaning to its Hebrew audience (unlike "Bamoth" to us). I prefer "*owners/lords of the high places of Arnon* [*ba'ălê bāmôt 'arnōn*]" (NET), a reference to cultic sites that fits contextually with the following mention of Moab's national and territorial God, "O people of Chemosh!" (v. 29). Although the precise functions of these "high places" (*bāmôt*) continue to be debated, they refer to publicly accessible (open air, but at times housed) stone constructions involved in cultic rituals for the Canaanite deities; they are distinct from, yet share similarities with, proximate altars (*mizbəḥôt*) and standing stones (*maṣṣēbôt*). Relevant to our text, Solomon set up *bāmôt* for other gods, including for Chemosh of Moab (1 Kings 11:7; 2 Kings 23:13), and *bāmôt* might have been installed first in Moab and then later incorporated into Cisjordan (Israel/Palestine) cultic sites in Iron I (see Zevit, *Religions*, 262–63). On Chemosh, see Burnett, "Transjordan," 342, 346–47.

42. MT: "We have demolished them as far as Nophah, which extends to Medeba" (*wannaššîm 'ad-nōpaḥ 'ăšer 'ad-mêdəbā'*). This is slightly awkward, possibly due to homophonic confusion, so here with some versions (ESV, NRSV) I draw from SP and LXX[ed], the latter of which can be translated "The women yet further ignited a fire against Moab" (NETS for *hai gynaikes eti prosexekausan pyr epi Mōab*). However, "women" (*hai gynaikes = nšym*) is an aural misreading of "We have demolished" (*wannaššîm*, a hiphil wayyiqtol + obj. suf.), and "which" (*'ăšer*) was

the Amorites.[43] [32]Moses sent spies to Jaazer,[44] and they captured its villages and dispossessed[45] the Amorites who were there. [33]Then they turned and went up the road to Bashan.[46] And King Og of Bashan and all his people came out to fight them, to go to war at Edrei. [34]Yahweh said to Moses, "Do not fear him[47] because I have delivered him and all his people and his land into your hand. You will do to him what you did to King Sihon of the Amorites, who lived in Heshbon." [35]So they defeated him, his sons[48] and all his people, until there were no survivors,[49] and they possessed his land.

Interpretation

21:1–3. The brief story begins when the Canaanite king of Arad, the eastern outpost of the arid Negev, hears that Israel is approaching on the road to Atharim,[50] although presumably they are still at Mount Hor (20:22; 21:4). So the king—probably like a tribal chieftain—attacks and captures some of them (v. 1).[51] Since leaving Sinai, Israel has faced opposing forces by cowering with fear (13:28–14:4) and rerouting to evade conflict (20:14–21). Now, in contrast, Israel responds by making a vow, a type of contractual oath, to Yahweh: "If you will indeed deliver this people into our hand, then we will completely destroy their cities" (v. 2; see the translation notes there).[52] Yahweh

heard accidentally as "fire" (*'ēš*); the definite article in SP, "the Nophah" (*hnph*), was probably an error. I interpret *nph* not as a toponym but as a qal qatal ptc. (*nōpēaḥ*) from **nph*, meaning, "to blow, set aflame" (*HALOT* 2:708–9). *'Ēš* (fire) and *nph* (blow) occur together in Job 20:26 and Isa. 54:16. In sum, I reconstruct this text to have originally read "We demolished them until fire set Medeba ablaze" (*wannaššîm 'ad nōpēaḥ 'ēš 'al mêdəbā'*). Considering ancient versions and Ugaritic, Althan ("Numbers 21,30b," 568–71) proposes "And we destroyed the throne of breathing out, Medeba quaked."

43. SP and LXX[ed]: "in (all) the cities of the Amorites."

44. The piel stem of **rgl* I means "to spy (out)" (*DCH* 7:410), which should be distinguished from the exploratory mission in Num. 13 (using "*twr*," *DCH* 8:610; see the first translation note on 13:2). Here an unidentified "them" is implied as the obj. of the main verb, which is modified by *l* + piel inf. of purpose, meaning "Then Moses sent them in order to spy out Jaazer" (*wayyišlaḥ mōšeh ləraggēl 'et-ya'zēr*).

45. Following the hiphil causative of SP and MT[qere], "dispossessed" (*wayyôreš* ≈ aor. *exebalon*, cast out, LXX[ed]), rather than the qal of MT[ketiv], "possessed, inherited" (*wayyîraš*).

46. "The road to Bashan" (*derek habbāšān*) is a metonym for "the King's Highway" (formally, *derek hammelek*; Num. 20:17; 21:22), also called the Transjordan Highway; see the fourth translation note on 20:17.

47. *'Al* + jussive expresses a specific or immediate prohibition: "Do not fear him" (*'al-tîrā'*; *GBHS* §4.2.3).

48. Probably due to homooarcton (*wə'et* . . . *wə'et*), SP omits "and his sons" (MT LXX[ed]).

49. Formally, "until a survivor did not remain for him."

50. Rasmussen, *Atlas*, 276.

51. Ashley, *Numbers*, 399; following Glueck, *Rivers in the Desert*, 114–15.

52. On oath-sworn contracts in the ANE, see Otto, "Covenant," 2047–51.

"listened to Israel's voice" (v. 3), just as the messengers recently informed Edom's king that Yahweh "heard our voice" in Egypt (20:16). Yahweh's favor is even more striking in light of Israel's failures, including Moses and Aaron's failing to listen to Yahweh's voice.[53] Yahweh keeps his word, handing over the Canaanites, and Israel keeps theirs, completely destroying them and their cities.[54] Their fresh toponym for that place—the region of Negev towns north of Mount Hor?—was Hormah, meaning "devoted to destruction" (see the second translation note on v. 3). Setting aside the preexistence of Hormah in 14:45, here the etiology of this toponym[55] not only represents the actualization of the divine protective favor envisioned in the Priestly Blessing (6:24–26) and Song of the Ark (10:35–36) but also gives a foretaste of Yahweh's victorious conquest of the rest of Canaan's prominent kings and cities (Josh. 6–Judg. 1).[56] The triumph of 21:1–3 marks a pivotal moment for Israel, as hereafter through Joshua they will win all their battles.[57]

21:4–9. To circumvent Edom's territory, the Israelites then travel from Mount Hor along the southeastern route to the Sea of Reeds, to the Gulf of Aqaba extension of the Red Sea.[58] It is never said why the Israelites, who successfully defeated the Canaanite king in the Negev, did not next move northward into the Negev to continue their campaign for Canaan. All that can be said is that, in God's providence, Israel had yet to experience a number of formidable and formative events in Transjordan (Num. 21:4–36:13→Deuteronomy→Josh. 2). Along the way to the Gulf of Aqaba, the people become impatient and assail God and Moses with an all-too-familiar invective (vv. 4–5; see the second translation note on v. 4).[59] The Egypt-nostalgia motif, which seems to drag on endlessly in the Moses story, finally comes to completion in Num. 21:5.

Below is a list of passages where the Egypt-nostalgia motif appears. The title identifies the issue that triggered the complaint.[60]

Egypt's Forces Advance (Exod. 14:11)
"Is it because there are no graves in Egypt that you have taken us to die in the desert? What have you done to us in bringing us out of Egypt?"

---

53. Num. 14:22–23; 20:10–13, 24; cf. 15:31.
54. See the "Implications" essay below, "Devotion to Destruction."
55. W. Lee, *Migratory Campaign*, 157–58.
56. See "Literary Genre and Structure" in the introduction.
57. Milgrom, *Numbers*, 172; Olson, *Death of the Old*, 149.
58. Rasmussen, *Atlas*, 108.
59. The inverse of Exod. 14:31 (Milgrom, *Numbers*, 173). Beyerle ("Eherne Schlange," 23–44) observes that the story advances by vacillating between narration (vv. 4–5a, 6–7b, 7e–8a, 9) and dialogue (vv. 5b, 7c–d, 8b–d).
60. The translations of the Scripture passages presented below are my own.

No Food (Exod. 16:3)
"If only we had died by the hand of Yahweh in the land of Egypt, when we sat by the meat pots and ate bread until we were full, because you have brought us out into this desert to kill this whole assembly with hunger."

No Water (Exod. 17:3)
"Why did you bring us up out of Egypt—to kill us and our children and our livestock with thirst?"

No Good Food (Num. 11:4–6)
"Who will give us meat to eat! We remember the fish we used to eat at no cost in Egypt, the cucumbers, melons, leeks, onions, and garlic. But now our throats are dry, and we see nothing but this manna!"

Canaan's Forces (Num. 14:2–3)
"If only we had died in the land of Egypt, or if only we had died in this wilderness! Why is Yahweh bringing us into this land to fall by the sword? Our wives and our children will become war captives. Wouldn't it better for us to return to Egypt?"

Moses's Authority (Num. 16:13)
"Isn't it enough that you have brought us up out of a land that flows with milk and honey in order to kill us in the wilderness? Now you are making yourself a prince over us?"

No Water or Good Food (Num. 20:3–5)
"If only we had died when our brothers died before Yahweh! Why did you bring Yahweh's community into this wilderness so that we and our cattle should die here?

No Water or Good Food (Num. 21:5)
"Why have you brought us up out of Egypt to die in the wilderness, for there is no bread or water, and we detest this horrible food."[61]

In contrast to Yahweh's gracious provision of water in Num. 20:11, here in chap. 21 Yahweh responds in judgment by sending venomous snakes to bite the people, and many Israelites die as a result (v. 6).[62] These snakes should not be overinterpreted as "fiery serpents" or "burning snakes" but are a species of venomous snake, such as a desert viper (see the translation note on v. 6).[63] Unexpectedly, the people confess their verbal sin: "We have sinned because we spoke against Yahweh" (v. 7). Within the desert wanderings of chaps. 11–25, this is the third and final communal confession, forming a recurring submotif

---

61. See the second translation note on 21:5. In Deut. 23:3–6, the lack of bread or water may allude to Num. 21:5, reinterpreted in the context of Num. 21–24 as Ammonite and Moabite inhospitality, which bars them from entering Yahweh's assembly (Kilchör, *Mosetora*, 259).

62. Leveen (*Memory*, 154) takes the perfunctory death notice in v. 6 as a sign of indifference and its own form of punishment.

63. Walton and Matthews, *Genesis–Deuteronomy*, 198.

(12:11; 14:40; 21:7).[64] Convinced that Moses, although disinherited (20:12), is still their mediator, the suffering people plead with Moses to pray to Yahweh to remove the snakes from among them (v. 7; see the first translation note there). This time, rather than retorting in anger and taking Yahweh's glory (20:10–12), Moses returns to his earlier pattern of graciously interceding for the people (v. 7).[65] Yahweh responds with a command that is executed precisely by Moses and Israel, resulting in deliverance:

> Make a venomous snake
>> and put it on a pole.
>>> When anyone who was bitten looks at it,
>>>> they will live. (v. 8)
> So Moses made a bronze snake
>> and put it on a pole,
>>> so that if a snake had bitten someone, when they looked at the bronze snake,
>>>> they lived. (v. 9)

In the Torah, Yahweh has repeatedly provided grace for humans by means of various forms of animals: animal skins to cover the shame of the first humans; a ram as a burnt offering in place of Isaac; bulls, billy and nanny goats, ewes, pigeons, and rams for purification and guilt offerings; a live billy goat for bearing iniquity; and now a venomous snake as an antidote to its bites.[66] Reading the story as is, Yahweh orders Moses to craft a venomous snake, echoing what Aaron did in Egypt;[67] that Moses chooses to forge a bronze snake is conceivable against the backdrop of snake cults and images in the ANE. Interestingly, at the tent-covered Hathor Temple in the Timna valley north of the Red Sea, near Israel's desert location in Num. 21:4–9, archaeologists discovered a votive bronze snake.[68] In the ANE, the snake was associated with sex, water, the bull, and the dove, signifying the fertility of the deity it represented.[69] However, the fact that Yahweh heals through this bronze snake indicates that he never intended it to be viewed as an idolatrous theriomorphic image (Exod. 20:4–5), although the people did later pervert

---

64. Here "we have sinned" (ḥāṭāʾnû). The verb *ḥṭʾ (to sin) occurs 17× in Numbers.

65. See Exod. 32:11–13; Num. 11:2; 14:13–19.

66. Gen. 3:21; 22:8, 13–14; Lev. 4:1–6:7; chap. 16.

67. Cf. Exod. 7:10–12.

68. Hess, *Israelite Religions*, 202–5, 207; Staubli, *Levitikus, Numeri*, 397. Timna was a site for mining and smelting copper (1200–900 BCE); by the close of the LBA, it had become common practice to add other metals, such as tin, to copper to harden it into bronze (Milgrom, *Numbers*, 175).

69. Joines, "Bronze Serpent," 246–50. See also Koenen, "Eherne Schlange," 353–72.

this bronze snake into an idol (2 Kings 18:4).[70] Also, in the ANE, snakebites were dealt with through incantation rituals, sometimes with amulets, but by implication this story opposes "the practice of snake incantation and magical-ritualistic acts."[71] The point here is that for divine healing, the Israelites must gaze at a deadly snake, evoking the memory of the snakes that have poisoned them, and invariably are still attached to some of them because of their sin against Yahweh.

In his *Poetics* Aristotle suggests that readers respond with *empathy* when they identify with the suffering of the tragic hero and with *fear* when they see themselves as vulnerable to the same human fate as the hero.[72] In our story, with no mention of anger from Yahweh or Moses, ultimately only intercession and saving grace, the storyteller lets us feel *empathy* for the suffering and dying Israelites but also *fear* that we too deserve to be punished with death for our own sins (1 Cor. 10:9; Rom. 6:23). An echo from the opening of the Torah can be heard as the snake in the garden, which became an agent of death, is now sent out by Yahweh as an agent of death (Gen. 3:1–15, 19).[73] Yet God cursed the snake to be defeated by the woman's offspring (3:14–15). In the end, Yahweh does not remove the snakes from Israel as the people had asked but provides a means of salvific healing for the sinners facing imminent death.[74] A future day would dawn when the God of Israel would provide a definitive means of salvific healing for sinners who face death: "Just as Moses lifted up the snake in the wilderness, so must the Son of Man be lifted up, so that everyone who believes in him will have eternal life" (John 3:14–15; cf. 12:32–34; 19:37).

21:10–20. The narrator next turns to recount how Israel proceeded incrementally around Edom to a valley in Moab near Pisgah, probably a mountain range near or coextensive with Mount Nebo.[75] The itinerary differs from that of Num. 33:5–49 in the stops it includes.[76] The discrepancies indicate two independent source documents plus the ancient sources inserted in vv. 14, 16–17, which collectively support the historicity of ancient Israel's basic route from the southern Negev to the Abarim Mountain range in what is

---

70. Joines, "Bronze Serpent," 250–56. Beyerle ("'Eherne Schlange,'" 23–44) argues that Num. 21:4–9 and the notice in 2 Kings 18:4 share the same literary origin. The desert creations, Aaron's golden calf and Moses's bronze snake, reappear thematically in the divided monarchy (1 Kings 12:28–33; 2 Kings 17:16; 18:4; 23:15–16); cf. Koenen, "Eherne Schlange," 353–72.

71. B. Schipper, "'Eherne Schlange,'" 369–87; one Ugaritic incantation list for snakebites identifies specific deities with their mountains or cult sites (Smith, *Monotheism*, 28).

72. Aristotle, *Poetics*, 23, 29, 32.

73. See Wénin, "Le Serpent," 545–54; Milgrom, *Numbers*, 174.

74. Wénin, "Le Serpent," 554; Seebass, *Numeri*, 2:327. Aster ("Num. 21:5," 341–58) concludes that the rhetorical aim of the story is Yahweh's dependability to protect and provide for his people in the desert.

75. Coextensive: Frevel, *Mit Blick*, 61; near: Rasmussen, *Atlas*, 296. See Num. 23:14; Deut. 3:17, 27; 4:49; 34:1; Josh. 12:3; 13:20. As a mountain range, see Milgrom, *Numbers*, 179.

76. On Mesopotamian travel itineraries, see Sparks, *Ancient Texts*, 377.

modern-day Jordan.[77] Also, the differences between the two itineraries reflect unique theological purposes.[78]

Table 21.1. Travel Itineraries Compared (I)

Numbers 21		Numbers 33	
Depart from →	Camp at	Depart from →	Camp at
Mount Hor →	*Way to the Sea of Reeds* (v. 4)	Mount Hor →	*Zalmonah* (v. 41)
		Zalmonah →	*Punon* (v. 42)
→	*Oboth* (v. 10)	*Punon* →	*Oboth* (v. 43)
Oboth →	*Iye Abarim, in the desert that faces Moab toward the sunrise* (v. 11; see the translation note there)	Oboth →	*Iye Abarim, Moab's border* (v. 44)
Iye Abarim →	*Wadi Zered* (v. 12; see the translation note there)	Iyim (= Iye → Abarim)	
Wadi Zered →	*the Arnon, the border of Moab and the Amorites* (v. 13)		
the Arnon →	*Beer* (v. 16; see the first translation note there)	→	*Dibon Gad* [north of the Arnon] (v. 45)
the desert (= Beer) →	*Mattanah* (v. 18)	Dibon Gad →	*Almon Diblathaim* (v. 46)
Mattanah →	*Nahaliel* (v. 19)		
Nahaliel →	*Bamoth* (v. 19)		
Bamoth →	*Valley in Moab, near Pisgah, which overlooks the wasteland* (v. 20; see the translation note there)	Almon → Diblathaim	*Abarim mountains, near Nebo* (v. 47)

The record integrates a fragment of an ancient topographical (cartographical?) source with the incipit "The Scroll of the Wars of Yahweh" (vv. 14–15; see the translation notes on v. 14).[79] Also, Israel's stop at Beer, meaning "Well

77. This is similar to how divergences in the four Gospel accounts reveal four distinct biographies of the remembered life of Christ (Keener, *Christobiography*, 1–24).

78. Dozeman, "Numbers," 164–65.

79. In v. 7, Christensen ("Num. 21:14–15," 359–60) repoints the two direct obj. markers of the MT (*'et*) as the verb "came" (*'ātā*), so that this source instead conveys Yahweh as divine warrior fighting in Moab: "[Yahweh] came in a whirlwind; He came to the branch wadis of the Arnon. He marched through the wadis; He marched/turned aside to the seat of Ar. He leaned toward the border of Moab; . . ." It may be tempting to adopt this reconstruction (with Staubli, *Levitikus, Numeri*, 288) since many have observed that the incipit does imply the religious nature

(of water)," was marked as the place where Yahweh told Moses to gather the people so Yahweh could give them water (v. 16; see the second translation note there). To commemorate Yahweh's water provision, the Israelites sang what may have been a well-digger's chant,[80] now embedded here in the itinerary (vv. 17b–18c):

> Spring up, O well! Sing to it!
> The well that the tribal chiefs dug,
> the nobles of the people opened
> with their scepters
> and with their staffs.[81]

As it stands now in its canonical placement, this aside in vv. 17–18 functions as a deferred denouement to the prior story when the Israelites complained of no water (v. 5). Some died of snakebites, others were healed, and now all who survived could quench their thirst. The itinerary is infused, therefore, with a positive emphasis on Yahweh's providential care. Even so, the rapid narration of this itinerary leaves the correct impression that Israel has made this journey all the way around Edom to the eastern border of the promised land in just a few months, indicating that their forty years in the desert were a tragic waste of time and lives (see 20:1; 33:38).

21:21–35. In this scene, the narrator depicts how Israel defeated Sihon, king of the Amorites, and Og, king of Bashan, and possessed their territories in Transjordan. Clarifying the extent and time frame of Israel's historical encounters with the Edomite, Moabite, and Amorite peoples and how this relates to Num. 20–24 remains a matter of debate due to the incomplete Late Bronze Age and Iron Age excavations and surveys of Transjordan.[82] The story at hand centers on Israel's conflict with the Amorites, a people group known in the Old Babylonian Mari archives as *Amurrû*. They were mobile pastoralists with an eponymous god Ammuru (Sumerian: Mar-tu).[83] The plotline tracks Israel's encounter with the Edomite king (20:14–21) but then diverges when Israel does not retreat but instead fights and destroys King Sihon of the Amorites, who controlled Moab.

---

of war with Yahweh as warrior (de Vaulx, *Nombres*, 241). However, with Levine (*Numbers*, 2:93–94): "It is as if he [Christensen] forced this brief poetic excerpt into an interpretive mold."

80. Knierim and Coats, *Numbers*, 241.

81. Comparing this to other Hebrew songs, see Levine, *Numbers*, 2:95–98.

82. Supporting Nelson Glueck's survey of a settlement gap between the EBA and end of the LBA, and between Iron Age II and the Persian period: Burnett, "Transjordan," 309–39; Grabbe, *Ancient Israel*, 110–15; but reconsidering the incomplete data to support Israel's interface with LBA kingdoms: Provan, P. Long, and Longman, *History of Israel*, 135–37; Kitchen, *Reliability*, 193–97.

83. D. Fleming, "Amorites."

Table 21.2. Battle Accounts Compared

King of Edom (20:14–21)	Sihon, King of the Amorites (21:21–32)
Israel sends messengers to the king (v. 14).	Israel sends messengers to the king (v. 10).
Reasons for benevolence to Israel (vv. 14–16).	
Messengers request passage through Edom's territory: "Let us pass through your land. We will not pass through a single field or vineyard, nor will we drink water from any well. We will follow the King's Highway. We will not spread out to the right or the left until we have passed through your territory" (v. 17).	Messengers request passage though Amorite-controlled land: "Let us pass through your land. We will not spread out into a single field or into a vineyard, nor will we drink water from any well, but we will follow the King's Highway until we pass through your territory" (v. 22; see the first and fourth translation notes there).
Edom refuses to grant Israel passage, including a verbal exchange with the messengers (vv. 18–20b, 21a).	Sihon refuses to grant Israel passage, without a verbal exchange (v. 23).
Edom comes out with a powerful force to attack Israel (v. 20c).	Sihon musters a comprehensive army to attack Israel (v. 23b–c; see the second and third translation notes there).
Israel turned away from Edom (v. 21b).	Sihon attacks Israel at Jahaz, but Israel defeats him and takes possession of his Amorite territory from the Arnon gorge to the Jabbok River (today's Zarqa River), formerly belonging to Moab (vv. 23d–30; see the translation notes on v. 24).

Ending at v. 24 would have sufficed to tell the story of Israel defeating Sihon and possessing his land from the Arnon gorge in the south (parallel to the middle of the Dead Sea) to the Jabbok River in the north, parallel to a third of the way up from the Dead Sea toward the Sea of Galilee (Kinnereth). Instead, in vv. 25–30 the narrator over-specifies to stress that this territory with its key fortified cities of Ar, Dibon, and especially Heshbon, where Sihon lived, had once belonged to the Moabites, but Sihon's Amorites destroyed and hegemonized the land, taking its sons as fugitives and daughters as war captives.[84] A proverbial Heshbon Ballad[85] is incorporated to vivify the brutal war imagery (vv. 27–30; see the first translation note on v. 27 and the translation note on v. 30). The mention of the destruction of the open-air cultic sites of Moab (*bāmôt*, v. 28; see the translation note there) and the defeat of Chemosh, the national god of Moab, points not overtly to Yahweh's victory but to Sihon's (v. 29). Without explicitly mentioning Yahweh in vv. 25–30, what then is the purpose of recounting these military actions here? Whatever the intent of the oral form of these stories, now they are edited into the canon of the Moses story and imply a triple victory for Israel: The Amorites defeated the

84. See Runge, *Discourse Grammar*, 387.
85. Levine, *Numbers*, 2:123–25; Dozeman, "Numbers," 166–67.

Moabites along with their cultic sites and god Chemosh, so by defeating the Amorites who had conquered the Moabites, Israel by extension also defeated the Moabites and their deity.

After the expansion of vv. 25–30, the narrator resumes the story line with Israel settling in the land of the Amorites and through Moses's espionage enveloping more Amorite territory, the villages of Jaazer (vv. 31–32; see the first translation note on v. 32). Israel then marches north on the King's Highway toward Bashan, and King Og marches south to fight Israel at Edrei (v. 33; see the translation note there). Yahweh, who has been ostensibly silent about the Amorite battles (vv. 21–32), at last interjects his voice by delivering a salvation oracle through his prophet Moses (v. 34; see the translation note there).[86] Again, irrespective of the shape of the original war stories, now Yahweh links Sihon to Og, implying that Yahweh is the providential force who delivered Sihon into Israel's hands, and he will do it again with Og. Yahweh's silence does not mean he has stopped working for his covenant people (Rom. 8:28–29). Yahweh the divine warrior accrues these new territories for his people, which correlates with ancient Near Eastern thought that the gods by their surrogate armies subjugated foreign peoples and amassed new land for their own people.[87] As with the total destruction of the king of Arad (21:1–3), so also with Israel's victories over Sihon and Og (21:21–35),[88] these battles anticipate—both in the macrostructure of Numbers and in the Hexateuch epic[89]—Yahweh's coming triumph over Canaan's ruling powers and core cities.[90] In a similar way, Christ's cross before his second coming and believers' present victories over sin by the Spirit before their glorification anticipate God's coming destruction of sin, evil, the powers of darkness, and death.[91]

Two questions naturally arise from this account. Have the boundaries of the promised land been expanded outside Canaan into the Transjordan? This text gives no reply. The reader must wait with a degree of cognitive dissonance until the episode of Num. 32 and the map of Num. 34.[92] The second question is Did Yahweh explicitly tell Israel to destroy Sihon and occupy his

---

86. Knierim and Coats, *Numbers*, 245.

87. See the "Implications" essay in chap. 29, "The Divine Gift of Land."

88. W. Lee (*Migratory Campaign*, 166) rightly perceives a *ḥrm concept underlying vv. 32–35.

89. The Deuteronomists repeatedly hold up Sihon and Og as precursors to Yahweh's/Israel's imminent domination and allotment of Canaan (Deut. 1:4; 2:24–26, 30–32; 3:1–13; 4:46–49; 29:7; 31:4; Josh. 2:10; 9:10; 12:4; 13:10–12, 21, 27–31). In Judges, Jephthah rejects the Ammonite claims to this territory by recounting Yahweh's defeat of Sihon (Judg. 11:19–23); cf. 1 Kings 4:19; Neh. 9:22; Pss. 135:11–12; 136:17–24; Jer. 48:45. Kosman ("Story," 157–90) traces Jewish haggadic retellings of the Og story.

90. See "Literary Genre and Structure" in the introduction.

91. Rom. 16:20; 1 Cor. 15:51–58; 2 Thess. 2:8; Heb. 2:14–15; 1 John 3:8; Rev. 17:14; chaps. 18–22.

92. See the "Implications" essays in chaps. 29 ("The Divine Gift of Land") and 31 ("How Big Is the Promised Land?").

domain? Later interpreters say yes (Deut. 2:24–37), but the present text is ambiguous. The Torah student might be inclined to infer divine orders, since the Amorites belong to the so-called anti-elect (Gen. 15:16–21), but we should not superimpose divine orders on this text but perceive divine providence.[93]

Implications

Devotion to Destruction

In the opening scene of Num. 21:2–3, Israel vows to "completely destroy" the cities belonging to the Canaanite king of Arad and then fulfills that vow. The verb for "completely destroy" occurring in vv. 2–3 is a weqatal form of the hiphil causative stem of the root *ḥrm*. These are the third and fourth appearances of this verb in the Pentateuch and the only ones in Numbers.[94] The meaning here is not exactly "dedicate to Yahweh" as in Lev. 27:28, and "proscribe" (NJPS) is too weak. The reader should not superimpose the Deuteronomistic orders in which *Yahweh himself* demands that Israel devote to destruction all the cities and peoples inhabiting Canaan.[95] I prefer to stick with the base meaning of the verb: "*we* [formally, "I"] *will completely destroy* [*wəhaḥăramtî*] their cities, . . . and *they completely destroyed* [*wayyaḥărēm*] them and their cities" (vv. 2–3).[96] With that said, the translations "consecrate their cities to their downfall/doom" (EÜ, my trans.) and "devote to destruction" (ESV) can be seen as anticipating Yahweh's more developed orders in Deuteronomy, where Yahweh demands *ḥrm* with two components: Canaan's cities and their residents will (1) become his exclusive property, necessitating that (2) no Israelite (or human) may plunder their spoils for themselves but must demolish them.[97]

The concept of *ḥrm* in Num. 21, Deuteronomy, and Joshua has a striking parallel in the Mesha Stele, also known as the Moabite Stone (ca. 840 BCE). This stone comes from Moab, the region to which Israel would next travel and fight (21:10–35) and reside (Num. 22:1–Josh. 2). On this meter-tall basalt slab, the Moabite King Mesha inscribed that their national god Chemosh (Kemosh) commanded him to recapture Nebo from Israelite occupation, and in his response, he destroys the "whole population" as an act of devoting them (*ḥrm*, the Moabite cognate) to the Moabite goddess, Ashtar-Chemosh (Ashtar-Kemosh). This stele also includes the earliest mention in an inscription of the name of Israel's deity, Yahweh, and reads as follows: "And Kemosh

---

93. This conclusion is based on v. 34 and the contrast with Yahweh's absence in the Amalekite-Canaanite war in 14:40–45.

94. Exod. 22:20 [22:19] (hophal); Lev. 27:29 (hophal).

95. Deut. 2:34; 3:6; 7:2; 13:15; 20:17.

96. See "*ḥrm* I," *DCH* 3:317. With NIV, NLT; similarly, "utterly destroy" (NRSV, NET).

97. Achenbach (*Vollendung*, 345–47, 636) suspects Num. 21:1–3 is pre-Deuteronomistic.

said to me: 'Go, take Nebo from Israel!' And I went in the night, and I fought against it from the break of dawn until noon, and I took it, and I killed [its] whole population, seven thousand male citizens(?) and aliens(?), and female citizens(?) and aliens(?), and servant girls; for I had put it to the ban for Ashtar Kemosh. And from there, I took th[e ves]sels of YHWH, and I hauled them before the face of Kemosh" (lines 14–18a).[98] Although the text is partially effaced, the account in this Mesha inscription shares the conceptual world of Num. 21:1–3 and later of Num. 31, with the divine (Moses's or Mesha's) vision to annihilate the "male citizens" and "female citizens" (cf. Num. 31:7–8, 14–17). But unlike the Mesha Stele and Num. 21:2–3, which involve a religious devoting of everyone to destruction,[99] in Num. 31 Moses allows the Israelites to spare the virgin women and girls (31:17–18).

In the ANE, the term *holy war* is redundant and anachronistic[100] because *ḥrm* in Num. 21 and the Mesha Stele illustrates that war was thought to be sanctioned by the gods. Of course, it does not resolve the ethical issue of biblical divine violence to say that Yahweh was simply acting like pantheons of the surrounding nations. Yahweh here clearly sanctions, and in Deuteronomy and Joshua demands, the annihilation of Canaan's residents.

Yet we must not overlook some important nuances. The king of Arad is identified explicitly as a Canaanite, and the Canaanites and Amorites were neither elect (Israel) nor nonelect (immigrants, Edomites, etc.) but *anti-elect*.[101] The narrative origins of the anti-elect reach back to Noah's curse on Ham's son, Canaan (Gen. 9:18–27), and the reality that the iniquity of the Amorites and Canaanites was polluting the land that belonged to Yahweh (Gen. 15:16; Lev. 18–20; 25:23). This Canaanite king living "in the Negev" is inside the borders of the promised land that Yahweh is giving to his covenant people (Num. 13:17, 22; 33:40; 34:3–5).[102] Furthermore, the king of Arad is not merely a victim but a perpetrator who pierced the proverbial apple of Yahweh's eye. The narrator tells us that "he attacked Israel and captured some of them," which shows that he is not innocent (v. 1; see the translation note there).[103] Now Israel responds just as Yahweh said he would respond in the negative colon of the Abrahamic blessing: "The one who treats you lightly I will curse" (Gen. 12:3).

Much ink has been spilled over the slaughtering of ancient Canaan's local residents, and we should not shy away from calling it genocide as defined by

---

98. "The Inscription of King Mesha," COS 2.23:138.

99. *Ḥrm* in Moabite and Hebrew.

100. Achenbach, "Divine Warfare," 1–27; Schwartz, "Warfare," 512.

101. See Kaminsky, "Election," 397–425.

102. See the "Implications" essay in chap. 29, "The Divine Gift of Land."

103. Similarly, the redaction of Joshua highlights that the Canaanites were destroyed not for their religion or ethics but for aggressively opposing Yahweh and his previous victories for his people (5:1; 10:1–2; 11:1–2): Stone, "Ethical and Apologetic," 25–35.

the United Nations: "Acts committed with intent to destroy, in whole or in part, a national, ethnical, racial or religious group."[104] We can conveniently leave Deuteronomy and Joshua for others to tackle, but we cannot hastily exonerate Israel and Yahweh in Num. 21:1–3 by calling this a defensive battle. As in Gen. 12:3b, so also in Num. 21:1–3, the punishment exceeds the crime: treating God's people lightly/contemptuously results in a formal curse, which seems proportionate; Arad's king attacks and captures some of Israel's people, and Israel retaliates by totally destroying all of their cities, which seems disproportionate. How is this retributive justice? Here I can only offer four encouragements to followers of Jesus today who rightly champion nonviolence (Matt. 5:38–40) but are also unwilling to become Marcionists by rejecting the theology and authority of the Torah (Matt. 5:17; Rom. 8:4).

1. Warfare and violence, formerly enacted in part through God's people in the Old Testament, belongs exclusively to the domain of God. God will destroy his enemies in the coming judgment,[105] and as God, he reserves the right to accomplish this by whatever means he chooses: Israel, foreign nations, natural elements.[106] As Jesus's followers, who do not enact vengeance but cry out to God for his vindication,[107] we must put the curse component of the Abrahamic blessing back into God's hands, as he originally articulated it (Gen. 12:3b). We do not take up arms in his name to destroy other humans but instead renounce sin and the spiritual forces of darkness.[108]

2. The suffering servant is our exemplar.[109] The Spirit may lead us to suffer at the hands of those who oppose God and his Son (Acts 20:22–24). If the Spirit is not leading us to suffer, then we should remove or defend ourselves from verbal or physical harm,[110] while relying on God's strength and wisdom to somehow bless and not harm the perpetrator.[111]

3. Yahweh has transformed the classification of anti-elect persons, formerly Canaanites and Amorites, into those who, if they trust in the Messiah Jesus, will transfer status from the anti-elect enemies of God into the elect and beloved children of God.[112]

4. We will be aided by the hermeneutical path of Augustine, later described by Anselm: "For I do not seek to understand that I may believe, but I believe in order to understand."[113] Personally, I have been helped by the Danish phi-

---

104. See https://www.un.org/en/genocideprevention/genocide.shtml.
105. Eph. 5:6; Phil. 3:18–19; 1 Thess. 2:16; Heb. 1:13; 10:13, 27; Rev. 16:19; 19:15.
106. Exod. 14–15; Hab. 1:5–11; Isa. 45:1–2; 2 Pet. 2:4–10; 3:5–10; Rev. 20:9–10, 14–15.
107. Matt. 5:38–40; Rev. 6:10; 19:2.
108. See the "Implications" essay in chap. 1, "Counting the Army."
109. John 10:11, 17–18; Rom. 5:8; Eph. 5:1–2.
110. Luke 4:29–30; Acts 9:23–25.
111. Luke 6:28; Rom. 12:14, 17–21.
112. Acts 10, 15; Rom. 5:10; Eph. 2:12–18; Col. 1:21–22.
113. Anselm, *Proslogium* 1, p. 31.

losopher Søren Kierkegaard, who wrestled with God's demand that Abraham sacrifice his beloved son (Gen. 22).[114] Because of his dynamic faith in God, Abraham suspended his ethical responsibility as a father to love and never harm his son. We, too, can suspend our ignorance and confusion about the ethics of biblical divine violence by reaching out in trust and love for the mysterious God who calls us to follow him.

114. Kierkegaard, *Fear and Trembling*, 265–72.

22

The Balaam Cycle

(22:1–24:25)

❧

Overview

By Yahweh's power, Israel recently defeated Canaanites in the Negev (21:1–3), Amorites, and the residents of Heshbon in Transjordan (21:21–31). Edited between those victories are stories and narration that underscore Yahweh's enduring commitment to his covenant with Israel by healing sinners bitten by the venomous snakes (21:4–9) and leading his people to the edge of the promised land (21:10–20). Now, at last, Israel arrives and camps at their penultimate destination in the Hexateuch, the desert valleys of Moab (22:1). Into this literary and geographical context, the editors have positioned the self-contained Balaam cycle.[1]

The story is a masterful work of literature. I frequently use a hyphenated title, God-Yahweh, since the divine name or appellative vacillates between Yahweh (*Yhwh*) and the angel of Yahweh (*mal'ak yhwh*), Elohim (*'ĕlōhîm*), and El (*'ēl*).[2] The cycle begins with the present Moabite king, Balak, who fears

---

1. See Olson, *Death of the Old*, 153–64.
2. Developing the conventional source analysis of Num. 22–24, Gray (*Numbers*, 309–79), Noth (*Numbers*, 171–75), Schmidt ("Bileam," 333–52), and Seebass ("Bileam-Perikope," 409–19) advance the opinion that the independent stories of J (Yahweh) and E (Elohim) were editorially combined and expanded (by the Pentateuch redactor: Scharbert, *Numeri*, 88ff.). Bickert ("Israel im Lande Moab," 189–210) argues that JE is not found in Num. 22–24. Instead, a pre-Deuteronomistic base narrative (using Elohim) with two parts and two oracles was expanded with a third oracle and redacted; then a Deuteronomistic revision integrated the story into Numbers and the donkey scene, fourth oracle, and other supplements were added. Similarly,

Israel's military might and calls on the non-Israelite prophet Balaam to curse the Israelites so that Balak can defeat them (22:1–6). Balak sends his messengers to commission Balaam to come and curse Israel, but Balaam obeys his deity, God-Yahweh, and so refuses to go with Balak's messengers (22:7–19). God-Yahweh then tells Balaam to go with Balak's officials, but God-Yahweh is angry with Balaam for going, so the angel of Yahweh opposes Balaam. While Balaam's donkey sees and fears the angel of Yahweh, Balaam does neither (22:20–30). Balaam confesses his sin and, in obedience to the angel of Yahweh, travels to meet Balak (22:31–41).

At Baal's high place in Kiriath Huzoth, Balak offers impressive sacrifices to God-Yahweh, and then Balaam mediates to Balak the first oracle of God-Yahweh, which asserts that Balaam cannot curse Israel, whom God has not cursed (23:1–12). Balak next offers impressive sacrifices at Pisgah, but Balaam delivers a second oracle, indicating that God will not be manipulated by divination to curse Israel, who is blessed (23:13–26). Then at Peor, Balaam, perceiving that seeking an omen against Israel is pointless, transmits a third oracle by God's spirit that honors Jacob-Israel's beauty, fertility, and military power, and honors God as Israel's redeemer (23:27–24:9).

Balak's anger reaches a boiling point, but Balaam conveys a fourth oracle, which predicts not only Israel's destruction of Balak's nation, Moab, by means of a star-scepter out of Jacob-Israel but also Israel's victory over other surrounding nations (24:10–19). Three more contracted oracles—about Amalek, the Kenites, and Assur—are incorporated (24:20–25). The purpose of this novella is to stress that God-Yahweh—interchanging divine names in the composite story—has irrevocably blessed Jacob-Israel, substantiating the Abrahamic blessing (Gen. 12:1–3).[3] Also, the story teaches that God-Yahweh is not a local deity confined to a single cultic site and that he cannot be manipulated by divination to reverse course and curse the blessed Jacob-Israel. Rather, God-Yahweh is sovereign over non-Israelite and Israelite nations alike, and he is resolute in keeping his promise to the patriarchs.

Robker ("Balaam Narrative," 334–66) argues that the Balaam story began as an independent work of literature before it was incorporated into a pre-Deuteronomistic/non-P narrative, which was expanded and redacted. Sutcliffe ("Unitate Litteraria," 5; "Numbers XXII," 439–42) argues that the story reflects a literary unity by a single, untrained author who left tensions unresolved. In basic agreement, Budd (Numbers, 259) takes only the donkey episode as an insertion into the whole. Achenbach (Vollendung, 389–424) assigns chaps. 22–24 to an older tradition with Hexateuch and Pentateuch redactions and additions.

3. Knierim and Coats (Numbers, 260–61) call the Balaam cycle an anti-legend about a foreign seer who tries to curse Israel and cannot defeat Israel in battle. Embedded are prophetic tribal oracles, particularly negative oracles of cursing and positive oracles of blessing (chaps. 23–24).

Translation

¹The Israelites traveled on and camped in the desert valleys of Moab along the Jordan River across from Jericho.⁴ **²**Balak, Zippor's son, saw everything the Israelites had done to the Amorites. **³**So the Moabites were terrified of the people because they were so numerous. The Moabites were deathly afraid because of the Israelites.⁵ **⁴**The Moabites said to the elders of Midian, "Now this mass of people⁶ will lick up⁷ everything around us, as the bull licks up the grass of the field." Zippor's son Balak was king of the Moabites at that time, **⁵**and he sent messengers to Balaam, Beor's son, at Pethor, which is near the Euphrates River in his native land,⁸ to summon him, saying, "A nation has come out of Egypt!⁹ They cover the face of the earth,¹⁰ and they are living next to me.¹¹ **⁶**Now come and curse these people for me because

4. "In the desert valleys of Moab" (*bəʿarbôt môʾāb*) in 22:1; 26:3, 63; 31:12; 33:48, 49, 50; 35:1; 36:13; Deut. 2:8; 34:1, 8; Josh. 13:32). The Hb. is normally rendered "plains of Moab," which most European and North American readers imagine as a large, flat grassland without mountains. Instead, these *desert valleys* (pl. *ʿarbôt*) formed the east bank of the Jordan River basin, in the Jordan Rift Valley, and were surrounded by the Transjordan and Cisjordan mountains visible to the east and west, respectively. The adjective *desert* valleys correlates with Israel's encampment in the area north of the Dead Sea, which is classified as desert, with only 0–4 inches of annual rainfall (Rasmussen, *Atlas*, 30). The Jordan Rift Valley is part of the Great Rift Valley, which stretches from the Beqaa Valley in Lebanon down to Mozambique. To the west of the desert valleys of Moab is the Jordan River, then the ancient oasis city of Jericho (Neolithic origins), later called "the city of palms" (*ʿîr hattəmārîm*; Judg. 1:16; 3:13). To the east is the plateau in Jordan, north to south, that is ca. 4,300 ft. above the Dead Sea. Just to the southwest of the desert valleys of Moab is the mouth of the Jordan River, which empties into the Dead Sea, about 1,365 ft. below sea level.

5. The Moabites' terror is stressed by the redundancy of two less common improper synonyms (rather than **yrʾ*), and the wayyiqtol forms may indicate that their fear resulted from what they saw in v. 2: "Balak, Zippor's son, saw everything the Israelites had done to the Amorites. So the Moabites *were terrified* [*wayyāgār*] of the people because they were so numerous. The Moabites *were deathly afraid* [*wayyāqāṣ*] because of the Israelites" (*GBHS* §3.5.1b). LXX^ed interprets the relationship between vv. 2 and 3 similarly: "*And when Balak son of Sepphor saw all that Israel had done to the Amorrite, also Moab feared the people very much . . .*" (NETS).

6. A contextual rendering of "the assembly" (*haqqāhāl*), with a referential article (*GBHS* §2.6.1) as in SP and LXX^ed, "*this* gathering."

7. A rare root (*lḥk**), often referring to destruction by fire, occurs five other times in the OT in the piel stem (Judges, 1 Kings, Psalms), but only in this verse (2×) in qal, meaning "lick up, eat" (*DCH* 4:532).

8. Formally, "the land of the sons of his people." Layton ("Num. 22,5," 32–61) reads *ʿammô* as a variant of *ʿammôn* (Ammon) for the reinterpretation "the land of the sons of Ammon." This, he notes, means not that Balaam was an Ammonite but that he was serving there when Balak summoned him.

9. Exclamation point renders *hinnē*, commonly "behold" or "look."

10. Formally, "They cover the eye of the land/earth" (*kissâ ʾet-ʿên hāʾāreṣ*). On the Mesopotamian and Israelite conception of the earth, see the third translation note on 12:3. Depending on the context, this conception can be expressed by either *hāʾāreṣ* or *hāʾădāmâ*.

11. More formally, "living *opposite me* [*mimmulî*]" (ESV).

they are too powerful for me. Perhaps I will prevail so I can conquer them[12] and drive them out of the land. For I know that whomever you bless is blessed, and whomever you curse is cursed."[13]

7So the Moabite elders and the Midianite elders departed with the fee for divination[14] in their hand. They came to Balaam and told him what Balak had said.[15] **8**He said to them, "Stay here tonight, and I will report back to you whatever Yahweh says to me."[16] So the Moabite officials[17] stayed with Balaam. **9**And God came to Balaam and said,[18] "Who are these men with you?"[19] **10**Balaam said to God, "Zippor's son Balak, king of Moab, has sent this message[20] to me: **11**'A nation has come out of Egypt![21] They cover the face of the earth.[22] Come now and put a curse on them for me. Perhaps I will be able to fight them and

---

12. Since the second yiqtol switches to a pl., I follow NET in reading the second verb not as complementary but as a logical result: "Perhaps *I will prevail* [*'ûkal*] so I [formally, *we*] can conquer [*nakkeh*] them." Against the other witnesses (4Q27 4Q23 MT SP LXX[mss]), LXX[ed] has two 1st pers. pls.: "since it is stronger *than we are*, if *we may be able* to strike some of them." The king as "an absolute monarch" regards his action as identical to "the will and action of the people" (Wevers, *Notes*, 363).

13. In Balak's allusion to Yahweh's blessing of Abraham in Gen. 12:3—"I will bless those who bless you, and the one who treats you lightly I will curse" (*wa'ăbārăkâ məbārkêkā ûməqallelkā 'ā'ōr*)—the piels are resultative, which correlates with the force of the pual: "For I know that whomever *you bless is blessed* [*tabārēk məbōrāk*, put into a blessed state], and whomever you curse *is cursed* [*yū'ār*, put into a cursed state]" (*GBHS* §3.1.3a).

14. Of the eleven OT occurrences of this noun, which normally means "divination," this is the only time it seems to mean "fee(s) for divination" (pl. of "*qesem*," *DCH* 7:272, gloss 2) since it is "in their hand," but it could mean "instrument(s) of divination" (*HALOT* 3:1115–16, gloss 3b).

15. Formally, "the words of Balak" (*dibrê bālāq*), which is a subjective gen., "what Balak had said" (*GBHS* §2.2.3).

16. Formally, "and I will return you a word just as Yahweh speaks to me."

17. Whereas in 21:18 *śar* I may be best translated "tribal chiefs" (*DCH* 8:187, gloss 2.4), here the term serves as a metonym for "the Moabite elders and the Midianite elders" (v. 7) who are Balak's representatives, so "officials" is more suitable (with *HALOT* 3:1350–52, gloss A1; or "courtiers" for EÜ). The term "princes" (ESV, NET) gives the wrong impression to modern readers, since these are not Balak's sons; nor are they clearly prospects for the Moabite kingship.

18. 4Q27 and LXX[ed]: "and said *to him*."

19. SP and LXX[ed]: "*What* are these people with you?"

20. "This message" is supplied from the context (many modern versions).

21. The MT attributive ptc. without a main verb is awkward: "*The nation who comes out* [*hā'ām hayyōṣē'*] of Egypt! They cover the face of the earth" (*hinnē* is typically intransitive). Instead, as a parallel to v. 5, the indefinite subject with a finite verb is preferred, since it is followed by the wayyiqtol: "A nation has come out [*'m yṣ'* ≈ *laos exelēlythen*] of Egypt! *They cover* [*wyks*] the face of the land" (4Q27 SP LXX[ed]).

22. See the third translation note on v. 5. 4Q27 and SP include the statement, probably as a harmonization to v. 5, "and they are living next to me" ([*mmwly*] *whw'h ywšb* 4Q27; *kai houtos enkathētai echomenos mou* LXX[ed]).

drive them out.'"[23] [12]But God said to Balaam,[24] "Do not go with them. Do not put a curse on the people because they are blessed."[25] [13]So Balaam got up in the morning and said to Balak's officials, "Go to your land,[26] for Yahweh[27] has refused[28] to let me to go with you." [14]So the Moabite officials returned to Balak and said,[29] "Balaam refused to come with us." [15]Balak again sent officials, more numerous and more distinguished than the first.[30] [16]And they came to Balaam and said to him, "This is what Zippor's son Balak[31] says: 'Do not let anything hold you back from coming to me.[32] [17]For I will highly honor you,[33] and whatever you tell me, I will do.[34] So come, put a curse on these people for me.'" [18]Balaam replied to Balak's servants, "Even if Balak would give me his palace full of silver and gold, I could not go beyond[35] the command of Yahweh my

23. The weqatal indicates the result: "I will be able to fight them *and* [as a result] *drive them out* [*wəgēraštîw*]" (GBHS §3.5.2b). 4Q27 and SP probably harmonize with v. 5, "and drive them out *from the land*."

24. The content of God's speech lends toward a disjunctive: "*But God said* [*wayyō'mer 'ĕlōhîm*] *to Balaam* . . ."

25. While the two *lō'* + yiqtol permanent or binding prohibitions (MT SP LXX[ed]) are probably original, the contextual meaning is captured by the two *'al* + jussive constructions of 4Q27, which indicate a specific or immediate prohibition: "*Do not go* with the men. *And do not put a curse* on the people" (*'l*[*tlk*] . . . *w'l* [*t'w*]*r*; GBHS §4.2.3, §4.2.11). Possibly to clarify the referent as those mentioned in v. 9 and to coordinate the impvs., 4Q27 reads: "Do not go with *the men* [(')*m h'nšym*]. *And do not* [*w'l*] put a curse on the people."

26. 4Q27 and LXX[ed] read instead "'Go to your *master*'" (*'dwn*[*y*]*kmh* 4Q27 ≈ *ton kyrion hymōn* LXX[ed]), probably attempting to be more precise, since the narrator next says, "So the Moabite officials returned to Balak."

27. LXX[ed] removes "for" and replaces "Yahweh" with "God," perhaps because the translator envisioned that Balaam would have used the generic, non-Israelite name for the deity with Balak's officials: "*God* [*ho theos*] does not allow me to go with you."

28. Always in the piel (16× in the Pentateuch); in Numbers **m'n* (DCH 5:119) occurs first when Edom refuses to allow Israel to pass through its territory and now twice to express Yahweh's refusal for Balaam to go with Balak's officials (22:13, 14).

29. A verbal hendiadys, formally, "*got up* [*wayyāqûmû*] *and went* [*wayyābō'û*]" (GBHS §4.3.3g.2); 4Q27 and LXX[mss], here and in v. 16, read "said *to him*," likely to improve the flow of the narration (see vv. 7, 32).

30. A niphal stative of **kbd* and near demonstrative, referring to the first group of Moabite officials in vv. 7–14, so more formally, "and honored more than these."

31. Probably to repeat the title used in v. 10, 4Q27 adds, "Zippor's son Balak, *king of Moab*" ([*m*]*lk*[*mw'b*]).

32. This root **mn'* (keep you) occurs three times in the Pentateuch, first in Gen. 30:2 (Jacob asserts that Yahweh *has withheld* from Rachel) and now here and in 24:11 in a contrasting *inclusio* around the Balaam cycle; see the second translation note on 24:11.

33. LXX[ed] omits the adv. "very highly," and renders the inf. formally: "For I will honor you honorably."

34. Probably to clarify Balak's intentions with a parallel obj., 4Q27 and LXX[ed] supply a dative of advantage: "I will highly honor you, . . . I will do *for you*."

35. Formally, "I am not able to cross over" (*la'ăbōr*), but if Balaam thinks himself to be a devoted Yahwist, maybe "I am not able *to transgress*" (NET).

god,[36] to do something small or great.[37] [19]Now stay the night here also, so that I may find out what more Yahweh might say to me."[38]

[20]God[39] came to Balaam that night and said to him, "If the men have come to call you, go with them,[40] but you must do exactly what I tell you."[41] [21]So Balaam got up in the morning, saddled his donkey, and went with the Moabite officials.[42] [22]But God became very angry[43] because he went, and the angel of Yahweh stood in the road to oppose him.[44] Now he was riding on his donkey, and his two servants were with him. [23]The donkey saw the angel of Yahweh[45] standing in the road with his sword drawn in his hand, so the donkey turned aside[46] from the road and went into the field. But Balaam beat the donkey to make her[47] turn back to the road. [24]Then the angel of Yahweh stood in a path among the vineyards, with a wall on either side. [25]When the donkey saw the angel of Yahweh, she pressed herself into the wall, and crushed Balaam's foot against the wall. So he beat her again. [26]Then the angel of Yahweh went ahead and stood in a narrow place, where there was no way to turn to the right or to the left. [27]When the donkey saw the angel of Yahweh, she crouched down[48] under Balaam. Balaam was angry and beat his

---

36. On the lowercase to indicate Balaam's self-identification as a devotee of Israel's deity, "Yahweh *my god* [*'ĕlōhāy*]," see the first translation note on 10:9. LXX[ed]: "the word of the Lord God."

37. Maybe harmonizing with 24:13, 4Q27 and LXX[ed] include "small or great *in my mind/ heart.*"

38. Likely perceiving the parallel plotline in v. 8 to be strangely absent here, 4Q27 adds "So the Moabite officials stayed with Balaam" (*wyšbw*]*śry* [*mw'b/ 'm bl'm*]).

39. Unlike 22:12, here SP envisions an intermediary or divine representative, "the angel of God."

40. A verbal hendiadys: formally, "*Get up, go* [*qûm lēk*] with them!" (*GBHS* §4.3.3g.2).

41. By left dislocation, the obj. is activated as the primary topic of the main clause: formally, "but only *the word that I speak to you,* it you must do" (*BHRG* §48.2.1).

42. After v. 20 in 4Q27 (col. XII), the rest of the line is blank, and the next line, all of v. 21, is written in red ink, suggesting that the scribe regarded v. 21 as introducing a new unit of discourse (Ulrich, *Qumran,* 152).

43. "*But God*" is contextual. Idiomatically, "But the anger/nose of God became hot/was kindled." Most likely to match "the angel of *Yahweh*" in v. 22b, SP (LXX[mss] MT[ms]) reads, "*Yahweh* became very angry."

44. The hithpael reflexive is followed by lameds of product and disadvantage, meaning "*stood himself* [*wayyityaṣṣēb*] in the road *as an adversary* [*ləśāṭān*] against him [*lô*]" (*GBHS* §3.1.5a; 4.1.10e.2, e.1).

45. In vv. 24–35, LXX[ed] reads "the angel of God" (vv. 23, 24, 25, 26, 27, 31, 32, 35). The exception is v. 34, "the angel of the Lord."

46. A consequential wayyiqtol, "*so the donkey turned aside* [*wattēṭ*]" (*GBHS* §3.5.1b).

47. "The donkey" (*hā'ātôn*) is a female donkey (cf. male *ḥămôr*) and grammatically fem. I preserve "her" (*ləhaṭṭōtāh*) and "whom" (*'ăšer,* v. 30) since she is a character in the narrative, a stereotype of one who is loyal yet undervalued and exploited (see Berlin, "Characterization," 69–85).

48. Or "then she lay down" (*wattirbaṣ*) or maybe even "then she fell down," a successive wayyiqtol (from "*rbṣ* I," *DCH* 7:407, glosses 1a, 2, 3).

donkey[49] with a staff. **28**Then Yahweh opened the donkey's mouth, and she said to Balaam, "What have I done to you that you would beat me these three times?" **29**Balaam said to the donkey, "You have repeatedly made me look stupid.[50] I wish I had a sword in my hand because I would kill you right now!" **30**The donkey said to Balaam, "Am I not your donkey, whom you have ridden all your life[51] until this day? Have I been in the habit[52] of doing this to you?" And he said, "No."

31Then Yahweh opened Balaam's eyes, and he saw the angel of Yahweh standing in the road with his sword drawn in his hand. So he bowed low and threw himself facedown.[53] **32**The angel of Yahweh said to him, "Why did you beat your donkey these three times? I came out to oppose you[54] because your way is perverse before me![55] **33**The donkey saw me and turned away before me[56] these three times. Maybe[57] if she had not turned away from me, by now I would have killed you[58] but let

---

49. A possessive article, "*his* donkey" (*hā'ātôn*; GBHS §2.6.7).

50. Commonly, "you have made a fool of me!" (*hit'allalt bî*). The hithpael of this root (*'ll*) is used in the six other texts to mean, "deal wantonly with," "make sport of," or "abuse (sexually)" (*DCH* 6:426). Based on the context of the donkey's repeated undesirable actions (vv. 23, 25, 27), I render the hithpael with an iterative nuance: "You have repeatedly made me look stupid" (*GBHS* §3.1.5c).

51. Formally, "from your still/continually."

52. The hiphil qatal and adverbial inf., probably emphatic (*GBHS* §3.4.2b2)—"have I habitually been in the habit?" (*hahaskēn hiskantî*)—come from the same uncommon root (*skn*), which occurs only here and in the Writings (6× in Job 15–35; Ps. 139:3; Eccles. 10:9).

53. Formally, "to his two nostrils" (*lə'appāyw* MT SP). 4Q27 and LXX^ed adjust to the more common idiom, "to his face."

54. By anacoluthon, "you" is inferred from common sense (cf. "him" stated in v. 22). Other manuscripts (4Q27 SP LXX^ed) add "you" for clarity.

55. A possessive article: formally, "the way is precipitous/steep before me" (*yāraṭ hadderek lənegdî*), in which the qal stative, **yrṭ* (is perverse), occurs only here, while in the verb's only other occurence (Job 16:11), the qal is transitive, "*and pushes me* [*yirṭēnî*] into the hands of the wicked" (*DCH* 4:297). LXX^ed: "your way was not pretty before me" (NETS; variant possibility: Ulrich, *Qumran*, 153). Other witnesses replace this rare verb with the more common stative: "*the (your) way is evil* before me" (*r'h hdrk* 4Q27); "*your evil way* is before me" (*hr' drkk* SP).

56. The formal "turned away *before me*" (*ləpānay*; ESV) may be preferred over "turned away *from me*" (*mlpny* 4Q27 SP ≈ *ap' emou* LXX^ed; NRSV, NET, NIV, NJPS), which can be seen as clarifying (with an ablative *min*) and forging a parallel with v. 33c, "if she had not turned away *from me*" (4Q27 MT SP LXX^AO; > LXX^BL).

57. Modern translations often omit the adv. "maybe, perhaps" (*'ûlay* MT 4Q27 SP), possibly to avoid representing Yahweh as one who deliberates or conjectures because he does not know his own course of action. Instead, I retain the adv. because the Hb. text adds complexity to Yahweh's character by disclosing his thoughts that reflect his dynamic interactions with Balaam and with his donkey. LXX^ed reads "and if" (*kai ei mē*), maybe from a separate Hb. source (*wlwly*, Ulrich, *Qumran*, 153).

58. Apparently to extend the *Leitwort* of *striking* (**nkh* in vv. 6, 23, 25, 27, 28, 32), SP reads "I would have *struck* you" (*'tk hkyty*) rather than "I would have *killed* [**hrg*] you" (4Q27 MT ≈ LXX^ed).

her live."[59] [34]Balaam said to the angel of Yahweh, "I have sinned because I did not know that you were standing to confront me[60] in the road. So now, if it is evil in your sight, I will go back."[61] [35]The angel of Yahweh said to Balaam, "Go with the men, but say[62] only what I tell you."[63] So Balaam went with Balak's officials. [36]When Balak heard that Balaam was coming, he went out to meet him at the Moabite town on the border of the Arnon at the edge of his territory. [37]Balak said to Balaam, "Didn't I deliberately send[64] for you to summon you? Why didn't you come to me? You really think[65] I am not able to honor you?" [38]Balaam said to Balak, "Look, I have come to you now. Am I really able to speak anything? Only the word that God puts in my mouth, that is what I must speak."[66] [39]Then Balaam went with Balak, and they came[67] to Kiriath Huzoth. [40]Balak sacrificed cattle and sheep, and sent them to Balaam[68] and to the officials who were with him. [41]The next morning Balak took Balaam, and brought him up to Baal's high place.[69] From there he saw a fraction of the people.[70]

[23:1]Balaam said to Balak, "Build[71] me seven altars here, and prepare for me here seven bulls and seven rams." [2]Balak did as Balaam had

---

59. Fronting activates both identifiable entities, contrasted by a disjunctive *wə*: "by now *even you* I would have killed, *but her* I (would) have let live" (BHRG §47.2.1[a]*b*; IBHS §39.2.3b).

60. Formally, "to meet me," but the context implies opposition (v. 32).

61. A reflexive *l*, formally, "I *myself* will go back" (*ʾāšûbâ lî*; GBHS §4.1.10m).

62. SP and LXX[ed]: "be careful to speak."

63. As in v. 20, here by left dislocation, the obj. is activated as the primary topic of the main clause: "but only *the word that I speak to you, it* you must do" (BHRG §48.2.1).

64. The adverbial inf. of the same root is emphatic, formally, "Didn't *sending I send* [*šālōaḥ šālaḥtî*]" (GBHS §3.4.2b2).

65. More formally, "*Really* [*haʾumnām*]? Am I not able to honor you?"

66. As in vv. 20, 35, by left dislocation, the obj. is activated as the primary topic of the main clause: "Only *the word that God puts in my mouth, that is what* I must speak" (BHRG §48.2.1). SP: "I must be careful to speak."

67. With a hiphil transitive and obj., SP presents Balaam as the guiding agent: "and *he* [Balaam] *brought him* [Balak] to Kiriath Huzoth" (*wyb'hw*).

68. The obj. of the piel transitive verb is not stated, but the slaughtered animals are likely implied: "and sent *them* to Balaam" (*wayšallaḥ ləbilʿām*; NRSV; cf. stated obj. 22:5). Many versions read "*some of* them," which is unnecessary; "sent for Balaam" (ESV) is unlikely, since that is typically expressed through the qal stem (DCH 8:378, gloss 3b).

69. *Bāmôt bāʿal* may be a toponym, "Bamoth-baal" (most versions), but even so, it means "Baal's high place," a public stone construction used ritually in the Baal cult in Moab. One recalls "*the high places* of Arnon" (*bāmôt ʾarnōn*, 21:28). Moabite King Mesha might be referring to this metonymically as a place he rebuilt: "I took *Beth-Bamoth* for it was destroyed" (Moabite Stele, line 27, https://www.worldhistory.org/Moabite_Stone_[Mesha_Stele]; Drey, "Bamoth, Bamoth-Baal," 145–46).

70. With ESV (≈ "part," NRSV; "portion," NJPS), forming a thematic *inclusio* with 22:3, where the Moabites feared the Israelite people who "were so numerous," yet different formal renderings of *qāṣēh* remain possible: "up to/as far as the people" (for EÜ), "*the extent* of the people" (see NET ≈ "outskirts," NIV).

71. For "build me" (*bənēh-lî*; *bnh* in vv. 14, 29), SP reads, "Make me" (*ʿśh ly*, see v. 30).

said. Balak and Balaam[72] then offered a bull and a ram on each altar.
[3]Balaam said to Balak, "Stay here by your burnt offering while I go off.
Maybe Yahweh[73] will come to meet me,[74] and whatever he shows me,
I will tell you."[75] ⌜So he left. Balak stood beside his burnt offering, and
Balaam went to meet with God,⌝[76] so he went off to a desert place.[77]
[4]And God met with Balaam,[78] who said to him, "I have arranged seven
altars,[79] and I have offered a bull and a ram on each altar." [5]Then Yahweh

72. LXX[ed] (MT[mss]) omits "Balak and Balaam," perhaps to continue the agency of v. 2a, insofar as only *"Balak* did as Balaam had said."

73. Probably to standardize to "God" throughout the Balaam cycle (*'ĕlōhîm* in MT 22:9, 10, 12, 20, 22, 38; 23:4, 27) and perhaps to try to remove the perception that Balaam could be a true prophet of Yahweh, Israel's covenant deity (see Balaam's rejection and death in 31:8, 16), SP and LXX[ed] inconsistently replace "Yahweh" with "God" (*'lhym* SP ≈ *ho theos* LXX[ed] in vv. 5 [SP *"angel of* Yahweh," *ml'k yhwh*], 8 [LXX[ed] reverses to Lord . . . God], 12 [LXX[ed] only], 16 [SP *"angel of* Yahweh," *ml'k yhwh*; "God" *ho theos* LXX[e]), 26.

74. "Yahweh will appear" (*yiqqārēh* MT 4Q27) from **qrh* is a niphal reflexive that recurs in chap. 23 (vv. 3, 4, 15, 16; also Exod. 3:18; 2 Sam. 1:6) and likely means Yahweh will allow himself to be encountered (*HALOT* 3:1137–38; *GBHS* §3.1.2c; prb. with LXX[ed] *phaneitai,* "appeared"; contra Ulrich, *Qumran,* 154), whereas the SP by homophony reads "Yahweh *will call* [*yqr'*]."

75. This hiphil causative with two objects—*"whatever* God causes *me* to see" (*ma-yar'ēnî*)—can be technical language of a prophet receiving a revelatory vision, as in Yahweh showing Moses the blueprints to the dwelling place (Exod. 25:9; 27:8; Num. 8:4) and his back but not his glory (Exod. 33:18–23; see *land* in Gen. 12:1; Deut. 34:1, 4). The Deir 'Alla inscriptions depict the prophet Balaam son of Beor as "a seer of the gods" (*ḥzh 'lhn,* https://www.livius.org/sources /content/deir-alla-inscription; Wilson, *Prophecy,* 132).

76. The text in half-brackets is absent from the MT and SP but present in 4Q27 and LXX[ed] ([*w*]*ylk wytyṣb blq 'l* ʿ[*w*]*ltw wbl'm* [*nqrh 'l 'lwhym*] ≈ *kai parestē Balak epi tēs thysias autou, kai Balaam eporeuthē eperōtēsai ton theon*). I include this plus (textual addition) because it is possibly original for three reasons: (1) the parallel scene in vv. 14–15 excludes this plus among the witnesses, so it is not likely a harmonization; (2) within vv. 3–4 this plus doesn't obviously attempt to clarify anything, nor is it needed to advance the plot; and (3) its absence in the MT can be explained by homoeoteleuton (skipping from *wylk* to *wylk*; see Wevers, *Notes,* 385–86).

77. "Desert place" (*šepî*) is used in the Pentateuch only here (10× elsewhere) and probably does not refer to "a bare/barren/deserted *height*" (NRSV, ESV, NIV) or "bare *hill*" (NLT; see glosses of *"šepî* I" excluding any explicit elevation in *DCH* 8:538). Earlier in this verse, SP reads "burnt offerings" (*'ltyk*), probably to match the plurality of sacrifices (vv. 1–2). Instead of "Yahweh" (MT), other witnesses read "God" (*'lhwym* 4Q27 SP ≈ LXX[ed]), probably to correlate with "God," the agent in v. 4.

78. On this niphal reflexive, now fulfilling Balaam's desire, see the second translation note on 23:3. Perhaps to distance the non-Israelite Balaam, who is later swept up in God's judgment against Midian (Num. 31:2, 8), from personally encountering God, 4Q27 and SP read "Then the angel of God encountered/found Balaam" ([*wymṣ'*]*ml*[*'k 'lwhy*]*m*[*'t b*]*l'm*).

79. Balaam's seven-altar arranging work (**'rk*) probably refers not to constructing the altars but to organizing the wood and sacrificial meat and organs of the bull and ram on the altars (see Elijah, who builds and then arranges in 1 Kings 18:31–33). Balaam's action recalls the prior cultic associations of this verb in the Pentateuch: Abraham arranges wood on the altar to offer his son to God (Gen. 22:9); Aaron and sons tend the lamps, arrange the bread table, arrange the wood and animal parts for burnt offerings (Exod. 27:21; 40:4, 23; Lev. 1:7, 8, 12; 6:12; 24:3, 4, 8). While Deut. 23:3–4 bars Balaam and the Moabites from entering the worshiping

put a word in Balaam's mouth and said, "Return to Balak, and say what I tell you."[80] [6]So he returned to him, and he was still standing by his burnt offering, he and all the Moabite officials. [7]Then Balaam spoke his saying:[81] "King Balak of Moab brought me from Aram,[82] from the eastern mountains, saying,[83] 'Come, put a curse on Jacob for me. Come, denounce Israel.' [8]How can I curse those God has not cursed, or how can I denounce those Yahweh has not denounced?[84] [9]For from the top of the rocks I see them; from the hills I watch them. A nation that lives alone and does not consider itself among the nations! [10]Who can count the dust of Jacob or number[85] the dust cloud of Israel?[86] Let me die the

---

"assembly of Yahweh" (*qəhal yhwh*; see Awabdy, *Immigrants*, 66–83), the Priestly vision in Num. 15:14–16 (also Lev. 17:8–9) allows non-Israelites, without disqualifying the Moabites, to bring burnt offerings among other offering varieties by fire to the Aaronic priest to offer to Yahweh. By arranging and sacrificing, the prophet Balaam, who receives oracles from Yahweh, now takes the prerogative of an Israelite priest (see Lev. 1:7–12; 6:12).

80. Formally, "and thus/so you must speak."

81. Formally, "Then he lifted his saying and said" (*wayyiśśā' məšālô wayyō'mar*), which is a superscript that recurs to introduce Balaam's speeches in chaps. 23–24 (23:7, 18; 24:3, 15, 20, 21, 23). The term *māšāl* can refer to a mocking song, byword, taunt, or indicting proverb, a common use by the Hebrew Prophets, which would correlate with Balaam's prophetic role (as Isa. 14:4; Jer. 24:9; Ezek. 14:8; Mic. 2:4; Hab. 2:6). However, the tone of Balaam's speeches is often uplifting (honoring Israel), and the typical meaning of *māšāl* is a proverb, saying, or wisdom saying, which could represent the prophet Balaam as a sage (see *māšāl* in Job 13:12; Prov. 1:1, 6; 10:1; 25:1; 26:7, 9; Eccles. 12:9). On the history of translating this idiom, see Vayntrub, "'*Take Up* a Parable,'" 627–45. Just before this, likely imported from the parallel introduction to Balaam's saying in 24:2, LXX[ed]: "And a divine spirit was upon him" (NETS).

82. LXX[ed] replaces the outdated toponym "Aram" (*'ărām*)—whose glory days in the ANE ended with the Achaemenid (Persian) Empire (332 BCE)—with the Greek name for the region, "Mesopotamia" (*Mesopotamias* LXX[ed]), meaning "between the rivers" of the Tigris and Euphrates.

83. I supply "saying" (LXX[ed], many versions) since this begins King Balak's direct speech reported by Balaam.

84. Balaam's speech includes three synonyms for cursing in vv. 7–8: the first is the most common verb (*'rr*, 63×); the second appears for the first time here in the OT (*z'm*, 12×); and the third appears first in the Balaam cycle and recurs throughout it but otherwise appears only in OT Wisdom literature (*qbb*, 10× in Num. 22–24; 4× in Job/Proverbs): "'Come, *put a curse* [*'ārâ*] on Jacob for me. Come, *denounce* [*zō'ămâ*] Israel.' How *can I curse* [*'eqqōb*] those God *has not cursed* [*lō' qabbōh*], or how *can I denounce* [*'ez'ōm*] those Yahweh *has not denounced* [*zā'am*]?"

85. This is a rare case of fusion, wrongly combining two words, in MT—formally, "*and a number* [*ûmispār*], the fourth of Israel [with direct obj. marker]." The original reading probably included the rest of the MT verse but with the finite verb of SP and LXX[ed], reconstructed as "and number the fourth of Israel" (*ûmî sāpar 'et-rōba' yiśrā'ēl*; cf. *wmy spr mrb't yśr'l* SP) and rendered by LXX[ed] as "and who will count Israel's multitudes" (*kai tis exarithmēsetai dēmous Israēl*).

86. Or "the fourth part of Israel" (ESV, NET, NIV for "*rōba'* I," *DCH* 7:406; with Tg[O] "from four," *mē'arba'*). I prefer "dust cloud of Israel" (*rōba' yiśrā'ēl*, from "*rōba'* II" *DCH* 7:406; *HALOT* 3:1181), suspecting the head noun to be a hapax synonymous with "dust of Jacob" (*'ăpar ya'ăqōb*; with NRSV, NJPS; Schmidt, *Numeri*, 119; Ashley, *Numbers*, 468; similarly, "[thick] cloud" for de Vaulx, *Nombres*, 276; Cazelles, *Nombres*, 112). Cognate support comes

death of the upright, and let my end be like theirs." [11]Balak answered:[87] "What have you done to me? I brought you to curse my enemies, but you have only blessed them!"[88] [12]Balaam replied, "Shouldn't I be careful to speak what Yahweh has put in my mouth?"[89]

[13]Balak said to him, "Come[90] with me to another place where you can see[91] them. You will see only a slim part of them,[92] but you will not see all of them. Curse them for me from there." [14]So he took him to the field of Zophim, to the summit[93] of Pisgah.[94] He built seven altars and offered a bull and a ram on each altar. [15]And Balaam said to Balak, "Stay here by your burnt offering while I meet someone over there."[95] [16]Then Yahweh met Balaam and put a word in his mouth and said, "Return to Balak, and say what I tell you." [17]When he came to him, he was still standing by his burnt offering, along with the officials of Moab. And Balak said to him, "What did Yahweh say?" [18]Then Balaam spoke his oracle: "Rise, Balak, and hear. Listen to me, son of Zippor. [19]God is not a human, that he would lie, nor a mortal, that he would change his mind.[96] Once he has said it, will he not do it? Once he has spoken, will he not make it happen?[97] [20]Yes, he has blessed, I have received. He has blessed, and

---

from the Akkadian "dust, dust heap, sand dune" ("*turbu'tu*," *CAD* 18:485). LXX[ed] eliminates the metaphor: "the descendants of Iakob . . . the divisions of Israel." A. Guillaume ("Numbers xxiii 10," 335–37) renders the bicolon "Who can count the warriors of Jacob / And who can number the people of Israel?"

87. Formally, "Then Balak said to Balaam."

88. A cognate adverbial inf. for emphasis: "But look! *You have blessed, blessing* [*bēraktā bārēk*]!" (*GBHS* §3.4.2b.2).

89. By left dislocation, the obj. is activated as the primary topic of the main clause: "Is it not *what Yahweh puts in my mouth, that* I will be careful to speak?" (*BHRG* §48.2.1).

90. Adopting MT[qere] as "*come* [*ləkâ-nā'*] with me" versus "*to you* [*ləkā-nā'*] with me" (MT[ketiv]; SP *lk n'*).

91. After v. 12 in 4Q27 (col. XVI, vv. 6–12 missing), the next line, v. 13a–b is written in red ink, marking what the scribe perceived to be the beginning of a new unit of discourse: "Balak said to him . . . see" (see Ulrich, *Qumran*, 154).

92. Formally, "you will see from there the end of their edge."

93. Formally, "head."

94. LXX[ed] tries to make sense of these toponyms: "*an outlook point* of a field, on the top of *Hewn Stone*" (*skopian . . . lelaxeumenou*; my trans.).

95. In this circumstantial *wa* clause (*GBHS* §4.3.3e), most versions add "with the Lord," but I supply "someone" to preserve the ambiguity of the Hb. text by which the narrator restricts Balak's knowledge: formally, "while I meet/encounter there" (similarly, "meet him" NIV).

96. These could be non-perfectives of capability that are hypothetical consequences: "God is not a human, *that he can lie* [*wîkazzēb*], nor a mortal, *that he can change his mind* [*wəyitnehām*]" (*IBHS* §31.4c). More likely, setting aside theological assumptions, the modal yiqtols are customary, depicting the human tendency toward lying and wavering: "God is not a human, *that he would* [be prone to] *lie*, nor a mortal, *that he would* [be prone to] *change his mind* (*IBHS* §31.2b).

97. Formally, "Has he himself said (it), but/and will not do (it)? (Has he) spoken, but/and he will not confirm it?"

I cannot reverse it.[98] [21]He has not observed misfortune in Jacob,[99] nor has he seen trouble in Israel. Yahweh their God is with them, acclaimed as king among them.[100] [22]God brought them out of Egypt, like the horns of a wild bull for them.[101] [23]For there is no omen against Jacob, nor divination against Israel. At this time it must be said of Jacob and of Israel, 'See what God has done!'[102] [24]Look, the people rise like a lioness, and like a lion raises himself up[103]—he does not lie down until he eats

---

98. Against many modern versions that seem to adapt the SP and LXX[ed] reading "See, I have received (a command) to bless" (*hn lbrk lqḥty* SP; *idou eulogein pareilēmmai* LXX[ed]), I rather prefer the MT, which is explainable as Hebrew poetry, a synonymously parallel bicolon:

| Yes, he has blessed, I have received | *hinnē* | *bārēk* | *lāqaḥtî* |
| He has blessed, and I cannot reverse it | *ûbērēk wəlō'* | *'ăšîbennâ* | |

Some repoint the verb as a qal pass. *luqqaḥtî*, meaning "I was taken/summoned to bless" (so Seebass, *Numeri*, 3:12; Levine, *Numbers*, 2:165), but most add an obj. for clarity, "received *a command/instruction*" or "a charge" (for Cazelles, *Nombres*, 112), but following the MT, I favor leaving the obj. ambiguous because (1) it could instead be "an oracle" (v. 18) or "what Yahweh has spoken" (v. 19); and (2) in parallel texts, the abstract obj. of *lqḥ* (receive) is either stated or clearly implied from the context (Exod. 22:11 [10]; Prov. 24:32; Jer. 2:30; contra Ashley, *Numbers*, 473).

99. The meaning "*misfortune, trouble* in Jacob" for this word is rare, with "iniquity, evil" being common ("*'āwen* I," *DCH* 1:154). Probably due to homophony (ayin for aleph), SP reads "*I have not looked on iniquity* [*l' 'byṭ 'wn*] in Israel, he has not . . ."

100. Formally, "and a shout/trumpet blast/joy of a king is among them" (*ûtərû'at melek bô*).

101. Balaam represents "Yahweh their God" (v. 21) as El/God (*'ēl*, v. 22), whose redemptive power on Israel's behalf is "like the horns of a wild bull" (*kətô'ăpōt rə'ēm*; LXX[ed]: "like *a unicorn's glory* [*doxa monokerōtos*] he was to them"!). The Hb. could mean "*They have* [*lô*], as it were, the strength of a wild bull" (NET), correlating with Israel as lion-lioness (v. 24), but more likely the bull metaphor completes the colon (poetic line) of God as redeemer, which correlates with his power for Israel's benefit in vv. 21, 23 (see duplication in Num. 24:8). The subject, a metonym of Yahweh, is *'ēl*, which in the Northwest Semitic cultures that surround Israel refers to the Canaanite God El ("*'l*," *DNWSI* 1:53–55); the name *'ēl* for Yahweh occurs in Num. 12:13; 16:22; 23:8, 19, 22, 23; 24:4, 8, 16, 23. In the Deir 'Alla inscriptions, the figure Balaam, son of Beor, receives a message from El, who has a cohort of amiable gods: "The gods came to him at night, and he beheld a vision in accordance with El's utterance" ("The Deir 'Alla Plaster Inscriptions," *COS* 2.27:140, 142). In Num. 23:22, the association with El is unmistakable, since one of his common epithets was "Bull El his Father" (*tr 'il 'abh KTU* 1.3 V 35–36; 1.4 I 4–15; etc.). El, Baal, and other gods were frequently represented iconographically (pictures, cult statues, figurines) as a bull in order to replicate their divine form, symbolize them, or display them with superhuman virility (see Smith, *History of God*, 41, 49–50; Hundley, "Golden Calf?," 560–62). Because v. 22 is presented as the word that Yahweh gives to Balaam for Balak (vv. 16–18), we should not be hasty to castigate this as syncretism like Israel's or Jeroboam I's golden calves (Exod. 32:4; 1 Kings 12:28) but rather should marvel at Yahweh for his resolve to *contextualize* the revelation of his perfect nature for Moabites and Israelites alike.

102. Formally, without interjection: "What God/El has done" (*ma-pā'al 'ēl*).

103. The second colon includes the common word *'ărî* (lion), while the term in the first colon is found only in poetry and means "lion" but sometimes also "lioness" (masc. "*lābî'*," *HALOT* 2:517; *DCH* 4:513, see examples). SP has a fem. second noun: "as a lion . . . as *a lioness* [*'ryh*]."

his prey[104] and drinks the blood of the slain." [25]Balak said to Balaam, "Do not curse them at all or bless them at all!" [26]Balaam replied to Balak,[105] "Didn't I tell you, 'Everything Yahweh says, I do'?"[106] [27]Balak said to Balaam, "Come, I will take you to another place. Perhaps it will please God[107] to let you curse them for me from there."[108] [28]So Balak took Balaam to the summit of Peor, which overlooks the wasteland.[109] [29]Then Balaam said to Balak, "Build seven altars for me here, and prepare seven bulls and seven rams." [30]So Balak did as Balaam said, and offered a bull and a ram on each altar.[110]

[24:1]Now Balaam saw that it pleased Yahweh to bless Israel, so he did not go as the other times to seek for omens,[111] but he set his face toward the wilderness. [2]Balaam lifted his eyes and saw Israel residing tribe by tribe, and God's spirit[112] came upon him. [3]Then he spoke his

---

104. The pronoun is implied: "*his* prey" (*ṭerep*).

105. Formally, "replied . . . and said."

106. By left dislocation, the obj. is activated as the primary topic of the main clause: formally, "'*Everything Yahweh says, it* I do'?" (*BHRG* §48.2.1). SP: "The entire word that God says, it I will do."

107. Anarthrous 4Q27 probably clarifies: "Perhaps it will please God [*'lwhym*]." Although the articular witnesses (*hoʾĕlōhîm* MT SP ≈ *tō theō* LXX^ed) can simply mean "God" (as 22:10), the MT/SP can also mean "the gods," which would fit the collection of Yahweh (throughout), Baal (22:41), and Chemosh (21:29) but does not fit the immediate context in which Balak inquires of Balaam what *Yahweh* says (v. 17) and which interchanges "God/El" (*ʾēl*, vv. 19, 22, 23) and "Yahweh" (vv. 17, 21, 26).

108. A consequential weqatal: "Perhaps it will please God [formally, be straight in God's eyes] *and as a result you will curse them* [*waqabbōtô*] for me from there" (*GBHS* §3.5.2b). In 4Q27 (col. XVI), after a gap in the text following vv. 22b–27c, v. 27d is written in red ink, indicating the scribal interpretation that a new discursive unit begins: "Perhaps it will please God . . . from there" (Ulrich, *Qumran*, 154–55).

109. With a referential article, "*the* wasteland" (*hayśîmōn*) refers to a particular desert or steppe proximate to Peor in Transjordan (*yaśîmôn* in Pentateuch: Num. 21:20; 23:28; Deut. 32:10; see *DCH* 4:333, gloss 3).

110. "On *each* altar" (for "on the altar," *bammizbēaḥ* MT 4Q27 LXX^ed) is a contextual addition (many versions); SP: "at the altar" (*ʾl mzbḥ*).

111. In Numbers only in 23:23 and here, the term is probably best rendered "omens" (*nəḥāšîm* from *naḥaš*; cf. "divination," NLT, NIV). On omens, see the "Implications" essay below, "The Irony and Satire of the Balaam Cycle." Perhaps influenced by 20:23, the broken text of 4Q27 here may have read something like "seek for omens against Jacob or divination against Israel" (conjecture by Ulrich, *Qumran*, 155); untranslated article, "(the) omens" (*hnḥšym* SP ≈ LXX^ed).

112. The gen. construction *rûaḥ ʾĕlōhîm* occurs in Numbers only here, although Moses uses a metonym in 11:29: "I wish that Yahweh would put *his spirit* [*rûḥô*] on them." The burden of proof rests on the majority, who capitalize this as "the Spirit of God" (ESV, NLT, NIV, NET, et al.) and seek to forge continuity with the third person of the Trinity revealed in the NT (*to pneuma tou theou*, and its inflected forms in Matt. 3:16; 12:28; Rom. 8:9, 14; 15:19 [or just *pneumatos*]; 1 Cor. 2:11, 14; 7:40; 12:3; Eph. 4:30; Phil. 3:3; 1 John 4:2). All faithful Christians confess the Triune God, expressed by the NT witnesses and defended by the First Council of Constantinople (381 CE), which rejected the heresy that denied the consubstantiality of the Holy Spirit with the Father (called pneumatomachianism, advanced today by Jehovah's Witnesses). At the same time, the progressive nature of God's revelation of himself frees interpreters to

saying:[113] "The prophecy[114] of Balaam, Beor's son, the prophecy of the man whose eye is opened,[115] **4**who sees a vision from the Almighty,[116] falling flat on the ground with eyes[117] uncovered: **5**'How beautiful are your tents, Jacob, and your dwelling places, Israel! **6**They are like date palms[118] spread out, like gardens beside a river, like aloes that Yahweh

admit that the Spirit as a person of the Godhead would not have been obvious to the ancient Israelites and the Jews of the Second Temple period. Here in 24:2, the gen. restricts us from reading this as "*a spirit of God*" because definite *'ĕlōhîm* makes *rûaḥ* determinate/definite (contra "a divine spirit," *pneuma theou* LXX^ed; "*ein*/der" by Seebass, *Numeri*, 3:13). Instead, a lowercase const. noun is the most honest and likely conception: "God's spirit" or "the spirit of God" (NRSV, NJPS; Levine, *Numbers*, 2:188; de Vaulx, *Nombres*, 282; Cazelles, *Nombres*, 113; Ashley, *Numbers*, 483). In the ancient Near East, a deity's spirit was an immaterial extension of that deity or a pantheon of deities: e.g., "As the spirit of my father Amun endures" ("Ramesses II," *COS* 2.25:36; cf. Job 27:3; 33:4) and "May the great gods of heaven and earth, all the Anunnaku deities together, the protective spirit of the temple" ("The Laws of Hammurabi," *COS* 2.131:353; cf. Ezek. 11:24). Other biblical texts present God's spirit (*rûaḥ 'ĕlōhîm*) as a force emanating from God that comes upon and possesses an individual, who then has an ecstatic experience (hithpael of **nb'*: 1 Sam. 10:10; 19:20, 23) and/or delivers a divine message (11:6; 2 Chron. 15:1; 24:20) or is granted wisdom/interpretation or skill (Gen. 41:38; Exod. 31:3; 35:31). "Possession by God's spirit" results in "the reception and delivery of the word of God" (Wilson, *Prophecy*, 145, locating this prophetic activity in the Ephraimite tradition). This is the Yahwistic (monotheistic) version of what one finds in places like Mari (Syria), Delphi (Greece), and, most relevantly, Deir 'Alla (Jordan), as shown in an Aramaic inscription (ca. 700 BCE), which undoubtedly refers to the same "Balaam son of Beor," who receives messages, probably oracles of doom, directly from the gods (see Wilson, *Prophecy*, 132–34). In this context, the gen. in 24:2 could be the source, "the spirit that comes from God," or more likely a possessive, "the spirit that belongs to God" or "God's spirit" (*GBHS* §2.2.1), like the spirit of a human being, insofar as *rûaḥ* (spirit) is a communicable attribute of God (see *rûaḥ* of a human in Gen. 45:27; 2 Sam. 13:39; 1 Chron. 5:26; Ezra 1:1; et al.).

113. Formally, "Then he lifted his saying, and he said."

114. See the comments below on "prophecy."

115. From the qal pass. "is open(ed)" (*šātum*). Its meaning is debated since it occurs in the OT only here in vv. 3 and 15 and without comparative Semitic evidence, but the visionary context here and in the opening of the Deir 'Alla inscription is informative, in which Balaam is "a divine seer" who "beheld a vision" ("The Deir 'Alla Plaster Inscriptions," *COS* 2.27:142). Contra Allegro ("*šetūm hā'ayin*," 78–79), who derives the meaning from the alleged Arabic cognate, *šatuma*: "the man, *the unrelenting one*." Such a rendering does not fit the direct context.

MT and LXX^ed include the same clause in v. 16, "the prophecy of the one who hears God's words" (*nə'um šōmēa' 'imrê-'ēl* MT; *phēsin akouōn logia theou* LXX^ed). I prefer the SP and 4Q27 (based on line spacing), which lack this clause. My reasons are as follows: (1) the SP MSS of Numbers and 4Q27 have a tendency to add rather than remove text from their Hb. source, which makes their lack of alignment with v. 16 significant; (2) it is more likely that MT/LXX^ed supplied the clause in v. 16 than that its absence from SP/4Q27 was caused by haplography due to either homeoarcton or homeoteleuton (skipping from *h'yn n'm šm' 'mry-'l 'šr*).

116. See the "Implications" essay below, "The Irony and Satire of the Balaam Cycle."

117. SP: "eye" (*'yn*).

118. Others take this as the common homonym "valleys" (NIV, NET; Cazelles, *Nombres*, 114), but that word most frequently connotes dry riverbeds, "wadis" ("*naḥal* I" *DCH* 5:657), and less frequently "streams" (Seebass, *Numeri*, 3:13). Instead, the point of Balaam's poetic oracle is that with the wilderness or desert in view (24:1), Jacob-Israel is surprisingly fertile, so I prefer

has planted,[119] like cedars beside the waters. [7]Water will flow[120] from their buckets, and their descendants will be like abundant water.[121] Their king will be greater than Agag, and their kingdom will be exalted. [8]God brought them out of Egypt, like the horns of a wild bull for them.[122] They devour hostile people,[123] break their bones and pierce them with arrows.[124] [9]They crouch[125] and lie down[126] like a lion, and as a lioness, who will rouse them? The one who blesses you is blessed, and the one who curses you is cursed!'"

[10]Balak was very angry at Balaam and clapped[127] his hands. Then Balak said to Balaam, "I called you to curse my enemies, but you have

---

the hapax "palm trees" (nəḥālîm, from "naḥal II," DCH 5:659) with the Arabic pl. naḥeel (date palms ≈ palm groves; de Vaulx, Nombres, 284; Levine, Numbers, 2:189; NRSV, ESV, NLT).

119. Other witnesses that are perhaps unfamiliar with "aloes" ("'ăhālîm II," HALOT 1:19) but have just read "your tents" in v. 5, aurally confuse "like aloes ['ăhālîm] that Yahweh has planted [nāṭaʿ]" (MT[L]) with "like tents ['ōhālîm, same consonants]) that Yahweh has pitched [nāṭâ]" (SP ≈ 4Q27 LXX[ed]; see v. 5).

120. This verb occurs in OT poetry, with only two other occurrences in the Primary History, namely, in summoning witnesses to the Yahweh-Israel covenant (Deut. 32:2) and in the Song of Deborah (Judg. 5:5).

121. LXX[ed] may reflect a separate Hb. source: "A person will come forth from his offspring, and he shall rule over many nations" (NETS for exeleusetai anthrōpos ek tou spermatos autou, kai kyrieusei ethnōn pollōn; Ulrich, Qumran, 155). Although it is hard to imagine that the first colon arose by an unintentional scribal error, the translator could have reinterpreted the text to center "the eschatological hopes of the people" on an individual future figure beyond the Alexandrian Jews of the third century BCE (Wevers, Notes, 406).

122. Like 23:22. On this adaptation of ANE bull imagery, see the brief excursus at the end of the comments on 23:27–24:9, "God . . . like the Horns of a Wild Bull." SP and LXX[ed]: "God/a god guided him out of Egypt" (nḥhw SP; hōdēgēsen LXX[ed]).

123. The grammar is sg. (formally, "he eats the nations/peoples of his enemies," yōʾkal gôyim ṣārāyw), but at least by the allusion to the Abrahamic blessing (Gen. 12:3) in v. 9d, the sg. refers collectively to all Israel ("The one who blesses you [sg.] is blessed, and the one who curses you [sg.] is cursed!"). Continuing the literary stress on a blessed Israel in vv. 5–7, I am inclined to identify God as the subject in v. 8a and then see a return to a collective Israel in vv. 8b–9; so following the Hb. word order: "God brought them out of Egypt, like the horns of a wild bull for them [lô = Israel]. They devour [yōʾkal = Israel] hostile people" (cf. NET: "God brought them out of Egypt. They have, as it were, the strength. . . . They devour . . .").

124. The final two verbs in v. 8 are used in Hebrew poetry to picture war violence: "break [yəgārēm] their bones and pierce [yimḥāṣ] them with arrows" (*grm 3× in the OT: here; Ezek. 23:34; Zeph. 3:3; *mḥṣ 14×: here and Num. 24:17; Deut. 32:39; 33:11; Judg. 5:26; 2 Sam. 22:39; Job [2×]; Psalms [5×]; Hab. 3:13).

125. Probably due to metathesis and perceiving an initial parallelism, 4Q27 likely means "as an enemy [cʿr, vocalized kaʿār], he lies down" (see "krʿ," HALOT 2:499; cf. "they/he crouch," kāraʿ: MT SP LXX[ed]).

126. Balaam's words here innerbiblically replicate Jacob's blessing of Judah (Gen. 49:9), which probably influenced the alternate Hebrew version here in Num. 24:9: "They crouch and lie down [rbṣ, as in Gen. 49:9] like a lion" (4Q27 SP[ms]; cf. škb MT SP with *škb in 23:24); maybe rbṣ or škn is the source of anepausato (LXX[ed]).

127. This verb (*spq I: DCH 6:182) appears in the Pentateuch only here but occurs five other times in the OT, where it is always negative: in Elihu's second speech, God strikes the wicked

only blessed them these three times![128] [11]Now, go back to where you came from![129] I said I would highly honor you, but now Yahweh has held you back[130] from honor." [12]Balaam said to Balak, "Didn't I also tell your messengers whom you sent to me: [13]'Even if Balak would give me his palace full of silver and gold, I could not go beyond Yahweh's command, to do anything of my own will, good or evil. Whatever Yahweh[131] says I must speak'? [14]So now, I am going back to my own people. Come, let me advise you[132] what this people will do to your people in days to come.'"[133]

[15]Then he spoke his oracle: "The oracle of Balaam, Beor's son, the prophecy of the man whose eye is opened, [16]the prophecy of the one who hears God's words and who knows knowledge from the Most High,[134] who sees a vision from the Almighty, falling flat on the ground with eyes uncovered: [17]'I see him, but not now. I look at him, but not near. A star will come out of Jacob, and a scepter will rise out of Israel. He will crush the foreheads of Moab[135] and the skulls of all the sons of Sheth. [18]Edom will become a possession, and Seir, his enemies, will become a possession, but Israel will act valiantly. [19]One from Jacob will reign.[136] He

---

even while the rebellious *clap* their hands without respect for God (Job 34:26, 37); Israel *strikes* its thigh in repentant shame (Jer. 31:19) and under Yahweh's judgment (Ezek. 21:12 [17]); and passersby clap to mock the ruined Jerusalem (Lam. 2:15).

128. A cognate adverbial inf. for emphasis: formally, "But look! You have *blessed them, blessing* [*bēraktā bārēk*], these three times!" (*GBHS* §3.4.2b.2). The SP, likely to standardize with the Balaam cycle, replaces the word "times" (*p'mym* MT) with the conventional word for "times" (*rglym*, as in 22:28, 32, 33).

129. Formally, "And now, flee/run away to your place."

130. After Gen. 30:2 (Jacob retorts to Rachel), the Pentateuch's other two occurrences of this verb—meaning "withhold, hold back, restrain, refuse" (qal of *mn': DCH 5:354)—are found in the Balaam cycle, forming a narrative reversal of Balak's demands on and promises to Balaam (Num. 22:16–17; 24:11).

131. LXX[ed]: "God."

132. This verb (qal of *y's) is a cohortative of wish in which Balaam expresses his desire to advise Balak, which requires Balak's consent (*GBHS* §3.3.3b). The only other time this verb appears in the Pentateuch is in Exod. 18:19, where another non-Israelite, Moses's father-in-law, Jethro (elsewhere called Hobab and Reuel), resolves to advise Moses on governing Israel (cohortative of resolve, qal of *y's: GBHS* §3.3.3a).

133. Formally, "in the latter/end of the days."

134. The first noun in the second colon is the verbal obj., "who knows *knowledge* [*da'at*]," modified by a gen. noun that is arguably not objective (e.g., "knows *the Most High*") but indicates authorship/origin: "knowledge *from the Most High* [*'elyôn*]" (see Joüon and Muraoka §129.f.10; *IBHS* §9.5.1c).

135. This is a dual, so more precisely, "the two temples [sides of the heads] of Moab" (*pa'ătê mô'āb*). I prefer "foreheads" (many versions) to avoid confusion with the homonym, temples, the dwelling places of gods.

136. The *min* of source marks the origin of the agent, "One from Jacob" (*miyya'ăqōb*), either a native Israelite or, less likely, a long-standing resident of Jacob, while the yiqtol announces a future phenomenon, "will reign, have dominion" (*wayērd; GBHS* §4.1.13a, 3.2.2a). The more common verb for ruling or reigning is *mšl* I (*DCH* 5:531), but the verb used here is *rdh* I (23×, *DCH* 7:419), which in the Pentateuch depicts the royal calling of the first humans ("They will

will destroy the survivors[137] of the city.'"[138] ²⁰Then he saw Amalek and
spoke his oracle: "Amalek was first among the nations, but their end
will be total destruction."[139] ²¹Then he saw the Kenites and spoke their
oracle: "Your dwelling place is secure,[140] and your nest is set in the rock.
²²Even so, the Kenites will be consumed. How long will Assur take you
captive?"[141] ²³Then[142] he spoke his oracle: "O, who will live when God
does this? ²⁴Ships[143] will come from the coast of Cyprus[144] and will afflict
both Assur and Eber,[145] and he will also be totally destroyed."[146] ²⁵Then
Balaam got up and returned[147] to his home, and Balak also went his own
way.

Interpretation

22:1–6. In this opening scene, fear of the size and military power of the Israelites grips the Moabites, and the Moabite king, Balak, summons the prophet
Balaam to curse the Israelites so that Balak can conquer them. The geographical

---

reign/have dominion over the fish," Gen. 1:26, 28), limitations on ruling other classes of humans
(Lev. 25:43, 46, 53), and Yahweh's curse against Israel if they violate the covenant ("Those who
hate you will reign over you," Lev. 26:17).

137. The "survivors" ("*śārîd* I," *DCH* 8:192, gloss 1) refers to human survivors, escapees,
refugees, or a remnant alive during or after a war, not to material "remains" (NET), which
perhaps was chosen to remove the image of unnecessary violence by this messianic figure, but
the oracle begins with and then is followed by militant imagery (vv. 17, 20–24).

138. Formally, "from a city" (*mēʿîr* ≈ LXX^{ed}), which ESV reads contextually as a pl. ("of
cities") and others take as a toponym in Edom's territory: "the survivors *of Ir* ['*îr*]" (NRSV,
NLT, NJPS); cf. Marx, "Nombres XXIV 19b," 100–104.

139. The gen. noun belongs to the larger group, "first *among* the nations" (*rēʾšît gôyim*; a
type of "partitive," *IBHS* §9.5.1k), followed by a contrasting idiom: formally, "but their end
will be as far as duration/forever" (*waʾaḥărîtô ʿădê ʾōbēd*). *ʾŌbēd* (duration) occurs only here
in vv. 20, 24 in the OT.

140. The base meaning of this adjective is "continuous" ("*ʾêtān* I," *DCH* 1:237).

141. SP: "the Kenites will be consumed *until* they take you captive *from* Assur" (my trans.).

142. LXX^{ed} adds "*And when he saw Og and took up his parable.*"

143. Scurlock ("Departure of Ships?," 267–82) argues that *ṣy* is not an Egyptian loanword
meaning "ships" but "coming forth," and so renders this: "Alas, who can survive except God has
willed it, the (military) expeditions (formally, "comings forth") from the hands of the Kittim?"

144. Formally, "from the hand of Kittim" (*miyyad kittîm*, omitted by SP), a toponym probably referring to the island of Cyprus (as in Isa. 23:1, 12), but in the Table of Nations it refers
more broadly to the Ionians or Greeks as descendants of Japheth (Gen. 10:4; 1 Chron. 1:7).
Kittim is probably what the Phoenicians called Kitti (*kty*) and Greeks, Kition, both referring
to a settlement near Larnaka, off the south-central coast of the island of Cyprus (Redditt,
"Kittim," 776–77). LXX^{ed} clarifies: "*And one will go out from/by the hand of the Kitieans.*"

145. Formally, "and will afflict Assur and will afflict Eber." Witfall ("Asher and Ḥeber?,"
110–14) argues that Eber should be read as Ḥeber (cf. Ḥeber the Kenite in Judg. 4:17).

146. For the same expression, see the translation note on 24:20.

147. A narrative sequence of three wayyiqtol verbs: formally, "Then Balaam got up and went
and returned to his place" (*wayyāqām bilʿām wayyēlek wayyāšāb limqōmô*).

inscription from the editors in v. 1 belongs to a different source than in 21:10–20,[148] so it is not clear if and how "the valley that is in the region of Moab, near the top of Pisgah, which overlooks the wasteland" (21:20) differs from the Israelites' new encampment "in the desert valleys of Moab along the Jordan River across from Jericho" (22:1).[149] This begins the Hexateuch's geographical theme, "in the desert valleys of Moab" (bəʿarbôt môʾāb), locating the Israelite camp in an arid zone (0–4 inches of annual rainfall) in the Jordan Rift Valley just north of the Dead Sea. This completes their trek from Sinai (10:11) and positions them to enter Canaan from the east (Josh. 3). In v. 2, Zippor's son Balak, later identified as Moab's present king (v. 4),[150] saw the ruins or heard about what the Israelites had done to the Amorites, likely referring intertextually to the Sihon story (21:21–32), but maybe also synecdochally including Og and Heshbon (21:33–35). Understandably, the Moabites are deathly afraid of the numerous Israelites, so the Moabites recite to Midian's elders—these distinct people groups are linked in the composition of Numbers[151]—a poetic simile of Israel as a ravenous bull (vv. 3–4; see the translation note on v. 3 and the second translation note on v. 4).

Balak sends messengers to Beor's son Balaam at Pethor, near the Euphrates River in his native land,[152] to employ him to formally curse the Israelites so that he can defeat them (vv. 5–6). Also on the Euphrates River, the city of Mari in the eighteenth century BCE had prophets especially concerned with conquering the enemy at war.[153] The site has yielded many texts of spoken oracles against foreign nations.[154] The figure of Balaam has attracted considerable scholarly attention since the 1967 discovery of the Aramaic inscriptions from Tel Deir ʿAlla, located about five miles east of the Jordan River, near the Zarqa (Jabbok) River.[155] As the inscriptions begin, one Balaam son of Beor,

---

148. Most attribute 22:1 to P or Pᵍ, and some see it as the ending of Pᵍ, but Frevel (Mit Blick, 81) shows that this would not be a sensible conclusion to a Pᵍ narrative.

149. See the translation note on 22:1.

150. Finkelstein, Naʾaman, and Römer ("Mesha Stele," 3–11) argue against André Lemaire's proposal of "House of David" (bt[d]wd) for line 31 of the Mesha Stele. They point out that there is no t and that a vertical line divider appears before the w, meaning that b begins a three-letter personal name, which they propose is "Balak" (blk), associated with the Moabite king in the Num. 22–24 narrative. The king's seat in line 31 was at Horonaim, a location that the Bible puts in relation to Moab, south of the Arnon gorge (Isa. 15:5; Jer. 48:3, 5, 34).

151. See the comments on 31:1–12.

152. Or "the land of the sons of Ammon" (Layton, "Num. 22,5," 32–61). See the first translation note on 22:5.

153. Hess, Israelite Religions, 89–90.

154. Hess, Israelite Religions, 89–90; Walton and Matthews, Genesis–Deuteronomy, 201.

155. An entry to the scholarship (in chronological order) is as follows: Naveh, "Deir ʿAlla Inscription," 236–38; Hoftijzer, "Prophet Balaam," 11–17; Hoftijzer and van der Kooij, Aramaic Texts; Wood, "Prophecy of Balaam," 121–24; McCarter, "Balaam Texts," 49–60; Levine, "Deir ʿAlla," 195–205; H. Müller, "Aramäische Inschrift," 214–44; Hackett, Balaam Text; Puech, "L'inscription," 354–65; Levine, "Balaam Inscription," 326–39; Lemaire, "Fragments," 26–39;

a divine seer, has a theophanic encounter, reports his visions, and warns the people; they listen, the evil gods are punished, and the goddess and the land are saved. This is how the story opens:

> The misfortunes of the Book of Balaam, son of Beor.
> A divine seer was he.
> The gods came to him at night,
> And he beheld a vision in accordance with El's utterance.
> They said to Balaam, son of Beor:
>
> > "So will it be done, with naught surviving,
> > No one has seen [the likes of] what you have heard!"[156]

In this study, we will be able to draw only a few comparisons with the Deir 'Alla inscriptions, concluding generally that the biblical and inscriptional accounts substantiate a historical Balaam figure.

Balak's message to Balaam rightly asserts that Israel has come out of Egypt, hyperbolically covers the face of the earth (or land), and is now encamped next to Balak (v. 5; see the third translation note there). Balaam has gained a reputation as a professional curser with a successful record: "For I know that whomever you bless is blessed, and whomever you curse is cursed" (v. 6). Ancient Near Easterners commonly believed that if a trained professional pronounced or inscribed the right combination of imprecatory words—either a direct formula ("I curse") or imperative ("curse!"), sometimes with an accompanying ritual—then automatically the deity or demon would put the individual or people into a cursed state.[157] Apparently unknown to Balak, perhaps even as the storyteller's dramatic irony against him,[158] his words echo Yahweh's blessing of Abraham: "I will bless those who bless you, and the one who treats you lightly I will curse" (Gen. 12:3). There are two sides to this allusion. Balak trusts in Balaam to put Israel into a cursed state, but the Torah reader knows that Yahweh has already resolved to put Abraham and his progeny, Israel, into a blessed state (see the second translation note on v. 6). At the same time, by merely intending to curse Israel, Balak is treating Israel lightly and becomes the object of Yahweh's curse. The allusion is, therefore, ominous.

Shea, "Inscribed Tablets," 21–37, 97–119; Lemaire, "Bala'am/Bela'," 180–87; Hoftijzer and van der Kooij, *Balaam Text*; Franken, *Tell Deir 'Alla*; Van Seters, *Life of Moses*, 408–13; Dijkstra, "Balaam," 43–64; Wood, "Balaam," 114; Franken, "Deir 'Alla," 137–38; Rösel, "Bileamgestalt," 506–24; Seow, "Deir 'Alla," 207–12; Sparks, *Ancient Texts*, 234–35; Robker, *Balaam*.

156. "The Deir 'Alla Plaster Inscriptions," COS 2.27:142, lines 1–7.

157. Johnston ("Magic," 143–44) notes that the third form of curse, wish formulas, does not presume an automatic response from the deity or demon.

158. See the "Implications" essay below, "The Irony and Satire of the Balaam Cycle."

22:7–19. In this next scene, Balak sends messengers to pay Balaam to come and curse Israel, but Balaam, in obedience to God-Yahweh his deity, refuses to go with Balak's messengers. So the Moabite and Midianite elders depart, carrying "the fee for divination," probably referring to Balak's commission for the professional curser (v. 7; see the first translation note there).

The messengers relay Balak's message to Balaam but must stay the night so that Balaam can find out and then report to them what Yahweh tells him (v. 8; see the second translation note there). As one of the dramatis personae, God comes to Balaam and asks who the men are, which Balaam answers indirectly by saying that Balak, king of Moab, has given him a message (vv. 9–10). Balaam recounts Balak's first propositions about Israel (out of Egypt, cover the earth), omits the third (living near me), and summarizes his royal orders to curse Israel so that Balak can fight them and drive them out (v. 11; see the first and third translation notes there). God then prohibits Balaam from going with the messengers and from putting a formal curse on the Israelites "because they are blessed" (v. 12; see the translation notes there). In obedience to God, Balaam tells the officials to return to their land because Yahweh has refused to let him go, which the officials adjust in their report to Balak, saying that Balaam "refused" to come with us (vv. 13–14; see the third translation note on v. 13 and the translation note on v. 14).

Dissatisfied with this rejection, Balak sends a second group of officials, even more numerous and distinguished, who come not explicitly with a divination fee (v. 7) but with a plea not to let anything hinder Balaam from coming, because Balak will highly honor him when he comes to put a curse on the Israelites (vv. 15–17; see the translation note on v. 15 and the second translation note on v. 16). Yahweh restricts Balaam—"Yahweh has refused to let me go with you"—while Balak entices: "For I will highly honor you, and whatever you tell me I will do." An echo of the voices in the garden can be heard, with Yahweh Elohim restricting and the serpent enticing (Gen. 3; Matt. 4:8–10). Balaam reasserts that he cannot go beyond the command of "Yahweh my god" to do anything, insignificant or significant (v. 18; see the first and second translation notes on v. 18). The straightforward implication is that this non-Israelite augur or diviner, Balaam from the Euphrates, is nonetheless seeking to be a loyal devotee of Israel's deity, Yahweh (cf. 2 Kings 5:17–18). Again, Balaam directs the messengers to stay the night with him so that he can ascertain what Yahweh will say (v. 19).

22:20–30. In this scene, God-Yahweh tells Balaam to go with the officials, but then God-Yahweh becomes angry with Balaam for going, and the angel of Yahweh opposes Balaam. The scene begins with a surprising turn of events: God comes to Balaam that night and tells him "If the men have come to call you, go with them, but you must do exactly what I tell you" (v. 20). In expressing this condition on Balaam, the Hebrew object is fronted for emphasis: formally, "but only *the word that I speak to you, it* you must do" (see the third translation note on v. 20). The next morning Balaam got up, saddled his donkey, and left with the Moabite officials, "but God became very angry because he went, and the angel of Yahweh stood in the road to oppose him" (vv. 21–22; see the translation notes on v. 22).[159] Why does God, who just told Balaam to go with the men, become angry and stand as an adversary against Balaam through the angel of Yahweh? Some resolve this by seeing v. 22 as a later addition.[160] In another view, God's anger arises *as* Balaam is going, not *because* Balaam is going,[161] but the sequence from v. 21 to v. 22 suggests causality. The traditional view has been that "Balaam's acquiescence indicates his eagerness to curse Israel, thereby arousing the anger of God."[162] In my view, the ambiguity of God's anger in v. 22 is intentional. It underscores God's sovereign right to become enraged with Balaam without giving an explanation, even though interpreters try to provide one. In a similar way, Yahweh never explains to Job why he experienced such painful and humiliating suffering (Job 38–42).

As Balaam rides his female donkey alongside his two servants, his donkey sees the angel of Yahweh standing in the road with his sword drawn, and naturally the donkey turns off the road and into the field (vv. 22–23). By instinct, donkeys need to see a clear path to move forward.[163] Balaam, oblivious to the angel of Yahweh, beats his donkey to coerce her to get back on the road (v. 23; see the third translation note there). The angel of Yahweh then stands in one of the rows of a vineyard, with a wall on either side. When the donkey sees the angel, she presses herself against one side, pinning Balaam's foot against the wall, and Balaam beats her once again (vv. 24–25). Next, the angel of Yahweh goes on ahead and stands in a space so narrow that it was impossible to turn aside. When the donkey sees the angel of Yahweh, she crouches or lies down, with Balaam still mounted on her, and a third time Balaam beats her with a staff (vv. 26–27; see the first translation note on v. 27). Yahweh, the creator of all land animals,[164] opens the donkey's mouth, and she engages in an intelligent dialogue with her long-standing master (vv. 28–30). By this remarkable exchange, the storyteller contrasts the character of the donkey with the character of Balaam (cf. 2 Pet. 2:16). From the implied narrator's point of view, Balaam's female donkey is a character in the narrative, not a full character per se, but a stereotype of one who is loyal, yet undervalued

---

159. Where was the second party of officials during Balaam's encounter with the angel of Yahweh in vv. 21–35? Sutcliffe ("Numbers XXII," 439–42) surmises that they could have been waiting for Balaam at a meeting place outside the city.

160. Gray, *Numbers*, 332.

161. Ashley, *Numbers*, 454–55.

162. Milgrom, *Numbers*, 199.

163. Personal conversation with Tonya Figg, owner of Donkeytown at Turner Farms, Heltonville, Indiana, July 29, 2021.

164. Gen. 1:24–25; 2:19–20.

and exploited.[165] By contrast, Balaam, a full character, is concerned with his image (not wanting to "look stupid," v. 29), is volatile and violent ("I wish I had a sword; . . . I would kill you right now!" v. 29), and ungrateful for his donkey, who has served him faithfully his entire life (vv. 28–30). In this way, Balaam violates the first colon of the proverb and embodies the second: "The righteous know the needs of their animals, but the mercy of the wicked is cruel" (Prov. 12:10 NRSV).

22:31–41. In this scene, after Yahweh opens his eyes, Balaam confesses his sin, and this time Balaam, in obedience to the angel of Yahweh, goes to meet with Balak.

Yahweh opens Balaam's eyes, and as a result he sees the angel of Yahweh standing in the road with a drawn sword, so Balaam, in a posture of subordination, bows and lies prostrate on the ground (v. 31). This time the angel of Yahweh replaces the donkey as Balaam's interlocutor, defending the donkey and condemning Balaam (vv. 32–35). The angel adds another dimension that highlights the dramatic irony that has just taken place: Balaam, known as a diviner, does not see the angel of Yahweh, but his donkey sees.[166] Saving her master's life from divine wrath is now added to the donkey's already-impressive record of faithful service (v. 33). Like the Israelites—who recently confessed their sin of complaining, which had led to Yahweh's release of lethal snakes among them (21:7)—now this non-Israelite confesses his sin, which appears to be bipartite: going with the officials (22:21–22, 34) and abusing his innocent animal (22:23–33). This scene shares features with Exod. 4:24–26: Both Moses and Balaam are sent to deliver a message to a foreign king, but both are hesitant. They are both met with hostility by Yahweh or the angel of Yahweh and are rescued by another (Zipporah; the donkey).[167]

This time, apparently in accord with the divine will, Balaam travels with Balak's officials, and Balak goes out to meet Balaam on the edge of his Moabite territory at the Arnon gorge (vv. 35–36; see 21:13). Balak is irate since he purposefully summoned Balaam and is baffled about why Balaam would refuse the honor Balak pledged to give him (v. 37; see the first translation note there). Balaam retorts, "Look, I have come to you now"—effectively, "At least I came"—and the reader knows how difficult Balaam's journey has been

---

165. See Berlin, "Characterization," 69–85.

166. See the "Implications" essay below, "The Irony and Satire of the Balaam Cycle."

167. Pettit ("Exodus 4.24–26," 163–77 [175]) identifies these and other parallels. Safren ("Balaam and Abraham," 105–13) sees a "mirror" relationship between the sacrifice of Isaac (Gen. 22) and Balaam's donkey episode, with the angel of Yahweh in both stories "reversing Divine intention as perceived by the protagonist" (113). Way ("Animals," 47–62) identifies parallels with the story of the prophet from Judah, the donkey, and the lion in 1 Kings 13: "The most intriguing of these similarities are the literary characterization of animals and the portrayal of animals as divine agents" (59).

(v. 38). Now in person, Balaam reasserts what he has already said to Balak's officials (v. 18) and what the angel of Yahweh has stipulated (v. 35): he can speak only the words that God puts in his mouth (v. 38; see the translation note there). The implication is that Balaam will not be able to pronounce a formal curse on the Israelites unless God puts that curse in his mouth. The two of them travel to Kiriath Huzoth,[168] where Balak sacrifices animals and from the meat feeds Balaam and the officials (vv. 39–40; see the translation note on v. 40). This is a gesture of ancient Near Eastern hospitality but is also perhaps in Balak's mind an alluring supplement to the divination fee (22:7). The next morning Balak escorts Balaam up to Baal's high place,[169] a vantage point from which "he," probably Balaam, can see "a fraction of the people" (v. 41; see the second translation note there). The implication is that Balaam now sees, presumably for the first time, what Balak has known, that Israel hyperbolically covers the face of the earth and is too powerful for Balak's military forces (22:5–6). The Torah reader knows what Balak does not and what Balaam might know, that Yahweh has begun to fulfill his promise to Abraham to make his descendants "as the stars in the sky and as the sand on the seashore" (Gen. 22:17). That fulfillment began to take shape in Egypt (Exod. 1:7) and was evident in Israel's extensive military census (Num. 1), and now it continues to be apparent, even though the old (exodus) generation has nearly died out in the desert.

23:1–12. The story takes an important turn as Balak offers impressive sacrifices to God-Yahweh at Baal's high place in Kiriath Huzoth, and then Balaam delivers God-Yahweh's message, which stresses that he is not capable of cursing Israel, whom God has not cursed.

The scene begins as Balaam directs Balak to construct seven altars, offer a bull and a ram on each altar, and wait for Balaam as he goes out to a desert place to encounter God-Yahweh and hopefully see a divine vision (v. 3; see the first and fifth translation notes there). Their location, noted in 22:41 (see the first translation note there), suggests the composite burnt offering on the seven altars is strategically offered on Baal's high place (bāmôt bāʿal), referring to the open-air stone construction used by the Moabites in the Baal cult (see 21:28 and the translation note there). Co-opting Baal's sacred zone, the deity they are trying to appease is not Baal, but Yahweh (v. 3). The undertone is syncretistic. God does meet with Balaam, and Balaam announces his arrangement and offering of sacrifices to God, calling attention to his devotion like Abraham, Moses, and Aaron before him, and implicitly invoking God's favorable response (v. 4; see the translation notes there). Yahweh puts a word in Balaam's mouth and orders him to convey it to Balak, so Balaam returns to find Balak "still standing by his burnt offering" along with all the Moabite

---

168. Unknown location in Moab (Rasmussen, *Atlas*, 290).
169. See the comments on 23:1–12.

officials (vv. 5–6). Their inability to do anything but wait around for Balaam and Yahweh seems comical.

The divine word given is ostensibly reformulated by Balaam into his own first-person prophetic "saying,"[170] which poetically inverts Balak's curse request (vv. 7b–8) and invokes a blessing on Israel (vv. 7b–10).[171] Balaam, whose native land is near the Euphrates in the eastern mountains of Aram (23:7; cf. Deut. 26:5),[172] self-identifies as a devotee of Yahweh (22:18). The issue of Balaam's faith is highly complex. First, as good readers of an unfolding story, we should not retroject the narrator's evaluation in 31:16 back onto the Balaam cycle or even the Num. 25 apostasy: "These women, on Balaam's counsel, caused the Israelites to be unfaithful to Yahweh in the matter of Peor, so that the plague came among the community of Yahweh!"[173] Rather, Num. 22–24 portrays Balaam as one who worships, depends on, and prophesies for Yahweh as his personal deity,[174] but his choices hint at a syncretism relating to his profession as a diviner or augur working in Assyria and Transjordan (cf. 2 Kings 5:18; cf. 2 Pet. 2:15; Jude 11). In one reconstruction, Balaam may have converted to Yahwism but then apostatized from it.[175] Although the narrator never discloses Balaam's access to Israel's sacred oral or textual traditions, the language of this revealed saying echoes Genesis and the Moses story. Verse 8 is the negative corollary of the Abrahamic blessing (Gen. 12:3) as well as the Priestly Blessing (Num. 6:24–26), while v. 9 flags Israel's independence from the nations, so characteristic of the signs and wonders, the exodus, and the Sinai legislation (Exod. 19:6; Lev. 26:45). Balaam's prayer in v. 10 uses a verb (*yšr*, upright, straight) that occurs once before in the Torah, when Moses charges Israel to be faithful to Yahweh and watch him deliver them from the imminent Egyptian army (Exod. 15:26; Ps. 49:14).

As expected, Balak is incensed that Balaam has done the exact opposite of what he ordered, blessing instead of cursing, but as if to say "I told you this would happen," Balaam rephrases his mantra as a question: "Shouldn't I be careful to speak what Yahweh has put in my mouth?" (vv. 11–12; see the translation notes there).

23:13–26. With the first attempt a total failure, Balak escorts Balaam to Pisgah to offer another set of impressive sacrifices to God-Yahweh, but from

---

170. See the first translation note on 23:7.

171. See the translation note on 23:8 and the second translation note on v. 10. Tostato ("Poems of Balaam," 98–106) argues that vv. 7–10 (E) reflect a concentric symmetry of ABA'.

172. See Rasmussen, *Atlas*, 17.

173. As different sources, see Frevel, "Book of Numbers," 32.

174. See Guyot, "Balaam," 235–42 (242).

175. Lutzky ("Ambivalence," 421–25) thinks Balaam was a diviner/prophet of Asherah who began to worship Yahweh alongside Asherah. But when the Judahite kings rejected Asherah worship (Hezekiah, Asa, Josiah, etc.), Balaam was castigated as a worshiper of a pagan deity and regarded as outside the Yahweh camp.

a second divine word, Balaam asserts that God cannot be manipulated by divination to curse his blessed people.

From the field of Zophim, the summit of Pisgah, Balak shows Balaam "only a slim part" of the Israelites, a mark of their vast size as an exhibit of Yahweh's blessing to Abraham (vv. 13–14). The Pisgah peak is not yet known as a Moabite cultic site, but the Israelites are below (21:20), and Moses will soon climb this peak to see the promised land, so Balak may be speculating that this is Yahweh's sacred mountain.[176] The same laborious sacrificial routine is followed: Balak builds the seven altars, offers a bull and a ram on each, and waits by his composite burnt offering; meanwhile Balaam leaves to "meet someone over there" (vv. 14–15; see the translation note on v. 15).

Yahweh again meets Balaam, puts a word in his mouth, and says to return to Balak and relay what Yahweh tells Balaam (v. 16). Once again, Balak is still standing by his burnt offering next to the officials of Moab,[177] but this time Balak impatiently interjects, "What did Yahweh say?" His question seems delusional since Balaam has emphatically reported that Israel cannot be cursed (23:7–10), but perhaps Balak hopes Yahweh is a fickle deity or on the precipice of anger against his rebellious people.[178] Balaam delivers the oracle in the first person as before (vv. 7–10), but this time the theology is even more profound. After the bicolon call to hear (v. 18b–c), the body of Balaam's oracle is bipartite.[179] Part one contains a series of four bicolons stressing that God is not like a human who might succumb to changing his mind about his prior verbal blessing of Israel (vv. 19a–b, 19c–d, 20a–b, 21a–b). In the case of Israel, no human has performed a speech act that generates their irreversibly blessed condition, but Yahweh has initiated this blessing himself (v. 20; see the translation note there; cf. Gen. 12:3; Num. 6:24–26). The mention of a human, a mortal (v. 19; cf. Mal. 3:6), may allude to the primordial history, when God distinguished himself from yet blessed his image bearers (Gen. 1:28), and later Israel obeyed and fulfilled his creation mandate (Exod. 1:7). A liar, a mind-changer (Num. 23:19; see the first translation note there), may allude to the first humans, deceived in the garden and now deceivers (Gen. 3:1–13; Rom. 9:6; Col. 3:9; 2 John 7). God sees no misfortune (*'āwen*) or trouble (*'āmāl*) in Jacob-Israel (Num. 23:21), a statement that might seem to conflict with the events recounted in Num. 11–21, but these terms are not used to depict Israel's misfortunes and troubles in the desert (see the first translation note on 23:21). From this perspective, not always replicated elsewhere, Israel is safeguarded by the faithful God in a perpetual state of blessing, irrespective of their sins and misfortunes (cf. Rom. 9:6; Eph. 1:2–14; 2:4–6; 2 Tim. 2:13; Heb. 6:18).

---

176. Deut. 3:17, 27; 4:49; 34:1.

177. "Princes" is probably a stylistic variation for the same officials in 23:6.

178. See the "Implications" essay below, "The Irony and Satire of the Balaam Cycle."

179. Tostato ("Poems of Balaam," 98–106) argues that vv. 18–24 (E) reflect a concentric symmetry of ABCB'A'.

Part two of the oracle contains a panegyric to Yahweh-God and Israel in three bicolons (vv. 21c–d, 22, 23a–b) with a poetic doxology about God and Israel's greatness and terrible power (vv. 23c–24). Yahweh as divine king (v. 21c–d) had recently decimated the king of Arad, Sihon king of the Amorites, and Og king of Bashan and now was terrifying the king of Moab (21:1–3, 21–35; 22:2–6). Balak had exclaimed, "A nation has come out of Egypt!" (22:5, 11), but now Balaam clarifies that God is the one who has carried out that nation's exodus (23:22). The imagery in v. 22 of God ('ēl) having "the horns of a wild bull" resembles the bull manifestations of El and Baal in Canaan and the Apis bull manifestation of Ptah of Memphis, Egypt (see excursus below). Yahweh now subsumes this image of virility "for them," probably meaning for Israel. No omen, no divination, is given from God-Yahweh against Jacob-Israel. Ideally, multiple spheres of ominous signs (celestial, terrestrial, by extispicy [interpreting animal entrails]) would increase the augur's confidence in the interpretation of a divine message, but here Balaam, in synonymous parallelism, asserts that not one omen can be found (v. 23a–b; see 24:1).[180] The greatness of God's work in Jacob-Israel (v. 23c–d) would be suspect in the eyes of the nations if the Balaam Cycle had been placed immediately after the stories of Num. 11, 12, 13–14, 16, or 20, but as we have seen, all four stories in Num. 21 magnify Yahweh's power and grace for Israel's benefit. Furthermore, the bloody leonine imagery of 23:24 can be taken as a metaphor for Israel's decimation of the Egyptians and their recent total destructions of Canaanites, Amorites, and people of Heshbon (Exod. 14–15; Num. 21:1–3, 21–31). At the same time, it echoes Jacob's leonine blessing of Judah in Egypt (Gen. 49:8–12). This echo, perhaps better classified as an allusion, culminates in Balaam's third oracle and is reappropriated by John in Rev. 5 (see below).

In the end, Balak understands the gist of the oracle, even if the import of the theology is beyond him. This can be seen in his reaching another level of exasperation and commanding Balaam to stop the undertaking: "Do not curse them at all or bless them at all!" (v. 25). Balaam counters with his mantra: "Didn't I tell you, 'Everything Yahweh says, I do'?" (see the second translation note on v. 26).

23:27–24:9. Balak makes yet another attempt from Peor, but Balaam, acknowledging now that seeking an omen against Israel is futile, delivers an oracle that magnifies Jacob-Israel's beauty, fertility, and destructive power and God's powerful deliverance. The reader now sees that Balak's ordering Balaam neither to curse nor bless Israel was capricious (v. 25) since he now guides Balaam up the summit of Peor that overlooks the wasteland, through which Israel apparently traveled (v. 28; see 21:20 and the translation note on 23:28). In his wishful thinking, Balak hopes that this famous cultic site of the

---

180. Walton, *Ancient Near Eastern Thought*, 225. See the "Implications" essay below, "The Irony and Satire of the Balaam Cycle."

Baal of Peor will allure God—against his revealed nature and his promise not to change his mind about his blessing on Israel (vv. 19–20)—to change his mind after all: "Perhaps it will please God to let you curse them for me from there" (v. 27; see the second translation note there; see Num. 25). Balaam directs the arduous sacrificial routine again, so Balak builds the seven altars and offers a bull and a ram on each (vv. 29–30). Whatever Balak and Balaam are thinking at this stage, the narrator seems to orient the reader to think "Not this again!" God-Yahweh comically lets the duo continue in their futile efforts, without a prophetic word such as "Stop bringing meaningless offerings!" (Isa. 1:13a NIV).

After three times hearing Yahweh's stance against cursing Israel (22:12; 23:7–10, 18–24), Balaam finally concedes that Yahweh has decided only to bless Israel, and Balaam makes no further attempts to ascertain omens against Israel (24:1; see the translation note there). Balaam turns his face toward the wilderness, lifts his eyes, and sees the tribes of Israel, and at that moment, God's spirit comes upon him and he utters another prophetic "saying" (vv. 1c–3a; see 23:7).[181] By saying "God's spirit came upon him" (v. 2), the narrator gives the reader no room for questioning the theological faithfulness of this and, by extension, the other oracles transmitted through this non-Israelite augur. Even so, Balaam's self-introduction in this oracle and the next could still be pretentious: "The prophecy of Balaam, Beor's son, the prophecy of the man whose eye is opened, who sees a vision from the Almighty, falling flat on the ground with eyes uncovered" (vv. 3b–4; see the third translation note on 24:3).[182] On the other hand, his profile reflects the reality that Yahweh has opened his eyes (22:31), and God's spirit has come upon him (24:2). Up until this point in the Pentateuch, the term "prophecy" or "prophetic utterance"[183] has referred to Yahweh's word to Abraham and to Moses (Gen. 22:16; Num. 14:28), but here the nuance shifts to a divinely inspired word spoken by the prophet Balaam. A parallel appears also in the Deir ʿAlla inscriptions: "The gods came to him at night, and he beheld a vision in accordance with El's utterance. They said to Balaam . . . Then his intimates entered into his presence. . . . Then he said to them: 'Be seated, and I will relate to you what the Shaddai-gods have planned, and go, see the acts of the gods!'"[184]

Balaam's prophetic saying in vv. 5–9 could be called an Ode to the Tents of Israel, which extols Israel, whom God has blessed. The first stanza of this bipartite ode paints a verbal portrait of Israel encamped in the arid Jordan River Valley (22:1) but nonetheless flourishing as Yahweh's lush orchard of

---

181. See the translation note on 24:2, where the original connotation of *God's spirit* is discussed.

182. A longer parallel appears in 24:15b–16.

183. See "*nəʾum*," DCH 5:579.

184. "The Deir ʿAlla Plaster Inscriptions," COS 2.27:142, lines 1–7.

diverse trees beside a voluminous and gushing river (vv. 5–7).[185] Echoes of Eden and of the covenant blessings of the fertile land of Canaan may be heard (Gen. 2–3; Lev. 26:4–6, 9–10). Thus the irrevocable blessing of Israel here and throughout Num. 22–24 cannot be disconnected from the patriarchal land promise (Gen. 12:1).[186] The second stanza is composed differently, with four bicolons (vv. 7c–d, 8a–b, 9a–b, 9c–d) surrounding one tricolon (v. 8c–e).[187] The focus of the second stanza is on the destructive power of Israel as God's divine blessing (see Lev. 26:4–6). The final bicolon (v. 9c–d), which alludes to the Abrahamic blessing and curse (Gen. 12:3a–b), serves as a coda for the whole ode, forming an *inclusio* with v. 5 (where the ode begins) by resuming the direct address to Jacob-Israel. The message of the entire ode is clear: Israel's fertility and power mean that anyone who opposes Israel does so to their own detriment, but whoever honors Israel flourishes.

The leonine image of v. 9 is a direct quotation of Jacob's blessing of Judah in Gen. 49:9 (see the second translation note on Num. 24:9). Because of this quotation, the interpreter is justified in identifying the leonine imagery in Balaam's second and third oracles as alluding to, or at least drawing from, Judah's blessing, whether Balaam in the story perceives this or not.[188] To appropriate the language of Judah's blessing is fitting within the book of Numbers since Judah has risen to prominence in the tribal confederation of Israel.[189] The apostle John has a vision of Jesus the Messiah that alludes to Jacob's blessing and Balaam's oracles.

Table 22.1. Judah's Blessings Compared

Genesis 49:8–9, 11b (NET)	Numbers 23:24; 24:9	Revelation 5:5, 9
[8]Judah, your brothers will praise you. Your hand will be on the neck of your enemies, your father's sons will bow down before you.	Look, the people rise **like a lioness**, and **like a lion** raises himself up—he does not lie down until he eats his prey and **drinks the blood of the slain** (see the first translation note on 23:24).	[5]Then one of the elders said to me, "Stop weeping! Look, the **Lion of the tribe of Judah,** the root of David, has conquered; thus he can open the scroll and its seven seals."
[9]You are a **lion's cub, Judah,** from the prey, my son, you have gone up.		

185. Leveen (*Memory*, 55) observes the contrast with the tents of Israel's rebellion in 11:10 and 16:26. Cf. LXX Num. 24:6, "like tents that the Lord has pitched," with Heb. 8:2, "the true tent, which the Lord has pitched."

186. Frevel, "Alte Stücke," 295.

187. The two verbs in v. 9a, "They crouch and lie down," can be read as a hendiadys in a single colon, as they are modified by one comparative, "like a lion."

188. Intertexts can be classified from most knowable to least knowable: citation→quotation→allusion→echo→trace (Stead, *Intertextuality*, 21–23).

189. Judah remained the largest tribe (74,600 [1:27] to 76,500 [26:22]), had the God-honored Caleb as a chieftain (13–14; 26:65; 32:12), led Israel's march in the signal position (2:3–9), and presented the first offering to dedicate the altar (7:11–17).

Genesis 49:8–9, 11b (NET)	Numbers 23:24; 24:9	Revelation 5:5, 9
He crouches and lies down like a lion; like a lioness—who will rouse him? . . .	⁹They crouch and lie down like a lion, and as a lioness, who will rouse them?	
¹⁰ᶜthe nations will obey him . . .		
¹¹ᵇhe will wash his garments in wine, his robes		⁹They were singing a new song: "You are worthy to take the scroll and to open its seals **because you were killed**, and at the cost of
in the **blood** of grapes. ¹²His eyes will be dark from wine, **and his teeth** white from milk.		**your own blood** you have purchased for God persons from every tribe, language, people, and nation."

John sees Jesus as the fullness of the Judah-leonine figure of the Torah. At the same time, what is most stunning is that Jesus subverts the conquering Judah-leonine figure by not taking the blood of other humans from the nations, but by giving his own blood *for* the nations.

Excursus: God . . . like the Horns of a Wild Bull (23:22; 24:8)

Balaam represents "Yahweh their god" as *ʾēl* (23:22; 24:8), whose redemptive power on Israel's behalf is "like the horns of a wild bull."[190] The Hebrew could mean, "*They have* [lô], as it were, the strength of a wild bull" (NET), correlating with Israel as lion-lioness (23:24; 24:9), but more likely the bull metaphor completes the bicolon, with God as redeemer from Egypt as the first colon. This correlates with his power for Israel's benefit in 23:21, 23 and implicit in 24:7c–9. The subject, a metonym of Yahweh, is *ʾēl*, which in the Northwest Semitic cultures that surround Israel refers to the Canaanite god El.[191] In the Deir ʿAlla inscriptions, the figure Balaam son of Beor receives a message from El, who has a cohort of amiable gods: "The gods came to him at night, and he beheld a vision in accordance with El's utterance."[192] Here in Num. 23:22 and 24:8, the association with El is unmistakable since one of his common epithets was "Bull El his Father."[193] Even so, Baal, Ptah (Egyptian), and other gods were also frequently represented as a bull in pictures, cult statues, and figurines. The bull image was intended to replicate their divine form, symbolize them, or display them with superhuman virility.[194] Because Num. 23:22 and 24:8 are

---

190. Hb. *kətôʿăpōt rəʾēm*; LXXᵉᵈ: "like *a unicorn's glory [doxa monokerōtos]* he was to them."
191. See "*ʾl*," *DNWSI* 1:53–55; the name *ʾēl* for Yahweh occurs in Num. 12:13; 16:22; 23:8, 19, 22, 23; 24:4, 8, 16, 23.
192. "The Deir ʿAlla Plaster Inscriptions," *COS* 2.27:140, 142.
193. Ugaritic: *ṯr ʾil ʾabh KTU* 1.3 V 35–36; 1.4 I 4–15, etc.
194. Smith, *History of God*, 41, 49–50; Hundley, "Golden Calf?," 560–62.

presented as the word that Yahweh gives to Balaam for Balak (23:16–18) and the saying that Balaam prophesies by God's spirit (24:2), I do not identify this as syncretism like the golden calves of exodus Israel or Jeroboam I clearly were (Exod. 32:4; 1 Kings 12:28). Rather, we may marvel at Yahweh for his resolve to *contextualize*, even through a *theriomorphic* metaphor, the revelation of his perfect nature for ancient Moabites and Israelites alike.

24:10–25. In this final scene of the cycle, Balak retorts in anger, but Balaam proceeds to deliver a final oracle that not only foretells Israel's decimation of Balak's nation, Moab, by a star-scepter out of Jacob-Israel, but of other powerful nations also. In response to Balaam's third oracle, an Ode to the Tents of Israel (24:3–9), Balak becomes extremely angry, lashes out by clapping his hands in Balaam's face as an apparent threat, and erupts: "I called you to curse my enemies, but you have only blessed them these three times!" (v. 10; see the translation notes there). His triple attempt to curse Israel has been reversed into a triple blessing of Israel. Balak detests this useless augur and tells him, "Go back to where you came from!" He also reminds Balaam for the third time that he would have highly honored him (22:17, 37; 24:11) and, without any grounds, claims that Yahweh has held Balaam back from honor (24:11; see the second translation note there). Balaam now recites the fullest form of his mantra to elucidate, one last time, why silver and gold cannot persuade him to do or say anything contrary to what Yahweh tells him (vv. 12–13). Verse 14 functions as an *inclusio* around the entire Balaam cycle, as Balaam returns to his home from which he was summoned, and as he explicitly addresses what the Israelites will do to the Moabites, the exact fear that Balak expressed in his opening monologue (22:4c–6). Balaam's oracle opens with his self-introduction, changing it—for stylistic and not genre variation—from "the prophecy of Balaam" (v. 3b) to "the oracle of Balaam" (v. 15b). He also expands it to include "the prophecy of the one who hears God's words and who knows knowledge from the Most High" (v. 16*; see the translation note there). Rather than a presumptuous Balaam claiming to know the Most High (an objective genitive), his assertion is that he has received knowledge of what God has said and how God will act (genitive of source). This is comparable to Balaam's knowledge of the gods in the Deir 'Alla inscription: "I will relate to you what the Shaddai-gods have planned, and go, see the acts of the gods!"[195]

In the body of the oracle (vv. 17–19), Balaam opens with the caveat that the person he sees in his vision is a future and distant entity: "I see him, but not now. I look at him, but not near" (v. 17). This deliberately ambiguous figure,[196] coupled with the star and scepter metaphors attached to him, is

---

195. "The Deir 'Alla Plaster Inscriptions," COS 2.27:142, lines 6–7.
196. Ashley, *Numbers*, 500.

suggestive of a Messiah. After quoting Num. 24:17, the Qumran sectarian scribes elucidate: "The sceptre is the prince of the whole congregation and when he rises he will destroy all the sons of Seth."[197] For the Qumran sect, the prince of the whole congregation was coextensive with the "shoot of David" and the "Messiah of Justice."[198] In its original context, Balaam depicts this person as a terrifying warrior king, who will one day crush Edom and Moab (24:17c–19). Maybe Balak was relieved by the future tense (like Hezekiah, 2 Kings 20:19), but Moab and Edom's present opposition to Israel is now a portent of their own destruction (Num. 20:14–21; chaps. 22–24). Balak's resolve to curse Israel in Num. 22–24 will bring judgment from Israel on his own people. This has a reflex in Deut. 23:4–6, which denies Ammonites and Moabites entry into Yahweh's assembly until the tenth generation. The Deuteronomic reason for this denial is inhospitality (cf. Edom in Num. 20:14–21) and Balaam's professional cursing (Moab in Num. 22–24).[199] Subsequent traditions will support this anti-Moabite stance (Neh. 13:1, 23), but others will dramatically make an exception for Yahweh-worshiping Moabites (Ruth; Isa. 56:1–7).[200]

As a Janus text in the canon, Balaam's oracle in vv. 17c–19 looks backward intertextually to the motif of Judah's royal scepter and domination and forward to Jesus's royal star, scepter, and domination:

Table 22.2. Royal Prophecies Compared

Genesis 49:8–12 (NET)	Numbers 24:17c–19	Matt. 2:1–2; Rev. 22:16 (NET)
[8]Judah, your brothers will praise you. Your hand will be on the neck of your **enemies**, your father's sons will bow down before you.	[17c]**A star will come out of Jacob**, and **a scepter will rise out of Israel**. He will crush the foreheads of Moab and the skulls of all the sons of Sheth.	After Jesus was born in Bethlehem in Judea, in the time of King Herod, wise men from the East came to Jerusalem [2]saying, "Where is the one who is born **king** of the Jews?
[10]**The scepter will not depart from Judah, nor the ruler's staff from between his feet**, until he comes to whom it belongs; **the nations will obey him.**	[18]Edom will become a possession, and Seir, his **enemies**, will become a possession, but Israel will act valiantly.	For we saw **his star when it rose** and have come to worship him" (see Matt. 2:7, 9, 10).
	[19]**One from Jacob will reign. He will destroy** the survivors of the city (see the translation note on v. 17 and the second translation note on v. 19).	"I, Jesus, have sent my angel to testify to you about these things for the churches. I am the root and the descendant of David, **the bright morning star!**" (see Rev. 2:28)

197. "The Damascus Document," in García Martínez, *Dead Sea Scrolls Translated*, 38.
198. See García Martínez, "Messianic Hopes," 115–75.
199. Cf. Kilchör, *Mosetora*, 259.
200. Moore, "Ruth the Moabite," 203–17; Awabdy, *Immigrants*, 81–83.

Finally, the narrator reports a rapid succession of three closing oracles: the first two Balaam saw as visions (like Num. 24:17–19), and this is probably implied for the third (vv. 20, 21–22, 23–24). Amalek, first among the nations, is doomed (v. 20; see the translation note there). Israel defeated Amalek in the Sinai desert (Exod. 17:8–16), saw them in Canaan (Num. 13:29; 14:25), and then were defeated by them (14:43–45), but the ultimate story will be of Israel's victory and Amalek's defeat. The Kenites, who live in safety in the rocks, will be consumed and held captive by Assur, which refers to the Assyrian city with the god by the same name (*Aššur*; vv. 21–22).[201] The final oracle discloses God's providential hand in all these wars and sets up the horror of the final onslaught: "O, who will live when God does this!" (v. 23). From Cyprus, the infamous Sea Peoples or Alexander's Grecian army or another force will injure and then destroy Assur and Eber, the descendants of Shem (v. 24; see the second translation note there and the translation note on v. 20).[202] The implication is that the Assyrian war machine and its deity, Assur, have hurt the Kenites and will not be immune. The invaders by sea will themselves, in the end, be destroyed by the divine warrior (vv. 23–24).

The ending of the story in v. 25 is anticlimactic. By going home, the subtext is that Balaam, and finally Balak, concede that they are powerless to turn Yahweh against Israel.

Implications

The Irony and Satire of the Balaam Cycle

It may be true that the Hebrew Scriptures do not show a proclivity toward irony or satire since they are constrained by divine interests—namely, revealing God, his engagement with his covenant people, and his dealings with the rest of creation.[203] However, it is a non sequitur to claim that the divine and human biblical authors would not or do not use irony and satire to make their divine interests more rhetorically compelling. One thinks of books like Jonah and Esther or the apocryphal novella of Daniel and the priests of Bel (Bel 1:1–22). The ark narrative of 1 Sam. 4–7 glitters with delightful irony and satire, as when the god Dagon is twice discovered prostrate in a posture of worship before the ark of Yahweh (1 Sam. 5:3–4). When reading the Moses story, we must be careful not to commit the same non sequitur by assuming that the Torah does not or would not express irony or satire. In this reflection, I define three types of literary irony, identify the ironies of the Balaam

---

201. See Judg. 4:11. On the link between the Kenites, Midianites, and early Yahwistic worship, see Cross, *Canaanite Myth*, 200–201.

202. See Levine, *Numbers*, 2:206.

203. Sternberg, *Poetics*, 135–36.

cycle, and show how from these ironies a satirical portrait emerges that has the power to reform the worldview of its audience.

The three primary forms of literary irony are verbal, situational, and dramatic. Verbal irony occurs when the ironist, whether a character or the narrator, knowingly says something that conflicts with reality.[204] In verbal irony, the ironist and the reader agree that a person can say one thing but intend something else, and that this is different from telling a lie.[205] In situational irony, the agents do not intend the irony, but it is "an event or occurrence that simply *happens* and that we consider ironic because of the way it occurred."[206] In dramatic irony, the implied author and audience see a larger significance to a character's words or actions but the character does not.[207] Individual ironies do not need to contribute to a larger work of satire, but they can: "When we speak of a satirical novel or a satirical play we probably have in mind a work of art which contains a sharp kind of irony or ridicule or even denunciation."[208] In the Balaam cycle, we find all three forms of literary irony, but only two of the forms are explored here.

The first irony we consider is *dramatic*: the storyteller, audience, and donkey know something that Balaam does not. On the way to serve Balak as a professional augur to see and influence the divine realm (22:7), Balaam cannot see the angel of Yahweh in the road, but his donkey can (22:7, 21–34). In the direct context, this illuminates God-Yahweh's sovereignty and human ignorance in the mystery of why God-Yahweh becomes angry when Balaam leaves with the messengers (22:20–22) and why Balaam is incapable of seeing the angel of Yahweh. This irony contributes to the Balaam cycle, which itself contributes to the Num. 11–25 composition concerning the prophetic role and knowledge of God. As the story unfolds, Balaam is transformed: "Then Yahweh opened Balaam's eyes, and he saw the angel of Yahweh standing in the road with his sword drawn in his hand" (22:31). Balaam bows low and confesses to the angel of Yahweh, "I have sinned because I did not know that you were standing to confront me in the road" (v. 34). It remains to be seen how pervasive this transformation is in Balaam's life, but this divine eye-opening and confession form the backdrop to his self-introductions of his two major oracles in chap. 24 (vv. 2, 3b–4, 15b–16). Balaam, who did not see, now sees, and who did not know, now knows. Interestingly, using the same verbal root of "who sees a vision from the Almighty" (*mḥzh šdy yḥzh*), the Deir ʿAlla inscription depicts the prophet Balaam son of Beor as "a divine seer" (*ḥzh ʾlhn*)[209] or, if an objective genitive, "a seer of the gods."[210]

---

204. Garmendia, *Irony*, 7–8.
205. Hutcheon, *Irony's Edge*, 17.
206. Garmendia, *Irony*, 5.
207. Garmendia, *Irony*, 6.
208. Elliot, *Power of Satire*, 101.
209. "The Deir ʿAlla Plaster Inscriptions," COS 2.27:142.
210. Wilson, *Prophecy*, 132. See Wiggershaus, "Man of Opened Eye."

Are Balaam's oracle introductions self-aggrandizing? It is hard to say. Since God-Yahweh opened his eyes, he assumes a prostrate position of reverence, and his oracles contain some of the most profound theology in the entire book of Numbers, even in the Pentateuch. According to Yahweh's classification in Num. 12:6–8, Balaam belongs with prophets to whom Yahweh reveals himself in dreams and visions, but about Moses Yahweh says "I speak with him face-to-face, in an appearance and not in riddles, and he looks at the form of Yahweh" (12:8a–b).[211] Moses, however, has recently rebelled against Yahweh and been disinherited (20:12). Although the Pentateuch editors have the final word in elevating Moses over all other prophets,[212] at this moment in the narrative, Moses has been humbled by Yahweh while Balaam is lifted high. Yahweh does not need Moses to reveal himself, and his revelation is not confined to Israel. He uses a non-Israelite augur to communicate to surrounding peoples profound theology that substantiates his blessing of the children of Abraham.

The second irony is *situational*: it comes from Balaam and Balak's joint attempt to coerce Yahweh. The Moabite king and his new prophet from the Euphrates imagine they can impress Yahweh by their sacrifices to obtain an omen against Israel. Twice at Balaam's explicit command and once without it, Balak builds *seven* altars and offers *seven* bulls and *seven* rams on them, which numerically symbolizes the fullness of their sacrificial performance for Yahweh (23:1–2, 14, 29–30). In the first two iterations, while the sacrifices are burning, Balaam retreats to consult with Yahweh for an omen against Israel (23:3, 15). In the third round, Balaam sees the futility of seeking an omen and instead sees Israel and prophesies by God's spirit (24:1–2). The narrator indicates that Balaam is seeking to be a faithful devotee of Israel's deity, whom he calls "Yahweh my god" (22:18; see the second translation note there). One thinks of Naaman, also from the Euphrates region, who claims to worship Yahweh, yet with a caveat (2 Kings 5:17–18). At no point does the narrator expressly state that Balak and Balaam are sacrificing to Yahweh, as a non-Israelite could potentially do, provided they followed the standard protocols of supplementary grain offerings and libations (Num. 15:1–16) and provided the blood is sprinkled in Yahweh's meeting tent (Lev. 17:1–9). Balak and Balaam do not follow Yahweh's protocols, and the surrounding language intimates that they are syncretizing by sacrificing to Yahweh in their own way and on indigenous cultic sites, such as Baal's high place at Kiriath Huzoth and the summit of Peor, known for a localized form of Baal worship (22:39, 41; 23:14, 28–30; 25:1–5).[213] It is conceivable that in his second attempt to obtain his desired omen, Balak sacrifices on the summit of Pisgah; no indigenous cult is

---

211. See the "Implications" essay in chap. 12, "Did Moses See Yahweh?"
212. See Deut. 34:10–12; Awabdy, "Holiness Contribution," 250–51.
213. See Spronk ("Baal of Peor," 147–48) and the comments on 25:1–5.

known to have been there, but Balak may be speculating that this is Yahweh's sacred mountain.[214]

Irrespective of why he chooses Pisgah, Balak seems to think that Yahweh might smell the sweet savor of the fourteen roasting animals, swarm around them like a fly,[215] and be enticed to swap sides, like certain deities would. Perhaps Yahweh is a fickle deity, like the bloodthirsty Ares (Latin Mars), who once backed the Achaeans but flipped sides to join Hector and the Trojans in taking revenge against Diomedes for injuring Aphrodite and pursuing Apollo.[216] Or maybe Israel has offended Yahweh (the reader knows that this is well within the realm of possibility, chaps. 11–21), and Yahweh will now, given the right feast, be convinced to slaughter his people all at once (cf. 14:11–16). In this regard, one thinks of the extensive divine curses that are commonplace in ancient contractual literature. The curses, carried out by both the gods and loyal human agents, apply not merely to foreigners or vassals but also to citizens.[217] Not only could a deity, for various reasons, turn against his own people, but the ancients also believed that certain magical incantations, specifically wish formulas or prayers, could compel a deity or demon to put a person or people into a cursed state.[218] These imprecatory prayers often included elements intended to convince the deity or demon to issue the curse: "I have given you sacrifices in the past."[219] With this in mind, Balak wants Balaam to pray to Yahweh and persuade Yahweh to curse the Israelites, but Balaam rejects this attempt since Yahweh orders him: "Do not put a curse on the people because they are blessed" (22:12). Thus Balaam repeatedly informs Balak that he can do only what God-Yahweh tells him to do and say only what God-Yahweh tells him to say.[220] Instead, Balaam pursues another mantic option, as indicated by his synonymously parallel bicolon: "For there is no omen against Jacob, nor divination against Israel" (23:20a–b). Likewise, the narrator's comment in 24:1 is suggestive: "so he did not go as the other times to seek for omens." This suggests that since formal *cursing* was not an option for Balaam, he could seek an *omen* from Yahweh against the Israelites.

In the ANE, an omen (Hb. *naḥaš*) referred to an observable event or phenomenon that signified a message from the gods that could potentially be interpreted by specialists like Balaam, who is among the skilled diviners and

---

214. Num. 21:20; 23:14; Deut. 3:17, 27; 4:49; 34:1.

215. As the gods swarmed Utnapishtim's sacrifice after the flood in "The Epic of Gilgamesh," *ANET* 68 (trans. E. A. Speiser).

216. Homer, *The Iliad* 5.30–39.

217. See "SAA 02 006. Esarhaddon's Succession Treaty [EST/VTE]," §14*, §58* (cf. §29), http://oracc.museum.upenn.edu/saao/saa02/corpus.

218. Johnston, "Magic," 143.

219. Johnston, "Magic," 143.

220. Num. 22:18, 35, 38; 23:3, 5, 8, 12, 16, 26; 24:12–13.

augurs mentioned in the Deir ʿAlla inscription.[221] Ascertaining more than one omen from different spheres—celestial, terrestrial, or by extispicy (interpreting animal entrails)—would strengthen the reliability of the augur's interpretation of the divine message.[222] But as God and Balaam and the narrator have indicated (23:23; 24:1), Balaam cannot obtain a single omen from Yahweh—whether by sky, earth, or animals—signifying that Yahweh has changed his mind and cursed Israel (cf. 23:20). Instead, Yahweh speaks through Balaam in seven oracles,[223] another ANE mode of divine communication,[224] and these speeches consistently support Israel and oppose Israel's enemies.[225] The situational irony is now describable. King Balak and his hired professional, Balaam, have offered excessive sacrifices that have not impressed the deity, they have been prevented from uttering formulaic curses, and the omens they have sought cannot be found.

From the two ironies we have discussed, the satire of the Balaam cycle emerges. By opening the eyes of a pathetic seer who cannot *see* the angel of Yahweh, God-Yahweh manifests both his authority to bypass the great Moses and raise up prophets from anywhere and to disseminate among the nations the knowledge that he has irrevocably blessed the Israelites. Moreover, Balak and Balaam's exhausting efforts that have occupied the whole novella of Num. 22–24 turn out to be a colossal waste not only of their time but of animals, altars, messengers, and heated emotions. Yahweh is neither a local deity nor affected by incantations or divination. Consequently, this Moabite king and his augur from the great Euphrates are impotent to subvert Yahweh's blessing of Abraham and his descendants (Gen. 12:3). To conclude this comical story of human impotence, the anticlimactic ending is quite fitting: "Then Balaam got up and returned to his home, and Balak also went his own way" (24:25).

---

221. Lines 1, 13–14: "The Deir ʿAlla Plaster Inscriptions," COS 2.27:143.
222. Walton, *Ancient Near Eastern Thought*, 225.
223. Hb. *māšāl*: 23:7, 18; 24:3, 15, 20, 21, 23; Hb. *nəʾum*: 24:3, 4, 15, 16.
224. For Egypt, see Kákosy, "Divination and Prophecy: Egypt," 372–73.
225. Num. 23:7–10, 18–24; 24:3–9, 15–19, 20, 21–22, 23–24.

23

Israelites Worship Baal of Peor

(25:1–18)

~~~

Overview

Since 22:1, the surviving members of the exodus generation have been stationed in the desert valleys of Moab, with a view of Canaan on a clear day. Encamped in the Jordan River Valley, they are now breathing the same arid air as the Judean desert of the land promised to their ancestors. What is more, Beor's son Balaam has recently and repeatedly blessed Yahweh's covenant people: "How beautiful are your tents, Jacob, and your dwelling places, Israel! They are like date palms spread out, like gardens beside a river, like aloes that Yahweh has planted, like cedars beside the waters. Water will flow from their buckets, and their descendants will be like abundant water" (24:5–7).[1] Does this mean Yahweh, after enacting his lethal judgment on Israel in Num. 11–21, has already fulfilled his curse against the exodus generation? Yahweh said, "In this wilderness your dead bodies will fall—all those of you who were enlisted in the census, twenty years old and up, who have complained against me" (14:29). He did concede to bring "your little ones" into the land (14:31). But with no statement by the narrator that the adults of the exodus generation have died off completely, do Balaam's oracles signal that grace is on the horizon for them? With these questions swirling in the reader's mind, the Israelites commit their final and ultimate act of unfaithfulness against Yahweh. In 25:1–5, the people commit sexual immorality with the Moabite women and bind themselves in covenant to their god, Baal of Peor; Yahweh and Moses in turn demand that the immoral Israelites be executed. Just then, in vv. 6–9, an Israelite man shamelessly leads a Midianite woman into his tent

---

1. Similarly, Olson, *Death of the Old*, 159; Ashley, *Numbers*, 515.

shrine to have ritual sex, but while they are in the act, Eleazar's son, Phinehas, thrusts a spear through them both, ending a plague against the Israelites. In vv. 10–13, Yahweh, by a performative speech act, enters into a covenant of peace and of a permanent priesthood with the family line of Phinehas because of his jealousy for his deity, Yahweh. As something of an appendix or denouement, the narrator in vv. 14–18 identifies by name and pedigree the Israelite man and Midianite woman who so brazenly sinned, and Yahweh commands Moses to treat the Midianites as enemies because they, as enemies, deceived the Israelites in the matter of Peor.[2] In the end, the Baal of Peor apostasy resurrects the plotline and essence of the golden-calf apostasy: worshiping other gods, averting Yahweh's wrath by slaying the guilty, and appointing the/a Levite for consecrated service to Yahweh in his sanctuary.[3]

Translation

1While Israel lived in Shittim, the people began to commit sexual immorality with the Moabite women.[4] **2**The women invited the people to the sacrifices of their gods, and the people ate and bowed down to their gods.[5] **3**So Israel joined itself[6] to Baal of Peor, and Yahweh's anger

2. Num. 25:1–5 is often assigned to J or JE and vv. 6–18 to P (Wellhausen, *Prolegomena*, 356–57; de Vaulx, *Nombres*, 299–301; Cross, *Canaanite Myth*, 316; Budd, *Numbers*, 281–82; Levine, *Numbers*, 2:282–91), but some see a Priestly redaction as finalizing vv. 1–5 also (Kim, "Finalization," 260–64; similarly, Schmidt, *Numeri*, 149). Knierim and Coats (*Numbers*, 265) read Num. 25 as an anecdotal report from the Yahwist; Noth (*Numbers*, 195) argues that a J account was reworked, but not by P. Others assign all of Num. 25 to P (Baden, "Violent Origins," 116) or to H along with the account's completion in Num. 31 (Knohl, *Sanctuary*, 96–98). However, since P/H does not clearly prohibit foreign marriage, but D does, Blum (*Komposition des Pentateuch*, 114–16) assigns Num. 25 to his K^D. Frevel ("High Priest," 152) spots in the story elements that are pre-Priestly (vv. 1a, 3, 5), non-Priestly (vv. 1b, 2, 4), and Priestly (vv. 6–19; cf. Seebass, *Numeri*, 3:125–27). Kislev ("P," 387–99) identifies three independent stories of different events, one Priestly and the other two non-Priestly, integrated by Priestly redactional verses. Achenbach (*Vollendung*, 637) assigns vv. 1–5 to the Hexateuch redactor (with Scharbert, *Numeri*, 103) and vv. 6–18 to phases one and three of his theocratic revision. Albertz ("Pentateuchal Redaction," 220–33; also Frevel, "Alte Stücke," 279) sees Num. 25–36 as the Pentateuch editor's replacement for the book of Joshua, but see my discussion under "Literary Genre and Structure" in the introduction.

3. Milgrom (*Numbers*, 211) notes these parallels: Exod. 32:8//Num. 25:2; Exod. 32:26–28//Num. 25:7–8; Exod. 32:29//Num. 25:11–13.

4. The opening wayyiqtol past narrative introduces a new section in the story line of the second wilderness generation (Num. 22–36), which I render like a temporal clause on which the second wayyiqtol and complementary inf. are dependent: "*While* Israel *lived* [*wayyēšeb*] in Shittim, the people *began to commit sexual immorality* [*wayyāḥel . . . liznôt*]" (*GBHS* §3.5.1c, e).

5. Probably to repudiate Moabite polytheism, the Jewish LXX translators render both references to "their gods" (*'ĕlōhêhen*) as "their idols" (*tōn eidōlōn autōn . . . tois eidōlois autōn*).

6. **Ṣmd* occurs only five times in the OT, here in vv. 3 and 5 with a reflexive meaning (niphal), as the Israelite men acted for themselves: "Israel joined themselves" (*wayyiṣṣāmed*) and "his

burned against Israel. **4**Yahweh said to Moses, "Take all the leaders of the people, impale and expose them[7] before Yahweh in broad daylight,[8] so that Yahweh's fierce anger may turn away from Israel."[9] **5**So Moses said to Israel's judges, "Each of you must execute[10] those of his men who were joined to Baal of Peor."

6Just then an Israelite man came and brought to his brothers[11] a Midianite woman in plain sight of Moses and of the whole Israelite community[12] while they were weeping at the entrance of the meeting tent. **7**When Phinehas son of Eleazar, the son of Aaron the priest, saw it,[13] he got up from the assembly, took a spear[14] in his hand, **8**and went

---

men who were joined" (*'ănāšāyw hanniṣmādîm*). The incident is also alluded to in Ps. 106:28, "Then they joined themselves to Baal of Peor" (*wayyiṣṣāmdû* [niphal] *ləba'al pə'ôr*; *GBHS* §3.1.2c). Elsewhere we read that Joab's sheath *was fastened* (2 Sam. 20:8, pual pass.) and "*Yoke* your tongue to deceit" (Ps. 50:19 NJPS, hiphil).

7. The imperatival weqatal, dynamically "impale and expose them" (*wəhôqa' 'ôtām*; *GBHS* §3.5.2c), has a verbal root (**yq'*) that occurs eight times in the OT with the base meaning "be dislocated"; in the hiphil it means something like "expose with broken limbs" (*DCH* 4:274; hiphil also in 2 Sam. 21:6, 9). Not using the normal verb for hanging (**tlh*) or mentioning the means of a tree/pole (Deut. 21:22; Josh. 8:29; 10:26), wall (2 Sam. 4:12; 1 Sam. 31:10), or gallows (Esther 7:9), the verb **yq'* (hiphil) instead in context connotes execution by impaling on a stake, documented in Old Babylonia, Ugarit, Egypt, Neo-Assyria, and Achaemenid Persia. See the comments on 25:4.

8. Formally, "before the sun" (*neged haššāmeš* ≈ LXX[ed]). SP, likely to harmonize to v. 5, reads "Instruct that they may execute those of his men who were joined to Baal of Peor."

9. Impaling and exposing the corpses of Israel's leaders will result in averting Yahweh's wrath, as expressed by this weqatal following the volitives: "Take . . . impale . . . *so that* Yahweh's fierce anger *may turn away* [*wəyāšōb*] from Israel" (*GBHS* §3.5.3b).

10. "Execute" (ESV ≈ "put to death" for Cazelles, *Nombres*, 118) is a contextual rendering of the verb **hrg*, which means "kill" (many versions), since a breach of the covenant with Yahweh is a capital offense.

11. Others render this dynamically: "(in)to his family" (NRSV, ESV); "into his tent" (NLT); "into the camp" (NIV); "to his companions" (NJPS). I prefer the formal rendering "to his brothers" (*'el-'eḥāyw*, with Schmidt, *Numeri*, 145; NET, et al.), the most common meaning of the noun ("*'āḥ*," *DCH* 1:173). This does not imply polyandrous sex or gang rape by the males of the family. Rather, in a communal culture, the Israelite needs the approval of his brothers by the same father to engage in sexual intercourse with the Midianite woman (v. 8); hence, the dynamic translation, "and presented the Midianite woman to his kinsmen" (Levine, *Numbers*, 2:281).

12. Formally, "to(ward) the eyes of Moses and to(ward) the eyes of the whole community of Israelites."

13. The five wayyiqtols foreground the narrative events (J. Cook, "*Wayyiqtol* and *Weqatal*," 247–73). This translation also reflects the possibility that the first wayyiqtol (v. 7a) is followed by four consequential wayyiqtols (vv. 7b–8b), indicating that Phinehas's string of actions result from seeing the perversity: "*When* Phinehas son of Eleazar, the son of Aaron the priest, *saw it* [*wayyar'*], he got up [*wayyāqām*] . . . took [*wayyiqqaḥ*] . . . went after [*wayyābō' 'aḥar*] . . . and thrust it through [*wayyidqōr*] . . ." (*GBHS* §3.5.1b).

14. Or a "lance" (*rōmaḥ*), as both spears and lances were thrust at the enemy, whereas javelins were thrown at medium distance. *Rōmaḥ* and *ḥănît* are not always easy to translate specifically, but they include spears, lances, and javelins (King and Stager, *Life*, 225). The spear, designed for stabbing, contained a sharp blade attached to the end of a wooden shaft. "Bigger

after the Israelite man[15] into his tent shrine[16] and thrust it through[17] the two of them, the Israelite man and the woman into her stomach. Then the plague against the Israelites stopped.[18] **9**But those who had died in the plague came to 24,000.

10Then Yahweh spoke to Moses: **11**"Phinehas son of Eleazar, the son of Aaron the priest, has turned my anger away from the Israelites. He was jealous for me[19] among them, so I did not finish off[20] the Israelites in my jealousy. **12**Therefore tell him that I am giving[21] to him my covenant of peace. **13**That is, he and his descendants after him have a covenant of a permanent priesthood,[22] because[23] he was jealous for his god[24] and made atonement for the Israelites."

---

and heavier than a javelin, the spear was the main weapon of the infantry and of the chariotry" (King and Stager, *Life*, 225–26).

15. A referential article, "*the* Israelite man" (*'îš-yiśrā'ēl*, 2× v. 8), the same Israelite man of v. 6 who brought in the Midianite woman (*GBHS* §2.6.1).

16. A possessive article, "*his* tent shrine" (*haqqubbâ*; *GBHS* §2.6.7). This noun—often rendered "tent" (most) or "chamber" (NJPS, ESV), "alcove" (Cazelles, *Nombres*, 118), or "inner room" (for Schmidt, *Numeri*, 145)—is not the common word for tent (*'ōhel*), but a hapax; hence, the honesty of the transliteration by de Vaulx, *Nombres*, 289; and "*qubbah*-tent" by Levine, *Numbers*, 2:281). In nonreligious settings, it could refer to the inner room of a tent, particularly the women's room ("*qubbâ*," HALOT 3:1060, gloss a ≈ "*qubbâ* I," DCH 7:170), but since this is a cultic context (25:2–3, 5), it is more likely to be a tent sanctuary for cultic prostitution, a "tent shrine" ("*qubbâ* II," DCH 7:170 ≈ HALOT 3:1060, gloss b).

17. The verb (**dqr*), occurring only here in the Pentateuch (11× in the OT), in the qal can mean "pierce" or "thrust through" (*DCH* 2:461), but "thrust through" is preferred since the spear penetrated both his body and her stomach (v. 8). The obj. "it" is elided (absent) in Hb., but readers know he thrust the "spear" (*rōmaḥ*, v. 7; *IBHS* §11.4.3).

18. The niphal may be a middle verb with a quasi-active meaning, but contextually it implies divine agency: "the plague . . . *stopped* [by Yahweh]." Its wayyiqtol aspect could simply indicate a temporal sequence but seems to convey the result of Phinehas's actions: "When Phinehas saw it, . . . he got up . . . took . . . went after . . . and thrust it through. . . . *Then* the plague against the Israelites *was stopped* [*wattē'āṣar*]" (*GBHS* §3.5.1a, b). More formally, this verb means "was restrained" or "was held back" ("*ṣr*," HALOT 2:870–71).

19. Formally, "by the jealousy of him for/with my jealousy."

20. This euphemism for annihilation, "finish, complete" (**klh*), is marked by a simple *wǝ* and can be understood as the apodosis (result) of a conditional statement beginning with a causal clause (piel inf. const.): "*Because* he was jealous for me . . . , *therefore* I did not finish off . . ." (*GBHS* §4.3.3f; and §4.1.5f, esp. Exod. 16:7). I adapt this meaning to Eng. style: "He was jealous for me . . . , *so* I did not finish off . . ."

21. This qal act. ptc., with a continuing aspect, probably implies a present tense, meaning "I am giving and continue to give to him" (*GBHS* §3.4.3; cf. imminent future tense: ESV).

22. I interpret the weqatal here as epexegetical, meaning that it is subordinate to the ptc. in v. 12 (functioning as the main verb) and explains Yahweh's gift of the covenant of peace: "*I am giving* [*nōtēn*] to him my covenant of peace. *That is, he and his descendants after him have* [*wǝhāyǝtâ lô ûlǝazar'ô 'aḥărāyw*] a covenant of a permanent priesthood" (*IBHS* §32.1.3e).

23. *Taḥat 'ăšer* (because) is a less common but idiomatic way to express an explanation in Hb. (just over 10× in the OT).

24. It is possible not to syncretize and render this as a lower case, "for his *god*" (*lē'lōhāyw*), forming a contrast between Phinehas's loyalty to Yahweh, his personal and national deity, and

¹⁴The name of the Israelite who was speared—who was speared to death²⁵ with the Midianite woman—was Salu's son Zimri, a chieftain in the tribe of Simeon.²⁶ ¹⁵The name of the Midianite woman who was killed was Cozbi, daughter of Zur, a tribal chief of a Midianite family.²⁷ ¹⁶Then Yahweh spoke to Moses:²⁸ ¹⁷"Treat the Midianites as enemies and kill them, ¹⁸because they treated you as enemies when they deceived you²⁹ in the matter of Peor, and in the matter of Cozbi, a Midianite chieftain's daughter, their sister, who was killed when the plague came as a result of Peor."³⁰

Interpretation

25:1–5. The Israelites committed sexual immorality with the Moabite women and joined themselves to their god, Baal of Peor, so Yahweh and Moses order the execution of the immoral Israelites. Encamped since 22:1 in the desert valleys of Moab, Israel was living specifically at Shittim (a.k.a. Abel-Shittim), which may have been Tell el-Hammam on Wadi Kafrein.³¹ There "the people began to commit sexual immorality with the Moabite women" (v. 1; see the translation note there). This appears to refer to the Israelite men indulging in prostitution (*znh qal) with "the daughters of Moab" (bənôt mô'āb), that is, with the unmarried young women of Moab.³² As the story unfolds, it becomes clear that some of the men were already married (vv. 4–5), while others were bachelors still in their father's household (v. 6). The disgraceful legacy of Lot's older daughter, who had sex with her father and gave birth

---

the cultic prostitution of the Moabite women and Israelite men who sacrificed to and worshiped "their gods" (’ĕlōhêhen, 2× in v. 2). See the first translation note on Num. 10:9.

25. This is a contextual rendering (like "stabbed," NET) in light of the spearing in vv. 7–8, expressed by a hophal (pass.) that means "to be struck dead" ("nkh," HALOT 2:698).

26. Formally, "a chieftain of the patriarchal house (belonging) to the Simeonite(s)."

27. Formally, "who is the head of the peoples of the patriarchal house in Midian."

28. Colon for "saying"; see the third translation note on 1:1. Other witnesses include "Speak to the Israelites and say."

29. Formally, "they were your enemies in their deception by which they deceived you"; LXXᵉᵈ: "in deceitfulness."

30. This is a causal preposition, interpreting the plague to be the result of the sexual and spiritual infidelity at Peor: "when the plague came *because of* the matter of Peor" (’al-dəbar-pəʿôr; GBHS §4.1.16d).

31. Aharoni, Land, 34, 203; Rasmussen, Atlas, 108; Walton and Matthews, Genesis–Deuteronomy, 205. Shittim is mentioned again as the place of departure for Joshua's spies (Josh. 2:1; 3:1); also Joel 3:18; Mic. 6:5 (recollecting Num. 22–25).

32. In the Torah, the verbal and nominal forms of *znh marks the woman, not the man, as the prostitute (Gen. 34:31; 38:15, 24; Lev. 19:29; 21:7, 9, 14; Deut. 22:21); but see the second translation note on Num. 15:39 regarding *znh as spiritual. A separate term, "dog" (keleb), refers metonymically to a male prostitute (Deut. 23:18 [19]): "keleb," HALOT 2:476. Kilchör (Mosetora, 243) sees Deut. 23:18–19 as drawing on Num. 25 and 30.

to Moab, is perpetuated in Num. 25 by these subsequent daughters of Moab (Gen. 19:37). By this introduction in v. 1, the narrator implies that the men were guilty of illicit sex with the presumably unmarried daughters (Deut. 22:13–19; 1 Cor. 7:2, 9), even though it is not clear from this text alone if they could have, theoretically, made restitution by marrying the daughters (Exod. 22:16; Deut. 22:28–29). The ambiguous, sometimes negative, view of the Moabites earlier in the book (21:11–24:17) does not automatically preclude exogamous marriage with Moabite women, and later biblical traditions are split on the issue (cf. Deut. 23 with Ruth).[33] Of course, there is a literary tension between the Exodus tradition of Moses's wife as a Midianite,[34] a people who also are resident in Moab, and the enticing Midianite women of Num. 25.[35] But the governing concern of the narrator of our story is not intermarriage or alliances per se but idolatrous cultic sex.[36] Elsewhere in the Torah, *znh refers not to intermarriage but to spiritual prostitution, breaking covenant with Yahweh through cultic worship of other gods, which may simultaneously involve engaging in temple prostitution.[37] Here, with *znh only in v. 1, the sequence of events suggests that their illicit sex (v. 1) was in tandem with or led to illicit worship: "The women invited the people to the sacrifices of their gods, and the people ate and bowed down to their gods" (v. 2 ; cf. Rev. 2:14, 20; 1 Cor. 10:8).[38] The Moabite sacrificial feasts involved performing sexual rites (see below).[39] The most famous sequence, about which Yahweh warns elsewhere, is intermarriage leading to the worship of other gods (Exod. 34:14–16; Deut.

---

33. Against: Deut. 23:3–6; 1 Kings 11:1, 7, 33; Ezra 9:1; Neh. 13:1–3. For: Ruth the Moabite (cf. Isa. 56:1–6). Krause ("Aesthetics," 422–25) argues that the story of Rahab the prostitute in Josh. 2 counters the negative view of Num. 25, Deuteronomy, and the rest of Josh. 1–11 by presenting a God-fearing foreign woman who joins the Israelite community.

34. See Exod. 2–4; 18:1; cf. Moses's wife as Cushite (Num. 12:1).

35. See Dor, "Well in Midian," 141–61. Contra Fleurant ("Phinehas," 285–94), who oversteps the textual evidence to argue that the original story identified the Midianite woman of 25:6–8, 14–18 not as Cozbi but as Moses's Midianite wife, but the priestly redactor obfuscated this connection because he was uncomfortable with the prophet Moses being in such a dilemma.

36. With Frevel, "High Priest," 157; W. Lee, *Migratory Campaign*, 174; Douglas, *Wilderness*, 100, 191, 201; Olson, *Death of the Old*, 159–60. Contra Levine (*Numbers*, 2:294–97) and Pettit ("Expiating Apostasy, 457–68), who believe the "real sin" or central violation of Num. 25 is foreign intermarriage; and contra Blenkinsopp ("Baal Peor," 97), who rereads Num. 25 as "a 'covenant of kinship' between Israelites and Midianites resident in Moab, sealed by marriage between high-status individuals from each of these lineages. The violent repudiation of this transaction by the Aaronid Phineas is in marked contrast to the Midianite marriage of Moses."

37. The verb *znh (qal) is frequently used of spiritual prostitution, in which men, women, or both are the agents who ritually worship other gods: Exod. 34:15–16; Lev. 17:7; 20:5, 6; Num. 15:39; 25:1; Deut. 31:16 (on *znh, see the second translation note on Num. 15:39 and the note to the comments on 25:1).

38. Contra Origen, who conjectures that the people bowed down to the idols but did not worship them (Lienhard, *Numbers*, 250).

39. Noth, *Numbers*, 196.

7:1–4),[40] but these verses stress a related but opposite sequence: "sexual immorality" (*znh*) also leads to spiritual infidelity (vv. 1–2).

In Exod. 34:14–16 there is an explicit warning against making a covenant with the people of the land lest it lead to spiritual infidelity; here a covenant seems to have been made directly with a local Moabite deity: "So Israel joined themselves to Baal of Peor, and Yahweh's anger burned against Israel" (v. 3). The imagery of *joining themselves*, or fastening or yoking themselves (*ṣmd* niphal; see the translation note on v. 3), to Baal of Peor contrasts with Israel's orders to *hold fast* (*dbq* qal) to Yahweh and his covenant stipulations,[41] with Isaiah and Zechariah's visions of foreigners joining themselves (*lwh* niphal) in covenant to Yahweh,[42] and with Jeremiah's vision of the postexilic Judeans *joining themselves* (*lwh* niphal) to Yahweh in an eternal covenant (Jer. 50:5). Here the narrator envisions a rejection of Yahweh by those performing the cultic ritual that formally declares their allegiance to the Moabite god, Baal of Peor.[43] Baal is the god, and the mountain Peor is his residence and where Balaam instructs Balak to offer sacrifices (Num. 23:28–30).[44] The name Peor probably relates to the verbal root *pʿr* (open wide), which in Isa. 5:14 refers to the *mouth* of the underworld, so that Baal of Peor likely "represents there the chthonic [relating to the underworld] aspect of the Canaanite god of fertility," the god Baal, who in Ugaritic mythology reigns from Mount Zaphon.[45] This association with the underworld appears to be supported by Ps. 106:28, which alludes to the Num. 25 episode: "Then they joined themselves to the Baal of Peor, and they ate sacrifices (offered) *to the dead* [*mētîm*]."[46] After centuries in Egypt, this was Israel's first encounter with Canaan's most important agricultural deity.[47] The Israelite men failed to resist not only their sexual impulse toward the foreign women but also the prospect of fertile women, animals, and crops associated with the deity.[48]

Yahweh responds, just as he has throughout the wilderness wanderings, with burning anger against his unfaithful people (v. 3).[49] Yahweh then demands that Moses orchestrate the execution of all Israel's leaders (*kol-ro'šê*

---

40. Staubli, *Levitikus, Numeri*, 306.

41. Deut. 4:4; 10:20; 11:22; 13:4 [5]; 30:20; Josh. 22:5; 23:8 (cf. 23:12).

42. Isa. 14:1; 24:2; 56:3, 6; Zech. 2:11.

43. Beth-Peor in Deuteronomic tradition: Deut. 3:29; 4:46; 34:6; Josh. 13:20.

44. In Numbers, Baal is associated with other sites, Baal of Meon (32:38) and Baal of Zephon (33:7); Milgrom, *Numbers*, 212.

45. Spronk, "Baal of Peor," 147–48.

46. See de Vaulx, *Nombres*, 299.

47. Mari, Ugarit, and Egypt records indicate that Baal did not become a prominent deity in Canaan until the Late Bronze Age/New Kingdom Egypt (Milgrom, *Numbers*, 212).

48. See Hess, *Israelite Religions*, 333.

49. See Num. 11:1, 10, 33; 12:9; 16:46; cf. 22:22. Later Yahweh's anger at the Baal of Peor apostates is recollected in Num. 31:16; Josh. 22:17; Ps. 106:28–31; Hosea 9:10.

hā‘ām)—apparently including the chieftains (*nəśî’îm*)[50]—by impaling and exposing them "before Yahweh," that is, at his meeting tent so Israel is cognizant that Yahweh is witnessing the execution, and "in broad daylight" as a public exhibition (see the first and second translation notes on v. 4).[51] Elevating the bodies of war victims on a stake is the most common form of impaling,[52] but the public impaling here is for illicit sex with Moabite women and spiritual infidelity, which invites two ANE comparisons. First, in Mesopotamia in the Isin-Larsa period (ca. 2004–1763 BCE), an adulterous woman was punished by impalement. Second, a collection of Ugaritic letters refers to a citizen of Ugarit who committed a "great sin" of blasphemy against the storm god of Sidon (apparently by entering the most holy place of his temple unauthorized), and the Sidonians (Phoenicians) demanded the man's execution by stoning and impaling him.[53] The purpose of impaling and exposing the corpses of the leaders was not just to deter the rest of the community from continuing in their infidelity but also "so that Yahweh's fierce anger may turn away from Israel" (v. 4). In v. 5 Moses appears to augment Yahweh's orders by commanding Israel's judges (*šōpəṭê yiśrā’ēl*; see Exod. 18:22, 26) to execute the men under their governance who had joined themselves to Baal of Peor (v. 5; see the translation note there). The implication of vv. 4–5 together is that purging the evil must be comprehensive, leaders and followers alike, to assuage Yahweh's wrath.

25:6–9. As the death sentences are being delivered by judge Yahweh and Moses (vv. 4–5), "*just then*" (*wəhinnēh*) an Israelite man presents a Midianite woman to his brothers, presumably for approval to take her as his bride and perform ritual sex with her (v. 6; see the first translation note there).[54] This takes place while Moses and the community are weeping at the entrance of the meeting tent (v. 6), apparently because their leaders, husbands, and fathers have just been executed at the tent (vv. 4–5).[55] The situational irony is apparent: while the community is mourning the death of their unfaithful men, an Israelite man who seemingly has not yet had ritual sex shamelessly brings a Midianite woman to meet his family "in plain sight of Moses and of

---

50. Earlier *nəśî’îm* in Num. 1, 2, 3, 4, 7, 10, 13, 16, 17.

51. Similarly, Milgrom (*Numbers*, 213) suggests that the impalement of Saul's sons likely occurred before the renowned altar at Gibeon (2 Sam. 21:6; 1 Kings 3:4). Thus, the possibility remains that the impaling here was in hopes of expiating for the Israelites and ending the plague (Milgrom, *Numbers*, 476–80).

52. See the relief of Assyrian soldiers impaling conquered Israelites at Lachish: https://www .worldhistory.org/image/15849/lachish-relief-at-nineveh.

53. Tetlow, *Women*, 34; Singer, "History of Ugarit," 670.

54. Milgrom, *Numbers*, 214.

55. Milgrom (*Numbers*, 214) argues that the narrator subtly indicts Moses, who instead of weeping as a penitence rite, should have been hunting down the Israelite man and the Moabite woman.

the whole Israelite community" (v. 6; see the second translation note there).[56]
Is this man naive or so sexually aroused that he has convinced himself that
he can evade the lethal wrath of Yahweh, Moses, and the judges?

Phinehas son of Eleazar, the son of Aaron the priest, now enters the scene
(v. 7). The appellative indicates that Phinehas comes from the line of Levites
who slaughtered the golden-calf worshipers (Exod. 32:26–28)[57] and from
Aaron, who made atonement after the Korah rebellion (16:46–50). It also
means that he is next in line to become the high priest (v. 7; Exod. 6:25).[58]
Phinehas makes his debut here in the Moses story with five foregrounded
actions (wayyiqtols) that dramatically advance the plot: Phinehas sees the
Israelite and Midianite woman pass, rises from the assembly (of mourn-
ers?), grasps a spear or lance crafted for thrusting at an enemy, goes after the
man into his tent shrine—probably a tent sanctuary constructed for cultic
prostitution[59]—and thrusts his spear through them both (vv. 7–8; see the
first translation note on v. 7 and the third translation note on v. 8). As the
probable leader of the sanctuary guard, he would have been armed in this
way.[60] His single spear penetrates "through the two of them, the Israelite man
and the woman into her stomach," implying that they were in the sexual act
when they were killed (v. 8). The situational irony appears to be grounded
in the *lex talionis* principle, "eye for an eye, tooth for a tooth": penetrating
in intercourse is rewarded with being penetrated by the spear.[61] The judges
impale the erring men publicly (vv. 5–6), the Aaronic priest impales these
two privately (v. 7), and the theological implication is that no guilty person

56. Situational irony occurs simply because of the way the events happen or unfold (Garmendia, *Irony*, 5).

57. See Deut. 33:8–11. Baden ("Violent Origins," 116) observes that Num. 25 and 2 Chron.
23, where the Levites militarily defend the king and temple, share the same tradition of Levitical
violence found in Deut. 33:8–11 and Exod. 32.

58. This is a canonical reading, but the title "high priest" or "great priest" (*hakkōhēn
haggādōl*) occurs in the book only in Num. 35 and may belong to a different editorial stratum
than the Eleazar-Phinehas texts of Num. 25; 27 and 31: Frevel, "Book of Numbers," 13–14.

59. Frevel ("High Priest," 157) sees this act as defiling the inner sanctuary of Yahweh's
dwelling "if one may assume *hkbh* [the Israelite's tent shrine] as the *hykl*, or even the *dbyr*,
that is the "holy of holies."

60. Milgrom, *Numbers*, 215.

61. This does not mean the narrator symbolizes Phinehas as penetrating Cozbi sexually, rap-
ing her with his spear, contra the suppositious reasoning of Sivan ("Rape," 74): "Phinehas kills
Cozbi by piercing her belly. Her mode of death is clearly symbolic, as has been often observed.
But the symbolism must be fully appreciated. By wielding a spear Phinehas uses a weapon that
resembles a male sexual organ. By selecting her womb as a target, he rapes her. To be precise,
he impregnates her in a manner calculated not only to inflict death but also to degrade her legal
relationship to a level of arbitrary passion." Following Sivan is Rees, "Numbers 25," 167–69; in
a similar spirit are subversive readings by Gafney, "Numbers 25:1–18," 189–98; and Vaka'uta,
"Indicting YHWH," 179–87.

can evade divine judgment (Heb. 4:12–13; 2 Pet. 3:10).[62] The sequence, not the syntax, indicates that Phinehas's spearing puts an end to "the plague" (definite) previously unmentioned, signaling the end of the scene (v. 8; see the fourth translation note there).[63] This epidemic could have been one of many diseases known in the ancient world, such as typhoid, malaria, cholera, tuberculosis, anthrax, bubonic plague, or diphtheria.[64] The narrator adds that 24,000 died in this plague, probably symbolizing an exhaustive judgment of 2,000 from every tribe.[65]

25:10–13. Yahweh now speaks to Moses to praise Phinehas and establish with him a covenant of peace and a permanent priesthood, because he was jealous for Yahweh. The Jewish rabbis were concerned that Phinehas acted as a vigilante above the law, but Yahweh's endorsement ultimately vindicates him in these verses.[66] Yahweh's tribute to Phinehas is shaped as a concentric structure, highlighting Phinehas's actions in the frames (vv. 11, 13b–c), Yahweh's actions in the center (vv. 12–13a).[67] Applying the same appellative to Phinehas as the narrator did in v. 7, Yahweh opens by calling attention to his lineage, intimating that Phinehas will inherit the high-priestly office, which has passed from Aaron (Lev. 8–10)—bypassing Nadab and Abihu, who died—to Eleazar (Num. 20:25–28) and one day to Phinehas (Josh. 24:33).[68] As the narrator suggests, Phinehas's spearing of the immoral Zimri and Cozbi stops the plague against the Israelites (vv. 8–9). From Yahweh's vantage point, Phinehas has presented Zimri and Cozbi as a blood sacrifice that atones for (*kpr piel) the Israelites and thus averts Yahweh's wrath from the Israelites (vv. 11, 13).[69] Yahweh honors his jealousy and rewards Phinehas with a covenant of peace and perpetual priesthood (vv. 12–13), which, along with Phinehas's atoning work, are discussed in the "Implications" essay below ("The Legacy of Phinehas"). For the Israelites, Phinehas's jealousy and atoning sacrifice also result in more significant grace than just stopping the plague. In a canonical reading, Yahweh's statement "*so I did not finish off the Israelites* in my jealousy" (*wəlōʾ-killîtî ʾet-bənê-yiśrāʾēl*, v. 11)[70] refers euphemistically to not annihilating the *children* of the exodus generation (14:31), since their

---

62. While unstated in this story, Frevel ("High Priest," 157) perceives that Phinehas defiled himself by contacting, at least with his spear, their dead bodies (Num. 5:1–4; 6:9–12), and in Lev. 21:10–12 the high priest is commanded not to touch a corpse; hence, Phinehas rather than Eleazar executes the couple.

63. Zeelander, "Closural Conventions," 338.

64. Walton and Matthews, *Genesis–Deuteronomy*, 205.

65. Excluding Levi, but counting Ephraim and Manasseh separately (see, e.g., 13:4–15); cf. 1 Cor. 10:8.

66. Greengus, *Laws*, 228; Milgrom, *Numbers*, 215.

67. See the "Implications" essay below, "The Legacy of Phinehas."

68. See also Josh. 22:13, 30–33.

69. See the comments on 31:48–54; cf. Frevel, *Desert Transformations*, 425–34.

70. See the second translation note on 25:11.

parents (with the exception of Joshua and Caleb) were already condemned to "be finished off" (*yittammû*) in the desert (14:35; see vv. 20–38).[71] In the end, by Yahweh's mercy, the children will "experience the land that you have rejected" (14:31).

25:14–18. The narrator names the shameless Israelite man and Midianite woman (of vv. 6–9), specifying their pedigrees, and Yahweh tells Moses to kill the Midianites for deceiving the Israelites into worshiping Baal of Peor. It is not superfluous that the narrator names the two who were speared to death as Zimri son of Salu, a Simeonite chieftain, and Cozbi daughter of Zur, a tribal chief from a Midianite family (vv. 14–15; see the first translation note on v. 14).[72] Nowhere else in the OT do we learn about these two or their stock,[73] so the narrator's purpose here is to personalize the story and reveal that the fathers of the sinful couple were chieftains, rendering the foolish actions and tragic fate of their children even more shocking. To the violence of Jacob's son Simeon (Gen. 34; 49:5), Zimri adds a second stain to the tribe's legacy, while Cozbi defames one of Midian's prominent families, not just their immoral women (see the second translation note on v. 14 and the translation note on v. 15). The editorial placement of vv. 14–18 after Yahweh's covenant with Phinehas (vv. 10–13) indicates not merely the secondary nature of this couple[74] but offers a character contrast between Phinehas, jealous for Yahweh and worthy of perpetual honor and a hierocratic role in Israelite society (vv. 10–13), and Zimri and Cozbi, unfaithful to Yahweh and worthy of perpetual shame and extermination from Israelite society (vv. 14–16).

The discursive unit ends with Yahweh's directive to Moses to reciprocate by treating the Midianites as enemies, just as they treated the Israelites as enemies (vv. 16–18). This echoes and fulfills the spirit of the Abrahamic covenant and Balaam's oracles (Gen. 12:3; 22:17; Num. 22:12b; 25:17). The Midianites treated the Israelites as enemies, Yahweh says, by deceiving the Israelites in two ways (v. 18). They deceived Israel in the matter of Baal of Peor (vv. 1–5) and in the matter of Cozbi (vv. 6–9; see the first translation note on v. 18). Calling Cozbi "a Midianite chieftain's daughter, their sister" (v. 18) further personalizes the shame on Midian's families. Also, only here does Yahweh synchronize the events and assert causation: Cozbi "was killed *when* the plague came *as a result of Peor*" (see the second translation note on

---

71. Similarly, Olson, *Death of the Old*, 84, 89, 123.

72. Lutzky ("Name 'Cozbi,'" 546–49) argues the name Cozbi (*kozbî*) may reflect a play on two Semitic roots, *kzb* I (to lie, deceive), shaming the false goddesses at Peor (Astarte or Asherah?), and *kzb* II (to be luxuriant, magnificent). While Cozbi allures (*kzb* II) the Israelite man, she is only a delusion (*kzb* I).

73. The OT mentions Cozbi only here, but Zimri is named here and in 1 Macc. 2:26; see the "Implications" essay below, "The Legacy of Phinehas."

74. Achenbach (*Vollendung*, 440–42, 637) thinks that vv. 14–18 were added by the third and final theocratic revision of the Torah.

v. 18).[75] Israel is held accountable and punished (vv. 7–9), but the Midianites will also be punished for their deception (v. 17). The first humans (the deceived) as well as the serpent (the deceiver) were cursed for their actions (Gen. 3:12–19). Here again, no one is let off the hook, and the righteous justice of Yahweh is upheld. However, the editors of Numbers force the reader to wait until chapter 31 to see divine retributive justice against Midian. But God is not slow in keeping his promises (2 Pet. 3:9), and as the people of God await his sure judgment of the nations, we must first slaughter the infidelity that arises in our own hearts: "Put to death, therefore, whatever belongs to your earthly nature: *sexual immorality*, impurity, lust, evil desires and greed, which is *idolatry. Because of these, the wrath of God is coming*" (Col. 3:5–6 NIV, emphasis added).

Implications

The Legacy of Phinehas

Just as Yahweh venerated and validated Moses as his prophet without equal (12:6–8), now Yahweh venerates and validates Aaron's grandson, Phinehas, as his priest par excellence.[76] Like Yahweh's tribute to Moses, his tribute to Phinehas in 25:10–13 takes the form of a concentric structure,[77] repeating Phinehas's actions in the frames (vv. 11, 13b–c) and positioning Yahweh's actions in the center (vv. 12–13a):

> [11]"Phinehas son of Eleazar, the son of Aaron the priest,
> > has turned my anger away from the Israelites.
> > > He was *jealous for me* among them, so I did not finish off the Israelites *in my jealousy*.
> > > > [12]Therefore tell him that I am giving to him my covenant of peace.
> > > [13]That is, he and his descendants after him have a covenant of a permanent priesthood,
> > because *he was jealous for his god*
> and made atonement for the Israelites."

This monologue by Yahweh functions as a performative speech act, bringing about a new relationship with Yahweh for Phinehas and all his priestly

---

75. Cf. vv. 6–8 with vv. 9 and 18.
76. Leveen, *Memory*, 47–48.
77. See the comments on 12:6–9.

descendants.[78] In v. 12, the verbal aspect is continuous: "I am giving and continue to give him my covenant of peace" (see the translation note on v. 12). The genitive construction "my covenant *of peace*" (*bərîtî šālôm*) occurs in three other passages in the OT, all of which point to Yahweh's promise to redeem his covenant people from exile and personally protect them in their secure land (Isa. 54:10; Ezek. 34:25; 37:26).[79] By his actions, Phinehas averts Yahweh's anger and makes peace between Yahweh and his people, and now Yahweh reciprocates this by making peace with Phinehas and his descendants forever. It is simplest to read "a covenant of a permanent priesthood" (*bərît kəhunnat 'ôlām*) not as a second covenant but as expounding the covenant of peace (see the first translation note on Num. 25:13). Nearly forty years earlier, at Sinai, Yahweh pledged to make Aaron and his male descendants a permanent priesthood (Exod. 29:9; 40:14–15).[80] What is distinctive here is that Yahweh apparently enters into a bilateral treaty with a single priest, Eleazar's son Phinehas, and with his descendants. Every ANE treaty was not only *bilateral* (between two parties) but also *binary* (with promises and obligations),[81] and we can identify Yahweh's promise of a permanent priesthood as Yahweh's obligation (v. 13). Phinehas, however, fulfilled his promise and obligation before the treaty of peace was ratified, having already through his actions convinced Yahweh of his lifestyle of loyalty (vv. 7–8, 11). How this covenant relates to the Priestly instructions of Num. 1–4 and 18 remains an open question,[82] but synchronically we can say that the Phinehas covenant marks a maturation in Yahweh's relationship with the Aaronic priests. This covenant of a perpetual priesthood echoes the enduring covenant that Yahweh established with Abraham and would later establish with David (Gen. 17:7, 13, 19; 2 Sam. 7:8–16; Ps. 89:29). A psalmist later depicts Yahweh as making an oath to David's son, who was also a priestly warrior for Yahweh (Ps. 110:4–7).

Why would Yahweh make such weighty promises to this young priest, who was not even the current high priest? The concentric frames described above explain the reason: Yahweh peers into Phinehas's actions, narrated from a human perspective in vv. 6–9, and uncovers *motives* and *results* that resonate with Yahweh's own nature and actions. First, in the inner frames of the concentric speech, Yahweh reveals Phinehas's motives: he was jealous for Yahweh, just as Yahweh himself was jealous (vv. 11b, 13aβ; see the first translation note on v. 11). The verbal root "to be jealous" (*qn'*) first appeared in Numbers as a *Leitwort* in chap. 5, referring to a husband's jealous suspicions that his wife

---

78. See Austin, *Do Things with Words*, 4–11, etc. See Frevel, "High Priest," 152–56.

79. Probably stronger than the connotation of "pact of friendship" (Milgrom, *Numbers*, 216).

80. Frevel, "Book of Numbers," 153–54.

81. Arnold, *Genesis*, 101–2.

82. Frevel, "Book of Numbers," 32.

had been unfaithful.[83] A conjugal connotation is also evident here in 25:11–13 as Phinehas, a loyal lover of his deity, Yahweh, was jealous for Yahweh and his covenant with Israel. However, he was not merely suspicious of Israel's infidelity with the Moabite women and their gods but saw it (vv. 1–5) and was even eyewitness to an Israelite in the act of cultic sex (vv. 7–8). Phinehas is devoted (holy) to Yahweh not just formally as a priest but also as a loyal devotee of Yahweh, his personal deity. Thus "jealous *for his god/God* [*lēʾlōhāyw*]" (v. 13) contrasts with the Israelite men who "bowed down *to their gods* [*lēʾlōhêhen*]," the gods of the Moabite women (v. 2; see the translation note there). This means that Phinehas self-identifies as personally responsible to shame and purge Yahweh's unfaithful bride, Israel (cf. Lev. 18–20, 26; Num. 5).

Second, in the outer frames of the concentric speech, Yahweh reveals the results of Phinehas's actions: he has averted Yahweh's wrath and made atonement for Israel (vv. 11a, 13b). Surprisingly, by sparing the couple Phinehas has sacrificed the guilty (Zimri-Cozbi) for the guilty (Israel), which inverts the prototypical innocent-for-guilty sacrifice, as articulated by Milgrom: "Therefore, there exists a strong possibility that all texts that assign to *kippēr* [atone, ransom] the function of averting God's wrath have *kōper* [a ransom] in mind: innocent life spared by substituting for it the guilty parties or their ransom."[84] As a priest, Phinehas is holy to Yahweh (25:10–11a), but it seems that his spearing was accepted as an atoning sacrifice because he was emphatically *jealous* for Yahweh, his God (vv. 11b–13).[85] Consequently, Yahweh did not "finish off" or annihilate the Israelites but fulfilled his patriarchal land promise to the new generation (see the comments above).

The legacy of Phinehas continues after Num. 25. It is only fitting that Phinehas, in charge of transporting the sanctuary's articles and trumpets for signaling, leads the military attack on the Midianites to enact Yahweh's vengeance for the Baal of Peor apostasy (31:6, 16). In Joshua, probably because of Phinehas's reputation at the Baal of Peor apostasy (22:17), the Israelites send Phinehas to lead a tribal coalition and purge Yahweh's people again (22:13). However, no blood is shed that day because he concludes that the Reubenites, Gadites, and half-tribe of Manasseh have remained loyal to Yahweh (22:13–33). In Judges, Phinehas reappears in a strange editorial aside: "The ark containing God's covenant was there [Bethel] in those days, and Phinehas son of Eleazar son of Aaron was serving before Yahweh in those days" (Judg. 20:28, my trans.). The implication seems to be that, with no king

---

83. Piel stative of *qn'* in Num. 5:14 [2×], 30; noun *qinʾâ* (jealousy) 7× in 5:14–30.

84. Milgrom, *Leviticus*, 1:1082. See also Sklar, *Sin*, 47.

85. Monroe ("Phinehas' Zeal," 211–31; "Disembodied Women," 39–45) has made the case that for the Priestly authors, Cozbi has become a female scapegoat, expiating and propitiating the deity as in Hittite and Neo-Assyrian human scapegoat rituals. This does not seem to be the driving conceptuality, however, since only 25:18 focuses on Cozbi; everywhere else (vv. 6–8) the Israelite man is the primary agent, listed first, and the focus of Phinehas's pursuit.

in Israel to enforce Yahweh's justice (Judg. 17:6; 18:1; 19:1; 21:25), not even Phinehas, jealous as he is for Yahweh, can prevent the infidelity and chaos that characterizes Judg. 17–21. The namesake and priestly lineage of Phinehas is traced later in the Hebrew Bible,[86] and the biblical songwriters and scribes honor him as an exemplar when they retell Israel's history.[87] This is not to say that Phinehas is the main point of the stories that bear his name. Rather, "he stands for, even identifies, the validity of a particular action in the context of the proper worship of Yahweh."[88]

Beyond these OT references, I will mention two later "disciples of Phinehas" who saw themselves as taking up the mantle of Phinehas.[89] The first was Mattathias, an aged priest of the Second Temple period. When the Seleucid ruler Antiochus IV invaded the northwest Judean town of Modein, he brought abusive and shameless desecrations, not only prohibiting sacrifices and festivals to Yahweh but also building altars and shrines for idols on which pigs and other unclean animals were sacrificed (1 Macc. 1:44–49). But the scribe of this tragic account offers a glimmer of hope because of the zeal of Mattathias (1 Macc. 2:23–27, 50–54). In the LXX the Greek verb *zēloō* and noun *zēlos* are used of both Phinehas (Num. 25) and Mattathias, although one can see a slight semantic shift from being "jealous for Yahweh" (Phinehas) to being "zealous for the law" (Mattathias).[90] Just as Phinehas, in his jealousy for Yahweh, spears the apostate Zimri (and Cozbi) to purge the Israelite community of their infidelity, so Mattathias in his zeal for the law kills the apostate to purge the Jewish community of their infidelity. It appears that, just as Yahweh interprets Phinehas's spearing as an atoning sacrifice, so Mattathias views his slaughter of the Jew on the altar as an atoning sacrifice that will avert God's wrath and spare the Jewish people.[91] From Mattathias came Judas Maccabeus, "the hammer" (1 Macc. 2:4, 66; 3:1), who purified the temple (4:41–51; cf. 2 Macc. 10:1–8), and later the Zealots, described in Josephus and the Gospels, who dreamed of replicating the miraculous Maccabean revolt and overthrowing Rome.[92]

Finally, it appears that Saul, who later became the apostle Paul, imagined himself to be a type of Phinehas. Paul describes his former way of life as a devotee of Yahweh: "in regard to the law, a Pharisee; *as for zeal* [*kata zēlos*], *persecuting the church*; as for righteousness based on the law, faultless" (Phil.

86. By a contrast of character, Eli's sons, Hophni and Phinehas (1 Sam. 2:34), and probably namesakes (1 Esd. 8:62; 2 Esd. 1:2). Priestly lineage of Phinehas: 1 Chron. 6:4, 50; Ezra 7:5; 8:2, 33; 1 Esd. 5:5.

87. Ps. 106:30; 1 Chron. 9:20; Sir. 45:23; 4 Macc. 18:12.

88. Organ, "Pursuing Phinehas," 217.

89. Cf. 1 Sam. 15:32–33, where Samuel hacks King Agag into pieces in a display of total devotion to Yahweh (Ashley, *Numbers*, 522).

90. *Zēloō*: LXX[ed] Num. 25:11, 13; 1 Macc. 2:24, 26, 27, 50, 54, 58 (Mattathias about Elijah); *zēlos*: Num. 25:11 [2×]; 1 Macc. 2:54, 58 (Mattathias about Elijah).

91. Cf. atonement/propitiation in 4 Macc. 4:11–13; 6:27–29; 17:22.

92. See N. Wright, *People of God*, 176–81.

3:5e–6 NIV). Like Phinehas and Mattathias and a select few other heroes of the faith, Paul's zeal for the law impelled his mission to purge the Jewish people from a defiling sect, that of Jesus of Nazareth, who claimed to be the Messiah.[93] As a result of encountering the crucified and risen Messiah, Paul conceived of his Phinehas-like mission in a radically different way.[94] Although Paul never portrays Jesus as a second Phinehas, Paul would have endorsed the analogy articulated by Cyril of Jerusalem in the fourth century: "If Phinehas by his zeal in slaying the evildoer appeased the wrath of God, shall not Jesus, who slew no other but 'gave himself a ransom for all,' take away God's wrath against humanity?"[95] In light of Christ's *self*-sacrificial zeal, Paul exhorts Jesus followers not to be jealous of others (*zēloō*)[96] but to be zealous (*zēloō/ zēlos*) for spiritual gifts, for what is truly good, and for the well-being of other believers.[97] Perhaps alluding to Num. 5 and 25 as he writes to the believers in Corinth, Paul models a Phinehas-like jealousy, emulating God's jealousy, to purify Christ's bride, but he does so not with violence but with rhetoric and tough love: "*I am jealous* [*zēlō*] for you with *a godly jealousy* [*theou zēlō*]. I promised you to one husband, to Christ, so that I might present you as a pure virgin to him" (2 Cor. 11:2 NIV, emphasis added; cf. Eph. 5:25–27). Like Phinehas, zealous believers today still collaborate with God in the purification of Christ's body;[98] we accomplish this not by sacrificing the guilty but by being self-sacrificing for the guilty (James 5:19–20).

---

93. See also Acts 8:1–3; 9:1–5; Rom. 10:2; 1 Cor. 15:9; Gal. 1:13, 23; 1 Tim. 1:13; cf. Heb. 10:27.

94. See Dunn, *New Perspective*, 11–12.

95. Lienhard, *Numbers*, 251.

96. Rom. 13:13; 1 Cor. 3:3; 13:4; 2 Cor. 12:20; Gal. 4:17; 5:20; James 3:14, 16; 4:2.

97. 1 Cor. 12:31; 14:1, 39; 2 Cor. 7:7, 11; 9:2; Gal. 4:18.

98. Synergistic sanctification (Phil. 2:12–13).

24

Census of the New Generation

(26:1–65)

∽∾

Overview

Since the Israelites left Sinai in Num. 10:11, they have become the story's antagonists: wandering, complaining, rebelling, and dying in the wilderness. This does not end when they arrive at the desert valleys of Moab adjacent to the promised land (22:1) but continues through the apostasy in Moab in Num. 25.[1] So after the literary break at 10:11 (departing Sinai), a geographical transition in the book of Numbers occurs at 22:1,[2] but a more meaningful, albeit soft break (compared to 10:11), occurs here with the second census in chap. 26, from which point the narrators say nothing of Israel complaining or revolting again.[3] On a smaller scale, the hard break at chap. 26 divides Israel's time at the Moabite plains into two subsections: chaps. 22–25 and chaps. 26–36.[4] On a larger scale, Num. 26 to Josh. 21 forms an expanse of the Hexateuch narrative that anticipates and fulfills the conquest and settlement of the land through kinship ties and allotment.[5] The opening collection of Num. 26:1 [25:19]–27:23, with the tribal census of the second generation and thematically related short stories, is not a law collection[6] but rather

---

1. With Seebass, "Eigene Komposition," 96.
2. Cf. Artus ("Numbers 32," 372–75), who sees a tripartite division, with a strong break when Israel arrives in the desert valleys of Moab: 1:1–10:36; chaps. 11–21; 22–36.
3. Frevel, "Alte Stücke," 268n54.
4. Schmidt, *Numeri*, 155.
5. See von Rad, *Priesterschrift*, 162. On Num. 26–36* as post-P[g], and as not incomplete without the conquest and settlement in Joshua, see Frevel, *Mit Blick*, 378–79.
6. Contra Milgrom, *Numbers*, xv.

the next scenes in the narrative that introduce the *children* of the exodus generation, now stationed as families in hopeful anticipation of life in the land of Canaan.[7] At the same time, the censuses of chaps. 1 and 26 organize the entire composition of Numbers, moving from the old exodus generation, which dies in the wilderness (Num. 1/11–25), to the birth of a new generation destined to inherit the land (Num. 26–36).[8] The chapter is divided into four units, but the last two are connected by the narrator thematically. In vv. 1–51, Yahweh directs Moses and Eleazar alone, without the chieftains, to take the second census (vv. 1–4), which they do faithfully. The canonical shape of the census is more familial than the first census, forming the basis for the distribution of territory in Canaan among Israel's tribes (vv. 5–51). In vv. 52–56, Yahweh orders Israel to assign each tribe a territory relative in size to the population of the tribe (vv. 53–54) but then stipulates that this must be done by casting lots (vv. 55–56). This is followed in vv. 57–62 with a unique census of the families of Levi, which is connected to the ensuing postscript in vv. 63–65 by the theme of those who were *not listed* in the second census of 26:5–51.

Translation

1a [25:19]After the plague, **1b [26:1]**Yahweh said to Moses and to Eleazar son of Aaron the priest,[9] **2**"Take a census[10] of the entire Israelite community, twenty years old and up, by their patriarchs' households,[11] everyone eligible for military service."[12] **3**So Moses and Eleazar the priest spoke with them in the desert valleys of Moab along the Jordan River across from Jericho: **4**"Take a census[13] of the people twenty years old and up, just as Yahweh commanded Moses and the Israelites who came out of the land of Egypt."

5Reuben was Israel's firstborn. The Reubenites: from Hanoch, the Hanochite family; from Pallu, the Palluite family; **6**from Hezron, the Hezronite family; from Carmi, the Carmite family. **7**These were

---

7. Seebass, "Eigene Komposition," 101; Douglas, *Wilderness*, 123. Classically, the censuses in chaps. 1 and 26 have been attributed to P as reflecting the community of the Second Temple period (Scharbert, *Numeri*, 106) or, more specifically, to the first phase of a theocratic revision of the Torah that centers in chap. 26 on the land claim (Achenbach, *Vollendung*, 441–72, 638).

8. Olson, *Death of the Old*, 55, 198; Leveen, *Memory*, 37–39.

9. Comma for "saying," and colon in vv. 3, 52. See the third translation note on 1:1.

10. Formally, "lift up a head."

11. Formally, "by the house of their fathers"; on the Iron Age Israelite *bêt-'āb* extended family, see Stager, "Archaeology," 1–35; Schloen, *House of the Father*.

12. Formally, "all who go out for war [or, in the army]"; LXX[ed]: "everyone who goes out to do battle in Israel" (as 1:3, etc.).

13. The clause "take a census" (*śǝ'û 'et-rō'š*) is elided but assumed from v. 2.

Reubenite families, and of them those who were enlisted came to 43,730.[14] [8]Pallu's son was Eliab. [9]Eliab's sons were Nemuel, Dathan, and Abiram.[15] It was Dathan and Abiram who were chosen by the community[16] and fought against Moses and Aaron, with Korah's followers, when they fought against Yahweh.[17] [10]The earth opened its mouth and swallowed them and Korah when his followers died, when the fire consumed 250 men,[18] and they became a warning sign.[19] [11]But the sons of Korah did not die.[20]

[12]The Simeonites by their families:[21] from Nemuel, the Nemuelite family; from Jamin, the Jaminite family; from Jakin, the Jakinite family;

14. A qal pass. ptc. from *pqd (HALOT 3:955–58, gloss 3; DCH 6:737–45, gloss 3b), with a subject suffix that functions as a predicate adjective: "The ones who were enrolled of them [pəqudêhem] came to 43,730."

15. Pronounced "Abirom" ('byrwm) by 4Q27.

16. Formally, "chosen of the community" (qərî'ê hā'ēdâ), with a subjective gen., meaning the community chose Dathan and Abiram; "chosen by the community" (GBHS §2.2.3). There is no need to amend the text to a qal pass., "who were chosen/called" (qərû'ê MT^qere), because the received text can be read, as in 16:2, as an adjective: "who were called/chosen by the community" (qərî'ê MT^ketiv SP ≈ adj. epiklētoi LXX^ed).

17. "Fought against" (*nṣḥ I), five times in the Pentateuch and in Numbers only here, is a hiphil intransitive: "It was Dathan and Abiram who were chosen by the community and fought against Moses and Aaron [hiṣṣû 'al-mōšeh wə'al-'ahārōn] with Korah's followers, when they fought against Yahweh [bəhaṣṣōtām 'l-yhwh]" (DCH 5:737). SP apparently replaced this root to match the language of Korah's rebellion elsewhere: ". . . gathered together [hw'dw] against Moses and Aaron with Korah's followers, when they gathered together [bhw'dtm] against Yahweh" (from "y'd," see HALOT 2:419, niphal gloss 2; cf. 14:35; 16:11; 27:3). LXX^ed: "who banded together . . . in the insurrection . . ."

18. Probably to match 16:35, 4Q27 includes "250 men who offered the incense."

19. "Warning sign" (NIV, or "warning" in many versions) is a dynamic rendering of a generic nēs, referring to something elevated and visible ("flag, standard": HALOT 2:701). Of the three other occurrences in the Pentateuch, Moses in the first calls Yahweh his banner raised to honor Yahweh after the victory over the Amalekites (Yhwh nissî, Exod. 17:15). Then this term refers to the pole (nēs) on which the bronze snake of healing was placed (Num. 21:8, 9). Now here the visible, supernatural deaths of Korah and his followers, who rebelled, become a "warning sign" to the second wilderness generation who survived (Num. 26:10). On the addition of subjects in the other witnesses (4Q27, SP, LXX^ed), probably for clarity but without exegetical significance, see Ulrich, Qumran, 157.

20. In contrast to the tone of divine judgment against Korah and his followers in v. 10, this is an exception marked by a disjunctive wə: "But the sons of Korah did not die" (ûbənê-qōraḥ lō'-mētû; IBHS §39.2.3b). This brief contrasting clause may be a later addition, not simply because it does not fit with v. 10, but because it does not align with the Num. 16 narrative to which vv. 10–11 refer, which describes the death of the sons of Korah (16:27, 32). The "Sons of Korah," musicians to whom a collection of psalms are attributed, may have been responsible for this addition of Num. 26:11 to trace their roots back to Korah of Num. 16, implying that Num. 16:27–32 was hyperbolic (cf. hyperbolic Josh. 11:23 versus Josh. 13:1–6; 23:13; Judg. 1:1; 2:3; 3:1). In any case, Num. 26:11 presents the continuation of Korah's line, as in the genealogy of 1 Chron. 6:22–24 [7–9]; 9:19 (so Achenbach, Vollendung, 121).

21. SP: "The Simeonites by the families of the Simeonites" (SP ≈ LXX^ed).

¹³from Zerah, the Zerahite family; from Shaul, the Shaulite family. ¹⁴These were the Simeonite families: 22,200.

¹⁵The Gadites by their families: from Zephon, the Zephonite family; from Haggi, the Haggite family; from Shuni, the Shunite family; ¹⁶from Ozni, the Oznite family; from Eri, the Erite family; ¹⁷from Arod, the Arodite family; from Areli, the Arelite family.²² ¹⁸These were the Gadite families, and of them those who were enlisted came to 40,500.

¹⁹Judah's sons were Er and Onan, but Er and Onan died in the land of Canaan. ²⁰The Judahites by their families were, from Shelah, the Shelahite family; from Perez, the Perezite family; from Zerah, the Zerahite family. ²¹The Perezites were, from Hezron, the Hezronite family; from Hamul,²³ the Hamulite family. ²²These were Judah's families, and of them those who were enlisted came to 76,500.

²³The Issacharites by their families: from Tola, the Tolaite family; from Puah, the Puite family;²⁴ ²⁴from Jashub, the Jashubite family; from Shimron, the Shimronite family. ²⁵These were Issachar's families, and of them those who were enlisted came to 64,300.

²⁶The Zebulunites by their families: from Sered, the Sardite family; from Elon, the Elonite family; from Jahleel, the Jahleelite family. ²⁷These were the Zebulunite families, and of them those who were enlisted came to 60,500.

²⁸The Josephites by their families: Manasseh and Ephraim. ²⁹The Manassites: from Machir, the Machirite family, and Machir was Gilead's father; from Gilead, the Gileadite family. ³⁰These were the Gileadites: from Iezer,²⁵ the Iezerite family; from Helek, the Helekite family; ³¹from Asriel, the Asrielite family;²⁶ from Shechem, the Shechemite family; ³²from Shemida, the Shemidaite family; from Hepher, the Hepherite²⁷ family. ³³Now Hepher's son Zelophehad had no sons, only daughters. The names of Zelophehad's daughters²⁸ were Mahlah and Noah, Hoglah, Milcah, and Tirzah. ³⁴These were the Manassite families, and of them those who were enlisted²⁹ came to 52,700. ³⁵These were the Ephraimites by their families: from

---

22. Also pronounced "from *Arodi* [*'rwdy* SP ≈ LXX^{ed}] . . . from *Aril* [*'ry'l* 4Q27 LXX^{ed}] . . . *Arilite* [*'ry'ly* 4Q27 LXX^{ed}] family."

23. Pronounced "Hamuel" by others (LXX^{ed} *Iamouēl*; vocalized SP *ḥāmûʾēl*, likely 4Q27, because later it is *ḥḥm*]*w'ly*).

24. Adjusting MT "Punite" (*happûnî*, ESV, NRSV, NJPS), I prefer "Puite" (*hpw'y* 4Q27 SP LXX^{ed} [*ho Phouai*] NLT, NET, NIV), the gentilic form of "Puah" (Gen. 46:13; Exod. 1:15; Num. 26:23; Judg. 10:1; 1 Chron. 7:1).

25. Or "Achiezer" (*'hy'zry* 4Q27 SP LXX^{ed}).

26. Or "Asrel . . . Asrelite" (*'s*]*r'l* 4Q27; and *śr'ly* 4Q27 MT).

27. Or "Hopher . . . Hopherite" (*ḥwpr* . . . *ḥwpry* 4Q27 ≈ LXX^{ed}).

28. Formally, "*the name* [*šm*] of Zelophehad's daughters" (MT SP), which is idiomatic and is adjusted to 27:1 (Josh. 17:3) by other witnesses, "*These are the names* of Zelophehad's daughters" (4Q27 LXX^{ed}).

29. I follow the pattern with other witnesses, "and *of them those who were enlisted*" (*lpqdyhm* 4Q27 MT^{mss} SP LXX^{ed}; cf. "and those who were enlisted," *wpqdyhm* MT).

Shuthelah, the Shuthelahite family; from Beker, the Bekerite family; from Tahan, the Tahanite family. **36**And these were the Shuthelahites: from Eran, the Eranite family. **37**These were the Ephraimite families, and of them those who were enlisted came to 32,500. These were Joseph's descendants by their families.

38The Benjaminites by their families: from Bela, the Belaite family; from Ashbel, the Ashbelite family; from Ahiram, the Ahiramite family; **39**from Shupham, the Shuphamite family; from Hupham, the Huphamite family. **40**Bela's sons were Ard and Naaman.[30] From Ard, the Ardite family; from Naaman, the Naamanite family. **41**These were the Benjaminites by their families, and of them those who were enlisted came to 45,600.

42These were the Danites by their families: from Shuham, the Shuhamite family. These are Dan's families by their families. **43**As for all the Shuhahite families, those who were enlisted came to 64,400. **44**The Asherites by their families: from Imnah, the Imnahite family; from Ishvi, the Ishvite family; from Beriah, the Beriahite family. **45**From the Beriahites:[31] from Heber, the Heberite family; from Malkiel, the Malkielite family. **46**Now the name of Asher's daughter was Serah. **47**These were Asherite families, and those who were enlisted came to 53,400.

48The Naphtalites by their families: from Jahzeel, the Jahzeelite family; from Guni, the Gunite family; **49**from Jezer, the Jezerite family; from Shillem, the Shillemite family. **50**These were Naphtali's families by their families, and of them those who were enlisted came to 45,400.

51The enlisted Israelites came to 601,730.[32]

52Then Yahweh said to Moses: **53**"To these the land must be divided as an inheritance based on the number of names.[33] **54**To a larger tribe you must give a larger inheritance, and to a smaller tribe you must give a smaller inheritance. To each one its inheritance must be given based on the number of those who were enlisted.[34] **55**But the land must be divided by lot;[35] they will inherit[36] according to the names of their ancestral tribes.[37]

30. SP and LXX^ed omits "Bela's sons were Ard and Naaman."

31. SP and LXX^ed omit "From the Beriahites."

32. Formally, "the ones who were enlisted of the Israelites were . . ."

33. The first preposition *b* marks the essence or identity, the second marks the numerical standard: "To these the land must be divided *as an inheritance* [*bǝnaḥălâ*] *based on the number of names* [*bǝmispar šēmôt*]" (IBHS §11.2.5d–e, nos. 21, 27–28).

34. Formally, "To the numerous/great you must make numerous/great their inheritance, and to the few/small you must make few/small their inheritance. Each according to the mouth of those who were enlisted of them must be given their inheritance."

35. Here and in v. 56, the focus is on "by lot," which is fronted: "But *by lot* must be divided the land, . . . *on the mouth of the lot* must be divided their inheritance" (BHRG §47.2.1[2]).

36. Probably assimilating to Num. 33:54 and 34:13, SP hithpael (*ytnḥlw*) means "they will maintain as a possession" ("*nḥl*," HALOT 2:686, gloss 1).

37. Formally, "the tribes of their fathers."

⁵⁶Their inheritance must be divided by lot among the larger and smaller tribes."³⁸

⁵⁷These were the Levites who were listed³⁹ by their families: from Gershon, the Gershonite family; from Kohath, the Kohathite family; from Merari, the Merarite family. ⁵⁸These were Levi's families: the Libnite family, the Hebronite family, the Mahlite family, the Mushite family, the Korahite family.⁴⁰ Kohath was Amram's father, ⁵⁹and the name of Amram's wife was Jochebed, Levi's daughter, who was born to Levi in Egypt. And by Amram she bore Aaron, Moses, and Miriam their sister. ⁶⁰And Aaron was the father⁴¹ of Nadab and Abihu, Eleazar and Ithamar. ⁶¹But Nadab and Abihu died when they offered strange fire before Yahweh.⁴² ⁶²Those of them who were listed came to 23,000, all males a month old and up. Since they were not listed among the Israelites, no inheritance was given to them among the Israelites. ⁶³These were listed by Moses and Eleazar the priest,⁴³ who listed the Israelites in the desert valleys of Moab along the Jordan River across from Jericho. ⁶⁴But no one among them had been listed by Moses and Aaron the priest when they listed the Israelites in the Sinai wilderness. ⁶⁵Because Yahweh had said of them, "They will definitely die⁴⁴ in the wilderness," not one of them was left,⁴⁵ except Jephunneh's son Caleb and Nun's son Joshua.

Interpretation

26:1 [25:19]–51. As the next scene in the narrative "after the plague" (v. 1a) of divine judgment that took 24,000 lives (25:9), Yahweh orders Moses and Eleazar to take a second census because the one taken nearly forty years ago has become obsolete (1:1–46). The Israelite parents who came out of Egypt

38. A niphal incomplete pass. with imperative force: "Their inheritance *must be divided*" (*tēḥāleq*). SP *yḥlq* is either an error (masc. niphal ≠ fem. subj.) or reads "he/one must divide their inheritance" (pronounced *yaḥălōq*).

39. Here and in v. 62, the qal pass. ptc. attributes the civilian Levites as "listed," whereas for the non-Levitical, military personnel, I prefer the military connotation of "enlisted." See also "listed" Levites, e.g., in Num. 3:16, 22, 34, 39, 42.

40. SP and LXX^ed transpose the order: "the Korahite family and the Mushite family."

41. A niphal pass., with the subjects marked with the definite direct obj. marker; formally, "*And born* [*wayyiwwālēd*] to Aaron *were Nadab and Abihu, Eleazar and Ithamar* [*'et-nādāb wə'et-'ăbîhû' 'et-'el'āzār wə'et-'îtāmār*]" (see IBHS §23.2.2e, example 12).

42. LXX^ed: ". . . before the Lord *in the wilderness of Sina*."

43. "These" (*'ēlleh*) could refer to only the Levites (vv. 57–62) but more likely refers to all the tribes with Levi, forming an *inclusio* with vv. 1–4 or specifically vv. 3–4. The gen. is subjective: "These were *listed by Moses* and Eleazar the priest" (*pəqûdê mōšeh* . . . ; GBHS §2.2.3).

44. An emphatic, cognate adverbial inf.: "They will definitely die" (*môt yāmutû*; GBHS §3.4.2b.1).

45. With de Vaulx (*Nombres*, 316), I take the explanatory *kî* clause as dependent on the ensuing independent clause marked by the simple *wə* + negated qatal: "*Because* [*kî*] Yahweh had said of them, 'They will definitely die in the wilderness,' *not* one of them *was left* [*wəlō'-nôtar*]" (rather than *wə* as "therefore," EÜ; or "and so," Seebass, *Numeri*, 3:152).

have died in the wilderness, and now their surviving sons must be counted and mustered for war to take the land of Canaan (26:1–51). After a generation of rebellion and death in the wilderness (Num. 11:1–25:18), Yahweh orders a second census, which soberly yet optimistically echoes his orders for the first census back in chap. 2:

Table 24.1. Censuses Compared

Census in Year 2 (1:1–20b)	Census about Year 40 (26:1–5)
¹Then Yahweh spoke to Moses in the Sinai wilderness inside the meeting tent, on day one of the second month in the second year after their exodus from the land of Egypt:	¹After the plague, Yahweh said to Moses and to Eleazar son of Aaron the priest,
²"Take a census of the entire Israelite community by their families, by their patriarchs' households, counting the name of every individual male. ³You and Aaron must enlist everyone eligible for military service, twenty years old and up, by their divisions.	²"Take a census of the entire Israelite community twenty years old and up, by their patriarchs' households, everyone eligible for military service."
[vv. 4–16: Named chieftains assist in taking the census] [vv. 17–19: Report of census completion by Moses, Aaron, and the named chieftains]	³So Moses and Eleazar the priest spoke with them in the desert valleys of Moab along the Jordan River across from Jericho: ⁴"Take a census of the people twenty years old and up, just as Yahweh commanded Moses and the Israelites who came out of the land of Egypt."
²⁰They were as follows: The descendants of Reuben, Israel's firstborn . . .	⁵Reuben was Israel's firstborn . . .

The innerbiblical formula in 26:4, "*just as Yahweh commanded* Moses and the Israelites who came out of the land of Egypt," orients the audience of chap. 26 to recall, compare, and contrast this census with the first census of the exodus generation in chap. 1.[46] Aside from flipping the sequence from Ephraim→Manasseh (1:32–35) to Manasseh→Ephraim (26:28–37), the tribes are listed in identical order in both censuses (see table 24.1). The differing narrative settings explain some of the differences (marked in bold). The first census was taken at Sinai, the second in the desert valleys of Moab across from Jericho. Aaron has died, and the mantle of high-priestly leadership had shifted to his oldest surviving son, Eleazar (Num. 20:23–29), who now partners with Moses to take the second census (26:1, 3). Moses and Eleazar together "spoke with them" (meaning the entire Israelite community) to direct the census. Yahweh's truncated mandate in 26:2 likely implies the components of 1:2–3:

46. See Fishbane, *Biblical Interpretation*, 44, 170–87.

"by their families" (1:2) can be presumed since this phrase recurs through-out chap. 26;[47]

"counting the name of every individual male" (1:2)—that is, not including men younger than twenty, women, and children—is indicated by the qualifying phrase "everyone eligible for military service" (26:2) and by the similar totals of chaps. 1 and 26 (on the totals see below);

the organization "by their divisions" (1:3) can probably also be inferred from the martial purpose of the count in 26:2 ("eligible for military service").

Naming Jericho in the frames around the second census (26:3, 63) increases excitement because the land promised so long ago is now in Israel's view.[48]

Nonetheless, there is a substantive difference beyond the narrative setting mentioned above: the first census has a *military* focus, whereas the second has a *family* focus that envisions real families with painful shortcomings and with children, grandchildren, and great-grandchildren now preparing to resettle together in the territories of Canaan allotted to them.[49] The second census, like the first, counts Israel's warriors eligible to fight for the promised land (26:2),[50] but chap. 26 says nothing of the chieftains, who are military "leaders of Israel's thousands" (1:16) and who played a pivotal role in directing the first census at the tribal level (1:4–19, 44). These chieftains, the reader infers from vv. 4, 63–65, have died off with the first wilderness generation, so that now the responsibility rests alone on Yahweh's prophet, Moses, and high priest, Eleazar, to direct the census, even if they must have pragmatically delegated the counting to representatives. Moreover, the form of the second census, as recorded in Numbers, is different and suggestive of its family focus (see the bold text in the table below).[51]

Numbers 1:22	Numbers 26:12–14
[22]From the descendants of Simeon:	[12]The Simeonites **by their families**:
according to the family history of their families and patriarchs' households, every male (of those who were enlisted) twenty years old and up, everyone eligible for military service, was listed individually by name.	from Nemuel, the Nemuelite **family**; from Jamin, the Jaminite **family**; from Jakin, the Jakinite **family**; [13]from Zerah, the Zerahite **family**; from Shaul, the Shaulite **family**.
[23]Those who were enlisted from the tribe of Simeon came to 59,300.	[14]These were the Simeonite **families**: 22,200.

47. Num. 26:12, 15, 20, 23, 26, 28, 35, 37, 38, 41, 42, 44, 48, 50.

48. P. Guillaume, *Land*, 151.

49. Levine (*Numbers*, 2:307) sees the second census as replacing the first wilderness census, mustering troops for conquest and settlement, and forming the basis for apportioning the land.

50. Formally, "enrolled," but as in chap. 1, I still prefer the contextual "enlisted" (vv. 7, 18, 22, etc.; see the translation note on v. 7).

51. Achenbach, *Vollendung*, 468.

413

With a few variations, the second census echoes the list in Gen. 46:8–27 of Israel-Jacob's descendants who migrated into Egypt.[52] As Israel's families settled in Egypt with Yahweh's blessing (Gen. 46:1–4), so Israel's families will settle in Canaan with Yahweh's blessing. The first census identifies only Israel's tribes, but the second census identifies by name seventy-nine family groups[53] descended from Jacob's grandsons, great-grandsons, and great-great-grandsons.[54] This implies that, in the narrative, the Israelite tribes can range from being undivided—as in the case of Dan, in which all its families trace their lines back to Dan's one son (vv. 42–43)—to seven subdivisions, as in the case of Gad, with its families tracing their lines back to each of his seven sons (vv. 15–18). Grandsons and great-grandsons, when mentioned, generate the same kinds of intratribal divisions (see the preceding note).

Adding to the family flavor of the second census are the anecdotal glosses in vv. 5a, 9b–11, 19, 33, 46, and 61. The concise remarks—about Reuben (neutral), Dathan and Abiram (negative), Er and Onan (negative), Zelophehad's daughters (raising questions), Serah (positive), and Nadab and Abihu (negative)—all play a rhetorical role in reshaping the message of the second census, in chap. 26. As the promised land looms large, these remarks warn the second wilderness generation of past family rebellion, to remember certain daughters, and to take heart that Yahweh has not abandoned his promises to Jacob's descendants (see the "Implications" essay below, "A Warning with Hope").

The count of the male fighters twenty years old and up from each tribe in the second generation is comparable to those in the first: Reuben (46,500 ≈ 43,730); Simeon (59,300 > 22,200); Gad (45,650 ≈ 40,500); Judah (74,600 ≈ 76,500); Issachar (54,400 < 64,300); Zebulun (57,400 ≈ 60,500); Manasseh (32,200 < 52,700); Ephraim (40,500 > 32,500); Benjamin (35,400 < 45,600);

---

52. Gray, *Numbers*, 387–88; Staubli, *Levitikus, Numeri*, 309–12; Douglas, *Wilderness*, 182–83. Levine (*Numbers*, 2:307) notes that the chap. 26 census correlates to a lesser degree with the Exod. 6:14–28 record of the Israelite families in Egypt (cf. 1 Chron. 2–9; Josh. 12–19). Kislev ("Census," 236–60) argues that the Num. 26 census reflects three stages: (1) close dependence on the Gen. 46 list, (2) an adaptation of the list for the allocation of the tribes by size, and (3) an additional adaptation by the MT to contextualize the list within its literary context in Numbers. Edelman ("Manassite Genealogy," 179–201) argues that to compose Manasseh's genealogy, the Chronicler in 1 Chron. 7:14–19 drew from an independent source along with Num. 26:29–34 and Josh. 17:1–3.

53. Contra Ziemer ("Erklärung," 271–87), the exact figure of seventy-nine is insignificant for interpreting chap. 26.

54. More often, families descended from sons are mentioned: from the sons of Simeon, Gad, Issachar, Zebulun, Dan, Naphtali. The additional tribal subdivisions are noted in the cases of families descended from each of Reuben's 4 sons (S), 1 grandson (GS) and 3 great-grandsons (GGS; vv. 5–11); Judah's 3 S and 2 GS (vv. 19–22); Manasseh's 1 S, 1 GS, 6 GGS, 1 GGGS, and 5 GGG daughters (vv. 29–34); Ephraim's 3 S and 1 GS (vv. 35–37); Benjamin's 5 S and 2 GS (vv. 38–41); Asher's 3 S, 1 daughter and 2 GS (vv. 44–47).

Dan (62,700 ≈ 64,400); Asher (41,500 < 53,400); Naphtali (53,400 > 45,400).[55] Asher's second generation, 53,400 strong, precisely replaces Naphtali's exodus generation, 53,400. The first and second censuses yield very similar combined totals for all the tribal warriors—from 603,550 to 601,730 (1:46; 26:51)—and the implication is theological. Setting aside the new sizes of each tribe, the second generation of warriors has effectively replaced the first. As a result, like the first census, the second equally imagines Israel's burgeoning population as a fulfillment of the Priestly creation mandate, "Be fruitful and multiply and fill the earth" (Gen. 1:28). Israel was fruitful and multiplied in Egypt (Exod. 1:7), and although an obliterated exodus generation called into question the Gen. 1 echo, the chap. 26 census reaffirms Israel's fruitfulness and that "God blessed them" again (Gen. 1:28a).[56]

26:52-56. With Israel's families counted and ready to move into Canaan (vv. 1–51), Yahweh addresses Israel's settlement by tribe in the land (vv. 52–56). Yahweh anticipates the potential problem that Israel's tribes could inherit a territory disproportionate to the population of their tribe—that is, land that is smaller or larger than needed for the tribe's numbers. Yahweh therefore issues orders to give a larger tribe a larger territory in Canaan and a smaller tribe a smaller territory: "to each one its inheritance must be given based on the number of those who were enlisted" (v. 54; see the translation note there). This clarifies the meaning of "based on the number of names [in the census]" (v. 53; see the translation note there), but it remains ambiguous whether this is a generic order (larger tribes receive larger territories and vice versa) or a specific order (the smallest tribe receives the smallest, the largest the largest, and every tribe is matched to its territory on a gradated scale). If the latter, then based on the census (vv. 5–50), the territories would be assigned in this order, from largest to smallest: (1) Judah (76,500), (2) Dan (64,400), (3) Issachar (64,300), (4) Zebulun (60,500), (5) Asher (53,400), (6) Manasseh (52,700), (7) Benjamin (45,600), (8) Reuben (43,730), (9) Gad (40,500), (10) Ephraim (32,500), (11) Simeon (22,200), and (12) Naphtali (45,400).

The vast disparity between Judah, with 76,500 men above age twenty, and Naphtali, with 45,400, obviously justifies Yahweh's orders in vv. 53–54, repeated in Num. 33:54. The great mystery of this unit, however, is the abrupt shift in vv. 55–56 demanding that "the land must be divided by lot" (see the first and second translation notes on v. 55). The order to cast lots is over-specified in v. 56 (see the translation note there), where Yahweh now covers the prior

55. See Milgrom, *Numbers*, 220. The figures show that Simeon dwindled nearly to 1/3rd the size of its exodus generation (!); Issachar is about 1/6th larger; Manasseh, 2/5ths larger; Ephraim, 1/4th smaller; Benjamin, 1/4th larger; Asher, 1/5th larger; and Naphtali, 1/5th smaller. For Levine (*Numbers*, 2:307–8), chap. 1 is a reflex to chap. 26 so that readers see the ascendancy of Manasseh (32K to 52K) and decline of Simeon (59K to 22K), revealing certain tribal traditions in Numbers.

56. See Specht, "Die Verfehlung," 295.

issue of tribal size: "among the larger and smaller tribes." As readers know, Num. 11–25 has been filled with dissenting minority factions, "enclaves" who claim to be led by consensus and who could potentially dissent over tribes not getting their fair share of the land, but casting lots has the power to settle such disputes.[57] Thus lots revealing Yahweh's selections would protect Israel's leaders involved in the proceedings.[58]

Lot casting is attested in Nuzi, Cappadocia, Assyria, and even today among some modern Arab tribes.[59] In Mari in ancient Mesopotamia, casting lots was how the king designated land estates to his vassals and military retirees.[60] Lots were typically, but not in every known case, cast in the presence of the deciding deities, as Shalmaneser III asserts on the Black Obelisk: "In my thirty-first year, I cast the lot a second time before Aššur and Addad."[61] Surveying the Hebrew terminology in the OT, Kitz clarifies the process of lot casting: "Each lot 'thrown into' (hûṭal bĕ-) a container. Someone 'shakes' (qilqal) the lots in a receptacle until one of them 'comes up' ('ālâ) and 'goes out' (yāṣā'). When the shaker has 'cast out' (hišlîk) a lot, it 'falls' (nāpal) to the ground. The meaning applied to that lot constitutes the mišpaṭ yhwh, 'the decision of Yahweh.'"[62] The lot caster had authority to shake the container, but this merely prepared the way for the deity to make a selection by causing the lot to jump from the container to the ground.[63]

So which is it in vv. 53–56? Execute Yahweh's orders, which have an imperative force,[64] and distribute the territories proportionately (vv. 53–54) or simply cast lots in Yahweh's presence and let Yahweh do the subdividing (vv. 55–56)? On the one hand, vv. 55–56 align with other Numbers texts where casting lots is ordered and with Joshua, where casting lots was the sanctioned modus operandi.[65] On the other hand, in the present literary form of the text, casting lots in vv. 55–56 is counterbalanced by human agency in vv. 53–54. The text never says how both divine and human actions are to be respected in the division of the land,[66] but it is reasonable to infer (with Seebass) that in fulfillment of Yahweh's will, the Israelites are involved in the decision but must not have the final word, even as Prov. 16:33 explains: "Into the lap the

57. Douglas, *Wilderness*, 45, 55.
58. Seebass, *Numeri*, 3:191; Procopius of Gaza (5th–6th cent. CE); Lienhard, *Numbers*, 253.
59. See de Vaulx, *Nombres*, 313.
60. Walton and Matthews, *Genesis–Deuteronomy*, 206.
61. Kitz, "Lot Casting," 214.
62. Kitz, "Lot Casting," 214.
63. Kitz, "Lot Casting," 214.
64. In vv. 53–54 are four imperatival yiqtols (*GBHS* §3.2.2d.4).
65. Num. 33:54; 34:13; 36:2; Josh. 14:2; 18–19*; 21*. Schmidt (*Numeri*, 161–62) sees vv. 55–56 as a late addition to bring Num. 26 into alignment with Joshua, whereas Seebass ("Versuch," 370–85) argues conversely that Num. 26 was the base layer to which Josh. 18:1–10 was supplied, presenting Joshua as the master of casting lots according to Yahweh's prior mandate.
66. Gray, *Numbers*, 394.

lot is cast, but from Yahweh is its every decision."[67] Or, from another perspective, as with the censuses where human warriors are numbered as agents of the divine warrior, so Israel's leaders who subdivide the land become agents of Yahweh, who reveals his choice to them by lot.

26:57–65. After the literary break of Yahweh's speech in vv. 52–56, which addresses land distribution among the tribes, the narrator resumes the census format of vv. 5–56 with Levi: "These were the Levites who were listed by their families" (v. 57a). So the census format continues in vv. 57–58a naming the core families descended from Levi, is put on pause with an inserted commentary about Aaron's family in vv. 58b–61, and then resumes in v. 62a with a conventional totaling of those listed: 23,000 (see the translation note on v. 57). The Levi census should strike readers as curious since Yahweh explicitly commanded Moses and Eleazar to count the eligible *fighters* twenty years old and up (vv. 2, 4) but said nothing of counting the Levites a month old and up, as he commanded back at Sinai (Num. 3:14–15).[68] In any case, as with the other tribes (vv. 5–56), the Levite census traces families descended from Levi—namely, the Gershonites, Kohathites, and Merarites (v. 57)—who Numbers readers know have been consecrated to Yahweh to serve in the meeting tent (chaps. 3–4). How Levi's families named in v. 58 are descended from Levi is surprisingly never told here but is recorded in the pre-exodus genealogy in Exod. 6:17–24: Libni was Gershon's son; Hebron, Kohath's son; Mahli and Mushi, Merari's sons; and Korah was the son of Izhar, who was Kohath's son. These families are mentioned probably because they were prominent in the editor's time, whereas other historic families from Levi have been effectively relegated to the past, including Shimei (Gershon's other son), Amram, Izhar, and Uzziel (Kohath's other son).

In vv. 58b–62, the detour tracing the line from Kohath to Aaron culminates with Nadab and Abihu's death, a frightening warning to the priesthood of the second wilderness generation (see the "Implications" essay below, "A Warning with Hope"). This negative word flows immediately into what is probably the main literary purpose of the Levi census in v. 62: "Those of them who were listed came to 23,000, *all males a month old and up, since they were not listed among the Israelites. No inheritance was given to them among the Israelites.*" A recount of the Levites was required, not to mobilize them for cultic service (as in Num. 1–4), but to clarify that the Levites will receive no territory. This is an important augment to the second census (vv. 5–51), which serves as the basis for dividing the land among the tribal families.[69] The number 23,000 is an increase of 1,000 from the first generation of Levites (22,000 in 3:39).[70]

---

67. Seebass, *Numeri*, 3:191; my trans. of Prov. 16:33.

68. Schmidt (*Numeri*, 162) attributes the Levi census to the Pentateuch redactor, who ties in this unit with the formulaic "These were the Levites who were listed by their families" (v. 57a).

69. Knierim and Coats, *Numbers*, 272.

70. With Procopius of Gaza (Lienhard, *Numbers*, 252).

This total may appear close to the tribe of Simeon (22,200), but the Levites are actually a much smaller tribe since their number includes all males one month or older rather than only males twenty years old and upward. Although it contrasts with the other tribes' count of warriors twenty years old and upward, this age span was not an innovation for the Levites (cf. 3:14–15). As with the first census, Levi was neither listed among the warriors nor given a territorial inheritance as the other tribes, which explains why the editor here segregates the Levi census (vv. 57–62) from the primary tribal census (vv. 5–51) by means of Yahweh's intervening speech on tribal allotments (vv. 52–56). This echoes the editorial arrangement of the Sinai materials in which Levi's census (Num. 3:14–39) was deferred and segregated from the other tribes of the first wilderness generation (Num. 1:20–43; cf. 1:44–53). Here, however, the narrator does not call attention to the positive explanation for the Levites' exclusion from the military census and lack of inheritance, which is that the Levites belong uniquely to Yahweh (8:15–16), serve Yahweh and the Aaronic priesthood in his meeting tent (1:48–53; chaps. 3* and 4*), receive Israel's tithes as an inheritance (18:21, 24), and, above all, receive Yahweh himself as their inheritance (18:20). By not recollecting this theological affirmation of the Levites but instead mentioning the deaths of Nadab and Abihu, the tone is sober and demands that Yahweh's cultic personnel live a different life, one that excludes them from fighting alongside their countrymen and denies them land but also must be marked by loyalty to Yahweh.

The Levi census (vv. 57–62) is linked to the next unit, the narrator's postscript (vv. 63–65), by the theme of those who are *not listed* in the census: the Levites "were not listed among the Israelites" in the first or second census (v. 62), and of the second generation, the children of those who died in the wilderness, it is said that "no one among them had been listed" in the first census except for Caleb and Joshua (vv. 64–65). The literary placement of vv. 63–64 *after* the Levi census (vv. 57–62) makes clear that Levi, while exceptional, belongs to Yahweh's covenant people. The postscript (vv. 63–64) forms an *inclusio* with vv. 3–4.[71] The *inclusio* around the first census repeated "twenty years old and up" (1:3, 20, 45), but here "twenty years old and up" (26:4) is not repeated in the closing frame (vv. 63–64), which effectively folds Levi into Moses and Eleazar's list (see the translation note on v. 63). Yet the main purpose of the postscript is to stress that Yahweh has lucidly fulfilled his emphatic word: "They will definitely die in the wilderness" (v. 65; see the first translation note there), which alludes to Yahweh's pronouncement in 14:35 (see 14:26–35). It has not only come to pass but has been substantiated by the second census. The narrator over-specifies by redundancy, first in v. 64 and again in v. 65, to emphasize that the entire generation of "the Israelites who came out of the land of Egypt" (26:4) had been put to death by divine judgment in the wilder-

---

71. W. Lee, *Migratory Campaign*, 177.

ness (v. 65; see the second translation note there). Joshua and Caleb are the noted exceptions.[72] Moses and Eleazar are also still alive, but Moses will soon die outside the land (20:12, 24; 27:14), and it is conceivable that Aaron's third son, Eleazar, was under twenty during the first census and so was not counted at that time. Highlighting Joshua and Caleb as the sole survivors from the exodus generation could give the impression that Yahweh was not completely successful in carrying out his word. Rather, the allusion to 14:35 reveals that the narrator is thinking in terms of Num. 14: the exception of these two God-fearing Israelites is also a direct fulfillment of Yahweh's word, "You will not enter into the land that I swore with a raised hand to settle you, except for Jephunneh's son Caleb and Nun's son Joshua" (Num. 14:30).[73]

Implications

A Warning with Hope: Family Stories within the Census

Unlike the first census, whose form is uninterrupted (Num. 1), five narrative asides are interwoven into the second census (26:5a, 9b–11, 19, 33, 46), and to these five, a sixth is inserted into the subsequent census of Levi (26:58b–61).[74] Without deictic particles—such as "It was *the same* Dathan and Abiram who . . ."—the author of these asides does not assume that the reader knows these stories from Genesis, Exodus, Leviticus, and Numbers. None of these asides belong to the census form (see 26:12–14 above), and they may have been later editorial insertions.[75] Readers apparently even needed to be told that "Reuben was Israel's firstborn" (v. 5a). In their present literary placement, these asides not only "highlight key points in the narrative"[76] but also play an important rhetorical role in the familial census of Israel's second generation.

The first role the asides in Num. 26 perform is to indirectly warn the new generation of families not to follow in the footsteps of their parents and ancestors who rebelled and reaped Yahweh's lethal judgment (vv. 9b–11, 19, 61). This is made explicit in the case of two Reubenites, Dathan and Abiram, and one Levite, Korah: "They became a warning sign" (v. 10; see the second translation note there). That is, looking soberly at the downfall of these men and their families in Num. 16 should deter the Israelites from fighting

---

72. Douglas (*Wilderness*, 194) argues that these two survivors, Joshua of Judah and Caleb of Ephraim, offer a parallel to the two tribes, Judah and Ephraim, who survived the Babylonian destruction of the temple and returned from exile, but there is little to no textual evidence that the northern tribe, Ephraim, was recognized with Judah as a surviving tribe.

73. Also Num. 14:38; 32:11–12.

74. Also a gloss, but for transitional purposes: "and Machir was Gilead's father" (v. 29).

75. Kuenen, *Hexateuch*, 100; Baden ("Source Stratification," 239n17, 244–45) sees these asides as post-redactional, independent, and basically midrashic insertions.

76. Leveen, *Memory*, 38.

against Yahweh or his leaders (see also the second and third translation notes on v. 9).[77] This warning is also implicit in the death of Aaron's oldest sons in v. 61, an aside from the census form in vv. 58b–61 that moves systematically to trace a single lineage: Kohath → Amram + Jochebed (Levi's Egypt-born daughter) → Aaron, Moses, and Miriam → Aaron fathers Nadab and Abihu (see the translation note on v. 60). Nothing is said of Moses's wife and children (Exod. 2:21–22) or of Aaron's other two sons, Eleazar and Ithamar (Num. 3:4). Instead, the narrator is undeterred from closing the account of this lineage with the lethal violation of Aaron's oldest sons: "But Nadab and Abihu died when they offered strange fire before Yahweh" (v. 61). If the aside about Dathan and Abiram warns all non-priestly Israelites (Reuben and by extension all the non-priestly tribes) and the mention of Korah warns the Levites (26:9b–11), here in v. 61 the implicit warning is aimed at Yahweh's priests of the second generation. This is what happens if you overstep your orders and attempt to manipulate Yahweh through his cultic system.[78] With regard to v. 19, the narrator does not expose the shame of Judah's having sex with a Canaanite woman or of his boys Er and Onan behaving wickedly in Yahweh's sight (Gen. 38). However, "but Er and Onan died in the land of Canaan" (v. 19) calls attention to the death of Judah's childless boys, communicating that "the land of Canaan" will not be immune, in the past or in the future, from stigmatizing death (cf. Lev. 26:14–44).[79]

A second function of the asides is to call the reader's attention to the names of eight Israelite women: Zelophehad's five daughters (Mahlah, Noah, Hoglah, Milcah, and Tirzah), Asher's daughter Serah (vv. 33, 46), and Amram's wife, Jochebed, and their daughter Miriam (v. 59).[80] This is surprising because the census does not require that women be mentioned, and ANE and OT cultures were predominantly patrilineal, patrilocal, and patrimonial.[81] The mention

77. Like Ps. 106:16–18, Num. 26:9b–11 refers to the narrative of Korah's rebellion in Num. 16 (Baden, "Source Stratification," 237–39).

78. G. Anderson ("Nadab and Abihu," 1–19) shows that the Priestly authors deliberately present Nadab and Abihu's violation as ambiguous—what was the "strange fire"?—in order to illustrate that the divine presence cannot be conjured magically by executing a ritual or legal formula.

79. King and Stager, *Life*, 46.

80. Amram married Jochebed, his father's sister (Exod. 6:20; Num. 26:59). Greengus (*Laws*, 26–27) argues that this intergenerational marriage was prohibited in subsequent law (Lev. 18:12–14), but the focus of that law is on prohibiting sexual relations, not actual marriage, with a parent's closest blood relatives (Milgrom, *Leviticus*, 2:1514–93). The argument of S. Levin ("Numbers 26,59," 25–33) is speculative that the precanonical Hebrew text matched the LXX, "The name of Amram's wife was Jochebed, Levi's daughter, who bore *these* ['*lh* / *toutous* = Gershon, Kohath, Merari] to Levi in Egypt," implying that Jochebed was her husband's aunt (Exod. 6:20) and his grandmother. Of course, the canonical Hebrew scribes (MT/SP, no Qumran reading) rejected such an incestuous relationship and by exchanging one letter corrected "bore *these* ['*lh*]" to "bore *to her* ['*th*]."

81. Patrilineal means descendants are traced through the male line. Patrilocal refers to the custom of settling as a married woman with the husband's family. Patrimonial means real estate is inherited from one's father or male ancestor.

of Serah remains mysterious,[82] and here for the first time in the Pentateuch readers learn that Miriam was Moses and Aaron's sister by the same mother.[83] In the case of Zelophehad's daughters, readers are supposed to question what will happen to Zelophehad's property in Canaan since he has no male heirs, which anticipates the events in Num. 27 and 36. At least we can say that while the census leaves countless daughters nameless, these three asides name and thereby honor these women within an androcentric Israelite society.[84]

Third, the asides imply that in spite of every shameful failure in Israel's families, Yahweh's covenant promises to Abraham of land, seed, and blessing have not been nullified but extend to the second generation, both in the wilderness and, soon, in their new home in Canaan (Gen. 12:1–3; 15:13–16). The contrastive clause is important: "and they became a warning sign. *But the sons of Korah did not die*" (v. 11). This makes plain what one might have wondered about the curious language of Num. 16:27, 32. Unlike the annihilation of Dathan and Abiram's entire family groups, Korah's descendants were preserved; only Korah, his immediate household, and his possessions were destroyed.[85] In fact, by an accident of archaeology, a record in the inscriptions from the southern city of Arad confirms that the "sons of Korah" (*bny.qrḥ*) were a surviving family group in preexilic Judah.[86] While the curious phrase of v. 11 may have been added later to the aside of vv. 9b–11 (see the translation note for v. 11), within the Num. 26 census it contributes a message of hope: even the notorious Korah has heirs living among the second generation who will inherit Yahweh's promises. Finally, the narrator speaks neutrally of Moses and Aaron in vv. 59–61, but readers of Numbers will recall that they too were guilty of rebellion against the covenant and suffered the curse of not entering the land of Canaan (Num. 20:12–13, 24; cf. Lev. 26:14–44). The message is substantiated: regardless of whether individual Israelites rebel, an entire generation rebels and incurs Yahweh's horrible judgment, or even Yahweh's leaders rebel, Yahweh has resolved to fulfill his covenant promises to his people who trust and obey him. This hopeful warning from Numbers is revived by the author of Hebrews to urge Jesus's followers to persevere in their test of faith and obedience (Heb. 3:16–19; 4:11).

---

82. Also Gen. 46:17; 1 Chron. 7:30. Shectman (*Women*, 152) notes that growing out of the mystery, Serah became prominent in rabbinic legends in which she is considered a miracle worker, immortal, and even crucial to Israel's exodus from Egypt.

83. See Douglas, *Wilderness*, 197.

84. Cf. Shectman, *Women*, 18–19.

85. Blum, *Komposition des Pentateuch*, 264.

86. Arad 49.1: "Sons of Betzal, 3 Sons of Korah, 2 Son of Gilgal, 1 Sons of Koniah [. . .] 1 [. . .]1 [Yeh]oaz, 1 Obad[iah] Yehoab [. . .]iah, 1 [so]n of Tzemach, 1 [. . .]D-el [. . .]A, 2 Shuʿal, 1 Pedaiah, H?, 11 Sons of Aha, H?, 3" (Schniedewind and Holmstedt, *Hebrew Inscriptions*).

25

Zelophehad's Daughters to Inherit Land; Moses Disinherited and Succeeded by Joshua

(27:1–23)

∞

Overview

In the census of the second generation (chap. 26), the narrator's aside that Zelophehad of Manasseh had "no sons, only daughters" (26:33) exposed a structural problem that put these daughters and the land claim of Zelophehad's family at risk. This problem is addressed in Num. 27:1–11 through an "oracular novella" with these components: Zelophehad's daughters communicate this legal loophole to Moses and the leaders (vv. 1–4), Moses brings the case to Yahweh for a decision (v. 5), and Yahweh redresses the daughters' case at hand with an oracle (vv. 6–7) and then issues an enduring decree for all Israel (vv. 8–11). The case ruling of Zelophehad's daughters is later revised and expanded in Num. 36, forming an *inclusio* that encompasses the final major block of discourse in Numbers, from the second census (chap. 26) to the close of the divine instruction through Moses at Moab (36:13).[1] The legal adjustments found in Num. 27 and 36 reflect later, yet integral, supplements to Yahweh's instructions to Moses at Sinai.[2] The second, third, and fourth units of chapter 27 are separate speeches, but because they share the same

---

1. Olson, *Death of the Old*, 175; Milgrom, *Numbers*, 296; Leveen, *Memory*, 178.
2. See Frevel, "Book of Numbers," 24–31. Also, most view either 27:1–11 or 36:1–12 as a supplement to the other story; see Seebass, *Numeri*, 3:195–212, 450–63; Achenbach, *Vollendung*, 567–73; Frevel, "Book of Numbers," 28–29.

topic—Israel's leadership transition—they can be taken together as a single dialogue between Yahweh and Moses, concluded by Moses's obedience (vv. 12–23).[3] Yahweh speaks first to direct Moses to climb a certain mountain and look across into Canaan, but he reminds Moses that like Aaron he will die outside the land because of their rebellion against Yahweh at Meribah (vv. 12–14). Moses speaks next (vv. 15–17). Knowing that his life and role as Israel's leader is coming to a close, Moses asks Yahweh to choose his successor (vv. 15–17). Yahweh responds to Moses by ordering him to install Joshua, who will assume a royal function among the Israelites (vv. 18–21). Eleazar and Moses then obediently commission Joshua (vv. 22–23).[4]

Translation

[1]Then the daughters of Zelophehad son of Hepher,[5] the son of Gilead, the son of Machir, the son of Manasseh from the families of Manasseh,[6] the son of Joseph, came forward.[7] These were his daughter's names:[8] Mahlah, Noah, Hoglah, Milcah, and Tirzah.[9] [2]And they stood before Moses and Eleazar the priest and the chieftains of the whole assembly at the entrance to the meeting tent and said,[10] [3]"Our father died in the wilderness, but[11] he was not part of the following who gathered themselves together against Yahweh among Korah's followers. Instead,[12] he died for his own sin, and he had no sons. [4]Why should our father's

3. Seebass (*Numeri*, 3:216–17) calls 27:12–23, "The appointment of Joshua as preparation for the death of Moses." The thematic unity of 27:12–23 does not negate its compositional layers, as even the shifts in the LXX Greek vocabulary may indicate (Kislev, "Vocabulary," 59–67).

4. Blum (*Komposition des Pentateuch*, 227, 276) has argued that a Priestly composition (KP), which integrated Priestly and non-Priestly texts, concluded in Num. 27*. Others have argued that the conventional Priestly narrative ended at Num. 27:23; Janowski, *Gottes Gegenwart*, 214–46; Ska, *Pentateuch*, 147–51; Noort, "Bis zur Grenze des Landes?," 99–119.

5. 4Q27 pronounces this name "Hophar" (*ḥwpr*, vocalized *ḥôper* 4Q27 ≈ *hopher* LXX[cd]) or maybe "Huphar" (*ḥûper*).

6. Probably to eliminate a perceived redundancy of the term Manasseh, LXX[ed] removes "the son of Manasse(h)" (see 32:39, 40; 36:1; but 26:29).

7. These "women approached" (*wattiqrabnâ*) Moses, Eleazar, and the chieftains at the entrance to the meeting tent (v. 2).

8. Perhaps to remove the redundancy, LXX[ed] reads "And these were their names."

9. The daughters are listed in this order in three texts (Num. 26:33; 27:1; Josh. 17:3), suggesting that this is likely their birth order, but in Num. 36:11, in a story that revisits Zelophehad's daughters, the order is Mahlah, Tirzah, Hoglah, Milcah, and Noah, perhaps because the narrator is recalling their names from memory. 4Q27 pronounces the second name "Torzah" or "Turzah" (*twrṣh*; cf. *tirṣâ* MT); see Ulrich, *Qumran*, 159.

10. Formally, "saying."

11. A disjunctive, specifically concessive, *wə*: "Our father died in the wilderness, *but* he was not part of the following . . ." (*IBHS* §39.2.3).

12. I read the *kî* as a restrictive adv.: "*Instead* [*kî*] he died for his own sin" (*IBHS* §39.3.5d, no. 16). SP clarifies, "but *our father* [*'bynw*] died for his own sin."

name disappear[13] from among his family because he had no son? Give us a possession among our father's brothers."[14] **5**So Moses brought their case[15] before Yahweh.

6Yahweh said to Moses:[16] **7**"What the daughters of Zelophehad are saying is right. You absolutely must give them[17] possession of an inheritance among their father's brothers,[18] and you must transfer[19] their father's inheritance to them. **8**And you must tell the Israelites: 'If a man dies and has no son, then you must transfer[20] his inheritance to his daughter. **9**And if he has no daughter, then you must give his inheritance to his brothers. **10**And if he has no brothers, then you must give his inheritance to his father's brothers. **11**And if his father has no brothers, then you must give his inheritance to his closest relative from his family, and he will possess it. This will be for the Israelites a legal requirement,[21] as Yahweh commanded Moses.'"

12Yahweh said to Moses: "Go up this mountain in the Abarim range, and see the land[22] I have given to the Israelites. **13**When you have seen it, you will be gathered to your people, as Aaron your brother was gathered,[23] **14**because you rebelled against my word in the Zin

---

13. *Gr‘ occurs in the OT seven times in the niphal, all in the Pentateuch (Exod. 5:11; Lev. 27:18; Num. 9:7; 27:4; 36:3 [2×], 4). As a passive it could mean "be taken away" (ESV), but a middle voice is more likely: "Why should our father's name disappear [yiggāra‘ šēm-'ābînû] from among his family" (Cazelles, Nombres, 125; EÜ, NIV, NLT; GBHS §3.1.2b).

14. Formally, "our father's brothers" ('ăḥê 'ābînû), but it could mean "our father's relatives"; also v. 7.

15. "Their case" (mišpāṭān) is 3rd per. fem., referring to the daughters' case (vv. 1–4).

16. Colon here and in vv. 8, 15 for "saying"; see the third translation note on 1:1.

17. A dynamic rendering of the emphatic adverbial inf. preceding the yiqtol command of the same root (*ntn): "You absolutely must give [nātōn tittēn] them possession of an inheritance among their father's relatives" (GBHS §3.4.2b1; §3.2.2d4).

18. The pronouns referring to the daughters are masc. (IBHS §6.5.3), but SP tries to improve this with fem. forms: "give them [lhn] possession . . . among their ['byhn] father's relatives."

19. This hiphil weqatal conveys the same obligatory force of the preceding yiqtol: "and you must transfer [wəhaʿăbartā] their father's inheritance to them" (GBHS §3.5.2c).

20. This hiphil causative is a weqatal that expresses a command if the condition is met, "If a man dies and has no son, then you must transfer [wəhaʿăbartem]" (GBHS §3.5.2d). Formally, the verb means "cause to cross over," whereas SP and LXX[ed] replace this with the more common "you must give/confer."

21. Formally, "a statute of a decision/judgment" (ḥuqqat mišpāṭ); so Cazelles, Nombres, 126; de Vaulx, Nombres, 320. With Seebass (Numeri, 3:196), I take the gen. noun as an attributive ("a legal requirement"), although an attributed gen. is possible ("a statutory ordinance"; Ashley, Numbers, 541) or "an applicable law" (EÜ).

22. Likely to clarify that Yahweh's command here (repeated in Deut. 3:23–29) would be fulfilled when Moses ascends Mount Nebo (Deut. 32:49; 34:1), LXX[ed] adds "Go up into the mountain that is on the other side (that is, Mount Nabau), and see the land, Chanaan."

23. An ellipsis: "When you have seen it, you will be gathered to your people ['el-ʿammêkā], as Aaron your brother was gathered (to his people)." This refers euphemistically to Aaron's death in 20:24, which expressed this complement, "Aaron will be gathered to his people ['el-ʿammāyw]," followed by a similar ellipsis in 20:26 (BHRG, 277n15). To elucidate this reference

wilderness when the community rebelled against me, by failing to honor me as holy[24] before their eyes at the waters." (These were the waters of Meribah in Kadesh in the Zin wilderness).[25]

15Then Moses said to Yahweh: **16**"Let Yahweh, the god[26] of the breath of all living things, appoint someone[27] over the community, **17**who will go out before them and come in before them, and who will lead them out and bring them in, so that Yahweh's community will not be like sheep that have no shepherd." **18**Yahweh said to Moses, "Take Nun's son Joshua, who has spirit,[28] and lay your hand on him. **19**Have him

---

to Aaron's death on Mount Hor in 20:22–29, LXX[ed] adds, "Aaron your brother was added *in Hor the mountain.*"

24. Hiphil *qdš* means "to treat, consider God as holy" (*HALOT* 3:1072–75, gloss 4.a) or "regard, treat, praise Y. as holy" (*DCH* 7:194, gloss d.2). As an inf. const. it explains the preceding verbal action: "when you rebelled against my word . . . *with regard to honoring me as holy*" (*bimrîbat hā'ēdâ ləhaqdîšēnî*; *IBHS* §3.4.1g, example 31). "Failing" is inferred. The language and theology reflect H (see Lev. 17–26), which "is principally concerned that Israel's leaders uphold Yahweh as holy, using the derived stems of *qdš* in the perception of the entire Israelite community" (Awabdy, "Holiness Contribution," 253).

25. This parenthetical gloss reflects the phrasing in Deut. 32:51 and clarifies for readers who either may not have made the connection with the Meribah story in Num. 20:1–13 or, before Numbers was fully composed, were unaware of the story (see de Vaulx, *Nombres*, 321–22; Schmidt, *Numeri*, 166–67).

26. A gen. of source: "Yahweh, the god (who causes/creates) the breath of living things" (*IBHS* §9.5.2c); "living things" (NIV) is a better rendering of *bāśār* than the archaic "flesh." Traditionally, this is rendered "the Lord, *the God* of the spirits of all humankind." First, I prefer Yahweh, without "the" because it is a personal name (and we do not know how to vocalize Yahweh). Second, I render a lowercase, "Yahweh, *the god of the breath* ['ĕlōhê hārûḥōt] . . . ," because at this stage in Yahweh's progressive revelation, he presents himself not as the only existing deity (see Exod. 20:2–3) but as the only deity worthy of exclusive devotion (similarly, "Yhwh, *divine ruler*" by Levine, *Numbers*, 2:343). A parallel construction occurs in 16:22 with the personal name "God" (*'ēl*) followed not by a second personal name but by an appellative describing God's nature: "O God, the god of the breath of all living things" (*'ēl 'ĕlōhê hārûḥōt ləkol-bāśār*). The noun *'ĕlōhîm* can function as a proper name, but that is not the most natural understanding when in const. with a gen. (a descriptor or enclitic pronoun). See Deut. 4:7 and the first translation note on Num. 10:9.

27. Not until v. 18 is the man Joshua identified, so "someone" is preferable here for *'îš* (NJPS, NIV; *HALOT* 1:43–44, gloss 9).

28. Formally, "a man/person who has a spirit in him(self)" (*'îš 'ăšer-rûaḥ bô* MT ≈ LXX[ed]; SP: "*the* man/person . . ."). The word "spirit" (*rûaḥ*) is indeterminate and so does not clearly refer to *the* Spirit (de Vaulx, *Nombres*, 324; ESV, NLT) or "the spirit" (Cazelles, *Nombres*, 126; RSV [Noth, *Numbers*, 212]; Ashley, *Numbers*, 547; Budd, *Numbers*, 304). It lacks a qualifying gen. attested elsewhere, such as "the S/spirit of God" (*rûaḥ 'ĕlōhîm*, Gen. 41:38; Exod. 31:3; 35:31), "a spirit of wisdom" (*rûaḥ ḥokmâ*, depicting Joshua in Deut. 34:9; cf. Exod. 28:3), or "a spirit of jealousy" (*rûaḥ-qin'â*). The narrator portrays Caleb similarly but with an adjective: "because *he has a different spirit* [hāytâ rûaḥ 'aḥeret 'immô] and follows me completely" (Num. 14:24). With no qualifier, I am hesitant about guesses like "the spirit of leadership" (NIV) or "such a spirit" (NET), although these come closer to the contextual meaning. My more formal rendering, "Joshua, who has spirit," connotes the kind of courageous spirit that we see in Joshua (Josh. 1:6, 7, 9, 18; 10:25), which contrasts with the discouraged

stand before Eleazar the priest and before the whole community, and commission him in their sight.[29] **20**Then you must give some of your majesty[30] to him, so that the whole Israelite community will obey.[31] **21**And he will stand before Eleazar the priest, who will inquire for him before Yahweh by the decision of the Urim.[32] At his command they will go out, and at his command they will come in, both he and all the Israelites with him, the whole community."[33] **22**So Moses did as Yahweh commanded

---

spirit of the Canaanites, who are afraid of Joshua and Yahweh: "and there was no spirit left in anyone" (*wəlō'-qāmâ 'ôd rûaḥ*, 2:11) and "there was no longer any spirit in them" (*wəlō'-hāyâ bām 'ôd rûaḥ*, 5:1). Dynamic translations of Num. 27:18 that fit this connotation are "an inspired man" (NJPS) and "a man gifted with spirit" (for EÜ), but "a person possessed of spirit" (Levine, *Numbers*, 2:343) probably implies something too much like ANE spirit possession.

29. Formally, "and command him before their eyes." "Commission" (ESV, NET, et al.) is the contextual meaning in vv. 16–23.

30. "Your majesty" (*mēhôdəkā*) from **hôd* I, "splendor, majesty, beauty" (*DCH* 2:500; similarly, *HALOT* 1:241). LXX[ed]: "your glory" (*tēs doxēs sou*). It is the only time this word appears in the Hexateuch, but elsewhere it describes the king's majesty (Pss. 21:5 [6]; 45:3 [4]; Jer. 22:18), as noted by Gray (*Numbers*, 402). Some render this "your authority," which is not a lexical gloss and likely was chosen to overcome the theological problem (or strangeness) of Moses having splendor by reducing this to Moses's authority, a reality well-attested in the Moses story ("by the authority of Moses," *bəyad-mōšeh*; 10× in Numbers). I prefer the basic meaning, with the high probability that Moses's "majesty" in Num. 27:20 refers to Exod. 34:29–34, in which the skin of Moses's face radiates brilliantly (Haran, "Moses' Face," 165–67; Van Seters, *Life of Moses*, 359).

31. Joshua is probably the implied obj. of Israel's obedience: "The whole Israelite community will obey *him*" (many versions). However, the Hb. does not state an obj. (*yišmə'û*), allowing either "obey Joshua" or "obey Yahweh" who is speaking (vv. 18–21) or both. In this way, Joshua emulates Moses by leading the people to obey his (Joshua's) voice, which conveys Yahweh's directives (see Josh. 22:2–5).

32. "The Urim" (*hā'ûrîm*), as in 1 Sam. 28:6, is probably a synecdoche for the binary phrase "the Urim *and* the Thummim" (*hattummîm*). These cultic objects were fixed onto the "breast-piece of decision" worn over Aaron's heart when he entered the meeting tent to ascertain Yahweh's decision about a matter (Exod. 28:30) or to gain knowledge of the future (1 Sam. 28:6). This form of divination is prescribed by Yahweh for the Aaronic priests (Exod. 28:30; Lev. 8:8); elsewhere cleromancy, casting of lots, is sometimes prescribed for Israel's leaders (Lev. 16:8–10; Num. 26:55–56; 33:54; 34:13; 36:2; Josh. 14:2; 18:6, 8, 10; 19:51). Other means of divining in the ANE are banned, such as necromancy (i.e., consulting the spirits of the dead through a medium; Lev. 19:31; 20:6; Deut. 18:11; 1 Sam. 28:7–25). Although the OT does not explicitly prohibit the common practice of extispacy—examining animal entrails for divinely inspired knowledge—this would have been rejected as a form of "coercion, manipulation, or even somehow bypassing God" (Walton, *Ancient Near Eastern Thought*, 248). By homophony, LXX[ed] misinterprets this priestly implement as "the decision *of the clear ones*" (*tōn dēlōn* LXX[ed] for *h'wrym* as masc. pl. subst. **'yr*, brightness, light).

33. An epexegetical *wə* makes sense of the MT/SP: "both he and all the Israelites with him, [*that is*] *the whole community*" (*wəkol-bənê-yiśrā'ēl 'ittô wəkol-hā'ēdâ*; *GBHS* §4.3.3d). Probably attempting to improve the syntax, reconstructed 4Q27 reads "and all the Israelites, and the whole community with him"; LXX[ed] reads "he and all the sons of Israel of one accord and all the congregation" (NETS).

him. He took Joshua[34] and had him stand before Eleazar the priest and before the whole community. **23**He laid his hands[35] on him and commissioned him, as Yahweh commanded by the authority of Moses.[36]

Interpretation

27:1–11. The brotherless daughters of one Manassite, Zelophehad, express their fear to Moses that their father's name and land inheritance will not be preserved within their tribe (vv. 1–4), so Moses brings this to Yahweh (v. 5), and Yahweh addresses this legal loophole (v. 7) and establishes a statute for the future (vv. 8–11).[37] The Priestly genre of the unit has been called "oracular novella," which includes three parts: (1) a short story as the daughters present their case (vv. 1–5); (2) an ensuing divine oracle with a case ruling for the daughters (v. 7); and (3) a formal statute for the Israelite community at large (vv. 8–11).[38] The short story begins in v. 1 with a "static introduction"[39] by the narrator to name the main characters—Zelophehad's daughters Mahlah, Noah, Hoglah, Milcah, and Tizrah—which are probably listed in their birth order (see the fifth translation note on v. 1)—and identify their family relationship, Zelophehad of "the families of Manasseh" just enumerated in the census (26:29–34). This pretemporal information about Zelophehad and his daughters was already given in the census (26:29–34), but there the narrator clarified: "Now Hepher's son Zelophehad had no sons, only daughters" (26:33a). By this comment, the narrator created a gap in the reader's knowledge about the precarious future of these daughters. This may only make us curious today, but for ancient readers who knew the culture, it would have gripped them with suspense.[40] In their patri*lineal* culture, what will happen

---

34. Most likely to assimilate to the common appellative, 4Q27 reads "*Nun's son* Joshua" (see 26:65; 27:18; 32:12, 28; 34:17).

35. Yahweh had commanded Moses, "You must lay *your hand* [*yādkā*] on him" (v. 18). Here the switch to pl., "his hands" (*ydyw* 4Q27 MT[L] LXX[ed]), may be insignificant, but it raises the possibility that Moses did not execute Yahweh's command precisely, as in Num. 20:7–12. Probably to realign the text to v. 18, some witnesses read "his hand" (*ydw* SP MT[mss]).

36. Formally, "by the hand of Moses." Most likely to duplicate Deut. 3:21–22, using the standard superscription for a more seamless insertion, 4Q27 and SP read as follows (the plus in bold): "[Then **Mose**]s said to him, "Your eyes have seen what Yahweh did to these two ki[4Q27 breaks off here]ngs, so Yahweh will do to all the kingdoms where you are crossing over (there). You must not fear them because Yahweh your God, he will fight for you."

37. Cf. Cocco, *Women*, 117–66.

38. Chavel, *Oracular Law*, 196–256. Also Lev. 24:10–23; Num. 9:6–14; 15:32–36. Knierim and Coats (*Numbers*, 275) call this genre "case report," stressing a judicial precedence that gives rise to legislation; cf. Weingreen, "Daughters," 518–22.

39. Alter, *Biblical Narrative*, 80.

40. Knowledge gaps about past events foster curiosity, while knowledge gaps about the future foster suspense (Sternberg, *Poetics*, 265–66).

to Zelophehad's family lineage and honor? In their patri*monial* culture, will Zelophehad's family's claim to a plot of land in Canaan vanish because he had no male heir? In their patri*local* culture, will his daughters, before they marry and settle with their husbands' families, have any land to call their home in Manasseh's territory?[41] These tense questions, intimated by 26:29–34 and 27:1, are now addressed by 27:2–11.[42]

In v. 2, the daughters come forward collectively and stand before Israel's powerful male leaders—Moses, Yahweh's prophet; Eleazar, Yahweh's high priest; and the chieftains, Israel's tribal representatives—at the meeting tent, the place where Yahweh meets with his people (see the third translation note on v. 1).[43] With one voice, the daughters present their case for adjudication (vv. 3–4). They start with the crucial background that Moses and the leaders need to know: Zelophehad died among the exodus generation in the wilderness, but he was emphatically not among his contemporaries who were guilty of rebellion against Yahweh (v. 3; see the translation notes there). The main point the daughters articulate is clear: "And he had no sons" (v. 3d), but before they get to that point, the daughters foreground their father's innocence (vv. 3a–c). This foregrounding is intended to have a "primacy effect," that is, to precondition Moses and the leaders and to impress upon readers that Zelophehad's sonless predicament (v. 3d) was not the result of a curse for any rebellion on his part (vv. 3a–c).[44] In contrast to his contemporaries in the wilderness who received fatal retribution for their transgressions (v. 3b), Zelophehad "died in the wilderness" (v. 3a), which is explained in the *inclusio* as "Instead, he died for his own sin" (v. 3c). This does not clearly refer to being punished with the nation after the explorers returned from Canaan (14:29)[45] but more straightforwardly connotes that he died a "natural death as a sinner with the rest of humankind."[46] The daughters stress this point because in both the HB and the ANE, a patriarch with no male heir was commonly thought to be under a divine curse.[47] In a hymn to the sun god Shamash, the people curse a fraudulent person and as a result, "No heir will (there be) to take over his property, Nor will (there be) kin to succeed to his estate."[48] Two Old Babylonian rulers curse anyone who tampers with their rock inscription

41. The distinction in meaning among these patri- compounds is explained in a note to the "Implications" essay in chap. 24, "A Warning with Hope."

42. Seebass, "Eigene Komposition," 96, 98, 106–7.

43. Hundley, "Tabernacle or Tent of Meeting?," 3–18.

44. See Resseguie, *Narrative Criticism*, 209.

45. Contra Milgrom, *Numbers*, 231.

46. Awabdy, "Holiness Contribution," 257; possibly 27:3 alludes to Gen. 2:16–17; 3:3–5, 19, 22–24; later Paul teaches that human sin results in death (Rom. 5:12).

47. Lev. 20:20–21; Jer. 22:30; cf. Abram in Gen. 15:2–3; also cf. the Ugaritic Aqhat Epic, in which the sonless Danel requests that the God El provide him with a son to be his heir; see "The Tale of Aqhat," *ANET* 149–55 (trans. H. L. Ginsberg).

48. "The Shamash Hymn," *COS* 1.117:418.

for the goddess Eshtar: "May they [the named gods] not grant him heir or offspring."[49] This was also one of the divine curses of breaking Hammurapi's laws: "May the goddess Nintu, august mistress of the lands, the mother, my creator, deprive him of an heir and give him no offspring."[50]

In v. 4a, while the daughters could have decried their own predicament within the patrilineal, patrilocal, and patrimonial system (noted above), they wisely play to their androcentric audience by pointing out the threat to the continuation of their father's reputation: "Why should our father's name disappear from among his family because he had no son?" (see the first translation note on v. 4). The daughters, listed by their *names* (*šəmôt*), redirect the focus to their father's *name* (*šēm*).[51] Their father's "name" here is a metonym for the title to his land,[52] as shown by the daughters' directive to Moses and the leaders: "Give us a possession among our father's brothers" (v. 4b; see the second translation note there). The meaning could be: "Give us the registration of our father's land in Canaan among his blood brothers" (never named) or "among the land of the Hepherite family" to which Zelophehad belonged (26:32) or even "among the land of the tribe of Manasseh" (26:29–34). However, based on the straightforward meaning of "his brothers" in v. 9, "our father's brothers" in v. 4b probably refers to Zelophehad's own biological brothers.[53] Next, following the form of an oracular novella, Moses brings their case to Yahweh for his adjudication (see the translation note on v. 5).[54] This presumably means that the daughters stay in place at the meeting tent's entrance while Moses enters the holy place to ask Yahweh, in the most holy place, to speak an oracle to settle the daughters' case (see Num. 7:89).[55]

In vv. 6–11, Yahweh delivers his oracle to Moses. Although Yahweh's verdict closes out the story, readers can infer that Moses relayed the verdict to the daughters and the leaders present. As with other oracular novellas in the Torah, Yahweh's oracle is bipartite: Yahweh first deals with the case at hand (v. 7) and then institutes an enduring statute for Israel more broadly (vv. 8–11). Here Yahweh honors the daughters and their request in the strongest possible terms. First, he does not mention preserving their father's name, the issue the daughters raised before the male leadership (v. 4), but instead exclusively defends the daughters themselves. Second, Yahweh publicly endorses the daughters' words, "What the daughters are saying is right" (v. 7b), which must be understood within their honor-shame culture. The person with power,

49. "Simurrum–Iddi(n)-Sin," COS 2.106:255.
50. "The Laws of Hammurabi," COS 2.131:353.
51. Levine, *Numbers*, 2:341.
52. Levine, *Numbers*, 2:346.
53. See the "Implications" essay in chap. 33, "Daughters Who Become Heiresses."
54. See Lev. 24:12; Num. 9:8; cf. Num. 15:34.
55. Unlike the cases of Lev. 24:12 and Num. 15:34, the daughters are not guilty and so do not need to be placed in custody until Yahweh issues a verdict. Rather, like Num. 9:8, the daughters wait at the entrance to the meeting tent for Moses to return with the divine response.

Yahweh, publicly *ascribes honor* to the women, and in turn Moses, Eleazar, and the chieftains are forced to acknowledge this conferred honor because of Yahweh's superior rank.[56] Next Yahweh forcefully commands Moses not only to grant the daughters' specific request for land, echoing v. 4b, but goes beyond this to ensure that the daughters become the legal proprietors of their father's real estate (vv. 7c–d; see the first and third translation notes there). Yahweh's expansion of the daughters' request includes the rare phrase "possession of an inheritance" (elsewhere only in Num. 32:32), which has two aspects: "While *'ḥzt* [possession] indicates land ownership or tenure as in Lev. 25 and Lev. 27, the term *nḥlh* [inheritance] indicates inheritance in the land allocation process proper."[57] As with other oracular novellas, Yahweh further expands his case ruling beyond the immediate scenario by issuing a statute for all the Israelites (vv. 8–11).[58] Now that the loophole of Zelophehad's daughters has been closed, Yahweh proceeds to close related loopholes that will arise in the different types of nuclear and extended families.

Man with no son	→	daughter inherits (v. 8)
Man with no son or daughter	→	man's brothers inherit (v. 9)
Man with no son, daughter, or brothers	→	man's paternal uncles inherit (v. 10)
Man with no son, daughter, brothers, or paternal uncles	→	closest family relative inherits (v. 11)

This contingency plan[59] for the transfer of land inheritance is contained literarily by the quotative frames in v. 8a and v. 11c: "And you must tell the Israelites," and "This will be for the Israelites a legal requirement, as Yahweh commanded Moses" (see the translation note on v. 11).[60] Ancient Israel would remain a patrimony, meaning that by default land inheritance belonged to the patriarch and would be passed on to his son. However, Yahweh's legal provisions here (vv. 8–11) make clear that patrimony is not the only God-honoring way to structure the society of the covenant people. Deuteronomic law raises a question: How can this custom of daughters as heiresses here in Num. 27 and 36 coexist with the custom of levirate marriage ordered in Deut. 25:5–10 (cf. Deut. 21:15–17)? They both appear to accomplish the same end of perpetuating the father's name (Num. 27:4; Deut. 25:10) by establishing an heir to the family

---

56. See Malina, *New Testament World*, 34.
57. Frevel, "Book of Numbers," 27.
58. See Lev. 24:15–22; Num. 9:9–14; 15:37–41.
59. See the translation note on v. 8.
60. "As Yahweh commanded Moses" could be Yahweh speaking of himself and Moses in the third person for future Israelites or a shift back to the editor's voice, since Yahweh would naturally say to Moses "as I commanded you" (e.g., Exod. 29:35; 31:6, 11).

estate.[61] Moreover, the Bible is not alone in transferring the title for family land to daughters. In a Nuzi contract (Hurrian-influenced Akkadian language) and in the Laws of Hammurapi (Akkadian) and of Lipit-Ishtar (Sumerian), the land inheritance of a sonless patriarch was transferred to daughters and other relatives (see the "Implications" essay in chap. 33, "Daughters Who Become Heiresses"). Thus the casuistic (case) law of Num. 27:6–11 is not a novelty but is Yahweh's gracious contextualization of ANE case law for his covenant people, to whom he has promised a land. Divine promise becomes reality for the daughters in Josh. 17:3–6, displaying Yahweh's faithfulness yet again.

27:12–14. Yahweh orders Moses to climb a certain mountain, see the land of Canaan, and then die as Aaron did because Moses and Aaron rebelled and did not honor Yahweh as holy among the people. In this speech, Yahweh's directive and rebuke echoes his words to Moses and Aaron back in Num. 20:12–13, 23–29:

Table 25.1. Aaron and Moses Disinherited[a]

Numbers 20:12–13, 23–29	Numbers 27:12–14
[12b]"Because both of you did not trust me **by honoring me as holy in the sight of the Israelites**, therefore you will not bring this community into the land I have given them." [13]**These are the waters of Meribah (contention)**, because the Israelites contended with Yahweh, and he showed himself to be holy among them.	[12]Yahweh said to Moses: "Go up this mountain in the Abarim range, and see **the land I have given to the Israelites.**
[23]Yahweh spoke to Moses and Aaron at Mount Hor, by the border of the land of Edom:	[13]When you have seen it, **you will be gathered to your people, as Aaron your brother was gathered,**
[24]"**Aaron will be gathered to his people,** for he will not enter the land I have given to the Israelites **because both of you rebelled against my word at the waters of Meribah.**	[14]**because you rebelled against my word** in the Zin wilderness when **the community rebelled against me, by failing to honor me as holy before their eyes at the waters." (These were the waters of Meribah** in Kadesh in the Zin wilderness).
[vv. 25–28b = Eleazar succeeds Aaron] [vv. 28c–29 = Aaron dies, Israel mourns]	

a. On their disinheritance, see the "Implications" essay in chap. 20, "What Was the Sin of Moses and Aaron?"

Even with the echo of Aaron's death report, Yahweh's speech to Moses in vv. 12–14 can hardly be called a death report.[62] More accurately, the elements of

61. See Gray, *Numbers*, 397–98; Budd, *Numbers*, 301; and esp. Kilchör, *Mosetora*, 297; Kilchör, "Levirate Marriage," 429–40.

62. Ashley (*Numbers*, 549) draws from Coats's Genesis commentary to summarize the elements of a death report: (1) formulaic summary with the age and date of death; (2) death

vv. 12–14 come closer to the genre of a judgment speech conveying a death sentence.[63] Because Moses and Aaron did not display Yahweh's holiness in the eyes of his covenant people (see the first translation note on v. 14), Yahweh's great prophet, Moses, does not have impunity but will suffer a parallel fate to Yahweh's great priest, Aaron.[64] Together they broke the covenant, and together they suffer the covenant curses, which Yahweh announced in Lev. 26:14–39, of losing their claim to live in the land and of dying in the land of their enemies (see the translation note on v. 13).[65]

Unlike Mount Hor in Edom where Aaron died, the mountain that Moses climbs in the Abarim range affords him a view of Canaan. Forming the northwestern perimeter of the Moabite plateau, the Abarim range reaches from the edge of the Jordan River around the northeastern end of the Dead Sea; only later is the mountain identified as the 2,740-foot-high Mount Nebo (Deut. 32:49; cf. Num. 33:47).[66] From there, on any given day, Moses could even taste the dry wind from the Judean desert, intensifying both the pain of his infraction and the reality that Yahweh would soon fulfill his covenant promise to the children of Abraham, Isaac, and Jacob.[67] Strikingly, the same could be said regarding the position of the rebellious Israelites when they were at Kadesh in the Zin wilderness (v. 14) at Canaan's southern border: "You can hardly get any closer to the cultural land border without being in the land yourself."[68] Furthermore, the literary placement of vv. 12–14 after the episode involving the daughters of Zelophehad is striking: the vulnerable daughters, who have not broken the covenant with the rebels of the exodus generation, are emphatically guaranteed their own plot of land in Canaan, while Israel's great leaders, who rebelled among the exodus generation, are barred from entering the land.[69] Finally, unlike the account of Aaron's death and unlike Moses's own habit of immediate obedience to Yahweh in the book of Numbers, Moses does not die immediately here in fulfillment of Yahweh's orders. In fact, the

---

notice; (3) burial notice; (4) mourning notice; (5) notice of the perpetuation of the deceased person's line. Contra Ashley (*Numbers*, 549) and W. Lee (*Migratory Campaign*, 180), vv. 12–14 do not clearly contain any of these elements of a death report, which come only in Deut. 34*.

63. With Knierim and Coats (*Numbers*, 278), but they also associate this with a death report.

64. See chap. 20 and the "Implications" essay in chap. 3, "Is There a Hierarchy within the People of God?"

65. Awabdy, "Holiness Contribution," 251–56. However, Cooper and Goldstein ("Entrance to the Tent," 215) move beyond the textual evidence to claim a subversive intent: "In Numbers 20 and 27, H has co-opted and neutralized the Moses tradition, effectively stating that Mosaic leadership is not a model to be followed after Moses's death."

66. Walton and Matthews, *Genesis–Deuteronomy*, 206.

67. Boorer, *Priestly Narrative*, 561. See Gregory the Great's theological application (Lienhard, *Numbers*, 255).

68. My trans. of Frevel, *Mit Blick*, 76n30.

69. Lienhard, *Numbers*, 255.

scribes of Deuteronomy's prologue and epilogue, with their own theological emphases, also report Yahweh's orders to Moses to climb the mountain and visualize the land without entering it.[70] Readers must wait expectantly until Deut. 34, where the editors at last recount Moses's final mountain climb, his looking over the promised land, his death outside the land, Israel's ritual mourning at his death, and the official transition to Joshua.[71]

27:15–23. In the wake of Yahweh's pronouncement that Moses's death is imminent (vv. 12–14), Moses requests that Yahweh appoint his successor (vv. 15–17). Yahweh selects Joshua and explains his royal role (vv. 18–21); in obedience, Eleazar and Moses commission Joshua (vv. 22–23). As the echo of Aaron's death (20:23–29) reverberates in Yahweh's words to Moses in 27:12–14 (see above), three elements are conspicuously absent: (1) Aaron died, and (2) Israel mourned over him (20:28c–29), but Moses's death and Israel's mourning over him are deferred until Deut. 34*; (3) Eleazar succeeds Aaron as high priest (20:25–28b), but Yahweh says nothing of Moses's successor. So Moses naturally implores Yahweh to select an individual to lead Yahweh's people after he dies (27:15–17). Moses appeals to Yahweh on the basis of his sovereignty as the creator, "the god of the breath of all living things" (v. 16; as in Num. 16:22; cf. Heb. 12:9). In v. 17, Moses casts a vision for his replacement with both military and royal overtones, intimating an authoritative, kingly commander who will lead Yahweh's people in the conquest of Canaan.[72]

In vv. 18–22, Yahweh discloses his selection of "Nun's son Joshua, who has spirit," which likely connotes a courageous spirit that Caleb and Joshua exemplify elsewhere (Josh. 1; 14:6–9; and elsewhere in the book of Joshua; see the translation note on Num. 27:18). Yahweh instructs Moses to perform the first five steps (vv. 18– 20) of the ritual to commission Joshua as Israel's next leader: (1) "Take" Joshua as Moses once had to "take" Aaron and Eleazar (20:25),[73] (2) lay hands on Joshua, (3) stand Joshua before Eleazar the priest and the whole community, (4) commission Joshua in their sight, and (5) give "some" of Moses's "majesty" to Joshua "so that the whole Israelite community will obey" (v. 20; see the second translation note there). Moses's majesty or splendor (*hôd*), which elsewhere describes kings, may refer to the episode in which Moses's face radiated brilliantly from being in Yahweh's presence (Exod. 34:29–34; see the first translation note on Num. 27:20). A ritual, as we find here in vv. 18–20, functions as "a privileged activity system that is believed to carry out a transformation process involving

70. Deut. 3:23–28 is Deuteronomistic, Deut. 32:48–52 duplicates Num. 27:12–14, and both likely stem from H (Awabdy, "Holiness Contribution," 254–56).

71. See Frevel, *Mit Blick*, 73, 348; Ashley, *Numbers*, 550.

72. See the "Implications" essay below, "Joshua, a Divinely Appointed Royal Shepherd?"

73. Otto ("Priesterschrift," 19) posits Num. 27:15–23 as a post-Priestly redaction that presents Joshua's installation (Deut. 3* and 34*) as analogous to the process of Eleazar's installation (Num. 20*).

interaction with a reality ordinarily inaccessible to the material domain."[74] In particular, laying on of hands signifies the transfer of intangible entity (see Lev. 16:21); in this case, some of Moses's splendor is transferred to the next leader, Joshua (cf. Num. 8:10). In the El Amarna rock tombs (ca. 1400–1350 BCE), for example, Pharaoh extends his arms over his officials to install them for service.[75] The Deuteronomists reflect on Moses's hand-laying ritual in Num. 27* and imply that it was effective because "Moses had placed his hands on him [Joshua], *and the Israelites obeyed him* [Joshua] and did just as Yahweh had commanded Moses" (Deut. 34:9). The effectiveness of this ritual is ultimately illustrated in the book of Joshua, in which the Israelites are characterized by obedience to Joshua's military leadership in the conquest of Canaan.[76] In v. 19 the order was already given to Moses to stand Joshua before Eleazar, so I am inclined to see vv. 21–23 as a projection into the future to highlight an essential component of Joshua's role: "And he will stand before Eleazar the priest, who will inquire for him before Yahweh by the decision of the Urim. At his command they will go out, and at his command they will come in, both he and all the Israelites with him, the whole community" (see the second translation note on v. 21).[77] The Hebrew verbs in these verses probably have a continuous aspect,[78] meaning Joshua's ongoing or customary responsibility will be to consult with Eleazar the high priest for divine direction. Clearly in v. 21c–d, Yahweh grants Moses's request for a successor "who will go out before them and come in before them, and who will lead them out and bring them in" (v. 17). However, while Joshua and not Eleazar is probably the commander in v. 21c–d ("at his command"), Yahweh has subtly adapted Moses's request by subjecting Joshua to Eleazar (v. 21a–b).[79] Eleazar alone was sanctioned to employ the Urim and Thummim as the priestly mode of ascertaining Yahweh's decisions, especially now Yahweh's decisions for Israel at war (v. 21c–d; see the first translation note there).[80] "As this episode affirms, in the larger scheme of things within Numbers it is the priest, not the prophet or his successor, who becomes ever more crucial to the future rule of the community."[81] This integral role for Eleazar the high priest is reaffirmed in Numbers,

---

74. Gane, *Cult and Character*, 15.

75. Walton and Matthews, *Genesis–Deuteronomy*, 207.

76. The sole exception is Achan's sin in Josh. 7.

77. It is also possible that v. 21a is redundant for emphasis, meaning that v. 21 was part of this ritual, so that Eleazar, by the Urim (and Thummim), authenticates Joshua as Israel's leader (Dozeman, "Numbers," 220).

78. This yiqtol probably has a continuous aspect (*GBHS* §3.2.2).

79. P. Guillaume, *Land*, 171. Kislev ("Investiture of Joshua," 429–45) argues that a Persian-era editor inserted v. 21a–b (and other lines in vv. 12–23), assigning Eleazar the high priest a higher status than Joshua. Similarly, Noquet, "NB 27, 12–23," 655–75.

80. See de Vaulx, *Nombres*, 323.

81. Leveen, *Memory*, 54; cf. Zeelander, "Closural Conventions," 344.

and in the book of Joshua Eleazar collaborates with Joshua to distribute the land.[82]

In vv. 22–23, Moses obeys Yahweh by publicly installing Joshua in his place in a manner that echoes Moses's installation of Eleazar in Aaron's place (20:27–28a). Unlike the Aaron-to-Eleazar transition, Moses does not clothe Joshua with high-priestly attire, but by laying his hands on Joshua, Moses commissions Joshua with authority to lead Yahweh's people (see the translation notes on v. 23). In the Yahweh-Moses interchange of vv. 15–21, Joshua "has spirit" (v. 18b) before Moses lays hands on him (v. 23), which correlates with other texts that stress Joshua's preexisting, exemplary character.[83] From another perspective, the Deuteronomists seem to trace the origins of Joshua's spirit, or at least a new dimension of it, back to this event of Moses placing his hands on Joshua (Deut. 34:9).

Implications

Joshua, a Divinely Appointed Royal Shepherd?

In a very personal dialogue with Yahweh, Moses implores Yahweh to raise up Moses's successor (Num. 27:15–17). Noticeably, Moses addresses Yahweh directly (v. 15) in the third person, "Let Yahweh" (v. 16), which in the ANE may suggest that Moses invokes Yahweh as the great king. To give one of countless examples, Abdi-Heba, the administrator of Jerusalem (14th cent. BCE), pleads with the Egyptian monarch in the third person: "May the king turn his attention to the archers so that archers of the king, my lord, come forth."[84] Moses's epithet for Yahweh reveals an extremely high view of Yahweh not only as the covenant deity of "the community" (v. 16) or "Yahweh's community" (v. 17) but as the sovereign deity over all creation: "Let Yahweh, the god of the breath of all living things" (v. 16; see the first translation note there). The only other time this title occurs in the OT is in Num. 16:22, when Moses and Aaron plead with the sovereign Yahweh to be gracious and not annihilate the whole community because of Korah, Dathan, and Abiram's rebellion.[85] The epithet "the god of the breath of all living things" (v. 16) also appears in Egyptian theology, in which it was common to laud the Pharaoh as the source of life for Egyptians, vassal states, and even for everyone. This eulogy to Rameses II, who is coextensive with the god Re (or Ra), illustrates

---

82. See Num. 32:2; 34:17; Josh. 14:1; 19:51; 21:1; cf. Frevel, *Mit Blick*, 37–39. Artus ("Numbers 32," 377–78) shows that in contrast to Josh. 1–12, the high priest/Eleazar plays a preeminent role in Josh. 13–22.

83. Num. 14:30, 38; 26:65; 32:12.

84. "EA 286, A Throne Granted, Not Inherited," *Amarna Letters*, 326–27 (trans. William L. Moran).

85. See Ashley, *Numbers*, 551.

this well: "We come to thee, lord of heaven, lord of earth, Re, life of the whole earth . . . who fashioned the people, giver of breath into the nostrils of all, making all the gods live . . . maker of the great, fashioner of the lowly, whose word produces food . . . beloved of truth, in which he lives by his laws."[86] The divine king Yahweh—not Re or Re's pharaonic manifestation on earth or any other national god—is the source of all life.

Consequently, Moses understood that only the divine king Yahweh holds the prerogative to appoint a human leader over his covenant people (vv. 16–17; see the second translation note on v. 16). Like Moses's epithet for Yahweh in v. 16, the portrait of the role that Moses paints for his successor has strong royal overtones, even though neither Moses nor Yahweh use the title "king" for the one soon identified as Nun's son Joshua (v. 18). It is telling that to begin, Moses asks for one who will be "over the community" (v. 16), not merely over the army or troops. Yahweh agrees to this request (v. 20), and Moses actualizes it (vv. 22–23).

The next expressions, "who will go out before them and come in before them, and who will lead them out and bring them in" (v. 17), have the military connotations of one who leads troops in and out of battle.[87] This can refer to a general or commander, and in the ANE and OT, kings sent their generals into battle.[88] However, ANE kings and princes were strong warriors in their own right, and they frequently claimed that they led their troops into the battlefront and safely home, even if their claims were for propaganda and not grounded in reality.[89] Once again, Yahweh grants Moses's request: "At his [Joshua's] command they will go out, and at his command they will come in" (v. 21c–d). What tips the scales to show that Moses depicts a royal figure is the purpose clause, "so that Yahweh's community will not be like sheep that have no shepherd" (v. 17). In ANE thought, gods were frequently called shepherds, and gods regularly appointed kings as shepherds to lead the flock of their people. So the hymnist celebrates Amun, who merged with the sun god Re, as a "valiant shepherd who drives his flock, / Their refuge, made to sustain them."[90] In the Atra-Ḫasis epic, "Ishtar [was looking for] a shepherd and searching high and low for a king. Inninna [was looking for] a shepherd and searching high and low for a king."[91] Famously, Hammurapi (18th cent. BCE) self-identifies as one such divinely appointed royal shepherd over Sumer and Akkad, but before him King Lipit-Ishtar (19th cent. BCE)

---

86. Niehaus (*Themes*, 41), quoting Breasted, *Records of Egypt*, 3:108 (§265).

87. The word pair "to go out" and "come in" in the OT commonly refers to going to war as a commander (van der Lingen, "BWʾ-YṢʾ," 59–66).

88. Trimm, *Warfare*, 129 and throughout. King Saul's general was Abner, David's was Joab, Nebuchadnezzar's was Nebuzaradan.

89. Trimm, *Warfare*, 288.

90. "Two Hymns to the Sun-God," *COS* 1.27:44.

91. "Atra-Ḫasis," *COS* 1.130:453.

had already made that claim: "At that time, I, Lipit-Ishtar, the pious shepherd of the city of Nippur, the faithful husbandman of the city of Ur . . . king of the lands of Sumer and Akkad, the heart's desire of the goddess Inanna, by the command of the god Enlil, I established justice in the lands of Sumer and Akkad."[92] Before both of them, however, Sargon I (24th cent. BCE) of Akkad was venerated as the royal shepherd: "Bless Sargon, who holds fast to the hem of your garment, the shepherd of Assyria, who walks behind you!"[93]

The theme of the divinely appointed royal shepherd is significant not only in the ANE[94] but also in the OT, probably beginning with Judah's *ruler's staff* (Gen. 49:10) and centering on Judah's descendant David. The shepherd boy of his father's flock became the shepherd king of God's people.[95] As with the ANE literature, the OT fluidly alternates between divine royal shepherd and human royal shepherd, especially in the Psalms and Prophets.[96] A few biblical texts allude to Num. 27:17 in particular, leading to the words of Jesus in the Gospels.[97] Like Yahweh's faithful shepherds Joshua and David, but unlike his unfaithful shepherd Ahab, Jesus was and is God's appointed royal shepherd over Israel and his body, the church, and the NT authors are consistent in affirming this claim.[98] But even the obedient shepherds Joshua and David cannot be compared to the great shepherd, Jesus, who is perfectly faithful to guard, sustain, and lay his life down for his flock.[99]

The NT writers repeatedly testify that Jesus was the long-awaited messianic king, the *son of David of the tribe of Judah*, who has come to suffer in his first coming and will later return to reign over all nations in God's kingdom on the new earth. So when Jesus, son of David, comes onto the scene of history, he embodies the role of Yahweh as divine shepherd, who with compassion gathers and feeds his covenant people, Israel (Ps. 23; Matt. 9:36; Mark 6:34; John 10). But did the NT authors move away from Num. 27:17, a key source text that envisions *Joshua* (vv. 18–21) as Yahweh's provision so that Israel would not be like sheep without a shepherd? One could conjecture that they did because Joshua, while clearly a war commander in the book that bears his name, is never called a king, and because the Messiah would not come from his tribe, Ephraim, but from Caleb's tribe, Judah (cf. Num. 13:6, 8; Gen. 49:8–10). Even so, the NT authors knew well that Joshua in Canaan,

92. "The Laws of Lipit-Ishtar," *COS* 2.154:411.
93. "A Hymn to Nanaya with a Blessing for Sargon II," *COS* 1.141:473.
94. See Niehaus, *Themes*, 34–55.
95. See 1 Sam. 16:11; 17:34–36; 2 Sam. 5:2; 7:7; 1 Chron. 17:6.
96. Either divine or human royal shepherds: Gen. 49:24; Pss. 23:1; 28:9; 49:14; 78:71; 80:1; Eccles. 12:11; Isa. 40:11; 44:28; Jer. 17:16; 22:22; 31:10; 43:12; 49:19; 50:44; 51:23; Ezek. 34:5, 8, 12, 15, 23; 37:24; Amos 3:12; Mic. 5:4, 6; 7:14; Zech. 10:2; 11:4, 7, 9, 15–17; 13:7.
97. See 2 Sam. 5:1–2 (cf. 1 Chron. 11:2); 1 Kings 22:17 (cf. 2 Chron. 18:16); Matt. 9:36.
98. Matt. 2:6; 9:36; 25:32; 26:31; Mark 6:34; 14:27; John 10:2, 11–12, 14, 16; Heb. 13:20; 1 Pet. 2:25; 5:2, 4; Rev. 7:17.
99. John 10:1–21; Heb. 13:20; 1 Pet. 2:25; Rev. 7:17.

like Moses in Egypt, was an unforgettable savior of God's people. In fact, Joshua's birth name, Hoshea (*hôšēaʿ*, Num. 13:8, 16), derives from the causative imperative, which means "Deliver!" or "Save!" (*hôšaʿ*). Moses, however, called him the name that stuck, Joshua (*yəhôšuaʿ*), which means "Yah(weh) saves." The form of Joshua's name in the Septuagint, the authoritative Greek Scriptures used by the NT authors, was none other than "Jesus" (*Iēsous*).[100] By an explanatory clause, Matthew reveals that he sees this connection between Nun's son Jesus (Joshua), savior of Israel from its enemies, and Joseph and Mary's son Jesus, savior of Israel from their sins: "She will give birth to a son and you will name him *Jesus* [*Joshua*] *because he will save his people from their sins*" (Matt. 1:21 NET).[101] This second savior, not from Ephraim but from Judah, was Yahweh's ultimate "ruler who will shepherd my people Israel" (Matt. 2:6 quoting Mic. 5:2).

---

100. Auld titles his LXX commentary *Joshua: Jesus Son of Nauē in Codex Vaticanus*.
101. Naming the boy Jesus/Joshua was fitting "*because* [*gar*] he will save his people from their sins" (Wallace, *Greek Grammar*, 673).

26

Sacrificial Calendar

(28:1–29:40)

⁓

Overview

As Num. 9–10, 15 prepared the first wilderness generation to worship Yahweh through appointed festivals and sacrifices, so now Num. 28–29 prepares the second generation with its own updated sacrificial calendar.[1] The English chapter divisions separate Num. 28 and 29, but there are at least four internal reasons to conclude that Num. 28–29 was intended to be read as a single collection.[2] First, the *inclusio* of 28:2 and 29:39 encompasses the divine instructions of chaps. 28–29: "Be careful to offer me at its appointed time" (28:2) and "These you must present at your appointed times" (29:39 [40]). The term "appointed time" (*mô'ēd*) occurs characteristically here and in three passages that Num. 28–29 expands innerbiblically: Lev. 23*, Num. 9–10*, and Num. 15*.[3]

1. On the "cultic calendar" as a blended genre, see Knierim and Coats, *Numbers*, 288–89.
2. Many perceptively treat Num. 28–29 together: Staubli, *Levitikus, Numeri*, 318–25; Achenbach, *Vollendung*, 602–11; Seebass, *Numeri*, 3:232–64; Schmidt, *Numeri*, 171–81; Scharbert, *Numeri*, 114–19; Budd, *Numbers*, 309–19; W. Lee, *Migratory Campaign*, 181–85. Thematically, but without literary justification, de Vaulx (*Nombres*, 326) perceives a larger section of *sacrifices and vows* from chaps. 28–30.
3. On Num. 28–29 expanding Lev. 23, see Nihan, "Festival Calendars," 177–232; Achenbach, *Vollendung*, 602–11; Achenbach, "Heiligkeitsgesetz," 147, 167; Otto, "Priesterschrift," 1–50 (throughout); Schmidt, *Numeri*, 177–81; Levine, *Numbers*, 2:394–95; de Vaulx, *Nombres*, 326–45; Douglas, *Wilderness*, 114–15. For this reason, many have argued that Num. 28–29 reflect one of the latest additions to the Pentateuch (Noth, *Numbers*, 219; Schmidt, *Numeri*, 3–10; Frevel, "Alte Stücke," 274). Blum (*Komposition des Pentateuch*, 224, 227) sees Num. 28–29 as supplements that connect Numbers to Joshua, while Achenbach (*Vollendung*, 602–11) puts Num. 28–29 in the second phase of the late, theocratic revision of the Torah, which resonates

Second, the structural pattern of the units in chap. 28 continues through chap. 29. Yahweh identifies the appointed time, the day and month, when the Israelites must offer sacrifices or begin the festival, and he then gives the protocols for the complex sacrifices and festival celebrations. These units flow in this order: continual burnt offering (28:1–8); burnt offering on the Sabbath day (28:9–10); monthly burnt offering (28:11–15); seven-day Passover starting on day 14 of the first month of the exodus calendar (28:16–25); firstfruits offering during the Festival of Weeks (28:26–31); blowing trumpets on day one of the seventh month (29:1–6); humbling (that is, Atonement) on day ten of the seventh month (29:7–11); an eight-day Festival of Booths starting on day fifteen of the seventh month (29:12–35).[4]

The third reason why Num. 28–29 coheres as a collection is that the composition of the offerings overlaps throughout; for example, see the unmistakable resemblance between the offerings for Passover (28:16–25) and humbling/Atonement (29:7–10).

Fourth, and finally, the narrator says nothing at the end of chap. 28 but reserves his voice for 29:40 [30:1], implying that Moses conveyed the divine instructions from 28:1–29:40 [30:1] in one sitting: "Moses told the Israelites everything, just as Yahweh had commanded him." The festival calendars of the Pentateuch are multifaceted and nuanced,[5] but Num. 28–29 must not be overlooked for its integral theological contribution.

Translation

[1]Then Yahweh spoke to Moses: [2]"Command the Israelites:[6] 'My offering, my food as an offering by fire to be my pleasing scent, be careful to offer to me at its appointed time.'[7] [3]Say to them, 'This is the offering by fire

---

with the prince's offerings in Ezek. 45–46 (cf. Gray, *Numbers*, 403), even if Ezekiel is obviously not constrained by the procedural order of the sacrifices (Rainey, "Order of Sacrifices," 495). Knohl ("Priestly Torah," 65–117; *Sanctuary*, 8–14) views Lev. 23 as a combination of P and H, but Num. 28–29 as entirely P; cf. Stackert, "Composition," 183. I find convincing the work of Rhyder (*Centralizing the Cult*, 57, 104, 284–86, 336, 368), who argues that H in Lev. 23 *centralizes time* in the festal calendar and instructions for regular offerings, and Num. 28–29 represents a post-H priestly supplement to Lev. 23 with much more detail regarding the festival and regular offerings (Lev. 23 is unaware of Num. 28–29).

4. I retain the language of Num. 28–29; e.g., 29:7–11, with its "humbling," refers to the Day of Atonement, but this title is never expressed here (cf. Lev. 23:27–28; 25:9).

5. For a survey of the calendars in Exod. 23*, 34*, Lev. 23*, Deut. 16*, and Num. 28–29*, see Staubli, *Levitikus, Numeri*, 321–25.

6. The second quotative frame is translated as a colon, formally "*Command* the Israelites, *and say to them.*" Perhaps to uphold Yahweh's authority (20:9–12), SP reads, "Then Yahweh spoke to Moses *and commanded* the Israelites."

7. The obj. is fronted as the focus: "*My offering, my food as an offering by fire to be a pleasing scent* be careful to offer to me at its appointed time." To refer more precisely to the *multiple*

that you will offer to Yahweh: two unblemished lambs a year old, every day as a continual burnt offering.[8] [4]The first lamb[9] you must offer[10] in the morning, and the second lamb you must offer at twilight,[11] [5]with one-tenth of an ephah of finely ground flour as a grain offering mixed with a quarter hin of pressed olive oil.[12] [6]It is a continual burnt offering, which was instituted on Mount Sinai[13] as a pleasing scent, an offering by fire to Yahweh. [7]Its libation must be a quarter hin for each lamb. Pour out brandy as a libation[14] to Yahweh in the sanctuary. [8]And the second lamb you must offer at twilight. As you offered the grain offering and its libation in the morning, so you must offer it as an offering by fire, as a pleasing scent to Yahweh.

[9]"On the Sabbath day, you must offer[15] two unblemished lambs a year old, and two-tenths of an ephah of finely ground flour as a grain offering, mixed with olive oil, with its libation. [10]This is the burnt offering for every Sabbath,[16] along with the continual burnt offering and its libation.[17]

[11]"On day one of every month, you must offer as a burnt offering to Yahweh two young bulls, one ram, and seven unblemished lambs a year old, [12]with three-tenths of an ephah of finely ground flour as a grain offering, mixed with olive oil, for each bull,[18] and two-tenths of an

---

designated times requiring sacrifice in chaps. 28–30, SP reads "at their appointed times," and LXX[ed] "at my feasts."

8. Formally, "by/for the day a burnt offering continually."

9. "The first lamb" and "the second lamb," and again "the second lamb" in v. 8—these are all fronted to reactivate these as the topics of vv. 4–7 and v. 8, respectively (*BHRG* §47.2.1[1]).

10. The verb is, formally, "you must do/perform" (*ta'ăśeh*); also 28:8, 15 [niphal pass.], 20, 21, 24, 31; 29:2, 39.

11. Idiomatically, "between the two evenings" (and v. 8), meaning, "the time between sunset and nightfall" ("*'ereb*," *HALOT* 2:877–78).

12. Probably because only here is the "olive oil" (*šemen*) explicitly to be "pressed" or "beaten" (*kātît*), SP and LXX[ed] remove this adjective ("olive oil," 9× in chaps. 28–29).

13. This qal pass. ptc. as an attributive adj.—formally, "which was made on Mount Sinai" (*hā'ăśuyâ bəhar sînay*)—functions as an innerbiblical citation formula, calling the reader's attention back to the first set of instructions at Mount Sinai for the same daily offerings (Exod. 29:38–43). See Fishbane, *Biblical Interpretation*, 170–87.

14. A gen. of material and *l* of advantage: "libation *made out of* brandy *for* Yahweh" (*nesek šēkār lyhwh*; *GBHS* §2.2.10; §4.1.10e1). For *šēkār* as brandy, see the second and third translation notes on 6:3. While serving in and around the meeting tent (Lev. 10:9), the Aaronic priests and anyone under a Nazirite vow (Num. 6:3) were prohibited from drinking wine (*yayin*) or brandy (*šēkār*), whereas here Yahweh instructs that, in coordination with the continual burnt offering, the Israelites must pour out for Yahweh a brandy drink offering.

15. "You must offer" is elided and assumed from its twofold use in the preceding verse (*ta'ăśeh*, v. 8; also 2× in v. 4; *IBHS* §11.4.3d2, 4).

16. Formally, without a copula, "A burnt offering of a Sabbath by its Sabbath."

17. SP: "and their libations"; see the first translation note on v. 14 and the translation note on v. 15.

18. This is a contextual rendering considering the two calves of v. 11, but formally, "for the one bull" (MT LXX[ed]).

ephah of finely ground flour as a grain offering, mixed with olive oil, for the ram, [13]and a tenth ephah of finely ground flour as a grain offering, mixed with olive oil, for each lamb, as a burnt offering for a pleasing scent, an offering by fire to Yahweh. [14]Their libations[19] will be a half hin (of wine)[20] for a bull, a third hin for a ram, and a fourth hin for a lamb.[21] This is the burnt offering for every month[22] throughout the months of the year. [15]Also one male goat as a purification offering must be offered to Yahweh, along with the continual burnt offering and its libation.[23]

[16]"On day fourteen of the first month is a Passover for Yahweh.[24] [17]And on day fifteen of this month is a festival. For seven days bread made without yeast must be eaten.[25] [18]And on day one there is to be a sacred assembly.[26] You must not do any business work,[27] [19]but you must offer an offering by fire:[28] a burnt offering to Yahweh of two young bulls, one ram, and seven lambs a year old. They must be without blemish in your estimation.[29] [20]Their grain offering is to be of finely ground flour mixed with olive oil. You must offer three-tenths of an ephah for each

19. Likely to match to the sg. elsewhere (i.e., vv. 7, 8, 9, 10), LXX[ed] reads "their libation."

20. The gen. of content, "of wine" (*yyn*), is placed in parentheses because it is an ellipsis in MT and LXX[ed], which express the copula (*hyh* / *estai*); SP replaces the copula with "of wine" (*yyn*).

21. Most correctly leave untranslated the article attached to the animal names (generic: *GBHS* §2.6.5), and the *l* seems to be association, although this is a rare use (yet "a great many uses of *l* remain to be elucidated": *IBHS* §11.2.10e). In the ANE there is evidence of libations offered to deities *in association* with an animal, as in Mesopotamia: "A libation was made while the king held a sheep against his breast or presented a fish" (Sigrist, "Sacrifice," 330–32). Likely to align with the typical description, SP includes "of *each* bull . . . of *each* lamb" (see "each" in vv. 7, 12, 13, 21, 28, 29).

22. Formally, "a burnt offering of a month by its month."

23. Probably to harmonize with the pl. in v. 14, SP reads "with their libations."

24. Rather than "Yahweh's Passover," probably a *l* of advantage, "a Passover to/for Yahweh" (*pesaḥ lyhwh*; see the third translation note on 9:10; cf. also 9:14).

25. This niphal incomplete pass. implies obligation: "must be eaten" (*yēʾākēl*; *GBHS* §3.1.2a). Perhaps for clarity, SP and LXX[ed] revise this to a command: "You (all) must eat" (*GBHS* §3.2.2d.4).

26. Formally, "an assembly of sacredness/holiness" (*miqrāʾ-qōdeš*), understood as an attributive gen., "*a sacred* assembly" (*GBHS* §2.2.5), which recurs throughout chaps. 28–29 (28:18, 25, 26; 29:1, 7, 12). Deverbal *miqrāʾ* (**qrʾ* I "to call, summon, invite"), meaning "convocation" or "assembly," is almost completely concentrated in the Priestly festival instructions in the Moses story (Exod. 12:16 [2×]; 11× in Lev. 23; Num. 10:2; 6× in Num. 28–29; also Isa. 1:13; 4:5; but the "reading" of Torah in Neh. 8:8).

27. Formally, "any business of work" (*kol-maleʾket ʿābōdâ*; vv. 18, 25, 26), which is fronted as the focus (*BHRG* §47.2.1.2bi) and which I take as an epexegetical gen., meaning "any *business* work" (*IBHS* §9.5.3c). Not all forms of work are prohibited during this and other festivals but only work that is *malāʾkâ*, which frequently refers to one's business, occupation, or trade ("*malāʾkâ*," *HALOT* 2:586, gloss 2).

28. Here and in v. 27, the volitional weqatal contrasts the preceding, permanent prohibition: "Any business work *you must not do* [*lōʾ taʿăśû*], *but you must offer* [*wahiqrabtem*] an offering by fire" (*GBHS* §3.5.2c, §4.2.11).

29. The predicate adjective is fronted as the focused constituent, and the *l* is estimative, formally, "*Without blemish* they must be *to you*" (*BHRG* §47.2.1[2]; *GBHS* §4.1.10k).

bull and two-tenths for the ram.[30] [21]You must offer[31] a tenth of an ephah for each of the seven lambs, [22]with one goat for a purification offering[32] to make atonement for you. [23]You must offer these in addition to the morning burnt offering, which is for a continual burnt offering.[33] [24]In this way you must offer daily for seven days the food offering made by fire as[34] a pleasing scent to Yahweh. It is to be offered with its libation[35] in addition to the continual burnt offering.[36] [25]On day seven you must have a sacred assembly. You must not do any business work.

[26]"On the day of the firstfruits, when you bring a new grain offering to Yahweh in your weeks,[37] you must have a sacred assembly. You must not do any business work, [27]but you must offer a burnt offering as[38] a pleasing scent to Yahweh: two young bulls, one ram, seven lambs a year old,[39] [28]with their grain offering of finely ground flour mixed with olive oil: three-tenths of an ephah for each bull, two-tenths for the one ram, [29]with a tenth for each of the seven lambs, [30]with one male goat[40] to make atonement for you. [31]You are to offer them in addition to the continual burnt offering and its grain offering. They must be without blemish in your estimation, along with their libations.

[29:1]"On day one of the seventh month, you must have a sacred assembly.[41] You must not do any business work.[42] It will be your day for

30. Here and in v. 21, the obj. is fronted as the focused constituent: "*Three-tenths of an ephah for each bull and two-tenths for the ram* you must offer" (*BHRG* §47.2.1[2]).

31. SP removes this verb, "you must offer/do," reading instead a verbless clause, "will be."

32. Likely adjusting to the formulation of this phrase in chap. 7 (12×; then 15:24; 28:15), SP here and throughout chaps. 28–29 reads "also/with one male goat from the goats as a purification offering" (also in 28:30; 29:5, 11, 16, 19, 22, 25, 28, 31, 34, 38).

33. Here and in v. 31, the clause is fronted as a backward pointing deictic reference, clarifying that the Passover lambs do not replace the continual burnt offering (vv. 3–8): "*In addition to the morning burnt offering, which is for a continual burnt offering,* you must offer these" (*BHRG* §47.2.1.2c[#b]). Using a different construction, vv. 10, 15 provide a similar clarification, "*along with* ['l] the continual burnt offering and its libation."

34. SP omits "as" (*l*) and so reads as an appositional phrase: "food offering made by fire, a pleasing scent to Yahweh."

35. SP: "with their libations"; see the first translation note on v. 14.

36. Following NJPS, the libations are not those of the continual (regular) burnt offering but those of the Passover burnt offering, which otherwise would strangely lack accompanying libations.

37. Formally, "in your weeks," but probably alluding to the seven-week computation of Lev. 23:15 (Nihan, "Festival Calendars," 206).

38. Like v. 24, SP omits "as" (*l*) and so reads as an appositional phrase: "a burnt offering, a pleasing scent to Yahweh."

39. Arguably to match the qualification elsewhere in chaps. 28–29, SP includes "They must be whole/without blemish for you," and LXX[ed] includes "without blemish."

40. See the translation note on v. 22.

41. On the recurring attributive gen. construction "a sacred assembly" (*miqrā'-qōdeš* in 28:18, 25, 26; 29:1, 7, 12), see the first translation note on 28:18.

42. As in 28:18, 25, in this recurring construction, the verbal obj. is always fronted for stress: "*Any business work* you must not do" (29:1, 12, 35). On "business work," see the second translation note on 28:18.

blowing trumpets.[43] **2**You must offer[44] a burnt offering as a pleasing scent to Yahweh: one young bull, one ram, and seven lambs a year old without blemish. **3**Their grain offering is to be of finely ground flour mixed with olive oil, three-tenths of an ephah for the bull, two-tenths of an ephah for the ram, **4**and one-tenth[45] for each of the seven lambs, **5**with one male goat as a purification offering to make atonement for you. **6**These are in addition to the monthly burnt offering with its grain offering, and the continual burnt offering with its grain offering and their libations[46] as specified,[47] as a pleasing scent, an offering by fire to Yahweh.

7"On day ten of this seventh month, you must have a sacred assembly. You must humble yourselves. You must not do any business, **8**but you must offer a burnt offering as a pleasing scent to Yahweh:[48] one young bull, one ram, and seven lambs a year old. They must be without blemish in your estimation. **9**Their grain offering must be of finely ground flour mixed with olive oil, three-tenths of an ephah for the bull, two-tenths for the ram, **10**a tenth for each of the seven lambs, **11**with[49] one male goat as a purification offering, in addition to the purification offering for atonement and the continual burnt offering with its grain offering[50] and their libations.[51]

12"On day fifteen of the seventh month,[52] you must have a sacred assembly. You must not do any business work, but you must celebrate a festival to Yahweh for seven days.[53] **13**You must offer a burnt offering, an offering by fire as a pleasing scent to Yahweh: thirteen young bulls, two rams, and fourteen lambs a year old. They must be without blemish.

43. A gen. of purpose, "day *intended for* blowing trumpets" (*yôm tərû'â*; GBHS §2.2.8), in particular, for "blast[ing], sounding of horn or trumpet, on first day of seventh month as feast day" (*DCH* 8:768, gloss 2).

44. As in chap. 28, formally, "you must do/perform"; also see 28:4, 8, 15 (niphal pass.), 20, 21, 24, 31; 29:39.

45. To match the idiomatic repetition of "a tenth" throughout chaps. 28–29, SP and LXX[ed] read "a tenth, a tenth."

46. SP: "with *its* libations" (*wnskyh*).

47. Formally, "according to their ordinance" (cf. *bəšābu'ōtêkem* in 28:26; *DCH* 5:561, gloss 3).

48. As in 28:19, 27 and 29:12, 35, a volitional weqatal is contrasted (contextually) by the preceding, permanent prohibition: "*Any business you must not do* [*kol-məlā'kâ lō' ta'ăśû*], *but you must offer a burnt offering* [*wəhiqrabtem 'ōlâ*] as a pleasing scent to Yahweh" (*GBHS* §3.5.2c, §4.2.11).

49. Twice in chaps. 29–30, "(with) one male goat" is asyndetic (without the conjunction *wə*: 28:30; 29:11), but normally it is coordinated, "with one male goat" (*ûśə'îr*), throughout 28:15–29:38 (*BHRG* §31.1.1.2d).

50. Probably to assimilate to v. 9 (et al.), several manuscripts read "with *their* grain offering" ([*w*]*mnḥtm* 4Q27 11Q19 MT[mss]).

51. SP and LXX[ed] read "with *its* libations," and LXX[ed] adds the common qualifying phrase of chap. 29 (8 other times): "according to the interpretation, as a smell of fragrance, a sacrifice to the Lord."

52. SP and LXX[ed] specify "of *this* seventh month."

53. Following the pattern of chaps. 28–29, a volitional weqatal is contrasted (contextually) by the preceding permanent prohibition; see the translation note on v. 8.

14Their grain offering must be of finely ground flour mixed with olive oil, three-tenths of an ephah for each of the thirteen bulls, two-tenths of an ephah for each of the two rams, **15**a tenth for each of the fourteen lambs,[54] **16**with one male goat as a purification offering, in addition to the continual burnt offering with its grain offering and its libation.

17"'On day two:[55] twelve young bulls,[56] two rams, fourteen lambs a year old, all without blemish, **18**and their grain offering and their libations for the bulls, for the rams, and for the lambs, according to their number as specified, **19**with one male goat as a purification offering, in addition to the continual burnt offering with its grain offering and their libations.[57]

20"'On day three: eleven bulls, two rams, fourteen lambs a year old, all without blemish, **21**and their grain offering and their libations for the bulls, for the rams, and for the lambs, according to their number as specified, **22**with one male goat as a purification offering, in addition to the continual burnt offering with its grain offering and its libation.

23"'On day four: ten bulls, two rams, and fourteen lambs a year old, all without blemish, **24**and their grain offering and their libations for the bulls, for the rams, and for the lambs, according to their number as specified, **25**with one male goat for a purification offering, in addition to the continual burnt offering with its grain offering and its libation.

26"'On day five: nine bulls, two rams, and fourteen lambs a year old, all without blemish, **27**and their grain offering and their libations for the bulls, for the rams, and for the lambs, according to their number as specified, **28**with one male goat as a purification offering,[58] in addition to the continual burnt offering with its grain offering and its libation.'"

29"'On day six: eight bulls, two rams, and fourteen lambs a year old, all without blemish, **30**and their grain offering and their libations for the bulls, for the rams, and for the lambs, according to their number as specified, **31**with one male goat as a purification offering, in addition to the continual burnt offering with its grain offering and its libation.'"

32"'On day seven: seven bulls, two rams, and fourteen lambs a year old, all without blemish, **33**and their grain offering and their libations for the bulls, for the rams, and for the lambs, according to their number as specified, **34**with one male goat as a purification offering, in addition to the continual burnt offering with its grain offering and its libation.'"

---

54. SP adds "with their libations."

55. The colon (vv. 17, 20, 23, 26, 29) stands for an elided verb that can be supplied from the prior weqatal command "you must offer" (*wahiqrabtem*, v. 13, also in v. 8; *IBHS* §11.4.3d2, 4); cf. the ellipsis of *ta'áśeh* (you must offer) in 28:9.

56. Formally, "twelve young bulls, *sons of the cow* [i.e., from the herd]" (*bny bqr* MT SP), which is omitted in 4Q365, 11Q19, and LXX[ed], probably to harmonize with the absence of this qualifier in the subsequent days (vv. 20, 23, 26, etc.).

57. SP: "and *its* libations."

58. Likely assimilating to this phrase elsewhere (28:22, 30; 29:5), 4Q27 reads "with one male goat *of the goats for* a purification offering *to make atonement for yourselves*," while SP and LXX[ed] read "with one male goat *of the goats for* a purification offering."

³⁵"'On day eight, you must have a closing ceremony.⁵⁹ You must not do any business work, ³⁶but you must offer a burnt offering, an offering by fire, as a pleasing scent to Yahweh: one bull, one ram, seven lambs a year old, all without blemish. ³⁷Their grain offering and their libations for the bull, for the ram, and for the lambs, according to their number as specified, ³⁸with one male goat as a purification offering, in addition to the continual burnt offering with its grain offering and its libation.

³⁹"'These you must present to Yahweh at your appointed times, in addition to your vow offerings and your freewill offerings,⁶⁰ as your burnt offerings, your grain offerings, your libations, and your sacrifices for peace.'" ⁴⁰ [³⁰:¹]Moses told the Israelites everything, just as Yahweh had commanded him.

Interpretation

28:1–8. The quotative frame in 28:1 introduces Yahweh's lengthy instructions to Moses, which extend from 28:2 through 29:39. The opening and closing discourse, both from the narrator and from Yahweh, forms an *inclusio* with three frames:

> Then Yahweh spoke to Moses:
> > "Command the Israelites:
> > > 'My offering, my food as an offering by fire to be my pleasing scent, *be careful to offer to me at its appointed time*'" (28:2).
>
> > "'These *you must present to Yahweh at your appointed times*, in addition to your vow offerings and your freewill offerings, as your burnt offerings, your grain offerings, your libations, and your sacrifices for peace.'"
> > Moses told the Israelites everything,
> just as Yahweh had commanded him (29:39–40 [30:1]).

---

59. This "closing ceremony" (*ʿăṣārâ*, 11× in the OT, 3× in the Pentateuch) is not identical to the recurring "sacred assembly" (*miqrāʾ-qōdeš*, 6× in Num. 28–29) but is an improper synonym. Thus, on day 8 of the festival (*sukkōt* inferred from Lev. 23:36), the Israelites were to convene, not exactly for a "holiday" ("*ʿăṣārâ*," *HALOT* 2:871, gloss 1) or "a solemn assembly" (ESV, NJPS), but more precisely for "a closing assembly of festival" (suggested as possible by *DCH* 6:540, gloss 1), given that it often refers elsewhere to the eighth and final day of a festival to Yahweh (Lev. 23:36; Deut. 16:8 [seventh day]; Neh. 8:18), the dedication of Yahweh's temple (2 Chron. 7:9), or "a great sacrifice to Baal" (2 Kings 10:20).

60. As in 15:3, no protocols are supplied for "your vows/vow offerings and your freewill offerings" (*minnidrêkem wanidbōtêkem*), because the author assumes that the reader knows how to execute these from Yahweh's prior revelation through Moses on Mount Sinai (see "vow," *neder*, Lev. 7:16; 22:18, 21, 23, 38; 27:2; Num. 6:2; 5, 21; "freewill offering," *nadābâ*, Lev. 7:16; 22:18, 21, 23, 38; "appointed feasts of Yahweh," *môʿădê yhwh*, Lev. 23:2, 4, 37, 44).

This *inclusio* orients readers to see, first, that these sacrificial instructions are *for all the Israelites*,[61] not just the priests, and second, that the sacrifices and festivals are *for Yahweh* and so must be performed at the times he fixes with every sacrifice he prescribes. Cultic worship must be executed by the community, not just the priestly hierarchy, for Yahweh and on Yahweh's terms. Although Israel offers the array of sacrifices, they belong to Yahweh for his enjoyment, which the opening metaphor underscores, "My offering, my food as an offering by fire to be my pleasing scent" (28:2).[62] In Gen. 1:14, God created the markers of "appointed times, days, and years," and now in Israel's sacrificial cult, God claims appointed times for himself, creating an important distinction between the common and the sacred.[63]

Without the preface "when you enter the land" (Num. 15:2, 18), the basic sense of chaps. 28–29 is that the sacrifices and festivals that began at Sinai must continue to be celebrated, but now with several key expansions. The first subunit (vv. 3–8), in which Yahweh orders Israel to offer a continual burnt offering, is an expansion of Exod. 29:38–42 and Lev. 6:9–13. The citation formula, "which was instituted on Mount Sinai" (Num. 28:6aα), points back to Exod. 29* and Lev. 6*, but now Num. 28* moves into new territory (see the translation note on 28:6). The Lev. 6* law (and probably Exod. 29* law) was directed to the Aaronic priests, whereas Num. 28:3–8 makes clear that the continual burnt offering was to be, in some way, the responsibility of all the Israelites (vv. 2a, 3a). Without mentioning Yahweh, how many burnt offerings, or of what type (cf. Lev. 1:1–17), Lev. 6:9–13 is focused instead on the role of the priests in keeping the fire burning constantly (vv. 9, 11, 12, 13), changing into and out of their clean priestly garments (vv. 10–11), and removing fatty ashes from the altar (v. 11). By contrast, Exod. 29:38–42 and Num. 28:3–8 specify and focus on the offering of two lambs, one lamb in the morning and one in the evening (vv. 4, 8; see the first translation note on 28:4). Accompanying each lamb will be the same combination of a raw grain offering with olive oil and a libation of brandy (see the translation note on 28:7, the first translation note on 15:5, and the second translation note on 5:15). From Israel's perspective, the burnt offering expresses costly, total devotion to Yahweh, as everything is consumed on the altar (LXX: "whole burnt offering," *holokautōma*), and it ascends up for Yahweh to smell (Hb. *'ōlâ* related to **'ālâ*, go up). The other shift in focus is from the priests as central agents (Lev. 6:9–13) to Yahweh as the central recipient (Num. 28:3–8). As Num. 28:2 already preconditions readers, the continual burnt offering is emphatically for Yahweh alone: "offer to Yahweh" (v. 3), "an offering by fire to Yahweh" (v. 6), "a libation to Yahweh in the sanctuary" (v. 7), "an offering by fire, as a

---

61. With Scebass, "Eigene Komposition," 96.
62. See the "Implications" essay below, "Does Yahweh Eat the Sacrifices of His People?"
63. See Dozeman, "Numbers," 234–36; also see 4:1–14 for **qdš* as what belongs to the deity (Clines, "*Qdš*," 481–502).

447

pleasing scent to Yahweh" (v. 8). As the Israelites encamp around the meeting tent (Num. 2:17), and in the future as they make pilgrimage triannually to the Jerusalem temple (see Deut. 16:16; Isa. 33:20), they will visualize the *axis mundi*[64] as they see the smoke rising from the continual burnt offering to Yahweh in the heavens, reminding them that pleasing Yahweh, with whom they are bound in covenant, is the most important calling on their lives.

28:9–10. The instructions zoom out from the continual burnt offering (vv. 3–8) to the weekly burnt offering on the Sabbath day (vv. 9–10). The weekly burnt offering, presented presumably in one session, was identical to the continual burnt offering presented in the morning and evening: two unblemished yearling lambs (= one lamb 2×), two-tenths of an ephah of a fine-flour grain offering (= one-tenth 2×), but with a single libation (cf. a libation with each lamb, vv. 7–8). Prescribing this weekly burnt offering for Yahweh is an innovation: no other Sabbath instruction in the Pentateuch even hints at presenting weekly sacrifices.[65] The sacred assemblies of the festivals in chaps. 28–29 repeatedly demand "You must not do any business work" (28:18, 25; 29:7, 12, 35).[66] Surprisingly, this prohibition, so characteristic of the Sabbath elsewhere (Exod. 20:10; 31:14; Num. 15:31–41; et al.), is not found in these Sabbath directives in vv. 9–10. The simplest explanation is that vv. 9–10 innerbiblically assume and expand the Holiness instructions, which use the same language of no business work during the sacred assemblies as we find in chaps. 28–29.[67] Leviticus 23:2–3 envisions the Sabbath as a weekly festival to or for Yahweh, so it is only fitting in Num. 28* that this festival include sacrifices for Yahweh. Within the broader Pentateuch, the expansion of Num. 28:9–10 takes on theological import: the weekly Sabbath ritual of remembering Yahweh as creator of the universe (Exod. 20:8–11) and as redeemer of Israel from bondage in Egypt (Deut. 5:12–15) is now inculcated ritually into the Israelites when they express to Yahweh their total devotion through burnt offerings and their gratitude and enjoyment through grain and drink offerings.[68]

28:11–15. By mandating a burnt offering on the first day of every month, Yahweh orients Israel's life toward him through the bidaily, weekly, and now monthly sacrificial rituals. The concentric rings are now obvious:

64. See the "Implications" essay in chap. 2, "The Centrality of God's Presence"; Levenson, *Sinai & Zion*, 122–25.

65. Cf. Exod. 16, 20, 31, 35; Lev. 23, 24, 25; Num. 15; and Deut. 5.

66. See the comments on 15:32–36.

67. Contra P. Guillaume (*Land*, 88), offering sacrifices on the Sabbath (Num. 28:9) does not subvert the human rest, which is from business work, not from the cultic work of sacrifices to Yahweh. In the teaching of Jesus, the priests desecrate the Sabbath and yet remain innocent of violating the Torah (Matt. 12:5), which may mean that they do not perform business work but perform prescribed cultic work of a different nature that enables the Sabbath rest of the community.

68. To our knowledge, the Sabbath was a novelty of ancient Israel. Levine (*Numbers*, 2:404) points out that the Mesopotamian *šapattu* is a dubious parallel.

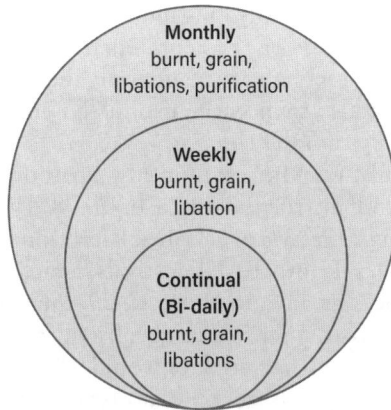

Figure 26.1. Offering Times

As with the continual and weekly burnt offerings, the monthly sacrifice is a single, albeit complex, burnt offering. The "burnt offering" hypernym subsumes its associated grain offerings and libations, as the *inclusio* makes plain: "On day one of every month, you must offer *as a burnt offering* to Yahweh. . . . This is *the burnt offering* for every month throughout the months of the year" (vv. 11, 14). The monthly burnt offering exceeds the size of the continual and weekly burnt offerings since it requires (1) two young bulls, a ram, seven unblemished lambs a year old (v. 11); (2) grain offerings proportionate to the size of each animal: three-tenths of an ephah of fine flour for each bull, two-tenths for the ram, one-tenth for each lamb (vv. 12–14); (3) and accompanying libations, now probably of wine (as 15:5, 7, 10) rather than brandy, which is not mentioned here (v. 14; cf. v. 7).[69] After the "burnt offering" *inclusio* (vv. 11, 14) closing off the unit, Yahweh adds the requirement of a purification offering, although the effect of atonement is only implicit here (cf. "atonement" in 28:22, 30; 29:5, 11). Presumably this monthly burnt offering would be signaled by the blast of trumpets (Num. 10:10). In northern Mesopotamia, worship of the moon god Sin was common, and the new moon at the start of every month displayed the moon god's enduring reign.[70] In Ugarit, the lunar cult centering on the god Yariḫ and his consort, the goddess Nikkal, was prevalent.[71] Unlike Sin and Yariḫ, Yahweh is not confused ontologically with the moon; Num. 28:11–15 elevates Yahweh alone as sovereign over the earth's

69. See the second and third translation notes on 28:14 and the second translation note on 15:4. Achenbach ("Complementary Reading," 209) sees a motif from the grape cluster in Num. 13:23, connoting the gift of wine in Canaan, to the wine libations throughout Num. 15* and 28–29*. The offering list is not identical but parallel to those in Num. 7* and 15* (Olson, *Death of the Old*, 87).

70. Walton and Matthews, *Genesis–Deuteronomy*, 208.

71. Levine, *Numbers*, 2:405.

domain (cf. Gen. 1:16–18). Finally, this monthly burnt offering is a novelty among the divine commands of the Pentateuch, and its contribution is to orient and reorient the Israelites to view not only their daily lives and weekly work-rest rhythms but also their entire exodus-based year as a continuous display of their worship of Yahweh.

28:16–25. The daily, weekly, and monthly burnt offerings (28:2–15) are fronted before the festival instructions of 28:16–29:38. The literary effect arguably grounds readers in a *lifestyle* of sacrificial devotion to Yahweh before the *seasonal* festivals arise. Like other ANE festivals, Israel's festivals were based on its agricultural calendar; here in Num. 28–29, they occur in the first and seventh months of the year.[72] Yet, strikingly absent from Num. 28–29 is any sense that these festivals and sacred days would influence Yahweh to fertilize the agriculture of ancient Israel, in contrast to many ANE agricultural festivals, such as the Mesopotamian Akitu New Year's celebration aimed at procuring the gods' fertile blessings in the coming year.[73] At Sinai, the Israelites celebrated their second Passover, a year after the exodus (Num. 9:1–14; cf. Exod. 12), but since then the narrative gives no indication that they have been observing the Passover throughout their wilderness journeys otherwise marked by disobedience. Even as Yahweh in Num. 9:6–14 expands the Passover law (Exod. 12*) to accommodate unclean, travelers, and immigrants,[74] now Yahweh again expands the Passover festival (1) to ensure that Passover and the Feast of Unleavened Bread are conjoined as a single festival (as in Lev. 23:5–6) and (2) to add to the household ritual of lamb slaughter (Exod. 12*) a collection of festival sacrifices *for Yahweh* in his meeting tent and later in the temple (see the translation note on Num. 28:16).[75] In particular, Num. 28:16–25 repeats verbatim the Passover orders of Lev. 23* (normal font in the table) and then supplies "the offering by fire," which Lev. 23:8 mentions but never defines (boldfaced in the table):

Leviticus 23:4–8	Numbers 28:16–25
[5]On day fourteen of the first month, **at twilight,** is a Passover for Yahweh. [6]And on day fifteen of this month is a festival of bread made without yeast to Yahweh. For seven days you must eat bread made without yeast.	[16]On day fourteen of the first month is a Passover for Yahweh. [17]And on day fifteen of this month is a festival. For seven days bread made without yeast must be eaten.

72. Wagenaar ("Calendar Innovations," 3–24) observes that the Babylonians held two New Year's festivals each year, in the first month and seventh month, which is not clear in Exod. 23, 34 and Deut. 16 but resembles the festival calendars of Exod. 12, Lev. 23, and here in Num. 28–29.

73. Walton and Matthews, *Genesis–Deuteronomy*, 207.

74. See the "Implications" essay in chap. 9, "Numbers 9:9–14 in the Progressive Theology of Passover."

75. Cf. Ezra 6:19–20; Ezek. 45:21.

Leviticus 23:4–8	Numbers 28:16–25
[7]And on day one there is to be a sacred assembly for you. You must not do any business work, [8]but you must offer an offering by fire	[18]And on day one there is to be a sacred assembly. You must not do any business work, [19]but you must offer an offering by fire: **a burnt offering to Yahweh** . . .
	[vv. 19aβ–23, 24b: **burnt offering, grain offering, libations, purification offering, with the continual burnt offering**]
to Yahweh for seven days.	[24a]**In this way you must offer daily** for seven days the **food offering made by fire as a pleasing scent** to Yahweh.
On day seven there is to be a sacred assembly. You must not do any business work.	[25]On day seven you must have a sacred assembly. You must not do any business work.

The evidence indicates that Num. 28–29 was intended not to replace but to supplement H's vision in Lev. 23 to centralize time in the festal calendar and regular offerings.[76] The overlapping instruction (normal font) reinforces the authority of Lev. 23*, while the new instruction (boldface) expands Lev. 23* to detail the quality and quantity of the festival offerings.[77] In both Lev. 23* and Num. 28*, the seven-day Passover-Unleavened Bread festival is bookended by sacred assemblies, with no business work on the first and seventh days (see the first translation note on 28:18). Throughout these seven days, bread without yeast is to be eaten, recalling the Israelites' hurried exit from Egypt, which required them to carry their dough with them before they had time to add the yeast (Exod. 12:34; see the translation note on Num. 28:17). The festival is marked by eating: Israel and Yahweh eat the Passover lamb (cf. Exod. 12:1–13), and Israel eats bread without yeast "for seven days" (Num. 28:17) while Yahweh eats "daily for seven days the food offering made by fire" (28:24).[78] Syntactically, not performing any business work is contrasted with performing Yahweh's offerings by fire (see the first translation note on v. 19). In particular, the Passover festival's complex burnt offerings, with grain offerings and libations, are identical to those of the monthly burnt offering (vv. 11–15) but multiplied by seven for each of the festival's seven days (see the translation note on v. 20). The lambs must be without blemish in Israel's estimation (v. 19; see the second translation note there), while the libation formulas for these sacrifices can be supplied from v. 14 (v. 24b; see the third translation note there). Like the daily, weekly (implied), and monthly burnt offerings, the burnt offerings for the Passover-Unleavened Bread festival delight Yahweh as "a pleasing scent" (28:24). The purpose of the purification offerings at the Passover festival is "to make atonement for you" (28:22), which is restated in the Festivals of Weeks (28:30), Trumpets (29:1), and the

---

76. With Rhyder, *Centralizing the Cult*, 57, 104, 284–86, 336, 368.
77. Nihan, "Festival Calendars," 177–232, esp. 228.
78. See the "Implications" essay below, "Does Yahweh Eat the Sacrifices of His People?"

Day of Atonement (29:11). Based on other Priestly texts, atonement refers to removing (expiating) sin and transgression, resulting in divine forgiveness of the Israelites, and to removing physical impurity, resulting in the ritually clean state of the Israelites (see the first translation note on 6:11 and the third translation note on 18:1).[79]

Finally, vv. 16–25 make an important contribution to a biblical theology of the Passover. Just as Yahweh slaughtered the firstborn sons and livestock of Egypt, sparing Israel's firstborn, so in collective memory, Israel slaughtered the lambs and smeared their blood on the doorframes. Augmenting this custom, Israel must now also *slaughter* a complex burnt offering for Yahweh their deliverer at his dwelling place. Likewise, as the Israelites left Egypt in haste and ritually enact that formative experience by eating bread *without yeast* for an entire week, so now Israel offers grain offerings of fine flour *without yeast* as an expression of gratitude to Yahweh their deliverer (see Lev. 2:11).

28:26–31. The temporal marker "*On the day* of the firstfruits" follows Yahweh's pattern of demarcating the sacrificial instructions (28:3, 11, 16; 29:1, 7, 12). The allusion to Lev. 23 is clear: "You must count fifty days until the day after the seventh Sabbath, and then *you must bring a new grain offering to Yahweh* [Lev. 23:16]. . . . On the day of the firstfruits, *when you bring a new grain offering to Yahweh* during your Festival of Weeks" (Num. 28:26). In fact, Num. 28:26–31 repeats or assumes all of Lev. 23:15–22, including the one-day sacred assembly without business work at the Festival of Weeks (Lev. 23:21; Num. 28:26).[80] Also, the composition of the Festival of Weeks burnt offering is identical to that of the monthly burnt offering (28:11–15) and Passover burnt offering (28:19–22), and the text assumes that the reader has knowledge of these preceding instructions.[81] Furthermore, Num. 28:26 alludes to the fifty-day time lapse between the firstfruits ritual at the beginning of the barley harvest in March (Lev. 23:9–14) and the start of the Festival of Weeks (23:15–22). These can be seen in the two shorthand expressions, respectively, "*On the day of the firstfruits*, when you bring a new grain offering to Yahweh *in your weeks*" (Num. 28:26).[82] In Yahweh's prior instructions at Sinai, the Israelites were ordered to perform a firstfruits ritual at the inception of their first harvest in Canaan (Lev. 23:9–14), and then after seven weeks they were to celebrate the Festival of Weeks by a grain offering, a complex burnt offering

---

79. Contra Albertz (*Israelite Religion*, 2:464), atonement was not essentially "prophylactic," preventing disease, but theological, removing impurities so that Yahweh could forgive the offender (see "and he/she will be forgiven" in Lev. 4:20–6:7).

80. In view of its tendency to expand rather than replace Lev. 23, it is likely that Num. 28 assumes the mandate to leave harvest gleanings for the poor and immigrants (Lev. 23:21–22).

81. From the Passover ritual, "one goat *for a purification offering* to make atonement for you" (28:22; cf. 29:11) is implied here in "one male goat to make atonement for you" (28:30). As with Passover (28:24b), for the Festival of Weeks, the deictic "their libations" (28:31) required that the Israelites use the libation formula given for the monthly burnt offering (v. 14).

82. Nihan, "Festival Calendars," 206; cf. Ashley, *Numbers*, 567.

with its libations, a purification offering, and by raising the lambs (of the burnt offering) and bread (of the "firstfruits") as an elevation offering to Yahweh (Lev. 23:15–22). Now by the shorthand language of 28:26, the firstfruits ritual and Festival of Weeks are conjoined as a continuous celebration of Yahweh's benevolence to his covenant people as they harvest their grain.

29:1–6. The pattern of the Passover and Weeks festivals is repeated at the Festival of Trumpets, opening with the date, day one of the seventh month, on which Israel would gather in a sacred assembly while ceasing any business work (v. 1; see the first and second translation notes there). The composition of the complex burnt offering is identical to the burnt offering offered monthly and at the Passover and Festival of Weeks.[83] In Num. 10:1–10, the Aaronic priests held the sole responsibility to blow trumpets to gather the community, launch the Israelites on a journey, initiate a military attack, celebrate festivals, and perform sacrifices. The distinctive characteristic of this festival, however, was that Yahweh designates one day of the year to the express purpose of "blowing trumpets" (29:1; see the third translation note there). Once again Lev. 23* is the source of the Festival of Trumpets that Yahweh expands on in Num. 28*. In contrast to the Festival of Weeks in Lev. 23* and Num. 28* (see 28:26–31, above), what is glaringly absent in Lev. 23:23–25 is the nature of Israel's sacrifices to Yahweh: "You must not do any business work, but you must present *an offering made by fire to Yahweh*." This absence is the focus of Yahweh's teaching in Num. 28–29: "My offering, my food as an offering by fire to be my pleasing scent, be careful to offer to me at its appointed time" (28:2).[84] So Num. 29:1 repeats Lev. 23:24–25a, and then Num. 29:2 picks up where Lev. 23:25b left off: "But you must present an offering made by fire to Yahweh. . . . You must offer a burnt offering as a pleasing scent to Yahweh." This day for blasting the sound of a trumpet, whether made of hammered silver (Num. 10:2) or a ram's horn (Josh. 6:5), was to be a "memorial" (Lev. 23:24), probably of the day the Israelites blasted the horn when the holy Yahweh descended on Mount Sinai and terrified the Israelites, with whom he then entered into covenant (Exod. 19:13, 16, 19; 20:18). Yahweh resided on Mount Sinai, towering above his people, and now in the meeting tent in the center of his people. Through the Num. 29:1–6 legislation, the centrality of the holy Yahweh is safeguarded by converting the Day of Trumpets into a day saturated with sacrificial worship of Yahweh at his dwelling place amid his covenant people.

29:7–11. Just ten days after the Festival of Trumpets (vv. 1–6), that is, on day ten of the seventh month, Israel must reconvene for another sacred assembly, conducting no business work (v. 7). What marks this day is the imperative "You must humble yourselves" (v. 7c). The broad, if elusive, directive could

---

83. For analysis, see the comments on 28:11–15 above.
84. See the "Implications" essay below, "Does Yahweh Eat the Sacrifices of His People?"

even mean to oppress themselves (piel of *ʿnh) but was later interpreted as a communal fast (Isa. 58:5; cf. Joel 2:15).[85] This corporate self-humbling or self-denial ritual was first introduced in the addendum to the Day of Atonement ritual in Lev. 16:29–34 and was then reemphasized in Lev. 23:26–32. As we have seen above, the primary source text of Num. 29:7–11 is Lev. 23, where Yahweh, with over-specified rhetoric, will himself execute anyone who does any business work on this unparalleled Sabbath day of self-humbling (Lev. 23:29–32). Only in the Holiness collection does Yahweh call this "the Day of Atonement" (yôm hakkippurîm, Lev. 23:27, 28; 25:9), a title not used in Lev. 16* or here in Num. 29*. Once again, the source text of Lev. 23* leaves a gap about the nature of this day's "offering by fire to Yahweh" (Lev. 23:27), which Num. 29:8–11 fills: "But you must offer a burnt offering as a pleasing scent to Yahweh: one young bull . . ." (v. 8; see the translation note there). The Day of Atonement's complex burnt offering—with accompanying grain offerings, libations, and the purification offering—is identical to that of the monthly burnt offering and preceding festivals (see analysis of 28:11–15). In 28:11 Yahweh stresses that this is to be in addition to Israel's continual burnt offering (28:3–10) and "in addition to the purification offering for atonement" (29:11), an innerbiblical reference ensuring that Israel will not neglect the crucial, multifaceted Day of Atonement ritual of Lev. 16:1–28. In Lev. 16* Yahweh underscores the purification of his dwelling, his priests, and the entire community of Israel by purifying their sin, transgressions, and physical contagions. Then Lev. 23* and Num. 29* together add a second theological dimension: The Day of Atonement is intended not only to cleanse and restore Israel to Yahweh so he can dwell in their midst but also to bring delight to Yahweh through the expressions of self-humbling and diverse sacrifices from his cleansed people at his cleansed dwelling place.

29:12–38. Only five days after the Day of Atonement, on day fifteen of the seventh month every year, Israel regathers for a sacred assembly and ceases all business work (v. 12). The imperative "You must celebrate a festival to Yahweh for seven days" (v. 12; see the second translation note there) reveals that the festival described in vv. 12–38 is the seven-day Festival of Shelters (ḥag hassukkôt, Lev. 23:34, 42–43; Deut. 16:13, 16), even though the title is absent here, just as the name "Day of Atonement" is absent from vv. 7–11.[86] In Lev. 23:33–43 Yahweh commands Israel to camp out for seven days in temporary shelters ("booths," NRSV) made of tree branches in memory of their ancestors who lived in temporary shelters in the wilderness when Yahweh brought them out of Egypt (23:42). Here Yahweh has another concern,

---

85. Later the rabbis envisioned other forms of self-denial, such as abstaining from eating, drinking, wearing sandals, bathing, and sexual intercourse (Milgrom, *Numbers*, 246–47).

86. The Festival of Shelters is also referred to as the Festival of Ingathering (Exod. 23:16; 34:22; see Ashley, *Numbers*, 570).

to clarify the sacrifices that must be offered on every day of this seven-day festival. In Lev. 23:27 the "offering by fire to Yahweh" is only broadly defined as "a burnt offering, grain offering, sacrifice [probably sacrifice for peace], and drink offerings, *each on its proper day* [*dəbar-yôm bəyômô*]" (23:37). Now Yahweh fills out what "each on its proper day" means by the expansive sacrificial protocols of Num. 29:13–38. Not unlike the chieftains' twelve-day procession of sacrifices to dedicate Yahweh's altar (Num. 7), Israel must offer seven successive days of offerings by fire to Yahweh. The text is highly repetitive, which may burden modern readers, but this is an emphatic way of declaring Yahweh's worthiness to receive such a prodigious, systematic succession of animal and grain sacrifices on his altar (see the comments on 7:10–83). The pattern of sacrifices recurs for each of the seven days (e.g., vv. 17–19). The only daily change is the descending number of bulls: thirteen bulls on day one, twelve bulls on day two, eleven bulls on day three, successively decreasing to the clean and complete number of seven bulls on day seven, for a total of seventy bulls offered over the week. Every day the Israelites are to offer double the number of rams and lambs that they offer for their monthly burnt offering and prior festivals: two rams instead of one, fourteen lambs instead of seven. The purification offering stays the same, and the continual burnt offering must not cease (v. 19). The seven-day festival, which commences with a sacred assembly of no business work (v. 12), concludes with a unique "closing ceremony" on the eighth day, with no business work and only the sacred work of presenting pleasing sacrifices to Yahweh (vv. 35–38; see the translation note on v. 35; cf. Lev. 23:35–36).

It remains a mystery why Yahweh chooses to infuse the Festival of Shelters with so many sacrifices rather than the formative Passover-Unleavened Bread festival that also entails seven days of sacrifices (28:14). One explanation is that this ritual echoes the *zukru*-festival of LBA Emar, Syria (ritual text: Emar 6, 373).[87] The two versions of this festival, annual and septennial, resemble the Num. 29* Festival of Shelters in that they began on the fifteenth of the month (v. 12),[88] lasted for seven days (vv. 13–34), and included seventy sacrifices in all (vv. 13–34). The seventy sacrifices in Emar were offered one for each of seventy gods, representing the whole pantheon. There is no mention of a pantheon in Num. 29*, only Yahweh, who alone receives Israel's seventy young bulls along with many other types of sacrifices. Finally, if it were possible to dilute the Festival of Shelters into an anthropocentric ritual that simulates Israel's transience and discomfort in the wilderness (à la Lev. 23:42–43), Num. 29:12–38 destroys that possibility by proliferating the sacrifices *for the*

87. Ayali-Darshan, "Seventy Bulls," 9–19.

88. Also, the *zukuru*-festival was a New Year's celebration (Ayali-Darshan, "Seventy Bulls," 13–17), and as Wagenaar ("Calendar Innovations," 3–24) notes, the Babylonians had a second New Year festival in the seventh month, which seems to be reflected in the month-seven festivals of Exod. 12, Lev. 23, and Num. 28–29.

pleasure of Yahweh. In so doing, Num. 29* reconditions the suffering Israelites to "rejoice before Yahweh your God for seven days" (Lev. 23:40).

29:39–40 [30:1]. As noted above, the *inclusio* with three frames (28:1–2; 29:39–40 [30:1]) encloses Yahweh's speech (28:2–29:38) and depicts it as centering on offering Yahweh's sacrifices at the appointed times specified in his speech. The final frame in v. 40 [30:1] stresses Moses's obedience to communicate Yahweh's sacrificial calendar to the whole Israelite community, for whom it is intended. Yahweh's closing words do not mention the purification offering or atonement, perhaps because these derive from the foundational offerings: burnt, grain, and greetings (Lev. 4:1–6:8; 6:25–37; Lev. 1–3). Instead, in v. 39 Yahweh clarifies that the Israelites must not forget to freely respond to Yahweh's goodness by also offering their vow offerings (for vows they have made) and freewill offerings expounded in Num. 15:1–16 (see the translation note on 29:39).[89] Mentioning these additional offerings here follows the parlance of chaps. 28–29: Yahweh reminds the Israelites of offerings "*in addition to the* morning burnt offering, . . . continual burnt offering, . . . monthly burnt offering, . . . purification offering" (13×). One can read this from two perspectives, depending on the disposition of the heart: countless sacrifices to Yahweh are an overwhelming burden, or countless sacrifices are still not adequate to praise Yahweh. Yahweh is disgusted with the first perspective of multiplying sacrifices without a right relationship with Yahweh and others (Ps. 40:6–8; Isa. 1:11–13). There are, however, examples of the second perspective, such as when the people under Nehemiah's leadership joyfully dedicated Jerusalem's rebuilt walls with great sacrifices to God (Neh. 12:43).

Implications

Does Yahweh Eat the Sacrifices of His People?

A number of cultic sites in the Levant dating to the Late Bronze and Iron Ages have been discovered with sacrificial remains. To give two examples, the Canaanite Fosse Temple at Lachish (later Judah) contained the bones of sacrificial sheep, goats, oxen, birds, and fish. At Ugarit, archaeologists have discovered bird bones (cf. Lev. 1–7*),[90] and libations were offered at both locations. Israel was no stranger to ancient sacrificial rituals, yet as we have seen above in Num. 28–29, the array of prescribed sacrifices displayed different aspects of Israel's relationship with Yahweh, from expressing total devotion (burnt offering) to removing the impurities of sin and physical contagions (purification offering) and showing gratitude for abundance (grain offerings and libations). This does not mean, however, that Israel's sacrifices to Yahweh

89. On vows, see Lev. 27; Num. 6 and 30.
90. Kitchen, *Reliability*, 408–9.

were only for Israel's benefit. In the opening frame of the *inclusio* around Num. 28–29, the described identity, the verbal object, is fronted as the focus of Yahweh's speech: "*My offering, my food as an offering by fire to be my pleasing scent* be careful to offer to me at its appointed time" (Num. 28:2).[91] Can "my food"[92] and "my pleasing scent" actually mean that Yahweh eats and smells Israel's sacrifices to his delight? A famous parallel appears in the Epic of Gilgamesh when Utnapishtim survives the flood and sacrifices to the gods:

> The gods smelled the savor,
> The gods smelled the sweet savor,
> The gods crowded like flies about the sacrifice.[93]

In Mesopotamian cults, a mouth-opening (*pīt pî*) and mouth-washing (*mīs pî*) ritual transforms the cult image into a divine being, as this incantation states: "This statue without its mouth opened cannot smell incense, cannot eat food, nor drink water."[94]

Back in Num. 4:7, "the table of the Presence" (*šulḥan happānîm*) seems to avoid an anthropomorphic Yahweh eating food at his table, like other deities would. The substantive "the Presence" (*happānîm*) may be a way to avoid naming Yahweh as Israel's deity seated to eat at the table in his house, which stands in contrast to the ANE deities who were thought to consume meal offerings via their cult images.[95] Here in Num. 28:2 "my food" (*laḥmî*) can give the impression that Yahweh enjoys eating Israel's sacrifices offered by fire on the platter of his bronze altar.[96] We find similar language in the instructions for the Aaronic priests in Lev. 21–22, calling Yahweh's sacrifices "the food of their/your [sg., pl.]/his god."[97] As for Num. 28:2, one may retort that "my food" is defined as "my pleasing scent" (*rêaḥ nîḥōḥî*), but smelling involves inhaling food particles, and this does not explain why, if Yahweh wants to dissociate himself from eating, he would say "my food."

Conceptual metaphor theory can help us at this interpretive impasse. "Conceptual" metaphor means that metaphors operate on the level of thoughts, not just words; they use a concrete concept to point to a more abstract concept, and not vice versa.[98] Also, an audience may no longer be aware of the concrete source for the metaphor (so-called killjoy theory), appreciating only the

---

91. *BHRG* §47.2.1b.
92. "My food" can, in other contexts, mean "my bread" (*laḥmî*).
93. The Epic of Gilgamesh, in *ANET* (trans. E. A. Speiser), 68.
94. Sommer, *Bodies of God*, 19.
95. See the first translation note on 4:7; Oppenheim, *Ancient Mesopotamia*, 183–98.
96. Knohl (*Sanctuary*, 30) attributes 28:2b to H scribes not averse to presenting Yahweh anthropomorphically.
97. Hb. *leḥem ʾĕlōhêhem/- êkem/-êkā/-āyw* (Lev. 21:6, 8, 17, 21, 22; 22:25).
98. S. Pinker, *Stuff of Thought*, 238–49.

abstract message, or they may be well aware of the source (so-called "messianic theory").[99] In our case, ancient readers of Numbers were well aware of the concrete concept of the metaphor: the human phenomenon of eating, drinking, and smelling foods at a meal in a home. We see this concrete concept made explicit in Lev. 21–22: just as sacrifices for Yahweh are called "the food of their/your/his god," so also his human representatives, the Aaronic priests, eat Israel's sacrifices as "his/their food" (*laḥmô*, Lev. 22:7, 11; cf. 22:13). More important, in Num. 28–29 all the sacrifices are edible or drinkable and enjoyed by humans in daily life outside the sacrificial cult: finely ground flour mixed with olive oil, brandy, grilled lamb, beef (bull), mutton (ram), and goat.

The difficulty, then, is not in perceiving this concrete concept of the metaphor, but the abstract to which the concrete points, because Yahweh does not physically eat, drink, or smell. Right? There are instances when the biblical narrators state that Yahweh's fire physically consumes (formally, "eats," *'kl*) sacrifices, such as at the inauguration of the priests (Lev. 9:24) and at Elijah's contest with the prophets of Baal (1 Kings 18:38). Typically, however, eating, drinking, and smelling the sacrifices are anthropomorphic activities attributed to Yahweh, which point to an abstract concept of how Yahweh relates to his covenant people. That abstract concept cannot be that Yahweh is physically needy. Unlike other gods, the biblical authors are consistent that Yahweh needs no sustenance, and he has no cult image to mediate his care through daily feeding, clothing, and housing.[100] There is no illusion in the Hebrew Scriptures that Yahweh needs food and drink or that his priests need to feed him (Ps. 50:12–13). In Mesopotamian temple cults, by contrast, the priests, especially in public spaces, sought to maintain the impression that the gods were eating and drinking the sacrifices in their houses.[101] In the satirical Jewish story of Bel and the Dragon, the Babylonian priests of Bel, with their wives and children, are exposed as illusionists (Bel 1:13). To be fair, there were ancient Mediterranean thinkers who openly acknowledged that the gods do not dine as humans do, as the implied narrator of Homer's *Iliad* remarks in a surprising aside: "For the gods do not eat bread nor drink wine, hence they have no blood such as ours, and are immortal."[102]

Furthermore, the abstract concept cannot be that Yahweh's food serves to empower and protect Yahweh, as in Egyptian temple worship: "Once properly prepared, the deity may then partake of the various offerings presented to it. Analogous to but far more than human nourishment, the food offerings are charged with divine potencies through the medium of ritual, both to protect and to empower the divine image."[103] Numbers has already testified to the

---

99. S. Pinker, *Stuff of Thought*, 238–49.
100. Ps. 50:12–15; Acts 17:24–25; see Walton, *Ancient Near Eastern Thought*, 100.
101. Hundley, *Gods in Dwellings*, 275n334.
102. *Iliad* 5.341–42 (trans. Butler, 33).
103. Hundley, *Gods in Dwellings*, 197.

aniconic Yahweh as the victorious divine warrior who needs no protection and employs his power both to punish and protect his covenant people.[104]

In closing, I argue that the concrete concept of Yahweh's eating, drinking, and smelling Israel's sacrifices points to the abstract concept of Yahweh's enjoyment of the devotion of his covenant people. As Num. 11–25* has shown, Israel's devotion cannot be merely cultic worship devoid of gratitude for Yahweh's goodness, obedience to his commands, and trust in his power to provide and deliver (1 Sam. 15:22). At the same time, faithfully offering food and drink offerings to Yahweh at their appointed times and according to their protocols was still essential to expressing devotion to Yahweh. Yahweh delights in cultic devotion only from those restored to him and to others, as the final form of Ps. 51:16–19 envisions. Jesus understood the reality that the Father delights in sacrificial gifts at his altar only when the devotee has first sought reconciliation (Matt. 5:23–24).

At the climax of history, Yahweh took great delight in the sacrifice of his Servant, his Son, the Messiah Jesus (Isa. 53:10; Phil. 2:8–11). When Jesus, the great high priest, offered his own body as the definitive atoning sacrifice, no more sacrifice for sins remains (Heb. 10:12–18, fulfilling Lev. 4:1–6:8, 25–30; 7:1–7). Yet until the second temple was destroyed (70 CE), Jewish followers of Jesus could have theoretically and orthodoxly still have offered the sacrifices of Lev. 1–3, which are central to Num. 28–29, not to deal with sin but to express their total devotion to (burnt), gratitude for (grain), and fellowship with (sacrifice of greetings) God, who has reconciled them to himself in Christ. After all, Jesus's followers today still offer "real and tangible sacrifices to God, only by a different mode, by the priestly mediation of Christ and the power of the Holy Spirit."[105] Echoing the language of Yahweh's burnt and grain offerings as "a pleasing scent"—eleven times in Num. 28–29—Jesus's own sweet-smelling sacrifice has become a model of love for all of his disciples to please the Father as he did: "And walk in love, as Christ loved us and gave himself up for us, a fragrant offering and sacrifice to God" (Eph. 5:2).[106]

---

104. Punishment is prominent throughout Num. 11–25*, while protection features in Num. 6:24–26; 10:35–36; chaps. 21, 22–24, 31.

105. Awabdy, *Leviticus*, 25.

106. See also the "Implications" essay in chap. 8, "The Levites, a Living Sacrifice."

27

Vows to Yahweh

(30:1–16)

◈

Overview

The reason for the literary placement of Num. 30's teachings on vows and oaths after the centralized festival sacrifices of Num. 28–29 is debated.[1] Although Num. 29:39 provides a thematic bridge—"in addition to your vow offerings and your freewill offerings" (cf. Lev. 23:38)[2]—a more robust connection is apparent: vows typically involve sacrifices or valued gifts (Num. 15:3; Lev. 27:1–33),[3] and the pilgrimage festivals are opportune times to offer such vow sacrifices or gifts.[4] For the first time in the Torah story, Moses communicates Yahweh's teaching to Israel's tribal leaders (30:1 [2]), who are patriarchal representatives of Israel's families. The instructions are casuistic (case law) in form, possibly emerging implicitly from legal precedents (cf. explicitly Num. 15*, 27*, 36*).[5] These case laws deal with the vows and oaths made by Israel's men (v. 2) but then quickly move on to center on keeping or nullifying pledges and vows made by Israel's women: a young woman in her father's house (vv. 3–5), a woman when she transitions into marriage (vv. 6–9), and a married woman in her husband's house (vv. 10–15). One may hear an echo of the vow

---

1. As elsewhere in this commentary, I follow Eng. verse numbering (Num. 30:1–16) in this chapter; the equivalent versification in the HB is 30:2–17.
2. Schmidt, *Numeri*, 182; Milgrom, *Numbers*, 250; Budd, *Numbers*, 324.
3. See de Vaulx, *Nombres*, 346–47; Sturdy, *Numbers*, 209.
4. Ashley, *Numbers*, 575.
5. Ashley, *Numbers*, 574; Knierim and Coats, *Numbers*, 293.

of the Nazirite first given to exodus-generation men and women (6:2), even as now the Nazirite vow remains a possible option for men, daughters, and wives of the second generation.[6] The unit here is enclosed by the *inclusio* of the narrator's voice (vv. 1, 16), and the closing frame of v. 16 recasts this chapter to be not primarily about vows or oaths but about the solidarity of Israel's family relationships: the husband and wife, and the father and daughter. This chapter offers a prime example of Yahweh's tendency to contextualize his revelation within a patriarchal society to promote the cohesion of Israel's families (see the "Implications" essay below, "Patriarchal Family Structure").[7]

Translation

1 [2]Then Moses told the Israelite tribal leaders:[8] "This is what Yahweh commands:[9] **2 [3]**If a man makes a vow to Yahweh or takes an oath to put an obligation on himself,[10] he must not break his word, but must do everything he said.

3 [4]"If a young woman[11] still living in her father's house makes a vow to Yahweh or pledges herself to an obligation, **4 [5]**and her father hears about her vow[12] or the obligation she has taken on herself, and her father says nothing to her, then all her vows will stand, and every obligation she has taken on herself will stand.[13] **5 [6]**But if her father opposes[14] her when he hears about it, then none of her vows or her

---

6. Olson, *Death of the Old*, 87.

7. Most agree that Num. 30 belongs to the latest additions to the Torah: Scharbert (*Numeri*, 119–21) attributes Num. 30 to the Pentateuch redactor; Achenbach (*Vollendung*, 612–14) assigns it to the third and final supplementary phase of the theocratic revision of the Torah.

8. Formally, "the heads of the tribes (belonging) to the Israelites."

9. Or "has commanded" (NET, ESV), after the notice of 29:40 [30:1]. The verb describes a speaking action (*ṣwh*), thus a performative qatal: "This is what Yahweh *commands* [ṣiwwâ]" (EÜ, NIV).

10. This *l* inf. clause gives the purpose of taking the oath, with a cognate accusative: "in order to bind a binding obligation on his life" (*leʾsōr ʾissār ʿal-napśô*; *GBHS* §4.1.10d).

11. The text envisions a young woman living in her father's household, not yet married or engaged: formally, "If a *woman* [ʾiššâ] vows a vow to Yahweh or pledges a pledge (while) *in her father's house, in her youth* [babêt ʾābîhā binʿurêhā]" (single and not betrothed: "naʿûrîm," *HALOT* 2:704, gloss 2; cf. vv. 9–15).

12. Even so, it is conceivable that he hears her make the vow audibly, which is the direct obj.: formally, "and her father hears *her vow* [ʾet-nidrāh]."

13. After "on herself," the manuscripts differ: "(every obligation . . .) will stand" (*yqwm*, MT); "her father will confirm it" ([ʾbyh yq]ymnw wth, hiphil, 4Q27); "(?) they will stand" (*yqwmw* 11Q19 SP); "(her determinations . . .) will remain for her" (*menousin autē*, LXX^ed).

14. This rare verb (*nwʾ*), with six of its eight OT occurrences here in Num. 30 and 32 (30:5 [2×], 8, 11 [6 (2×), 9, 12]; 32:7, 9), means "oppose" in the hiphil in this setting (*DCH* 5:633, gloss 1a; ESV). In context, the father or husband does not exactly "restrain" (*DCH* 5:633, also gloss 1a) or "forbid" (NIV) her, since she has already successfully pronounced the vow (vv. 5, 8, 11 [6, 9, 12]); nor does he "overrule" (NET) or "disavow(ed)" (Levine, *Numbers*, 2:426) her,

461

obligations that she has taken on herself will stand,[15] and Yahweh will release her from it, because her father opposed her.[16]

6 [7]"And if she marries a man while under a vow[17] or after carelessly speaking[18] an obligation that she takes on herself, **7 [8]**and her husband hears about it, but says nothing to her when he hears about it,[19] then her vows will stand and her obligations[20] that she has taken on herself will stand. **8 [9]**But if, when her husband hears about it, he opposes her, then he nullifies[21] the vow that obligates her, along with whatever she spoke carelessly that she has taken on herself. Yahweh will release her from it.[22] **9 [10]**But every vow made by a widow or by a divorced woman,[23] which she has taken on herself, will be binding on her.

10 [11]"If she makes a vow in her husband's house or takes on herself an obligation with an oath, **11 [12]**and her husband hears about it, but says nothing to her, does not oppose her, then all her vows will stand, and every obligation that she has taken on herself will stand. **12 [13]**But if her husband clearly nullifies them[24] when he hears them, then[25] whatever came out of her lips, whether her vows or an obligation taken on herself

---

since Yahweh holds that prerogative: "and Yahweh will release her from it/them" (vv. 5, 8, 12 [6, 9, 13]). Rather, once she has spoken the vow, her father (v. 5 [6])—and/or, later in life, her husband (vv. 8, 12 [9, 13])—can oppose her by expressing disapproval of the vow she has taken and so prevent its establishment (v. 12 [13]), resulting in Yahweh's release of the vow.

15. Although the sg. is acceptable, SP and LXX[ed] adjust to pl.: "they will (not) stand" (also v. 12 [13]).

16. This "her" is absent in LXX[ed]: "because her father withheld consent" (NETS).

17. With a circumstantial *wa*: formally, "And if she indeed becomes a man's *while* her vow is on her" (*GBHS* §4.3.3e); LXX[ed]: "But if, when she grows up, she becomes a man's wife" (NETS).

18. The noun here occurs only in vv. 6, 8 [7, 9] in the OT and means something like "impetuous utterance" ("*mibṭā*'," *DCH* 5:126), deriving from "to speak impetuously" (*bṭ*' piel, 3× only). The gen. is subjective, "an impetuous utterance *by* her lips," which I render as "after carelessly speaking" (*mibṭā' śapātêhā*; *GBHS* §2.2.3).

19. I follow the word order of 4Q27 and LXX[ed]—"but says nothing to her when he hears about it"—although the meaning is the same in MT/SP: "but when he hears about it, he says nothing to her."

20. Although it may be secondary, as the more contextual reading, which is parallel with the pl. "her vows," I prefer "and her obligations" (*w'sryh* 4Q27 MT[ms] SP LXX[ed]; cf. "her vow," *w'srh* MT[L]).

21. The verb recurs in the hiphil in vv. 8, 12, 13, 16 [9, 13, 14, 17], with a concrete meaning, "to break, destroy" ("*prr* I," *HALOT* 3:974–75, gloss 1), but with oath-sworn contracts like covenants and treaties and with vows, it can mean "nullify" (many versions) or "annul" ("*prr* I," *DCH* 6:782, gloss 1c).

22. Probably to harmonize with the language of v. 8 [9], 4Q27 and LXX[ed] in v. 9 [10] share three plusses: "*all* her *vows* and *her obligations*" (MT Syr: sg. "vow").

23. These genitives are understood as subjective: "But every vow made *by* a widow or *by* a divorced woman" (*wanêder 'almānâ ûgarûšâ*; *GBHS* §2.2.3).

24. The adverbial inf. of the same root is emphatic, "if her husband *clearly* nullifies them" (*hāpēr yāpēr 'ōtām*; *GBHS* §3.4.2b.1).

25. Asyndeton here, but contextually an apodosis: ". . . , *then* whatever . . ."

will not stand.[26] Her husband has nullified them, and Yahweh will release her. **13 [14]**Any vow or sworn obligation that results in her affliction, her husband can confirm or nullify.[27] **14 [15]**But if her husband says nothing about her from day to day, then he confirms all her vows or all her obligations which she is under. He confirms them since he said nothing to her when he heard them. **15 [16]**But if he nullifies them after he has heard them, then he will bear her iniquity."

16 [17]These are the statutes that Yahweh commanded Moses, regarding the relationship between[28] a husband and his wife, and between a father and his young daughter still living in her father's house.

Interpretation

30:1–2 [2–3]. The vow instructions open with two surprises in v. 1: the narrator does not report any direct speech from Yahweh to Moses as one normally finds (28:2; 31:3), and Moses transmits Yahweh's commands, not to the Israelites generally, but specifically to the leaders of Israel's tribes (see the translation notes on 30:1 [2]).[29] This group was identified earlier by four descriptors, "Israel's chieftains, the heads of their patriarchs' households, . . . the chieftains of the tribes; they were the ones in charge of those who were enlisted" (7:2). This twelve-man group, consisting of one representative from each tribe, plays an integral role as Israel's war commanders and as cultic liaisons between the priests and Levites, on the one hand, and the community, on the other.[30] As a result of the Baal of Peor apostasy, these leaders were supposed to have been executed (25:4–9), and surprisingly their successors, the tribal leaders of the new generation, are not called on to assist Moses and Eleazar in the second census (Num. 26; cf. 1:4–19). Despite this elusive recent history, the tribal leaders of the second generation are now Israel's salient patriarchs (as

---

26. Although the sg. is acceptable, SP and LXX[ed] adjust to pl.: "they will not stand" (also v. 5 [6]).

27. Formally, "her husband will confirm it or her husband will nullify it" (*'îšāh yaqîmennû wa'îšāh yapērennû*), but the yiqtol verbs here indicate permission granted by Yahweh to her husband: "her husband *can* confirm or *can* nullify" (using "can" in current usage for "may"; GBHS §3.2.2d.2). LXX[ed]: "her husband will establish *for her*, and her husband will cancel."

28. For clarity, I supply *"regarding the relationship"* (with Cazelles, *Nombres*, 135; Levine, *Numbers*, 2:427; NIV, NLT).

29. Frevel (*Mit Blick*, 172) notes that "This is what Yahweh commands" (30:1 [2]) is exclusively Priestly parlance (Exod. 16:16, 32; 35:4; Lev. 8:5; 17:2; Num. 30:1; 36:6).

30. Based on Num. 10:4, Moses would have had to blow a single trumpet blast to summon the tribal leaders here. These named leaders are commanders of Israel's army divisions (1:16), assisted Moses and Aaron in counting the exodus generation (1:4–19; 4:34, 46), dedicated Yahweh's altar (chap. 7), and brought their tribe's staff to Yahweh's meeting tent to witness the budding of Aaron's staff (chap. 17). A separate group of named leaders explored Canaan (13:3–13).

7:2) and are therefore suitable communicators of Yahweh's orders in vv. 2–15 [3–16], which are intended to protect the family structure in ancient Israel (see the "Implications" essay below, "Patriarchal Family Structure").

The tribal leaders must first teach all patriarchs, Israel's men, regarding two kinds of formal commitments they may make: either "a vow to Yahweh" or "oath to put an obligation on himself" (see the translation note on v. 2 [3]). Vows in the Hebrew Bible and ANE were "consistently conditional"[31] and so could involve executing a particular task (sacrifice in Lev. 27*; ark transport in Ps. 132:1–5) or negotiating with the deity to get a desired outcome (Jephthah's vow for victory in Judg. 11:30–31).[32] In Num. 21:2–3c, Israel's exodus generation made and fulfilled their obligation concerning a conditional vow to Yahweh. By distinction, an oath was simply a pledge or promise to do something, as the Israelite spies pledged to protect Rahab and her family (Josh. 2:12–14). However, any vow or oath was regarded as "a religious act, drawing the deity into a pact with the worshipper, it may not be broken under penalty of God's displeasure (see Ex 20:7 . . .)."[33] One can read Num. 30 as a supplement to Lev. 27, in which Yahweh specifies the cost value of specific vows, the cost of redeeming vowed people, animals, houses, fields, firstborn, and people or things permanently dedicated to Yahweh by a vow.

Here in Num. 30:2 [3] the purpose of Yahweh's directive is not to recall the types of vows or oaths a man may choose to make but to exhort Israelite men to integrity when making a formal commitment. Jesus understood this spirit of Num. 30:2 when he quotes this text and calls his disciples to live lives, not of empty promises, but of perfect integrity (Matt. 5:33, 48). In our text here, by using a rhetorical point-counterpoint set—first the prohibition, then its inverse command—Yahweh ardently insists on every man's faithfulness to keep his word: "He must not break his word, but must do everything he said."[34] Promises were taken seriously in Mesopotamian ritual, as this confession by a sick person shows: "I promised then reneged; I gave my word but then did not pay."[35] Deuteronomy 23:22–23 relates intertextually to Num. 30:2 [3] and possibly also Lev. 5:4[36] but is unique in two primary ways: (1) delaying fulfillment is effectively tantamount to breaking a vow (and Yahweh "will surely hold you accountable as a sinner"),[37] and (2) the "freewill offering" (as in

31. Cartledge, *Vows*, 134–35; but see the argument for unconditional Nazirite vow: Cocco, *Women*, 168–81.

32. Walton and Matthews, *Genesis–Deuteronomy*, 209.

33. Walton and Matthews, *Genesis–Deuteronomy*, 209.

34. See Runge, *Discourse Grammar*, 386.

35. Lambert, "Dingir.šà," 280, line 124, cited by Milgrom, *Numbers*, 251.

36. Römer ("Urkunden," 20) and Frevel ("Alte Stücke," 282; cf. Budd, *Numbers*, 322) argue that Num. 30* is an addendum to Deut. 23:22–23, whereas Kilchör (*Mosetora*, 273–74) argues that Deut. 23* expands Num. 30:3 [4] and Lev. 5:4.

37. See also the harsh judgment for delaying the fulfillment of a vow in Eccles. 5:4–6.

Num. 29:39) illustrates one available vow that they must be careful to fulfill. Formally, Num. 30:2 prohibits the man from failing to fulfill his promise: "He must not *profane* his word" (hiphil of *ḥll*), indicating that breaking vows was not only a legal liability but also a desecration of cultic purity.[38] One can see, then, how Procipius of Gaza (ca. 465–528 CE) could infer from Num. 30* that breaking a vow is equivalent to lying to God.[39] Moreover, integrity in oath- and vow-taking may also explicate the Holiness prohibition, "You must not swear falsely in my name, so that you do *not profane* the name of your god. I am Yahweh" (piel of *ḥll*, Lev. 19:12; cf. Exod. 20:7).[40] As Num. 30:2 [3] appears to expound Lev. 19:12, so Jesus expounds Num. 30:2 [3] by exposing the spirit of this law, its latent divine ideal of verbal fidelity, by locating it within a larger theological framework (Matt. 5:33–37).

30:3–5 [4–6]. The audience turns from men to young women still living in their father's house (v. 3; see the translation note there). Although the young women in view may have been betrothed,[41] they are implicitly unmarried because in patrilocal cultures like ancient Israel, married women move into the patriarchal compound of their husband's family.[42] The language parallel with v. 2 makes clear that just like Israelite men, these Israelite daughters have the same prerogative to make a vow to Yahweh or pledge themselves to another obligation. And like the males (v. 2 [3]) and married women (vv. 6–15 [7–16]), the daughters of Israel can make vows anywhere, which we may infer from the lack of "before Yahweh" throughout Num. 30 (cf. 5:16–6:20).[43] Yet the stress of this text is on the daughter's position under the authority of her father, in whose home she lives. Her father alone holds the power to sanction or nullify her vow or obligation (vv. 4–5). Her father, probably not hearing her pronounce anything audibly but hearing that she has made a vow or taken an obligation while under his roof, validates her decision if he does not say anything (v. 4 [5]; see the first translation note there). The text is vague, allowing her father to remain either purposefully silent, meaning he positively affirms her choice, or negligent, meaning that he does not affirm her choice but has failed to say anything.

The disjunctive in v. 5 [6], "But if her father opposes her when he hears about it" (see the first translation note on v. 5 [6]), results in the cancellation of her vow or obligation, and her father's opposition will be automatically endorsed by Yahweh: "and Yahweh will release her from it, because her father opposed her" (v. 5bβ [6bβ]). By her performative speech act, "the vow took

---

38. Levine, *Numbers*, 2:428; Shectman, *Women*, 168n85; Milgrom, *Numbers*, 251.

39. Lienhard, *Numbers*, 258.

40. Intertextuality between Lev. 19:12 and Num. 30:2 cannot be validated, but both demand oral integrity in the act of the niphal of *šbʿ* (to swear, take an oath; *DCH* 8:240–43 §Ni. 1).

41. Budd, *Numbers*, 322.

42. See King and Stager, *Life*, 39–40.

43. Goldstein, "Women," 60.

on a life of its own,"[44] but now by the second speech act of her father, that living vow can be terminated.[45] Noth infers, "Because the woman, dependent on the man's decision, is subjectively innocent, Yahweh will 'forgive' her."[46] Since a person falsely swears a vow or oath to one's own destruction (see above), the paterfamilias backed by Yahweh can use his power to prevent daughters from making formal commitments that they would not be able to keep.[47] Since daughters and wives were financially dependent on their fathers or husbands, in many scenarios the patriarch felt the weight of the vow as the one liable to pay for the sacrifices or offerings for the women to fulfill their vows.[48] The letter of this law would not prevent a cruel father from unnecessarily restricting his daughter from expressing her devotion to Yahweh, but Deuteronomic law ensured that daughters were equal celebrants of the weekly Sabbath rest and of Yahweh's festivals.[49] In Deut. 10:17–19, Israel's patriarchs are to emulate Yahweh as the exemplary paterfamilias,[50] and for Num. 30 one may infer a similar *imitatio dei* principle from the framing chapters of Num. 27 and 36: As Yahweh emphatically endorses the claim of the unmarried daughters of Zelophehad, so human fathers should be inclined to endorse their unmarried daughters when they make vows and obligations.[51]

30:6–9 [7–10]. Yahweh turns next to the scenario of a woman who enters marriage having made a prior vow to Yahweh or obligation (see the first translation note on v. 6 [7]). This section makes the most sense if it is not a redundancy with the teaching about the already-married woman in vv. 10–15 [11–16]. The protasis, then, contains a main classification with two subordinate situations:

> And if she marries a man
>> while under a vow
>> or after carelessly speaking an obligation that she takes on herself (v. 6 [7])

Presumably, just before she gets married, the woman has made a vow, by implication to Yahweh (vv. 2, 3 [3, 4]), which is commendable but binding at the start of her marriage, or "after carelessly speaking an obligation," that vow is imprudent and hangs over her marriage (vv. 6, 8 [7, 9]; see the second

---

44. Dozeman, "Numbers," 236.
45. See Austin, *Do Things with Words*, 4–11, et al.
46. Noth, *Numbers*, 225.
47. As indicated by "carelessly speaking" in v. 6 [7].
48. Levine, *Numbers*, 2:436; Olson, *Numbers*, 175.
49. Exod. 20:10; Deut. 5:14; 12:12, 18; 16:11, 14.
50. See Awabdy, *Immigrants*, 49–60.
51. Cf. Seebass, *Numeri*, 3:276; and the comments on Num. 27:7b.

translation note on v. 6 [7]). The language reflects Lev. 5:4, "thoughtlessly takes an oath," which brings guilt that requires confession and a purification offering (Lev. 5:5–19). The newly married woman's pledge, even though spoken rashly, is still binding, and her husband will feel an obligation to respond.[52] Both kinds of commitments, positive and negative, her new husband can validate by his silence or invalidate by voicing his opposition (vv. 7–8 [8–9]; see the first translation note on v. 8 [9]). These verses clarify the woman's ambiguous situation: If she makes a vow or obligation while still in her father's house (vv. 3–5 [4–6]), when she gets married she fully transfers from being under the authority of her father to being under the authority of her new husband.[53] This law ostensibly draws a theological inference from the primal vision that the husband and wife form a new and separate family unit (Gen. 2:24).

This conceptuality is reinforced by the classes in v. 9 [10] introduced by the disjunctive clause: "But every vow made by a widow or by a divorced woman, which she has taken on herself, will be binding on her" (see the translation note on v. 9 [10]).[54] The widow and divorced woman are both husbandless, no longer under a paterfamilias with authority over the residents of his patriarchal household.[55] Against the ANE and Israelite stigma and vulnerability of being a widow or divorced,[56] v. 9 [10] elucidates that these classes of women are under no patriarch's authority, such as an uncle or brother, and so their formal commitments are always binding, just as those of Israelite males (v. 2 [3]). Beyond this, what is shocking is that in contrast to Torah texts that limit divorced women,[57] here the divorced woman is endowed with the privilege to make unchecked, binding vows to Yahweh or commitments to others. The conception is implicit: As with the widow and orphan in Deut. 10:18, so also the divorced woman is under the protective authority of Yahweh as her divine paterfamilias.[58]

30:10–15 [11–16]. Finally, Yahweh turns to women who are already married at the time they take a vow or pledge an oath; this status is implied in the descriptor, "If she makes a vow in her husband's house" (v. 10 [11]). Once again, the same language is repeated from vv. 3–5 [4–6] and vv. 6–9 [7–10], now making plain a common structure for vv. 3–15 [4–16]:

---

52. Gray (*Numbers*, 416) draws this conclusion from Num. 30:6 [7] while considering Lev. 5:4; Ps. 106:33; Prov. 12:18; 20:25; Eccles. 5:3–6; Sir. 18:23.

53. Cf. Eph. 5:22; de Vaulx, *Nombres*, 348.

54. As a disjunctive, v. 9 [10] might have been supplied later (de Vaulx, *Nombres*, 347).

55. Conversely, the patriarch's extended family includes both his wife and daughters (Awabdy, *Immigrants*, 44–45).

56. King and Stager, *Life*, 53, 57.

57. Lev. 21:7, 14; 22:13; Deut. 24:1, 4.

58. For Yahweh as "surrogate paterfamilias" in Deut. 10:17–19, see Awabdy, *Immigrants*, 55.

Table 27.1. Women Making Vows

	Unmarried daughter (vv. 3–5 [4–6]) "A young woman still living in her father's house" (v. 3 [4])	Woman who marries (vv. 6–9 [7–10]) "If she marries a man while under a vow" (v. 6 [7])	Married woman (vv. 10–15 [11–16]) "If she makes a vow in her husband's house" (v. 10 [11])
She makes a vow or pledge and patriarch hears about it.	vv. 3–4 [4–5a]	vv. 6–7a [7–8a]	vv. 10–11a [11–12a]
Patriarch says nothing, which validates the vow or pledge.	v. 4 [5b]	v. 7b [8b]	v. 11b [12b]
Patriarch opposes her, which invalidates the vow or pledge.	v. 5a [6a]	v. 8a [9a]	v. 12a [13a]
Yahweh releases her from the vow or pledge.	v. 5b [6b]	v. 8b [9b]	v. 12b [13b]

The three classes (boldface in the table above) theoretically cover all women in ancient Israel, since if one is not a minor in her father's house, then "it was presumed that all adult women were married."[59] Widows are the ambiguous exception.

There are three noteworthy developments in vv. 10–15 [11–16]. (1) Verse 12 [13] appears to conflate the husband's two acts of opposing and nullifying in v. 8 [9] into one emphatic act: "But if her husband clearly nullifies them when he hears them" (v. 12 [13]; see the first translation note there). (2) "Whatever came out of her lips" (v. 12 [13]) seems to be shorthand for "the vow that obligates her, along with whatever she spoke carelessly that she has taken on herself" (v. 8 [9]). The phrase "whatever came out of her lips" may also connote her self-commitment in a juridical context, even as Yahweh self-commits to his people in Deut. 8:3b.[60] (3) When one sees the pattern of vv. 3–15 [4–16], one immediately notices the addition of vv. 13–15 [14–16], which appear to be tightly communicated as a chiasm.[61] By redundancy, these verses over-specify the husband's power to confirm or nullify his wife's vows and obligations.[62] As with the ritual for a wife suspected of adultery (Num. 5:12–31), the vowing or pledging wife is also positioned under the authority of her husband. However, the main purpose of vv. 10–15 [11–16] is to prevent the wife from affliction: "Any vow or sworn obligation that results in her affliction, her husband can confirm or nullify" (v. 13 [14]; see

59. Milgrom, *Numbers*, 250.
60. Kiss, "Der Mensch," 510–25.
61. Staubli, *Levitikus, Numeri*, 327.
62. See Runge, *Discourse Grammar*, 388.

the translation note there). The husband may nullify his wife's oath right after he hears it, but if he delays, "he will bear her iniquity" (v. 15 [16]; cf. 5:31). This means the husband would face the consequences of her offense (cf. Num. 18:1),[63] possibly because "the sacredness of the name of God that was pronounced at the time of swearing the vow has been violated."[64] The husband, then, can prevent his wife from making a destructive oath like King Saul, who depleted the energy of his troops while in pursuit of the enemy and unknowingly put his son Jonathan under a curse (1 Sam. 14:24–30), or like Jephthah, whose vow resulted in the slaughter of his own daughter (Judg. 11:29–40).[65] To be clear, a husband could also choose to "confirm" an oath that leads to his wife's affliction, so this law does not protect a woman who makes a dangerous vow and has a fiendish husband who does nothing to stop her. However, a God-fearing husband could allow his wife to go through with a painful oath. For example, a woman could take a Nazirite vow to display her love for Yahweh (Num. 6:2), but it could be an act of self-denial, even affliction, especially if she must shave off her hair.[66] A painful vow could also more deeply inculcate the Yahweh worshiper, man or woman, in the history of Yahweh's sustenance through, and deliverance from, affliction (Deut. 8:1–3; 16:3). Hannah must have felt the emotional agony of giving away her boy, Samuel, to Yahweh, but all Israel could thank her husband Elkanah for not stopping Hannah from fulfilling her painful vow (1 Sam. 1:1–2:21).[67]

30:16 [17]. The narrator's subscript forms an *inclusio* with v. 1 [2] and encloses vv. 2–15 [3–16] as a single unit of divine instruction that Moses relays to the tribal leaders. The narrator's synopsis of Yahweh's statutes forms a chiasm: first, "regarding the relationship between a husband and his wife" (v. 16aβ [17aβ]) refers to the second block of instructions (vv. 6–15 [7–16]); and second, "between a father and his young daughter still living in her father's house" (v. 16aγ [17aγ]) refers to the first main block of instructions (vv. 3–5 [4–6]). Surprisingly, the narrator says nothing about vows or oaths or about the oath-taking man at the start (v. 2 [3]), but summarizes the divine statutes of vv. 2–15 [3–16] as fundamentally about the husband-wife relationship and father-daughter relationship (see the translation note on v. 16 [17]). This suggests that, in the narrator's perspective, Yahweh's commands are not about vow- and oath-taking per se but about protecting the cohesion of patriarchal Israelite families.

---

63. Levine, *Numbers*, 2:433.

64. Knohl, *Sanctuary*, 229.

65. Contra Douglas (*Wilderness*, 171, 199), Num. 30 is not a metaphor for the divine-Israel relationship: Israel's covenant with Yahweh takes the form of a vow, while Yahweh may disapprove and cancel the vow if Israel makes vows to, and covenants with, false gods.

66. See the comments on 6:18.

67. Cf. Budd, *Numbers*, 324.

Implications

Patriarchal Family Structure: Accommodating to a Post-Fall World

On the surface, Num. 30 pertains to making vows to Yahweh and pledging commitments to others, but the instructions are clearly focused on enforcing the patriarchal structure of the home in ancient Israel, in which the daughter remains under the authority of her father and the married woman under the authority of her husband (vv. 3–15). Even the narrator perceives the social depth of Yahweh's instructions by asserting that they are ultimately about the husband-wife and father-daughter relationships (v. 16; see above). Cartledge goes so far as to claim that "male dominance becomes the controlling rule" of Num. 30.[68] Although his claim is a non sequitur, the evidence does indicate that Num. 30 aims to reinforce the *patriarchal hierarchy* in the family. First, as Cartledge rightly observes,[69] the teaching of Num. 30 does establish the power of the woman's father, and then husband, to either affirm or nullify the woman's vows to Yahweh and pledges to others (vv. 3–15 [4–16]). Second, throughout the chapter, Moses addresses not the women making the vows but Israel's male tribal leaders (v. 1 [2]), who are "the heads of their patriarchs' households" (7:2). The national patriarchs teach the local patriarchs how to validate and invalidate the oaths of the Israelite women. Third, the unit uses the rhetorical device of divergence,[70] dealing quickly first with the non-focus to get to the focus: the teaching opens with a single verse about men (v. 2 [3]), followed by thirteen verses about women (vv. 3–15 [4–16]); this imbalance cannot be accidental. Numbers 30 ensures the subordination of women to their patriarchs, just as Numbers elsewhere ensures the subordination of the Israelites to Yahweh's priests.[71]

To understand the origins of patriarchy in Num. 30, in the entire biblical narrative, and in our world today, we must go back to the opening chapters of Genesis. In Gen. 1:26–28, Elohim, God, makes human beings in his image and likeness for the express purpose of governing the aquatic, avian, and terrestrial animals. As Elohim's image bearers and the first humans, man and woman together are equal not only in value but also in their function as his royal representatives on earth. Male and female (*zākār ûnəqēbâ*) refer to distinct genders, each with distinct biology and behavioral tendencies, but together the male and female display the glory of God to the rest of creation over which they rule (Ps. 8:3–8). This pattern of equal value and function continues in Gen. 2, albeit from a different perspective. In the garden of Eden, the narrator explains, "Yahweh Elohim took the man and put him in the garden

---

68. Cartledge, *Vows*, 34–35.
69. Cartledge, *Vows*, 34–35.
70. See Arnold, *Genesis*, 116.
71. Leveen, *Memory*, 172.

of Eden to work it and keep it" (Gen. 2:15), but presumably before the man has any chance to begin farming this orchard, Yahweh Elohim says just three verses later "It is not good for the man to be alone. I will make him *a helper as his partner* ['ēzer kənegdô]" (Gen. 2:18). The proximity of vv. 15 and 18 means that burden of proof rests on anyone who attempts to argue that Yahweh Elohim does not envision the woman as an equal partner in working and keeping the garden. Elsewhere, God is called a "helper" ('ōzēr, e.g., Ps. 118:7), but God is omnipotent (function) and is of infinite worth (value), so it is a non sequitur to argue that the woman in the Gen. 2 narrative is not equal to the man in both value and function.[72] This stands in contrast to the patriarchalism that governs other ANE creation stories.[73]

This original and good creation order of the male-female relationship is tragically fractured in Gen. 3. In response to the rebellion of the first humans in the garden, Yahweh Elohim curses the serpent, woman, and man (Gen. 3:14–19). The narrator recounts: "To the woman he [Yahweh Elohim] said, 'I will intensify your pain in bearing children. In pain you will have children. Your desire will be for your husband, but he will rule over you'" (Gen. 3:16). I do not want to dive into the complementarian-versus-egalitarian debate here, but I would like hopefully to find common interpretive ground relating to the man's actions toward the woman. Although different verbal stems are used, it is possible that "and he will rule over you" (*mšl in 3:16) could allude to "so they may rule over" (*rdh in 1:26), indicating that Elohim's good design of his male and female image bearers ruling over the animals now has been distorted to include the man ruling over the woman. In any case, *as a part of the divine curses*, "and he shall rule over you" (3:16) reflects a new world that is fractured in the way men relate to women, husbands relate to their wives, and—we can infer—fathers relate to their daughters. In a healthy biblical theology, male dominance over women (à la Gen. 3:16) is a curse resulting from the fall and is one of the reasons for creation's groaning (Rom. 8:19–23). In the end, the curse of male dominance will be overturned in the consummation of all things (Rev. 22:3). God's image bearers with glorified physical bodies "will neither marry nor be given in marriage" but will be "like the angels of heaven" (Matt. 22:30 NIV), and they will together delight in the worship of the slaughtered Lamb, the King from the tribe of Judah, the Lord Jesus Christ.

Until that day, we must extend Francis Schaeffer's question: "How should we then live *now in a post-Genesis 3:16 world*?"[74] It is a deeply personal and many times painful experience for women to hear a myopic man attempt to answer this question, and this is not the place for directing families and

---

72. Arnold, *Genesis*, 60; similarly, Ashley, *Numbers*, 578.
73. Trible, "Depatriarchalizing," 30–48; cited by Arnold, *Genesis*, 59.
74. Schaeffer, *How Should We Then Live?*

churches in how to work this out. I want only to offer a few thoughts on the enduring significance of Num. 30 for Jews and Christians today.

First, the patriarchal culture of Num. 30 should not be seen simply as Yahweh enforcing his curse, "He shall rule over you" (Gen. 3:16), but neither should it be seen as disconnected from the fall of Gen. 3. Before discussing Israel's patriarchal, patrilineal, and patrilocal culture, Sandra Richter incisively challenges her readers: "God did not *canonize* Israel's culture."[75] We must not *canonize the patriarchy* of Num. 30 because it reflects an Israelite society within the cursed world of Gen. 3:16. Until God fully redeems his image bearers in the new creation (Rev. 21–22), we repeatedly find that he accommodates his ideal vision of Gen. 1–2 to husband-wife and father-daughter relationships in a world disordered by sin.[76]

Second, although God in Num. 30 condescends from his ideal, God also elevates Israel to something closer to his ideal than that reflected in the surrounding ANE cultures.[77] There are no close ANE parallels to the instructions of Num. 30, although as in Num. 30, ANE women were under the authority of their deity and their husband. This New Hittite story remarks about the ideal woman: "She is dependent on the authority of the god. She stands in woman's subordination, and she does not disobey (her) husband's word."[78] Within this patriarchal world, Num. 30 opens strikingly by holding Israel's men accountable to their word (v. 2 [3]) and closes by forcing them, if they do not speak in time, to bear the full weight of their wife's vow or oath decision (v. 15 [16]). From this we perceive that "vows imply the active presence of God in the life of people. . . . Ancient Israel expected God to be faithful to the contract. They also held themselves accountable."[79] Furthermore, Num. 30 orients Israel's men to protect the women under their authority. As Cartledge acknowledges, "A vow to Yahweh was considered to be a serious matter, not to be made rashly (Prov. 20.25),"[80] and this seriousness is apparent in the recurring phrase "and Yahweh will release her from it" (vv. 5, 8, 12 [6, 9, 13]). The implication is that the father or husband of v. 2 [3] is responsible to guard his unmarried daughter or wife from making vows or oaths that result in her "affliction" (v. 13 [14]) or that of others. In the Damascus Document (before 66 BCE), the Qumran scribes interpret Num. 30 as preventing women from violating the Torah, Israel's covenant terms with Yahweh, which could result not only in her own affliction but in that of the whole community (CD XVI, 10–12).[81] In the HB, the God-fearing husband uses his power to stop

---

75. Richter, *Epic of Eden*, 23.
76. See Goldingay, *Models for Interpretation*, 116; Brauch, *Abusing Scripture*, 247–49.
77. See Webb, *Slaves, Women, and Homosexuals*.
78. "The Sun God and the Cow," COS 1.59:156.
79. Dozeman, "Numbers," 236.
80. Cartledge, *Vows*, 13.
81. Noted by Staubli, *Levitikus, Numeri*, 327.

women and men in his household from the dangerous folly of making vows to other deities, like the Queen of Heaven (Jer. 44:24–25); vowing to Yahweh but offering him defective sacrifices (Mal. 1:14); and using prostitution money to fulfill one's vows to Yahweh (Deut. 23:19; Prov. 7:14).[82]

In sum, in a post-Gen. 3:16 male-dominant world, the enduring and redemptive ethic of Num. 30 is an invitation to males to employ their power to protect the women entrusted to them by Yahweh. Any man can distort Num. 30 to his own destruction (à la 2 Pet. 3:16), but he can also use his power self-sacrificially to love and safeguard the women of his household, as the apostle Paul urges: "Husbands, love your wives, as Christ loved the church and gave himself up for her," and "Fathers, do not provoke your children to anger, but bring them up in the discipline and instruction of the Lord" (Eph. 5:25; 6:4).

82. Levine, *Numbers*, 2:435.

28

War with Midian and Its Aftermath

(31:1–54)

∽∾ ꞏ ∾∽

Overview

Israel's ongoing encampment in the desert valleys of Moab since Num. 22:1 forges a bridge between the exodus generation (Num. 1–25*) and the new generation (Num. 26–36*). Consequently, although the new generation was not indicted for the apostasy with the Baal of Peor and Moabite women, the sins of their fathers in Moab endure not only in their living memory but also in Yahweh's unsatisfied vengeance. The plague of divine judgment killed 24,000 Israelites for their sin (25:8–9), but at that time Yahweh also demanded that Israel "destroy" the Midianites, a metonym for the Moabites (25:16–18). Although not fundamentally culpable, the second generation must now carry out these orders, which Yahweh reiterates as an act of double vengeance, both Israel's (v. 2) and Yahweh's (v. 3).[1] The placement of chap. 31 after the sacrificial calendar (chaps. 28–29) and vows to Yahweh (chap. 30) is sensible for at least four reasons considered below.[2]

---

1. Gray (*Numbers*, 418–19) regards Num. 31 as a late addition to P, while Noth (*Numbers*, 229) sees it as a post-Priestly supplement to the entire Pentateuch. Levine (*Numbers*, 2:445) sees Num. 31 as P filling the gap of JE, which offered no accounts of hostile relations with the Midianites (cf. Num. 22–24). For Knohl (*Sanctuary*, 96–98), Num. 25 and 31 were post-P contributions specifically of H; for Schmidt (*Numeri*, 186) and Scharbert (*Numeri*, 121), Num. 31 depends on Num. 25 and must be assigned to a final Pentateuch redaction. Achenbach (*Vollendung*, 615–22) sees Num. 31 as a midrash concerning the Torah-based Yahweh war against Midian incorporated in the last phase of the theocratic revision of the Torah.

2. See the "Implications" essay below, "War Tribute in the ANE and Numbers 31."

As a unit of discourse, the battle report[3] of chap. 31 can be broken down into six subunits:

1. Yahweh commands vengeance against the Midianites, and Israel's warriors kill Midian's men (vv. 1–12).
2. Moses in anger demands the execution of the nonvirgin women and purification of all involved (vv. 13–20).
3. Eleazar further instructs purification procedures (vv. 21–24).
4. Yahweh orders the division of the war spoils (vv. 25–31).
5. The narrator enumerates the war spoils (vv. 32–47).
6. The chieftains offer their gold and ornamental tribute to Yahweh (vv. 48–54).[4]

Translation

[1]Then Yahweh spoke to Moses:[5] [2]"Take the Israelites' vengeance on the Midianites[6]—after that you will be gathered to your people."[7] [3]So Moses said to the people:[8] "Arm some of your men to go to war against the Midianites[9] and to execute Yahweh's vengeance on Midian. [4]Send into battle a thousand men from every tribe, from all Israel's tribes."[10] [5]So from Israel's thousands, twelve thousand armed for battle, a thousand from every tribe, were supplied. [6]Moses sent them into battle, a thousand from every tribe, with Phinehas, son of Eleazar[11] the

---

3. Knierim and Coats, *Numbers*, 297.

4. Contra Milgrom (*Numbers*, 491–92) and Staubli (*Levitikus, Numeri*, 331), vv. 48–54 can hardly be called a battlefront flashback that chiastically correlates with vv. 1–12; see the critique by W. Lee (*Migratory Campaign*, 191–92), who instead sees a bipartite structure of the battle (vv. 1–12) and its aftermath (vv. 13–54) with three subsections (vv. 13–24, 25–47, 48–54). Seebass (*Numeri*, 3:209–318) perceives six sections: vv. 1–12, 13–18, 19–24, 25–31, 32–47, 48–54.

5. Regarding the colon for "saying" here and in vv. 3 and 25, see the third translation note on 1:1.

6. Formally, "Avenge the vengeance of the Israelites from the Midianites." Many versions render the gen. as a *l* of advantage, "Take vengeance *for* the Israelites," but this would be atypical. A possessive gen. is more probable, "Take *the Israelites' vengeance* [*nəqōm niqmat bənê yiśrāʾēl*] on the Midianites," which is how most versions rightly, but inconsistently, render the parallel in v. 3, "execute *Yahweh's vengeance* [*nqmt-yhwh*]" (*GBHS* §2.2.1). The cognate construction has no additional semantic value (*BHRG* §33.3[5]), but it is noteworthy that this is the only place in Numbers (31:2–3) where either this verb (**nqm*, avenge, take vengeance; 35× in the OT) or noun (*nəqāmâ*, vengeance; 27× in the OT) appear (see *DCH* 5:751, 753).

7. Formally, "your peoples," which SP and LXX[ed] adjust to "your people."

8. 4Q27 has "So Moses said to *the Israelites*."

9. Formally, "men for battle, and they will be against Midian."

10. The obj. is fronted as the focused constituent: "*A thousand men from every tribe, from all Israel's tribes* send into battle" (*BHRG* §47.2.1[2ab]).

11. LXX[ed] adds "Eleazar *son of Aaron* the priest."

priest, who was in charge of the sanctuary's articles and the trumpets for signaling.[12] **7**They fought against the Midianites, as Yahweh had commanded Moses, and they killed every man.[13] **8**They killed the Midianite kings[14]—in addition to others slain by them—Evi, Rekem, Zur, Hur, and Reba, the five Midianite kings. They also killed Beor's son Balaam with the sword.[15] **9**The Israelites captured the Midianite women with their children,[16] and plundered all their animals, all their cattle, and all their wealth.[17] **10**They burned[18] all their towns where they settled and all their enclosures.[19] **11**They took all the plunder and spoils, both people and animals. **12**They brought the captives and the spoils and the plunder to Moses, Eleazar the priest, and the Israelite community,[20] to the camp in the desert valleys of Moab, along the Jordan River across from Jericho.

12. Numbers presents the Levites' "cultic service" (*ṣābā'*, 6× in Num. 4) as analogous to the nonpriestly Israelites' "military service" (noun *ṣābā'*, 36× in Num. 1–2). Here Phinehas is presented as Yahweh's *priestly warrior*, transporting the cultic accoutrements into the war. The text can also be read: "Moses sent them *into battle* [*laṣṣābā'*], a thousand from every tribe, with Phinehas, son of Eleazar the priest, *into battle* [*laṣṣābā'*], and the sanctuary's articles and the trumpets for signaling *were in his hand/charge* [*bəyādô*]" (similarly ESV).

13. Formally, "every male" (*kol-zākār*; ESV, NJPS, NET), but "every man" (NIV, NLT; see 31:7) is preferred for clarity, because (1) the "women and *their little ones* [*ṭap*]" includes male children and younger men, who have also been spared, as 31:17 reveals (see the first translation note on 31:9); and (2) "every male" (*kol-zākār*) can also include male animals, which must be killed according to Deuteronomy (13:15; 20:16) but in this scene have been spared (Num. 31:9, 11).

14. The obj. is fronted as the focused constituent: "*And the Midianite kings* they killed" (*BHRG* §47.2.1[2ab]).

15. The obj. is fronted as the focused constituent: "*And Beor's son Balaam* they killed with the sword" (*BHRG* §47.2.1[2ab]).

16. *Ṭap* can mean "little ones" or "little children" (*HALOT* 1:378, gloss 1; NET, ESV), but in the context of Num. 1 and 31 it refers more broadly to "children" (*DCH* 3:372; NIV, NLT, NJPS), spanning from infant boys with their mothers (v. 9) to young Moabite men who had not gone out to fight the Israelites (vv. 7–8). In Israel, young men under 20 were not yet eligible for military service (Num. 1).

17. The obj. is fronted as the focused constituent: "*And all their animals, all their cattle, and all their wealth* they plundered" (*BHRG* §47.2.1[2ab]). On *bəhēmâ* as "animals" (not *beasts* of burden or draft animals) and *miqneh* as "livestock" (not *animals* more broadly or *flocks* more narrowly) here and Gen. 34, 36, and Num. 31, 32, see Mastin, "*Miqneh* and *Bᵉhēmâ*," 491–515. The last category that they took, the noun *ḥayil*, has a broad range of meanings—faculty, power, army, upper class of a city—but here means "goods" (many versions) or "wealth, property" (*HALOT* 1:311–12, gloss 2). I prefer the rendering "wealth," since the Israelite soldiers would have selectively taken the most valuable items, whereas "goods" could include less valuable material culture, and "property" could be misunderstood today as real estate.

18. Formally, "they burned with fire."

19. The obj. is fronted as the focused constituent: "*And all their towns where they settled and all their enclosures* they burned with fire" (*BHRG* §47.2.1[2ab]). On the rare term "enclosures" (**ṭîrâ*), see P. Guillaume, *Land*, 131n17.

20. Likely assimilating to common usage, SP reads "and the *whole* Israelite community" (as, e.g., in 25:6; 27:19, 20, 22; 31:27).

[13]Moses, Eleazar the priest, and all the chieftains of the community went out[21] to meet them outside the camp. [14]But Moses was angry with the military officers,[22] the commanders over thousands and commanders over hundreds, who had come from service in the war. [15]Moses said to them, "Have you let all the women live?[23] [16]These women, on Balaam's counsel,[24] caused the Israelites to be unfaithful to Yahweh[25] in the matter of Peor, so that the plague came among the community of Yahweh! [17]So now, kill every boy, and kill every woman who has had sex with a man.[26] [18]But all the young women who have not had sex with a man, keep alive for yourselves.[27] [19]As for you all, anyone who has killed someone or touched a corpse must remain outside the camp for seven days.[28] You and your captives must purify yourselves[29] on the third day and on the seventh day. [20]You must purify every garment and everything made of leather, everything made of goat's hair, and everything made of wood."[30]

[21]Then Eleazar the priest said to the men of war who had gone into battle, "This is the statute of the law that Yahweh commanded Moses: [22]'Only the gold, the silver, the bronze, the iron, the tin, and the lead,

21. I prefer the SP/LXX[ed] reading, with a sg. verb and compound subject: formally, "Moses *went out* [*wyṣ'* SP; *Kai exēlthen* LXX[ed]], as well as Eleazar the priest and all the chieftains of the community, to meet" (*BHRG* §35[9]; see the second translation note on 32:25).

22. Formally, "those appointed over the army."

23. A resultative piel, meaning, "Have you preserved every female?" (*haḥiyyîtem kol-nəqēbâ*; *GBHS* §3.1.3a). Soon after this, we learn that Moses does allow female virgins, young women, and girls to live (31:18).

24. A subjective gen. and possibly a causal *b*, meaning, "These women, *because of the word that Balaam spoke* [*bidbar bil'ām*], caused the Israelites to be unfaithful" (*GBHS* §2.2.3, §4.1.5f).

25. "To be unfaithful to Yahweh" (*limsār-ma'al byhwh*, v. 16) occurs only here and in Num. 5, which prohibits unfaithfulness to Yahweh or to one's husband (**m'l* with cognate *ma'al* in 5:6, 12, 27). Since it does not appear in the Num. 25 episode to which it refers, Num. 31 exhibits a theological exegesis of the sin with the Moabite women and their gods as a fundamental breach of Israel's covenant with Yahweh (see Knohl, *Sanctuary*, 109n165, 184).

26. A fronted obj. as the focused constituent: "*And every woman who has known a man by lying with a male* kill" (*BHRG* §47.2.1[2ab]).

27. Beginning with a disjunctive *wa* clause, in contrast to v. 17, the obj. here again is fronted as the focused constituent: "*But all of the children (girls) among the women who have not known the bed/lying of a male* keep alive for yourselves" (*BHRG* §47.2.1[2ab]).

28. The impv. is directed to the whole Israelite community (pl., "And you all must remain outside," *wə'attem ḥānû*) but is then restricted to individuals, anyone who has killed or touched a corpse.

29. This hithpael impv. conveys a resultative force, meaning, "You and your captives must put yourselves into a pure state" (*tiṭḥaṭṭə'û . . . 'attem ûšəbîkem*; *GBHS* §3.1.5, §3.1.3a). "And your captives" is an expanded subject of the reflexive verb, not a direct obj., as many versions wrongly imply: "Purify yourselves and (purify) your captives."

30. The obj. is fronted as the focused constituent: "*Both every garment and everything made of leather, everything made of goat's hair, and everything made of wood* you must purify" (*BHRG* §47.2.1[2ab]).

23everything that can withstand the fire,[31] you must pass through the fire, and it will be clean,[32] but it must still be purified with the purifying water.[33] Anything that cannot withstand the fire you must pass through the water.[34] **24**You must wash your clothes on the seventh day, then you will be clean, and afterward you may enter the camp.'"

25Then[35] Yahweh said to Moses: **26**"You and Eleazar the priest and the community's family leaders, count the plunder that was captured,[36] both people and animals. **27**Divide the plunder between the war captors[37] who went out to battle and the whole community. **28**You must exact[38] a share[39] for Yahweh from the warriors who went out to battle: one life out of five hundred, from the people, the cattle, the donkeys, and the sheep.[40] **29**Take it from their half and give it to Eleazar the priest as an offering of tribute to Yahweh. **30**But from the Israelites' half[41] take

31. Formally, "Everything that enters into the fire."

32. A weqatal expresses the result of obedience: "everything that can withstand the fire *you must pass through the fire* [*taʿăbîrû bāʾēš*], *and (as a result) it will be clean* [*wəṭāhēr*]" (*GBHS* §3.5.2b).

33. Formally, "waters of impurity" (*mê niddâ*), which I understand as an instrumental *b* and gen. of purpose, "*by means of* waters *intended for removing* impurity" (*bəmê niddâ*). See the second translation note on 19:9.

34. The result clause in v. 23b, which here again we might infer, is supplied by 4Q27: "Anything that cannot withstand the fire you must pass through the water]s for purification [and it will be clean]" (. . .] *y ndh* [*wṭhwr yhyh*] ≈ LXX^mss; see Ulrich, *Qumran*, 163).

35. After 31:24, the rest of the line in 4Q27 (col. XXVI) is broken but likely blank, and the next line that contains vv. 25–26aα—"Then Yahweh said . . . people and animals" (excluding at the end in Hb. "You and Eleazar . . .")—is written in red ink, denoting the scribal view that v. 25 introduces the next unit of discourse (Ulrich, *Qumran*, 162).

36. Formally, "lift the head of the war spoils of the captives."

37. A substantival ptc. and objective gen., meaning "those who capture/seize the war" (*tōpəśê hammilḥāmâ*; *IBHS* §37.1c; *GBHS* §2.2.4).

38. A contextual rendering of the hiphil weqatal command from *rwm: "*You must raise* [*wahărēmōtā*] a tribute" (*DCH* 7:445, gloss 8; *GBHS* §3.5.2c).

39. "Share" (*mekes*) occurs 6× in the OT, all here in Num. 31 (vv. 28, 37, 38, 39, 40, 41). Many translate it "tribute," which is fine (*DCH* 5:270), but I prefer "share" (NLT). First, it is distinct from its improper synonym *tərûmâ* (tribute; 18× in Num. 5, 6, 15, 18, and in 31:29, 41, 52), with "share" as the source and "tribute" as the product; see, for example, "exact a *share* [*mekes*] for Yahweh" (v. 28), which then "you must give to Eleazar the priest *as an offering of tribute* [*tərûmat*] to Yahweh" (v. 29; see the translation note on 5:9). This indicates that the otherwise redundant gen. in v. 41 expresses purpose: "Moses gave *the share as Yahweh's tribute offering* [*mekes tərûmat yhwh*]" (*GBHS* §2.2.8). Second, an Akkadian cognate refers to a "share of the yield of a field" or "customs dues," that is, a tax on imports ("*miksu*," *CAD* 10.2:63–65; so also Hb. *mekes* is an i-class segholate: see *miksām*, "their share," in vv. 38, 39, 40). Possibly one could think of the *mekes* for Yahweh as an import tax on the foreign (Moabite) spoils, as similarly *miksu* in an Old Babylonian text refers to "the share of the [customs] toll to be paid by the individual persons, delivered to the temple of Ningal" (*CAD* 10.2:65, gloss 2).

40. Probably influenced by 31:30, SP adds "and the sheep *and from every animal*," whereas LXX^ed adds "and from the goats."

41. The fronted constituent is reactivated in contrast to the portion that Yahweh receives as his tribute in v. 19: "Take it from their half . . . as an offering of tribute to Yahweh. *But from the Israelites' half* take . . ." (*BHRG* §47.2.1[1c]).

one portion out of fifty, from the people, the cattle, the donkeys, and the sheep[42]—from every animal—and give them to the Levites who are responsible for the care[43] of Yahweh's dwelling place." [31]Moses and Eleazar the priest did as Yahweh had commanded Moses.

[32]The spoil that remained[44] from the plunder that the troops[45] had taken was 675,000 sheep, [33]72,000 cattle, [34]61,000 donkeys, [35]and as for people,[46] 32,000 young women who had never had sex with a man. [36]The half share of those who went to war numbered[47] 337,500 sheep, [37]and[48] Yahweh's share from the sheep was 675. [38]There were 36,000 cattle, of which Yahweh's share was 72. [39]There were 30,500 donkeys, of which Yahweh's share was 61. [40]There were 16,000 people, of which Yahweh's share was 32 people. [41]Moses gave the share as Yahweh's tribute offering to Eleazar the priest, as Yahweh had commanded Moses. [42]From the Israelites' half, which Moses had separated from the warriors[49]—[43]from the community's half—there were 337,500 sheep, [44]36,000 cattle, [45]30,500 donkeys, [46]and 16,000 people. [47]From the Israelites' half Moses took one of every fifty people and animals and gave them to the Levites who were responsible for the care of Yahweh's dwelling place, just as Yahweh had commanded Moses.

[48]Then[50] the officers[51] who were over the thousands of the army,[52] the commanders of thousands and the commanders of hundreds,[53] approached Moses [49]and said to him,[54] "Your servants have counted the men who were in the battle, who were under our authority,[55] and not

---

42. 4Q27 has an inverted order: "and from the ca]ttle[,]from[ ]the[she]ep, from the donkeys" (≈ LXX[ed]); later the order is sheep, cattle, donkeys (vv. 37, 38, 39).

43. Formally, "those who guard the guarded things."

44. LXX[ed] conflates the noun and appositional phrase: "*And the abundance* of the plunder."

45. Formally, "the people of the army."

46. Formally, "and a life/soul of people."

47. Here the Hb. copula is used: "*were (in) number [wattəhî . . . mispar]*."

48. After 31:36, the rest of the line in 4Q27 (col. XXVI) is blank, and the next line that contains vv. 37–38a—"Then they approached, the officers . . . who came"—is written in red ink, denoting the scribal view that vv. 37–38a introduce the next unit of discourse (Ulrich, *Qumran*, 163). This is a rare instance in which I do not follow (by indenting) the ancient scribe's paragraph.

49. Formally, "the men who had gone to war."

50. After 31:47, the rest of the line in 4Q27 (col. XXVII) is blank, and the next line that contains most of 31:48—"Then they approached, the officers . . . who came"—is written in red ink, denoting the scribal view that v. 48 introduces the next unit of discourse (Ulrich, *Qumran*, 163).

51. Formally, "the ones who were appointed" (*happəqudîm*). 4Q27 and LXX[ed] include "Then *all* the officers," which correlates with the extensive nature of their census (v. 49) and of the tribute they brought to Yahweh (v. 52).

52. Instead of the more obvious selection of *'al* (over), here the choice of *l* could indicate specification or possession, but by implication, authority: "the officers who were *in relation to/belonged to* the thousands of the army" (*GBHS* §4.1.10h, f).

53. Probably to assimilate to v. 14, 4Q27 adds "commanders over hundreds *of those who had come from service in the war.*"

54. Hb. restates the name "Moses" (*mōšeh*).

55. Formally, "who were in our hand."

one of us is missing. **50**And we have brought Yahweh's offering, what each of us found:[56] gold ornaments, armlets and bracelets, signet rings, earrings, and necklaces,[57] to make atonement for ourselves before Yahweh."[58] **51**Moses and Eleazar the priest received[59] the gold from them, all in the form of crafted articles. **52**All[60] the gold of the tribute that they offered up to Yahweh, from the commanders of thousands and the commanders of hundreds, weighed 16,750 shekels.[61] **53**The soldiers had all taken plunder for themselves. **54**So Moses and Eleazar the priest received the gold from the commanders of thousands and of hundreds and brought it into the meeting tent as a memorial for the Israelites before Yahweh.[62]

56. Formally, "each what he has found."

57. In the ANE, ornaments and jewelry were worn by women and men for various reasons: as a sign of one's status and affluence, as a form of currency, and for religious uses, such as adorning one's neck with an amulet or charm having apotropaic power to avert evil spirits (King and Stager, *Life*, 276). In v. 50, the placement of the conjunctions may have been to couple related types of jewelry, "armlets *and* [*wə*] bracelets, signet rings, earrings *and* [*lə*] necklaces" (4Q27 [broken] and LXX^ed probably add "and" to every element).

58. The purpose inf. *ləkappēr* (to make atonement; MT SP ≈ *exilasasthai* LXX^ed) gives the desired end for which the officers brought Yahweh's offering, whereas the broken 4Q27 appears to contain a weqatal (*wkp*[*r*]), likely implying Eleazar as their priestly intermediary (v. 41): "*so that he will* make atonement" (probably not "he would/used to make atonement," *IBHS* §32.2.3e). In the Priestly texts of the Pentateuch, the **kpr* piel (to atone) typically refers to the act of purging or removing sin, guilt, or ritual impurity (see the translation note on 5:8, and "to make expiation [for]" in *DCH* 4:455; also Büchner, "Appeasing God," 237–60). The gold-jewelry tribute to Yahweh (vv. 48–54) was at least thought to effect atonement without an animal blood sacrifice (v. 50). Other nonsacrificial means of atonement in the Pentateuch include money from the Israelite men older than 20 as a census tax (Exod. 30:15–16), Moses's intercessory prayer (Exod. 32:30), a grain offering from the poor (Lev. 5:13), the scapegoat of Yom Kippur (the Day of Atonement; Lev. 16:10), and incense on burning coals brought into the Israelite community (Num. 16:46–47). It is possible to perceive human sacrifice as the means of atonement in at least two texts: Phinehas's spearing of the Israelite man and Midianite woman while they were having sex (Num. 25:7–8, 13); and capital punishment, a human blood sacrifice, for murder, human bloodshed (Num. 35:33). Other examples include Deut. 21:4, 8 (by merely breaking the neck of a cow?) and 32:43 (by war?).

59. Formally, "took" (*wayyiqqaḥ*), but "received" represents the textual focus on the gift and givers, who had announced "We have brought Yahweh's offering" (v. 50).

60. SP and MT^mss omit "all," perhaps because "all" might imply that there was other gold not offered to Yahweh.

61. Approximately equal to the weight of 420 pounds of gold. Shekels of precious metals were weighed using silver weights, with one shekel (of silver) weighing 11.4 grams (190,950 grams = 420 lbs.; see the fourth translation note on 3:47). Contra Ashley (*Numbers*, 601), who inflates this number to 600 pounds of gold.

62. A closing *l* of advantage and *lipnê* of location, so that this plundered gold, now in Yahweh's meeting tent, is to be a historic reminder of this occasion, "*to*/*for the benefit of* the Israelites (*stationed*) *in the presence of* Yahweh" (*libnê-yiśrā'ēl lipnê yhwh*; *GBHS* §4.1.10e.1, §4.1.12a).

Interpretation

31:1–12. Through Moses, Yahweh commands the Israelites to take vengeance on the Midianites, and the Israelite warriors respond by killing all the Midianite men. This will be Moses's final battle before he is "gathered to his people," a euphemism for his death, which fulfills Yahweh's word to him (27:13) and echoes the death of his brother Aaron (v. 2; cf. Num. 20:24, 26; 27:13). The command to "take the Israelites' vengeance on the Midianites" (v. 2; see the first translation note there) is revoiced metonymically as "execute Yahweh's vengeance on Midian" (v. 3), which reveals the interrelationship of Yahweh and his covenant people. Although the initial sin at Peor was with the Moabite women (25:1–5), the grotesque scene of infidelity with the Midianite woman, Cozbi, ensued (25:6–15), and Yahweh demands that Israel destroy the Midianites (25:16–18). The Midianites and Moabites are distinct people groups in Transjordan (see 22:4, 7),[63] but in both Num. 25:16–18 and Num. 31 it appears that Midian functions as a surrogate for the original offenders, the Moabite women.[64] With five chapters in between, the editors envision Num. 31 as returning to and finally enacting Yahweh's orders to kill the Midianites for deceiving the Israelites to commit apostasy (25:16–18).[65]

Moses must order 12,000 men, 1,000 from every tribe, to execute Yahweh's marching orders (vv. 4–5; see the translation note on v. 4).[66] Assuming the second census of Num. 26, the twelve fighting tribes include Manasseh and Ephraim separately (26:28–37), but exclude Levi (26:57–62). Of Levi, however, Eleazar's son Phinehas is to oversee the transport of the dwelling place sancta and trumpets for signaling the call to war (v. 6; see the second translation note there).[67] The sancta include the ark (10:35–36) and perhaps the high priest's

---

63. Biblical Midian has come to be associated with Qurayya pottery and culture in Northwest Arabia (Graf, "Arabia," 433–34), while the Moabites were thought to be linked in LBA–Iron I to Dibon (modern Dhiban, east of the Dead Sea and south of Amman) and Butartu (Rabbah/Rabbat, modern Amman) and later to Madaba (Medeba) and other Transjordan towns under King Mesha's control (Burnett, "Transjordan," 322–25).

64. Gafney, "Numbers 25:1–18," 193. Levine (*Numbers*, 2:445) offers the reasonable explanation that the Priestly authors augmented the Baal of Peor episode involving the Moabite women (25:1–5) with Midianite perpetrators (25:6–15) and a divine call to destroy them (25:16–18), and now P presents the fulfillment of their destruction in Num. 31.

65. The divine orders in 31:2 repetitively resume those in 25:16–18: Gray, *Numbers*, 420; Olson, *Death of the Old*, 182–83; Milgrom, *Numbers*, 255; cf. Kuhl, "Die 'Wiederaufnahme,'" 1–11.

66. Milgrom (*Numbers*, 256) notes other attestations of 12,000 troops: Solomon's cavalry (1 Kings 10:26); Ahithophel advises Absolom to select this number to chase David (2 Sam. 17:1); and based on our verse, the Temple Scroll orders the king to choose 12,000 (i.e., 1,000 from each tribe) to function as his bodyguard (11Q19 LVII, 9–11).

67. In Qumran's War Scroll (1QM, ca. mid-first cent. BCE to early first cent. CE), the priesthood plays a significantly increased military role (Milgrom, *Numbers*, 257, 372–73).

garments, golden frontlet, or Urim and Thummim.[68] Lugging these cultic objects through the battlefield ensures Yahweh's presence with Israel in the fight.[69] Armies in the ANE included priests and diviners (e.g., Mari archives), prophets (2 Kings 3), and transportable sacra (e.g., Shalmaneser III's annals), so that the king and his military could consult their deities in the battle and invoke them to bring about the victory.[70] So why did Yahweh choose Phinehas for this crucial task of superintending the sacra? While any surviving sons or grandsons of Aaron could blow the trumpets at war (10:9), Eleazar, not Ithamar, was appointed over the entire sanctuary, its furnishings, and the Levite stewards (3:32; 4:16). Commander Joshua would also be subject to Eleazar's military guidance (27:21). Now Yahweh gives Phinehas, not his father the high priest, the esteemed military position, possibly for three reasons. First, Eleazar needs to continue his high-priestly service in the tent (3:4; 20:28). Second, as high priest, Eleazar must avoid touching a corpse altogether, an obvious problem in warfare (Lev. 21:10–12).[71] Third, it was Phinehas who, in his zeal for Yahweh, averted Yahweh's anger against the Israelites who were unfaithful with the Baal of Peor (Num. 25:7, 11; cf. Josh. 22:13–32).

The subunit of vv. 5–12 is framed by Moses's agency: he sends the troops into battle (vv. 5–6), then with Eleazar and the chieftains he meets the troops coming from the battle with their spoils (v. 13). In the center, the Israelites, in obedience to Yahweh, fight the Midianites (v. 7), which the narrator then in vv. 8–12 elucidates with a succession of foregrounded (primary) events and fronted (emphasized) conquered entities.[72] They kill every man,[73] the five Midianite kings, and Beor's son Balaam (vv. 7–8; see the translation notes there), capture the Midianite women and their children, plunder their livestock and wealth (v. 9; see the translation notes there), burn all their settlements and enclosures (v. 10; see the translation notes there), and carry all the war spoils, people, and animals, to Moses, Eleazar the priest, and the Israelite community encamped in the desert valleys of Moab (vv. 11–12). Israel's relatively small army of twelve thousand suffers no casualties.[74] The death

---

68. Milgrom, *Numbers*, 257.

69. Leveen, *Memory*, 52.

70. Walton and Matthews, *Genesis–Deuteronomy*, 210.

71. Milgrom, *Numbers*, 256, following Ramban (Nachmanides, 13th cent. CE).

72. In vv. 7–12, the five Hb. wayyiqtol verbs foreground the main events of the story, while the deviations of the perfective qatal verbs are due to word order—fronting the objects of those killed, the goods plundered, and towns and encampments burned (vv. 8 [2×], 9, 10); see J. Cook, "*Wayyiqtol* and *Weqatal*," 261–64.

73. Kilchör (*Mosetora*, 241) notes the thematic proximity of killing every male in vv. 7, 14–18 with 21:1–3; Deut. 20:13, 16–18 (he cites other texts that to me are not clearly proximate). The language can be understood as hyperbolic, which would explain how the Midianites arise later as a foe in Gideon's day (Judg. 6–8; so de Vaulx, *Nombres*, 355; cf. Ashley, *Numbers*, 589).

74. Milgrom, *Numbers*, 255.

notice of Beor's son Balaam (v. 8)[75] will disappoint readers who entertained
the possibility that Balaam, nowhere to be found in the Baal of Peor scene
(Num. 25), had become a non-Israelite devotee of Yahweh (cf. Num. 15:13–15;
Exod. 12:48–49).[76] After all, Balaam confessed his sin to the angel of Yahweh
(22:34), received visions from the Almighty, and felt compelled to speak only
what Yahweh told him (chaps. 22–24), prepared to sacrifice to God (23:4),
repeatedly blessed Yahweh's blessed people, echoing the Abrahamic promise
(i.e., 23:11, 20; 24:9–10; Gen. 12:3), fell flat on the ground in a posture of
reverence or worship (24:4, 16), and had a high view of Yahweh (23:21–22).
But, sadly, the final word of Balaam's legacy is a warning of judgment: "The
death of the once obedient messenger of God, Balaam, in Num. 31 reminds
the new generation that God is a jealous God who will not allow disobedience
to go unpunished" (cf. 2 Pet. 2:15–16; Jude 11; Rev. 2:14).[77]

31:13–20. Moses and the leaders meet the chieftains outside the camp
(v. 13), preempting any public reception and celebration by the civilian families inside the camp, which early readers would have expected of triumphal
processions in the ANE (1 Sam. 18:6–7; 2 Chron. 20:27–28; cf. Exod. 15).[78]
Also, it was conventional for kings, upon returning home, to erect a monument to commemorate their victory (cf. Exod. 17:15; 1 Sam. 7:12; 15:12).[79]
Later Moses and Eleazar demand ritual purification before the troops reenter the camp (vv. 19–20, 21–24), but here the lack of a welcome home
and a monument at least creates curiosity about what Moses is thinking
when he exits to meet the troops outside the camp (see the translation note
on v. 13).[80] The narrator immediately reveals (v. 14) that Moses is irate that

---

75. Alongside 31:8, see Josh. 13:20, which Blum (*Komposition des Pentateuch*, 270) argues
marks the Priestly link between Josh. 13 and texts at the end of Numbers like Num. 31 (cf.
Robker, "Balaam Narrative," 352–54). It is conventional to think of the negative death notice
of Balaam in v. 8 (also v. 16) as reflecting a later Priestly perspective to the non-Priestly Num.
22–24*: Cross, *Canaanite Myth*, 318; Budd, *Numbers*, 350; Frevel, "Book of Numbers," 32;
Robker, "Balaam Narrative," 350, 355.

76. With Cross (*Epic to Canon*, 61), who concludes that in the JE (non-P) narrative, Num.
22–24, "Balaam is treated in effect as a convert."

77. Olson, *Death of the Old*, 157–63, esp. 162. Dozeman ("Numbers," 246) concludes, "The
priestly writers [Num. 31] are much less generous about granting Balaam an authentic relationship with God outside of the Israelite cult than were the non-Priestly writers [Num. 22–24]."
This may be true of the Priestly writers, but the H Priestly writers, like D, were arguably open
to non-Israelite Yahweh worshipers (Awabdy, *Immigrants*, 205–7, 214–26). The judgment and
death of Balaam became a recurring warning to God's people: Deut. 23:4–5 (Neh. 13:2); Josh.
13:22; 24:9–10; Mic. 6:5; 2 Pet. 2:15–16; Rev. 2:14.

78. Before New Kingdom Egyptian troops received the gift of their spoils, they marched
triumphantly home, were officially received, arrived prominently at the quay (landing stage on
the Nile) of Karnak, and presented a sacrifice to Amun: Spalinger, "New Kingdom Triumphs,"
102, cited by Trimm, *Warfare*, 414.

79. Trimm, *Warfare*, 413, cf. 21, 162, 201, 300, 320.

80. See Sternberg, *Poetics*, 265–66.

the military officers have let the Midianite women live and demands that they execute every boy and nonvirgin woman, but take the virgins as wives. Moses's anger is directed at the officers who spared the lives of the women, the very women who caused the Israelites to be unfaithful to Yahweh at Peor, resulting in a plague that killed 24,000 Israelites (vv. 15–16; see the translation notes there; cf. 25:9). His anger may have surprised the troops because their divine orders to *take vengeance* (*nqa/*ntn + nəqāmâ, vv. 2, 3) did not specify that they should totally destroy (*ḥrm I) the Midianites, which he commanded Israel to do to the cities of the Canaanite king of Arad (Num. 21:2–3; cf. Deut. 7, 13, 20*; 1 Sam. 15:3). For readers, the death of Balaam (v. 9) also comes as a surprise or even a disappointment within the chaps. 22–25 story line, but here Moses finally gives clear justification: "These women, *on Balaam's counsel*, caused the Israelites to be unfaithful" (v. 16; see the first translation note there).[81] Moses, therefore, demands that the officers kill every Midianite boy and every woman who has had sex with a man, which would include married women and unmarried women who had cultic sex (v. 17; see the translation note there; cf. 25:1–2). Then, using an imperative verb (hiphil *ḥyh), Moses orders the officers to spare the Midianite virgins and take them as their wives (v. 18; see the translation note there). Moses's exogamous orders in v. 18 differ from Deuteronomic law, which gives men the option of taking a wife from one of Israel's war captives (Deut. 21:10–14).[82] According to Exod. 2:21, Moses himself married a Midianite virgin, Zipporah, and now he demands Israelite men to follow his own life path.[83] Even so, the positive perspective on Moses's Midianite wife and father-in-law in Exod. 2, 4, 18 stands in contrast to his scathing tone against the Midianite women, men, and children in Num. 31.[84] It is conceivable that the stories of Num. 25 and 31 influenced the editors of

---

81. See Frevel, *Desert Transformations*, 155–88; cf. Douglas, *Wilderness*, 218, 22.

82. Also, in 31:17 nonvirgin women and male children are to be killed and female virgins spared, while in Deut. 20:14, women and children are to be taken as prisoners (see Weinfeld, *Deuteronomic School*, 238–39; Seebass, *Numeri*, 3:315, 317; Kilchör, *Mosetora*, 242). Kilchör contends that Deut. 20:14–18 supplements Num. 31:17 by specifying how the women are to be treated. For the inverse, taking Deut. 20 and 21:10–14 as the background for the Priestly work of Num. 31, see Dozeman, "Numbers," 245–46.

83. Budd (*Numbers*, 333) concludes that "the author of Numbers, like Ezra, has no sympathy for foreign marriages, and is anxious perhaps to close any loopholes in which the example of Moses is cited." Against Budd, v. 18 is a glaring exception that stands in contrast to the exclusivism against Moabite and other foreign wives in Num. 25; Deut. 23:3–6; Ezra 10; Neh. 13:1–3, 23–27; cf. the War Scroll I, 1–3, depicting the "sons of light" in their offensive battle against Edom, Moab, and Ammon. Augustine draws out this positive perspective of v. 18 to establish that virgins, like Mary the mother of Jesus, can be called women in Scripture (Lienhard, *Numbers*, 260).

84. Dor, "Well in Midian," 141–61.

Num. 12:1 to identify Moses's wife not as Midianite (Exod. 2:16, 21), but as a Cushite (Num. 12:1; see the third translation note there).[85]

Israel's burning down of the Midianite tented villages (31:10) and slaughter of the civilian population while taking the virgin women as prisoners of war (31:18) corresponds to Assyrian war practice against nomadic enemies like the Arabs.[86] Does this mean that Yahweh and Israel are blindly, to their shame, imitating ANE violence? And what about these women? One could conclude that the patriarchal family structures on display in chap. 30 (women's vows) are grossly exploited in chap. 31, as Moses, the chieftains, and the priests subjugate the Midianite women as carnage and virgins as captives forced to become wives of the foreign men who killed their fathers, mothers, brothers, uncles, and aunts (vv. 9, 15–18). There is a noticeable omission, however. Against the widespread ANE practice of battlefield rape,[87] there is no hint whatsoever that the Israelite men were to rape the Midianite women. Also, Yahweh's violence against these Midianite women and the whole society to which they belonged is directed at punishing them for deceiving Israel to be sexually and religiously unfaithful (vv. 16–17); in this sense Yahweh fulfills his Abrahamic curse (Gen. 12:3). These points, however, do not fully resolve the moral issue of Yahweh's/Israel's vindictive violence, especially for those who strive to obey the ethic of Jesus to "love your enemies" (Matt. 5:44).

Another path is to try to absolve Yahweh of Moses's vengeance (vv. 14–18). Since Moses rebelled earlier (Num. 20:12; 27:13–14) and since the massacre here was never explicitly ordered by Yahweh (vv. 13–18) but was Moses's attempt to execute Yahweh's vengeance (see vv. 2–3), one may wonder whether Moses is carrying out Yahweh's will or his own.[88] Even while Moses's vindictive actions are questionable, the narrator or editor does not evaluate Moses negatively (as in 20:12; 27:13–14; Deut. 32:48–52), and Yahweh's silence is followed only by his orders to divide up the plunder (vv. 25–30), suggesting his approval of the vengeance taken.[89]

Our visceral responses to Num. 31 are legitimate and painful, but we must not eradicate this chapter from our biblical theology, not simply because it is part of "all scripture" (2 Tim. 3:16), but also because doing so would neglect the central messages of Yahweh's lethal holiness and Yahweh's worthiness to

---

85. Habakkuk 3:7 puts "the tents of Cush" and "dwellings of Midian" in synonymous parallelism; see Achenbach (*Vollendung*, 275).

86. Staubli, *Levitikus, Numeri*, 332. See esp. Stol, *Women*, 331–38.

87. Washington, "Violence," 203.

88. Brown ("Vengeance," 65–84) argues that Moses's call for slaughter is a questionable enactment of Yahweh's command (v. 2) and instead that the honor of the story rests on the officers who give generously to Yahweh's sanctuary (vv. 48–54).

89. See Sternberg, *Poetics*, 54.

receive the international spoils of the wars of his people.[90] The delay between Num. 25 and 31 illustrates that God does not forget human acts of perversity and deception leading to covenant infidelity. His future judgment is inevitable for the unfaithful who do not repent, not only for the nations who have committed adultery with the great prostitute, Babylon, but also for his people who do not obey his voice (Rev. 18:4). But even as Jesus pronounces judgment on physical and mental adultery and other forms of sexual promiscuity,[91] he also offers himself as life-giving living water to the Samaritan woman who has had five husbands, and he takes great delight in the excessive devotion of the woman who "lived a sinful life."[92]

In vv. 19–20, Moses demands that after the second round of slaughter, the warriors and their captives who have killed someone or touched a corpse must undergo a seven-day purification ritual (see the translation notes on v. 19). Moses's instructions rely on and align with the corpse decontamination ritual instructions of Num. 19:11–22.[93] The one difference is that the warriors returning from the fight must quarantine outside the camp (as Num. 5:1–4; Deut. 23:10–15), whereas civilians in 19:11–22 could remain in the camp for their purification.[94] Because the soldiers are at war, they are not responsible for bloodshed (murder), which defiles (35:33–34),[95] but of corpse contamination, which would still pollute the sanctuary where Yahweh lives in the camp (Num. 5:3).[96] The details are sparse here, but the contaminated must remain outside the camp for seven days, presumably purifying their bodies on the third and seventh days and at some point purifying their clothes and any leather, hairy, or wooden items carried out of the war (see the translation notes on vv. 19–20). Ceramics are not listed among the washables because they must be smashed (Lev. 15:12).[97] The importance of purity not only explains why Moses, Eleazar, and the chieftains meet them *outside* the camp, eliminating any triumphal entry into the camp, but also reveals a second element to Moses's anger: entering the camp unclean would violate Yahweh's

---

90. See the "Implications" essays in chap. 4 ("The Holiness of God Is Lethal") and chap. 28 ("War Tribute in the ANE and Numbers 31").

91. Not to mention many texts on sexual immorality, these deal with adultery: Matt. 5:27–32 (cf. 2 Pet. 2:14); Mark 10:2–12//Matt. 19:3–9//Luke 16:18; Mark 7:21//Matt. 15:19; cf. Rom. 13:9; James 2:11; Rev. 2:22; 18:1–24.

92. John 4; Luke 7:36–50//Matt. 26:6–13//Mark 14:3–9//John 12:1–8; cf. the interpolation of John 7:53–8:11.

93. D. Wright, "Purification," 214–16.

94. D. Wright, "Purification," 223; Murray, "Yнwн's Veto," 471; Milgrom, *Numbers*, 258.

95. Murray, "Yнwн's Veto," 471. He argues that the Chronicler (1 Chron. 22, 28) draws ideationally from the legislation of Num. 31 (war purification) and 35 (murder) to disqualify David, a shedder of blood, from building Yahweh's temple.

96. Milgrom, *Numbers*, 260.

97. Milgrom, *Numbers*, 260.

prior instructions and inferably incite his wrath (Num. 5:1–4; 9:1–14; cf. Lev. 5:3–6 and Lev. 13–15*).[98]

31:21–24. Moses's war purification instructions are incomprehensive (vv. 19–20), so now Eleazar extends "the statute of the law that Yahweh commanded Moses" (v. 21).[99] By this formula, Eleazar appears to refer to Moses's preceding orders (vv. 19–20) that effectively correlate with Yahweh's instructions for corpse decontamination delivered to Moses and Aaron in Num. 19:11–22.[100] Eleazar's authority to offer such an extension recollects his calling as Aaron's son to distinguish what is holy from common, clean from unclean, and "to teach the Israelites all the statutes that Yahweh has spoken to them through Moses" (Lev. 10:10–11). Here Eleazar fulfills his calling, teaching the warriors to purify by fire, then by water, the metallic items brought home from the battle that can withstand the fire (vv. 22–23; see the second translation note on v. 23). The metals are listed from most to least valuable: gold, silver, bronze, iron, tin, and lead.[101] Withstanding the fire does not mean melting and removing dross, but sanitizing while preserving the integrity of each object's form; the chieftains later present intact gold jewelry from the war that must have been so purified (vv. 48–54).[102] This correlates with what we know about metallurgy today. While a wood fire can eventually exceed 2,000°F, a wood fire auto-ignites at 260°F, at which point or soon thereafter these metals can be inserted and removed from the fire without melting. Tin, lead, and alloys with a low melting point would need to be inserted at a lower temperature or be removed more quickly.[103] The metals must also be purified with "the purifying water," that is, water for the designated purpose of removing impurities, like contagions such as blood and other unsanitary elements such as dirt (v. 23; see the third translation note there; cf. 19:9). All meltable objects brought back from the war must be washed with this water (v. 23; see the fourth translation note there). The Baal Cycle may offer an image of postwar washing with purifying waters. After bathing her hands in the blood of warriors, the West Semitic goddess 'Anatu "gathers water and washes, dew of heavens, oil of

---

98. Frevel ("Alte Stücke," 290) sees Num. 9:1–14 and Num. 31 as paradigmatic Torah discussions.

99. "This is the statute of the law [zō't ḥuqqat hattôrâ]" is rare (also 19:2) and probably reflects a later stage in which "tôrâ is oscillating between the whole law of Moses as a self-referential term and the statute of a single law" (Frevel, "Book of Numbers," 23–24).

100. D. Wright, "Purification," 223.

101. Milgrom, *Numbers*, 261.

102. With Joüon ("Notes," 44, my trans.), who renders v. 23: "Any object that can be *immersed* in fire, you must '*immerse*' it in fire, . . . cannot be immersed in fire, you must '*immerse*' in water."

103. Melting points in degrees Fahrenheit: gold (1,947.52), silver (1,763.2), bronze (copper-tin-aluminum alloy; 1,881–1,900), iron (2,800), tin (449.47) and lead (621.43) (American Elements, "Melting Point of Common Metals, Alloys, & Other Materials," https://www.american elements.com/meltingpoint.html).

earth, the showers of Cloud-Rider. The dew (that) the heavens pour down, the showers (that) the stars pour down. She beautifies herself."[104]

In vv. 19–20, Moses specifies a seven-day quarantine outside the camp, with self-purification on the third and seventh days and a washing of clothes and items (leather, wool, wood) at an unspecified time during that week. These instructions ostensibly presume the seven-day purification ritual of Num. 19.[105] Here Eleazar further specifies that this clothes washing must occur on the seventh day, and as a result Eleazar in Priestly parlance declares them physically and ritually clean: "Then you will be clean, and afterward you may enter the camp" (v. 24). This echoes the protocols for the skin-diseased persons now healed: after their seven-day quarantine outside the camp, the priest examines and pronounces them clean (Lev. 13:6, 34; 14:9). Before the skin-diseased persons who are declared clean can reenter the camp, they must perform an extensive eight-day purification ritual, but the warriors here do not (cf. Lev. 14; cf. Num. 5:1–4). As with Moses's preceding orders (vv. 15–20), here again the narrator does not tell us that the Israelites obeyed Eleazar's orders (vv. 21–24), leaving a degree of narrative tension unresolved (cf. v. 31).

31:25–31. Yahweh commands Moses to divide the plunder between the war captors and whole Israelite community, and to give 1/500th of the warriors' share of the plunder to Yahweh, but 1/50th of the people's share to the Levites. To begin, Moses, Eleazar, and the community's family leaders must count the plunder, including people and animals, but not the metals to be purified (v. 22), which will later be offered as tribute to Yahweh (v. 50). They must then "divide" (*ḥṣh) the spoils, giving 50 percent to the war captors and 50 percent to the civilians; this becomes clear in the spoil list of vv. 32–47 (v. 27; see the translation note there). The intent of delineating these two groups, the warriors and the civilians, relates to the fact that a portion of the warriors' share must go to Yahweh (vv. 28–29; see the first and second translation notes on v. 28), while a slightly smaller portion from the civilians' share must go to the Levites (vv. 30; see the first translation note there).

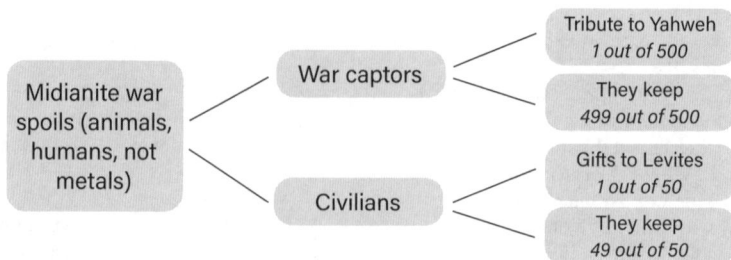

Figure 28.1. Spoils of War

104. "The Ba'lu Myth," COS 1.86:251. With Trimm, *Warfare*, 424.
105. Gray, *Numbers*, 242.

This means that Israel's war captors would keep 99.8 percent (499/500) of their share and Yahweh 0.2 percent (1/500). The civilians would keep 98 percent (49/50) of their share and the Levites 2 percent (1/50). These figures are stunning in their ANE environment.[106] Indicative of the ANE more broadly, Rameses III, the last great New Kingdom monarch, claims that the war spoils are "stamped with my name"; that is, they belong exclusively to him.[107] The divine king Yahweh holds the exclusive rights to the Midianite war spoils—indicated by the fact that he decides their distribution (vv. 25–30)—but reserves proportionately almost nothing for himself.[108] Also, it is remarkable that Yahweh split the spoils 50/50 between the warriors who risked their lives and homebound Israelite families. This sharply contrasts with the trend of kings, who rarely if ever distributed spoils to commoners but frequently to their soldiers. The pharaohs conventionally rewarded soldiers with a portion of the plunder they presented to him, and Cyrus the Great dispersed spoils based on the achievements of his troops.[109] The Mari ruler Yasmah-Adad was advised regarding his spoils: "Feed your troops spoils so they will bless you."[110] Moses and Eleazar rightly distribute the spoils (v. 31), which comes as a relief to ANE readers who regard one who embezzles spoils as "breaking an oath to the gods and to the king."[111]

31:32–47. The narrator depicts the dividing up of the spoil with a focus on the tribute to be given to Yahweh for Eleazar's use (from the warriors' half) and to the Levites (from Israel's half), the keepers of Yahweh's dwelling place. The narrator first lists the inventory of "the spoil that remained from the plunder that the troops had taken" (v. 32), where "the plunder the troops had taken" apparently refers to their leather, hairy, and wooden items; clothes (v. 20); and their stockpile of metals (v. 22). From the inventory, the four parties are assigned their due shares of the animal and human spoils, based on Yahweh's previously stated proportions (vv. 25–30).

Eleazar the high priest was commanded to be both a distributor and receiver of spoils (vv. 25–31), but here Moses alone distributes (vv. 41, 47), while Eleazar receives the tribute offering for Yahweh (v. 41). The Levites here are justified as recipients by their common appellative, "who were responsible for the care of Yahweh's dwelling place" (v. 47). These spoils supplement the Levites' regular remuneration for their service to Yahweh, the Israelites' tithe

---

106. See Elgavish, "Spoils of War," 247–73. Milgrom (*Numbers*, 262) argues that the Temple Scroll from Qumran, by giving the clergy their share first, harmonizes with David's distribution of war spoils in 1 Sam. 30 and with Moses's in Num. 31:25–47.

107. Trimm, *Warfare*, 318.

108. In the Qur'an (surah 8.42), one-fifth of the war spoils are to be distributed to God, Muhammad, his family, orphans, the poor, and travelers (Gray, *Numbers*, 423).

109. Trimm, *Warfare*, 320, 344.

110. Sasson, *Mari Archives*, 187, cited by Trimm, *Warfare*, 330.

111. Trimm, *Warfare*, 328.

Table 28.1. Sharing the Spoils of War

Spoils Inventory (31:32–34)	Warriors' Spoils (31:36–41)	→ Yahweh's Tribute	Civilians' Spoils (31:42–47)	→ Levites' Portion
675,000 sheep	337,500 sheep	→ 675 sheep	337,500 sheep	→ [6,750 sheep][a]
72,000 cattle	36,000 cattle	→ 72 cattle	36,000 cattle	→ [720 cattle]
61,000 donkeys	30,500 donkeys	→ 61 donkeys	30,500 donkeys	→ [610 cattle]
32,000 female virgins	16,000 people	→ 32 people	16,000 people	→ [320 people]

a. The bracketed totals in this column are implied by 31:47.

of their sacrifices and offerings (18:21–32). The notices of Moses's obedience to Yahweh in distributing the spoils faithfully (vv. 41, 47) are a redundancy since he and Eleazar were already said to have distributed the spoils (v. 31). The literary effect turns Moses's anger (vv. 14–18) and the warriors' lack of obedience (vv. 15–24) into a memory and stresses the reception of spoils as a divine blessing reminiscent of the days of old when they plundered the Egyptians as they left Egypt.[112]

31:48–54. The episode culminates with the military officers presenting to Yahweh a huge collection of gold to make atonement for themselves. The scene begins as the military officers, who were rebuked for sparing the Midianite women who caused the Israelites to sin (vv. 14–16), approach Moses (v. 48; see the third translation note there). At this point, the careful reader wonders why the narrator has not reported that the officers obeyed Moses's orders to "kill every boy, and kill every woman who has had sex with a man" (v. 17).[113] Precise obedience to Yahweh's war commands is crucial (i.e., Num. 14:40–45; cf. Josh. 7; 1 Sam. 15). The question of whether the officers are lingering in disobedience continues with what first comes out of their mouths: They have counted their troops and have found "not one of us is missing" (v. 49). David incited divine wrath and a plague when he counted his troops (2 Sam. 24), and every military census must be supported by a ransom to prevent a plague (Exod. 30:12).[114] The officers are on shaky ground, but then again, "not one of us is missing" suggests that no Israelite soldier or any mercenaries have died (vv. 7–12). Israel's total domination implies that the blessing of the divine warrior rests on the officers and their men (cf. Lev. 26:7–8; Num. 6:24–26; 21:21–35). Concerns about the officers are put to rest as they bring the valuable jewelry, plundered from the Midianite women (v. 9; see the second translation note on v. 50), and presumably purified by fire and water (vv. 21–24; no narration of obedience), to Moses as Yahweh's offering (v. 50). The officers are portrayed

112. Exod. 3:22; 12:35–36; cf. Gen. 49:27; Lev. 26:1–13. Later the Israelites encounter the Midianites' wealth again in Judg. 6:5; 8:24–26 (Ashley, *Numbers*, 598).

113. Sternberg, *Poetics*, 265–66.

114. Dozeman, "Numbers," 247–48.

as generous Yahweh worshipers, like the chieftains of the first generation who gave lavishly to the Levites and to dedicate Yahweh's altar (Num. 7). Offering these precious metals and stones from war to the king is well-attested in the ANE;[115] the implication is that the officers regard Yahweh as Israel's king, worthy of such costly devotion (as in Exod. 12:35; 35:22–29). What is distinctive here is that they intend by this non-blood sacrifice "to make atonement for ourselves before Yahweh" (v. 50; see the third translation note there). While blood is foundational for atonement in Holiness theology (Lev. 17:11), there are precedents for bloodless atonement offerings in the Torah. Particularly relevant is the census tax ransom that the Israelite men older than twenty were to give to Yahweh to make atonement for their lives (Exod. 30:12–16). Although the officers could be aiming to effect atonement for unknown or unexposed sin, as with a burnt offering (Lev. 1:4),[116] in this case the officers may be seeking atonement specifically for the apostasy at Peor by which their fathers had broken the covenant with Yahweh (cf. Phinehas's ransom in 25:13), for their own at least initial failure to kill the Midianite women who had caused the Israelites to be unfaithful (31:14–16), or possibly to pay the ransom price for taking a census of their troops (as Exod. 30:11–16).[117]

Moses and Eleazar receive and offer up to Yahweh the officers' lucrative and pluriform gift, indicating that they, too, believed this bloodless offering could effect atonement (vv. 51–52, 54; see the translation note on v. 51). The total weight of the offering came to approximately 420 pounds of gold (v. 52; see the second translation note there)! In v. 53 the narrator contrasts the officers' unselfish act of devotion to Yahweh with the soldiers, as the NJPS clarifies: "*But* in the ranks, everyone kept his booty for himself." In the synopsis of v. 54, the narrator adds to atoning "offering" (v. 50) and "tribute" (v. 52) a third aspect: Moses and Eleazar "brought it into the meeting tent as a memorial for the Israelites before Yahweh" (v. 54; see the translation note there). It is astonishing that Moses and Eleazar enter the tent together, pointing to a later stage in the transition from Moses to the high priest's authority in the theocracy of Israel.[118] The memorial they haul into Yahweh's presence resonates with priestly imagery elsewhere in the HB,[119] and its purpose comes into focus when we contemplate its ANE religious and political context. The Moabite King Mesha boasts: "And from there, I took th[e ves]sels of YHWH, and I hauled them before the face of Kemosh (Chemosh)."[120] In the ANE,

115. See the "Implications" essay below, "War Tribute in the ANE and Numbers 31."
116. Milgrom, *Leviticus*, 1:172–77.
117. Noth, *Numbers*, 232; Dozeman, "Numbers," 247–48; Ashley, *Numbers*, 599.
118. Frevel, *Mit Blick*, 172; Frevel, "Book of Numbers," 22.
119. Utzschneider (*Heiligtum*, 169–71) identifies Exod. 28:12, 29; 36–38; 30:11–16; 39:9; Zech. 6:14; Ezra 2:69; Neh. 2:20.
120. "The Inscription of King Mesha," *COS* 2.23:138. See the "Implications" essay below, "War Tribute in the ANE and Numbers 31."

importing a foreign enemy's cult statue into the temple of one's own deity symbolized the native deity's victory and supremacy.[121] Although Yahweh is not to be represented iconographically, the articles of his dwelling place, such as the ark and other sacra, symbolize his powerful presence on the battlefront (31:6; cf. 10:35–36). These items, along with Yahweh's cache of silver and gold, could be captured and imported into another deity's temple.[122] No command in Num. 31 is given to import Chemosh's cult statue into Yahweh's meeting tent, which would break the formal meaning of the Decalogue's first word,[123] but what v. 54 indicates is that the cache of gold from the officers, now in Yahweh's dwelling place, visibly reminds the Israelites of the supreme power of their deity over Chemosh and the other gods of Transjordan.

Implications

War Tribute in the ANE and Numbers 31

The ancient text of Num. 31 conveys Yahweh's vengeance through violence against Midianite women, children, and men. This, of course, is a painful saga that modern readers are tempted to throw out, but in doing so they place humans at the center of the story. This common response to Num. 31, I argue, fails to see the primary Yahweh-centered, cultic message of the story. The literary placement of chap. 31 provides an entry into its message. We may never definitively explain why the editors of Numbers positioned chap. 31 after the sacrificial calendar (chaps. 28–29) and vows to Yahweh (chap. 30), but I proffer three plausible reasons. (1) Yahweh worship, as directed in chaps. 28–29, always has corequisites; in this case, Israel must take vengeance against the Midianites and then purify Israel's warriors and spoils or, by implication, Yahweh worship will be adversely affected (31:2–3, 13–20). (2) Phinehas the priest presumably signals the charge as Israel's warriors take their formation around Yahweh's ark and sancta (31:6, 13; cf. 2:17; 10:8–9, 35–36). (3) The Midianite war results in considerable tribute to Yahweh and resources for Eleazar the high priest, which effectively honor and finance Yahweh's sacrificial cult (31:21–54).

Although the narrative tension rises to its pinnacle with Moses's anger in v. 14, one can argue that the narrator is most concerned to move readers to the second half of the story (vv. 21–54), which centers on the purification and distribution of war spoils, culminating with the impressive tribute given

---

121. See Hundley, *Gods in Dwellings*, 215.

122. See 1 Sam. 4:1–7:2; 2 Sam. 6:1–20; Jer. 52:16–19; Dan. 1:2; 5:2–3, 23; Ezra 1:5–11; 5:14–15; 6:5; Neh. 13:4–9.

123. Formally, "You must not have *other gods before my face*"; cf. 2 Chron. 33:7; Ezek. 8:3; 2 Macc. 6:2. Solomon presumably avoids this violation with Chemosh but commits another (1 Kings 11:7).

to Yahweh (vv. 32–54). In the context of the ANE, perhaps the first striking absence from the story is that Yahweh does not order the Israelites to capture and relocate the foreign gods of Moab. The Moabite Stone illustrates this contrast. King Mesha announces that he has devoted the Israelite occupation of Nebo to destruction for the goddess Ashtar Kemosh (*ḥrm*), like Israel devoted the Canaanite cities to destruction in Num. 21:2–3, but ostensibly unlike Num. 31*, in which the Moabite virgins could be spared (v. 18).[124] Mesha then declares: "I took th[e ves]sels of YHWH, and I hauled them before the face of Kemosh."[125] Similarly, Tiglath-Pileser I (12th–11th cent. BCE) subordinates the foreign deities to serve in the temples of the Assyrian goddesses and gods: "At that time I donated the 25 gods of those lands, my own booty which I had taken, to be door-keepers of the temple of the goddess Ninlil, beloved chief spouse of the god Aššur, my lord, (the temple) of the gods Anu (and) Adad, (the temple of) the Assyrian Ištar, the temples of my city, Aššur, and the goddesses of my land."[126] Likewise, Adad-ninari II (10th–9th cent. BCE) boasts that he "gave their gods as gifts to Aššur, my lord."[127] Not merely peoples, but also gods were subjugated as vassals of Assyria. By contrast, in Num. 31 Yahweh has ordered Israel to take vengeance because the Moabite women enticed the Israelites to worship the Baal of Peor (Num. 25:1–3, 17–18; 31:1–3), so capturing Moab's cult icons and implements, however cogent this would be as a symbol of Yahweh's sovereignty, would only entice Israel again to spiritual and physical infidelity. That fidelity to Yahweh is at the fore of the Midianite war is revealed in Moses's tirade (31:15b–16a).

If the Moabite cult images are conspicuously absent, the importance of Israel's deity, Yahweh, is conspicuously present in the distribution of the war spoils in Num. 31*. In the ANE, captors commonly devoted their war spoils to the god or gods.[128] In certain accounts, however, the gifts, usually sacrifices, to the deity are appended or inserted later in the record, rather than central to it. For example, the New Kingdom Pharaoh, Thutmose III (15th cent. BCE) records the spoils of his famous Battle of Megiddo but says nothing of any tribute gifts to the gods. Later, after his fifth Asiatic campaign, he records that he gave offerings to Amun-Re (see below), but this comes across as entirely self-motivated, to receive "life, prosperity, and health" (reconstructed) as "Menkheper[re] [Thut. III], given life forever" (in the text).[129] This contrasts with the conviction of the narrator in Num. 31 that Yahweh's share is fully integrated into the distribution of the war spoils, reflecting his boundedness to his covenant people and cultic representatives to whom he generously bestows

---

124. See the "Implications" essay in chap. 21, "Devotion to Destruction."
125. "The Inscription of King Mesha," *COS* 2.23:138.
126. Grayson, *Assyrian Rulers*, 20.
127. Grayson, *Assyrian Rulers*, 144.
128. Levine, *Numbers*, 2:470–72.
129. "The Annals of Thutmose III," *COS* 2.2A:13.

the vast majority of the spoils. Nonetheless, Thutmose III's annals of his Megiddo campaign offer a close parallel context and genre to that of Num. 31:32–47. I have placed certain phrases in bold font to underscore a contrast of who receives the glory through these lists.[130]

Table 28.2. List of Spoils Compared

Spoils from the Midianite War (Num. 31:32–47)	Spoils from Thutmose III's Battle of Megiddo
The spoil that remained from the plunder that the troops had taken was:	[The list of booty which **his majesty** carried off from the city of] Megiddo:
675,000 sheep	3,400 prisoners-of-war
72,000 cattle	83 hands
61,000 donkeys,	2,041 horses
and as for people, 32,000 young women who had never had sex with a man.	191 foals
The half share of those who went to war numbered	6 stallions
337,500 sheep,	. . . colts
and Yahweh's share from the sheep was 675.	The gold decorated chariot and golden (chariot) pole of that enemy.
There were 36,000 cattle,	The fine, gold decorated chariot of the chieftain of [Megiddo].
of which Yahweh's share was 72.	[. . .]
There were 30,500 donkeys,	892 chariots of **his feeble army**, totaling 924.
of which Yahweh's share was 61.	The fine, bronze mail coat of that enemy.
There were 16,000 people,	The fine bronze mail coat of the chieftain of
of which Yahweh's share was 32 people.	Meg[iddo].
Moses gave the share **as Yahweh's tribute offering to Eleazar the priest, as Yahweh had commanded Moses.**	20 mail [. . .] coats of **his feeble army**.
From the Israelites' half, which Moses had separated from the warriors—from the community's half—there were:	502 bows
	7 fine silver decorated tent poles of the tent of that enemy.
337,500 sheep	Now [**his majesty's**] army captured [the livestock of this city]
36,000 cattle	[. . .]
30,500 donkeys	387 [. . .]
and 16,000 people.	1,929 cows
From the Israelites' half Moses took one of every fifty people and animals and gave them **to the Levites who were responsible for the care of Yahweh's dwelling place, just as Yahweh had commanded Moses.**	2,000 goats
	20,500 sheep
	The list of that which was **carried away afterwards by the king** of the possessions of the palace of that enemy from Yenoam, from Inuges, from Herenkaru, and the property of those cities which had been **loyal to him** which were **carried away because of** [the awe of his majesty].[a]

a. "The Annals of Thutmose III," COS 2.2A:12–13. After the quoted text, Thutmose III enumerates wives, children, male and female servants, surrenderers, and defectors.

130. I also removed verse numbers and adjusted punctuation to show the parallel genre.

"Yahweh's share" and Yahweh's authority to command stand in contrast to Pharaoh's majesty and military power. Thutmose III goes on to detail an impressive collection of "precious stones, gold, bowls, and a variety of vessels," which provides an analogy to the Israelite chieftains' offering to Yahweh consisting of "gold ornaments, armlets and bracelets, signet rings, earrings and necklaces" (Num. 31:50; cf. 7:10–88). The difference is that Israel's chieftains give their gift *to Yahweh* expressly "to make atonement for ourselves before Yahweh" (31:50). The Yahweh-centered nature of their tribute recurs throughout this subunit.[131] On the contrary, Thutmose III's spoils list functions to enhance "his majesty"[132] as a monomaniacal king who was fixated on maintaining the Egyptian empire's hegemony over the land of Canaan. The ensuing annals of Thutmose III's fifth Asiatic campaign do include his sacrifices to the Egyptian gods, but again this serves to enhance his own reputation as the ideal king:

> Now his majesty plundered the city of War[t]et. [. . .] *Giving praise to his majesty* [Thutmose III] by his army. Giving adoration to [Amun] *for the victories* [*which he*] *had given to his son. They were happy and pleased with his majesty more than anything.* Thereafter, *his majesty* proceeded to the offering storehouse. Giving offerings to [Amun]-Re-Harakhty consisting of oxen, fowl, short-horned cattle [. . .] [*on behalf of life, prosperity, and health, the king of Upper and Lower Egypt*], Menkheper[re], given life forever.[133]

It is telling that the last phrase of these annals, before the text breaks off, exalts not the Egyptian pantheon, but the divine monarch as the one worthy of the war tribute: "*because of the awe of his majesty* . . ."[134] At the finale of history, only one eternal, divine, and majestic king, the victorious Lamb, will receive the impressive tribute of the nations (Rev. 21:23–27).

---

131. Esp. vv. 50 (2×), 52, 54.

132. Hoffmeier ("The Annals of Thutmose III," COS 2.2A:12–13) reconstructs "his majesty" based on its preponderance throughout the annals.

133. "The Annals of Thutmose III," COS 2.2A:13.

134. "The Annals of Thutmose III," COS 2.2A:13.

29

Gadites and Reubenites Inherit Transjordan Territory

(32:1–42)

⁂

Overview

As Num. 26–36 prepares the second generation for life in the promised land, the war with Midian in Num. 31 has prepared the way literarily for Num. 32. By executing vengeance on the Midianites for leading Israel to sin with the Baal of Peor (Num. 25), Yahweh expands his hegemony over territories in Transjordan, adding to his control over the former domains of Sihon and Og (Num. 21:21–35). The Gadites and Reubenites see this as a prime opportunity to ask Israel's leaders for "the land that Yahweh conquered" (32:4), which is ideally suited for their copious livestock (vv. 1–5). Moses reacts furiously because he has concluded that the Gadites and Reubenites are, by their request, disobeying Yahweh's orders to conquer and inhabit Canaan, which was promised to the patriarchs (vv. 6–15). The Gadites and Reubenites respond to Moses by reaffirming their motive—the land is good for their cattle—but now promise to fight in Cisjordan before rejoining their families east of the Jordan (vv. 16–32). Moses accepts their request contingent on the obedience of the two tribes (vv. 20–24). Through a back-and-forth dialogue, it appears that Moses directs the two tribes to make a formal oath and pledge their loyalty to Israel and to Yahweh (vv. 25–27, 28–29, 31–32). Finally, Moses grants to the two tribes and, surprisingly, to half of Manasseh's tribe the domains of the defeated kings Sihon and Og (vv. 33–42). The chapter thereby serves as an etiology for how these tribes came to settle in Transjordan.[1] Or more

---

1. Zeelander, "Closural Conventions," 335. The composition of Num. 32 is notoriously complex and has invited many reflections (see Budd, *Numbers*, 337–41), but here I summarize

precisely, there are two etiologies: the story's frames narrate the settlement and city-building of the three tribes in Transjordan (vv. 1–5, 33–42), while in the center Moses demands their loyal participation in the holy war as the precondition to occupying Transjordan (vv. 6–32).[2] In the end, there is no rebellion, and the intertribal dispute is resolved positively, as in chaps. 27 and 36, thus enhancing the motifs of obedience and hopefulness in the discourse of chaps. 26–36.[3]

Translation

[1]Now the Reubenites and Gadites owned a very large number of cattle. When they saw[4] that the land of Jazer and the land of Gilead was a good place for cattle,[5] [2]the Gadites and the Reubenites[6] came and

---

only a few. De Vaulx (*Nombres*, 362–71) sees three layers in chap. 32: ancient tribal traditions of Gad and Reuben (vv. 34–38), an Elohistic story (vv. 1–32*), and a unifying redaction that includes vv. 6–15. Schmidt ("Ansiedlung," 497–510; cf. *Numeri*, 191–202) also identifies three layers: a base E(lohist) layer (parts of vv. 1–38*), which assumes the Sihon and Balaam narratives; a Pentateuch redaction (parts of vv. 4–33*), which stresses fighting in the Cisjordan conquest as prerequisite to possessing Transjordan land and adapts the account to Deut. 3:12–20; and a later editor (parts of vv. 17–36*), who links the awarding of Transjordan land to the two tribes with the distribution of Cisjordan land to the other tribes. Seebass ("Erwägungen," 33–48) identifies early reflections (vv. 3, 34–38*) transformed by the Yahwist (v. 3) and augmented by later layers. Van Seters (*Life of Moses*, 436–50) contends that the Yahwist adapted the simple Deut. 3:12–20 report to fashion the Num. 32 story, which stresses the "colonization" of the eastern lands. Scharbert (*Numeri*, 125) regards the Pentateuch redactor as unifying JE and P materials. For Achenbach (*Vollendung*, 369–88), verses conveying the theme of land conquest and settlement belong to the Hexateuch redaction (vv. 1–2a, 5–6*, 20–22*, 25–27, 33, 40), but to this layer a theocratic revision was added, stressing Eleazar's high-priestly authority and exhorting the community to fidelity (vv. 2b–4, 7–15, 16–32*; and later, 34–39, 42); similarly, Artus ("Numbers 32," 370–71, 380–81). Frevel ("Alte Stücke," 276) sees in the Num. 32* settlement of the Transjordan a pre-Priestly tradition (cf. Deut. 1–3*, 9–10*), which was infused with Priestly supplements (vv. 1*, 4–6, 20, 22, 25, 28–30; Frevel, *Mit Blick*, 38). Isolating vv. 7–15 as an enigmatic secondary insertion, Marquis ("Composition," 408–32) distinguishes from the remaining verses (vv. 1–6, 16–42) a Priestly story and an Elohist story, originally independent but now intertwined into a disunified narrative. Kislev ("Gadites and Reubenites," 619–29) argues that the Priestly verses (e.g., v. 29) in Num. 32 were written as additions to the non-Priestly verses (e.g., vv. 20–21). Knohl (*Sanctuary*, 98) sees H as unifying the heterogeneous materials of Num. 32.

2. Dozeman ("Numbers," 248) assigns these frames to the pre-Priestly source stressing inheritance and the core to the Priestly source stressing holy war as the precondition for inheritance.

3. Olson, *Death of the Old*, 123.

4. The second wayyiqtol past narrative indicates a consequence, so I render the first wayyiqtol: "*When they saw* [*wayyir'û*] . . . , [then] *the Gadites and Reubenites came* [*wayyābō'û bənê-gād ûbənê rə'ûbēn*]" (*GBHS* §3.5.1a).

5. A gen. of purpose: "They saw the land, . . . and look/behold the place was *a place of* [*intended for*] *cattle*" (*wayyir'û 'et-'ereṣ . . . wəhinnēh hammāqôm məqôm miqne*; GBHS §2.2.8).

6. Perhaps to adjust to the natural birth order of v. 1, LXX[ed] reads "the Reubenites and Gadites" throughout chap. 32 (vv. 2, 6[with SP], 25, 29, 31, 33[with SP]). Probably to assimilate

said to Moses, Eleazar the priest, and the chieftains of the community:[7] **3**"Ataroth, Dibon, Jazer, Nimrah, Heshbon, Elealeh, Sebam, Nebo, and Beon—**4**the land that Yahweh conquered[8] before the Israelite community is a land for cattle,[9] and your servants have cattle." **5**Then they said, "If we have found favor in your sight, let this land be given to your servants as a possession. Do not make us cross the Jordan."

6But Moses said[10] to the Gadites and the Reubenites, "Must your brothers go to war while you remain here? **7**Why do you discourage the heart[11] of the Israelites to cross over into the land that Yahweh has given them? **8**Your fathers did this when I sent them from Kadesh Barnea to see the land.[12] **9**When they went up to the Wadi Eshcol and saw the land, they discouraged the heart of the Israelites from entering the land that Yahweh had given them. **10**Yahweh's anger was aroused that day, and he swore, **11**'None of the men[13] who came from Egypt, twenty years old and up, will see the land that I swore to give to Abraham, Isaac, and Jacob,[14] because they did not follow me completely,[15] **12**none except Caleb, Jephunneh the Kenizzite's son, and Nun's son Joshua because they followed Yahweh completely.' **13**So Yahweh's anger burned against the Israelites, and he made them wander[16] in the wilderness for forty years, until the entire generation that had acted wickedly in Yahweh's

---

to v. 33, SP repeatedly inserts "and the half-tribe of Manasseh" among Reubenites and Gadites who would inherit Transjordan land (vv. 1[with 4Q27], 2, 6, 25[with 4Q27], 29[with 4Q27], 31).

7. Colon here and commas in vv. 10, 25, 31 for "saying" (see the third translation note on 1:1).

8. Formally, "struck down" (*hikkâ*, hiphil of *nkh), but understood to imply "subdued" (NET, NIV) or "conquered" (NLT, NJPS) because it is now available as "land for cattle" (*'ereṣ miqneh*).

9. Formally, "a land of cattle" (*'ereṣ miqneh*), probably a gen. of purpose, "a land *good for* cattle" (*GBHS* §2.2.8; see v. 1).

10. The wayyiqtol is sequential, but the content of Moses's response implies a disjunction: "*But Moses said* [*wayyō'mer mōšeh*] . . . , 'Must your brothers go to war . . . ?'"

11. Following MT*qere* hiphil, "Why do you *discourage* [*tanî'ûn*] the heart/mind of the Israelites?" (in place of MT*ketiv* qal, possibly meaning "Why do you *hinder* [*tanû'ûn*] the heart . . . ?").

12. A *l* + inf. const. of purpose. This reference to Israel's expedition in Num. 13 indicates exploration, not espionage: "when I sent them from Kadesh Barnea (in order) *to see the land* [*lir'ôt 'et-hā'āreṣ*]" (*GBHS* §3.4.1c). See the first translation note on 13:2.

13. LXX*ed*: "none of *these* men who . . ."

14. In this allusion to 14:26–35, the patriarchs are a noteworthy addition: "the land that I swore to give to Abraham, Isaac, and Jacob" (*hā'ădāmâ 'ăšer nišba'tî la'abrāhām layiṣḥāq ûlaya'ăqōb*).

15. A causal *kî* clause, giving the reason for Yahweh's judgment, formally, "because they did not fill after me" (*kî lō'-mil'û 'aḥărāy*), with piel **ml'* + '*aḥăr*, meaning "remain true" (*HALOT* 2:583–84, gloss 7; *GBHS* §4.3.4b). The same construction is repeated, but positively, for Caleb and Joshua in v. 12; see Num. 14:24; Deut. 1:36; Josh. 14:8, 14; 1 Kings 11:6.

16. This verb (**nw'* I) occurs forty-one times, but only four times in the Pentateuch. Here Moses presents Yahweh as the ultimate cause of Israel's wandering in the wilderness, as expressed by the hiphil causative of this root, meaning "*He made them wander* [*wayni'ēm*] in the wilderness for forty years" (see *DCH* 5:644, gloss 3; *GBHS* §3.1.6a.2). Similarly, Deut. 8:2–3.

sight was finished.[17] [14]And here you are standing in your fathers' place, a brood of sinners,[18] to increase again Yahweh's fierce anger[19] against the Israelites.[20] [15]Because if you turn away from following him, he will abandon them again in the wilderness, and you will destroy this entire people."

[16]Then they came close[21] to him and said, "Let us build[22] sheepfolds here for our flocks and cities for our children,[23] [17]but we[24] will arm ourselves for battle and go before the Israelites until we have brought them to their place. Then our children can live[25] in towns fortified from the inhabitants of the land.[26] [18]We will not return to our homes until every Israelite has received their inheritance.[27] [19]For we will not accept any inheritance with them on the other side of the Jordan and beyond, because our inheritance has come to

17. A temporal clause with inf. const., formally, "until the finishing of the entire generation that had acted wickedly in the eyes of Yahweh."

18. The head noun is a hapax, meaning "brood, increase" (*"tarbût,"* DCH 8:674), and is modified by a gen. of material, "a brood *composed of* sinful men" (*tarbût 'ănāšîm ḥaṭṭā'îm*; GBHS §2.2.10).

19. "Yahweh's fierce anger" combines two nouns, formally, "the burning/anger of the anger of Yahweh" (*ḥărôn 'p-yhwh*). In Moses's charged rhetoric, *l* + inf. const. appears to express the purpose of the verb: "And here *you are standing* [*qamtem*] in your fathers' place, a brood of sinners, *in order to increase* [*lispôt*] again Yahweh's fierce anger" (GBHS §3.4.1c).

20. Formally, "*toward* the Israelites" (*'l* 4Q23 MT), which apparently SP and LXX[ed] sought to improve, "*against* the Israelites" (*'l* SP; *epi* LXX[ed]).

21. The wayyiqtol past narrative is sequential and uses a verbal root (*ngš), as often in the Priestly writings for approaching Yahweh's sacred space or offerings: "Then they came close to him" (*wayyiggəšû 'ēlāyw*; see Num. 4:19; 8:19).

22. A cohortative of wish, by which the Reubenites and Gadites express their desire to act with Moses's consent: "*Let us build* [*nibneh*] sheepfolds" (GBHS §3.3.3b).

23. Maybe "our children" (*ṭappēnû*) is a metonym for "Our children, our wives" (*ṭappēnû nāšênû*) in v. 26; hence, the various dynamic renderings of v. 16: "our women/wives and children" (NIV, NLT), "our families" (Schmidt, *Numeri*, 192; NET), "our dependents" (Budd, *Numbers*, 336), or "our ones not able to march" (for Seebass, *Numeri*, 3:321). Perhaps more likely, "cities for our children" (*'ārîm ləṭappēnû*) does not have their wives in view, but refers to rooting their childrens' future in Transjordan (with EÜ; de Vaulx, *Nombres*, 366; Cazelles, *Nombres*, 142; "young children," Levine, *Numbers*, 2:481; "little ones," Ashley, *Numbers*, 603; NRSV, ESV).

24. The identifiable entity is reactivated by fronting in contrast with v. 16: "Let us build sheepfolds here for our flocks and cities for our children, *but we* will arm ourselves for battle" (BHRG §47.2.1; IBHS §39.2.3b).

25. Following the volitive in v. 16, probably a result weqatal: "*Let us build* [*nibneh*] sheepfolds here for our flocks and cities for our children. . . . *Then our children can live* [*wəyāšab*] in towns fortified" (GBHS §3.5.3b).

26. "*In towns fortified* [*bə'ārê hammibṣār*] from the inhabitants of the land" reflects the common fortification of a town or city by an encompassing wall with towers, in distinction from an open village (King and Stager, *Life*, 231). Within this region, during the Late Bronze–Iron I periods, the city of Amman illustrates the ideal protection for the families of the two and a half Israelite tribes: it was "well fortified and easily defended by a system of surrounding wadi approaches" (Burnett, "Transjordan," 314).

27. Formally, "until the Israelites, each one, inherits his/their inheritance."

us on this eastern side of the Jordan."[28] **20**Then Moses replied, "If you do this,[29] and if you arm yourselves for battle before Yahweh, **21**and all the armed men you have cross the Jordan before Yahweh until he drives out his enemies from his presence, **22**and the land is conquered[30] before Yahweh, then after that you may return and will be free[31] of obligation to Yahweh and to Israel. This land will then be your possession before Yahweh. **23**But if you do not do this, then you have sinned against Yahweh, and know that your sin will find you out. **24**So build towns for your little ones and folds for your sheep,[32] but do what you said you would do."[33]

25The[34] Gadites and the Reubenites said[35] to Moses, "Your servants will do as my lord commands. **26**Our little ones, our wives, our cattle,[36] all our animals, will be there[37] in the towns of Gilead, **27**but your servants will cross over, everyone armed for war, to do battle in Yahweh's presence, just as my lord says."[38] **28**So Moses gave orders about them to Eleazar the priest, to Nun's son Joshua, and to the leaders of the families of the Israelite tribes. **29**Moses said to them: "If the Gadites and the Reubenites cross the Jordan with you, everyone armed for battle in Yahweh's presence, and the land is conquered, then you must give

28. Formally, "from across the Jordan to(wards) the east/sunrise."

29. Formally, "Then Moses said *to them*, 'If you do *this thing*.'"

30. Considering the preceding syntax, the niphal incomplete pass. (from **kbš*, "subdue") probably implies Yahweh as the agent: "until <u>he drives out his enemies</u> *from his presence* [*hôrîšô ʾet-ʾōyəbāyw mippānāyw*], <u>and the land is conquered [by him]</u> *before Yahweh* [*wənikbəšâ hāʾāreṣ lipnê yhwh*]."

31. An apodosis-marking *wə*, permissive yiqtol, and apodictic weqatal express the results of obeying the preceding three conditions: "If you do this, and if you arm yourselves . . . and all the armed men you have cross . . . , and after that *you may return* [*tāšubû*], *and you will be free* [*wihyîtem nəqiyyîm*] from Yahweh and from Israel, *and this land will be yours* [*wəhāytâ hāʾāreṣ hazzōʾt lākem*]" (*GBHS* §3.2.2d.2, §3.5.2d, §4.3.3f).

32. M[L] spells "for your sheep" erroneously (*lṣnʾkm*) by transposing the letters ʾ and *n* (from "*ṣōʾn*," *DCH* 7:59–63). The correct spelling (*lṣʾnkm*) is found in 4Q23 MT[mss] SP.

33. Formally, "But what comes out from your [pl.] mouth [sg.], you must do."

34. After v. 24 in col. XXVIII of 4Q27, the rest of the line is blank, and the next line containing v. 25 ("[They said, the Reub]enites . . . a[s my lord commands]") is written in red ink, marking the scribe's interpretation that v. 25 initiates the next discursive unit (Ulrich, *Qumran*, 165).

35. With a sg. predicate (*wayyōʾmer*), the compound subject acts as one agent: "The Gadites said, as well as the Reubenites" (*wayyōʾmer bənê-gād ûbənê rəʾûbēn*; *BHRG* §35[9]). SP and LXX[ed] equalize them: "The Gadites and the Reubenites [all] *said* to Moses."

36. Against MT[L] "our cattle/livestock" (*miqnēnû*), perhaps not appreciating the asyndeton and collective potential of this noun, other witnesses read "and our cattles" (*umqnynu* 4Q27 MT[ms] LXX[ed] [*ta ktēnē hēmōn*]; pl. in 20:19; 31:9; see Wevers, *Notes*, 540–41).

37. LXX[ed] omits "there" since they are speaking in Transjordan.

38. The identifiable entity is fronted in contrast to the entity in v. 26: "Our little ones, our wives, our cattle, all our animals, will be there in the towns of Gilead, *but your servants* will cross over, everyone armed for war, to do battle in Yahweh's presence, just as my lord says" (*BHRG* §47.2.1[a]*b*; *IBHS* §39.2.3b).

them the land of Gilead as a possession. [30]But if they do not cross over with you armed,[39] they must accept possessions among you in Canaan." [31]The Gadites and the Reubenites answered, "What Yahweh has spoken to your servants, we will do.[40] [32]We will cross over armed in Yahweh's presence into the land of Canaan, but the possession that we inherit will be ours[41] on this side of the Jordan."

[33]So Moses gave to the Gadites and the Reubenites, and to half the tribe of Manasseh, Joseph's son, the domain[42] of King Sihon of the Amorites, and the domain of King Og of Bashan, the land[43] with its towns and the territories of the surrounding towns. [34]The Gadites rebuilt Dibon, Ataroth, Aroer, [35]Atroth Shophan,[44] Jazer, Jogbehah, [36]Beth Nimrah, and Beth Haran as fortified cities and folds for sheep. [37]The Reubenites rebuilt Heshbon, Elealeh, Kiriathaim, [38]Nebo, Baal Meon—some names being changed[45]—and Sibmah, and they renamed the towns they rebuilt.[46] [39]The descendants of Manasseh's son Machir[47]

39. A large plus is inserted here by 4Q27 and LXX[ed], perhaps to clarify what should be done with the possessions and wives (see v. 5). Here is LXX[ed] with 4Q27 in brackets: "[for the war before the Lord, then you shall carry over their chattel and their]wives[and their animals, ahead of you into the land of Chanaan]" (NETS; see Ulrich, *Qumran*, 166).

40. The obj. is fronted as the focused constituent: "*What Yahweh has spoken to your servants* we will do" (*BHRG* §47.2.1[2ab]).

41. A subjective gen., formally, "And/but with us will be the possession *of our inheritance*" (*wəʾittānû ʾăḥuzzat naḥălātēnû*; *GBHS* §2.2.3).

42. The const. noun *mamleket* can also be translated "*the kingdom* of King Sihon of the Amorites, and *the kingdom* of King Og of Bashan" (so ESV, NIV, NJPS). However, I prefer "domain" (or "territory," NLT; "realm," NET) for two reasons. First, their "domain" (*mamlākâ*) is explained geographically by the appositional accusatives: "the domain of . . . the domain of . . . [that is] *the land with its towns* [*hāʾāreṣ ləʿārêhā*] and *the territories of the surrounding towns* [*bigbulōt ʿārê hāʾāreṣ sābîb*]." Second, the term "kingdom" might wrongly imply that these kings, associated in Numbers with Amorites in Transjordan, were powerful forces like the New Kingdom of Egypt (ca. 1550–1069 BCE) or New Hittite Kingdom (ca. 1500–1180 BCE). Although the Amorites intermittently posed a threat to their neighbors during their elusive history in the third and second millennia BCE, they were consistently known as mobile pastoralists, shepherding flocks over great distances (see D. Fleming, "Amorites"). This explains how, by Yahweh's power, the reign of Sihon and of Og could come to an end in a single battle each (21:21–32, 33–35).

43. Indefinite SP: "land" (*ʾrṣ*).

44. Pronounced "Shophim" (*špym*) by SP, and "Sophar" (*sōphar*) by LXX[ed], which also omits "Atroth."

45. A hophal (pass.) fem. pl. ptc. from *sbb, modifying the first two listed names: formally, "Nebo, Baal Meon, *being turned around of name* [*mûsabbōt šēm*], and Sibmah."

46. The wayyiqtol and its predicates indicate a renaming, whereas the qatal verb simply means "they built": "*And they called by names* [*wayyiqrəʾû bəšēmōt*] the [preexisting] names of the towns that *they built* [*bānû*]." However, contextually "rebuilt" is understood, since the two and a half tribes settled in and rebuilt the preexisting yet war-torn towns and territories of Sihon and Og in Transjordan (v. 33; see 21:21–35).

47. 4Q27 adds "Machir, son of Manasseh, *son of Joseph*."

went to Gilead, captured it,[48] and dispossessed the Amorites[49] who were in it. **40**So Moses gave Gilead to Manasseh's son Machir, and he lived there. **41**And Manasseh's son Jair went and captured their tent camps and named them Tent Camp of Jair (Havvoth Jair).[50] **42**And Nobah went and captured Kenath and its villages and named it Nobah after his own name.

Interpretation

32:1–5. The Gadites and Reubenites request that Israel's leaders make a concession to allow these two tribes with their many cattle to settle in Transjordan territories, which were recently conquered by the Israelites and would be suitable for cattle, referring to livestock comprising all kinds of hoofed, domesticated animals.[51] In v. 1, the narrator begins with a pretemporal, static introduction,[52] which informs readers that the lands of Jazer and Gilead appealed to the Reubenites and Gadites because "they saw" (past narrative of *yr') that it was a "good place for cattle," which they possessed in abundance (see the translation notes on v. 1). The dyad subject of this introduction is "the Reubenites and Gadites" (v. 1; as Deut. 3:12, 16), but all seven of the ensuing references place Gad first, then Reuben, which probably reflects the older tradition (vv. 2, 6, 25, 29, 31, 34, 37).[53] These two tribes ask Israel's leaders—Moses, Eleazar the priest, and the chieftains—to make an exception for them to inherit land outside Canaan (vv. 3–5). While the reason for their request is that this land is fitting for their sizeable herds of cattle (v. 4; see the second translation note there), the logic of their request hinges on the reality that the nine Transjordan towns they recount are "the land that Yahweh conquered before the Israelite community" (vv. 3–4; see the first translation note on v. 4). This was the expanse of land under the domain of King Sihon of the Amorites and King Og of Bashan (Num. 21:21–35; cf. Deut. 29:7–8). The narrator then reported that Israel, by Yahweh's power, defeated these kings, and the Israelites settled in the land of the Amorites (21:31) and possessed

---

48. Before Canaan, Israel captures land from different Transjordan peoples (*lkd in Num. 21:32; 32:39, 41, 42; Deut. 2:34, 35; 3:4; then 24× in Joshua).

49. While the hiphil transitive of *yrš can refer to an obj. possessed—such as land (14:24), a mountain, a city, or a name—here the Amorite inhabitants of Gilead are "driven out" or "dispossessed" (*DCH* 4:303 [2]; *HALOT* 2:441, gloss 2). Dispossessing peoples occurs in 14:12 (Israel).

50. Jair captured "their tent camps" (ḥawwōtêhem), which gives rise to the toponym "Havvoth Jair" (ḥawwōt yā'ir), meaningless to Eng. readers (many versions, but see NLT). I prefer to express its meaning as "tent camp, tent village" modified by "Jair" as a possessive gen.: "Tent Camp of (belonging to) Jair" (ḥawwōt yā'ir; "ḥawwâ," *HALOT* 1:296).

51. Milgrom, *Numbers*, 266.

52. See Alter, *Biblical Narrative*, 80.

53. Noth, *Numbers*, 236.

the land of Bashan (21:35). In a canonical reading, then, Num. 32 explicates 21:31, 35. The Gadites and Reubenites reassert that the divine conquest of this region is over, and nine towns are effectively open for new settlers (v. 3; cf. 21:26, 35).[54]

Their request, however, can be heard as an echo of two preceding Torah stories that did not end well, the first being Abram and Lot (Gen. 13:10–12). Like Lot, the Reubenites and Gadites have great livestock. Like Lot, they see that the land east of the Jordan would be good for their livestock (cf. Gen. 13:5–6, 10). Like Lot, they leave Abraham or Abraham's descendants to choose land outside "the land of Canaan," which, according to Num. 13:2, 17, means land outside the borders of the land pledged by Yahweh (also Num. 34).[55] Consequently, is the narrator implying that two tribes are making an ominous choice, even as Lot settled as far as Sodom, full of wickedness and destined for divine judgment (Gen. 13:10c, 12–13; cf. Gen. 19)? After all, as recently as Num. 31, Moses had vividly reminded Israel of the women in Transjordan who "on Balaam's counsel, caused the Israelites to be unfaithful in the matter of Peor" (31:16) and faced Yahweh's vengeance.

The second story, which Moses explicitly recalls (vv. 8–12; see below), is that of the twelve explorers, ten of whom returned with a discouraging report (Num. 13). Like those ten ("We are not able to go up against those people," 13:31b), the Gadites and Reubenites appear to be shirking Yahweh's command to fight in Canaan for the land: "Do not make us cross the Jordan" (32:5). Additionally, although Num. 32 does not echo Num. 16 overtly, it was the same Reubenite tribe whose Dathan and Abiram, with Korah of Levi, led the insurrection resulting in Yahweh's horrible wrath.[56] The Reubenite tribe's history in the wilderness and the echoes of Gen. 13 and Num. 13 leave the reader with knowledge gaps about the future, creating a suspenseful moment:[57] Will Yahweh react in terrible judgment once again?

32:6–15. In anger Moses lambastes the Gadites and Reubenites, believing they have turned away from Yahweh and are planning to evade their calling to inhabit the land of Canaan that Yahweh promised to give to the descendants of Abraham, Isaac, and Jacob. In the opening and closing frames of Moses's tirade, he rhetorically expresses three reasons why the two tribes must not stay in Transjordan (vv. 6–7, 14–15).

---

54. Of the nine towns in v. 3, three were conquered in the Num. 21 stories—Dibon (21:30), Jazer (21:32), Heshbon (6× in 21:25–34)—while the other six were not mentioned before: Ataroth, Nimrah, Elealeh, Sebam, Nebo, and Beon. On archaeology and topography of sites identified with these towns, see Milgrom, *Numbers*, 267–68; Ashley, *Numbers*, 607–8; Walton and Matthews, *Genesis–Deuteronomy*, 212. These nine towns differ from the account in Num. 21 (Noth, *Numbers*, 237) and from Deut. 3:8–17 and Josh. 13:8–13 (Dozeman, "Numbers," 248).

55. See Ashley, *Numbers*, 606n26.

56. Leveen, *Memory*, 65–66.

57. Sternberg, *Poetics*, 265–66.

First, they are evading their military orders to fight with their brothers in Cisjordan (v. 6). Moses thinks that their selfishness will not only fracture the solidarity of Israel's tribal alliance but evade Yahweh's orders to Abraham and his descendants to fight with Yahweh to conquer Canaan (Gen. 22:17).[58] Loyalty to Yahweh is at stake, a motif with a Janus effect in the Hebrew Bible, looking back to the disloyal explorers (Num. 13–14) and forward to Josh. 22, which again calls into question the political and spiritual loyalty of the two and a half tribes.[59] Later Reuben and Gilead (Gad) are indicted in the Song of Deborah for failing to fight with their Cisjordan countrymen (Judg. 5:15d–17a).[60] Later still, the God of Israel motivates Tiglath Pileser III to deport the Reubenites, Gadites, and half-tribe of Manasseh to several Assyrian cities because of their unfaithfulness (1 Chron. 5:6, 25–26).[61]

Second, Moses is irate that, by refusing to enter Canaan, the Gadites and Reubenites will discourage the rest of Israel from taking hold of Yahweh's promise, just like the ten frightened explorers initiated the downfall of the entire exodus generation (Num. 13–14). The prophet-scribe Moses now acts as a wise rhetor, innerbiblically exegeting the language of the narrated events of Num. 13–14 to move the two tribes toward repentance.[62] I have placed in italicized bold font Moses's present exhortation, which he infers from how the Num. 13–14 events unfolded forty years prior.

Table 29.1. Intertextuality of Moses's Exhortation

Numbers 13–14*	Numbers 32:6–14
	[6]*Must your brothers go to war while you remain here?* [7]*Why do you discourage the heart of the Israelites to cross over into the land that Yahweh has given them?*
13:1–33	[8]Your fathers did this when I sent them from Kadesh Barnea to see the land.
13:21–24	[9]When they went up to the Wadi Eshcol and saw the land,
13:28–29, 31–33; 14:1–4, 10a	they discouraged the heart of the Israelites from entering the land that Yahweh had given them.

---

58. See the "Implications" essay in chap. 1, "Counting the Army." On their selfishness, see Sprinkle, *Leviticus and Numbers*, 403–5.

59. Artus ("Numbers 32," 371–81) believes these three stories present the two and a half tribes as a symbol for the diaspora Jews, who were still subject to the authority of the high priest in the Persian period.

60. Ashley, *Numbers*, 609.

61. Staubli, *Levitikus, Numeri*, 336.

62. Moses's speech exemplifies *haggadic* exegesis, a precursor to rabbinic *haggadah*, which involved "moral and theological homilies, didactic expositions of historical and folk motifs, expositions and reinterpretations of ethical dicta and religious *theologumena*, and much more" (Fishbane, *Biblical Interpretation*, 281).

Numbers 13–14*	Numbers 32:6–14
14:10b–12	[10]Yahweh's anger was aroused that day,
14:21–24, 28–30; cf. 26:63–65	and he swore, [11]"None of the men who came from Egypt, twenty years old and up, will see the land that I swore to give to Abraham, Isaac, and Jacob, because they did not follow me completely, [12]none except Caleb, Jephunneh the Kenizzite's son, and Nun's son Joshua because they followed Yahweh completely."
14:10–25:18	[13]So Yahweh's anger burned against the Israelites, and he made them wander in the wilderness for forty years, until the entire generation that had acted wickedly in Yahweh's sight was finished.
	[14]*And here you are standing in your fathers' place, a brood of sinners, to increase again Yahweh's fierce anger against the Israelites. [15]Because if you turn away from following him, he will abandon them again in the wilderness, and you will destroy this entire people.*

The new generation had not witnessed the great events of the exodus and Sinai, and most would not have witnessed the explorers (Num. 13–14), so they had to depend on Moses's testimony of the past to compel them to trust in Yahweh's promises for the future.[63] Moses looks back to the Num. 13–14 catastrophe as a precedent through which to interpret Israel's present relationship with Yahweh. Moses, or more precisely the scribes who convey Moses's speech (v. 6, "But Moses said . . ."), concisely redeploys the language of the Num. 13–14 narrative. In just two verses, 32:11–12, Moses reuses multiple lemmas from 14:21–24, 28–30 to underscore that the explorers disloyal to Yahweh were rewarded with death outside the land, while Joshua and Caleb, fully devoted to Yahweh, were promised life in the land (see the third translation note on v. 11; cf. Lev. 26:1–13). Moses summarizes the explorers' actions: "They discouraged the heart of the Israelites from entering the land" (Num. 32:9). This, of course, illustrates exactly what Moses believes the Gadites and Reubenites are now doing: "Why do you discourage the heart of the Israelites to cross over into the land that Yahweh has given them?" (v. 7; see the translation note there). They are ostensibly rejecting Yahweh's good promise to the patriarchs, just as the exodus generation did (v. 11; see the second translation note there).

The first two rhetorical reasons for not staying in Transjordan—evading their military service and discouraging the Israelites—cause the third reason: rebellion against Yahweh that incites his lethal anger once again. When Moses shames and condemns the two tribes for "standing in your fathers' place, a brood of sinners" (v. 14; see the first translation note there), he means that the two tribes of the new generation are tantamount to the ten rebellious explorers of the old. Because of the ten explorers, "Yahweh's anger was aroused that day . . . against the Israelites" (vv. 10, 13); now Moses believes the two tribes

---

63. Olson, *Death of the Old*, 151.

have again increased "Yahweh's fierce anger against the Israelites" (v. 14; see the second translation note there). Yahweh's people are a communal culture, meaning that Yahweh will cause the entire community to suffer for the rebellion of a subset of its members (v. 13; see the first translation note there).[64] The Hebrew Scriptures are polyphonic: the scribal tradents of Num. 32 warn that Yahweh "will abandon them again in the wilderness" (v. 15) while the Deuteronomists declare that Yahweh "will never leave you nor forsake you" (Deut. 31:6, 8; Josh. 1:5; 1 Kings 8:57). In the end, a fresh census (Num. 26), even Yahweh's reaffirmation of his covenant promise of land (26:52–56; chap. 27*), does not grant the second generation a license to sin or impunity from divine judgment (cf. Rom. 6:1–2; 2 Cor. 5:10; Heb. 10:26–27; 1 Pet. 4:17). Another cycle of forty years of rebellion and death outside the land hinges on what the two tribes do next.

32:16–32. The Gadites and Reubenites draw near to Moses, probably aiming to pacify Moses's anger (see the first translation note on v. 16). Immediately they restate their motive, seeking to convince a distrusting Moses. They do not merely rescind their prior request for war exemption (v. 5); they pledge to become shock troops, the vanguard leading their countrymen in the fight for Canaan: "Let us build sheepfolds here for our flocks and cities for our children, but we will arm ourselves for battle and go before the Israelites until we have brought them to their place" (v. 16; see the second translation note on v. 16 and the first translation note on v. 17).[65] Their admirable new proposal is enhanced further by three additions. (1) They desire the land not just for their cattle (as vv. 1, 4) but also for their children, whom they can protect in fortified cities from the land's inhabitants (vv. 16–17; see the second and third translation notes on v. 17). (2) They will not return to their homes until every Israelite receives their inheritance, and they will not take any Cisjordan land for themselves (vv. 18–19). (3) Having already stated that Yahweh has conquered this desirable land (v. 4), the two tribes now seem to imply divine providence by explaining, *"Our inheritance has come to us* on this eastern side of the Jordan" (v. 19).[66]

Moses accedes to their request if they are extremely careful to do what they have promised (vv. 20–24; see the second translation note on v. 22). One senses an ongoing skepticism on Moses's part, which resembles other stories, like Joseph's first interaction with his grown brothers (Gen. 42:9–20). To modern readers the verbal interchange in vv. 3–32 feels highly redundant,[67] but this has the power to slow down the discourse to underscore the precarious nature of

---

64. Cf. Josh. 7, 22; 2 Sam. 24. Kilchör (*Mosetora*, 316) contends that Deut. 17:2 alludes to Num. 32:13b: those "who acted wickedly in Yahweh's sight."

65. Milgrom, *Numbers*, 270.

66. See the "Implications" essay below, "The Divine Gift of Land."

67. Milgrom (*Numbers*, 492–94; followed by Douglas, *Wilderness*, 106) and Staubli (*Levitikus, Numeri*, 334–36) remove vv. 7–15 as an interpolation to expose a chiasm in vv. 1–38.

the path the two tribes are pressing to take (see vv. 6–15 above).[68] The unit contains nearly four sets of dialogues between Moses and the Transjordanians that give structure to vv. 1–42,[69] although vv. 33–42 are not a speech.[70] This back-and-forth debate between Moses and the two tribes reflects an ANE oath-taking ritual performance to enter into a contract, or vassal treaty, or loyalty oath.

Table 29.2. Oath-Taking Rituals Compared

Moses Lets a Few Tribes Take Transjordan Land (Num. 32:1–32)	Joshua's Covenant Treaty at Shechem (Josh. 24)
Moses excoriates the two tribes for their unfaithfulness to Yahweh (vv. 6–15).	Joshua excoriates the people for their unfaithfulness to Yahweh (vv. 2–15).
Two tribes pledge their loyalty (vv. 16–19).	The people pledge their loyalty (vv. 16–18).
Moses repeats the terms and warns of consequences of disloyalty (vv. 20–24).	Joshua warns of the consequences of disloyalty (vv. 19–20).
Two tribes repeat the terms and repledge their loyalty (vv. 25–27).	The people repledge their loyalty (v. 21).
Moses directs Eleazar, Joshua, and the patriarchal leaders regarding the pledge the two tribes have taken, as Moses will not be there to enforce it (vv. 28–30).	Joshua identifies the people as their own witnesses to the covenant treaty (v. 22a–b).
	The people assume the role of witnesses (v. 22c–d).
	Joshua gives a final charge of loyalty to the people (v. 23).
Two tribes repeat the terms and repledge their loyalty (vv. 31–32).	The people repledge their loyalty (v. 22).

The Joshua-Israelites exchange at Shechem overtly establishes a covenant treaty (Josh. 24:25–27), while Num. 32 does not, but both accounts distinctively oscillate several times between the leader's warning and the people's pledge. This suggests that the narrator envisions the Num. 32 interchange as a formal loyalty oath-taking ritual.[71] One can hear, for instance, resonances with the late Assyrian loyalty oaths, in which Assyrian state officials

---

68. Cf. Runge, *Discourse Grammar*, 388. Contra W. Lee (*Migratory Campaign*, 196), who sees the shift from public (vv. 1–15) to private (vv. 16–27) to public (vv. 28–32) as explaining the redundancy in the story.

69. Jobling, "Jordan a Boundary," 94–96.

70. Critique by W. Lee, *Migratory Campaign*, 196.

71. Milgrom (*Numbers*, 272–73) also perceives an oath-taking ritual, and Ashley (*Numbers*, vv. 613–14) calls this a formally ratified agreement and a covenant ceremony, while Knierim and Coats (*Numbers*, 301) classify the chapter's genre as a dialogue of negotiations ordered by speech formulas. I am suggesting even more specifically that a loyalty oath is in view.

and vassal states swear their loyalty to the Assyrian king's successor.[72] For example, in Esarhaddon's Succession Treaty (EST and VTE), Esarhaddon demands loyalty to his son and successor, Assurbanipal, then the subordinates collectively swear a loyalty oath to Esarhaddon.[73] Like Esarhaddon, who makes his subjects swear allegiance to his successor, Moses makes the Gadites and Reubenites swear allegiance to Yahweh since Moses knows he will not be alive to hold them accountable, and later the aging Joshua makes the Israelites swear their allegiance to Yahweh at Shechem now that they have settled in the land. Like Esarhaddon's subordinates, the Gadites and Reubenites also collectively and redundantly confess their complete loyalty to Moses and Yahweh: "Your servants will do as my lord commands . . . to do battle in Yahweh's presence, just as my lord says. . . . What Yahweh has spoken to your servants, we will do. . . . We will cross over armed in Yahweh's presence" (vv. 25, 27, 31, 32; see the second translation note on v. 25 and the translation notes on vv. 27 and 31).

32:33–42. The narrator brings the story to a close by recounting that Moses gives the former lands of kings Sihon and Og to Gad and Reuben and the half-tribe of Manasseh, Joseph's son (v. 33).[74] Strikingly, nothing is said of Yahweh here, with the implication that Moses has full authorization to reenvision the borders of Israel's inheritance! This soon will come into literary tension with the Cisjordan boundaries of the promised land in Num. 34.[75] The literary implication here, however, is that Moses is satisfied with the pledge of the Gadites and Reubenites to fight in Canaan, and readers of the Numbers narrative can infer that Yahweh approves this expanded land inheritance in his customary discourse with Moses (7:89; cf. Deut. 3:12, 16; 29:7–8).[76] By Moses's endorsing action in vv. 33 and 40, "The promise and hope of the new generation, though momentarily threatened, remains intact."[77] Moreover, within the Torah story, Moses does not allow Jacob's curse of Reuben to inhibit his land claims (Gen. 49:3–4).[78] Along with an expanded promised land, also perplexing is the inclusion of the half-tribe of Manasseh (Num. 32:33) with the other two tribes, most simply indicating that vv. 39–42

---

72. See Otto, "Covenant," 2047.

73. See Parpola and Watanabe, *Neo-Assyrian Treaties*, online.

74. Schmidt ("Ansiedlung," 497–510; "Sihon und Og," 328–29) isolates an older narrative (vv. 1–2*, 4–5*, 6, 16–17, 20, 24, 33–38*), which presupposes the defeat of Sihon and Og (Num. 21). Even so, Noth (*Numbers*, 237) observes that Num. 32 does not harmonize with Num. 21, which instead focuses on the plateau farther south, reaching to the Arnon, as the territory Israel conquered.

75. See the "Implications" essay in chap. 31, "How Big Is the Promised Land?"

76. Kilchör (*Mosetora*, 322) observes that Deut. 12 also presumes, with Num. 32 and Deut. 3, that Israel has already conquered the Transjordan territories.

77. Olson, *Death of the Old*, 93.

78. Douglas, *Wilderness*, 183.

were supplied later to the text as the scribes of the Torah explain Manasseh's presence in Transjordan.[79]

First, the etiology of vv. 1–32 explains the origins of Israel's settlements in Transjordan; yet it speaks only of the Gadites and Reubenites and says nothing of the three Manassite families (Machir, Jair, Nobah) who are called the half-tribe of Manasseh.[80] The Gadites and Reubenites go to great lengths to persuade Moses that they will fight with their Israelite brothers in Canaan (vv. 16–32), so it is surprising that Moses gives the half-tribe of Manasseh the land of Gilead without any pledge on their part (vv. 33, 40).

Second, the half-tribe of Manasseh appears to be tagged on in v. 33, which is repeated again in v. 40 as if to ensure readers against the absence of Manasseh in the story to that point. Specifically, the half-tribe descends from Manasseh's sons Machir, Jair, and Nobah, although mysteriously only Machir is recorded as his son in the second census (26:29).[81] In that census Gilead is Machir's son, but here Gilead is Machir's new home (26:29; 32:39–40). Readers will also recall that Zelophehad was a descendant of Machir's son Gilead (Num. 27:1).[82]

Third, the tag of vv. 39–42 noticeably breaks the pattern. Manasseh does not rebuild cities as the Gadites and Reubenites do (vv. 34–38) but captures and dispossesses the people (see the second translation note on v. 38 and the third translation note on v. 39). It is unclear what the renamed toponyms in Reuben's territory are (v. 37), but those in Manasseh's territory are linked to their conquests: Jair and Nobah choose their eponyms and are remembered forever by "Tent Camp of Jair" (Havvoth Jair; see the translation note on v. 41) and "Nobah" (v. 42).

The transfer of the "domain" of kings Sihon and Og to the two and a half tribes of the people of Yahweh reflects the struggle of ANE kings to expand the earthly domain of their deity as land for their people (v. 33; see the first translation note there). The "land with its towns and the territories of the surrounding towns" is a synecdochic triad for the whole domain of the Amorite and Bashanite king. The Gadites rebuild eight towns into "fortified cities and folds for sheep" located throughout Transjordan, in the southern, northern, and northwestern regions of Gilead and Bashan (vv. 34–36).[83] The

---

79. Levine (*Numbers*, 1:496–98) attributes vv. 39–42 to an early Yahwistic record; Seebass (*Numeri*, 3:359–62) sees a base layer in v. 39a, 41–42, with a Dtr layer in vv. 39b–40; de Vaulx (*Nombres*, 370) regards these as old memories the redactor has incorporated; Noth (*Numbers*, 240), Scharbert (*Numeri*, 128), and others are undecided about the origins of vv. 39–42. All these share the consensus that vv. 39–42 reflect a tradition that is distinct from vv. 1–38 (also Dozeman, "Numbers," 250; Milgrom, *Numbers*, 492–94; Ashley, *Numbers*, 606).

80. Milgrom, *Numbers*, 275, 494–96.

81. Cf. Seebass, "Machir," 496–503.

82. From Num. 32:33–42 and Josh. 17:1–6, Snaith ("Daughters," 126) infers that the story of the daughters of Zelophehad (Num. 27) is an etiology for how Manasseh held land in Transjordan.

83. Walton and Matthews, *Genesis–Deuteronomy*, 212.

Reubenites rebuild six towns, and distinctively, "they renamed the towns they rebuilt," particularly in Heshbon on the northwestern edge of the Madaba plain (v. 37; see the translation notes on v. 38).[84] The editor gives the last word to Manasseh's sons, Machir, Jair, and Nobah, safeguarding the memory of their names by their cities[85] and substantiating Manasseh's descendants' claim to Transjordan land. Unlike the negative connotation of city naming in other stories—like Babel, where the nameless "whole earth" resolved to make a name for themselves but are now remembered embarrassingly by Yahweh's power to "confuse" (*bll) their languages (Gen. 11:4, 9)—the city founders from the two and a half tribes now have eponyms like legends such as Romulus, the mythic founder of Rome, and Alexander the Great, who renamed many cities Alexandria.

Implications

The Divine Gift of Land

The narrator of Num. 32 is consistent that if the tribes of Reuben and Gad are to inherit land in Transjordan outside of the circumscribed promised land of Canaan, they must convince Israel's leaders that (1) Yahweh has decisively conquered that land (vv. 4–5, 7, 9), (2) they will lead their brothers in the fight to conquer Canaan (vv. 17–18, 20, 29–30), and (3) their land inheritance has shifted to Transjordan (vv. 19, 20–22, 27, 29–30). Even as the narrator does not shy away from Israel's very human struggle to displace indigenous peoples and to redefine the boundaries of the promised land,[86] a strong theological undercurrent in Num. 32 overlaps significantly with the thinking of Israel's neighbors. In ANE thought, the gods reigned from heaven over an earthly kingdom through a human king, so a god would give specific territories to the king to expand the god's kingdom on earth. In obedience, kings would defeat and claim ownership of the new land but always conceived of it ultimately as a divine gift. Echoes of such a divine land gift are heard in the ANE contractual literature,[87] and one might particularly see parallels between Num. 32 and 34 and the promissory royal grant of land and dynasty to an individual.[88] The giver is the great king, Yahweh, and the individual is Abraham (Lev. 26:42; Num. 32:11). What seems to differ is that Abraham was not given a royal dynasty (cf. Gen. 14–15 and 2 Sam. 7), and Yahweh's gift was more precisely

---

84. Walton and Matthews, *Genesis–Deuteronomy*, 212. Artus ("Numbers 32," 369) posits vv. 34–38 as a gloss on v. 33.

85. One might recall the fear of Machir's great-great-granddaughters, that their father's name would be erased (Num. 27:4).

86. See the "Implications" essay in chap. 31, "How Big Is the Promised Land?"

87. See Otto, "Covenant," 2047–51.

88. Weinfeld, "Covenant of Grant," 184–203.

to Abraham's descendants, an entire people, who are called "a *royal* priesthood" (Exod. 19:5–6) with a warrior leader.[89]

An illustration of a divine gift of land comes from the Middle Assyrian king, Tukulti-Ninurta I (reign ca. 1243–1207 BCE), whose name means "My trust is in Ninurta," the warrior god.[90] Like the oral map of Num. 34, Tukulti-Ninurta describes the topography and settlements of the divine land gift he claims to have received. Earlier in the book of Numbers, Yahweh conquers and subsumes certain Transjordan cities through Israel's military: "When he [King Sihon] came to Jahaz, he fought against Israel. But Israel defeated him in battle and took possession of his land. . . . 'Woe to you, Moab. You are destroyed, O *people of Chemosh!* He has made his sons fugitives, and his daughters war captives of King Sihon of the Amorites. We have overpowered them. Heshbon has perished as far as Dibon'" (Num. 21:23–24, 29–30). In the Num. 32 story, the Gadites and Reubenites refer to nine defeated cities dominated by Yahweh: "Ataroth, Dibon, Jazer, Nimrah, Heshbon, Elealeh, Sebam, Nebo, and Beon—*the land that Yahweh conquered* before the Israelite community is a land for cattle, and your servants have cattle" (32:3–4). The implication of Num. 21* and 32:3–4 is that Yahweh has defeated Chemosh and the pantheon of Moab and subsumed the royal domain of Sihon and Og (see the first translation note on v. 33).

Now the fulfillment notice of 32:33–42 takes this one step further, making clear that Yahweh has not only conquered but has also given their domain to his own covenant people. The Deuteronomists reaffirm these expanded borders of the promised land (Deut. 3:12, 16). In a wonderful accident of archaeology, three cities mentioned in Num. 21* and 32* appear in a ninth-century BCE inscription of the words of Moabite King Mesha, who boasts that he obeyed his god Chemosh by taking back land that Israel had captured.[91] Mesha's inscription reveals a deep political and theological clash: both kingdoms claimed to own the same specific sites east of the Jordan because both claimed that their deity, Chemosh (Kemosh) or Yahweh, had given them the same expanse of land.

Through Jesus the Messiah, the domain of God extended once again beyond the Jordan River to the east. This time, however, the expansion was not political hegemony over the eastern and northeastern Roman provinces of Syria, Perea, and the Decapolis. Rather, according to Matthew, Jesus fulfilled Isa. 9:1–2 by his own life-giving invasion into the personal lives of those who lived beyond the Jordan River (Matt. 4:24–25).[92] This royal son of David led

---

89. See the "Implications" essay in chap. 25, "Joshua, a Divinely Appointed Royal Shepherd?"

90. Grayson, *Assyrian Rulers*, 236–37.

91. "The Inscription of King Mesha," *COS* 2.23:138. See Tebes, "Mesha Inscription," 286–92.

92. John the Baptist prepares the way for the Messiah in towns and country around the Jordan such as Bethany in Perea, east of the Jordan (Luke 3:3; John 1:28; 3:26), and even baptizes Jesus

God's people, not to overthrow the Roman occupation of Transjordan, but to repentance as God's means of expanding God's reign in the world (Matt. 4:17). Transjordan was only the beginning. All who follow Jesus gladly obey his royal decree of discipling "all nations" (Matt. 28:19–20) even "to the ends of the earth" (Acts 1:8).

in the Jordan (traditionally on its east side; Mark 1:9). Jesus ministers "beyond the Jordan" (Matt. 19:1; Mark 10:1; John 10:40).

30

Travel Itinerary from Egypt to Moab

(33:1–56)

∼⤳∽

Overview

In Num. 33, the unidentified narrator meticulously reports Israel's travel itinerary from Egypt to the desert valleys of Moab, where the Israelites have been encamped since Num. 22:1. Interpreters continue to debate why the editors of the materials in Num. 26–36 have located Num. 33 here, after the episode with the two and a half tribes in Transjordan, rather than immediately following Num. 22:1. The literary effect of its placement is that at the completion of Num. 32, Israel's problems at Moab—international (chaps. 22–24), rebellious (chap. 25), sociological (chap. 27), militant (chap. 31), and intertribal (chap. 32)—have effectively been dealt with, and now Israel can recount God's faithfulness while fixing its gaze on entering Canaan, the final phase of its travel itinerary. The traditions underlying the itinerary remain a matter of ongoing discussion,[1] but it does fit within the genre of formulaic itinerary lists preserved from the ANE. The narrator prepares readers to interpret the travel itinerary through three lenses: (1) Moses and Aaron as Israel's guides,

---

1. The itinerary attributed to Moses (v. 2) has been reported by authors or editors after Moses (vv. 1–49). Some see the itinerary as Deuteronomistic (G. Davies, "Composition of the Pentateuch," 1–13; cf. Olson, *Death of the Old*, 115), others as Yahwistic (Budd, *Numbers*, 350–53), and others as Priestly (Cross, *Canaanite Myth*, 308–21; Baden, *Redaction*, 133; cf. Frevel, "Book of Numbers," 14), post-Priestly (Van Seters, *Life of Moses*, 153–64), or as a late collation of sources (Gray, *Numbers*, 443–44; Noth, *Numbers*, 242; Coats, "Wilderness Itinerary," 139–52). In this scholarly morass, others are more tentative about the tradition but still characterize it as a "learned study" (Holzinger, *Numeri*, 160, cited by Frevel, "Alte Stücke," 291n130; cf. Ashley, *Numbers*, 624–25).

(2) the report as recorded by Moses himself, and (3) Yahweh exhibiting his lethal force by defeating the Egyptians and their gods as Israel left Egypt (vv. 1–4). The core component of the unit is the summary of the places where Israel traveled and camped, bringing God's people, over the course of forty years, from the Egyptian Nile Delta to the Moabite desert valleys on the verge of their new homeland (vv. 5–49). The geographical trajectory of the chapter moves from *Egypt* (vv. 1–4), through the *Sinai wilderness* and *Transjordan*, to *Moab* (vv. 5–49) and into *Canaan*, where Israel must remain resolute to expel Canaan's residents, destroy the local cultic sites, and apportion the land by lot relative to the size of each of Israel's tribes (vv. 50–56). This last unit in the chapter (vv. 50–56) initiates the last segment within chaps. 26–36—namely, 33:50–36:13, which centers entirely on what is to occur in Canaan.[2]

Translation

[1]These[3] were the travels of the Israelites, who went out of the land of Egypt by their divisions under the authority of Moses and Aaron.[4] [2]Moses recorded[5] their departures, stage by stage, at Yahweh's command. So these are their travels according to their departures. [3]They departed from Rameses in the first month, on day fifteen of the first month. The day after the Passover[6] the Israelites went out

2. Milgrom, *Numbers*, 277; Ashley, *Numbers*, 634.

3. After 32:42 on col. XXVIII of 4Q27, the rest of the line is blank, and the next line, containing 33:1–3—"These were the travels . . . Moses recorded"—is written in red ink, indicating that the scribe regarded 33:1 as beginning a new unit of discourse (see Ulrich, *Qumran*, 166).

4. Formally, "by the hand of Moses and Aaron," where "hand" is a metaphor for a "(sphere of) power, rule, control, . . . authority (e.g., Gen. 41:35)" ("*yād* I," *DCH* 4:82, gloss 4a).

5. Within the Pentateuch story, the written Mosaic corpus of (1) "all Yahweh's words" (*kol-dibrê yhwh*, Exod. 24:4) is called "the Book of the Covenant" (*sēper habbərît*, 24:7), which may refer to the Covenant Code (20:23–23:19), whereas the Decalogue of 20:2–17 was written by God's finger; (2) "these words" (*haddəbārîm hāʾēlleh*, 34:27) referring to the so-called Ritual Decalogue (34:11–27), but the unstated agent of *ktb* in v. 28 is probably Yahweh; (3) "each man's name" and "Aaron's name" on their respective tribal staffs (*ʾîš ʾet-šəmô . . . šēm ʾahărōn*, Num. 17:17–18); here (4) "their departures, stage by stage" (*môṣāʾêhem ləmasʿêhem*, Num. 33:2), in Israel's travel itinerary from Egypt to Moab (Num. 33:3–49); (5) "all the words of this instruction" (*kol-dibrê hattôrâ hazzōʾt*, Deut. 27:3, 8), referring back to some form of Deuteronomy's legal core, either chaps. 5–26 or 12–26 or a putative original form (see Arnold, "Number Switching," 163–80); (6) "this instruction" (*hattôrâ hazzōʾt*, Deut. 31:9), possibly incorporating the blessings and curses of chap. 28 (whereas chap. 27 appears to have been inserted later between chaps. 26 and 28: Alt, "Die Heimat," 250–75; Otto, *Deuteronomium 23,16–34,12*, 1930–35); (7) "this song" (*haššîrâ hazzōʾt*, Deut. 31:22), presumably the forthcoming Song of Moses (Deut. 32:1–43); and finally (8) Moses finished writing "the words of this instruction" (*dibrê hattôrâ-hazzōʾt*, Deut. 31:24), an even fuller form of Deuteronomic instruction, perhaps including the Song of Moses (Deut. 12–26*, 28*, 32*).

6. Anaphoric article, "*the* Passover" (*happesaḥ*), refers to the first Passover, in Exod. 12 (*GBHS* §2.6.1).

defiantly in plain sight of all the Egyptians,[7] [4]while[8] the Egyptians were burying all their firstborn, whom Yahweh had killed among them. Yahweh also executed judgments on their gods.[9]

[5]The Israelites traveled from Rameses and camped in Succoth. [6]They traveled from Succoth and camped in Etham, on the edge of the wilderness. [7]They traveled from Etham and turned to Pi-hahiroth, which is to the east of Baal Zephon,[10] and they camped near Migdal (Tower).[11] [8]They traveled from Pi-hahiroth and crossed through the middle of the sea into the wilderness. They went three days' journey in the Etham wilderness and camped in Marah (Bitterness). [9]They traveled from Marah and came to Elim, and in Elim there were twelve springs of water and seventy palm trees, so they camped there.[12] [10]They traveled from Elim and camped by the Sea of Reeds.[13] [11]They traveled from the Sea of Reeds and camped in the Zin wilderness. [12]They traveled from the Zin wilderness and camped in Dophkah. [13]They traveled from Dophkah and camped in Alush. [14]They traveled from Alush and camped in Rephidim, where there was no water for the people to drink. [15]They traveled from Rephidim and camped in the Sinai wilderness. [16]They traveled from the Sinai wilderness and camped at Kibroth Hattaavah. [17]They traveled from Kibroth Hattaavah and camped in Hazeroth. [18]They traveled from Hazeroth and camped in Rithmah. [19]They traveled from Rithmah and camped in Rimmon Perez. [20]They traveled from Rimmon Perez and camped in Libnah. [21]They traveled from Libnah and camped in Rissah. [22]They traveled from Rissah and camped in Kehelathah. [23]They traveled from Kehelathah and camped at Mount Shepher. [24]They traveled from Mount Shepher and camped in Haradah. [25]They traveled from Haradah and camped in Makheloth. [26]They traveled from Makheloth and camped in Tahath. [27]They traveled from Tahath and camped in Terah. [28]They traveled from Terah and camped in Mithcah. [29]They traveled from Mithcah and camped in Hashmonah. [30]They traveled from Hashmonah and camped in Moseroth. [31]They traveled from Moseroth and camped in Bene Jaakan. [32]They traveled from Bene Jaakan and

7. A spatial *l* and probably *b* of manner: idiomatically, "The Israelites went out *with a raised hand toward the eyes of all Egypt/the Egyptians*" (*bəyād rāmâ lə'ênê kol-miṣrāyim*; *GBHS* §4.1.10a; §4.1.5i; see Num. 15:30).

8. A circumstantial *wə*: "the Israelites went out defiantly . . . , *while the Egyptians were burying* [*ûmiṣrayim məqabbərîm*] all their firstborn" (*GBHS* §4.3.3e).

9. The obj. is fronted as the focused constituent marked by an adversative *b*: "*And against their gods* [*ûbē'lōhêhem*] Yahweh executed judgments" (*BHRG* §47.2.1[2]).

10. A contextual rendering of "before the face of (opposite) Baal Zephon" ('*al-pənê ba'al ṣəpôn*).

11. Formally, "before Migdol" (*lipnê migdōl* MT). I repoint the vowel as "Migdal" (with NET), meaning "tower" ("*migdāl*," DCH 5:131).

12. Rendering the wayyiqtol as the logical result: "*so they camped there* [*wayyaḥănû-šām*]" (*GBHS* §3.5.1b).

13. On the "Sea of Reeds" (*yam-sûp* MT), instead of "Red Sea" (LXX), see the second translation note on 14:25.

camped in Hor Haggidgad. ³³They traveled from Hor Haggidgad and camped in Jotbathah. ³⁴They traveled from Jotbathah and camped in Abronah. ³⁵They traveled from Abronah and camped in Ezion Geber. ³⁶They traveled from Ezion Geber and camped in the Zin wilderness,¹⁴ namely, Kadesh.

³⁷They traveled from Kadesh and camped at Mount Hor, on the edge of the land of Edom. ³⁸Aaron the priest climbed¹⁵ Mount Hor at Yahweh's command, and he died there in the fortieth year after the exodus of Israelites¹⁶ from the land of Egypt on day one of the fifth month. ³⁹Aaron was 123 years old when he died on Mount Hor. ⁴⁰The Canaanite king of Arad, who lived in the southern region of Canaan,¹⁷ heard the Israelites were coming.¹⁸ ⁴¹They then traveled from Mount Hor and camped in Zalmonah. ⁴²They traveled from Zalmonah and camped in Punon. ⁴³They traveled from Punon and camped in Oboth. ⁴⁴They traveled from Oboth and camped in Iye Abarim, on Moab's border. ⁴⁵They traveled from Iim and camped in Dibon Gad. ⁴⁶They traveled from Dibon Gad and camped in Almon Diblathaim. ⁴⁷They traveled from Almon Diblathaim and camped in the Abarim mountains, near Nebo.¹⁹ ⁴⁸They traveled from the Abarim mountains and camped in the desert valleys of Moab, along the Jordan River across from Jericho. ⁴⁹They camped by the Jordan River, from Beth Jeshimoth as far as Abel Shittim in the desert valleys of Moab.

⁵⁰Then Yahweh spoke to Moses in the desert valleys of Moab along the Jordan, across from Jericho, and said:²⁰ ⁵¹"Speak to the Israelites and tell them, 'When you cross the Jordan into the land of Canaan, ⁵²you must drive out all²¹ the land's inhabitants before you. Destroy

14. Presumably to add back in the stop that appeared missing from 13:1, LXX^ed inserts "in the Sin wilderness. *And they set out from the Sin wilderness and camped in the Pharan wilderness,* that is, Kades." This aligns with 13:27, where there is another LXX^ed plus (Wevers, *Notes*, 561).

15. Formally, "he went up" (*wayya'al*). I render this wayyiqtol dynamically, "he climbed," because the southern Transjordan highlands, east of the Arabah (southern Dead Sea basin), are composed of Nubian sandstone on a granite foundation and are higher than 5,000 feet (Aharoni, *Land*, 40). The identity of Mount Hor is unclear, but in any case, Josephus's (*Ant.* 4.83) description matches the topography of Edom's highlands: "There [Josephus thought at Petra], *being surrounded by high mountains,* Aaron went up onto it" (*entautha hypsēlou periechontos orous auto anabas Aarōn ep' auto,* my trans.).

16. A specification *l,* meaning, "in the fortieth year *with regard to the exiting* [*lǝṣēʾt*] of the Israelites from Egypt" (*GBHS* §4.1.10h).

17. Here the meaning is "(in) the southern region" (*bannegeb*), but more frequently elsewhere this was a toponym, "the Negev," in southern Canaan. On the Negev, see the comments on 13:17.

18. The *b* (+ inf. const.) marks the obj. of a verb of sense perception: formally, "he heard the coming of the Israelites" (*wayyišmaʿ . . . bǝbōʾ bǝnê yiśrāʾēl; GBHS* §4.1.5b).

19. Formally, "before Nebo" (*lipnê nǝbô*) but known geographically to be "in the vicinity of Nebo on the road from Dibon to the plains of Moab by the Jordan at Jericho" (Aharoni, *Land*, 202).

20. Colon for "saying" (see the third translation note on 1:1).

21. At the beginning of vv. 52, 53, the identical weqatal, **yrš* hiphil, is used as a command but translated differently due to different objects: "*You must drive out* [*wǝhôraštem*] all the

all their carved images, destroy their cast images,[22] and demolish all
their high places.[23] **53**You must take possession of the land and live in
it because I have given you[24] the land[25] to possess it. **54**You must divide
the land by lot as an inheritance for your families. To a larger tribe you
must give a larger inheritance,[26] and to a smaller tribe you must give
a smaller inheritance. Wherever anyone's lot falls, it will be theirs. You
must inherit according to your ancestral tribes.[27] **55**But if you do not
drive out the land's inhabitants before you, those you allow to remain
will be barbed hooks in your eyes and thorns[28] in your side. They will
treat you with hostility[29] in the land where you will be living. **56**And what I
intended to do to them I will do to you."

Interpretation

33:1–4. With these opening words (vv. 1–4), the narrator introduces the ensuing record of Israel's travel itinerary from Egypt to the promised land (vv.
5–49). This introduction has been literarily crafted to stress four realities.

1. Moses and Aaron have been Israel's authoritative leaders out of Egypt
(v. 1). "Under the authority of Moses and Aaron" (see the second translation
note on v. 1) recalls not the subsequent failures of Moses and Aaron (Exod.
32:2–6; Num. 20:12; 27:14) but their famous work of rescuing the Israelites
from Egypt, just as the Deuteronomists eulogize Moses as the one "who did

---

land's inhabitants before you. . . . *You must take possession* [wəhôraštem] of the land." 2Q7
and one LXX[ms] omit "all," probably harmonizing to v. 55.

22. A gen. of material: formally, "their images of cast metal" (ṣalmê massēkōtām).

23. As with the first weqatal in v. 52, "You must drive out," the second weqatal and two ensuing yiqtols are imperative and pl., indicating that they are for all Israelites to enact: "*Destroy*
[wə'ibbadtem] all their carved images, *destroy* [tə'abbēdû] their cast images, and *demolish*
[tašmîdû] all their high places."

24. In the causal kî clause, which gives the reason why Israel must take possession of the
land, the indirect obj. is fronted as the focused constituent: "*because to you* I have given the
land" (BHRG §47.2.1[2a]; GBHS §4.3.4a).

25. A possessive article, "*their* land" (= LXX[ed]).

26. Likely to make the first yiqtol parallel to the second, SP alters the first to a sg.: "*you must
give* [trbh] . . . *you must give* [tm'yt]. . . ."

27. Formally, "To the larger you must increase its inheritance, and to the smaller you must
decrease its inheritance. To where goes (to it there) the lot, it will belong to him/them. According to the tribes of your fathers you [pl.] must inherit."

28. The pl. noun śikkîm (barbed hooks) is an OT hapax and could instead be a homonym
that means "thorns" ("śēk I" or "śēk II," DCH 8:147). The following noun, ṣənînîm (thorns,
pricks), occurs only here and in Josh. 23:13, a text that also speaks metaphorically of the ir-
ritation of any surviving inhabitants of Canaan but adds the covenantal warning "They will
trap and ensnare you" ("ṣānîn," DCH 7:136).

29. The verb means "treat with hostility, attack" ("ṣrr II," HALOT 3:1058, qal gloss 1) and
can refer to hostility against Israel's enemies (Exod. 23:22; Num. 25:17–18) or, as here in Num.
33, against Israel (Num. 10:9).

all those signs and wonders the LORD sent him to do in Egypt" (Deut. 34:11 NIV).[30]

2. "Moses recorded" every stage of Israel's journey directed by Yahweh (v. 2). The redundant literary bridge, "So these are their travels according to their departures" (v. 2b), asserts that the travel itinerary of vv. 3–49, or the formulaic itinerary of vv. 5–49, reproduces the content of Moses's record (v. 2). Over the course of the Moses story, the Pentateuch's editors narrate that Moses "recorded" or "wrote down" (qal of *ktb) eight texts. Most were explicitly revealed to Moses by Yahweh and span from the Book of the Covenant at Sinai (Exod. 24:4) to an earlier form of Deuteronomy at Moab (Deut. 31:24).[31] As part of this amassing Mosaic corpus, Israel's travel itinerary is the scribal production of Yahweh's prophet and, therefore, a valid document, worthy of integration into the Torah.

3. The focus is on Israel's traveling "at Yahweh's command" (v. 2), which recalls the narrator's altogether positive preview in Num. 9:23 but sets aside Israel's rebellions along the way (Num. 11–25*).[32]

4. Israel began its mass migration as a people by defiantly exiting Egypt as Yahweh manifested his deadly power over the Egyptians and their gods (vv. 3–4). If one isolates the aside of vv. 3b–4, the result may be the original form of the itinerary (vv. 3a, 5–49), which reads smoothly: "They departed from Rameses in the first month, on day fifteen of the first month. The Israelites traveled from Rameses and camped in Succoth."[33] However, so formative was the Passover event that the narrator or editor inserted it as an Archimedean point from which all must interpret the early history of the Israelites before they receive a land of their own.[34] After the inaugural Passover in Egypt on the fourteenth of the month (Exod. 12:6), the narrator here conceives of Israel's departure, not at night (cf. Exod. 12:31–33), but the next day, on the fifteenth (v. 3a), probably because Exod. 12:33 envisions the daily *morning* phase of forming dough, even before the yeast, for that day's bread.[35]

As an innerbiblical exegesis of Israel's departure narrated in Exod. 12:34–36 and 14:8, the narrator remarks that "the Israelites went out defiantly in plain sight of all the Egyptians," or formally, "The Israelites went out *with a raised*

---

30. On the contrasting perspectives on Moses (and Aaron) in Numbers, see Awabdy, "Holiness Contribution," 250–56.

31. For all these texts, see the translation note on v. 2.

32. Douglas, *Wilderness*, 125.

33. Cf. Scharbert, *Numeri*, 129; Schmidt, *Numeri*, 205. Van Seters (*Life of Moses*, 160) sees vv. 2–4 as Priestly. De Vaulx (*Nombres*, 373) perceives v. 4 as supplementary, while Seebass (*Numeri*, 3:377) views all of vv. 2–4 as supplementary.

34. See Staubli, *Levitikus, Numeri*, 337; see also the first translation note on v. 3 and the "Implications" essay in chap. 9, "Numbers 9:9–14 in the Progressive Theology of Passover."

35. King and Stager, *Life*, 17–18, 65–67.

hand toward the eyes of all Egypt/the Egyptians" (see the second translation note on v. 3). The narrator may be mocking a long history of Egyptian kings famous for their dominating right hand raised in war, as for example Pharaoh Rameses II (19th dynasty, reign ca. 1279–1213 BCE) depicts himself on the wall reliefs in the Great Temple at Abu Simbel, near the border of Egypt and Sudan.[36] From the death of Egypt's firstborn sons and male cattle (Exod. 12:29–33), the narrator extrapolates that Israel departed "while the Egyptians were burying all their firstborn, whom Yahweh had killed among them" (Num. 33:4a; see the first translation note there). The narrator presumably understands that, although preparations for burial probably began that night to prevent disease (Exod. 12:29–30),[37] the next morning, when the Israelites fled, the Egyptians were still performing their extensive funerary rituals of embalming the body (Gen. 50:26), pronouncing incantations by the priests, and depositing in the tomb practical and valuable items essential for one's afterlife.[38] The final word of the aside, "Yahweh also executed judgments on their gods" (v. 4b; see the second translation note there), is the narrator's way of saying that Yahweh fulfilled his promise to the suffering Israelites: "and on all the gods of Egypt I will execute judgment. I am Yahweh" (Exod. 12:12c–d). The narrator may be incisively linking the burial of the firstborn boys *and animals* (v. 4a) with Yahweh's judgment on Egypt's gods (v. 4b), whom the Egyptians represented as theriomorphic.[39]

33:5–49. Continuing in the voice of the narrator, the formal itinerary alternates between Israel's traveling (**nsʿ*) and camping (**ḥnh*) in a circuitous route from Rameses in the Egyptian Nile Delta to the desert valleys of Moab in sight of Canaan. A number of itineraries have been preserved from the ANE and Greece, suggesting that Num. 33:5–49 belongs to the same literary genre used by royal administrations in antiquity.[40] An Old Babylonian itinerary, The Road to Emar, follows a slightly different pattern: "'Day X, place Y,' where 'Y' refers to an overnight station along the route and 'X' refers to the number of days at the site. In most cases 'X' is a single day."[41] The Old Assyrian king Shamshi-Adad I records in a letter: "After the 20th day of the month [Mam] miturn, on the second day, I will leave for Mari. The day when I shall have sent this my tablet to you, on the second day from Shubat-Enlil, in the direction of Mari, I will depart. In the evening . . . from (ihu) Shubat-Enlil to (ana) Tilla, from Tilla to Ashihim, from Ashihim to Iyati, from Iyati to Lakushir, from

---

36. See Spero ("Gods of Egypt," 86) for other connotations of Israel's exodus as a humiliation of its oppressor, Egypt, and its gods. Also, Num. 33:3b could allude to the associated Festival of Unleavened Bread (Hepner, "The Morrow," 393).

37. Hepner, "The Morrow," 394.

38. See Kuhrt, *Ancient Near East*, 1:123, 132–33, 135, 140–43.

39. See Spero, "Gods of Egypt," 85.

40. G. Davies, "Wilderness Itineraries," 81; Knierim and Coats, *Numbers*, 309.

41. Sparks, *Ancient Texts*, 377; cf. G. Davies, "Wilderness Itineraries," 54–57.

Lakushir to Sagaratim."[42] New Kingdom Egyptian annals included different royal excursions and military domination in Syria-Palestine,[43] with Thutmose III's first war campaign being illustrative: "'Year 23, 1st month of the third season, day 16—as far as the town Yehem.'"[44] Similarly, Neo-Assyrian kings in the ninth and eighth centuries BCE depicted their war campaigns by the places where they stopped and the cities they defeated.[45] Here is one pattern used in these Assyrian itineraries: "From City A I departed, in city B I spent the night."[46] From these itineraries, the pattern of Num. 33:5–49 differs slightly: "They traveled from X and camped in Y. They traveled from Y and camped in Z." With forty-two stops and forty-one legs, Israel's journey is divided into three main phases: from Rameses to the Sinai wilderness (vv. 5–15), from the Sinai wilderness to Kadesh (vv. 16–36), from Kadesh to the desert valleys of Moab (vv. 37–49).[47]

Table 30.1. Travel Itineraries Compared (II)

Moses Story Correlation	Numbers 33 Itinerary	
	Depart from →	Camp at
Exod. 12:37	Rameses →	Succoth (v. 5)
Exod. 13:20	Succoth →	Etham (v. 6)
Exod. 14:2, 9	Etham →	Pi-hahiroth (v. 7)
Exod. 15:23	Pi-hahiroth →	Marah (Bitterness) (v. 8)
Exod. 15:27	Marah →	Elim (v. 9)
—[a]	Elim →	*Sea of Reeds*[b] (v. 10)
Exod. 16:1	*Sea of Reeds* →	Zin wilderness (v. 11)
—	Zin wilderness →	*Dophkah* (v. 12)
—	*Dophkah* →	*Alush* (v. 13)
Exod. 17:1	*Alush* →	Rephidim (v. 14)
Exod. 19:2	Rephidim →	Sinai wilderness (v. 15)
Num. 10:12 (called Paran wilderness); 11:34	Sinai wilderness →	Kibroth Hattaavah (v. 16)
Num. 11:35	Kibroth Hattaavah →	Hazeroth (v. 17)

---

42. G. Davies, "Wilderness Itineraries," 71.
43. G. Davies, "Wilderness Itineraries," 60–63.
44. G. Davies, "Wilderness Itineraries," 61.
45. G. Davies, "Wilderness Itineraries," 57–59; cf. Walton and Matthews, *Genesis–Deuteronomy*, 213.
46. Sparks, *Ancient Texts*, 377; G. Davies, "Wilderness Itineraries," 57; Knierim and Coats, *Numbers*, 309.
47. Milgrom, *Numbers*, 277.

—	Hazeroth →	Rithmah (v. 18)
—	Rithmah →	Rimmon Perez (v. 19)
—	Rimmon Perez →	Libnah (v. 20)
—	Libnah →	Rissah (v. 21)
—	Rissah →	Kehelathah (v. 22)
—	Kehelathah →	Mount Shepher (v. 23)
—	Mount Shepher →	Haradah (v. 24)
—	Haradah →	Makheloth (v. 25)
—	Makheloth →	Tahath (v. 26)
—	Tahath →	Terah (v. 27)
—	Terah →	Mithcah (v. 28)
—	Mithcah →	Hashmonah (v. 29)
—	Hashmonah →	Moseroth (v. 30)
—	Moseroth →	Bene Jaakan (v. 31)
—	Bene Jaakan →	Hor Haggidgad (v. 32)
—	Hor Haggidgad →	Jotbathah (v. 33)
—	Jotbathah →	Abronah (v. 34)
—	Abronah →	Ezion Geber (v. 35)
Num. 20:1	Ezion Geber →	Zin wilderness, Kadesh (v. 36)
Num. 20:22	Kadesh →	Mount Hor, edge of Edom (v. 37)
—	Mount Hor →	Zalmonah (v. 41)
—	Zalmonah →	Punon (v. 42)
Num. 21:10	Punon →	Oboth (v. 43)
Num. 21:11	Oboth →	Iye Abarim, Moab's border (v. 44)
Cf. Num. 21:30 (Dibon)	Iim →	Dibon Gad (v. 45)
—	Dibon Gad →	Almon Diblathaim (v. 46)
Cf. Num. 27:12; Deut. 32:49	Almon Diblathaim →	Abarim mountains, near Nebo (v. 47)
Num. 22:1	Abarim mountains →	Desert valleys of Moab along the Jordan River across from Jericho (v. 48)

a. Blank lines indicate that the location is not mentioned in Scripture prior to Num. 33.
b. Italicized names identify locations not previously mentioned in the Moses story.

The above chart does not include the descriptive landmarks and intermittent routes between encampments (see vv. 5–49). Also, the itinerary raises questions of lesser exegetical importance. For instance: Is Iim (ʿyym, v. 45) a shorthand (removing the middle letters) for Iye Abarim (ʿyy hʿbrym, v. 44)? Also, does the editor of this itinerary make historical inferences to

521

incorporate otherwise unmentioned stops?[48] For instance, the editor may have inferred that after Elim and before the Zin wilderness Israel would have naturally stopped beside the Sea of Reeds (vv. 10–11). Likewise, Moses and the people did arrive at the Abarim mountain range (Num. 27:12), which was "near Nebo" (see the translation note on v. 47), so the editor could infer that they set up camp there before finally encamping in the desert valleys of Moab (vv. 47–48).[49]

There are, however, three key interpretive issues.

1. The itinerary begins and ends by recapitulating many of Israel's journeys recorded in Exodus and Numbers,[50] but twenty-four toponyms (most of the italicized names above) were *never mentioned* as stops for Israel in the Moses story, and seventeen of those are never referred to anywhere else in the Hebrew Bible.[51] This has baffled not only Moses story readers, but also historical geographers who try to match the Bronze and Iron Age settlements with the toponyms of this itinerary.[52] Some are persuaded that the Num. 33 itinerary reflects fifteenth or thirteenth century BCE Egyptian, Sinai, and Transjordan settlements,[53] while others see a historical core in Num. 33 that has been edited to reflect the realities of the seventh or eighth centuries BCE, including sites not occupied until the Iron II period.[54] Others see Num. 33 as interacting with the itineraries of Num. 21:10–20 and Deut. 10:6–7,[55] or even incorporating settlement patterns of the Persian era.[56] In any case, we should not overlook the literary effect of Num. 33: The narrator, reporting Moses's record (vv. 1–2), fills in many gaps of the Moses story by informing us of twenty-seven additional stops in Israel's migration to the promised land. This implies that the Moses story has not told readers every leg of the journey, but narrated a selection of pivotal stops where, through one or

---

48. On Plutarch's use of historical inference, educated guesses based on other sources, and his own wider knowledge when constructing his biographies, see Bishop, "Historiography," 80–157.

49. See Frevel, *Mit Blick*, 60.

50. On the complex relationship between the Num. 33 itinerary and the exodus and wilderness traditions in the Moses story, see Coats, "Wilderness Itinerary," 139–52; Cross, *Canaanite Myth*, 308–21. Walsh ("Egypt to Moab," 20–33) argues from the Exodus and Numbers materials that there were originally two independent itinerary chains.

51. Regarding the toponyms unattested elsewhere, some count sixteen (Dozeman, "Numbers," 252), others seventeen (Ashley, *Numbers*, 623; W. Lee, *Migratory Campaign*, 197), and others eighteen (Milgrom, *Numbers*, 499).

52. See van Bekkum, "Geography," 93–117; Tebes, "Desert Place-Names," 65–96. For an entry into historical geography, see Rainey and Notley, *Sacred Bridge*.

53. Hoffmeier, *Ancient Israel*, 35–176, 235–49; Kitchen, *Reliability*, 191–99; 254–75.

54. Grabbe, *Ancient Israel*, 95–96.

55. G. Davies, "Wilderness Itineraries," 47–52; Kallai, "Wandering-Traditions," 175–84. G. Davies ("Wilderness Itineraries," 49) is typical in that he sets aside the non-itinerary recapitulations of Deut. 1:6–3:29 and Judg. 11:16–23.

56. Achenbach (*Vollendung*, 622–29) places 33:1–49 in the final phase of the theocratic revision of the Torah, which he dates to the fourth century BCE.

several accompanying stories, Israel's relationship with Yahweh had either progressed or regressed.[57]

2. Israel encamped *twice* in the Zin wilderness associated with the settlement of Kadesh (vv. 12, 36). Kadesh, also called Kadesh Barnea, was the southern border of Canaan (34:4) and therefore an optimal place of departure for Israel's twelve tribal leaders to explore Canaan (13:26; 32:8). Without noting that Israel stopped at Mount Sinai (!; see below), the literary implication of the laborious list of travels and encampments, spanning vv. 12–36 and representing nearly forty years from Exod. 16:1–Num. 20:1, could have been eliminated. This especially evokes the memory of Israel's wandering and the death of that first generation in the wilderness (Num. 11–25*).

3. On the one hand, there is an intriguing collection of asides inserted into the itinerary,[58] and on the other hand, there is a shocking omission of formative events. Regarding the omissions, nothing is said of Israel's exodus from Egypt by crossing the Sea of Reeds (see the second translation note on 14:25) or receiving Yahweh's covenant instructions (*tôrōt*) at Mount Sinai. The Sea of Reeds in vv. 10–11 does not refer to crossing the sea by Yahweh's power (Exod. 14*), since it is mentioned as a stop *after* Marah and Elim of Exod. 15–16*. So also "the Sinai wilderness" does not refer to Mount Sinai in particular, which could easily have been said, but advances the motif of the book of Numbers, "Yahweh spoke to Moses in the Sinai wilderness . . ." (Num. 1:1; see the introduction to the commentary). If the editor had not incorporated other asides into the itinerary (see below), these omissions would not be so glaringly obvious. Some have argued they were omitted for source-critical reasons, but if Num. 33 reflects a later addition to the Pentateuch materials, it is more likely that the editor simply wanted to highlight other issues. In particular, the editor saw fit to recollect the Passover event, both Israel's defiant exodus and Yahweh's destruction of the Egyptian firstborn (vv. 3–4 → Exod. 12*). The editor recalls Elim's springs and palms (v. 9 → Exod. 15:27), Rephidim's lack of drinking water (v. 14 → Exod. 17:1), and the Canaanite king of Arad who heard Israel was approaching (v. 40 → Num. 21:1).[59] We may never be able to fully answer why these asides were incorporated, but

57. Stories are associated with Rameses, Succoth, Etham, Pi-hahiroth, Marah, Elim, the Zin wilderness, Rephidim, the Sinai wilderness, Kibroth Hattaavah, Hazeroth, the Zin wilderness (again), namely, Kadesh, Mount Hor. Only Oboth and Iye Abarim (Iim) are stops without accompanying stories.

58. The asides were probably added later to the preexisting formulaic itinerary (Noth, *Numbers*, 243). G. Davies ("Composition of the Pentateuch," 1–13) argues that the itinerary properly reflects older sources and P, while the inserted asides reflect Deuteronomic and Deuteronomistic ideas.

59. See the translation notes on v. 40, which alludes to 21:1 in not so many words; v. 9 probably quotes Exod. 15:27, omitting "and there" (*wašām*); and v. 14 slightly modifies the syntax of Exod. 17:1. In all three instances, these small adjustments may indicate a *memorized reuse* of the Exodus source texts (see Bergland, *Reading*, 103–4).

they point to the historiographical axiom: "It is not sufficient to recall the past. The past must be recalled in specific and polemically useful ways."[60] In my estimation, the asides collectively attest to Israel's precarious early history through which Yahweh preserved and protected his people, sometimes leading them out of their awful context (Egypt) to rest at a desert oasis (Elim), other times meeting their physical and military needs right where they were (Rephidim, Mount Hor).[61] The battle with the Canaanite king of Arad (v. 40) may have been recalled because after that fight, Israel conquered every subsequent enemy on their route to Canaan.[62] Maimonides (12th cent. CE) rightly sees a theological purpose in these asides.

The most expansive aside in vv. 38–40 derives from Num. 20:27–21:1, relaying the death of Aaron and the interface with the king of Arad, already noted above.

Numbers 20:27–30	Numbers 33:38–39
[23]And Yahweh spoke to **Moses** and Aaron at Mount Hor . . . [25]**Take** Aaron and his son Eleazar, and **lead them** up Mount Hor. [26]**Remove** Aaron's garments and **put them** on his son Eleazar, and **Aaron will be gathered** to his people and will die there."	
[27]So **Moses** did as Yahweh commanded, and **they went** up Mount Hor in the sight of the whole community. [28]**Moses** removed Aaron's garments and put them	[38]**Aaron the priest** climbed Mount Hor at Yahweh's command,
on his son Eleazar. So **Aaron died** there on top of the mountain. And **Moses and Eleazar** came down from the mountain. [29]When **the whole community** saw that Aaron had died, the **whole house of Israel** mourned for Aaron for thirty days.	and **he died** there in the fortieth year after the exodus of Israelites from the land of Egypt on day one of the fifth month. [39]**Aaron was** 123 years old when he died on Mount Hor.

Comparing the two narrations of Aaron's death illuminates a contrast between their main subjects. In Num. 20* Moses is the primary agent acting on Aaron, while Eleazar and the community of Israel are secondary agents responding to Aaron, but other than climbing with Moses and dying, Aaron is only a passive subject (i.e., "Aaron will be gathered," v. 26). By stark contrast, in Num. 33* Aaron is not just *the only* active subject; he is highly honored in three ways. (1) Aaron climbs Mount Hor in personal obedience to Yahweh (33:38a; see the first translation note there), with nothing said of Yahweh's command to Moses or Moses's obedience to Yahweh (20:23, 27). (2) His death—forty years, or one full generation, after the exodus—is now and forever officially commemorated on Israel's calendar (v. 38b). (3) Dying at age 123 on Mount Hor means that Aaron exceeded the ideal three-generation life

---

60. Leveen, *Memory*, 42.
61. Similarly, Maimonides (12th cent. CE), cited by Milgrom (*Numbers*, 277).
62. Leveen, *Memory*, 43.

span of 120 years (v. 39), and later readers will see that Aaron exceeded the 120-year life span of Moses (Deut. 34:7). The final form of Num. 33 therefore stresses the enduring legacy of Yahweh's high priest, Aaron, and by implication compels the Israelites to honor Aaron's successor, Eleazar, Yahweh's new priestly intermediary in the emerging theocratic kingdom of Israel.[63]

33:50–56. Yahweh now speaks through Moses to the Israelites at Moab to reassert three of his prior orders: Israel must (1) drive out the inhabitants of the land, (2) destroy their Canaanite cultic objects and sites, and (3) divide the land by lot proportionately among the tribes according to their size. Some see a literary break at 33:50,[64] but even if this is so, the editors responsible for positioning vv. 50–56 seem to have done so deliberately: The narrator has painted an undeterred and overwhelmingly positive picture of Israel's journey to the edge of the land (vv. 1–49, both itinerary and asides), and now Israel must be warned sternly about what lies ahead (vv. 50–56). In v. 50 the geographical marker is unnecessary since Yahweh has been intermittently speaking to Moses "in the desert valleys of Moab along the Jordan, across from Jericho" (v. 50)[65] since at least 25:10, but we can infer that it has been happening since they arrived at those plains in 22:1 (see 7:89). The marker, therefore, serves to intensify readerly awareness of Israel's nearness to the land, which Moses himself will not enter (20:12), but in which Israel must enact Moses's words from Yahweh: "When you cross the Jordan into the land of Canaan" (v. 51c). This condition for entering the land, contingent on Yahweh's power (Num. 15:18) and Israel's obedience (26:64–65),[66] must be accompanied by Israel's purging Canaan of its people, cultic images, and open-air worship sites before Israel takes up residence (vv. 51–53, 55–56). Yahweh's iconoclastic orders involve the obliteration of three Canaanite cultic objects: carved images, cast images, and high places (v. 52).[67]

Yahweh's directive to drive out the land's inhabitants frames the subunit by *inclusio* of a point-counterpoint set, first positively, "drive out" (v. 52; see the first translation note there), then negatively, "But if you do not drive out . . . " (v. 55).[68] Expelling the local residents must be linked to filling the

---

63. Eleazar features prominently in Numbers: 3:2, 4, 32; 4:16; 16:37, 39; 19:3, 4; 20:25, 26, 28 [2×]; 25:7, 11; 26:1, 3, 60, 63; 27:2, 19, 21, 22; 31:6, 12, 13, 21, 26, 29, 31, 41, 51, 54; 32:2, 28; 34:17.

64. A case can be made for 33:50–36:13 as the book's final segment, concerned exclusively with what takes place in Canaan (Milgrom, *Numbers*, 277; Ashley, *Numbers*, 634). Also, some argue that 33:50–34:12 does reflect a source distinct from 33:1–49, namely, the Priestly base layer (Frevel, *Mit Blick*, 39).

65. This geographical marker for Yahweh's or Moses's speeches occurs in 26:3; 33:50; 35:1; 36:13.

66. See the "Implications" essay in chap. 1, "Counting the Army."

67. See the "Implications" essay below, "Canaanite Cultic Sites."

68. See Runge, *Discourse Grammar*, 386; and the "Implications" essay in chap. 21, "Devotion to Destruction."

land with Israel's tribes because Yahweh has given this land exclusively to Israel (v. 53; see the first translation note there). The language resonates with other texts (see below) where Yahweh orders the Israelites *to destroy* the peoples of the land, but here the command is *to drive them out*.[69] The locals to be expelled, however, would not include non-Israelite immigrants (*gērîm*),[70] a social class who lived among the Israelites and could offer sacrifices to Yahweh (15:14–16) and even celebrate Passover (see 9:14 and the first translation note there). The curse of not driving out the land's inhabitants is not only that they would become "barbed hooks in your eyes and thorns in your side" (v. 55; see the first translation note there) but also that Yahweh himself would tragically turn his hostility away from the peoples of Canaan and toward his covenant people (vv. 55b–56; see the "Implications" essay below, "Canaanite Cultic Sites").

Last, v. 54, which abruptly changes the topic to distributing the land proportionately among the tribes, was most likely inserted into the preexisting discourse of vv. 51–56 with its *inclusio* of driving out the land's inhabitants (vv. 52, 55).[71] The insertion of v. 54 is a curtailed duplication of 26:53–56, combining the human responsibility of assigning each territory in Canaan in proportion to the size of every tribe, with the divine guidance of assigning each territory by casting lots.[72] Now within the vv. 51–56 discursive unit, v. 54 takes on new significance: Israel must *empty the land* of its residents with their enticing cultic practices (vv. 51–53, 55–56) and synchronously *fill the land* with new residents, Israel's tribes, who submit to Yahweh's guidance to distribute the land equitably (v. 54).

Implications

Canaanite Cultic Sites: Destroy Them or Be Destroyed by Them

After retelling Israel's journey to the edge of the promised land (vv. 1–56), Yahweh then warns the Israelites about the next leg of their journey, their future settlement in the land now filled with non-Yahwistic worshipers (vv. 50–56). "Indeed, even when the people at last settle in the land, the full promise may still elude them (Num. 33:55–56)."[73] The expulsive and iconoclastic commands of Num. 33 (vv. 51–53, 55–56) are not anomalous, but resonate with similar ominous admonitions in the Book of the Covenant (Exod. 23:20–33), in the renewed covenant through Moses at Sinai (Exod. 34:13), the Holiness

---

69. A. Lee, "Iconoclastic Stipulations," 222.
70. See Douglas, *Wilderness*, 242.
71. Staubli, *Levitikus, Numeri*, 340.
72. See the second translation note on v. 54.
73. Olson, *Death of the Old*, 183.

Code,[74] Deuteronomy's prologue and legal core,[75] and the covenant through Joshua at Shechem (Josh. 24:11–24). One also perceives lucid connections with King Josiah's thorough cultic reforms toward centralized Yahweh worship in Judah.[76] When we take a closer look at Num. 33:52, in particular, we find that Yahweh issues a string of imperatives, which Israel must obey: "*Drive out . . . Destroy* all their carved images, *destroy* their cast images, and *demolish* all their high places" (33:52; see the third translation note there). Three Canaanite cultic objects are banned. "Carved images" (*maśkît*) were representations of deities carved in stone or silver that looked like animals (theriomorphic), humans (anthropomorphic), or a combination of both (therianthropic).[77] In distinction, "cast images" (*ṣalmê massēkōtām*) were images of deities constructed by pouring melted metal into a mold, either an openside mold or open sand casting.[78] Last, "high places" (*bāmôt*), while not identical to altars or standing stones, were open-air cult platforms,[79] typically stone constructions raised above the ground and used in cultic rituals for the Canaanite deities (see the translation note and comments on 21:28). These three are not an exhaustive list, as shown by analogous texts in Deut. 12:2–4 and Lev. 26:1, 30.[80] One point of clarity that is added in Deut. 12:4 can be assumed here also: "You must not worship Yahweh your God in their way" (*lōʾ-taʿăśûn kēn lyhwh ʾĕlōhêkem*). The issue is not merely that Israel must worship Yahweh alone (Exod. 20:3; Deut. 5:7); Israel must also not worship Yahweh using the preexisting forms of Canaanite and other non-Israelite cults.

The intense tone of Yahweh's orders in 33:52 raises questions about Israel's trustworthiness to obey the orders when they interface with the peoples and religious practices of Canaan. Throughout the Moses story up to this point, Israel has shown a mixed record of cultic faithfulness to Yahweh: syncretisticly constructing a golden calf to worship Yahweh (Exod. 32*),[81] obediently devoting to destruction the Canaanite city called Hormah (Num. 21:2–3), committing infidelity with the Moabite/Midianite women and Baal of Peor (Num. 25*), and most recently executing Yahweh's judgment on the Midianites (Num. 31*). This sobering history looms in the background of the rhetoric of Num. 33. In particular, in 33:55 the curse that Israel will reap if they disobey is that the

---

74. Lev. 18:24–30; 20:22–24; 26:1, 30. Following Wellhausen (in *Composition* and in *Prolegomena*), Knohl (*Sanctuary*, 98, 106n157) contends that Num. 33:52–53, 55–56 reflects the language of H, but vv. 50–51, 54 appear to reflect the Priestly Torah, which H expanded.

75. Deut. 4:23–28; 7:1–5, 16–26; 12:2–4; cf. Judg. 2:2.

76. See 2 Kings 22–23. See Staubli, *Levitikus, Numeri*, 341.

77. "*Maśkît* I," *DCH* 5:504.

78. See Mettinger, *No Graven Image?*

79. Levine, *Numbers*, 2:523.

80. On the connection of 33:50–56 to the Deuteronomic tradition, see Seebass, "Eigene Komposition," 97; Levine, *Numbers*, 2:522. Budd (*Numbers*, 360–61) sees a Priestly author supplementing Deuteronomistic themes with Lev. 26:1, 30.

81. See Hundley, "Golden Calf?," 559–79.

land's inhabitants will become "barbed hooks in your eyes and thorns in your side" (v. 55; see the first translation note there), which recollects the painful curses that Yahweh already portended at Sinai (Lev. 26:14–39) and anticipates the tragic story line of Judges. "They will treat you with hostility" (*ṣrr, v. 35) is profoundly not the way it was supposed to be. The devastating result of Israel's disobedience is that Yahweh would invert the Abrahamic blessing:

> I will bless those who bless you, but the one who treats you lightly I will curse. (Gen. 12:3a–b)

> They will treat you with hostility in the land where you will be living. And what I intended to do to them I will do to you. (Num. 33:55b–56)

In the end, Num. 33:50–56 becomes a presage to the Israelites to frighten them into choosing a life of exclusive covenant loyalty to Yahweh. We might question such frightening rhetoric as manipulative, but that entirely misses the point: Yahweh petrifies Israel with the horrors of divine judgment *so that* Israel will choose the path that leads to life in the land. A militant break from Canaan's local cults was essential for Israel's self-preservation.[82] We may easily neglect that the language used throughout this same frightening unit, vv. 50–56, also implies that, in contrast to the exodus generation, Yahweh is intent on blessing the second generation with life in their land inheritance (vv. 50, 51, 53, 54 [2×]).

Deuteronomy, conveying the last will of Moses, develops this rhetoric into a blessing-curse polarity to motivate Israel toward life-giving obedience in the land: "for he/it is your life" (Deut. 30:20). The referent of the pronoun ($h\hat{u}$') remains elusive, either "for *it* is your life," referring to Israel's act of "obeying his voice and holding fast to him," or "for *he* is your life," referring to Yahweh himself. Markl concludes that this ambiguity may be intentional: "While it means life for Israel to engage actively in the relationship with Yahweh, which includes obedience, it is also true that finally the living God from Horeb ([Deut.] 5:26) is the source of all human life (8:3, cf. 32:39)."[83] The alternative to life-giving obedience to Yahweh (Deut. 28:1–13) is disobedience, resulting in the curse of petrifying divine retribution (28:14–16). This is not relegated only to the Old Testament. Jesus also stresses the terrifying judgment of God in order to urge his disciples to honor Christ and so be accepted by their heavenly Father on the day of judgment (Matt. 10:27, 32–33). As Jesus's followers, we must develop the habit of repenting as often as we become aware of our sin (Luke 13:3). In love, we must also urge not only unbelievers to repent in view of God's coming wrath (Acts 17:30–31) but also our own family members in the body of Christ to return to the truth and be rescued from death (James 5:19–20).

82. A. Lee, "Iconoclastic Stipulations," 225.
83. Markl, "This Word," 86.

31

Borders of Israel's Inheritance in Canaan

(34:1–29)

Overview

Transjordan territory has been allotted to Reuben, Gad, and the half-tribe of Manasseh (Num. 32*; 34:13–15), and the travel itinerary from Egypt to Canaan has been reviewed, with the Israelites encamped at the edge of the promised land (Num. 33*). Next, as one would expect in the ANE context in which deities give specific territories to their people, Yahweh demarcates the region in which his covenant people will live, ideally permanently. Through his intermediary prophet Moses, Yahweh creates an oral map of the southern, western, northern, and eastern borders of Israel's inheritance in the land of Canaan (vv. 1–12). The implication of v. 13 is that Moses communicates Yahweh's map to the Israelites and then reasserts the outcome of Num. 32* that Reuben, Gad, and the half-tribe of Manasseh inherit land in Transjordan, not in Canaan (vv. 13–15). The discursive unit concludes as Yahweh authorizes Eleazar the high priest, Joshua, Israel's new leader, and ten chieftains from Israel's western tribes to assign the recently demarcated land of Canaan to the ten and a half Israelite tribes (vv. 16–29). The lead words "inheritance" and "inherit" govern chap. 34, accentuating the transition from the wilderness (Num. 1–25) to Israel's imminent migration into the land (Num. 26–36).[1] Numbers 35 can be seen as a supplement to the oral map (Num. 34) by designating towns for the Levites within the boundaries

---

1. Leveen, *Memory*, 36. See "inheritance" (*nḥlh*) in vv. 2, 14, 15; and "inherit" (**nḥl*) in vv. 13, 17, 18, 29.

of the land (35:1–8) and asylum towns for involuntary homicide (35:9–34).[2] Although the borders of Canaan are smaller than what God promised to the patriarchs and their descendants, the language of Num. 34 points to Yahweh's determination to fulfill his land promise to Abram/Abraham and his descendants (Gen. 15:7–21).[3]

Translation

[1]Then Yahweh spoke to Moses: [2]"Command the Israelites, and tell them: 'When you enter the land of Canaan,[4] this is the land that will be allotted[5] to you as an inheritance, the land of Canaan with its borders: [3]your southern border[6] will extend from the Zin wilderness along the side of Edom, and your southern border will run eastward to the edge of the Salt Sea,[7] [4]and then your border will turn from the south to the Scorpions' Ascent,[8] cross to Zin, and its southern limit will be to Kadesh Barnea. Then it will extend to the settlement of Addar[9] and cross to Azmon. [5]Then the border will turn from Azmon to the Wadi of Egypt, and its limit will be to the Sea. [6]Your western border will be the

2. Milgrom, *Leviticus*, 282; W. Lee, *Migratory Campaign*, 202.

3. See the "Implications" essay in chap. 29, "The Divine Gift of Land."

4. Formally, in apposition, "into the land, Canaan" (MT LXX^ed). SP has a gen., "into the land of Canaan."

5. Formally, "the land that *will fall* [*tippōl*] to you as an inheritance," which may allude to the way the lots fall when cast in Yahweh's presence to distribute the land inheritance among the tribes (see Josh. 18:1–10).

6. Here SP reads "side to the south" with LXX^ed "side that is *to* the southwest" (NETS). Throughout the chapter, SP suffixes toponyms and directions with the directive *hē'* (a.k.a. *hē'* locale, *BHRG* §28.1) differently from MT (see vv. 3, 5, 6, 7, 8, 9, 11).

7. "Salt Sea" (*yām-hammelaḥ*) was called this because of its extremely high salinity (34.2% in 2011) and salt (halite) deposits (today on its western coast); see Gen. 14:3 ("valley of Siddim, that is the Salt Sea' *'ēmeq haśśiddîm hû' yām hammelaḥ*) and 19:26 (where Lot's wife turned to salt). This body of water is confidently identified in the Jordan Rift Valley as the Dead Sea, whose surface and shoreline today is at 1,365–1,412 feet (416–430.5 meters) below sea level, the lowest elevation on the land surface of the earth.

8. Instead of "the ascent of Akrabbim" (NRSV, ESV, NJPS), "Scorpions' Ascent" (*ma'ălēh 'aqrabbîm*) preserves for English readers the meaning of this southern toponym that would have been apparent to Hebrew readers. On the historical geography, see Görg, "Zum 'Skorpionenpass,'" 508–9.

9. Most render this "Hazar Addar," but early readers would have perceived that the first noun in const., even as a fixed toponym, means "settlement, village" (const. *ḥăṣar* from *ḥāṣēr*, see Gen. 25:16; *HALOT* 1:345, gloss A1; *DCH* 3:296 gloss 3). This is also true of "settlement of Enan" in vv. 9–10 (cf. "Hazar Enan"). LXX^ed "to the village of *Arad*" was probably an aural error in its Hebrew source text (*'ārād* for *'addār*) or reflects deliberate modification in its source because Hazzar Addar appears only here in the Pentateuch. The king of Arad has already been mentioned twice in Numbers (21:1; 33:40), and Arad was the more well-known site—a famous Early Bronze Canaanite settlement until ca. 2650 BCE, deserted, then occupied from the 11th cent. until 587–577 BCE, when it was destroyed by the Neo-Babylonian king Nebuchadnezzar II.

Great Sea and its coast.[10] This will be your western border. [7]And this will be your northern border: from the Great Sea you will draw a line[11] to Mount Hor; [8]from Mount Hor you will draw a line to Lebo Hamath, and the border's limit[12] will be to Zedad. [9]The border will extend to Ziphron, and its limit will be to the settlement of Enan. This will be your northern border. [10]For your eastern border draw a line[13] from the settlement of Enan to Shepham. [11]The border will go down from Shepham to Riblah, on the east side of Ain, and the border will go down and reach[14] the east side of the Sea of Kinnereth. [12]Then the border will go down along the Jordan,[15] and its limit will be to the Salt Sea. This will be your land by[16] its borders that surround it.'"

[13]Then Moses commanded the Israelites: "This is the land that you will inherit[17] by lot, which Yahweh has commanded to give[18] to the nine and a half tribes,[19] [14]because the Reubenite tribe by their patriarchs' households, Gadite tribe by their patriarchs' households, and half the Manasseh tribe have received their inheritance. [15]The two and a half tribes have received their inheritance on the other side of the Jordan,[20] east of Jericho, toward the sunrise."

[16]Yahweh said to Moses: [17]"These are the names of the men who are to assign[21] the land to you as an inheritance: Eleazar the priest and

---

10. In place of "the Great Sea *and coast*" (*ûgəbûl*), formally, "and border," SP and LXX[ed] read "the Great Sea *will determine the border*."

11. This piel imperatival yiqtol (*GBHS* §3.2.2.d.4) has a verbal root (*t'h*) that appears in the OT only here in 34:7, 8, meaning "to mark (out a boundary)" (*DCH* §8:581) or "to signify, delineate, mark a boundary" (*HALOT* 4:1673).

12. SP and LXX[ed]: "*its* [pron.] outlet *shall be* [sg.] the borders . . ." Similarly, see vv. 9, 12.

13. This hithpael imperatival weqatal (*GBHS* §3.5.2.c) is from "desire" (*'wh*), but contextually it must refer to boundary marking (*t'h*, vv. 7, 8), so its spelling should probably be emended to *wəhit'êtem*, meaning "draw a line" (*DCH* §8:581).

14. This weqatal command, "reach" (*ûmāḥā*), is an OT hapax and denotes something like "to strike against, i.e., reach, meet" ("*mḥḥ* II," *DCH* 5:215; *HALOT* 2:568).

15. Formally, "down *to the Jordan*" (*hayyardēnâ*, with *hē'* locale, *BHRG* §28.1), but the syntax may allow "down along the Jordan" to express the drop in elevation from the Sea of Kinnereth (Galilee, 686–705ft/209–215m below sea level) to the Salt Sea (Dead Sea, 1,365–1,412ft/416–430.5m below sea level).

16. A normative *l* that marks the division of the land into parts (*GBHS* §4.1.10.i).

17. This hithpael imperatival yiqtol has a reflexive meaning, but in this root (*nḥl*) the subject (you pl.) is not the direct obj. (the land) but the indirect obj., meaning "which you must inherit (it) for yourselves" (*GBHS* §3.2.2.d.4; §3.1.5.a).

18. LXX[ed] reads, "commanded *Moyses* [*tō Mōusē*] to give," which illuminates that the MT/SP may assume Moses as the obj. by ellipsis (*IBHS* §11.4.3), and therefore I render the inf. with an act. voice: "commanded [Moses] *to give* [*lātēt*]" (NRSV, ESV; contra NLT, NIV, NET, NJPS).

19. LXX[ed] adds "half-tribe *of Manassē*," probably to harmonize with v. 14 (Wevers, *Notes*, 578; also see 32:33).

20. Formally, "'(from) across the Jordan" (*mē'ēber ləyardēn*) (NJPS) or "beyond the Jordan" (ESV, NRSV), but not "on this side of the Jordan" (NET).

21. Formally, "inherit for you [pl.]."

Nun's son Joshua. **¹⁸**You must take one chieftain from every tribe to assign the land as an inheritance. **¹⁹**These are the names of the men: from the tribe of Judah, Jephunneh's son Caleb; **²⁰**from²² the Simeonite tribe, Ammihud's son Shemuel; **²¹**from the tribe of Benjamin,²³ Kislon's son Elidad; **²²**and from the Danite tribe, a chieftain, Jogli's son Bukki. **²³**From the Josephites, Ephod's son Hanniel, a chieftain from the tribe of Manasseh; **²⁴**from the Ephraimite tribe, a chieftain, Shiphtan's son Kemuel; **²⁵**from the Zebulunite tribe, a chieftain, Parnach's son Elizaphan; **²⁶**from the Issacharite tribe, a chieftain, Azzan's son Paltiel; **²⁷**from the Asherite tribe, a chieftain, Shelomi's son Ahihud; **²⁸**and from the Naphtalite tribe, a chieftain, Ammihud's son Pedahel." **²⁹**These are the ones whom Yahweh commanded to assign the inheritance among the Israelites in the land of Canaan.

Interpretation

34:1–12. In this speech, Yahweh paints an oral map for the Israelites of the southern, western, northern, and eastern borders of Israel's inheritance in the land of Canaan.²⁴ The editors introduce the monologue with the standard superscription (Yahweh→Moses) and two additional quotative frames ("command the Israelites" and "tell them"), which slow down the discourse in anticipation of Yahweh's words intended for all the Israelites. The oral map of Israel's borders (vv. 3–12b) is itself bordered literarily by the narrator's *inclusio* (vv. 2c, 12c).²⁵ The early audiences of Num. 34* presumably knew the contours and toponyms of that land, but for many today, reading Num. 34* is like reading for the first time the place names and topographical markers on a detailed map of an unfamiliar country. When we can confidently identify the meaning of a toponym in vv. 3–12 that was apparent to the original Hebrew-speaking audience, I translate that meaning. For example, in v. 4, "ascent of Akrabbim" (many versions) means "Scorpions' Ascent," and "Hazar Addar" is "the settlement of Addar" (see the translation notes on v. 4). This verbal map revealed by Yahweh ostensibly matches the northern extent of the exploration of the twelve (Num. 13:21–26)²⁶ and, with detail similar to Num. 34*, the maps given to Joshua and later to Ezekiel in his vision of the land of the restored temple community.

22. This asyndetic translation matches SP and LXX^ed (vs. MT conjunctive waw).
23. On SP's spelling of Benjamin, see the translation note on 2:22.
24. Specific language that supports such an oral map could be the directive "draw a line" (see the translation notes on vv. 7 and 10).
25. See Runge, *Discourse Grammar*, 387; see also the "Implications" essay below, "How Big Is the Promised Land?"
26. See Olson, *Death of the Old*, 143; Levine, *Numbers*, 2:539.

Table 31.1. Oral Maps Compared

	Israel in Canaan (Num. 34:3–12)	Judah (Josh. 15:2–12)	Restored Temple Community (Ezek. 47:13–20)
Southern Border	Zin wilderness (v. 3) Side of Edom Edge of the Salt Sea (see the second translation note on v. 3) Scorpions' Ascent (v. 4) Zin Kadesh Barnea	Southern tip of the Salt Sea South of Scorpions' Ascent Zin Kadesh Barnea Hezron	Tamar Meribath Kadesh, the river
	Settlement of Addar Azmon (v. 5) Wadi of Egypt the Sea	Addar Karka Azmon Wadi of Egypt the Sea	the Great Sea
Western Border	the Great Sea and its coast (v. 6)	the Great Sea	the Great Sea, opposite Lebo Hamath
Northern Border	the Great Sea (v. 7) Mount Hor Lebo Hamath (v. 8) Zedad Ziphron (v. 9) Settlement of Enan	north of the Salt Sea at the mouth of the Jordan Beth Hoglah north of Beth Arabah Stone of Bohan (son of Reuben) Debir from the Valley of Achor Gilgal (opposite the Adummim Pass south of the valley) waters of En Shemesh En Rogel Ben Hinnom Valley Slope of the Jebusites on the south (Jerusalem) top of the hill opposite the Ben Hinnom Valley spring of the waters of Nephtoah Cities of Mount Ephron Baalah (Kiriath Jearim) Mount Seir Slope of Mount Jearim (Kesalon) Beth Shemesh Timnah Slope of Ekron Shikkeron Mount Baalah Jabneel the Sea	the Great Sea Hethlon Zedad Hamath Berothah Sibraim (between the border of Damascus and Hamath) Settlement of Hattikon Hauran Settlement of Enan (border of Damascus)

	Israel in Canaan (Num. 34:3–12)	Judah (Josh. 15:2–12)	Restored Temple Community (Ezek. 47:13–20)
Eastern Border	Settlement of Enan (v. 10) Shepham Riblah (east side of Ain; v. 11) East side of the Sea of Kinnereth [Galilee]	the Salt Sea	
	Along the Jordan (v. 12; see the first translation note there) the Salt Sea	mouth of the Jordan River	the Jordan River (between Hauran and Damascus, between Gilead and Israel)

In Num. 34*, the eastern border is marked off by more sites along the Great Rift Valley, whereas in Josh. 15* and even Ezek. 47*, the northern border is delineated in far greater specificity, but overall Ezekiel reduces the toponyms.[27] In all three lists, by leaving off the boundaries of the territories of Reuben, Gad, and the half-tribe of Manasseh in Transjordan, these tribes are segregated outside "Canaan" proper (Num. 34:2; cf. vv. 14–15), which calls into question their solidarity with the majority of the Israelite tribes. This rift began in the narrative in Num. 32* when, to Moses's consternation, the eastern two and a half tribes choose their own land outside of Canaan, and it reemerges in Josh. 22*, when the eastern tribes innovate by constructing a second altar to Yahweh.

These political tensions form a substratum to vv. 1–12 that remain a matter of speculation; but with clarity, the map of Israel's borders implies that Yahweh demarcates the territory that he will give to his covenant people, just as ANE deities gave specific expanses of land to the nations that belonged to them.[28]

34:13–15. Moses reiterates that the land must be inherited by lot and clarifies that Reuben, Gad and the half-tribe of Manasseh will not inherit any land in Canaan. In a synchronic reading, the deictic adjectives—"*This* is the land that you will inherit by lot, *which* Yahweh has commanded to give to the nine and a half tribes" (v. 13)—refer back to vv. 2–12, implying that Moses delivers Yahweh's map of Israel's future land borders (vv. 2–12). Just after the second census (chap. 26), Yahweh already ordered that Israel subdivide their land specifically by lot (26:55–56), and just before he gave the land's map, he reiterated the order to cast lots (33:54). Casting lots means that it is ultimately Yahweh who subdivides the land inheritance among the nine and a half tribes of his people (see the first translation note

---

27. See Hutchens, "Boundaries," 215–30; Y. Levin, "Numbers 34:2–12," 56–61; P. Guillaume, *Land*, 152–58.

28. See the "Implications" essay in chap. 29, "The Divine Gift of Land."

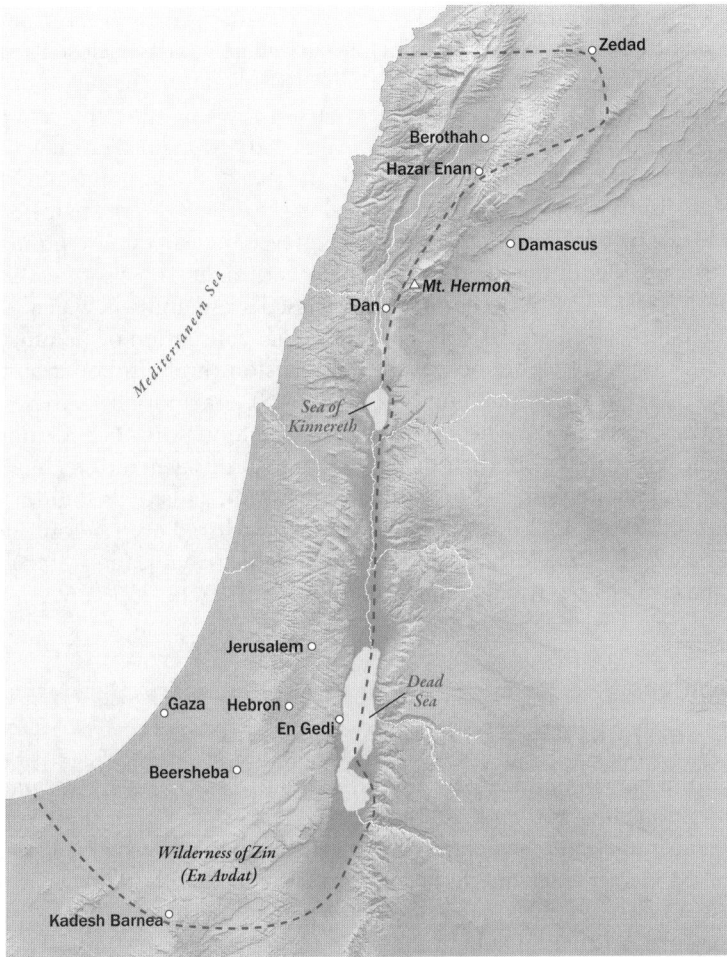

Map 31.1. Approximate Borders of the Promised Land (according to Num. 34:3–12)

on v. 13).[29] In v. 14, Moses over-specifies by repeating the decision in Num. 32* that the remaining two and a half tribes—the Reubenites, Gadites, and the other half of Manasseh—would not inherit land within the boundaries of Canaan just detailed (vv. 1–12) since they have already received their inheritance to the east, in Transjordan.[30]

34:16–29. Yahweh appoints Eleazar, the high priest; Joshua, Israel's new leader; and chieftains from the nine and a half tribes to assign to the Israelite

29. See the comments on 26:52–56.
30. Artus ("Numbers 32," 374) sees the Transjordan tribes, explicitly outside the boundaries of Canaan (vv. 1–12), as representative of the Jewish diaspora living outside the land.

tribes the land of Canaan, which Yahweh has just mapped out (vv. 1–12).[31] The name list of vv. 19–27 reflects a distinct literary genre[32] and is enclosed as a unit by the narrator's *inclusio* (vv. 17a, 29). This list includes the names of the men who would assign the land inheritance, each man's father's name and tribe, which recollects the list of chieftains who assisted Moses and Aaron in count-ing the first generation of fighters (1:4–16) and that of the explorers of Canaan (13:4–16). Except for Jephunneh's son Caleb (13:6; 34:19),[33] the names of the tribal leaders differ on all these lists, which prevents, even if unintentionally, a nepotistic transfer of the chieftaincy from fathers to their own sons (cf. 1:5–15 and 34:16–28). "The old generation has passed away, and a new generation of leadership has emerged."[34] In fact, the social convention of naming each chieftain's father—Jephunneh, Ammihud, Kislon, Jogli, Ephod, Shiphtan, Parnach, Azzan, Shelomi, Ammihud (vv. 19–28)—memorializes these men, but at the same time recollects that they were among those condemned to die in the wilderness with their own rebellious exodus generation (14:26–35; 26:64–65). Having replaced his late father, Aaron, as Israel's high-priestly leader (20:25–28), Eleazar features prominently, listed even before Joshua (34:17; cf. 27:19–22). Joshua is no longer Judah's tribal leader ("Hoshea," 13:8), but Israel's pantribal commander (34:17; cf. 27:12–23).

Implications

How Big Is the Promised Land?

The oral map in Num. 34:2–12 is self-contained by the narrator's *inclusio* that mentions the land and its borders (vv. 2c, 12c).[35] Within these frames, the narrator uncovers the details of Yahweh's map of the promised land (vv. 3–12b). Modern readers might become overwhelmed with the esoteric place names and miss the ANE echo of a deity, here Yahweh, revealing a specific territory of land that he will give to a king and his people.[36] Moses was not a king receiving Yahweh's gift, but he was Yahweh's prophet par excellence (Num. 12:6–8; Deut. 34:10–12), and as such he was in ongoing dialogue with

31. Ten chieftains from the nine and a half tribes excludes the tribe of Levi, which is given Yahweh in lieu of land inheritance (Num. 18:20–24; 26:62), and Reuben and Gad, who inherit Transjordan land (Num. 32; 34:13–15), but includes half the tribe of Manasseh (34:23); the other half of Manasseh will settle in Transjordan.

32. Knierim and Coats, *Numbers*, 320.

33. Caleb, who survived his predecessors, serves to symbolize Yahweh's enduring promise and warning; remarks about Caleb are nearly always coupled with the memory of the unfaithfulness of the explorers in the exodus generation (Olson, *Death of the Old*, 94).

34. Olson, *Death of the Old*, 94.

35. Kilchör (*Mosetora*, 221) argues, "When you enter the land" (34:2) is linked intertextually with Deut. 18:9 but not with the similar construction in Lev. 25:2.

36. See the "Implications" essay in chap. 29, "The Divine Gift of Land."

Yahweh about the Israelites, who were the heirs of Yahweh's promises to patriarchs Abram/Abraham, Isaac, and Jacob.[37] It was first to Abram that Yahweh mapped out the borders of the land for Abram's descendants: "On that day Yahweh made a covenant with Abram: "To your descendants I give this land, from the Wadi of Egypt to the great Euphrates River, the land of the Kenites, Kenizzites, Kadmonites, Hittites, Perizzites, Rephaites, Amorites, Canaanites, Girgashites, and Jebusites" (Gen. 15:18–20). Other texts reiterate this vast stretch of land as far north as the Euphrates in modern-day Syria (Exod. 23:31; Deut. 1:7; Josh. 1:4). In other Hexateuch passages, Yahweh even articulates borders that reach southward beyond the Wadi of Egypt (Num. 34:5) to "the Sea of Reeds" (*yam-sûp*, Exod. 23:31) at Egypt's border and northward to "the great Euphrates river, *all the land of the Hittites*" (*kōl 'ereṣ haḥittîm*, Josh. 1:4; cf. 13:1–6) in modern-day Turkey![38] It was not Israel's commander Joshua but warrior King David who stretched Israel's domain beyond the Abrahamic parameters, namely, over the Euphrates River (2 Sam. 8:3; cf. 10:9–19). His son Solomon powerfully "ruled all the kingdoms from the (Euphrates) River to the land of the Philistines, as far as the border of Egypt" (1 Kings 4:21),[39] but this seems to imply that Israel did not claim ownership of these kingdoms.[40] For example, Tiglath-Pileser I claims for Assyria: "I gained control over lands, mountains, towns, and princes who were hostile to [the god] Aššur. . . . I added territory to Assyria and people to its population. I extended the border of my land and ruled over their lands."[41]

Within the Hexateuch story (Genesis through Joshua), the oral map of Num. 34 poses a problem to the interpreter: the northern border does not touch the Euphrates in Mesopotamia or Hittite country in Anatolia. We may try to harmonize Num. 34 with the other far-reaching maps of the promised land, but in my judgment, it cannot be done with honesty. Rather, in my view the editors of Num. 34 have, under the inspiration of the Spirit, updated the borders of the promised land for a new era in the life of God's people.[42] This

---

37. See the patriarchal triad—Abraham, Isaac, and Jacob—in Exod. 2:24; 3:6, 15–16; 4:5; 6:3, 8; 32:13; 33:1; Lev. 26:42; Num. 32:11; Deut. 1:8; 6:10; 9:5, 27; 29:13; 30:20; 34:4.

38. Artus ("Numbers 32") argues that Josh. 13:1–6 expands the boundaries of Num. 34 for theological and political reasons.

39. By Jehoiakim's reign (late 7th cent. BCE), Babylon had gained control of the expanse from the Wadi of Egypt to the Euphrates (2 Kings 24:7).

40. At no time in Israel's history did their territory correspond cleanly to Num. 34 (Milgrom, *Numbers*, 284).

41. Grayson, *Assyrian Rulers*, 13.

42. Y. Levin ("Numbers 34:2–12," 55–76, esp. 75–76) sees the Priestly composers (hence, the Ezekiel overlap) as incorporating the southern border, both the Edomite border and fortress of Kadesh Barnea, from the Deuteronomistic map of Josh. 15:1–4. The northern border with Lebo Hamath and Riblah, he argues, betrays "the Levantine dominions of [Egyptian Pharaoh] Neco II, killer of Josiah, preserved by Nebuchadrezzar II, destroyer of Jerusalem" (76). Hutchens ("Boundaries," 215–30) contends that the Priestly compositions of Num. 34 and Ezek. 47 betray

may be difficult for some to hear, but the words of Yahweh in the Torah may best be characterized as "the covenantal instructions of dynamic YHWH to his dynamic people, creating a dynamic covenant adaptable to various circumstances and settings."[43] Furthermore, a careful reading of Num. 34* indicates that its editors wrote from a Cisjordanian perspective, that is, from inside Canaan. That narratorial perspective from within the land is probably not revealed by the demonstratives "this is/will be (your) the land" (vv. 2, 7, 12), which can refer internally to the verbal map (vv. 2–12), but later by v. 15: "The two and a half tribes have received their inheritance *on the other side of the Jordan, east of Jericho, toward the sunrise*" (see the translation note on v. 15). This stands in literary tension with the expansion of Israel's land inheritance into the Transjordan domain of Sihon and Og, which is given to the tribes of Reuben, Gad, and half the tribe of Manasseh (Num. 32*). Also, the text here begins with the third-person superscription, not hiding the reality that later editors transmitted 34:1–12, "Then Yahweh spoke to Moses . . ."); the discourse itself seems to imply that the audience knows not only mountain names but even smaller settlements: "From Mount Hor you will draw a line to Lebo Hamath, and the border's limit will be to Zedad. The border will extend to Ziphron, and its limit will be to the settlement of Enan" (v. 8). The Mount Hor mentioned here is not the Mount Hor where Aaron died (Num. 20:22–21:4) but a northern peak, possibly Mount Hermon in the Anti-Lebanon range. The point here is that the Israelites have never been to these places in the far north, so then why does Yahweh not use geographical descriptors so the Israelites will recognize the boundaries?

Attempting to reconstruct the historical vantage point of the editors can be valuable, but it can also miss the theological cogency of the discourse. Although the spacious borders of Num. 34:3–12 were never realized in Israel's history,[44] they do approximate the territorial borders that the New Kingdom Egyptian pharaohs laid claim to in Canaan before Israel arrived.[45] Subverting Egypt's hegemony, Yahweh now claims this land for his people. Consequently, "The Israelites were the legitimate successors of the Egyptians."[46] Further-

---

a temple aspiration to be "a pan-Israelite institution" (229), and "a Priestly demarcation of the clean land of Israel may have operated alongside, or even competed with, more political drawings of Israelite boundaries" (229). Levine (*Numbers*, 2:540) argues that late "priestly writers were informed by a vision of the Promised Land that included all of Egyptian-dominated Canaan, as it was just before the beginning of the Iron Age."

43. Bergland, *Reading*, 44.

44. See Olson, *Death of the Old*, 96.

45. De Vaux ("Le pays," 23–29). In particular, the Num. 34 borders correlate with the 18th dynasty of Egypt in Canaan (15–14th cent. BCE), also noted by Seebass ("Eigene Komposition," 97); Walton and Matthews, *Genesis–Deuteronomy*, 213. Then in the 13th cent. BCE, Rameses II and the Hittites established Egypt's northern border, including Damascus, by a peace treaty (Milgrom, *Numbers*, 284, 501–2).

46. Levine, *Numbers*, 2:540.

more, the borders of Canaan are revealed to Israel from the divine warrior, who has no need of human cartographers because he intimately knows and cares for the land that he owns and will give to his people. The Deuteronomists assert this truth from Moses (as Deut. 11:11–12). In the metanarrative of redemptive history, God will one day dry up the great Euphrates River in his judgment (Rev. 16:12), but the borders of the second promised land, the new earth, will contain a far greater river, bringing the Abrahamic blessing once and for all to the nations (Rev. 2:7; 22:1–2, 14, 19).

32

Towns for the Levites; Towns for Refuge

(35:1–34)

❧

Overview

Now that the route to and boundaries of the promised land have been defined (Num. 33 and 34, respectively), the editors next keenly position Yahweh's divine speeches, which designate towns and pastures for the Levites (35:1–8) and towns of refuge for those who kill someone accidentally (35:9–34).[1] Although the Levites have no land inheritance in one tribal region, they of course needed to reside somewhere. In Yahweh's initial speech, Moses must give the Levites forty-two towns and surrounding pastures for their herds and an additional six towns for any Israelite, Levite or not, to flee to if they have accidentally killed someone (vv. 1–8). Yahweh's ensuing speech clarifies the nature of the six towns for refuge—three in Canaan, three in Transjordan—where any person who kills another by accident may take refuge from the blood avenger until the killer stands trial (vv. 9–15). Yahweh then explains and illustrates

---

1. Knierim and Coats (*Numbers*, 327) conclude that the divine-speech form of chap. 35 is editorially "incorporated like anecdotal tradition into the wilderness itinerary." Gray (*Numbers*, 464–76) designates 35:1–8 as a supplement to P (P^s) and vv. 9–34 as P (typo, "9–24" on 469). Noth (*Numbers*, 253) attributes this unit to the redaction that unified the Pentateuch and DtrH, since he sees Num. 35 as dependent on Josh. 20:1–21:42. Knohl (*Sanctuary*, 99–100) and Stackert (*Rewriting*, 57–96) identify in both 35:1–8 and 35:9–34 the language and conceptuality of H (also Stackert, "Composition," 193n64; but cf. Nihan, "Priestly Laws," 118–19). Achenbach (*Vollendung*, 594–600) puts Num. 35–36 in the first phase of the high-priestly, theocratic revision of the Torah.

the types of homicide that bar the killer from the towns of refuge, demanding their execution (vv. 16–21). These include involuntary manslaughter (vv. 16–17; see table 32.1 below) and what might be classified as either voluntary manslaughter or first- or second-degree murder (vv. 20–21). Next, Yahweh exemplifies the types of accidental killing that permit the killer to flee to the nearby town of refuge until their trial (vv. 22–28). Finally, Yahweh ratifies the instructions for the towns of refuge (vv. 9–28) as statutory law for the Israelites (v. 29). He dictates that there be multiple witnesses prior to sentencing a suspect to death (v. 30), and he proscribes any ransom for a murderer (vv. 31–32). Yahweh closes with the theological reason he prohibits homicide: murder profanes with blood the land where Yahweh resides among his covenant people (vv. 33–34).

Translation

> **1**Then Yahweh spoke to Moses in the desert valleys of Moab by the Jordan River across from Jericho:[2] **2**"Command the Israelites to give the Levites towns to live in from the inheritance that the Israelites will possess.[3] Also give the Levites pastures around the towns. **3**So they will have towns to live in, and their pastures[4] will be for their cattle, for their possessions,[5] and for all their animals. **4**The pastures around the towns[6] that you give to the Levites must extend 3,000 feet[7] from the town wall. **5**You must measure from outside the town 3,000 feet[8] to the east side,

2. "*Across from* Jericho" is absent, inviting readers to supply it from their geographical knowledge or from 34:15 (anacoluthon); LXX[ed] supplies "opposite."

3. Formally, "from the inheritance of their possession" (*minnaḥālat 'āḥuzzātām*). "Israelites" is added for clarity since the Levites will not possess a land inheritance (Num. 18:20–26; 26:62).

4. SP's "*their* pastures" (*mgršyhn*) refers grammatically to the towns' pastures, while 4Q27/ MT's "*their* pastures" (*migrəšêhem*) refers to the Levites' pastures (LXX[ed], *autōn*, m. or f.). SP may have harmonized to v. 7 (similarly v. 4): "pastures of the towns"; v. 2 relates the pastures to both towns and Levites: "Also give the Levites pastures around the towns" (*ûmigrāš le'ārîm səbîbōtêhem tittənû laľwiyyim*).

5. LXX[ed] omits "for their possessions," possibly due to homeoarcton (Wevers, *Notes*, 585).

6. "Around" (*sābîb*) in v. 2 is absent here, but the possessive gen. (also v. 5), "pastures belonging to the towns" (*GBHS* §2.2.1), is probably a shorthand for v. 2, meaning "pastures *around* the towns."

7. The number 3,000 feet is based on LXX[ed], "*two thousand [dischilious]* cubits all around," where 1 cubit = ca. 1.5ft. MT/SP reads "a thousand cubits all around" (*'elep 'ammâ sābîb*); I address such problems in the comments. The Hb. text possibly reflects haplography by homophony with the following doubled *m* in *'ammâ*, "cubit" (even more so with an original accusative case ending on an a-class segolate:*'alpa 'ammati* for *'alpayim 'ammati*; cf. Akkadian *ammatu: CAD* 1.2:70–75).

8. Formally, "two thousand by the cubit (measurement)" (*'alpayim bā'ammâ*), where 1 cubit = ca. 1.5 ft.

541

3,000 feet to[9] the south side, 3,000 feet to[10] the west side, and 3,000 feet to the north side, with the town in the middle. This will belong to them[11] as pastures around the towns. **6**From these towns that you give to the Levites, you must choose six towns for refuge[12] to which a person who has killed someone may flee, and give them[13] forty-two other towns. **7**So the total number of towns, with their pastures, that you will give to the Levites comes to forty-eight. **8**The towns you give them must come from the property of the Israelites. From the larger tribes take more, and from the smaller tribes take fewer.[14] Each must give some of its own towns to the Levites in proportion to the size of its inheritance."[15]

9Then Yahweh said to Moses: **10**"Speak to the Israelites and tell them, 'When you cross over the Jordan into[16] the land of Canaan, **11**you must then select some towns as towns for refuge for you, so that a person who has killed someone accidentally[17] may flee there. **12**The towns will be a refuge for you from the avenger so that the killer may not die before they stand trial before the community.[18] **13**These towns

---

9. As in chap. 34, SP and LXX[ed] read ". . . *to* the east side [= MT], 1,000 yards *to* the south side, 1,000 yards *to* the west side [= 4Q27], and 1,000 yards *to* the north side" (SP with *hē'* locale, *BHRG* §28.1; and LXX[ed] with attributive prep. phrase *to pros* . . .). I render v. 5 consistently with this directional force because the MT implies the meaning of the SP/LXX text.

10. Here I prefer the harder reading "to the west" (*ymh*, with *hē'* locale, *BHRG* §28.1) in 4Q27 SP LXX[ed] (*pros thalassan*) over the MT "the west" (*yām*). It may be more likely that MT omitted the *h* (vocalized as a long *â*) by homophony (*yāmâ 'alpayim*) and presumed the contextual reading (without a *hē'* locale), than that the Qumran-SP-LXX "to the west" (*yāmâ*) harmonized to 34:5 (*hayyāmmâ*, "to the west").

11. SP and LXX[ed]: "to you [pl.]." Because these pastures surrounding the towns are to be given to the Levites, MT and T[O] is preferred: "to them" (MT: *lāhem*; Tg[O]: *ləhôn*).

12. A gen. of purpose, meaning "towns *intended as a* refuge" (*GBHS* §2.2.8).

13. MT masc. pronoun "and to *them*" (*wa'ălêhem*) refers syntactically to the Levites, whereas SP and LXX[ed] contain a fem. pronoun, "in addition to *these*," which refers to the "six *towns* for refuge" (*šēš-'ārê hammiqlāṭ*); the variant may reflect an attempt to correct a gender disagreement in MT between *these* and *towns* that could have arisen since "town" (*'îr*) is "morphologically masculine, syntactically feminine and semantically neuter" (*BHRG* §24.2.1.4d).

14. Formally, "from the larger you must increase, and from the smaller you must decrease."

15. Formally, "each [tribe], according to the mouth of its inheritance that they possess, must give from its cities to the Levites." SP brings the subject and verb into a number (sg.) agreement, "each . . . that *it possesses*," while the MT shift to pl. is logical (*ad sensum*), since a tribe (sg.) was made up of people (pl.).

16. "Cross over *into* the land of Canaan" follows the meaning of the SP (*'l*) and LXX[ed] (*eis*), which is implied in MT, "cross over *to/toward* the land of Canaan" (*'arṣâ*).

17. The *b* of manner (*GBHS* §4.1.5i) describes the way that the individual kills another human, "by accident" (*bišgāgâ*). As noted for 15:24–29, I follow Milgrom (*Leviticus*, 1:228–29) in that we can be more precise than a lexicon can ("*šəgāgâ*," *HALOT* 4:1412–13; *DCH* 8:262–63), insofar as the noun *šəgāgâ* appears to refer to "inadvertent wrongdoing" committed by conscious negligence—"accidentally" as here in 35:11, 15—or by exposed ignorance (in error) and expiated by a purification offering (*ḥṭ't*), whereas the "reparation offering" (*'šm*) was offered to make atonement for sin committed unintentionally (see Lev. 5:17–19; Num. 5:6–7).

18. Formally, "until his standing before the community for judgment."

that you give will be your six towns for refuge. **14**You must give three towns beyond[19] the Jordan, and you must give three towns in the land of Canaan; they will be towns for refuge. **15**These six towns will be places for refuge for the Israelites, for the immigrant, and for the settler among them,[20] so that anyone who kills a person accidentally may flee there.

16"But if someone hits another with an iron object, and it results in death, that person is a murderer. The murderer must be put to death. **17**If someone hits another with a handheld stone that could kill,[21] and it results in death, that person is a murderer. The murderer must be put to death. **18**Or[22] if someone hits another with a handheld wooden object[23] that could kill, and it results in death,[24] that person is a murderer. The murderer must be put to death. **19**The avenger of blood must kill the murderer himself; when they meet, the avenger will put the murderer to death.[25] **20**If someone pushes another out of hatred or throws something intentionally so that the person dies,[26] **21**or with hostility

19. "Beyond" (*mē'ēber*, NRSV, ESV) indicates a perspective from within the land (Cisjordan), rather than from Transjordan, where the Israelites are presently in the narrative (*not* "on the east side," NLT; or "on this side," NIV, NET).

20. This dyad of non-landowning residents, "and for the immigrant and for the settler" (*walaggēr walattôšāb*), represents the language of the priestly texts in Exodus–Leviticus–Numbers, whereas "immigrant who is within your towns [formally, gates], orphan, and widow (and Levite)" is characteristic of Deuteronomy (see Awabdy, *Immigrants*, 117–18, 187).

21. Formally, "a stone of hand that kills."

22. SP and LXX^ed "but if." Contextually "or" (MT Tg^O) is preferred because the text reaches a disjunction only at v. 22: "*But if* [*wa'im*] someone pushes another suddenly, *without hostility* [*balō'-'êbâ*], . . ."

23. An "iron object" (gen. of material: *kalî barzel*, "object [*made out*] of iron," v. 16), a "handheld stone" (*'eben yād*, formally, "a stone of hand," v. 17), and a "handheld wooden object" (gen. of material: *kalî 'ēṣ-yād*, "object [*made out*] of wood of hand," v. 18)—all of these are generic descriptors of instruments for war *and* for farming. So rather than call them tools (ESV, vv. 16, 18; NJPS, vv. 17, 18) or weapons (NRSV, NET in v. 18), I prefer the hypernym "object" (with NLT, NIV). This versatility is presumed in the prophetic pleas "Beat your swords into plowshares" (Isa. 2:4) and "Beat your plowshares into swords" (Joel 3:10); we might think of examples like Shamgar, who kills six hundred Philistines with a cattle prod (*malmad habbāqār*, Judg. 3:31; see Snyman, "Shamgar," 125–29). By analogy, the Assyrians used various daggers (see Urartu excavations) apparently not primarily for war, but for rituals and celebrations; although they fought with axes, they mainly employed them as tools (Seevers, *Warfare*, 229). The archaeological evidence in the 11th–10th cent. BCE, as Israel appears in the land (see Merenptah Stele, ca. 1208), reveals iron agrarian implements at both Philistine and Israelite sites but iron weaponry at only the Philistine sites (Muhly, "Iron Technology," 52).

24. 4Q27 adds "The striker must be put to death" (*mwt*] ywmt hm[kh, see Ulrich, *Qumran*, 170–71). This may be a harmonization to v. 21, but that would be odd, since it creates a redundancy later in the verse: "The murderer must be put to death."

25. "Avenger" and "murderer" have been supplied for clarity; formally, "when he meets him, he must kill him."

26. 4Q27 transposes the final words, which could mean "so that the person dies intentionally" (*wymwt bṣdyh*), which is nonsensical, so the MT/SP/LXX^ed word order more naturally conveys the meaning.

hits another by hand and the person dies, the striker must be put to death. That person is a murderer.[27] The avenger of blood[28] must kill the murderer when they meet. **22**But if someone pushes[29] another suddenly, without hostility, or throws something at him unintentionally, **23**or throws any stone[30] that can kill, but without seeing the other person, and the person dies, even though they were not enemies and no harm was intended, **24**then the community must judge between the killer and the avenger of blood according to these regulations. **25**The community must rescue the killer[31] out of the hand of the avenger of blood, and the community must restore the killer to the town of refuge they had fled, and the killer will live there until the death of the high priest, who was anointed with the holy oil. **26**But if the killer leaves the border of the town where they fled for refuge, **27**and the avenger of blood finds the killer[32] outside the border of the killer's town for refuge, and the avenger of blood kills the killer, the avenger will not be guilty of blood,[33] **28**because the killer must remain in the designated town for refuge until the death of the high priest. But after the death of the high priest, the killer may return to their own land. **29**So these things must be a statutory law for you throughout your generations, wherever you live.[34]

30"Whoever kills a person must be put to death as a murderer on the testimony of multiple witnesses;[35] but no one will be put to death on the testimony of only one witness.[36] **31**Also, you must not accept a ransom for the life of a murderer who is guilty of death. They must be put to

27. 4Q27 and LXX^{ed} add "The murderer must be put to death," probably assimilating to vv. 16, 17, 18.

28. 4Q27 includes "The avenger of blood, he [*hw'*] must put him to death," maybe assimilating to v. 19.

29. The verb (**hdp* qal) can mean "thrust, push (away), drive out" (*DCH* 2:491), but in the context of v. 22 probably just means "push" (*HALOT* 1:239) with the sense of "runs into someone."

30. Instead, 4Q27 reads "*a stone object*" (*b^{k}ly*, superscript ^{k}), which is more contextual but may be an assimilation to vv. 16, 18.

31. MT reads "killer" (*hārōṣēaḥ*), with LXX^{ed} (**phoneuō* always renders the Hb. **rṣḥ* in Numbers, all 13× in chap. 35), but SP reads "striker" (*hmkh*, vocalized *hammakkeh*), perhaps assimilating to "striker" from v. 24 because this individual did not intend to kill and so was not to be indicted as a murderer.

32. Although I have included "the killer" (*hārōṣēaḥ*) because the text is gender neutral (not just male killers), this clarifying reading might be attested in 4Q27 (*wm*]*ṣ' gw'*[*l hdm 't hrwṣḥ*, similar to v. 27b).

33. Formally, "he will not have blood" (*'ên lô dām*), with the implication that he will not have the blood of another person on his hands or on his account; cf. pl. his/their "bloods" (*dāmîm*) as personal blood guilt: Exod. 22:2–3; Lev. 20:9, 11, 12, 13, 16, 27.

34. Formally, "in all your settlements."

35. Formally, "by the mouth of witnesses." My dynamic translation of the pl. as "multiple witnesses" is inferred from the contrast with "one witness" (*'ēd 'eḥād*) in v. 30b.

36. Formally, "but one witness must not answer against a life to die" (*wa'ēd 'eḥād lō'-ya'āneh bᵊnepeš lāmût*); SP has a qatal form, "but one witness *has not even answered* [*w'nh*] against a life to die," which might reflect influence of the qal qatal (**'nh*) in the witness law of Deut. 19:18.

death. [32]And you must not accept a ransom for anyone who has fled to a town for refuge, to allow them to return to live in their own land before the death of the high priest.[37] [33]You must not pollute the land where you live.[38] Blood defiles the land, and the land cannot be purified of the blood that is shed there except by the blood of the person who shed it. [34]Do not defile[39] the land where you will live, in which I live, because I Yahweh live among the Israelites."

Interpretation

35:1–8. By the agency of Moses, Yahweh enjoins the Israelite tribes to give forty-eight towns to the Levites: forty-two towns and their pastures for Levites and their herds and six towns of refuge for anyone who has killed someone but is not subject to the death penalty. The topography of the superscription, "in the desert valleys of Moab by the Jordan River across from Jericho," occurs nine times in Num. 22–36 and accentuates Israel's encampment on the brink of entering the promised land.[40] When Israel does enter, however, the Levites have no allotted place to live, so Yahweh orders that the Israelites give, from their own tribal lands, towns for the Levites to live in, along with those towns' surrounding pasturelands for the Levites' cattle, possessions, and animals (vv. 2–3; see the first translation note on v. 4). The Jubilee law in Lev. 25 presupposes that these Levitical towns, if sold, will revert to the Levites' possession every fiftieth year (25:32–34).[41] Canaan had settlements fortified with walls (25:29), which may be called cities or towns, and settlements without walls, which may be called villages (25:31). Here in Num. 35:2–8 the towns are walled and surrounded by pasturelands, enabling protected residents to go out and work nearby as agropastoralists (farming

37. I supply the attributive adj. from SP and LXX[ed], "the *high* priest" (SP: *hkhn hgdwl*; LXX[ed]: *ho hiereus ho megas*), which is probably a harmonization to vv. 25 and 28 (with de Vaulx, *Nombres*, 402). MT's "the priest" (*hakkōhēn*), with a referential article (*GBHS* §2.6.1), implies "the *high* priest," mentioned in vv. 25 and 28.

38. MT lacks the ptc. "where you live," but modern versions are reasonable in adopting this ptc., which is attested in SP and LXX[ed] (also Syr Vulg[ed] Tg[PJ Neo]; here a fut. continuous: *GBHS* §3.4.3). While the ptc. could be a harmonization to the Pentateuch's only two other occurrences of the phrase in Num. 33:55; 35:34, the MT minus would reflect an ellipsis of the ptc. in the idiomatic Hebrew construction: "where" (relative pron. *'ăšer*) + "you live" (ptc. *yōšəbîm*) + "in it" (resumptive pron. *bāh*); see // ellipsis Exod. 34:12, *IBHS* §11.4.3.d.1; on resumption, *BHRG* §36.3.1.1.4.

39. MT is sg.: "you (sg.) must not defile" (*tətammē'*); SP and LXX[ed] are pl.: "you (pl.) must not defile," continuing the pattern of *lō'* + 2nd pers. pl. yiqtols in vv. 31, 32, 33.

40. Num. 22:1; 26:3; 26:63; 31:12; 33:48, 49, 50; 35:1; 36:13. For "desert valleys," see the translation notes on 22:1 and 35:1. Many assign 35:1–2a to the Priestly redactor (de Vaulx, *Nombres*, 391).

41. Block, "'Meeting Places,'" 97–99. Achenbach ("Heiligkeitsgesetz," 167; *Vollendung*, 594–600) agrees but still sees Num. 35 as composed later. See Levine, *Numbers*, 2:569–71.

and raising livestock), not as transhumant pastoralists migrating seasonally with their households.[42] The dimensions prescribed for the pasturelands are notoriously difficult to interpret. If one follows the MT/SP, how can the pastures extend 1,500 feet (1,000 cubits) from the town wall (v. 4), but at the same time extend from outside the town 3,000 feet (2,000 cubits) in every direction (v. 5)? Verse 4 envisions a circular city, while v. 5 portrays a "square of common land around the city. The city itself is in effect envisaged as being only a point."[43] The proposals to harmonize the meaning of the MT/SP in vv. 4 and 5 have been unsatisfying.[44] I adopt (with EÜ) the Septuagint reading of 3,000 feet (2,000 cubits) in v. 4, which could have been a harmonization to v. 5,[45] but equally plausible in this instance, the MT/SP text could have arisen by haplography (see the second translation note on v. 4 and the second translation note on v. 5).

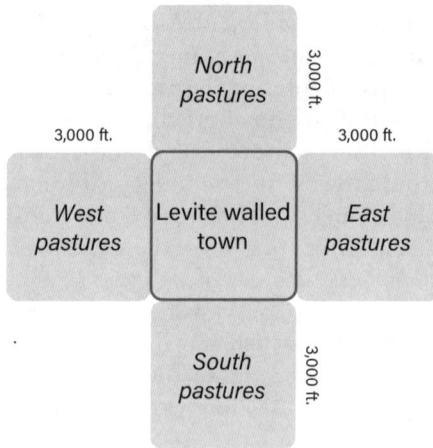

Figure 32.1. Layout of a Levitical Town

The arrangement echoes that of Israel's military encampment and order of departure: Yahweh's ark, carried by the Levites, resides in the center of the tribes (2:17), surrounded by the tribes on the east, south, west, and north, in clockwise order (2:3–31); now, upon entry into Canaan, the Levites will reside in their designated towns, surrounded by their cattle, possessions, and

42. King and Stager, *Life*, 112–13.
43. Sturdy, *Numbers*, 238.
44. See Seebass, *Numeri*, 3:440–41. Requiring a big assumption is Budd (*Numbers*, 376): "It may be best to assume that the cubits of the Levitical pasture lands are cubit frontages of land—in other words on each side of the city there was a block of land with a frontage of two thousand cubits (v 5), and a depth of 1000 cubits (v 4)."
45. Wevers, *Notes*, 586.

other animals on the east, south, west, and north, in that order (35:4–5).[46] In both configurations, the Levites are in the center, whether serving the central sanctuary (Num. 1–4, 8, 18) or living in their towns throughout Israel (Num. 35). But how can the Levites be in both places at once? As Frevel concludes, "Either the Levitical cities are intended only for the women, the children, and the age-related men who are no longer fit for service (which may include alternate shifts for the Levite as described in Num. 8:26), or the construction of Levitical cities produces ghost towns."[47] One solution is to see the Levitical towns as a "deliberately centrifugal religious strategy," so that the Levites maintain the central sanctuary *and* advance the religious life of the Israelites living throughout the land.[48] Not only would constant travel be logistically almost impossible, but more importantly, neither the centralized worship instructions (Num. 1–4, 8, 18) nor the Levitical town instructions (Num. 35) imagine such an itinerant existence for the Levites. My approach is to see these as separate sources, but each with its own theological contribution: the Levites are bound to Yahweh and his meeting place *and* Israel must provide towns for Yahweh's servants.[49] How these two visions work out pragmatically was of little concern to the final editors of Numbers, although Ezekiel seems to combine them in his vision of the restored temple community (48:10–14).[50] What is apparent here is that the divine call to give towns and pasturelands to the Levites in Num. 35 can be seen as an expansion of the landless Levite theology in Num. 18:20–24 and 26:62. The forty-two Levitical towns, with another six intended for refuge where "a person who has killed someone may flee" (v. 6; see the first translation note there), are not the Levites' land inheritance from Yahweh, but Israel's. Now, by repeating the order to "give" (*ntn) nine times in the discursive unit (vv. 2–8), an *imitatio Dei* principle emerges. Just as Yahweh *has given* the tithe portion of Israel's offerings to the Levites for their food (18:20–24, *ntn 2×), so now Israel must *give* forty-eight of its towns to the Levites for their residence (see the second translation note on v. 6).[51] Placing towns under priestly control was practiced by the Hittites and by Egypt in its hegemony in Canaan, and designating sacred and royal towns with an elevated status is attested broadly in the ANE.[52]

---

46. Or perhaps a rectangular arrangement with nine sections, the Levitical town in the middle, and Israelite agricultural land in the corners (sections 1, 3, 7, 9): Block, "'Meeting Places,'" 98–99; following Milgrom, "Levitical Town," 185–88; Milgrom, *Numbers*, 502–4.

47. Frevel, "High Priest," 139n2.

48. Block, "'Meeting Places,'" 93–121, esp. 117.

49. Similarly, Dozeman, "Numbers," 264.

50. See de Vaulx, *Nombres*, 396.

51. Cf. Olson, *Death of the Old*, 87.

52. Walton and Matthews, *Genesis–Deuteronomy*, 214.

Since the number forty represents fullness or entirety in the HB and ANE,[53] a total of forty-eight may represent a surplus, that is, more than enough towns for the Levites.[54] The Levites, in six of their forty-eight towns, will host Israel's asylum seekers (v. 6).[55] At the same time, the explicit mention of forty-two towns exclusively for the Levites could offer an elite emulation of the forty-two nomes, or administrative districts, of Upper and Lower Egypt in the glory days of its dynastic origins.[56] Instead of an Old Kingdom Egyptian nomarch over the districts, Yahweh is Israel's monarch, who directs the allocation of his land to his people.[57] In any case, while forty-two is a prime number, forty-eight is a composite number, meaning that the twelve tribes—with Ephraim and Manasseh counted separately (26:28–37)—could be enjoined to give four towns each to the Levites (48/12 = 4). Instead, just as Israel's leaders must subdivide their land inheritance in Canaan in proportion to the size of every tribe (26:52–56; 33:54), so the number of towns that every tribe gives to the Levites is to be proportionate to the size of each tribe (35:8). Every tribe must give some of its towns to the Levites, but the larger tribes must give more towns, the smaller tribes give fewer towns (v. 8). This directive, without casting lots for Yahweh's verdict (26:55–56; 33:54), could open the door for intertribal disputes regarding how many towns each tribe should relinquish to the Levites. The tribes, however, have not been left without exemplars of generosity toward the Levites. Yahweh's vision to meet the needs of the Levites was already embodied by the chieftains of the exodus generation, who resourced the Levites in their meeting-tent services (7:1–9), and by Moses and Eleazar, who gave the Levites one-fiftieth of the Israelites' spoils from the Midianite war (31:30–31, 47). Following the second census (see 26:51, 62), the 601,730 soldiers, who will fight to inherit the towns of Canaan, must give a relatively small number of those towns to the 23,000 Levites and their families, who will not fight but will ensure through their meeting-tent services that Israel's relationship with Yahweh remains intact. At the very

---

53. Cf. Roscher, *Die Zahl 40*. A. Pinker ("Number 40," 165) notes that in a Babylonian inscription, *kissatum* ("aggregate, the whole, universe, set, fullness, or entirety") occurs with number 40 (*ni-mi-in*) as well as with 7 and 50.

54. Gosse ("42 Generations," 146, 148) observes that the number 42 in the Egyptian Book of the Dead correlates to a malediction, which could be altered into a benediction. Also, Balaam, hired to curse Israel, offered a total of 42 sacrifices (Num. 23:1, 14, 29). These points are interesting but irrelevant to Num. 35.

55. See Leveen, *Memory*, 177–78.

56. Upper Egypt in the south had twenty-two nomes; Lower Egypt in the north included Memphis and nineteen other administrative units; see Kuhrt, *Ancient Near East*, 1:151–52). On Priestly elite emulating the literature of the surrounding empires, see Sparks, "*Enūma Elish*," 625–48. Gosse ("42 Generations," 146–47) does not connect the forty-two nomes with Num. 35 (cf. 147n25) but does see it forming part of the backdrop for the forty-two generations from Abraham to Jesus the Messiah (Matt. 1:1–17).

57. See the "Implications" essay in chap. 29, "The Divine Gift of Land."

end of the Hexateuch story, the Levites assert themselves, and Joshua and the tribal leaders, in obedience to Yahweh's command to Moses, assign the Levites their forty-eight towns and pasturelands (Josh. 21:1–41; cf. 1 Chron. 6:54–81 [3–66]).[58] The Levitical towns become the last proof that "not one of all the good promises that Yahweh had made to the house of Israel had failed. Everything came to pass" (Josh. 21:45).

35:9–15. Through Moses Yahweh defines for the Israelites the six towns for refuge—three in Canaan, three in Transjordan—into which anyone who kills another accidentally may flee for protection from the avenger until the killer's trial. In this second speech (vv. 6–34), Yahweh explicates the nature of the towns of refuge mandated tersely in v. 6. The only criterion for choosing the six towns for refuge is that three must be in Transjordan, three in Cisjordan (v. 14). In contrast to the proportionate distribution of the forty-two Levitical towns (v. 8), this even three-to-three distribution is disproportionate to the tribal populations recorded in the chap. 26 census: the two and a half Transjordan tribes represent roughly 25 *percent* of Israel's population (ca. 110,580), while the 9.5 Cisjordan tribes make up about 75 *percent* (ca. 492,970).[59] The effect of this disproportion is twofold. First, this overprotects the Israelites belonging to the Transjordan tribes, since they are geographically segregated from Canaan proper and subject to being misunderstood by the 10.5 tribes (Num. 32; Josh. 22). Second, this disproportion substantiates the Transjordan region annexed by the two and a half tribes as part of the promised land, now with three towns belonging to Yahweh's sacred Levites but designated as refuges for Reuben, Gad, and the half-tribe of Manasseh (Num. 32; 34:14–15; 35:6).[60] Deuteronomy names the three Transjordan towns chosen for refuge (4:41–43) and reiterates with its own theological parlance the order to establish three Cisjordan towns for refuge (19:1–13), which Joshua then fulfills (Josh. 20:1–9).[61]

---

58. Without intertribal dispute, Israel's giving (*ntn) in Josh. 21 is seen as an act of fulfilling Num. 35 (Hutton, "Levitical Diaspora," 60). Most tribes give four towns; Judah and Simeon, nine; Naphtali, three (see Block, "'Meeting Places,'" 95–97). On the literary relationship between Num. 35 and Josh. 20:1–21:42, see proposals by Schmidt ("Leviten," 103–21; *Numeri*, 217) and by Seebass (*Numeri*, 3:426–31).

59. See Num. 26:7, 18, 34. My projected numbers are based on dividing Manasseh's count, 52,700 (Num. 26:34) in half, but this is indeterminate because there is no biblical census of the Transjordan and Cisjordan populations of Manasseh.

60. See the "Implications" essay in chap. 31, "How Big Is the Promised Land?"

61. Stackert (*Rewriting*, 57–96) argues that the asylum law of Num. 35:9–34 is H's adaptation of Deut. 19:1–13 (see also Kislev, "Cities," 249–64), but Nihan ("Priestly Laws," 118–19) is hesitant to assign Num. 35* to H. Kilchör (*Mosetora*, 224–38) argues the reverse, that Deut. 19* presupposes and supplements Exod. 21:12–14 and Num. 35*. Mattison ("Contrasting Conceptions," 232–51) argues that for H (Num. 35:9–34), bloodguilt results from shedding any human blood; whereas for D (Deut. 19:1–13), bloodguilt results only from homicidal intention.

The towns for refuge are intended to be safe havens for anyone who has killed someone by accident (v. 11; see the translation note there). In the ideal world of obedience to Yahweh's *tôrâ*, the killer, before standing trial, could relocate to one of three refuge towns on their side of the Jordan and live in protective custody without fear of being killed by the family members of the deceased (vv. 11–12; see the translation note on v. 12). Remarkably, by this law Yahweh protects not only his covenant people, the Israelites, but also two other social classes: immigrants and settlers (v. 15). The historical referent of these classes will be debated, but they are grouped here as a dyad as residents in Israel's settlements who do not own land but who are granted certain rights and protections in other Torah legislation (see the translation note on v. 15). These must be differentiated from the foreigner class (*ben-nēkār, nokrî*) and the so-called nonelect class, the Amalekites and the Canaanites,[62] who are not to be granted asylum in the towns of refuge.

35:16–21. Continuing his speech, Yahweh elucidates the violent crimes that necessitate capital punishment, and by obvious implication, disqualify the criminal from taking asylum in one of the towns of refuge. In casuistic (case-law) form, Yahweh gives three examples of involuntary manslaughter (vv. 16–19) and three examples of what could be either voluntary manslaughter or first- or second-degree murder (vv. 20–21).[63] Probably as a deliberate act of innerbiblical exegesis,[64] the scribes who recorded Yahweh's words in vv. 16–21 illustrate the generic directive of the Covenant Code: "Whoever strikes a person and they die must be put to death" (Exod. 21:12). The cadence of the first subunit, vv. 16–18, is predicated on the threefold recurrence of four elements:

Table 32.1. Manslaughter Cases

Casuistic Protasis Examples of Involuntary Manslaughter	Casuistic Apodosis no. 1 Yahweh's Verdict	Casuistic Apodosis no. 2[a] Capital Punishment
If someone hits another with a(n) • iron object (35:16) • handheld stone (35:17)[c] • handheld wooden object (35:18)[d] and it results in death,	"that person is a murderer"	"The murderer must be put to death"[b]

a. Apodoses 1 and 2 are both asyndetic.
b. The construction "be put to death" (*môt yûmat*) is characteristic of H (Stackert, "Composition," 193n64).
c. See the translation note on 35:17.
d. See the second translation note on 35:18.

62. See Deut. 7:1–2; 13:16; 20:17; 25:19; 1 Sam. 15:1–3. On the anti-elect, see Kaminsky, "Election," 397–425; and the comments on 10:29–32.
63. These scenarios that disqualify one from asylum are set off by the disjunctive "but" (*wə*) in v. 16.
64. Kilchör, *Mosetora*, 224–31.

These examples are best classified as involuntary manslaughter because, although the killer did not act intentionally or out of hostility (as in vv. 20–21), by carelessly handling dangerous objects—iron, stone, wooden—they show a "failure to perform a legal duty expressly required to safeguard human life."[65] The three examples are not exhaustive, but from them the community can extrapolate to other scenarios (see v. 24). The cadence is broken in v. 19, where Yahweh dictates that "the avenger of blood" (*gō'ēl haddām*)—formally, "the redeemer of blood"—must kill the murderer when they meet. In the ANE, "the blood of the slain was avenged by his nearest kinsman, called *go'el*, either by taking the blood of the slayer or of a member of the latter's family or by accepting monetary compensation."[66] In Israel, Yahweh makes clear that neither a family member's blood nor monetary compensation can be accepted (vv. 31–32), but only the blood of the killer (vv. 19, 21, 26–27, 33–34). The nearest kinsman is now obligated to avenge the blood of his deceased relative.[67] This authorized blood vengeance reflects the principle of *lex talionis* (a life for a life),[68] illustrated and legislated in the Holiness oracular novella of the blasphemer against the Name (Lev. 24:10–23).[69]

The reason for breaking the pattern in v. 19 becomes clear in vv. 20–21, which turns to examples of either voluntary manslaughter, second-degree murder, or even first-degree murder. The language—"out of hatred" (*bəśin'â*), "intentionally" (*biṣdiyyâ*), and "with hostility" (*bə'êbâ*)—distinguishes these scenarios from vv. 16–19 as *willful* acts of homicide.[70] These scenarios, however, do not disclose whether the one who pushes out of hatred (v. 20), throws an object intentionally (v. 20), or punches (v. 21) acted to kill the victim intentionally with premeditation (first-degree murder), intentionally without premeditation (second-degree), or impulsively without premeditation (voluntary manslaughter). The issue of premeditation is irrelevant to Yahweh, who denies refuge and demands the capital punishment of every killer who acts carelessly (vv. 16–19) or intentionally (vv. 20–21).[71] Here again, the avenger of blood is the agent who carries out the death sentence ordered by Yahweh (v. 21, as in v. 19).

---

65. *Merriam-Webster.com Dictionary*, s.v. "involuntary manslaughter."

66. Milgrom, *Numbers*, 291; also W. Lee, *Migratory Campaign*, 206.

67. Other obligations toward the dead in ancient Israel included burying and mourning and protecting a dead man's name and inheritance through levirate marriage (Deut. 25:5–10) or intratribal marriage (Num. 27, 36); see Shemesh, "Do Not Bare," 37–38.

68. Budd, *Numbers*, 384; Ashley, *Numbers*, 655. See Levine, *Numbers*, 2:561–65.

69. See Chavel, *Oracular Law*.

70. W. Lee (*Migratory Campaign*, 206–7) rightly calls vv. 16–21 cases of "deliberate homicide," but this makes his label "involuntary homicide" for vv. 10b–34 inaccurate. See Levine, *Numbers*, 2:565–69.

71. I part with Milgrom (*Numbers*, 291), who sees Num. 35 as innovative in restricting asylum to only *unpremeditated* manslaughter.

35:22–29. In the next segment of his speech, Yahweh illustrates the kinds of accidental killing that allow the killer to escape to a town of refuge. These words appear to explicate the terse Covenant Code law: "If it [a person's death by striking] was not premeditated, but came about by an act of God, then I will appoint for you a place to which the killer may flee" (Exod. 21:13 NRSV).[72] The subunit here offers only a soft literary break, because vv. 22–23 repeat the scenarios of vv. 20–21, but now *without intentionality*. In these three scenarios, the killer neither intended to kill (as in vv. 20–21) nor acted in a patently careless manner (as in vv. 16–19).[73] The replacement of punching (v. 21) with throwing a lethal stone without seeing the victim (v. 23) may be because there is no unintentional form of punching.[74] In any case, these scenarios result in death from actions that could be misinterpreted as intentional, so the community where the death occurs must interject its judicial power.[75] First, the community apparently must pronounce an innocent verdict for the killer so that the avenger of blood will have no legal right to execute the killer (v. 24). Second, the community must physically rescue the killer from the avenger of blood and ensure the killer's safe passage to the town of refuge (v. 25). In Num. 35 nothing is said about the killer's family. Would they join the killer in relocating? What is clear is that Yahweh is redundant—and thus emphatic in vv. 25, 28, and 32—in forbidding the killer to leave the town of refuge until the death of the acting (anointed) high priest,[76] after which they may return to their hometown, and no one is allowed to harm them (vv. 25, 28; see v. 32). The important role of the high(est) priest is implicit in Num. 17 and 35 but explicit at the end of Numbers (35:28, 32), "with the installation of a high priest who reigns in genealogical succession."[77] The implication may be that the death of the high priest serves to atone for the blood shed by the manslayer.[78] If so, this anticipates the suffering servant of Isa. 52–53 and Jesus the Messiah as a substitutionary sacrifice.[79]

One of Yahweh's desires is that by following the legal protection of vv. 22–28, the community will decrease the number of honor killings of unconvicted persons and protect the land from pollution by innocent blood (see vv.

---

72. Kilchör, *Mosetora*, 224–31.

73. See the translation note on 35:22.

74. Formally, "hits another by hand" (see v. 21).

75. This location is implied by the separate town of refuge where the killer has fled (v. 26). There is no useful ritual here to convict or exonerate the killer of guilty intentions as there is in Num. 5:5–31 for a woman suspected of adultery (see Douglas, *Wilderness*, 161).

76. On the anointed high priest, see the entire title in Lev. 21:10, 12; cf. 4:3, 5, 16; 6:22; 16:32. For other references in the HB, see Ashley, *Numbers*, 654n21.

77. Frevel, "High Priest," 158–60, esp. 160. This anticipates the elevated position of Eleazar the high priest in Josh. 13–22: see Num. 32:2; 34:17; and the comments on 27:15–23.

78. Ashley, *Numbers*, 656; Walton and Matthews, *Genesis–Deuteronomy*, 215.

79. See 4 Macc. 6:28–29. In the same spirit, Ambrose (4th cent. CE) and Paterius (6th–7th cent. CE) offer tropological and christological interpretations (Lienhard, *Numbers*, 273).

27, 33–34).[80] If, however, the killer exits the borders of the town of refuge, the avenger of blood may kill him without incurring guilt (v. 27; see the second translation note there). Even as obedience to Yahweh's words ensures the covenant blessing of safety in the land (Lev. 26:1–13; cf. Deut. 28:1–14), so also the killer's obedience to Yahweh's words here (vv. 26–28) ensures the killer's safety in the land. The theological message of this unit reverberates throughout both Testaments: just as God, by this law, protects those who faithfully remain in a town of refuge, he protects his covenant people who remain under his protection,[81] and he ultimately protects those who faithfully remain in his Son, Jesus the Messiah (John 10:1–18; Jude 21–25).[82] Finally, in v. 29 Yahweh uses the plural "these things" (*'ēlleh*) most likely to conclude both of the preceding discursive units: the towns for the Levites (vv. 1–8) and the towns for refuge (vv. 9–28).[83] In Lev. 18–26 and Num. 9, Yahweh's *ḥuqqōt* and *mišpāṭ* are separate entities that Israel must uphold, but v. 29 combines them (as in the case law of Zelophehad's daughters, 27:11) into a binding "statutory law" (*ḥuqqat mišpāṭ*).[84] The towns for the Levites and for refuge must, therefore, be maintained among Israel's settlements throughout Israel's history (v. 29; see the translation note there). Here the use of *mišpāṭ* may also hint at Yahweh's own *justice* in securing the survival of the Levites and punishing the heinous act of murder while protecting the innocent. Similarly, Abraham was convinced that Yahweh would protect the innocent even as he must punish the wicked: "Will not *the judge* [*hăšōpēṭ*] of all the earth do what is *just* [*mišpāṭ*]?" (Gen. 18:25).

35:30–34. After the literary closure of v. 29, Yahweh further qualifies the instructions about the towns of refuge by demanding multiple witnesses before anyone is sentenced to death (v. 30), prohibiting a ransom for a murderer or one accused of murder (vv. 31–32), and teaching that bloodshed pollutes the land in which Yahweh himself lives among his people (vv. 33–34). First, Yahweh qualifies the statutory law of the towns for refuge by requiring multiple witnesses before executing someone accused of homicide (v. 30; see the translation notes there).[85] It is not clear if they must be eyewitnesses of the murderous act itself or if they provide corroborating evidence about the murder. In either case, Yahweh delegitimizes all independent false accusations

---

80. Milgrom (*Numbers*, 291) identifies six distinctive features of the Num. 35 asylum law compared to common ANE practice. See Greengus, *Laws*, 147–87.

81. Burnside ("Exodus and Asylum," 243–66) argues that the Num. 35 asylum towns thematically and structurally echo Israel's own asylum-seeking from Egypt (Exod. 2:11–22 [Moses]; Exod. 14–15 [Israel]); cf. taking refuge in Yahweh from enemies in Pss. 2, 20, 28, 110.

82. John 17:11, 15; Rom. 8:31–39; 2 Thess. 3:3; 1 Pet. 1:5; 3:13; 1 John 5:18; Rev. 3:10.

83. Cf. the sg. "*This* is the instruction" (*zō't hattôrâ*; Num. 5:29; 6:13, 21; 19:14).

84. Cf. "This is the statute of the law" (*zō't ḥuqqat hattôrâ*: Num. 19:2; 31:21), which could likewise be rendered "This is the statutory law."

85. Another formulation of the law of multiple witnesses occurs in Deut. 17:6–7; see Kilchör, *Mosetora*, 69, 233–35, 238, 316.

of murder (cf. Exod. 20:16 NLT; Deut. 5:20). This law, on one hand, aims to protect the innocent from being put to death unjustly (cf. Exod. 23:7); on the other hand, it prevents the Israelite community from executing the innocent and incurring bloodguilt and land defilement (Num. 35:33).

The second way Yahweh qualifies the instructions about the towns of refuge is by forbidding the Israelites from accepting a ransom (*kōper*, i.e., a bribe) to pardon a murderer who must be put to death (v. 31) or free someone from the obligation to flee to a town of refuge and remain there until the current high priest dies rather than returning to their own land (v. 32, as in v. 28; see the translation note on v. 32).[86] In Num. 3 Yahweh declares that he has taken, and the Israelites must take, the Levites as a ransom, a living substitute instead of a sacrificial one, in place of all the firstborn Israelites (vv. 11–13, 40–51). Here the ransom is rejected for those *accused* of murder (v. 31) or *guilty* of murder (v. 32) because by implication this would violate Yahweh's *mišpāṭ*, which his covenant people must uphold in their society. The NT authors present Jesus the Messiah as the final "ransom" (*lytron*), echoing the role played by the Levites as a sacrificial ransom for God's people.[87] Elsewhere the NT authors teach that Jesus ransoms the guilty, which in one sense, overturns the prohibition of giving or accepting a ransom for guilty murderers in Num. 35 (see 1 Pet. 1:18–19; Titus 2:14).

The final way that Yahweh qualifies the law regarding the towns of refuge is by providing an ecological and theological motivation never to murder another human being (vv. 33–34; cf. Deut. 19:10). Only here in the Hebrew text is the land, in which Yahweh lives among his people, the explicit direct object that bloodshed pollutes.[88] Dozeman concludes: "The priestly writers' laws of homicide arise from their vision of a new creation. Life has sanctity, and blood defiles the earth. . . . Not a single life is expendable in God's land, according to the priestly writers."[89] This theology reverberates from the story to Cain: "And the LORD said, 'What have you done? The voice of your brother's blood is crying to me from the ground. And now you are cursed from the ground, which has opened its mouth to receive your brother's blood from your hand'" (Gen. 4:10–11 ESV). Noah's generation had filled the land

---

86. S. Wong ("Notion of [*kpr*]," 81–82, with Sklar, *Sin*, 56–61) remarks that primarily *kōper* designates a legitimate ransom, but five times it means an illegitimate payment, a bribe: Num. 35:31–32; 1 Sam. 12:3; Job 36:18; Amos 5:12.

87. Mark 10:45; Matt. 20:28; LXX: Num. 3:12, 46, 48, 49, 51; 18:15; 35:31, 32. Also cf. Jubilee ransom (*lytron*) in Lev. 25*; 27:31. The Levites were marked as *servants* of Yahweh in his meeting place (Num. 3–4, 18), and they were to become a *ransom* for the firstborn Israelites (3:40–51). In 1 Tim. 2:5–6 Paul uses the related term *antilytron* (ransom), a NT hapax.

88. Frevel, "Purity Conceptions," 377. Mattison ("Contrasting Conceptions," 237) makes the case that *unintentional* bloodshed also pollutes the land since the manslayer cannot return to normal life until expiation by the death of the high priest occurs (v. 32). See this theme also in Deut. 32:43; Ps. 106:38; Ezek. 9:9; 36:18.

89. Dozeman, "Numbers," 267.

with violence (*ḥāmās*, Gen. 6:11), so after the flood, God prohibited Noah's descendants from committing murder because every person is made in the image of God (*baṣelem 'ĕlōhîm*, Gen. 9:6). When Israel is in the wilderness, they also cause blood guilt if someone slaughters an animal but does not present it as an offering to Yahweh at the central meeting tent (Lev. 17:3–4; cf. Gen. 9:4–6). One may also hear an echo of the pervasive blood that in Exod. 7:14–25 contaminated Egypt's primal elements, its water and land.[90] The language of Num. 35:33–34, however, resonates most deeply with Num. 5:2–3.[91] Because of Yahweh's presence among the Israelites, Israel must not defile its wilderness camps by means of physical contagions that belong to the realm of death[92] or defile the prospective land through murder, which also belongs to the realm of death (35:33–34).[93] The only means of purifying the polluted land is to put to death the murderers, to take the blood of perpetrators because they took the blood of the victim (35:33; cf. Gen. 9:5–6). In context, the kinsman blood avenger is the one who effects this purgation by executing the murderer (vv. 19, 21, 27). Israel's motivation to purge the land should be not vengeance but devotion to their deity, Yahweh, who lives amid his people's camps and promises to live in Canaan by localizing his presence in the central meeting tent (Exod. 25:8; 29:45–46; Lev. 26:11; Num. 35:34).[94] A conceptual *inclusio* encloses chap. 35 as a unit of discourse: give towns to *the Levites to live among the Israelites* (v. 2), and do not defile the land because *Yahweh lives among the Israelites* (v. 34). Yahweh cannot live in a land polluted by physical contagions or bloodshed.

This is graphically depicted later by Ezekiel's prophetic visions of the glory of Yahweh abandoning his temple and land because of his people's bloodshed and perversity (Ezek. 9:9; 10:4, 18; 11:23). At the consummation of all things, the new Jerusalem will be a land unstained by bloodshed or unrepentant murderers (Rev. 21:8; 22:15; cf. 18:24; 19:2) or anything else unclean (21:27). It will also be a land without a manufactured dwelling place for God because God and his Lamb, whose own blood was shed in the former land (5:9; 7:14; 12:11), will reign in glory forever (21:22–23).

---

90. See Boorer, *Priestly Narrative*, 256.

91. See Frevel, "Purity Conceptions," 384, 404–5.

92. See the comments on 5:1–4.

93. Stackert (*Rewriting*, 63) has also argued that here in vv. 33–34 "the concern for blood pollution in the land (. . .) is conceptually analogous to H's [concern about] pollution of the land by sexual transgressions" (see even Frevel, "Book of Numbers," 16). As a rule, to the defiling contagions identified by P (Lev. 1–16, et al.), H adds and stresses moral impurities (Lev. 17–26; here in Num. 35:30–35): Goldstein, "Women," 51.

94. Knohl (*Sanctuary*, 99) contends that Yahweh residing (*škn*) among his people is distinctive of texts he assigns to H: Exod. 25:8; 29:45–46; Lev. 15:31; 26:11; Num. 5:3; 16:3.

33

Daughters of Zelophehad
Keep Their Land; Colophon

(36:1–13)

❧

Overview

The final chapter of Numbers returns to the inheritance problem of the daughters of Zelophehad from chap. 27, forming a thematic *inclusio* around the material in chaps. 27–36 that prepares the freshly counted second wilderness generation (chap. 26) to inherit the promised land.[1] This return to the daughters, giving the impression of an ongoing saga, may surprise modern readers since in 27:6–11 Yahweh appeared to sufficiently close the loophole by granting Israel's daughters, without a brother to inherit their father's real estate, full legal status as heiresses. However, ancient readers aware of Israel's patrimonial culture may have wondered about a second loophole, which Num. 36 exposes. In this consummative episode of the book, the patriarchal leaders from Zelophehad's tribe, Manasseh, approach Moses and the chieftains with their concern. They explain that if the daughters marry men from a different tribe, then the daughters' land will become the property of their husband's tribe (vv. 2–4). Moses concurs and by the word of Yahweh formulates a law of endogamy that requires female Israelite landowners, such as Zelophehad's daughters, to marry only men from their own tribe so that no tribe's property will be transferred to another tribe (vv. 5–9). In obedience to Yahweh, the daughters marry men from their own tribe, which, the narrator tells us in advance, will keep their father's inheritance inside the Manassite

1. Olson, *Death of the Old*, 175; Milgrom, *Numbers*, 296; Leveen, *Memory*, 178.

tribe (vv. 10–12).[2] The editors of Numbers have the final word, and they have chosen to stress the consummation, and thus the sufficiency, of Yahweh's commands and legal decisions for the Israelites, who are still in the desert valleys of Moab (since 22:1) and have yet to realize Yahweh's land promise to the patriarchs (v. 13).

Translation

1Then the leaders of the patriarchs' families of the people of Gilead, son of Machir, son of Manasseh, from the Josephite families, approached and spoke before Moses[3] and the chieftains who were leaders of Israel's patriarchs.[4] **2**They said, "Yahweh had commanded[5] my[6] lord to give the land as an inheritance by lot to the Israelites, and my lord was commanded by Yahweh to give the inheritance of our brother Zelophehad to his daughters. **3**But if they marry one of the men from another Israelite tribe, their inheritance will be taken away[7] from the

2. Achenbach (*Vollendung*, 567–73, 638) puts Num. 27 in phase one and 36 in phase three of the theocratic revision of the Torah; Scharbert (*Numeri*, 138) assigns it to the Pentateuch redactor. Frevel ("Book of Numbers," 28–29, following Kuenen, *Hexateuch*, 98) makes the case that chaps. 27 and 36 belong to the same layer as final supplements to chaps. 26–36. Most regard chap. 36* as an appendix/supplement to 27* (Noth, *Numbers*, 257; Schmidt, *Numeri*, 223) and/ or to the entire book (Cross, *Canaanite Myth*, 317; Budd, *Numbers*, 389; Levine, *Numbers*, 2:575). Kislev ("Numbers 36,1–12," 249–59; similarly, Milgrom, *Numbers*, 511–12) interprets Num. 36* as a second author's innovation to what was lacking in 27*; Seebass (*Numeri*, 3:205–7) sees Num. 27*, based on 26*, as secondary to 36*. Building on Knohl (*Sanctuary*, 100), Awabdy ("Holiness Contribution," 256–58) argues that 36:1–11 belongs to H, not only because of the need to engage with the authoritative Jubilee law (Lev. 25) but also because of the conception with Num. 27* that the daughters, as second-generation members obedient to Yahweh's covenant, will inherit the covenant promise of blessing in the land (Lev. 26:1–13).

3. 4Q27 adds "and before Eleazar the priest," probably imported from 27:2 to harmonize the accounts of the daughters of Zelophehad. It is unlikely that MT/SP/LXX *Vorlage* omitted the phrase by homeoarcton caused by the repetition of *wlpny*.

4. Formally, "the chieftains, heads of *fathers* belonging to the Israelites." SP is smoother: "the chieftains, heads of *the fathers* belonging to the Israelites," while LXX[ed] replaces "chieftains" with "houses," which smooths the text further: "the rulers of the paternal *houses* of the sons of Israel" (NETS; see Wevers, *Notes*, 601).

5. The piel qatal can be translated "*had* commanded" (*ṣiwwâ*) because in the already past-tense narrative, the daughters speak about a prior event (*BHRG* §19.2.1.2[2]).

6. "My lord" (*'et-'ădōnî*) is fronted as the focused constituent. The daughters may recall the divine decision in 27:1–11 by using the appellative "my lord" to focus on Moses as mediator (*BHRG* §47.2.1[2]). LXX[ed]: "The Lord commanded *our* lord, . . . and the Lord instructed *the lord*."

7. The niphal weqatal "will be taken away" (*wənigraʿâ*) is a simple pass. with no concern to identify an agent (*GBHS* §3.1.2a), in this case because *primogeniture* is established in other *torah* instruction (esp. Deut. 21:15–17; see Exod. 13:2–15; 22:29; 34:20) and 36:3 presumes a *patrilocal* society in which the husband brings his wife into his father's extended household (see King and Stager, *Life*, 38).

557

inheritance of our fathers and be added[8] to the inheritance of the tribe into which they marry. So it will be taken from the lot of our inheritance. [4]And when the jubilee of the Israelites takes place, their inheritance will be added to the inheritance of the tribe into which they marry. So their inheritance will be taken away from the inheritance of our patriarchal tribe."[9]

[5]Then Moses commanded the Israelites by the word of Yahweh: "What the tribe of the Josephites is saying is right. [6]This is what Yahweh has commanded for Zelophehad's daughters: 'Let them marry[10] whomever they desire,[11] only they must marry within the families of their father's tribe. [7]Then[12] an inheritance belonging to the Israelites will not pass from tribe to tribe, for every one of the Israelites must hold on to their fathers' tribal inheritance. [8]Every daughter who possesses an inheritance from any of the tribes of the Israelites must marry a man from one of the families in her father's tribe, so that every Israelite will hold on to[13] their fathers' inheritance. [9]No inheritance may pass from tribe to[14] tribe, for every one of the tribes of the Israelites must hold on to its own inheritance."

[10]The daughters of Zelophehad did just as Yahweh had commanded Moses. [11]Mahlah, Tirzah, Hoglah, Milcah, and Noah[15]—Zelophehad's daughters—married the sons of their uncles on their father's side.

---

8. SP fem. verb (*wnwsph*) is preferred here since the subject and its passive verb agree syntactically: *nhltn* [fem.] . . . *wngr'h* [fem.] . . . *wnwsph* [fem.], "their *inheritance . . . will be taken away* . . . and *be added*"; MT gender disagreement (fem. . . . fem. . . . masc.) can be understood as a default to the masc. gender; *BHRG* §24.2.3(3), cf. §35(7) on *ad sensum* shift to masc.

9. 4Q27 includes a long plus that can be reconstructed based on 36:1b–2: "[And they spoke before Moses and before] Eleazar the [priest and before the chieftains who were leaders of the Israelite paternal households. They said, "Yahweh commanded my lord, Joshua son] of Nun and Ca[leb son of Jephunneh to give the land as an inheritance]" ([*wydbrw lpny mwšh wlpny*] *'l'zr h*[*khwn wlpny hnśy'ym r'šy h'bwt lbny yśr'l wyw'mrw 't 'dwny w't yhšw' bn*] *nwn w't k*[*lb bn ypwnyh swh yhwh ltt 't h'rs bnhlh*] > MT SP LXX^(ed)); Ulrich, *Qumran*, 171. Considering the lengthening tendency of 4Q27 and the absence of any phrasal indicators of haplography, it is improbable that the MT/SP/LXX *Vorlage* accidentally omitted this reading.

10. 4Q27 adds "Let them *indeed* marry," possibly influenced by 30:7.

11. Formally, "'(to) the one that is good in their eyes" (*lattôb ba'ênêhem*); the masc. possessive pronoun, "*their* eyes," refers to the daughters' eyes (semantically, not syntactically); see *BHRG* §24.2.3(3).

12. The simple *w* on the negated yiqtol functions like an apodosis if the prior impv. (in v. 6) is obeyed: ". . . only they must marry ['*ak . . . tihyênâ lanāšîm*] . . . Then [*wa*]"; *GBHS* §4.3.3(f).

13. Formally, "will possess" (*yîrašû*; NIV, ESV), but contextually "keep" (NJPS), "continue to possess" (NRSV), or "retain" (NET).

14. SP uses a synonymous preposition ('*l* vs. MT *l*), which may be a harmonization to the phrase in v. 7.

15. The order and connecting conjunctions of the daughters differ among the witnesses:

(MT Tg) Mahlah, Tirzah and Hoglah and Milcah and Noah

(SP) Mahlah and Noah, Hoglah, Milcah and Tirzah

(LXX^(ed)) Thersa and Hegla and Melcha and Noua and Maala (NETS)

(Vulg) Maala et Thersa et Egla et Melcha et Noa

[12]They married into the families of the Manassites, the descendants of Joseph, and their inheritance remained in the tribe of their father's family.
[13]These are the commandments and the decisions that Yahweh commanded the Israelites by the authority of Moses, in the desert valleys of Moab by the Jordan River across from[16] Jericho.

Interpretation

36:1–4. The patriarchal leaders from Gilead of Manasseh explain to Moses that Yahweh's orders for Zelophehad's daughters, delivered in 27:6–11, leave open a loophole that will inevitably result in every tribe's loss and every tribe's acquisition of real estate in the promised land. Each tribe will be assigned an expanse of land proportionate to their size and by means of casting lots (26:52–56; 33:54), but now a pressing question arises: How can each tribe maintain generational possession of their allotted land? The Gileadite family leaders are presumably a constituency of younger fathers belonging to the new generation, excluding patriarchs of the first exodus generation, who died in disobedience (e.g., 13:11) or in obedience like Zelophehad (27:3). They approach Moses and the chieftains and articulate the loophole: If Zelophehad's daughters marry outside their tribe, then in the Year of Jubilee, the daughters' land will transfer into the permanent possession of their husband's tribe (vv. 2–4). They begin by acknowledging their subordinate rank to Moses—a double "my lord" (*'ădōnî*) address, which has royal overtones—and by affirming the *stare decisis* of Yahweh's judicial ruling to give the land inheritance of Zelophehad, who had no sons, to his daughters as their property (v. 2; see the translation notes there). Even if we may imagine the distress of these patriarchs in their monologue, they are hardly complex characters but typify the singular trait of devotion to the preservation of their tribe.[17] This can be seen in their divergence from the daughters' scenario (v. 2) and convergence on the ensuing land losses for their tribe (vv. 3–4).[18] Their over-specified fixation on losing some of their allotted inheritance (vv. 3–4) should be interpreted not as chauvinistic neglect of the daughters' own predicament but as tenacity to advocate for their tribe at large, and Moses and Yahweh come to endorse their stance (vv. 5–9).[19] Using the same verbal root and stem, the daughters are concerned that their father's name *would be lost* (**gr' niphal*, 27:4) with

16. As in 35:1, "*across from* Jericho" is absent, inviting readers to supply it from their geographical knowledge or from 34:15 (anacoluthon).
17. See Berlin, "Characterization," 76–78.
18. See the first translation note on v. 3 and the translation note on v. 4.
19. See Runge, *Discourse Grammar*, 387. *With* Frevel ("Book of Numbers," 28n106) but contra Kislev ("Numbers 36,1–12," 251), the daughters' inheritance does not become "almost valueless in practice according to chapter 36."

his inheritance, while the patriarchs are concerned that their tribe's land *will be lost* (*gr*ʿ niphal, 36:3–4).[20] Thus the patriarchs are seeking a more generalized law so that Manasseh, and by implication every tribe, can maintain the original dimensions of its land inheritance for posterity.[21]

The patriarchs say that the timing of the transfer of land out of the original tribe's possession and into the new tribe will occur in the Year of Jubilee; this alludes to the fiftieth year decreed in Lev. 25:8–16 and 27:16–24, the only Jubilee instruction in the Pentateuch (v. 4). Referring to the Jubilee has been enigmatic to interpreters because the Jubilee law refers specifically to land debts, not exactly to inheritance.[22] Also, Num. 36:4 "suggests that in the year of jubilee everything remained unaltered; one would expect, rather, that in the year of jubilee the original conditions of possession would be reinstated."[23] For example, a poor Israelite who works as an indentured servant will, in the Jubilee year, "go back to his own clan and return to the possession of his fathers" (Lev. 25:40). Applying this legal precedent to Num. 36:4, the land forfeited to another tribe by the daughter's marriage would be restored to the daughter's family and tribe. However, a residential house in a walled city, if one sells it but does not redeem it within one year, becomes the permanent possession of the buyer in the Jubilee year (Lev. 25:29–30). In the spirit of this law, others have conjectured that 36:4 points to a previously unknown Jubilee custom.[24] Most likely, the patriarchs' concern is precisely that there is no provision in the Jubilee law for these daughters and their tribes to receive back their inheritance land, and without such a provision for redemption (*gəʾullâ* in Lev. 25*), the land in the Jubilee year would become the permanent possession of the tribes into which the daughters had married.[25]

36:5–9. Agreeing that the Josephites have identified a legal loophole, Yahweh through Moses issues a new law that restricts female Israelite landowners, like Zelophehad's daughters, to marry only within their tribe so that no tribe's land inheritance will be transferred to another tribe. The story contains all the elements of an "oracular novella," with a short story (vv. 1–4) followed by a divine oracle with a case ruling and formal legislation (vv. 5/6–9).[26] The divine oracle, however, is less overt here since the narrator first says "Moses

---

20. Leveen, *Memory*, 179. Kislev ("Numbers 36,1–12," 249–59) argues that the author of Num. 36* innovatively stresses *tribal* inheritance, which was absent in chap. 27* as it stresses *familial* inheritance.

21. W. Lee, *Migratory Campaign*, 208.

22. Dozeman, "Numbers," 266.

23. Noth, *Numbers*, 257.

24. Sturdy, *Numbers*, 244; de Vaulx (*Nombres*, 405) calls it an "unprecedented provision."

25. With Levine, *Numbers*, 2:578.

26. With de Vaulx (*Nombres*, 405), Knierim and Coats (*Numbers*, 275, 330, "case study" genre) see the other oracular novellas in Lev. 24:10–23; Num. 9:6–14; 15:32–36; 27:1–11. However, Chavel (*Oracular Law*, 8), whose term "oracular novella" I am using, excludes Num. 36* from this genre because the Gileadites in Num. 36* approach Moses not about a new subject

commanded the Israelites by the word of Yahweh" (v. 5) and only later appears to recount the ruling in Yahweh's wording: "This is what Yahweh has commanded for Zelophehad's daughters: '*Let them marry . . .*'" (vv. 6b–9). Ostensibly this reflects the transition in the later part of the book from Moses as mediator to Moses as lawgiver[27] and correlates with the shape of Deuteronomy, which is saturated with Moses's words rather than Yahweh's words (but cf. Num. 36:13). So here and in Num. 32, although Moses himself is doomed to die outside the land, he exercises his authority with Yahweh to make a far-reaching decision on Israel's land inheritance.[28] Moses and Yahweh begin by honoring Zelophehad's daughters with the stunning prerogative to select husbands, when the custom of the day always gave the male and his family this prerogative (see the second translation note on v. 6).[29] Their choice of a spouse must be endogamous, marrying within their tribe, but could also be exogamous by marrying outside their clan, affording them a prospect pool within the tribe of Manasseh of 52,700 men who are twenty years old and above, not to mention the younger men (26:34).

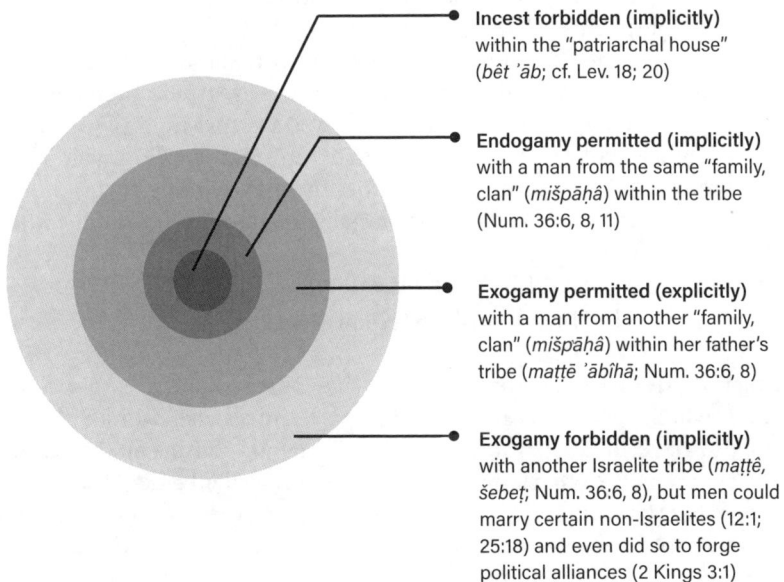

Incest forbidden (implicitly) within the "patriarchal house" (*bêt 'āb*; cf. Lev. 18; 20)

Endogamy permitted (implicitly) with a man from the same "family, clan" (*mišpāḥâ*) within the tribe (Num. 36:6, 8, 11)

Exogamy permitted (explicitly) with a man from another "family, clan" (*mišpāḥâ*) within her father's tribe (*maṭṭē 'ābîhā*; Num. 36:6, 8)

Exogamy forbidden (implicitly) with another Israelite tribe (*maṭṭê, šebeṭ*; Num. 36:6, 8), but men could marry certain non-Israelites (12:1; 25:18) and even did so to forge political alliances (2 Kings 3:1)

Figure 33.1. Forbidden and Permitted Marriages

---

or scenario but about the prior ruling in Num. 27. In my view, this is an inadequate reason to exclude it from the genre.

27. Frevel, "Book of Numbers," 29–30.

28. Seebass, "Eigene Komposition," 98.

29. Awabdy, "Holiness Contribution," 257. See, i.e., Gen. 2:24; chaps. 24; 28–29; 34; 38; Num. 12:1; Deut. 22:13; 24:1.

To bring this episode to a close, the narrator uses the closural convention of shifting from the past (the patriarchs and Zelophehad's daughters, vv. 1–6) to the reader's future (vv. 7–9), which suggests that the whole episode functions as an etiology, explaining the enduring-heiress custom in Israel.[30] This final part of Yahweh's speech, like that of the patriarchs' (vv. 2–4), becomes highly redundant with point-counterpoint sets in order to make only two points.[31] First, female landowners (v. 8), apparently not all women, must practice endogamy by marrying only men from their own tribe (vv. 6, 8). Second, their endogamy is crucial only because it will prevent any tribe from acquiring some of another tribe's land or losing some of its own (vv. 7 [2×], 8, 9 [2×]; see the translation notes on vv. 7 and 8). The law does not prevent Israel's tribes from acquiring or forfeiting territory by other means, such as civil war (Judg. 12:4–6; 20–21; 1 Kings 16) or diplomatic treaties (cf. Josh. 9–10; 1 Kings 5:12; 9:10–14; Obad. 7).

36:10–12. The daughters of Zelophehad obey the endogamy law by marrying within their tribe, which keeps their father's land inheritance within the Manassite tribe. In scene 1 of their textualized story, 27:1–11, the daughters *spoke* what was right in Yahweh's estimation (27:6–7), and now the narrator recounts that they "*did* just as Yahweh had commanded Moses" (36:10). Throughout chaps. 27 and 36, the narrator characterizes these daughters as the ideal type of Israelite women, assertive and given a surprisingly powerful voice in a patriarchal world, yet also obedient to Yahweh their God, who honors them in return.[32] The narrator also honors them by naming them, this time in an order that differs from their presumable birth order repeated earlier:

Mahlah, Noah, Hoglah, Milcah, and Tirzah (26:33; 27:1)

Mahlah, Tirzah, Hoglah, Milcah, Noah (36:11)[33]

The metathesis of Tirzah and Noah here may relate to underlying social factors, but what is clear is that these named daughters also avoided the ANE humiliation of celibacy[34] by marrying their unnamed cousins on their father's side. Zelophehad, were he alive, would have received a bride-price from his nephews, but the ambiguity of the recipient here is overshadowed by the pan-Israelite concern of preventing the intertribal transfer of real estate.[35] The daughters' obedience to Yahweh's new marital law (vv. 5–9) ensures, at least

---

30. Zeelander ("Closural Conventions," 343) notes Berlin's descriptor, "time bridge," to lead the narrative into the present time (Berlin, *Poetics*, 108–9).

31. Point-counterpoint sets occur in vv. 7, 9; see Runge, *Discourse Grammar*, 386; cf. Douglas, *Wilderness*, 237, 244.

32. Berlin, "Characterization," 76–78.

33. See the translation note on v. 11.

34. King and Stager, *Life*, 56; see Isa. 4:1; Jer. 16:2.

35. King and Stager, *Life*, 54; on bride-price, see Gen. 34:12; Exod. 22:16–17; 1 Sam. 18:25.

through their lifetime, that their father's land inheritance will remain the exclusive possession of their father's tribe, Manasseh (v. 12). So the penultimate word of the Numbers narrative is obedience, strengthening hopes that the promise of divine blessing will ensue for the second generation as it settles the land of Canaan and the Transjordan (cf. Lev. 26:1–13; Num. 6:24–26). This report (vv. 10–12) is anachronistic, of course, in that it projects into the future when Israel is in the land and the daughters' inheritance "remained in the tribe of their father's family." This provides literary closure to the episode, not requiring the Hexateuchal fulfillment that one finds in Josh. 17:3–4, which serves another function at that juncture.[36]

36:13. The editors conclude the composition of Numbers with this colophon, which forms an *inclusio* with 35:1, collecting the refined protocols of landholdings in chaps. 35–36,[37] and an *inclusio* with 22:1, enclosing the story of Israel in the desert valleys of Moab by the Jordan River across from Jericho.[38] This ending to the book may feel abrupt to modern readers, but we should ask if it offers a "satisfying consonance" with the book that it concludes.[39] The nominal clause of identification—"These are *the commandments and the decisions* [*hammiṣwôt wəhammišpāṭîm*] that Yahweh *commanded* [*ṣiwwâ*] by the authority of Moses"—is a satisfying ending in that it resonates with the language of Lev. 27:34, forming an *inclusio* around the book of Numbers: "*These are the commandments* [*hammiṣwôt*] that Yahweh *commanded* [*ṣiwwâ*] Moses for the Israelites on Mount Sinai."[40] At the same time, Num. 36:13 is a partially dissonant ending, since the material relating to the Moabite desert valley opened (22:1) and closed (36:12) as *a narrated story* that incorporates, but is certainly not limited to, Yahweh's commands and legal decisions.[41] Here the editors redefine the 22:1–36:12 narrative as Yahweh's commandments and legal decisions, which suggests that they were working at a later time, when the Moses Story with its embedded divine instructions (*tôrâ*) had already come to be characterized as an authoritative Torah.[42] While the unique materials in Num. 1–10 and 26–36 distinguish

---

36. Thus, Awabdy ("Holiness Contribution," 258n66) attributes 36:(10), 11–12 to the Pentateuch redaction.

37. Leveen, *Memory*, 177.

38. The topographical triad—desert valleys of Moab–Jordan River–Jericho—occurs in Num. 22:1; 26:3, 63; 31:12 [with *"that is* (*'šr*) across from Jericho"]; 33:48, 50; 35:1; 36:13; and Josh. 13:32 (cf. partial mentions in Num. 33:48; 34:15). For the anacoluthon of *"across from* Jericho," see 36:13 and the translation note there.

39. Leveen (*Memory*, 173), citing Kermode, *Sense of an Ending*, 17.

40. Otto, "Ende der Toraoffenbarung," 194–97; Kilchör, *Mosetora*, 8.

41. See *GBHS* §5.1.1a.

42. Kislev ("Numbers 36:13," 115) sees 36:13 as a Priestly Persian-era addition. Robker ("Balaam Narrative," 345) contends that 36:13 and the other inscriptions with the formulaic "in the desert valleys of Moab across from the Jordan River" (see the second note in the comments on 36:13) belong to the same editorial layer.

Numbers from Leviticus and Deuteronomy, the editorial inscriptions attribute the composition to Moses—"by the authority of Moses" (see the translation note on 4:37)—as equally authorized revelations from Yahweh during Israel's migration to the land.[43] Finally, this formulaic colophon is the last of its kind in the continuum of superscriptions in Exodus–Leviticus–Numbers;[44] by its *anaphoric* nature, it does not create a literary bridge into Deuteronomy. The fissure is expanded by Deuteronomy's opening superscription, which is *anticipatory* in nature:[45]

Num. 22:1–36:12 ← 36:13	Deut. 1:1 → Deuteronomy[a]
These are the commandments	*These are the words*
and the decisions that Yahweh	*that Moses spoke to*
commanded . . .	*all Israel . . .*

a. Or to a form of the speeches within Deut. 1:6–33:29.

The story line of Numbers is vital to the larger Hexateuch epic since Numbers incessantly anticipates when Yahweh will fulfill his land promise to the patriarchs. However, by the 36:13 colophon, the editors end the composition with their backward-pointing message: "Right now you have everything you need to obey Yahweh's word through Moses even while you are still outside the land waiting for Yahweh to fulfill his promise."[46] This consummative message resonates throughout the canon and in the lives of God's people today: "Today, if you hear his voice, do not harden your hearts as you did in the rebellion, during the time of testing in the wilderness" (Heb. 3:7–8 NIV).[47]

Implications

Daughters Who Become Heiresses

Moses's ruling in Num. 36:5–9 demands that Israel's daughters who inherit land marry endogamously, within their tribe, so that every tribe will maintain possession of its own allotment of territory in the promised land. However, this is not the only way, according to Pentateuchal law, to keep a tribe's real

---

43. Achenbach, *Vollendung*, 23, 600–601.

44. In Numbers, the editorial inscriptions appear in 1:1 ("in the Sinai wilderness in the meeting tent"); 12:16 ("in the Paran wilderness"); and in 22:1; 26:3; 33:50; 35:1; 36:13 ("in the desert valleys of Moab").

45. With Otto ("Ende der Toraoffenbarung," 193–94), the geographical setting and the reporting of the words of Moses provide a thematic link between Num. 36:13 and Deut. 1:1–5, but Numbers' colophon clearly looks back, while Deuteronomy's superscription looks forward. Kilchör (*Mosetora*, 8) argues that Deut. 29:1 [28:69] alludes to Lev. 27:34, Num. 36:13, and Deut. 4:44 so that Deuteronomic law presents itself as interpreting the expanse of Exod. 20:1–Num. 36:13.

46. Cf. Leveen, *Memory*, 180–81.

47. Quotation from Ps. 95:8; see also Heb. 3:15; 4:7.

estate from passing out of their possession to another tribe. In Deut. 25:5–10, Moses institutes the custom of levirate marriage. This law, appearing later in the Torah story, would have rectified the predicament of Zelophehad's daughters. From Hepher, Zelophehad's father, descended an entire family group within Manasseh's tribe, giving the impression that Hepher would have had sons other than Zelophehad (26:32–33). The only reason Zelophehad is mentioned and not any of his brothers is that he distinctively "had no sons, only daughters" (26:33; 27:33). The daughters do refer to "our father's brothers" (vv. 4b, 7), which could refer to his relatives or, based on the restrictive meaning in v. 9, his own biological brothers (see the comments on these verses). If Zelophehad's anonymous widow had followed the levirate marriage law (Deut. 25:5–10; cf. 21:15–17; Ruth 4:10–11), she could have married one of Zelophehad's brothers to bear a male heir and preserve Zelophehad's name (Num. 27:4; Deut. 25:6–7), thus protecting the patrilineal transmission of the land inheritance within Manasseh's tribe.[48]

Interpreters have debated what is going on between these ostensibly competing laws in Numbers and Deuteronomy. Conceptually, they appear to be incompatible, since "the institution of Levirate marriage implies that daughters play no role in passing down the clan name in the patriarchal agnatic society."[49] In one view, since the Priestly scribe of Num. 27 and 36 makes no provision for levirate marriage, this possibly indicates that he disapproved of such marriages (cf. Lev. 18:16; 20:21),[50] but this is an *argumentum ex silentio*. Others go farther, saying that the late Priestly authors of Num. 27 and 36 abrogate the Deuteronomic levirate marriage principle,[51] but Num. 27 and 36 give no linguistic indication of overturning a precedent, and the literary placement of Deut. 25 after Num. 27 and 36 gives Deut. 25 the final synchronic word. Another option is to regard Deut. 25 as a moral obligation but not a legal obligation, whereas Num. 27 and 36 are compulsory law,[52] but this disregards the eventual status—at least by the Persian era—of the Deuteronomic collection as an authoritative Mosaic Torah.[53] Others have argued the inverse, that the levirate custom of Deut. 25 was given not to replace the Numbers laws but to supplement their gap and make an exception

---

48. Embry ("Legalities," 31) argues that Num. 36 illuminates certain ambiguities in the book of Ruth, including "why Ruth is required in marriage in order for the kinsman-redeemer to act or why Naomi is the beneficiary of the marriage between Boaz and Ruth. Furthermore, the regulation of Zelophehad's daughters helps explain the unique combination of levirate marriage and the actions of the kinsman-redeemer found in Ruth 4."

49. Frevel, "Book of Numbers," 25.

50. Gray, *Numbers*, 397–98. Rather, since Zelophehad was deceased, his widow would be free to marry his brother without violating Lev. 18:16; 20:21 (Rom. 7:1–3; but cf. Kilchör, "Levirate Marriage," 429–40).

51. Budd, *Numbers*, 301.

52. Schmidt, *Numeri*, 164.

53. Römer and Brettler, "Deuteronomy 34," 401–19.

to Lev. 18*, 20*, and Deut. 5:21a so that marrying one's deceased brother's wife does not qualify as adultery.[54] Even though this view is a non sequitur due to the lack of convincing anaphora in Deut. 25 that would link it intertextually to Num. 27 and 36, this view cannot be ruled out on principle. At this interpretive impasse, I take another path forward by seeing the primary influences on the formulation of Num. 27 and 36 as ANE and, ultimately, theological.

Across the ANE, there were several laws and contracts that presented certain scenarios in which a daughter could become an heiress in a patriarchal world. To the convention that only men could inherit the family estate, Gudea (ca. 22nd cent. BCE), ruler of Lagash in Mesopotamia, granted an exception in his city: "From the house that had no son I allowed his daughter to act in the capacity of its son (and) heir."[55] Other texts support this conception that a daughter could become an heiress "under the guise of being a man."[56] In a Sumerian law of Ur-Nammu (21st cent. BCE) or maybe of Lipit-Ishtar (20th or 19th cent. BCE), "If a man dies without male offspring, an unmarried daughter shall be his heir."[57] In a series of inheritance laws, the Old Babylonian Code of Hammurapi (18th cent. BCE) presents several scenarios in which a daughter from certain classes of persons would receive the benefits of "her inheritance" land, but ultimately "her estate/inheritance belongs only to her brothers."[58] However, three special classes of daughters could become heiresses along with her brothers: "If, during a father's lifetime, his daughter becomes an *ugbabtu*, a *nadîtu*, or a *qadištu*, they (her brothers) shall divide the estate considering her as an equal heir."[59] An *ugbabtu* was a "female devotee of a male deity";[60] a *nadîtu* was a "woman dedicated to a god, usually unmarried, not allowed to have children";[61] a *qadištu* was a "woman of special status."[62] Since a *nadîtu* would be without a biological heir, she had the prerogative of choosing someone else to inherit her estate.[63] A man could also give his wife "a field, orchard, house, or movable property" by leaving her an official contract, so that when he died, her children could not reclaim the land from her, and "the mother shall give her estate to whichever of her children she

54. Kilchör, *Mosetora*, 279; Kilchör, "Levirate Marriage," 429–40.

55. From the Gudea Statue B vii 44–46, cited by Stol, *Women*, 301; http://oracc.museum .upenn.edu/etcsri/Q001541.

56. Stol, *Women*, 302.

57. "Laws of Lipit-Ishtar," *Law Collections* (trans. Roth), 26, law §b. Roth attributes the law to Lipit-Ishtar; Stol (*Women*, 301) and others credit Ur-Nammu.

58. "Laws of Hammurabi," COS 2.131:346, laws §§178 (37.61–38.19), 180 (38.43–45), 181 (38.60–75); Roth, *Law Collections*, 117–18.

59. "Laws of Hammurabi," COS 2.131:412, law §179 (38.20–24).

60. "*Ugbabtu*," CAD 20:33.

61. "*Nadîtu*," CAD 11:63.

62. "*Qadištu*," CAD 13:48.

63. "Laws of Hammurabi," COS 2.131:346, law §182; Roth, *Law Collections*, 118.

loves, but she will not give it to an outsider."[64] The term "children" (*māru*) in the plural can refer to both male and female,[65] suggesting that the mother could designate an heir or an heiress to acquire her field or other property.

In ancient Egypt, the individuality of every human, male and female, can be found in its inheritance laws and in very early marriage contracts.[66] Staubli concludes, "It was no coincidence that Queen Hatshepsut, in particular, had to legitimize herself in her position as a pharaoh, particularly through inheritance law regulations. In doing so, she insists on the typical Egyptian stipulation that the heir to the heir must also be worthy, that she is a competent administrator."[67] Although Middle Assyrian Law says nothing of heiresses, in two Middle Assyrian (ca. 14th–12th cent. BCE) wills it appears to have been possible for a daughter, alongside her brothers, to inherit movable and maybe immovable property from her father.[68] Job, likewise, gave to his beautiful daughters an inheritance among their brothers (Job 42:15). Finally, as a helpful segue we may consider a contract (ca. 15th cent. BCE) from the city of Nuzi on the Tigris. The text reads "If Gilimninou does not give birth to a son, then his daughter must take a share in the inheritance," and to this the contract adds a matrilocal custom in which the husband of the heiress enters her clan by marriage (*errebu*).[69] By contrast, in Num. 27 and 36, the daughters do not receive a *share*, but all the shares of their father's entire inheritance were presumably divided equally among the sisters; if one daughter is the heiress, she receives the entire estate (27:8). Also unlike the Nuzi contract, the cousins whom the daughters married were already part of their clan or extended family, Gilead (36:1); Moses's ruling of endogamy within each tribe (36:5–9) does not convert Israel from a patrilocal to a matrilocal culture.[70]

What is noteworthy about all these ANE examples is that a woman living in a patriarchal society could, under certain conditions, be formally conferred the legal status of heiress. These vestiges of societal openness stand in contrast to the tendency of the ANE that "points to land inheritance by males only; and in the exceptional cases, where land was given to women, such women were not allowed to marry outside of their father's kindred."[71] Of course, these favorable inheritance laws do not expose what happened to

---

64. "Laws of Hammurabi," *COS* 2.131:345, law §150. See the normalized Akkadian text by Roth, *Law Collections*, 109–10. The Widow's Plea ostracon has a debated provenance but, as a subform of a letter, details the legal petition of a sonless widow to receive an inheritance promised orally: "The Widow's Plea," *COS* 3.44:86; http://biblelandpictures.com/product/5387-widows-plea-ostracon.

65. Huehnergard, *Akkadian*, 10; "*māru* 1b," *CAD* 10:313, gloss 6b.

66. Staubli, *Levitikus, Numeri*, 316.

67. Staubli, *Levitikus, Numeri*, 316, my trans.

68. Démare-Lafont, "Inheritance Law," 6–7.

69. De Vaulx (*Nombres*, 319) quotes C. Gordon, "Parallèles nouziens," 34–41 (38), my trans.

70. See Block, "Marriage and Family," 40.

71. Ahiamadu, "Female Inheritance," 211.

most women in real life.[72] In my view, Yahweh and the authors of Num. 27 were well aware of ANE jurisprudence, and they regarded the rare custom of an heiress solution to the tribal inheritance problem to be essentially good and adaptable into ancient Israelite society. In addition, Num. 36 draws out the ANE preference of endogamy, marrying one's close relatives or within one's clan or tribe, over exogamy, marrying outside those boundaries.[73] Also, marrying too close, incestuously, is prohibited in the Torah (Lev. 18, 20) and unpopular in the ANE.[74]

In distinction from the ANE milieu, the stories of Num. 27 and 36 are shaped by two theological messages: Yahweh highly values both the solidarity of every Israelite tribe *and* the honor of Zelophehad's daughters. The threefold repetition in Moses's speech in chap. 36 cannot be clearer: "for every one of the Israelites must hold on to their fathers' tribal inheritance" (36:7, with variations in vv. 8 and 9). At stake is the possibility that tribes over generations could incrementally lose not just their allotted homeland but also their tribal solidarity and, worse yet, their tribal loyalty (*ḥesed*). "Tribal dynamics routinely involve competing territorial claims in both ancient and modern contexts," yet in ancient Israel, "tribal loyalties (*ḥesed*) run deep and ultimately prevail."[75] Endogamy within one's tribe will mitigate against tribal disloyalty (36:5–12).

If the message of the *inclusio* of Num. 33:51–56 is that *loyalty to Yahweh* by exterminating the locals (vv. 51–52, 55–56) is pivotal to taking possession of the land (vv. 53–54), the message here is that *loyalty to your tribe* by marrying internally is pivotal to maintaining possession of the land. Said another way, "Here it becomes clear that the preservation of family property holdings was one of the highest values in Israelite society. That is because the land was the gift of the covenant, so each family's allotment was its share in the covenant."[76] The theology of Num. 27 and 36 centers on Yahweh, who by his legal provisions preserves his people and their loyalty to each other as constituents of his covenant. God's nature remains consistent in this matter: "This inheritance is kept in heaven for you, who through faith are shielded by God's power. . . . Love one another deeply, from the heart" (1 Pet. 1:4b, 22).

---

72. See different scenarios identified by Stol, *Women*, 302–3.

73. King and Stager, *Life*, 38, 55. The preference of endogamy over exogamy continued into the first-century Mediterranean world (Malina, *New Testament World*, 119). See Frevel, *Desert Transformations*, 357–78.

74. There are exceptions; e.g., one Neo-Babylonian daughter was forced to marry one uncle after another to maintain the family wealth (Stol, *Women*, 273–74). Conversely, in the story of Tob. 6:12, Tobias is charged to marry one daughter, Sarah, and so gain her father's possessions (see Stol, *Women*, 273).

75. Petter, "Tribes and Nomads," 393.

76. Walton and Matthews, *Genesis–Deuteronomy*, 215.

In at least six ways, Yahweh, Israel's sovereign deity, attributes honor to the vulnerable daughters of Zelophehad and the future daughters of Israel.

1. The editors of Numbers incorporate three texts in Numbers (26:33; 27:1; 36:11), when one would have sufficed,[77] that list the daughters *by their names*, which "confers being, even status, without defining personality" (cf. Isa. 56:5).[78]

2. Publicly, in front of the male elders of the community, Yahweh emphatically endorses Zelophehad's daughters' claims (27:7) and, by extension, the future claim of all Israel's daughters (27:8–11).[79]

3. Yahweh seals his ruling on the daughters' behalf as a "legal requirement," a statutory law that resists being overturned in the future (27:11).

4. In a literary contrast to Moses, who rebels and loses his land inheritance (27:12–14), the daughters and their father did not rebel with the first generation and are regarded as worthy of the covenant blessing of the land.[80]

5. Departing from the ANE and biblical custom of men and/or their families choosing wives for themselves,[81] Yahweh transfers the agency to Zelophehad's daughters, requiring only that their choice be endogamous (36:6).[82]

6. The narrator lifts up Zelophehad's daughters as exemplars of obedience to Yahweh, resulting in the blessing of preserving their tribe's inheritance (36:10–11).[83]

Also writing in an extremely patriarchal culture, the apostle Peter admonishes husbands to honor their wives "since they too are also *heirs of the gracious gift of life*" (1 Pet. 3:7 NRSV, emphasis added). For the apostle Paul,

77. See Runge, *Discourse Grammar*, 387.

78. Sternberg, *Poetics*, 330. Leveen (*Memory*, 176) sees the threefold naming as a way of reassuring the new generation that they, unlike their parents, will be preserved.

79. See the comments on 27:7.

80. Awabdy, "Holiness Contribution," 256–58. Contra Aaron ("Zelophehad's Daughters," 1–38), who argues that Num. 27 and 36 reflect fictional events that were intended to subvert the ancient custom of granting a father or mother the right, if they so chose, to assign their daughter(s) an inheritance. This parental right is attested in the ANE (see above examples), but there is insufficient data to claim that it was a "stable social custom" in either the ANE or ancient Israel.

81. E.g., Gen. 24; Exod. 21:4; Lev. 21:13; Num. 31:18; Deut. 21:11–12a.

82. This reveals a "concern for inclusiveness, and the flexibility of the tradition and the need for reinterpretation" (Olson, *Death of the Old*, 175).

83. Although Mary was presumably from the tribe of Levi (Luke 1:5, 36) and Joseph was from Judah (Matt. 1:2, 16, 20; Luke 3:23, 33), Eusebius (3rd–4th cent. CE) makes the argument that she was "virtually" from the same tribe in alignment with the endogamy law of Num. 36 (Lienhard, *Numbers*, 273).

godly mothers and grandmothers are also worthy of praise because they pass on their own inheritance of faith to their children and grandchildren: "I remember your genuine faith, which first lived in your grandmother Lois and in your mother Eunice and now, I am sure, lives in you also" (2 Tim. 1:5, my trans.).

Bibliography

Aaron, David H. "The Ruse of Zelophehad's Daughters." *Hebrew Union College Annual* 80 (2009): 1–38.

Abela, Anthony. "Shaming Miriam, Moses' Sister, in Num 12,1–16: Focus on the Narrative's Exposition in vv. 1–2." In Römer, *Leviticus and Numbers*, 521–34.

Achenbach, Reinhard. "Complementary Reading of the Torah in the Priestly Texts of Numbers 15." In Frevel, Pola, and Schart, *Book of Numbers*, 201–32.

———. "Divine Warfare and Yhwh's Wars: Religious Ideologies of War in the Ancient Near East and in the Old Testament." Pages 1–27 in *The Ancient Near East in the 12th–10th Centuries BCE: Culture and History; Proceedings of the International Conference Held at the University of Haifa, 2–5 May, 2010*. Edited by G. Galil et al. Alter Orient und Altes Testament 392. Münster: Ugarit-Verlag.

———. "Das Heiligkeitsgesetz und die sakralen Ordnungen des Numeribuches im Horizont der Pentateuchredaktion." In Römer, *Leviticus and Numbers*, 145–75.

———. "Lex Sacra and Sabbath in the Pentateuch." *Zeitschrift für altorientalische und biblische Rechtsgeschichte* 22 (2016): 101–10.

———. *Die Vollendung der Tora: Studien zur Redaktionsgeschichte des Numeribuches im Kontext von Hexateuch und Pentateuch*. Beihefte zur Zeitschrift für altorientalische und biblische Rechtsgeschichte 3. Wiesbaden: Harrassowitz, 2003.

Aejmelaeus, Anneli. "What We Talk about When We Talk about Translation Technique." Pages 531–52 in *X Congress of the International Organization for Septuagint and Cognate Studies, Oslo, 1998*. Edited by B. A. Taylor. Society of Biblical Literature Septuagint and Cognate Studies 51. Atlanta: Society of Biblical Literature, 2001.

Aharoni, Yohanan. "Excavations at Tel Beer-sheba." *Biblical Archaeologist* (1972): 111–27.

———. *The Land of the Bible: A Historical Geography*. Rev. ed. Translated by A. F. Rainey. Philadelphia: Westminster, 1979.

Ahiamadu, Amadi. "Assessing Female Inheritance of Land in Nigeria with the Daughters of Zelophehad Narrative (Numbers 27:1–11)." In Brenner and A. Lee, *Leviticus and Numbers*, 199–212.

Albertz, Rainer. "Das Buch Numeri jenseits der Quellentheorie: Eine Redaktionsgeschichte von Num 20–24 (Teil I)." *Zeitschrift für die alttestamentliche Wissenschaft* 123 (2011): 171–83. "(Teil II)." *Zeitschrift für die alttestamentliche Wissenschaft* 123 (2011): 336–47.

———. "The Formative Impact of the Hexateuch Redaction: An Interim Result." Pages 53–74 in *The Post-Priestly Pentateuch: New Perspectives on Its Redactional Development and Theological Profiles*. Forschungen zum Alten Testament 101. Edited by F. Giuntoli and K. Schmid. Tübingen: Mohr Siebeck, 2015.

———. *A History of Israelite Religion in the Old Testament Period.* Vol. 1, *From the Beginnings to the End of the Monarchy.* Vol. 2, *From the Exile to the Maccabees.* Old Testament Library. Translated by J. Bowden. Louisville: Westminster John Knox, 1994.

———. "A Pentateuchal Redaction in the Book of Numbers? The Late Priestly Layers of Num 25–36." *Zeitschrift für die alttestamentliche Wissenschaft* 125 (2013): 220–33.

———. *Pentateuchstudien.* Forschungen zum Alten Testament 117. Edited by J. Wöhrle with F. Neumann. Tübingen: Mohr Siebeck, 2018.

———. "Wilderness Material in Exodus (Exodus 15–18)." Pages 151–68 in *The Book of Exodus: Composition, Reception, and Interpretation.* Supplements to Vetus Testamentum 164. Edited by T. B. Dozeman, C. A. Evans, and J. N. Lohr. Leiden: Brill, 2014.

Alcorta, Candace S., and Richard Sosis. "Ritual, Emotion, and Sacred Symbols: The Evolution of Religion as an Adaptive Complex." *Human Nature* 16 (2005): 323–59.

Allegro, J. M. "The Meaning of the Phrase *šetūm hāʿayin* in Num XXIV 3,15." *Vetus Testamentum* 3 (1953): 78–79.

Alt, Albrecht. "Die Heimat des Deuteronomiums." Pages 250–75 in *Kleine Schriften zur Geschichte des Volkes Israel.* Vol. 2. München: Beck, 1978.

Alter, Robert. *The Art of Biblical Narrative.* New York: Basic Books, 1981.

Althan, R. "Numbers 21,30b in the Light of the Ancient Versions and Ugaritic." *Biblica* 66 (1985): 568–71.

American Elements. "Melting Point of Common Metals, Alloys, & Other Materials." No pages. https://www.americanelements.com/meltingpoint.html.

Amr, Zuhair S., and Ahmad M. Disib. "Venomous Snakes and Snakebites in Jordan." Pages 251–73 in *Clinical Toxinology in Asia Pacific and Africa.* Edited by P. Gopalakrishnakone et al. Toxinology 2. Dordrecht: Springer, 2015. https://link.springer.com/content/pdf/bfm%3A978-94-007-6386-9%2F1.pdf.

Anderson, Bradford A. "Edom in the Book of Numbers: Some Literary Reflections." *Zeitschrift für die alttestamentliche Wissenschaft* 124 (2012): 38–51.

Anderson, Gary A. "The Interpretation of the Purification Offering [*ḥṭʾt*] in the Temple Scroll (11QTemple) and Rabbinic Literature." *Journal of Biblical Literature* 111 (1992): 17–35.

———. "'Through Those Who Are Near Me, I Will Show Myself Holy': Nadab and Abihu and Apophatic Theology." *Catholic Biblical Quarterly* 77 (2015): 1–19.

Anselm. *Proslogium.* Translated by S. N. Deane. Chicago: Open Court, 1926. Online copy, Grand Rapids: Christian Classics Ethereal Library, 2002. https://ccel.org/ccel/a/anselm/basic_works/cache/basic_works.pdf.

Aristotle. *The History of Animals.* In *The Complete Works of Aristotle: The Revised Oxford Translation.* Edited by J. Barnes. Bollingen Series 71/2. Princeton: Princeton University Press, 1984.

———. *Nicomachean Ethics.* Translated by H. Rackham. Loeb Classical Library 73. Cambridge, MA: Harvard University Press, 1926. http://www.perseus.tufts.edu/hopper/text?doc=Perseus%3Atext%3A1999.01.0054.

———. *Poetics: A New Translation by Anthony Kenny.* Oxford World's Classics. Oxford: University of Oxford, 2013.

Arnold, Bill T. *Genesis.* New Cambridge Bible Commentary. Cambridge: Cambridge University Press, 2008.

———. "Genesis 1 as Holiness Preamble." Pages 332–44 in *Let Us Go Up to Zion: Essays in Honour of H. G. M. Williamson on the Occasion of His Sixty-Fifth Birthday.* Supplements to Vetus Testamenum 153. Edited by I. Provan and M. J. Boda. Boston: Brill, 2012.

———. "The Holiness Redaction of the Primeval History." *Zeitschrift für die alttestamentliche Wissenschaft* 129 (2017): 483–500.

———. "Number Switching in Deuteronomy 12–26 and the Quest for *Urdeuteronomium.*" *Zeitschrift für altorientalische und biblische Rechtsgeschichte* 23 (2017): 163–80.

———. "A Singular Israel in a Pluralistic World." Pages 1–17 in *Distinctions with a Difference: Essays on Myth, History, and Scripture in Honor of John N. Oswalt.* Edited by B. T. Arnold and L. G. Stone. Wilmore, KY: First Fruits, 2017.

Arnold, Bill T., and Brent A. Strawn, eds. *The World around the Old Testament: The People and Places of the Ancient Near East.* Grand Rapids: Baker Academic, 2016.

Artus, Olivier. *Études sur le livre des Nombres: Récit, Histoire et Loie en Nb 13,1–20,13.* Orbis Biblicus et Orientalis 157. Fribourg: Editions Universitaires; Göttingen: Vandenhoek & Ruprecht, 1997.

———. "Numbers 32: The Problem of the Two and a Half Transjordanian Tribes and the Final Composition of the Book of Numbers." In Frevel, Pola, and Schart, *Book of Numbers,* 367–82.

Ashley, Timothy R. *The Book of Numbers.* 2nd ed. New International Commentary on the Old Testament. Grand Rapids: Eerdmans, 2022.

Aster, Shawn Zelig. "'Bread of the Dungheap': Light on Num 21:5 from the Tell Fekherye Inscription." *Vetus Testamentum* 61 (2011): 341–58.

Astour, Michael C. "The Origin of the Terms 'Canaan,' 'Phoenician,' and 'Purple.'" *Journal of Near Eastern Studies* 24 (1965): 346–50.

Auld, A. Graeme. *Joshua: Jesus Son of Nauē in Codex Vaticanus.* Septuagint Commentary Series. Leiden: Brill, 2005.

Ausloos, Hans. *The Deuteronomist's History: The Role of the Deuteronomist in Historical-Critical Research into Genesis–Numbers.* Oudtestamentische studien 67. Boston, Brill, 2015.

Austin, J. L. *How to Do Things with Words.* 2nd ed. Cambridge, MA: Harvard University Press, 1975.

Awabdy, Mark A. "Did Nadab and Abihu Draw Near before Yhwh? The Old Greek among the Witnesses of Leviticus 16:1." *Catholic Biblical Quarterly* 4 (2017): 580–93.

———. "The Holiness Composition of the Priestly Blessing." *Biblica* 99 (2018): 29–49.

———. "The Holiness Contribution to the Hexateuch in Numbers 20–36* and Deuteronomy 32*." *Zeitschrift für altorientalische und biblische Rechtsgeschichte* 25 (2019): 247–58.

———. *Immigrants and Innovative Law: Deuteronomy's Theological and Social Vision for the [gr].* Forschungen zum Alten Testament 67. 2 Reihe. Tübingen: Mohr Siebeck, 2014.

———. *Leviticus: A Commentary on Leueitikon in Codex Vaticanus.* Septuagint Commentary Series. Leiden: Brill, 2019.

———. "Yнwн Exegetes Torah: How Ezekiel 44:7–9 Bars Foreigners from the Sanctuary." *Journal of Biblical Literature* 131 (2012): 685–703.

Awabdy, Mark A., and Fredrick J. Long. "Mark's Inclusion of 'For All Nations' in 11:17d and the International Vision of Isaiah." *Journal of Inductive Biblical Studies* 1 (2014): 224–55.

Ayali-Darshan, Noga. "The Seventy Bulls Sacrificed at Sukkot (Num 29:12-34) in Light of a Ritual Text from Emar (Emar 6, 373)." *Vetus Testamentum* 65 (2015): 9–19.

Baden, Joel S. "The Documentary Hypothesis." Pages 13–33 in *The Composition of the Pentateuch: Renewing the Documentary Hypothesis.* New Haven: Yale University Press, 2012.

———. *J, E and the Redaction of the Pentateuch.* Forschungen zum Alten Testament 68. Tübingen: Mohr Siebeck, 2009.

———. "The Narratives of Numbers 20–21." *Catholic Biblical Quarterly* 76 (2014): 634–52.

———. "Source Stratification, Secondary Additions, and the Documentary Hypothesis in the Book of Numbers: The Case of Numbers 17." Pages 233–47 in *Torah and the Book of Numbers.* Edited by C. Frevel, T. Pola, and A. Schart. Forschungen zum Alten Testament II. Tübingen: Mohr Siebeck, 2013.

———. "The Structure and Substance of Numbers 15." *Vetus Testamentum* 63 (2013): 351–67.

———. "The Violent Origins of the Levites: Text and Tradition." In Leuchter and Hutton, *Levites and Priests,* 103–16.

Baker, David W. "Law and Legal Systems in Ancient Israel." In Greer, Hilber, and Walton, *Behind the Scenes,* 492–98.

Bar-Ilan, Meir. "'They shall put my name upon the people of Israel' (Num. 6:27)." [In Hebrew.] *Hebrew Union College Annual* 60 (1989): 19–31.

Barnett, Richard David, and Amelto Lorenzini. *Assyrian Sculptures in the British Museum*. Toronto: McClelland & Stewart, 1975.

Barnouin, M. "Les recensements du livre des Nombres et l'astronomie babylonienne." *Vetus Testamentum* 27 (1977): 280–303.

Baumgarten, Albert I. "The Paradox of the Red Heifer." *Vetus Testamentum* 4 (1993): 442–51.

Beale, G. K. *The Temple and the Church's Mission: A Biblical Theology of the Dwelling Place of God*. New Studies in Biblical Theology. Downers Grove, IL: IVP Academic, 2004.

———. *We Become What We Worship: A Biblical Theology of Idolatry*. Downers Grove, IL: IVP Academic, 2008.

Beale, G. K., and D. A. Carson. *Commentary on the New Testament Use of the Old Testament*. Grand Rapids: Baker Academic, 2007.

Beirne, D. "A Note on Numbers 11,4." *Biblica* 44 (1963): 201–3.

Bell, Catherine. *Ritual Theory, Ritual Practice*. Oxford: Oxford University Press, 1992.

Ben Asher, Bahya. *Commentary*. https://www.sefaria.org/Numbers.21.9?lang=en& with=Rabbeinu%20Bahya&lang2=en.

Ben Bezalel, Judah Loew. *Gur Aryeh on Bamidbar*. https://www.sefaria.org/Numbers .20.12?lang=bi&with=Gur%20Aryeh%20on%20Bamidbar|Quoting&lang2=en.

Bennett, Brian H., David L. Parker, and Mark Robson. "Leprosy: Steps along the Journey of Eradication." *Public Health Reports* 123, no. 2 (March–April 2008): 198–205. https://journals.sagepub.com/doi/pdf/10.1177/003335490812300212.

Bergland, Kenneth. *Reading as a Disclosure of the Thoughts of the Heart: Proto-Halakhic Reuse and Appropriation between Torah and the Prophets*. Beihefte zur Zeitschrift für altorientalische und biblische Rechtsgeschichte 23. Wiesbaden: Harrassowitz, 2019.

Berlejung, Angelika. "Der gesegnete Mensch: Text und Kontext von Num 6,22–27 und den Silberamuletten von Ketef Hinnom." Pages 37–62 in *Mensch und König: Studien zur Anthropologie des Alten Testaments*. Herders biblische Studien 53. Edited by A. Berlejung and R. Heckl. Freiburg im Breisgau: Herder, 2008.

Berlin, Adele. "Characterization in Biblical Narrative: David's Wives." *Journal for the Study of the Old Testament* 23 (1982): 69–85.

———. *Poetics and Interpretation of Biblical Narrative*. Sheffield: Almond, 1983. Repr., Winona Lake, IN: Eisenbrauns, 1994.

Bernstein, Moshe J. "What Has Happened to the Laws? The Treatment of Legal Material in 4QReworked Pentateuch," *Dead Sea Discoveries* 15 (2008) 24–49.

Betz, Hans Dieter. "Das Problem der Grundlagen der paulinischen Ethik (Röm 12,1–2)." *Zeitschrift für Theologie und Kirche* (1988): 199–218.

Beyerle, Stefan. "Die 'Eherne Schlange': Num 21,4–9: Synchron und diachron gelesen." *Zeitschrift für die alttestamentliche Wissenschaft* 111 (1999): 23–44.

Bibb, Bryan D. *Ritual Words and Narrative Worlds in Leviticus*. Library of Hebrew Bible/Old Testament Studies 480. London: T&T Clark, 2009.

Biblia sacra: Iuxta Vulgatam versionem. 5th rev. ed. Edited by R. Gryson. Stuttgart: Deutsche Bibelgesellschaft, 2007.

Bickert, Rainer. "Israel im Lande Moab: Die Stellung der Bileamerzählung Num 22–24 in ihrem redaktionellen Kontext." *Zeitschrift für die alttestamentliche Wissenschaft* 121 (2009): 189–210.

Birdsall, J. Neville. "The Codex Vaticanus: Its History and Significance." Pages 33–41 in *The Bible as a Book: The Transmission of the Greek Text*. Edited by S. McKendrick and O. A. O'Sullivan. London: British Library/New Castle, DE: Oak Knoll, 2003.

Bishop, Paul Bernard. "Historiography in Lives: Plutarch's Use of Thucydides in the Lives of Pericles and Nicias." MA thesis, Durham University, 2016.

Blenkinsopp, Joseph. "The Baal Peor Episode Revisited (Num 25,1–18)." *Biblica* 93 (2012): 86–97.

Block, Daniel I. "Eden: A Temple? A Reassessment of the Biblical Evidence." Pages 3–30 in *From Creation to New Creation: Biblical Theology and Exegesis; Essays in Honor of G. K. Beale*. Edited by D. M. Gurtner and B. L. Gladd. Peabody, MA: Hendrickson, 2013.

———. "Marriage and Family in Ancient Israel." Pages 33–102 in *Marriage and Family in the Biblical World*. Edited by K. M. Campbell. Downers Grove, IL: InterVarsity, 2003.

———. "'The Meeting Places of God in the Land': Another Look at the Towns of the Levites." In Gane and Taggar-Cohen, *Current Issues*, 93–121.

Blum, Erhard. *Studien zur Komposition des Pentateuch*. Beihefte zur Zeitschrift für die alttestamentliche Wissenschaft 189. Berlin: de Gruyter, 1990.

Boorer, Suzanne. "The Place of Numbers 13–14* and Numbers 20:2–12 in the Priestly Narrative (P^g)." *Journal of Biblical Literature* 131 (2012): 45–63.

———. *The Vision of the Priestly Narrative: Its Genre and Hermeneutics of Time*. Ancient Israel and Its Literature 27. Atlanta: SBL Press, 2016.

Brauch, Manfred T. *Abusing Scripture: The Consequences of Misreading the Bible*. Downers Grove, IL: IVP Academic, 2009.

Breasted, James H., ed. and trans. *Ancient Records of Egypt: History Documents from the Earliest Times to the Persian Conquest*. 5 vols. Chicago: University of Chicago Press, 1906.

Brendsel, Daniel J. *"Isaiah Saw His Glory": The Use of Isaiah 52–53 in John 12*. Berlin: de Gruyter, 2014.

Brenner, Athalya. "Introduction." In Brenner and A. Lee, *Leviticus and Numbers*, 1–6.

Brenner, Athalya, and Archie Chi Chung Lee, eds. *Leviticus and Numbers*. Texts @ Contexts Series. Minneapolis: Fortress, 2013.

Brichto, Herbert C. "The Case of the ŚŌṬĀ and a Reconsideration of Biblical 'Law.'" *Hebrew Union College Annual* 46 (1975): 55–70.

Bridge, Edward. "Polite Israel and Impolite Edom: Israel's Request to Travel through Edom in Numbers 20.14–21." *Journal for the Study of the Old Testament* 35 (2010): 77–88.

Brin, Gershon. "Numbers XV 22–23 and the Question of the Composition of the Pentateuch." *Vetus Testamentum* 30 (1980): 351–54.

Brown, Ken. "Vengeance and Vindication in Numbers 31." *Journal of Biblical Literature* 134 (2015): 65–84.

Brueggemann, Walter. *The Land: Place as Gift, Promise, and Challenge in Biblical Faith*. 2nd ed. Overtures to Biblical Theology. Minneapolis: Fortress, 2002.

Büchner, Dirk L. "[*exilasasthai*]: Appeasing God in the Septuagint Pentateuch." *Journal of Biblical Literature* 129 (2010): 237–60.

Budd, Philip J. *Numbers*. Word Biblical Commentary 5. Waco: Word, 1984.

Buis, Pierre. "Le Livre des Nombres." *Cahiers évangile* 78 (1991): 5–58.

———. "Qadesh, un lieu maudit?" *Vetus Testamentum* 24 (1974): 268–85.

Burnett, Joel S. "Transjordan: The Ammonites, Moabites, and Edomites." In Arnold and Strawn, *The World around the Old Testament*, 309–52.

Burnside, Jonathan P. "Exodus and Asylum: Uncovering the Relationship between Biblical Law and Narrative." *Journal for the Study of the Old Testament* 34 (2010): 243–66.

———. "'What Shall We Do with the Sabbath-Gatherer?' A Narrative Approach to a 'Hard Case' in Biblical Law (Numbers 15:32–36)." *Vetus Testamentum* 60 (2010): 45–62.

———. "Why Was Moses Banned from the Promised Land? A Radical Retelling of the Rebellions of Moses (Num 20:2–13 and Exod 2:11–15)." *Zeitschrift für altorientalische und biblische Rechtsgeschichte* 22 (2017): 111–60.

Butler, Samuel, trans. *The "Iliad" of Homer and the "Odyssey."* 1898. Great Books of the Western World 4. Chicago: Encyclopedia Britannica, 1952. Cf. Perseus online.

Calvin, John. *Harmony of the Law*. Translated by C. W. Bingham. Vol. 4. Grand Rapids: Christian Classics Ethereal Library, 1998. https://ccel.org/ccel/c/calvin/calcom06/cache/calcom06.pdf.

Caplice, Richard I. "Participants in the Namburbi Rituals." *Catholic Biblical Quarterly* 29 (1967): 346–52.

Cardellini, Innocenzo. *Numeri 1,1–10,10: Nuova versione, introduzione e commento.* I Libri Biblici Primo Testamento 4.1. Milano: Figlie di San Paolo, 2013.

Carr, David M. *Writing on the Tablet of the Heart: Origins of Scripture and Literature*. Oxford: Oxford University Press, 2005.

Cartledge, Tony W. *Vows in the Hebrew Bible and the Ancient Near East*. Journal for the Study of the Old Testament Supplement Series 147. Sheffield: JSOT, 1992.

———. "Were Nazirite Vows Unconditional?" *Catholic Biblical Quarterly* 51 (1989): 409–22.

Cazelles, Henri. *Les Nombres*. Sainte Bible 4. Paris: Cerf, 1952.

Chavel, Simeon. "Numbers 15:32–36: A Microcosom of the Living Priesthood and Its Literary Production." Pages 45–55 in *The Strata of the Priestly Writings: Contemporary Debate and Future Directions*. Edited by S. Shectman and J. S. Baden. Abhandlungen zur Theologie des Alten und Neuen Testaments 95. Zürich: Theologischer Verlag Zürich, 2009.

———. *Oracular Law and Priestly Historiography in the Torah*. Forschungen zum Alten Testament 2/71. Tübingen: Mohr Siebeck, 2014.

Childs, Brevard S. *The Book of Exodus: A Critical, Theological Commentary*. Old Testament Library. Louisville: Westminster John Knox, 2004.

———. *Introduction to the Old Testament as Scripture*. Philadelphia: Fortress, 1979.

Christensen, Duane L. "Num 21:14–15 and the Book of the Wars of Yahweh." *Catholic Biblical Quarterly* 36 (1974): 359–60.

Christian, Mark A. "Middle-Tier Levites and the Plenary Reception of Revelation." In Leuchter and Hutton, *Levites and Priests*, 173–97.

Choi, John H. *Traditions at Odds: The Reception of the Pentateuch in Biblical and Second Temple Period Literature*. Library of Hebrew Bible/Old Testament Studies 518. New York, London: T&T Clark, 2010.

Clines, David J. A. "Alleged Basic Meanings of the Hebrew Verb *Qdš* 'Be Holy': An Exercise in Comparative Hebrew Lexicography." *Vetus Testamentum* 71 (2021): 481–502. https://www.academia.edu/28065748/Alleged_Basic_Meanings_of_the_Hebrew_Verb_qd%C5%A1_be_holy_An_Exercise_in_Comparative_Hebrew_Lexicography.

Coats, George W. *Genesis: With an Introduction to Narrative*. Grand Rapids: Eerdmans, 1983.

———. "The Wilderness Itinerary." *Catholic Biblical Quarterly* 34 (1972): 135–52.

Cocco, Francesco. *Women in the Wilderness: The "Female Legislation" in the Book of Numbers (Num 5,11–31; 27:1–11; 30:2–17)*. Forschungen zum Alten Testament 138. Tübingen: Mohr Siebeck, 2020.

Cohen, Chaim. "The Biblical Priestly Blessing (Num 6:24–26) in the Light of Akkadian Parallels." *Tel Aviv* 20 (1993): 228–38.

Comprehensive Aramaic Lexicon [CAL]. Online: http://cal.huc.edu/index.html.

Cook, John A. "The Semantics of Verbal Pragmatics: Clarifying the Roles of *Wayyiqtol* and *Weqatal* in Biblical Hebrew Prose." *Journal of Semitic Studies* 49 (2004): 247–73.

———. *Time and the Biblical Hebrew Verb: The Expression of Tense, Aspect, and Modality in Biblical Hebrew*. Linguistic Studies in Ancient West Semitic 7. Winona Lake, IN: Eisenbrauns, 2012.

Cook, Stephen L. "Innerbiblical Interpretation in Ezekiel 44 and the History of Israel's Priesthood." *Journal of Biblical Literature* 114 (1995): 193–208.

Cooke, Gerald. "The Sons of (the) God(s)." *Zeitschrift für die alttestamentliche Wissenschaft* 76 (1964): 22–47.

Cooper, Alan M., and Bernard R. Goldstein. "At the Entrance to the Tent: More Cultic Resonances in Biblical Narrative." *Journal of Biblical Literature* 116 (1997): 201–15.

Cross, Frank Moore. *Canaanite Myth and Hebrew Epic: Essays in the History of the Religion of Israel*. Cambridge, MA: Harvard University Press, 1973.

———. *From Epic to Canon: History and Literature in Ancient Israel*. Baltimore: Johns Hopkins University Press, 1998.

Curzer, Howard J. "Spies and Lies: Faithful, Courageous Israelites and Truthful Spies." *Journal for the Study of the Old Testament* 35 (2010): 187–95.

Davies, Eryl W. "A Mathematical Conundrum: The Problem of the Large Numbers in Numbers I and XXVI." *Vetus Testamentum* 45 (1995): 449–69.

Davies, G. I. "The Wilderness Itineraries." *Tyndale Bulletin* 25 (1974): 46–81.

———. "The Wilderness Itineraries and the Composition of the Pentateuch." *Vetus Testamentum* 33 (1983): 1–13.

Dawkins, Richard. *The God Delusion*. Boston: Mariner Books, 2008.

de Boer, P. A. H. "Numbers VI 27." *Vetus Testamentum* 32 (1982): 3–13.

DeGuglielmo, Antonine. "What Was the Manna?" *Catholic Biblical Quarterly* 2 (1940): 112–29.

de Hoop, Raymond. "The Interpretation of Isa 56:1–9: Comfort or Criticism." *Journal of Biblical Literature* 127 (2008): 671–95.

Deir ʿAlla Inscription. https://www.livius.org/sources/content/deir-alla-inscription.

del Olmo Lete, Gregorio. "Sacrifice, Offerings and Votives: Syria-Canaan." In Johnston, *Religions of the Ancient World*, 332–33.

Démare-Lafont, Sophie. "Inheritance Law of and through Women in the Middle Assyrian Period." Paper presented at the Women and Property conference of the Center for Hellenic Studies at Harvard University. Cambridge, MA, August 2003. https://chs.harvard.edu/wp-content/uploads/2020/07/women_property_lafont.pdf.

de Regt, Lénart J. "Partial Repetition in Sections of Numbers 4 and the Translator." In Römer, *Leviticus and Numbers*, 417–22.

de Tarragon, Jean-Michel. *Le Culte à Ugarit: D'après les Textes de la Pratique en Cunéiformes alphabétiques*. Cahiers de la Revue biblique 19. Paris: Gabalda, 1980.

de Troyer, Kristin. "When Did the Pentateuch Come into Existence? An Uncomfortable Perspective." Pages 269–86 in *Die Septuaginta—Texte, Kontexte, Lebenswelten*. Edited by M. Karrer and W. Kraus. Wissenschaftliche Untersuchungen zum Neuen Testament 219. Tübingen: Mohr Siebeck, 2008.

de Vaulx, J. *Les Nombres*. Sources bibliques. Paris: Gabalda, 1972.

de Vaux, Roland. "Le pays de Canaan." *Journal of the American Oriental Society* 88 (1968): 23–29.

Dever, William G. *Who Were the Early Israelites, and Where Did They Come From?* Grand Rapids: Eerdmans, 2003.

Dietrich, Manfried, Oswald Loretz, and Joaquín Sanmartín. *The Cuneiform Alphabetic Texts: From Ugarit, Ras Ibn Hani and Other Places (KTU)*. 2nd ed. Abhandlungen zur Literatur Alt-Syrien-Palästinas und Mesopotamiens 8. Münster: Ugarit-Verlag, 1995.

Dijkstra, Meindert. "Is Balaam Also among the Prophets?" *Journal of Biblical Literature* 114 (1995): 43–64.

Dor, Yonina. "From the Well in Midian to the Baʿal of Peor: Attitudes to the Marriage of Israelite Men and Midianite Women." In Brenner and A. Lee, *Leviticus and Numbers*, 141–61.

Dorival, Gilles. *Les Nombres*. Paris: Cerf, 1994.

Douglas, Mary. *In the Wilderness: The Doctrine of Defilement in the Book of Numbers*. Rev. ed. Oxford: Oxford University Press, 2004.

———. *Leviticus as Literature*. Oxford: Oxford University Press, 1999.

Dozeman, Thomas B. "The Book of Numbers." Pages 3–268 in *The New Interpreter's Bible*. Vol. 2. Edited by L. E. Keck. Nashville: Abingdon, 1998.

———. *Exodus*. Eerdmans Critical Commentary. Grand Rapids: Eerdmans, 2009.

———. "Geography and Ideology in the Wilderness Journey from Kadesh through the Transjordan." Pages 173–89 in *Abschied vom Jahwisten: Die Komposition des Hexateuch in der jüngsten Diskussion*. Beihefte zur Zeitschrift für die alttestamentliche Wissenschaft 315. Edited by J. C. Gertz, K. Schmid, and M. Witte. Berlin: de Gruyter, 2002.

———. "Inner-Biblical Interpretation of Yahweh's Gracious and Compassionate Character." *Journal of Biblical Literature* 108 (1989): 207–23.

Drey, Philip R. "Bamoth, Bamoth-Baal." In Freedman, *Eerdmans Dictionary*, 145–46.

Driver, S. R. *The Book of Exodus: In the Revised Version with Introduction and Notes*. Cambridge: Cambridge University Press, 1911.

Dunn, James D. G. *The New Perspective on Paul*. Rev. ed. Grand Rapids: Eerdmans, 2008.

Edelman, Diana. "The Manassite Genealogy in 1 Chronicles 7:14–19: Form and Source." *Catholic Biblical Quarterly* 53 (1991): 179–201.

Eissfeldt, Otto. *Hexateuch-Synopse: Die Erzählung der fünf Bücher Mose und des Buches Josua mit dem Anfange des Richterbuches*. Darmstadt: Wissenschaftliche Buchgesellschaft, 1962.

Elgavish, David. "The Division of the Spoils of War in the Bible and in the Ancient Near East." *Zeitschrift für altorientalische und biblische Rechtsgeschichte* 8 (2002): 247–73.

Eliade, Mircea. *Patterns in Comparative Religion*. New York: Meridan, 1958.

Elliger, Karl. "Sinn und Ursprung der priesterlichen Geschichtserzählung." *Zeitschrift für Theologie und Kirche* 49 (1952): 121–43.

Elliot, Robert C. *The Power of Satire*. Princeton: Princeton University Press, 1972.

Embry, Brad. "Legalities in the Book of Ruth: A Renewed Look." *Journal for the Study of the Old Testament* 41 (2016): 31–44.

Eng, Milton. *The Days of Our Years: A Lexical Semantic Study of the Life Cycle in Biblical Israel*. Library of Hebrew Bible/Old Testament Studies 464. London: T&T Clark, 2011.

Enns, Peter. *Inspiration and Incarnation: Evangelicals and the Problem of the Old Testament*. 2nd ed. Grand Rapids: Baker Academic, 2015.

Evans, Trevor V. "Numbers." Pages 58–67 in *The T&T Clark Companion to the Septuagint*. Edited by J. K. Aitken. London: Bloomsbury, 2015.

———. "Some Alleged Confusions in Translation from Hebrew to Greek." *Biblica* 83 (2002): 238–48.

Feinstein, Eve Levavi. "The 'Bitter Waters' of Numbers 5:11–31." *Vetus Testamentum* 62 (2012): 300–306.

Feldman, Louis H. "Philo's Version of the Biblical Episode of the Spies." *Hebrew Union College Annual* 73 (2002): 29–48.

Fensham, F. Charles. "Salt as Curse in the Old Testament and the Ancient Near East." *Biblical Archaeologist* 25 (1962): 48–50.

Feucht, Christian. *Untersuchungen zum Heiligkeitsgesetz.* Theologische Arbeiten 20. Berlin: Evangelische Verlagsanstalt, 1964.

Findlay, James. "The Priestly Ideology of the Septuagint Translator Numbers 16–17." *Journal for the Study of the Old Testament* 30 (2006): 421–29.

Finkelstein, Israel, Nadav Na'aman, and Thomas Römer. "Restoring Line 31 in the Mesha Stele: The 'House of David' or Biblical Balak?" *Tel Aviv* 46 (2019): 3–11.

Fishbane, Michael A. "Accusations of Adultery: A Study of Law and Scribal Practice in Numbers 5:11–31." *Hebrew Union College Annual* 45 (1974): 25–45.

———. *Biblical Interpretation in Ancient Israel.* Oxford: Oxford University Press, 1985.

Fleming, Daniel E. "The Amorites." In Arnold and Strawn, *World around the Old Testament,* 1–30.

———. *The Legacy of Israel in Judah's Bible.* Cambridge: Cambridge University Press, 2012.

Flesher, Paul V. M., and Bruce D. Chilton. *The Targums: A Critical Introduction.* Studies in the Aramaic Interpretation of Scripture 12. Leiden: Brill, 2011.

Fleurant, Josebert. "Phinehas Murdered Moses' Wife: An Analysis of Numbers 25." *Journal for the Study of the Old Testament* 35 (2011): 285–94.

Frankel, David. "Two Priestly Conceptions of Guidance in the Wilderness." *Journal for the Study of the Old Testament* 81 (1998): 31–37.

Franken, Hendricus J. "Deir 'Alla, Tell." Pages 137–38 in *The Oxford Encyclopedia of Archaeology in the Near East.* Vol. 2. Edited by E. M. Meyers. Oxford: Oxford University Press, 1997.

———. *Excavations at Tell Deir 'Alla: The Late Bronze Age Sanctuary.* Louvain: Peeters, 1992.

Freedman, David Noel, ed. *Eerdmans Dictionary of the Bible.* Grand Rapids: Eerdmans, 2000.

Fretheim, Terence E. *Exodus.* Interpretation: A Bible Commentary for Teaching and Preaching. Louisville: Westminster John Knox, 1991.

Frevel, Christian. "Alte Stücke—späte Brücke? Zur Rolle des Buches Numeri in der jüngeren Pentateuchdiskussion." Pages 255–99 in *Congress Volume Munich 2013.* Supplements to Vetus Testamentum 163. Edited by C. M. Maier. Leiden: Brill, 2014.

———. "The Book of Numbers—Formation, Composition, and Interpretation of a Late Part of the Torah. Some Introductory Remarks." In Frevel, Pola, and Schart, *Book of Numbers,* 1–37.

———. *Desert Transformations: Studies in the Book of Numbers.* Forschungen zum Alten Testament 137. Tübingen: Mohr Siebeck, 2020.

———. "Ending with the High Priest: The Hierarchy of Priests and Levites in the Book of Numbers." In Frevel, Pola, and Schart, *Book of Numbers,* 138–63.

———. *"Mit Blick auf das Land die Schöpfung erinnern": Zum Ende der Priestergrundschrift.* Herders biblische Studien 23. Freiburg im Breisgau: Herder, 2000.

581

———. "Numeri." Pages 212–301 in *Stuttgarter Altes Testament: Einheitsübersetzung mit Kommentar und Lexikon*. 3rd ed. Edited by E. Zenger. Stuttgart: Katholisches Bibelwerk, 2005.

———. "Practicing Rituals in a Textual World: Ritual and Innovation in the Book of Numbers." Pages 129–50 in *Ritual Innovation in the Hebrew Bible and Early Judaism*. Beihefte zur Zeitschrift für die alttestamentliche Wissenschaft 468. Edited by N. MacDonald. Berlin: de Gruyter, 2016.

———. "Purity Conceptions in the Book of Numbers in Context." Pages 369–411 in *Purity and the Forming of Religious Traditions in the Ancient Mediterranean World and Ancient Judaism*. Edited by C. Frevel and C. Nihan. Boston: Brill, 2013.

———. "Understanding the Pentateuch by Structuring the Desert: Numbers 21 as a Compositional Joint." Pages 111–35 in *The Land of Israel in Bible, History, and Theology: Studies in Honour of Ed Noort*. Supplements to Vetus Testamentum 124. Boston: Brill, 2009.

———. "Von der Unvollkommenheit des Vollkommenen: Anmerkungen zur Anthropologie der Rituale im Buch Numeri." Pages 215–44 in *Die Erfindung des Menschen: Person und Persönlichkeit in ihren lebensweltlichen Kontexten*. Theologie–Kultur–Hermeneutik 21. Edited by S. Beyerle. Leipzig: Evangelische, 2016.

Frevel, Christian, Thomas Pola, and Aaron Schart, eds. *Torah and the Book of Numbers*. Forschungen zum Alten Testament 2/62. Tübingen: Mohr Siebeck, 2013.

Frymer-Kensky, Tikva. "The Strange Case of the Suspected Sotah (Numbers V 11–31)." *Vetus Testamentum* 34 (1984): 11–26.

Gabriel, Richard A. *The Great Armies of Antiquity*. Westport, CT: Praeger, 2002.

Gafney, Wil. "A Queer Womanist Midrashic Reading of Numbers 25:1–18." In Brenner and A. Lee, *Leviticus and Numbers*, 189–98.

Galbraith, Deane. "Interpellation, not Interpolation: Reconsidering Textual Disunity in Numbers 13–14 as Variant Articulations of a Single Ideology." *The Bible & Critical Theory* 10 (2014): 29–48.

Galil, Gershon. "The Sons of Judah and the Sons of Aaron in Biblical Historiography." *Vetus Testamentum* 35 (1985): 488–95.

Gallagher, Edmond L. "Is the Samaritan Pentateuch a Sectarian Text?" *Zeitschrift für die alttestamentliche Wissenschaft* 127 (2015): 96–107.

Gane, Roy E. "'Bread of the Presence' and Creator-in-Residence." *Vetus Testamentum* 42 (1992): 179–203.

———. *Cult and Character: Purification Offerings, Day of Atonement, and Theodicy*. Winona Lake, IN: Eisenbrauns, 2005.

———. "Didactic Logic and the Authorship of Leviticus." In Gane and Taggar-Cohen, *Current Issues*, 197–221.

Gane, Roy E., and Ada Taggar-Cohen, eds. *Current Issues in Priestly and Related Literature: The Legacy of Jacob Milgrom and Beyond*. Atlanta: SBL Press, 2015.

García Martínez, Florentino, ed. and trans. *The Dead Sea Scrolls Translated: The Qumran Texts in English*. 2nd ed. Translated by W. G. E. Watson. New York: Brill; Grand Rapids: Eerdmans, 1996.

————. "Messianic Hopes in the Qumran Writings." Pages 115–75 in *LDS Perspectives on the Dead Sea Scrolls*. Edited by D. M. Pike and D. W. Parry. Provo, UT: Foundation for Ancient Research and Mormon Studies, 1997.

Garmendia, Joana. *Irony*. Key Topics in Semantics and Pragmatics. Cambridge: Cambridge University Press, 2018.

Garroway, Kristine Henriksen. *Growing Up in Ancient Israel: Children in Material Culture and Biblical Texts*. Society of Biblical Literature and Biblical Studies 23. Atlanta: SBL Press, 2018.

Garton, Roy E. *Mirages in the Desert*. Beihefte zur Zeitschrift für die alttestamentliche Wissenschaft 492. Berlin: de Gruyter, 2017.

Geiger, Michaela. "Synergie zwischen priesterlichem und göttlichem Handeln im Aaronitischen Segen (Num 6,22–27)." *Vetus Testamentum* 68 (2018): 51–72.

Gerhards, Meik. "Über die Herkunft der Frau des Mose." *Vetus Testamentum* 55 (2005): 162–75.

Gertz, Jan Christian. "Kompositorische Funktion und literarhistorischer Ort von Deuteronomium 1–3." Pages 103–23 in *Die deuteronomistischen Geschichtswerke: Redaktions- und religionsgeschichtliche perspectiven zur "Deuteronomismus"—Diskussion in Tora und Vorderen Propheten*. Edited by M. Witte, K. Schmidt, D. Prechel, and J. C. Gertz. Beihefte zur Zeitschrift für die alttestamentliche Wissenschaft 365. Berlin: de Gruyter, 2006.

————. "The Miracle at the Sea: Remarks on the Recent Discussion about Origin and Composition of the Exodus Narrative." Pages 91–120 in *The Book of Exodus: Composition, Reception, and Interpretation*. Supplements to Vetus Testamentum 164. Edited by T. B. Dozeman, C. A. Evans, and J. N. Lohr. Boston: Brill, 2014.

————. *Tradition und Redaktion in der Exoduserzählung: Untersuchungen zur Endredaktion des Pentateuch*. Forschungen zur Religion und Literatur des Alten und Neuen Testaments 186. Göttingen: Vandenhoek & Ruprecht, 2000.

Glatt-Gilad, David A. "The Re-interpretation of the Edomite-Israelite Encounter in Deuteronomy II." *Vetus Testamentum* 47 (1997): 441–55.

Glueck, Nelson. *Rivers in the Desert: A History of the Negev; Being an Illustrated Account of Discoveries in a Frontierland of Civilization*. New York: Farrar, Straus & Cudahy, 1959.

Goldingay, John. *Models for Interpretation of Scripture*. Grand Rapids: Eerdmans, 1995.

Goldstein, Elizabeth W. "Women and the Purification Offering: What Jacob Milgrom Contributed to the Intersection of Women's Studies and Biblical Studies." In Gane and Taggar-Cohen, *Current Issues*, 47–65.

Goodfriend, Elaine Alder. "Leviticus 22:24: A Prohibition of Gelding for the Land of Israel?" In Gane and Taggar-Cohen, *Current Issues*, 67–92.

Goodman, David. "Note on Seraphim and Fiery Serpents." In Douglas, *In the Wilderness*, 213–15.

Gordon, Cyrus H. "Parallèles nouziens aux lois et coutumes de L'Ancien Testament." *Revue biblique* (1935): 34–41.

Gordon, Robert P. "Compositeness, Conflation and the Pentateuch." *Journal for the Study of the Old Testament* 51 (1991): 57–69.

Görg, M. "Zum 'Skorpionenpass' (Num XXXIV 4; Jos. XV 3)." *Vetus Testamentum* 24 (1974): 508–9.

Gosse, Bernard. "The 42 Generations of the Genealogy of Jesus in Matt. 1:1–17, and the Symbolism of Number 42, Curse or Blessing, in the Bible and in Egypt." *Studia Biblica Slovaca* 10 (2018): 143–51.

Grabbe, Lester L. *Ancient Israel: What Do We Know and How Do We Know It?* Rev. ed. New York: T&T Clark, 2017.

Graf, David F. "Arabia and the Arabians." In Arnold and Strawn, *World around the Old Testament*, 417–65.

Gray, George B. *A Critical and Exegetical Commentary on Numbers*. International Critical Commentary. New York: Charles Scribner's Sons, 1903.

Grayson, Albert K. *Assyrian Rulers of the Early First Millennium BC: I (1114–859 BC)*. Royal Inscriptions of Mesopotamia 2. Toronto: University of Toronto Press, 1991. https://ia804706.us.archive.org/26/items/AssyrianRulersOfTheEarlyFirst MillenniumBc11114-859Bc/A.Kirk_Grayson_Assyrian_Rulers_of__Early_First _MBookFi.org.pdf.

Greengus, Samuel. *Laws in the Bible and in Early Rabbinic Collections: The Legal Legacy of the Ancient Near East*. Eugene, OR: Cascade, 2011.

Greer, Jonathan S. "The 'Priestly Portion' in the Hebrew Bible: Its Ancient Near Eastern Context and Its Implications for the Composition of P." *Journal of Biblical Literature* 138 (2019): 263–84.

Greer, Jonathan S., John W. Hilber, and John H. Walton, eds. *Behind the Scenes of the Old Testament: Cultural, Social, and Historical Contexts*. Grand Rapids: Baker Academic, 2018.

Gressmann, Hugo. *Altorientalische Texte und Bilder zum Alten Testamente*. 2 vols. Tübingen: Mohr: 1909.

Griffith, Sidney H. *The Bible in Arabic: The Scriptures of the "People of the Book" in the Language of Islam*. Princeton: Princeton University Press, 2013.

Guillaume, Alfred. "A Note on Numbers xxiii 10." *Vetus Testamentum* 12 (1962): 335–37.

Guillaume, Philippe. *Land and Calendar: The Priestly Document from Genesis 1 to Joshua 18*. Library of Hebrew Bible/Old Testament Studies 391. London: T&T Clark, 2009.

Gunkel, Hermann. *The Psalms: A Form-Critical Introduction*. Facet Books, Biblical Series 15. Philadelphia: Fortress, 1967. Translated from vol. 1 of *Die Religion in Geschichte und Gegenwart: Handwörterbuch in gemeinverständlicher Darstellung*. 2nd ed. Tübingen: Mohr Siebeck, 1930.

———. *The Stories of Genesis*. Vallejo, CA: BIBAL, 1994. Translation of *Die Sagen der Genesis*. Göttingen: Vandenhoeck & Ruprecht, 1901.

Gunneweg, A. H. J. "Das Gesetz und die Propheten: Eine Auslegung von Ex 33,7–11; Num 11,4–12,8; Dtn 31,14f.; 34,10." *Zeitschrift für die alttestamentliche Wissenschaft* 102 (1990): 169–80.

Gurtner, Daniel M. "'Atonement Slate' or 'Veil'? Notes on a Textual Variant in Exodus XXVI 34." *Vetus Testamentum* 54 (2004): 396–98.

Guyot, Gilmore H. "Balaam." *Catholic Biblical Quarterly* 3 (1941): 235–42.

Hackett, Jo Ann. *The Balaam Text from Deir ʿAllā*. Harvard Semitic Monographs 31. Chico, CA: Scholars Press, 1984.

Hagelia, Hallvard. *The Dan Debate: The Tel Dan Inscription in Recent Research*. Sheffield: Sheffield Phoenix, 2009.

Hallo, William W. "Compare and Contrast: The Contextual Approach to Biblical Literature." Pages 1–30 in *The Bible in the Light of Cuneiform Literature*. Ancient Near Eastern Texts and Studies 8. Edited by W. W. Hallo, B. W. Jones, and G. L. Mattingly. Vol. 3 of *Scripture in Context*. Lewiston, NY: Edwin Mellen, 1990.

Hanson, Howard E. "Num XVI 30 and the Meaning of *BĀRĀʾ*." *Vetus Testamentum* 22 (1972): 353–59.

Haran, Menahem. "The Shining of Moses' Face: A Case Study in Biblical and Ancient Near Eastern Iconography." Pages 159–73 in *In the Shelter of Elyon: Essays on Ancient Palestinian Life and Literature in Honor of G. W. Ahlström*. Journal for the Study of the Old Testament Supplement Series 31. Edited by W. B. Barrick and J. R. Spencer. Sheffield: JSOT Press, 1984.

Harrington, Hannah K. "Intermarriage in the Temple Scroll: Strategies of Neutralization." In Gane and Taggar-Cohen, *Current Issues*, 463–82.

Heinzerling, Rudiger. "On the Interpretation of the Census Lists by C. J. Humphreys and G. E. Mendenhall." *Vetus Testamentum* 50 (2000): 250–52.

Hepner, Gershon. "The Morrow of the Sabbath Is the First Day of the Festival of Unleavened Bread (Lev 23,15–17)." *Zeitschrift für die alttestamentliche Wissenschaft* 118 (2006): 389–404.

Hess, Richard S. *Israelite Religions: An Archaeological and Biblical Survey*. Grand Rapids: Baker Academic, 2007.

Hilber, John W. *Old Testament Cosmology and Divine Accommodation: A Relevance Theory Approach*. Eugene, OR: Cascade, 2020.

Hobbs, T. R. "Hospitality in the First Testament and the 'Teleological Fallacy.'" *Journal for the Study of the Old Testament* 26 (2001): 3–30.

Hobson, Nicholas M., Juliana Schroeder, Jane L. Risen, Dimitris Xygalatas, and Michael Inzlicht. "The Psychology of Ritual: An Integrative Review and Process-Based Framework." *Personality and Social Psychology Review* 22 (2018): 260–84.

Hoffmeier, James K. *Ancient Israel in Sinai: The Evidence for the Authenticity of the Wilderness Tradition*. Oxford: Oxford University Press, 2005.

———. *Israel in Egypt: The Evidence for the Authenticity of the Exodus Tradition*. Oxford: Oxford University Press, 1999.

Hoftijzer, Jacob. "The Prophet Balaam in a 6th century Aramaic Inscription." *Biblical Archaeologist* 39 (1976): 11–17.

Hoftijzer, Jacob, and K. Jongeling. *Dictionary of the North-West Semitic Inscriptions*. 2 vols. Leiden: Brill, 1995.

Hoftijzer, Jacob, and G. van der Kooij, eds. *Aramaic Texts from Deir ʿAlla*. Leiden: Brill, 1976.

———, eds. *The Balaam Text from Deir ʿAlla Re-evaluated: Proceedings of the International Symposium Held at Leiden, 21–24 August 1989*. Leiden: Brill, 1991.

Holy See Press Office for Pope Francis. "Audience with Seminarians of the Diocese of Agrigento, 24.11.2018." https://press.vatican.va/content/salastampa/en/bollettino/pubblico/2018/11/24/181124h.html.

Holzinger, Heinrich. *Numeri*. Kurzer Hand-Commentar zum Alten Testament 4. Tübingen: Mohr, 1903.

Homan, Michael M. *To Your Tents, O Israel! The Terminology, Function, Form, and Symbolism of Tents in the Hebrew Bible and the Ancient Near East*. Culture and History of the Ancient Near East 12. Leiden: Brill, 2002.

Homer. *See* Butler, trans.

Howerton, Amanda, Ross Burnett, Richard Byng, and John Lennox Campbell. "The Consolations of Going Back to Prison: What 'Revolving Door' Prisoners Think of Their Prospects." *Journal of Offender Rehabilitation* 48 (2009): 439–61.

Huehnergard, John. *A Grammar of Akkadian*. 3rd ed. Eisenbrauns: Winona Lake, IN, 2011.

Humphreys, Colon J. "The Number of People in the Exodus from Egypt: Decoding Mathematically the Very Large Numbers in Numbers I and XXVI." *Vetus Testamentum* 48 (1998): 196–213.

———. "The Numbers in the Exodus from Egypt: A Further Appraisal." *Vetus Testamentum* 50 (2000): 323–28.

Hundley, Michael B. *Gods in Dwellings: Temples and Divine Presence in the Ancient Near East*. Atlanta: Society of Biblical Literature, 2013.

———. "Tabernacle or Tent of Meeting? The Dual Nature of the Sacred Tent in the Priestly Texts." In Gane and Taggar-Cohen, *Current Issues*, 3–18.

———. "What Is the Golden Calf?" *Catholic Biblical Quarterly* 79 (2017): 559–79.

Hutchens, Kenneth D. "Defining the Boundaries: A Cultic Interpretation of Numbers 34.1–12 and Ezekiel 47.13–48.1, 28." Pages 215–30 in *History and Interpretation: Essays in Honour of John H. Hayes*. Edited by M. P. Graham, W. P. Brown, and J. K. Kuan. Journal for the Study of the Old Testament Supplement Series 73. Sheffield: JSOT Press, 1993.

Hutcheon, Linda. *Irony's Edge: The Theory and Politics of Irony*. London: Routledge, 1995.

Hutton, Jeremy M. "The Levitical Diaspora (II): Modern Perspectives on the Levitical Cities Lists (A Review of Opinions)." In Leuchter and Hutton, *Levites and Priests*, 45–81.

Janowski, Bernd. *Gottes Gegenwart in Israel*. Beiträge zur Theologie des Alten Testaments. Neukirchen-Vluyn: Neukirchener Verlag, 1993.

Jeon, Jaeyoung. "The Zadokites in the Wilderness: The Rebellion of Korach (Num 16) and the Zadokite Redaction." *Zeitschrift für die alttestamentliche Wissenschaft* 127 (2015): 381–411.

Jobling, David. "The Jordan a Boundary: Transjordan in Israel's Ideological Geography." Pages 88–134 in *The Sense of Biblical Narrative: Structure and Analysis in the Hebrew Bible II*. Journal for the Study of the Old Testament Supplement Series 39. Sheffield: Sheffield Academic, 1986.

Johnston, Sarah Iles. "Magic." In Johnston, *Religions of the Ancient World*, 139–52.

———, ed. *Religions of the Ancient World: A Guide*. Cambridge, MA: Harvard University Press, 2004.

Joines, Karen Randolph. "The Bronze Serpent in the Israelite Cult." *Journal of Biblical Literature* 87 (1968): 245–56.

Josephus. Translated by H. St. J. Thackeray et al. 10 vols. Loeb Classical Library. Cambridge, MA: Harvard University Press, 1926–65.

Joüon, Paul. "Notes Philologiques sur le Texte Hébreu d'Exode 8,22; 7,13; 40,38; Lévitique 23,29; 26,16; Nombres 31,23; Deutéronome 8,4 (et Néhémie 9,21); 8,15; 28,47, 68; 29,14." *Biblica* 9 (1928): 41–46.

Kákosy, László. "Divination and Prophecy: Egypt." In Johnston, *Religions of the Ancient World*, 371–73.

Kallai, Zecharia. "The Wandering-Traditions from Kadesh-Barnea to Canaan: A Study in Biblical Historiography." *Journal of Jewish Studies* 33 (1982): 175–84.

Kaminsky, Joel S. "Did Election Imply the Mistreatment of Non-Israelites?" *Harvard Theological Review* 96 (2003): 397–425.

Kazen, Thomas. "Purity and Persia." In Gane and Taggar-Cohen, *Current Issues*, 435–62.

Keel, Othmar. *Die Welt der altorientalischen Bildsymbolik und das Alte Testament: Am Beispiel der Psalmen*. 3rd ed. Zürich: Benziger, 1980.

Keener, Craig S. *Acts: An Exegetical Commentary*. Vol. 3, *15:1–23:35*. Grand Rapids: Baker Academic, 2014.

———. *Christobiography: Memory, History, and the Reliability of the Gospels*. Grand Rapids: Eerdmans, 2019.

———. *Romans: A New Covenant Commentary*. New Covenant Commentary Series 6. Eugene, OR: Cascade, 2009.

Keller, Sharon R. "An Egyptian Analogue to the Priestly Blessing." Pages 338–45 in *Boundaries of the Ancient Near Eastern World: A Tribute to Cyrus H. Gordon*. Journal for the Study of the Old Testament Supplement Series 273. Edited by M. Lubetski, C. Gottlieb, and S. Keller. Sheffield: Sheffield Academic, 1998.

Kellermann, Diether. *Die Priesterschrift von Numeri 1,1 bis 10,10 literarkritisch und traditionsgeschichtlich untersucht*. Beihefte zur Zeitschrift für die alttestamentliche Wissenschaft 120. Berlin: de Gruyter, 1970.

Kermode, Frank. *The Sense of an Ending*. New York: Oxford University Press, 1967.

Kierkegaard, Søren. *Fear and Trembling* [excerpt]. Edited and translated by H. V. Hong and E. H. Hong. Princeton: Princeton University Press, 1983. Repr., pages 265–72 in *Nineteenth-Century Philosophy*. Vol. 4 of *Philosophic Classics*. Edited by F. E. Baird and W. Kaufmann. Upper Saddle River, NJ: Prentice Hall, 1997.

Kilchör, Benjamin. "Levirate Marriage in Deuteronomy 25:5–10 and Its Precursors in Leviticus and Numbers: A Test Case for the Relationship between P/H and D." *Catholic Biblical Quarterly* 77 (2015): 429–40.

———. *Mosetora und Jahwetora: Das Verhältnis von Deuteronomium 12–26 zu Exodus, Levitikus und Numeri.* Beihefte zur Zeitschrift für altorientalische und biblische Rechtsgeschichte 21. Wiesbaden: Harrassowitz, 2015.

Kim, Young Hye. "The Finalization of Num 25,1–5." *Zeitschrift für die alttestamentliche Wissenschaft* 122 (2010): 260–64.

King, Philip J., and Lawrence E. Stager. *Life in Biblical Israel.* Louisville: Westminster John Knox, 2001.

Kislev, Itamar. "The Census of the Israelites on the Plains of Moab (Numbers 26): Sources and Redaction." *Vetus Testamentum* 63 (2013): 236–60.

———. "The Cities of Refuge Law in Numbers 35:9–34: A Study of Its Sources, Textual Unity and Relationship to Deuteronomy 19:1–13." *Zeitschrift für altorientalische und biblische Rechtsgeschichte* 26 (2020): 249–64.

———. "The Investiture of Joshua (Numbers 27:12–23) and the Dispute on the Form of the Leadership in *Yehud.*" *Vetus Testamentum* 59 (2009): 429–45.

———. "Joshua (and Caleb) in the Priestly Spies Story and Joshua's Initial Appearance in the Priestly Source: A Contribution to an Assessment of the Pentateuchal Priestly Material." *Journal of Biblical Literature* 136 (2017): 39–55.

———. "Numbers 36,1–12: Innovation and Interpretation." *Zeitschrift für die alttestamentliche Wissenschaft* 122 (2010): 249–59.

———. "Numbers 36:13: The Transition between Numbers and Deuteronomy, and the Redaction of the Pentateuch." Pages 113–24 in *From Author to Copyist: Essays on the Composition, Redaction, and Transmission of the Hebrew Bible in Honor of Zipi Talshir.* Edited by C. Werman. Winona Lake, IN: Eisenbrauns, 2015.

———. "P, Source or Redaction: The Evidence of Numbers 25." Pages 387–99 in *The Pentateuch: International Perspectives on Current Research.* Forschungen zum Alten Testament 78. Edited by T. B. Dozeman, K. Schmid, and B. J. Schwartz. Tübingen: Mohr Siebeck, 2011.

———. "The Story of the Gadites and the Reubenites (Numbers 32): A Case Study for an Approach to a Pentateuchal Text." Pages 619–29 in *The Formation of the Pentateuch: Bridging the Academic Cultures of Europe, Israel, and North America.* Forschungen zum Alten Testament 111. Edited by J. C. Gertz, B. M. Levinson, D. Rom-Shiloni, and K. Schmid. Tübingen: Mohr Siebeck, 2016.

———. "The Vocabulary of the Septuagint and Literary Criticism: The Case of Numbers 27,15–23." *Biblica* 90 (2009): 59–67.

Kiss, Jenö. "Der Mensch lebt nicht vom Brot allein, sondern . . ." *Vetus Testamentum* 58 (2008): 510–25.

Kitchen, K. A. *On the Reliability of the Old Testament.* Grand Rapids: Eerdmans, 2003.

Kitz, Anne Marie. "The Hebrew Terminology of Lot Casting and Its Ancient Near Eastern Context." *Catholic Biblical Quarterly* 62 (2000): 297–14.

Kline, Moshe. "Structure Is Theology: The Composition of Leviticus." In Gane and Taggar-Cohen, *Current Issues,* 225–64.

Knierim, Rolf P., and George W. Coats. *Numbers.* Forms of the Old Testament Literature 4. Grand Rapids: Eerdmans, 2004.

Knipping, Burkhard R. *Die Kundschaftergeschichte Numeri 13–14: Synchrone Beschreibung, diachron orientierte Betrachtung, fortschreibungsgeschichtliche Verortung.* Theos: Studienreihe theologische Forschungsergebnisse 37. Hamburg: Kovač, 2000.

Knohl, Israel. "The Priestly Torah versus the Holiness School: Sabbath and the Festivals." *Hebrew Union College Annual* 58 (1987): 65–117.

———. *Sanctuary of Silence: The Priestly Torah and the Holiness School.* Minneapolis: Fortress, 1995. Repr., Winona Lake, IN: Eisenbrauns, 2007.

Köckert, Matthias. *Leben im Gottes Gegenwart: Studien zum Verständnis des Gesetzes im Alten Testament.* Forschungen zum Alten Testament 43. Tübingen: Mohr Siebeck, 2004.

Koenen, Klaus. "Eherne Schlange und goldenes Kalb: Ein Vergleich der Überlieferungen." *Zeitschrift für die alttestamentliche Wissenschaft* 111 (1999): 353–72.

Kosman, Admiel. "The Story of a Giant Story: The Winding Way of Og King of Bashan in the Jewish Haggadic Tradition." *Hebrew Union College Annual* 73 (2002): 157–90.

Krašovec, Jože. "Is There a Doctrine of 'Collective Retribution' in The Hebrew Bible?" *Hebrew Union College Annual* 65 (1994): 35–89.

Krause, Joachim J. "Aesthetics of Production and Aesthetics of Reception in Analyzing Intertextuality: Illustrated with Joshua 2." *Biblica* 96 (2015): 416–27.

Kselman, J. S. "A Note on Numbers XII 6–8." *Vetus Testamentum* 26 (1976): 500–505.

Kuenen, Abraham. *An Historico-Critical Inquiry into the Origin and Composition of the Hexateuch.* Translated by P. H. Wicksteed. London: MacMillan, 1886.

Kugler, Gili. "The Threat of Annihilation of Israel in the Desert: An Independent Tradition within Two Stories." *Catholic Biblical Quarterly* 78 (2016): 632–47.

Kugler, Robert A., and Kyung S. Baek. *Leviticus at Qumran: Text and Interpretation.* Supplements to Vetus Testamentum 173. Boston: Brill, 2017.

Kuhl, Curt. "Die 'Wiederaufnahme'—Ein literarkritisches Prinzip?" *Zeitschrift für die alttestamentliche Wissenschaft* 64 (1952): 1–11.

Kuhrt, Amélie. *The Ancient Near East: c. 3000–330 BC.* 2 vols. New York: Routledge, 1995.

Lambdin, Thomas O. *Introduction to Biblical Hebrew.* New York: Scribner, 1971.

Lambert, W. G. "Dingir.šà.dib.ba. Incantations." *Journal of Near Eastern Studies* 33 (1974): 280.

Lauinger, Jacob. "The Neo-Assyrian *adê*: Treaty, Oath, or Something Else?" *Zeitschrift für altorientalische und biblische Rechtsgeschichte* 19 (2013): 99–115.

Layton, Scott C. "Whence Comes Balaam? Num 22,5 Revisited." *Biblica* 73 (1992): 32–61.

Leal, Robert Barry. *Wilderness in the Bible: Toward a Theology of Wilderness.* Studies in Biblical Literature 72. New York: Peter Lang, 2004.

Lee, Archie C. C. "Reading Iconoclastic Stipulations in Numbers 33:50–56 from the Pluralistic Religious Context of China." In Brenner and A. Lee, *Leviticus and Numbers,* 213–26.

Lee, Won W. *Punishment and Forgiveness in Israel's Migratory Campaign.* Grand Rapids: Eerdmans, 2003.

Lehming, Sigo. "Massa und Meriba." *Zeitschrift für die alttestamentliche Wissenschaft* 73 (1961): 71–77.

———. "Versuch zu Num 16." *Zeitschrift für die alttestamentliche Wissenschaft* 74 (1962): 291–321.

Lemaire, André. "Balaʿam/Belaʿ fils de Beʿôr." *Zeitschrift für die alttestamentliche Wissenschaft* 102 (1990): 180–87.

———. "Fragments from the Book of Balaam Found at Deir Alla: Text Foretells Cosmic Disaster." *Biblical Archaeology Review* 11 (1985): 26–39.

LeMon, Joel M. "Egypt and the Egyptians." In Arnold and Strawn, *World around the Old Testament*, 169–96.

Leuchter, Mark A., and Jeremy M. Hutton, eds. *Levites and Priests in History and Tradition*. Ancient Israel and Its Literature 9. Atlanta: Society of Biblical Literature, 2011.

Leveen, Adriane B. "'Lo We Perish': A Reading of Numbers 17:27–20:29." In Frevel, Pola, and Schart, *Book of Numbers*, 248–72.

———. *Memory and Tradition in the Book of Numbers*. Cambridge: Cambridge University Press, 2008.

———. "Variations on a Theme: Differing Conceptions of Memory in the Book of Numbers." *Journal for the Study of the Old Testament* 27 (2002): 201–21.

Levenson, Jon D. *Sinai & Zion: An Entry into the Jewish Bible*. HarperCollins: New York, 1985.

Levin, Saul. "An Unattested 'Scribal Correction' in Numbers 26,59?" *Biblica* 71 (1990): 25–33.

Levin, Yigal. "Numbers 34:2–12, The Boundaries of the Land of Canaan, and the Empire of Necho." *Journal of Near Eastern Studies* 30 (2006): 55–76.

Levinas, Emmanuel. *Ethics and Infinity: Conversations with Philippe Nemo*. Translated by R. A. Cohen. Pittsburgh: Duquesne University Press, 1985.

———. "God and Philosophy." Pages 153–74 in *Collected Philosophical Papers*. Translated by A. Lingis. Dordrecht: Martinus Nijhoff, 1987.

Levine, Baruch A. "The Balaam Inscription from Deir ʿAlla: Historical Aspects." Pages 326–39 in *Biblical Archaeology Today: Proceedings of the International Congress on Biblical Archaeology Jerusalem, April 1984*. Edited by J. Amitai. Jerusalem: Israel Exploration Society, 1985.

———. "The Deir ʿAlla Plaster Inscriptions." *Journal of the American Oriental Society* 101 (1981): 195–205.

———. "The Descriptive Tabernacle Texts of the Pentateuch." *Journal of the American Oriental Society* 85 (1965): 307–18.

———. *Numbers*. Vol. 1, *1–20: A New Translation with Introduction and Commentary*. Anchor Bible 4. New York: Doubleday, 1993.

———. *Numbers*. Vol. 2, *21–36: A New Translation with Introduction and Commentary*. Anchor Bible 4A. New York: Doubleday, 2000.

Levine, Baruch A., and William W. Hallo. "Offerings to the Temple Gates at Ur." *Hebrew Union College Annual* 38 (1967): 17–58.

Levinson, Bernard M. *Deuteronomy and the Hermeneutics of Legal Innovation.* Oxford: Oxford University Press, 1997.

Levison, John R. "Prophecy in Ancient Israel: The Case of the Ecstatic Elders." *Catholic Biblical Quarterly* 65 (2003): 503–21.

Lienhard, Joseph T., SJ, ed. *Exodus, Leviticus, Numbers, Deuteronomy.* Ancient Christian Commentary on Scripture: Old Testament 3. Downers Grove, IL: InterVarsity, 2001.

Lim, Johnson Teng Kok. *The Sin of Moses and the Staff of God: A Narrative Approach.* Studia Semitica Neerlandica 35. Leiden: Brill, 2018.

Lipton, Diana. "Bitter Waters (Numbers 5), Flood Waters (Genesis 6–9), and Some Theologies of Exile and Land." In Brenner and A. Lee, *Leviticus and Numbers,* 121–39.

Lohfink, Norbert. *Theology of the Pentateuch: Themes of the Priestly Narrative and Deuteronomy.* Translated by L. M. Maloney. Minneapolis: Fortress, 1994.

Lutzky, Harriet C. "Ambivalence toward Balaam." *Vetus Testamentum* 49 (1999): 421–25.

———. "The Name 'Cozbi' (Numbers XXV 15, 18)." *Vetus Testamentum* 47 (1997): 546–49.

Lynch, Matthew J. "Neglected Physical Dimensions of 'Shame' Terminology in the Hebrew Bible." *Biblica* 91 (2010): 499–517.

MacDonald, Nathan. "Edom and Seir in the Narratives and Itineraries of Numbers 20–21 and Deuteronomy 1–3." Pages 83–103 in *Deuteronomium: Tora für eine neue Generation.* Edited by G. Fischer, D. Markl and S. Paganini. Beihefte zur Zeitschrift für altorientalische und biblische Rechtsgeschichte 17. Wiesbaden: Harrasowitz, 2011.

Machinist, Peter. "The Question of Distinctiveness in Ancient Israel: An Essay." Pages 196–212 in *Ah, Assyria . . . : Studies in Assyrian History and Ancient Near Eastern Historiography Presented to Hayim Tadmor.* Scripta Hierosolymitana 33. Edited by M. Cogan and I. Eph'al. Jerusalem: Magnes, 1991.

Malina, Bruce J. *The New Testament World: Insights from Cultural Anthropology.* Rev. ed. Louisville: Westminster John Knox, 1993.

Mallon, Alexis. "La Mer Rouge et L'Exode." *Biblica* 6 (1925): 396–400.

Markl, Dominik. "This Word Is Your Life: The Theology of 'Life' in Deuteronomy." Pages 71–96 in *Gottes Wort im Menschenwort: Festschrift für Georg Fischer SJ zum 60. Geburtstag.* Edited by D. Markl, C. Paganini, and S. Paganini. Österreichische biblische Studien 43. Frankfurt: Peter Lang, 2014.

Marquis, Liane M. "The Composition of Numbers 32: A New Proposal." *Vetus Testamentum* 63 (2013): 408–32.

Marx, Alfred. "A propos de Nombres XXIV 19b." *Vetus Testamentum* 37 (1987): 100–104.

Mastin, B. A. "What Do *Miqneh* and *Bᵉhēmâ* Mean in Genesis XXXIV 23, XXXVI 6; Numbers XXXI 9, XXXII 26?" *Vetus Testamentum* 45 (1995): 491–515.

Matthews, Victor H. "Marriage and Family in the Ancient Near East." Pages 1–32 in *Marriage and Family in the Biblical World.* Edited by K. M. Campbell. Downers Grove, IL: InterVarsity, 2003.

591

Mattison, Kevin. "Contrasting Conceptions of Asylum in Deuteronomy 19 and Numbers 35." *Vetus Testamentum* 68 (2018): 232–251.

McCarter, P. Kyle, Jr. "The Balaam Texts from Deir ʿAlla: The First Combination." *Bulletin of the Schools of Oriental Research* 239 (1980): 49–60.

McEvenue, S. "A Source-Critical Problem in Nm 14,26–38." *Biblica* 50 (1969): 453–65.

McGovern, Patrick E., Stuart J. Fleming, and Solomon H. Katz, eds. *The Origins and Ancient History of Wine: Food and Nutrition in History and Anthropology.* New York: Routledge, 1996.

McGrath, Alister, and Joanna Collicutt McGrath. *The Dawkins Delusion? Atheist Fundamentalism and the Denial of the Divine.* Downers Grove, IL: InterVarsity, 2007.

Mendenhall, George E. "The Census Lists of Numbers 1 and 26." *Journal of Biblical Literature* 77 (1958): 52–66.

———. "Covenant Forms in Israelite Tradition." *Biblical Archaeologist* 17 (1954): 50–76.

Mettinger, Tryggve N. D. *The Dethronement of Sabaoth: Studies in Shem and Kabod Theologies.* Coniectanea Biblica: Old Testament Series 18. Lund: Gleerup, 1982.

———. *No Graven Image? Israelite Aniconism in Its Ancient Near Eastern Context.* Stockholm: Almqvist & Wiksell, 1995.

Meyer, Esias E. "Ritual Innovation in Numbers 18?" *Scriptura* 116 (2017): 133–47.

Michalowski, Piotr. "Carminative Magic: Towards an Understanding of Sumerian Poetics." *Zeitschrift für Assyriologie* 71 (1981): 1–18.

Middleton, J. Richard. *A New Heaven and a New Earth: Reclaiming Biblical Eschatology.* Grand Rapids: Baker Academic, 2014.

Migsch, Herbert. "Zur Bedeutung von [*mlʾ*] Nipĥʿal in Num 14,21 und Ps 72,19." *Biblica* 82 (2001): 79–83.

Milgrom, Jacob. "The Alleged Wave-Offering in Israel and the Ancient Near East." *Israel Exploration Journal* 22 (1972): 33–38.

———. "The Case of the Suspected Adulteress, Numbers 5:11–31: Redaction and Meaning." Pages 69–75 in *The Creation of Sacred Literature.* Edited by R. E. Friedman. Berkeley: University of California Press, 1981.

———. "Confusing the Sacred and the Impure: A Rejoinder." *Vetus Testamentum* 44 (1994): 554–59.

———. "The Levitical Town: An Exercise in Realistic Planning." *Journal of Jewish Studies* 33 (1982): 185–88.

———. *Leviticus.* Vol. 1, *1–16: A New Translation with Introduction and Commentary.* Anchor Bible 3A. New York: Doubleday, 1991.

———. *Leviticus.* Vol. 2, *17–22: A New Translation with Introduction and Commentary.* Anchor Bible 3B. New York: Doubleday, 2000.

———. *Leviticus.* Vol. 3, *23–27: A New Translation with Introduction and Commentary.* Anchor Bible 3C. New York: Doubleday, 2001.

———. *Numbers.* JPS Torah Commentary. Philadelphia: JPS, 1990.

———. "On Decoding Very Large Numbers." *Vetus Testamentum* 49 (1999): 131–32.

———. "The Paradox of the Red Cow (Num XIX)." *Vetus Testamentum* 31 (1981): 62–72.

———. "The Rationale for Biblical Impurity." *Journal of the Ancient Near Eastern Society* 22 (1993): 107–11.

———. "The Shared Custody of the Tabernacle and a Hittite Analogy." *Journal of the American Oriental Society* 90 (1970): 204–9.

Miller, J. Maxwell. "The Korahites of Southern Judah." *Catholic Biblical Quarterly* 32 (1970): 58–68.

Miller-Naudé, Cynthia L., and Jacobus A. Naudé. "The Translation of Quotative Frames in the Hebrew Bible." *Folia orientalia* 52 (2015): 249–69.

Mirguet, Françoise. "Numbers 16: The Significance of Place—an Analysis of Spatial Markers." *Journal for the Study of the Old Testament* 32 (2008): 311–30.

Moabite Stone. https://www.worldhistory.org/Moabite_Stone_[Mesha_Stele].

Monroe, Lauren A. S. "Disembodied Women: Sacrificial Language and the Deaths of Bat-Jephthah, Cozbi, and the Bethlehemite Concubine." *Catholic Biblical Quarterly* 75 (2013): 32–52.

———. "Phinehas' Zeal and the Death of Cozbi: Unearthing a Human Scapegoat Tradition in Numbers 25:1–18." *Vetus Testamentum* 62 (2012): 211–31.

Monson, James M. *Geobasics in the Land of the Bible*. Rockford, IL: Biblical Backgrounds, 2008.

Moore, Michael S. "Ruth the Moabite and the Blessing of Foreigners." *Catholic Biblical Quarterly* 60 (1998): 203–17.

Moran, William L., ed. and trans. *The Amarna Letters*. Baltimore: Johns Hopkins University Press, 1992.

Moreno García, Juan Carlos. "Economies in Transition: Trade, 'Money,' Labour and Nomads at the Turn of the 1st Millennium BC." Pages 1–39 in *Dynamics of Production in the Ancient Near East: 1300–500 BC*. Edited by J. C. Moreno García. Oxford: Oxbow, 2016.

Morgenstern, Julian. "Two Additional Notes to 'The Suffering Servant—A New Solution.'" *Vetus Testamentum* (1963): 321–32.

Moxnes, Halvor. "Honor and Shame." Pages 19–40 in *The Social Sciences and New Testament Interpretation*. Edited by R. L. Rohrbaugh. Peabody, MA: Hendrickson, 1996.

Muhly, James D. "How Iron Technology Changed the Ancient World and Gave the Philistines a Military Edge." *Biblical Archaeology Review* 8 (1982): 40–54.

Müller, Hans-Peter. "Die aramäische Inschrift von Deir ʿAllā und die älteren Bileamsprüche." *Zeitschrift für die alttestamentliche Wissenschaft* 94 (1982): 214–44.

Müller, Reinhard, and Juha Pakkala. *Insights into Editing in the Hebrew Bible and the Ancient Near East: What Does Documented Evidence Tell Us about the Transmission of Authoritative Texts?* Contributions to Biblical Exegesis and Theology 84. Leuven: Peters, 2017.

Murray, Donald F. "Under YHWH's Veto: David as Shedder of Blood in Chronicles." *Biblica* 82 (2001): 457–76.

Na'aman, Nadav. "'Hebron Was Built Seven Years before Zoan in Egypt' (Numbers XIII 22)." *Vetus Testamentum* 31 (1981): 488–92.

Naveh, J. "The Date of the Deir 'Alla Inscription in Aramaic Script." *Israel Exploration Journal* 17 (1967): 236–38.

Neo-Assyrian Treaties and Loyalty Oaths. *See* Open Richly; Parpola

Ngo, Robin. "Miniature Writing on Ancient Amulets." *Biblical Archaeology Society: Bible History Daily*, March 3, 2022. https://www.biblicalarchaeology.org/daily /biblical-artifacts/inscriptions/miniature-writing-ancient-amulets-ketef-hinnom.

Niehaus, Jeffrey J. *Ancient Near Eastern Themes in Biblical Theology*. Grand Rapids: Kregel, 2008.

Nietzsche, Friedrich. *On the Genealogy of Morality* [excerpt]. Edited by K. Ansell-Pearson. Translated by C. Diethe. Cambridge: Cambridge University Press, 1994. Repr., pages 457–74 in *Nineteenth-Century Philosophy*. Vol. 4 of *Philosophic Classics*. Edited by F. E. Baird and W. Kaufmann. Upper Saddle River, NJ: Prentice Hall, 1997.

Nihan, Christophe. *From Priestly Torah to Pentateuch: A Study in the Composition of the Book of Leviticus*. Forschungen zum Alten Testament 25. 2 Reihe. Tübingen: Mohr Siebeck, 2007.

———. "Israel's Festival Calendars in Leviticus 23, Numbers 28–29, and the Formation of 'Priestly' Literature." In Römer, *Leviticus and Numbers*, 177–232.

———. "The Priestly Laws of Numbers, the Holiness Legislation, and the Pentateuch." In Frevel, Pola, and Schart, *Book of Numbers*, 109–37.

———. Review of R. Achenbach, *Die Vollendung der Tora: Studien zur Redaktionsgeschichte des Numeribuches im Kontext von Hexateuch und Pentateuch*. *Review of Biblical Literature*. 2006. http://www.bookreviews.org.

Nissinen, Martti, ed. *Prophecy in Its Ancient Near Eastern Context: Mesopotamian, Biblical, and Arabian Perspectives*. Symposium Series 13. Atlanta: Society of Biblical Literature, 2000.

Noam, Vered. "Corpse-Blood Impurity: A Lost Biblical Reading?" *Journal of Biblical Literature* 128 (2009): 243–51.

Noort, Ed. "Bis zur Grenze des Landes? Num 27,12–23 und das Ende der Priesterschrift." In Römer, *Leviticus and Numbers*, 99–119.

Noquet, Dany. "NB 27,12–23, La succession de Moïse et la place d'Éléazar dans le livre des Nombres." In Römer, *Leviticus and Numbers*, 655–75.

Noth, Martin. *A History of Pentateuchal Traditions*. Englewood Cliffs, NJ: Prentice-Hall, 1972. Translation of *Überlieferungsgeschichte des Pentateuch*. Stuttgart: Kohlhammer, 1948.

———. *Numbers: A Commentary*. Old Testament Library. Philadelphia: Westminster, 1968.

———. *Das System der zwölf Stämme Israels*. Beiträge zur Wissenschaft vom Alten und Neuen Testament 4.1. Stuttgart: Kohlhammer, 1930.

Novick, Tzvi. "[h'myn] in Jud 11,20 and the Semantics of Assent." *Zeitschrift für die alttestamentliche Wissenschaft* 121 (2009): 577–83.

Olson, Dennis T. *The Death of the Old and the Birth of the New: The Framework of the Book of Numbers and the Pentateuch.* Brown Judaic Studies 71. Chico, CA: Scholars Press, 1985.

———. *Deuteronomy and the Death of Moses.* Minneapolis: Fortress, 1994.

———. *Numbers.* Interpretation: A Bible Commentary for Teaching and Preaching. Louisville: John Knox, 1996.

Open Richly Annotated Cuneiform Corpus. "SAA 02 006. Esarhaddon's Succession Treaty (VTE)." http://oracc.museum.upenn.edu/saao/saa02/corpus.

Oppenheim, A. Leo. *Ancient Mesopotamia: Portrait of a Dead Civilization.* Rev. ed. Chicago: University of Chicago Press, 1977.

Oppenheim, A. Leo., et al., eds. *The Assyrian Dictionary of the Oriental Institute of the University of Chicago.* Chicago: Oriental Institute, 1956–.

oracc. *See* Open Richly; Neo-Assyrian Treaties and Loyalty Oaths; Parpola

Organ, Barbara E. "Pursuing Phinehas: A Synchronic Reading." *Catholic Biblical Quarterly* 63 (2001): 203–18.

Origen. *The Song of Songs: Commentary and Homilies.* Ancient Christian Writers 26. Translated by R. P. Lawson. New York: Paulist Press, 1957.

Oswalt, John N. *The Bible among the Myths: Unique Revelation or Just Ancient Literature?* Grand Rapids: Zondervan, 2009.

Oswalt, Wolfgang. "Die Revision des Edombildes in Numeri XX 14–21." *Vetus Testamentum* 50 (2000): 218–32.

Otto, Eckart. "Covenant." Pages 2047–51 in *Encyclopedia of Religion.* Vol. 3. 2nd ed. Edited by L. Jones. Detroit: Macmillan Reference, 2005.

———. *Deuteronomium 23,16–34,12.* Vol. 4. Herders Theologischer Kommentar zum Alten Testament. Freiburg: Herder, 2017.

———. "Das Ende der Toraoffenbarung: Die Funktion der Kolophone Lev 26,46 und 27,34 sowie Num 36,13 in der Rechtshermeneutic des Pentateuch." Pages 191–201 in *Auf dem Weg zur Endgestalt von Genesis bis II Regum: Festschrift Hans-Christoph Schmitt zum 65. Geburtstag.* Edited by M. Beck and U. Schorn. Beihefte zur Zeitschrift für die alttestamentliche Wissenschaft 370. Berlin: de Gruyter, 2006.

———. "Forschungen zur Priesterschrift." *Theologische Rundschau* 62 (1997): 1–50.

Pardee, Dennis. "*Mārîm* in Numbers V." *Vetus Testamentum* 35 (1985): 112–15.

———. *Ritual and Cult at Ugarit.* Society of Biblical Literature Writings from the Ancient World 10. Atlanta: Society of Biblical Literature, 2002.

Park, Song-Mi Suzie. "Census and Censure: Sacred Threshing Floors and Counting Taboos in 2 Samuel 24." *Horizons in Biblical Theology* 35 (2013): 21–41.

Parker, Simon B., ed. *Ugaritic Narrative Poetry.* Society of Biblical Literature Writings from the Ancient World 9. Atlanta: Scholars Press, 1997.

Parpola, Simo, and Kazuko Watanabe. *Neo-Assyrian Treaties and Loyalty Oaths.* State Archives of Assyria 2. Helsinki: Helsinki University Press, 1988. http://oracc.org/saao/Q009186/. http://oracc.museum.upenn.edu/saao/saa02/corpus.

Paterson, J. A. *The Book of Numbers.* Leipzig: Hinrichs'sche, 1900.

Payne, Philip B., and Paul Canart. "The Originality of Text-Critical Symbols in Codex Vaticanus." *Novum Testamentum* 42 (2000): 105–13.

Pearce, Sarah J. K. *The Words of Moses: Studies in the Reception of Deuteronomy in the Second Temple Period.* Texts and Studies in Ancient Judaism 152. Tübingen: Mohr Siebeck, 2013.

Petrie, W. M. Flinders. *Researches in Sinai.* London: J. Murray, 1906.

Petter, Thomas D. "Tribes and Nomads in the Iron Age Levant." In Greer, Hilber, and Walton, *Behind the Scenes*, 391–95.

Pettit, David P. "Expiating Apostasy: Baal Peor, Moses, and Intermarriage with a Midianite Woman." *Journal for the Study of the Old Testament* 41 (2018): 457–68.

———. "When the LORD Seeks to Kill Moses: Reading Exodus 4.24–26 in Its Literary Context." *Journal for the Study of the Old Testament* 40 (2015): 163–77.

Pinker, Aron. "The Number 40 in the Bible." *Jewish Bible Quarterly* 22 (1994): 163–72.

Pinker, Stephen. *The Stuff of Thought: Language as a Window into Human Nature.* London: Penguin, 2008.

Piper, John. *Fifty Reasons Why Jesus Came to Die.* Wheaton: Crossway, 2005.

———. *Let the Nations Be Glad: The Supremacy of God in Missions.* 3rd ed. Grand Rapids: Baker Academic, 2010.

Pola, Thomas. *Die ursprüngliche Priesterschrift: Beobachtungen zur Literarkritik und Traditionsgeschichte von P^G.* Wissenschaftliche Monographien zum Alten und Neuen Testament 70. Neukirchen-Vluyn: Neukirchener Verlag, 1995.

Provan, Ian, V. Philips Long, and Tremper Longman III. *A Biblical History of Israel.* Louisville: Westminster John Knox, 2003.

Puech, É. "L'inscription sur pl tre de Tell Deir Alla." Pages 354–65 in *Biblical Archaeology Today: Proceedings of the International Congress on Biblical Archaeology Jerusalem, April 1984.* Edited by J. Amitai. Jerusalem: IES, 1985.

Rainey, Anson F. "The Order of Sacrifices in Old Testament Ritual Texts." *Biblica* 51 (1970): 485–98.

Rainey, Anson F., and R. Steven Notley. *The Sacred Bridge: Carta's Atlas of the Biblical World.* Enhanced ed. Jerusalem: Carta, 2015.

Rashi (Rabbi Shlomo Yitzchaki). "On Numbers 20:12." In *Pentateuch with . . . Rashi's Commentary.* Translated by M. Rosenbaum and A. M. Silbermann. London: Shapiro, Valentine, 1929–1934. https://www.sefaria.org/Rashi_on_Numbers.

Rasmussen, Carl G. "Encountering the Holy Land, Session 1: Introduction to the Middle East." July 30, 2019. https://www.youtube.com/watch?v=eXC2VOKsXPc&feature=emb_title.

———. *Zondervan Atlas of the Bible.* Rev. ed. Grand Rapids: Zondervan, 2010.

Ratzinger, Joseph Cardinal. *The Spirit of the Liturgy.* Translated by J. Saward. San Francisco: Ignatius, 2000.

Recht, Laerke. *Human Sacrifice: Archaeological Perspectives from around the World.* Cambridge: Cambridge University Press, 2019.

———. "Human Sacrifice in the Ancient Near East." *Trinity College Dublin, Journal of Postgraduate Research* (2009): 168–80.

Redditt, Paul L. "Kittim." In Freedman, *Eerdmans Dictionary*, 776–77.

Redford, Donald B. *Egypt, Canaan, and Israel in Ancient Times*. Princeton: Princeton University Press, 1992.

Redmount, Carol. "Bitter Lives: Israel in and out of Egypt." Pages 58–89 in *The Oxford History of the Biblical World*. Edited by M. D. Coogan. Oxford: Oxford University Press, 1998.

Rees, Anthony. "Numbers 25 and Beyond: Phinehas and Other Detestable Practice(r)s." In Brenner and A. Lee, *Leviticus and Numbers*, 163–77.

Reis, Pamela Tamarkin. "Numbers XI: Seeing Moses Plain." *Vetus Testamentum* 55 (2005): 207–31.

Rendsburg, Gary A. "An Additional Note to Two Recent Articles on the Number of People in the Exodus from Egypt and the Large Numbers in Numbers I and XXVI." *Vetus Testamentum* 51 (2001): 392–96.

Resseguie, James L. *Narrative Criticism of the New Testament: An Introduction*. Grand Rapids: Baker Academic, 2005.

Reviv, Hanoch. "The Traditions concerning the Inception of the Legal System in Israel: Significance and Dating." *Zeitschrift für die alttestamentliche Wissenschaft* 94 (1982): 566–75.

Rhyder, Julia. *Centralizing the Cult: The Holiness Legislation in Leviticus 17–26*. Forschungen zum Alten Testament 134. Tübingen: Mohr Siebeck, 2019.

Richter, Sandra L. *Epic of Eden: A Christian Entry into the Old Testament*. Downers Grove, IL: IVP Academic, 2008.

Robinson, Bernard P. "Moses at the Burning Bush." *Journal for the Study of the Old Testament* 75 (1997): 107–22.

Robinson, H. Wheeler. "The Council of Yahweh." *Journal of Theological Studies* 45 (1943): 151–57.

Robker, Jonathan Miles. *Balaam in Text and Tradition*. Forschungen zum Alten Testament 131. Tübingen: Mohr Siebeck, 2019.

———. "The Balaam Narrative in the Pentateuch/Hexateuch/Enneateuch." In Frevel, Pola, and Schart, *Book of Numbers*, 334–66.

Roi, Micha. "The Law of the Sotah and the Cup of Wrath: Substantive and Adjective Law in the Hebrew Bible." *Revue biblique* 124 (2017): 161–79.

Römer, Thomas C. "L'arche de Yhwh: de la guerre à l'alliance." *Études théologiques et religieuses* 94 (2019): 95–108.

———, ed. *The Books of Leviticus and Numbers*. Bibliotheca ephemeridum theologicarum lovaniensium 215. Leuven: Peeters, 2008.

———. "De la périphérie au centre: Les livres du Lévitique et des Nombres dans le débat actuel sur le Pentateuque." In Römer, *Leviticus and Numbers*, 3–34.

———. "Egypt Nostalgia in Exodus 14–Numbers 21." In Frevel, Pola, and Schart, *Book of Numbers*, 66–86.

———. "Israel's Sojourn in the Wilderness and the Construction of the Book of Numbers." Pages 419–45 in *Reflection and Refraction: Studies in Biblical Historiography in Honour of A. Graeme Auld*. Edited by R. Rezetko, T. H. Lim, and W. B. Aucker. Supplements to Vetus Testamentum 113. Leiden: Brill, 2007.

————. "Mose in Äthiopien: Zur Herkunft der Num 12,1 zugrunde liegenden Tradition." Pages 203–15 in *Auf dem Weg zur Endgestalt von Genesis bis II Regum: Festschrift Hans-Christoph Schmitt zum 65. Geburtstag*. Edited by M. Beck and U. Schorn. Beihefte zur Zeitschrift für die alttestamentliche Wissenschaft 370. Berlin: de Gruyter, 2006.

————. "Nombres." Pages 196–210 in *Introduction à l'Ancien Testament*. Edited by T. Römer, J.-D. Macchi, and C. Nihan. Le Monde de la Bible 49. Genève: Labor et Fides, 2004.

————. "Nombres 11–12 et la question d'une rédaction deutéronomique dans le Pentateuque." Pages 481–98 in *Deuteronomy and Deuteronomic Literature: Festschrift C. H. W. Brekelmans*. Bibliotheca ephemeridum theologicarum lovaniensium 133. Leuven: Peters, 1997.

————. "Zwischen Urkunden, Fragmenten und Ergänzungen: Zum Stand der Pentateuchforschung." *Zeitschrift für die alttestamentliche Wissenschaft* 125 (2013): 2–24.

Römer, Thomas C., and Marc Z. Brettler. "Deuteronomy 34 and the Case for a Persian Hexateuch." *Journal of Biblical Literature* 119 (2000): 401–19.

Römheld, Diethard. *Wege der Weisheit*. Beihefte zur Zeitschrift für die alttestamentliche Wissenschaft 184. Berlin: de Gruyter, 1989.

Roscher, W. H. *Die Zahl 40 in Glauben, Brauch und Schrifttum der Semiten: Ein Beitrag zur vergleichenden Religionswissenschaft, Volkskunde und Zahlenmystik*. Leipzig: Teubner, 1909.

Rösel, Martin. "Wie einer vom Propheten zum Verführer wurde: Tradition und Reception der Bileamgestalt." *Biblica* 80 (1999): 506–24.

Ross, A. P. "Paronomasia and Popular Etymology in the Naming Narratives of the Old Testament." PhD diss., University of Cambridge, 1982.

Roth, Martha T. *Law Collections from Mesopotamia and Asia Minor*. Society of Biblical Literature Writings from the Ancient World 6. Atlanta: Scholars Press, 1995. http://www.g2rp.com/pdfs/LawCollectionsFromMesopotemiaAndAsiaMinor.pdf.

Rowe, Ignacio Márquez. "Review of M. Yon and D. Arnaud, eds. *Études ougaritiques*, I. *Travaux 1985–1995*." *Orientalia* 74 (2005): 136–45.

Ruikar, Shilpa S., Pallavi R. Rajopadhye, S. C. Kale, and Snehal A. Masurkar. "Formulation of Ash Based Dish Wash Bars and Their Studies on Bacteria Removal Efficiency." *International Journal of Advanced Science and Technology* 29 (2020): 1256–63.

Runge, Steven E. *Discourse Grammar of the Greek New Testament: A Practical Introduction for Teaching and Exegesis*. Peabody, MA: Hendrickson, 2010.

Ruprecht, Eberhard. "Das Zepter Jahwes in den Berufungsvisionen von Jeremia und Amos." *Zeitschrift für die alttestamentliche Wissenschaft* 108 (1996): 55–69.

Ruwe, Andreas. *"Heiligkeitsgesetz" und "Priesterschrift": Literaturgeschichtliche und rechtssystematische Untersuchungen zu Leviticus 17,1–26,2*. Forschungen zum Alten Testament 26. Tübingen: Mohr Siebeck, 1999.

Safren, Jonathan D. "Balaam and Abraham." *Vetus Testamentum* 38 (1988): 105–13.

Šagi, Janco. "Problema Historiae Codicis B." *Divus Thomas: Commentarium de philosophia et theologia* 85 (1972): 3–29.

Sakenfeld, Katharine D. "The Problem of Divine Forgiveness in Numbers 14." *Catholic Biblical Quarterly* 37 (1975): 317–30.

Sasson, Jack M. "About 'Mari and the Bible.'" *Revue d'Assyriologie et d'archéologie orientale* 92 (1998): 97–123.

———. "An *Apocalypticizing Vision* from Mari? Speculations on ARM X:9." *Mari: Annales de recherches interdisciplinaires* 1 (1982): 151–67.

———. *From the Mari Archives: An Anthology of Old Babylonian Letters.* Winona Lake, IN: Eisenbrauns, 2015.

———. "Numbers 5 and the 'Waters of Judgment.'" *Biblische Zeitschrift* 16 (1972): 249–51.

Schaeffer, Francis A. *How Should We Then Live? The Rise and Decline of Western Thought and Culture.* L'Abri 50th Anniversary edition. Wheaton: Crossway, 2005.

Schaff, Philip, and Henry Wace, eds. *Eusebius Pamphilius: Church History, Life of Constantine, Oration in Praise of Constantine.* Vol. 1. of *A Select Library of the Nicene and Post-Nicene Fathers.* Series 2. Edinburgh: T&T Clark, 1890. Repr., Grand Rapids: Eerdmans, 1982.

Scharbert, Josef. "Israel's Sojourn in the Wilderness and the Construction of the Book of Numbers." Pages 419–45 in *Reflection and Refraction: Studies in Biblical Historiography in Honour of A. Graeme Auld.* Edited by R. Rezetko, T. H. Lim, and W. B. Auker. Leiden: Brill, 2007.

———. *Numeri.* Die neu Echter Bibel: Kommentar zum Alten Testament mit der Einheitsübersetzung. Würzburg: Echter Verlag, 1992.

———. "Der Sinn der Toledot-Formel in der Priesterschrift." Pages 46–56 in *Wort, Gebot, Glaube: Beiträge zur Theologie des Alten Testaments; Festschrift für W. Eichrodt.* Edited by H. J. Stoebe, J. J. Stamm, and E. Jenni. Abhandlungen zur Theologie des Alten und Neuen Testaments 59. Zürich: Zwingli Verlag, 1970.

Schart, Aaron. "The Spy Story and the Final Redaction of the Pentateuch." In Frevel, Pola, and Schart, *Book of Numbers,* 164–200.

Schenker, Adrian. "Once Again, the Expiatory Sacrifices." *Journal of Biblical Literature* 116 (1997): 697–99.

Schinkel, Dirk. "Mirjam als Aussätzige? Zwei Bemerkungen zu Num 12." *Zeitschrift für alttestamentliche Wissenschaft* 115 (2003): 94–101.

Schipper, Bernd U. "Die 'eherne Schlange'—zur Religionsgeschichte und Theologie von Num 21,4–9." *Zeitschrift für die alttestestamentliche Wissenschaft* 121 (2009): 369–87.

Schipper, Jeremy. "Interpreting the Lamb Imagery in Isaiah 53." *Journal of Biblical Literature* 132, no. 2 (2013): 315–25.

Schloen, J. David. *The House of the Father as Fact and Symbol: Patrimonialism in Ugarit and the Ancient Near East.* Winona Lake, IN: Eisenbrauns, 2001.

Schmid, Hans Heinrich. *Der sogenannte Jahwist: Beobachtungen und Fragen zur Pentateuchforschung.* Zürich: Theologischer Verlag Zürich, 1976.

Schmidt, Ludwig. "Die Ansiedlung von Ruben und Gad im Ostjordanland in Numeri 32,1–38." *Zeitschrift für die alttestamentliche Wissenschaft* 114 (2002): 497–510.

————. "Bileam: Vom Seher zum Propheten Jahwes; Die literarischen Schichten der Bileam-Perikope (Num 22–24)." Pages 333–52 in *Gott und Mensch im Dialog.* Edited by M. Witte. Boston: de Gruyter, 2013.

————. "Die Kundschaftererzählung in Num 13–14 und Dtn 1,19–46." *Zeitschrift für die alttestamentliche Wissenschaft* 114 (2002): 40–58.

————. "Leviten- und Asylstädte in Num XXXV und Jos. XX; XXI 1–42." *Vetus Testamentum* 52 (2002): 103–21.

————. "P in Deuteronomium 34." *Vetus Testamentum* 59 (2009): 475–94.

————. "Sihon und Og in Num 21,2ff.* und Dtn 2,24ff.*: Ein Beitrag zur Entstehung des Buches Numeri." In Frevel, Pola, and Schart, *Book of Numbers*, 314–33.

————. *Studien zur Priesterschrift.* Beihefte zur Zeitschrift für die alttestamentliche Wissenschaft 214. Berlin: de Gruyter, 1993.

————. *Das vierte Buch Mose: Numeri 10,11–36,13.* Das Alte Testament Deutsch 7/2. Göttingen: Vandenhoeck & Ruprecht, 2004.

Schniedewind, William M. *How the Bible Became a Book: The Textualization of Ancient Israel.* Cambridge: Cambridge University Press, 2004.

Schniedewind, William M., and Robert D. Holmstedt. *Hebrew Inscriptions (English Translation).* Version 3.5. n.p.: OakTree Software, 2018. https://mcarasik.files .wordpress.com/2021/06/41-pinchas-5781.pdf.

Schwartz, Mark. "Warfare in the World of the Bible." In Greer, Hilber, and Walton, *Behind the Scenes,* 506–14.

Scurlock, Joann. "Departure of Ships? An Investigation of [ṣy] in Numbers 24.24 and Isaiah 33.23." *Journal for the Study of the Old Testament* 33 (2010): 267–82.

Seebass, Horst. "Edom und seine Umgehung nach Numeri XX–XXI: Zu Numeri XXI 10–13." *Vetus Testamentum* 47 (1997): 255–62.

————. "Erwägungen zu Numeri 32:1–38." *Journal of Biblical Literature* 118 (1999): 33–48.

————. "Machir im Ostjordanland." *Vetus Testamentum* 32 (1982): 496–503.

————. *Numeri.* 3 vols. Biblischer Kommentar Altes Testament. Neukirchen-Vluyn: Neukirchener Verlagsgesellschaft, 2003–12.

————. "Numeri als eigene Komposition." In Frevel, Pola, and Schart, *Book of Numbers,* 87–108.

————. "Num XI, XII und die Hypothese des Jahwisten." *Vetus Testamentum* 28 (1978): 214–23.

————. "Versuch zu Josua xviii 1–10." *Vetus Testamentum* 56 (2006): 370–85.

————. "YHWH's Name in the Aaronic Blessing (Num 6:22–27)." Pages 37–54 in *The Revelation of the Name YHWH to Moses: Perspectives from Judaism, the Pagan Graeco-Roman World, and Early Christianity.* Edited by G. H. van Kooten. Leiden: Brill, 2006.

————. "Zu Num X 33f." *Vetus Testamentum* 14 (1964): 111–13.

————. "Zur literarischen Gestalt der Bileam-Perikope." *Zeitschrift für die alttestamentliche Wissenschaft* 107 (1995): 409–19.

Seevers, Boyd. *Warfare in the Old Testament: The Organization, Weapons, and Tactics of Ancient Near Eastern Armies.* Grand Rapids: Kregel Academic, 2013.

Segal, Michael. "The Text of the Hebrew Bible in Light of the Dead Sea Scrolls." *Materia giudaica* 12 (2007): 5–20.

Seitz, Christopher R. "The Prophet Moses and the Canonical Shape of Jeremiah." *Zeitschrift für die alttestamentliche Wissenschaft* 101 (1989): 3–27.

Sénéchal, Vincent. "Quel horizon d'écriture pour Nb 14,11–25? Essai de sondage des soubassements de cette péricope." In Römer, *Leviticus and Numbers*, 609–29.

Seow, C. L. "Deir ʿAlla Plaster Texts." Pages 207–12 in *Prophets and Prophecy in the Ancient Near East*. Edited by M. Nissinen. Society of Biblical Literature Writings from the Ancient World Series 12. Atlanta: Society of Biblical Literature, 2003.

Seybold, Klaus. *Der Segen und andere liturgische Wort aus der hebräischen Bibel*. 2nd ed. Zürich: Theologischer Verlag Zürich, 2005.

Shea, William H. "The Inscribed Tablets from Tell Deir ʿAlla." *Andrews University Seminary Studies* 27 (1989): 21–37, 97–119.

Shectman, Sarah. "The Social Status of Priestly and Levite Women." In Leuchter and Hutton, *Levites and Priests*, 83–99.

———. *Women in the Pentateuch: A Feminist and Source-Critical Analysis*. Hebrew Bible Monographs 23. Sheffield: Sheffield Phoenix, 2009.

Shemesh, Yael. "Do Not Bare Your Heads and Do Not Rend Your Clothes" (Leviticus 10:6): On Mourning and Refraining from Mourning in the Bible." In Brenner and A. Lee, *Leviticus and Numbers*, 33–54.

Sigrist, Marcel. "Sacrifice, Offerings and Votives: Mesopotamia." In Johnston, *Religions of the Ancient World*, 330–32.

Simkins, Ronald A. "Paran." In Freedman, *Eerdmans Dictionary*, 1009.

Singer, Itamar. "Chapter Fifteen: A Political History of Ugarit." Pages 603–733 in *Handbook of Ugaritic Studies*. Edited by W. G. E. Watson and N. Wyatt. Leiden: Brill, 1999.

Sivan, Helena Zlotnick. "The Rape of Cozbi (Numbers XXV)." *Vetus Testamentum* 51 (2001): 69–80.

Ska, Jean-Louis. *Introduction to Reading the Pentateuch*. Translated by P. Dominique. Winona Lake, IN: Eisenbrauns, 2006.

———. "Old and New in the Book of Numbers." *Biblica* 95 (2014): 102–16.

Sklar, Jay. *Sin, Impurity, Sacrifice and Atonement: The Priestly Conceptions*. Hebrew Bible Monographs 2. Sheffield: Sheffield Phoenix, 2005.

Smith, Mark S. *The Early History of God: Yahweh and Other Deities in Ancient Israel*. 2nd ed. Grand Rapids: Eerdmans, 2002.

———. *The Memoirs of God: History, Memory, and the Experience of the Divine*. Minneapolis: Augsburg, 2004.

———. *The Origins of Biblical Monotheism: Israel's Polytheistic Background and the Ugaritic Texts*. Oxford: Oxford University Press, 2001.

———. "Ugarit and the Ugaritians." In Arnold and Strawn, *World around the Old Testament*, 139–67.

Smoak, Jeremy D. *The Priestly Blessing in Inscription and Scripture: The Early History of Numbers 6:24–26*. Oxford: Oxford University Press, 2016.

Snaith, Norman. "The Daughters of Zelophehad." *Vetus Testamentum* 16 (1966): 124–27.

———. "A Note on Numbers XVIII 9." *Vetus Testamentum* 23 (1973): 373–75.

Snyman, S. D. "Shamgar Ben Anath: A Farming Warrior or a Farmer at War?" *Vetus Testamentum* 55 (2005): 125–29.

Sommer, Benjamin D. *The Bodies of God and the World of Ancient Israel*. New York: Cambridge University Press, 2009.

———. "Reflecting on Moses: The Redaction of Numbers 11." *Journal of Biblical Literature* 118 (1999): 601–24.

Sonnet, Jean-Pierre. "NB 20,11: Moïse en Flagrant Délit de 'Main Levée'?" In Römer, *Leviticus and Numbers*, 535–43.

Spalinger, Anthony J. "Egyptian New Kingdom Triumphs: A First Blush." Pages 95–122 in *Rituals of Triumph in the Mediterranean World*. Edited by A. Spalinger and J. Armstrong. Culture and History of the Ancient Near East 63. Leiden: Brill, 2013.

———. *War in Ancient Egypt: The New Kingdom*. Oxford: Blackwell, 2005.

Sparks, Kenton L. *Ancient Texts for the Study of the Hebrew Bible: A Guide to the Background Literature*. Peabody, MA: Hendrickson, 2005.

———. "*Enūma Elish* and Priestly Mimesis: Elite Emulation in Nascent Judaism." *Journal of Biblical Literature* 126 (2007): 625–48.

———. *God's Word in Human Words: An Evangelical Appropriation of Critical Biblical Scholarship*. Grand Rapids: Baker Academic, 2008.

Specht, Herbert. "Die Verfehlung Moses und Aarons in Num 20,1–13* P." In Frevel, Pola, and Schart, *Book of Numbers*, 273–313.

Speiser, E. A. "The Background and Function of the Biblical *nāśîʾ*." *Catholic Biblical Quarterly* 25 (1963): 111–17.

Spencer, John R. "*PQD*, the Levites, and Numbers 1–4." *Zeitschrift für die alttestamentliche Wissenschaft* 110 (1998): 535–46.

Sperling, David S. "Miriam, Aaron and Moses: Sibling Rivalry." *Hebrew Union College Annual* 70–71 (1999–2000): 39–55.

Spero, Schubert. "'And against All the Gods of Egypt I Will Execute Judgements . . .'" *Jewish Bible Quarterly* 27 (1999): 83–88.

Sprinkle, Joe M. *Leviticus and Numbers*. Teach the Text Commentary Series. Grand Rapids: Baker Books, 2015.

Spronk, Klaas. "Baal of Peor." Pages 147–48 in Karel van der Toorn, Bob Becking, and Pieter W. van der Horst, eds. *Dictionary of Deities and Demons in the Bible*. 2nd extensively rev. ed. Leiden: Brill; Grand Rapids: Eerdmans, 1999.

Stackert, Jeffrey. "The Composition of Exodus 31:12–17 and 35:1–3 and the Question of Method in Identifying Priestly Strata in the Torah." In Gane and Taggar-Cohen, *Current Issues*, 175–96.

———. *Rewriting the Torah: Literary Revision in Deuteronomy and the Holiness Legislation*. Forschungen zum Alten Testament 52. Tübingen: Mohr Siebeck, 2007.

Stager, Lawrence E. "The Archaeology of the Family in Ancient Israel." *Bulletin of the American Schools of Oriental Research* 260 (1985): 1–35.

———. "Forging an Identity: The Emergence of Ancient Israel." Pages 90–131 in *The Oxford History of the Biblical World*. Edited by M. D. Coogan. Oxford: Oxford University Press, 1998.

Staubli, Thomas. *Die Bücher Levitikus, Numeri*. Neuer Stuttgarter Kommentar 3. Stuttgart: Katholisches Bibelwerk, 1996.

Stead, Michael. *The Intertextuality of Zechariah 1–8*. New York: T&T Clark, 2009.

Stein, Bernhard. "Der Engel des Auszugs." *Biblica* 19 (1938): 286–307.

Stern, Ephraim. *Archaeology of the Land of the Bible*. Vols. 1–2. Anchor Bible Reference Library. New York: Doubleday, 1990–2001. New Haven: Yale University Press, 2007.

Sternberg, Meir. *The Poetics of Biblical Narrative: Ideological Literature and the Drama of Reading*. Indiana Studies in Biblical Literature. Bloomington: Indiana University Press, 1985.

Stol, Marten. *Women in the Ancient Near East*. Translated by H. Richardson and M. Richardson. Berlin: de Gruyter, 2016.

Stone, Lawson G. "Early Israel and Its Appearance in Canaan." Pages 127–64 in *Ancient Israel's History: An Introduction to Issues and Sources*. Edited by B. T. Arnold and R. S. Hess. Grand Rapids: Baker Academic, 2014.

———. "Ethical and Apologetic Tendencies in the Redaction of the Book of Joshua." *Catholic Biblical Quarterly* 53 (1991): 25–35.

Strawn, Brent A. *The Old Testament Is Dying: A Diagnosis and Recommended Treatment*. Grand Rapids: Baker Academic, 2017.

Sturdy, John. *Numbers*. Cambridge Bible Commentary. Cambridge: Cambridge University Press, 1976.

Sumner, W. A. "Israel's Encounters with Edom, Moab, Ammon, Sihon, and Og according to the Deuteronomist." *Vetus Testamentum* 18 (1968): 216–28.

Sutcliffe, E. F. "A Note on Numbers XXII." *Biblica* 18 (1937): 439–42.

———. "De unitate litteraria Num XXII." *Biblica* 7 (1926): 3–39.

Taggar-Cohen, Ada. "Covenant Priesthood: Cross-Cultural Legal and Religious Aspects of Biblical and Hittite Priesthood." In Leuchter and Hutton, *Levites and Priests*, 11–24.

Teall, Ed. *Introduction to Logic: Evaluating Arguments*. Cincinnati: Atomic Dog, 2001.

Tebes, Juan Manuel. "Desert Place-Names in Numbers 33:34, Assurbanipal's Arabian Wars and the Historical Geography of the Biblical Wilderness Toponymy. *Journal of Northwest Semitic Languages* 43 (2017): 65–96.

———. "The Mesha Inscription and Relations with Moab and Edom." In Greer, Hilber, and Walton, *Behind the Scenes*, 286–92.

Tengström, Sven. *Die Toledotformel und die literarische Struktur der priesterlichen Erweiterungsschicht im Pentateuch*. Coniectanea biblica: Old Testament Series 17. Lund: Gleerup, 1981.

Tetlow, Elisabeth Meier. *Women, Crime, and Punishment in Ancient Law and Society*. Vol. 1, *The Ancient Near East*. New York: Continuum, 2004.

Thomas, Matthew A. *These Are the Generations: Identity, Covenant, and the "To-ledot" Formula*. London: T&T Clark, 2011.

Tiffany, Stephen T. "Cognitive Concepts of Craving." *Alcohol Research & Health* 23 (1999): 215–24.

Tostato, Angelo. "The Literary Structure of the First Two Poems of Balaam (Num xxiii 7–10, 18–24)." *Vetus Testamentum* 29 (1979): 98–106.

Tov, Emanuel. "Nature of the Samaritan Pentateuch." *The Israelite Samaritan Version of the Torah: First English Translation Compared with the Masoretic Version.* Edited by B. Tsedaka and S. Sullivan. Translated by B. Tsedaka. Grand Rapids: Eerdmans, 2013.

———. "The Relevance of Textual Theories for the Praxis of Textual Criticism." Pages 23–35 in vol. 1 of *A Teacher for All Generations: Essays in Honor of James C. VanderKam*. Supplements to the Journal for the Study of Judaism 153. Edited by E. F. Mason et al. 2 vols. Leiden: Brill, 2011.

———. "The Septuagint of Numbers as a Harmonizing Text." Pages 181–201 in *Die Septuaginta—Geschichte, Wirkung, Relevanz: 6. Internationale Fachtagung veranstaltet von Septuaginta Deutsch (LXX.D), Wuppertal 21.–24. Juli 2016*. Wissenschaftliche Untersuchungen zum Neuen Testament 405. Edited by M. Meiser et al. Tübingen: Mohr Siebeck, 2018.

———. *Textual Criticism of the Hebrew Bible*. 2nd rev. ed. Minneapolis: Fortress, 2001.

———. *Textual Criticism of the Hebrew Bible*. 3rd rev. ed. Minneapolis: Fortress, 2012.

———. *Textual Criticism of the Hebrew Bible, Qumran, Septuagint: Collected Essays*. Vol. 3. Supplements to Vetus Testamentum 167. Boston: Brill, 2015.

———. "Textual Harmonization in Exodus 1–24." *TC: A Journal of Biblical Textual Criticism* 22 (2017): 1–16.

Trible, Phyllis. "Depatriarchalizing in Biblical Interpretation." *Journal of the American Academy of Religion* 41 (1973): 30–48.

Trimm, Charlie. *Fighting for the King and the Gods: A Survey of Warfare in the Ancient Near East*. Society of Biblical Literature Resources for Biblical Study 88. Atlanta: SBL Press, 2017.

Tropper, Josef. "The Divine Name *Yahwa*." Pages 1–21 in *The Origins of Yahwism*. Edited by J. van Oorschot and M. Witte. Beihefte zur Zeitschrift für die alttestamentliche Wissenschaft 484. Boston: de Gruyter, 2019.

Tsevat, M. "God and the Gods in the Assembly." *Hebrew Union College Annual* 40–41 (1969–70): 123–37.

Tucker, Paavo N. *The Holiness Composition in the Book of Exodus*. Tübingen: Mohr Siebeck, 2017.

Turner, Victor. *The Ritual Process: Structure and Anti-Structure*. Chicago: Aldine, 1969.

Tyson, Craig W. *The Ammonites: Elites, Empires, and Sociopolitical Change (1000–500 BCE)*. London: Bloomsbury T&T Clark, 2014.

Ulrich, Eugene. *The Biblical Qumran Scrolls: Transcriptions and Textual Variants.* Supplements to Vetus Testamentum 134. Leiden: Brill, 2010.

———. "An Index of the Passages in the Biblical Manuscripts from the Judean Desert (Genesis–Kings)." *Dead Sea Discoveries* 1 (1994): 113–29.

US Department of Health and Human Services. "Infant Mortality in the United States, 2019." *National Vital Statistics Reports* 70, no. 14, December 8, 2021. https://www .cdc.gov/nchs/data/nvsr/nvsr70/nvsr70-14.pdf.

Utzschneider, Helmut. *Das Heiligtum und das Gesetz: Studien zur Bedeutung der sinaitischen Heiligtumstexte (Ex 25–40; Lev 8–9).* Orbis biblicus et orientalis 77. Freiburg: Universitätsverlag; Göttingen: Vandenhoeck & Ruprecht, 1988.

Vaka'uta, Nāsili. "Indicting YHWH: Interpreting Numbers 25 in Oceania." In Brenner and A. Lee, *Leviticus and Numbers*, 179–87.

Valbelle, Dominique. "Les recensements dans l'Egypte pharaonique des troisième et deuxième millénaires." *Les cahiers de recherches de l'institut de papyrologie et d'égyptologie de Lille* 9 (1987): 37–49.

van Bekkum, Koert. "Geography in Numbers 33 and 34 and the Challenge of Pentateuchal Theory." Pages 93–117 in *Torah and Traditions: Papers Read at the Sixteenth Joint Meeting of the Society for Old Testament Study and the Oudtestamentisch Werkgezelschap, Edinburgh, 2015.* Oudtestamentische Studiën 70. Leiden: Brill, 2017.

VanderKam, James, and Peter Flint. *The Meaning of the Dead Sea Scrolls: Their Significance for Understanding the Bible, Judaism, Jesus and Christianity.* London: T&T Clark, 2002.

van der Lingen, Anton. "BW'-YṢ' ('To Go Out and to Come In') as a Military Term." *Vetus Testamentum* 42 (1992): 59–66.

van der Louw, Theo A. W. *Transformations in the Septuagint: Towards an Interaction of Septuagint Studies and Translation Studies.* Contributions to Biblical Exegesis & Theology 47. Leuven: Peeters, 2007.

van der Meer, Michaël N. "The Next Generation: Textual Moves in Numbers 14,23 and Related Passages." In Römer, *Leviticus and Numbers*, 399–416.

van der Toorn, Karel. *Scribal Culture and the Making of the Hebrew Bible.* Cambridge, MA: Harvard University Press, 2009.

Van Seters, John. *The Life of Moses: The Yahwist as Historian in Exodus–Numbers.* Louisville: Westminster John Knox, 1994.

Vartejanu-Joubert, Madalina. "Les 'anciens du peuple' et Saül: Temps, espace et rite de passage dans Nombres XI et 1 Samuel X." *Vetus Testamentum* 55 (2005): 542–63.

Vayntrub, Jacqueline. "'To *Take Up* a Parable': The History of Translating a Biblical Idiom." *Vetus Testamentum* 66 (2016): 627–45.

von Rad, Gerhard. *Die Priesterschrift im Hexateuch.* Beiträge zur Wissenschaft vom Alten und Neuen Testament. Stuttgart: Kohlhammer, 1943.

von Soden, Wolfram. "Mirjām-Maria '(Gottes)-Geschenk.'" *Ugarit-Forschungen* 2 (1970): 269–72.

Vosté, Jacques-M. "Les Oracles de Balaam d'après Mar Išoʿdad de Merw (c. 850)." *Biblica* 29 (1948): 169–94.

Wagenaar, Jan. "Post-Exilic Calendar Innovations: The First Month of the Year and the Date of Passover and the Festival of Unleavened Bread." *Zeitschrift für die alttestamentliche Wissenschaft* 115 (2003): 3–24.

Wagner, Siegfried. "Die Kundschaftergeschichten im Alten Testament." *Zeitschrift für die alttestamentliche Wissenschaft* 76 (1964): 255–69.

Waite, Jerry. "Short Note: The Census of Israelite Men after Their Exodus from Egypt." *Vetus Testamentum* (2010): 487–91.

Wallace, Daniel B. *Greek Grammar beyond the Basics: An Exegetical Syntax of the New Testament*. Grand Rapids: Zondervan, 1996.

Walsh, Jerome T. "From Egypt to Moab: A Source Critical Analysis of the Wilderness Itinerary." *Catholic Biblical Quarterly* 39 (1977): 20–33.

Waltke, Bruce K. *The Book of Proverbs: Chapters 15–31*. New International Commentary on the Old Testament. Grand Rapids: Eerdmans, 2005.

Walton, John H. *Ancient Near Eastern Thought and the Old Testament: Introducing the Conceptual World of the Hebrew Bible*. 2nd ed. Grand Rapids: Baker Academic, 2006.

———. *Genesis 1 as Ancient Cosmology*. Winona Lake, IN: Eisenbrauns, 2011.

———. *The Lost World of Genesis One: Ancient Cosmology and the Origins Debate*. Downers Grove, IL: IVP Academic, 2009.

Walton, John H., and Victor H. Matthews. *The IVP Bible Background Commentary: Genesis–Deuteronomy*. Downers Grove, IL: InterVarsity, 1997.

Washington, Harold C. "'Lest He Die in the Battle and Another Man Take Her': Violence and the Construction of Gender in the Laws of Deuteronomy 20–22." Pages 185–213 in *Gender and Law in the Hebrew Bible and the Ancient Near East*. Edited by V. H. Matthews, B. M. Levinson, and T. Frymer-Kensky. Sheffield: Sheffield Academic Press, 1998. 2nd ed. London: T&T Clark, 2004.

Way, Kenneth C. "Animals in the Prophetic World: Literary Reflections on Numbers 22 and 1 Kings 13." *Journal for the Study of the Old Testament* 34 (2009): 47–62.

Webb, William J. *Slaves, Women, and Homosexuals: Exploring the Hermeneutics of Cultural Analysis*. Foreword by Darrell L. Bock. Downers Grove, IL: InterVarsity, 2001.

Webster, Brian. "Chronological Index of the Texts from the Judaean Desert." Pages 351–446 in *The Texts from the Judaean Desert: Indices and an Introduction to the Discoveries in the Judaean Desert Series*. Discoveries in the Judaean Desert 39. Edited by E. Tov. Oxford: Clarendon, 2002.

Wefing, Sabina. "Beobachtungen zum Ritual mit der roten Kuh (Num 19.1–10a)." *Zeitschrift für die alttestamentliche Wissenschaft* 93 (1981): 341–64.

Weil, Simone. *Waiting for God*. Translated by E. Craufurd. New York: Putnam's Sons, 1951. Repr., New York: Harper & Row, 1973.

Weimar, Peter. "Die Toledot-Formel in der priesterschriftlichen Geschichtsdarstellung." *Biblische Zeitschrift* 18 (1974): 65–93.

Weinfeld, Moshe. "The Covenant of Grant in the Old Testament and in the Ancient Near East." *Journal of the American Oriental Society* 90 (1970): 184–203.

———. *Deuteronomy and the Deuteronomic School.* Oxford: Oxford University Press, 1972. Repr., Winona Lake, IN: Eisenbrauns, 1992.

Weingreen, Jacob. "The Case of the Daughters of Zelophehad." *Vetus Testamentum* 16 (1966): 518–22.

Weisman, Ze'ev. "The Personal Spirit as Imparting Authority." *Zeitschrift für die alttestamentliche Wissenschaft* 93 (1981): 225–34.

Weitzman, M. P. *The Syriac Version of the Old Testament: An Introduction.* University of Cambridge Oriental Publications 56. Cambridge: Cambridge University Press, 1999.

Wellhausen, Julius. *Die Composition des Hexateuchs und der historischen Bücher des Alten Testaments.* 3rd ed. Berlin: Reimer, 1899.

———. *Prolegomena to the History of Ancient Israel.* New York: Meridian Books, 1957. Reprint of *Prolegomena to the History of Israel.* Translated by J. S. Black and A. Enzies, with preface by W. R. Smith. Edinburgh: Adam & Charles Black, 1885. Translation of *Prolegomena zur Geschichte Israels.* 2nd ed. Berlin: Reimer, 1883.

Wells, Bruce, F. Rachel Magdalene, and Cornelia Wunsch. "The Assertory Oath in Neo-Babylonian and Persian Administrative Texts." *Revue internationale des droits de l'antiquité* 57 (2010): 13–29.

Wenham, Gordon J. "Aaron's Rod (Numbers 17.16–28)." *Zeitschrift für die alttestamentliche Wissenschaft* 93 (1981): 280–81.

———. *The Book of Leviticus.* New International Commentary on the Old Testament. Grand Rapids: Eerdmans, 1979.

———. *Numbers.* Sheffield: Sheffield Academic, 1997.

Wénin, André. "Le serpent de Nb 21,4–9 et de Gn 3,1: Intertextualité et élaboration du sens." In Römer, *Leviticus and Numbers*, 545–54.

Wesley, John. *Wesley's Notes on the Bible.* Grand Rapids: Francis Asbury Press, 1987. Grand Rapids: Christian Classics Ethereal Library. https://ccel.org/ccel/wesley/notes.

Westermann, Claus. *Praise and Lament in the Psalms.* Atlanta: John Knox, 1981.

Wevers, John William, ed. *Notes on the Greek Text of Numbers.* Society of Biblical Literature Septuagint and Cognate Studies 46. Atlanta: Scholars Press, 1998.

———. *Numeri.* Vol. III,1 of *Septuaginta Vetus Testamentum Graecum.* Göttingen: Vandenhoeck & Ruprecht, 1982.

Wible, Andy. "Inflation of Conflict." Pages 280–81 in *Bad Arguments: 100 of the Most Important Fallacies in Western Philosophy.* Edited by R. Arp, S. Barbone, and M. Bruce. Oxford: Wiley Blackwell, 2019.

Wiggershaus, Benjamin. "The Man of Opened Eye: Ancient Near Eastern Revelatory Convention and the Balaam Cycle (Numbers 22–24)." PhD diss., Asbury Theological Seminary, 2021.

Wilson, Robert R. *Prophecy and Society in Ancient Israel.* Philadelphia: Fortress, 1980.

Witfall, Walter, Jr. "Asshur and Eber, or Asher and Ḥeber? A Commentary on the Last Balaam Oracle, Num 24.21–24." *Zeitschrift für die alttestamentliche Wissenschaft* 82 (1970): 110–14.

Witherington, Ben, III. *Paul's Letter to the Romans: A Socio-Rhetorical Commentary.* Grand Rapids: Eerdmans, 2004.

Wittmer, Michael E. *Heaven Is a Place on Earth: Why Everything You Do Matters to God.* Grand Rapids: Zondervan, 2004.

Wolters, Albert M. *Creation Regained: Biblical Basics for a Reformational Worldview.* 2nd ed. Grand Rapids: Eerdmans, 2005.

Wong, Ka Leung. "'And Moses Raised His Hand' in Numbers 20,11." *Biblica* 89 (2008): 397–400.

Wong, Sonia K. "The Notion of [*kpr*] in the Book of Leviticus and Chinese Popular Religion." In Brenner and A. Lee, *Leviticus and Numbers*, 77–95.

Wood, Bryant G. "Balaam Son of Beor." *Bible and Spade* 8 (1995): 114.

———. "Prophecy of Balaam Found in Jordan." *Bible and Spade* 6 (1977): 121–24.

Wright, Benjamin, III. "The Letter of Aristeas and the Question of Septuagint Origins Redux." *Journal of Ancient Judaism* 2 (2011): 303–25.

Wright, David P. "Profane versus Sacrificial Slaughter: The Priestly Recasting of the Yahwist Flood Story." In Gane and Taggar-Cohen, *Current Issues*, 125–54.

———. "Purification from Corpse-Contamination in Numbers XXXI 19–24." *Vetus Testamentum* 35 (1985): 213–33.

Wright, N. T. *The New Testament and the People of God.* Vol. 1 of *Christian Origins and the Question of God.* Minneapolis: Fortress, 1992.

Yadin, Azzan. "[*Qwl*] as Hypostasis in the Hebrew Bible." *Journal of Biblical Literature* 122 (2003): 601–26.

Yarden, Leon. *The Tree of Light: A Study of the Menorah, the Seven-Branched Lampstand.* Ithaca, NY: Cornell University Press, 1971.

Zeelander, Susan. "The End of Korah and Others: Closural Conventions in Priestly Narratives of Numbers." In Gane and Taggar-Cohen, *Current Issues*, 325–67.

Zevit, Ziony. *The Religions of Ancient Israel: A Synthesis of Parallactic Approaches.* London: Continuum, 2001.

Ziemer, Benjamin. "Erklärung der wichtigsten 'demographischen' Zahlen des Numeribuches aus ihrem kompositionellen Zusammenhang." *Vetus Testamentum* 60 (2010): 271–87.

Zimmerli, Walther. "Zur Vorgeschichte von Jes 53." Pages 213–21 in *Studien zur alttestamentlichen Theologie und Prophetie.* Theologische Bücherei: Neudrucke und Berichte aus dem 20. Jahrhundert 51. Munich: Kaiser, 1974.

Zuckschwerdt, Ernst. "Zur literarischen Vorgeschichte des priesterlichen Nazir-Gesetzes (Num 6:1–8)." *Zeitschrift für die alttestamentliche Wissenschaft* 88 (1976): 191–205.

Subject Index

Author Index

Index of Scripture
and Other Ancient Writings